Sepik Heritage

Sepik Heritage
Tradition and Change in Papua New Guinea

Edited by

Nancy Lutkehaus

Christian Kaufmann
William E. Mitchell
Douglas Newton
Lita Osmundsen
Meinhard Schuster

Carolina Academic Press
Durham, North Carolina

Carolina Academic Press
700 Kent Street
Durham, North Carolina 27701
919–489–7486

Contents

Part Nine: Conveying the Past

Preface

History for whom, and for what? To me that is the crucial point. I have become interested in history because of development in the Sepik. History for the villager, as was clearly shown during the Sepik symposium's first session, has to do with land and with the autonomy of the clan and the village. We Iatmul always have two sets of references, one to condemn and belittle others and one to promote ourselves.

I hope that a more considered effort can now be made to work out a new kind of history. As a former provincial premier, I would like to see a history for planning purposes, both provincial and national. We are so diversified, and we tend to feel that each clan or village is an island. Perhaps we can somehow gain an inkling that we are of the same flesh and blood—that we have a common ancestry and because of it are in fact as close as blood relatives. A history pointing to common factors and thereby moderating and minimizing the accumulated differences would contribute to village, community, provincial, and national unity and progress.

Timbunke, January 4, 1988   FATHER CHERUBIM DAMBUI

Prologue

Meinhard Schuster

For a variety of reasons, the 1960s and '70s saw a considerable increase in ethnological fieldwork in the Sepik area. Some of these reasons were, like the majority of researchers involved, of foreign origin: the growing general interest in the West in non-European cultures, the increasing number of young people studying anthropology, and the increasing availability of research funds in Western countries associated with the economic growth of the times. Other reasons emerged within Papua New Guinea itself: the opening up of the last restricted areas, the continued diversity, richness, and authenticity of the traditional cultures, and the activities of the new nation's own institutions, such as the National Museum, the Institute of Papua New Guinea Studies, and the University of Papua New Guinea.

This intensification of research meant that young (for the most part) scholars of both sexes came to the country for extended periods of fieldwork. Some of them were attached to universities or museums that had a tradition of Sepik field research or of studies based on their institutions' Sepik collections, which dated back to pre-World War II or even German times; others came on individual projects without such backing and the wider contacts it involved. Given this situation, a need was increasingly felt for better communication, which was sometimes restricted by language barriers, among colleagues from outside Papua New Guinea and between them and Papua New Guinean scholars and the foreign anthropologists working in Papua New Guinean institutions.

It was Bill Mitchell who first advanced the idea of a Wenner-Gren symposium devoted to Sepik anthropology, but as we in Basel were occupied with other tasks (most of them also connected with Papua New Guinea) at the time it was a number of years before the idea matured into action. During a visit to New York in 1982, Christian Kaufmann had the first talks with Lita Osmundsen, the Wenner-Gren Foundation's Director of Research. Afterwards our American colleagues, first of all Douglas Newton, offered their support. When I saw Mrs. Osmundsen nine months later, the outline of the symposium was agreed upon.

This included the establishment of an organizing committee (consisting of Kaufmann, Mitchell, Newton, Nancy Lutkehaus, and myself) and the criteria for the invitations, leaving the details to later correspondence and phone calls.

The idea of the conference, as gradually developed and eventually expressed in its subtitle "The Study of Sepik Cultures in and for Modern Papua New Guinea," was to offer a framework for reflecting, through precirculated papers, discussions, and this publication, on the role that the anthropological research done so far or planned for the future in the Sepik might play in the young nation of Papua New Guinea. This was not, of course, seen as a matter of reducing anthropology to economic development, social work, or politics. Rather, the idea was to consider what the study of traditional Sepik cultures, including historical questions, could contribute to an understanding of the present situation and, from a broader perspective, to the building of a multiethnic nation.

This topic might have been treated by a small group of scholars on the basis of examples drawn from their own or other people's research, but because there was so much anthropological fieldwork going on in the Sepik we considered it more appropriate to put the question implied by the phrase "in and for modern Papua New Guinea" to everyone who had done research in the Sepik in recent times. By doing so, we felt, we could highlight the national framework within which all anthropological research now takes place and at the same time obtain a relatively complete picture of the state of Sepik research that would also be of interest to the Papua New Guinea authorities.

It was decided that every anthropologist, geographer, art historian, and linguist who had done fieldwork in the Sepik since about 1960, published about it, and remained actively in contact with the discipline would be invited. We defined "Sepik" as covering the whole triangle between the north coast (including the Schouten Islands), the border with Irian Jaya, and the lower northern slopes of the central mountain range, thus excluding the Telefomin area even though it is part of the West Sepik Province but going beyond the East Sepik Province into the Ramu area of Madang

Province. As the list of participants shows, political authorities of both Sepik provinces were also invited. Unfortunately, His Honor the Prime Minister Michael Somare, himself from the East Sepik Province, was prevented from attending by duties requiring his presence in Papua New Guinea.

Ten of the participants came from Papua New Guinea (including foreign anthropologists employed by Papua New Guinea institutions), fifteen from Australia, fourteen from the United States, and twenty-two from Europe. With the total number of participants exceeding sixty, plus the Wenner-Gren staff and senior anthropology students from Basel interested in Papua New Guinea, the conference developed into something between a traditional Wenner-Gren symposium (usually a much smaller affair) and a small regionally defined anthropological congress. As our contacts since then have demonstrated, this size allowed the participants to establish a kind of scholarly community made up, with few exceptions, of anthropologists and other researchers occupied with and fascinated by the Sepik and to gain a much better picture of the research, the people behind it, and the perspectives guiding it. It also formed a base from which to survey and record the efforts of participants to date with regard to publications, museum collections, maps, films, audio recordings, and other materials of documentary and other value for the Sepik people and Sepik researchers.

I am grateful to the Wenner-Gren Foundation for Anthropological Research, Inc., and, in particular, to its President and Director of Research, Lita Osmundsen, for the support that made this symposium possible, especially since it came to be much larger than was originally conceived. My thanks also go to the Schweizerische Akademie der Geisteswissenschaften, Berne, and to the Kanton Basel-Stadt for their substantial contributions, as well as to the Deutscher Akademischer Austauschdienst for enabling us immediately after the conference to show our guests from overseas the major old Sepik collections in German museums. Last but not least, I thank my colleagues of the organizing committee in Switzerland and the United States and all the collaborators of the Ethnologisches Seminar der Universität Basel and the Museum für Völkerkunde und Schweizerisches Museum für Völkerkunde Basel for their help before, during, and after the Sepik symposium.

Prologue

Lita Osmundsen

In the early 1970s, Margaret Mead introduced William Mitchell to me so that he could present to the Wenner-Gren Foundation for Anthropological Research his idea for a conference on the Sepik. Even at that early date, we recognized the potential scope and significance of this idea and responded with enthusiasm and encouragement, aware of the richness of historical data on the Sepik and the burgeoning and varied body of contemporary research. The preliminary idea offered a unique opportunity to foster the sort of international and cross-disciplinary communication that the Foundation had always supported.

The long-standing program of the Foundation for sponsoring and organizing international and interdisciplinary conferences was well established, and its conference themes were shifting to include more regional and areal studies. More significant, such conferences involved as active participants not only the researchers but the subjects of their research, who were themselves becoming scholars of their own culture. This added dimension gave new vigor to conventional scholarly discussion and subsequently to anthropological studies in general.

The original concept for a conference on the Sepik eventually became a full-blown proposal, with valuable input and collaboration first from Mitchell's Swiss co-organizers, Meinhard Schuster and Christian Kaufmann, and then from his American colleagues Douglas Newton and Nancy Lutkehaus. In its final form, the proposal embraced the plan to include several Papua New Guineans, both scholars and government officials, among the participants.

The Foundation sponsored the conference with its financial resources and its organizational expertise. Implementation of the conference structure fell to its organizing committee, which worked with the Foundation over many months to refine a series of topics that could bridge the diversity of research interests, approaches, and styles represented by so large a number of scholars of such varied geographical and conceptual backgrounds. Over time, a dynamic, problem-oriented format emerged to maximize interpersonal interaction and stimulate plenary discussion. It drew together a wide array of ethnographic and other data and took advantage of the many perspectives reflected in the contributed papers. Discussions were to alternate between plenary sessions and three smaller, randomly mixed groups that permitted more direct and interpersonal exchanges, the results of which could be shared by everyone on a daily basis.

With almost seventy participants and only nine days to cover the range of issues on the program, the organizers eliminated the customary formal presentations of prepared papers (which had previously been distributed among the participants). At the opening session, participants were told that they were expected to act as total resources, utilizing the whole of their experience rather than concentrating on the portions of it represented by their contributed papers. While this decision was almost certain to produce some discomfort, the organizers recognized that the conference served a different purpose from the eventual publication. The primary goals of the conference were to expose the basic issues, stimulate discussion, establish interconnections among individual scholars, and intensify good relations for future research "in and for Papua New Guinea."

As a conclusion to the sessions, three participants were invited to summarize the results from their different points of view and comment upon future research possibilities. Anthony Crawford commented on problems and prospects of documentation, and Andrew Strathern attempted a synthesis of some of the various issues (tradition, power and politics, belief systems and expressive culture). David Lea commented on the legacy of the colonial period and development and evaluated the problems and successes of the conference process. Lea stated that the management of the program was surprisingly effective and that there was ample opportunity to raise issues of mutual concern in our specialties, but he expressed regret that the papers were not "systematically discussed or delivered in a conventional way. . . . They were an underutilized but rich resource." This comment reflected participants' desires to have their papers given their due, and it is this aim that we hope this publication will now serve.

A tour of Sepik collections of artifacts in museums of West and East Germany capped the conference for those participants who were able to attend. Especially for the representatives of Papua New Guinea, this was an exciting opportunity to view historical materials diligently collected earlier in the century.

One palpable impact of both the conference and the tour has been the establishment of institutional and human contacts that have continued to thrive. Another is the ongoing collaborative documentation of bibliographies, audiovisual materials, and museum collections on the Sepik. Adding to this vast wealth of references, this publication of the papers prepared for the conference and since revised extends and, it is hoped, provides some coherence to the inventory of Sepik research. The organizers, now functioning as editors, have struggled to find the most satisfying structure for assembling the diverse papers in terms of a meaningful set of themes and relationships. The Foundation has performed the by no means easy task of securing a publisher willing to undertake so sizable, complex, and specialized a work. Much time, energy, and funding have been invested in its production. We are hopeful that it will further advance research and thereby not only serve the needs of Sepik peoples and specialists but also attract the attention of scholars in their comparative studies of other areas.

I add my voice to that of Meinhard Schuster and on behalf of the organizers/editors in thanking the many contributing and funding agencies, those already mentioned above as well as the Institute for Intercultural Studies (founded by Margaret Mead) for its support of the representatives of Papua New Guinea. With the organizers/editors, I thank the members of the Swiss staff— Brigit Obrist and the senior students who assisted in the logistics of the conference and afterwards helped to develop segments of the published material. Thanks go also to the Wenner-Gren staff, particularly Nina Watson, my right hand throughout the preparations for the conference and subsequent publication planning meetings. Barbara Metzger, copy editor of the international journal *Current Anthropology*, took on the added massive task of copy-editing this volume. We are in her debt. I am especially grateful to both Meinhard Schuster and Christian Kaufmann for suggesting the charming city of Basel as the venue for the conference and for arranging for the Institute of Ethnology, the Museum of Ethnography, and the Swiss Museum of European Folklife to host and accommodate the sessions and other conference activities. Their management of the local conference arrangements always balanced efficiency with gracious hospitality. Throughout, their efforts, ever sensitive to the social as well as intellectual needs of the group, contributed greatly to the success of the conference. Lastly, I extend my gratitude to the organizers/editors, whose collaboration, commitment, and hard work over several years have brought this project to its fruition with the publication of this volume on the Sepik.

Foreword

Douglas Newton

Long ago, in a place far away, someone remarked to me, almost grudgingly, "This bloody country, it gets to you." She was using "bloody," of course in that peculiar case the laudatory pejorative, as in New Guinea we say, "Man no-good tru," or, in New York, "Man, that cat is baaaad."

The place was the Sepik, and indeed the Sepik is, in many ways, a bloody country. It is always excessive in one way or another; too hot, too dry, too humid. The river area boasts, as Brigitta Hauser-Schäublin says, mainly "fish, water, and mosquitoes"—she could have added that the hills have mainly rocks, roots, and other kinds of mosquitoes. There is no natural comfort or even simple convenience. Its bad points are hard on the outsider, who all the same can bring necessities from home; they are worse for the inhabitant, whose responsibilities and livelihood depend on the place itself. On the other hand, the Sepik is not a green hell; it is not even particularly unhealthy compared to other parts of the tropical world; it returns a reasonably easy living for relatively little labor.

It is not a place for which we have nostalgia but also not one we ever forget. As a landscape it has overwhelming beauty—in one of his last public statements, Gregory Bateson (1978:77) said he still thought the Sepik was one of the most beautiful places in the world. It must be one of the most physically vivid and sensuously acute. I doubt if anyone here cannot summon up in an instant the sensations of the texture of the soil, the crackle of palm leaves, the different smells of burning wood. And the people. It was the opinion of a well-known anthropologist that "we aren't here to make friends." But alas, we do, and we remember equally sharply their personalities, their voices, their expressions. It is perceptions like this that make the Sepik one's second nature, one's second homeland. It becomes a part of our lives, and we should pay our respects to that.

Like good Sepik people, we should also pay homage to our ancestors. I mentioned Bateson, and I will mention others. The Basel symposium "Sepik Research Today: The Study of Sepik Cultures in and for Papua New Guinea," out of which this publication emerges, occurred within a few months of the centenary of the day in May 1885 on which Finsch took a whale boat twenty miles up the Sepik, the first European vessel on the river. If the symposium had been held fifty years ago, it would have been a much smaller gathering of people with very different conceptions of what they were doing. One might have seen the great dinosaurs of Kaiser-Wilhelmsland: Reche, Schultze-Jena, Behrmann, Thurnwald, joined by the somewhat later generation of Speiser, Höltker, Kirschbaum; and some twenty-five years after that, the even younger generation which included Mead, Bateson, Fortune, Kaberry, Wedgwood, and Hogbin—not a complete roll call, but names that immediately come to mind.

There were remarkably few of them. As late as the 1960s, Haberland (1965) could say, in an article on urgent research needs, "it seems hardly credible [that the Sepik] is a relatively unknown territory in the ethnological sense and even worse in the linguistic one . . . our knowledge about the territory is amazingly small." He named about thirty-five scholars, not all anthropologists, who had published since 1900. The presence of some sixty participants at the 1984 Basel symposium—and there could have been more—was in itself an indication of how times have changed. One must add that the changes are largely due to the launching from the Basel Museum of the latest, most thorough, and best-coordinated campaign of Sepik research, inspired by Alfred Bühler and led by Meinhard Schuster.

We now know a vast amount more than we did in 1965. Very much to the point, we know it within a series of conceptual frameworks, differing greatly from those of the earlier researchers, which have to do not only with the Sepik, or New Guinea, or Melanesia, but with the Pacific Basin as a whole. These partly derive from recent research but will also direct its future. One of the questions implicit or explicit in some of this volume's papers is whether or not the Sepik Provinces are a distinct, discrete area. If there is an answer, it probably must be yes and no. Intuitively speaking, it is hard not to feel that this triangle of land decisively bounded by sea and mountains, inhabited by people speaking a quarter of the languages of New Guinea, producers of many vigorous art styles, and with a turbulent, introverted history, displays a distinctive quality all its own: the sum of the distinctiveness of dozens of small to large groups. While intuition is a useful signpost, it does not constitute proof, and the question will no doubt continue to arouse discussion.

Variety is a starting point, not an end, to our studies. Unfortunately, researchers' perceptions of it have generated political debate. Anthropologists have often been accused (particularly in recent years) of having fostered the concept of variation in collusion with administrative interests—the divide-and-rule principle—at the expense of a now-desirable concept of national unity. This was never really the case, from the very beginning, even though, through a study of differences, Reche early proposed expanded Sepik culture areas (1913: 465–67, 475–76) and Behrmann did much the same with studies of architecture and tribal divisions (1918, 1924, 1933)—all implying larger affiliations than the village or even the linguistic unit. Mead in particular, Hogbin, Gewertz, May and Tuckson, McDowell, Lutkehaus, Schindlbeck, and the encyclopedic Tiesler—to name only a few—have stressed interrelationships of groups through trade and warfare. Though we should not exaggerate the extent of such contacts, even in the precolonial past certainly every group knew of several other groups—which is not to say that coastal people followed the weekly head-hunting scores of the May River.

But at a higher level than the communication chain, one may think of what Dark (1979:130) calls "themes": "a particular subject, such as a myth, event, or custom, and its expression in a set of artistic forms . . . there may be variations in the expression of the forms as one compares different cultures, but a theme should have basic underlying forms throughout an area." Bateson, like Mead, saw the Sepik as a sort of cultural jigsaw puzzle, with the bits available to all groups to fit together as they would. Surely something of this kind exists rather intensely in the Sepik, to an extent which justifies its being called an "area." As such, it is part of a greater New Guinea area, which again forms part of realms, increasingly larger, which span the Pacific Ocean. This conception of a Pan-Oceania is not particularly new but is surely becoming increasingly and more accurately powerful.

The most remarkable work toward defining the Sepik as an area has been done by Laycock and his colleagues first with the discovery of the Ndu-family languages (Laycock 1965) and more recently with the formulation of the Sepik-Ramu phylum and the lesser phyla between it and the sea (Wurm 1975, 1976, 1977a), all bracketed by the Trans–New Guinea phylum. What they have done in effect is to create nothing less than a metacartography on which we orient ourselves as much by languages as by geographical features.

J. Peter White's discovery of the Kosipe site in the mountains of the Central Province, with its C^{14} date of 26,000 B.P., was the first event to revolutionize our view of New Guinea's history, and it opened the door to further research, mainly in highland areas. The northern lowlands have not received anything like the same attention. Swadling's work on Sepik prehistory is thus almost as revolutionary, not so much for its treatment of sparse facts and objects as for an interdisciplinary approach including a synthesis of linguistic history and geology in the Sepik. This opens another door to research in New Guinea; it also exemplifies the kangaroo-like leaps that characterize New Guinea history. From the landforms and their associated populations of 6000 B.C., we take a giant jump almost without pause to a matter of a couple of hundred years ago, when living traditions begin. The study of oral history has begun rather late in New Guinea, compared to Africa, owing perhaps to a skepticism inherited from both British and American anthropologists. But among their other achievements the Basel team of scholars, precisely by employing oral traditions, has begun to make sense of Middle Sepik history. One hopes that for an ever wider field it will be possible to do the sort of study combining archaeology with oral tradition that Golson, Lampert, and Oram (1969) pioneered in the Port Moresby area.

In more recent periods, probably the most imposing part of the Sepik's cultural heritage is its art. At last the music, so far underrated both for itself and for its cultural significance, is being studied, as reflected in this volume, as it deserves. Famous as they are, the visual arts are still relatively neglected. We need studies not only of taxonomies of the styles, iconography, and iconology but of what aesthetics mean to these immensely productive people. The career of the individual artist has barely been considered. Above all, studies are needed on what Stanek calls the "mysticism" of the religions, which may be very different from our Western conception of the sacred but evidently compellingly vital.

The charter of the Basel symposium was the discussion of Sepik research "in and for" modern Papua New Guinea. The meaning of "in" seems reasonably clear, but how are we to understand "for"? The word implies action, the dictionaries tell us, preferably beneficial or favorable to someone or something; what sort of action are we to take? The answer may not entirely depend on the anthropologists. A directing force in research has been, and will no doubt continue to be, the consequences of the establishment of independence in Papua New Guinea. The role of the anthropologist has been vigorously debated with a mind-boggling range of arguments, too numerous to single out for quotation. Every point of view anyone has presented has been countered by an equal and opposite view. In the 1970s, it became clear that a body of younger Papua New Guinean intellectuals took a very poor view of anthropologists, and so did an unexpected number of older people in general. Many specific resentments were aired, and in some cases anthropologists responded in rather self-flagellatory terms, as became the climate of the time. It was, after all, a period when a sincere, however newly found, concern with ethics nearly led some archaeologists and anthropologists to question whether they should be practicing their disciplines at all (Jorgensen 1971; Meighan 1984:208–13).

What, in point of fact, is the use of anthropology? Anthropologists might ask in return, why should it have a use and why should it need one? They might reply that there is a long-accepted principle that research into anything may come in handy for someone, someday, and that in any case they enjoy doing it. These are not really inadequate answers, but they may need expansion and elucidation.

At present the official stance of the government, expressed through the appropriate agencies, is that researchers are welcome enough as long as their work does not present the country in an unfavorable light and is "relevant." The conditions for mandatory affiliation to the University of Papua New Guinea, for example, hint at the desirability of a degree of activism: they require "quarterly reports from the field emphasizing practical issues and what the researcher might do and has done about them" (Conditions 1982:3, 4, 5). This is what might be called "service anthropology" as against "salvage research," in Soroi Eoe's phrase. It can, of course, provide short-term benefits, as in studies of health, nutrition, land rights, and so on. Programs of this kind have obvious attractions for government, as they inform and therefore assist it.

Probably the most important aspect of salvage research is the preservation for the future of a country's cultural heritage. This, anywhere, is a backbreaking and probably heartbreaking task with many conflicting interests involved. New nations usually start out acutely aware that there are aspects of their cultures that differentiate them from the rest of the world, and paradoxically—in view of what I remarked earlier—the distinctive qualities of national culture are nearly always recognized as a means of self-definition. This kind of awareness is not new; Bernal (1980:72–77) describes it as a powerful instrument of national aspiration in Mexico from the seventeenth century on. The politicians therefore make excellent plans for institutions which will preserve and publicize those aspects, but after a time they forget them and go about the business of development which will enrich the country but further sap its cultural heritage. Criticism of this policy is not always understood or enjoyed (Lévi-Strauss 1985:xiii–xv), and Eoe describes the difficulties facing anyone who tries to work under such conditions.

Apart from suffering financial and bureaucratic obstacles, the would-be preserver becomes embroiled in a worldwide problem. Two aspects are especially conspicuous on the material level. The devastation of archaeological sites, for instance, through looting, overbuilding, and public works is as rapid and violent in Europe, Asia, and the New World—including the United States—as it could ever be in the Pacific. Any attempt to counter it anywhere comes up against powerful influences indeed. Exportation of the national heritage of objects to the deprivation of the country of origin has malign effects, but they may be more easily combatted. Aggressive action against it can be remarkably effective, not only by legality but by a less obvious yet still powerful weapon: the arousal of public opinion. Neither museums nor new private collectors, with very few exceptions, want the embarrassment of owning what a government has claimed to be an illegal export; in other parts of the world it has done a great deal to inhibit the illegal flow of antiquities.

The preservation of the nonmaterial sector of any culture forms a different, sensitive, and infinitely more difficult project. By its nature it is elusive and ephemeral. Adolf Bastian, as early as 1881, lamented the loss of ethnographic information; "our generation will rightly bear the brunt of blame for the irretrievable loss" (Koepping 1983:217). Margaret Mead tells us how she and her contemporaries were desperate to get to the field: the last old man who knew something about the past of a culture might be dying at that moment. When we recollect that she started her Sepik fieldwork only a few years after the government established control of the river, that sounds almost quaint. Many of us have really seen some of the last old men—the men of the German time—die with their memories sealed.

Bateson remarks somewhere that Iatmul men divided three-quarters of their lives equally between performing ceremonies, thinking about ceremonies, and sexual adventure; daily business took up the rest of their time. I doubt if Iatmul life is compartmented in the same way now; if not, how different must be the Iatmul men's perception of their culture! We understand, I think, that a good deal of any research we try to do now about the past is already a filtration of memory through a couple of generations which are increasingly out of touch with the pre-Westernizing past.

Unofficial conservation can be embodied in the natural processes of a culture. Tuzin, as an anthropologist, describes here the transmission of knowledge from generation to generation of children. Interference from without, however well-intentioned, may have dubious aspects. Robert Paul Smith, a novelist, writes about the same phenomenon and its interruption among American children. He describes how some boys had forgotten the game of mumbly-peg. "When I was a kid," he says, "it was our theory that the grownup was the natural enemy of the child, and if any father had come around being a pal to us we would have figured he was either a little dotty or a spy. What we learned we learned from another kid." And, he goes on, "I taught those kids to play mumbly-peg, and for all I know, if I hadn't happened to be around that day, in another fifteen years they would have to start protecting mumbly-peg players like rosy spoonbills or the passenger pigeon" (Smith 1957:8–9). There is conservation of culture in a nutshell, with all its hints of interference and paternalism.

It is only when cultures are in decline, or changing radically, whichever one prefers, that we have to think about conserving them. By the time it needs conserving, a culture, like a work of art, is in a bad way. It will never revert to its pristine stage, which other stages will replace. The past scene of Papua New Guinea has certainly changed radically. On the other hand, one can hardly say it is dead. What emerges from some of the papers of this publication is that, in the midst of their present distress, the Sepik people have three options: business, cargo cults, and custom. When one is unsuccessful, they try another for a while, in a cycle. Evidently custom, in some form or another, will very likely persist as an important part of the cultural repertoire, even if in far from pristine form, for the foreseeable future.

At the same time, whether the acquisition of such knowledge by outsiders will take place is another question. This has already been said here, but it seems worth further detail. For those raised in the Western scientific tradition, knowledge is inexhaustible because as it answers questions it exposes, one hopes, a prospect of further questions to be answered. In much of the western Pacific knowledge, it seems, is finite, and the person who attains its limit becomes an almost transcendental being, or starts to wither. Knowledge is also power; power can be wealth, or the other way round. What lies behind the resistance of many New Guineans to researchers, then, is the conviction that the researchers are removing a precious asset—and why? To make enormous profits for themselves. Numerous examples have been described recently, and some incidents have also shown that those being researched, in recent years, were quite indifferent about the researcher's ethnic origins. Arguments that research and recording are for the ultimate good of future generations, no matter who does them, may or may not be heard sympathetically. In addition, Sepik people, like others anywhere, may simply change their minds about what they want (e.g., Bowden 1985, Kaufmann 1984b).

Can we in spite of this make some sort of contribution to Papua New Guinea by studying Sepik history? If it comes to that, what is the use of history, or rather historiography? There have been several grand designs, cyclic theories which purport to show that history has patterns the meaning of which is, say, "Nations which do not learn from the errors of the past are bound to repeat them" or that inevitable political processes will ultimately validate a particular set of social theories. The latter used to include evolutionary schemes which demonstrated national destiny. English children used to be taught a version of English history designed to explain how the parliamentary system came about, the formation of the United Kingdom, the Kingdom's acquisition of an empire which—this was before 1939—was being modulated into a worldwide benevolent commonwealth. It was an elegant artifact, full of powerful iconic figures of big men, a tool explaining the world in which many of my generation expected to find duties and employment. No doubt the educators of other nations used similar tools.

Does Papua New Guinea want to create something of this kind in the interests of national unity? The technical problems seem to be vast; Bragge's and Wassmann's work gives us some insight into their dimensions and the further problems of reconstructing a national history. Westerners have easy models—waves of migrations, invading forces, which may be applicable to the Sepik only in a rather inaccurate sense if at all. When one considers the sheer number of communities in the Sepık Provinces, each with its own history, it begins to seem unlikely that a full record of them will ever be made. If it were, it is hard to tell how it could ever be handled on conventional Western lines without falsification. It may be necessary for Papua New Guineans to invent a new model—a fascinating prospect.

The question may be one which applies to further realms of knowledge. Perhaps the ultimate contribution of research and researchers in Western modes will be not so much a dogma or a regimen but the exemplification of alternative ways of investigation and comprehension. This is perhaps a question of stance rather than program, a willingness to resign the assumed hegemony of Western thinking, if it seems inappropriate to a given situation, without abandoning its empirical foundation.

Meanwhile we should not forget that the Sepik cultures, or what remains of their integrity, may have remarkable endurance and stamina but are nonetheless desperately fragile. There is no escaping the fact that in spite of all advances the tasks of research are still urgent, if anything more than ever. Severe disruptions of the ecosystem— the plague of *Salvinia molesta* gives a hint of their potential—or the introduction, however inadvertent, of new strains of disease and the exigencies of industrial development could sweep away what still exists in short order.

For the many who sense that the cultures of the Sepik Provinces represent a rare human achievement, this can only be a tragedy, even if the inevitable tragedy of all human history—all the more reason to record while we can as much as we are able of the achievements of the ancestors for the sake of their descendants.

Introduction

Nancy Lutkehaus

This volume's title and organization reflect the editors' belief that its contribution to Papua New Guineans and to Melanesian studies is the description and analysis of the Sepik region's rich cultural heritage. By "cultural heritage," in this case, we mean first of all history—prehistory, oral history, cultural history, and colonial and postcolonial history. Knowledge of past people, places, and events can be useful in understanding and directing the development of the future. "Cultural heritage," however, also means living and past cultural and social traditions—the rituals, beliefs, values, customs, and cultural institutions (systems of land tenure, forms of political leadership, marriage, and exchange) characteristic of particular Sepik societies. Finally, there is the rich legacy of material and nonmaterial culture traditionally identified in the West as "the arts." Best-known, of course, are the visual arts of the Sepik—the magnificent carved masks and ancestral figures, shields, bark paintings, netbags, and pottery—examples of which are found in museum collections and galleries throughout Europe, Australia, and the United States. Less well-known to outsiders but no less appreciated by those familiar with them are the stately men's houses, architectural masterpieces characteristic of much of the Sepik region, and the design motifs and symbols associated with them. The verbal arts of political oratory, song, magic, myth, and metaphor—important sources of power and persuasion in Sepik societies—and the more ephemeral arts of dance and music ought not to be forgotten in considering the region's repertoire of artistic creations.

The volume begins with a section on history—"Concepts of the Past"—containing ethnohistorical accounts of events both of the period of recorded history and of the mythological past. While some papers attempt to correlate information in oral accounts with that from historical documents, the overall focus is on Sepik constructions of the past.

The Sepik region is characterized by widespread cultural interconnections both among indigenous groups and between these groups and outsiders. The papers in the next section—"Intercultural Connections"—describe links of widely varying nature, historical depth, and geographic scope and include discussion of language and systems of cultural meaning.

The most dramatic intercultural connections, in terms of their long-term social and cultural effects and depths of impact, have been those between Sepik peoples and various representatives of the West. The papers in the section "Impact of the West" describe different dimensions of this experience including, among others, the involvement of missionaries and colonial and postcolonial government administrators, the development of cash-cropping, and the effects of tourism.

The next five sections cover a broad range of social and cultural topics. "Social Relations and Authority" focuses on the analysis of traditional and new forms of Sepik leadership. It also presents descriptions of often overlooked aspects of social interaction such as gestures that express amity and reinforce social cohesion. "Person and Socialization" describes some of the culturally specific ways in which individuals learn to become particular adult members of their society, the nature of childhood in Sepik societies, different concepts of the person associated with different domains of social life, and the importance of adolescent experience in shaping an adult's world view and sense of cultural identity. Again focusing on the individual, the papers in the next section, "Engendering Gender," explore the social and cultural dimensions of being male or female in a number of Sepik societies. The section "Sickness and Health" encompasses a wide range of issues having to do with both physical and psychological phenomena. Sorcery figures prominently in several of the papers, as do the interface between indigenous medical practices and Western medicine and cultural attitudes toward food and nutrition. The section "Visual and Aural Arts" includes papers that deal with either geographic areas or topics that have previously received little or no attention. The new information they present on indigenous architecture and music, in particular, is an important addition to the existing corpus of data on other traditional arts in the Sepik.

The final section, "Conveying the Past," includes discussion of various projects and government proposals aimed at protecting objects and preserving knowledge about traditional Sepik crafts and skills. Preservation, however, is not the final goal; ultimately, the aim is to disseminate information to be used in new and creative ways and to foster an interest in and appreciation of the Sepik's cultural heritage both within and beyond Papua New Guinea. The volume concludes with Andrew Strathern's comparison of aspects of the history and ethnography of the Sepik and of the New Guinea highlands and Papua New Guinea at large. Strathern points to the need for more comprehensive historical and contemporary ethnographic data from the many cultures of the region as the basis for study of present and future change.

The large number of contributors and the sheer mass of the new information presented reflect the growth in the corpus of ethnographic data about Sepik societies over the past twenty-five years. Of the more than fifty contributors, most are sociocultural anthropologists, but there are also archaeologists, art historians, geographers, political scientists, and both former and present government officials among them. Although they were given considerable freedom in their choice of subject matter, some consensus on important issues and themes can be detected. Among these are a focus on some of the common Sepik cultural traits identified by Mead (1938), who noted that the region was characterized by a diversity based on a self-conscious diffusion of nonmaterial cultural elements, such as secret names and forms of magic, and local variations on common cultural themes, such as initiation rituals, sorcery, and masks and masked-dancer performances (which gives rise to speculation as to the significance of "place" and "voice" in the development of ethnography and anthropological discourse [see Appadurai 1988]). As Strathern notes, some new generalizations about the region have also emerged, such as that power in the Sepik is vested not only in control of material objects—shells, boars' tasks, etc.—but in control over esoteric knowledge as well.

Other topics, such as trade and exchange, male initiation rituals, and the nature of leadership in stateless egalitarian societies, are significant throughout Melanesia. Still others reflect the theoretical and analytic perspectives of current interest within sociocultural anthropology in general. One such is reflexivity on the part of anthropologists concerning the role they play—as individuals and as representatives of Western society—in the cultural scenarios they investigate. Another is notions of personhood in different cultures. Yet another is the culture of colonialism, the aim being not only to look at Westerners' reasons for going to "savage frontiers" or their impact on indigenous cultures but to examine the social structure and symbolic behavior of the colonial cultures themselves. Finally, there is a focus on the psychosocial effects of rapid or far-reaching social change. Questions concerning the emotional salience of cultural authenticity or the nature of cultural identity in situations of extreme social change bear directly on issues of importance both to the Sepik and to Papua New Guinea as a whole.

The East and West Sepik are just two of the country's nineteen provinces. We hope that the ethnographic and historical information about them that is presented in this collection will further Father Dambui's goal of minimizing the sense of difference among peoples and provinces. Insight into the cultural and historical similarities among societies and the experiences of individuals may help to foster an understanding that Papua New Guineans from all parts of the nation share elements of a common history and cultural ancestry. It may also contribute to the growing Pan-Pacific nationalism that aims to unite Pacific Islanders of all nations through a sense of a Pacific cultural identity in efforts to deal with problems. The wonderfully rich and creative cultural heritage of the Sepik is not just of and for Sepik peoples alone. It belongs to the contemporary nation of Papua New Guinea and to all Pacific peoples.

Sepik Heritage

Part One
Concepts of the Past

Introduction

Meinhard Schuster

As we know from history and observe in the present, nations need more to exist than some kind of political organization and an adequate socioeconomic base; they need an idea of their distinctiveness from their neighbors. This idea, closely related to what is called "national identity," may make use of linguistic or geographic boundaries, but, as the case of Switzerland shows, these are often insufficient to distinguish a political body. National identity is more a diachronic than a synchronic category. In most cases it refers to the values of a common past; in others it invokes an ideal future itself designed in relation to the past or the present. Papua New Guinea, well on its way toward an understanding of its identity as a modern nation on the Melanesian model, is no exception to the rule of the dominance of history in the shaping of identity, whether individual, local or regional, or national. It is understandable, therefore, that history has been given broad attention in this symposium, as is apparent not only in the papers of this section (devoted not so much to historical data as to the different ways of conceptualizing the world and the intellectual tools available for the cultural construction of history) but also in the abundance of historical references in the papers elsewhere in this volume.

"History," of course, is not restricted to the linear Western model based on chronology and, for the most part, written documents but includes other modes of structuring the past that are considered equally valid and valuable even though they may tell truths about the past and its relation to the present other than those that we in the West are used to. This understanding is reflected in the following papers, all concerned with local or regional ways of constructing history. Particular though they may be, along with a multitude of other such studies they constitute the elements of a comprehensive picture of Papua New Guinea's past.

On the basis of his broad experience in settling land disputes as assistant district commissioner at Ambunti and numerous detailed versions of migration histories collected from the villages involved, Lawrence Bragge studies the repeated migrations up the Sepik of people from Japandai, the westernmost Nyaula village, that finally resulted in the settlement of the Japandai outlier Brugnowi between 1924 and 1927. Combining different ways of recording the past, he presents the sequence of major events with regard to land tenure, settlement, and conflict up- and downriver from Ambunti between about 1830 and 1973.

Also concerned with migrations recorded by the Nyaula, the Western Iatmul of the Middle Sepik, Jürg Wassmann concentrates on the ancient wanderings of the mythical founding clan and village ancestors from their general place of origin (near Gaikorobi) into the areas of their present settlement. He separates these "mental" migrations from actual historical ones (of, at maximum, the last two hundred years) but also points to their common core in spatial terms. The ancient movements are considered to legitimize present-day land claims, and from a broader perspective they constitute the main instrument for articulating the past, forming a spatiotemporal grid that is the basis of a system of interlinkages also expressed through names, songs, and a special form of knotted cord.

The use of spatial elements and the sequence of generations to construct time and history is also central to Gisela Schuster's and my papers on the historical thinking of the Aibom, on the southern border of the Central Iatmul. After discussing the technical prerequisites for our Western chronology-based history, which is readily demonstrated to be subject to reductive selection, varying emphases, and changing interpretations of events, we show that the conception of the past and its relation to the present in the Aibom's nonchronological patterning of history is characterized by a strong tendency to classify supposedly earlier and later events, as well as events with the same type of action occurring on different levels, as not only equivalent but identical. History, according to the Aibom, is predominantly iterative and confirmative, and order in time is given, if at all, as a sequence of localities associated with the events and persons or other beings involved. Combined with genealogical knowledge that usually covers the last eight generations, this sequence makes it possible—in spite of difficulties arising from name-giving and adoption customs—to outline a linear account of this period with emphasis on movement to and from former settlements on the Aibom hill.

Beginning with an eyewitness account by a Neligum (Samukundi Abelam) man of the violent recruiting practices in the Sepik of a German recruiter, Richard Scaglion examines the general structure of Abelam historical narratives. He points particularly to the shortening of the time between major events, the general vagueness of statements about the length of time periods, and the episodic view of history, which is place-oriented rather than time-oriented. Despite these limitations, this autobiographical text, which refers to relatively recent historical events, can be related to Western-type data of the same time to establish a coherent picture of the period of first contact.

Also speaking about history since the white man came, Sasha Josephides reports that the Boroi, who live east of the mouth of the Ramu River in two older and two newer settlements, divide the past into two sharply opposed periods: the now abolished bad old days, a time prior to and including about five decades of Catholic missionary efforts, and the good modern period of "business," the years since 1954, when Seventh-Day Adventist missionaries began to dominate village life. Here history also finds a spatial expression.

According to Josephides, the Boroi "put their past in the old village" (Bak)—where, in contrast to the situation in the modern coastal places, traditional ritual is still much practiced—and keep it alive there.

In summary, the papers in this section seem to show that the later part of the past up to the present is mainly arranged in a linear order based on the memory of one's own life, on the sequence of generations before those of the living, and on events connected with the coming of the Europeans—these latter events often being located on a Western chronological scale. Biography and genealogy appear to be the only traditional linear ways to overcome the year as the maximal unit of time. Nevertheless, the past two hundred or so years are characterized by locally specific modes of structuring or accentuating time. These are sometimes obvious extensions of the kind of conceptualization that organizes the more distant times and, therefore, integrates the two dimensions of the past into a coherent whole. Concepts of the distant past, however, are difficult to characterize in general terms. These can only be properly analyzed as components of local linguistically based cognitive systems of the universe, in particular, of the categories of time and space, and it is the latter, as the locus of events, that apparently plays the dominant role.

1/ Aspects of the Aibom Concept of History

Meinhard Schuster

This paper aims to describe the way in which the people of Aibom, a Iatmul village south of the Middle Sepik, conceive of their past. It is based on personal experience during four periods of fieldwork on various themes in the Sepik basin (1961, 1965–67, 1972–73, and again later in 1973) that included several stays in Aibom. Since 1965, I have worked together with my wife, Gisela Schuster; I am most grateful for her critical comments, now integrated into this paper, on the basis of her own broad knowledge and thoughtful evaluation of Aibom historical data.

The Aibom concept of history—as we may call the past in its structured form—cannot simply be described as such; the English terms which need to be used for this purpose inevitably have European connotations. Also, having been brought up in Europe I have no choice but to start with my own Western notions about history and then try to replace them with Middle Sepik ones as far as I have become acquainted with them. Therefore, it seems appropriate to begin—with Aibom in mind—with a critical examination of the Western idea of history to the extent that may be useful in explaining the contrasting picture of history in traditional Aibom.

There is, however, a more important reason for contrasting the two concepts of history. Aibom is no longer a world of its own; it is now a village of the East Sepik Province of Papua New Guinea. Tok Pisin has been added to its local language as a widely used means of communication, and English is known by more and more of its inhabitants. The modern nation is structured politically on the Western model, and it has a Western-style university which includes the academic study of history in terms of Western concepts and methods. Therefore, the official picture of national history cannot but be of the Western type, with a prehistoric stratum, a period of early contact and discovery, a colonial period including the two World Wars, and the era of independence. On the other hand, there is a rural, village, Melanesian type of historical thinking which does not, and

should not, perish with the appearance of these modern institutions and modes of handling the past. This kind of history is not a lesser alternative, though it may prove the weaker one in confrontation with the other under modern conditions and with regard to modern interests. Traditional ways of thought about the past are basically of another order insofar as they meet human needs other than the Western ones.

In the present situation we may therefore expect that traditional concepts will remain alive for a time in a certain tension with the kind of history taught in the schools but will finally be forced either to be integrated into this modern history or to be classified as "mythology" or "folklore," as has happened in other parts of the world. Since Papua New Guinea has declared its aim to preserve its Melanesian heritage, it seems suitable to devote some attention to a particular aspect of this heritage which may in its general lines be representative for other Papua New Guinean villages.

I shall refrain, therefore, from using either the chronological data on the Middle Sepik recorded since the early German expeditions, the indications given by prehistory (still very few in this region), or the results of linguistic analysis and comparison. I shall, however, include a kind of statement that has definite historical value in Aibom, namely, the mythical. In doing so I am trying to approach more directly the picture of history as Aibom people seem to have it, the data they furnish, and the use they make of their kind of knowledge of the past. In general, it seems advisable not to attempt to connect their history piece by piece with our chronological system but to reconstruct their system as fully as possible before approaching the difficult task of correlating the two, i.e., to write "history from within," though necessarily with our own intellectual tools, before comparing it with the "history from outside" imported by Western science. The following pages, directed more to the formal aspects of the Aibom concept of history than to the wealth of data organized by it, can only represent the first steps in this direction.

The Process of Tradition

Every human society has its history. Though the size of the society and its ways of conducting research on history or of preserving historical knowledge have to be taken into account, there is no minimum size or technical level for the existence of history. A Sepik village with a few hundred inhabitants, then, can just as well have history as a European nation. But is it the same kind of history?

In order to answer this question, we have to start from a wider base, for apparently we have to distinguish in principle—and not forget to do so in practice—between two meanings of the word "history." First, there is the full account of the major and minor events within such a society or associated with it from outside during the whole past of the society or its parts—a practically unlimited mass of material that can scarcely be conceived of, let alone handled. Secondly, there is the particular selection of data out of this stream of life through hundreds and thousands of years that we make use of in constructing a sequence of interrelated events. The reasons for this selection are various, but perhaps three major ones may be pointed out.

In all phases of known history, a contemporaneous selection was already at work, deciding which of the events of the time were worth commemorating and giving them—ideally—a durable shape by structuring a formless memory as narrative, by writing it down, by erecting some kind of monument, etc. Thus not only technical skills, such as the presence or absence of writing or stoneworking, but also cultural values define the contents and limits of what we can hope to know afterwards.

This already reduced corpus of data, while generally preserved by memorization, ritual repetition, or its sheer material existence, is reduced further by material destruction, partial loss of memory, reinterpretation or adaptation, errors in transcription and translation, etc. In addition, in this second phase as well, the interests of the period are highly influential: no small part of the material and intellectual heritage is—sometimes literally—discarded as useless or unwelcome under the new circumstances.

With the rest, then, modern research tries by a variety of methods to reconstruct history by linking the fragments together in a way that makes sense according to modern judgment—guided, of course, by the nature of these remains themselves but also by the more general scientific and, of course, political conditions under which such research takes place. This is obvious if we remember, for example, that history for a long time concentrated upon the political dimension of the past: the rise and fall of nations and empires, the sequence of rulers and their dynasties, the varieties of political systems, wars and the peace treaties ending them but leading to new wars, etc. Now the picture has, to a certain degree, changed, and new realms of past human existence—everyday life, social stratification, economic conditions—have reached the level of academic historical interest. History has, one might say, come to include an ethnographic perspective; having formerly looked at events mainly "from above," it now looks at them also "from below." More important, in retrospect, is that such major fields of human life had to wait so long before they were accepted within the range of professional historical interests; this indicates that the earlier pictures given by historians, despite their claim to be comprehensive with regard to the past, have obviously been far from it. The existing store of documents, diminished as it may be, apparently contains sufficient data to support new approaches to the past, and we may safely predict that still other approaches will follow.

This abbreviated survey is intended to show that history—understood as scientifically organized knowledge of the past, not as the past itself—cannot, given the nature of its documents and the way in which they are used, offer more than a picture of the past in the form of a system of traits selected as important first by contemporaneous standards, secondly by the interests of those who have preserved them, and thirdly by the changing focus of research. Thus history is subject to continuous cultural evaluation and reevaluation throughout the three main stages of its formation sketched above. It mirrors basic cultural values and central cultural questions, and there is no such thing as an objective assembly of historical data. The known history of a society as projected against the background of its full but unknown former life is a rather arbitrary selection of data, even in regions with a long documenting tradition such as Europe. History is not the result of a more or less self-developing research process that leads us—through the discovery of more and more old facts and their assignment to their proper places—to an ever better understanding of the past; the most we can achieve is a "concept," "picture," or "image" of history. This unsatisfactory situation is not due to the lack of sources or of research but reflects a basic condition which can never be overcome.

Turning to the question whether this three-stage reduction process occurs in a cultural tradition without written records and without a wide range of durable documents of other kinds, like that of Aibom, I offer the following general observations: First, there is no doubt that, here too, only a highly selected part of all the events happening is considered important enough to be recorded in a formalized (or other durable) way for the next generation. Secondly, however, in a cultural tradition which seems to have been characterized by a less rapid sequence of major changes, the pressure on oral tradition—once texts are established as such—to adapt to new conditions by being reinterpreted and therefore changed seems less than in areas where cultural (or political) breaks succeed each other at shorter intervals. This increases the possibility that even rather old oral traditions will be preserved intact. Regarding the third stage, i.e., the present-day evaluation of the—mostly oral—heritage of early times, it is quite obvious again that different needs (for instance, those created by broader and farther-reaching contacts or by new types of conflict) will lead to different ways of handling the corpus of historical data as a whole or of stressing parts of it considered to be of particular importance for a modern problem.

We may conclude, therefore, that the greater cultural stability during the phase in which a certain volume of established knowledge of the past is handed down from generation to generation serves, to a certain degree, as a counterweight to the absence of documenting techniques such as writing and that, mutatis mutandis, the basic attitudes toward the history of one's own society can be considered, with regard to the questions of tradition discussed so far, basically the same across cultures. In literate as well as in nonliterate cultures, the resulting picture of history is strongly determined not primarily by an abstract need to be as complete and balanced as possible but by a preference for a certain set of aspects dictated by one's own cultural conditions both in former periods and in the present.

Coming back, now, to our initial question whether we are dealing with the same kind of history in a Western nation and in a traditional Middle Sepik village, we must also be aware of the differences. In examining them we shall again, as

before, argue not about the quantities of recorded data but about what we do with them. For the same reason, we shall leave aside the apparent inequality between history on the village level and that on the nation level and shall not—though it might be interesting—introduce the Western village as the other side of the comparison. The justification for this omission lies in the fact that the Western picture of history as it is transmitted through education and as it forms the basis of public opinion and debate takes the nation—or its perhaps smaller antecedents—as its conceptual unit, and villages are always seen and treated as parts of this larger social entity. The nation, not the village, provides the framework for Western history, and it may be doubted—given the very early date of social stratification of the feudal type in Western political organization, leading to the early formation of regional sovereignties—that the village ever served this purpose. But in the traditional Middle Sepik world the village, with its proud insistence upon autonomy, provided this framework: there was no political or other authority above this local unit, which was also the answer to the question where an individual came from.

This equivalence—for our problem of historical thinking—of the Western nation and the Sepik village also includes, on both sides, a perception of the outside world as being organized on the same level: other nations here, other villages there. These surrounding foreign units are integrated into the picture of history mainly by referring either to the more permanent relations between them and one's own social unit (such as trade or political alliance) or to individual, perhaps repeated, actions in both directions (such as attacks), or as places of one's own origins (i.e., starting points of migrations or emigrations), but very rarely with a major interest in the foreign history in its own right, at least not on the popular, nonscientific plane.

Western Chronological History

Let us discuss, then, necessarily in an abbreviated and generalized way, and without fully entering into man's concepts of time and history, some conditions of Western history insofar as they seem relevant to our approach to Aibom history, "history" now being understood as referring to historical research as well as to the picture resulting from it. The basic and dominant instrument of this history is, of course, the chronological scale, and I shall consider it with regard to the technical suppositions it is built upon and to its effects upon the concept of history as a whole.

First of all, there is the construct of a linear, endless numerical progression (in German, *Zahlenreihe*) in which each successive number is attained from the preceding one by the same logical step; this concept perhaps has its roots, in the ancient Near East, in astronomical contexts but was, as a general counting instrument, not confined to these purposes.

Secondly, chronology calls for a conceptualization of time which is quite opposite to what everyday and life-long experience might suggest: namely, that it is not an uninterrupted flow without beginning and end but can be divided into parts of equal length and is to be understood as a chain of units which are formally identical but may be associated with different contents.

Time, then, is not just another expression for continuity; actually, our own word "time" is, on the contrary, derived—via the Latin *tempus*—from the Greek verb (first person singular) *temno* (τέμνω), "to cut off, to divide, to limit" (Sticker 1958). But apparently the division of time represented by the ubiquitous sequence of day and night was not sufficient for a chronology, perhaps mainly for practical reasons if we consider the already completely unmanageable number of days (or nights) in a normal human lifetime. Larger units such as months, years, or groups of years had to be conceived of on the basis of seasonal and astronomical observations, and their proper lengths had to be defined in a rather precise way.

Thirdly, these abstract devices had to be combined in order to count time-units in an endless sequence with ever increasing numbers. But two logical questions still needed to be answered: when to start and how to handle the possibilities of repetition—whether to allow them only within the main time-unit (having the same month appear again in the next year) or to count these time-units themselves up to a fixed number (such as fifty-two) and then start again. The two questions do not condition each other but do tend to be connected: linear systems must have a starting point, cyclical systems—those with the second kind of repetition mentioned—may have one. In practice they will if there is a tendency to reach linearity on the next level by counting the cycles.

Now, Western chronology, as used habitually by historians, is of the linear kind; its starting point, however, was not—and could not be—derived from logical-calendrical operations of the

kind described but was established by a religious event, technically similar, though with different contents, to other ancient models such as the Roman one, counting *ab urbe condita*, since the (mythical?) date of the founding of Rome.

This means, for our context, that Western chronology represents the combination of a mathematical concept, a specific interpretation of time, and a central religious event; this last element may well be classified with events of comparable weight in other religions, represented prominently in their sacred texts, i.e., their myths, but if the other two indispensable constituents of chronology are lacking, such events will not become the pivot of history in a chronological sense. In addition, it is difficult to imagine how such a chronology could work without any kind of writing or pictographic technique, but this would not necessarily be impossible.

Apparently, as is shown by other calendar systems in human history, this particular chronological model is far from being the only one possible. Western chronology is not "absolute," as its year numbers are, almost paradoxically, qualified in contrast to other events being arranged only "relatively" as "earlier" and "later," and it is not the only right or true or even natural instrument for orientation in time that it is generally, often naïvely, taken to be. On the contrary, Western chronology is basically "relative" in its dependence on the highly specialized principles and assumptions just mentioned. It represents one arbitrary way to approach the past, its interpretation and structuring, but it has proved a very powerful one, at least in the Western world, and is now spreading over the rest of the world along with Western culture in general.

In this strong position, Western chronology is also responsible for two other generally accepted ideas about time that are of particular interest in relation to the Aibom attitude toward time: first, that time is irreversible and that, with each new year gone by, we are farther from the mentioned starting point or from even an earlier point which is usually defined negatively, by its position before zero, or from any event in the past assigned to a certain year; and secondly, that there are distances between two points on the time scale measurable by the number of time units in between—distances which can never be eliminated and need to be filled with events, or persons representing events, in order to obtain a satisfying picture of the past. The so-called dark ages between the fall of the Roman empire and the beginning of Merovingian rule are an example of such an uncomfortable gap in European history and illustrate at the same time the degree to which chronology has assumed dominance over content.

This system of chronology has in the course of time developed into not only the backbone of the Western concept of history—which can surely not be imagined to exist without counting the years—but also, to a considerable degree, its raison d'être. When a thing happened has become a basic question, and associating a relic from the past with the most probable date for its production according to our chronology is considered, if not the aim, a necessary first step in the research process. This is not, of course, to underestimate other major aims of historical research that are well known and therefore need not be listed here.

What I want to stress is that history in the Western scientific world is conceptualized mainly in its temporal dimension, as a sequence of related events along a strong guiding line consisting of rather small time-units arranged in a linear order; this guiding line, the Christian chronology, is considered the only correct one and sufficient and appropriate for the whole world in the present, the past, and the future—as is shown, for example, by the considerable efforts made to correlate other calendars such as the ancient Mesoamerican ones with our own. This makes perfect sense as long as the relations between the events arranged in this order are obvious—as they may be in a limited region or within a group of nations continuously acting or reacting upon one another—or can at least be shown to be highly probable and to represent a meaningful aim of research; but things become meaningless when isolated events from different continents and distant times are assembled in the same way on the same scale. This rather absurd development—providing answers to such questions as "What was happening in Caesar's time in New Zealand?"—is, nevertheless, only the logical extreme of a concept of history dominated by the chronological perspective and therefore shows with particular transparency its limitations and its principal fallacy.

This notion of the linearity of history did not, however, arise immediately and simultaneously with interest in the events of former times. The word "history" (see Rupp and Köhler 1951) is derived—again, via a Latin connecting link—from Greek *historeo* (ἱστορέω), meaning originally "to know something by one's own experience" and then the activities necessary for obtaining such knowledge; consequently, Greek *historia* (ἱστορία) came to designate such knowledge, eventually with connotations of what we today call "science" in its broad sense and, within the sciences, of history as forming logically a part of what can be known. But Greek *historia* always included also the meaning of "narrative." *Historia* in classical Latin not only preserved but even enlarged this wide variety of meanings, which was retained through late (= Medieval) Latin times (though paralleled by other words such as *chronica, gesta,* or *annales* to express the specific meaning of our "history") into the early stages of the Romance languages.

On the whole, we can observe a process which started with "histories" in the form and with the content of what we might call today "stories," told mostly with regard to some high-ranking, heroic personality, and ended by combining these originally unconnected narratives of various kinds into a single "history"—of course, with the help of the concept of a chronological order; this was not difficult to establish in the Christian Middle Ages, when events were preferably determined by their general position in the Christian framework, including their distance from the birth of Christ. History was, as we may phrase it, "temporalized" as it was unified.

But the closeness of the English terms "history" and "story" and, to give another example, the continuing double use of the German *Geschichte* with exactly these two meanings show that the range of contents of the Tok Pisin word *stori,* as it is used in modern contexts in the Sepik, is not at all foreign to Western historical thinking but only restricted and overshadowed there by a strong tendency toward chronological unilinearity.

This short sketch of some aspects of the Western concept of history and its development has also shown that we must—for logical reasons as well as with regard to the comparison with other cultures—refine our original opposition of the past as such and our picture of it and distinguish three categories which are relevant for the whole range of "history" and "histories" and tend to be mixed in general use.

First, there is a "past" in the principal meaning of the universe of events before the present; as this past remains inconceivable, the "past" tends to be understood as the corpus of what we know—or may know—of former times. In both meanings, the "past" has no structure of its own.

Secondly, there is "time" as a category of orientation on the basis of everyday experience, also having no structure but open to structuring in quite a number of ways, as the variety of time-organizing and time-measuring systems in human history shows (Sticker 1958). Time is only in a very general way connected with the category of the past—i.e., by being used, if at all verbalized directly, to designate the distance between the present and an event that has occurred or that will occur; all more precise qualities of "time," including in particular its relation to other categories of thinking, remain to be defined for each cultural system.

Thirdly, there is "history" as the organized way in which cultures conceive their past. This may be done by heavy use of a system of structured time such as Western chronology or in some other way. Such an alternative can be studied in Aibom.

Aibom Nonchronological History

Aibom has no chronology, but it has a known past which is fully entitled to be classified as history; it is not an unstructured mass of isolated, fortuitous data in the form of random stories and incoherent statements telling something about what happened here and there in former times but applies several principles of organization.

One of these can be recognized in the clear tendency to arrange events in groups which either take the form of sequences or are conceived as layers, perhaps representing sequences themselves; both aggregates include and are the expression of the basic order of an "earlier" and "later" which is in Aibom—as generally in the Iatmul region—the equivalent, on a generalized temporal level, of the gradation between a first-born and a second (or later) son. This relation is felt to be a very important one and constitutes, in the form of a pair of events, the minimal unit of any temporal order—the more so as it reflects, additionally, not only the strong dualistic tendency immanent in Aibom (and general Iatmul) in all aspects of thinking but also the primeval mother-son relation of the *nyame* and *nyaui* moieties.

Two other organizing principles may be mentioned. First, Aibom history, like Western history, is "linear" insofar as its lines end up in the present or are projected backward from the present. At the same time, however, it can be described as "iterative" in two respects. One is demonstrated, for example, by the ceremonial reenactment of events which are said to have happened long ago but are also conceived by those involved to be

happening right now—not as mere duplication or repetition but as the same action with its full intellectual content and intensity. In this well-known case of the ceremonial evocation of *illud tempus*, with its also well-known difficulties for our understanding, which are not at all overcome by our usual recourse to the concept of a "symbolic" performance, the linear distance between the former event and the present one is reduced to zero, contracted into one point on the hypothetical time-scale: history may be concentrated in the extreme, but this does not make it nonexistent. The other iterative process can be seen in the return of the same "motif," the same type of action (not the action itself), at various points in the past; though the events are described as different, a tendency toward their equation can be clearly observed.

Secondly, Aibom history concedes a broad parallelism in that the necessity to arrange different events in a chain of "earlier" and "later," the later always being the earlier of the next pair, is not strongly felt. This is at least the public, exoteric view; on the esoteric level, however (which in Aibom and the Iatmul region in general means within mythology), such parallelism may be suspended by the superior knowledge of leading wise men who are aware of the principal identity of central persons called by different names or described elsewhere as being different or of important events referred to in various ways in different traditions (what we may sometimes classify as "versions" [Stanek 1983]). If we were to try to draw a sketch of the past in the form of a rectangular system with one dimension symbolizing the course of time and the other the space for contemporaneous (or parallel) actions, then the processes described above could be conceived as two types of contraction: a "longitudinal" one in the case of the iterations and a "transversal" one in the case of different events' being identified as the same at another conceptual level.

These two processes can also be seen at work where a kind of stratification, as mentioned above, has taken place. Apparently the dividing horizons between these strata of events are always kept permeable, and the tendency is strong not to accentuate the separating element contained in such an order but to combine, or even integrate, the strata by conceiving them as constituents of one comprehensive system, a homogeneous whole.

In all these cases, however, the positions at both ends of the described range, representing two possibilities of conception, always remain discernible to the Aibom mind: the events of the past can be understood either as following one another or, in their contracted form, as being the same. The two types of conception are, with regard to precisely the same events, not only coexistent but equally "true"—comparable, perhaps, to a certain degree, to the picture of social organization which the village of Aibom offers: to be at the same time a single local unit, proud of its identity as "Aibom," and a cluster of clans of various origins and with vivid claims of autonomy as well.

This intellectual elasticity—which is not chaos—represents a particular dynamic aspect of the Aibom attitude toward the data of the past; together with their permeation by truths from the level which we separate from history as being mythology and therefore, at best, only partly historical, it is primarily responsible for the difficulties which European observers—trained to work with one-level events at fixed, never reappearing points of time—confront in the study of Aibom historical thinking.

For Aibom people, however, this mobility—though not arbitrary—offers the chance to neutralize contradictions within certain limits; but we must not forget that there is a strong tendency in Aibom thinking to integrate seemingly incompatible statements so as to form one truth. This can be achieved by adaptation or reinterpretation of traditional knowledge—as is impressively shown by the integration of a white younger brother into the two-brothers myth of the well-known Melanesian type in order to explain the obvious existence of white people and the hopeful question whether we white people did not have the same story, i.e., history, aimed at demonstrating its truth. This adaptation was, of course, based on the assumption that the younger brother had always been white but people telling this history had not realized it or had forgotten about it. In Aibom eyes, myths, including, of course, their historical dimension, contain the truth, and there can be only one truth.

In examining these structural features of Aibom historical thinking and their ways of interacting with or permeating one another in two of the major areas of Aibom history, we have to keep in mind a circumstance which separates Aibom from other Iatmul villages of the Middle Sepik, namely, the change of its identity in a particular period not very long ago; this break in continuity, which prevents Aibom history from showing the long-range grandeur known from other Iatmul places (Wassmann 1982), may also have provided

a reason for the attention of the present Aibom people to what I have called stratification, and it makes it understandable that Aibom identity is constituted less by long genealogical lines or migration records than by a local element: the hill.

The Two Aiboms

Aibom history consists of two layers: an older, non-Iatmul one and a younger Iatmul one. This assumption is generally accepted historical knowledge at least among the older people. The "Iatmulization" that took place, according to Aibom informants, some generations ago was not a single event of the hostile type which is so often referred to in Middle Sepik histories but a continuous process of intermarrying, mainly of Aibom men with Iatmul women (but also vice versa, with a double effect upon Aibom insofar as Iatmul men who married Aibom women—perhaps among other wives—would live temporarily or permanently in Aibom and leave their children there). This can be traced through the origin histories of various clans. On the whole, the usual phrasing, telescoping history and at the same time reflecting the strong attachment of a male to his mother prefigured by the basic nyame-nyaui relation mentioned above, is "We speak the language of our mothers." As these mothers (and the less prominent outside fathers) are said to have come mainly from Malingei,[1] the nearest Iatmul village a few canoe hours north of Aibom and just south of Palimbei (Parambei), the language spoken in Aibom came to be Central Iatmul—the vernacular of the villages which, like Malingei, are according to mutual traditions descended from Palimbei.

But this ancestral sequence Palimbei-Malingei-Aibom is crossed by a second association which links Malingei with Soatmeli (Suapmeri), one of the first generation of Iatmul villages on the Sepik, situated northwest of Malingei on the south bank of the river. Whereas this old Soatmeli is said to have contributed, with emigrants after its destruction, to the population of Malingei, the present-day village of Soatmeli—situated not far upriver from the old settlement, with its remarkable megalithic remains—was refounded, in turn, two or three generations ago by Malingei people (see Schuster 1973). Aibom considers itself primarily connected with Malingei and Soatmeli and classes Palimbei, like Chambri, on the hostile side. The relations between Aibom and Soatmeli, though (or because?) they are not immediate neighbors, are particularly close. In Soatmeli oral records they are said to date back to the times of old Soatmeli; for example, the stones on the old village site are said to have been transported by Aibom people from the Aibom hill to the bank of the Sepik, where there were no such stones, and old Soatmeli is said to have made gifts in return. We may conclude from these texts that Aibom people are considered to have already been living on the Aibom hill during the—very early—active period of old Soatmeli.

This leads us to the older stratum of Aibom history. In contrast to the more recent relations between these villages, traceable through intermarriage and other kinds of contact such as joint ceremonies in Malingei or Soatmeli, the preceding phase of Aibom's past is, on the whole, much less clear, at least on the basis of what is known about it in present-day Aibom.

First of all, people say that pre-Iatmul Aibom spoke a language similar to Chambri; some clans tell of their former close connections with Wombun, the northeasternmost part of the three-part village of Chambri (see, e.g., Gewertz 1983) and therefore next to Aibom, by tracing their genealogies back to a Chambri man or by referring to other elements common to Aibom, Chambri, and even the wider southern region. Detailed linguistic analysis may show that such an ancient relationship existed; at the moment, before ancient texts of both places have been thoroughly compared, it can only be stated that according to Aibom information this former language died out in Aibom quite a while ago and that the Aibom people of today do not understand present-day Chambri. But on the other side, we observed on one occasion, serving as a kind of test, that a text which was sung by some Aibom men in Chambri and classified by them as being "old Aibom" was apparently partially understood by Chambri people present.

In any case, this Chambri connection is only one of quite a number of southern relations of Aibom or, more precisely, of parts of Aibom in the past. They point, for instance, to the region of the old place of Mensuat south of Chambri on top of a rather steep hill, where we found this village still in 1966. According to later Mensuat information, the earlier Aibom had been situated on a mountain named Dougual, lying to the west of old Mensuat near Mali and Sangruman and accessible from Timbunmeli, apparently to the southwest; on the side of this mountain there was clay, and early Aibom—itself also called Dougual—had already made pottery from it as it does

today. Its language is said to have been the old Mensuat one, not that of Chambri, and this Aibom had no canoes. This latter remark corresponds very precisely with the Soatmeli's claim that they had given the first canoe to their Aibom friends and shows the difference between river-going Iatmul and walking mountain villagers quite clearly. After a conflict with Mali, this early Aibom is said to have been abandoned for the Aibom hill.

Such southern relations also point to the mountains around the Govenmas lake south of the Kapriman region, which are collectively named Kumbranggaui and are, in Aibom mythology, considered to be the places of origin and of various actions of important mythical personalities in the beginning of time; Kumbranggaui represents the southern of the two world hemispheres resulting from the breakthrough of the Sepik in the primeval past. The northern one, Ampiangei, comprises mainly the Sawos region but also the whole country between the northern bank of the Sepik and the seacoast and culminates, symmetrically to the Govenmas mountains, in the Maprik hills.

Further, these relations point to several places in and around the Kapriman river system (made up of the Korewori, the Korosemeri, and the Blackwater in between) such as, first of all, Masantoni (Masantenai), situated northeast of the Middle Korewori and said to have been the aim of an early, more or less "backward," migration of parts of old Aibom (but already the one on the Aibom hill) on a southern land route via Chambri and a northern water route along the Sepik. Our hope of finding, in a rather backward place like Masantoni, as Aibom people had supposed, at least traces of the old Aibom language was, however, disappointed, though Masantoni people confirmed the one-time migration from Aibom; they said that, like the Aibom people, they had lost their old language and adopted the Korewori-type language they speak today.

These old southern and southeastern connections of Aibom, which cannot be discussed here in full, seem an important key to Aibom history, but to evaluate them the historical knowledge of the Kapriman people and of the more southern villages must be properly collected and analyzed. From Aibom knowledge alone these old events will be difficult to reconstruct. The Dougual narrative obtained from Mensuat, for instance, was confirmed in Aibom but only in a general way, and it was clearly more because of our questions from outside than because of its importance in

Aibom historical thought that information about this phase of Aibom came forward.

This southern orientation—also apparent in the location of Aibom wild sago swamps in the direction of the Korosemeri and the general feeling that this direction is especially associated with Aibom—forms a layer of history retained in the form of several actions which, seen from outside, obviously belong to different time levels but are not to our knowledge arranged in a coherent sequence. Seen together, they provide a contrasting sphere to the Iatmul style of modern Aibom life, imported from the north, and a useful argument for claiming a pre-Iatmul age for the settlement on the Aibom hill, the right to settle there and to use the adjacent plains and their ponds for various purposes—but this former stage was not comprehensively conceived of as being the great old time of true Aibom.

The unifying function which could be provided by such a vision, is—on the contrary, but not in contradiction—associated with the Iatmul stratum which furnished the language spoken every day and was personalized in the Malingei women who came to Aibom to marry there, thus bridging, on the personal as well as on the symbolical level, the gap between the two historical periods.

This tendency toward unification is also shown in a surprising but nevertheless typical way by the fact that the topos of Kumbranggaui is apparently not part of the old Aibom repertoire but Iatmul in origin. But in spite of that, pointing to the Kumbranggaui mountains in Aibom is pointing to the pre-Iatmul southern past of the village—for instance as the region that Yuman Wusmangge, the founding goddess of Aibom pottery (Schuster 1969a), unknown in general Iatmul mythology and therefore probably a leading figure of the old Aibom religion, came from. The goddess has been integrated into the Iatmul type of social organization which is followed today in Aibom, though in ritual she continues to play an outstanding role through the bamboo flute orchestra representing her voice (Spearritt 1979) and by her necessary appearance in the event of general Aibom malaise. On the whole, the two layers of mythohistorical tradition are blended so as to confirm each other, but, again, without denying or suspending the existence of either.

Aibom on the Hill

A much smaller problem in another main area of Aibom history is the attachment of the village to its hill. In the generally flat Middle Sepik landscape, the hills of Aibom, Chambri, and Tambunum are prominent and visible from far away, and the same is, of course, the case with the long hill chains to the south that are part of the Kumbranggaui hemisphere.

In Aibom cosmology, these hills are mainly interpreted in two ways. They are considered, understandably in this swampy region, as islands which even moved, "swimming," in early times and are therefore simply another, though particularly solid, form of the general Iatmul concept of *agwi*, the first island in the primeval sea. On the other side, they are personalized in the usual dual pattern already mentioned: the Chambri and Aibom hills or, again, the two tops of the Aibom hill are said to be sisters, the Aibom hill representing the transformed body of the above-mentioned goddess, who is herself split into two female beings and is present in each piece of Aibom pottery, as the clay for it comes from the Aibom hill.

The Tambunum hill, together with the Paliagwi hill south of Chambri, forms another pair, raising the number of "sisters" to four but apparently not joined, as far as we know, by a separate common history of their own. Still, since they are mountains, the Aibom consider them theirs. It was, therefore, probably not by chance that, similar to the records mentioning Chambri men as Aibom clan founders, a Paliagwi yet unborn was brought to Aibom to found a clan group; and the Paliagwi flutes now in Aibom, together with several known persons, are considered the spoils of the war in which Aibom extinguished Paliagwi—where Mensuat now stands—not long ago.

On the other hand, the Tambunum hill is said to have split off from the Aibom hill and to have drifted down the Kumalio (see below) and then the Sepik to its present place. The migration of the Sui clan—one of the four most ancient clans in Aibom—to Masantoni (see above) is explicitly said to have followed the old route of the Tambunum hill, showing them almost naturally where to settle, notwithstanding the geographical distance between this mountain and the places of old as well as present-day Masantoni. This reasoning demonstrates again the iterative aspect characteristic of Aibom historical thinking; it was also considered, in a modern conflict over land between Tambunum and Masantoni, to be the historical foundation—and therefore proof—of the Masantoni claim to the Tambunum hill.

These events and views may be sufficient to illustrate the deep-rooted Aibom feeling toward mountains in general; there is no other place for Aibom to exist, and a hill necessarily has something to do with Aibom. But there are still more specific thoughts regarding the Aibom hill, with its peculiar ridge, characterized by a notch in about the middle of its south–north extension. This saddle is explained in the following way: The Kumalio River, now following the southern border of the hill and serving as main connection between Lake Chambri, Aibom, and the Sepik, or, in another version, the Kumbrameli brook, flowing down the middle of the western hillside, tried to break through the Aibom hill but succeeded only in producing this notch in the middle. This action obviously reproduces, on a minor scale, the breakthrough of the Sepik resulting in the formation of Kumbranggaui and Ampianggei, as described before; the resemblance to the name Kumbrameli is not meaningless, the less so as this name belongs, in the highly elaborated name system of the Middle Sepik (see Wassmann 1982, Stanek 1983), to the Mboui clan, another of the four original Aibom clans and therefore especially closely associated with that early time.

That the two instances of a river breaking through a landmass and splitting it into halves characterized mainly by the mountains upon them are seen as essentially the same event in Aibom historical thinking shows the two kinds of contraction, transversal and longitudinal, working together in one example. The former can be seen in the circumstance that both events are considered to have happened in the same period in the very beginning of time, that is, contemporaneously; in another version, they are even linked, together with a similar attempt by a third river, in a single set of actions. On the other hand, because things connected with southern hills, such as Kumbranggaui, tend to belong to the older Aibom history, whereas events on the Aibom hill are related in general (but not without important exceptions) to the more recent history, a certain temporal distance cannot be denied, although it is eliminated by equating the two events with the same motif, the breakthrough of a river in primeval times.

The hill of Aibom, then, is the world in its most concentrated form. In this quality, it gives stability to Aibom, but, logically, as a whole, for Aibom has changed its actual location on the hill ridge or slopes in an astonishingly rapid sequence which stands in sharp contrast to the stability of the big Iatmul villages on the banks of the river.

At many places, the river is no longer there, having been reduced to a lagoon, but the village remains in its old place. The mobility of Aibom on its hill can, therefore, hardly be considered Iatmul settlement behavior; and since pragmatic reasons such as the changing war situations often mentioned can also not be considered plausible for all these movements (enemy villages did not change their own locations and did not alternate between friendly and hostile in a comparable rhythm) we may be allowed to take this local instability, in general, as a relic of the southern Aibom past, resembling, with clearly less amplitude, what we hear from other villages there.

The settlement history on the Aibom hill, as shown to us by Aibom people at these various localities, is marked by six major names in this temporal order: Wereman, Suinggei, Awanggei I, Kumbuimalinggei, Awanggei II, Aibom (fig. 1). The settling of the present village was witnessed by persons still living and happened just before World War II—which assumed, as can easily be imagined, a prominent place in the conception of history of senior people. The preceding settlement, Awanggei II, was situated just above present-day Aibom in about the middle of the southeastern slope of the hill; the place before that, however, Kumbuimalinggei, lay at quite a distance on the northeastern slope and was itself abandoned for Awanggei II when the few oldest people living in Aibom ten years ago were still very small children.

According to genealogical information, people had stayed in Kumbuimalinggei for about two generations—about as long as later on in Awanggei II; before that, they had moved to this northern place from Awanggei I, which, as the name shows, lay near the place of the later Awanggei II but a little above it. In this southern part of the hill early Suinggei was also to be found, on the southernmost part of the ridge itself, just where it starts to turn downward. This piece of land still carries its name, referring to Sui, an ancient clan which has already been mentioned as migrant to Masantoni.

Probably about this time, there was also a settlement on the southeastern edge of the hill, beyond the southernmost house of present-day Aibom; it was said to have been established by people of Pasko, another of the four early clans, and is referred to in various records by the name of its men's house, Nongruimbit. Wereman, finally, is also a men's-house name. It is said to have been the very first men's house to exist; it was not built by man but appeared together with

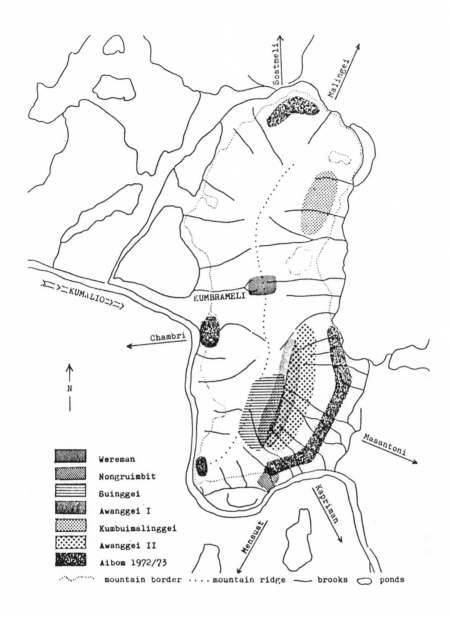

Fig. 1. The settlements on the Aibom hill.

the earth. It was situated, therefore, in the landscape of primeval events, right in the notch between the two Aibom hilltops, and when the river waters tried to break through the mountain at this place it was swept down on the other side. Now its parts are hidden but may be seen—as water spirits—at the bottom of the Kumalio River running there; its former place on the ridge—perhaps even higher before the notch was made by the water—retains its name and is owned by the Yogum clan that, together with the Mboui, Sui,

and Pasko clans already mentioned, formed the early Aibom population.

Combined with what we have heard before, the origin, position, and fate of Wereman indicate that it marks, in the Aibom view, the very beginning of history on the hill, but it was not known in Aibom what kind of people—or beings—actually sat on the benches in the primeval Wereman men's house. The name Wereman was not used again, at least not for a men's house; this is particularly surprising in that other men's-house names, such as Nongruimbit, Kosimbi, Fondim-bit, and Tangruimbit, appear again and again. They are ascribed to the later villages or to phases within the settlement period of a village, mostly in groups of three, sometimes overlapping. The repetition of the same names for new buildings at mostly new places not only connects these build-ings—as being the same ones—with one an-other but also links the settlements as such in one long chain. Of this chain, the first member is not Wereman but probably Suinggei, together with Kaluawanggu, just north of it on the ridge, which was, as is suggested by the name of its men's house, Tengglembit, also mainly a Sui place. Wereman was, to conclude, a men's house on the Aibom hill but not of the Aibom people.

The other places on the hill pose no conceptual problems either for Aibom or for us. As surface potsherds of various types in the Suinggei-Awanggei region as well as at the Kumbuima-linggei place indicate, Aibom had been, as was to be expected, a pottery place for a number of gen-erations (Kocher-Schmid 1980). For the two most recent places before present-day Aibom, Kum-buimalinggei and Awanggei II, the memories are still remarkably precise and allow not only the lo-cation of early house sites on a map but also the listing of their former inhabitants or at least of the clans they belonged to. Kumbuimalinggei pro-vides an important additional clue to history: it was probably the place where the aforementioned Iatmulization took place or continued, as is sug-gested by its name ("Malinggei flying-fox"), its northern position in the direction of Malingei, memories, and genealogical data (cf. G. Schus-ter's contribution below).

Some Comparative Remarks

Without summing up what has been said or will be said in G. Schuster's paper below, we may consider Aibom history, understood as the Aibom picture of history, basically as a spatial system; the order in time is given as the sequence of lo-calities associated with events, and even geneal-ogy has its temporal aspect—already contained in the sequence of persons—enhanced by the as-sociation of persons with events in designated places. History becomes precise where it is at the same time geography; the temporal order is sub-ject to the spatial one, which may, however, itself be suspended when events in different places are classified as the same.

This shows that, on the whole, quality is the decisive category of Aibom historical thinking, and the difference between "earlier" and "later" is much more one of quality than one of time. Contractions as outlined above are made in var-ious directions on the basis of the assumption that the two things being condensed into one are of the same quality in the aspects considered important in Aibom. This is also shown by the totemic sys-tem, which has been left almost untouched in this paper; it provides an efficient conceptual frame for drawing identifying lines into the prehuman past as well as into the nonhuman environment. In such a concept of history, a chronology of the Western type is simply not needed and would, if present, only disturb the system by establishing differences—because of the association of per-sons or events with different points of time—where Aibom thinking conceives identity. The strength of this identifying tendency is shown in particular on the level of the smaller family, in which the grandfather and the grandchild may clearly be seen existing and acting as two differ-ent persons but are, on the important level of the naming system as well as in social contexts (see below), conceived as the same person in a clas-sification of a higher order.

Such an attitude shows a basically static con-cept of human events everywhere, including those of the past, our history. In contrast to the chronological model, Aibom history is not con-ceived as a sphere in which in principle only new things ever happen (notwithstanding some at-tempts to establish linear or cyclic patterns or laws of history); on the contrary, history is prin-cipally a field of iterative actions reenacting the same events in most of their details, as on the cer-emonial level, or repeating earlier actions in other places or with other actors, or with other differ-ences. Along these lines of interpretation, history means the same thing happening again.

The function of history in Aibom, then, is not to explain how a later event developed from a for-mer one—giving history a causal dimension run-ning in small steps parallel to the temporal one—but to confirm the basic relations between the parts of the world (between two clans, two vil-lages, two hemispheres, but also between a vil-lage and its land, etc.) by new actions. This pro-vides the background for the considerable role of history (including, of course, what we are accus-tomed to call mythology) on the juridical and po-litical level: nothing can happen outside of this all-encompassing frame. History in Aibom does not unfold a picture of wide variations taken as absolute; instead, it has to prove that the basic orientation marks remain the same in spite of variations in outer form. The human need, then, which history in Aibom meets may be described as the need for stability of essential relations and associations or, more generally, the world order, whereas the chronological type of history reflects the desire for change.

This static aspect characterizes the underlying attitude and the lines of interpretation of the Aibom concept of history; therefore, it needs to be kept in mind as possibly permeating and influencing statements about the past. But the Aibom picture of history cannot be reduced to this structuring element: there is, as has been seen, considerable movement as well. This dynamic aspect, as shown by movements in space and by actions of people on different time levels, is incorporated in a wealth of "histories"; by collecting them and paying particular attention to their connecting links in the form of, mostly, persons and places, we can establish a rather coherent aggregate of events which may well be called a system. However, this system seems not be present, as far as we know, in its entirety in the mind of any one of the knowledgeable persons in Aibom—not so much because of the lack of writing as an aid to memory as because of the traditional competitive relationship between the clans: they have their own preferences in the broad area of history and their own versions of the more general topics. This makes it necessary for people from outside

or those whose youth places them at a certain distance from the traditional social system to take on this task. It seems an essential one with regard to the Melanesian heritage of modern Papua New Guinea—a point which was also stressed with great authority by Dambui in this symposium; village histories, seen in the light of the concepts structuring them and illuminated by comparisons on the regional level, offer the only possibility of obtaining individualized information on the time before the white man came. There is still time to preserve these complex autochthonous systems of organizing the past operating simultaneously on several planes of imagination, one of which is our "history."[2]

Notes

1. "Malingei," the name of the village, is written as on most maps; in other cases, the -nggei ending is written, more correctly, with two g's (pronounced as in "finger," not as in "singing").

2. Of particular interest for comparison with this paper and that of G. Schuster below are the contributions to this volume of Scaglion and Wassmann with regard to Sepik concepts of history, space, and time and of Bragge with regard to village migrations in the Sepik basin. The necessity of combining individual villages' systems of history was also convincingly shown by Dambui's work on Timbunge historical traditions, offering valuable correspondences to some of the Aibom data.

2/ Aibom Genealogy as History

Gisela Schuster

In considering to what degree and in what way Aibom genealogy represents history, we may start with some characteristics of the Aibom (and mostly also wider Iatmul) way of naming individuals and assigning them clan membership that cause difficulties for us in reconstructing sequences of ancestors but nevertheless illustrate some central aspects of the Aibom conception of the individual's position and mobility within the genealogical framework:

1. As every Iatmul has a number of names, some of which are used at the same time, it is difficult to designate a person with certainty by a name, especially in earlier generations.

2. As grandfather and grandchild tend to have the same name, particularly in the line of the first-born, it is difficult to identify the generation; this repetition of names—and therefore of persons—is basic to Iatmul historical thinking not only on the personal level but also on others. In the age-group system which regulates initiation and proceeds by half-generation steps, the grandfather leaves the system when the grandchild achieves the active level in it.

3. The custom of keeping clans or clan groups from dying out or strengthening them anew by the adoption of people from other clans or clan groups adds considerably to the difficulty of tracing genealogical lines as we understand them. Other changes of persons from one clan to another occur because of conflicts on issues such as concurrent claims to names, drum signals, etc. It may happen that someone has been given a name which he should not have because it belongs to another clan. In one such case, the man insisted on retaining his name and was therefore considered a member of both clans involved, though not on the same level. In another, the persons involved simply left both clans and were accepted by a third and given new names—which did not, however, exclude completely the use of the former ones. Such irregularities seem to be particularly frequent in Aibom compared with other Iatmul places, probably because of the late introduction of the Iatmul name system and the difficulties of adaptation of the former to the new one.

4. Because the Iatmul show a particular appreciation of everything that was first and being

adopted necessarily includes the notion of being secondary and therefore minor, adoptions tend to be concealed in records. Under these conditions, showing a great mobility of individuals with regard to their clan membership—in contrast to the general importance of just this membership, in particular membership by birth—it is difficult to obtain long genealogical sequences in Aibom. Though there exists, as with all Iatmul, an admirable capacity for the memorization of large numbers of names in ceremonial contexts, Aibom interest is not just directed toward keeping in mind long lists of ancestor names in their proper order. Instead, names—and therefore their former bearers—tend to be connected with events, actions, or places, which, however, do not imply a strict temporal order by themselves. This involves a tendency to assume, in cases where actual knowledge is incomplete, that such cases repeat earlier ones or that little-known former events happened in exactly the same manner as well-known later ones; on such assumptions, even the lost name of a husband or wife may be made up according to the names of another couple provided that other conditions, such as the two clans involved, were the same.

Though, for these reasons, some uncertainties may remain, it was possible to obtain in Aibom genealogical lists with an average of eight generations for most of the clans. This corpus of sequences represents, if parallel generations (counted backward from the present) are supposed to have lived at about the same time, a linear system which should be able to provide additional information on the process through which Aibom took over the Iatmul language and culture, doubtless one of the crucial developments in Aibom history. This sequence of events will therefore be taken as an example of the picture of history which is provided by Aibom genealogical data and others directly associated with them.

As Meinhard Schuster has pointed out above, a former Aibom settlement named Kumbuimalinggei was probably the main place where the Iatmulization proceeded; how long Kumbuimalinggei had been settled can be imagined from the information that someone had been brought there as a baby from the preceding settlement (Awanggei I) and died, very old, at the succeeding one (Awanggei II). The Kumbuimalinggei period in between can therefore be estimated to have been less than a long human lifetime. This calculation is confirmed by the information that three generations died there.

Kumbuimalinggei is said to have been founded by two men: Kauli, of the Ngglagen clan, and Mebran, of the Weinkuante. Kauli was born in Malingei, Mebran in Awanggei I (i.e., Aibom) but of a Chambri father and an Aibom mother. Neither settlement founder, then, was descended from an Aibom father or belonged to one of the four ancient clans (Sui and Yogum of the nyame and Mboui and Pasko of the nyaui moiety). Kauli was placed, in the Ngglagen genealogy, six generations ago and Mebran, in the Weinkuante sequence, seven—consistent with what may otherwise be estimated for the founding of Kumbuimalinggei.

Kauli and Mebran not only founded, or refounded, their own clans in Aibom but also are considered founding fathers by other present-day clans. Apparently, this reinforcement of the major social units was done deliberately in Kauli's case: he is said to have bought an unborn child in Paliagwi to become the first Weinkuantshab man and a Nggalma clan man from Chambri to whom today's Aibom Nggalma trace their origin, whereas Mebran's four sons became, by the usual process of clan splitting, the founding fathers of Pasko and Nongusime, Weinkuante and Samaniak clans. These efforts also included an exchange of women between the Weinkuante and Ngglagen clans: Mebran's son married a Ngglagen woman from Malingei, Kauli the daughter of Mebran.

Mebran's son is also said to have killed a Chambri woman classified as a sister of his—a case which gave rise to the generally hostile and today still unfriendly relations with Chambri. That Kumbuimalinggei was established at the far end of the Aibom hill from Chambri may have been a consequence of this event. Still, Aibom settled back into the former Awanggei region near the hill and pointing toward Chambri while hostilities were still in full swing.

The Aibom renewal in Kumbuimalinggei was apparently not a development aimed against the four ancient clans. The genealogies show that one Mboui girl was also married by Kauli and another given to another man from Malingei who was urged by the Mboui to settle in Kumbuimalinggei. The Pasko clan history continued through Kumbuimalinggei, but in addition one of Me-

bran's grandchildren was apparently incorporated into the Pasko line that is the only one to persist up to the present in Aibom. The Yogum and Sui, though threatened by extinction in more recent generations, were also still present in Kumbuimalinggei, the Sui clan with several lines and its own men's house.

There can be little doubt that these ancient clans will have insisted upon their privileges by priority rights; that the newcomers from Chambri and Malingei could achieve, in spite of this, such importance in the Aibom picture of history may be due to their outstanding personalities but surely also to the fact that nearly two-thirds of the adult men of today consider themselves descended from them and that we see these details of the Aibom village past only with their eyes. Moreover, there may have been a general decline in Aibom population in those times that offered room for immigration or even made it desirable. Such a loss of population was not directly reported for any of the settlement places, but there is a record telling in a more general form of a conflict between the Mboui, Yogum, and Pasko clans, on one side, and Sui clan, on the other, that caused a sizable emigration. Pasko clan members went via Chambri to Masantoni, Sui via the Sepik; Mboui also headed in this direction but came back via Chambri; and Yogum left Aibom too. Personal names of some of the eight clan leaders participating (two from each clan) are to be found in the genealogies just one generation before that of the founders of Kumbuimalinggei.

The data of this last record suggest that of the Aibom population of the time, which was made up almost entirely of the four ancient clans, a considerable part seems to have emigrated after a fight within the village, most probably Awanggei I. This unstable situation then offered an opportunity for two able and enterprising men from the immediate neighboring villages, Malingei and Chambri, to settle there, perhaps quite welcome to the remaining population as reinforcements of the local defense in such a headhunting area. Proximity to Malingei may have led to much closer contact with the north and to an increasing use of the Malingei language, Iatmul, which perhaps had been partially known before because of the still older Soatmeli connection. While these Malingei contacts intensified, mainly through intermarriage which led to Iatmul's being called "our mothers' language," almost naturally the Chambri contacts became weaker and deteriorated to hostility. Aibom switched from a general southern orientation, probably still prevalent in the early hill period, to the northern one dominant since.

Whereas we may reconstruct, in this manner, the Kumbuimalinggei events with a certain probability and satisfy our desire for a European-style picture of this part of Aibom history—which may be accentuated by the estimate that the Kumbuimalinggei settlement period probably lasted from 1850 till 1900—the Aibom themselves are not satisfied with such a view. In several accounts they connect the emigration to Masantoni—as part of a more widespread emigration from Aibom—directly with a particular event which is said to have happened in Kaluawanggu, on the southern ridge of the Aibom hill. There lived in a small lake a water spirit named Tumtummeli in the shape of a big fish; it killed a child but was afterwards killed by one of the child's parents and his or her kin. In some accounts this killing leads to—or is conceived as expression of—a conflict between the father's and the mother's side: when Tumtummeli is described as an ancestral water spirit of the paternal clan, it is killed by the mother's brothers. In return, then, the paternal relatives kill a water spirit of the mother's clan, a crocodile. But even without this social opposition, the child's being killed by a water spirit—in most versions, while taking a bath, with its mother not far away—and the subsequent killing of this water spirit are considered to raise enough tension and general bad feeling to cause the large-scale emigration immediately following.

If this narrative is structured according to the dual pattern, then the two sides are said to be Sui and Mboui, which means, on the moiety level, nyame and nyaui; this structure of a paternal nyame and a maternal nyaui aspect allows variations in detail, such as the classification of the child and its father as Nggalma (another nyame clan) or—as we have seen—the grouping of the Mboui with the Pasko (also nyaui), but also with the Yogum (being nyame). This last detail does not fit completely into the picture, nor does the opposition between three clans and only one instead of two against two; both elements may, however, have the function of underlining the prominent and singular position of the Sui, on whose land and primarily against whom these events happen—no doubt a decisive condition by Aibom standards. The close Sui connection to Tumtummeli is also shown by the fact that the canoe by which they went to Masantoni was also called Tumtummeli—as was, again, the first canoe ever built (by the Soatmeli) for the Aibom, perhaps because of the prominent position of the Sui—as the dominant nyame clan—in the early Aibom time.

Of course, the introduction of the ancestral water spirits into the story raises it to a higher level, as does its location in Kaluawanggu, on the ridge between Suinggei and Wereman; this geographical association implies a temporal one with the early settlements of Aibom on the hill and therefore with the early time, as recorded in the myths, in a broader sense. This aspect is also shown by the indication that the Tumtummeli killing happened at a time when coconut palms did not yet exist and when people were still very small; in general, narrators never forgot to mention that all this happened long, long ago in the time of the early ancestors.

We may conclude, then, that to Aibom reasoning about the past, the explanation of an emigration of parts of clans—which had apparently happened not too long ago and was, as such, nothing very unusual—simply in terms of an intravillage conflict between clans did not seem intellectually sufficient; major events like these need to have a prefiguration on, a foundation in, and a relation with an event of the same type on a higher—and, therefore, former—plane. The two events are seen as the same, as is shown by the habitual combination of the Tumtummeli killing with the pre-Kumbuimalinggei emigration, which was probably also a historical event as we understand the word "history."

3/ The Nyaura Concepts of Space and Time

Jürg Wassmann

Do connections exist between apparently divergent parts of Nyaura (Iatmul) culture, between spirits and genealogies, between names and flutes, between totems and songs, between ancient beings and landownership today–that can be represented systematically? Bateson (1958 [1936]:127) called attention to the existence of such a system of relationships among the Central Iatmul, pointing to a link between myths and the names of things and persons. His writings also contain a description of the idea of a migration in ancient times (1932:407). However, he could not adduce evidence of this system or present an account of it, for, as he said, "the system is in a terribly muddled state," characterized by "fraudulent heraldry" and "tangle" (1958[1936]:128). Today, more than fifty years later, it is possible, with due caution, to answer this question. Two incidents from my fieldwork throw light on the matter.[1]

On the way from Wewak to Maprik with a handful of men and women from Kandɨngei, the first village of the Nyaura, I alighted at Winge, some 15 kilometers from Maprik, and in the apparently deserted village took a few photographs of a typical Abelam cult house in the course of construction. Suddenly an elderly woman appeared and ran toward me in a fury. "Tourists," she cried, "must pay 2 kina for every photograph." I was nonplussed and not a little vexed. An elderly man from Kandɨngei saved the situation with masterly aplomb. All the men in the truck, he said in Tok Pisin, were members of the Nyaura clan,[2] whose ancestors, as everyone knew, had passed through Winge long before. Consequently, they were all entitled to take photographs there. The old woman, obviously greatly embarrassed, apologized.

When I had been in Kandɨngei for three months, I noticed in tape recording and translating certain songs (sui) that their contents revolved around a certain totem, that the text of a song consisted of a short story whose protagonist was the totem, and that hundreds of names were mentioned which were familiar to me as the names of members of the village, districts, men's houses,

and dogs. One day an informant, bursting with pride, declared that his own name not only occurred in the songs but also possessed a related secret name in the "knotted cord" (kɨrugu). This was the first time that there had been any talk of the knotted cord, and some weeks were to elapse before I set eyes on one.

Order out of Chaos: The Nyaura as Strict Systematists

Is there a link between these two incidents? I shall argue that there is, offering not a theory introduced from outside but a Nyaura theory. I shall describe an abstract system of order comprising numerous nexuses of meaning that makes it possible to interpret aspects of the culture which at first sight appear disparate and to show how they are linked.

Formally this system has three characteristics:

1. It is secret. Knowledge of the links and ties is part of the secret knowledge of a small number of important men whose influence stems precisely from this knowledge. There is a difference in principle between the multiplicity of the exoteric culture as it exists in a more or less pronounced form in the consciousness of most clan members and the fundamental cultural unity existing in the esoteric knowledge of certain important men. On the one hand are the bewilderingly large number of totems, the thousands of names, the innumerable myths and fragments of myths which outwardly stand in no relation to one another, on the other the knowledge held by only a few men of the interconnections which simplify everything. It is therefore not so much the mythological tales as such that are secret—some of them are even familiar to children as bedtime stories (wapuksapuk)—as their precise geographical locations and the true identities of their protagonists.

2. It is related to clan groups. Clans are gathered together in groups of varying size. A primary distinction is made between the moieties,

sky and earth; each moiety is divided into clan associations, each consisting of two clan groups of two, three, four, or more clans each. Each clan group has its own system, which differs from others in content but not in structure.

3. The secret interconnections form a dynamic system, although it is claimed that they represent an attempt to establish a static order. It follows that the praxis of this system—its daily application by the important men—is also dynamic. There is continuous rivalry among the important men over the legitimate ownership (i.e., ownership derived from the system) of names and totems. The ownership of a name is equated with the power to dispose of the object designated by the name as one pleases. The climax of these disputes over the correct interpretation of the system is a public contest in which names are argued over at the ceremonial stool (*pabu*).[3]

So much for the formal characteristics of the system. In terms of content, each relational system revolves around two principal themes: the creation and the subsequent mythological migration of the ancient people. Implicit in the process of creation and the ancient migration is a space-time grid.

The Conception of Space: The Long March of the Crocodiles

The stories of ancient times can be summarized as follows: Before creation there was water everywhere. Then a crocodile appeared and split in two, its lower jaw becoming the earth, its upper jaw the sky. This cleavage explains the subsequent division of society into earth and sky moieties. Then the first pair of brothers came into existence, and from them sprang other pairs of brothers by repeated issue. These pairs of brothers were the founders of the present clan associations. The first brother of the pair is the founder of the first clan group of an association, the second brother that of the second clan group. Their sons and grandsons founded the numerous individual clans one or two generations later.

The locale of these events is an area to the north of the Middle Sepik near the village of Gaikorobi[4] (fig. 1). In the beginning all the ancient people were gathered there. Then the founders of the clan groups and their relatives left the village, following in the tracks of crocodiles which cleared the way for them, and thus brought about the most important event of ancient times: the

severance from the place of origin and the migration into the areas of present settlement. The path of the migration was through the bush around Gaikorobi to the Sepik River and across it through the district of the present Central Iatmul into the villages now occupied by the Nyaura (fig. 2). During this journey, always in the tracks of the crocodiles, possession was taken of tracts of land, parts of the bush, lakes, and watercourses, and villages and hamlets were founded. The land taken and the villages founded at that time determine present claims to possession. The scraps of food and the excrement left behind on the migration were the origin of the water spirits (*wanjimout*).

Two points are of crucial importance: The two brothers of a pair behaved in different ways, and the migrations of the various clan associations had their own typical patterns. The second brother of each pair was the dynamic one, the one who first crossed the Sepik. The first brother, by contrast, at first adhered to the bushland and the place of creation. This contrast is made through the set expressions "by canoe" and "on foot", both brothers ultimately covering the same path.[5] A further point: The ground covered by the migration of a clan association centered on a particular area in which it founded a particularly large number of villages and which was either not touched at all by the other pairs of brothers or explicitly used only as a "transit corridor." Each pair of brothers, and thus each clan association, had its own area. It is typical that the regions of the fraternal pairs of the earth moiety lay mainly above (to the west of) the Middle Sepik and those of the sky moiety mainly below it (to the east). These two features explain the correspondence between the earth moiety and the upper course of the river and the sky moiety and the lower course and, ideally, that between the first clan groups and the areas on the left bank of the Sepik and the second groups and the areas on the right bank (see table 1).[6] The allocation of areas at that time is shown in table 2. As may be seen from figure 2, Winge is one of the villages in the sphere of influence of the Nyaura clan association (in Malingwat district, north and northwest of Pagwi). This explains the reaction of the woman from this village in the example given in the introduction.

At this point we are confronted with the question whether there is in fact a connection between the "mental" migration in ancient times and the actual history of Nyaura settlement as it is beginning to be reconstructed.[7] In other words, is the

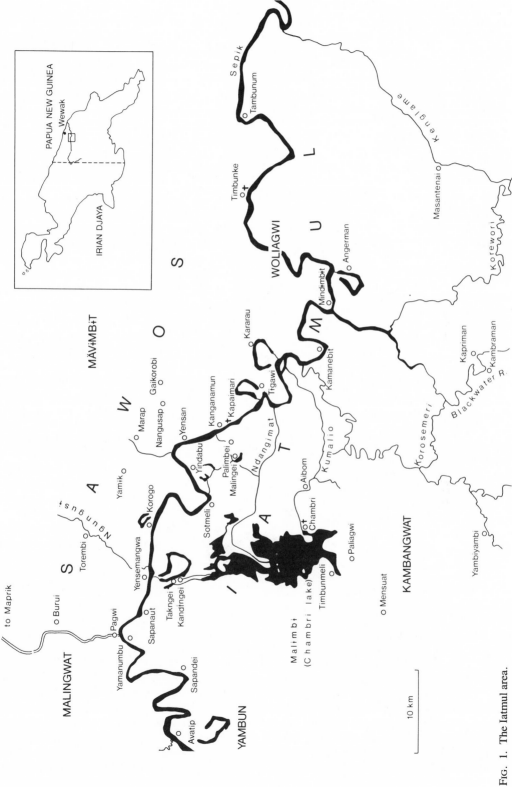

Fig. 1. The Iatmul area.

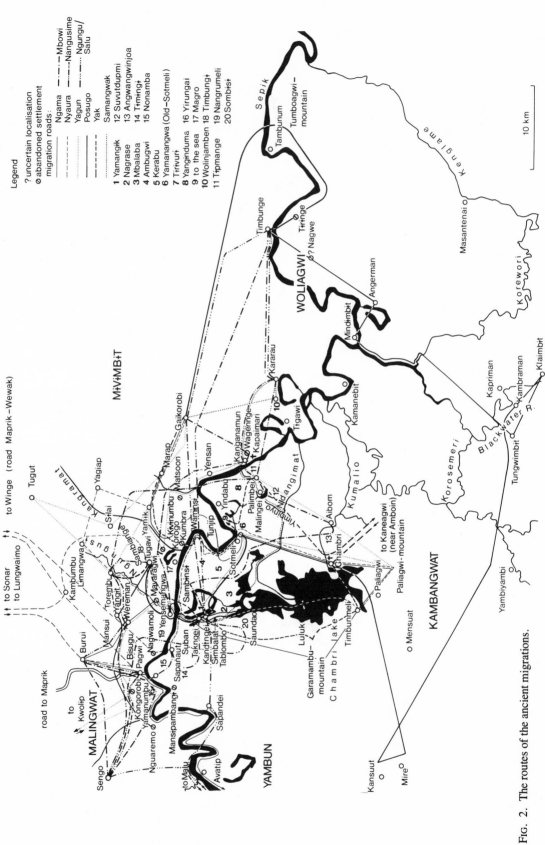

Legend

? uncertain localisation
⊘ abandoned settlement
migration roads:

— · — Ngama   — · · — Mbowi
— — — Nyaura   · · · · · · Nangusime
— · · — Yagun   — · · · Ngungu/
· · · · · Posugo   Salu
— — — Yak
· · · · · · · Samangwak

1 Yamangik   12 Suvutdupmi
2 Nagrase   13 Angwangwinjoa
3 Mbalaba   14 Timingi
4 Ambugwi   15 Nonamba
5 Kerabu   16 Yirungai
6 Yamanangwa (Old–Sotmeli) 17 Magro
7 Tirivuri   18 Timbungi
8 Yanginduma   19 Nangrumeli
9 to the sea   20 Sombisi
10 Wolinjamben
11 Tipmange

Fig. 2. The routes of the ancient migrations.

TABLE 1
GEOGRAPHIC REPRESENTATION OF NYAURA SOCIAL ORGANIZATION

	RIGHT BANK (KAMBANGWAT), SECOND BROTHER	LEFT BANK (MALINGWAT/ MɨVɨMBɨT), FIRST BROTHER
Upper course (Yambun), earth moiety	Samblak	Ngama
	Wango	Nyaura
	Pulau	Tɨpme Yagun
Lower course (Woliagwi), sky moiety	Nangusime	Posugo
	Nolim	Yak
	Smat	Mbowi
	Samangwak	Mandigo

TABLE 2
DISTRIBUTION OF REGIONS AND VILLAGES AMONG CLAN GROUPS

CLAN GROUP	AREAS ASSIGNED
Earth moiety	
Ngama association	
1. Ngama	Mɨvɨmbɨt region
2. Samblak	Sepik upper course (Yambun), Garamambu mountain
Nyaura association	
1. Nyaura	Malingwat region (Ambiange), Kandɨngei (Nyaurangei) village
2. Wango	Lake Chambri (Malɨmbɨ)
Yagun association	
1. Tɨpme Yagun	Mɨvɨmbɨt region, particularly Yensan village, Ngungusɨ watercourse
2. Pulau	Paliagwi mountain
Sky moiety	
Posugo association	
1. Posugo	Timbunge, Mɨndɨmbɨt villages
2. Nangusime	Tonagwanmeli sago swamp (near Timbunmeli), Kambangwat region
Yak association	
1. Yak	the sea
2. Nolim	Sepik lower course (Woliagwi)
Mbowi association	
1. Mbowi	Kanganamun, Aibom villages
2. Smat	the sky, Palimbei village
Samangwak association	
1. Mandigo[a]	?
2. Samangwak	the region "under the water," Kalelo (Kararau) village, Ndangimat watercourse

[a] This group has died out.

spatial aspect of the system just described of historical quality?

The place of origin of the present Nyaura population is unanimously and very emphatically declared to be Gaikorobi. Three stages in its migration may be distinguished: In the first stage, with Gaikorobi as a center, various branch villages were founded in its vicinity, including Nangusap, Marap, and Yamɨk.[8] Part of the population, however, left the bush around Gaikorobi and reached

the Sepik. There the settlement of Yamanangwa (Old Sotmeli) was founded as the first village on the river. Bateson named "Tshuotmali" as the "traditional first village of Iatmül on the Sepik" (1932:256). The villages of Timbunge and Tambunum, lying downriver, are said to have been founded from Yamanangwa. Hostilities with the bush village of Yamɨk led to Yamanangwa's being abandoned after a short time, and the population split into two migratory groups. At the beginning of the second stage, the first group founded the settlement of Palimbei, which subsequently led to the foundation of the branch settlements of Malingei, Yensan, and Kanganamun. Malingei was the center from which present-day Sotmeli was founded only a short distance above the earlier settlement of Yamanangwa, which had been abandoned. The second group initiated the third stage by migrating upriver and founding the village of Nyaurangei (today Kandɨngei and Takngei, i.e., lower and upper villages), finally radiating out from there to settle the whole of the present Nyaura region.

The first village, established in great-great-grandfather's time,[9] was Yensemangwa, which guards the entrance to the watercourse Ngungusɨ, leading to the market village of Torembi. Shortly after this came Sapanaut, which controls the entrance to the watercourse Sambaragwan, the link between the Sepik and the sago village of Wereman. Subsequently Yamanumbu was founded as the third village, followed by the fourth, Sapandei, facing the watercourse Maliwei, leading to the sago village of Lɨmao. The fifth village was Korogo, originally sited just below the mouth of the Kamangawi watercourse that links Takngei with the Sepik at a place called Malimbo but later relocated downriver in its present position. At the same time two more villages were founded from the branch villages. These were Tɨgawi, on the lower course of the Middle Sepik, established from Yensemangwa, and Brugenowi, on the upper course, established from Sapandei. During World War II, Timbunmeli, on the south shore of Lake Chambri, was established from Kandɨngei. In the early seventies two new settlements were established in Lake Chambri, one on the island of Arinjon (with inhabitants from Takngei), the other on the island of Luluk (with inhabitants from Sapanaut).

From comparison of the conjectural histories of migration, the details of which were elicited through genealogies[10] and direct questions, with the stories of ancient migrations, it is clear that, in spatial terms, the historical pattern of events could very well constitute the core of the ancient pattern. However, in the way it is presented by the system, the second and third stages of the historical migration, which were contemporaneous, occurred in sequence. The core of the historical and the "mental" migrations, which may be common to the two, is shown in figure 3.

Statements concerning the historical migrations never contain any detailed information on the precise routes followed, for example, the ac-

tual paths taken between the villages. By contrast, stories about the ancient migrations are as a rule very precise as to whether a village was actually founded or simply visited or passed through. It is striking that the districts only visited in passing (for example, the area of the Korewori River, the upper course of the Sepik, or the Malingwat area) are all on the outer margins of the region through which the migration took place. The sea is even explicitly mentioned as a "thought place," i.e., as a place only imagined. According to the system, the villages actually founded become more numerous along the course of the Middle Sepik. They include settlements still inhabited today and those that have since been abandoned. The places said to be abandoned settlements, at least those that I have been able to examine, show signs of previous occupation. Schuster (1973) draws attention to the ruined remains of Yamanangwa or Old Sotmeli, and within the Nyaura area I have visited the former settlement sites of Tablombo, Mavaragwi (Yambunmangɨ), Mansɨpambangɨ, Kongorobi, and Nguaremo. All show traces of settlement, such as rows of palms, ceremonial mounds, and, in some cases, even potsherds.

Thus, the question whether ancient migrations are historical may be provisionally answered in the affirmative, at least as far as the general spatial aspects of the migration are concerned. However, no final answer is yet possible. To permit such an answer, genealogies from other villages would have to be studied systematically and the remains of settlements throughout the Sepik region assessed in terms of archaeological history.[11]

To what extent does the system have practical relevance? The question is whether all the land rights and claims can in fact be derived from the course of the migrations—as all informants vehemently assert—or whether the system is only a general frame of reference, practice being infinitely more complicated. This point is particularly pertinent because one of the features of the system is, of course, its dynamic character; it is the locus of deliberate manipulations by the important men to provide retrospective legitimation for an existng state of affairs.

For the Nyaura, when they visualize the area in which they live in terms of space, the central feature is the Sepik River (see fig. 4). In the central section of the river live the Nyaura nɨmba (the Nyaura people from Sapandei to Korogo; see fig. 1), the Palimbei nɨmba (from Sotmeli to Kanganamun), and the Woliagwi nɨmba (from Kararau

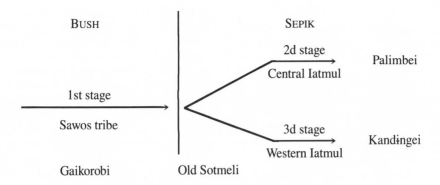

FIG. 3. The possible common core of the historical and "mental" migrations.

to Tambunum). These three groups feel that there are cultural, linguistic, and historical bonds among them.[12] The space surrounding this middle section is divided into regions marked off to form individual districts (known as *ndɨmba*, "enclosures") inhabited by specific people. Each of these districts is occupied by *numungi* ("aliens" or "ignorant people").[13] Yambun is the district surrounding the upper course of the river beyond Sapandei; Malingwat (or Ambiange) the district north to northwest of Pagwi; Mɨvɨmbɨt the bush region north of the central course of the river (with Gaikorobi as center); Woliagwi the entire lower course of the river (all the way from Kararau to the sea); and Kambangwat the whole region south of the Sepik, from the south shore of Lake Chambri (not counting Timbunmeli) to the Korewori River. To these must be added, as purely mythological regions, the area "under the water" (*ngungu ndɨmba*) and that of the stars (*sɨngut ndɨmba*). The fact that the lower course begins at Kararau and that consequently the more remote Eastern Iatmul are actually "outside" shows how very much such divisions are determined by a particular geographical viewpoint. Each of these districts falls within the orbit of a clan association; they are the specific areas of the migrating pairs of brothers.[14]

The system is of practical importance, however, only within the area belonging specifically to the Nyaura, that is, within their sphere of influence. The attitude adopted toward settlements outside those limits is one of fine distinctions in some cases and of diffuseness and uncertainty in others. As might be expected from the course and nature of the migrations, places within the areas of the Central and Eastern Iatmul—insofar as they are affected by the system at all—are regarded as cofounded settlements which were then abandoned by some of their own people, as are those between Gaikorobi and the Sepik River (but here with perceptible aloofness). All the others are rather "story places," although certain informants deny this and stress that they were actually visited by the Nyaura groups. It would be interesting to know whether the inhabitants of these places are at all familiar with the Nyaura migrations, as is presumably the woman at Winge.

When, early in my stay, I systematically recorded the haunts of the water spirits around Kandɨngei, asked about the names and owners of the districts, and investigated where particular women were allowed to fish, a picture emerged which could be interpreted only very much later when I had come to know the system. These places and specific areas of land were located—in the majority of cases—on the routes of these migrations.[15] The only exception concerned the gardens laid out on the lagoon of Kandɨngei, where no specific order could be ascertained. For example, on the shores of Lake Chambri (Malɨmbɨ), of the nine areas in the northwest corner (Tablombo), six belong to the Ngama group (Ngama association); of the twenty-six on the western side, five belong to the Nyaura group and fifteen to the Wango (Nyaura association); the whole of the southern shore is Nangusime territory (Posugo association). No possessions are recorded around the village of Chambri itself, whereas the areas around the Ndangimat watercourse are, in nine out of fourteen cases, Smat and Samangwak possessions (Smat and Samangwak associations). These results should be compared with the migrations shown on figure 2. (The route followed by the Yak association does run through Lake Chambri but explicitly only as a route of "transit.") The lake as a whole, with the exception of the small area on the shore near

Chambri, lies within the orbit of the village of Kandingei. The Wango group (Nyaura association) has authority here. This example is of interest in that it is diametrically opposed to what Gewertz (1983:137) asserts to be true from the viewpoint of the Chambri.[16]

How land rights are in fact distributed can be reconstructed only from innumerable case studies of land disputes, and not only with reference to the statements of Kandingei informants, which are biased by their own interests. It seems evident, however, that migration routes and the actual possession of land (and thus also of fishing places and the haunts of water spirits) are conceived of as being interdependent even though this relationship may assume ideological features.

The Conception of Time: Names Make Persons

If the relationship between the past, as the period of ancient migrations, and the present can be conceived of as a spatial continuum, the following interrelationship can be readily visualized: In the past the world and its people came into being; the latter gave themselves their specific social order. According to the system, the present is nothing but a precise reflection of the situation created at that time, which forms the basis and the still valid model for present circumstances. In other words, the present social order and system of landownership are legitimated simply and solely by the fact that they originated and were set up in ancient times. All present members of the clan are direct progeny of the people of ancient times, and it is this genealogical link alone that confers on them the right to represent their ancestors in ceremonies and to narrate their actions in contemporary myths.

Both the past and the present have a certain temporal depth or duration. The past becomes articulated through the spatial pattern of the migration. The beginning is indicated by the creation of the world and the end by the founding of the present-day villages; in between there are the migrations as the successive occupations of places of settlement. True, very careful distinctions are made between the succeeding generations within the ancient or primal personnel, but it is rare for more than two or three to be mentioned. The present is historical or genealogical time, four or, rarely, five or six generations. Events are fixed in time by reference to genealogies or are linked with external events. "At the time of the Japanese" or (less accurately) "when I was working in Rabaul" are standard phrases, although there is always the possibility (never utilized) of counting the years. The year (*naambi*) itself comprises two sections, the dry season (*nyagange*) and the flood season (*sambiangu*). The beginning of the year is marked by the start of the dry season, roughly in June according to our reckoning. Each section is divided into six "moons" (*mbap*) which, at least with regard to the dry season, are closely correlated with garden activities (i.e., preparation for forest clearing, actual clearing, planting, growth of the plants, ripening of the plants, harvest). The tripartite division of days (which was important until a few years ago and also in ancient times), by which the days are divided into two days for fishing (*kwosera, sasiba*) followed by the day on which the fish are bartered at the market (*wengasiba*), has lost importance since the government established daily markets at Pagwi and other centers (these are particularly large on Thursdays).

Thus there is a clear distinction between past and present time, but the flow of time within each period is not particularly important; interest is focused on the precise spatial (geographical), not the temporal, positions of events. For the past, in particular, actual duration plays hardly any part at all.[17] Nor does the image of the succession of past and present, reasonable enough in our eyes, characterize their relationship in all respects. Inquiry into the historical accuracy of the system in its temporal aspects shows that there is no equivalence between the ancient and the postulated historical migration. For example, the founding of the village of Kandingei (Nyaurangei) took place four generations ago;[18] it was founded by ancestors whose actual names are still known and recorded in the genealogies. Yet its founding is also part of mythological events. Now, it is possible to argue that oral traditions are always foreshortened, i.e., that the distance between the past and the generation living today invariably remains the same, mythical events always being advanced to correspond to historical ones. Whereas such foreshortening may well apply to the first part of the Nyaura migration, it does not apply to the second and third stages. That the founding of the village of Kandingei (and other settlements) is fixed both genealogically and mythologically shows that no very precise dividing line can be identified between historical and ancestral events. The distant past is on the one hand distinguished from the present but on the other not only brought up to it

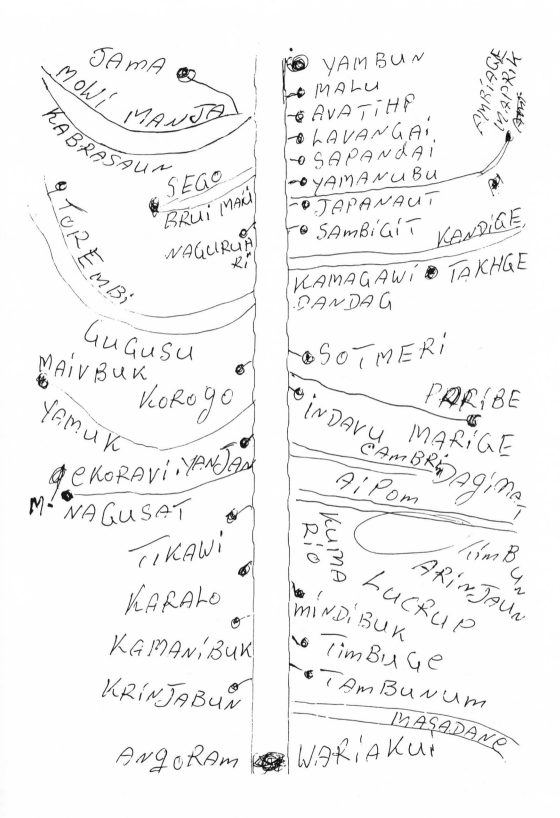

FIG. 4. The villages of the Middle Sepik (by David Kisondemi, Kandingei).

but brought into it. Mythological events are extended into the present.

If we look at names, we obtain another picture. At each place visited by the migration (and, as I have explained, the places vary with the clan association), the clan group founder leaves behind a few men and women. He assigns them an animal, plant, or some other object into which they can transform themselves; thus each place has its own "totem." This "totem" and all the objects of the place receive names of their own, which are arranged in pairs in long lines. The inhabitants of the village are also given names. The "totems" assigned in this way form the basis of the present totem system. Most important of all, the names used at that time form the stock of present names. The whole stock of names from the past is used for the present; persons, men's houses, dwellings, canoes, dogs, and pigs all bear names drawn from this stock. Thus there is a close identification between all persons and things of the present with those of the past. The person of today is defined by his (ancient) name in the sense that he figures as a reincarnation—albeit a frail one—of the primal being of the same name. He also bears responsibility for each "totem" into which his ancestor could change himself in the past. The use of names causes the two periods to coincide and expunges the linear-genealogical succession. This is made very clear when, for example, one of the important men of Kandingei, Wolindambwi (the name is that of one of the ancient migrants), rises to his feet during a heated debate in the men's house and calls out excitedly, "I, I, Wolindambwi, I took part in the ancient migration!"

Thus time regarded as the past is not merely the events linearly preceding the present (genealogies) any more than it is merely time repeating itself in cycles (cult). It is closer to the truth to say that past and present are both equally periods of time which require duration; the events taking place in them are (also) parallel in course and permit a constant movement back and forth between the juxtaposed times. Furthermore, through the use of ancient names the person of today finds himself simultaneously in both times.

Visual and Aural Representation of the Space-Time System

The system of interlinkages is also represented visually and aurally.

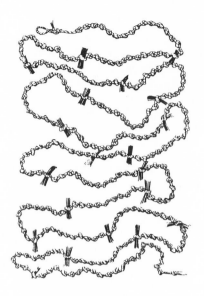

FIG. 5. The Palingawi kɨrugu.

The visual representation takes the form of the *kɨrugu*, "knotted cords." Each cord is between 6 and 7 meters in length and has knots of different sizes at regular intervals. Each kɨrugu represents one of the ancient migrations; it "is" that migration.[19] Each of the large knots in a kɨrugu represents a place along the migration route; the smaller knots contain the secret names of the "totems" associated with each spot. For example, the knotted cord of the Pulau clan group (Tɨpme Yagun association) is called Palingawi. Palingawi is the crocodile that cleared the way for the clan group founder Wolindambwi. This particular knotted cord has twenty large knots and on average ten smaller knots between every two large ones (see fig. 5). The informant who first mentioned the knotted cord to me was referring to one of his secret names, contained in the knotted cord of his clan group.

Aurally, the parts of the system intended for the public are recited in song cycles (*sagi*). Each cycle consists of a fixed sequence of songs and lasts between twelve and sixteen hours. A cycle exhibits three features: localities, names, and tales.

Localities. The cycle as a whole reproduces the course of the migration. Each individual song marks a place on the migration, with a few songs that refer to the creation being sung *before* the first place (always Gaikorobi),[20] and thus each song corresponds to a large knot in the knotted cord. For example, the song cycle of the Pulau follows the migration of this group (fig. 2). The first songs relate to the creation of the earth; later the first place, Gaikorobi, came into being.

Names. Each song revolves around a specific "totem" whose names are given in pairs in long lists. In each cycle hundreds of names are mentioned. These lists of names are regarded as official lists. The secret or "shadow lists" are those which are represented in the knotted cord by small knots. The etymology of both the public and the secret names refers to the "totem" or to past events centered on the "totem" of the place in question. For example, the third song on the creation (at the subsequently created place Gaikorobi) mentions twenty-two public names for the primeval crocodile, twenty names for the first place to come into existence (Gaikorobi or Mivimbit), and eight names for the first women of ancestral times. The primeval crocodile Kabakmeli emerges from the primal sea; it turns in a circle and the earth comes into being; it goes on turning and the earth solidifies on the parts of its body. The earth or the crocodile—since the two are equated—lies there, shaking a little at first and then gradually becoming firmer. The "totem" is the primeval crocodile (the newly arisen earth). The etymology of the names (earth, place, women) refers to the events attendant on the creation of the earth. Some of the names of the primeval crocodile (or of the earth) are (1) Andi-kabak-meli and (2) Kipma-kabak-meli (*andi, kipma*, "earth"; *kabak*, "primeval crocodile"; *meli*, masculine ending), meaning "The crocodile is the primeval crocodile which is also the earth"; (3)Lisi-nyo-mbu-ndemi and (4) Kasi-nyo-mbu-ndemi (*lisi, kasi*, "shake, earthquake"; *nyo*, "mother of pearl, seashell"; *mbu*, break open or to pieces"; *ndemi*, masculine ending), meaning "The crocodile or the earth has just emerged from the sea and is rocking to and fro"; (5) Pat-nawi-gumbangi and (6) Nganga-nawi-gumbangi (*pat = pet*, "spittle"/*nganga*, "lower jaw"; *nawi*, masculine ending (?); *gumbangi*, masculine ending), meaning "The crocodile has spittle in its throat." Some names of the first place are (7) Lili-lipma and (8) Kwakwa-lipma (*lili*, "slip away"/*kwakwa*, "stand up and fall down"; *lipma*, "coconut palm" [here a metaphor for "place"]), meaning "The newly created place still rocks"; and (9) Man-mbo and (10) Tamba-mbo (*man*, "foot, leg"/*tamba*, "hand, arm"; *mbo = mbao*, "dust, morning mist"), meaning "The place is now dry and the dust settles on the hands and feet of the people of the first place."

Tales. Each song relates a short tale in which the "totem" of the place accomplishes a particular action. The texts recited in the song are simply small, harmless extracts from the secret myths.[22] For example, the third song on the creation (at the later first place) bears the title "The Song to the Crocodile That Split in Two." The contents revolve around the primeval crocodile that rises to the surface of the water with a rotary motion, bringing with it a piece of earth, and later splits in two, its upper jaw becoming the sky while its lower jaw becomes the earth: in this way the sky and the earth come into being, and soon it will be light. The first women dance with joy at the coming of the light. Extracts of the text of the song are as follows (Wassmann 1982: 347–49):

> Father, your upper jaw (became the sky)
> Father, your upper jaw,
> Ancestor, your lower jaw (became the earth),
> Father, your jaw,
> . . . .
> Father, you Andikabakmeli,
> Andikabakmeli, Kipmakabakmeli, O you (my) water spirit!
> Father, in this place,
> in the place Lililipma,
> near the coconut palm Kwakwalipma,
> you lay down,
> and then your upper jaw became the sky.

The whole interlinked pattern can be understood only when the events which in the past took place at this subsequent first place are known. At present they are described in the following myth (only extracts of which are presented here). The passages forming the background of the song are in italics; those relating to names are underlined as well.

Once there were no men, there were no women, there were no things of any kind on the earth, the earth had not yet come to be, there was only an endless empty stretch of water, only water. Only water, *ngu* (water), *kongu* (the water from which everything arose). The stretch of water lay there and did not move.

Suddenly the water foamed, it foamed for a long time, and a small thing was washed up, it was a tiny crocodile. Only a tiny thing, only rubbish. Some time passed and it grew legs, it grew arms, it grew a tail, it grew jaws, it grew eyes, it was a proper crocodile. There it lay, and its skin, its back and its legs were those of a crocodile, but its face was that of a man, its head was that of a man. It moved and swam along and lay in the endless stretch of water. There it lay deep in the water, in the great darkness. There it lay, it grew bigger and bigger and a mighty crocodile took shape. There it lay. It thought: "How shall I manage? There is no place where I can sit or sleep or rest, why is that so?" It lay there and pondered.

It wanted it to be so and thus it happened: its *spittle* [cf. Names 5 and 6] (air bubbles) sank down below, it did not drift upwards, no, its spittle sank down to the bottom of the sea. It was dark and the spittle sank and sank and sank down to the bottom of the sea, this spittle sank and sank and then rose again, rose up, rose and stuck to its breast, such a little thing. Then the crocodile said in surprise: "What thing drifted back there? O, my child, come back!" So it spoke and thought and lay there. Then it moved and *together with the little thing it floated up*, it floated up, it reached the surface of the water, and there everything was lit up with the light of day. Day had dawned, it was bright day, and *the earth had come up, the earth had come up* [cf. Names 1 and 2, 3 and 4], only a little piece, it is true, but this little piece lay there.

The crocodile slid back into the water and it swam round it, it swam round this little piece of earth and circled round it, and *the earth grew in size*. And so it continued for a time and the earth became fairly big, like an island, a little island [cf. Names 7 and 8].

... The crocodile had come up together with the water, and after a short time it opened its jaws, the upper jaw rose up, the earth rose up, a man rose up, it was the sun Nyagonduma (which had come into being). *It opened its jaws, "Ahhhhhhh!" it went and split in two parts* [cf. song]; the sun Nyagonduma was thrown up, and it became light. It was Nyagonduma, and the day broke. And so it remained. Nyagonduma was the child of the water spirit Wanjimoutnagwan, Kabak. The crocodile looked around, around about it looked, and all the mountains, the parts of the bush, the grass, the plants, all things of the earth came into being. It went on looking, and the insects and all other things came into being and were there. *All things came into being and were there* [cf. Names 9 and 10]. And so it remained. . . .

I have attempted to answer the question whether connections capable of systematic description can be established between two, at first sight, unrelated incidents, one involving an embarrassed woman at Winge and the other an involuntary reference to the knotted cord. The answer consists in the description of a culture-immanent system of interlinkages known in its totality only to the important men that allows them to bring the most disparate things together in thought within a space-time grid. These mental networks of interrelationships are represented visually and aurally in the knotted cords and the song cycles. Both types of representation mention thousands of names, follow a fixed sequence of geographical places, and refer in shorthand to events which occurred in ancient times and on which the present Nyaura world order is based. Bateson's supposition of a system of relationships is thus confirmed.

That a description such as this one is possible at all is principally due to improved linguistic knowledge (through the work of Staalsen 1965, 1966a,b, 1969, 1971, n.d. a,b) and the development of Nyaura society. The decay of the traditional force of social pressure has led to the partial opening of the secret domain and hence to easier access to the secret knowledge of the important men and the system of interlinked meanings.[23] The formal, order-creating aspect of the system has been presented here. However, further studies are needed that deal with the application of this abstract system in practice, for, as Bateson (1932:413) noted, "such a diagram could never represent the practice of the people, though it might illustrate their theory of genealogical organization. Indeed, the name songs constitute such a diagram." With the examples of the name dispute or the land conflict with other villages (Chambri), there is good reason to believe that the static order and exemplary character claimed for the system and presented here can be shown not to be absolute and to afford an opportunity for political manipulation.

Notes

1. My fieldwork was done in Kandingei, a Western Iatmul (or Nyaura) village, in 1972–73 under the direction of Meinhard Schuster and with the generous financial support of the Swiss National Fund for the Promotion of Scientific Research. This article is based on materials published in 1982 (an English version of which will soon be published). The texts of five song cycles (*sagi*) have just appeared (Wassmann 1988),

along with another article on the system described here (Wassmann 1987). In 1983 and 1984 I returned to Kandɨngei for a few months in order to check the findings from 1972–73. At that time, the texts of the song cycles recorded in Kandɨngei were returned to the individual clan associations in written form. The ethnographic material presented here is reproduced with the authorization of the important men of Kandɨngei. D. Q. Stephenson prepared the translation.

2. "Nyaura" is the name the Western Iatmul give themselves; it is also the name of one of their clans. The Western Iatmul villages are Sapandei, Yamanumbu, Sapanaut, Yensemangwa, Korogo, Takngei and Kandɨngei (earlier a village known as Nyaurangei), and Timbunmeli (see fig. 1).

3. In this article the system is described solely as a static order.

4. The spellings of place names are those of the various members of the Sepik expedition of 1972–73 working in particular areas.

5. Although the two brothers of each pair are ascribed different areas (the left and right banks of the Sepik), their routes are, as a rule, identical; the first brother always follows the second after some delay. Thus only one route (that of the second brother) is marked on figure 2. There are, however, two exceptions: The two clan groups in the Posugo association (Posugo and Nangusime) show diverging routes; consequently both are marked. Within the same association a single clan (Ngungu/Salu) has an autonomy which finds its expression in a route of its own.

6. In fact the system is very much more complex. Specific districts are assigned not only to individual clans and lineages but also to individual clan members within the framework established by their own association.

7. Research conducted in other villages by different investigators has come to basically the same conclusions (Kaufmann 1984c; Laycock 1965, 1973; Newton 1967; Schuster 1973); (see Schuster and Schuster, Bragge in this volume).

8. Schindlbeck (1984) adds to the historical depth of the reconstruction by naming other settlements *before* Gaikorobi.

9. Reckoned from 1972–73; cf. Bragge in this volume.

10. I am aware that the extent to which genealogies can be considered reliable historical sources is controversial.

11. The first work done in this direction has been undertaken by Swadling (in this volume) and Kocher-Schmid (1980).

12. Nevertheless, the Nyaura form a distinctly independent group within the Iatmul. This is illustrated by the fact, among others, that any particular name may be borne by only one individual at a time within the Nyaura, whereas it is immaterial if anyone within the Palimbei group bears the same name.

13. In Nyaura the inhabitants of Mɨvɨmbɨt are called Sauas (Sawos). Strictly speaking, this expression is used only for the people with whom the Nyaura barter sago. (Kandɨngeians can therefore refer to the Timbunmeli people as Sauas without reservation.)

14. Namely (with the relevant association in parentheses), Yambun (Ngama), Malingwat (Nyaura), Mɨvɨmbɨt (all clans, but especially Yagun), Woliagwi (Yak), Kambangwat (Posugo), the sky (Mbowi), and the region "under the water" (Samangwak) (cf. table 2). The fenced enclosures set up for the most important ceremonies, within which the long flutes (*sagi wabi*) are blown, correspond to these "enclosures." At the end of each performance the sisters of the pair of brothers—whose voices have been audible through the flutes—return to their "region."

15. Within the region of Kandɨngei. The situation in the other village areas was not investigated.

16. Whether the stringing together of historical narratives and myths in Gewertz's work justifies the subtitle "A Historical Ethnography . . . " may be doubted.

17. Plumb (1978) makes a distinction which is useful here in sharply differentiating between "past" and "history." The "past" embraces all those concepts which man uses to explain and justify to himself the creation of the world and himself and existing social institutions. Time has no part to play in it. "History," on the other hand, is an academic discipline of our Western world that seeks to describe with the greatest possible objectivity what actually happened in the past (cf. also the works of Ernest Gellner).

18. Cf. n. 9.

19. In the region of the Nyaura there are twelve knotted cords, as many as there were migrations.

20. Actually the sequence of the songs (in relation to ancient times) is complicated by the fact that they are regularly interrupted by the insertion of recitatives which relate to the *current* purpose of the performance of the cycle. The different time planes contained in songs and recitatives are felt to be the same during the performance.

21. This is a selection of public names. Secret names are not to be published, especially as their structure is the same as that of the public.

22. The fundamental dilemma is that as many of the clan's "totems," ancient beings, and names as possible should be mentioned to enable clan members to identify with their clan and justify to members of other clans their claim to their possessions while at the same time revealing as little as possible of the secret knowledge of the relationships between the clans, "totems," names, and ancient beings.

23. The knotted cords and the song cycles provided a relatively concrete approach to the system. Beyond them were the hundreds of fragments of information—the casual "dropping" of a brief sentence is typical of the transmission of (mythological) knowledge—which had to be linked together into a whole by laborious work with informants.

4/ The Japandai Migrations[1]

Lawrence Bragge

As assistant district commissioner at Ambunti from 1970 to 1974, I was responsible for the good government of the district. Part of the law-and-order function was knowing what was going to happen in time to defuse the issue; this is known as preventive justice. Because the main source of potential conflict in Ambunti seemed to me to be land problems, my research was aimed at documenting migrations and settlement patterns for all the groups administered from Ambunti. The mass of disputes were placed in a historical context in this way. I did not set out to resolve disputes; I sought to have the best possible data on hand when a dispute approached a law-and-order flashpoint. The procedure then was to become involved with all parties to the dispute and assist with registration of the dispute with the Lands Titles Commission for hearing.[2]

Ambunti Land-Tenure Types: A Regional Perspective

After recording hundreds of pages of oral history (see appendix) I wondered if there was ever to be an end to the stories of ancient wandering clans traveling giant distances and doing amazing things. More than once informants discussed the problem Wassmann (in this volume) describes as the relationship between the "'mental' migration in ancient times and the actual history of . . . settlement." This distinction was made for me by Kolion of Nogosop as being the people's "old and new testaments," respectively, and took on more meaning for me later. Variations of what Kolion had said appeared time and again in the interview material; headhunting and related practices, for example, were something which had started only "recently." Kolion said that it had started when they killed the culture hero Mai'imp (Moem in Schindlbeck's [1980] spelling), and Gwolai of Tegoi said that it was when they killed Jesus. Some Kandingai people said that the ancestral heros Magisaun and Tangweiyabinjua had started it. The point is that it is widely accepted that this vital element in traditional religion was not present in the people's "old testament."

A restatement of this concept in slightly different words by Guanduan of Kanganaman altered my view of the ancient migrations:

> In the distant past there was no fighting. There were few people. They made it free, and they came up plenty of people. They came and went as they pleased and fished and gathered as they liked. There became more and more of them and the time came when they started to establish land ownership and boundaries and to mark out villages. This was the time fighting started . . . headhunting started.

It seemed to me that he was speaking of a hunter-gatherer utopia. I immediately thought of the paper Hatanaka and I had just written (1973) concerning the Hewa people. To this point I had thought of the ancestral migrations in terms of displaced persons, as in the Japandai, Sengo, and Tegoi migrations to be discussed here. Now I decided that we were probably talking about a nomadic or seminomadic Hewa-style existence, with migration as a way of life.

Scaglion's discussion in this volume of the episodic concept of history is important here. I think that Iatmul and Sawos people in particular distinguish between "new"- and "old"-testament migrations and lifeways. The "new" includes all memory of a village life "as it has always been" with events more or less known and remembered. The "old" testament is an ancient memory of an earlier time. The telescoping of time in oral histories would eliminate the gradual transition from nomadic to sedentary existence, and thus we have "a total restructuring of reality" in people's views of "old" and "new." This, then, was the hypothesis that prompted me to seek further land-tenure links and transitions in my notes, and what emerged was a repeated pattern of four types of land tenure. Most groups recall at least one transition from one type to another, always in a set order. I do not have space here to document cases for and against a theory of the evolution of land tenure (but see Bragge n.d.). For background to the Japandai migrations, I will state only that all Ambunti landowning groups can be classified into one of four land-tenure types, that there is a tendency for simpler forms to change into more complex ones, and that the developed military power and alliances of the complex groups often threaten the existence of smaller and/or less complex ones. The four types are as follows:

1. *Rei.* "The primary social group, an extended family with patrilineal core called *rei*, is a residential unit. . . . It was basically a foraging band. . . . The largest *rei* has 23 members" (Hatanaka and Bragge 1973:51). "The size of community in which men are able to live is controlled by the supply" (p. 40). "The residential house or base . . . lasts for one to two years. Then the people move on" (p. 46).

2. *Established villages with a maximum of one ceremonial house and related simple clan structure.* The Wagu described by Dye in this volume would fall into this category. The example I had in mind was Kagiru, a two-clan village on the April River. Each clan has its separate residential area in the village and its own land, streams, and sago stands. Kagiru has one ceremonial house. The lifeways and legends of these people indicate they are not too far removed from their southern cousins, the "Hewa."

3. *Established villages with more than one ceremonial house and established residential wards.* Typical of this category are the Upper Sepik villages from Swagup to Tauri. Each village has between two and four wards. Ward settlement follows a pattern, with the first-arrived clan being regarded as *papa bilong graun* ([Tok Pisin] father of the ground). Other clans then arrived and were granted usufruct rights that solidified through time but never quite equaled the rights of the original clan. The ward population has a single ceremonial house and in former times of war developed a high degree of military efficiency, with strategies involving clan-owned war canoes (see Ambunti Patrol Report no. 11a, 1973–74, appendices I and P, for details).

4. *Nimba.* Wassmann (in this volume) defines *nimba* (enclosure) as an individual district inhabited by specific people. I use the term to designate a group of villages claiming known and remembered migration from a central mother village or adoption by conquest. The fragmentation of the original village is usually along the lines of the wards described above. Land tenure takes on a new complexity with conflict between mother and daughter villages over rights to lands within the ancestral boundaries. Hostilities within the nimba are restricted; people recognize their unity against outsiders as well as their common

origins. While endogamy is not a rule, people nearly always marry within the nimba.

Yambon

From the beginning of memory, Yambon (fig. 1) has attracted wanderers. Because it was the place where the Japandai ancestors saw their future, I will start the story there.

Five Yambon informants told stories of ancestors coming from underground and from lakes in a form part-human, part-animal, and part-stone. The first and most prominent was Apwimendi, who originated at a hill called Ianimbunimbir. Nine of an unknown number of ascending generations to Apwimendi were recorded; suffice it to say that Yambon has a long history on the land around Ianimbunimbir. The stories tell of the wandering ancestors gathering together, for example: "They met an ancestor of Garu's called Yanbunmis [see appendix for estimated date]. They . . . told him they had brought a language for him to use . . . the language we all now speak [Manambu]. His old language is lost" (informant Tagapwi/Mebukumbi) Not all the ancestors came with sacred gifts. According to Sangai, "My ancestor [Kagaramar, see appendix] . . . made a canoe and was curing it by burning the new wood. . . . The fire burned all the yam and *mami* [a particular species of yam] gardens of the Avatips. He thought it best to go to Yambon." Outside opinion on Yambon's mixed heritage is not always favorable. According to Nauwi Sauinambi of Bangwis, "Yambon came from up near Swagup and Alakai, some came from Garamambu. They did not paddle canoes. They just hid and had sing-sings when they used to oil their bodies with tree sap. . . . If a man makes trouble he will leave his village and live with another village. A mixed village is a poor village." This and other comments about forming into clans indicate to me that Yambon probably consisted of a number of rei-type groups forced together into a simple village situation by the Manambu threat. The language change and the statement about not previously using canoes indicate changes in Yambon lifeways under the influence of the Manambu who absorbed them.

The first of a number of large migrations to Yambon had its origin at Parembei. According to Gaui of Sengo,

The reason why our ancestors moved was that crocodiles were finishing all the young men and women. My ancestor killed all our

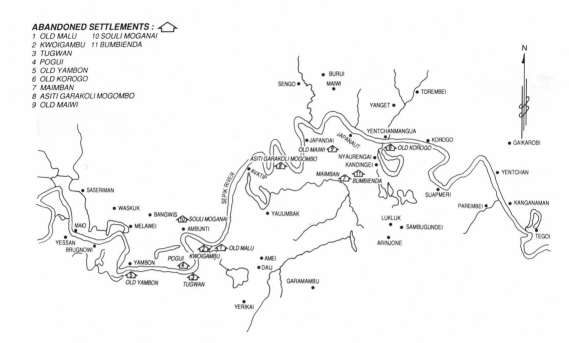

ABANDONED SETTLEMENTS :

1 OLD MALU   10 SOULI MOGANAI
2 KWOIGAMBU   11 BUMBIENDA
3 TUGWAN
4 POGUI
5 OLD YAMBON
6 OLD KOROGO
7 MAIMBAN
8 ASITI GARAKOLI MOGOMBO
9 OLD MAIWI

FIG. 1. The Chambri Lakes.

pigs and said, "If we stay here we will be finished." . . . They married off all the single girls. . . . They doubled canoes and paddled upriver away from Parembei to find new land [see appendix]. . . . They went ashore at Yambon and the Yambons wanted to fight us. . . . The Parembeis hastily broke camp and went downriver. . . . In their haste they left two young women behind, Damdagwa and Mabisaunogwi . . . they were asleep and were left by accident.

An area of land near Malingai was pointed out to me as the place where the Sengo ancestors lived. I assume that this was a residential ward similar to the sections of Parembei discussed by Coiffier in this volume.

Why did the Sengo ancestors go to Yambon? Wassmann (in this volume), describing the Iatmul world, says that "the central feature is the Sepik River . . . in the central section of the river are the Nyaura nɨmba (the Nyaura people from Sapandei to Korogo . . .), the Palimbei nɨmba (from Soatmeli to Kanganamun), and the Woliagwi nɨmba (from Kararau to Tambunum)." To this I will add that upriver of the Nyaula nɨmba is the Manambu nɨmba based on Avatip. To acquire land within any of these four areas would have meant a confrontation (usually a life-and-death

situation for the newcomer) with a multivillage alliance. Yambon at that time, being a small group without alliances, must have been far more attractive.

The next move involving Yambon started at what is now Avatip. According to Kwatauwi/Vivigamei of Avatip,

When Asiti overpopulated they made Mogombo and Garakoli villages nearby. They stayed there a long time and through many fights, and the waterways silted up and left Asiti, Mogombo, and Garakoli too far inside . . . [When] Yabsit [see appendix] came and started Avatip . . . we divided the people to set up Malu and Avatip. Big brother to Avatip, small brother to Malu . . . all the clans were represented in both places. Malu is the name of the mountain, but the people are Avatips.

The Manambu expansion illustrates the development of a nɨmba-type group from a single village. The site of Asiti, Garakoli, and Mogombo was a continuous residential area extending for about two miles, similar to present-day Nyaurengai and Kandingai.

Lisindu of Malu continued the story: "Upon arriving at Malu, my ancestor saw fires at Ambunti, which indicated enemy people close by. . . . The enemy was called Souli Moganai." Nauwi Sauinambi of Bangwis explained that the Malu, unable to paddle close to shore for fear of arrows, attempted a raid but withdrew when one of their men lost an arm trying to open the stockade gate. The Souli Moganai (Kompom Nggalla is the Kwoma name for them) cooked and ate the arm, and the Malu sought Kwoma assistance. Lisindu described the outcome: "Waskuk [Kwoma] killed them all. . . . we Malu wanted to fight too, but when we came in the morning the fight was over." The outcome was bad for Malu, as Nauwi explained: "Our men patrolled the river bank from Malu to Melawei. We prevented the river people collecting bush materials . . . cutting sago or hunting. Trespassers were shot to the extent that Malu would not paddle on this side of the river . . . They had no land with sago on it, so . . . were forced to trade with the bush people [Kwoma]."

The Souli Moganai apparently had a number of garden hamlets between the Melawei lagoon and Mount Ambunti. Their main settlement was the stockaded village on top of Mount Ambunti. According to Nauwi, it had a single ceremonial house called Mankap. I therefore suggest that this was a simple one-ceremonial-house village. I think it fair to say the Souli Moganai's fate was sealed by the Manambu expansion to Malu. The Kwoma moved against the Souli Moganai when they learned of Malu intentions to take the Souli Moganai lands; they simply got in first.

That failure to control sago resources necessitates trade is a common feature for a river-based nɨmba (see Ambunti Patrol Reports nos. 8, 1972–73; 5, 1973–74; 13, 1972–73; see also Gewertz 1983).

Lisindu of Malu took up the story: "Malu met again, and it was decided we should extend our land holdings further upriver by destroying Yambon." Karandaman of Malu gave the reason for this fight as the murder of two Malu men by Yambon. He went on: "Domogwai's ancestor [of Malu] said, 'Their big man Kugiaweni sent me a *tanget* [(Tok Pisin) shrub used to send a message][3] . . . he will come tomorrow to trade.' . . . he came . . . and they speared him with a paddle. He cried out . . . 'Do not kill me quickly . . . they are hunting at Ianimbunimbir . . . for a feast over killing the Malus.'" Lisindu continued: "They were smoking the pig meat when the Malus arrived . . . two or three survived . . . these are the ancestors of the present Yambon people. Malu settlers went and established a camp at Yambon to protect their new lands." Yambon consider this an overstate-

ment, and I agree. According to Garu, "Yambon by this time had developed into clans which claimed the land. . . . The clans came and set up camp on the point where the Summer Institute of Linguistics is now, because the Malus had established a camp at Mount Malu." Garu's story of Kugiaweni and the fight generally confirmed the above. He went on: "Next morning the Yambons went down and saw the bodies of their relatives, met the Malu fighting force, and fought with them."

Malu and Yambon versions agree that Yambon then abandoned their village in favor of a succession of bush camps. My assumption is Yambon reverted to rei-type foraging groups for this period in the bush. This called for a revision of my understanding of the "conquest" of Yambon. Yambon's language changed to Manambu, but this seems to have happened [see appendix] some thirty to forty years prior to the existence of Malu. Further, the Malu settlement on Yambon land reflected a division within Malu more than a desire to claim land. Malu's next move, we find, was to attack Garamambu, south of the river, but, as Karandaman explained, a Malu elder called Sangurandaman, angry over a bride-price, had put a curse on the raid: "'This line . . . will be finished at Gumbanawur.' All the fights of the past the Malus had won, but they lost this fight against Garamambu because of Sangurandaman's curse. . . . Benjindum [see appendix] came back to Malu defeated. . . . He said 'No, I will not live more at Malu, I will go upstream.' He made camp where I live now [three miles upstream of Ambunti near Tugwan Pogui and Ianimbunimbir]." My information indicates that even then, Garamambu was a nɨmba-type group (combining with Yerikai). Stories tell of the crushing of two small groups, Amei and Dau, located between the Manambu and Garamambu nɨmbas, and the absorption of the survivors.

Another migration was about to take place, this time from the Nyaula nɨmba village Japandai. I suggest that the situation Japandai was about to enter involved a divided Malu that had recently tried and failed to gain land north and south of the Sepik and had failed to press home its advantage against Yambon, still in hiding in the forest.

The First Japandai Migration

Opinion varies as to why the Japandais migrated. Yakabus Kami of Maiwi said, "In fear of fighting from Maiwi"; Kwatauwi of Avatip said, "They had it in their minds to migrate"; Kwonji of Burui said, "The Nyaurengais went up to Japandai and stole their women and pigs and made sorcery and native customs against them"; and Karandaman of Malu said, "We . . . wanted them to come . . . because they were our trade source for pottery and baskets. Between friends . . . trade is cheap and easy, between enemies prices are high and trade slight." Informants from Japandai and Brugnowi (settled by the third Japandai migration) did not talk of reasons for the migration beyond describing events concerning Maiwi village. Malingot/Ongwinjambi of Brugnowi described how his great-great-grandfather Gumbeli of Maiwi killed a Maiwi man who had committed adultery with Gumbeli's wife. Gumbeli and his brother fled to the protection of Japandai. Then, some time afterward,

> Maiwi wanted to attack Nyaurengai, and they came upriver to give ginger to [seek an alliance with; see n. 3] Avatip. The Japandais saw the war canoe coming . . . and said, "Don't bother to go to Avatip, we will help you." [They] gave Maiwi a long tanget, and the Maiwis went home. The Japandais then prepared a short tanget and gave it to Yessan Maio and Saseriman, and they came . . . to Japandai.

Yakabus Kami of Maiwi continued the story:

> A Maiwi man died, and they had a sing-sing for him. They marked a day in advance, and the Japandais . . . were advised. The Japandais took ginger up to near Ambunti . . . the people mourning were not suspicious . . . there were no enemies around. . . . near dawn . . . a woman went up a coconut tree and she called, "Maiwi enemies approach." They called back, "We have no enemies, Maiwi is safe." "Is that so?" [she said]. She was unable to change their thinking so . . . climbed down . . . took her children and belongings and paddled them in a canoe to the middle of the lake. . . . The spears did not miss. Maiwi was badly beaten.

Yakabus told of Maiwi's flight to Japanaut and then across the Sepik toward Burui. Malingot mentioned follow-up raids and compensation paid for the death of a Saseriman warrior. He went on, "After the fight Gumbeli and Japandai men Paligumban and Avagien moved upriver to obtain new land. . . . [They] settled at Kwoigambu . . . near the Malu Rest House. Gumbeli gave four women to Malu."

The reason for the migration was probably the unlimited hostility exercised against a fellow Nyaula nɨmba village. Nyaurengai and other Nyaula nɨmba villages could be expected to take reprisals for such an action; this could be what Kwonji was talking about. (This hostility could also be the reason some Japanaut and Nyaurengai men felt free to take part in the massacre of the second Japandai migration; see below.) Karandaman had the following to say about the Japandai settlement on Malu land at Kwoigambu:

> the Japandais . . . came to live near the . . . waterway to Yerikai. A Malu man . . . [called] Winjiba washed sago and fenced the sago off. The pig of a Japandai man Abakien ate the sago. The Malu came . . . and speared the pig. He said, "Ah, yes, I speared the pig because it ate my sago. The sago was well fenced, but the pig broke down the fence. . . . I would not have speared the pig if the sago had been unfenced." The pig owner agreed with this and cut the pig up and gave it to the Malus to eat. . . . The Japandais then got up and said, "We will not live here!"

Malingot's story continued:

> Then [Gumbeli] . . . went upstream beyond Yessan to Kusai Lagoon; then he came back to settle at Yessan. But Paligumban was afraid of the Swagup and Waskuk people. He felt they were too far from home, so they drifted down to Pogui. . . . Malu's ancestor Benjindum was there. The Yambons had been attacked by Malu and were wild in the bush. Our ancestor saw footprints of a man. . . . Malu said it was their enemy Yambon, and suggested that Malu and Japandai lay an ambush . . . but my ancestor said, "No, we will become their friends." They found the Yambons and established them at Suaigai. Then they called out for more Japandais to come . . . and make camp opposite Gumbeli's camp, Pogui, at Tugwan. Gumbeli gave two women (Mangandawa and Tuganmangiwanga) to Yambon with shell money to make . . . friends.

Yambon does not acknowledge Japandai assistance, asserting that the Malus invited them to come and live at Malu and they finally came and set up camp at Tugwan. Nauwi's Kwoma version supports the Japandai version: "[Japandai] . . . pulled Yambon down to the river a little upstream of where Karandaman lives now, Tugwan." The Malu-Japandai debate about the Yambon future is fascinating because in retrospect Japandai took the course which was to do them most harm.

Malingot went on:

Gumbeli's line put its first market at Mino and then at Dwagup at Waskuk. Then our ancestor decided he should have a separate market from the combined Japandai-Malu market. He arranged a private market at Tirim . . . [Benjindum] gave ginger to Waskuk to kill Gumbeli. Gumbeli . . . met the Waskuks, and they told him. . . . So Gumbeli gave them ginger to kill Benjindum. Tangets were exchanged and confused . . . both tangets indicating the same day for Waskuk to kill Benjindum on behalf of Gumbeli and to kill Gumbeli on behalf of Benjindum. The Waskuks attacked and killed them both.

Karandaman's version adds detail: "Kalimi, my uncle, married Gumbeli's first daughter Kavebimanga. They all went . . . [to the market with Waskuk] Gumbeli, Kainimba, Benjindum [and others] all fell."

Malingot continued: "There was a payback. Japandai, Malu Yessan, and Maio fought the Waskuks at the Dwagup market site. The Waskuks were beaten. Japandai had their sing-sing at Tugwan, Malu had their sing-sing at Malu." (It seems significant that, with Benjindum dead, activity for Malu people again centered on Malu, not Tugwan. Warfare would seem to have reunified Malu.)

Karandaman told how his father used Saseriman intelligence reports to attack Waskuks gathering fish and tortoises in the Waskuk lagoon at low water. After killing these, they killed women and children in Waskuk gardens until driven back to the water by Waskuk warriors, who had the advantage of the higher ground.

Malingot picked up the story at a time apparently some months later:

An argument [about fishing and gardening rights] developed between Japandai and Yambon. Yambon sent ginger to Malu and Waskuk. The men [of Japandai] were away, and the fight came in their absence. . . . They killed two elders . . . two children and a woman. . . . In the afternoon the Japandais returned and found the village burned, and the dead. They slept outside and then prepared food and double canoes and drifted downriver to Japandai.

The Yambon version of this fight, as told by Garu, stated, "Yaunimbir, the wife of Jaimbendu, was at the mouth of the waterway . . . and Yeramai [of Japandai] exposed his penis to her. Malu and Yambon killed the [Japandais]." Nauwi Sauinambi's Kwoma version is similar: "Jaimbendu of Yambon had a wife . . . who was like a prostitute. She was the mistress of a [Japandai] man Nagwanmeri. . . . Malu agree to ferry the Waskuks to the fight. The survivors went downriver on rafts and broken canoes. My ancestor then took Yambon up to their present village site and set them up there."

It is difficult to say at exactly what point Yambon became a unit within the Manambu nimba. It represents a case, like Aibom and Suapmeri within the Parembei nimba, of an alien group's being absorbed rather than being wiped out. In seeking Malu assistance to remove Japandai (who so recently had argued with Malu for the continued existence of Yambon), Yambon acknowledged its position as a Manambu village.

Leadership, in my opinion, was the key to the initial success and ultimate failure of the first migration. Gumbeli established his group securely at Tugwan. He became a peacemaker who brought Yambon out of hiding and argued against Malu's plan to annihilate Yambon. He commenced trade, which obviously developed into a fluid interchange among half a dozen villages. Benjindum was a leader of apparent equal strength. Without the division he created within Malu, I doubt whether the Japandais would have succeeded as they did. But with Gumbeli's and Benjindum's leadership gone, the fabric unraveled.

The combined losses from the two fights against the first Japandai migration were compiled by Malingot and the Brugnowis as follows (I will not list names): nine men, seven women, and three youths, fourteen of them Japandais and five Maiwis.

Between Migrations

An old land file at Ambunti contains an undated interview with two Japandai elders, Wagi/Banduwan and Mariandei/Kaneiman, according to whom "more than half the Japandais went upriver and settled at a place called Tugwan . . . The Tugwan settlement lasted for some time, perhaps as long as a generation." When the survivors reached Japandai, "the permanent Japandais suggested that the Tugwan Japandais go and settle at Maiwi. The permanent Japandais were having some trouble with Korogo, Yentchanmangua, and Nyaurengai. The Tugwan Japandais went to Maiwi, but . . . were . . . badly treated so . . . returned to Japandai."

Malingot elaborated on this: "We retreated to Maiwi. We did not think of the old fight against Maiwi, but the Maiwis made sorcery against us and killed us to pay back the fight we made against them years ago." The Japandai "payback" for Tugwan was aimed at Malu. It started with a raid which, according to Malingot, burned a hamlet called Manji. The next raid killed four women tending fish traps at dawn. Following this four people were killed while rolling sago logs near Lake Kwoigambu. "Malu was feeling the results. . . . They said, 'We were not the source of the ginger. Yambon is the place where the fight started.' Malu gave us a war canoe called Kabandingei and said, 'Go in this canoe and kill Yambon.' . . . The Malus gave the Japandais a tanget to mark the Yambon market day with Saseriman." Japandai prepared an ambush for this trading party and fought at Yambon on their way back downstream. Malingot continued: "They [Japandai] went to Tugwan and decorated themselves and sang their way downriver. Malu asked, 'How many did you kill?' We replied, 'Seven.' Malu replied, 'Good, you have ended the fight now.' They explained that they had been afraid and that women and children had died of starvation." Malingot told of two more raids on Yambon, resulting in four additional deaths, before peace was made. Malu Avatip and Yambon informants were not asked directly about these raids or the gift of the war canoe. None of the informants from these villages offered acknowledgment or details.

The Second Japandai Migration

According to Malingot of Brugnowi, "There was interchange and movement back and forth. Malu and Yambon came and invited us to come back to live at Yambon at the old place south of the Yambon gate [the narrowest point on the Sepik's navigable length]." The old land-file interview with Wagi and Mariandei was more specific:

They [Japandai] stayed there for years and the population grew. The Tugwan branch wanted to return again to Tugwan, but they were opposed by the permanent Japandais, who did not want to reduce village strength. However, an influential man of the Tugwan faction went to Yambon and discussed matters with an influential Yambon man [Mangoimeri spoke to Kwanggambi of Yambon about forty years ago]. Both these men were in their prime and of considerable standing in their respective communities. Mangoimeri proposed that the Japandai people return to the Yambon area. Kwanggambi was agreeable . . . but suggested that instead of settling as a unit on their own land they come to Yambon and settle into the village and become absorbed in the Yambon community. . . . Mangoimeri went back to Japandai and the move was arranged.

Malingot and the other informants from Japandai had little to say about the second migration beyond that it "was quickly followed by a big fight that finished Japandai." The Yambon version of what happened, as told by Garu Jam, was as follows:

[Japandai] asked if they might come back and live with Yambon again. Our fathers agreed, but said, "You must not behave as you did last time." They came back, but they behaved as they had before. If our women went anywhere they made to kill them, the same with small parties of men. They disputed our rights to use the lagoons. Yuwandu sent ginger to Waskuk, Avatip, Nyaula, Nyaurengai, Malu, and they came and finished the place. Few . . . survived to return to Kambaramau. Their bodies were thick like dead fish in the water. The priest Father Kirschbaum [at Marienberg] . . . saw the bodies and sent word to Madang.

In another discussion Garu added:

We took no prisoners. Some men thought about taking children to raise as their own, or young girls and women to take as wives. But they feared . . . if they did . . . later when they grew up they would know where their place was and go back and leave the Yambons. Plenty of men caught such people and hid them, but others found them and they were killed. There has not been a third fight against Brugnowi because we are at peace now and our children are growing up well and we know if the fight came we would be running in the bush and our children would die of starvation as they did in the past during fighting times.

The Malu version, as told by Lisindu, was as follows:

The [Japandai] commenced disputing the Yambon rights to fish in lagoons. The Yambon big men . . . sent ginger down to our fathers at Malu. The problem of the [Japandai] presence had concerned us for some time. We sent tangets down to the big men of Nyaula, Sugundambwi, and Yabisaun of Nyaurengai Kandingai. They came in their big war canoes. The combined force went and finished them. We beheaded them and threw the bodies in the river.

The Avatip involvement was described by Kwatauwi:

> Parakau of Avatip and Yabisaun [of Japanaut] were friends; although they were of different groups, they came to see each other on village business. . . . This was the sort of relationship through which ginger is passed to start a fight. . . . Yambon did not send the ginger [to Avatip] . . . it came to Avatip from Nyaula. . . . In this fight we did not take heads. The bodies went into the . . . water. Avatip was happy to fight because they [Japandai] were on Yambonjandu, which is Yambon land, part of Avatip land.

Both Malu and Avatip statements indicate a degree of proprietary interest in Yambon land. The removal of Japandai made the Manambu nɨmba a true "enclosure."

Malingot said of the survivors, "Few were able to escape by canoe or floating logs on the Sepik. The Malus came out and fought them as they drifted by. In the night they came to the passage into Avatip and waited until dawn, then Noganmeri . . . called out to the Avatips of his clan . . . 'Will you fight us? If you will, come and kill us now. Yambon killed us and few of us are left.'" The clan associations described by Wassmann are significant here; the survivors were able to seek protection of clansmen at Avatip on the very day after warriors from that village had taken part in the massacre. Later we will see the Tegoi people of Nyaula nɨmba seeking clan-association protection in the enemy Parembei nɨmba. Similar clan relationships exist between Iatmul and Sawos villages and, I would guess, throughout the Ndu language family.

Malingot continued: "The Avatip slit-drums were beaten, and Avatip canoes came out to get them. The Avatips ferried us down. They pulled out the broken spears and arrows and fixed our wounds. . . . Movements on the river were at night. . . . Malu and Yau'umbak [another Avatip daughter village] were still after us." Kwatauwi of Avatip enlarged on this: "We were sorry for them and took them ashore and put oil and banana leaves on their wounds and cut their skin with bamboo knives to let the bad blood out. . . . When they were repaired we sent them down to their old place Kambaramau." Malingot told the story of some less fortunate survivors:

> Bumbienda was the place [from] where the Japanauts came and fought us. This is inland from the present Japandai, on the Chambri side of the swamp. The [Bumbienda] *haus tambaran* [(Tok Pisin) ceremonial house] was called Jriabei. The captured children were Dumison and Jumibangwa. They were about nine years old. Sugurap, a child of Yabisaun's, [attacked] one with a spear; his father killed him. . . . This is done so the child may wear black paint and be initiated. When the children were dead they were placed one in each of the main post holes of the haus tambaran and the post put in on top of them, and the ground is called after them, by their names. This gives the ground power. This is how we establish ownership. If we have named land in this way it is ours and no one can touch it. If we are trying to win new land and a fight starts, we must always return to the old place with a name.

This touches on deeper shades of ownership and belief that I will go into elsewhere.

Indirect Consequences of the Massacre

Opinion on the action against Japandai within the Nyaula nɨmba was mixed, with some strongly in favor and some strongly against. Two new migrations resulted. Of the Tegoi migration, Gwolai of Tegoi said,

> Men of Japanaut . . . and Nyaurengai . . . killed the Japandais. Four of our fathers . . . [of Samiangwat clan, Yentchanmangua village] opposed this attack on Nyaula people by Nyaula people. They said, "Japandai was a good place, they were our source of canoes and paddles, why did you kill them?" Their opposition was clear and open, and it was evident that they intended to back this fight. . . . Two [cousins from Seliambu] clan said, "We are few who think this way. . . . We cannot pay back this big fight. . . . It would be better if you went back to where you buried Bonguwan [an ancestor

killed by Korogo and buried at his widow's village Kaminimbit in a burial plot purchased with a girl called Malinjoa]. Mainbwan agreed with the idea. The two cousins came and helped him make a double canoe. . . . They left in the night and said nothing to the village as a whole. Maimbwan changed his mind and decided to try his luck at Kanganaman. . . . They had plenty of clansmen there, Samiangwat, Naua, Masam. . . . At dawn the next day the Kanganaman leader Malingingin . . . sent talk to Parembei, Malingai, and Yentchan to come. "Our enemies are here . . . Nyaulas from Yentchanmangua; come and kill them." It was a challenge to the whole Parembei [nɨmba]. . . . They all came, including Aibom. Malingingin had a great understanding of the Parembei people. Also, he made magic so that the strength of the Parembeis for fighting would be gone. . . . The Parembeis said, "No, we will not kill them, we will give them sago." It is a custom that if a clan gives food to people they are making a truce.

Gwolai went on to say that a later dispute caused a shift from Kanganaman to Tegoi.

Nyaula Settlement of the Chambri Lakes

According to Weindumbanga of Lukluk, grandson of Yabisaun,

> While living at Bumbienda . . . Yabisaun went with the Yau'umbaks and participated in the massacre. Some other Japanauts went also. The Nyaurengais were very angry about this, as [Japandai] were of our language and were a good source of paddles and canoes . . . but the Japanauts protected them [the killers] . . . to be safe Yabisaun left Bumbienda, which was close to the way the Nyaulas came and went, and went to Mambangaui.

Weindumbanga went on to talk of the development of sago trade with Garamambu and the eventual settlement of Sambugundei and Lukluk Islands in the Chambri Lakes.

Another view was offered by Maganjui of Nyaurengai:

> I put the Japanauts by Lukluk. The Japanauts went to kill the Japandais . . . The

Nyaulas got up to kill the offending Japanauts in a payback. I went with my elder brother and collected the offenders Yabik, Wabiengaui, Gumbiagwan [of Japanaut] and from Nyaurengai, Ambaimeri, Kamburi, Kubeliwan, Mondindimba, Ambundimi, and Kanabimeri and we took them to Maiban [Maimban to the Avatips and presumbly Mambangaui to Lukluk] on the Yau'umbak waterway. We did this because they were our family and we wanted to help them. We cleared the bush for them. Later we took them to Sambugundei, and then, when they killed the prospectors at Korosameri, they ran away and we put them at Lukluk.

There is, of course, more background to Nyaula land claims and counterclaims in the Chambri area, but it is not significant for this topic.

The Tegoi migration resulted from the opposition of a Nyaula group to the involvement of Nyaula people in the Japandai massacre; the Sambugundei/Lukluk migration resulted from participation in it. This and the repeated mention of Nyaula people fighting Nyaula people indicates the upheaval the incident obviously caused within the Nyaula nɨmba. The accepted code within the nɨmba is strictly limited hostility; the Japandai massacre was outside the accepted code.

Australian Involvement

The Melbourne newspaper *The Age* for March 3, 1924, reported tales of horror brought back from New Guinea by passengers on the steamer *Mataram*:

> Mrs O'Brien, a woman who had travelled extensively in New Guinea, visited the Sepic River District and there it was alleged she witnessed the result of a frightening massacre of sleeping blacks. Mrs O'Brien arrived at the camp of a Malu tribe on the morning after the atrocities had taken place. It was then learned that a tribe of kanakas had made a friendly visit to a Malu tribe from Avanky and Yambu. But in the middle of the night they were set upon by their hosts and murdered in their sleep. Mrs O'Brien saw 68 bodies scattered around while hundreds of spears and stakes pinned them to the ground. There were 37 survivors but all had been frightfully mutilated. These included 15 men 12 women and 10 babies.

Mrs O'Brien said that such stories never reach the outside world, and were scarcely credible but the things she had seen in the space of a few months she would not care to see again during the remainder of her lifetime.

Her story caused debate in the Australian Commonwealth Senate. In *Senate Debates* for Friday, March 28, 1924, we read:

Senator Grant asked the Minister for Home and Territories

1. Has the Minister received information to the effect that during a night attack by one native tribe upon another on the mainland of New Guinea 68 Kanakas were killed and a considerable number wounded?

2. If so, will he inform the Senate what steps, if any, have been taken to punish the participants?

Senator Pearce: The answers are—

1. The only information so far received is based entirely upon hearsay. The informants had no personal evidence to offer and did not even visit the scene of the alleged tragedy. They claim however to have seen some of the survivors of a tribal fight which is stated to have taken place two months earlier in a portion of the Sepik River valley outside the area under effective Government control.

2. An expedition in the charge of an experienced District Officer, consisting of four Europeans and 30 native constables, has been despatched to the Sepik river to make an investigation, and, if possible, to arrest the culprits and bring them to trial. The expedition is in no sense punitive, and one of its objectives is the establishment of a permanent Government station 250 miles up the river as a preliminary step to bringing the surrounding area under control.

Townsend (1968:97) describes this expedition and the establishment of Ambunti as follows:

Japondai had so grown in numbers that they felt strong enough to spare a number of families to take up . . . land where they once lived but had been hunted from 10 to 15 years before. To do this they had to go upstream about 40 miles, passing their old enemies, the Avatips and the Malus, and stopping within sight of other enemies, the Jambons. They chose a time for this migration when they knew that the men of these

villages would be occupied away from the river; and so . . . arrived safely . . . and commenced to build new houses. Several months went by without any of their traditional enemies showing any signs of displeasure and, indeed, it is easy to see why the Japondai began to feel that they were going to get away with it. Their feeling of security was strengthened even more by the unusual behavior of the Jambons who . . . began to send them gifts in the form of timber and other building materials. They did this by constructing rafts of logs and by sending a lone man in a canoe to call out to the Japondai people and point out what was floating down stream. The Japondai, no doubt wary at first, eventually relaxed their guard and became careless and when one day, a number of rafts appeared, spread out over the surface of the river, some of their men put out in canoes to collect them as usual. These were therefore helpless spectators when the Avatip and Malu allies of Jambon attacked from the rear of the village. . . . In all 28 Japondai lost their heads.

The apparent conflict between what is said by Townsend and the people's story may, I think, be attributed to two causes: (1) In such a primitive situation, without adequate interpreters in the initial stages, it would have been nearly impossible to establish exactly what happened. (2) Townsend and the others undoubtedly wanted the matter taken out of the political arena as quickly as possible so that they could get on with establishing the station and making friendly contact with the Ambunti people. Even in the post-Self-Government period, there was a recognition of the fact that the people in initial and early contact stages lived according to a set of rules, and it was hardly their fault if some such rules broke government laws. In late 1974 I made murder arrests in an initial-contact situation among Hewa people, and in the national court hearing I spent far more time as a witness for the defense than I did for the prosecution. In the interest of justice it was essential that the judge be fully aware of the antecedents of the people upon whom he was to pass sentence. These Hewa murderers were sentenced to terms varying from eighteen to twenty-four months. In Townsend's day, willful murder was punished by hanging. His position of first explaining the law that would apply from then on was the best course of action open.

No arrests were made for the Japandai massacre, and no one came to trial. Headhunting after that date was brought to trial, and persons convicted were hanged. Garu of Yambon explained how the situation was handled:

> The *kiap* [(Tok Pisin) government officer] came then to teach Yambon the law. We scattered, some to Yessan, some to Waskuk, some to Melawei and Saseriman . . . and stayed a long time in the bush. Vaginap, the *luluai* [(Tok Pisin) appointed chief] of Avatip, spoke to us and tried to grease the Yambons. . . . They took two men to Ambunti, Ganbank, and the other ran away. Ganbank came back without being jailed, and they took two more to Ambunti, Yebindu and Marikwat, and gave them salt and rice and other things. . . . They made peace like this and became friends . . . and brought them back to Yambon.

The Brugnowi list of dead from the raid on the second migration shows sixty-eight: fifteen men, nineteen women, fifteen girls, eighteen youths, and one small boy, sixty of them Japandais and eight Maiwis. I have no doubt that the number was sixty-eight, not twenty-eight as Townsend (1968) has it. This was the number listed by name, sex, age, and village for me in 1972 and also the number mentioned in the 1924 newspaper article and the government debate, neither of which I read until 1983.

The Third Japandai Migration

Reference to Townsend (1968) indicates that the third Japandai migration occurred prior to Townsend's posting to Kavieng in 1927. Malingot's story continued:

> We wanted to go and fight again to pay back our defeat . . . but kiap Townsend came. . . . At the Yessan invitation to once again go upriver, there was varying opinion at Japandai . . . some said enough of our people had been killed up there. Nine men got up, including Tultul Imingaui, and made camp at Brugnowi. We purchased the land from Yessan. . . . The Japandais and the Yessans saw kiap Townsend at Ambunti, and he said the Yessan talk was OK. They gave us land and cleared the bush for us and made houses for us without floors, a roof over our heads. . . . The nine men prepared payment for the land and gave it to the Yessans. There were two heaps of pay plus a pig and a dog,

and they cut the pig and the dog up for food and distributed the pay at Yessan. The Yessan got up and killed four women, Kimbeinmange, Yambungwun, Ambai, and Wanio, to make Brugnowi a strong place. The land deal was settled. We needed a lake to fish and find food in; Ailambari they . . . purchased, Juigogo, an island, they paid for. They sold this land to us. Lombugu Banglaga lakes also we purchased. The tributaries and waterways we have purchased. We will eat together without boundaries, was what Yessan said.

Yessan ruefully confirmed this. Said Yingir, "Brugnowi was our mistake. We invited them to come and live on our land. We sent them decorated lime gourds as gifts down to Japandai, after the Yambons had twice defeated them, and they came at our invitation."

The land-file interview with Japandai elders Wagi and Mariandei ends:

> With the Government established at Ambunti the Japandais again went upriver and settled where they are now. . . . The Tugwan migrants feel they have a strong claim through their payments for ground and their previous heavy losses. Just after the war, fighting broke out between Yambon and Brugnowi over disputed hunting rights. The Yambons were sent to jail at Angoram for their part in it.

The final Brugnowi list of dead contains five names: two men and three women killed at Lake Swokawit upstream of Yessan after the war with Japan.[4]

Reports of conflict between Yessan and Brugnowi over the years include District Court depositions dated June 23, 1954, to the effect that seven Brugnowis and seven Yessans had been jailed for riotous behavior two to four months each. The dispute was over canoes and trees, with Brugnowi offering compensation and Yessan refusing to accept it. A Japandai village book notation from 1960 records Japandai fears that Brugnowi would plant tree crops on their former lands, their concern being that they would not be able to retain their present lands if the matter went to court. In Ambunti Patrol Report no. 11, 1967–68, R. Treutlein says,

> Yessan Maio own the land upon which Brugnowi live. The Yessan Maio describe the Brugnowi as thieves and rogues, who encroach on land and water rights without permission and ignore *tambu* [taboo] signs.

There are also some marriage disputes mainly brought about by customary differences. Brugnowi work on a reciprocal gift exchange while Yessan Maio have a one-way payment system. . . . Brugnowi is prepared to make a special effort . . . to get back on a friendly footing. . . . Feeling is high and Yessan Maio would like to push Brugnowi back to Japandai.

In Ambunti Patrol Report no. 4, 1968–69, J. Corrigan and P. den Ousten assert that

[Brugnowi] do not hold any land apart from that of their village site and acquire their food, building materials, canoe timber from other villages. They have a reputation for living off their wits and are much "sharper" than their immediate neighbours, especially the people of Yessan Maio, who have lost considerable numbers of young girls to the more sophisticated Brugnowi men. . . . trouble arises due to different attitudes to bride price.

And in Ambunti Patrol Report no. 8, 1972–73, I report that "this Brugnowi land has now been registered with the Lands Titles Commission for hearing. As a result the Brugnowis have sent two families back to Japandai to guard their land holdings there." This just-in-case attitude interested Avatip, who then sought to register a claim on all Japandai lands on the ground that they had been abandoned by their rightful owners when the third Japandai migration went upriver. D. B. Robertson, G. Swainson, and Lands Titles Commissioner Page, in Ambunti Patrol Report no. 15, 1972–73, summarize the LTC's decision:

Land belongs to Brugnowi. But Yessan Maio retain sago gathering and hunting rights. Originally 9 Japandai families came at the invitation of Yessan Maio to live. Others came later. Payment made for land and various rights. Yessan Maio evidence told of migrations from Nukuma area through Tongwinjamb Mino and Melawei then back to Yessan. Maio was the same group living on the other side of the Sepik. Yessan Maio came to live with the ancient group Naiuri who took them in five generations ago, just as the Yessan took in Brugnowi in the 1930s.

In a district court case dated March 12, 1973, five men were fined $10 each for carrying offensive weapons in a public place after the LTC decision. Forty-four Yambon and Malu men, some wearing black war paint, were intercepted on the

Ambunti airstrip. This is the last document in my Japandai file. I doubt that it is the end of the story.

Notes

1. This paper is about oral history and land tenure. Scaglion's paper in this volume made me realize that I had addressed a number of problems in recording oral histories and found my own solutions. I agree with all the points he raises and will not repeat them here. My reading of the textbooks indicates that land tenure can only be understood in the context of the culture as a whole, and this points firmly in the direction of microstudies. My interests and responsibility as an administrator were regional, however, and May's advocacy of macro-studies and the symposium's interest in regional issues and trends are heartening. I hope that this regional approach to land tenure will offer something new and complement other papers in this volume. (The one I see as most closely related to my own is that of Wassmann.) While I will concentrate on land tenure, I recognize that other cultural aspects (religion in particular) are involved. In this regional context, then, I suggest that the variations in land tenure described would also indicate variations in social structure and religious complexity.

2. The Australian administration was quick to acknowledge that difficulties over land were increased with the establishment of law and order. Native Administration Regulation 59 of 1924 gave district officers the authority to adjudicate land disputes and remained in force until 1957. Under the Native Land Registration Ordinance of 1952, lands commissioners, drawn from senior officer ranks, were appointed to adjudicate disputes, and in 1962 the Lands Titles Commission was established.

At the District level, there were always problems. At the time of the hearing of the Brugnowi dispute reported here, for example, there were only seven lands titles commissioners; no officer thought this was enough. Registration of disputes demanded a full chain-and-compass traverse of the land. Near the Sepik and other major rivers, this was often impossible because of deep swamps, lakes, etc.; the land was physically under water or the cement markers had vanished in the mud. The area between Yessan and May River presented a special problem; here the river was forever changing course, and even where boundaries were settled the river had a habit of making adjustments.

Then there was the matter of acceptable evidence. A culturally aware officer recognizes the importance of myths and legends to the land tenure system. Western evidence-taking tends, however, to be skeptical about tales, for instance, of birds dropping a huge *kwila* tree to create a lake containing water spirits. With luck the commissioner might agree that myths indicated a claim, but then he would learn that the Sepik had broken into the lake and the spirits had escaped, expanding the clan's claim. He was far more interested in known and remembered material with a degree of reality that he could identify. He could hardly give great weight to evidence that would appear ludicrous if brought to appeal. A decision in these circumstances that went against the mythical claim would not be accepted.

To some extent, then, the problem was a cultural one. The only persons with enough experience were senior officers, all Australian. The problem was indigenous. The Lands Titles Commission Act established "demarcation committees," groups of local leaders appointed to specific demarcation areas. An aim of this was to place land-dispute settlement in the hands of the best men available, indigenous leaders. The necessary records were kept in a register at the district office that also contained all previous administrative decisions. From 1974 to 1976 at Koroba in the Southern Highlands, I worked with these committees from time to time. Some disputes were mediated in this way, and a degree of success could be claimed for the system, particularly where official interest and supervision adequately supported it. Most officers would, I think, agree that land disputes were best left alone—that the only time to step in was when not to meant a breakdown in law and order.

3. According to Nauwi Sauinambi of Bangwis, 'fastening a tanget' is the same as giving a note. Periods of time are marked, if there are five tangets [croton leaves] . . . meet us on Friday . . . Monday, Tuesday, Wednesday, Thursday, Friday [one leaf for each day] . . . If you have trouble in your place . . . you would take wild taro, ginger, cook black face paint, bamboo shavings from sharpening a spear point and wrap them up into a package and give them [with the sharpened spear] to an enemy group. . . . This means, 'If you are a true man you will come and destroy this place.' You have to give it to a man of power in the place. This man will then decide either to attack or to let it go. [He] may report back to the village to be destroyed, 'We have received this bundle . . . but we have been good friends in the past, so look after this man, or we will be obliged to come and kill you.' A group receiving such a bundle generally rejoices . . . everyone likes to fight. If I received a bundle . . . I would take all the men to the haus tambaran and . . . I would throw it onto the floor at the foot of one of my kin. He would pick it up. This is the acceptance of the invitation to fight. He may not pick it up if he has relatives in the village. He will allow another to pick it up. The people who accept the invitation divide the contents of the bundle and tie their portion to the spears they will use in the fight. The black paint supplied will be put on their faces. When the fight is over and the survivors see the ginger on the spears, they will know the source of the fight came from within their own village. The man who sent the bundle may . . . live with the aggressors, or pretend not to know. If he is discovered he will be killed. The man who sent the spear he had sharpened will expect that particular spear to kill his specified enemy in the village."

4. The Tegoi migration, the third Japandai migration, and the Nyaula settlement of the islands in the Chambri Lakes all suggest that the notion of "frozen land boundaries" resulting from the establishment of law and order needs a closer look. These migrations and a number of others not mentioned occurred after the so-called freeze.

Appendix

The Recording of Oral History

The main tool I developed in dealing with oral history was a cross-reference index, a portion of which is set out in table 1. I used a tape recorder and transcribed the interview material from the tapes. Translation from Tok Pisin to English was done between the headphones and the typing fingers; English expression was allowed to suffer in favor of literal meaning. Double meanings and *tokbokis* ([Tok Pisin] secret terms) were typed in Tok Pisin as well. I learned to limit my questioning and allow the informant to tell his story his way. I found that the index classified the information the way I wanted it without altering the words of the informant's story and that it generally served as an adequate reminder without reading the actual transcripts. At the end of an interview and during breaks I asked questions to establish some form of chronology. This usually involved genealogy or dated events. I made a conscious effort to do this wherever possible but find in rereading the material that I should have recorded more such information. I am considering recording the indexed data on a computer to facilitate analysis.

What follows is my best attempt to establish a time schedule for the events described above. Where years are mentioned, in most cases they are very approximate. I first constructed a simple genealogy linking the ancestor involved in the event under discussion with my informant and then computed the approximate year of the event by taking into consideration the age of the informant in 1970, the guessed age of the ancestor, and an estimate of twenty years per generation. I decided on a generation gap of twenty years on the assumption of conscious effort of villages under stress to build up their numbers. I think that under more normal conditions the span would be longer.

The Yambon language change: Yanbunmis-Paligumban-Kawapi-Jugunbendi-Eimangauwi-Kitimbai-Jam-Garu. Assuming that both Yanbunmis (also known as Yingunmis) and Garu were fifty years of age, the language change occurred in about 1830.

TABLE 1
SAMPLE PAGE OF INDEX FOR ORAL HISTORY INTERVIEWS

Page	Subject	Village	Myth Le	Prehis	German	Aust	Japanes	Postwar	SG & Ind	Cult
	Cr Gwolai of Tegoi									
275	Leader's body buried at Kaminimbit	TGOI			*					
275	Land rights purchased with girl Malinjoa	TGOI			*					
275	Return ex-Kaminimbit to Yentchanmangua	TGOI			*					
275	Fight against Korogo	TGOI				*				
275	Migr—Politics Brugnowi massacre	TGOI				*				
275	Kanjanaman takes in migrants	TGOI				*				
275/6	Offering/acceptance of food→Peace	TGOI			*	*				
276	Women trouble move Tegoi ancestral land	TGOI				*				
276/7	Raid Tipmauawi 2 kills establish village	TGOI				*				
277	Creation of land in the Sepik	TGOI	*							
277	Origins Iatmul groups Angoram area	TGOI		*						
277	Kaminimbit migr after Magaro fight	TGOI		*						
277	Fighting started when Jesus was killed	TGOI	*							*

NOTE: Time periods distinguished are Mythical-legendary, Prehistoric, German, Australian, Japanese, Postwar, Self-Government and Independence, and Cult.

Sangai's ancestor's migration: Kagaramar-Sounkebi-Nyebindimi-Yepi-Sangai-married children. Kagaramar joined Jugunbendi in Garu's genealogy, Sangai said. Assuming that both Kagaramar and Sangai were forty-five, the former's migration dates to about 1890.

The Parembei (Sengo) migration: Tagungwi-Wolindumba-Watjoan-Tubwi-Gaui and Growmbanga-Paiambilwa-Melisugwan-Gumawan-Kwolowiwan-Paiangaui. Assuming that Gaui and Paiangaui were fifty, Growmbanga and Tagungwi fifty and thirty, respectively, the migration took place in about 1870.

The establishment of Avatip and Malu: Yabsit-Bwiandimi-Pelam-Komasungwa-Naukwan-Olimal-Wama (child). Assuming that Yabsit was forty-five and Olimala fifty-five, these settlements date to about 1860. Another opinion is based on the fact that Gutubi was one of the first Malu settlers: Gutubi-Kamai-Irembu-Dangwan-Lisindu. Assuming that Gutubi was forty and Lisindu sixty, the settlement dates to about 1870.

Benjindum's settlement on Yambon land: Kabaigumban-Kungwienmeri-Karandaman. Kabaigumban died in the Garamambu fight, and Kungwienmeri was a small child at the time; Karandaman was born about 1905; thus the settlement took place 1890–95.

The end of the Tugwan settlement: According to Garu, "When we lived at Tugwan the Germans came up. The Germans went back from Ambunti [1913] and the Yambons moved to the old place [south of Yambon gate]." Townsend (1968: 97) indicated in 1924 that the Japandais had been there ten to fifteen years before. The end of the Tugwan settlement, then, dates to about 1913.

The Japandai massacre at Yambonjandu: The Senate debate indicated that it was two months before the informants heard about it. Assuming another two months for them to have boarded the steamer and reached Sydney on about March 1, 1924, the massacre occurred in about November 1923.

5/ Reconstructing First Contact: Some Local Effects of Labor Recruitment in the Sepik

Richard Scaglion

As the highly acclaimed film *First Contact* vividly displays, incidents of first contact have had profound and lasting effects on the Melanesian consciousness. Unfortunately, there is very little literature on Melanesians' views of first contact. Most of Sepik history has been written from a European viewpoint, partly because only recently have Melanesians begun to write their own history and partly because relatively few historians or anthropologists have concentrated on ethnohistorical topics. In another generation, many of the elderly Sepik people who witnessed or participated in these events will be gone, and we will have lost the opportunity to record their view of these events. This paper presents an account of first contact by an Abelam participant,[1] together with an attempt to reconstruct the events described by him from a Western historical viewpoint. Broader effects of the event of first contact on the Samukundi Abelam population are also explored.

The Abelam population was apparently first contacted in the Wosera area by Richard Thurnwald during his 1913 exploration of the Sepik foothills. His contacts appear to have been generally friendly, if somewhat strained. Thurnwald (1914) writes:[2] "Our reception in the individual villages was not unfriendly even if frequently the inhabitants, on the approach of the sinister strangers, had made themselves scarce and only gradually returned when they saw that there was no danger. Then they brought coconuts, yams, taro, breadfruit kernel, bananas, and tobacco in great quantities." Samukundi Abelam, unfortunately, had a markedly different experience. Their first contacts with Europeans were generally with labor recruiters, many of whom were notorious for their excesses. Since neither the administration nor the missions had yet established any significant presence in the area, Samukundi had no formal recourse against the depredations of recruiters. In Neligum village, at least, contacts with labor recruiters led the elder generation of

Abelam to view Europeans as powerful intruders able to impose their will on villagers. Active resistance was thought to be fruitless.

Attitudes such as these had a marked effect on various aspects of socioeconomic development during the colonial period. For example, in another paper (Scaglion 1985) I describe how, until recently, Samukundi Abelam viewed traditional conflict management as being quite different from the system of introduced courts. Villagers tended to stress the adjudicatory, coercive elements of Western law rather than the mediatory elements which would have been more in keeping with traditional notions of justice. As a result, Samukundi Abelam viewed introduced court litigation as something to be suffered in silence. They rarely brought cases to court and almost never appealed unfavorable decisions. I believe that this attitude was related to the view of European magistrates as powerful individuals able to impose their will on the Abelam just as the recruiters had done. Again, resistance was thought to be pointless. This paper explores the historical basis for such attitudes.

Historical Background

First contact in Neligum apparently occurred in the early 1920s. Labor recruitment had already had a long history in the Pacific, and the evidence for questionable recruiting techniques is incontrovertible. While a few authors make a strong case for the labor trade, asserting that recruiters were for the most part attracting willing laborers for the mutual benefit of both employer and employee (see, e.g., Wawn 1973), the consensus is that many recruiters employed inhumane techniques. In 1884, for example, the recruiting agent and the boatswain of the *Hopeful* were convicted in Australia for their part in the mass kidnapping of "recruits" in New Guinea, in an incident in which at least thirty-eight New Guineans were killed (Docker 1970:219; Giles 1968:12). While these mass murders were sufficient to have caused a public outcry in Australia, the practice of kidnapping unwilling recruits continued unabated.

In the Sepik area, recruitment was rather sporadic and limited in extent until around the turn of the century. After the German imperial government assumed administrative control from the Neu Guinea Kompagnie, attention turned toward copra plantations, trade, and the use of local labor. After coastal regions had been seriously depleted of labor potential, inland areas, which previously had been virtually ignored, were penetrated and organized for labor. The explorer and anthropologist Richard Thurnwald virtually ensured the interest of labor recruiters in the Sepik foothills through the published account of his 1913 exploratory expedition and his observation that "I have nowhere in the South Sea come on a country with as dense a population as this, even when I consider the thickly populated south end of Bougainville. . . . From a practical viewpoint, recruiting would be a primary consideration in this region. To introduce recruiting with skill and without violence would be well worth the trouble for those interested in it."

Unfortunately, the next decade saw considerable violence linked to the labor trade in the foothills. Allen (1976:63–64), for example, describes a 1918 incident in the Dreikikir area in which two German labor recruiters of dubious reputation were killed. Villages were burned in reprisal, and police subsequently killed twelve men who had attacked a patrol. Curtain (1980) provides narratives from residents of several villages in the foothills which describe abductions by recruiters. Tuzin (1976:25) graphically describes how a recruiter was speared to death in Lehinga village "while employing recruiting methods of dubious legality." Paul Roscoe (personal communication) has indicated that kidnapping by European recruiters was reported to him by Boiken informants. Reed (1943:146) also mentions the practice of kidnapping men from villages that had refused to furnish recruits.

These same patterns were being replicated elsewhere in the Sepik. According to Rowley (1958:202–5),

> The most ambitious punitive expedition of the A.N.M.E.F. was one despatched by Johnson to the Sepik. In September 1918, he sent to Trumble an account of how, during a visit he had paid to Madang, he met at the Station a German recruiter named Fritsche, who stated that while he had been recruiting

about 250 miles from the mouth of the Sepik, his native assistants had been attacked. With the ever-increasing demand for plantation labor there was no question of prohibiting recruiting so far inland; and Johnson considered an expedition necessary. . . . Johnson issued an operation order placing Olifent in charge of a large expedition to assemble at Angoram. The steamer *Sumatra*, armed with a three-pounder and two machine guns, was made available. The party included three regimental officers, a medical officer, ten "other ranks," and seventy-five native police.

This expedition caused considerable destruction along the river. Villages were shelled, houses burned, and ceremonial houses destroyed. Several villagers were killed. The expedition prompted further reprisals, with subsequent counterreprisals, and according to Rowley (1958:205) "the Sepik River area remained troublesome, probably because of the increasing pressure being applied by recruiters."

Townsend (1968:110–13) gives an account of what was probably the first government patrol near Neligum. It was made in July 1924 in response to rumors of recruiting abuses. Accompanied by six policemen, Townsend followed a "trail of broken clay pots, smashed plants, and tales of abduction" to a group of Samukundi villages which had not yet been contacted either directly or indirectly by the government. In Kulingai he found a man who was dying from "an array of pellet holes" apparently fired from the shotgun of a recruiter. Townsend reported widespread fear and hostility from Abelam throughout the area.

It is obvious from reading the early Australian *Reports to the League of Nations on the Administration of the Territory of New Guinea* that the control of labor recruitment in the territory was a major concern of the administration at this time. The first immediate aim of the native policy of the administration stated in the *Report* for 1914–21 was "to stop evils which in the past had been connected with recruiting."

It is clear, then, that the Samukundi were first contacted by labor recruiters who were not above kidnapping recruits in new areas. Furthermore, owing to the rather recent killings of several recruiters in the foothills area alluded to above, first contact was made by recruiters who were not unaware of the possibilities of retaliation by villagers. Given this historical milieu, I proceed to an account of first contact as related by Mambil of Neligum, an eyewitness to and participant in the events described. At this time the Neligum Abelam had heard of the existence of *tuang* (pale and powerful human-like beings), but no one had actually seen one.

The Narrative

Mambil's acount is as follows:

Two men from Imbia,[3] who previously had worked on the coast, brought the Germans. During a huge downpour, while many young men were sleeping in the *haus tambaran* at Suaapel, the whites surprised the village. Tomuk, Yamukundi's father, was captured, tied up like a pig, and carried off to Ndinge,[4] where his captors sought shelter in the *haus tambaran* which had been deserted. At the time he was captured, I was in my garden.

My younger brother came and told me the news about Tomuk. At the time I was somewhat of a runt, and furthermore, I had ringworm which had ruined my skin. I wasn't very highly regarded in the village. Tomuk, however, was a valuable member of our kinship group. We didn't know what the whites were going to do with him; we assumed that he would be killed or was being held hostage for some purpose which we didn't understand. Because he knew I was unhappy in the village and didn't have much to lose, my brother suggested that we go and attempt to exchange me for Tomuk. I agreed. The whites also agreed.

At this time the recruiting party consisted of the German (*Masta* Kristall),[5] another *masta* (a Malay), a large party of men from the coast who worked for the German, the two men from Imbia, and one man from Mamembel. The party set off toward Kuminibus.[6]

After a while we stopped to rest. While some of the men were constructing a rough shelter of coconut leaves, some people from Kuminibus detected our presence. Two of the men from the coast, who had guns, tried to convince two of the men from the Kuminibus party to come along with us. The Kuminibus men, however, were afraid and cautious. One went back to warn the village, and the rest of the people kept their distance. Anticipating trouble, the Malay went off into the bush with several of his men and all

the cargo to construct another shelter some distance away.

By this time Kuminibus had been alerted, and we heard them strike the log slit-drum sounding the village to arms. Emboldened by the prospect of reinforcements, one of the Kuminibus men, Kiyandu, threatened our party with his spear, whereupon one of the men from Arabumi[7] shot and killed him. His wife, Seberamu, tried to run, but the coastal man caught her and carried her off. When we arrived at the new campsite, the German, fearing a reprisal, decided to push on.

We traveled for some time, and eventually rested at the base of a mountain. The coastal men stood up two stakes in the ground. They tied the woman from Kuminibus to these stakes, with her legs spread apart. The men from the coast, the two whites included, took turns raping her all night until just before daylight.

Since the man from Kuminibus had been killed, we were all still afraid of an attack, and left at five in the morning. Eventually we arrived at the coast. After a time we came upon a huge house in the bush, where a pig had just been roasted, and we all ate. The party split up afterward. One large group set off down one path, but the two whites and some of the rest of us went to the house of a coastal man named Kwaalin. When we arrived there, his wife cooked dinner and we slept.

The next day we set off again, and by lunchtime we had come to the junction of the two rivers, where we ate. Shortly afterward, we came up to a village called Suain. *Masta* Kristall had a house in this area, at a place called Ulau; the Malay also lived near here at a place called Yakamul. We stayed for two weeks.

During this time *Masta* Kristall decided to give the Kuminibus woman to the Malay as a wife. He had her washed and dressed in a new *laplap* and presented her to the Malay. They also roasted a pig.

When we left the area, we met the first part of our party en route to Aitape. We reached Aitape at night. The next day we "signed" our labor contracts by putting our fingerprints on a piece of paper. We didn't know what we were doing.

The next morning we caught a boat for "Tamalio" Island, where we stayed for about a month waiting for another ship. It was during this time that some men stole some food from the Catholic mission. When the theft was discovered, the two men ran away. However, the next morning everyone was lined up and, when it was obvious that these two men were missing, their belongings were searched. Some of the stolen pork was found in their string bags. After the men were caught, they were tied to a case and given ten lashes each with a *kanda*, which was heated, so that the skin came off with each lash.

When the ship finally arrived, a German schooner took us to her. The large ship, named *Simutura*, was anchored in Wuvulu Harbor. We stopped at an island where cargo was unloaded and copra was taken on. We offloaded the copra at Kavieng. After about a year, we arrived at Manus, where I worked for several years.

I remember there were two white men there at Manus, *Masta* Kipina and *Masta* Meron. We worked at a place called Silamen. We were lined up and issued a bushknife and ax and told to stay awake until we were told otherwise. Anyone caught sleeping would be beaten. We set off before dawn, walking by torchlight to the workplace, which we reached at dawn. We cut and burned the bush, eating rice and tinned fish for lunch. Since I looked small, I was given easy work, mostly planting things.

After a while I began to understand Pidgin. Before this all the workers could only talk with hand gestures. I was the first person from Neligum to learn Pidgin, and later I taught the people back home.

After a while our contract was finished, and we were taken to Rabaul, where we were told that we should contract again. A clerk asked us where we wanted to go, and we told them Aitape.[8]

It was at this time that the English[9] took over from the Germans. Most of the Germans took off for Sydney on a large ship. While most of them were gone, some of us broke into the government store and stole some goods, which we buried. Later an English ship came and took us to Madang, where the Germans were working with the English.

Many of the men left at this time to go back home to Aitape, but they couldn't find my papers, so I stayed for a while along with

one of the men from Imbia. Eventually a clerk found our papers, and we were sent back to Aitape, where we were paid five pounds.[10]

I worked for a while at Malol, and then at Walis and Mushu, and eventually returned to the village. People were really surprised to see me; they all thought that I was dead. I convinced Uliambu to go to the coast with me, to a place called But. We brought back all sorts of things—bushknives, axes, etc. I paid bride-price for my wife, and we gave some of the things as presents to encourage others to go and work for the English. Several agreed, and we all set off for the coast. When we reached the beach, we built a big fire so that the ship could see us and pick us up. Some of the men worked at Walis Island, and some worked at Mushu. I returned with *Masta* Rapis to recruit other men. At this time we were "buying" them with steel tools and other presents.

The task of translating and organizing this narrative without seriously distorting the meaning of the original was made difficult by differences between Abelam and Europeans in perceptions of "historical time," beliefs about the nature of "knowledge," and conventions for narrative organization. Very briefly, Abelam tend to telescope or foreshorten time periods between significant events in keeping with their episodic view of history (Scaglion 1985). They are also less concerned with and consequently less precise about periods of time. As a result, estimates of time periods by Abelam informants are extremely unreliable by Western standards. Furthermore, Abelam assign much more reliability to eyewitness accounts than to secondhand information. Indeed, their very language often forces the speaker to reveal the source of his knowledge or reason for his lack of it. For example, there is *veknwu* (to know by hearing), *ve* (to know by seeing), *kwutndeng* (to know without having just heard or seen), etc. One can say "I don't know" in numerous ways: *kaapuk veknwuwuren* (I don't know because I didn't hear), *kaapuk vewuren* (I don't know because I didn't see), *yangeikwak* (I don't know because I had no way of knowing), etc.[11] As a result, Abelam narratives rarely contain hearsay information that would logically link particular episodes to their broader historical context. Finally, since Abelam narratives are place-oriented rather than time-oriented, they are sometimes not related in chronological order. Consequently, I have taken some liberties in loosely translating Mambil's narrative and have chosen to present it in chronological order.

Reconstruction of Events from a Western Historical Viewpoint

Despite the cautions about interpretation just offered, events described by Mambil are still at variance with the construction of Western history. The most disturbing fact from a Western point of view is the time frame. A Western historical account is expected to express precisely *when* an event occurred. While Mambil insists that his recruiter was a "German" and that these were "German times," I have placed the incident in the early 1920s, long after the Germans were displaced following World War I. Mambil claims to have worked for one contract period (generally three years) before "the English took over from the Germans." If this statement referred to the Australian takeover in 1914, the date for first contact would be put back to about 1910. However, if Mambil were about fifteen at the time, he would have been eighty-eight in 1983 when the narrative was collected, and he did not look eighty-eight. Furthermore, Richard Thurnwald's previously cited account implies that labor recruitment had not been conducted in the area before 1913 at the earliest.

Obviously, Mambil's age is critical to a historical reconstruction of these events. Mambil, however, does not know his age. Any pre–World War II village books for Neligum that existed were destroyed in the war, and patrol officers in the postwar period were obliged to reconstruct census information. The earliest reconstruction I have been able to locate was compiled by K. A. Brown in 1955 and revised for tax purposes by J. W. Frawley in 1957. Judging by the different colors of ink used in the the original, Mambil's name was not entered until 1957. In any case, elderly Abelam are simply listed as "aged," and no attempt was made to estimate a year of birth. A revised village register was compiled by W. T. Brown in 1963 in which Mambil's estimated year of birth is listed as 1920.

However, other evidence suggests that this date must be much too late. If it were correct, and if Mambil were fifteen or so at the time of first contact, the event would have taken place around 1935. However, the first patrol through the Samukundi Abelam area probably occurred in 1924 (Townsend 1968:110–13), and by the mid-1930s

patrols were being made fairly regularly through this area in response to the demands of European prospectors. Thus, in the 1930s, Europeans were no longer totally new to the area, and first contact must have occurred much earlier.

Mambil's mention of "German times" suggests a possible earliest birth date of roughly 1895. In 1963, when the estimate of a 1920 birth date was made, Mambil's estimated age would have been roughly forty-three. While a patrol officer might have underestimated Mambil's age by as much as fifteen years, making him actually fifty-eight at the time, it is difficult to imagine his having been over sixty and estimated to be in his early forties. Thus patrol records suggest an "earliest" birth date of about 1905 for Mambil. Working from this date, first contact would logically have occurred between 1920 and 1925.

If we accept this date, long after the Australians had assumed administrative control of the Sepik, how can we explain the "Germans" in Mambil's account? Evidence suggests that, despite a formal change of colonial governments, life in the Sepik continued much as it had before the war, certainly until the Australian civil administration began in 1921 (Mair 1948:95):

> Between the occupation of New Guinea by Australia in September, 1914, and the armistice with Germany in November, 1918, the majority of German owners of plantations remained in occupation of their properties and carried on business subject only to the restriction that they might not remit money to Germany. Some land transactions which had been partially completed by the German Government were put through and new applications were entertained, though grants were confined to annual leases. This policy was continued under the mandatory administration until the Land Ordinance was enacted in 1922.

In 1918, two German labor recruiters, Stendel and Kommling, were killed in the Sepik foothills by Kombio villagers (Allen 1976:63), and, throughout the early years of the 1920s, Germans continued to be active in labor recruitment and labor supervision. In fact, it was not until 1924–26 that expropriated German properties were offered for sale (Mair 1948:95). Thus, it is likely that the "English takeover" to which Mambil refers was actually expropriation.

Other evidence from Mambil's narrative provides clues for refining the above time reconstruction. He states that the large vessel which took him to Manus was the *Simutura*. According to Townsend (1968:87–88), the *Sumatra* was an Australian administrative vessel in the early 1920s. This was the very same vessel that was used in the previously described punitive expedition up the Sepik River following the attack on a German labor recruiter's party. While I am still researching the ship's history, Townsend does mention that she was lost at sea in 1923, which would set an upper limit for the date of first contact, if this indeed was the vessel in question. However, Mambil could easily have been taken aboard the *Sumatra* in 1921 or 1922, worked for "several years" at Manus, and witnessed the change of hands of the plantation during the expropriation of 1924–26.

For the most part, the place names given by Mambil are "confirmed" by historical records. Suain, Ulau, and Yakamul are all large villages along the north coast of the East Sepik. "Tamalio" Island is almost certainly Tumleo Island. The Society of the Divine Word had established a station at Tumleo around the turn of the century. Jacobs (1972:496) states, "from the first a distinctive aspect of its work was the emphasis given to the teaching of German in its schools in an attempt to overcome linguistic fragmentation and to forestall Pidgin English." Since Mambil spent the first month of his contract period in this environment, it is not surprising that he assumed that Germany was still in power.

Reconciliation of the Narrative with Other Abelam Accounts

Mambil did not witness the capture of Tomuk when the recruiter's party first surprised the village. In fact, he initially intended to begin his narrative at the point where his brother met him in the garden. However, I asked him to describe the capture for the record, and this resulted in the brief paragraph which opens the narrative. In two previous papers (Scaglion 1983, 1985) I have presented a brief version of the events of first contact from the combined perspectives of several other informants who were children at the time. This version differs from Mambil's account in several important particulars: it does not mention Mambil's being exchanged for Tomuk (which led me to believe that it was Mambil himself who actually was captured); it does not mention rain, but rather implies that initiation ceremony preparations were in progress at the time of the intrusion;

it does not mention any of Mambil's experiences except his time on Mushu, where some of these informants subsequently worked; and, finally, it seriously underestimates or telescopes the time period between his departure and his return to the village.

These discrepancies are explainable given both the age of the informants at the time and the cautions concerning the nature of traditional Abelam views of "historical time," "knowledge," and narrative organization offered earlier. There was no overlap between the eyewitness knowledge of Mambil and that of the other informants. He did not see the initial intrusion or the villagers' reactions following his departure; they did not see the hostage exchange or his labor experiences. Consequently, from an Abelam point of view, there is no real contradiction. It was in asking informants to speculate about events that they did not actually see that confusion was created.

The other informants remembered the excitement of the initiation preparations, the fear and shock of initially seeing the strange white beings and hearing gunshots, the subsequent village meetings, the grief of Mambil's relatives, the speculation about his fate, and his subsequent return. I have had to reconstruct the actual capture from secondhand accounts.

Discussion

While Europeans knew of the existence of local peoples and were prepared for their first meetings with them, the very existence of whites was unknown to many of the people they met. Surprise and shock must have been frequent.

The generous offerings of food to Thurnwald's party demonstrate the Abelam practice of kind treatment of strangers. Abelam view strangers as potential allies. Unfortunately, the actions of labor recruiters initially established whites as enemies of the Samukundi. Thus it is not surprising that Townsend's contact patrol was met with hostility. He reports "narrowly escaping" from the village in which the "potential recruit" had been killed.

Despite an initial hostility toward whites, however, it soon became clear to the Samukundi that active resistance was pointless. Recruiters were known to shoot unwilling laborers, and the Samukundi were aware of the power of firearms. Where their neighbors had retaliated against recruiters, quick and severe retribution had been the result. Furthermore, by the 1930s, the administration had established a significant presence in the area in order to protect gold miners. In building Maprik station in 1938, considerable numbers of laborers were impressed into service by the administration, and, again, resistance was shown to be futile. Any lingering thoughts of active resistance against whites were definitely eliminated during World War II, when Europeans showed awesome strength and firepower.

Thus, for better or worse, the Samukundi felt that they were stuck with whites, whose directives were thought to be something to be suffered in silence. As a result, during the post–World War II colonial period, Abelam rarely directly refused to obey white directives. However, evidence suggests that the Samukundi may have engaged in a form of "passive resistance" which seriously hindered socioeconomic development in the area and of which government officials were often ignorant. Patrol reports, medical reports, and agricultural extension officers' reports are replete with complaints of villagers' initially agreeing to do something but then doing nothing. Frequently, the "lack of influence" of village officials is cited as the cause. For example, Patrol Officer M. R. Duncan (Maprik Patrol Report no. 2, 1954–55, p. 4) stated, "The people of the area do not seem to realise the importance the Luluai and Tultul should carry with their position. Hence most of the officials have very little influence." J. M. Wearne (Wosera Patrol Report no. 8, 1953–54, p. 5) called village officials "mostly incapable or unco-operative." In remarking on specific village officials, Patrol Officer K. A. Brown (Maprik Patrol Report no. 5, 1954–55) made notations of the following kind: "Elderly with little support from villagers but does what he can," "Likeable old fellow who does little," and "Strong man in village. More interested in observing village ceremonies. Pays little attention to his duties unless pressed."

While Samukundi were extremely active and energetic in areas that were of interest to them and did not conflict with traditional custom, in other areas they remained suspicious of the administration, cautious, and uncooperative. A report from one of the very first postwar patrols (Maprik Patrol Report no. 2, 1945–46, p. 9) perceptively identified one of the main causes of these problems: "In those villages previously censused, new names were added to the census. These natives had hidden in the bush. They seemed to think that by giving their name and having it recorded they were likely to be called up for forced labour."

This sort of anxiety, rooted in labor recruitment, created serious difficulties throughout the 1950s and 1960s. It proved very difficult for government officers to distinguish between proposed development projects about which Samukundi were genuinely enthusiastic and those which, in the end, they would passively resist. This made it virtually impossible to discuss the genuine concerns of Abelam or to meet their valid objections to proposals. Samukundi would generally agree with proposals advanced by Europeans, then do what they wished. In another paper (Scaglion 1985) I have shown how the acceptance of a Western form of justice was delayed until the introduction of village courts, which the Samukundi themselves could structure. In other areas of development, similar patterns resulted. Thus, I would argue that the nature of first contact had broad and long-lasting effects in the Samukundi region and, by extension, in other areas of the Sepik as well.

Epilogue

As I worked on the initial draft of this paper for the symposium in Basel in 1984, I began to feel guilty for not having given Mambil a suitable present for all the hours he had spent with me the previous summer relating his story. Consequently, I sent him a handsome Smith and Wesson hunting knife with a pachmayr grip, which I knew he would appreciate. I believe he died before it reached him. The implications are obvious: the reconstruction of the Melanesian version of early Sepik colonial history must be done immediately.

Notes

1. Credit for this account should properly go to Mambil. I should also like to thank Malemole, who initially interested me in first contact, as well as Yalinyinge, Jimmy, and Kori, who listened to Mambil's account with me and who helped with the translation and interpretation. I am also indebted to Mary Taylor, Nancy McDowell, Buck Schieffelin, Jim Roscoe, and Deborah Gewertz for useful comments and suggestions at various stages of this research. Mambil's narrative was collected under the auspices of a grant from the Faculty Research Grants Committee, University of Pittsburgh.

2. This and other passages from Thurnwald's account are adapted from a translation generously provided by David Lea.

3. Imbia is a neighboring Arapesh village. Since Mountain Arapesh have cultural affinities with the

north coast, it is not surprising that men from Imbia would have had contact with Europeans before their more hinterland-oriented Samukundi Abelam neighbors.

4. Ndinge is a hamlet in Neligum located near the previously mentioned Suaapel. For the relative locations of these hamlets as well as Mamembel (below), see Scaglion (1976:72–77).

5. "Kristall" is a pseudonym. Because of the historical nature of this paper I have used actual names throughout, except, because of the sensitive nature of the incidents described, in the cases of "Kristall," "Kiyandu," and "Seberamu." Masta Kristall's real name is clearly of German origin.

6. Kuminibus is a large Abelam village roughly three kilometers west of Neligum.

7. Arabumi was said to be a coastal village, although I have not been able to find a village by that name in the Sepik. It may be a hamlet or a regional designation.

8. Under the Australian administration, laborers who intended to sign new contracts were required to be returned to their place of recruitment for at least one month's leave for each year of service (*Report to the League of Nations* 1921–22:58).

9. The term "English" here refers to the Australians, who took over the administration of the Territory of New Guinea from the Germans after World War I. That Mambil called Australian administrators "English" is not really surprising. Read (1947) describes how German-speaking missionaries referred to Australian and other English-speaking Europeans as "English," causing indigenous people to adopt the usage. Mambil's early contacts with Europeans were with German-speakers, and this fact, coupled with the close identification of Australia with the British Empire at the time, probably led to the confusion.

10. At this point in the narrative there was a lengthy delay while Mambil attempted to remember and calculate just how much money he actually got. To his best recollection, his rate of pay was two shillings per month, but he seemed to be very unsure of this figure. At this rate, his work period would have been less than three years. Minimum wage under the Australian administration was five shillings per month (*Report to the League of Nations* 1921–22:52).

11. There is also the expression most familiar to this anthropologist: *awuknwak* (I don't know, and don't ask me again).

6/ Seventh-Day Adventism and the Boroi Image of the Past[1]

Sasha Josephides

Many Papua New Guineans today are concerned with notions such as "new" and "old," "traditional" and "modern," "the age of the ancestors" and "the age of business." Increasing efforts are being made by the administration to preserve the past by keeping artifacts from leaving the country, teaching traditional skills in the schools, and attempting to persuade young people to participate in traditional dances and take pride in their heritage. Villagers as well as townspeople are aware that many high-ranking politicians are "for" traditional custom. At the same time, villagers are being pushed to develop along Western lines, improve their homes and gardens, change the crops they grow, alter their diet, learn modern skills, and so on.

That this two-way pull between tradition or *kastam* and modernity is occurring throughout Papua New Guinea is clear from the literature, and the Sepik is no exception. The tension between kastam and modernity is a recurring theme in this volume and takes many forms. Allen, for example, concludes his discussion of new movements that Sepik villagers have become involved in with what looks like a return to kastam, but he points out that some years later, while villagers still believed that kastam was good, since it did not bring in any money they had no plans for further ceremonies. Schindlbeck, taking up the issue of what is meant by kastam and examining its relationship to Christianity and economic development, reports that Kwanga men are still experimenting with both ways—doing business in one season and dancing for *kwaramba* the next.

In the Boroi villages where I worked, concern with these issues took the form of a total rejection of kastam and an attempt to cut off all links with the past. This led to a particular way of talking about the past that stressed how different it was from the present. In this paper I will concentrate on this picture of the past.

Ethnographic and Historical Background

The Boroi are located in the lower Ramu area of the Bogia Sub-District, which is administratively within Madang Province but borders on the East Sepik. The Boroi, who are Gamei-speakers (Z'graggen 1971), number some 480 and at the time of my fieldwork inhabited four areas: two new villages on the coast on either side of a river and two old villages an hour to an hour and a half upriver by canoe. The old villages, Bak and Gabun, are the villages from which the coastal Boroi came. The people of Gabun started moving to the coast about fifty years ago, while the people of Bak started moving much later and stayed on the opposite side of the river, thus reestablishing the original situation of two villages with a river between them. The administration has named these two new villages Boroi 1 and Boroi 2, but it is closer to local usage to call them by the same names as the old villages and to reserve the name "Boroi" for the people. The distribution of the Boroi at the time of fieldwork was as follows: 16 in old Gabun, 209 in new Gabun, 102 in old Bak, and 152 in new Bak.[2].

In addition to the division into Bak and Gabun, a division which involves descent as well as locality, the Boroi are divided into eight named *ngomor* or clans, four of which are associated with Bak and four with Gabun. As elsewhere in this area (Meiser 1955), the term that can be translated as "clan" refers to both a structure (a platform with a roof on it) and a group of people. In the new villages the structures are absent. Although these clans are thought of as kinds of descent groups, the relationship stressed is not the lineal one but that between brothers. The idiom used to conceptualize a clan is that of a group of brothers living together, fighting together, and carrying out joint rituals. These brothers do not have to be particularly close genealogically, and the rules of recruitment are extremely loose. However, since inheritance is largely patrilineal and residence patrivirilocal, there are in fact more agnates than anything else in a clan—a situation that, following Barnes (1971:100), could be described as one of "cumulative patrifiliation." These clans are the landowning units in Boroi, but as a result of usufruct and convention, most land accrues to individuals and their descendants.

Another way of looking at the clans is as groups of brothers exchanging sisters. The Boroi are endogamous and have a rule of clan exogamy (though there are a few "wrong" marriages). There is a preference for real sister exchange, and in this kind of marriage bridewealth, which in any case is small, is not paid. Women do not belong to a clan in the same way as men do, but every woman is associated with a clan through her father, brother, or husband.

Boroi ritual is intimately connected with the clans, each clan having its own deities, sacred animals, sacred flutes, and other ritual objects, all of which have a role to play in the male cult. The most powerful of the deities are the *murup* (Tok Pisin *tumbuan*)—ancestor spirits and the founders of the clans. The tumbuan, in the form of masked dancers, played a crucial part in the puberty rites that were performed for both sexes and in boys' initiation into the male cult. The different clans also have special characteristics the most important of which is whether they are peace clans or war clans. This is linked with a system of hereditary chiefs.[3]

The changes brought by the arrival of Europeans in the area are profound and touch on every aspect of Boroi life. The first Europeans to arrive were German planters and traders. At least two planters settled in the area before the turn of the century and started plantations on Boroi land. Some of the older villagers remember working on those plantations, which have now been returned to the clans. The planters were followed by missionaries, who arrived at the beginning of the twentieth century and set up a station in the hills behind Bogia, the present government station. These were German Catholics (Society of the Divine Word), and although their patrols must have taken them to the Boroi villages fairly early on, a permanent mission station within easy reach of Boroi was not set up until the thirties.

By this time, the Boroi were coming into regular and significant contact with Europeans and even moving to the coast in order to be close to the mission and government stations. Many Boroi were recruited to work in the gold mines at Wau and Bulolo and on plantations throughout the country. This phase of contact ended with the Boroi's being sent home just before war broke out.

The war had a devastating effect on the Boroi. The Japanese occupied their villages; most people fled to the bush, but a few men stayed behind and made gardens for the Japanese soldiers. (One of these men was later imprisoned as a collaborator by the Australian administration.) After the defeat of the Japanese, the Boroi emerged from the bush and rebuilt new Gabun, which had been destroyed.

The next major upheaval was in 1954, when the Seventh-Day Adventist mission established itself in the area. About half of the Boroi in the new villages converted right away, and many others eventually followed.[4] Although the majority of people were nominally Catholic at that time, there was no Catholic missionary in the village, and even in Kaian, the mission station, there was only a brother rather than a priest. Some Boroi implied that they had been abandoned by the Catholics and had therefore changed their church. Other reasons given by people for converting were that this was a new church and they wanted to try it and that they realized that it was the "true" church. A few, including Magau, the present church elder, and Tatao, the deacon, converted after their prayers had been answered; Magau's dying son had recovered, while Tatao himself had survived critical illness. Other people converted because they were afraid of burning in hell and still others because their friends and relatives had converted and they did not want to be left out. Most of the older people who converted did so in order to join their children.

These conversions had a profound effect on the village. The Seventh-Day Adventists are fundamentalists; they recognize no interpretation of the Bible, believing the whole of it to be strictly factual and relying especially on the Old Testament. They keep the Sabbath, observe the various food taboos of Leviticus, and believe literally and vehemently in the Last Judgment. Boroi describe the Day of Judgment as the time when Christ will come again and "finish this ground," rewarding the followers of Seventh-Day Adventist doctrine and destroying the rest.

It is therefore not surprising that the Boroi who converted put an end to initiation, ritual, and everything else to do with the ancestors and the male cult. The men of new Gabun stored all the paraphernalia connected with the tumbuan in their men's house, and it was later set afire by a man who "went mad."[5] The same man (now the councillor) also set fire to a men's house in old Bak, but the people there rebuilt it and made new sacred flutes so that they could continue with their initiation ceremonies. The people of new Gabun decided not to do so. These decisions reflected the strength of the Seventh-Day Adventist church in each of the villages.

Major developments since that time are connected with economic changes. The first Boroi coconut plantation was started by the present councillor in 1965; three years later another man, with official help, started a sizable cooperative and later took over the plantation for himself. These two men, along with a third businessman, have in recent years been making a good profit from their plantations. Most other Boroi have planted coconuts since then, and everyone now has some kind of income. Boroi have also opened trade stores, acquired trucks, and experimented with some other cash crops. In August 1979 an all-weather road to the new villages was completed—a big step forward from most people's point of view and an opportunity to get more seriously involved in "business."

The recent history of the Boroi has been a tempestuous one, with regular major upheavals, and therefore it is only to be expected that they should keep talking about the differences between the past and the present. However, the particular way in which they talk about these matters warrants detailed investigation.

The Past

There are in fact two distinct Boroi pasts: a good past and a bad one. The good past is linked with the Day of Judgment and with the view that the world is getting worse and worse. The present world is seen as a hard and evil place, the past as a Golden Age. "In the good old days," the story goes,

the ground was new. There was a lot of fish in the sea and river, and the mangroves were full of game animals and birds. To get sago you just had to put a bucket under the sago palm and the sago would flow into it. Men were tall in those days, one and a half times the height they are today [there is a tree in the bush where a Boroi and his Manam exchange partner marked their heights]. These

distant ancestors did not fight or use *poison*[7] to kill or any such thing.

This story of an idyllic past did not emerge until after I had been in the village for some time, and even then it was not much talked about. What the Boroi constantly talked about was the "bad old days," and I felt that this was the official version of the past. This bad past was not linked with the Last Judgment but appeared to be inseparable from the coming of the Seventh-Day Adventist mission. This inseparability expressed itself in language, since Boroi, like other New Guineans, rarely talk about "the past" or even "the old days" but construct sentences using the word "before"[6] and some major event. When the bad past was being talked of, what usually came after the word "before" was "Seventh-Day Adventism." In other words, Seventh-Day Adventism was fitted between the past and the present, serving to distinguish the two. I must stress here that it was not just people who had joined the church who talked in this way but *all* Boroi. The coming of the Seventh-Day Adventist mission was important for every Boroi, and there is even a possibility that Christianity is equated with Seventh-Day Adventism and Catholicism with traditional religion. Boroi use the word "mission" to refer to the Seventh-Day Adventist mission, apparently forgetting that it is not the only one.

The picture of the bad past that I put together over the months is expressed in snippets of conversation, some heard many times and from different people, others only two or three times and in confidence. Some things I was told in answer to a question, but most of what follows sprang from a desire on the part of my informants to tell me how different it was in the past.

Before the mission came we were devil worshippers. Yes, that's all the tumbuan are, fallen angels; we worshipped fallen angels. We also worshipped insects. We brought insects to the village from the bush, decorated them, and worshipped them. [People say all this with bitterness and laugh at what they consider to be their own stupidity.] You see, we didn't know any better, we didn't know about the Big Man. We weren't clear on anything. We worshipped graven images. We didn't keep the Sabbath.

Before the mission came we didn't have good lives, and there weren't many of us because we kept dying. The tumbuan kept killing us [this said in a whisper]. The power of the ground is not good power. We used to be ruled by the power of the ground. The power of the ground is very strong.

Five of my sons were killed by this power [the power of the ground], before the mission came. Now I only have one son. Now I go to church. It was a very bad time, the time before the mission, a very wild, evil time.

Before the mission came everyone knew how to perform sorcery, *poison*, and magic. There were many ways of killing men, of ruining their lives. Before the mission came we were so frightened. We couldn't go to the bush at night because there were so many bad things. Oh friend, if you'd come to our village before the mission came, oh my! you wouldn't have lived to see your mother and father again, no! you wouldn't have been able to go back to your school and tell them about us. In fact, if we weren't Christians you would have to say "goodbye" to your own place right now because you wouldn't see it again. You can laugh, but it's a good thing you came to the village after the Seventh-Day Adventists and not before!

We were always at war with our neighbors before the mission came. That was the time of war and fighting. It wasn't a good time. We would go out in our canoes; we would go to the Ramu villages and kill as many people as we could lay our hands on. We would cut off their heads and bring them back. If there were any children that looked healthy and good we would bring them back and raise them. That old man [referring to an old villager], why do you think he is like that? He hasn't got over the taste of human blood yet.

Flesh too. He's already tasted it and he can't forget it. That's what the rituals were really about, you know; what they do now sometimes, it's for show, it's got no meaning. Before, we were very frightened of our neighbors. You see that bit of the river? It used to go all the way to Awar, that branch of the river, but our ancestors blocked it so that the Awar wouldn't come and kill us in retribution. Those were very bad times. We never married people from outside the village because we were too scared of them.

We were always playing tricks on the women before the mission came. What funny tricks we used to play on them! [This is one of the rare occasions on which men laughed in their account of the bad old days.] When we were carving a new *garamut* [slit-drum], we would get the women to cook for the garamut spirits. They would cook all sorts of things, and we would take the food to the bush for the spirits to eat, but do you know what? It wasn't really the spirits who ate it; there weren't really any spirits. We, the men, ate the food. That was a very good trick. We did the same with the first *pitpit* [wild sugarcane] of the season. We took it to the men's house for the tumbuan to eat, but it wasn't really the tumbuan who ate it, it was the men. That was very funny. If the women had known, they would have been very angry. The women never found out. If a woman had come to the bush or to the men's house while we were feasting, she would have been torn to bits and thrown in the bush. Then we would say the tumbuan had got her. The mission put an end to that. It wasn't right to treat the women in that way.

Before the mission came, men and women would sin together in the spirit house. They would leave their *laplap* [loincloths] and their grass skirts outside and go inside naked, and inside, oh man! Well, we know better now.

In the old days we wasted our time and food on the rituals which were nothing more than devil worship. We didn't know any better. We didn't have good tools, and we didn't know how to work properly. We were quite ignorant. We are getting a bit clearer now.

By their own account, since becoming Christian/Seventh-Day Adventist, the Boroi live better (although, of course, they still have to watch out for sorcerers and *poison* men from other villages, who have either not heard the good news or chosen to ignore it, and for the tumbuan, who are not so happy at the conversion). The mission, by teaching the Boroi about God, has given them the chance of going to heaven instead of burning in eternal flames and also improved their lot here on earth. They can now make money and achieve a higher standard of living because they no longer waste their time and energy on activity which "bears no fruit."[8] The mission has also brought good schools to the area so that the Boroi can learn to read, write, and speak English and do business.

Of course, this way of talking about the past and of looking at the past is not peculiar to the Boroi, nor is the apparently contradictory memory of both "good old days" and "bad old days."

What is special to them is a near obsession with the past (mostly the bad past) and a tendency to oppose the past and the present. Almost every question I asked was answered in two parts: what they did in the past and what they do now. If both accounts were not available, I was told what they did in the past and almost in the same breath that they no longer do it, or I was told what they do now, with the additional information that the ancestors did not do this. It eventually became obvious that a great deal of what the Boroi said about the past had more to do with wanting to present the past as different from the present than with factual accuracy. It also became apparent that many of the things people said about the present were misleading and that the account of the present could be manipulated in order to make it appear different from the past.

What first alerted me to this was a misleading assertion concerning the present. Some old men told me that before the mission came they had had a very strong law against eating sago leached by their wives but that the mission had taught them that they had to love their wives and give up these foolish taboos. When I later discovered that a certain young man (a very good Seventh-Day Adventist) did not eat sago leached by his wife, I asked all the young men, and it turned out that none of them ate sago leached by their wives. I then asked older men and found that among them Seventh-Day Adventists and Catholics alike ate their wives' sago. It was not difficult to see that men started eating their wives' sago after their marriages had stabilized and that no change in the practice over time was involved.

The claim that men were no longer keeping the sago taboo contrasted the past and the present indirectly by suggesting that a custom present in the one was absent in the other. Some of the direct contrasts made or implied can be seen when we put together the Boroi pictures of the bad old days and of the present. Here are some of the more important ones with indications as to their factual accuracy:

Now the Boroi worship God and are God-fearing. In the past they worshiped the tumbuan, who are the devil.

In fact, many Boroi still worship the tumbuan, and all Boroi have some sort of relationship with them. Many Boroi no longer worship God.

Now the Boroi are civilized and peace-loving. In the past they would kill for nothing and were absolute savages. Had any white person come to the village before the mission he would have been killed.

In fact, the Boroi fight all the time and recently had a large-scale fight with a neighboring village that resulted in a court case. I cannot be sure whether in their "savage" past they would have killed any visiting white, but the ancestors obviously had not killed the plantation owner near old Bak, who went home at a ripe old age to die in Germany. However, even if there had been this risk, it would have been over long before the Seventh-Day Adventist mission appeared in 1954.

Before the mission came, everyone practiced sorcery, magic, and other evils. Now they do not do any of these things, although their neighbors perform them against the Boroi.

Most and possibly all Boroi know some magic and use it, and there have been a few cases of *poison* in the village. As for sorcery, few New Guinean peoples admit that there is sorcery in their village, and had I gone to Boroi two hundred years ago I would probably have been told that the Boroi did not practice sorcery but that their neighbors did.

Before becoming Seventh-Day Adventists, Boroi wasted food and labor through exchange and ritual. Now they just look after their own families and are better-off.

There is a certain amount of truth in this, but a lot of work is still done for rituals, and the family is not the independent unit people sometimes like to suggest.

In the past the Boroi were stupid and ignorant. To join the Seventh-Day Adventist church is to be smart and progressive.

This last contrast is obviously not of the same type as the others, and I cannot comment as to its factual accuracy. It is, however, a very important contrast and possibly the key to all the others.

Obviously, it is quite possible that some of my data are wrong because I misunderstood or because people did not tell me certain things or lied to me about others. Another possibility is that the reason the recent past is described as such a bad time is that missionaries and administrators have given Boroi this picture of their past and they have accepted it. It is also possible that old Boroi do not know what young Boroi are doing and vice versa. However, all these kinds of explanations only account for each individual misrepresentation of the past, while what is indicated here is a systematic representation of the past or, where more convenient, of the present in such a way that the two appear completely different. The contrast may be with a golden past, a savage past, or less often, just a past that is "opposite."

Other Places and Other Dimensions

The Boroi are not the only New Guineans to oppose present and past in this way. Something remarkably like the Boroi perception of the past but considerably more formalized has been described by Errington (1974*a, b*) for the Karavarans. The Karavarans are preoccupied with achieving social order, especially in their ritual, and not slipping into a state of chaos. They believe that their ancestors lived in an anti-society called the *momboto* (literally, "failure to see clearly"). During this time men looked and behaved like wild animals and did not abide by any rules. The momboto is considered to have ended a few days after the arrival of George Brown, a Methodist missionary who came to the area in 1876 (Errington 1974*b*:19–21). The Karavarans' view of their past is much closer to a myth of reversal (though masquerading as history) than the Boroi's. It therefore shows what is likely to happen to the Boroi perception of the past when the events that it is apparently based on have become remote: what now appears to be an inaccurate memory of events with many obvious exaggerations and inconsistencies (which people sometimes admit to) could become a full-fledged antithesis.

Parallels with the Boroi perception of the past can also be found in other dimensions within Boroi culture itself. One other important opposition is that between the old and the new villages. The contrasts here are similar to the contrasts made regarding the past and the present, and these too grossly simplify and misrepresent the situation. When people talk about the old village, they usually mean old Bak, as old Gabun is too small to be of much significance.

Old Bak is a dirty bush village. They keep pigs there, so there is pig's mess everywhere and the people get diseases. In the old village they are continuing with the traditional religion, and they have ritual objects. They do not go to church, and the children do not go to school. They are all rather thick in the bush village ["bush kanaka" is one of the worst insults in the area], and the only thing they know how to do is prepare sago. New Gabun and new Bak, on the other hand, are clean coastal villages without any pigs. The people are sophisticated and work copra. They have given up the traditional ritual and are good Seventh-Day Adventist Christians. They are interested in progress and in developing their business.

Although there are differences between old Bak and the new villages, there are not quite as many as is claimed. Physically old Bak does look very different from the new villages; it is much more compact, and the houses are larger and of an older style. There are also men's houses, and the village is structured around them although the men do not sleep in them. Traditional ritual is more important in old Bak, but it is also visited quite regularly by a Catholic priest, and many people attend church on these occasions. Even if Catholicism is classified with the traditional religion, the opposition is not quite as clear-cut as presented. Moreover, many of the things which are supposed to have ceased to exist in the new villages do still exist there, so the contrast is not what the Boroi claim it to be.

Where the differences between the two villages are indeed what they are claimed to be, a misrepresentation is brought into play. It is true that there is very little ritual activity in either of the new villages, but one reason for this is that people living in the coastal villages go to old Bak when they want to perform any ritual; the medium for one of the tumbuan lives in new Bak but goes to old Bak to enter into trance. (This is partly because he can use a men's house there.) Even though it is true that more traditional ritual takes place in old Bak, then, it is not necessarily the inhabitants of that village who perform it. Similarly, although children cannot easily go to school from old Bak, as it is too far, they get around the problem by staying with relatives in new Gabun or new Bak. The copra and sago situation is the same. Most coconut palms are planted on the coast, and the majority of sago palms are in the bush. Some people from old Bak have palms on the coast and go there to prepare their copra, while nearly all Boroi go to the bush to cut sago and often sleep either in old Bak or in bush houses while they are doing so. People from old Bak preparing copra usually go back at night. The old and the new villages may be very different, and different things may happen in them (though they are not as different as people make out), but very often it is the same people who do these different things.

The similarities between what people say about the past and what they say about the old village are obvious. In a way, having the old village may mean that the Boroi can keep alive their past without admitting to it, since they can put it in the old village. It is almost like having spatial expression for a temporal entity.

Yet another contrast that is constantly drawn is between the old and the young. The theme is the same as that of the past and the present and of the new and old villages, and in this case too the differences are exaggerated in an attempt to show that the two have nothing in common. It is also claimed that recent changes have produced the generational opposition, but judging from the nature of Boroi initiation ritual and from a general hostility which exists between adjacent generations, it is likely that this kind of opposition has always been there.

The Destruction of the Past

Many contrasts are either made or implied in the way the Boroi talk about themselves, of which the following are the most important: present–past, new village–old village, young–old, Christian/ Seventh-Day Adventist–tumbuan worshipper/ Catholic, civilized–savage, copra–sago, coast– bush, clean–dirty, smart–stupid, Westerner– kanaka, Tok Pisin–Boroi. There are many ways of looking at these oppositions. It is, for example, likely that the Boroi have always used the idiom of opposition to construct and describe their universe.[9] The importance of duality in their social organization would certainly suggest this. What is to the point here is that by creating an opposition between the past and the present they are denying that there is any continuity between the two. By denying continuity, they are effectively saying that they have destroyed the past. Furthermore, they make it very clear that they have done so because of the Seventh-Day Adventist mission. They have "given up" certain things because of this mission, and in opposing the bad past and the good present they place the mission between them.

It will be remembered that this is not the only destruction linked with the coming of the Seventh-Day Adventist mission: the ritual objects and the spirit house were also destroyed. After this destruction, the Boroi tried to get rid of many other things as well. Some Boroi men say that when the ritual objects had been destroyed they decided that they would have nothing more to do with the ancestors, so they cooked a lot of food and took it to the cemetery and gave it to the ancestors, saying, "This is it, now. It's all finished now. We've completely finished with you now." In fact, it was not so easy to get rid of the ancestors, and the Boroi are still troubled by them. Other things from the past were even more difficult to prevent from entering into the present, and therefore it was necessary to alter the past to erase them from it or to turn a blind eye to them in the present.

The destruction of the past was a response to the coming of the Seventh-Day Adventist mission, and it involved an attempt to destroy the past physically by burning traditional objects and abandoning the ancestors and intellectually by creating oppositions suggesting that all nonphysical aspects of the past had also been destroyed. Since the Boroi live in an area famous for cargo-cult activity, their destruction of the past must be looked at in the light of that activity. Boroi, not very communicative on the matter, would only tell me that cargo activity was "rubbish" and that they had never destroyed their crops, built stores for the cargo, or done any of those things. Yali, the foremost of the cargo prophets of the Madang area, had spent a night with Boroi and told them his laws, but according to an old man whom he had appointed as his village leader he had never told them to destroy anything other than what was bad for people, such as sorcery.

It would hardly be surprising if people thought that they were taking part in some sort of cargo cult in becoming Seventh-Day Adventists, for the Christian element is marked in cargo thought and Seventh-Day Adventist doctrine is considerably closer than any other form of Christianity to cargo cultism. For example, Mambu, an early prophet, told his followers that if they would do as he advised "a ship laden with manufactured goods for all would arrive in due course. Those who ignored his advice would be swallowed in a holocaust" (Burridge 1971:65). This is very close to Seventh-Day Adventist threats concerning the Day of Judgment. Burridge makes the point that "Adventist teaching is not uncomplementary to cargo expectation—in particular, at the time, in regard to the second coming of Yali" (Burridge 1960:234). There are, furthermore, echoes of the Boroi refrain that in the past they did not know, that they were not clear on anything, and so on, in the Tangu myth's characterization of the ancestor of black men as "dull" (Burridge 1971:64) and the myth retold by Lawrence (1964:77) that speaks of New Guineans as "lost in the darkness." As has already been indicated, for many

Boroi the Seventh-Day Adventist church was revealed as the "true" church that would rescue people from ignorance, and in cargo thought also knowledge is something that can be revealed or withheld.

Although Burridge sees the connection between Seventh-Day Adventism and cargo activity, he says that few Manam Islanders joined the church because "tobacco, betel nut, feasting, dancing, pork, all must be eschewed. Life becomes literally one long wait with nothing to do in the meantime except talk, quietly meditate, and eat vegetables" (1960:234). In fact, even Seventh-Day Adventists would have had to do more for the cargo than wait for it, and the church's worship can hardly be characterized as "quiet meditation." Seventh-Day Adventists go to church very regularly, where they sing, pray, and make speeches covering everything from the state of the water holes in the bush to the latest government bulletins to be heard over the radio. They also have many meetings, bazaars, marches, and various special rituals such as full baptism dressed completely in white and a "Last Supper" ceremony which involves washing one another's feet. The cargo rituals described by Burridge as having been instigated by Mambu appear mild in comparison. It is not, however, ritual that is to bring the cargo to the Seventh-Day Adventists. Although the church's ritual is very well developed, the Boroi consider themselves to have given up ancestor ritual not for Seventh-Day Adventist ritual but for business: "We're just going to work business from now on." In response to the question why they had given up the ancestor ritual, one young man said that it "didn't bear fruit; it was a waste of time and food, we could never get rich with those rituals"; then, as an afterthought, he said that they "couldn't hold the name of God" if they practiced those things and that God might punish them.

While Seventh-Day Adventism fits in with cargo thought, it is a more pragmatic and less enthusiastic phenomenon. Two important differences betwen the cargo situation and what is happening in Boroi can be pointed out in particular. First, early cargo myths legitimized cargo expectations by saying that the New Guineans had been stupid and therefore forfeited their right to the cargo but that the Europeans, if they are the brothers of New Guineans, should share with them (Lawrence 1964:77); the Boroi start from the same premise but legitimize their right by disowning their stupid ancestor. I suspect that in time and with changing political consciousness,

they will begin to play down their bad past and ignorant ancestor and bring the noble first ancestor of the Golden Age to the forefront. It is likely that this will have to happen before any nationalist sentiment can develop. The second difference is that whereas the cargo cult relies on ritual to bring about success, the Boroi seem to be much more dependent on business.[10]

Both Seventh-Day Adventism and the cargo cult promise a better tomorrow both on earth and in heaven for giving up everything one has. The idea is to close the door on the past, but this has not been and cannot be done. Certain events which took place shortly before I left the village suggest that the Boroi may soon stop trying. Someone carved the mask of one of the Gabun tumbuan, thus giving the spirit a channel of expression. After claims that several people had been killed and others threatened by this spirit, the men of Gabun jointly carved a slit-drum for it and held a full-scale ritual to honor this drum. They have promised that they will build a men's house in the near future so that the tumbuan will be appeased. At the same time, I was told that many of the people from new Bak are moving to old Bak because they want to revive the rituals. Does this mean that since it is business[12] which is seen as bringing the Boroi a better way of life, they can now abandon Seventh-Day Adventism and acknowledge the presence of the past?

I do not know what combination of kastam, business, and Christianity the Boroi are now pursuing, but these are three elements that they are juggling in the hope of a brighter future. A fourth element that has not yet fully entered many villagers' consciousness is the degree to which they can succeed in the modern world given the odds against them as small-scale cash-croppers at the mercy of world markets. Research in Papua New Guinea must also look at the external constraints and consider whether there is any possibility of villagers' ever getting this particular jigsaw puzzle right.

Notes

1. The fieldwork on which this paper is based was carried out between August 1978 and September 1979 and funded by the British Social Science Research Council.

2. Based on my own census, carried out in June 1979.

3. These types of clans and chiefs are also reported by Meiser (1955) for the Kaian.

4. At the time of fieldwork, out of 233 adults 145 were affiliated to the Seventh-Day Adventist church. This figure excludes former converts who have now left the church completely but includes those who have temporarily lapsed.

5. Although this story is told as a straightforward factual account of the result of one man's madness, it obviously has to be understood in relation to similar events elsewhere (e.g., McSwain 1977:85; Williams 1978:38).

6. This is partly linguistic, but it is possible to express "the past" in both Tok Pisin and Boroi if necessary.

7. The Tok Pisin term for certain types of witchcraft.

8. The English expression "bears no fruit" was often introduced into Tok Pisin sentences.

9. This is especially so in the way the Boroi look at the passage of time, which is similar to what has been reported by Errington for the Karavarans. Errington follows Gellner in distinguishing an "evolutionary" view of history such as that prevalent in the Western world, which looks at change as cumulative and gradual, and an "episodic" view, such as that of the Karavarans and other non-Western societies, which looks at history as "a series of discrete and static states" (Errington 1974a:257). Although Errington does not talk of oppositions, it is clear that he is dealing with that kind of material and that what demarcates each episode is an event around which an opposition is created (see Errington's account of the coming of the Methodists).

10. This shift is not confined to the Boroi (cf. May 1982:440).

11. What exactly is understood by "business" is another story (see Josephides 1982).

Part Two
Intercultural Connections

Introduction

Meinhard Schuster

The mosaic of world cultures has long stimulated anthropologists first to study each culture as a whole, second to look for similarities among particular cultures, neighboring or distant, that will allow their classification in terms not of geography but of type, and third to establish the order of cultures in time, including—once evolutionist simplifications have been overcome—the connections that may once have existed among them or can still be traced at the time of the research. This latter task is, of course, of particular interest—and difficulty—in a region like the Sepik, where, as in Papua New Guinea in general, the cultural mosaic is extremely rich, especially in terms of linguistic diversity. Although some may object to defining a culture by the language spoken, pointing to the diffusion of nonlinguistic culture traits and words and to the possibility of language replacement, no one will deny that there is no way to speak seriously about, say, French culture without including the French language as an integral part of the picture. We should also keep in mind what has been said ever since von Humboldt's time about the close relationship between language and thought, particularly on the level of abstract concepts.

Irrespective of the linguistic situation, the Sepik shows an astonishing degree of cultural diversity that can only partly be attributed to environmental differences among the Sepik Hills in the south, the northern coastal ranges, the river plains, and the coast. It makes sense, therefore, not only to study its (mostly small) cultural units by themselves but also, as the following papers do, to pay attention to their relationships within and outside the Sepik basin and to the contributions of these relationships to their present forms. These papers should also provoke us to consider the broader significance of such connections.

Investigating the roots of the present cultural diversity in the Sepik, Pamela Swadling presents the limited archaeological evidence available so far for the geomorphic events that have shaped the landscape at various stages, such as the early flooding of the Sepik-Ramu basin by the sea and the numerous earthquakes that have occurred continuously up to the present. She also discusses the influence on the Sepik of the Southeast Asian

kingdoms and, later, of traders who reached Irian Jaya and the north coast of Papua New Guinea from Indonesia and Malaysia. In addition to these external influences, internal human movements also shaped the Sepik region—developments such as the concentration in the northwest of Torricelli-language-speakers whose ancestors, probably the initial Pleistocene occupants of most of the Lower and Middle Sepik area, were displaced as a result of the northward movement of Sepik-Ramu language groups from their supposed southeastern homelands.

Hushang Philsooph also examines the possible cultural influence of Southeast Asia, in this case from the perspective of historical linguistics. Besides dealing with the relatively recent Malay contacts in the Torricelli Mountains both prior to and during the colonial period, he focuses on lexical evidence from more than 150 languages, including words for trade goods, kinship terms, personal names, and terms with sexual and religious meanings. The etymological relationships among these terms found in South Asian, Southeast Asian, and New Guinea languages (in particular Au, a Torricelli-phylum language spoken near Lumi), Philsooph suggests, support the argument for very early intercultural connections via the Indonesian archipelago between the Indian and Islamic worlds and the northern Sepik.

Looking inland and southward and using a quite different kind of evidence—that of arrows, shields, and smoking tubes—Barry Craig discusses the apparent relationship, via long-distance trade, between the Mountain Ok culture area and numerous groups in the western Sepik all the way down the Sepik River to the coast. He refers primarily to the similarity of the graphic designs on these three artifact types and shows that the distribution of related forms is independent of the linguistic distribution of the groups; whereas arrow designs cross several language boundaries, those of shields and smoking tubes tend to be specific to particular language groups. Further, within groups speaking the same language the designs on the three types of artifacts are not necessarily the same.

Dealing with intercultural connections within the Sepik basin, Anthony Forge investigates the reasons for the cultural dominance of the Abelam over their neighbors in the southern Prince Alexander Range. This dominance, Forge argues, is seen in their expansion to the north and west, the copying of their artistic styles by surrounding groups, and the sale and/or "lease" to others of elements of their ritual corpus. In addition, Forge points to the Abelam's high population density, the large size of their villages, their (former) effectiveness in warfare, and their skill in cultivating yams for both subsistence and ceremony. He ascribes major weight to the Abelam's social system, characterized by exchange, balance, and flexibility, which has permitted adaptation and innovation and—most important—led to their being admired and feared by their neighbors for their superior ritual access to supernatural power.

In his reflections on the high degree of linguistic and cultural diversity in the Sepik and on intercultural processes, Colin Filer also focuses mainly on Abelam-Arapesh relations. He questions in principle the equation of language groups with culture groups. By separating for analytic purposes the different levels of what is understood as "culture" and then outlining an alleged contrast between a stage of rather isolated small groups and a later stage of large, more uniform and expansive groups of greater complexity such as the communities formed by Ndu-speakers, Filer shows that cultures (or parts of them), languages, and peoples may spread independently of one another and promote cultural distinctions, not continuities. This emphasis on distinctions, he asserts, is characteristic of the Sepik peoples as a whole.

Examining the ritual of Wamu village, the northernmost Anggor-speaking settlement, Peter Huber is concerned to transcend the village as the traditional frame of reference of ethnographic research and the unit of culture typically isolated for study by ethnographers. By comparing spells, chants, and parades with masked figures (*tumbuans*), all integral features of the local religious system, with other formally similar features of Wamu and other villages, he shows that only a complementary analysis on the regional level (in his case, including most of the Border Mountain region to the north and people speaking different languages) can lead to insight into the meaning of symbolic forms, especially forms peripheral to the local culture studied.

Taken as a whole, the papers in this section have two major concerns, both of which depart from the dominant pattern characteristic of ethnographic study, i.e., a focus on small, mostly local groups. This pattern, in part a response to the exigencies of field research, has meant that little attention has usually been paid to the local group's position as part of a larger regional system or as a node in a network of far-reaching intercultural connections. With the specific aim of overcoming this limitation, some of the contributors to this section have sought to place the diversity of the Sepik in broader perspective in time and space by bridging the distance between the first settling of the area and the present, tracing the links between northern New Guinea and Southeast Asia, or illustrating some of the cultural relationships between the Sepik basin and the central mountain range that divides New Guinea lengthwise. The other concern, geographically more circumscribed, is to throw light on the processes operating between neighboring peoples that result in cultural exchanges either on the basis of equality or, as with the Abelam and Iatmul and their neighbors, in a relationship of dominance and subordination. As a result of these concerns, these papers show us that the cultures of the Sepik are not the closed systems that local analyses sometimes seem to suggest.

7/ Sepik Prehistory[1]

Pamela Swadling

The current cultural diversity of the Sepik suggests a complex past. This paper attempts to examine some of the factors responsible for this complexity. The information will be presented in three parts: landscape changes, possible outside influences, and internal developments.

Landscape Changes

The cultural history of the peoples of the Sepik has not taken place in a static physical environment. Dramatic changes have occurred both in the Sepik-Ramu basin and on the north coast. Unlike Torres Strait, which became dry land during the cold phases of the Pleistocene, the north coast of New Guinea gained little additional land because of the steep offshore drop to the ocean bottom (see Löffler 1977: fig. 36). There were, however, major changes during the last low sea level, some twenty thousand years ago, in the Sepik-Ramu basin.[2] At times of low sea level, rivers cut into their old alluvium and form deeply cut embayments. When the sea level rises, these bays and inlets are drowned and then rapidly fill with sediment and organic matter, producing a more regular coastline (fig. 1). The very steep offshore drop beyond the mouth of the Sepik River means that twenty thousand years ago the Sepik and Ramu river systems would have had greatly increased gradients. This would have allowed the surface of the Sepik-Ramu basin to be eroded to a much lower base level than that of today. Calculations for the Sepik River indicate that the estimated drop in sea level of 140 meters (Chappell 1982) which took place at this time would have allowed the downcutting by the then river system as far upstream as the May River area. Some evidence of this remains; many of the valleys on the southern edge of the Sepik-Ramu basin are downcut much lower than the present level of erosion (Löffler 1977).

The situation began to change when the snow and ice began to melt at the end of the Pleistocene fourteen thousand years ago. When the sea level began to rise, the Sepik and Ramu river systems were unable to infill the downcut basin at the same rate as the incoming sea. This meant that a large area of the basin was flooded by salt water when the sea reached slightly above its present level six to five thousand years ago. By then the Sepik-Ramu basin had been transformed into a huge presumably mangrove-fringed inlet with a large island, now the Bosmun Plateau, at its entrance.

The maximum extent of the flooding would not have been greater than the area of the post-Pleistocene sediments recorded in the Sepik-Ramu basin (fig. 2). The last flooding of the Sepik-Ramu basin would not have extended over the area of Pleistocene sediments now found along the base of the central range from east of Aiome to east of Amboin and on the Bosmun Plateau. Estuarine conditions would have prevailed around the drowned shoreline. The myths some Sepik-Ramu groups have about a time when the Sepik-Ramu swamplands were one big sea may relate to this time. This may explain why a devasting flood is the greatest disaster imaginable to the Arapesh, who live in an area where earthquakes, fires, droughts, warfare, and pestilence are the local disasters (Tuzin 1977: 203–4).[3] Sediment studies around the edge of the Sepik-Ramu basin should reveal, as they did at the Aitape skull-fragments site, the former presence of intertidal mudflats, characterized by blue, sandy muds, carbonized wood, and marine and intertidal shellfish.[4] The presence of the shellfish *Polymesoda* (*Geloina*) *coaxans*, *Batissa violacea*, *Placuna placenta*, and *Saccostrea* spp. in the lower Jimi rock-shelter recently excavated by Pawel Gorecki also suggests the nearby presence of estuarine conditions (Swadling and Anamiato n.d.).

After the basin had been flooded, it gradually began to fill with the sediments being brought down by the Sepik and Ramu river systems. Over time this resulted in the slow outward movement of the delta and associated beach-ridge systems of these rivers. Meanwhile, behind the deltas and beach ridges and beyond the levees being built up by the rivers, the basin was also being filled by the growth of organic matter. This organic growth and seasonal flooding probably blanketed the former beach ridges. Peat associated with unweathered alluvium in the Wewak–Lower Sepik

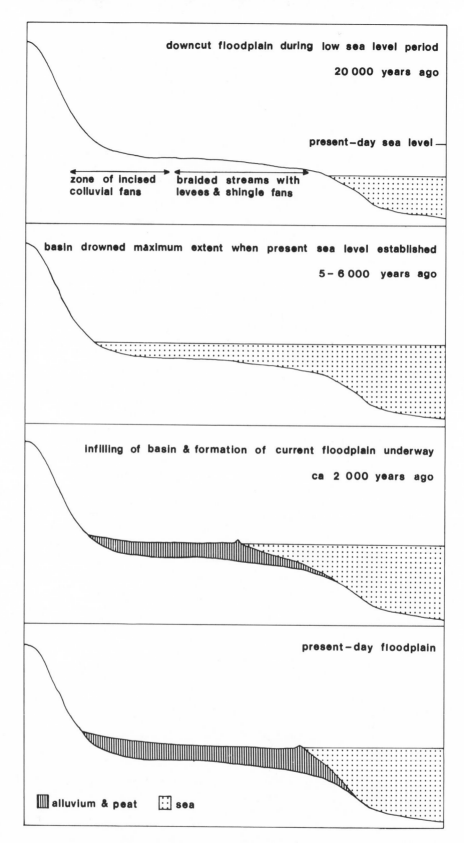

FIG. 1. The main landscape changes in the Sepik-Ramu basin in the last 20,000 years.

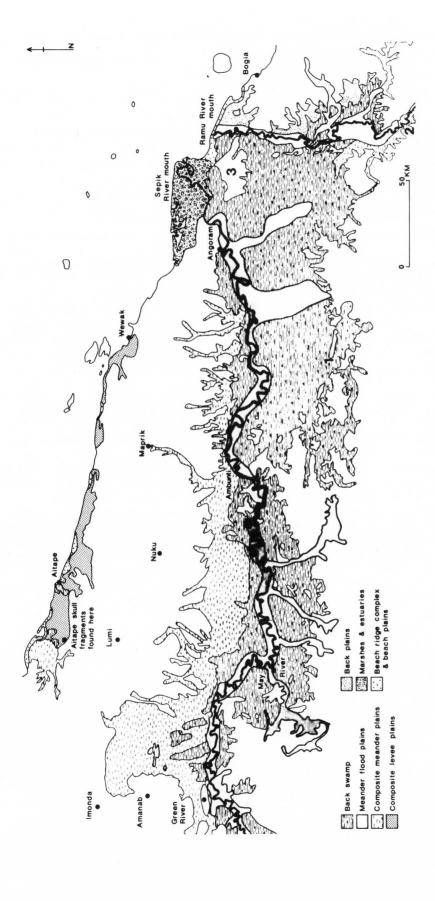

FIG. 2. Recent (post-Pleistocene) deposits in the Sepik-Ramu basin (adapted from Löffler 1974). 1, Amboin; 2, Aiome; 2, Bosman Plateau.

area has been dated at 1,800 and 3,500 years B.P. (Haantjens and Bleeker 1970:165). Once more information is available, geomorphic studies should be able to produce a model for the filling of the Sepik-Ramu basin.

Today the southern part of the Sepik meander plain consists of a series of nearly continuous swamps that extend right up to the foot of the abruptly rising central mountains. Within the swampland belt, more or less isolated hills and mountains, for example, the Aibom and Chambri hills, stand out like islands. Sago stands occur at the grassland/bush fringes within the swamps. There are also large areas of grassland swamp and river levees without sago palms in the vicinity. Peoples that inhabit localities with extensive sago stands supply sago to those areas where sago does not grow; Gewertz (1977) and Schindlbeck (1980) describe this trade in the Middle Sepik area. Levees within the meander floodplains of the Sepik and Ramu Rivers provide suitable sites for many villages. In the Middle Sepik, levees provide good short-term gardening land for up to six months of each year, whereas the grass country of the Lower Sepik is flooded for up to nine months of each year (Cox 1979). Apart from seasonal flooding, the people on the Sepik floodplain sometimes face dramatic changes when a river moves across its floodplain. Mead (1935) describes how the Yuat changed its course by 25 kilometers to flow through the area occupied by the Mundugumor (Biwat), who a few generations later were still adjusting to the change. Löffler (1977: fig. 35) shows the channel change.

North of the Sepik River extensive swamps are rare or absent. Instead, low-angle fans cover much of the area between the river and the mountains. The formation of these fans was probably largely independent of sea-level changes. It is likely that their buildup is due to the large sediment supply coming down from the rising mountains to the north (Löffler 1977:104). Inland from Sissano Lagoon, the Torricelli Mountains appear to have risen at the rate of 8 millimeters per year within the last five thousand years. Apart from building up alluvial fans, this uplift has brought about other changes. In 1929 part of a human skull was found by geologists searching for oil. The find was made at an altitude of 52 meters (170 feet) in a lens in the bank of Paniri Creek where it emerges onto the coastal plain from the Barida Range, about 12 kilometers (8 miles) inland from Sissano Lagoon. Figure 3 shows the stratigraphy where the skull fragments were found; a location map can be found in Hossfeld (1965). The area

around the site is now tropical rain forest. Less than five thousand years ago, this lens was a hollow scoured in an intertidal mudflat which had filled with blue, sandy muds rich in carbonized wood. The deposit contained not only the human skull fragments but also coconut shell and fiber, driftwood, marine and intertidal shellfish, land snails, and foraminifera.

Three of the skull fragments could be joined together to reproduce the brow and front cranial section of a skull.[5] Because of their location, it was initially thought that these skull fragments, usually referred to as the Aitape skull, were of Pleistocene age. The post-Pleistocene radiocarbon dates for the site and a reexamination of the fragments indicate that they belong to modern man (*Homo sapiens*) and not to the earlier *H. erectus*. They remain the earliest human remains so far found in New Guinea (Fenner 1941; Hossfeld 1949, 1964–65, 1965; Gill 1968). This find indicates the difficulties archaeologists will face in locating early coastal sites along the north coast. Today there is a tendency for human settlements on the north coast to be clustered at river mouths, where fishing is more rewarding than off the exposed sandy beaches that make up the greater part of the coast. Although a similar pattern probably existed in the past, it will not be an easy task to locate early coastal sites unless they have been exposed in the banks of present-day streams.

Today the area between the coast and the Aitape skull site consists not only of depositional material from slope wash but also of debris brought down by earthquake-induced slumping in the mountain hinterland. Earthquakes are frequent in this area; 5–10 percent of the world's earthquakes occur along the north coast of New Guinea and in the Bismarck Archipelago (Brooks 1965). After the severe 1935 earthquake in the Lumi area of the Torricelli Mountains, Stanley et al. (1935) reported the dislodgement of more than 60 percent of the soil, subsoil, and tropical jungle in the area of the epicenter, in some places exposing the underlying bedrock. Former V-shaped valleys below these slopes were filled with debris to heights of 15–18 meters above the old valley floor. Earlier, the earthquake of 1907 had caused the huge subsidence of earth that produced Sissano Lagoon.[6] Marshall (1937:490–91, 493), traveling from the coast to the Lumi area some four months after the 1935 earthquake, described the scene as follows:

> In the disaster great piles of debris had crashed into the valleys, creating brimming dams which had finally burst, loosing a tor-

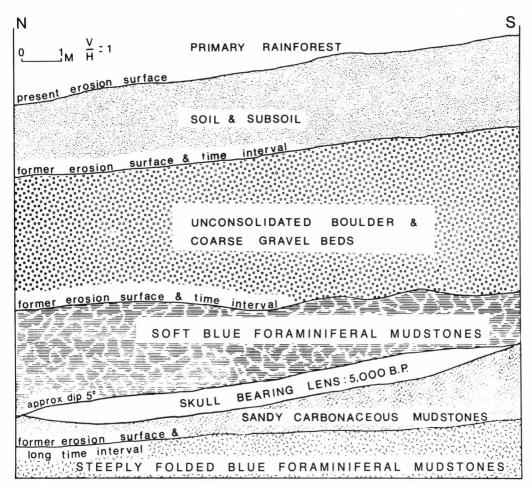

N   S

PRIMARY RAINFOREST

present erosion surface

SOIL & SUBSOIL

former erosion surface & time interval

UNCONSOLIDATED BOULDER &
COARSE GRAVEL BEDS

former erosion surface & time interval

SOFT BLUE FORAMINIFERAL MUDSTONES

SKULL BEARING LENS : 5,000 B.P.

approx dip 5°

SANDY CARBONACEOUS MUDSTONES

former erosion surface &
long time interval
STEEPLY FOLDED BLUE FORAMINIFERAL MUDSTONES

FIG. 3. Stratigraphic position of the Aitape skull fragments, found in the east bank of Paniri Creek about 12 kilometers inland from Sissano Lagoon (based on Hossfeld 1965).

rent of pent-up floodwater which had flowed into the lowlands, menacing the property and lives of the river natives. We saw huge piles of torn timber, stripped logs half buried at muddy river bends, hundreds of acres of wrecked jungle along the banks. In places the floor of the forest is buried in 150 to 180 centimetres of silt, and the trees which remain erect are sadly battered and stripped of every vestige of foliage. . . . The track over the mountains, a traditional trading route of the Wapei natives, was almost completely destroyed. Hillsides had slid away, carrying with them millions of tons of earth and timber, revealing bare rocky ridges completely devoid of vegetation. As the line of carriers climbed higher into the ranges we saw where ridge after ridge had crashed into the valleys. Great slices, hundreds of acres in extent, had been shaken out of the heavily timbered mountains. The ruined valleys below presented an awe-inspiring spectacle. . . . In Wapei many lives were lost in the earthquake. The villages on the ridges were all badly shaken, and houses and people were often carried away when the hillsides slipped into the valleys. Everywhere I saw signs of industry on the part of the inhabitants, the rebuilding of burnt or fallen houses, and the occasional re-establishment of unsafe or abandoned villages on neighbouring ridges.

The coastline and landscape changes that have occurred in the Sepik-Ramu basin and on the north coast have certain implications for the prehistorian. It is obvious that areas covered with post-Pleistocene deposits cannot be expected to yield surface Pleistocene remains. However, we can expect to find Pleistocene sites on the plains and in the foothill and mountain areas provided they have not been removed by slips or buried by alluvial fans and landslides.

Outside Influences

We can still only speculate whether the morphological similarities observed between certain prehistoric artifacts from Papua New Guinea and those from the Jomon period in Japan (12,000–2,000 B.P.) arise from actual links. Certainly some of the pottery (Joyce 1912), especially from the Middle and Lower Sepik, and the stone clubs are remarkably similar.

The Lapita pottery tradition, which is widespread in Oceania and has an antiquity of at least four thousand years in New Guinea (Bafmatuk, Egloff, and Kaiku 1980), ceased to be made and used about the time of Christ. The one potsherd found near Aitape (Swadling 1981:66) on what was probably an island in prehistoric times indicates that Lapita was used on the north coast. My efforts to locate other sites on Kairiru and Muschu Islands off Wewak were unsuccessful, but this may reflect the extensive erosion now occurring on this part of the coast. Whether or not Lapita pottery will be found on the Bosmun Plateau, which was an island six to five thousand years ago, remains a tantalizing question.

One thousand years before the birth of Christ, another ceramic tradition appears in Melanesia. Unlike the makers of Lapita, who managed to maintain considerable uniformity in the style and decoration of their pots over a large geographic area for a considerable period, the people making incised and applied-relief pottery soon established clear geographic styles. This possibly reflects the breaking down of close personal links with distant communities as local groups established their own identities and found suitable raw materials in their own localities. One as yet unrecognized geographic style of the incised and applied-relief pottery may have developed in the Sepik region. Like traditional Sepik pottery, incised and applied-relief pots excavated from elsewhere in Melanesia have baggy shapes and were made by coiling or ring building (Bellwood 1978:258–59). The coiled pottery excavated by Susan Bulmer at Wanlek, which dates from 4,000–3,000 B.P. (Bulmer 1982:181), gives some indication of the antiquity of this production technique in the Sepik-Ramu basin. Bulmer also found a small red-slipped sherd and sand-tempered red pottery dating before 3,000 B.P. (Bulmer 1977:68). Wanlek is an open site on a headland overlooking the main ford of the Kaironk River at an altitude of 1,675 meters (fig. 4). The traditional track west to the Sal and Jimi Valleys passed by the site, and the track down to the lowland Rao of the Ramu area passes near it. The pottery found at Wanlek is probably trade ware brought up from the Ramu. In this respect it is surprising that Pawel Gorecki (personal communication, 1984) found no pottery in the rock-shelters he excavated along the lower Jimi, which becomes the Yuat. Future work by Gorecki along the Yuat may reveal whether coastal communities that produced pottery lived at the western end of the Pleistocene alluvial (see fig. 2) some six to three thousand years ago.

From after the time of Christ, New Guinea may have become the outer fringe of a number of trade networks which extended out of the various trading kingdoms in Southeast Asia. Culture contact between the professional traders from these kingdoms and the people of New Guinea may have stimulated certain changes in Melanesia. In much the same way as Europeans brought Christianity to New Guinea, these traders may have introduced their own religious ideas and practices. Secondary burial in pots (probably from the Philippines), stone monuments, and artistic motifs such as interlocking spirals (probably from western Indonesia) may have been introduced in this way and spread eastward in Melanesia by local trade networks. By A.D. 700, the time of the earliest written records in Indonesia, the trading kingdom of Srivijaya in southwestern Sumatra was well established. Srivijaya certainly had trade links with New Guinea and the Moluccas as early as the eighth century; a Srivijayan maharaja presented bird-of-paradise plumes to the Chinese emperor of the time. At the New Guinea end, trade links with South Asia are clearly attested by the bronze finds made on the Cenderawasih Peninsula and in the Lake Sentani area. In this respect it is probably not a coincidence that these two areas were the major export areas for bird-of-paradise plumes during the first European plume boom from 1908 until the declaration of World War I (Swadling n.d.).

Although undated, the surface artifacts found at a fortified site called Jembekaki on the north coast of Batanta Island, off the western tip of New Guinea, may be all that remains of one former Southeast Asian trading station (Galis and

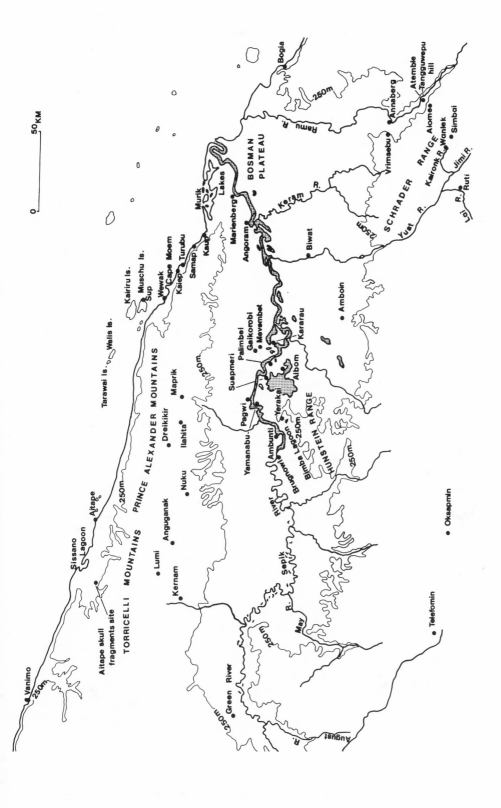

Fig. 4. The Sepik, including sites mentioned in the text.

Kamma 1958, Soejono n.d. [1963]). The fragments of a bronze spearpoint mold and other remnant bronze raw material found there indicate that it was occupied by people with knowledge of metallurgy. The pottery (fig. 5) is decorated by means of incisions, impressions, and appliqué, with spiral and geometric motifs as well as faces or masks. Some sherds are from small cooking pots, others from large urns. A terracotta head was also found. There are decorative similarities between some of the pottery from Jembekaki and old Aibom pottery in the Sepik. Some of the pottery made at Lake Sentani, where many bronze artifacts have been recovered, also has appliqué decorations similar to those produced by some industries in the Sepik.

The Bronze Age links with New Guinea probably ceased once Indonesia fragmented into a number of smaller-scale political units. Ternate was established as a vassal Javanese state in A.D. 1222 but like Tidore later became independent of Java. In the seventeenth century neither sultanate had any real control over New Guinea, and certainly there was no control over the coast east of the Mamberamo River until a garrison was established at what became Hollandia (now Jayapura) in 1852. This suggests that perhaps from the time of Srivijaya's decline and probably from the time Tidore and Ternate were established all direct Asian influence ceased on the north coast of New Guinea east of Cenderawasih Bay. Asian traders did not return until after the establishment of the garrison at Hollandia in 1852 (Swadling n.d.). The speakers of Sko languages who inhabit the north coast and some inland areas from east of Vanimo to Jayapura may in part be descendants of the Bronze Age traders. The rate of change on this part of the coast once contact with the Asian

traders was lost was probably slower than on the Cenderawasih Peninsula, where links with the Moluccas and farther west were maintained. This may explain in part why languages similar to Sko are not now found on the Cenderawasih Peninsula.

Austronesian-language-speakers may have established a chain of settlements along the north coast in the hope of reestablishing links with the Asian traders who came no more or for other reasons (for example, to escape volcanic eruptions in New Britain). A chain of related languages extends from Sarmi, some 90 kilometers east of the mouth of the Mamberamo River, to the Kove west of the Talasea Peninsula in West New Britain (Ross 1977). The available archaeological evidence from the Wewak region suggests that the Austronesian settlements established there date after the direct impact period of Asian traders; the pottery excavated at the base of a midden mound at Sup on Muschu Island (one of the major Austronesian trading villages in the Wewak region) dates to 710 ± 95 B.P. (SUA 704). The Sup pottery is like that still made by Austronesian-speaking potters at Kaiep and Turubu and in the former Austronesian-speaking village of Samap. Related but probably older pottery collected at Cape Moem[7] on the mainland just east of Wewak and at Kaup near the Murik Lakes is in some ways similar to the late Hangan pottery of Buka (Specht 1969:232), which ceased to be made there about A.D. 1000.[8] None of the pottery from Sup bears any resemblance to the pottery from the inland Sepik, and this in itself suggests that the ancestors of the Austronesian-speakers on this part of the north coast settled there after contact with eastern Indonesia had ceased or gone into decline. However, some of the pottery from the

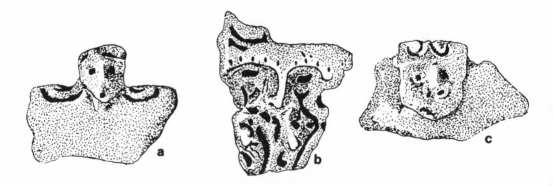

FIG. 5. Potsherds with faces from Jembekaki (Galis and Kamma 1958), widths 8 centimeters (a), 10.3 centimeters (b), and 11 centimeters (c). (Now in the Rijksmuseum voor Volkenkunde, Leiden.)

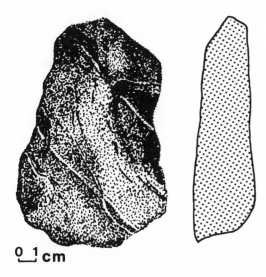

0 1 cm

FIG. 6. Waisted blade found at a depth of about 2.5 meters in alluvial gravel downstream of Yerakai village near Bimba Lagoon, some 20 kilometers southeast of Ambunti (PNG National Museum, Cat. No. 79.2.CBH.4).

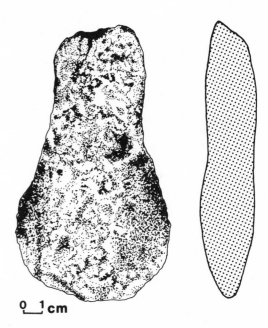

0 1 cm

FIG. 7. Tanged blade found at Lumi in the Sandaun Province (PNG National Museum, Cat. No. 83.2. REL.1).

oldest known Sawos and Iatmul sites, which ethnohistorical evidence suggests may be up to a thousand years old (Kaufmann in this volume), has punctate decorations like those found in the Hangan style and comb decoration similar to that of the subsequent Malasang style on Buka (Kocher-Schmid 1980:39). Such decorations are not a feature of historic Middle Sepik pottery.[9]

Internal Developments

Three artifacts which are probably Pleistocene in age have so far been found in the Sepik region. Gold prospectors found a waisted blade (fig. 6) in alluvial gravel downstream of Yerakai village near Bimba Lagoon, some 20 kilometers southeast of Ambunti, in the early 1970s. Paul Wumbun reported to Laurie Bragge at the Ambunti District Office that it had been found at a depth of about 2.5 meters (8 feet). The waisted blade is of sedimentary rock with distinct banding and is relatively small. The heavy, blunt working edge appears to be more water-rolled than the waist and upper part of the implement. Its lack of overall water-rolling suggests that it has not traveled very far. As a northeastern extension of the Hunstein Range arcs around Bimba Lagoon and Yerakai village, it is likely that the implement has been washed out from this area of high ground. A tanged blade (fig. 7) was found in 1982 by Alphonso Carapas and brought to the National Mu-

seum by Emese Bagley. The field where it was found has been in cultivation for four or five years. The jawbone of what is probably an extinct Pleistocene animal was found in Pa'am Creek near Kernam village, some 25 kilometers southwest of Lumi (A. D. Stevens, Lumi Patrol Report no. 2, 1967–68, Papua New Guinea National Archives); unfortunately, the current whereabouts of this find is unknown. A unifacial chert blade which was found by Laurie Bragge in the headwaters area of the Green River may also date from the Pleistocene period. It was found in 1964 on a track near a cave east of Terauwi village on the southern slopes of the Border Mountains. The blade was sent to Port Moresby in the same year for the PNG Museum collection, but was never catalogued. Its current whereabouts is unknown.

Although these tantalizing finds provide a glimpse of what archaeologists can expect to find from the Pleistocene, language groups at present provide the best means of examining the cultural diversity of the Sepik. Linguistic research, especially that of Laycock and Z'graggen (Laycock 1965, 1973, 1975; Laycock and Z'graggen 1975), has not only revealed a complex linguistic picture but also made evident that about a third of the languages found in Papua New Guinea are spoken in the Sepik-Ramu region. When using linguistic data to reconstruct cultural history, it is necessary to acknowledge that individuals and groups sometimes abandon their language in favor of a new one for reasons of economic, social, or political expediency. Accepting this, the present-day linguistic distribution within the Sepik-Ramu region, when considered along with other data, appears to hold promise of reflecting a great deal about the history of human settlement in the area.

Of all the language groups in the Sepik, only the Torricelli, Kwomtari, Left May, and unclassified ones seem in general terms to have any likelihood of being solely descendants of the initial Pleistocene occupants of the Sepik-Ramu region. Our attention will be focused on the Torricelli phylum because of its size (over seventy thousand speakers) and the lack of data on the smaller groups. Unlike the Torricelli-phylum groups, peoples speaking languages within the Sepik-Ramu, Sko, and Austronesian groups seem to be descended from, at least in part, or influenced by various visitors and colonists to the north coast, whereas the Trans–New Guinea-language-speakers (for example, Mianmin and Gadio Enga) have migrated out of the highlands to settle the northern slopes of the central mountain range.

The Torricelli phylum consists of the languages of the peoples now occupying the Torricelli and Prince Alexander Mountains, the Angoram hills, and the western tip of the Adelbert Range (near Bogia). Unrelated to any of Papua New Guinea's other languages, these languages may constitute one of the country's oldest language groups. Hence it is possible that their speakers may be the descendants of the first settlers of the Lower-Middle Sepik basin, coastal mountains, and shoreline. They may have occupied this region for the greater part of the time people are thought to have been in New Guinea, but this remains to be demonstrated archaeologically. The recent discovery of a tanged blade at Lumi is the first indication that human settlement in this area may have considerable antiquity.

A speculative reconstruction of the cultural history of the Torricelli-phylum groups based on their current distribution and other data is as follows: Their ancestors had probably been in the area since Pleistocene times. When the sea level was some 140 meters below the present level, they may have occupied the extended plains, hills, and coast of the Sepik. Although occupying a considerable area, their numbers may not have been great. When the sea level reached its present level about six to five thousand years ago, the Bogia group was cut off from the others by a rising sea which flooded the Sepik-Ramu basin. The Mo-numbo stock of the Torricelli phylum in the Bogia area is no more distantly related to the rest of the phylum than are other stocks to each other. This observation suggests that the Torricelli phylum probably extended from west of Lumi to east of Angoram by six to five thousand years ago.

In the Sepik-Ramu basin, most of the peoples speak languages grouped in the Sepik-Ramu phylum, which, like the Torricelli phylum, has no relationships with languages found elsewhere in New Guinea. The wide distribution of ceramic industries among what are now fragmented groups and what appears to be a regular sound correspondence for the word "pig" within the Ndu family of the Sepik subphylum (see Laycock 1965) suggests that pottery and pigs were known to the speakers of the common ancestral language. One of the many questions which at present cannot be answered is whether the ancestors of the Sepik-Ramu-phylum groups were immigrants into this area or originated in contact between foreign pottery-bringing immigrants and people already settled or moving down into the Sepik-Ramu basin from the highlands.

If the speakers of the ancestral Sepik-Ramu language were resident in the Sepik-Ramu basin some six to five thousand years ago, their settlements were part of a landscape very different from the one found there today. Much of the Sepik-Ramu basin would have been flooded, as the sea reached its present level at this time. Within this extensive inlet there would have been a number of potential settlement localities. Above high water would have been the alluvial plains of Pleistocene age located along the base of the central mountains from east of Amboin to east of Aiome. In the middle of the inlet entrance there would have been an island of the same formation, now the Bosmun Plateau. Also available would have been the eastern Ramu slopes and perhaps some areas farther west. The Middle Sepik plains and Angoram hills would probably have been avoided, being occupied at the time by ancestors of the present-day Torricelli-phylum groups. During prehistoric times, however, the latter seem to have been encouraged by the northward-expanding Sepik-Ramu peoples to move to their present foothill, mountain, and coastal localities.

The Sepik and Ramu subphyla, which today account for some 92 percent of all speakers of Sepik-Ramu languages, probably diverged from a common ancestral language spoken by settlers along the southeastern shores of the flooded Sepik-Ramu basin. The other small subphyla may have developed their present high degree of divergence from the Sepik and Ramu subphyla through long isolation or subsequent foreign influence. The former may be the case with the Leonhard Schultze subphylum, whereas bronze-using traders may have had some impact on the Lower Sepik and Gapun subphyla. Alternatively, perhaps these latter developed a separate identity on what was then Bosmun island.

Today the largest group of closely related languages within the Sepik-Ramu phylum is the Ndu family, representing some 47 percent of all Sepik-Ramu-phylum-speakers. Within the Ndu family, four languages—Abelam, Boiken, Iatmul, and Sawos—account for 46 percent. People speaking Ndu-family languages today occupy a number of different environmental zones. For example, the Iatmul occupy the Sepik floodplain, the Sawos the sago-rich lower North Sepik plains, and the Maprik Abelam and Boiken the foothills of the Prince Alexander Mountains. Their linguistic similarity, however, presupposes a common settlement history up to their separation.

Linguistic work and recorded oral traditions suggest that there has been a large but gradual migration of speakers of Sepik-subphylum languages from some point south of the Middle Sepik toward the coast (Laycock 1965). If this is the case, the alluvial plains of Pleistocene age from east of Aiome to east of Amboin could be a likely homeland. Located behind extensive back swamps, these areas are now poorly drained, though this may not have begun to be the case until about two thousand years ago. Whether these alluvial plains were the homeland of people now speaking Sepik-subphylum languages will remain a matter of speculation until they and the land above high water in the Karawari and Korosemeri River areas have been surveyed by archaeologists for evidence of early settlement.

Within Papua New Guinea, the Sepik-Ramu region has the greatest known range of artifacts that have evident links not only with the highlands but also with other coastal and lowland areas. The discovery of a tanged obsidian ax (fig. 8) somewhere between the Sepik and the mountains south of Wewak is one of many tantalizing finds. It suggests comparison with similar artifacts reported from Talasea (J. Specht, personal communication; Swadling 1981:67), from near Huahlil at Gimi Routonua on the Arawe coast of West New Britain (PNG National Museum, Cat. No. 81.53.14), from the Yodda Valley in the Northern Province (Casey 1934:98), and from Manus (Bühler 1946–49:230). Unfortunately Eric Schell, who purchased the Sepik example

from villagers selling artifacts at the Windjammer Hotel in Wewak, was unable to get any further details as to where it was found. Similar stone artifacts, though not made of obsidian, are known from the Simbu area of the highlands, among them the ax (fig. 8a) found at Bomai south of Gumine (Bulmer and Tomasetti 1970:38–41). Another tantalizing find is the thin slate (?) digging tool (fig. 9c) found by a woman fishing in the lagoon south of Brugnowi village in 1973 (Barry Craig, personal communication, 1983). Its form warrants comparison with that of similar artifacts (fig. 9a,b) from Wanlek (Bulmer 1982:196–97; 1973), Waghi Valley (Allen 1970), and Wurup, 9 kilometers southeast of Mt. Hagen (Christensen 1975). Until the filling of the Sepik basin can be modeled, it is difficult to assess the land-use potential of different parts of it over time. There is the possibility that when the delta was in the vicinity of Pagwi the steeper river gradient of that time made the vicinity of Brugnowi more suitable for agriculture than it is today.

Along with disc, ovoid, pineapple, and star clubs (Höltker 1940–41), mortars and pestles have also been found in the Sepik-Ramu region. One of the largest mortars known from Papua New Guinea (fig. 10a) was found at Vrimsebu, an old village site in the hilly country at the foot of the Schrader Range about four walking hours west of Annaberg on the Ramu River (Kasprusch 1940–41). A similar mortar was found farther up the Ramu on Tangguwepu hill at Atemble. Other mortars are reported from Atemble and the Keram River. A spectacular bird pestle (fig. 10b) was probably collected in the Marienberg area of the Lower Sepik. Other stone pestles have been found on the hilly island in the lagoon south of Brugnowi, at the old Yamanambu site just upstream of the present village of the same name, and on Kairiru and Muschu Islands.

If we accept for the present the hypothesis that the Pleistocene alluvial plains were the homeland of the speakers of Sepik-subphylum languages, we can consider the consequences of such a location when local drainage conditions deteriorated and back swamps began to develop. As the physical environment changed, people may have been encouraged to migrate to better-drained settlement sites in the mountains to the south (where today there are speakers of Sepik Hills languages), to the plains and hills of the Upper Sepik (now the home of speakers of languages of the Upper Sepik superstock, the Yellow River stock and the Bikisi stock), and along the levees of the Sepik meander floodplain, as well as competing

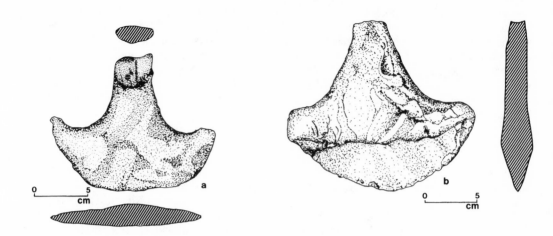

FIG. 8. Artifacts suggesting highland-coast links. *a*, tanged stone ax found at Bomai airstrip, south of Gumine in Simbu Province (Bulmer and Tomasetti 1970); *b*, tanged obsidian ax found between the Sepik and the mountains south of Wewak (PNG National Museum, Cat. No. 84.7.1.CLW.1).

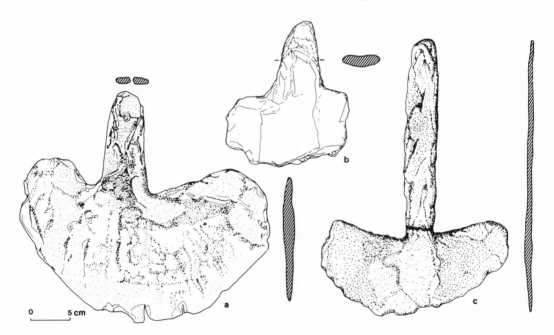

FIG. 9. More artifacts suggesting highland-coast links. *a*, from Wurup, Western Highlands (Christensen 1975; PNG National Museum, Cat. No. E14774.MNO.1); *b*, from Wanlek, Madang Province (Bulmer 1982); *c*, from Brugnowi, East Sepik Province (collected by Barry Craig, 1973; PNG National Museum, Cat. No. 83.123.61.CLU.1).

with the ancestors of the Torricelli-phylum groups for the Middle Sepik plains (now inhabited by speakers of languages of the Middle Sepik stock).

Once any gardening group was established on the northern bank of the Sepik River, a slow, continual movement to the north was probably encouraged by the nature of the plains between the Sepik River and the Prince Alexander Moun-

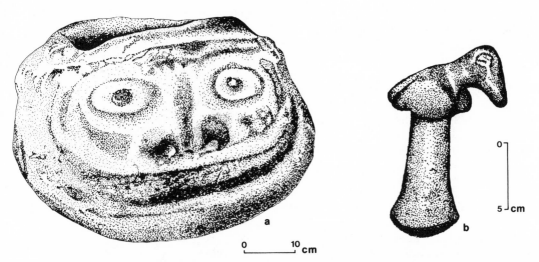

FIG. 10. Stone mortar and pestle from Sepik-Ramu basin. *a*, mortar from Vrimsebu village in the hilly country at the foot of the Schrader Range (Kasprusch 1940–41; PNG National Museum, Cat. No. E16320. JDN.1); *b*, pestle probably from the vicinity of Marienberg (Höltker 1951: 236–38, Plate 19.1; Newton 1979: 46, 50). Now in the Lateran Museum, Rome. A similar artifact now at the Anthropos Institute in St. Augustin, Federal Republic of Germany, was found in the Tokain River on the mainland coast opposite Karkar Island (Höltker 1968).

tains. Extensive grasslands are found there today. Recent land-use studies indicate that when people first cleared the area for gardens the original forest was probably already in precarious balance. Most of the soils are poor. The upper plains have thick sandy and gravelly soils, whereas those to the south have heavy plastic clays. Land clearing on these soils was probably rapid. The low yields gained would have required unusually large gardens, and their quick loss of soil fertility would have caused early abandonment. These infertile, physically poor soils combined with a rather low annual rainfall of about 100–150 centimeters (40–60 inches), with a seasonal dry spell, would have restricted forest regeneration. Moreover, drought conditions and the level nature of the countryside would have promoted the rapid expansion of grassland by fire in poor regrowth. This sequence continues today where forest remnants in the north of the plains are now being cleared. The formation of the grasslands probably encouraged people to follow the retreating forest fringe northward until they reached the foothills of the Prince Alexander Mountains (Robbins 1968, Reiner and Robbins 1964, Haantjens, Mabbutt, and Pullen 1965).

Unlike the areas of the Middle Sepik plains now under grasslands, the southward-flowing tributary floodplains and the lower plains terrace have younger, chemically more fertile soils. Most

of these richer soils are under forest. All the villages within the Sepik grasslands belt today are found near these valley strips of forest, which do include sago. Their gardens are likewise concentrated in these forest areas. After clearing and gardening, forest regeneration is rapid and normal in these tributary floodplains, to the extent that much of the forest today lacks secondary characteristics (Haantjens, Mabbutt, and Pullen 1965). Groups unable to gain access to such tributary floodplains had no alternative but to move on.

When forest clearance and grasslands formation began on the Middle Sepik plains is unknown. The presence of certain geomorphological features on the low hilly terrain of the northern grassland plains suggests that the grasslands may have some antiquity. The features concerned are stone stripes and associated microrelief produced by the combined activities of earthworms and slope wash. The former brought the coarse gravel and fine material to the surface as worm casts, and the action of water has caused a downslope orientation and rough sorting of the material (Haantjens 1965, 1969; Löffler 1977). Such features could not develop under forest cover and presumably would take considerable time to form.

From prehistoric times until the area came under government control, land-hungry Wosera

(Abelam) villages expanded into the relatively sparsely populated areas to the north and west, pushing back the Arapesh and Kwanga, who were comparatively well off for land. Periodic fighting took place throughout Wosera territory, especially at its northern and western frontiers. Each village was concerned with protecting what it had at the expense of its neighbors. Wosera warfare was intense and characterized by high casualty rates that were probably sufficient to reduce the population's rate of increase. The end result of such fighting was a continual change of land boundaries and even of village sites (Lea 1965:205). For example, in the late 1920s and early 1930s the Abelam-speaking Nungwaia villagers, under pressure from their neighbors, surprised and massacred most of the inhabitants of a Kwanga-speaking village and took over their village site and land (Forge 1966:24–25).[10]

While the Maprik (Abelam) and Wosera were generally able to push the Torricelli-phylum groups before them, there was one area where the Arapesh seem to have been able to fend off their advances. In this area the Wosera found their way blocked by the large and densely settled Southern Arapesh-speaking Ilahita villages. These communities were probably the creation of the Abelam themselves, who for generations had been encouraging the northward movement of weaker peoples. These Torricelli-phylum migrants apparently swelled the ranks of the populations among which they found refuge until they became a defensive match for the Wosera invaders. From about 1880 onward the Ilahita people adopted certain of the socially integrating practices of their aggressors. In Tuzin's (1976:75) view, "the adoption of the *tambaran* cult as the ritual basis of village organization[11] demonstrated that a degree of initiative borrowing occurred as the Arapesh contended with integrative problems of unprecedented proportions."

There seems little doubt that, prior to the advance of the Ndu-family groups, Torricelli-phylum groups were sparsely distributed across the face of the Torricelli and Prince Alexander foothills. It is likely that they then lived in mobile communities of not more than one to two hundred persons, subsisting on sago[12] and the products of hunting and gathering. Tuzin believes that their agriculture would have been rudimentary and marginally productive compared to what the Southern Arapesh-speakers, for example, achieve today (Townsend 1971:23, cited by Tuzin 1976:83):

In fact, groups of precisely this description still inhabit large areas of the Torricelli Mountains and also the hills south of the Sepik River in its upper reaches. The Sanio, a group of the latter region, display this form of ecological adaptation, as well as the sociological characteristics that seem often associated with it. They are highly mobile, not because their subsistence activities demand it, but because they move to avoid or resolve the conflicts which arise in the close living of a hamlet. Political leadership is too weak to resolve such conflicts within the group. This type of social structure seems to be widely characteristic of hunting and gathering peoples.

Tuzin continues,

For the Ilahita Arapesh, contact with the southern invaders changed all that, propelling them along a different line of social and cultural development. [A major introduction seems to have been, if not yam cultivation itself, the mass of beliefs and ritual practices currently surrounding yam production and competition (Tuzin 1976:79)] And yet remnants of the old order remain, in their liberal attitude toward land rights within the group (cf. Mead 1947:220), in parts of their ritual, mythology, and economy—and, curiously, in their attitude toward war. . . .

. . . Ilahita, though not lacking inter-personal aggressive capabilities, did not glorify war despite its objective importance to them. This is highly reminiscent of the Mountain Arapesh (Mead 1935) and vividly contrastive with the Middle Sepik head-hunting cultures. From this it would seem that, just as the emergence of large villages was associated with the Abelam and Gawanga contact, so too was the pattern of large-scale fighting. This style of warfare was an entailment of *village* life, and it is not surprising that it was waged in the name of the *village's* tutelary spirits, themselves a creation of Middle Sepik imagination.

To the west of the crowded Wosera live the Kwanga. They have on their west a vast area of forest. In this area it is likely that pressure from the south ceased once the Kwanga had seized as much land as they could hold. Consequently, the Torricelli-phylum Bumbita to their north did not experience the same pressure from the south as the Ilahita Arapesh. Tuzin suggests that this is why the Bumbita settlements have not been compelled to amalgamate into larger units. The smaller political and residential units of the Bumbita may thus provide us with a glimpse of how the Ilahita once lived: "West of the territory of the Ilahita Arapesh, human populations thin out rapidly, and ever larger tracts are given over to tall, primeval forests. By the time one has reached Lumi . . . the vegetation is predominantly luxuriant ancient stands of palm, ficus and sago. Settlements are small and widely scattered" (Tuzin 1976:12). The northward expansion of the Sepik-Ramu-phylum groups probably encouraged the Torricelli-phylum groups to withdraw from the plains to the foothills and mountains. This northward movement toward the Lumi and Nuku area, as well as the movements of others shunted northwest by the expansions of the Kwanga and Abelam, may explain the profusion of small linguistic groups in the area between Lumi and Maprik.

In the area south of Lumi and Nuku, northward migration would not have been encouraged by the rapid formation of man-induced grasslands, as was the case to the east, since considerable areas of uninhabited forest can still be found. Mainasin Yempeti (personal communication, 1977) found during his oral history recording at Anguganak village that his people have traditions about ancestors occupying land near the Sepik River more than eight generations ago. Their explanation for their northward movement is concerned with floods. Perhaps these were caused by the sudden release of rivers dammed by earthquake debris; alternatively, they may reflect the joining of settlement traditions to a distant dreamtime event such as the drowning of the Sepik-Ramu basin some six to five thousand years ago. Another explanation for their northward movement may be the westward expansion of such Sepik-Ramu-phylum groups as the Karawa, Bouye, Autu, Namie, Ak, and Awun, the latter slowly moving into the plains country as they withdrew. Other representatives of the Sepik-Ramu phylum were also moving west up the Sepik basin; for instance, the Abau-speakers who now occupy the August and Idam River areas and the nearby part of the Sepik River claim that they migrated to their present territory from the mouth of the May River (Barry Craig, personal communication).

In the Prince Alexander Range area to the east of the Abelam, the northward-advancing Sepik-Ramu-phylum groups apparently absorbed the Torricelli-phylum groups in their path. According to Laycock (cited by Tuzin 1976:73), the language of the Boiken-speaking people who now inhabit the Prince Alexander Mountains is an in-teresting blend with a basically Ndu pattern and Torricelli additives. This suggests that the original inhabitants were absorbed by the Boiken intruders. It is perhaps not surprising, in this respect, that the settlement traditions of this area are concerned with conquests and the redistribution of territory. Boiken-speakers were to settle such offshore islands as Tarawai and Walis and later the nearer island of Muschu.

An old site called Mevəmbət near the Sawos village of Gaikorobi is the ancestral site for Iatmul and many Sawos. Ethnohistorical data (see Kaufmann in this volume) indicate that it dates to about seven hundred years ago. When the ancestors of the Iatmul split from the Sawos at Mevəmbət they founded the Iatmul villages of Suapmeri, Palimbei, Kararau, and Timbunge from which the twenty-seven present-day Iatmul villages were established. In 1973 the Iatmul numbered almost ten thousand. If they have gained their own cultural identity only within the last seven hundred years, this has considerable implications for Sepik and Papua New Guinea art studies, as other major art-producing groups such as the Gogodala and Elema also seem to be expanding ones that have acquired their specific cultural identities in relatively recent times (see Swadling 1983a).

Conclusion

The apparent prehistoric cultural links between the peoples of the Sepik and both the highlands and other lowlands of Papua New Guinea will undoubtedly stimulate other archaeologists to face the rigors of Sepik fieldwork. Geomorphic studies of the swamplands and their formation will be an important complementary study to the search for and investigation of Pleistocene and post-Pleistocene sites. I hope that other scholars will assist our efforts to understand recent prehistory by making detailed records of the settlement and migration traditions found throughout the Sepik region. Ceramic sequences also need to be established for all the main pottery industries in the Sepik. Key ceramic study areas would include the Abelam heartland, the dry-land areas of the Sawos, the Bosmun Plateau, the area of Pleistocene sediments east of Aiome and east of Amboin, and the Aiome-Atemble area.

Postscript

Data from exploratory oil wells, stratigraphic drill holes, other geomorphic observations, and archaeological finds indicate that the Sepik-Ramu floodplain is less than six thousand years old. Contrary to the appraisal given above, a former floodplain was not inundated by the last marine transgression. The rise in sea level only increased the depth of the existing Sepik-Ramu bay. Floodplain deposits were only laid down in the Middle and Lower Sepik-Ramu after the last marine transgression some six thousand years ago. For further information, see my paper in the forthcoming *Sepik Culture History: Innovation, Variation, and Synthesis*, edited by Shirley Lindenbaum and Anthony Forge.

Notes

1. I wish to thank Tukul Kaiku of the National Archives for her help, David Gillieson and Jim Rhoads for their constructive comments, Anton Gideon for drawing figures 3–10, and Mary Rei for her typing.

2. As Löffler (1977:96) observes, it is likely that the lowering and subsequent drowning and infilling of the Sepik-Ramu basin took place repeatedly during the Pleistocene.

3. Tuzin reports that the Arapesh have a fairly matter-of-fact account of a devastating flood and its impact. However, the story of one survivor then enters the realm of magic and supernatural: "In Arapesh mythology, whenever a calamity befalls mankind, it is invariably that of a devastating flood, sometimes accompanied by a great wind. The usual scenario is that all save one man are destroyed by the waters. After the flood recedes this lone survivor wanders about until he encounters a village that has been (inexplicably) unaffected by the recent deluge. The protagonist is by now youthful and superhumanly beautiful, possessed of culturally esteemed qualities in ideal measure, and his popularity with women provokes their menfolk into plotting his murder. The hero is forewarned by his magical omniscience, and in a stirring climax he flies away, gorgeously caparisoned, to the northern mountains, where he remains to this day. His departure is still lamented, because with it man was deprived forever of the secrets of eternal youth and beauty and knowledge."

4. Some indication of these may already have been recorded by the various oil exploration companies that have worked in the region. These companies are now being asked whether they would make available to the National Museum any data they have on the geomorphic history of the Sepik-Ramu basin during the past twenty thousand years.

5. Now Cat. No. 2933, Australian Institute of Anatomy, Canberra (Gill 1968:142).

6. Eiby (1957:192) gives the date as 1906, whereas Haantjens and Alpine (Haantjens 1972:9) give 1907. The latter is correct.

7. Five obsidian samples from Moem were all found to be from the Lou Island source in Manus. Five of the six obsidian flakes from Wom, just west of Wewak, were from Lou; the other was from Talasea (Ambrose 1976:359). The results for the obsidian from the Sup excavation are not yet available. Parkinson (1907:351) reports that he observed two Manus trade canoes in the Schouten Islands.

8. The decoration of pottery from the Madang coast from about A.D. 1000–1600 also seems, like that from the Wewak region, to be characterized by linear and nubble appliqué and incision (Egloff 1975:14).

9. Was the two-brothers myth, widely distributed in Oceania, incorporated into the Sepik heritage when the ancestors of the present north-coast Austronesian-speaking communities expanded along the northern New Guinea coastline?

10. See Gorlin (1973:28) for another description of Wosera expansions.

11. Forge (1972a) notes that the basic residential unit among the Abelam is the ritual group. He looks at the population sizes these groups can maintain and how "cell-division-like" splits occur once they become too large. Clearly the village splits of the Abelam and Iatmul are very different from the complex small migrations which give rise to new settlements in the Nuku area (for the latter, see Filer in this volume). A comparative study of these may provide valuable information about social process and change in the Sepik.

12. Sago palms would not occur naturally in the Torricelli and Prince Alexander foothills, hence it is likely that they were introduced from the Sepik swamplands to the south (Lumi Agricultural Patrol Report no. 2, 1962–63, cited by Fountain 1966). In other words, the sago palms which occur in those parts of the Sepik where natural forest succession would choke them out have also been introduced, and their presence is dependent on the human maintenance of an open canopy (J. Rhoads, personal communication, 1984; Rhoads 1982; Schindlbeck 1980:551).

8/ Open Structures:
Aspects of Cross-Cultural Influence in the Sepik in Relation to Southeast Asia, India, and the Middle East[1]

H. Philsooph

The relationship between Southeast Asia and New Guinea has a long but neglected history. For example, a maharaja of the Malay kingdom of Srivijaya, centered upon Palembang in Sumatra, is said to have presented bird-of-paradise plumes to an 8th-century Chinese emperor (Swadling in this volume), and it is claimed that "long ago, probably before the Christian era, the gorgeous feathers of one or two species of birds of paradise drifted mysteriously via Malaysia to Western Asia" (Gilliard 1969:21; see also Bellwood 1976, Hughes 1977). In the past, this contact perhaps involved Malay-speaking people, in particular, but this did not greatly limit its cultural scope. The Malay-speakers who came into contact with New Guinea were not always Malays, because Malay in its pidgin form was for centuries a lingua franca. Moreover, Malays and other Southeast Asian peoples had been assimilating elements of major Asian cultures, especially the Indian and the Islamic, for a long time. Indian culture began to be assimilated in Southeast Asia in the early Christian era and was the main external influence until the end of the Middle Ages. Islam began to be established during the thirteenth century and was introduced into some parts of the area—including western New Guinea (now called Irian Jaya)—even earlier. Indian and Islamic cultural influence was preceded and accompanied by trading relationships between Southeast Asians, Indians, Middle Easterners, and, later, Muslims from India and elsewhere, relationships that to some extent continued after European contact in the sixteenth century. The renowned maritime trade routes linking China, India, and the Middle East passed through Southeast Asia, the peoples of which were skillful navigators. Southeast Asians voyaged as far as Australia, on the one hand, and Madagascar, on the other.

Although Indian and Middle Eastern influence on Southeast Asia has been the subject of much historical and some linguistic research,[2] this article is intended as a further contribution to its study. The lexical evidence given for Middle Eastern influence comes mainly from Hindi/Urdu and Malay, but an attempt is made, within the limitations of space, to show that the influence is far more widespread than is usually recognized. Beyond this, a lexical item in the field of taboo whose supposed origin has been taken for granted for over a century is reconsidered in the light of indigenous ideas. In most instances the lexical evidence given regarding Indian influence consists of new findings. Elsewhere the sources are specified whenever possible. The linguistic influence of India is often equated with Sanskrit influence, to the point that if a Southeast Asian word is not of Sanskrit origin it is sometimes assumed to have nothing to do with India. This study, however, takes into account other languages that have been living languages of India for centuries and sometimes millennia, such as Bengali, Gujarati, and Tamil.

The evidence for early Southeast Asian influence (and its origin in India and the Middle East) is chiefly lexical; more precisely, it consists of lexical items of the noun class relating to the domains of trade, sexual taboos, magic, kinship, and personal names. The lexical aspect of a language, in particular its noun class, is usually more susceptible to change and borrowing than any other part. As a result, nouns are of special significance in recording external influence and some of its direct effects. Moreover, lexical items, and nouns in particular, have another virtue: they can be means by which the past may be caught as present. As will be seen, they can be used as evidence for the past that seems so inaccessible in preliterate cultures, but they differ from archaeological artifacts in that they are part of the present, living culture.

Two further points must be borne in mind with regard to the lexical data that form the basis of this study. The first is their sheer quantity. Resemblances among a few lexical items in a small number of languages may simply be said to be due to chance, but resemblances among many items in many languages cannot be so explained. The second is a tendency in the word lists presented here, drawing upon more than 150 languages, for unrelated languages to recur frequently, indicating that the suggested lexical relationships between them are numerous and hardly attributable to chance.

Theoretically, this study seeks to draw attention to the external aspect of what various writers have called "structure," "totality," "system," and the like. Since the beginning of the development of the structural approach, that is, since Hegel asserted that "the truth is the whole," it has often suffered two major shortcomings. First, there is a tendency to divorce the synchronic and the diachronic aspects of a structure, sometimes (as in the nineteenth century) at the expense of the former and sometimes (as in the twentieth century) of the latter. Second, there is a less challenged and more persistent tendency, beginning with Hegel himself, to conceive of a structure as a closed, self-contained, and self-explanatory whole and to regard external factors as either destructive and undesirable or insignificant and dispensable. In contrast, this study was inspired by the conviction that a structure is actually or potentially open and that its formation, survival, and transformation partly depend on and cannot fully be understood apart from its relationships and opposition with the outside world, namely, other structures.

The lexical data from the Sepik compared with those from Southeast Asia and India in this study are often limited and sometimes confined to a single example from the Au language. At present, at least in the published sources, pertinent Sepik data are far from sufficient. The Au-speakers frequently mentioned here are the Sepik people among whom I carried out fieldwork (September 1971–September 1973). They live in Au East and Au West Census Divisions, Lumi Sub-District, numbered 4,098 in 1972, and are divided into nineteen "villages" with an average population of 215. Their economy is traditionally based on shifting cultivation and sago production, supplemented by gathering, hunting, and fishing. They traditionally lack village headmen, and their political system is egalitarian and noncentralized. Au is one of the forty-eight languages forming the Torricelli phylum, the third-largest phylum of Papuan languages in New Guinea (Laycock 1973, Wurm 1982). There are five other lan-

guages of that phylum in the two Au census divisions, but in terms of number of speakers and villages Au is more widespread than the others. It has more than one dialect; the dialect employed here is that spoken in Puang, the village that was the main site of my fieldwork.

Lexical items are written as they appear in the sources concerned, though in a number of cases the spelling, whether transliteration or transcription, is somewhat simplified for the sake of easy comparison or typographical simplicity. In a few cases Dutch orthography is altered to fit English spelling conventions, for example, Dutch *j* to English *y*. There are also instances in which it was found useful to add the original non-Roman scripts (in parentheses) or a broad phonetic transcription (in brackets). Likewise, the names (and their spelling) of the Southeast Asian languages given here are the same as those in cited sources. Whenever possible such works as Lebar (1964, 1972*a*, 1975), Voegelin and Voegelin (1977), Llamzon (1979*b*), and Omar (1983) are also taken into account, and sometimes alternative names and spellings are added.

A source of potential confusion is the languages spoken by the aboriginal peoples (now nonpejoratively called Orang Asli) of the Malay Peninsula; the classification adopted here is Benjamin's (1976; cf. Diffloth 1974), and it corresponds with earlier and less accurate classifications as follows: Northern Aslian = Jahaic = Semang; Central Aslian = Senoic = Sakai; Southern Aslian = Semelaic = Sakai.

No references are given for the lexical items in Arabic and Indian languages; the references are already copious, the words are widely known, and sources on India and the Middle East are, compared with those on the Sepik and Southeast Asia, considerable and more easily accessible. Since the Southeast Asian languages referred to are numerous and frequently cited, to avoid repetition their locations are specified in the appendix.

Recent Contact

Recent Southeast Asian contact with the Sepik will be discussed only briefly, partly because of limitations of space and partly because the study of such contact in earlier times is far more neglected and recent contact is greatly overshadowed by European influence. It is generally accepted (e.g., Cheesman 1938[?]; Lea 1972: 1034), though not sufficiently recorded, that the first outsiders to come into contact with the Sepik peoples were often Malays (and sometimes Chinese). This is shown to be true, for instance, for the Dreikikir (Allen 1976:56–63) in the East Sepik Province and the Umeda (Gell 1975:2–4) in the West Sepik. It is also true for the Gnau (Lewis 1980:200–215) and the Au. With regard to Wapei, another census division in the Lumi Sub-District, a patrol officer observes, "From old village books and discussion with elderly men it would seem initial contact in the area was with Malay Bird of Paradise shooters . . . " (Lumi Patrol Reports, no. 4, 1970–71). In 1936, A. J. Marshall traveled with a recruiter through some parts of the Lumi Sub-District and the Au area, and, using the term "Wapei" in its broad sense, referring to most of the sub-district's peoples, including the Au, he observes, "Long before the first European ventured over the Torricelli ranges the Malay bird shooters knew the country, and had established friendly trading relations with the Wapeis . . . " (1937:495).[3]

Among the Au, elderly men have certain vivid recollections of Malay contact that had begun prior to the early 1920s, that is, before the beginning of European contact with the Au. For example, they describe the difference between the muzzle-loader, the type of gun used by the Malays, and the gun introduced later by Europeans. It may be that the first time the Au saw and tried to use a European gun their reaction was similar to that of the Sepik villagers described by Reed (1943:92), whose contact with Malays was pre-European:

As a surveyor for Oil Search Ltd., Eve visited many villages in the northwest Sepik District during 1935 to 1939 which, so far as is known, had never seen a white man. Here he was greeted by those unknown primitives in Malay expressions. A few terms in the same language were used to designate the recognized trade goods with which he purchased food for his line of carriers. Although the natives recognized guns for what they were, they pantomimed their use as if they were muzzle-loaders, a type of gun whites have never used in New Guinea.

The Au say that the Malays who used to visit them were mainly interested in shooting the lesser bird of paradise (*Paradisaea minor*) or purchasing its plumage. The following occurrence is related by Au villagers in Puang: Once two Malay men named Soba and Jinka came to Puang across the Torricelli Mountains from somewhere to the west of Lumi in Dutch New Guinea. One of the men climbed a tree to shoot a bird called *teghepen* (Au) and was struck by lightning, fell out of the tree, and died. The same thing happened to the other man, who had climbed a mango tree to shoot a bird of paradise. These trees are said to be near Meisi, the previous site of the Nikis hamlet in Puang. It is also said that the men came when the people of Nikis were still living in Meisi. Since these people moved to Nikis in 1935, the events of the story, if factual, must have taken place before that date. At least one of the names attributed to the above-mentioned men is Malay. *Sobat*, sometimes pronounced *soba*, is Malay for "friend" or "companion." In the Sepik this word, like *tuan* (master), was one of the best-known Malay words (excluding those in Tok Pisin) and as a friendly term was sometimes used in first encounters with Europeans. In 1935, J. K. McCarthy, an experienced patrol and district officer, visited some of the people living near the Yellow River for the first time accompanied by a New Guinean corporal named Yongas. Describing his visit and the fact that for some time they did not encounter any local inhabitants, McCarthy writes that at one point Yongas said, "We should find men to-morrow." He continues: "The next morning we did—three of them, sitting around a fire cooking a tree-climbing kangaroo. 'Soaba! Soaba!' Yongas called gently. The men were trembling. But soon they were pacified, and even delighted, when they realized they could converse with us" (McCarthy 1964:161–62).[5] It is noteworthy that the term has entered some local languages in Irian Jaya, indicating earlier Southeast Asian contact with that part of New Guinea: in Awya, Kwime, and Taikat, *sobat* means "friend."[6]

This term and *sahabat*, another Malay term of the same derivation, have further bearing on the themes of this paper. First, they are, with minor variations in form, found in a number of other Southeast Asian languages, indicating that their presence in a New Guinea language is not in itself evidence for Malay contact as against contact with other Southeast Asians[7]:

Malay	sobat; sahabat	friend
Javanese	sobat; sahabat/ sakabat	friend
Buginese	soba	friend
	sahaba	friends
Iban	sabat	friend
Madurese	sobat	friend
Sundanese	sobat	friend
Mandar	sobaq	friend

Tidore	*sobat*	friend
Gane	*sobat*	friend
Masarete	*sabate*	friend
Sapolewa	*sopate*	friend
Piru Seram	*sohobate*	friend
Suwawa	*sahabati*	friend
	sahabati beba	woman friend
Gorontalo	*sahabati*	friend; woman friend
Atinggola	*sahabati*	friend; woman friend
Kaidipang	*sahabato*	friend; woman friend

Second, the two terms are known to be Arabic in origin (Marsden 1984[1812]:201; Matthes 1874: 769, 1102; Klinkert 1930[1882]:643), and since they or related forms are also found in India it is not unlikely that at least in some cases they reached Southeast Asia through India:

Gujarati	*sobat*	companionship
	sobati	friend, companion
Bengali	*sohobot*	companionship
Punjabi	*sohbat*	companionship
	sohbati	friend, companion
Hindi	*suhbat*	companionship
	suhbati	friend, companion, sociable
Urdu	*suhbat*	companionship
	suhbati	friend, companion
	sahabat	companionship
	sahaba	companions
	sahiba	woman friend, lady
Arabic	*suhba(t)*	friendship, companionship, friends
	sahaba(t)	friendship, companionship, friends, companions
	sahiba(t)	woman friend or companion
	sahibat	woman friends or companions

Recent Southeast Asian contact with Sepik peoples, including the Au, is, of course, closely connected with European contact. Especially in uncontacted or uncontrolled areas, Malays were often employed by Europeans to shoot birds of paradise for commercial purposes. Soon after 1828, when Dutch rule began in West New

Guinea, the birds' skins became an "important product" there (van der Veur 1972:280). Sometimes Malays, as Dutch employees, crossed the border to shoot the birds in the Sepik, even during German rule.[8] In the period of German administration (1885–1914), a considerable number of Malays were imported, mainly as unskilled and semiskilled laborers who also occasionally acted as bird-of-paradise shooters. The party of Germans that founded the colony in New Guinea consisted of 5 Europeans and 37 Malays. In Kaiser-Wilhelmsland, including the Sepik, the Malay population was as much as 757 in 1892 and reached its all-time peak, about 900, in 1893 (Biskup 1970:85–86; Hempenstall 1978:164). The peak of the plume trade was between 1880 and 1920. Soon afterward Australian and later Dutch administrations prohibited the shooting of the birds and the export of skins. There is, however, evidence that the sale of skins and the crossing of the Dutch border by Malay shooters did not entirely stop for some years (Marshall 1938:198; Champion 1967:105; Townsend 1968:66; see also Cheesman 1938[?]:41–44).

In 1971–73 the Au had a favorable attitude toward Malays and sometimes referred to them as *paʔab* (mother's brother) or as *kandere* ([Tok Pisin] matrilateral kin). In Au society matrilateral relatives and in particular the mother's brother are, on the one hand, ideally protective and caring and, on the other, conceived as outsiders, that is, outside the patrilateral clan to which a person belongs by birth. Other Sepik peoples also seem to have a good image of Malays. L. E. Cheesman, who traveled through the Sepik region in 1940, discovered by chance that before the arrival of Europeans Krissa village was regularly visited by Malay traders (1941:184–85): "I was passing the hut of one of the oldest men of the village. . . . I conversed with him, using Sorn as an interpreter, and asked whether Malay traders used to come there. . . . He was delighted to talk about the traders who came no more, only his generation remembers them. . . . I asked whether the villagers liked the traders. The old man beamed, there was no doubt about his feelings: 'Abidi wai-ai' (traders good), he repeated several times."

This attitude toward Malays did not, however, necessarily obtain in the past, that is, during actual contact. It goes without saying that one's image of the past may be colored by one's present needs, interests, and problems and that perhaps the older generation in the Sepik—like the old villager referred to in the above quotation—somewhat idealizes its lost youth. The available evidence, though very limited, suggests that the relationship between Malays and local peoples in various parts of New Guinea was not without conflict. In the time of German administration, it is said, "In July 1887 the people of Dugumor and Tombenam villages attacked the twelve Malays working at Hatzfeldhaven while the station superintendent was down with malaria. Six Malays were wounded and eventually died" (Biskup 1970:90). It was also observed that "bird of paradise hunters . . . had been murdered or involved in murderous incidents. An official statement in 1912 had dealt with the special risks of bloodshed incurred, and the need for special restrictive regulations created by the "ever widening range of the hunt," and stated that the work was "regularly carried on by coloured hunters' [Malays and Chinese]" (Rowley 1958:193). In 1932, in the south of Lumi, E. W. Oakley, assistant district officer for Aitape District, and the surveyor H. D. Eve had an unfriendly reception by the local people exactly because they had been mistaken for Malays. In his patrol report the officer writes, "a party of approximately 50 natives armed with spears and arrows rushed into camp. . . . Two constables from Vanimo recognised a few words of Malay pidgin and enquiries revealed we had encountered natives formerly in touch with Malay bird hunters" (Allen 1976:57; see also p. 60 and Flinders 1803:231–32; Warner 1932; and Worsley 1955).

Early Contact

Trade and Lexical Borrowing

Lexical evidence for earlier Southeast Asian influence on the Sepik may first be found in the names of articles of trade. Sometimes such names travel with the articles to regions where other languages are spoken. Tobacco (table 1), for example, undoubtedly reached Southeast Asia and New Guinea by diffusion and trade; it is of American origin and was not grown in any part of the Old World before the sixteenth century. It was introduced into Southeast Asia probably in the mid-seventeenth century and from there into New Guinea in that century or the next (Cranstone 1972:734; Womersley 1972:224–25). Terms for tobacco similar to those in table 1 are also found elsewhere in New Guinea and its environs: in the Madang Province, Angaua *sokay*, Atemple *jokay*, and Paynamar *sukwai* (all these languages belonging to the Trans–New Guinea phylum and the first two to the Atan family) (Z'graggen 1980*c*: 38; see also 1980*b*:76), and in Truk Trukese (Austronesian phylum) *suuqa* (cigarette) (Dyen 1965*b*:16–17, 20).[9]

Likewise, terms similar to the terms for salt in table 2 occur in languages outside the Sepik region: in the Madang Province, Isabi *sia*, Biyom *sei*, and Tauya *sia* (all Trans–New Guinea phylum) (Z'graggen 1980*c*:29) and in Irian Jaya Sentani (West Papuan phylum) *se* (Stokhof 1983*a*: 137). By tradition salt is an important article of trade in both New Guinea (Hughes 1977:77–106) and Southeast Asia (Lebar 1964, 1972*a*, 1975). For example, in Southeast Asia the salt trade has long been a factor in creating links between peoples of the interior and the commercially minded seafaring "coastal Malays." In Au *siak* is the word for the local salt, ashes of stems of the sago palm. The Au consider the color of *siak* to be black (*niba?ak*); in a myth in which two women attempt to become birds of paradise (*Paradisaea minor*), for example, the first thing they do is mix sago ashes with water and rub the paste on parts of their necks and heads to make them black. Plant-ash salt, which tends to be grey or dark because of its impurities, is a traditional form of salt in the Sepik and throughout New Guinea and Southeast Asia. In the But village of Wewak it is the ashes of the sago palm; in Bogia, a similar swamp palm is used (Wills 1958:170–72, 176), and among the Gnau, in the Lumi area, it is those of "some aromatic tree barks (including *Planchonia timorensis*) or the pods of the native winged bean" (Lewis 1975:60). Elsewhere in New Guinea the plants used for salt making include grass, vines, shrubs, and ferns (Hughes 1977:94–98). Swamp palms are also among the plants used in Southeast Asia in this connection (Harrisson 1970:300–304; Morris 1953:48; Roth 1968:386–87). *Coix gigantea*, a grass from which trade salt is made in the eastern highlands, is said to have probably been introduced from Southeast Asia for this purpose (Hughes 1977:77).

Rock salt, a type of salt for which India is well-known, is colorless in its pure form, but it is often impure and its color depends on the impurities. These impurities frequently include bituminous matter, which is black. Hence Indian rock salt is, as seen in table 3, closely associated with bitumin. It is of interest that plant salt is sometimes rocklike in consistency.[10] In the past India most likely traded its rock salt with Southeast Asia,

TABLE 1

Sepik and Irian Jayan Words for "Tobacco" and Their Suggested Origin in Southeast Asian and
Indian languages

Language	Phylum or Family[a]	Lexical Item	Denotation
Au	A	*sauke*	tobacco
Olo[b]	A	*sauke*	tobacco
Telefol[c]	B	*suuk*	tobacco
Digul Mappi	C	*smoke/sumge*	tobacco
Malay	D	*sugi/sugeh*	quid of tobacco or betel
Iban	D	*sugi*	quid of tobacco or betel
Melanau	D	*sugi*	quid of tobacco
Kayan	D	*sugi*	quid of tobacco
Toradja	D	*sugigi*	quid of tobacco
Toba Batak	D	*sugisugi*	quid of tobacco
Hindi	E	*sukha*	dry; dry tobacco (eaten with betel-leaf)
Urdu	E	*sukha*	as above
Marathi	E	*suka*	dry; tobacco
Gujarati	E	*sukko*	tobacco
Ho	F	*sukul*	tobacco
Malayalam	G	*cukka*	tobacco
Pali	E	*sukkha*	dry
Sanskrit	E	*śuṣka*	dry

Sources: Olo, McGregor and McGregor (1982:113); Telefol, Healey and Healey (1977: 154, 330); Digul Mappi, Stokhof (1982*d*:136); Melanau, Mulder et al. (1930:113); Kayan, Rousseau (1974:132–33).

[a] A, Torricelli (Papuan); B, Trans–New Guinea (Papuan); C, West Papuan; D, Austronesian; E, Indo-Aryan; F, Austroasiatic; G, Dravidian.
[b] Spoken in Lumi Sub-District.
[c] Spoken in Telefomin Sub-District.

which, like New Guinea, does not have this type of salt.

If the words for salt in table 2 are of Indian origin, this is not the only case in which an Indian word, being the name of an article of trade, has influenced languages outside India. Basham (1979:230) notes that "Indian loan-words in Greek and Latin are nearly all of articles of trade," such as emerald, beryl, ginger, pepper, sugar, rice, and cotton. Moreover, there is another group of lexical items, all with the meaning "saltpeter," whose Indian origin has been noted: Malay, Javanese, Sundanese, and Melanau *sendawa*, Sasak and Ngaju Dayak *sandawa*, Makassar *sundawa*, Buginese *sunrawa*, Tagalog *sangyawa* (Gonda 1973[1952]:95, 438, except for Melanau, Mulder et al. 1930:116; for Tagalog, see also López 1939:72)). The origin of these items is the Sanskrit *saindhava* (produced in the Indus or Sind; rock salt from Sind), (e.g., López 1939:72, Gonda 1973[1952]:95, 438), and similar forms are found in other Indian languages: Pali *sindhava*, Prakrit *sendhava*, Gujarati *sindhava*, *sindha lun* (*lun*: salt), Bengali *soindhovo lun* (*lun*:

salt), Marathi *sendhya mith* (*mith*: salt). These items derive from *Sind* (Sanskrit *Sindhu*), the name of the region near the Indus where the rich rock-salt deposits of India are located.

Taboo, Sex, and Magic

One part of the vocabulary which is especially susceptible to change and borrowing consists of taboo words, words avoided for religious, moral, political, or other reasons. The first category of taboo word with which we are concerned relates to sexual intercourse. Words of this type are sometimes replaced by words from foreign languages, in particular languages to which esteem and prestige are attached. This may explain, in the case of the examples in table 4, why the Au seem to have borrowed from Southeast Asian languages, which in turn seem to have borrowed from Indian ones or from Arabic. The Au penis sheath in question is one of two kinds (fig. 1) and consists of a seashell; the other, *weiken*, is the fruit of a wild tree of the same name. *Pilir/pirir* seems to be more recent than *weiken* but well-integrated into the culture, being used in adornment

TABLE 2

"SALT" IN AU AND VARIOUS SOUTHEAST ASIAN
LANGUAGES

LANGUAGE	PHYLUM OR FAMILY[a]	LEXICAL ITEM
Au	A	*siak*
Northern Aslian[b]	C	*siak; siya? seya?; seya?*
Central Aslian[c]	C	*siah*
Malay[d]	B	*siah*
Melanau	B	*siah; chia*
Solorese	B	*sia*
Sanggau	B	*sia*[e]
Toradja	B	*sia*
Taman	B	*sia*
Buginese	B	*sia*
Kajaman	B	*siya*
Sasak	B	*sije*
Endeh	B	*si-eh*
Palaung	C	*se?*
Danaw	C	*ts'a*
Achinese	B	*sira*
Karo Batak	B	*sira*
Fordata	B	*sira*
Jamdena	B	*sire*
Malay[f]	B	*sirah*
Dusun	B	*silan*
Rejang	B	*siley*
Moken[g]	B	*chela; selak*
Makassar	B	*sela*[h]

SOURCES: Aslian, Benjamin (1976:114), Skeat and Blagden (1966:702); Malay, Skeat and Blagden (1966:702); Melanau, Clayre (1972:40), Mulder et al. (1930:116), Ray (1913:101, 185), Roth (1968: appendices, lx, xci); Solorese, Sasak, and Endeh, Stokhof (1983b:120, 162, 262, 273); Sanggau, King (1976:142, 159), Ray(1913:143); Toradja, Stokhof (1984:60, 78); Taman, Hudson (1970:313); Kajaman and Dusun, Ray (1913:185); Palaung and Danaw, Luce (1965:114–15); Achinese and Moken, Lewis (1960:54); Fordata and Jamdena, Stokhof (1981a:38, 56); Rejang, Blust (1984:431); Makassar, Lewis (1960:54), Stokhof (1984:154, 172; see also 190, 218, 236).

[a] A, Torricelli (Papuan); B, Austronesian; C, Austroasiatic.
[b] Jehai, Kensiu, Kintaq Bong, and Mendriq.
[c] Semnam and/or Sabum.
[d] Melano Dayak dialect.
[e] In another dialect *zia*.
[f] Brunei dialect.
[g] Also called Selung.
[h] In another dialect *chila*.

and as part of bridewealth and included, to represent the heart, in spirit images made for sing-sings (Au *ghanja*).

With regard to table 5, the following comments are in order: In Hindi, Urdu, and Southeast Asian languages such as Malay, *f*, *q*, and *gh* occur in loanwords, especially Arabic ones, and are often pronounced *p*, *k*, and *g* respectively (e.g.,

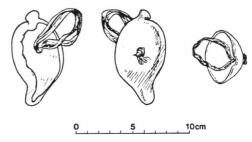

FIG. 1. Au penis sheaths. *A, pirir/pilir; B, weiken.*

Arabic *faqir*, Hindi and Urdu *phakir*, Malay *pakir* [religious mendicant]; Arabic *rafiq*, Hindi and Urdu *raphik*, Malay *rapik* [friend]; Arabic *ghalat*, Hindi and Urdu *galat*, Malay *galat* [wrong]).[11] Hindi and Urdu differ from Malay in that their *p* and *g* are sometimes aspirated, as in the above examples. In Malay, as in many other Austronesian languages, the lexicon tends to be basically disyllabic, and borrowed monosyllabic words are often transformed into disyllabic ones (e.g., Arabic *qabr*, Malay *kubur* [grave]; Arabic *hukm*, Malay *hukum* [order]; Arabic *qalb*, Malay *kalbu* [heart]).

The argument of table 5 is more tentative than the others so far presented. The etymologies of Hindi/Urdu *kulpa* and *gilaf* raise no problem. *Kulpa* derives from Arabic *qulfa* and *gilaf* from Arabic *ghilaf*. The origins of Au *ghelpa* and Southeast Asian *kulup* are, however, not easily identifiable. The Au word is similar to Hindi/Urdu *kulpa* but not to any Southeast Asian word; this may be due to a gap in my data or in the available data or an indication of possible direct Indian-Sepik contact, but it may also point to the weakness of the etymological assumptions. Likewise, Southeast Asian *kulup* is similar to some Arabic words but not to any Indian one, and this gap may have similar implications. As the data of this paper indicate, it is often through India that Arabic words have reached Southeast Asia (cf. Fatimi 1963, Drewes 1968).

There are further problems associated with *kulup*. For too long it has been taken for granted that in Malay, if not other languages, *kulup* derives from Arabic *ghulf/qulf* (Marsden 1984[1812]: 275; Klinkert 1930[1882]:832; Wilkinson 1957:622; Richards 1981:169). This etymology is not, however, as self-evident as it appears. First, we have just seen that *ghulf* does not occur in Indian languages. Secondly, the denotations of the two words are not as similar as is often assumed. Wilkinson writes: "*kulup*: (Arabic *ghulf* = prepuce) . . . Used of the prepuce" (1957:622). But in Arabic *ghulf* is not singular

TABLE 3
SUGGESTED ORIGIN FOR AU AND SOUTHEAST ASIAN "SALT" TERMS IN INDIAN LANGUAGES

LANGUAGE	FAMILY[a]	LEXICAL ITEM	DENOTATION
Hindi	A	*saila-lun*	rock salt
		sila	rock
		sila-jit	bitumen, stone lac
Sinhalese	A	*saileya*	rock salt
		sila	rock
		sila-jatu	bitumen
		saila-ja	rock-produced, mixed with bitumen
Nepali	A	*sila*	rock
		sila-jatu	bitumen
Marathi	A	*sila*	rock
Telugu	B	*saileyamu*	rock salt
		sila-jittu	bitumen
Tamil	B	*cilam*	rock salt
		(< sila)	
		sila	rock
		sailam	mountain, hill
		cila-tailam	bitumen, as exuding from rocks
Sanskrit	A	*saileya*	rock salt, rock-produced, bitumen
		saileyam	rock salt
		sila	rock
		saila	rocky, rock, hill, mountain, bitumen
		sila-ja	rock-produced, bitumen
		saila-ja	rock-produced, bitumen
		sila-jam	bitumen
		saila-jam	bitumen

[a] A, Indo-Aryan; B, Dravidian.

and does not mean "prepuce"; it is the plural of *aghlaf* (uncircumcised) and of *ghilaf* (sheath, cover). Thirdly, it is unusual for an Arabic plural to be used as singular in Malay. Fourthly, *kulup* may just as well derive from Arabic *ghuluf*. But *ghuluf* has the same disadvantages as *ghulf*: it is not used in India and is plural. To complicate matters further, the origin of *kulup* cannot be sought in the other Arabic words in table 5 either. For example, if Malay had borrowed *ghulfa* (prepuce) or *qalafa* (prepuce) it would not have changed them to *kulup*, as such sound changes do not seem to accord with the ways in which Arabic words undergo sound modification after being incorporated into Malay.

Consideration of certain indigenous ideas goes some way toward an alternative or complementary etymological view. In many Indian languages there are indeed words formally similar to, though semantically different from, *kulup* and *ghelpa*, all meaning "lock" and/or "padlock": Bengali *kulup*, Marathi *kulup*, Gujarati *kulup*, Kashmiri *kuluph*, Punjabi *kulph/kulpha*, Ho *kulpu*, Hindi *kulaph/kulph*, Urdu *kulph*, Brahui *kulf*. The Hindi term *kulphi*, which derives from *kulaph*, is figuratively used for "a handsome young boy" and the expression *shore ki kulphi* (*shore ki*: of salt) for "a fair youth." Similar terms and expressions may well occur in other Indian languages but, being vulgar or taboo, are not traditionally recorded in dictionaries. Likewise, in Southeast Asia *kulup* or related forms may have similar usage: Javanese *kulup* (young boy [literary or formal term of address]); Iban *ulup*, term of endearment addressed to son-in-law, familiar term of address to younger man; Malay *kulup* (usually shortened to *lup*, *lop*, or *yop*), familiar name often given to eldest son of a good family. Furthermore, in many Southeast Asian languages terms for the genitalia or similar terms are employed in addressing youngsters. In Sadanese, *laso* denotes "penis" and *laso?* and *aso?* are terms of address for boys (Sirk 1978:270). In Javanese, *nduk*, the affectionate term of address for "little girls," is "thought to derive from a word meaning vagina" (Geertz 1961:102). In

TABLE 4

SUGGESTED ORIGIN FOR AN AU TABOO WORD IN SOUTHEAST ASIAN AND INDIAN LANGUAGES

LANGUAGE	PHYLUM OR FAMILY[a]	LEXICAL ITEM	DENOTATION
Au	A	*pirir/pilir*	penis sheath
Malay	B	*pelir*	penis
		buah pelir	testicle (*buah:* fruit)
Iban	B	*pelir/peler*	testicle; scrotum
		telu pelir	testicle (*telu:* egg)
		igi peler	testicle (*igi:* seed)
		pelirir	to castrate
Banjar	B	*peler*	penis
Javanese	B	*peli*	penis
Roti	B	*pelibolok*	penis
Madurese	B	*peller*	scrotum
Sanggau	B	*parer*	penis
Hindi	C	*pelar/pelra*	testicle
		phal-kosak	scrotum (*phal:* fruit; *kosak:* sheath, shell), testicles
Punjabi	C	*pehla/pihla*	testicle
Sinhalese	C	*pella*	testicle
		pelli	testicles, trunk
		pelli-dandu	lit. "testicles-wood"[b]
Tamil	D	*pelam*	testicle
Sanskrit	C	*pelam/pelakah*	testicle
		phalam	testicle; fruit
		phal-kosa	scrotum (*phal:* fruit; *kosa:* sheath, cover)

SOURCES: Roti, Stokhof (1983b:20, 38); Madurese, Nothofer (1985:296; see also 1975:187–88); Sanggau, King (1976:157). See also Austronesian words for different types of shell in Mike (1968:150), Blust (1980c:73–74, and Wurm and Wilson (1983: 46–47, 185–86).

[a] A, Torricelli (Papuan); B, Austronesian; C, Indo-Aryan; D, Dravidian.

[b] Two pieces of wood used in squeezing a young bull's testicles to produce the same effect as castration.

Ma'anyan *butoh* means "youngster," while *butuh* and its cognates are among the most widespread terms for "penis" in Southeast Asia (Sirk 1978:270; Wurm and Wilson 1983:150). In Hanunóo, *ʔutin* means "penis" and is also "a masculine proper name" (Conklin 1953:58); *luluʔ* is "a masculine proper name" and also means "pulling back of the foreskin, penis . . . " (p. 172); and *binbin* is "a feminine proper name" and also denotes "vagina; vulva; external parts of the female genital organs; this term usually refers to the genitalia of children" (p. 83).

Again, a lock or padlock, considered here not in relation to the key but to the trunk or the door on which it is hanging, is not symbolically inappropriate for the male genitalia. In Southeast Asia the same term is sometimes used for the male genitalia and for "lock" (e.g., Javanese *kontol* [scrotum]; Sundanese *kontol* [testicles, scrotum]; Malay *kontol* [short, thick, pendulous object]; Madurese *kontol* [padlock] [Nothofer 1975:70]). In Malay, *kontol* is also used, figuratively, for "a testicle or the penis" (Wilkinson 1957:610). In

Javanese, *le*, the affectionate term of address for little boys, is "thought by Javanese to derive from the word *kontole*, meaning penis" (Geertz 1961:102).

In Southeast Asia, *kulup* is also used in the sense of "lock." In Cebuano Visayan, *lukub*, which seems to be a case of metathesis, means "lock" (Cabonce 1983:591). The denotations of the same word in Hanunóo, another Filipino language, are "skin, bark, cover, outer layer"; *lukub ʔutin* (*ʔutin:* penis) means "foreskin" and *lukub mata* (*mata:* eye) "eyelid" (Conklin 1953:172). In Bontok, *koyop* means "eyelid" as well as "prepuce" (Reid 1976:169).

The Indian *kulup*, to which the Southeast Asian *kulup* (with its cognates) seems to be related, is itself known to be of Arabic origin, namely, from Arabic *qufl* (lock, padlock). We have already seen that in Southeast Asia monosyllabic borrowed words tend to become disyllabic. The same is true to some extent of India. Thus sometimes monosyllabic Arabic words had al-

TABLE 5

SUGGESTED ORIGIN FOR ANOTHER AU TABOO WORD IN SOUTHEAST ASIAN, INDIAN, AND ARABIC LANGUAGES

LANGUAGE	PHYLUM OR FAMILY[a]	LEXICAL ITEM	DENOTATION
Au	A	*ghelpa*	penis
		ghelpa yiniu	testicle (*yiniu:* egg)
Hindi/Urdu	C	*kulpa*	prepuce
		gilaf	prepuce; sheath, cover
Bengali	C	*gilap*	sheath, cover
Arabic	D	*ghulfa/qulfa*	prepuce
		qalafa	prepuce
		ghilaf	sheath, cover
Malay	B	*kulup*	prepuce
		ber-kulup	uncircumcised
Iban	B	*kulup*	prepuce
		be-kulup	uncircumcised
Madurese	B	*kulup*	uncircumcised
Sundanese	B	*kulup*	prepuce
Banjar	B	*kulup*	prepuce
Karo Batak	B	*kulup*	prepuce; uncircumcised
Dairi Pakpak	B	*kulup*	prepuce; uncircumcised
Isneg	B	*silup*	prepuce; uncircumcised
Bontok	B	*koyop*	prepuce; uncircumcised
Arabic	D	*ghulf/ghuluf*	pl. of *ghilaf*
		ghulaf/qulaf	pl. of *ghulfa/qulfa*
		qalaf/qalafat	pl. of *qalafa*
		ghulf/qulf	pl. of *aghlaf/aqlaf*

[a] A, Torricelli (Papuan); B, Austronesian; C, Indo-Aryan; D, Semitic.

ready been disyllabized in Indian languages before reaching Southeast Asia. Southeast Asian and Indian words for "age, lifetime" compared with the Arabic *umr*—Malay, Javanese, Iban, Manobo *umur*, Melanau *umor* (Clayre 1972: 107), Hindi *umr/umur*, Bengali *umor*, Punjabi, Malayalam *umar*, Nepali *umar/umer*—constitute a case in point.

Hindi *kulphi* simply consists of Arabic *qulf* (lock, padlock) and the adjectival suffix *i* (relating to). Other denotations of this term, which also occurs in Bengali, Nepali, and so forth, do not seem to be without Freudian implications. In Bengali and Nepali as well as Hindi it denotes "a mold for ice, jelly, etc.," and the mold may be cylindrical or conical. In Nepali it also denotes "a cigarette holder." In Southeast Asia, in Ilokano, *kuliap* means "straw (for sucking up a beverage); cigar holder" (Carro 1956:153).

Another type of word which may be taboo or subject to avoidance relates to magic. Magic is of course often associated with mystical or supernatural danger, secrecy, and fear of retaliation. Lexical borrowing in magic may result from these features of magic or from circumstances in which the magic itself, or one of its parts, is of foreign origin. Here we must confine ourselves to

two examples from East Sepik languages. One is the word *ngimbim* (B. J. Allen, personal communication, 1984), which is possibly of Southeast Asian origin. The other is *ndjambi* (S. Harrison, personal communication, 1984), which, as Harrison points out, may derive from Malay *jampi* or *jampi-jampi*. It is also possible that *ndjambi* derives from Southeast Asian languages other than Malay, since *jampi* and related forms are widespread in Southeast Asia (table 6). Sometimes it is assumed that *jampi* is itself a Sanskrit word (e.g., Wilkinson 1957:442), but, as Gonda (1973[1952]:302–3, 307–8) points out, there is no evidence for this assumption. In his view, if *jampi* is of Sanskrit origin it may derive from *japa* (uttering prayers, spells, or names of a deity in a low voice) or *japin* (one who utters prayers, etc., in a low voice). The formal differences between *jampi* and the above words, such as nasalization, are found in many Sanskrit words and their borrowed forms in Southeast Asian languages (Gonda 1973[1952]:chap. 4). Nasalization is, of course, a widespread phenomenon in lexical borrowing. Four possible New Guinean examples are given above: *ngimbim* and *ndjambi* from *jambi* (table 6) and *somke/sumge* from *sugi/sugeh* (table 1). Further suggestions for the pos-

TABLE 6
SEPIK TERMS ASSOCIATED WITH MAGIC AND THEIR SUGGESTED ORIGIN IN SOUTHEAST ASIAN LANGUAGES

LANGUAGE	PHYLUM OR FAMILY[a]	LEXICAL ITEM	DENOTATION
Manambu	A	*njambi*	protective magic for trees and their fruits
Urat	B	*ngimbim*	magic: *poison* (Tok Pisin)
Malay	C	*jampi*	spell, invocation
		jampi-jampi	spell, invocation
		men-jampi	to utter *jampi*
Sasak	C	*jampi*	chants (in healing ritual)
Javanese	C	*jampi*	medicine
		dukun jampi	specialist in herbs and local medicine
Old Javanese	C	*jampi*	medicine, cure
Minangkabau	C	*jampi*	ritually potent medicine
Sundanese	C	*njampe*	spell used in exorcism
		tukang jampe	specialist in protective amulets and love magic
Madurese	C	*jampe(h)*	a medicine used with spell
Balinese	C	*pe-nyampi* (base:*jampi*)	styptic, invocation uttered over wounds
Batak[b]	C	*pa-njampi*	styptic
Iban	C	*sampi*	prayer, invocation
		sampi nugal	*sampi* used at planting
Bisaya[c]	C	*dampi*	medicine
Dairi Pakpak	C	*jampi*	a medicine used with spell
Semai[d]	D	*jampi'*	spell (for healing)
Batek[e]	D	*jampi'*	spell (for healing and fruit trees)
Jehai[e]	D	*jampi*	exorcism

SOURCES: Malay, Skeat (1965), Gimlette (1971:44, 54, 77); Sasak, Krulfeld (1972:68); Javanese, Koentjaraningrat (1972:52); Minangkabau, Batak, and Bisaya, Gonda (1973 [1952]:307–8); Sundanese, Wessing (1974:151, 308), Koentjaraningrat (1972:56), Gonda (1973 [1952]:307–8); Iban, Jensen (1974:67–68, 178–81); Semai, Dentan (1979:88); Batek, Endicott (1979:59, 99); Jehai, Schebesta (1973:194).

[a] A, Sepik-Ramu (Papuan); B, Torricelli (Papuan); C, Austronesian; D, Austroasiatic.
[b] Spoken in Sumatra.
[c] Spoken in the Philippines.
[d] A Central Aslian language.
[e] A Northern Aslian language.

sible origin of *jampi* in Sanskrit and other Indian languages are as follows:

Sanskrit	*jalpi*	inarticulate or low speech; uttering prayers and formulas in a low voice
Prakrit	*jamp*	to utter in a low voice
Hindi	*jap*	uttering prayers, spells, or names of a deity in a low voice
	japi	uttering prayers, etc., in a low voice; one who does so
Sinhalese	*japa*	uttering prayers, etc., in a low voice
Bengali	*jop*	to utter in a low voice
Kodagu	*jamsi*	to utter (spells or prayers)

Kannada	*japa*	repeating prayers, spells, or the names of gods
Tamil	*jepam*	spell; prayer
	jepi	to utter sacred formulae or spells
	tampi	to counteract by spells or invocations

Kinship Terminology

Tables 7–12 display the formal similarities in terms for "father," "mother," "child," and/or "sibling's child" in various languages of the Sepik, Southeast Asia, and India. The terms given here are not always the only pertinent ones in the languages concerned, and their denotations are not necessarily exhaustive.[12]

TABLE 7
"Father" in Sepik Languages

Language	Term	Phylum[a]	Family	Sub-District
Aru	*aya*	A	Palei	Lumi
One	*aya*	A	West Wapei	Lumi, Aitape
Seta	*aya*	A	West Wapei	Lumi
Seti	*aya*	A	West Wapei	Lumi
Yis	*aya*	A	Wapei	Lumi
Abau	*ayo*	B	Abau	Amanab[b]
Amal	*aya*	B	Biksi	Lumi
Bouye	*aya*	B	Ram	Lumi
Karawa	*aya*	B	Ram	Lumi
Namei	*eya*	B	Yellow River	Lumi, Ambunti
Aroup	*ayi*	A	Palei	Lumi
Elkei	*aiye*	A	Wapei	Lumi
Yau	*aiye*	A	Wapei	Lumi
Auwan	*aiya*	B	Yellow River	Lumi
Umeda	*aiya*	C	Waris	Amanab
Lou	*ayan*	A	Komio	Maprik
Autu	*naya*[c]	B	Ram	Lumi
Iatmul	*nyai*[c]	B	Ndu	Angoram, Ambunti
Galu	*ataya*	A	Wapei	Lumi
Kapriman	*aytya*	B	Sepik Hill	Angoram
Sanio	*ayte*	B	Sepik Hill	Ambunti
Urat	*yai*	A	Urat	Maprik
Olo	*yai*	A	Wapei	Lumi, Aitape
Yil	*ya*	A	Wapei	Lumi
Aiku	*yaya*	A	Palei	Lumi
Nambi	*yayak*	A	Palei	Lumi
Wiaki	*yaye*	A	Wiaki	Lumi
Ningil	*ya'ai*	A	Wapei	Lumi
Au	*gha'ai*[d]	A	Wapei	Lumi

Sources: For most terms, Laycock (1965:151; 1968:52); for Urat, B. J. Allen, personal communication, 1984; Iatmul, Bateson (1958:305); Sanio and Kapriman, Dye, Townsend, and Townsend (1969:152); Umeda, Gell (1975:56); Auwan (also called Awun [Laycock 1973:23, 75]), Kelm and Kelm (1980:240–43); Olo, McGregor and McGregor (1982:137–55).

[a] A, Torricelli; B, Sepik-Ramu; C, Trans–New Guinea (all three Papuan).
[b] And Irian Jaya.
[c] Note that addition of nasal element also occurs in "mother" in this language (see table 9).
[d] *gh* represents a voiced velar fricative.

It may be argued that these terminological similarities have nothing to do with lexical borrowing. First, it may be suggested that kinship terms for close relatives such as parents are part of "basic vocabulary" and consequently unborrowable. The claim made in glottochronology is, however, simply that for basic vocabulary the rate of change or replacement by borrowing is less than that for other lexical items (Hymes 1960:4–15). Also, with regard to the borrowing of kin terms some of the evidence given here is unquestionable: whether Indian kin terms have been borrowed by Southeast Asian and Sepik languages or not, it is known from Indian studies that they have been subject to borrowing within India. As is illustrated in tables 8 and 10, identical or similar kin terms are used not only in different lan-

guages of the same family but also in languages of unrelated families, Indo-Aryan, Dravidian, and Austroasiatic. More fundamentally, there is some doubt whether kin terms are part of basic vocabulary. For example, in his first test list (215 items) Swadesh included six kin terms (Hoijer 1956:49–50). In his second test list (100 items), however, he eliminated kin terms altogether and said that words like *papa* and *mama* are "sometimes widely borrowed among neighboring languages, even when ordinary cultural borrowings do not take place" (Swadesh 1955:126). Rather than eliminating kin terms from the basic vocabulary, however, perhaps we should reconsider the assumption that the rate of borrowing for the terms or the vocabulary is necessarily low. This assumption, which in its earlier forms seems

TABLE 8
AYYA AND RELATED FORMS IN IRIAN JAYAN, SOUTHEAST ASIAN, AND INDIAN LANGUAGES

LANGUAGE	PHYLUM OR FAMILY[a]	LEXICAL ITEM	DENOTATION
Awya	A	*ayo*	F
Jautefa	B	*ai*	F
Malay	B	*ayah*	F
Banjar	B	*ayah*	F
Mah Meri[b]	C	*ayah*	F
Temoq[b]	C	*ʔayah*	F
Minangkabau	B	*ayah*	F
Old Javanese	B	*yayah*	F
Pagu	A	*aya*	F
Iban	B	*aya*	FB
Kayan	B	*aya*	aged, old
Tamil	D	*ayyā, ayyan*	F
Telugu	D	*ayya, aya*	F
Kannada	D	*ayya, aya*	F
Toda	D	*eyi, eya*	F
Gondi	D	*ēyāl*	F
Kota	D	*ayn*	F
Malayalam	D	*ayyan*	F
Pali	E	*ayyaka*	F
Parengi	C	*ayan*	F
Koya	D	*ayya*	F
Kodagu	D	*ayye*	FB
Kolami	D	*ayyā*	MF
Irula	D	*ayyan*	FFF
Tulu	D	*ayye*	priest, teacher, master

SOURCES: Awya, Stokhof (1983*a*:143); Jautefa, Stokhof (1982*d*:109); Mah Meri and Temoq, Benjamin (1976:106), Skeat and Blagden (1966:599); Minangkabau, Josselin de Jong (1980:48); Pagu, Stokhof (1980*b*:191); Iban, Freeman (1960:86); Kayan, Blust (1977:95, 104), Rousseau (1974:118, 129), Roth (1968: appendices, cvi); see also Leach (1950:60–61), Douglas (1911:84, 100, 104–5).

[a] A, West Papuan; B, Austronesian; C, Austroasiatic; D, Dravidian; E, Indo-Aryan.
[b] A Central Aslian language.

somewhat ethnocentric, that is, associated primarily with European languages and cultures (cf. Hoijer 1956, Hymes 1960), may well not be applicable to every case. For instance, it may be that kin terms are sometimes more readily borrowed than other items or other basic items or that the rate of borrowing for the entire basic vocabulary is significantly high. Wurm (1982:260), the leading authority on the Papuan languages which constitute more than 90 percent of Sepik languages, observes that "a special trait of Papuan languages is the ease with which basic vocabulary items and features generally thought to be 'unborrowable' or at least not readily borrowable seem to have been exchanged between languages to a very great extent" (see also Wurm 1982:65).

A second objection that may be raised is that there is a universal tendency for parental kin terms to be similar irrespective of the language to which they belong. That this is indeed the case has been statistically confirmed by Murdock

(1959) on the basis of his world ethnographic sample and theoretically elucidated by Jakobson (1960). Furthermore, as a glance at Murdock's and Jakobson's contributions will show, the parental kin terms in tables 7–10 are in accord with this tendency in a number of respects. It does not follow, however, that the terminological resemblances are unrelated to lexical borrowing. The individual does not usually invent parental kin terms but learns them from those around him, and this is not inconsistent with Jakobson's view that these terms originate in nursery words and children's language. It could indeed be said that a basic reason the Indian terms in tables 7–10 may have been borrowed by Southeast Asians and Sepik peoples is precisely that they are subject to the universal tendency just mentioned and are therefore simple and agreeable to children as well as adults. It could also be hypothesized that, generally speaking, being subject to this tendency is an important factor in the diffusion of some kin

TABLE 9
"MOTHER" IN SEPIK LANGUAGES

LANGUAGE	TERM	LINGUISTIC PHYLUM[a]	FAMILY	SUB-DISTRICT
Seta	*ama*	A	West Wapei	Lumi
Seti	*ama*	A	West Wapei	Lumi
One	*ama*	A	West Wapei	Lumi, Aitape
Yau	*ama*	A	Wapei	Lumi
Olo	*ema*	A	Wapei	Lumi, Aitape
Auwan	*amai*[b]	B	Yellow River	Lumi
Tangu	*amai*	B	Ataitan	Bogia[c]
Manambu	*amay/amei*	B	Ndu	Ambunti
Bouye	*ami*	B	Ram	Lumi
Karawa	*ami*	B	Ram	Lumi
Autu	*nami*	B	Ram	Lumi
Iatmul	*nyamei/nemay*	B	Ndu	Angoram, Ambunti
Mountain Arapesh	*jame-ku*[d]	A	Arapesh	Wewak, Maprik, Aitape

SOURCES: For most terms, Laycock (1965:151; 1968:52); for Iatmul, Bateson (1958:305); Tangu, Burridge (1969*b*:71); Manambu, S. Harrison, personal communication, 1984; Auwan, Kelm and Kelm (1980:240–43); Olo, McGregor and McGregor (1982:137–55); Arapesh, Fortune (1977 [1942]:19, 88).

NOTE: In Aekyom, spoken across the southern border of the West Sepik Province in Awin Census Division, Western Province, the term for "mother" is *aemae*. What makes this the more significant is that the terms for "father" (*ai*) and "mother's brother" (*mom*) (R. Depew, personal communication, 1986) are also similar to those given in tables 7 and 13 respectively. Aekyom belongs to the Trans–New Guinea phylum.

[a] A, Torricelli; B, Sepik-Ramu (both Papuan).
[b] Mother's sister.
[c] In its broad sense, as used by Laycock (1978), the Sepik culture region covers the Western Madang Province, where Bogia is located.
[d] *ku* is a suffix; the term for "mother's sister" is *amake-ku* (Fortune 1977 [1942]: 17–21, 88).

terms as against others in different languages. A case in point is the Indian term *mama* (MB, etc.), which is perfectly consistent with the above tendency and the child's early linguistic ability.[13] In India this term is more widespread than any other, and it is also fairly well distributed in Southeast Asia and even found in the Sepik.

The diffusion of the kin terms under consideration is also linked to the fact that for the past two millennia or so Indians have not only had economic and cultural contact with Southeast Asia but also lived and intermarried there. Not much is known about the possibility of intermarriage between Southeast Asian and Sepik peoples in the past, but at least in recent times Southeast Asians have sometimes married local women. According to the 1966 census, there were 2,484 persons of "mixed race" in Papua New Guinea, 50 percent of whom were the result of intermarriage between non-Europeans, especially Malays and Chinese, and local women (Tudor 1969:33). In Puang, elderly Au men recall that two visiting Malays married two women from the village and took the women away with them. In physical characteristics Au are occasionally somewhat Mongoloid or Malay-like, and this observation has also been made of other peoples inside and outside the Sepik (Wedgwood 1934:380; Hogbin 1935:313;

Thomas 1941:165; Champion 1967:105). Marshall, during his 1936 trip to the Au area, observed that Malay influence could "easily be traced in the pale-faced, slit-eyed people we occasionally saw in the otherwise pure bush communities" and reported that in Yankok, an Au village, there were two such women and that he had seen and photographed them in other places as well (1938:49–50). The relevance of such physical features should not, however, be overemphasized; specialists maintain that Mongoloids and Australoids have coexisted in New Guinea and sometimes interbred for five thousand years (Bellwood 1979:25–51).

The data of tables 7–12 should be evaluated not in isolation but in relation to additional kin terms in the Sepik and/or Southeast Asia that show suggestive resemblances to their Indian equivalents. For example, tables 13 and 14 are concerned with the Indian kin terms *mama* and *mami* and what seem to be their borrowed forms in Southeast Asian and Sepik languages.[14] In table 13 the Sepik terms are few, probably because the majority of Sepik kinship terminologies are not yet fully recorded or published. For instance, for most of the Sepik languages mentioned in table 7 the kin terms pertinent to table 13 are unknown. The observed variations in the denotations of

TABLE 10
AMMA AND RELATED FORMS IN IRIAN JAYAN, SOUTHEAST ASIAN, AND INDIAN LANGUAGES

LANGUAGE	PHYLUM OR FAMILY[a]	LEXICAL ITEM	DENOTATION
Dem	A	*ama*	M
Kapauku	A	*amei*	M
Jautefa	B	*ame*	M
Malay	B	*ema?*[b]	M
Minangkabau	B	*amai*	M
Sundanese	B	*ema*	M
Solorese	B	*ema*	M
Tagalog	B	*ima*	M
Makassar[c]	B	*ama*	M
Pampangan	B	*ima*	M
Semai[d]	C	*ame?*	M
Tamil	D	*amma*	M
Malayalam	D	*amma*	M
Kannada	D	*amma, ama*	M
Telugu	D	*amma, ama*	M
Kolami	D	*amma*	M
Tulu	D	*amma*	M
Naikri	D	*amma*	M
Pali	E	*amma*	M
Sinhalese	E	*amma*	M
Hindi	E	*amma*	M
Urdu	E	*amma, ammi*	M
Sindhi	E	*amma*	M
Punjabi	E	*amma*	M
Brahui	E	*amma*	FM
Pengo	E	*ama*	FZ

SOURCES: Dem and Kapauku, Stokhof (1983a:208, 220; see also 6); Jautefa, Stokhof (1982d:109); Minangkabau, Josselin de Jong (1980:47); Sundanese, Koentjaraningrat (1972:55); Solorese, Barnes (1972:93), Stokhof (1983b:271); Tagalog and Pampangan, López (1939:38); Makassar, Stokhof (1984:234); Semai, Benjamin (1976:111), Dentan (1970:360).

NOTE: In Austronesian languages the most usual words for "mother" are terms such as *ina* or *tina* and for "father" terms such as *ama* or *tama* (Wurm and Wilson 1983; Blust 1979; 1980a:216). This makes it more likely that *ama* (mother) in the Austronesian languages shown here is of foreign origin. Similar terms are also found in many Tibeto-Burman languages; whether or not these have any bearing on the origin of the Southeast Asian or Indian terms here awaits investigation.

[a] A, Trans–New Guinea (Papuan); B, Austronesian; C, Austroasiatic; D, Dravidian; E, Indo-Aryan.

[b] Malays tend to pronounce the last element as a glottal stop, but it is usually written as *k(emak)*.

[c] In the Bonthain dialect.

[d] A Central Aslian language.

mama and *mami* can often be readily explained in the light of kinship studies in anthropology. In India *mami* in the sense of MBW is, like *mama* in the sense of MB, used in various kinship terminologies, including the symmetrical type especially characteristic of Dravidian languages. A symmetrical system of terminology which expresses bilateral cross-cousin marriage can be expected to have the following equations: MB = FZH = WF = HF and MBW = FZ = WM = HM. Hence *mama* and *mami* are equated with the same or some of the same relatives in a number of Indian languages. Terminologies that are more or less symmetrical are also found in Southeast Asia. Southeast Asia is also associated with a tendency toward the generational type of termi-

nology, which implies the following equations: MB = FB = F and FZ = MZ = M. Malay terminology is of course basically generational, but no reflection of this is found in the terms listed in table 13. The reason is that *mama* and *mami* are not much used by Malays and not integrated into their terminological system.[15] The Malay term *bapak* (or *pak*) used for F is also the basic term for FB and MB, to which the qualifier *penakan* or *saudara* ("collateral") may be added. Likewise, *emak* (or *mak*), used for M, is also the basic term for MZ and FZ, which may be qualified by *penakan* or *saudara*.[16]

It is of interest that the Malay word *saudara*, which has related forms in many other Southeast Asian languages, is Sanskrit in origin (Gonda

TABLE 11
"Child" and/or "Sibling's Child" in Sepik and Southeast Asian Languages

Language	Phylum or Family[a]	Lexical Item	Denotation
Au	A	*nikan*	S, ZS
		niki	D, ZD
Elkei	A	*ninan*	C
Yau	A	*nini*	C
Lou	A	*lenan*	C
Olo	A	*nanke*	S, eBS (m.s.), eZS (w.s.), DH
		nankio	D, eBD (m.s.) eZD (w.s.), SW
Iatmul	B	*nian*	C, BC
Melanau	C	*nakan*	BC, ZC
Bisaya[b]	C	*nakon*	BC, ZC
Iban	C	*akan*	BS, ZS
Ma'anyan	C	*aken*	BC, ZC
Ngaju Dayak	C	*aken*	BC, ZC
Manobo	C	*enaken*	BC, ZC
Tausug	C	*anakun*	BC, ZC
Murik	C	*anak aken*	BC, ZC
Sanggau	C	*anak manakan*	BC, ZC
Malay	C	*anak penakan*	BC, ZC
		kemanakan	BS, ZS
Balinese	C	*keponakan*	ZC
Javanese	C	*keponaqan*	eBC, eZC
Ilokano	C	*kaanakan*	BC, ZC
Tagalog	C	*pamangkin*	BC, ZC
Bajau Laut	C	*kamanakan*	BC, ZC, PGCC

SOURCES: Elkei, Yau, and Lou, Laycock (1968:52); Olo, Laycock (1968:52), McGregor (1982:137–55); Melanau, Morris (1953:109–10; 1978:56), Mulder et al. (1930:107–8); Bisaya, Peranio (1972:165); Iban, Freeman (1960:86); Ma'anyan, Hudson (1972:64); Ngaju Dayak, Miles (1971:214); Tausug, Kiefer (1972:34); Murik, Blust (1974:162); Sanggau, King (1978:213); Malay, Banks (1974:49; 1983; cf. Djamour 1959); Balinese, Geertz and Geertz (1975:171); Javanese, Koentjaraningrat (1960:108); Ilokano, Constantino (1971:227); Tagalog, Llamzon (1979a:135); Bajau Laut, Sather (1978:191); see also Leach (1950:60–61), Needham (1954, 1955).

[a] A, Torricelli (Papuan); B, Sepik-Ramu (Papuan); C, Austronesian; for families to which the Sepik languages belong, see table 7.

[b] Spoken in Sabah and Sarawak.

1973[1952]:102, 428, 521–22). In Malay *saudara* denotes B, Z, C as well as the relatives specified above. Related forms (e.g., *sudara, sedara*) are found in languages such as Javanese, Achinese (Gonda 1973[1952]:102, 119), Ai, Sekola, Ambon Maleis, Tonsea (Stokhof 1982a: 156, 172, 186, 202; 1983d:66, 80), and some Aslian languages (Skeat and Blagden 1966:547–48, 558). In Sanskrit we find *sodara* (born from the same womb), *sodaraḥ* (uterine brother), *sodarā* (uterine sister). The same terms with minor variations in form occur in many other Indian languages, e.g., Pali *sodariya* (uterine brother), Hindi *sahodar*, (born of the same womb, uterine brother), Bhojpuri [Sadani] *sahodar* (born of the same womb, uterine brother), Nepali *sahodar* (born of the same womb), Sinhalese *sahoda* (born

of the same womb), *sahodara* (uterine brother), *sahodari* (uterine sister).

Finally, some comments on the denotations of *mama* and *mami* in the Sepik language of which I have firsthand knowledge:[17] One of the features of Au terms *mama* and *mami* is that they are used for both sexes. This feature, relating to the role of gender in the Au language, is found in many Au kin terms, such as *tata* (FyB, MyZ) and *ghita?am* (CEF, CEM). When Au kin terms are employed referentially, they are suffixed by possessive pronouns which specify the sex of the person referred to. Thus while both FF and MM are addressed as *mama*, the former is referred to as *mama kai* (my male grandparent [grandparent-he-mine]) and the latter as *mama pai* (my female grandparent [grandparent-she-mine]).[18] As may

TABLE 12
"CHILD" AND/OR "SIBLING'S CHILD" IN
(DRAVIDIAN) INDIAN LANGUAGES

LANGUAGE	LEXICAL ITEM	DENOTATION
Tamil	makan	S, BS (m.s.), ZS (w.s.)
	makal	D, BD (m.s.), ZD (w.s.)
	marumakan	BS (w.s.), ZS (m.s.), DH
	marumakal	BD (w.s.), ZD (m.s.), SW
	maka	C
	makkal	C (plural)
Malayalam	makan	S, ZS (w.s.)
	makal	D, ZD (w.s.)
	marumakan	ZS (m.s.)
	marumakal	ZD (m.s.)
	makkal	C (plural)
Tulu	mage	S, BS (m.s.), ZS (w.s.)
	magal	D, BD (m.s.), ZD (w.s.)
	makkal	C (plural)
Kannada	maga (nu)	S, BS (m.s.), ZS (w.s.)
	magalu	D, BD (m.s.), ZD (w.s.)
	moga	C
Irula	mage	S, BS, ZS
	maga	D, BD, ZD
	marumage	DH
	marumaga	SW
Gondi	maghi	S, BS (m.s.), ZS (w.s.)
Kuwi	maka	D (vocative)
Malto	maqe	boy
	maqi	girl

be seen in the equations implicit in the following examples, some of the features of Au terminology accord with the symmetrical type mentioned earlier: pa'ab (FZH, MB), ta'ait (FZ, MBW), wokna (FZS, MBS), wokni (FZD, MBD), ghanmok (ZH, WB). But Au terminology does not reflect marriage with first cross-cousins, which is forbidden in the Au area. For the Au, the ideal marriage is with one's FMBSD, that is, asymmetrical and between second cross-cousins. Hence, as seen in table 13, the term mami equates WF and WM not with FZH/MB and FZ/MBW but with FMBS and FMBSW (and the parents of some other second cross-cousins).

As noted above, the Au employ only one term for each of the following pairs of relatives: FZH/MB, FZS/MBS, and ZH/WB. Such terms are, however, sometimes modified by certain phrases

which differentiate the members of each pair and consequently bring this aspect of the terminology more into accord with an asymmetrical system. The phrase added to the terms for MB, MBS, and WB is ka miak (of meat) and that added to the terms for FZH, FZS, and ZH ka pawak (of shell rings). These phrases reflect the fact that the most characteristic gift presented by wife givers to wife receivers is smoked meat and by wife receivers to wife givers shell rings. Similarly, nikan is employed for ZS as well as S and niki for ZD as well as D, but these terms are sometimes modified by swara (chicken) and applied exclusively to the ZS and ZD (m.s.).

A significant asymmetrical distinction made in Au terminology is that between WF and WM, on the one hand, and HF and HM, on the other. While the former two are called mami, the latter two are called gha'ai (primarily denoting F) and mi:ja (primarily denoting M) respectively. The puzzling Au usage of mama for persons of a different generation, namely, grandparents, is partial evidence for the equation in the Au area of WF and WM with grandparents in contrast to the equation of HF and HM with parents. Further evidence is that mami, closely related to mama, is employed for WF and WM by the Au and for FF and MF by their neighbors the Gnau, who use mama for FM and MM. The main evidence is, however, that in a number of Au villages the same term, ma'am, is employed for WF and WM as well as grandparents. Au kin terms sometimes vary from village to village, mama and mami, for example, being used only in some villages, such as Wulukum (Fountain 1966:fig. 3.1), while in others, such as Puang and Tumentonik (Scorza 1974), ma'am corresponds to mama and mami combined.

The equation of wife givers like WF, WM, and, of course, MB (who is sometimes WF as well), on the one hand, and grandparents, on the other, is also found in Southeast Asia, where mama/mami or related forms are sometimes used for grandparents (e.g., Lio mamo [grandparent] [S. Howell, personal communication, 1986; Stokhof 1983b:173]; Lima meme manawa [manawa: male] [grandfather], meme mapina [mapina: female] [grandmother] [Stokhof 1981a:150, 166]; Tagalog mamay [grandfather], mama [mother's brother]; Bikol and Sebu mamay [grandfather] [López 1939:56]). This equation is further expressed by another set of cognate words that has already been subjected to perceptive comparative examination pertinent to the present issue (Barnes 1979, Blust 1979). Examples of this cog-

TABLE 13
MAMA AND *MAMI* IN SEPIK AND SOUTHEAST ASIAN LANGUAGES

LANGUAGE	PHYLUM[a]	LEXICAL ITEM	DENOTATION
Au	A	*mama*	FF, MF, FM, MM
		mami	WF, WM, FMBS, FMBSW
Auwan	B	*mam*	FZH, FMBDH
		mamei	MBW, FZ, FMBD
Gnau[b]	A	*mama*	FM, MM
		mami	FF, MF
Urat	A	*mamiyen*	HM
Kwoma[c]	B	*mem*	MB, MBS, MBSS
Telefol	C	*mom*	MB
Malay	D	*mama?*[d]	MB
		mami	MBW
Luhu	D	*meme*	MB
Garo	E	*mama*	MB, FZH, WF, HF
		mami	MBW, FZ, WM, HM
Karo Batak	D	*mama*	MB, WF
		mami	MBW, WM
Rembong	D	*mama*	MB, FZH, WF, HF
Rejang	D	*mama*	MyB, FyB
Sangir	D	*meme*	FZ, MZ
Minangkabau	D	*mama'*	MB
Pangasinan	D	*mama*	MB, FB
Kerinci	D	*mama*	MB
Semaq Beri[e]	F	*mama*	MyB, FyB
Ngaju Dayak	D	*mama'*	MB
Atayal	C	*mama?*	MB, FB

SOURCES: Auwan, Kelm and Kelm (1980:240–43); Gnau, Lewis (1980:44, 177; personal communication, 1984); Urat, B. J. Allen, personal communication, 1984; Kwoma, Bowden (1983b:747); (Williamson 1980:533); Telefol, Healey and Healey (1977:334); Luhu, Collins (1983:80); Garo, Needham (1966:144); Karo Batak, Singarimbun (1975:202); Rembong, Needham (1985:278–79); Rejang, Blust (1984:431); Sangir, Stokhof (1982c:94, 124, 152, 174, 210, 234); Minangkabau, Josselin de Jong (1980:47); Kerinci, Steinhauer and Hakim Usman (1978:489, 493); Semaq Beri, Jensen (1977–78:173); Ngaju Dayak, Miles (1971:214).

[a] A, Torricelli (Papuan); B, Sepik-Ramu (Papuan); C, Trans-New Guinea (Papuan); D, Austronesian; E, Sino-Tibetan; F, Austroasiatic.
[b] Spoken in the Lumi Sub-District.
[c] Spoken in the Ambunti Sub-District.
[d] Usually written *mamak*; see table 10, n. b.
[e] A Southern Aslian language.

nate set in various Austronesian languages are *appo*, *ipo*, *ompu*, *ambo*, *upu*, *pu*, *tepu-n*, *tabu (-na)*, *tibu*, *upun*, and *eppu?*, glossed as "grandparent (ancestor)" and/or "grandchild." Sometimes terms of this set are used for various affines, especially wife givers. In Kedang, according to Barnes (1979:20) "it is not just male and female wife-givers whom the Kedang call *epu*, but also all members of either sex of the second ascending genealogical level" (see also Barnes 1974, 1977).[19] In Lio *pu* means "trunk" and is used for WB; it may also be used with various prefixes to mean true MBD and other important members of the wife-giving group such as WF (S. Howell, personal communication, 1986). Further examples are Katingan *epu*, Dohoi *upu*, Tabojan *umpu*, Dusun Dejah *ampu*, Murung

ompu, Ngaju Dayak *empu* (parents-in-law) (Hudson 1967:82–110; Blust 1979:206). The following Au terms are worth considering in connection with those of the above set that are concerned with "grandparent/grandchild": *ma?am nepu* (great-grandparent [*ma?am*: grandparent]), *nepani* (grandchild, great-grandchild), *nepanyak* (grandson, great-grandson), *nepanya* (granddaughter, great-granddaughter). As with these Au terms, in some Southeast Asian languages the terms for "grandparent" and "grandchild" are not identical and/or have *n* as the initial element (e.g., Sula Fagudu *nopa fina* [*fina*: female] denotes "grandmother" and *ana nopa* [*ana*: child] "grandchild" [Stokhof 1980b:69–70], Toba Batak *ompung* "grandparent" and *pahompu* "grandchild" [Brineman Bovill 1985:39–43], and Ce-

TABLE 14
MAMA AND *MAMI* IN INDIAN LANGUAGES

LANGUAGE	FAMILY[a]	LEXICAL ITEM	DENOTATION
Tamil	A	*mama, maman*	MB, FZH, WF, HF
		mami	MBW, FZ, WM, HM
Irula	A	*mama, mame*	MB, FZH, WF, HF
		mami	MBW, FZ, WM, HM
Naikri	A	*mama*	MB, FZH, WF, HF
		mami	MBW, FZ, WM, HM
Naiki (Ch.)	A	*mama*	MB, FZH, WF, HF
		mami	MBW, FZ, WM, HM
Hindi	B	*mama*	MB
		mami	MBW
Marathi	B	*mama*	MB
		mami	MBW
Gujarati	B	*mama*	MB
		mami	MBW
Bengali	B	*mama*	MB
		mami	MBW
Punjabi	B	*mamma*	MB
		mammi	MBW
Sinhalese	B	*mama*	MB, FZH, WF, HF
Telugu	A	*mama*	MB, FZH, WF, HF
Tulu	A	*mami*	MBW, FZ, WM, HM
Kui	A	*mama*	MB, FZH
Brahui	A	*mama*	MB, WF
Nahali	C	*mama*	MB, FyZH
		mami	MBW
Santali	C	*mama, mamo*	MB
		memi	MBW
Munda	C	*mama*	MB
		mami	MBW

[a] A, Dravidian; B, Indo-Aryan; C, Austroasiatic.

buano Visayan *apohan* "grandparent" [and "great-grandparent"] and *apo* "grandchild" [Cabonce 1983:450; Yap and Bunye 1971:28]).[20]

Why wife givers and grandparents are equated is a very complex issue. The equation is found not only in Southeast Asia and Oceania (in both Austronesian and Papuan languages) but also in Africa (Radcliffe-Brown 1971) and historically in Europe (Benveniste 1973:18–92). Also, it is only one of the many forms assumed by the "skewing rule," the rule concerned with the formal equivalence of relatives of different generations (Lounsbury 1969). As far as its sociopsychological roots are concerned, it seems to be at least sometimes an expression of the superiority of wife givers over wife receivers in systems of asymmetric alliance or generalized exchange (cf. Barnes 1979). This idea, which may well lead to much deeper insights, is in need of further research and development. Here I confine myself to a brief ethnographic account of this superiority,

which is a significant feature of both kinship and world view, in the Au area.

Wife receivers are indebted to wife givers primarily because the latter are conceived of as life givers. It is often said by a MB of his ZS: "He did not come out of a tree-hole"; the rest, which is well-known and usually left unsaid, is "He came out of the genitalia of my sister." Life depends on wife givers not only for its *emergence*, through the mother, but also for its *maturation*, through the MB. The protagonist of the puberty rites that are considered vital for physical growth is the MB, who smears his penile blood on his ZS or ZD's body and, after mixing it with specially prepared food, gives it to the child to eat.

When wife givers are spoken of, it is their rights which are stressed, whereas with regard to wife receivers it is their duties. In marriage it is the right of the former to give women and the duty of the latter to receive them. It is the MB's right, not duty, to perform the puberty rites, and it is the ZH's duty to invite him to do so and to present him shell rings afterward. It is also the MB's right to determine how many shell rings he wishes to receive; no matter how many rings are given, the MB's rights are encroached upon if he has not been consulted beforehand. Shell rings, which are given by F, ZH, and FZS to MB, WB, and MBS, respectively, as offerings on various occasions, never circulate in the opposite direction. They express respect, indebtedness, and submission in many different contexts. They are offered to the ancestors as propitiation, paid to acquire the right to perform certain healing rituals connected with powerful spirits, and presented by the novice to his master after learning the art of pointing magic (Au *manmin*). They are also offered by a murderer as compensation and to express his desire to appease the victim's ghost and close relatives.

If wife receivers do not fulfill their duties, they may be penalized, through the use of destructive magic or otherwise, by wife givers. If the ZS does not fulfill his duties in giving the plumes of the first bird of paradise he shoots to his MB, the MB is entitled to resort to magic or to use the bones of his ancestors to make his ZS ill. In contrast, if the MB does not reciprocate as he ought to by giving his ZS meat, the ZS and his father do not and are not entitled to use destructive magic or have the support of their own ancestors to harm him. The attitude of wife givers toward wife receivers, if the former are matrilateral kin, is at the same time protective and caring (this is frequently reflected in Au mythology). Attitudes are, of course, often complex and have different if not contradictory components. If the MB is demanding, he is also benevolent. When the ZS is the victim of destructive magic, retaliatory action may be taken by his MB. When the ZS is in conflict with his father or someone else, he may seek protection from his MB. "Chicken son" used by the MB for his ZS is a term of endearment.

Personal Names

There are some striking formal resemblances between Au personal names and certain Southeast Asian, Indian, and/or the Middle Eastern words that are also personal names and are used for the same sex as their Au equivalents. A few examples must suffice here; additional ones will call for more data on names in the Sepik that will permit the separation of fortuitous lexical correspondences from real ones. Anis is a male name among the Au and also in Southeast Asia, India, and the Middle East; its Arabic origin is clear from the fact that *anis* [ʔani:s] is Arabic for "close com-

panion" and also a male name in that language. Anis is a male name among the Wapei of the West Sepik (McGregor 1975:20,62) and, in the form of Alis, among the Arapesh (Mead 1947a:269; 1947c: 416); it is reported to be very common in the Sepik region as a whole (Townsend 1968:261). Another Arabic male name, *mahdi* (rightly guided), is used in India and Southeast Asia and by the Wapei (Mitchell 1978b:206, 236), in whose language, Olo, the terms for parents and children also seem to be of Southeast Asian and/or Indian origin (tables 7, 9, and 11). Yet another Arabic male name, *khamis* [xami:s], appears in Au as Kamis and in similar forms in India (*khamis*) and Southeast Asia (*kamis/ kemis*).[21] It means "Thursday" (of ritual importance in many Muslim communities) and is related to the word for "five" [xamsa]. In Southeast Asia, as in India, it retains these meanings in a variety of languages (e.g., Malay *kamis/kemis*, Tiruray and Banjar *kamis*, Mandar *kammis*, Madurese *kemmes*, Lio *kamis* [S. Howell, personal communication, 1986], Buginese *kammisik*, Balinese *kemis* [Thursday]; Javanese [Becker 1979:199] and Sundanese [Wessing 1974:218] *kemis* [five]).

Some of the (Southeast) Asian-like names used by the Au may well be the result of recent Malay contacts, but this cannot be said of all the names of this type, as they are found among the names of ancestors as well as the living generations. Anis, for example, is the name of the FFFB of a man called Wananap who is in his thirties. Because Au genealogies are traditionally shallow, covering no more than two to five generations, Asian-like names may have existed in Au culture even earlier than this, and where found they can be assumed to be genuine. The Au do not attempt to invent genealogical connections even with the many nonagnates and nonrelatives often found in an Au clan. Another Asian-like Au name is Yakub, a well-known Muslim name in Southeast Asia, India, and, in the form of [yaʔqu:b], the Middle East. Yakub does not, however, occur among the names of past generations in my collected genealogies, and, being a Christian name as well (with Dutch/German pronunciation), may have been introduced by the missionaries into the Au area. A puzzling issue requiring further research in this connection is that *yakub* is also a kind of banana tree associated with what seem to be traditional beliefs and rituals.[22] These beliefs and rituals may have developed, at least in part, in recent times, or, alternatively, they may be genuinely traditional and the banana tree or its present name of recent origin and somehow related to the missionaries.

One question raised by the existence of Asian-like Sepik names is whether or not they are indicative of intermarriage between Southeast Asians and the people of the Sepik. We have already seen that in their recent contacts Southeast Asians have married local people, and they may have done so in earlier times as well. Another reason for the existence of Asian-like names, at least in the Au area, may be that the adoption of foreign names does not conflict with local beliefs and customs. The first time the mother breast-feeds her newborn, she mentions a series of names to it, and the one she is saying as the baby begins to suck at the breast becomes its name. Among the names she mentions are ideally first and foremost those of the baby's patrilateral and matrilateral ancestors, but, as genealogies show, this rule is not much observed. Genealogies also indicate, at least as far as they go, that names are not usually repeated inter- or intragenerationally. The Au have a large stock of names, and this may be partly because until very recently they have been rather mobile, mixing with peoples of other languages.

The Interstructural Approach and Other Issues

I have tried to provide evidence for the influence upon each other of certain structures, here cultures and their languages. A study on this scale may well contain errors of judgment. Gonda (1973[1952]:57), whose research into Sanskrit influence on Southeast Asia is monumental, observes: "It must be borne in mind that everyone who writes on cultural and linguistic borrowings in ancient times, and especially when dealing with South-East Asia, stands a good chance of making many mistakes." I have attempted, within the limitations of space, to reduce the significance of such mistakes by providing numerous cases of lexical borrowing and illustrating them at length. Apart from the preceding fourteen tables, there are certain other cases that can be considered only briefly here.

Laycock (1975b) has briefly discussed some grammatical and lexical resemblances between Torricelli-phylum languages and the aboriginal languages of the Malay Peninsula (Senoi, Semang) and suggested the possibility of a genetic link between the two groups. I have presented further evidence for lexical resemblances between the two groups, calling the aboriginal languages "Aslian." These items, however, while perhaps indicative of lexical influence, do not strengthen the possibility of the genetic link in question. Whether of Indian origin or not, most of them are Austronesian or also occur in Austronesian languages (Wurm and Wilson 1983). The depth and the nature of the connections between Papuan and Southeast Asian languages have not yet, however, been fully uncovered and understood, and credit is due to Laycock and others (Greenberg 1971, Wurm 1977b, Wurm et. al. 1977) for trying to place the Sepik and New Guinea in a broader perspective.

Theoretically I have sought to draw attention to interstructural relations. Thus I have related some aspects of different and widely scattered cultures to each other and tried to show that the data form significant patterns. The study is certainly more extensive than intensive, partly because of the nature of the data, but some of the cultures considered do seem to have had far-reaching connections. When loanwords include not only terms for articles of trade, personal names, and sexually and magically taboo words but also so-called unborrowable words, namely, parental kin terms, external cultural influences cannot be described as superficial. The idea that structures are open and their external relations and oppositions are no less important than their internal ones challenges some fundamental assumptions in the social sciences and requires detailed examination in its own right. To conclude the discussion here, I want to show its critical bearing on Austronesian culture history and early Austronesian social structure.

Austronesian languages, numbering five hundred or more, are widely distributed in Southeast Asia and Oceania and are also found in the coastal areas of the Sepik and other parts of New Guinea. In an important recent work on Austronesian culture history, Blust (1976; see also 1980b:240–41) has advanced the hypothesis that the original Austronesian-speakers (ca. 4000 B.C.) had a relatively advanced culture, with domesticated pigs, rice, pottery, needle and thread, and perhaps the loom, iron, and an indigenous script. Since some of these, such as rice, iron, and a script, are not known to have existed in Oceania, he argues that the Austronesian-speakers who moved eastward from Southeast Asia to Oceania must have lost a number of their cultural possessions. His hypothesis is based on the assumption that the Austronesian terms for the cul-

TABLE 15
"Iron" in Austronesian and Indian Languages

Language	Lexical Item	Denotation
Kenyah	*bari*	iron
Batak (Palawan)	*baribari*	iron, metal
Squliq Atayal	*bali*	iron, metal
Sanggau	*basi*	iron
Malay	*besi*	iron
Kadazan	*bosi*	iron
Hindi	*beri*	irons, fetters
Bengali	*beri*	irons, fetters
Sindhi	*bberi*	irons, fetters
Punjabi	*beri*	irons, fetters
Marathi	*bidi*	irons, fetters
Gujarati	*bedi*	irons, fetters

Sources: Batak, Squliq Atayal, Blust (1976:28); Sanggau, King (1976:149).
Note: In these Indian languages *r* is flapped and *d* retroflex; the former is a modification of the latter.

TABLE 16
"Rust" in Austronesian and Indian Languages

Language	Lexical Item	Denotation
Malay	*karat*	rust
Balinese	*karat*	rust
Madurese	*karat*	rust
Batak (Palawan)	*karat*	rust
Kerinci	*kahat*	rust
Tamil	*karai*	rust, stain, blackness
Malayalam	*kara*	rust, stain, blackness
Telugu	*kara*	rust, stain, blackness
Toda	*kar*	rust, stain, blackness
	kart-	to become black
Kodagu	*kara-, karat-*	to become black

Sources: Batak, Blust (1976:30); Kerinci, Prentice and Hakim Usman (1978:152).
Note: Blust (1976:30) reconstructs the proto-form for the Austronesian words as **kara (Ct)*.

tural items in question are not of foreign origin. In a few cases he briefly deals with the possibility of external origin, pointing out that **surat* (write) "is not a Sanskrit loanword," rejecting the idea that **zawa* (millet) derives from Sanskrit, and observing of **pajay* (rice plant, paddy) that if it were "a loanword acquired within the past two or three millennia one would expect some evidence for a source language on the Asian mainland. To date no one has suggested a candidate" (1976:32–33).

It seems to me, however, that a significant number of the terms in question are of foreign and especially Indian origin. Because of limitations of space and the complexity of the matter, the examples must be few, brief, and without much comment. Words for "salt" have been discussed in some detail. Words for "iron," "rust," and "ax/adz" may be taken as further examples (tables 15–17).

This lexical evidence regarding the suggested Indian origin of some Austronesian words does not, of course, necessarily indicate that the objects to which the words refer are also of Indian origin. It does, however, indicate that Austronesian culture history cannot be adequately studied without taking external influences into account. As early as 1964, Murdock put forward a hypothesis diametrically opposed to Blust's (Murdock 1964). In the light of Dyen's (1965*a*[1963]) lexicostatistical contribution to Austronesian studies, he argued that the original Austronesian-speakers lacked agriculture and lived by fishing and gathering, but when they moved westward from their homeland in Melanesia they came into contact with the more materially advanced cultures of mainland Southeast Asia and acquired domesticated pigs, cultivation, iron, and writing. He also made brief reference to the later influence of China, India, and the Middle East on Austronesian culture history. Murdock's hypothesis is of interest here for the extent to which it draws attention to mainland Asia; whether the Austronesian homeland was in Melanesia or not is another matter (cf. Blust 1982). The hypothesis, however, requires further development and a

TABLE 17
"Ax/Adz" in Austronesian and Indian Languages

Language	Lexical Item	Denotation
Buginese	*wase*	ax
Sanggau	*wase*	ax
Kayan	*asei*	ax
Ilokano	*wasay*	ax
Pangasinan	*wasay*	ax
Bontok	*wasay*	ax
Sinhalese	*wasi*	adz
Tamil	*vacci*	adz
Malayalam	*vacci*	adz
Kannada	*baci*	adz
Bengali	*basi*	adz
Sanskrit	*vasi*	adz

Sources: Sanggau, King (1976:162); Ilokano, Pangasinan, and Bontok, Zorc (1978:76, 80); Kayan, cf. Southwell (1980:8, 90) with Rousseau (1974:98).
Note: Blust (1970:145) reconstructs the proto-form for "ax" as **wasay*; on the proto-form, see also Zorc (1978) and Wurm and Wilson (1983).

more solid factual basis. At any rate, it is not backed by any lexical evidence. Blust (1976:36) is right in saying that in it "no attempt is made to identify a possible source language for any of these putative loans."

In another comparative study, Blust (1980*a*) deals with early Austronesian social structure, and this article is of particular interest in that it is accompanied by critical comments from both anthropologists and linguists. Blust argues, in agreement with Goodenough (1955, 1956) and in opposition to Murdock's earlier work (1949), that early or original Austronesian social structure possessed unilineal descent groups, and he tries to demonstrate, in the light of van Wouden's and Lévi-Strauss's works, that the groups had an asymmetric-alliance or generalized-exchange system based on matrilateral cross-cousin (MBD) marriage. Here again his hypothesis pivots on the study of lexical items, in this case, kin terms, and on the assumption that they are not loanwords. This and the preceding hypotheses have bearing on Papuan cultures in the Sepik and Oceania because Austronesian- and Papuan-speakers have interacted and interbred since the remote past. We have seen, for example, that sometimes the two groups have basic vocabulary items in common and that among the Au people the marriage rule, partly reflected in the kinship terminology, is asymmetrical.

Without intending to belittle Blust's hypothesis, I wish to show that a significant number of the kin terms discussed in it could be of Indian origin. This is not, of course, to suggest that asymmetric alliance as an institution was imported from India. It does mean, however, that if the kin terms are shown to be Indian loanwords, first, they cannot by themselves be evidence for asymmetric alliance as a characteristic of original Austronesian social structure, and secondly, they will shed further light on the far-reaching nature of the past relationship between Southeast Asia and Oceania, on the one hand, and India and mainland Asia, on the other. Terms for "elder sibling," "younger sibling," and "mother's brother" in Austronesian and Indian languages are shown in tables 18–20. A few Sepik terms are worthy of note: Manam *a'a*, Kwoma *laka, lega*, Boikin *ace* (eZ [w.s.], eB [m.s.]).[23] The Austronesian terms for "elder sibling," like the rest of the Austronesian words mentioned in this paper, are taken from western Austronesian languages spoken in Southeast Asia, but, significantly enough, similar terms for "elder sibling" are also found in Oceanic or eastern Austronesian languages (see

TABLE 18
"ELDER SIBLING" IN AUSTRONESIAN AND INDIAN LANGUAGES

LANGUAGE	LEXICAL ITEM	DENOTATION
Malay	*kaka?*	eZ, (sometimes) eB
Iban	*aka*	eZ, eB
Kadazan	*aka, taka*	eZ, eB
Ilokano	*kaka*	eZ, eB
Ami	*kaka*	eZ, eB
Kedang	*aqe*	eZ, eB
Tamil	*akka, akkal, akkan*	eZ
Malayalam	*akka*	eZ
Kannada	*akka*	eZ
Telugu	*akka*	eZ
Tulu	*akka*	eZ
Sinhalese	*akka*	eZ

SOURCES: Iban, Freeman (1960:86); Ami, Mabuchi (1960:134); Kedang, Barnes (1974:266–67).

Blust 1979, Wurm and Wilson 1983): Proto-Austronesian **kaka* (eZ, eB), Proto-Polynesian **tuqaka*, Proto-Oceanic **kaka* (eZ [w.s.], eB [m.s.]).

The last example is concerned with a puzzling series of terms which Blust believes to be a single set of words, deriving from the same etyma,

TABLE 19
"YOUNGER SIBLING" IN AUSTRONESIAN AND INDIAN LANGUAGES

LANGUAGE	LEXICAL ITEM OR ETYMON	DENOTATION
Toba Batak	*anggi*	yZ (w.s.), yB (m.s.)
Fijian	*taci*	yZ (w.s.), yB (m.s.)
Proto-Austronesian	**a (n) ji*	yZ, yB
Proto-Austronesian	**qa (n) ji*	yZ, yB
Proto-Oceanic	**ta (a) ji*	yZ (w.s.), yB (m.s.)
Proto-Oceanic	**tansi*	yZ (w.s.), yB (m.s.)
Kannada	*tangi*	yZ
Tulu	*tangi*	yZ
Tamil	*tankai*	yZ
Malayalam	*tanka*	yZ
Irula	*tange*	yZ
Kui	*tangi, angi*	yZ

SOURCES: Toba Batak, Brineman Bovill (1985:39–43); Fijian, Capell (1963); Proto-Austronesian and Proto-Oceanic, Blust (1979), Wurm and Wilson (1983), Dempwolff (1969).

TABLE 20
"Mother's Brother" in Austronesian and
Indian Languages

Language	Lexical Item or Etymon	Denotation
Dusun Dejah	*matua*	MeB, FeB, FeZH, MeZH
Malay	*mintuha/mentua*	WF, WM, HF, HM
Bajau Laut	*mato'a*	WF, WM, HF, HM
Mukah	*tua?*	MB, FB, FZH, MZH
Proto-Oceanic	*matuqa*	MB
Proto–Western Malayo-Polynesian	*ma(n)tuqa*	MB, WF, (HF?)
Hindi	*matula*	MB
Marathi	*matula*	MB
Bengali	*matula*	MB
Pali	*matula*	MB
Sinhalese	*matula*	MB, WF, HF
Tamil	*matulan*	MB, WF, HF

Sources: Dusun Dejah, Hudson (1967); Bajau Laut, Sather (1978:191); Mukah, Blust (1980a:212); Proto-Oceanic and Proto–Western Malayo-Polynesian, Blust (1980a), Wurm and Wilson (1983). Proto–Western Malayo-Polynesian is defined by Blust (1980a:208) as "the Malayo-Polynesian languages of western Indonesia and the Philippines, including Chamorro, Palauan, Chamic, and Malagasy."

Note: Related terms for MBW in Indian languages are Hindi *matulā, matulāni, matuli*, Sinhalese *matulā*, Tamil *matuli*, Bengali *matulāni, matuli*, Sanskrit *matulā, matulāni, matuli*. The Indian terms for MB, not much used at present, derive from Sanskrit *matula* (MB), which is related to Sanskrit *matri* (M). As is shown by some of the commentators on Blust's article, the above series of Austronesian words and their original denotation(s) and form(s) need far more investigation. As a result, the suggested Indian origin should be viewed with caution.

namely, *aya*. The terms most often denote either "mother" or "father" and are sometimes used for "father's sister," "nursemaid," and so forth. Blust unconvincingly concludes that the denotation of *aya* is "father's sister," and in this regard he is criticized, factually and otherwise, by Chowning and Fox. None of his critics, however, questions his assumption that the terms belong to a single set. I suggest that the terms in question are members of at least three distinct sets, which are probably of external origin and which have been confounded because of their similarity in form. First, there is a set of terms denoting "father," such as Malay *ayah* and Sundanese *aya*, which may derive from Indian terms with identical denotation such as Tamil *ayya* and Kannada *ayya* (table 8).

Second, there is a set of terms denoting "mother," such as Abui *ia*, Atayal *y-aya*, and Buli *aye* (and other examples in Blust's article), similar terms to which are also found in India.[24] Terms like Tamil *ayya* (father), whether traced back to Sanskrit or not, are mostly found in Dravidian languages of India. The same family of languages also has strikingly similar terms for "mother" (cf. tables 8 and 10): Tamil *āyi, yāy, āy*, Kannada *āyi, tāyi*, Telugu *tāyi*, Tulu *tāyi*, Gondi *ayal, yāyāl, iyāl*, Pengo *aya, iya*. Further similar terms are found in two other major linguistic families in India, namely, Indo-Aryan and Austroasiatic, the last of which is also widespread in Southeast Asia: Indo-Aryan, Bengali *āi*, Gujarati *āyi*, Sindhi *āi*, Marathi *āi*, Pali *ayyakā*; Austroasiatic, Parengi *aya*, Asur *aya*, Santali *ayo*, Munda *ayo*, Nahali *ay*.

The third set consists of words that mean "nursemaid" and are widely thought to be of Portuguese origin, e.g., Malay *ayah* (Indian nursemaid), Tagalog *yaya*, Cebuano Visayan *yaya, aya* (nursemaid). In his Malay-English dictionary, perhaps the most commonly used Austronesian dictionary in Southeast Asia, Wilkinson (1957: 55) writes: "*ayah* 1. Father . . . 2. (Hindustani, from Portuguese *aia* = governess or nursery governess) Indian nurse or maid servant. . . . " Whether the Portuguese influence was indirect, through India, or not, similar words are more widespread in Indian languages and are usually specified in Indian dictionaries to be of Portuguese origin: Hindi *āyā*, Urdu *āyā*, Sindhi *āyā*, Nepali *āyā*, Bengali *āyā*, Gujarati *āyā*, Tamil *āyā* (nursemaid).

It is no accident that a scholar of Blust's caliber overlooks the available information on the Portuguese origin of some of the words in question. It is no accident that in another publication (1970:145) he loses sight of the fact that, as pointed out in Wilkinson's dictionary (1957:1280; see also Winstedt 1949[1913]:230), *waris* is of Arabic derivation (and this despite his assertion that he has "relied on Wilkinson and Winstedt for the identification of most non-Austronesian loans in Malay, and on Gonda [1952] for information regarding the Sanskrit element in all of the languages used in the present comparison" [1970:113–14]). It is no accident that, in the last few decades, although the contributions made by Blust and others to the lexical aspect of Austronesian languages are immense, the identification of loanwords in these languages has remained underdeveloped. And it is no accident that the specialists who comment on Blust's article neither refer to the Portuguese origin of the above words nor question that the kin terms under study are anything but indigenous. Behind all these seeming accidents lies the long-standing domination of a scientific ideology or paradigm insisting that structures are closed, self-contained, and self-explanatory and that external factors are either destructive and undesirable or insignificant and dispensable.

Postscript

Since this article was completed I have continued my research and now find it necessary to make the following brief remarks:

1. There is far more, sometimes more persuasive, lexical evidence for Indian/Southeast Asian influence not only in the Sepik and the rest of New Guinea and Melanesia but also in Micronesia and Polynesia. So far the Sepik has, however, shown the greatest degree of influence. This seems to be connected with a number of its other special characteristics. The Torricelli phylum is typologically very distinctive and forms "a genetic group in itself; that is, no other languages in the New Guinea area appear to be even distantly related to it" (Laycock 1975:768). The Sepik, in its broad sense, is linguistically an extremely heterogeneous area (Laycock 1978:246), and its physical environment has undergone exceptional and dramatic changes in the past (see Swadling in this volume).

2. I have talked of Southeast Asian contacts, but in the Sepik and especially in Oceania as a whole the Indian/Southeast Asian influence is sometimes too widespread and fundamental to be the result of limited contacts in Oceania even if they were as repetitive as those between the Makassarese of eastern Indonesia and the aborigines of Arnhem Land in northern Australia (Macknight 1976). It may be that at times the influence was exerted when some of the peoples of Oceania were still in Southeast Asia, in which case it sometimes dates back to before the Christian era.

3. It should be emphasized that lexical (or other) influence has not always been unidirectional, from India through Southeast Asia to the Sepik or Oceania. Austroasiatic-speakers were already in Southeast Asia and eastern India when Dravidians and Indo-Aryans, who are culturally more dominant, moved to India, and it is now established that Austroasiatic languages have, however limitedly, influenced the vocabularies of both Dravidian and Indo-Aryan languages. Also,

when Austronesian-speakers (and perhaps some Papuan-speakers) were in Southeast Asia, whether as their original home or not, they and Austroasiatic peoples must have exerted influence on each other, lexically and otherwise.

It may well be that some of the words said to be of Indian origin in this article are in fact Austroasiatic or Austronesian or even Papuan, but whatever the outcome of future studies of these neglected issues it will not affect the basis of this article, which is primarily concerned with interstructural influence, irrespective of its direction. Nor will it basically affect the discussions on early Austronesian culture history and social organization, both of which need to be studied interstructurally. If some of the kin terms prove to be Austronesian, that result will have been achieved only after studying their possible relationships with Indian and other kin terms.

4. There is further evidence for the lexical connection between Torricelli languages and the Aslian languages of Malaysian aborigines. This is worth mentioning because, first, the words concerned, unlike those cited in this article, do not occur in Austronesian languages and consequently could not have been borrowed from them by Torricelli-speakers. Thus one may suggest that sometime in the past Torricelli-speakers were probably in Southeast Asia, as it is unlikely that Malaysian aborigines have come into contact with them in the Sepik or other parts of Oceania. Secondly, the evidence is such that it seems to leave no doubt about the lexical connection in question.

5. There is a great deal more to be said about the kin terms, to which further terms can now be added. Here I limit myself to a few remarks on *mama* and *mami*. In Oceania, chiefly to the east of the Sepik, *mama* usually means "father" and seems to derive from *ama*, which is the most common Austronesian term for "father" and which takes a number of other initial segments, as in *kama, hama, fama, dama*, and especially *tama*. Also, as in Motu, it is sometimes the child's term of address for "father." But there seems to be another *mama*, and the lack of differentiation between the two is one reason the Indian/Southeast Asian aspect of the matter keeps being overlooked (e.g., Blust 1980:212). Apart from not being a child's term, the *mama* discussed in this article usually denotes "mother's brother," "father-in-law," etc., all of which are related meaningfully and contrast with "father" in various ways. Besides, it is frequently associated with *mami*, as its feminine form, an associ-

ation some manifestations of which have reached as far as the Sepik. And what is more, it is mainly found to the west of the Sepik, in Southeast Asia and India, where it is employed in Dravidian, Indo-Aryan, and Austroasiatic as well as Austronesian languages.

6. This article does not take into account some pertinent Asian cultures, especially Chinese; apart from the limitations of space, the reason is simply my lack of knowledge of these cultures. The suggested etymologies of Au *pirir/pilir* and especially Au *ghelpa* remain very doubtful unless supportive evidence is found in other Sepik languages. The relation between Southeast Asian *jampi* and Sanskrit *japa* is more promising than Gonda thought. In Rejang, an Austronesian language in Sumatra, an almost identical word, *japai*, means "spell, incantation" (Jaspan 1984:20).

Notes

1. I thank Donald C. Laycock for commenting on part of the first draft of this paper and Bryant J. Allen, Colin S. Filer, Simon J. Harrison, Gilbert Lewis, and David Lipset for word lists from the languages of the Sepik peoples among whom they have carried out anthropological research. The relevant words, though few, are included here with acknowledgment. The languages in question may well contain more words relevant to my theme, because I inquired about only ten words or so in the lists and did so at a time when the paper was still in its initial stages. Thanks are also due to Signe Howell and Robert Depew for their word lists, which, being more recent, are longer; again, a few words are included with acknowledgment. Howell has carried out research among the Chewong of the Malay Peninsula and the Lio of eastern Indonesia; only the Lio words were relevant to this paper. Depew did his fieldwork among the Aekyom-speaking people of the Western Province. Last and not least, I thank M. Malek for his invaluable help in the preparation of the manuscript by word processor.

The comparative study with which this paper is concerned is being continued and is intended for publication, after further fieldwork in the Sepik, in a more developed and satisfactory form. An attempt will also be made to base the study on deeper familiarity with the languages concerned, including Dutch and German, of which my knowledge is very limited at present.

The Southeast Asian dictionaries consulted are listed below in alphabetical order of the names of the languages concerned. To avoid repetition, no further reference will be made to these dictionaries (except where unavoidable), even when they are the only sources for the lexical data cited: Atayal, Egerod (1980); Balinese, Barber (1979); Banjar, Hapip (1977); Batak (in Palawan), Warren (1959); Buginese,

Ide Said (1977), Matthes (1874); Cebuano Visayan, Cabonce (1983), Yap and Bunye (1971); Dairi Pakpak, Manik (1977); Hanunóo, Conklin (1953); Iban, Richards (1981), Scott (1956), Howell and Bailey (1900); Ilokano, Constantino (1971), Carro (1956); Isneg, Vanoverberch (1972); Javanese, Horne (1974); Old Javanese, Zoetmulder and Robson (1982); Kadazan, Antonissen (1958); Kayan, Southwell (1980); Kenyah, Galvin (1967); Madurese, Asis Safioedin (1977), Kiliaan (1904); Malay/Indonesian, Echales and Shandily (1975), Wilkinson (1957), Winstedt (1949[1913]), Klinkert (1930[1882]), Marsden (1984[1812]); Mandar, Muthalib (1977); Manobo, Elkins (1968); Pangasinan, Benton (1971); Tagalog, Ramos (1971); Tiruray, Schlegel (1971); Toba-Batak, Warneck (1977[1906]); Toradja, Tammu and van der Veen (1972).

2. For the history of Southeast Asia and the Indian and Middle Eastern influence on it see, for example, Fatimi (1963), van Leur (1955), Hall (1968), Meilink-Roelofsz (1962), Wheatley (1973), and Wolters (1967). For anthropological and historical findings on pre-European Southeast Asian contact with Australia and New Guinea, see Berndt and Berndt (1951), Hughes (1977), McCarthy (1938–40), Sopher (1965), Warner (1932), and Worsley (1955). The major work on the linguistic influence of India on Southeast Asia is that of Gonda (1973[1952]); see also van Buitenen and Ensink (1964).

3. Similar observations are made by Marshall (1938:49–50). On recent Southeast Asian contact, see also Seiler (1982), which was not available to me at the time of writing this section, as well as the papers by Allen, Haiveta, R. J. May, and Scaglion in this volume.

4. What the Au themselves say is that these people moved to Nikis "after the earthquake." Remembered by the Au as a turning point in their history, this earthquake took place in 1935 (Stanley et al. 1935). An eyewitness account of it is given by McCarthy (1964:156–58), and some of its effects on the Lumi Sub-District and the Au area are described by Marshall (1938:12–13, 16–19, 38–39).

5. See also Marshall (1937:500) and Champion (1967:4, 60–78, 101–28) and cf. *sambio*, *samo*, and *seno*, translated by Champion as "peace word."

6. These three lexical items are from Stokhof (1983a:143, 151, 159). Taikat is considered under "Arzo and Tami area" (p. 157).

7. Tidore and Gane, Stokhof (1980b:218, 316); Masarete, Stokhof (1982b:22); Sapolewa, Stokhof (1981b:196); Piru Seram, Stokhof (1982a:4); Suwawa, Gorontalo, Atinggola, and Kaidipang, Stokhof (1983c:6, 94, 186, 222).

8. The border between Dutch and German New Guinea was inadequately defined and controlled and was never the subject of a formal treaty between the two administrations. See also Huber (1983:42–43).

9. It has recently come to my attention that similar words for tobacco are recorded for several other Sepik languages, among them Sissano *sauke* or *saue*, Wu-

tung *sa'ei*, Puare *savke*, and Krisa *sakkoi* (Laycock 1976:256, 268). Sissano, spoken in the Aitape Sub-District, is Austronesian; the other three, spoken in the Vanimo Sub-District, are Papuan, members of the Sko phylum (Laycock 1973).

10. Horsburgh (cited by Roth 1968:386), referring to the Dayaks of Sarawak, observed in 1858: "The chief condiment of the (Balau) Dayaks is salt, which they procure from the nipa palm, and which they much prefer to that obtained by evaporation from sea water. The boughs of the nipa are cut, dried, and burnt, and their ashes washed in water, so as to dissolve the salt contained in them. . . . It is a dirty grey and often black-looking substance, possessing a slightly bitter taste . . . and as it is generally produced in masses of considerable size and as hard as a stone, it has much the appearance of a mineral that has been dug out of the earth."

11. On the phonology of loanwords in Malay/Indonesian, see, for example, Stokhof (1975) and Mahdi (1981).

12. The kin-type notation employed is as follows: F, father; B, brother; M, mother; Z, sister; P, parent; G, sibling; e, elder; y, younger; H, husband; W, wife; S, son; D, daughter; E, spouse; C, child; m.s., man speaking; w.s., woman speaking.

13. See Jakobson (1968) as well as Murdock (1959) and Jakobson (1960). See also Leach (1971), in which he applies and develops Jakobson's views in relation to relatives other than mother and father. Leach's article is of further interest in that some of the Sinhalese kin terms he examines, namely, *amma*, *mama*, and *akka*, are also considered in this paper.

14. The Indian origin of *mama* and/or *mami*, at least in Malay, has been pointed out by a number of philologists (Hamilton 1919:35; Winstedt 1950[1947]:72; 1949[1913]:27; Wilkinson 1957:732–33). It was a matter of controversy in the 1930s and used or misused in naive diffusionist theories (Josselin de Jong 1980:24–25). In the last few decades, anthropologists and linguists have either rejected this etymology or, more often, overlooked it (Josselin de Jong 1980; Blust 1980*a*:212; see also the comments by anthropologists and linguists on Blust's 1980*a* article).

15. On the Malay kinship terminology and its variations, see Banks (1974, 1983), Djamour (1959), Swift (1965), and Wilder (1982).

16. The Malays have another term for F, *ayah* (see table 8), that is used in limited contexts only. In the hill regions of Kedah, Malaysia, *ayah* is used "for individuals who have greater status pretensions, such as those who are wealthy or have taken the *Hajj*" (Banks 1983:56), and in Singapore "in polite speech Malays refer to, and sometimes address, their father as *ayah*" (Djamour 1959:26).

17. For an analysis of Kwoma kin terms, see Bowden (1983*b*) and Williamson (1980). In Urat and Au the terms for MB are *puap* (B. J. Allen, personal communication, 1984) and *pa'ab* respectively. The term *pap* is used for MB in Iwan, another Sepik language (Rehburgh 1974:212).

18. The possessive pronoun of any animate object indicates its sex: *napara kai* denotes "my male dog," *napara pai* "my female dog."

19. In Oceanic languages *apu* is said to be a protoform for MB (Grace 1969:46).

20. Examples of this set also occur in some other Sepik languages: Warapu (Sko phylum, Papuan) *tyapu* (prefix + *apu*) (grandfather), *kwopu* (prefix + *apu*) (grandmother); Sissano (Austronesian) *apuk* (grandmother) (Laycock 1976:256, 265). Two other Austronesian languages provide us with further examples: Wogeo *tubu* (grandfather/grandchild) (Hogbin 1964:308), Manam *tubu* (grandparent/grandchild) (Wedgwood 1959:247–48). Wogeo *tubu* is included by Blust in his illustration of the above set, along with *tubu* as used in two other Austronesian languages of Melanesia: Tanga, where it denotes "grandparent," and Nali, where it denotes "grandparent/grandchild" (Blust 1979:208). With regard to *mama*/*mami* as well as *tubu* in Manam it should be noted that children more often use *meme* than *tubu* as a term of address for "grandparent"; that *meme* and *tina* denote "mother" and *mama* and *tama* "father"; that *meme* = HM, WM and *mama* = HF, WF; and that Manam kinship terminology is Hawaiian (Wedgwood 1959; cf. Hogbin 1964).

21. In Southeast Asia and India, [*x*] is often pronounced as *k* or aspirated *k* [*k*ʰ], being rare in the indigenous languages and found mostly in loanwords, especially from Arabic. Another example is Arabic *khabar* (news), appearing in Malay, Javanese, Iban, Balinese, and Sundanese *kabar*, Madurese (Stevens 1968:16–18, 40) *kabhar*, Hindi/Urdu, Nepali, Gujarati, and Marathi *khabar*, Bengali *khobor*, Tamil *kapar* (news). (In the transliteration of Indian lexemes, *kh* stands not for [*x*] but for aspirated *k*.)

22. According to myth, a remote ancestor named Wajeki was transformed on his death into a yakub and returned in a dream to say, "When you plant this banana tree, call my name, and I will help it to grow well." There are many magical spells for the growth of yakub and other banana trees, and in some of them the name of the mythical ancestor is mentioned. The full name of the yakub is *yakub metik*, which could be translated as "yakub the husband," and it is conceived to be the husband of another banana tree that is called *wisan meta*, "wisan the wife." It is said that the yakub bananas grow upward and are hard and large, whereas the wisan bananas hang down and are relatively small. Yakub is called *namba wan* ("number-one") banana in Tok Pisin.

Sometimes yakub bananas are eaten communally, as they are believed to promote physical growth. A great many bananas are roasted, mixed with such things as meat and coconut, and formed into a large image (called *qimin*) of a man with a penis. The image is decorated with seashells (also used as penis sheaths) and shell rings and kept in the men's house. Yakub bananas are not only the most powerful but also potentially the most dangerous and are often found on the list of food taboos in many contexts. Yakub must not be eaten, for example, by pregnant women, by men engaged in making a new slit-gong, or by men who have eaten *kepna*, a magical mixture associated with pointing magic, raiding magic (Au *ghiwa?ak*, Tok Pisin *sanguma*), and hunting. A man may not eat of the yakub planted in the village by his MB or FMBS. The wife and children of a man who plants yakub may eat its bananas, but he may not.

23. Manam, Wedgwood (1934:386–87); Kwoma, Bowden (1983b:747), Williamson (1980:533), and Whiting and Reed (1938:201); Boikin, Laycock (1965:151). Southeast Asian terms for "elder sibling" may even be more similar to that in Manam, such as Sawu *a'a* (Stokhof 1983b:6), Niala *aa* (Stokhof 1981b:164), Semaq Beri *?e?e?* and Semelai *?i?i?* (Benjamin 1976:116). (The last two languages are Austroasiatic [Aslian].)

24. Abui, Lebar (1972b:96); Atayal, Buli, Blust (1979:224–25; 1980a:216). For the spelling of the Atayal term, see also Egerod (1980).

Appendix

Southeast Asian Languages Referred to in Text and Their Locations

Abui	Island of Alor
Achinese [= Achehnese]	Northern Sumatra
Ai	Central Moluccas [= Maluku]: Banda
Ambon Maleis	Central Moluccas: Ambon
Ami [= Amis]	Eastern Formosa
Atayal	North Central Formosa
Atinggola [= Bulanga-Uki]	Northern Sulawesi [= Celebes]
Bajau Laut	Sabah
Balinese	Bali and Western Lombok
Banjar [= Banjarese]	Kalimantan [= Borneo]
Batak	Philippines: Northwestern Palawan
Batak	Northern Sumatra
Batek	Malay Peninsula
Bikol [= Bicol]	Philippines: Luzon
Bisaya	Sabah, Sarawak
Bisaya	Philippines: Bisayan Islands
Bontok	Philippines: Luzon
Buginese [= Bugis]	Southern Sulawesi
Buli	Southern Halmahera
Cebuano Visayan	Philippines: Cebu, Bohol, Leyte, Negros
Dairi Pakpak [= Dairi]	Northern Sumatra
Danaw	Burma
Dohoi	Southern Kalimantan
Dusun	Southwestern Kalimantan
Dusun Dejah	Southwestern Kalimantan
Endeh [= Ende]	South Central Flores
Fordata [= Fordat]	Southern Moluccas: Tanimbar
Gane [= Giman]	Southern Halmahera
Garo	now part of Assam
Gorontalo	Northern Sulawesi
Hanunoo	Philippines: Mindoro
Iban [= Sea Dayak]	Sarawak, Kalimantan
Ilokano [= Iloko]	Philippines: Northwestern Luzon, Mindoro
Isneg	Philippines: Luzon
Jamdena [= Jamden]	Southern Moluccas
Javanese	Eastern and Central Java
Jehai	Malay Peninsula
Kadazan	Western Sabah
Kaidipang	Northern Sulawesi
Kajaman	Kalimantan
Karo Batak	Northern Sumatra
Katingan	South Central Kalimantan
Kayan	Sarawak, Kalimantan
Kedang	Solor Archipelago: Lombata [= Lomblen]
Kensiu	Malay Peninsula
Kenyah	Sarawak
Kerinci [= Kerinchi]	South Central Sumatra
Kintaq Bong	Malay Peninsula
Lima	Central Moluccas: Seram [= Ceram]
Lio [= Lionese]	Central Flores
Luhu	Central Moluccas: Seram
Ma'anyan	Southwestern Kalimantan
Madurese [= Madura]	Madura and Northeastern Java
Mah Meri	Malay Peninsula
Makassar [= Makassarese]	Southern Sulawesi
Malay/Indonesian	Malaysia, Indonesia
Mandar [= Mandarese]	Southern Sulawesi
Manobo [= Bukidnon]	Philippines: Mindanao
Masarete	Central Moluccas: Ambon
Melanau	Sarawak
Mendriq	Malay Peninsula
Minangkabau	Sumatra and Malay Peninsula
Moken [= Selung]	Mergui Archipelago
Mukah	Sarawak
Murik	Sarawak
Murung	Southern Kalimantan
Ngaju Dayak	Southern Kalimantan

Pagu	Northern Halmahera	Semai	Malay Peninsula
Palaung	Burma	Semaq Beri	Malay Peninsula
Pampangan	Philippines: Luzon	Semnam	Malay Peninsula
Pagasinan	Philippines: North Central Luzon	Solorese [= Solor]	Islands of Solor, Adonara, Lombata
Piru Seram	Central Moluccas: Seram	Squliq Atayal	North Central Formosa
Rejang	Southwestern Sumatra	Sula Fagudu	Island of Sula
Rembong	Western Flores	Sundanese [= Sunda]	Western Java
Roti [= Rotinese]	Islands of Roti and Timor	Suwawa	Northern Sulawesi
		Tabojan (Lawangan)	Southwestern Kalimantan
Sabum	Malay Peninsula		
Sadanese	Southern Sulawesi	Tagalog	Philippines: Central Luzon, Mindoro
Sanggau [Embaloh = Maloh]	Western Kalimantan		
		Taman	Southern Kalimantan
Sangir	Islands of Sangi and Talaud	Tausug [= Taw Sug]	Philippines: Palawan
		Temoq	Malay Peninsula
Sapolewa	Central Moluccas: Seram	Tidore [= Tidorese]	Northern Halmahera
Sasak	Islands of Lombok and Sumbawa	Tiruray	Philippines: Mindanao
		Toba Batak	North Central Sumatra
Sebu	Philippines: Cebu	Tonsea (Minahasa)	Northern Sulawesi
Sekola	Central Moluccas: Banda	Toradja	Central Sulawesi

9/ Diversity of Cultures or Culture of Diversity?[1]

Colin Filer

If an epitaph were to be inscribed on the grave-stones of all the anthropologists who had become thoroughly mystified while doing fieldwork in the Sepik region, it would surely be that the exception proves the rule. In this paper I shall discuss the application of this worthy principle to the problem of linguistic and cultural diversity, which has formed the constant backdrop of ethnographic research in this region even when it has been resolved as much by assumptions as by evidence.

As a starting point for my argument, I should like to enlist a point made almost fifty years ago by an anthropologist whose writings are nowadays somewhat unfashionable, Margaret Mead: "If it were possible to demonstrate that the peoples who speak . . . related languages also have related cultures, the proof would not be decisive that the present culture was, in any sense, anciently connected with these languages, and had been retained by the peoples who retained that speech" (1970[1938]:17). In a paper written shortly before her death, when the linguistic and ethnographic evidence about the Sepik "culture area" was considerable, she returned to a similar point: "In fact, we have no way of knowing whether any apparently unique quality is part of some larger pattern of behavior which a people share with another, as yet unrecorded, culture, within the geographical area or outside it, or even whether it is very ancient or comparatively recent" (1978:71). Such an agnostic position, which few would associate with this author, has been regularly shunned by those scholars who have wandered in her footsteps.

Subsequent ethnographic research in this region has largely proceeded on the assumption that the shape or pattern of linguistic variation is indeed the fundamental matrix of a broader cultural diversity. The linguists, for their part, have assumed that the shape of linguistic diversity is broadly identical in all the relevant dimensions of linguistic description and have thus been able to produce maps which not only show the boundaries between individual languages but also reveal the degree to which one language is related to an-other.[2] Few anthropologists feel qualified to question the assumption which is necessary for this exercise, and most prefer to read such maps as valid statements of the most enduring form of cultural variety—the rule by which exceptions are to be assessed. When they encounter two neighboring communities whose members speak quite unrelated languages but have cultures which are otherwise remarkably alike, they promptly look for evidence that each item of shared cultural property has been begged, stolen, or "borrowed" by one group from the other. If they look hard enough, the evidence is usually found.

In this way, the problem of linguistic and cultural diversity has been cast in a definite mold. If the linguists can explain why there are so many languages in this region, then the anthropologists are inclined to accept this as an explanation of why there are so many "cultures." The ethnographic contribution to the problem is to show how certain "culture traits" have gained release from their original and natural association with a given language-group or group of languages and thus to show the way in which a pattern of "exchange" (or gift or theft) between communities has brought about a number of exceptions to the rule that language-groups *are also* "cultures" and that families of languages *are also* "culture areas." Even Mead's agnostic sentiments can almost be accommodated by this understanding of the problem, so long as one allows for an indefinite number of exceptions.

I wish to propose a rather different way of approaching the problem. I suggest that the degree of linguistic diversity in the Sepik region is sufficiently remarkable, even by Melanesian standards, that it requires some *special* explanation, over and above the one that has been offered by the linguists. I also suggest that their account of the phenomenon requires assumptions which are somewhat inconsistent with the ethnographic evidence and should therefore be excluded from the special explanation that we seek. If our search leads us, in the first instance, to the realm of "culture," then it leads us to a word that suffers from an overload of ambiguity. But if we can resolve such ambiguity before we start the search, then we stand a chance of showing not only that the degree of linguistic diversity in this region is related to a form of cultural diversity, in one sense of the word "culture," but that both are partly explained, in another sense of the word, by a type of cultural *uniformity*.

Three meanings of the word "culture" are relevant to our discussion: (1) *Material* culture comprises the concrete, tangible qualitites of *manufactured* objects, the more durable of which are fit to populate museums. (2) *Symbolic* culture comprises the *arrangement* of a range of objects—tangible, visible, or audible—through which each comes to stand for something other than itself. (3) *Spiritual* culture comprises that part of human discourse which is devoted to the *interpretation* of symbols. The syntax and vocabulary of ordinary, "natural" language may be regarded as the core component of symbolic culture, not just because it is the most pervasive medium of communication but also because it is excluded by definition from the realms of both material and spiritual culture.

The tendency to elide or conflate these three senses of the word "culture" is a function of the fact that it is only the first and the third which are mutually exclusive. This point can be established by means of an example drawn from our present area of interest. A flute is an item of *material* culture. If it is decorated with a carving which represents the identity of a particular spirit, then it is also an item of *symbolic* culture, its meaning given by the "language" of the art employed to make it. The music played on this flute belongs to another segment of *symbolic* culture but one which is excluded, as is ordinary language, from the realm of manufactured forms because its elements are sounds. If this music represents the movement of the spirit represented by the carving, and this movement is an episode within a myth, the myth itself is an item of *spiritual* culture, insofar as it translates the meaning of the music into ordinary language. But such a myth may also be an item of *symbolic* culture if it is constrained by certain narrative conventions which set myths apart from ordinary language and thus make it possible to formulate their meaning in another type of conversation.[3]

If these are all the things we mean by "culture," what is meant, in each case, when we speak of "cultures" in the plural? In the *material* sense, a single culture is a concrete form of manufacturing activity. In the *symbolic* sense, it is an ordinary language or an orchestrated set of sig-

nifiers of another, special type. And in the *spiritual* sense, it is a form of thought, a sense of meaning, or a spirit of existence—a principle by which significance is granted to the symbols of a "language." In each sense, taken separately, we may also say that there are cultures which combine such things to make a larger whole—a manufacturing technology, a system of communication, or a set of guiding principles. And at a higher level still, we may be able to distinguish cultures that are systematic combinations of such sets. But there is *no* sense in which it can be taken for granted that *each culture in a certain region occupies a unique and exclusive space by virtue of belonging to a unique and exclusive local group*. And yet it is precisely this assumption which a language atlas tends to foist on unsuspecting anthropologists.

Green People/ Orange People

Let us now consider the type of assumption that is made by those who would deduce the prehistoric formation of Sepik "cultures" from the present distribution of Sepik languages. For this purpose, we may restrict our attention to the area which is roughly defined by a line joining Lumi, Yangoru, Timbunkie, and Edwaki (Yellow River) and which I propose to call the "Central Sepik region."[4] According to Laycock (1981), the many languages indigenous to this area belong either to the Sepik-Ramu phylum (and the Sepik subphylum) or to the Torricelli phylum. There is no space in this article to question the validity of the criteria by which Laycock and his fellow linguists have arrived at their classification. In this section I only wish to indicate the "cultural" significance implicitly bestowed on certain "deep" grammatical criteria which have been taken as the basis for distinguishing the Sepik-Ramu from the Torricelli languages. I now propose to rename these the Green and the Orange Languages (these being the colors by which they are depicted in the language atlas) to make a serious point about the interpretation of the boundary between these "groups." I wish to question the tendency of Sepik scholarship to reconstruct the prehistory of this region and its present form of cultural diversity in terms of the interaction between Green (Sepik-Ramu) and Orange (Torricelli) *people*— and their several linguistic subdivisions.

Much of the blame for this tendency must be attached to the Canberra "circle" of linguists to which Laycock himself belongs. According to Laycock (1973:54–55),

It is only the large languages of the Maprik area . . . that prevent the Sepik language figures from degenerating into complete incredibility. Is there an explanation for this situation of extreme linguistic complexity? The tentative explanation that suggests itself is that the Sepik area represents, on the one hand, a natural migration route (so that many diverse populations have passed through it), and, on the other hand, a backwater area into which smaller groups have been forced by the intrusion of large dominant groups. . . . Among the earliest arrivals were speakers of languages ancestral to the present Torricelli [Orange] Phylum. . . . At a later date, speakers of Sepik-Ramu [Green] Phylum languages entered along the border area, reaching the Sepik River and proceeding downstream. . . . Speakers of languages of the Sepik Sub-phylum . . . seem to have swung to the south. . . . At a later date, they returned to the Sepik, with one branch (the Ndu family) forcing its way through land occupied by Torricelli Phylum speakers to the north coast.

Elsewhere in the same article (pp. 7, 57) he argues,

The Torricelli group appears to have no related languages outside of the Sepik-Ramu area, but the occurrence of a rare genetic factor in both the Torricelli areas and the Markham areas suggests that languages in this type may originally have extended up the Ramu and across the divide into the Markham Valley, being later absorbed by Austronesian immigrants—a hypothesis that awaits further testing by looking for Torricelli Phylum features in the substratum of Markham Valley Austronesian languages. . . . If the original bearers of the gene [Gerbich-negative blood-type] could be associated with the ancestors of speakers of Torricelli Phylum languages (a not unlikely hypothesis), then we would be one step further in our reconstruction of the prehistory of New Guinea.

In a subsequent publication, this "genetic factor" is magically transformed into "a unique characteristic of speakers of Torricelli Phylum languages" (Wurm et al. 1975:939).[5]

Of course, as Laycock himself admits, such reconstructions are purely speculative, and I have

absolutely no quarrel with speculation. What bothers me is the complex of assumptions that lies behind this instance of it. Together these comprise what might be described as the naturalistic model of prehistory, the very model Mead was apparently seeking to challenge in the remarks previously quoted. Its component assumptions can be conveyed in the form of a myth which divides the prehistory of Melanesia, like that of humanity in general, into two periods or stages. I shall designate these as "Babel-time" and "Sodom-time," the turning point between them being represented by the conversation between Abraham and Pharaoh (Genesis 12:16), since this was the moment of first contact between what had hitherto been mutually isolated language-groups or speech communities.

In Babel-time, these were natural communities precisely in the sense that the forms of linguistic and genetic diversity were identical. Blood and language went together, as the song says, like a horse and carriage. Each natural community developed as a world unto itself, adapting to its own environment in ignorance of any other possibility and limited in size by technical constraints which guaranteed the reproduction of its isolation. Within these fundamental limits (symbolized by the Tower), every aspect of the life of a community was subject to a gradual and constant rate of change. If such communities were moving, they were moving slowly, and the small environmental changes which resulted brought about a constant adaptation in those aspects of their life which were dependent on the quality of the environment. In other aspects of their life, where variation over time was relatively "free" of such determination, it was still determined by some natural law of evolution, free of any conscious intervention on the part of the community itself. In all such communities, genetic changes occurred at roughly the same rate, in accordance with the laws of biology, and the rate of linguistic change, though perhaps more rapid, was equally constant, random, and universal. Where space permitted, such communities might gradually grow, divide, and multiply; but this expansion of the total population made no difference to the conditions under which the life of each community was ultimately given by its genealogy and its ecology. The languages and dialects of Babel-time were thus related to each other by degrees which were approximated by the distance and the difference between the habitats of the communities which spoke them.

In Sodom-time, the story goes, this natural economy of tidy correspondences was interrupted by the start of "international relations." Some individual communities became unnaturally "dominant" as a result of some material or "cultural" invention which enabled them to pass beyond the limits of their natural isolation. Once through this looking glass, they multiplied more rapidly, moved greater distances, acquired new territories and exploited them more thoroughly. In the course of their expansion, they encountered groups still lurking in the backwardness of Babel-time, which they either fought and routed or converted to their novel way of life. And so it came to pass that the size and mutual relationship of languages and dialects no longer held a mirror to their spatial and environmental distribution. In this lack of correspondence it is possible to see the progress and the triumphs of the Sodomites, because there is *one* law which does *not* change from Babel-time to Sodom-time—the law which states that people always speak a language which diverges slightly from the language of their parents, and this alteration always takes place at a constant rate.

When this model is applied to the Central Sepik region, it naturally gives rise to a particular reading of its prehistory. Such are the differences between the Green and Orange languages that their speakers are assumed to have no common ancestors within this region, and it is assumed that one of these two populations must be the original inhabitants. Since the places now occupied by Orange people could have been inhabited for a much longer period than some of the places now occupied by Green people (see Swadling in this volume), and since the technology of the Orange people is generally regarded as the more rudimentary of the two, it is argued that the Orange people are the aboriginals and have been squeezed into their present territory by invasions emanating from the river and the coast. Since the languages of the invaders now appear to be as diverse as the Orange languages themselves, it is considered that this process of displacement has been going on for several millennia, presumably involving many small transitions to Sodom-time, most of which have now been lost to view. And most of these could only have been temporary aberrations from the norm, because the present pattern of diversity can hardly be explained except on the assumption that most of the language-groups in this region, whatever their color, continued to languish in Babel-time. Otherwise, we must resort to Laycock's somewhat contradictory suggestion that the diversity of Orange languages is the result of Orange people's being squeezed

into a "backwater" (in the hills), while the diversity of Green languages is the result of Green people's inhabiting a "natural migration route" (on the water).

However great the overall diversity of language in the Central Sepik region, it is still true that this diversity is much reduced in certain areas. There are seven languages which, at the last count, boasted more than nine thousand speakers. Three of these are Orange (Wape, Southern Arapesh, and Mountain Arapesh) and four of them are Green (Kwanga, Abelam, Sawos, and Iatmul). The "families" to which they belong are also unusually large by the standards of the region. The Wapei and Arapesh families each had over twenty-three thousand speakers, while the Nukuma family (including the Kwanga and Kwoma languages) had over sixteen thousand. But the Abelam language alone had thirty-three thousand speakers, and the Ndu family, to which it belongs, had almost ninety-two thousand (Laycock 1981). It is not surprising, therefore, that attempts to find a recent and more permanent example of the change from Babel-time to Sodom-time have been directed to this latter family of languages—so much so that much of what is said about relationships between the Green and Orange "people" as a whole, through centuries of interaction, seems to be implicitly derived from evidence of recent Abelam invasions of the Arapesh environment. Meanwhile the problem of diversity—linguistic, "cultural," and structural—becomes a question of what Abelam and other types of Ndu do to each other and their neighbors.

Ndualism and Imperialism

If people speaking languages of the Ndu family have stolen the limelight of Sepik ethnography, this is not just because anthropologists are naturally attracted to large language-groups but also because these language-groups appear to be distinguished from the others in the region by the surplus quantity and value of their "culture"—in all senses of the word. Not only has their "art" been taken (literally) as the special prize of the collectors roaming through the area, but, as Bateson said of the Iatmul, "their social organization, kinship, and religious systems are developed to an extreme of complexity" (1958[1936]:4). Other students of Ndu communities and "cultures" have persistently endorsed this view, while those who have concerned themselves with the surrounding language-groups argue that their cultures have been more or less diluted by the imitation or appropriation of Ndu inventions.[6] The cultural configuration of the region is accordingly regarded as a series of concentric spheres of influence, radiating from the Ndu ideal toward an outer edge of darkness, and the number of speakers of each Ndu language seems to reflect the complexity and centrality of the culture to which it is attached. Unless it can be argued that this pattern of hegemony was one by which the Ndu were able to divide as well as dominate their neighbors or that what they were exporting, paradoxically, *was* a form of cultural diversity, then it looks as if they were engaged in the destruction, not the reproduction, of the most distinctive feature of the region as a whole. From this point of view, *the degree of linguistic diversity is to be explained by a degree of cultural poverty or cultural dependence*, which consists in *the absence of whatever magical ingredient explains the type of uniformity engendered by the Ndu.*

When anthropologists discuss what Sepik cultures "do," they know that they are talking in a sort of shorthand, since these "cultures" are collections of autonomous communities, each of which was more or less unique in its construction and behavior. If there is a special factor which explains the greater uniformity and local domination of Ndu culture(s), it should therefore be apparent in the volume and variety of the external links between these smaller local groups, which constitute the evidence of their transition to Sodom-time. At this point, the ghost of Adam Smith encourages the anthropologist to find this special factor in the realm of trade or, to be less precise, "exchange."

The territory occupied by Ndu communities ranges northward from the banks of the Sepik River through swamps and sparsely populated grasslands to the foothills of the Torricelli Mountains. Ndu cultures are distinguished from each other as the superstructures of subsistence systems which exploit these different environments to different effects. These distinctions were constructed and elaborated in the consciousness of local people through the separation of two categories of exchange. Between communities that occupied the same environmental zone, there was symmetrical exchange of like for like, the delayed reciprocity of prestation or the negative reciprocity of feud. For instance, Abelam communities knew others of their kind as those with which they either exchanged yams or "exchanged" spears (Forge 1972*b*:538), while Iatmul communities

balanced their accounts with collections of Iatmul heads (Bateson 1958[1936]:139). These symmetrical exchanges were conducted in a spirit of equivalence, a spirit which was quite unlike the one that animated the relationships of trade or barter which took place between communities in different environments. When Iatmul communities exchanged their fish for the sago produced by Sawos communities, they were not only reinforcing a sense of cultural distinction but also violating the canons of classical political economy, for the two sides seem to have agreed that this exchange was premised on the superiority of the Iatmul over the Sawos, despite their shared recognition that the Iatmul needed the sago more than the Sawos needed the fish (Gewertz 1983:36–37).

This kind of "false consciousness" appears to be a widespread feature of Melanesian trading relationships, and it was a constant theme of "intercultural" exchanges in the Sepik area.[7] The Arapesh communities which made shell rings to trade for pigs produced by Abelam communities construed their craft monopoly as a dependence on the Abelam for a commodity which they could equally supply themselves (see Forge in this volume). And it was this paradoxical imbalance of trade which provided the motive and the means for the diffusion of *some* aspects of the Abelam and Iatmul "cultures." Abelam and Iatmul communities, within their separate spheres of influence, were able to sell or lease a wide variety of items from their own *symbolic* culture in exchange for items of material (but nonsymbolic) wealth. While this encouraged the buyers of symbols to "borrow" much of the *material* culture with which their purchases were associated, their "creditors" were further assured of their own superiority by the knowledge that their *spiritual* culture, which contained the hidden "value" of their symbols and their styles, was still their own monopoly (see Forge in this volume).

It is perhaps because the efflorescence of this double-dealing *spirit* of exchange, symmetrical and asymmetrical, does not make sense in strictly economic terms that anthropologists have not been wholly satisfied with the idea that a greater *volume* of exchange along the trade routes linking coastal Arapesh communities with Sepik River peoples to the south suffices to explain the greater uniformity of language in this sector of the region. It is not enough to say that economic diversity has been substituted for linguistic and cultural diversity, because the artificial development of a local division of labor does not explain the artificial "domination" of some products over others, the development of symbolic "production" as a local specialty, or the forces which have led the Abelam to intensify their surplus yam production with a view to giving yams away. In order to deal with these additional oddities, attention is diverted to the factors which unequally distribute the appearance and reality of *power* between communities and thus, perhaps, between the cultures which contain them.

Ultimately, what makes it possible for one community to dominate another is presumably the threat of force, and the substance of this threat presumably resides in a disparity in quantity and quality of the fighting strength which each can muster. If the terms of unequal exchange are terms dictated by relatively large communities to relatively small communities, then it may be argued that the dominant position of a language-group (or group of languages) reflects the average size of the communities which it contains, while the size of a community reflects the complexity of its internal organization, which may in turn be derived from the spirit of the culture to which it belongs. It is this kind of reasoning which leads Gewertz to conclude that Iatmul communities survived and flourished by "keeping their sago-suppliers trapped in the double bind between organizational capacity and political autonomy" (1983:34—35). However, there seems to be a certain circularity in such reasoning, and this has been exaggerated and obscured by the confusing terminology which anthropologists have used in their analysis of local group formation.

A case in point is Forge's (1972a) attempt to demonstrate that the size of "settlements" in Melanesia generally and in the Sepik region in particular is not simply determined by the density of population or the violence accompanying population pressure but also a function of "normative factors." Having supported this argument with a contrast between the scattered settlement patterns of certain high-density highlands societies and the nucleated settlement patterns typical of high-density Sepik societies (p. 368), he proceeds to contradict it by contrasting the typical size of settlements in "'rich' cultures," like the Abelam and Iatmul, with those in "'poor' cultures," like the Mountain Arapesh—the difference between the two apparently being nothing other than the density of population and its differential consequences for the system of production and exchange (pp. 370–71).

The Mountain Arapesh, whose poverty of "culture" was related to the poverty of their environment, were forced to live in small and scattered hamlets but would evidently have preferred to occupy the type of "basic residential unit" which is said to be the norm for Neolithic cultivators in New Guinea. The norm in question is a population of between 150 and 350—enough, but not too many, to engage in satisfying status games with its collective surplus product (p. 374). Among the Abelam, this unit was a nucleated and stockaded string of hamlets which Forge calls a "ritual group," reserving the word "village" for the basic *military* unit of society, made up of from one to eight such "basic" groups, the number varying according to the presence of, once again, population density and the intensity of fighting which resulted from it (p. 372).

This choice of terminology implies a proposition which the highlands evidence would not appear to warrant, since it links the size of the political community not merely to the *density* of population but also to its relative *concentration*. Thus (pp. 372–73):

> where the pressure of war is mitigated (as in the Mamblep [northern Abelam], a valley system protected by mountains on three sides, which has about 2000 inhabitants forming a single confederation against two very large villages to the south), the ritual group emerges as a separate unit, not contiguous to other like units for protection. However, land holdings and old residence sites show that until the stable confederation was formed, these now spatially separate ritual groups were grouped together . . . like the rest of the Abelam.

In other words, "ritual groups" *are* "villages" *except* where population pressure dictates the transformation of "confederation" into residential concentration. As if to underline the point that this coagulation is a more important feature of political communities than their internal unity, Forge cites Bateson's evidence that "ritual groups" in Iatmul "villages," which also reached remarkable proportions, feuded with each other in a manner that was "comparable to killing enemies" (p. 369).

Despite the title of his article, Forge here refrains from arguing that *variation* in the size of Sepik "villages" can be ascribed to variation in the norms or principles which motivate their internal structure and in turn can be construed as variable properties of Sepik cultures. Despite the evidence that most Abelam people live in large, concentrated settlements (p. 373),

> the same range of figures is to be found among the neighbouring southern and plains

Arapesh, although their language is totally unrelated and the institutions on which they found their settlements different. Indeed a southern Arapesh village, Ilahita, is one of the largest traditional villages in lowland New Guinea, 1200 plus, apparently having been formed under the pressure of Abelam expansion. Although the housing appears almost continuous, this complex is made up of at least six ritual groups each of which maintains its identity. It is only when the Arapesh reach the cold and poor soils of the higher parts of the coastal range that their settlement size falls to eighty and less.

This suggests that the capacity of Abelam communities to dominate Arapesh communities depended on a temporary imbalance in the density and concentration of the respective populations, *not* upon the mutual acknowledgment of an imbalance in the power of their respective spiritual cultures. However, Tuzin's subsequent (1976) study of Ilahita seems to have persuaded Forge (in this volume) that the size and power of Abelam communities *can* partly be deduced from the distinctive organizing principles which their inhabitants espouse.

The Ilahita Syndrome

By 1969, Ilahita had a population of almost fifteen hundred. According to Tuzin, this not only made it the second-largest "village" in the whole of the Sepik region but also constituted a radical and unique departure from the normal size of Orange settlements. "From what little is known of them," he says, "all Torricelli cultures favor small villages (200 inhabitants at most) or dispersed hamlets" (1976:77), and the "hamlet-based" settlements of Orange people, such as the Arapesh, were no military match for "the predatory expansion of village-based peoples," such as the Abelam (p. 76). The size of Ilahita therefore has to be explained as the result of special measures which the Orange people took to overcome their culturally limited capacity to organize themselves in larger local groups: "Given . . . the defensive urgency in maintaining large settlements, the need arises for alternative conventions to bind the individual to non-kin members of the community; to fill, as it were, the remaining, extra-familial space" (p. 78). For Ilahita, this necessity was the mother not of invention but of imitation: "In fact, the adoption of the Abelam Tambaran Cult as the ritual basis of village organization demonstrates

that a degree of imitative borrowing occurred as the Arapesh contended with integrative problems of unprecedented proportions" (p. 75). To Ilahita, the symbolic culture of the Abelam brought with it the complexity of social structure which was vital to expansion. In other words, the size of Arapesh communities provides us with a measure of their cultural dependence. Insofar as it reflects the density or productivity of their component populations too, these are factors which can also be attributed to Abelam expansionism: "Abelam diffusion influences, together with the demographic consequences of their intrusion, contributed much to the Arapesh shift from an economy based on sago and hunting-and-gathering to one based on an elaborate garden technology centered on the yam" (p. 79). The circle linking language, culture, and political economy is thereby closed.

By rewriting Forge's distinction between "rich" and "poor" cultures as a distinction between "village-based" Green cultures and "hamlet-based" Orange cultures, Tuzin places a much heavier load on the criteria used to define a "village." The six component parts, or "wards," of Ilahita count not as "basic residential units" but as "intermediate-level communities" (p. 56), and the "enigmatic" size of Ilahita as a whole is to be contrasted with the "upper limit for the average, autonomous, nucleated settlement [of] 300 to 400 inhabitants" (p. 305). In other words, the "village" *is* the "basic residential unit" *in those cultures which possess the norms or principles required to integrate or unify such entities*. But what precisely is the measure of this unity? If we revert to the vocabulary advocated by Hogbin and Wedgwood (1953), why should Ilahita be counted as a "parish" rather than a "galaxy"? Tuzin himself observes that the so-called wards have "a fair amount of autonomy over their internal political and ritual affairs" (p. 56) and "*as such* rarely if ever interact" (p. 123). If it is the mere contiguity of settlement which makes Ilahita into a single "village," then I cannot see why Tuzin argues that the neighboring Bumbita Arapesh, who numbered well over two thousand in 1969, "did not, however, aggregate into large villages. Their political units are small (100 to 200 persons), *even though all the villages of the group are nearly contiguous along a single ridgetop*" (p. 77n, emphasis mine). And if the key criterion is military unity, we may additionally note that "there was no history of warfare between Bumbita villages" and the whole group might therefore be regarded, like Ilahita, as a defensive confederation of autonomous war-making groups (p. 59).

While Tuzin sees fit to chastise the unobservant patrol officers who once divided Ilahita into a number of distinct "villages" (p. 87n), it is not at all clear to me that their use of the word did greater violence to common sense or the English language than does Tuzin's own. While it may be true that the "normative factors" which set limits to the size of manageable census units in the eyes of colonial officials were indeed quite different from the ones which Forge believes to have constrained the size of "basic residential units" in the precolonial era, the numerical results of these two sets of factors are much the same. I therefore suggest that we abandon the terminology of "wards" and "parishes" altogether, since both these entities are the creations of colonial administration, and agree to call Ilahita (and perhaps Bumbita too) a *community* made up of *several* villages, just as it appeared to the original census takers. If villages are nucleated groups of hamlets, and communities are nucleated *or* non-nucleated groups of villages *or* hamlets, then we do not beg the question whether villages or hamlets are the basic residential units in a given area or the question whether residential concentration is essential to the unity of the community. A contrast between village-based and hamlet-based communities may still be warranted, but we shall not be tempted to attribute quite so much importance to the difference between the size of a large, nucleated, village-based community and the average size of the groups officially listed in the *Village Directory*.

Whether or not we regard the sheer size of Ilahita as a problem in its own right, we may still be led to wonder how the complexity of its internal structure is measured. According to Tuzin, this concentration of population resulted from the assimilation of "refugees" in the period between 1880 and 1940 (pp. 44, 53), and this "startling" expansion was the cause or the consequence of its "measurably greater complexity of socio-cultural forms" (p. 307) as compared with neighboring communities. While it may be true that immigrants outnumbered emigrants during this period (p. 72), it does not seem likely from Tuzin's figures (pp. 54, 355–56) that the net gain to the total population could have amounted to more than two hundred individuals at most—in which case it must be presumed that Ilahita was already a sizable village-based community in 1880. And if it was the complexity of its internal constitution which facilitated its further expansion, then it is surely rather odd that the larger of the two immigrant villages took no part at all in the political

and ceremonial relationships which expressed this constitution (p. 266), while the smaller one was incorporated only at the expense of its symmetry (pp. 217–18).

When we consider this constitution in its pure and ancient form, we discover that it consisted in the division of the original community into two moieties, each of which was divided into two villages, each of which was divided into two "submoieties," each of which was divided into two "clans." In the biggest of the four villages, each clan was divided into two more clans, and the biggest of these was also divided in two. Every clan was divided into two "subclans," most of which were identical with hamlets. No one would deny that this was dualism with a vengeance. But the flexibility of this system and even its "complexity" are not immediately evident. One might equally explain the patent *difficulty* of incorporating immigrant groups by reference to its obsessive rigidity—a factor which might also explain why Ilahita became a community of traditionalists in the colonial era (pp. 35, 39, 42). Perhaps, as Tuzin claims, this form of structural schizophrenia was "borrowed" from the Abelam as a device to keep the Abelam at bay, but since its origins are evidently lost beyond the bounds of living memory, this must remain a matter of speculation.

The collective memory of Ilahita proves intractable to Tuzin's thesis on another point, for its inhabitants apparently have no idea that they or other Orange people in the neighborhood have suffered or survived the consequences of a constant Abelam expansion. Tuzin reckons this to be an instance of false consciousness: "In short, Arapesh informants in saying that *they* have never been defeated are correct only if they ignore the possibility that significant numbers of them are descended from Arapesh who *were* defeated and who yielded large tracts of land to the Abelam" (p. 75). If indeed the Ilahita people failed to see or to recall the forces which obliged their predecessors to transform their social structure, it could be because they had no common border with an Abelam community, but it might also be because the boundary which separated Green and Orange people as a whole had no political significance. The precolonial network of alliances and enmities paid no attention to this boundary, and, as Tuzin himself informs us, many of the "refugees" who swelled the size of Ilahita were not Orange people at all but the remnants of a Green (Kwanga) community (pp. 80–81). And while Tuzin reports that these people were the *acknowl-*

edged victims of Abelam "expansion," this fact may be less significant than their subsequent assimilation into an *Arapesh* community.

To take this point a little farther, the distinction between Green and Orange communities may be less significant than the fact that two of the villages in the vicinity of Ilahita—one an ally, one an enemy—either comprised a mixture of Green and Orange people or had populations that were thoroughly bilingual (p. 54). If communities and villages were growing, scattering, and recombining in a manner which allowed or forced their members to exchange one language for another, we should hardly be surprised if they did not attach deep historical significance to language boundaries.

Forms of Circulation

One of the most puzzling features in the standard portrait of Ndu expansionism is the extraordinary rate at which the population of this language-family is said to have increased. The naturalistic model tells us that the present distribution of Ndu languages and dialects points to the existence of a "proto-Ndu" group occupying what is now a part of Sawos territory, and the present population speaking Abelam or Iatmul is supposed to be descended from individuals who left this area within the last few hundred years (see Swadling in this volume). If thirty thousand Abelam appeared from nowhere in the space of fifteen generations, then they must have been very fertile indeed, all the more remarkable when one considers that they may have suffered more than any other Sepik population from the ravages of holoendemic malaria and internecine warfare—both, as Forge points out (in this volume), side effects of their excessive density. Forge's argument that Abelam still multiplied at an astounding rate draws rather less from any demographic evidence to this effect than from the common-sense assumption that high density *implies* a rapid rate of growth and an imperative to territorial expansion, all three being seen as features of a single population which is otherwise distinguished by its language and its spiritual culture.

This could be taken as the final step in a chain of reasoning that aims to solve the problem of diversity by first inverting it and then explaining the *reduction* of diversity by reference to all the features which supposedly distinguish Sodom-time from Babel-time. Beneath the uniformity of language lies a cultural elaboration which enables

bigger language-groups to dominate the smaller language-groups beyond their boundaries because it is associated with a greater structural complexity—a greater volume and variety of links between a set of local subdivisions whose internal constitution has already reached a more intensive and extensive level of cooperation. If there is a problem in defining the "communities" whose strength of numbers warrants this suggestion, it can still be argued that the dominant position of a language-group reflects not so much the *size* of the communities which it contains as the *rate* at which these groups expand, segment, migrate, and ultimately seize new territory from their benighted neighbors. The strength of Abelam communities was thus reflected in a spirit of expansion and aggression, while the strength of Arapesh communities of comparable size resided in a spirit of consolidation and defense.

The density of population and degree of residential concentration, the rate of population growth and population movement, the intensity and productivity of labor, and the quantity and quality of manufactured and symbolic products—this mass of interacting variables could be said, in Marxist language, to be part and parcel of the "forces of production." Should we therefore say that the "explosion" of the Ndu, and in particular the Abelam, resulted from the higher level of development of Ndu productive forces? Forge does not seem happy with this neat reductionism, since he claims (in this volume) that the Abelam acquired their present system of production *from the people they supposedly displaced*. The magical ingredient which they brought with them from their rather dismal homeland in the floodplain was the military and artistic spirit which enabled them to beat their predecessors at the Orange game of cultivating and exchanging yams by adding a degree of "superstructural" elaboration which struck fear and deference into the minds of Orange people. Such was the critical invention which brought Abelam to Sodom.

I think that Forge is right to shy away from ecological or technological determinism and correct in his assertion that we have to understand the "power of culture" if we wish to make sense of the mass of cultural distinctions in the Sepik region. But I believe he fails to stand the problem of diversity the right way up because he will not countenance the thought that *cultures may have genealogies which do not match the genealogies of local populations*. Once we concede this possibility, the way is open to another view of Abelam "expansion," one which may be no less hypothetical than that espoused by Forge and Tuzin but has the merit of establishing a space wherein the power of culture may be reinterpreted. In this perspective, "Abelam" may have been not a swarm of locusts sweeping through the Sepik hills but a swarm of moths attracted to a deadly flame.[8]

Tuzin tells us that the Ilahita people *did not realize* (if it was actually true) that the Abelam were closing in on them, *ignored* the possibility (or fact) that many of their ancestors had been evicted from their homelands by the Abelam, yet "borrowed" much of their technology and ideology from enemies they did not recognize as such, the better to defend themselves against an unknown threat. Another instance of false consciousness? Perhaps; but we should not assume that this is so without considering a question Tuzin does not ask. If Ilahita people had been steadily adopting the symbolic culture of the Abelam, *why should there not have come a time at which they took the language too*?

There is some evidence that quite a number of communities within the Sepik region have "exchanged" one language for another (even unrelated) language, sometimes with surprising speed (see Laycock 1973:16). I do not know of any detailed study of the way such switches have occurred, but for our present purposes it is enough to note that they may change the boundaries of language-groups *without any alteration in the size or spatial distribution of the population*. In other words, the Ilahita people may be right. The southern Arapesh need not include descendants of an Orange population which the Abelam displaced; *the Abelam themselves may be descended from the Arapesh*. Once languages, like other local products, are admitted to the sphere of circulation, we are not obliged to read the Sepik language map as evidence of an astounding birth rate in the largest language-group, and we are not obliged to argue, as Forge does (in this volume), that "areas of high density were expanding and areas of low density being compressed."

However, this is only half the story. The demographic puzzle may have changed its shape a little, but the riddle of the reproduction of diversity remains. If we grant the possibility that Abelam—the language and the culture—was extending its domain across a dense but relatively static population, we may wonder whether there were any counteracting forces *limiting* this tendency toward uniformity.

Although there may be instances in which entire communities had reasons to adopt a novel language, this was surely not the standard way for individuals to cross linguistic boundaries. As we have seen, the Ilahita population was enlarged by Kwanga-speaking refugees who left their tongues behind them when their bodies were incorporated by an Arapesh community. The evidence of oral history throughout the Sepik region indicates that such events were relatively common, all the more so where the scale of warfare was apparently intensified by population pressure. In this sense, there is no denying a degree of population movement, *but it does not follow that the movement was centrifugal*. The Kwanga refugees assimilated into Ilahita could instead have removed themselves to what is virtually virgin forest in the opposite direction. Why should we think that Abelam communities were any less receptive to the foreign-speaking refugee than Ilahita was, *unless* we have assumed that they were permanently overpopulated by their own fertility? If we do not make this assumption, then we have a way of understanding how the language and the culture of the Abelam could have been spatially restricted through a lengthy period in which it acted as a magnet to the many border-crossers who increased its population.

But why should people be attracted to an overpopulated area? The reason may be nothing other than the previously noted *popularity* of what this area produced: these things were popular within a wider sphere of influence because they were perceived to be the products of the power of population. And this is not as circular an argument as it may sound. If we grant the possibility that Abelam—the *area*—exported something of its culture, *not* its language, in return for an addition to its labor power, this would have been a process which had limits of its own. Indeed, the ethnographic evidence suggests that there may well have been a growing contradiction in the Abelam productive system. If local labor was increasingly diverted from the tasks of food production to the cultivation of *inedible* symbolic yams and to the manufacture of a range of other symbols needed to appease the spirit of exchange, and if this was happening because it was the only way to bind communities together in the face of mounting population pressure but had the paradoxical effect of adding foreign immigrants to these communities, then we may readily imagine that this pressure would have finally become unbearable, and something would have snapped.[9] On this extreme hypothesis, the ferment of artistic creativity which so attracts the Western connoisseur could be regarded as a sign that Abelam was not *ex*ploding but *im*ploding.

The naturalistic model of prehistory invites us to believe that, even in a region like the Sepik, there was only one dynamic form of international relations that did *not* consist in the exchange of objects (or ideas) between the members of communities whose languages were fixed possessions. On this account, the normal pattern of exchange (or trade) could be disrupted only when people and their languages *together* colonized new territories and absorbed, if they did not displace, the previous inhabitants. But now we see that there are other possibilities which cannot simply be discounted. People may adopt new languages and language-groups adopt new people; languages may be "exchanged" without their speakers, and speakers may cross boundaries without their languages. If *all* forms of cultural identity, including ordinary language and the basic organizing principles of social life, could move about quite independently both of each other and of their producers, *who were also relatively mobile*, what *were* the fixed points in this sphere of circulation other than those features of the physical environment which simply could not be removed from one place to another?

Within the Abelam environment, the uniformity of language may have simply been a function of the density of population and communication, but this may not tell us very much about the constitution of diversity within the consciousness or practice of the people thus united. As Forge himself points out (in this volume), those who have lived within the boundaries of Abelam in this century have been "in a ferment of creation in ritual and art. New forms of ritual and hence social organization have spread across the Abelam area, along with changes in art style," and these processes have "*naturally tended to produce diversity*" (emphasis mine). Forge claims that all these forms of innovation and diffusion, whether cultural or structural, are features of a single overarching "metaculture," hence a single Abelam *mentality*. But why should we suppose that spiritual "cultures" were coterminous with language boundaries? If ordinary language is regarded as a single and elastic form of cultural identity, we should perhaps be skeptical of evidence that there was anything especially distinctive about the Abelam, as *people*, other than their language. Forge says that they "were conscious" of themselves as the possessors of a "culture" which they did not share with others. But was this *all* the consciousness they had of cultural identity, or was it only one of several dimensions of perceived diversity?

There may be *some* dimensions of diversity for which it can be said that Sepik "cultures," like communities, were strictly *local* entities, the common and exclusive property of those who lived and moved within the confines of a single boundary. There may be *other* kinds of "culture" which had rather different attachments—which were *not* the "private" properties of local populations but reflections of the form and level of development of certain *branches of production*. In the present instance, one might argue that there was no spiritual culture of the "Abelam" but only one of the *yam*—the forces and relations of production which the yam was understood to signify within a multilingual mixture of communities in which it was *more or less* important as an item of subsistence or exchange. *Some* cultural distinctions may have been a mirror to the separation of discrete productive systems in discrete environments, while *others* may have been reflections of technologies combined in different degrees in different communities, regardless of the language in which these distinctions were discussed.

In that case, there is no need to assume, as Tuzin does, that "Arapesh" were forced to choose between annihilation and another spiritual "culture" or to argue that the Ilahita yam cult was "imported" from a language-group in which the yam was only *relatively* more important and the population *correspondingly* more highly concentrated. The boundary which separated "Abelam" from "Arapesh" was a *material* division, insofar as there was some exchange across it or a noticeable difference between the systems of production which these names connoted, and *symbolic*, insofar as this was an exchange of symbols for each other or another type of product or was simply given in the minds of local people as a difference between the speakers of two radically unrelated languages. The boundary which separated "Abelam" from "Sawos," on the other hand, was less symbolic and *perhaps* less real. Forge says that there was no clear boundary between "what we call Abelam and what we call Sawos," but he appears to be referring mainly to a chain of *dialects* which linked the local groups which spoke these languages. If we then take the point of view of individual *communities*, be they "Sawos," "Abelam," or "Arapesh," it might be true to say that if one had a sense of being different from other groups in one direction and in one respect, one would be likely to possess a sense of continuity in *that* respect with groups in the opposite direction. An "Abelam" community might share a sense of continuity with nearby "Arapesh" communities in some respects *apart* from the criterion of ordinary language and in *these* respects might have a sense of being different from other "Abelam" communities. The "Abelam" might not exist, in practice or in consciousness, *except* as a collection of communities which seem in *some* directions to possess a common tongue. Other forms of culture may have other points of separation.

Conclusion

Despite the questions which this article has sought to raise, I cannot claim to have provided any better explanation of the ethnographic facts than that provided by the naturalistic model of prehistory. The "Abelam" in particular and the "Ndu" in general may be exceptions to the rules which govern the reproduction of linguistic *and cultural* diversity in the remainder of the Sepik region, but a solution to the problem of diversity would be more persuasive if it could show how these "exceptions" proved these rules. And I suggest that this solution should be sought in the discovery of rules which "naturally" tend to *reproduce exceptions*.

The first step which ethnographers have normally taken in their approach to the problem of diversity has been to study or construct a map which shows the spatial distribution of languages, cultures, or communities; the second step has been to probe the internal and external relations of *one* of these entities with a view to casting some fresh light on the general problem from a particular point of view. I have tried to produce a set of arguments which might encourage the adoption of a rather different approach, a method of proceeding which might profitably be compared to that which Marx adopted in his study of the capitalist system.

The starting point of *Capital* appears to be a statement of the obvious: "The wealth of societies in which the capitalist mode of production prevails appears as an 'immense collection of commodities'; the individual commodity appears as its elementary form. Our analysis therefore begins with the analysis of the commodity" (Marx 1976[1867]:125). As Marx proceeds to show, the *form* of the commodity is only superficially a simple thing, containing as it does the central contradictions of an *ideology*, the "fetishism" of commodities, which both reflects and hides the "real laws" of capitalist production. Marx's

method of analysis may still be valid as a way of understanding "culture," even in societies where capital does *not* prevail, provided we can specify and justify a starting point which takes the place of the commodity.

Considering the problem dealt with in this paper, one is tempted to suggest that the traditional wealth of the Sepik region appears as an "immense collection" not of commodities but of "languages" and "cultures." But while this statement may be obvious enough to linguists and ethnographers, whose own perceptions cannot be entirely liberated from the form of the commodity, *was it so obvious to the producers of this wealth, whose own experience of the commodity form was far more limited*? Should we not be trying to avoid the tendency to think of "languages" or "cultures" as the private properties of local groups, at least until it can be shown that this was how the Sepik people mainly thought about their many local differences? Would it not be less tendentious to begin with the idea that Sepik people saw their world as a collection not of "languages" and "cultures" but of cultural *distinctions*, reproduced and reinterpreted at many levels and in many ways without becoming "things" associated with collections of communities?

A buried model of commodity exchange may constitute the greatest single obstacle to ethnographic understanding of the local form of cultural diversity within the Sepik region. To quote again from Marx, "the *exchange* of *commodities* begins where *communities* have their *boundaries*, at their points of contact with other communities, or with members of the latter" (p. 182, emphasis mine). It may well be the case that there was *some* commodity exchange at *some* points of contact between Sepik communities. But the subjective form of cultural diversity may not have given any special privilege to this relationship or to the boundaries which it established or transformed. Our problem is to specify the *many other ways* in which the "boundaries between communities" were understood, traversed, and realigned, for if there is a single Sepik system of beliefs which tends to generate a multiplicity of cultural distinctions, it is likely to be one in which the "boundaries," and therefore the *identities*, of local groups are necessarily and centrally confused. Our task is therefore to investigate the possibility that such a *spiritual* culture of diversity goes some way toward explaining the evident diversity of cultural identities and then to ask if this "folk model" has internal contradictions which deserve the name of ideology.

Notes

1. This article is a revised and expanded version of the first half of the paper which I originally prepared for the Basel symposium. That paper was itself incomplete, and I have subsequently realized that it could not be brought to a conclusion within the space available to me here. I have consequently deleted that section of the paper which dealt specifically with the "cultural configuration of Nuku District," and I hope to publish an extended discussion of this subject in due course. The present article should therefore be regarded as a theoretical prologue to that discussion, and its title is intended to reflect the importance which I attach to the views put forward by Anthony Forge (in this volume).

2. I refer here to the maps contained in the *Language Atlas of the Pacific Area* (Wurm and Hattori 1981). Within this collection, the map which currently concerns us is Map 6, "Sepik Provinces," compiled by Donald Laycock. The linguists to whom I refer are those whose work is cited as source material for this particular map.

3. The distinction made here between symbolic and spiritual culture is not to be confused with Bateson's distinction between *eidos* and *ethos*. The risk of confusion exists because the original meaning of these words in Ancient Greek is as close to the distinction made here as it is to the manner in which Bateson chose to use them. Bateson himself conceded that he had translated the two words quite freely for his own purpose, to convey what most anthropologists nowadays describe as the distinction between "structure" and "sentiment" (see Bateson 1958[1936]:26–34, 218–20).

4. The "Central Sepik region," as defined here, is considerably larger than the area which is conventionally described as the "Middle Sepik." The "Middle Sepik" peoples are those that live on or near that stretch of the Sepik River which runs from Ambunti to An-

goram. They all speak languages belonging to the Sepik-Ramu phylum and are renowned for the quality of their arts and crafts.

5. There is in fact very little in the way of biological evidence to support statements of this kind. Indeed, such evidence as exists runs counter to the hypothetical correlation of linguistic and genetic boundaries, both in this particular region (Simmons et al. 1964–65) and in Papua New Guinea as a whole (Serjeantson, Kirk, and Booth 1983). I am grateful to Bryant Allen for bringing these sources to my attention.

6. Apart from the authors whose work is discussed elsewhere in this article, there have been several detailed ethnographic studies of communities or "cultures" which fall into one or the other of these categories. In respect of the Ndu-speakers, see Gorlin (1973) on the Abelam, Schindlbeck (1980) on the Sawos, Stanek (1983) on the Iatmul, and Harrison (1982b) on the Manambu (related to the Iatmul). In respect of their neighbors, see Kaufmann (1968) and Bowden (1983a) on the Kwoma and Schindlbeck (1983) on the Kwanga. With the exception of Tuzin's work on Ilahita, the Orange neighbors have been curiously ignored.

7. The most sophisticated analysis of the "uneconomic" dimensions of Melanesian trading relationships is to be found in Sahlins (1972:277–314). Gewertz (1977a, 1978b, 1983) has explored this problem in the context of relations between Ndu and non-Ndu communities.

8. I have chosen the image of a "swarm of locusts" in order to capture the inferences which have been drawn from evidence that the Sepik grasslands, including those which lie to the south of the territory currently occupied by the "Abelam," are the result of human depredation (see Reiner and Robbins 1964, Haantjens, Mabbutt, and Pullen 1965). I do not wish to challenge the evidence itself, only the inferences.

9. Might this not be an explanation for the extremity of the restrictions on sexual activity in the "Abelam" yam-growing season? Might these not be interpreted as a response to population pressure? "Abelam" gender relations are discussed at length by Losche (1982).

10/ Is the Mountain Ok Culture a Sepik Culture?

Barry Craig

Is the Mountain Ok culture a Sepik culture? In a rough sort of way, the answer is no. The societies most like the Mountain Ok societies are to the west, in the central ranges and foothills of the easternmost interior of Irian Jaya (see Kooijman 1962, Craig 1969). In asking the question, however, what I want to do is call attention to the difficulties raised by referring to a "Mountain Ok" or a "Sepik" culture and the question of an appropriate methodology for the study of material culture in a polyglot country such as Papua New Guinea.

"Mountain Ok" is defensible as a term referring to a culture area, and the boundaries of "Mountain Ok culture" would be coincident with the boundaries of the Mountain Ok subfamily of the Trans–New Guinea phylum of languages and such geographically contiguous language groups as the Duranmin and Oksapmin to the east (fig. 1). "Sepik," however, is a geographical term for an area that includes remarkably diverse ecosystems, languages, and cultures. It would be meaningless to talk of a "Sepik culture," except perhaps in the most general of terms. At this stage in the study of "Sepik cultures" it would be presumptuous to generalize; the data available are insufficient to support such an approach. The linguists have done a magnificent job in determining language boundaries and analyzing family relationships among languages. Students of material culture lag far behind.

We cannot match the work of the linguists partly because our materials lie unstudied in museums scattered throughout the world and in vast quantities of unpublished field notes as widely dispersed and partly because many areas simply have not been given careful study. Many collections are poorly documented; for example, the H. D. Eve collection of bamboo smoking tubes in The Australian Museum attributes many pieces to villages which cannot be found on old or current maps, and no other data whatsoever are provided. It is time we began systematic distribution studies for certain artifacts from prescribed geographical regions. Even if the studies are incomplete because of the difficulty of accumulating sufficient data from some areas or processing the quantity of data, I believe it will advance our understanding of Sepik cultures to be able to note the distributions of certain artifact types and graphic styles in certain defined areas. Some patterns will suggest the relevance of language groupings, others trade and warfare; some may hint at relationships attributable to common origins. The exercise would also be helpful to museum curators by providing provenances for objects in their collections that lack them.

I have undertaken to examine, with particular attention to the Mountain Ok question, the distributions in the West Sepik and parts of the East Sepik Province of types/styles of three artifacts: arrows, shields, and smoking tubes.[1] My method is to examine the material available to me from each language group for each artifact and, by visual examination, measurement, and the like, to develop an understanding of the consistencies in (1) form (material, size, shape, etc.), (2) structures of the graphic designs executed on the artifact, (3) motifs or elements of these graphic designs, and (4) manner of execution of the graphic designs (curvilinear or rectilinear; use of relief bands, relief forms, incised lines; etc.). Ideally, a fifth category, content or meaning of the graphic designs, and a sixth, technique of manufacture of the artifact, should be included, but I have not done so because for these categories I have insufficient data.

The pattern of the distribution of the consistencies of form, structures, motifs, and manner of execution in relation to the pattern of language distribution is one consideration, but beyond this, each of these consistencies can be considered in relation to the others. For example, certain motifs may prove more widespread than any particular graphic design structure and certain design structures more widespread than any particular form of the artifact. A particular artifact may represent the coming together of several differing skill traditions, each with its own history and viability. The distributions of arrow types, shield types, and smoking-tube types in relation to one another are also of interest.

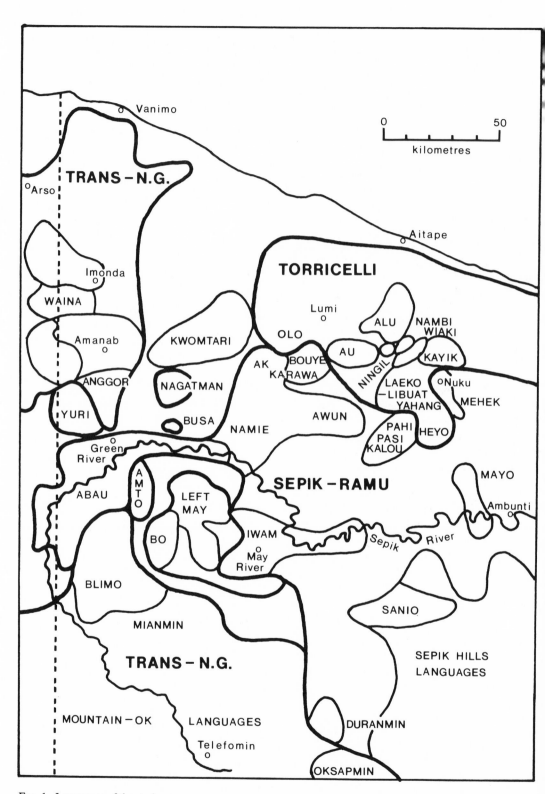

FIG. 1. Languages of the study area.

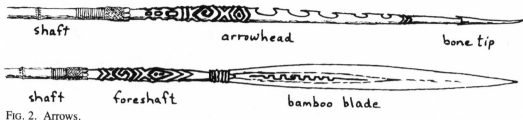

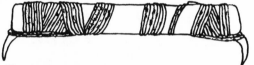

FIG. 2. Arrows.

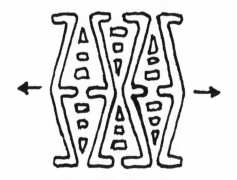

FIG. 3. Chiseling tool.

I do not pretend that this article represents a complete analysis of the distribution of the artifacts I have chosen for study; there are still too many gaps in my data. I intend this as a preliminary exercise, primarily testing a methodology and looking for the details that must yet be obtained so that something more fruitful may follow.[3]

Arrows

This study is only of the *designs* carved on hardwood arrowheads and on black-palm foreshafts of bamboo-bladed arrows. I do not have sufficient data at this time to study the *form* of various arrow types.

Arrows are generally around 150 centimeters long. Most of the arrows decorated with graphic designs are ones used for hunting wild pigs and cassowaries or for fighting (fig. 2). Arrows used for hunting small game are at best decorated with the most elementary designs. The designs are

chiseled into the wood using a tool made by binding halves of the lower jaw of a rat between the ends of two pieces of wood 8–12 centimeters long (fig. 3). The chiseled-out areas of the design are often filled with white lime or chalk and red ochre; the raised lines of the design (relief bands [Schefold 1966:259]) are thus left black or natural wood color. The hardwood points of arrows may be plain or intricately barbed, often with graphic designs chiseled in two or more bands with barbs or notches between them. A short piece of sharpened bone may sometimes be slipped over the point. Bamboo-bladed arrows usually have a black-palm foreshaft between the *pitpit* (wild sugarcane) shaft and the bamboo blade, the foreshaft usually being chiseled with designs painted with red and white. Barbs and hooks may be cut into the bamboo blade or a row of cane thorns fastened down the middle of it, designed to break off in the victim and promote death. The bone points are also designed to detach from the arrow in the victim's body.

Bows are usually about 180 centimeters long and of black palm with a string of split cane. In only one case—that of Waina-speakers of the Border Mountains—have I observed graphic designs chiseled into bows; otherwise they may be decorated with a few red parrot feathers or a wisp of bird-of-paradise plumage. Because black palm is a lowland material, it is not surprising that significant contacts exist along trade routes between the lowlands and the highlands and that both arrows and bows were frequently traded.

The universal presence of arrows specifically for use in warfare suggests that all groups experienced armed conflict fairly regularly, though probably with only modest loss of life. I was given many tales of fights after which shell valuables, stone tools, shields, and arrows were picked up and carried off or deliberately stolen from a body or a routed settlement.

I have, over the years, recorded the designs chiseled onto thousands of arrows, both in museum collections and in the field, by "rubbing"

FIG. 4. A widespread arrow design.

FIG. 5. Left May arrow designs that have Mountain Ok equivalents.

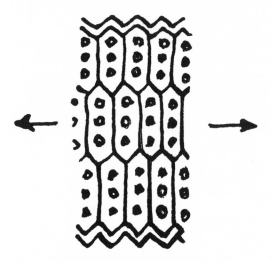

FIG. 6. Another widespread arrow design.

them with a large lumber crayon. A piece of paper is rolled around the arrow and held firmly while the paper is rubbed with the crayon; as the arrow is rolled, a three-dimensional design is transferred to the paper as a continuous two-dimensional rendering which is far more easily "read." I have sorted these design rubbings by language group and then by design type within language groups, and this has made it possible to examine the distribution of types of design struc-

ture and of motifs across several language groups. It may be possible one day to carry out this sort of analysis with a computer programmed for taxonomic analysis, providing the data fed into the computer are representative of the material that once existed in the field. It must be acknowledged that the distributions are probably not static and therefore a time factor may be involved.

There are far too many different designs to be discussed here. Some are rare and confined to one language group; others are widely distributed across diverse language boundaries. Two examples of the latter will have to suffice. One is the design in figure 4, which is found among all the Mountain Ok groups, the Amto, Blimo, and Bo of the West Range, and the Abau of the Upper Sepik west into Irian Jaya (covering speakers of languages of the Trans–New Guinea phylum and the Sepik-Ramu phylum and of one unclassified language). The design also occurs on bamboo ear tubes/paint containers of the Mountain Ok and on bamboo smoking tubes of the Abau and the Mayo-speakers near Ambunti. Left May designs also have their Mountain Ok equivalents (fig. 5). Another design (fig. 6), covering an even wider area, is found among the Mountain Ok, the Sanio of the Wogamush River (a Sepik Hills language

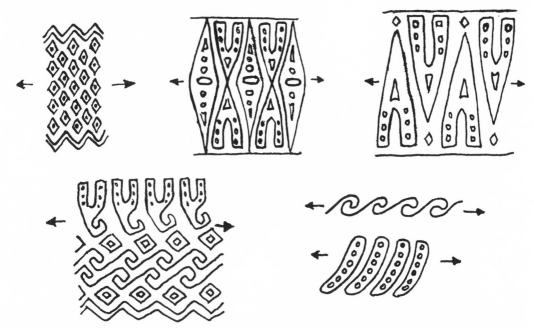

FIG. 7. Arrow designs illustrating the various structural principles. *Top left*, serial repetition; *center*, inversion symmetry; *right*, diagonally deflected symmetry; *bottom left*, agglutination; *right*, single asymmetric motifs.

TABLE 1
STRUCTURAL PRINCIPLES IN ARROW DESIGNS BY LANGUAGE GROUP

LANGUAGE GROUP	No. OF DESIGNS	STRUCTURAL PRINCIPLE (PERCENT)[a]					
		SR	IS	DDS	A	SAM	TOTAL
Mountain Ok							
Faiwol	85	3	24	34	19	20	100
Tifal	106	2	27	30	29	12	100
Telefol	263	2	22	27	35	14	100
Mianmin	246	2	18	8	61	11	100
Sugamin/Duranmin/							
Oksapmin	29	3	7	35	41	14	100
Total	729	2	21	22	41	14	100
West Range (Amto/Bo/Blimo)	35	20	17	14	49	0	100
Left May	23	9	9	26	35	21	100
Abau							
Idam/August Valley	66	18	14	48	15	5	100
Western	63	14	21	54	8	3	100
Central	94	22	14	58	3	3	100
Eastern	47	9	19	57	6	9	100
Total	270	17	16	54	8	5	100
Busa/Nagatman	70	4	27	64	3	2	100
Namie	21	19	19	33	24	5	100
Border Mountains							
Yuri	95	5	6	87	1	1	100
Anggor/Amanab/Wari	39	3	3	69	8	17	100
Total	134	4	5	82	3	6	100
Wapi (Olo-speakers?)	18	0	28	39	5	28	100
North Coast	57	0	23	42	2	33	100

[a] *SR*, serial repetition; *IS*, inversion summary; *DDS*, diagonally deflected symmetry; *A*, agglutination; *SAM*, single asymmetric motifs.

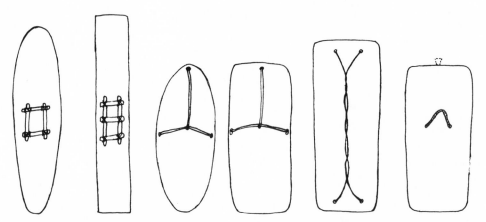

FIG. 8. Shield forms. *Left to right*, Sepik Hills, Iwam, Abau and Namie, Mountain Ok, North Coast.

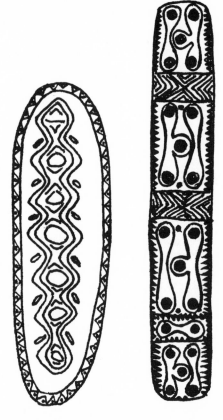

FIG. 9. Serial repetition of motifs. *Left*, Sepik Hills; *right*, Iwam.

FIG. 10. Relief bands outlining figure versus ground. *Left*, Namie; *right*, Abau.

group), the Abau of the Upper Sepik, and the Wapi (Lumi) of the Torricelli Range, as well as at Aitape on the north coast and even on Muschu Island near Wewak. Rendered somewhat differently, it may be found also in the highlands east of the Strickland Gorge. More detailed analysis is therefore necessary to differentiate a Mountain Ok version of this design from an Abau, Sanio, Wapi, or North Coast version.

This wide distribution of certain designs on arrows is understandable given the significance of trade and warfare. It is not considered remarkable that shells are exchanged over such vast distances, and the trade links that move stone tools around also extend widely despite the fact that the sources of their raw materials are more numerous and more local than the sources of shells. In 1983 I came upon a number of *febi* stone adze blades,

FIG. 11. Relief bands representing figure versus ground. *Left*, Namie; *Right*, Mountain Ok.

current in the Mountain Ok area and deriving from a quarry about ten days' walk west of the Sibil Valley in Irian Jaya (Kooijman 1962:23, 24), in the hands of men of Kambaramba near Angoram. I assumed that they had acquired them during patrols into the Mountain Ok area with patrol officers from Wewak or Ambunti, but they insisted that they did not know where they came from and that they had been passed on to them by their fathers and grandfathers. The trade routes that served to move these stone tools from Central

FIG. 13. Design elements of Namie and Mountain Ok shields. *Top left*, eye of bird or man, spiral tail of a bird of paradise; *right*, bent arm of man, leg of lizard, hornbill's beak, ribs; *center left*, moon, navel; *right*, pathway; *bottom left*, legs of crocodile; *right*, snake.

Irian Jaya to the Lower Sepik could also have served to distribute designs on arrows and smoking tubes.

The structural principles of the designs on arrows, most of which apply to designs on shields and bamboo smoking tubes as well, were found to be five (fig. 7): (1) serial repetition, the repeating of design elements or motifs from the proximal to the distal end of the design, whether inline or interlocking; (2) inversion symmetry or mirror image, bilateral symmetry around the "horizontal" axis (at right angles to the length of the arrow); (3) diagonally deflected symmetry, a special case of inversion symmetry in which the mirror image is deflected to one side so that an interpenetrating design is formed; (4) agglutina-

FIG. 12. Quartered design on Abau shield.

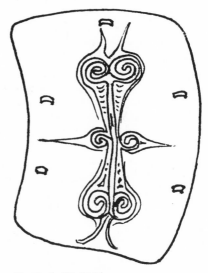

FIG. 14. Torricelli shield.

TABLE 2
DESIGN CHARACTERISTICS OF SHIELDS (PERCENT) BY LANGUAGE GROUP

	LANGUAGE GROUP					
DESIGN CHARACTERISTIC	SEPIK HILLS ($N = 43$)	IWAM ($N = 191$)	NAMIE ($N = 30$)	ABAU ($N = 181$)	MOUNTAIN OK ($N = 192$)	NORTH COAST ($N = 61$)
Structure						
Vertical symmetry	100	90	90	97	100	100
Horizontal symmetry	51	(70) 52	90	89	88	66
Serial repetition	47	(84) 15	3	8	0	6
Single asymmetric motifs	0	1	7	2	0	0
Manner of execution[a]						
Relief bands	[b]	100	100	100	100	97
Relief forms	[b]	100	7	14	0	95
Registers						
5 vertically	2	1	0	0	0	0
4 square	0	0	0	7	0	0
4 vertically	0	5	0	0	0	0
3 vertically	0	17	0	2	9	7
2 vertically	0	34	23	23	12	8
Single field	98	43	77	68	79	85
Elaborated subdivisions	0	47	23	6	0	2

[a] Sepik Hills, Iwam, Abau, and North Coast designs are curvilinear; Mountain Ok designs are rectilinear; Namie designs are both.
[b] Relief bands/forms with incised lines as well.

tion, the building of a design through the addition of differing and/or alternating motifs along the axis of the length of the arrow; and (5) single asymmetric motifs such as a line of linked spirals. The distribution of instances of these principles (table 1) shows some interesting commonalities and differences.

With regard to manner of execution, Mountain Ok and some related groups favor a rectilinear rendering of motifs while Upper Sepik groups prefer curvilinear rendering. North Coast and Wapi (Lumi) designs show both. This distinction is also significant for shield and bamboo smoking-tube designs. Fischer (1971), attempting to link certain characteristics of graphic designs with elements of social structure, has advanced some hypotheses concerning rectilinear and curvilinear styles. Rather than engage in such an analysis, I want to indicate an area for future research: the possibility that the structural principles of graphic designs are intellectual in origin, related to language and the way people structure their universe through language, while the manner of execution is emotional in origin, related to feeling and fantasy and therefore more existentially linked to environment and to the particular social adjustments influenced by environmental factors.

Of the various motifs, the spiral is common throughout the West Sepik, including the Moun-

tain Ok area (where it is the rectilinear version that is equivalent to the Asian "key" motif). This motif probably will be found to distinguish the Sepik and the highlands (east of the Strickland), since highlands arrows rarely have it.[2]

Shields

In a 1970 paper, I suggested that a sharper definition of "style" could provide the basis for more objective statements about similarities and differences in graphic design style and resolve some long-standing disagreements about the boundaries of certain style areas. Important preconditions for such an analysis are sufficient examples and, of course, precise provenance data. I want to explore the possibilities of this idea through an analysis of shield styles of the Sepik Hills, Iwam, Namie, Abau (all Sepik-Ramu phylum), Mountain Ok (Trans–New Guinea phylum), and North Coast (Austronesian and Sko phylum). (I will mention shields of the Lumi area here, but I do not have sufficient examples to include them in the analysis.)

The forms of shields (see Craig 1969:214) distinguish their provenance in all but one case (fig. 8). The Sepik Hills shields are an elongated oval with rigid handles on the back. I do not know if they are meant for use with bows and arrows or

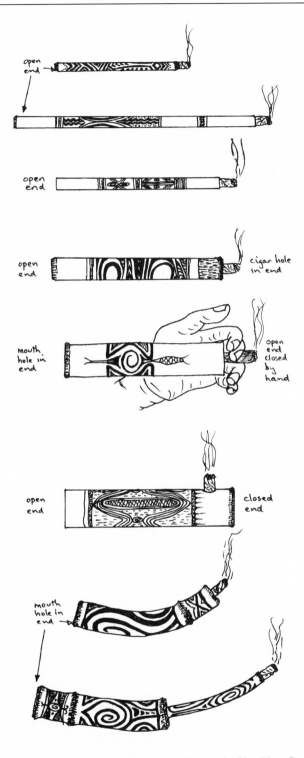

Fig. 15. Bamboo smoking tubes. *Top to bottom*, Central Range (Mountain Ok); River/Swamps (Abau, Namie, Bouye, Kalou, Busa, Nagatman, Amto); Southern Torricellis (Pahi, Heyo, Yahang, Mehek); Swamps and Southern Torricellis (Namie, Awun, Ningil); Border Mountains (Anggor, some Yuri); Torricellis (Wiaki, Nambi, Alu); Border Mountains (Yuri, some Anggor).

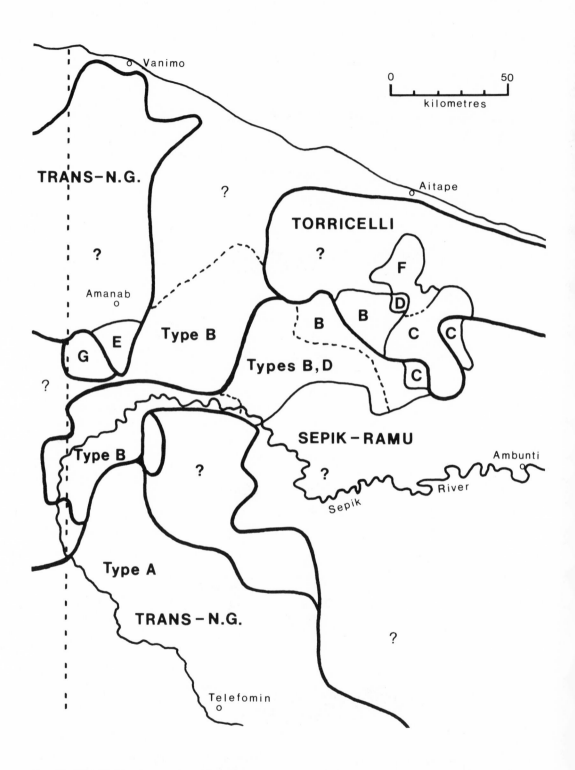

FIG. 16. Distribution of types of smoking tubes.

FIG. 17. Abau and Namie smoking apparatus.

spears, though I suspect the former. Iwam shields are relatively narrow and tall with rigid handles on the back and are used with spears. Mountain Ok shields are relatively broad and flat, with four holes to secure two vertically intertwining lengths of cane used as a carrying strap. Abau and Namie shields are also relatively broad and flat, but with a tendency toward an oval shape and with three holes to secure two lengths of cane secured at right angles to each other as a grip. Sepik Hills, Iwam, and Mountain Ok shields are planks split from a log; Abau and Namie shields are cut from the flat buttress root flanges of (usually) *Ficus* trees. Abau, Namie, and Mountain Ok shields are meant for use with bow and arrows.

Table 2 sets out the frequencies of various design characteristics by language group. ("Hori-

zontal symmetry" here is symmetry around the horizontal axis, equivalent to inversion symmetry for designs on arrows and smoking tubes.) It is apparent here that departure from symmetry around the vertical axis of a shield is rare for Sepik Hills, Abau, and Mountain Ok designs. In the case of Namie designs, the exceptions are the consequence of an asymmetric spiral design. The Iwam exceptions seem to have arisen from imperfect understanding of the design (particularly for some of the many shields carved in recent times for the tourist industry) or from the cooperation of two men in carving a shield, one to each side of the vertical axis. I have witnessed cooperative drawing of designs among Abau and Namie, but there one craftsman is likely to work on the lower half and another on the upper half, leading to departures from symmetry around the horizontal axis.

Mountain Ok departures from symmetry around the horizontal axis are a consequence of the particular design. For Sepik Hills designs, the frequency for horizontal symmetry of 51 percent can be altered to 70 percent if the central face motif is not considered asymmetric. Almost half of the Iwam shields are asymmetric around the horizontal axis, mainly because of the practice of placing different motifs in each of several fields or "registers" along the vertical axis of the shield. Abramson (1970) has suggested that this is a contemporary phenomenon reflecting the breakdown of a previously more structured society and the rise of virtuoso craftsmen.

Serial repetition of motifs along the vertical axis is rare or nonexistent for all groups except the Sepik Hills and Iwam, where the arrangement of designs is forced into a relatively narrow vertical field by the form of the shield itself (fig. 9).

Sepik Hills, Iwam, and Abau designs are predominantly curvilinear, Mountain Ok ones predominantly rectilinear (exceptions to the latter are to be seen in the rendering of spirals, which seem to have evolved in recent times from older, more angular forms). The Namie designs are particularly interesting. Where they are rendered by a relief band outlining a figure versus ground (fig. 10), they are more like Abau designs and are curvilinear. Where the relief band itself represents the figure versus ground (fig. 11), they are more like Mountain Ok designs. In fact, unless one is familiar with the entire corpus of Mountain Ok designs, it is almost impossible to distinguish these Namie designs; the main clue is the carrying strap of the shield itself.

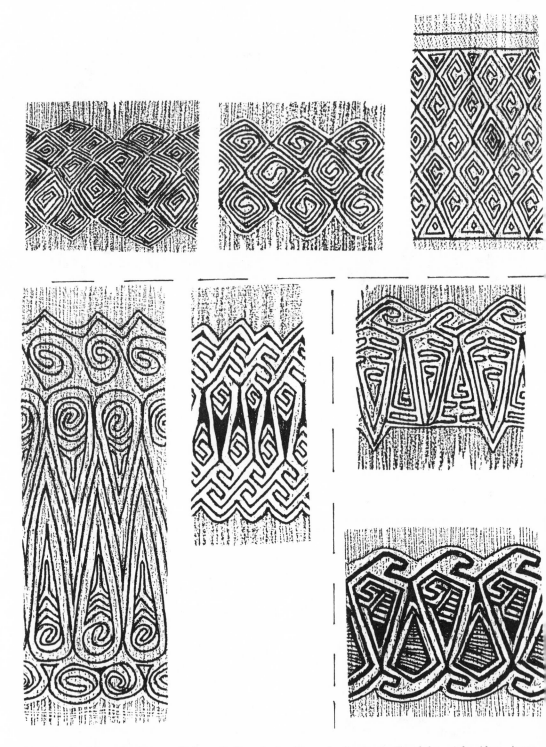

FIG. 18. Smoking-tube designs of Mountain Ok and other Upper Sepik groups. *Top, left to right*, Abau, Amto, and Mountain Ok; *bottom left*, Abau and Mountain Ok; *bottom right*, Abau and Mountain Ok.

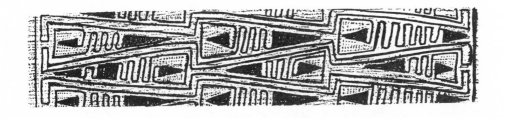

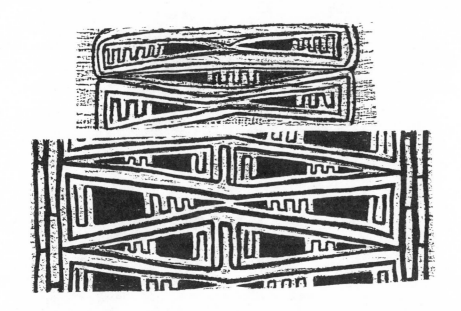

FIG. 19. A widespread smoking-tube design motif. *Top to bottom*, Mountain Ok, Abau, Namie, and Mayo.

All groups use relief bands, but only the Sepik Hills and Iwam make extensive use of relief forms to render the design. The tall, narrow form of Iwam shields is conducive to division into as many as five registers with elaborated divisions between them. The broader shields of the Namie, Abau, and Mountain Ok, however, are better suited to a single, integrated design; nevertheless, a quarter of Namie and Abau designs are divided into upper and lower registers, and a substantial number of Mountain Ok designs are divided into three, with primary emphasis on the center register. Some Abau designs are quartered (fig. 12).

The meanings of the design elements of Namie

FIG. 20. Pahi smoking-tube designs, Type C at left and right and Type B in the center.

FIG. 21. Anggor equivalent (*left*) of Namie Type D design (*right*).

FIG. 22. Type G and Type B designs compared. *Top right* and *top left*, *left to right*, Yuri and Namie; *bottom, left to right*, Yuri and Laeko-Libuat.

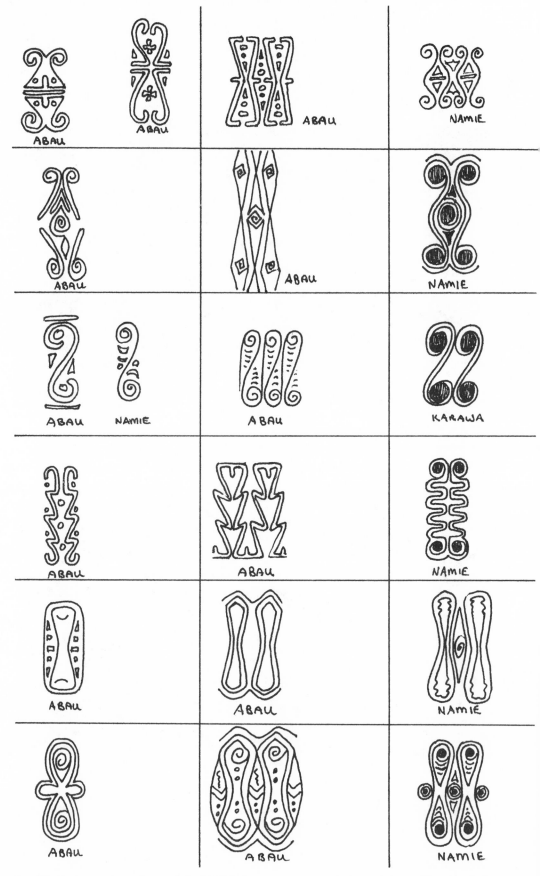

FIG. 23. Design correspondences. *Left*, shield designs; *center*, arrow designs; *right*, smoking-tube designs.

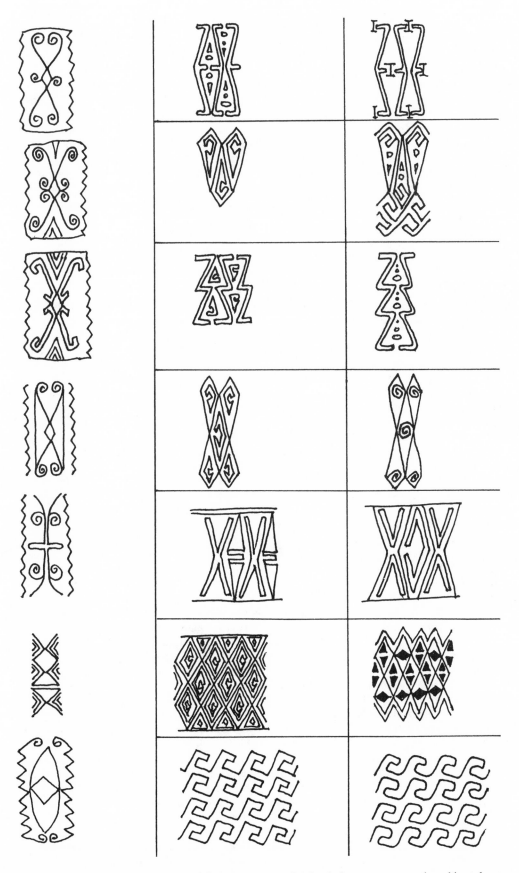

FIG. 24. Mountain Ok designs. *Left*, shield designs; *center and right*, designs on arrows and smoking tubes.

and Mountain Ok shields are surprisingly consistent (fig. 13). From the evidence presented so far, it is clear that if a direct connection exists between Mountain Ok and Namie shield designs, it cannot be via the Iwam of May River, whose shield designs are radically different; therefore it must be via the West Range. The study of arrow designs shows that there are similarities between Mountain Ok arrow designs and those of the Blimo, Bo, Amto, and Left May groups; furthermore, designs painted on sago spathes from Left May groups (Warumoi, Awai) are closely linked to both Mountain Ok and Abau-Namie designs (Schuster 1969b:pl. 23–29). Despite these apparent connections, they do not seem to me sufficient to explain the close similarity between Mountain Ok and Namie shield designs. The phenomenon requires detailed field investigation.

One shield design of the Tuwari-speakers of the upper Leonhard-Schultze River (Schuster 1968:pl. 34) is closely related to a Duranmin and Mountain Ok design. I do not know how far down the Leonhard-Schultze this influence extends, but shields of the lower river seem to be more closely related to Iwam shields (Schuster 1968:pl. 38–42).

I could find no evidence for the existence of shields among the Border Mountains peoples. However, five shields from Arso (Taikat-speakers [Trans–New Guinea phylum]), about thirty-five kilometers south of the north coast and fifteen kilometers west of the international border, have been illustrated by van der Sande (1907:pl. 26); three from the Vanimo area have been published by Schmidt (1929:pl. 14) and two others by Preuss (1899: figs. 4, 5). Tiesler (1970) illustrates seven of the Chicago pieces. These are all broad, flat shields, some with knoblike projections at the top (many Abau shields have this feature), described as cut from "the wall-like roots of large trees" (van der Sande 1907:253). They are decorated with relief bands and relief forms in mostly nonrepresentational designs that in certain instances are not unlike the designs of the Upper Sepik and Mountain Ok areas (e.g., cf. fig. 11 with Tiesler 1970:pl. 49).

Since the Busa- and Nagatman-speakers have shields like those of the Abau and Namie, it is possible that shields were possessed by Kwomtari-speakers. If this were also true for the Fas-speakers to the north in the Bewanis, this would establish a connection through to the north coast; however, there is no evidence available to me to confirm this.

The Torricelli language groups possessed small flat shields of a distinctive type (fig. 14; see also Tiesler 1970:pl. 36–41) with designs that are only remotely like Upper Sepik and Mountain Ok shield designs. To the east, a shield of the Torricelli Yapunda-speakers and another of the Sepik-Ramu Kwanga-speakers at Bongos (The Australian Museum, E.44367 and E.44366 respectively) are clearly related to the shields of the Abelam and Kwoma rather than to those of the Upper Sepik and Mountain Ok areas.

Smoking Tubes

In most of the study area, bamboo tubes are used for smoking tobacco. These are of various forms (figs. 15, 16 and table 3). Among the Mountain Ok, a small gourd rather than a bamboo tube was once seen used, and the people of the Fly–Ok Tedi headwaters (Western Province) commonly use a curved length of hollow branch, but the bamboo tube (Type A) is probably the most popular. Some groups, such as the Abau and Namie, use long gourd mouthpieces in conjunction with long bamboo tubes (Type B; see fig. 17). Everywhere the tobacco is rolled in a leaf to form a cigar about fifteen millimeters in diameter that is inserted into an appropriate hole in the apparatus or held between the fingers with the hand covering the open end of the apparatus. In almost all instances, the apparatus is decorated with design elements etched onto bamboo with a chisel or burned onto a gourd with glowing coconut-husk embers. In the latter case, the technique is the same for designs burned onto gourd lime pots (in the lowlands where the areca palm grows) and gourd phallocrypts; in the former case, the same technique is used to etch designs on bamboo lime pots (lowlands) and, in the Mountain Ok area, on bamboo paint containers that are also worn through holes in the earlobes.

The swamp dwellers adjacent to the Abau and Namie use the same long bamboo tubes (Type B); whether the long gourds are also used is not clear. In the eastern half of the distribution of this type, shorter, fatter bamboo tubes with a characteristic linked-spirals design (Type D) are also to be found. The Yuri-speakers of the Border Mountains use curved bamboo tubes (probably coming from near the roots of the plant rather than from the stem) that sometimes have two parts—a shorter, thicker section and a longer, thinner section that holds the cigar (Type G). The Anggor

TABLE 3
DESIGN CHARACTERISTICS OF SMOKING TUBES BY LANGUAGE GROUP

LANGUAGE GROUP	NO. OF ITEMS	TYPE	AVERAGE SIZE (MM)	MANNER	STRUCTURAL PRINCIPLE (PERCENT)[a]					
					SR	IS	DDS	A	SAM	TOTAL
Mountain Ok	25	A	206 × 12	R	16	16	44	0	24	100
Abau/Amto/ Nagatman/ Kwomtari	52	B	387 × 19	C	16	19	33	0	12	100
Namie/Ak/Awun	145	B	360 × 20	C	0	27	56	0	17	100
Bouye/Karawa/Au/ Kalou/Pasi	27	B	338 × 23	C	7	11	75	0	7	100
Laeko-Libuat/Pahi/ Heyo	35	C	302 × 22	CR	0	63	31	6	0	100
Kayik/Yahang/Mehek	9	C	261 × 22	R	0	56	0	0	44	100
Namie/Awun/Ningil/ Kalou	28	D	263 × 32	C	0	0	0	0	100	100
Anggor, some Yuri	58	E	245 × 51	C	0	21	15	0	64	100
Wiaki/Nambi/Alu	13	F	291 × 58	C	0	100	0	0	0	100
Yuri	34	G	245 × 30	C	3	9	74	0	15	100

[a] Key as for table 1.
[b] C, curvilinear; R, rectilinear; CR, both.

smoker of the Border Mountains uses a short, fat bamboo tube, holding the cigar in his hand clasped over the open end of the tube (Type E).

The tubes of largest diameter are those used by the Alu-, Nambi-, and Wiaki-speakers of the Torricelli Mountains (and probably other groups not represented in the collections I have examined). These tubes also differ in having an open mouth end and a hole for the cigar cut into the wall of the tube (Type F).

In the southern Torricellis, between the Wagasu and the Yimi river systems (tributaries of the Sepik), one again finds relatively long, thin bamboo tubes (Type C), generally somewhat shorter than the Abau/Namie type. The graphic designs peculiar to this region are rectilinear rather than curvilinear in character.

It would seem that Type B, characteristic of the river and swamp dwellers of the Upper Sepik, is also used by the Iwam-speakers of May River and the Sepik downstream from there (Kelm 1966b: pl. 190). In view of a tradition of origin of the Abau tracing them to immigrants from May River (Craig 1968:7, 8) and the intrusive nature of the distribution of their language, it is possible that the Type B apparatus of the Abau and Namie has its origin among the Iwam and has been adopted by neighboring language groups not of the Sepik-Ramu phylum such as the Amto, Nagatman, Busa, and Au. The Iwam designs, however, are quite different from any of those in the West Sepik Province.

Graphic designs along the length of the bamboo smoking tube exhibit the same basic structural principles identified for arrows. The distribution of these structural principles and the manner of execution (curvilinear/rectilinear) are given in table 3.

The types of tubes identified above in terms of form can usually be distinguished from one another on the basis of their designs as well. Connections do, however, exist between the designs on bamboo smoking tubes of the Mountain Ok (Type A) and those of the West Sepik Province language groups using Type B tubes (fig. 18). One particular motif is surprisingly widespread (fig. 19). I suggest that this is because of its similarity to certain arrow designs spread widely through trade and warfare. The designs on Mountain Ok smoking tubes are in fact closely related to certain designs on their arrows, and, as has been demonstrated, these in turn are related in motifs and structure to arrow designs widespread throughout the Upper Sepik area. This may suggest that the designs on Mountain Ok smoking tubes are derived from designs on arrows. Since decorated arrows no doubt predate the introduction of tobacco into New Guinea three or four centuries ago, it is not surprising that the Mountain Ok would look to their arrows for design ideas.

Type B designs, characteristic of the Abau, Namie, Ak, Awun, Bouye, Karawa, Kalou, and Pasi groups of the Sepik-Ramu phylum, are the most diverse of any of the types studied. The

Busa, Nagatman, and Kwomtari language groups (non–Sepik-Ramu) and the Au-speakers of the Torricelli phylum have also adopted Type B designs, and Pahi, of the Sepik-Ramu phylum, uses designs of both Type B and Type C. Type C is characteristic of the southern Torricelli-phylum groups and of Mehek (a Sepik-Ramu language related to Kalou, Pasi, and Pahi). Pahi tubes in fact often incorporate designs characteristic of Types B and C on the same tubes (fig. 20). Pahi tubes with Type C designs only are shorter than those with designs of Type B, and from table 3 it is clear that Type C tubes are shorter than Type B tubes.

The Amto and the Idam Valley Abau use some motifs clearly of Mountain Ok origin, and this can be ascribed to local borrowing. The same phenomenon is observed in the areas of common boundary between the Yuri and Anggor, each producing smoking tubes of the other's characteristic type. It is possible that intermarriage, with men moving to live among their wives' people, could account for this.

The existence of the Type D linked-spirals design on Anggor smoking tubes (fig. 21) suggests borrowing by the Anggor. However, except for one from "Fogoru" (which cannot be located on a map but could perhaps be Hogru, an Abau village on the Dio River quite close to Anggor territory), the farthest west I have recorded Type D is among the Namie.

Careful scrutiny reveals many correspondences in motifs and structural principles between Type G and Type C (fig. 22).

Thus there are instances of the use of designs characteristic of certain language phyla by groups belonging to neighboring language phyla. However, the distribution of smoking tubes is more like the language distribution than is the distribution of arrows. This is perhaps because smoking tubes are relatively new (three to four centuries old); arrows have been around for much longer, and the types/designs are more homogeneously distributed.

Comparison

The arrow designs are the hardest to analyze into distinct types. The distribution of designs is broad, crossing several language boundaries. The shield designs are quite specific to language groups, except for the widespread Abau/Busa/Nagatman/Namie type and the close similarity between Namie and Mountain Ok designs. The smoking-tube designs also tend to be specific to certain language groups, and I have suggested that this is at least in part the consequence of the relatively short time since smoking tubes were invented. It is possible that the shields, therefore, are also relatively recent artifacts, but it is more likely that because of their size they are not as readily exchanged as arrows or smoking tubes and may therefore be an older tradition than smoking tubes, their bulk producing the inertia that resists the tendency toward homogeneity.

Certain designs on arrows, smoking tubes, and shields of the Abau, Busa, Nagatman, and Namie can be shown to be consistent with one another (fig. 23). The designs on Iwam shields and smoking tubes are consistent, but the Iwam do not make arrows. Some Yuri arrow and smoking-tube designs are consistent, but the Yuri do not make shields. I could not check for correspondence between Torricelli arrows, shields, and smoking tubes, as I do not have examples of all three for any Torricelli group. Mountain Ok arrow and smoking-tube designs are consistent with each other, but the shield designs are different (fig. 24).

Generalizing from this, it appears that for most groups smoking-tube designs are consistent with arrow designs. For some groups, these designs are also consistent with shield designs; for others they are not. It is not surprising that arrow and smoking-tube designs should be consistent, since both these objects are cylindrical and three-dimensional, whereas shields are flat and two-dimensional.

Conclusions

I started out by suggesting that although the Mountain Ok culture is not a Sepik culture, it does have some relationships with Sepik cultures. Such links can be traced with regard to all three of the artifacts examined. Most puzzling is the similarity between certain Mountain Ok and Namie shield designs; only more field investigation will clarify the situation.

Careful examination along the lines suggested by this analysis should permit objects in museum collections to contribute to an understanding of the distribution patterns of artifacts. It is not too late to extend the breadth and depth of our understanding of this material by thorough field surveys, using photographs of objects collected long ago. It is only by such detailed study of particular artifacts (see also Haddon 1947) that we can hope to derive an understanding of the principles which will enable us to make our contribution to the history and prehistory of tribal relationships in Papua New Guinea.

Notes

1. Data for this study have been gathered by field research, museum studies, and a search of the literature. I first began collecting data for the Mountain Ok area in 1964, when I agreed to assemble and document a collection of material culture for the Australian Museum, Sydney. In 1967, a small grant from the Wenner-Gren Foundation and another from Jean Guiart enabled me to extend my work in the Mountain Ok area. I photographed almost all the houseboards and shields in the area and recorded hundreds of arrow designs. In 1968, a substantial grant from the Wenner-Gren Foundation make it possible for me to extend my ethnographic research into the Upper Sepik region, centered at Green River. Collections were assembled that are now housed in the state museums at Berlin and Leiden, The Australian Museum, and the Papua New Guinea National Museum in Port Moresby. In 1969 the museums of Berlin, Leiden, and Sydney financed a three-month expedition in the Upper Sepik to extend the 1968 research geographically, and ethnographic collections were assembled that are now housed in the three museums and the Papua New Guinea National Museum. During the 1968 and 1969 expeditions, designs on shields, arrows, and smoking tubes were recorded. In 1972–73, while under contract to the Commonwealth of Australia, I carried out further studies in the Upper Sepik region, mainly in the Idam Valley south of Green River. Over the years, several colleagues have sent me rubbings or drawings of arrow designs, and I have taken the opportunity to obtain photographs and rubbings of materials in various museums, among them The Australian Museum, Sydney; the British Museum, London; the Peabody Museum, Salem; the Field Museum, Chicago; the Museum für Völkerkunde, Berlin; the Los Angeles County Museum of Natural History, Los Angeles; and the Papua New Guinea National Museum, Port Moresby. Individuals who have been particularly generous with data include George Morren, Wilson Wheatcroft, Arnold Perey, and Pat Townsend.

2. This material warrants a more intensive and detailed analysis, but this is not the time or the place for it. For a study of highlands arrows, see Bush (1985).

3. Should any of my colleagues have data relevant to this study, I would be most grateful for the opportunity of including it to improve the analysis and extend the coverage.

11 / Masquerade as Artifact in Wamu

Peter B. Huber

In 1976, I had occasion to spend considerable periods of time in Wewak, residing in the Kreer Beach settlement among Koil Islanders and enjoying the acquaintance of sophisticated urban Papua New Guineans from a variety of backgrounds.[1] My business in Papua New Guinea, though not in Wewak, was to be an anthropologist, and my friends were aware of this. When we conversed I spoke as an anthropologist, but it was as often my part to give answers as to ask questions. The anthropology of Papua New Guinea, it proved, was of common interest to us. My interlocutors were as interested in my experience of human diversity in Papua New Guinea as was I in theirs.

This was a charming interlude in my Papua New Guinea fieldwork, and consequential: afterward the remote village of Wamu and its singular culture never appeared quite the same to me. The present essay grows out of these months in Wewak, filled with hours of leisure and aimless conversation. It concerns a shift in point of view on ritual, history, and the nature of culture in Papua New Guinea, the result of a chain of reassessments triggered in Wewak by encounters with urban Papua New Guineans.

These encounters are epitomized by a meeting with John Woichom of Aitape which occurred in Port Moresby in 1977, at the end of my last field trip. At that time, John was an M.A. student in anthropology at the University of Papua New Guinea. Our conversation, naturally, centered on Wewak. The persistence and/or resuscitation of traditional expressive forms was much in the air at that time, and eventually our conversation touched upon a ceremony that some Koil Islanders were attempting to revive and that had been described to me by them in some detail. The ceremony (also described by Hogbin 1970) is called *tangbwal* and features a *tumbuan* ([Tok Pisin] ancestral figure) called *leo*. To our mutual delight, John proved to be familiar with tangbwal and leo from his childhood in Aitape. In Aitape, the ceremony was rumored to have been "imported" in the not-too-distant past from Wogeo. One never really knows about historical hearsay, and it is pleasing to receive independent confirmation of the geography it invokes. But beyond this, I judge

that a more profound source of our mutual delight was the unexpected discovery of shared knowledge and experience, of shared *culture*.

Every fieldworker has this kind of experience, of course. Anggor-speakers from villages other than Wamu never failed to be satisfyingly surprised and impressed by my small displays of Anggor language and custom. Conversely, I was repeatedly gratified to meet Papua New Guineans in Wewak who played basketball skillfully or had informed opinions as to Carter's chances of being elected president. The striking thing about tangbwal was that learning about it had given me a link with John, who had grown up some 120 miles from Koil and had never been there; we both had seen the leo mask.

Papua New Guinea was a smaller place than I had imagined. This point, underscored by my conversations with John Woichom, was the implication of my many conversations with well-traveled Wewak acquaintances, though at the time I failed to recognize it. For these avocational anthropologists, Papua New Guinea was an intricate tapestry fashioned from the warp of the familiar and the weft of the bizarre. Yet it also presented different figures to each viewer, for its patterns varied with delineations of familiar and bizarre, and these delineations are a consequence of cultural experience. This realization suggested to me the possibility of patterns in the human landscape that transcend the units of culture isolated by ethnographers, and it led me to seek a third dimension of significance in the (to me) familiar facts of Wamu life: a regional significance superadded to the local and the theoretical.

In a way what is meant by "regional significance" is quite obvious, but snares abound. Assessing significance is largely a matter of placing things within a frame of reference, and on the regional level few exist. Anthropology has given little serious thought in recent years to spatial and temporal patterns in the distribution of ethnographic fact. Much energy, on the other hand, has been expended in identifying purely local patterns of association and linkage among ideas and activities. This actually interferes with the dialectical process of recognizing regional significance and building a regional frame of reference. Thus, in examining regional significance I shall find it necessary to keep local significance clearly in view. The main goal of my essay is not to propound a theory of regional analysis or to perform an illustrative regional analysis but simply to demonstrate that such an analysis is plausible, desirable, and surprisingly compatible with the ethnographic analysis of communities. I aim to demonstrate the complementarity of local and regional significance.

The vehicle for this demonstration will be a discussion of the ritual and ceremonial life of the Anggor of Wamu village in the West Sepik Province. Other topics—architecture or horticulture come to mind—might suit as well in principle, but the best and most voluminous published information available on the Anggor concerns ceremonial life.

In an earlier paper (Huber 1980) I defined ritual as "a determined mode of action informed by a scheme of symbolic classification which conceptually integrates the cosmos" and proceeded to examine it from that point of view. This definition led me to a discussion of the Anggor pig hunt as ritual and the discussion to the conclusion that certain events, by virtue of their symbolic load, have the capacity to "precipitate" or "realize" certain communities.[2] These events are what we ought to mean by "ritual" and analyze under that rubric. Among the Anggor it is the events associated with pig hunting and *only* those events that have this capacity; therefore pig hunting must be the subject of any study of Anggor ritual.

Conducted within this frame of reference, my study of Anggor ritual was a study from the point of view of local significance. It was concerned with the plans, memories, and intentions—states of knowledge—of community members interacting before my eyes. The past was relevant to my analysis only insofar as it was relevant to current action for contemporary actors; I was concerned only with those materials which seemed to be "put to work" in the service of "precipitation." The significance of these materials was limited to the work to which they were put. Consequently, a good bit of Anggor culture was perforce excluded from my account of Anggor ritual, including facts concerning ceremonial activities which would be considered "ritual" in common usage but not under my rather special definition. These ceremonial activities were certainly "determined modes of action" but appeared not to be "informed by a scheme of symbolic classification which conceptually integrates the cosmos." My definition of ritual, in other words, distinguished

phenomena fraught with local significance from those which seemed peripheral to community life and thus to beg regional interpretation.

Naturally, I do not mean to suggest that ritual so defined has *only* local significance and its counterpart ceremony has none. Ritual, rather, is central to community life and burdened with local significance, while ceremony is peripheral and present in the scene as much because of what has happened recently in the region as because of what is happening now in the locality. The periphery is a good place from which to launch a quest for regional significance, not just because it gives access but because one knows where it is in relation to the center. In what follows, I begin with this relation and try always to keep it clearly in view.

Anggor Religion

Anggor religious sensibility is concerned primarily with spirits and their encroachments upon the human world.[3] The Anggor are concerned to acquire knowledge about the disposition of the various different kinds of spirits with which they share their territory and to manage their relationships with those spirits to greatest advan These things are difficult to accomplis the landscape of each village terr lated by a plurality of spirit ty munities of any type and by i personalities within comm spirit individuals and types h and different inclinations. through time. There is a la tainty in the relationship b mitigated by omens, through which spirits mation as they wish spirits may cause ill the whole, however, general, they give form of aid in pig cery, and the sm harm men most of these benefit

Anggor rit cause pigs ar tinuing goo communiti govern ar these rel the An and go world. Impressionistically, pigs and spirits are daily preoccupations of the Anggor.

The activities linked with the supplication of spirits and the hunting of pigs include using spells (*sahwaf*), singing chants (*hoeli*), and parading with effigies (*sambero*). But these activities and the terms associated with them are also encountered in contexts which are not related to the central Anggor concern with pigs and spirits. There are a number of sahwaf, hoeli, and sambero which constitute distinct types of ceremony having nothing to do with pigs or spirits, with social relations, or with each other. These are the "leftovers" of purely local analysis and the subject of the present essay.

Sahwaf

The Tok Pisin word *sing-sing* is often translated as "ritual," yet the Anggor translate it as *sahwaf*, which means something more like "magic." The term *nimburisahwaf*, for example, refers to the magical spells used in cultivating gardens (*nimburi*). They are used privately, often not even whispered but silently thought. Yet they are referred to in Tok Pisin as *sing-sing bilong garden* (garden spells). The same could be said of pig and hearth magic. Powerful men and spirits have "sing-sing," meaning many spells; human activities which can be influenced by magic "have sing-sing" or sahwaf. Sahwaf are thus exceedingly personal and private, and it happens that ey can be dangerous to women and children (at same time, they are impaired by femininity). ord *sahwaf* is often uttered to children as a g to leave certain things alone, even things ot in fact have anything to do with magic. is way, the word *sahwaf* has some con- "taboo"; but the Anggor also have a stem of food taboos, properly so hese have little direct connection addition to all of these uses, the rs to one family of Anggor cer-

ils of the sahwaf ceremonies fr adepts, the details of their anon are widely disseminated. caused f Wok, a mythical being and corre e countryside destroy- wer which emanated er ended when two rom ambush and hwaf ceremonies ions. First came

Po, then Hwande, then Sahwaf Afund, and so on. In the context of discussing this myth and its cosmological implications, these sahwaf are spoken as of beings, but in all other contexts the names refer to the ceremonies only and may or may not be suffixed by the term *sahwaf*. The idea of a spiritual being that causes affliction and is mollified by the ceremony is not manifest in discussions of either illness or ceremony. It is more the case that the rituals themselves are cosmic elements that have an odd power of contagion: men become ill through improper contact with ritual substances or activities or through violation of food taboos associated with the rituals and then require a new performance of the ritual in order to be cured. Once cured they usually become adepts, while the performance of the ritual is likely to infect some new person who will later become a patient. Brought into being in mythical times, they are perpetuated by human activity but not by human design.

I can offer only fragmentary information on these ceremonies because I was unable to witness any and because the Anggor are reticent in speaking of them, even among themselves. Sahwaf appear generally to involve chanting and the application of red ochre and other substances to patient, adept, or spectator and to be dangerous. Some involve bloodletting, and all impose food prohibitions on varying categories of individuals. Everyone knows the names of the different rituals, but only a few know how to perform each one, and each has a different circle of adepts. Thus, they are mysterious and ill-defined to the Anggor community itself. They are "bought and sold"; the most frequently performed in 1970 was the Yafar sahwaf, which had recently been acquired from the neighboring Yafar-speakers (see Juillerat in this volume). Assimilated to the category sahwaf, it was performed frequently because it was considered not very dangerous. Others, such as the Yahate sahwaf, had been abandoned entirely because of their danger; many had died from Yahate, and the people had become afraid to perform it.

Finally, but not least important, sahwaf ceremonies include vocalization: singing, surely, and I believe also the use of spells, though informants are evasive and contradictory on this point. The texts of songs are more or less public knowledge and so were accessible to me. Of the many I collected, none contained recognizable words; rather, they were composed of strings of nonsense syllables. This was true also of the one spell which was vouchsafed to me.

The key to the Anggor concept of sahwaf, I believe, is the mysterious efficacy of *combinations*
of sounds.[4] These combinations are like elemen-
tal forces: their action is direct but not always reliable. They are known to men, revealed by spirits or taught by predecessors, but not understood.
Each person knows and uses his own sahwaf, has
been told how to use it by his teacher (father, uncle, elder brother, or guardian spirit), and has developed through trial and error some idea of how
best to use it. But because sahwaf are secret, men
never put these experiences in perspective by
comparing notes and so never achieve any real understanding of the system of forces which is
bound up with the patterning of sound.

Hoeli

In stark contrast to sahwaf, hoeli is essentially
poetry: filled with words, fraught with significance, elaborately structured, and public. The
term *hoeli* applies in general to certain performances of singing which would appear to any
non-Anggor little different from sahwaf chanting. But hoeli is a medium of communication,
while sahwaf is a mode of action.

The most common occasion for hoeli is the
completion of a successful pig hunt. In the evening, when the pig has been butchered and is
slowly smoking over every hearth, when the village is assembled and replete and the people have
heard the story of the hunt and are well pleased
with themselves, when the village boys have
completed their brief and impromptu performance of the *tupur* dance—then a handful of village men step forward for the hoeli. Side by side,
arms linked, they parade counterclockwise as
they sing. The men on the left more or less march
in place so that in effect the line swings slowly
around an axis.

Musically, the songs involve endless repetition
of a simple but pleasing pattern. Each passage begins with two short parallel phrases chanted rapidly and in a relatively high, almost falsetto voice
with a brief pause between them. A third phrase,
predicating the first two, moves from high pitch
down the scale, slowing in tempo until the phrase
concludes with a long-drawn-out "o," held for
several seconds and dipping at the end. There are
other contexts in which hoeli occurs—I shall discuss them below—and musical variations associated with each. What is common to all is some
form of repetition of passages, each moving from
high/brisk to low/drawn-out.

The following text represents two verses from
a hoeli set:

> *Ngarafe Maimur silin*
> *iuhur wor awoai*
> *nundiambamare*

> *Atungarafe Nungumapa silin*
> *ngamb wor awoai*
> *nundiambamare*

Strict translation is difficult because the passages are "poetic" in the double sense of assuming both semantic and morphophonemic license.
In addition to employing metaphor and idiom, the
passages distort the extremely complex verb
structure of Anggor by adding, deleting, or altering affix syllables to maintain cadence or achieve
harmony. But it is relatively easy to say how the
passages are performed, what they are about, and
where they fit within the corpus of hoeli.

Each of the passages represents one unit of the
repetitive musical pattern described above. The
first two lines are chanted in a high rapid mono-
tone, with a short break after *silin* and a slight
lengthening of the last syllable of this word and
also of *awoai*. *Nundiambamare* is chanted with
falling pitch and slightly slowing tempo, may be
followed by an extended *o*, which may slide
downward at the end, and may be repeated. Each
verse is accompanied by a complete circuit of the
dance ground.

The verses concern the houses (*wor*) of two local spirits: Ngarafe and her ancestor (*atu*, "grandmother"). The former is in the "valley of" (*silin*)
the Maimur River and the latter in the valley of
the Nungumapa River. Informants say that the
verses concern roofing new houses, though this is
not explicit in the text. Ngarafe is using *iuhur*, a
grass which humans plant to define boundaries
and never use as a roofing material. Her grandmother is using *bobor*, a succulent with colorful
leaves, also used as a border plant by humans and
never for roofing. The final line in each verse is a
complex form of a verb meaning "to occupy a
place," and its sense is "there you will reside."

These verses may be repeated several times
and then elaborated by others which introduce
new materials for the house-building and carry
the cycle of life forward through construction,
aging, and collapse. Informants allege that in a
given performance, the songs could focus on Animbi (another local spirit) as well as or instead of
Ngarafe and/or introduce different materials or
possibly different locations and still be the same
song. All Anggor verses are elaborations of

themes, the combined elaborations on any theme constituting a "song." Each song, in turn, is a liturgical unit.

I have written elsewhere of the Anggor ritual cycle which focuses on local spirits and pig hunting (Huber 1980). This cycle may occupy five or ten years. It culminates in an elaborate two-day costumed celebration. This celebration, however, is prepared in stages stretched out over years. Each stage has its song, such as the "hoeli of Ngarafe's house" discussed above. To complete the ritual cycle is thus to complete the cycle of songs.

In short, the opposition between hoeli and sahwaf is near perfect. Hoeli is religion, sahwaf magic. Hoeli is public, intelligible, and systematic, while sahwaf is private, senseless, and sporadic. Hoeli is safe, secure, and reassuring, while sahwaf, though it may confer benefits, is always dangerous and unreliable. It is important to the successful use of sahwaf that the phonetic patterns which compose the spells or chants be exactly reproduced each time; deviation may vitiate the effort, or worse. By contrast, it is virtually impossible to get hoeli wrong. Hoeli is not so much a corpus of texts as a tradition of oral performance not entirely dissimilar to that of the Slavic bards described by Lord (1976). Hoeli are to the Anggor what the Iliad was to the Greeks before Homer.

Sambero

It is easy to see how sahwaf is extraneous to the local frame of reference: it takes its sense from and incurs most of its practice in contexts which have nothing to do with pig hunting or local spirits. Hoeli seems the opposite, for I have yet to describe any contexts apart from those pertaining to pig hunting and local spirits in which hoeli is encountered. Sambero are like hoeli in this regard, closely linked with local-level religious practices aimed at cultivating friendly relations with spirits—indeed, hoeli and sambero are closely linked in all contexts. Some of these contexts, however, are extraneous to the community religion.

Anggor-speakers translate the term *sambero* into Tok Pisin as *tumbuan*. The sambero are the costumes for the two-day celebration mentioned above which culminates the Anggor ritual cycle. They are effigies, fabricated upon a frame of rattan and borne by human dancers whose torsos they completely encase. The stages in the ritual cycle are primarily stages in sambero production, and thus the hoeli are associated with different assembly points, materials, or costume elements. The two-day celebration is referred to as *sanindohoeli, sanind* being the collective term for the community of local spirits that were the object of religious life in Wamu in the 1960s and '70s. Individual spirits from within this community are named and known, associated with specific human families or lineages, and represented by distinctive effigies at the sanindohoeli. Ngarafe and Animbi, mentioned above, are the most "senior" of this group, and in consequence their effigies precede the others at the sanindohoeli. The distinctiveness of individual effigies is conferred almost entirely by *sir*, painted plaques that are the centerpieces of an essentially standard construction design.

The foundation for the effigy consists of an elongated conical framework of rattan over which a macrame sleeve has been stretched. The base of this cone should fit snugly around the bearer's shoulders and provide attachment for a bushy skirt made from the white inner bark found at the growing tip of certain palm species. The cone is perhaps three feet long, with rattan sides which continue another three feet above the tip, lashed together to form a single spike. The sir are attached to this spike so that they are carried above the cone and thus above the level of the human head. They are a foot wide by several feet long and are painted on two pieces of sago bark lashed back to back, with identical designs facing fore and aft. They are surmounted by cassowary plumes and sprays of decorative leaves (*Dracaena* and *Cordyline*), the entire assembly approaching ten feet in height. Once the sir and plumes are in place, each effigy is embellished by the addition of teeth and shells, fringe, plumes, and colored fruits to suit the taste of the bearer. A completed sambero is an imposing sight: magnificent in size and color and bewildering in its complexity, its human operator almost entirely obscured. Yet it can be known instantly as the sambero of a certain sanind because the simple and distinctive design of the sir stands out above all else.

Informants disagree whether the sanind are present in the sambero when they parade and dance or merely look on with approval, but other facts about the performance can be established. First, no man carries the sambero which he has fashioned and which represents his particular sanind. Instead, friends exchange services, bearing one another's effigies and receiving compensation for their labor. Second, the sambero parade and dance very briefly—only for minutes—at dawn, after a night of hoeli, dancing, and drumming. Third, the sir are the focal point of the performance. This is a point which might not be obvious if one observed only the finished effigy, for the sir is one of many elements. But years are devoted to the painting of the sir and only hours to the assembly of all the other costume elements. It is the stages in the preparation of the sir that are associated with the hoeli—one stage for building the enclosure in which to paint the plaques, another for building a roof under which to work, another for collecting the sago bark from which the plaques (*amongwan*) are fashioned, another for preparing the amongwan to receive the paint, yet another for the painting, and so forth.

Thus hoeli, sir, and sambero are linked and integrated into a complex liturgical system which is the focus of religious life from a local point of view. During the course of my fieldwork, I was never able to observe sanindohoeli itself because the timing was wrong, but I was able to observe work at several stages of sir preparation and to observe as well a daily preoccupation with sanind, pig hunting, and carrying the cycle forward. In addition, I was able to observe three elaborate ceremonies which include hoeli and employ sambero but have nothing to do with either pigs or spirits. These are the "leftovers" of local analysis, extraneous to the religious system yet constituted from similar liturgical elements.

The "Extraneous" Hoeli

When I assert that the three ceremonies I witnessed in 1970 are extraneous to the Anggor religious system, I mean that they are not informed by the body of public knowledge concerning sanind, sir, hoeli, pigs, and places that links events remote in space and time such as sanindohoeli, pig butchering, and séance and makes them part of a common collective enterprise. The three ceremonies are called *pou*, *ifiafohoeli*, and *kaimongwar*; each requires the production of a set cast of named sambero types, each having a distinctive appearance and style of performance. The designs of these sambero are similar to the design of the sanind sambero: the materials are the same (sometimes literally, for shells, plumes, rattles, fringe, and macrame sleeves are reused until they fall apart), and some specific characters in the casts are identical to the sanind sambero, save that they lack sir. The sambero for pou, kaimong-

war, and ifiafohoeli, however, do not represent or embody sanind or, indeed, spirits of any kind. They are types, or archetypes—often comic—and have names like *hond* ("mother") and *sagoeb* (wallaby), which in some instances relate to origin myths associated with the ceremony. Like sanind sambero, these parade briefly at dawn following a night of hoeli and/or dancing. But the hoeli are not sanind hoeli. They do not refer to spirits, nor do they refer to the surrounding landscape or to present time. The hoeli of these ceremonies do not connect with the current time, space, or religious life of the performing community, though musically they sound like the hoeli of sanind ritual and are composed of intelligible Anggor words rather than the nonsense syllables of the sahwaf.

In one respect, however, these three ceremonies are rather more like sahwaf than like hoeli: like spells, they are believed to act directly upon the world and effect specific desirable ends. Pou is good for the growth of children, for example. It acts against the chronic afflictions of yellow skin and swollen belly, protecting the healthy and curing the infirm. Although many of the roles in this ceremony are, in fact, acted by children (and the rest by young and adolescent men), the efficacy is felt by all in the village, especially toddlers too young to participate. Ifiafohoeli acts to cure men who have been afflicted with weakness and loss of breath as a consequence of improper contact with feminine things. Kaimongwar insures garden fertility, imparting a marvelous potency to the table scraps produced by adepts during the entire course of the performance. These mundane objects—leaf wrappings, sago ends, etc.—are shared out among senior men at the close of the festivities and rationed out over the coming years to anyone beginning a new garden. A small scrap the size of a fingernail, tossed among the debris of a burning garden plot, imbues an entire garden with an exceptional productive capacity. Of the three ceremonies, kaimongwar is "heaviest" and most like sahwaf in another respect: it can make people ill. The afflictions that can arise from kaimongwar are never terminal but are troubling and must be avoided through the observance of strict sexual and dietary restrictions. The good and bad consequences of these rituals, I must reiterate, are direct. Although the sambero associated with some of them have names like *ifiaf* ("ghost") and *pou hond* ("mother of pou"), and associated myths concern the activities of *ifiaf*, *pou hond*, and so on, informants emphatically deny that there are in reality any spirits which correspond to these names. Any suggestion that garden fertility is caused by spirits represented in the kaimongwar sambero or that illness is visited by such spirits on individuals who violate sexual prohibitions associated with kaimongwar is dismissed by informants as unwarranted reification.

From an Anggor point of view, these three ceremonies, like the sanind rituals, contain hoeli and sambero. In fact, one of them is called *hoeli*. Yet, they are also emphatically *not* a part of the liturgical system which culminates in the sanindohoeli, nor are they informed by its theology. In their instrumentalism, they are indeed more like sahwaf—which is, after all, the Anggor word used to translate the Tok Pisin term *sing-sing*. Where should one seek the sense and significance of these ceremonies? They are distinct from sanindohoeli. Do they then form a separate, cohesive and possibly complementary category? Does this category include sahwaf?

On the basis of similarities, differences, and continuities of detail too involved to explore here, it is tempting to answer yes to the first question and no to the second. Perhaps kaimongwar, pou, and ifiafohoeli are a set of symbolic variations on some characteristically Anggor themes. Kaimongwar and ifiafohoeli, for example, both employ an interesting choreographic feature absent from sanindohoeli. Using a bouncing, flat step which slaps the sole noisily on the packed earth of the dance ground, the company attempts to corner one or two dancers bearing the sambero. At the same time it avoids touching the effigies and so must give ground before a direct "charge," ranks parting to permit passage. All of this takes place in pitch darkness, and the effect is therefore one of a barely controlled melee (much like the pig hunt, in fact). The most interesting feature, however, is that in kaimongwar men chase the sambero, while in ifiafohoeli it is women and children who chase the sambero.

There are other points of contrast between the various ceremonies that suggest that they really need to be treated as a set. The sambero for ifiafohoeli, for example, are very different in materials (coconut fiber is used as a canvas rather than sago) and style (they are minute) from other sambero. The ifiafohoeli actors wear women's string skirts and dance backwards. In many respects, this ceremony, concerned with undoing the effects of uncontrolled reproductive power, is the inverse of kaimongwar, which is concerned precisely with intensifying reproductive power. The construction of the ceremonial house, the

night of chanting and dancing, the morning processional, the allocation of ceremonial roles, details of costume construction and self-enhancement, and relations among the various human purposes served by the ceremonies and the dangers to be avoided in them all suggest that they are elements of a single symbolic system, a system to which the sahwaf performances bear no discernible resemblance or connection.

Locating the Corpus

The corpus of this symbolic system is more extensive than the three ceremonies discussed briefly here. Other ceremonies than these, further permutations of the elements just described and presumably refractions of the same common symbolic system, were described to me in detail by Anggor informants. That I observed ifiafohoeli and not *kumao*, *tabari*, or *yufur* is purely a matter of chance. I think it right to treat all of these ceremonies as a category—partly because of similarities and continuities between them, partly because none of them seems to stand by itself as a matter of importance to the Anggor themselves. Yet, in spite of the fact that informants were liberal in supplying detail and background concerning ceremonies which did not actually transpire during my stay, the step away from what occurred during the years 1969 to 1972 and toward what could occur lands us on some rather shaky ground.

Among the three ceremonies which I witnessed, only one was sponsored by and occurred in Wamu. The other two involved Wamu but occurred in and for neighboring villages. Of the three ceremonies that informants described for me, two had been performed in Wamu in the past few years. One of these (*yufur*) might never happen again; informants speculated so, noting that they had no intention of ever performing it again. Against the temptation to write it off, we must consider that the other, *kumau*, had at that time been similarly "abandoned" by another village, a distant ally of Wamu. Yet when I returned to the Anggor five years later, in 1976, Wamu was making plans to aid this village by taking kumau to them and providing remedial instruction in performance. Kumau had been struck from the corpus of the other village but was being reinstated. This was possible because Wamu had kept the tradition alive in the interim, but rituals can "die" in the Anggor landscape. The Wamu territory is rife with places known to have been the sites of ceremonies of which now only the names and a few bizarre details are known. In that case, what of yufur? In 1970, the people of Wamu did not care if they ever saw it again. Was it dead? Is it?

An even more difficult problem is posed by the third ceremony described to me, for it had never yet been performed in Wamu. The people of Wamu had heard of it from their Anggor-speaking neighbors in Nai village and had witnessed performances in Nai. Nai had learned to perform the ceremony from people to the northeast who spoke a language entirely unrelated to Anggor. The people of Wamu considered this ceremony, called *tabari*, a "good thing." By this I believe they meant both that it had beneficial effects and that it was pleasing to behold. They observed, for example, that the tumbuan associated with it were extraordinarily tall and that this was a nice twist. They commented similarly on the large phallocrypts and observed that they found the songs pleasing. They noted with approval that the ceremony employed many fish motifs—though this did not mean that it would actually affect fish or fishing. In 1970, tabari was a ceremony some informants could describe; in 1976, several were actively studying it as apprentices, though it still had not been performed by the whole village. Has this ceremony come to life?

At this point, I am moving very rapidly toward the regional level of analysis, for once the question of temporal boundaries is introduced, the matter of spatial boundaries is only a step behind. Anggor informants have a collector's interest in liturgical forms. They speak of a variety of forms which are distinctly past and others which are potentially of the future—each attended by a haphazard collection of details. They speak with more certainty and elaboration of those which are present, in the sense of "for the moment." For many forms and details they know whence and whither; if ignorant of origins and destinations, it is not through lack of interest in the topic. The horizons within which they see ritual forms moving are broad: they name the Gagar, Kamberatoro, Amanab, Biaka, or Green River villages where different ceremonial forms originated. Certain of these names are social realities to informants. Depending which border of the Anggor territory is nearest, they have participated in rituals with the members of one or another of these alien villages, have exchanged food with them, have married their sisters and daughters. The degree to which any particular ceremonial form is present in a given community, in turn, depends on the re-

gional distribution of the form and the current extension of the community's social perimeter.[5]

In other words, to define the corpus of Anggor ceremonial forms extraneous to the local religious system, we must address a wider space and a longer time than the ethnographic here and now. The symbolic system which lies behind these forms is likely to be of a different order than that which ethnographic analysis in the local frame of reference permits us to discover. I am persuaded to this opinion, in part, simply because an analysis of the dynamics of Anggor religious life at the local level leaves bits left over, extraneous bits. These demand attention; but serious attention— as I have just indicated—leads one inexorably beyond the village and beyond the culture into alien territory which needs to be mapped.

In addition, however, there are the superficial but striking similarities between the figures which animate the Ida festival of the Wainis-Sowanda (Gell 1975) and the Anggor sambero. The Wainis-Sowanda do not come within the ambit of Anggor regional awareness, even in Wamu, the northernmost Anggor village. This is not surprising in that Wamu and Umeda are separated by a relatively broad territory containing some three thousand Amanab-speakers. What is surprising is that virtually every Ida tumbuan has a counterpart in an Anggor sambero, each encountered in a different Anggor ceremonial. The *teh* is similar to tumbuan found in pou and (somewhat less similar) to the wallaby tumbuan found in ifiafohoeli; it also bears a resemblance to the sanind tumbuan, though it lacks the sir. *Tamwa* and *ipele*, on the other hand, combine elements of very distinct tumbuan which the Anggor construct for ifiafohoeli, pou, and kaimongwar. The *ageli* is remotely similar to tumbuan created only for kaimongwar. And the *amov* wears an unusual and elaborate headdress which is not part of any Anggor tumbuan but is the standard dance costume of Anggor men adorning themselves for the tupur dance associated with the pig/sanind ritual cycle. For the Anggor, this is not a masquerade at all but a style of individual self-adornment; it is a new style, used by the middle-aged men but unfamiliar to the senior generation, having been copied within recent memory from the Amanab-speakers to the north.

Many other points of comparison are possible, of course—the Anggor use full body paint for tupur self-adornment but not in relation to tumbuan impersonation, whereas elaborate body painting codes are apparently critical in Wainis-Sowanda impersonation, for example (Gell

1975). But in this context, piling detail on detail serves no purpose. The point is that so many of the elements of an elaborate and integrated ritual system for the Wainis-Sowanda have been translated to the Anggor but in a disassembled form, as ceremony, and set on the periphery. What is amenable to a purely local analysis in Umeda requires a regional perspective in Wamu—and, perhaps, vice versa.

I hope it will not be thought that these observations in any way impeach Gell's analysis of the Ida. I do not propose that a local analysis is vitiated by the fact that its constituent units have regional distribution. I see no difficulty in the notion that the Wainis-Sowanda have assembled a number of disparate elements into a symbolic performance which focuses and precipitates (but does not exhaust) community life, while the Anggor have left these elements on the periphery, as it were, and focused their attention elsewhere.

The points I am making are simply these:

1. Anggor and Wainis-Sowanda plainly participate in a system of regional communication such that each is implicated in the past of the other, and a level must exist at which they are speaking related symbolic languages. "Constructing" this level is an operation which has great moment for the analysis of symbolic forms in communities throughout the area.

2. The relevance of this construction is greatest, the need most pressing, in dealing with peripheral rather than core symbolic forms. One can operate, as it were, in the vacuum of the ethnographic present at the core but not so at the periphery.

Clearly, the effort required to identify and explore the level at which Anggor and Wainis-Sowanda are speaking the same language is a collaborative one. I don't mean that Gell and I, or other anthropologists who have worked in the area, such as Juillerat (1981, 1982) or Peter (1979*a* and in this volume), need to sit down and prepare a concordance; nor do I mean that we ought to work out a schedule for publishing comparable information which we can expect will eventually provide the materials for achieving the goal. I mean simply that we all need to make some essays in that direction, as well as attending to our individual local-level concerns, and to respond to one another's attempts.

In a way, perhaps, this article should have been that kind of essay. The materials for making a start are surely there in the work of my colleagues. But an essay of that sort would be of interest only to those who are deeply immersed in the ethnography of the Border Mountains, while I think the point that lies behind such an exercise has relevance to all Sepik—and Papua New Guinea—studies. There is a growing interest among both Papua New Guinea intellectuals and anthropologists in a disparate family of topics collected under the rubric "history." Preeminent among these topics are archival accounts and native representations of the colonial encounter, local representations of change, and local representations of time, in short, the history of events and perceptions. What is missing, I would say, is the history of the *longue durée*. In a land devoid of archives, such a history may seem a dubious proposition; yet as the work of the Annalist school of French historians (Braudel 1967, Le Roy Ladurie 1974) shows us, records may be writ in architecture, in costume, in furniture, in the very face of the land.[6] I am convinced that the curve of precontact history in Papua New Guinea is so recorded. Though I have not stressed this point, the regional analysis I have sketched above would amount to a historiography of sir, of hoeli, and above all of tumbuan.

The chief difficulty that lies in our way is not the lack of material. After more than a hundred years of intensive ethnography, we have a good quantity on hand, and it is informative. But I think that the very ethnographic enterprise which has carried us so far predisposes us by its demands toward an inhibiting parochialism. I have focused my essay on the relationship between local and regional perspectives, and the interplay between the two, in order to establish in principle the possibility and the importance of dealing with both. We learned very well not to overlook the forest for the trees on the local level; we need now to achieve this trick of perspective on the regional level and duplicate through serious scholarship that feat which sophisticated Papua New Guineans seem to perform so easily.

Notes

1. The fieldwork on which this essay is based was carried out during three different visits to Papua New Guinea: October 1969 to April 1971, August and October 1976, and the summer of 1977. These trips were sponsored by the National Institute of Mental Health (Fellowship FO1 MH45391, Grant TO1 MH1229), by Princeton University, and by the National Science Foundation (Grant BNS76-83844), respectively. I was assisted during the first and last trips by Mary Taylor Huber and also in 1977 by Elliott Lee of Princeton University and Anton Gois of the University of Papua New

Guinea. For access to Kreer Camp, Wewak, and the people of Koil, I owe a large debt to Mary Taylor Huber, who maintained a house in Kreer and conducted ethnographic fieldwork in Wewak during 1976–77. The present paper represents a major revision of a paper presented at the American Anthropological Association meetings in Washington, D.C., in 1980. For critical reading of the present manuscript and for helpful suggestions, I am grateful to Margaret Williamson.

2. See also Wagner (1976), whose work introduced me to the notion of "precipitation" and greatly influenced my development of this line of thought.

3. The Anggor-speakers number slightly less than a thousand and are distributed unevenly among twelve villages located on the eastern slopes of the Border Mountains, north and east of the Dio (Faringi) River. This area is between Amanab and Green River Posts in the West Sepik Province. They practice mixed horticulture and silviculture, focusing on sago and *tulip*, heavily supplemented by taro, yams, and bananas. The social system is essentially encompassed by the village, which is divided into named patrilineal exoga-

mous groups. These matters are reported in some detail elsewhere (Huber 1975, 1978, 1979) and are mentioned only in passing here because they are not directly relevant to the matter in hand.

4. I stress "combination" because the syllables which compose sahwaf need not actually be uttered for the spell to work; just thinking of them is sufficient.

5. The same observations can be made of sahwaf. They do not enter into this discussion because they constitute a separate category, but also because local information on sahwaf is limited and regional information virtually nil.

6. Consider, for example, Le Roy Ladurie's remarkable study (1974) of the ebb and flow of populace, religion, social life, and money into rural Languedoc from the eleventh to the eighteenth century. It is grounded, of course, in written records—notably the *compoix* land registers for taxation purposes. But such movements as he describes leaves traces of other kinds—buildings and settlement sites, ecological deformations, distributions of style and, indeed, of religion.

12/ The Power of Culture and the Culture of Power

Anthony Forge

Are some cultures more successful than others? Apologizing in advance to the affected peoples and their ethnographers, I suggest that the Abelam have been more successful than their neighbors. The first question to be addressed is, of course, what is meant by success. Historians who write on the grand scale speak, if an invasion is successful, of the strengths of invaders and the weakness of the invaded, but of course they have the advantage of hindsight. In history there seems to be no criterion but survival. In the Sepik we have little recorded history, but the broad outline of the major population moves over the last few hundred years is fairly obvious. Wherever they originally come from, Ndu-family groups, among them those now known as the Abelam, came up from the Middle Sepik, probably creating the *kunai* plains by inappropriate cultivation methods. It seems likely that the groups now known as the Boiken, in the east, and the Kwanga, in the west, came up earlier and the Abelam later. Both Boiken and Kwanga live at lower density than the Abelam and are less closely related in language and culture than they are to the Sawos and the Iatmul. The Boiken went over the ranges down to the coast, but the Kwanga only approached the southern fall of the coastal mountains. Tuzin (1976) reports that some Kwanga clans were incorporated into Ilahita, which again suggests that such groups preceded the Abelam as inhabitants of that area. The Abelam stopped in the southern foothills of the Prince Alexander Range, leaving the Plains Arapesh with a thin band of villages on the upper southern fall of the range, very thin populations in tiny villages in the unpromising environment of the mountaintop (Mead's Mountain Arapesh), and larger villages on the northern fall of the range down to the coast. This latter group (Mead's Coastal Arapesh) seems to have made very little use of the seaside environment, turning the backs of its houses to the sea, disliking the sand, and so on (Mead 1938). Although the northern Abelam villages do not seem to have been making any further major attempts to expand higher into the mountains, the southwestern Abelam, known as

the Wosera, were still expanding to the west, into relatively lightly populated Kwanga areas. During the first decades of this century, they were also maintaining a degree of expansionist pressure on the Ilahita Arapesh and associated groups. The village of Ilahita, with a population density similar to that of the Abelam area to its south, seems to have formed a successful redoubt against further expansion in this direction (Tuzin 1976).

The crudest of the criteria of success is biological survival. Not only have the Abelam survived, but there seems to be reasonable evidence of population increase despite the fact that they inhabit the only confirmed area of holoendemic malaria on the island of New Guinea. Their infant mortality rate, before malaria control, was of the order of 450–500 per thousand (Peters 1960), a figure confirmed by the more extensive research of Schofield and Parkinson (1963). No doubt the holoendemicity was created by their population size and density, but the point is that there seems no sign that the population was declining; in fact, the opposite was the case. Kaberry (1957) gives the population of Kalabu village on the basis of her own total survey as 489 in 1940.[1] After a very hard time during the Japanese occupation and subsequent liberation, during which the Japanese executed a group of Kalabu men, the same collectivity of hamlets was enumerated at 633 in November 1958, before there were any effective malaria-control measures or much in the way of local medical services. This is a very high rate of increase, but Kaberry's census is certainly accurate, and the 1958 census patrol was more likely to get a low figure than a high one because taxation was known to be in the offing. This one village figure is the only one I know of from before the war. Kaberry's estimate of the total Abelam population in 1940 of twelve thousand is impossibly low, although the number of Abelam villages she gives ("about sixty") is about half the correct figure. In 1958 there were approximately thirty thousand Abelam, and with effective malaria control and gradually improving medical services the annual population growth rate averaged 4 percent, as opposed to the 1.8 percent suggested by the Kalabu figures before medical services were available. I have no intention of generalizing statistically from one village, but its experience is consistent with the history of villages known to me. Despite malaria and very severe warfare, the Abelam population as a whole was increasing before any effective colonial intervention, which took place for the northern Abelam in October 1937 with the founding of Maprik station.

The Abelam preferred the yam as a staple, although it was not usually available year-round. They devoted a great deal of energy and ingenuity to the growing of cultivars of the two main species *Dioscorea alata* and *D. esculenta*. These species were also cultivated by their neighbors, although the Arapesh villages to the northeast gave more attention to certain taro varieties. However, the Abelam were generally acknowledged to be supreme cultivators of the yam in the area. They had also discovered or developed a cultivar of *D. esculenta* called *asagwaka* which will tolerate saturated ground and even survive quite long periods under flood, thus enabling villages in the Wosera to make use of the fertile river flats to cultivate yams with very high returns. This appears to be an original development; I am not aware of any other reports of water-tolerant yams of any species. The botanical wisdom is that yam tubers rot when they come into contact with saturated soil, and indeed most Abelam cultivars do; elaborate techniques are used to drain the holes in which the long yams are planted. Lea (1964) has reported on the highly developed technology of yam cultivation and some measures of its very high productivity. The point I wish to make is that the Abelam, it would seem, must have initially acquired both the genetic material and the basic techniques of cultivation of yams from their neighbors but then developed both to a superior productivity and adaptability that enables them to live at a higher population density on not particularly good soils.[2] Not only was Abelam productivity greater, exceeding the FAO's standard figures (based mainly on West African and West Indian data), but according to Lea's figures some of their cultivars may have substantially higher protein content than the generally accepted values for yams.

Abelam cultivation practices for yams were under continuous pressure for refinement because of the vital role of exchange in the overall political economy. Up to 80 percent of a man's production would have to be publicly displayed and initially presented to exchange partners, affines, and matrilateral kin, and subsequently yams were included in village presentations to other villages, both allied and enemy. The public evaluation of each man's abilities in a series of competitive arenas undoubtedly contributed both to the overwhelming interest in yams, involving ritual and aesthetic factors, and to the development of a very intensive yam cultivation technology.[3] Unfortunately, there has been no published follow-up research on either the technology or the nutritional status of Abelam yams. Specimens collected by the U.S. Department of Agriculture are said to have yielded very promising results (Martin 1974), while other specimens taken to the Department of Agriculture, Stock and Fisheries test gardens in Lae were, after the director suffered a heart attack, mainly eaten by the convicts employed to cultivate them, though promising results had been obtained before this unhappy event.

Although, of course, the Abelam had no political unity, they were conscious of their culture as distinct from those of their neighbors. They recognized several dialects within their area and an almost continuous variation between villages, mainly conceptualized as differences in ritual, art, and yam-growing practices but also including what anthropologists would regard (although Abelam did not) as major differences in marriage practice and even kinship terminology. Their distinctness from the Arapesh, called by them Bugi, was always very obvious in their radically distinct languages, but they also distinguished themselves very clearly from other Ndu-family groups, regarding both the Kwanga and the Boiken and most of the Bugi as having only partial and inferior versions of Abelam ritual.

To the south the population density falls very sharply, and the widely dispersed villages of the kunai plains form a very wide transition zone between what we call Abelam and what we call Sawos, with, as far as I can make out, substantial variation between villages. The language too seems to change gradually, and Abelam going south for trade had little difficulty in making themselves understood even as far as the river. Even Sawos villages such as Aulimbit, within a few miles of the Sepik River, used Abelam motifs mixed with those of Iatmul origin for the decoration of their tambaran houses and displayed a healthy interest in yams and their cultivation. Thus Abelam influence could now be said to extend right across the plains.

From the distribution and sizes of villages in the Abelam area and its surroundings, it is obvious not only that the Abelam were living at a higher overall density but also that their villages were in general larger than those of their neighbors. I have argued (Forge 1972a) that there is a normative factor operating in such egalitarian cultivating societies that tends to produce a group of around a hundred fifty to two hundred as the basic political unit. Therefore these large villages require explanation. Among the Abelam the "ritual group," the prime unit of social intercourse and cooperation as well as the group which staged all ritual, was of this size, but most of the large Abelam villages consisted of two or three such groups. This amalgamation was clearly an artifact of warfare, the village being a defensive but not necessarily an offensive unit. In the Mamblep region northwest of Maprik station, most of the Abelam population was in a valley running up into the mountains and unthreatened by enemies except from the valley entrance, where the large villages of Apangai and Chiginangu stand. Inside the valley all the villages were single ritual groups and of the appropriate population size. For the rest of the Abelam, however, a single ritual group as a residential and defensive unit was in grave danger and either joined another village or was soon dispersed by warfare.

The large defensive units and high overall density undoubtedly made the Abelam efficient in warfare. The ability of ritual groups to live in the necessary close proximity for shared defense, without any form of centralized organization, was dependent on relationships expressed by vast exchanges of yams. There were also rules that allowed the expression of aggressive passions within the village by brawling between groups with clubs but not with spears. The distinction between aggressive yam exchange, which allowed alliance to continue, and war or feud is summed up in the Abelam contrast between *wi cambera* "those with whom we exchange spears," and *wapi cambera* "those with whom we exchange yams." The villages of the immediate neighbors of the Abelam are also sometimes larger, the most outstanding example being Ilahita, although Yamil to the northeast is also large. Ilahita is the only one for which we have a detailed study, and it is clear that here at least the principles that hold together the six wards are somewhat different from those typical of Abelam (Tuzin 1976). The point here is that the whole Abelam social organization contained elements which allowed several ritual groups to live in close proximity, thus forming a continuing large group effective for defense and often offense as well. Village warriors would collectively sweep the areas of gardens and the routes to them every morning to forestall ambush, and every man would turn out for a formal fight following a challenge by another village. This latter was, however, a public event and called for several days of preparation. The majority of casualties were inflicted by ambush, dawn raids on single hamlets, and other small-scale actions that required small groups recruited from only segments of a village and were carried out in great secrecy, sometimes against the interests of other members of the same village (Forge 1970a). All kills were, however, totaled and balanced on the basis of the village alone.

Abelam thus were in a better posture for war than most of their neighbors, and even though the majority of Abelam fought only against other Abelam, at the borders the pressure on neighbors to withdraw from the dense area of fighting Abelam, and thus allow expansion, must have been great and continuous. This process was still continuing until the late thirties and resumed as soon as the Japanese withdrew in 1945. In the Wosera, in particular, the densely packed central villages were putting great pressure on the western ones, which were in turn forcing back Kwanga groups to the west and the north. Areas of high density were expanding and areas of low density being compressed, producing a general redistribution of population density. It was always the Abelam who generated the high density which their social organization and exchange system could accommodate effectively and their yam and other productive technologies, as they gradually developed, permitted. Abelam villages therefore, if they did not have any advantage in warfare among themselves, had a decided advantage over their non-Abelam neighbors.

Effectiveness in warfare and skill in growing yams, particularly the phallic long yams, were in local terms merely the material manifestations of a more fundamental Abelam domination, that of power conceived essentially in magical and ritual terms. The Abelam were admired and feared for what was believed to be superior access to supernatural power in all forms and the concrete expression of this command of power in rituals, buildings, and an immense range of objects, decorations, and styles loosely classifiable as "art." In Sepik terms, it was the Abelam's superior access to supernatural power that made their long yams longer, their gardens more productive, and their occupation of land previously the undoubted property of others so conclusive. All their neighbors copied Abelam styles in ceremonial houses, decorations of man and yam, and overall ritual performances. For 10 to 15 miles from the western, northern, and eastern borders of the Abelam, all villages, whatever their language and culture, build ceremonial houses that look like Abelam houses, carve figures that look like Abelam figures, and so on. Farther from the border, the Abelam influences die away, although other aspects of the local cult remain. For instance, around Yangoru, Boiken have cults whose fundamental content is similar to those of Boiken on the Abelam border but whose figures, decorations, wealth items, and so on, are very different in form. Transfer of forms is undoubtedly significant, but transfer of names too presents an interesting pattern; almost all Abelam words are very closely related to Iatmul words and have the same range of meanings. Thus *wapi/wabi* refers in Abelam to long yams but in Central Iatmul to long flutes— not the sort of identity of meaning that linguists like, but since both objects are the central phallic objects of a cult from which women are excluded, an anthropologist can claim an identity of sense at least.[4] The only major ritual word I know in Abelam that has no cognate in Iatmul is *wala*. The word *wala* is used for a class of spirits conceived of as living in and controlling a specific territory, the only Abelam spirits with an essentially local tie. All other Abelam spirits are owned by a group of people, a clan, and go where the clan goes. Wala are also owned by a clan— indeed, there are no spirits that have a larger field of operation than a clan among the Abelam—but only by virtue of that clan's control of the land they inhabit. Wala are not represented in art (although they are associated with some of the basketry masks), but among the Arapesh immediately to the north of the northern Abelam (Mead's Plains Arapesh) the major spirit of each clan is called *walihas* and is represented in painting and carving exactly as are the Abelam *nggwalndu*. The wala of the Abelam are, I would suggest, possibly taken over from previous Arapesh occupiers of the land (see also Mead[1933–34]; the ending *-has* is a plural form [Fortune 1942]). Among the Ilahita Arapesh, however, the major spirits have not only the Abelam form but the Abelam name *nggwal*, a name cognate with the Iatmul *nggwail*, both meaning "father's father"; in Arapesh the word has no meaning apart from the class of spirit (Tuzin 1980).

Abelam ritual dominance of their immediate neighbors was not only a matter of copying, although that was certainly prominent particularly in art styles. Rights to hold ritual, objects to serve as the focus of secret ceremonies, ritual paraphernalia, spells, and instructions for ceremonies were sold to neighbors for many pigs and shellring wealth items. The sales were sometimes outright, but more usually attempts were made to "lease" ritual complexes and claim payment each time they were staged. Abelam were very cynical about this process. They did not consider that they were selling anything of real supernatural value, since they always left out parts that they considered vital but that were not publicly visible and, most important, they never parted with the secret formulae by which the nggwalndu were addressed or their secret names.[5] In fact, since all spirits are clan-related it would be impossible in theory for those not in the patriline to have access to such spirits. However, in contrast to Abelam theory, both my figures from 1958–59 and Kaberry's (1957) for 1939–40 show that only just over half of the adult men were actually members of the same subclan as their fathers, and patrilineality was by no means sacrosanct in practice. In sum, the access to the spirits to which Abelam attribute all prosperity and success cannot be said to be dependent on being born into the correct patriline. Attitudes toward this trade and export of ceremonial perhaps best illustrate Abelam views of their neighbors. Before considering the export of ritual, however, we must look at the internal trade.

Certainly during this century, a period for which I feel I have reasonably good documentation, the Abelam have been in a ferment of creation in ritual and art. New forms of ritual and hence social organization have spread across the Abelam area, along with changes in art style. For example, a *kumun/kwain* moiety system spread from the east, becoming fully assimilated in the Wingei/Bengragum/Sagisi area but only partially assimilated (being used to refer to groups that could be otherwise defined) in the Naramko/Yanuko region. This moiety system probably originated farther east and is reported by Mead (1938) among the Arapesh, although here again it does not appear to be of much importance. A new organization of the half-generation grades in the initiation system had been accepted in Gwalip about the time of white control and was tried out for the first time in Wambundu in 1959 at a ritual that I was able to attend. This new system, considered a great success, was regarded as rather "kinky" in that it involved sons' beating their fathers at one stage of the initiation. Again, the northern Abelam marriage system, permitting sister exchange and based on a six-shell-ring bridewealth, seems to have been slowly spreading to the southeast and southwest, replacing the asymmetrical system and the twenty-four-ring bridewealth. In art, the eastern style of sculpture changed radically around the turn of the century from one in which major carvings were essentially assemblages of elements with many pairs of opposed hooks (Forge 1973) to one that was essentially anthropomorphic. This change seems to have come from the west. In Kalabu village, now, at least, the home of the anthropomorphic style in its most classic form, Brigitta Hauser-Schäublin has recently been shown a carving in an old style which, while not the same as the old style in the east, is much more like it in conception than it is to the current style (personal communication). The flat-painting style of the east apparently did not change at the same time as the carving style. Some tentative changes were tried in the late fifties, but when a whole facade of a ceremonial house badly executed in what was meant to be the northern Abelam style was judged a disaster, further innovation in flat-painting style was discouraged.

Other changes were also taking place, though they are difficult to document in detail. What is certain is that a great deal of change in ritual and social organization was typical of the Abelam in the period of my informants' memories and no doubt long before that too. Much of this was fashion, the spread of more elaborate initiation systems at least in part motivated by a desire not to have a simple system while one's neighbors had a more complex one. It seems to me that there was also, however, a good deal of purposive change and microadaptation of the cultural and social apparatus available to the Abelam, who at the same time were expanding territorially and growing in numbers and in the number of their settlements— all processes that naturally tended to produce diversity. These changes passing between villages within the Abelam took place regardless of the state of warfare or alliance between contiguous villages. Ritual required truce, and enemies were essential participants (Forge 1966); further, the "roads" through which the big men obtained magical paint for yam growing and sorcery passed through enemy villages as well as those of allies (Forge 1962, 1970a). The process of transfer involved several factors. The major clan spirits, the nggwalndu or *cakindu* (nggwal is the public name) have, across the whole Abelam territory, only a very limited number of names

which constantly recur, and consequently neighboring villages will always have several clans that have the same major nggwalndu names. Whether nggwalndu that have the same names but are associated with clans in different villages that trace no sort of connection with each other are in any sense ultimately the same nggwalndu is a knotty problem to which neither I nor the Abelam can offer any definitive solution; basically some sort of identity is assumed if the occasion suits and denied if it does not. However, the same basic system of clan-based supernatural powers and the frequency of the same names undoubtedly helped in the transmission of ritual knowledge and esoteric practice between Abelam villages. Further, the initiation system allows youths and men to be initiated in ritual groups other than their own provided that their sponsors pay. This payment in itself confers rights in the ceremony on the initiated, who can initiate others in subsequent ceremonies. In these ways virtually perfect transmission of ritual innovations can take place.

In the export of ritual, either as items or as whole complexes, to members of other cultures mundane matters are very different. In addition, the conceptions of the spirits themselves and their relationship to the groups that claim them are unlikely to be the same.[6] The arrangements are made between villages and have a contractual form requiring long negotiation between big men. The sums demanded were very high, including large quantities of high-quality food while the work was being undertaken and a large number of pigs and shell rings of the finest type at the end of the ritual. Abelam attention centered on the preparation of the display, usually consisting of carving and painting but also including such things as basketry masks, headdresses, and other ornaments. Before contact most of the work of preparation was done in the selling village itself; this not only was safer but also helped to strengthen the sellers' view that what was being sold was the actual objects, not the right to reproduce them or the techniques and ritual of their manufacture. When all was ready the *maira* (a general Abelam term that corresponds to tambaran) were carried to the purchasers by an immense war party that devastated property along its way, cutting down young trees, raiding gardens, damaging fences, and even, according to some accounts, burning houses. At the outskirts of the receiving village the spearmen would throw their spears at a selected group of recipients chosen for their ability to dodge. The whole party would then sweep up to the ceremonial ground, throwing the remains of their pillage into the houses as they passed. These ritualized aggressions are typical of all ritual cooperation and aid between villages and occurred between Abelam villages as well. They were, however, intensified by the importance of what was being transported and in the case of the export of a whole major ceremony would have been very marked. The delivery having been made in a way that impressed everyone with the power of the objects being transferred, the whole party might stay and participate in the following ceremonials and dances, eating copiously and seducing its hosts' women, or simply collect its payment and leave.

In these transactions the Abelam did not consider that they were losing control of any supernatural power or giving anyone else control of any. Although all the preparations were done under full Abelam ritual conditions and taboos and in the name of the nggwalndu of the preparers, to whom the pigs they received were also dedicated, the release of the supernatural power engendered by the process of preparation took place outside the sphere of the nggwalndu operations, and it was inconceivable that one's nggwalndu could benefit strangers; they were in fact much more likely to do them harm. From the Abelam's point of view, they made objects which, when complete, were charged with power, but the recipients did not know how to use the power and were more likely to be damaged than blessed by the result. Some Abelam ritual experts conceded that in time Arapesh would learn how to use Abelam art and ceremonies to strengthen their own spirits and thus in the long run would get real benefit from their purchases. Yet because not all the spells and invocations had been transferred, they were certain that the full ceremonial power of their own rituals could not be equaled outside their own village.

I have endeavored to show that the Abelam have been not only successful but more successful than their neighbors. I have done this mainly in terms of the ability of the Abelam to maintain higher population density and larger villages, which requires a flexible social organization that uses equality-seeking exchange in preference to lineal principles (Forge 1972b). It also requires a more efficient productive system. With these materialist virtues the Abelam were able to push back their neighbors, who also accepted from the Abelam a view of Abelam ritual as intrinsically superior. These features combine to produce what

one might call a form of cultural domination that perhaps also manifests itself in another example I have not mentioned. Abelam wealth items were polished shell rings cut from huge shells of giant clam (*Tridacna gigas*) (Bühler 1957, Gardi 1958). The whole system of exchange and marriage, as well as payments for ritual services, depended on these shell rings, for which every Abelam, male or female, had an unending and insatiable lust. The rings were produced exclusively by a group of six small Arapesh villages and traded down to the Abelam in exchange for pigs. These Arapesh villages, which were not on the border with the Abelam, obtained the raw materials by means of long trade routes over the mountains and down to the coast and offshore islands. These villages had developed a ring-cutting and -polishing technology that gave them an effective monopoly. The villages, however, considered themselves totally dependent on the Abelam, and when I visited them at a time when they were having difficulties with shell supplies, they bemoaned their fate, seeing themselves as in danger of never eating pork again because of their inability to make enough rings. They nevertheless continued to behave very deferentially to those Abelam they visited with such rings as they could make and never suggested that because there was a shortage of rings the "price" of rings in terms of pigs should rise. This behavior is in our economic terms a complete misunderstanding of the "true" situation. These Arapesh villages and their ring production were essential for the long-term maintenance of the whole Abelam political and economic system. (Rings were also used as wealth by some of the immediate Arapesh neighbors of the Abelam but not by the Boiken, Sawos, or Iatmul.) The ring makers, however, could almost certainly have eaten more pork if they had diverted their labor into pig-food production and pig rearing and abandoned rings altogether. This failure to make any attempt to exploit their monopoly situation seems typical of the effect the Abelam had on their neighbors.[7]

If we admit that some cultures are more successful than others, in whatever terms, how are we to explain this? I have said that Abelam yam cultivation was more productive and efficient than that of their neighbors. Yet that cannot be due to anything they brought with them in the material sense, since they came from areas that were unsuitable for anything but the most amateur yam cultivation and could not have supported anything like the recent Abelam numbers. It is worth emphasizing that Abelam population expansion must have been very large and must taken place more or less where they are today. We have no accurate idea of how long all these movements took, but I would guess that Abelam occupation of their present area is only a matter of a few hundreds of years, with an absolute maximum of a thousand. Whatever the time period, it was within this limit that the Abelam took what their neighbors had and improved it. Similar considerations apply to the form of houses, both ceremonial and domestic; nothing like the Abelam form of house occurs to the south, either on the river or along the southern tributaries and in the hill country right up to the mountain wall. Abelam houses look like their neighbors' houses, yet Abelam ceremonial houses are bigger, often much bigger; they are more daringly raked forward and better-built, but in construction they are just a better version of the local type. In the case of houses we can say that the Abelam brought something with them, as I have argued before. Although Abelam and Iatmul ceremonial houses do not look alike, they are homologous at a more abstract level; that is, their symbolic functions and ritual forms are virtually identical (Forge 1966). One can also assume that in general outline the forms of social organization that I have argued were crucial to Abelam success came with them, as in many respects they were very similar to those reported from the Iatmul and other Ndu-family riverain groups. The major difference in social organization was the great intensification of exchange activities, obviously related to the development of the yam cult and the use of yam growing as a major means of acquiring and expressing prestige and hence political influence. I suspect that the Abelam's lack of respect for patrilineality as practice while they maintained it as ideology, found by both Kaberry and myself, is also more in evidence than among river groups. This certainly also contributed to the flexibility of Abelam on-the-ground dispositions and hence, I would argue, to their success.

In looking for possible explanations I shall start with a selection of materialist types. It would seem that any based on a simple conception of ecological systems as determinant are not very promising. The Abelam were occupying land previously used by those they displaced. The tool kits were identical, and the ancestors of the yam cultivars the Abelam used must have been initially acquired, together with the techniques of their cultivation, from the expropriated. I have of course assumed that the Abelam were under considerable "pressure" from rising population and,

perhaps, degraded garden lands to their south to intensify their horticultural practice; but surely the pressure must have been at least as great on the original occupants, who were losing ground as well as suffering increased population density as the displacement proceeded. As to political structures, it is difficult to see any substantial difference in the ability of big men to mobilize and control effective groups when comparing the Abelam with any reports of their neighbors. My impression from visits to many Plains Arapesh villages is that Arapesh had fewer big men per capita and on that measure may be presumed to have had a more effective leadership system. Certainly during the Japanese period and the postwar colonialist period, the only leaders in the area who had influence beyond their villages were Arapesh (individuals such as Loui, Simogun, and Pita Lus).

Again, although this must be subjective, it is difficult to see any particular group within Abelam society that could be said to have been exploited by anyone else on any consistent basis. Young men, after the ending of fighting, were in daily life a conspicuously leisured group, but in the preparation of ritual they worked very hard and consistently. It is, again, true that women did more work than men on the cultivation of domestic gardens and the rearing of pigs. If, however, one includes work in men's ritual yam garden, which contributed almost nothing to food but a great deal to technology, and men's huge ritual activities, the balance is restored. Whatever external authorities may think, there is no doubt that Abelam, both men and women, regarded these ritual activities as essential. Any attempt at numerical accounting in comparison between men and women can, in any case, only be indicative at best. Abelam male/female relations seem on the whole complementary and not markedly exploitive, and I have the impression that Arapesh women were more dominated. Events, I would suggest, even if dismissable as anecdotes, may tell us much. For instance, Tuzin (1980:21–23) gives an account of the honeymoon after Ilahita marriage which I do not question; yet on January 26, 1963, two freshly married Ilahita couples arrived in the northern Wosera village of Kwanimbandu, where the husbands set up a brothel in the empty government officer's patrol shelter and for three days their wives accommodated all the young bucks from the surrounding villages at two shillings a time, collected by their husbands. Such behavior by Abelam husbands was unthinkable. It may, of course, be just one of the benefits of civilization that the Abelam will eventually acquire; but certainly at that time Abelam women's bodies were their own to dispose of, sometimes in spite of their husbands. Another incident from the same village at much the same time illustrates this: A Protestant schoolboy caught *in flagrante delicto* by a husband was ordered by the village councillor to compensate the husband by the payment of three pounds; the wife openly gave her lover two pounds toward this on the ground that she had encouraged him and much enjoyed herself.

In short, I doubt that any case can be made for the Abelam's being more "advanced" in any Marxist sense than their neighbors; in fact, probably less real power over others in economic or political terms was vested in any individual or group among the Abelam than among their neighbors. The Abelam ritual system, as does the Iatmul, specifically excluded old men who had completed a full cycle as initiators from further ritual activity, thus preventing any chance of development of a gerontocratic system (Forge 1970*b*). The Abelam system of balance at every level, from the often very small subclan of a few adult men up to an alliance of villages capable of mobilizing three or four hundred men for a massive hostile exchange, staging an important ritual, or fighting a set battle, both limited the ability of any one big man continuously to hold together a large group of followers and permitted flexibility in responding to changes and opportunities in both ecological and social spheres. This flexibility was manifested in the many ways in which subclans could combine in different activities; for instance, a subclan would share landownership with other subclans of the same clan but be in opposition to them and allied with others in the ritual organization, presenting yams to each other in some exchange contexts but uniting to present yams to other groups in other contexts. In addition, the very free view taken of the patrilineal principle in recruiting group members and the use of exchange at every level to establish, maintain, or terminate relationships also promoted a responsive form of social organization. However, all was not anarchy; in the performance of major ritual the normally fluid organization crystallized, and the whole of the ritual group assumed, for the ritual season, the appearance of a textbook segmentary lineage system, with every man's actions determined by the purest of agnatic principles. Nor was this pretense; the fact that a man had been born into a particular subclan was irrelevant in comparison with the fact that he was at this major ritual behaving as a full member of that subclan, called by a name owned by the subclan, and working in the name of the subclan's nggwalndu. The practice of Abelam social organization was highly flexible, with the redistribution of men to exploit the available resources and maintain balance ensured by constant exchange. Major ritual, however, made the practice coincident with the ideology, and the sociology of that ritual group became perfect in terms of Abelam's beliefs about what their society should be. Major ritual could be successfully organized only if the component groups were more or less in balance at every level. In a real sense, such ritual returned Abelam society to a renewed original ideal state, and since the ritual would always have included the building of at least one new ceremonial house, the newness was physically expressed in a manner that dominated the settlement.

I mean "original" in the sense of "perfect," including, for instance, the absence of death. In 1959, a few days before the ritual climax of the most important ceremony at Kwimbu *amei* (ceremonial ground), Wingei village, I left the ritual ground, for once comparatively quiet, at dawn and met a man all alone dragging the body of his wife to the cemetery. She had died the previous evening, and the fact was simply not being acknowledged by anyone; there was no mourning, and her natal kin had refused to have anything to do with her burial, which they would ordinarily have performed, even though by so doing they abandoned all possibility of receiving the very substantial mortuary payment that was theirs by right. A death, as a sign of spiritual disfavor, should in fact have aborted the whole ceremony, but at such a time the momentum of the months of preparation and the immense stock of spiritual power waiting for release at the final ceremony made an interruption impossible.

The Abelam and their neighbors had no doubt where the secret of Abelam strength lies, and I have only looked at materialist theories in deference to their current popularity as explanatory mechanisms. With the Abelam, I believe that the secret of their success can only be ultimately located in that complex of beliefs, classifications, rituals, attitudes, and social relationships that we call their culture and, more particularly, in their ritual, which I take to be in much of its content a commentary on and distillation of the culture as a whole, a sort of metaculture. I have already made various attempts to analyze the "meanings" conveyed by or implicit in various parts of the art and ritual. Two of the very fundamental themes are the essential nature of men and women and the relation between violence and peace, and I shall concentrate on those.

The Abelam were an extremely violent people; warfare was chronic, and casualty rates appear to have been very high. Although such measures are full of danger, it appears that about 30 percent of deaths in the first ascendant generation from that of my mature adult informants in 1958 were killings by enemies. Such deaths are very likely better-remembered, but even so the rate of killing must have been very high. This figure is based on the complete genealogies of Bengragum village, and there is no reason to suppose that fighting was more frequent or intense there than anywhere else. Training boys to violence was considered essential, but this necessity started from the assumption that the will to kill had to be induced by cultural practice. Initiations into the various stages of the tambaran cult involved very little overt instruction in anything, although the initiates were beaten and rubbed with nettles at most stages. Puberty initiations for both boys and girls involved severe beatings, running the gauntlet carried by a mother's brother, and seclusion. Boys' seclusion was said to have been for up to two months, but nothing like the continuous bullying reported for the Iatmul took place (Bateson 1936), nor was there any scarification (although there was for girls). Boys were taught to bleed their penes and received instruction in a wide variety of male behavior including warfare, but the main purpose was to impress on them the importance of observing sex and other taboos and to fatten and strengthen them for their triumphant return to the village and reintegration into society. Actual training to kill was given in more secular contexts, both in pig hunting and in the actual killing of an unarmed refugee within the village. If it was decided to kill such a person, a group of unfledged young men would be assembled and instructed by older men. Usually the attack would take place in a garden where the refugee was working for his host. The attackers were expected to be horrified by what they had done and were treated with bespelled ginger and other magical substances to strengthen them and "heat their bellies" so that they could kill again.

The tambaran cult was full of symbols of male aggression and explicit and implicit identification of spear and phallus, but it also identified the phallus as a nutritive organ, while the long-yam cult reinforced this identity on a vast scale by equating the phallus, the yam, and the nggwalndu (Forge 1966). In the east, at least, the penultimate ritual of the tambaran sequence was considered the most violent, and beatings and nettle rubbings were severe. It is said that for this ceremony a dead enemy was painted and decorated like the carvings and set up with them. The last ritual of the cycle and the most important was, however, referred to as *yigen maira* (good tambaran), although this fact was concealed from the initiates, who to their amazement were not beaten and were rubbed only with dead nettles. Although in this final ceremony of the series they had various tricks played on them, there was a marked absence of aggression and no violence. This was the climax of the whole cycle of rituals and the point at which a man became fully adult and qualified to attend any ritual anywhere. The initiates were led to expect exactly the opposite of what they actually received. They had experienced increasingly dramatic, prolonged, and violent rituals during the rest of the cycle. At the end they found that the true nature of the nggwalndu was "good"—that violence, while necessary, was not an essential part of the ultimate nature of spiritual power.

The physical presence of women or their emanations was considered inimical to the performance of all tambaran ritual and to the cultivation of long yams; the reasons, however, were rather different in the two cases. In growing long yams, men were producing immense phallic symbols with which they identified very closely; to transfer their own virility successfully, it was believed, they had not only to preserve their own sexual power but also to scrupulously avoid any contact with aroused female sexuality. (An adulterous wife who served her husband food would ruin his yams.) In tambaran ritual, however, the men were in a "female" phase; they were imitating women's reproductive role, constructing a womb which contained their deepest secrets from which the initiates emerged streaked with the blood of rebirth. Until the initiates were reborn, the men observed a rigid taboo on sexual contact; in this case the rationale appears to have been that natural female sexuality would destroy the males' cultural creation of female sexuality. As soon as the initiation display had been seen, the all-night dances started, and vigorous sexuality was very much in evidence. Abelam men were not taught to be frightened of women, nor did any of their cults induce initiates to treat women with contempt, as Tuzin (1980) has reported for Ilahita. It is true that mothers sometimes warned their sons that leaving their semen in strange women rendered them liable to a devastating form of sorcery, but men did not seem to take this danger very seriously, and it certainly had no effect on their actions. Further, although women were physically excluded from ritual, I was told by senior men everywhere in Abelam territory that women knew all about the rituals because at least the senior ones attended them in the form of invisible flying witches (*kutagwa*). It is perhaps worth pointing out that to achieve their object, the male sex taboos required that women observe an equally stringent sex taboo for the same period, and it appears that they did.[8]

If we compare these aspects of Abelam ritual and art with Tuzin's admirably detailed reports from Ilahita, several points of interest emerge: the Abelam nggwalndu never required any killing within the village and was in the end revealed not to be essentially violent; the Ilahita nggwal does require intravillage killing and in the end is associated with death not just by physical violence but by sorcery as well. Abelam rituals imitated female reproduction and excluded women but did not even play at setting up womanless societies or encourage a low valuation of women; Ilahita rituals centrally promote sexual antagonism and do not appear to be based on the imitation of female reproduction, even though their overt forms and displays are very similar to those of the Abelam. In short, if for a moment we take Ilahita ritual as an imitation of Abelam, it has all the external form and little of the inner substance; the real core of Abelam ritual "meanings" has not been transferred but has been replaced by a new core that is an extrapolation from the apparent implications of the overt actions shared by both Abelam and Ilahita rituals.

I have argued that the Abelam symbolic system was peculiarly satisfying both in terms of social function and in the identification it provided for individual men, and it is at this level, I suggest, that we should look for the reason for Abelam success: their moral ascendancy over their neighbors and their superior morale. The symbolic system is efficient in directing aggressiveness outside the group and controlling aggression both between the sexes and between the component groups of the villages. My analysis and knowledge unfortunately apply only to the men; from what little I know of women's rituals, which really are effectively secret, they are certainly concerned with the management of sexuality and reproduction and are in that respect successful, since women show a great deal of confidence in the management of their sexual lives and no particular fear or hatred of men.

Abelam culture is in my view highly creative and innovative in both art and ritual; yet at a more abstract level, there are forms that Abelam share with other Ndu-family groups, notably the Iatmul and Sawos, which suggests that they brought into their present territory the basic orientation and beliefs about the fundamental nature of humanity that enabled them to respond more efficiently and with greater expressive vigor to the opportunities they found as they moved north. In this case, at least, it is precisely the members of the society that invests the most time, energy, and resources in ritual and art who are the most effective in materialist terms (the same might be said of the Iatmul), and it is in that society that we must look for the explanation. The conclusion that not all cultures are equally effective seems inescapable. We can add perhaps that if ritual and its expressive aspects can be regarded in some essential sense as an indigenous analytical process that combines perceived truths about the actual environment with fundamental beliefs about humanity, then it is understandable that the development of expressive systems that strike deep into the individual as well as serving the needs of society effectively embeds the individual in the culture, and if the symbolic systems remain both responsive to the changing situation and coherent to those who employ them, the culture will be more powerful than cultures that fail in this respect. In short, using the power of culture can produce a culture of power.

Notes

1. Kaberry completed a reanalysis of her Abelam data in October 1957 for a projected book to be edited by K. E. Read. She very kindly gave me a copy of this mimeographed paper before I left for my first visit to the Abelam later that year. As she says, this paper was based on "a detailed analysis of genealogical and residential material" and in some respects superseded her earlier report. The published version of this important paper was revised to take into account census and other data I had brought back from my fieldwork. I prefer to use the 1957 preprint of this paper, since all the data are clearly based exclusively on the material available to her in 1939–40.

2. Tuzin (1976, 1980) assumes that the Arapesh learned yam cultivation from the Abelam. While it is possible, even likely, that the ritualization of yam production in Ilahita owes much to Abelam practices, the initial technology and the cultivars must, I argue, have come from the Arapesh.

3. Another area where the yam production is very largely displayed and presented is the Trobriands, also

famous for the quality of their yams and the quantity of
their production.

4. D. C. Laycock (personal communication) believes the two words to be etymologically unrelated.
Bateson (1936), however, cites a Iatmul myth in which
the sacred flutes are invented by a man blowing on a
yam, and there is much similar evidence to support this
identity.

5. Some nggwal names listed by Tuzin are the
same as Abelam names, of which there is not a large
stock, but this transfer of the open names does not occur in the east.

6. The following material is based mainly on my
experience of eastern Abelam relations with Plains Arapesh and Boiken. For a related trade further west, see
Scaglion (n.d.).

7. The Abelam also had to import virtually all the
volcanic stone needed for axes (another similarity with
the Trobriands) and, similarly, to maintain the economy trade was more important than war and therefore
cultural domination more vital than domination
through violence. Abelam exports were mainly prod-

ucts of their culture, men's ritual and women's string
bags equally admired by their neighbors and highly
valued both on the coast and on the Sepik River. Non-
Abelam women apparently believed themselves unable
to produce such complex string bags, some with as
many as forty-eight floating threads. The skills for their
production were closely guarded secrets of Abelam
women and had magical as well as technical elements;
only the completed objects were traded (MacKenzie
n.d.). More mundane and less important Abelam exports were hunting dogs and tobacco, both reputed to
have extra bite and power. There is no space here to go
into Abelam stone dependence or string bags, an essentially female product symbolically related to human
fertility. But bags were both "imitated" by men in their
ritual painting and an essential item for inauguration of
a new ceremonial house, clearly expressing the male
Abelam view that complementarity of the sexes was at
the root of all success (Forge 1962, 1966).

8. Losche, elsewhere in this volume, on the whole
confirms this view of the balance between male and female in Abelam life.

Part Three
Impact of the West

Introduction

Christian Kaufmann

Papua New Guinea, independent since 1975, and its Sepik provinces are of special interest to students of the change brought about by the worldwide expansion of Western industrial society. The Sepik area contains the historical extremes of externally induced change. Whereas the islands and coastal areas became part of the German empire soon after its formal establishment in 1884 and the Sepik River system and its natural and human resources were evaluated for commercial potential before 1914, other parts of the region remained clouds on administrative maps until the 1950s and '60s.

Political, social, and historical studies of change on the national (and, earlier, the colonial) level are reasonably comprehensive. However, for an adequate understanding of Sepik history, says the political scientist R. J. May, we need to know much more from the perspective of villages, clans, local movements, and individuals. The fundamental questions that now need to be raised and answered, according to May, include what regional differences there are in attitudes toward development and change and how these attitudes were formed. Who were the regional leaders? What were their goals? What did their movements, be they *kago* (cargo) or *bisnis*, achieve? What has been the success of regional and district-level institutions such as local government councils? And, finally, how does village-level organization relate to provincial structures and goals and to commercial activities and social developments on the national level?

Bryant Allen attempts to begin to answer some of these questions by examining the role of certain dynamic individuals in several villages of the Torricelli foothills from the beginning of colonial influence in the region up to the present. This is the stuff history is made of for the majority of twentieth-century rural people worldwide, but the situation is especially complex in the Sepik area because many different sources of power have been involved in a relatively short period of time: the traditional power associated with access to esoteric knowledge gained through rituals of male initiation, the German and Australian colonial administrations, the Japanese and Allied military commands during World War II, and,

since 1975, the authority of elected government officials at both provincial and national levels. Whereas in the past initiation systems maintained basic equality among males, the result of contact with the West has been permanent inequality in the relationships between the world of Sepik villagers and that of leaders in provincial and national politics and economic enterprise.

What were the assumptions on which the contact was based? The opposition between the European—in the case of the Sepik, predominantly Roman Catholic—ideology governing missionaries' activities and the necessity to lay the material foundations for the church's spiritual goals through practical work is the subject of Mary Taylor Huber's contribution. Seen from this angle, the Sepik frontier presented its own historical peculiarities, but the gap between the activities of the mind in designing a locally rooted church and the activities engaged in as means to that end proves just as wide here as elsewhere.

The discussion of the impact of Western values is taken a step farther by Michael French Smith in his study of the attitudes of certain villagers with regard to the kind of community social organization that might serve the ends of business. According to Smith, villagers on Kairiru Island believed that their economic performance would improve if they could achieve what they interpreted to be a European style of communal cooperation in commercial activities. Their loyalty to a system that combined adherence to residential and patrilineal social groups with membership in one or two (sometimes three) ceremonial divisions for ritual activities, marriage, exchange, etc., prevented them from achieving this ideal form of social organization. The romanticization of communitywide cooperation in the service of business may well have to be abandoned to help keep village communities alive. We might note in passing that studies of the performance of village-level cooperative societies in both Sepik provinces would bridge an important gap in the evaluation of Western impact on the region.

In a semipermanent village community far off the main communication routes of the Sepik, the history of Western impact is different. From T.

Wayne Dye's historical sketch of change in Wagu village—change that stemmed in part from his family's presence in the area over a thirty-year period as representatives of the Summer Institute of Linguistics—we may learn about some basic developments at the stage of early intense contact under a colonial administration. Tracing more recent developments, Dye describes the determination of a core of villagers from Wagu to bring about change, even at the price of causing some individuals to drift away to more remote places. As a further development we should note that intravillage solidarity seems to have gradually diminished. Personal physical well-being and economic success thus seem to have become more important to individuals than the spiritual coherence of the community under the umbrella of either traditional religion (in its recently revived form) or Christianity.

The impact of the West has, of course, also brought attempts to control or at least limit it. In a movement that gained force when Michael Somare, with members of his Pangu party and their allies, first came to power under the transitional regime of self-government in 1972, traditional cultural values and practices became sources of renewed self-esteem at the village level and new identities at the provincial and national levels. Such movements almost always face two difficult questions: what aspects of the traditional heritage are worthy of reinterpretation or revival and how new ways of thinking, producing, and living with traditional practices are to be adopted without losing either one's roots or one's vitality. Just how demanding it can be to take traditional values seriously may be gathered from Markus Schindlbeck's report on individuals in Kwanga society who still submit to the old system of initiation.

There are, of course, basic conflicts between ceremonial activities and *bisnis*. One solution seems to be to divide one's time between commercial work and ritual activities. The Kwanga system of rituals is also opposed by noninitiates, however, for its interference with other traditional values such as the equal distribution of food and individual independence of movement.

Another way of reconciling a strategy for reinforcing traditional values with modern ways of earning a cash income in the village, also based on a temporal division of activities, is offered by tourism. In Jürg Schmid's paper small-group tourism on the Sepik River appears less an agent of change—which it may be in other places—than a way of retaining esteem for traditional values and skills in crafts, art, and rituals. At the same time, dealing with tourists provides an opportunity to experiment with new ideas and adapt these to local conditions.

The final case in this section shows how the development of small-scale agricultural (and related) projects by a government-sponsored center for agricultural research may serve as a focal point for initiating rapid change in traditional patterns of rural life. Such change is needed for several groups of villages in the area of the West Sepik Province that is of strategic importance because of its position along the international border with Irian Jaya. Many traditional ties exist between people on the two sides of the border. Hanns Peter, in his sketch of change among the Gargar of the Green River area, stresses the key question that confronts any government when the way of life of a people is about to change or be changed: Who will ensure that the identities of individuals and groups are not lost in the transition?

13/ Political and Social Change in the East Sepik: A Research Agenda

R. J. May

Most studies of social and political change in Papua New Guinea to date have been at broadly one of two levels. At one there is a collection of macro-studies, mostly by historians, political scientists, administrators, and geographers, which documents social and political "development" from a largely national perspective; at the other are numerous micro-studies, mostly by anthropologists, which focus on processes of change in one or a small group of villages. If it is a limitation of the macro-studies that they concentrate on the institutions of colonial government to the relative neglect of changes in conditions in villages (Rowley 1965 providing perhaps the major exception), it is a weakness of many micro-studies that in their concern with the internal dynamics of small societies the historical-contextual wood cannot be seen for the ethnographic trees; it is often as though the national and provincial governments did not exist.

Between these two levels, however, there is a smaller body of literature which describes change at an intermediate—roughly provincial or district— level and seeks systematically to relate change nationally to change in the village. The most substantial body of work by a single researcher in this context is that of Standish on Simbu; other, less comprehensive but substantial recent writings include that of Finney on *bisnis* in the Eastern Highlands, Donaldson and Good on class, and Gerritsen on "the terminal peasantry," the several volumes covering the country's five general elections, the studies of movements which I have labeled "micronationalist," and some of the writings of anthropologists such as Marie Reay and Andrew Strathern.

The great majority of these intermediate-level studies has drawn its data from highlands societies. Among the numerous studies of East Sepik societies, the work of the geographer Bryant Allen on innovation diffusion and, to a lesser extent, that of the geographer David Lea on land use and the sociologist Richard Curtain on labor migra-

tion are perhaps the only major contributions in this area, though some anthropological studies (for example, those of Scaglion, Smith, and Roscoe) have contained accounts of change, and we have studies of national elections in the East Sepik and of the Peli Association. Within the Australian National University's Department of Political and Social Change we have commenced a project on political and social change in the East Sepik the aim of which is to draw together what information we have for a comprehensive analysis of change in a lowland province from European contact to date.

Although the province is to some extent an arbitrary unit for analysis, it draws significance from the facts that from an early stage district administration created a sense of district/provincial entity; that the establishment of provincial governments institutionalized the province as a political entity and has tended to focus politics inward; and that in recent years there appears to have been an increasing "provincialization" (or at least "regionalization") of national politics. The East Sepik provides an interesting case study in this context for several reasons:

1. By most indices (e.g., Wilson 1975) it is a middle-level-of-development province and thus, if not "typical," at least not greatly unrepresentative of the country as a whole.

2. Capitalist penetration has not been extensive, and therefore a study of development might provide the basis for an examination of the validity for Papua New Guinea of currently fashionable dependency-type theses.

3. It has been the locus of economic development programs, first in connection with the "growth poles" concept and later as recipient of the country's first integrated rural development project.

4. For reasons not immediately obvious, it has been prominent in the development of "modern" political institutions.

Data for the project will be drawn from existing sources, including government records, oral histories (Papua New Guinean and foreign), and available secondary sources, supplemented where necessary and possible by further field-work.

The following summary outline seeks to indicate both the major sources of information now available and the gaps which need to be filled. A comprehensive East Sepik bibliography is being prepared as a separate exercise. This paper is thus in essence a tentative research agenda, to be modified and elaborated on the basis of further discussion within the province and with other Sepik scholars.

Early Contact

It is generally accepted that the first contact of Sepik peoples with the outside world was with Malay bird-of-paradise hunters. On present information it seems that the impact of these contacts—at least in the East Sepik—was slight, though Allen (1976:590–60) records that these hunters introduced shotguns and subsequently gained employment as "hired guns" in tribal conflicts (with obvious implications for the balance of political power), and Townsend (1968:65) comments that during the German regime "most of the plantations along the New Guinea north coast were made possible by means of the money obtained from the sale of the birds" and traders and missions also traded in bird-of-paradise skins (see also Philsooph in this volume).

Exploration of the interior commenced in 1885, when Otto Finsch entered the Sepik River; within two years a German steamer had traveled some 600 kilometers upstream. In 1902 von Schlechter became the first white man to cross the Torricellis, but it was not until the Behrmann expedition of 1912–13 that the area between the river and the coast was explored by Europeans. Meanwhile, following the establishment of a German trading station on Seleo in 1894, government and mission stations and plantations were set up along the coast and on the islands and subsequently at Marienberg and at Angoram on the river. With this penetration came the beginning of an expanded network of trade and contact generally. Village men were recruited, sometimes forcibly, to work on plantations on the coast and beyond the Sepik; mission influence spread into the villages, and the training of native catechists was begun.

After the Australians took over in New Guinea, there was little further exploration, and hence no substantial official contact with the interior, until the 1920s. With the establishment of civil administration in 1921, however, the Australian government committed itself to extending government control, among other things over labor recruiting, and to introducing new plants, extending education, and promoting the health and welfare of village people. A station was established at Ambunti, following the "Japandai massacre" (see Bragge in this volume), in 1924, and systematic patrolling of the hinterland began. During the 1930s both government and mission extended their influence. There was also oil exploration and gold prospecting. The discovery of gold around Maprik brought a minor gold rush to that area and resulted in the establishment of a patrol post at Maprik in 1937.

Some documentation of this early period is contained in government reports, in the writings of explorers and missionaries (notably the *Steyler Missionsbote*), and in a few more or less contemporary accounts by others (e.g., Beazley n.d., Cheesman n.d., Marshall 1938, Townsend 1968), and the situation in the province at the outbreak of the Pacific war is summarized in Allied Geographical Section (1943, 1944). Some of the material, together with oral histories of villagers, has been presented in several theses (notably Allen 1976 and Curtain 1980) and is summarized in May (n.d.c). There is also a useful collection of oral histories in volume 8, number 2 (1980) of *Oral History*. However, pending further installments of Wiltgen's history of the Roman Catholic church, the impact of the missions is only poorly documented (but see Smith and Taylor Huber in this volume), and we have virtually none of the sort of information on the effect of extended trade (except perhaps for Allen 1976) that Hughes and Strathern have provided for the highlands. The effect of the labor trade—the sort of relations it established between Sepik communities and outsiders, its significance in introducing the Sepik peoples to the wider world, and its effects on traditional social structures—has been documented to some extent by Allen (1976) and Curtain (1980), but considering its importance the record is still thin. Nor do we know much about the activities of the small group of planters, miners, and traders who operated in the province in the pre-1942 period.

From what evidence we do have, however, and judging from the more recent (and generally more benign) experience in other parts of the country, it is clear that the impact of early contact, even though geographically uneven and for the most part infrequent, was profound. It brought new technologies, new species, new ideas; it caused changes in trading patterns (see Allen in this volume) and in the political balance between communities; it launched an assault on traditional religions and associated forms of social organization, including gender relations; it took young men away from their societies and returned them (usually) with new skills and new visions; and, to quote Allen (1976:255), it "served to impress upon Papua New Guineans their inferior status relative to newcomers." Some of the effects of these changes have been recorded for a few Sepik societies, but we need generally to know more on such questions as the following:

What was the extent of resistance to the colonial intrusion by various communities? (We know that there was some violence and vengeance on both sides.)

How did contact, with its uneven impact on coastal and inland areas, affect the relations between communities?

How did exposure to the outside world—especially through recruitment to missions and government and through the indentured-labor system—affect social structures within communities? (I have in mind here questions of leadership and stratification as well as of the viability of traditional cultures. Allen [1976], for example, suggests that in appointing village officials both the German and the Australian administrations tended to favor younger men, who had traveled beyond their villages, over traditional leaders; if this is generally true—and my own information for the Yangoru area and for some river villages suggests that it is—then the Sepik situation contrasts with that described by several commentators on highlands societies, who suggest that the administration tended to support, and thus consolidate the position of, men of high traditional status. Another interesting question is whether government and missions tended to attract the same sort of person to positions of influence.)

What were the economic effects of early colonialism in terms of, for example, the introduction of new technologies and species, the impact of recruitment on the local labor supply and division of labor, and the extension of trade?

To what extent did mission activity in this period undermine traditional religions and their social and artistic manifestations?

The War and Early Postwar Years

Whereas initial contact came to the people of the Sepik in varying forms over a period of time, the impact of World War II was, if uneven, universal. Initially the principal effect of the war was the suspension of Australian administration. Subsequently, of course, Sepik villagers became substantially involved in the conflict, directly and indirectly, in and out of the province. The military aspects of the Papua New Guinea campaign have been well documented (Dexter 1961, Long 1963); concerning its impact on local communities, there is little published information (some archival material exists, along with some oral history) despite the fact that in parts of the province many people were killed, gardens destroyed, villages abandoned. Perhaps even more significant than the war itself, however, are the changes which wartime dislocation set in motion.

One outcome of the wartime experience in Melanesia was that a few forceful and farsighted individuals returned to their places after the war with visions of social, economic, and political change through communal organization and effort. The activities of Paliau Maloat on Manus and the New Men in the Gulf are widely known, thanks to the writings of Mead, Schwartz, and Maher. Pita Simogun's efforts at promoting cash-cropping in the Wewak-But-Boiken area have received some attention. Less well known is that in the early postwar years Simogun, Yauwiga, Beibi Yembanda, Kokomo Ulia, and a number of others (many of them ex-policemen) mobilized a large part of the province north of the river in a loosely coordinated, development-oriented, generally proadministration movement which promoted cash-cropping (especially rice and cacao) and other forms of business (notably, around Wewak, transport), road building, and education. At least some of the leaders of the movement also challenged the institution of the tambaran cult, and this brought them into conflict with traditional leaders and in some cases earned them the suspicious attention of administrative officers. The achievements of what might be called "the Simogun Movement" in organizing the planting of cash crops were considerable, as was its influence on the administration in promoting "development," but for a variety of reasons it failed to satisfy its supporters' (or its leaders'?) expectations of substantial monetary returns and within a few years gradually declined. Allen (1976) has documented the diffusion of Simogun's rice-planting program to the Dreikikir area, Maragau (1973) has provided a brief biography of Simogun, Gerstner (1952) mentions Yauwiga's activities, and I have collected data on the movement in the area between Wewak and Yangoru, but despite the significance of the movement to the broad process of change in the East Sepik I know of no other relevant study.

Several other movements, these of a more millenarian nature, also emerged in different parts of the province in this period, though the province's most extensive mass movement, the Peli Association, did not appear till 1969. Allen (1976:307–8) links inversely the political fortunes of *bisnis* (business) leaders and *kago* (cargo) leaders in Dreikikir: "[The failure of rice] opened further opportunities for other men. The leaders of the *kago* movement presented people with another vision, which was again enthusiastically accepted, and as the prestige and power of the *kago* men rose, that of the *bisnis* men fell." He goes on to observe, however, that "the *kago* vision was, as interpreted by the people, not vastly different from their early interpretations of the *bisnis* vision." For at least some of the leaders, too, the visions seem to have merged: Yembanda, for one, had a bet each way. Allen further argues that with the later introduction of coffee and the reestablishment of cooperatives bisnis leaders regained some of their lost status and that the establishment of local government councils provided other leadership opportunities for both kago and bisnis leaders.

The competition for leadership and influence in this early development period and the relationship between leadership and access to government services are certainly important topics for research, both for their relevance to an understanding of more recent politics in the province and for the potential contribution that Sepik studies might make to the ongoing debate about social stratification in postcolonial Melanesia.

The Transition to Independence

Lea (1972:1035) records that after the war "it took several years for the Australian New Guinea Administration Unit . . . and the civil Administration to re-establish effective control." Administration was, however, reestablished and patrolling extended. Social and economic development were pursued on a vastly expanded scale, cooperatives and local government councils were established, and, in the early 1970s, a belated attempt was made to prepare the people for imminent self-government and independence. The Catholic mission—having lost more than half its personnel in the conflict—also reestablished itself soon after the war, and a number of other denominations entered the competition for souls.

Although an agricultural station had been established at Bainyik in 1938 and some planting materials had been distributed to villages before 1942, there was little nonsubsistence economic activity in East Sepik villages until the 1950s. Before the war, a small cash income was derived from gold mining around Maprik, trading in crocodile skins along the river, and copra production, mostly on the coastal strip and islands north of Wewak. From the early 1950s on, cash-cropping was promoted, with limited success, through the Department of Agriculture, Stock and Fisheries. Initial emphasis was on peanuts, rice, and coffee; cacao, which was planted by Simogun and others in the early postwar years in defiance of government policy, subsequently received official support, and there was some experimentation with rubber and other minor crops and with fisheries and cattle. From the early 1960s on, the development of cash-cropping was linked to the spread of cooperatives and the extension of the road system; there were also limited attempts at population resettlement. Especially along the river, where the scope for cash-cropping was limited, artifact selling, tourism, and timber—all of which involved substantial foreign participation—also generated a limited cash income in this period, and some individuals and village groups sought wealth or prestige through trade stores and PMVs (public motor vehicles). As late as 1972, however, an official publication observed that "historically the Sepik area has been regarded as having little economic potential" (Department of Information and Extension Services 1972:56), and until the early 1970s the principal economic significance of the East Sepik, from a national viewpoint, continued to be as a source of plantation labor.

In 1974, in an almost symbolic preindependence gesture, the Central Planning Office published a "growth center study" for the East Sepik that listed priorities for development. These included a road between Angoram and Wewak, associated with the development of a business center in Angoram; the development of a business and community center based on Maprik; the development of tourism; and promotion of cacao and livestock around Wewak, the expansion of Wewak as a community and business center, and development of transport to the islands off Wewak (Philpott and the Central Planning Office 1974). But although the road to Angoram became a reality, little attempt was made to put this program into effect, and indeed it was soon superseded by a philosophy which emphasized decentralization, rural development, and the reduction of regional inequalities.

There is some record and analysis of agriculture in this phase of development in Shand and Straatmans (1974), Lea (1964, 1973), Lea and Weinand (1971), Seiler (1972), Allen (1976), Snowden (1978), and Stent (1979, 1984), as well as in the official statistical record; a wide-ranging study of transport needs was made in 1971–72 (Philpott 1972), and labor migration has been the subject of a major study (Curtain 1980), as has the artifact trade (May 1979, n.d.*a*). The overall impact of these externally generated economic forces has, however, so far received little systematic study: we know, for example, that the record with respect to cash-cropping generally was poor, but we do not fully understand the reasons for this; we have little knowledge of how such economic development as did occur affected existing economic and social structures; there is no comprehensive study of cooperatives; we have almost no record of foreign private interests; and so on.

An important aspect of the movements which proliferated throughout the country in the early postwar years was a demand not simply for material welfare but for development that would reduce the status inequalities between Papua New Guineans and Europeans and return to the former some of the autonomy they had enjoyed before contact. Colonial administrators and missionaries were not unaware of this: some were overtly sympathetic to such incipient nationalism, while others feared its political consequences and sought either to suppress it or to direct it into acceptable channels.

One such channel was native local government councils. The first councils were established in Papua New Guinea in 1950. The East Sepik got its first council in 1957, and by 1968 there were ten councils in the province; another two were added in the mid-1970s. The institution of local government clearly had important consequences for local authority structures throughout the province, even though the councils were for the most part heavily influenced by foreign advisors until well into the 1970s. Scattered information suggests that councils drew to some extent on traditional leadership and the established village-official structure but more on the emergent postwar bisnis leadership (Simogun became president of the But-Boiken council, Kokomo Ulia of the Dreikikir, Simogun-follower Tamindei of the Maprik, and so on) and on younger men of an emerging educated elite. The role of councils was circumscribed both by the limited functions allotted to them and by administration supervision; nevertheless, they played a significant role in mobilizing people at a supravillage level, and they were also used, tentatively, as a basis for communal bisnis ventures (notably in artifact trading).

The creation of local councils was matched at the national level by the institution of a legislative council consisting of appointed and elected members. Pita Simogun was appointed to the first legislative council in 1951 as member for New Guinea Coastal and remained in that position until 1961. Hughes (1965:10) records: "In the first four Legislative Councils between 1951 and 1961 the indigenous Members played a very minor part. Only Peta Simogen . . . served in all four Councils; he proved the most vocal indigenous Member. . . . " Simogun was also prominently involved in 1960–61 in the short-lived, foreign-dominated United Progress party, the first political party to be established within Papua New Guinea. In 1964 political development was taken a step farther with elections to the first House of Assembly. The East Sepik was covered by four open electorates as well as the Madang-Sepik special electorate. Tamindei won the contest in Maprik (Dewdney 1965); Simogun was successful in Wewak-Aitape; Dreikikir elected the young evangelist and bisnis man Pita Lus; Angoram returned the foreigner Pasquarelli; and Frank Martin of Wewak became the region's special member.

Political parties began to play a role only shortly before the next elections in 1968. The first of these to emerge, the Christian Democratic (subsequently United Democratic) party, was Sepik-based, organized by Simogun, Otto Kovingre, and Peter Maut and linked to the Catholic church. It eventually claimed four thousand paid-up members (Stephen 1972:75) and formally endorsed seven candidates (among them an ex-policeman and mission worker by the name of Matias Yaliwan) in the two Sepik provinces, though in Wolfers's (1972:940) view "probably a majority of Sepik candidates (and a few elsewhere) were party members." None of its candidates was successful, however, and the party soon faded away. The All People's party held its inaugural meeting in Angoram at the sawmill of one of its two foreign founders, Jim McKinnon (the co-founder was Frank Martin). Although McKinnon was elected in 1968 as member for Middle Ramu, the APP also had a fleeting existence, some half-hearted attempts at a UDP-APP alliance also coming to nothing (though the parties shared a general proadministration position).

More successful in establishing a lasting political organization were the founders of the Pangu party, among whom were Michael Somare (who in 1968 became leader of the parliamentary wing) and Pita Lus (who became party whip). Commenting on the 1968 elections, Wolfers says, "Political parties as such played no more than a very minor role . . . only in a minority of cases were a candidate's party affiliations revealed in public, or relevant to the number of votes that he received" (p. 940). Although we have no detailed study of the 1968 elections in the East Sepik, it seems certain from Wolfers's account that some of that minority was there, and the province has remained a source of Pangu strength and maintained party branch organization (not, admittedly, very robust organization, but probably about as robust as any mass party organization anywhere in the country). During the course of the 1968–71 House, Pangu became the most important single grouping in the parliament, declaring itself the "loyal opposition"; of minor historical importance, Loveday and Wolfers (1976:39–40), in their analysis of voting in that House, identify a "Sepik subgroup" on the other side. Apart from the material available on parties and elections, the autobiographies of Somare (1975) and Lus (1970) throw some light on political developments during these years.

Between 1968 and 1972 Pangu, under Somare's leadership, consolidated its position in the province, while constitutional development and political education steadily raised the level of understanding of and interest in national politics. In 1969, however, the failed CDP candidate Yaliwan had amassed another sort of following. The ongoing history of the Peli Association, in its various aspects, has been the subject of several studies (including May 1982b [1975]), and its electoral performance in 1972 and 1977 has been documented by Allen (1976) and Winnett and May (1983) respectively. It gives pause that had Yaliwan not been prevented, by educational qualifications, from contesting the East Sepik Regional seat in 1972, Papua New Guinea might not

have had Michael Somare to lead the country through self-government to independence.

Wewak had become the headquarters of the (combined) Sepik District in 1934, but up till World War II it had remained a small town. During the war it was for some time the largest Japanese base in Papua New Guinea (in 1943 containing 32,000 troops). Although it was largely destroyed by Allied bombing, reconstruction began in 1946. An expansion of government personnel and associated construction work in the early 1950s increased the foreign population, gave some scope for the establishment of service industries, and provided increased opportunities for local employment (some of which, however, were met by the import of more highly skilled labor from outside the province). The construction of the Wewak General Hospital and the Moem army barracks in the early 1960s gave a further boost to urban growth, and the extension of the Sepik Highway, on which construction began in 1962, increased the importance of Wewak as an administrative and commercial center and gave the rural population of the province substantially easier access to Wewak. There had been some in-migration to Wewak even before the war; in the 1950s, 1960s, and early 1970s in-migration accelerated. The urbanization of Wewak was examined in 1974 by Curtain and May (1979) as part of the ANU/UPNG Urban Household Survey. This survey (see also Garnaut, Wright, and Curtain 1977) provides comprehensive data on migration and on urban employment, income, and settlement that supplement data from the 1966, 1971, and 1980 censuses. A Wewak Development Plan (Taylor and Partners 1973) and a study by Lea (in Jackson 1976) provide additional information. I understand that a history of Wewak is "in press." The urban data of 1974 are supplemented by Curtain's more detailed studies (1976, 1978, 1980) of migration from the rural village end. The urban geography of Maprik in 1973–74 has been described by Allen (in Jackson 1976).

The Postindependence Period

As is perhaps true for the country as a whole, 1975 does not constitute an obvious watershed in the history of political and social change in the East Sepik. It is nevertheless a significant turning point in several respects. First and most obviously, it marks the final stage in the formal transfer of political power from the colonial

administration to Papua New Guineans and is associated with an increasing localization of "district administration" and other government services. Secondly, independence, and specifically
the citizenship provisions of the independence
constitution, accelerated the exodus of the foreign business community. Thirdly, the drafting of
the independence constitution initiated provincial
government.

In the East Sepik the process of establishing
the provincial government was a relatively
smooth one, and the record of the provincial government is one of the better ones in the country (in
1982 the East Sepik became the sixth province to
attain full financial autonomy). But while the process of decentralization has been the subject of
several studies, the operation of provincial government in the East Sepik has not, as far as I am
aware, received any systematic scholarly attention (an observation which would seem to be
about equally applicable to all provinces except
Simbu). Among the more obvious questions to be
addressed are the following:

What is the background of candidates in provincial elections, and what sorts of factors have
determined who succeeds? (I have some unpublished material on the provincial election of 1979
and subsequent by-elections, but as far as I know
there was no study of the 1983 election, in which
younger, better-educated candidates seem to have
done well. A question of particular interest to political scientists concerns the role of political parties: although the annual report of the province
asserts that there is no party system in the Provincial Assembly, clearly most candidates have
known political inclinations, and I suspect that
analysis of voting patterns in the Assembly would
reveal a discernible party vote even though region
appears to be more important.

What has the provincial government actually
done? What differences has provincial government made in policy making and the provision of
services within the province? (Education would
be a good point at which to start.)

What has been the state of relations between
the provincial government and (a) national politicians and (b) the public service in the province?
(The prominence of Pangu in the province gives
the first part of this question particular significance.)

What have been the effects of provincial government on politics within the province? (For example, there is some evidence of an emerging regional polarization, reflected in the existence, for
a while, of "area ministers," and before 1983

there appeared to be some resentment of the
"dominance" of national and provincial politics
by representatives of "river" Sepik communities.

Perhaps related to the rise of provincial government, there has been (in the East Sepik as in many
other provinces) a decline in the vitality of local
governments; the reasons for and implications of
this deserve study (in 1982 a working committee
on local-level government reported to the Provincial Assembly), as does the recent establishment
of community government in Wewak and moves
to establish a Boiken community government.

At the national level, there have been two elections since independence, in 1977 and 1982, both
of which have received some scholarly attention
(on 1977, Nyamekye 1983, Winnett and May
1983; on 1982, May n.d.*b*).

Apart from what information we have on
Pangu party organization and on the 1977 and
1982 election campaigns, we know little about
political leadership and networks beyond the village; nor do we have much information about the
political role of such organizations as, for example, the Wewak Local Association, the Angoram
Development Association, the Lus Corporation,
or the Sepik Producers' Co-operative Association. It has been suggested (see above) that in the
early colonial period village officials appointed
by the colonial governments were not frequently
traditional leaders—that colonialism created a
new class of big men. Later this "first generation" of new men of influence was largely replaced by bisnis and kago leaders who drew their
authority from yet other sources. Local government councils and national parliament opened additional fields of competition for leadership and
influence, and although bisnis and kago leaders
often filled these positions, increasingly they
have been replaced in turn by younger men more
deeply involved in the processes of change beyond the province. The introduction of provincial
government appears from casual observation to
have had mixed effects— reinstating some of the
"second-generation" leaders but increasingly
providing openings for a young, educated "third
generation" (including a large number of former
public servants and teachers) who are better
placed to act as brokers between the village and
the state. We are also seeing the emergence of an
urban-based elite, mostly dependent—as politicians or public servants—on the state.

Clearly the most important "event" in the eco-
nomic field since independence has been the
Asian Development Bank–supported East Sepik
Rural Development Project (ESRDP), which in

1976 became the first of several actual or planned integrated development projects at the provincial level throughout the country. The ESRDP consisted at the outset of six subprojects: Gavien land settlement, buffalo farming, inland fisheries, crop intensification, agricultural research, and agricultural and nutrition education. In the words of the initial ADB appraisal report (Asian Development Bank 1976:77), the project was intended to benefit

> farmers on the ill-drained grassland and the fishermen on the Sepik river, most of whom have so far hardly participated in the cash economy and are living at subsistence level.
> . . . families to be settled under the Gavien settlement subproject, the majority of whom are expected to be landless or having inadequate land resources. . . . farmers who have already entered the cash economy but whose incomes have remained low on account of poor cultivation and management practices.

It was further anticipated that the ESRDP would improve nutrition, raise the level of services (particularly in education), and establish rural industries in rubber, cacao processing, and fish marketing.

The ESRDP was subjected in 1979 to two examinations, one internal (Cairns, Takendu, and Sadler 1980) and one external, at the request of the provincial government (Curtain and May 1980); there have also been formal reviews of the separate subprojects as well as some critical comments from local observers (e.g., Cox 1979). The ESRDP has had at best limited success, a fact which perhaps has as much to do with factors beyond the control of the project planners (such as the *Salvinia* infestation and the delinquency of Australian quarantine procedures for buffalo stock) as with overly ambitious targets or failures in implementation. Having reached the end of its ADB funding, the project is due for assessment. Among the interesting questions to which we may or may not get answers are the following:

How effective is a large-scale, largely externally funded project of this type in lifting the level of "development" of a province, and what have been the specific achievements and failings of the ESRDP?

Who, in fact, have been the principal beneficiaries of the ESRDP? Has it reduced inequalities, particularly regional inequalities, within the province?

How does one account for the limited success of the crop intensification subproject, both in improving subsistence and in raising returns from cash-cropping? (This, it should be said, is a question which has been asked continuously, both in the East Sepik and elsewhere, since agricultural extension began.)

What have been the social and economic consequences of resettling families from various parts of the province at Gavien (especially in view of provincial government proposals for an expansion of resettlement)?

How effective have the government's efforts been in respect of nutrition education and nutrition-oriented agricultural extension work?

Assessment of the fisheries subproject will also provide some measure of the more general economic consequences of *Salvinia* (on which Gewertz [1980*a*] has also written).

Beyond the ESRDP, there is need to evaluate the performance of cash-cropping generally (the East Sepik being one of the few provinces in which the local people did not have foreign-owned plantations to take over after independence); to look at the state of Papua New Guinea private business—individual entrepreneurs and village groups (we do have the testimony of one businessman, Sani [1982]); to examine the question of foreign investment in the province; and perhaps to assess the performance of the provincial government's business arm in relation to those of older provinces (and in relation to the SPCA).

Since the 1950s the Catholic church, which before World War II had a virtual monopoly in the mission field, has been challenged not only by missionaries from some of the better-known Christian denominations (notably the Seventh-Day Adventists) but also by those of some evangelical groups of dubious origins (notably the New Apostolic Church). (Losche, in this volume, claims that in 1974 there were thirty-six denominations in the province.) There have also been substantial doctrinal changes within the Catholic church (see Smith in this volume) and important changes in the relative importance of religious and secular institutions as agents of change. I have already commented on the need for further research on the impact of the church in a historical context; we also need to know more about the contemporary role of the various missions at both village and provincial levels.

In recent years there appears to have been an increasing tendency on the part of anthropologists to address questions of contemporary social change rather than to dwell exclusively in the "ethnographic present." In directing attention to the impact of colonialism/incorporation-into-the-world-system on traditional social structures (specifically in relation to structures of authority, the role of women, and changing modes of production), anthropologists have come closer to some of the long-standing academic interests of political scientists, economists, human geographers, and others and to the practical concerns of Third World governments. In the Papua New Guinea literature, however, this tendency has so far been apparent more in the study of highlands societies than in the study of lowland ones such as those of the East Sepik.

The anthropological literature provides some description of traditional leadership in East Sepik societies, but apart from Hogbin (1978) on Wogeo and perhaps Lipset (1984) on the Murik Lakes the information is patchy and in the light of recent assessment of the big-man model perhaps deserves reexamination. We have little information on how traditional leadership structures have been affected by such factors as recruitment to missions, government and private foreign employment, the spread of new technologies and of cash-cropping (with consequent effects on land use, division of labor, etc.), education and outside employment experience, especially for younger people, and such modifications as have been made to traditional cultures (e.g., in relation to warfare, religion, and sorcery). Closely related to this is the broader question of social stratification generally—past, present, and future—and specifically its relationship to access to government services. Who now are the big men of the East Sepik? What is the basis of their high status? Do they represent the emergence of class interests?

As long ago as 1960, Bühler wrote of "Sepik: A Dying Culture." Undoubtedly elements of Sepik cultures have undergone rapid transformation (decline?) since contact, particularly, it would seem, among the Boiken and other, smaller groups in less thickly populated and/or longer-contacted areas. As against this, some cultures have proved either remarkably resistant to change or remarkably adept at accommodating "traditional" and "modern" elements; in some parts of the province traditional ceremonies are being revived. It would be interesting to know why different societies have been differentially affected by change (this question is addressed in Forge's contribution to this volume) and also (a smaller question) what impacts (positive and negative) tourism, the artifact trade, and the national government's cultural policies have had on tradi-

tional cultures (cf. Beier 1976). (The history of the East Sepik Cultural Council deserves a small monograph of its own.)

Until quite recently some of us regularly cautioned Bill Standish about talking about Papua New Guinea politics on the basis of his continuing study of Simbu, but in the past few years there appears to have been something of a "Simbuization" of the East Sepik: the emergence and escalation of large-scale lawlessness in Wewak, armed holdups of cacao buyers and less serious harassment of travelers along the Sepik Highway, widespread activity by *raskol* gangs in rural areas, and in at least one instance of which I am aware (around Yangoru) a virtual "tribal warfare" in which the men of one village, wearing traditional face paint and carrying fighting sticks and shields, attacked a traditional rival (according to one report, with the covert blessing of the local constabulary). For the Papua New Guinea highlands, *raskols* have been the subject of an important study (Reay 1982) and "tribal fighting" the subject of several scholarly studies as well as government reports. For the Sepik, so far as I am aware, there has been no major study of the apparently escalating lawlessness and the reasons for it and, indeed, little recognition outside the province of how widespread it has become. An important development throughout Papua New Guinea in recent years has been the growth of the village court system. For the East Sepik we have Scaglion's studies of village courts among the western Abelam, but I am not aware of any other research on this important subject.

Not entirely unrelated to the question of lawlessness is the subject of alcohol consumption. Between 1966 and 1980 the number of liquor licenses in the East Sepik Province increased from 21 to 140 (I have been unable to obtain later figures, but there has been a further substantial increase), largely as the result of a sympathetic official attitude toward village social clubs. It would be surprising if such dramatic statistics did not imply significant social repercussions, and casual observation suggests that they do. On this topic we do have papers by Roscoe, McDowell, and Smith as part of the Institute of Applied Social and Economic Research study of alcohol use and abuse (Marshall 1982), but further studies would be useful.

One of the more significant effects of colonial rule and postcolonial development has been their impact on demographic profiles. In 1980, 47.5 percent of the East Sepik Province's population was between the ages of five and twenty-five.

Given the limitations of the school system (in 1980, 79.5 percent of that age-group was not at school), the restricted employment opportunities within the province, the apparently declining demand for labor in traditional out-migration destinations, and the tendency for young people to drift into town, this poses significant problems for social planners in the East Sepik as elsewhere. Problems of youth are perhaps best considered under several broader headings (e.g., economic opportunities, social stratification, law and order), but the evidence of the national government's priorities (in 1980 a National Youth Movement Program was established; youth development was deemed to be a decentralized function) suggests that at least we need a baseline study of youth in the East Sepik. (A Youth Coordination Centre has been established in the East Sepik, though at the end of 1982 the province had received less in NYMP grants than any other province. There is now an Urban Youth Program in Wewak, in which some thirty groups [two thousand persons] were involved in early 1983.)

Some Big Questions

Before the 1970s, most political scientists writing about "political development" or "modernization" had in mind an essentially evolutionary model of change. In regarding development as a progression through historically determined phases, modernization theorists shared a Eurocentric intellectual tradition with Marx and with anthropologists of an earlier generation (cf. Hogbin 1958:15). The demise of evolutionary models, both of the right and of the left, has made analysis of change a more complex task. To avoid complexity, some recent commentators on Papua New Guinea have adopted what amounts to a *devolutionary* model, seeing the country as having been in a state of steady decline since independence; in support of this view they cite declining agricultural productivity, reduction in the level of provision of government services, increasing lawlessness, and a widening gap between a privileged few in the modern sector and the rural masses.

Most fieldworkers would probably acknowledge some elements of such a picture, but it is obviously not acceptable as a general description. In fact what we are now witnessing, in the East Sepik as elsewhere, is a complex process of change and adjustment in which developments set in train during the colonial period are working themselves out in relation to traditional cultural patterns and within the context of an independent Melanesian state. Colonialism had a profound impact on most Sepik societies: it destroyed institutions and patterns of behavior, some irrevocably, and it established new patterns of behavior, some irreversibly, and introduced new institutions. It is well to remember, however, that for most people the period of intense contact with the colonial regime was fairly short and its values and behavior patterns only poorly absorbed. Moreover, the level of activity sustained in the later preindependence and early postindependence days depended on a high level of external funding unlikely to last forever (especially considering the present climate of opinion on Australian aid to the region).

Whether the East Sepik is in, or approaching, what Howlett (1973) described for the Goroka Valley as "terminal development," "the infinite pause"; whether the conditions of village people will improve, as is envisaged by the ADB; or whether conditions will steadily deteriorate, as is suggested by some prophets of doom (within the village as well as beyond)— these are big questions. There are not likely to be any simple answers, but if Sepik research is indeed to be relevant to modern Papua New Guinea they are questions that must be addressed.

14/ The Importance of Being Equal: The Colonial and Postcolonial Experience in the Torricelli Foothills

Bryant Allen

Less than a hundred years ago a foreigner, probably a Javanese bird-shooter, crossed the Torricelli Mountains and encountered Kombio- and Wam-speaking peoples living along the northern edge of a strip of densely settled country on the southern fall of the coastal range. To the west his compatriots had for some years been penetrating deep into the Yellow, Sand, Horden, and North River catchments through the Bewani Mountains from Jayapura, camping for some months and shooting bird of paradise (Cheesman [n.d. (?1938)] and Aitape Patrol Report no. 3, 1932–33, South Wapi extending to the Sepik River, August to October 1932 [Commonwealth Archives AS13/26, Item 21]). By 1900 Chinese were established at Aitape, trading in competition with the Neu Guinea Kompagnie and "prepared to risk their necks trading well outside the competence of the law" (Rowley 1958:74). They were well known south of the coastal ranges; Loa, of Sambu village (Kombio), reports:

> When the Chinese, and later the white men, came here everyone ran away into the forest. They went and hid in various places in the forest. They said, "Shut up! Hide well and no talking. Quiet! No talking whatsoever! Hide!" When they came, if they heard us talking, they came into the forest and chased us. They chased the older men away and grabbed women and raped them, and held young boys to take them to the government station. They caught me like this.

Loa, then about eleven years old, was taken to Aitape and sent to sweep the streets of Rabaul.[1] The Chinese were followed over the Torricellis by the botanist Rudolf von Schlechter (1903) and by German recruiters, including two, Stendel and Kommling, who were killed in the Kombio area. This led to a bungled Australian-led punitive expedition in 1918 that resulted in the deaths of at least twelve villagers and the destruction of two villages (Brig. G. J. Johnson to the Secretary, Department of Defense, Ex-German New Guinea, Miscellaneous Reports, May-June 1918, January-March 1919, Australian War Memorial, Canberra; interview, Dosalai, Tong village [Kombio] 1972). These events sent a wave of fear rippling through villages to the south, as Kombio-speakers fled south and sought shelter with Urat. Urat-speakers in turn established substantial hamlets off the main ridges, which remained occupied until very recently. The last of a generation alive or born during this period of early colonial contact have died, and their children, preferring life in the larger villages, abandoned the former refuges and moved back to the main ridge in 1980.

These were experiences of such magnitude that I find it extremely difficult to imagine what they meant to the adults alive at the time and what effects they have had on subsequent generations. In the Sepik, until very recently, inadequate recognition has been given to the manner in which the colonial experience transformed traditional patterns of behavior and continues to influence the way in which the present generation confronts a world in which, from almost every viewpoint, the terms of exchange are unequal. Ethnographies justly renowned for their depth and richness of detail have concentrated on traditional life and passed over the colonial experience in a few pages, almost as if it were but a slight disruption of the normal train of events.[2] On the other hand, increasing numbers of Sepik researchers are incorporating modern historical perspectives. Gewertz (1983) has produced an excellent example of such a study, and a number of the articles in this volume discuss the influence of colonialism and rapid change on Sepik societies (e.g., Scaglion, Roscoe, Josephides, Lutkehaus, Errington and Gewertz, Smith, Dye, and Schindlbeck).

I wish to argue in this paper that colonialism is a critical explanatory variable in any attempt to understand modern village life, including contemporary "traditional" activities. I am using the term "colonialism" in the broadest possible sense to encompass all foreign intervention in local affairs, including the penetration of the market economy and the neocolonialism inherent in modern Papua New Guinea development.

The characterization of all Papua New Guinea societies as variants of Sahlins's (1962–63) "big-man" model has never sat comfortably on Sepik societies (Forge 1970a), and the characterization of them as falling along a continuum from "egalitarian" to "hierarchical" (Mitchell 1978) is not particularly satisfying. There is little doubt, however, that the foothills societies of the Sepik were deeply concerned with equality and balance between men and groups of men and with inequality and imbalance between men and women. From the Umeda in the west (Gell 1975) to Kairiru Island in the east (Smith 1978 and in this volume) and including the Wape (Mitchell 1978 and in this volume), the Urat (Allen 1976), the Ilahita Arapesh (Tuzin 1980 and in this volume), and the Abelam (Forge 1970a and in this volume, Scaglion 1981 and in this volume, Huber-Greub in this volume), village societies exhibited features of duality in which hypothetically identical groups were ritually opposed in exchanges and in many cases the men of one group were responsible for the initiation of the sons of the other. Theoretically, the exchanges between individuals within each group and between groups were to be equal and balanced; if the relationship was inherently always unbalanced, the superior-inferior positions were to be regularly passed back and forth between the groups. Within this pattern the struggle for leadership was often fierce and unrelenting, with no individual having any greater right than any other to positions of power and influence. On the other hand, men in all these societies were concerned with maintaining a superior position over women, many of them claiming that men had usurped the power that women once held over men.

While there are undoubtedly many exceptions to this general pattern (see, e.g., Lewis 1980), they are insignificant when compared with the attitudes and behavior of the foreigners with whom these societies came into contact as a result of colonization. Foreigners refused to enter into balanced and equal relationships and instead maintained, commonly by force, a superior and dominating position. This situation set in train a series of practical and intellectual crises in Sepik societies that continue into the present, when inequalities which first became apparent in the early 1900s have become entrenched and are

worsening. The history of the Sepik foothills from 1920 on is largely the history of individuals and groups attempting to meet these crises or take advantage of the opportunities they seemed to offer to redress the imbalances and inequalities created. It is important to understand how Sepik communities responded, which institutions were most vulnerable and which most resilient, and to seek in the historical pattern explanations of the reactions of Sepik people today to the policies and plans of their own provincial and national governments. To do this would certainly be to study Sepik cultures in and for a modern Papua New Guinea.

In an attempt to demonstrate the significance of the colonial experience, I will provide a description of events from immediately preceding and following colonization to the present and examine some responses to them in village communities of the Dreikikir District, on the western boundary of the East Sepik Province, with some minor forays into the surrounding region. Strathern (1982) studies this process in the Western Highlands by examining social inequalities between men and other men, between men and women, and between groups in precolonial times and then investigating to what extent colonialism resulted in changes. I will, with much less competence, examine the inequalities between villages and, within villages, between groups of men, men and other men, and men and women. I will do this in a historical context beginning with the immediately precolonial period.

Colonial contact across the coastal ranges was uneven in time and space, but in general it began along the crest of the ranges in the early 1900s and spread south. Well before face-to-face contact with foreigners occurred in the inland villages, however, quite radical changes took place. For example, it is almost certain that in the late 1800s smallpox spread inland. It is reported from Aitape in 1890 by Parkinson (Swadling 1979:43), and oral histories from Rauit (Lewis 1975 and personal communication) and from the Urat villages west of Dreikikir (Allen 1983) appear to be describing the disease. At Rauit it is said to have caused the abandonment of one hamlet and the scattering of some clans to other villages. In the Urat villages into which it spread it is credited with killing more than half of the people.[3] Such a disease must have had quite radical effects on village populations, social organization, and land use and settlement patterns.

In the Dreikikir area, another portent of the changes to come was the appearance of small pieces of sharpened steel, porcelain rings, and "dogs'" teeth. These were traded inland from the coast and gave coastal and mountain peoples increased influence over those to the south, bringing about a reversal of the existing situation. Prior to colonialism, most trade took place along an east-west axis inland of the ranges, and most small mountain communities, similar to that described by Mead in 1932, were peripheral to the trading and ceremonial exchanges centered on the more powerful and resource-rich Urat, Wam, Bumbita, and Muhiang villages located along the foothills at around two to four hundred meters above sea level (Allen 1976). This new north-south pattern was to become even more important following the imposition of colonial rule and was to remain in place until the end of World War II.

Another aspect of the increased influence of coastal communities over the inland area was blackbirding raids by Chinese, using coastal men armed with firearms. Young boys, properly speaking children, were taken by force by small parties of coastal men who held off anguished parents with shotguns. Girls were also taken and were married to men in the mountain and coastal villages or, in two cases, to Chinese. Whole villages scattered into bush hamlets and in at least one case were never reestablished (cf. Scaglion in this volume).

By 1912 German colonial control extended only to the crest of the coastal range, but young men from the uncontrolled southern villages who had been taken by raiding parties and who had worked on a plantation for three years and learned Tok Pisin were appointed *tultul* (interpreters) of their villages and sent home to spread the word about the power of the German empire. Some must have been less than twenty years old. Their appointment was the beginning of thirty years of struggle between individuals seeking power by taking advantage of opportunities generated by colonial intrusion and individuals who gained power through customary channels. In this immediate precolonial period, many traditional leaders were unable to comprehend the dimensions of the forces which they were confronting, and many accounts of contacts between villagers and Chinese and German recruiters contain descriptions of young tultul preventing and explaining the futility of a physical attack, acting as mediators between the two groups and gaining considerable prestige in doing so. Other accounts describe traditional leaders withdrawing totally from all contact with the intruders to avoid having to acknowledge the influence and power of the young upstarts. Other young men from the crest of the range were taught by Chinese how to use shotguns and returned home to shoot bird of paradise. "Hired" in a manner similar to sorcerers, they also used their guns on people. One, Mahetei of Arisili, later became a paramount *luluai* or *weitpus* (appointed local government official) and was described in 1950 as an outstanding traditional leader who "holds great sway" (Dreikikir Patrol Report, 5/6/50–13/6/50). He was in fact one of a new generation of leaders who were able to mediate between the village and the outside world and who, if shrewd and bold enough, were able to gain power well beyond the sphere of influence of leaders prior to colonial contact.

A village became officially "controlled" and part of the colony when its inhabitants were "lined," their names written into a census book, and officials appointed as representatives of the colonial power. Mahanung of Ngahmbole village recalls, "Thompson was a big man, fat with a beard. He took our names. He had police with him. They shot at that coconut there, you can still see the hole they made. The *kiap* [government officer] said, 'Don't try to fight us. We are too strong.'" Colonial "control" spread south from the crest of the range to reach all Urat villages by 1926, Urim and the two northernmost Kwanga villages by 1929, and all but the southernmost Kwanga villages by 1941. Today Urat men have two methods of describing their villages. The first, gradually disappearing as the old men who grew up with it die, refers to the precolonial village clusters; the second refers to the colonial pattern, which continues to be followed in all government activities such as censuses, tax collection, and elections.

The matter of "lining" and name taking goes deeper than is apparent at first glance. At the very first census, people did not understand what was occurring. They were lined up by police using an interpreter (one of the men discussed above) from a village to the north. The form of the line was set by the Australian patrol officer, and the interpreter and police pushed, shoved, and cuffed people into some semblance of what was required. Apart from the violence done to the villagers themselves, which previously no family leader would have accepted without retaliation, "lining" also did violence to the actual pattern of human life in the village, similar in many ways perhaps to the violence we do to it when we try and force it into some structuralist-functionalist model or other. The officer wanted biological families, and so men, women, and children, some of whom were now resident in other villages, had to come back and "line" with their "proper" families. Binghoiye of Ngahmbole village gives a good account of these happenings:

My father had died and I had gone to Musingwik to live with another father. . . . They called out. They wanted us to line. I wanted to give my name on top [at Musingwik] but Hautart from Whaleng [the paramount luluai responsible for all of the Urat at this time, a speaker of Yambes, Kombio, Urat, and Wam, resident at Whaleng] spoke. He said, "I think, child, you cannot stay here with your brothers and mother. You must go back to your father's village." Hautart had been to work at the coast. Now he came with the kiap. So they chased me out and I came back here. . . . We lined up. We were naked. Even our fathers and mothers stood there with their genitals exposed.

And what did the taking of names signify? Which names were given and why? Why did this apparently extremely powerful foreigner wish the names to be called at all? Even today, some people speak in esoteric ways about the names of the ancestors and their own names, which are held in "The Book." How does the knowledge that his name is written in the government book influence the behavior of a modern Sepik villager? I do not know, but I believe these are not unimportant questions. I have witnessed a small group of villagers angry that their names had been badly distorted during transcription to the electoral roll, but I could not later find the reason underlying their concern. They seemed, however, to have a quite mystical view of the purpose of the roll and the recording of names.

During the 1930s patrols from Aitape visited villages about once every three years, but even then the visits were unwelcome and people cooperated only because they had no alternative. Officers tried to settle disputes and enforce colonial regulations relating to housing, burial practices, and village hygiene. The "law" as it became known, was ill-understood. The Tok Pisin word *loa* now has connotations far beyond that of legislation and is commonly used in a mystical sense to refer to a body of revelatory knowledge in the possession of foreigners. People rebuilt houses and constructed latrines when required, but they went to some lengths to avoid burying their dead in deep trenches. Exposure of the body on an easily observable platform gave way to placing of the dead in shallow, open graves inside

houses (Allen 1983). Punishment for this practice was destruction of the house by fire, and the last house was burned for this offense in the Urat in 1953.

Close behind, or not uncommonly before, the kiap came the labor recruiter, now licensed and controlled. Boys and men volunteered to go see the world beyond the horizon, and others were "volunteered" by their elders. It was an act that took great courage. Ted Fulton, a gold miner on the Maprik field, went recruiting in the Wape in 1938 and knew better than to leave his new recruits alone at night to abscond, their courage evaporated (E. Fulton Papers, PMB Microfilm):

Monday 25th (Anzac Day) . . . 2 pm. Boys returned with 12 boys (5 from Wisa, 4 Koam, 1 Moonambil, 2 Muku). Fitted laplaps and completed purchase. Great excitement and many relatives accompanying. No signs of tears this time and villagers seem satisfied at seeing others return.

Tuesday 26th. Kept boys in house under supervision. 2 am went to inspect and guards Karti and Mangini fast asleep. . . . Rather a strain getting up at night to watch boys.

But even in 1937, on the fringes of controlled territory, men were prepared to face shotguns to prevent their children from being taken, as Charles Gough's death near Ilahita demonstrates.

A third group of foreigners to enter the arena during this period were German missionaries who visited temporary camps (see Taylor Huber in this volume). It is difficult to generalize about their behavior; while one raided ceremonial houses and pulled out secret paraphernalia and showed them to women, beat people, and burned houses, another is remembered as a quiet, nonviolent man. Again, I do not know what people perceived in the missionaries' activities. Some sent their children to the bible schools, but lessons were conducted in Tok Pisin, and the cane was used frequently enough to drive many children away after a few days. The missionaries selected and trained pastors whom they put back into the field to supervise the camps and run bible schools, thus creating another position with status and prestige outside of the traditional system of leadership.

A fourth group of foreigners who came into close contact with villagers during this period were the members of geological field survey parties employed by Oil Search Limited. Between 1934 and 1939 they surveyed an area from Matapau along the ranges north of Maprik and then south and west through the Wam, Kombio, Urat, and Wapi to Maimai. Although they also used local labor for their supply lines and purchased food from village people, they were interested neither in trying to enforce colonial regulations nor in buying and selling people. They were better-educated and more aware of their prejudices. Writing recently from his diaries of that time, Jack Fryer (personal communication) says, "It was humbling to realise that our new friends [carriers and laborers] had little or no vice, greed and lust, and no shame as we know it. Fear and anger, yes. What I particularly liked was their sense of humour." But men working for Oil Search were sometimes caned for offenses, and minor physical assaults occurred, not with any regularity but often enough for there to be no doubt over which group considered itself the superior.

Men who were indentured as laborers usually worked on either the Gazelle Peninsula plantations or the Morobe goldfields. During the period of their indenture they experienced a totally new form of social organization, worked to a clock (see also Smith 1982a), and learned a wide range of new skills. The great wealth of the foreigners, their numbers, and their links to sources of wealth overseas became apparent. The position of laborers at the very bottom of the colonial hierarchy was deeply impressed upon them; Misiaiyai (Anton) of Moseng village reports, "When I came out of the bush, I was like an idiot. When I saw how the Europeans lived my head spun. I saw their houses from the outside. Then, I became a servant and saw inside their houses. I saw their beds, their chairs and their tables. Their food and clothes. I thought these things were good. I saw the stores too. I was amazed at the things in them."

This period up until 1945 reinforced and deepened changes which had begun in the early 1900s. Coastal and mountain villages became more powerful, village officials gained more power, and, as old men died, the offices of village leader and appointed village official resided increasingly with the same men. Villagers seem to have selected men to be luluai who they believed would not become authoritarian and dictatorial, but the power of the office sometimes went to a man's head. The positions were semipermanent, and the kiap would change a luluai only with reluctance. A formerly fluid leadership situation became increasingly rigid; younger men challenging the rule of the luluai were challenging the rule of the colonial government. Physical challenges became outlawed. Ambitious young men commonly took repeated labor contracts and sought their fortunes elsewhere.

Little information exists about the effects on initiation and exchange of the loss of young men to the labor trade. Some men returned home between contracts to discharge their ritual obligations and to get married; others left and never returned. At Tumam their land and their positions in the ritual structures are still held for them in case they should return. An initiation I observed in 1978 at Kwatengisi, a Kwanga village, was interrupted when the elders of those being initiated protested that men who had not "seen the tambaran [spirits]" were assisting the initiators. This was unprecedented, but after some discussion it was decided that there was no alternative. The initiating group was so depleted by absentees and the elders so aged that the labor of uninitiated men was needed to continue the ceremony. Presumably other pragmatic adjustments were made to the pre-1945 traditions. The effect of changes on women during this period also remains a matter for speculation. It is likely that they were required to contribute more labor to subsistence production, and the loss of young men to the plantations almost certainly imposed stresses on mothers and sisters.

While individual communities faced their own crises and made accommodations in the period up to 1942, the war years of 1942–45 focused the crisis of colonialism for all communities. Although it was a uniquely horrifying event, it was in many ways merely the extreme extension and application of forces that had long been in play. People could no longer avoid facing the questions posed by colonial intrusion. What were the sources of the foreigners' power? Why did they refuse to engage in relationships based on equality? Was the superior-inferior relationship a permanent one? What could be done about it?

The way in which these questions were posed and explored by individuals and communities during the war is poorly researched and understood. Even at the superficial level of events, our knowledge is poor. We do know, for example, that Aitape was looted and coastal men came inland and terrorized villagers. Two priests were killed near But, and a European recruiter, Hook, was killed by coastal men near Dreikikir. This response to the withdrawal of Australian colonial control was not found elsewhere in Papua New Guinea, except in Oro Province. Australian officers blamed disruptions to village life on the missions (D. M. Fienberg [Fenbury], Aitape Patrol Report no. 4, 1944). Two years later local men who were involved were executed by firing squad before the assembled populations of all the nearby villages. Armed men attached to an intelligence-gathering operation abducted a number of southern Kwanga women, and when men tried to prevent another's being taken eight men were shot and killed. In 1943 dysentery caused declines in West Sepik village populations of up to 30 percent, and in battle zones sharp falls in populations occurred. Over fourteen hundred people died in the Urim and Urat census divisions alone between 1941 and 1945 (Allen 1983).

Elsewhere, Sepik indentured laborers trapped by the war on the Gazelle Peninsula were taken to Buna by the Japanese to work for them as carriers in their disastrous Kokoda Trail campaign. Others fought in the Papua and New Guinean Infantry Battalions. They were trained to use modern weapons to kill Japanese and took part in "disturbances" which resulted in proper uniforms and better pay rates; they saw inexperienced Australian troops fail their baptism by fire, mixed with Australian, American, and Japanese troops and with Papua New Guineans from all parts of the country, and experienced the military organization of large bodies of men and the massive amounts of ordnance which the war brought to Papua New Guinea (Nelson 1980).

The overall impact of the war in the Sepik is by no means clear. Wartime events suggest that people at first tried to gain the greatest advantage from an uncertain situation and then, when caught in the crossfire between two modern armies, tried to avoid, as much as possible, contact with either side. The psychological impact was considerable; at Dreikikir men still hyperbolize in speeches about the government by saying they will not yield on some point or another "even if they shoot us, like they did in the war." On the other hand, some men gained from their experiences. The war sharpened the differences between the generations that had developed before the war. Men who had achieved established positions of leadership before 1942 were confronted after the war by a group of young men with different experiences and ideas, determined to challenge the prewar patterns. Ex-servicemen and ex-policemen in particular refused to settle back under the old regime. They built new coastal-style houses on sites away from the main villages and almost immediately came into conflict with village officials and young Australian officers. They argued that the old traditions were no longer rel-

evant and that the power of the foreigners lay not in the old New Guinea spirits but in something known as *bisnis*. It was possible, they said, to produce commodities from village lands that could be exchanged for money. This was a source of the foreigners' power. If they did this successfully, they would achieve the respect of the foreigners who had formerly treated them like the "bush kanakas" they were.

The main commodity in question was rice. The full story of rice in the Sepik, too long to relate here, begins in the Northern Province and can be traced through the mixing of Sepik men and Papuans in the police and army. The driving force behind it was Pita Simogun of Dagau, a war hero and sergeant major of police who during the war had urged Sepik policemen to resign and return home to develop their village communities when the war was over. He sent information through a network of ex-policemen which spread from Dagau to Angoram, Ambunti, Lumi, and beyond.[4] At Supari another ex-policeman, Augen of Womsis, who was married to a woman from Wareli, started a small rice-growing enterprise with guidance from Simogun. He was assisted by Nalowas, an Albinama man.[5] The Dreikikir *bisnisbois*, as they were known, established their own hierarchies, which spread well beyond their own villages. Anton of Moseng village recalls,

> I looked for smart men in each village I visited. I told them, "I want a man who can withstand the scrutiny of everyone. Who can work, work hard. Who can speak well and who is intelligent. I am not concerned about flash clothes or a nice shiny skin. I want a good brain!" I looked for that sort of man and when I saw one I told him, "You are the committee man for this village. You organise them here. Organise rice growing."

Similarly, Kokomo of Emul village reports,

> We went around holding meetings and telling people about rice. I appointed committee-men in the Urat, Wam, and Bumbita areas. I didn't take rice around with me. I told them to go to Supari for that. I told them it was a good thing; that the government approved; that they should not listen to the luluais who did not like rice.

Within five years from 1950, all except the most distant mountain Anomakei villages had planted a crop of rice (Allen 1977). People were keen to challenge their village officials and the government, and many were just as pleased to reject, at least temporarily, all of the old ways.

Some younger officers supported the village officials and threatened the rice leaders with jail, but their superiors gave quiet encouragement to the new movement, together with warnings to stay within the law. According to Anton,

> Many of the big men were afraid of rice. They said it was bad. "What if this rice destroys our food gardens, the tambaran, the yam exchanges? Get rid of it, quickly." But we would not; so they ran to the kiap and told him, "It is bad, it is wrong. We will lose the ways of our ancestors." They were good men, but they were "stone-knives," men of the old ways.

Said Mwalhiyer of Ngahmbole village,

> I told them, "Listen to me. Now you are angry. But later you will be happy. If you don't listen now, later you will be sorry. You will remain as your mother and father lived. Stop these exchanges. Stop these initiations. Stop following the ways of our ancestors. That way is no longer any good. Now we must follow the way of the white men. That way we will become strong and rich." These were my own ideas. We had to stop the old ways and establish bisnis of our own if we were to succeed. . . . I was just a kanaka. I had never been away. But I could see what was happening.

Rice was the first crop cultivated solely for sale. New factors of access and location, which had begun to make their presence felt with the establishment of colonial control, became critical. Maprik, inland and to the east, had replaced Aitape as the administrative center, and a jeep road had been roughly pushed from Maprik to Dreikikir. The axis of trade and communications swung back to its precolonial orientation. The northern villages lost their positions as gateways to the coast and slipped into peripheral obscurity, while villages near the new road, which led to the rice-buying points and hullers, were advantaged in terms of marketing their rice. With no traditional sanctions or taboos to stop them, women as well as men became heavily involved in planting rice. Women were particularly important because only they could carry sufficient amounts of the harvest to the places where hullers had been set up by the fledgling cooperatives, the government's belated attempt to formalize the rice-growing activities.

Although some of the older generation joined the rice movement, many totally rejected it and, it is said, mounted a full-scale attack using sorcery on the rice leaders. The most important rice leaders hired their own *glasman* (clairvoyant) to sniff out the magical assaults before they could do any damage. The rice movement was brought down, however, not by the supernatural but by the laws of economics and marketing. The scale of production was minuscule and the marketing arrangements chaotic. Many gardens were planted communally by large numbers of people who received almost nothing when the harvest was sold and the proceeds divided among them. Finally, in many villages the women brought rice planting to a stop by refusing to carry the harvest to the buying points.

There is no doubt whatsoever that people had expected to transform their lives with this activity, and their disappointment was extreme. The appearance and rapid spread in 1956 of a spectacular millenarian movement involving mass hysteria, frenetic dancing, marching, the raising of the recently dead, and attempts to communicate with those already in the cemetery cannot have been solely fortuitous. Rice growing had caused people, particularly women, to travel farther from home than normal and mix more with people from other areas when camping around buying points. The leaders of the millenarian movement had been involved in the rice movement, some giving protection to the rice leaders, and their message was rapidly spread across the area. The source of most of the ideas in this movement, Wahute, of Selni village, had accompanied an Oil Search geologist-turned-guerrilla during the war and traveled widely in the Sepik. He had also come into conflict with the Catholic mission:

> The priest did not like me. I had argued with him before. He did not teach the children properly. He taught no English, only Pidgin. And hymn singing. He was stopping us from progressing. I threw the blackboard out the door. The father wrote to the kiap. He said I had told him I had died and had been resurrected. That was not true. God's spirit entered me at times, that was all. Then my eyes were clear. Now they are not.

Wahute also heard voices and had seizures, and these behaviors were contagious. People who did not spontaneously shake, collapse, and see visions could be induced to do so by jumping, deep breathing, and having leaves waved before their eyes. Customary sexual divisions did not apply. Women were deeply involved in all aspects of the movement. They proved more susceptible than men to hypnosis, and many of them saw visions. Only women were "raised from the dead." Some men and women experimented for a short time with sexual promiscuity in association with rituals, but they remain very secretive about this today. All bones, skulls, magical paraphernalia, and bodily decoration were supposed to be destroyed, but many men buried small durable items such as shells. Dreikikir Patrol Post was unmanned, and the activities were kept secret from the Evangelical missionaries who had established themselves at Dreikikir in 1952. Only when men at Bongos tried to kill the Catholic priest, who they believed was interfering in their attempts to contact the dead, did the movement come to the attention of the government. It was then swiftly put down, and the instigators were imprisoned for up to three years. A number of them served their sentences by extending the Telefomin airstrip. On their return from prison they had to walk from Maprik to Dreikikir. The journey coincided with a sudden outbreak of millenarian activity in villages all along their route, including Ilahita, where it took a government patrol to put a stop to things (Dreikikir Patrol Report no. 1, 1958–59).

After the suppression of the millenarian movement there appears to have been a period of adjustment and accommodation, almost as if the expenditure of energy first in rice, then in millenarianism had exhausted people. The leaders of both movements had failed publicly. The rice leaders had argued that Europeans had revealed the secret of their power and wealth in payment of the great debt of suffering created during the defeat of the Japanese, but most people now believed that the foreigners had deceived them. The millenarian leaders claimed that they had supernaturally had revealed to them the foreigners' secrets, but people now believed that either the revelations were wrong or the foreigners had acted quickly to suppress rituals which, if carried to their conclusions, would have been successful. During this period village officials regained some of their lost power through the enforcement of a program of road and bridge building which required the compulsory labor of all able-bodied adults. Some traditional activities were taken up again, but there was a significant increase in labor migration in the late 1950s, with many villages reported to be overrecruited.

It was decisions in Washington and Canberra that restored much lost prestige to the former rice leaders. On the recommendation of the World Bank, robusta coffee was introduced to lowland Papua New Guinea as a smallholder crop in 1964. Government extension officers rejuvenated the failed rural progress societies of the 1950s, and the bisnis leaders, now with full government backing, began to organize the planting of coffee. Rural progress societies became amalgamated into the Sepik Producers' Co-operative Association (SPCA), one of the most successful marketing cooperatives in the country, and the former bisnisbois became the directors.

By 1971 coffee sales were providing an estimated 60 percent of cash incomes in the East Sepik. Other sources of cash at that time were road work, gold mining, trading, food marketing, airstrip maintenance, and the sale of building materials (Weinand, Young, and Lea 1972). Because all coffee is sold to one of two cooperatives, it is possible fairly reliably to attribute coffee sales (and hence cash incomes from coffee) to villages in the Maprik Sub-Province (table 1, fig. 1). In 1971 and 1972 the highest per capita production of coffee was concentrated west of Maprik astride the Sepik Highway. Even then people in this area were receiving incomes from coffee fifty times greater than those in the areas of lowest production. In the ten years to 1981 this pattern of inequality intensified. Production increased three times in the highest-producing villages but fell in the lowest-producing ones, so that in 1981 the former were receiving per capita incomes from coffee three hundred times larger than the latter. While a recent increased interest in cacao may account for some of the decline in coffee production from some villages, areas such as Kaboibus, Tamaui, and the North Wosera were not heavily involved in cacao planting in 1981.

Despite the apparent success of coffee in some areas between Maprik and Dreikikir, per capita incomes remain low. The average per capita income from coffee in the top five coffee-producing census divisions in 1981 was around K29 (A$37). The rural minimum wage for 1981 was approximately K1,352 (A$1,750). Even if we assume that a rural laborer supported eight persons on his wage, per capita income in his family was still six times what a coffee producer in the highest-producing villages in the East Sepik received in 1981. In addition, coffee prices, and hence incomes, fluctuate with the market price. For much of 1980 coffee growers received over K1.10 per kilogram, but by August 1981 the price had fallen to 0.64 toea, about half that of the previous year.

Although the wage laborer must purchase food for his family from his wages, the village coffee

TABLE 1
PER CAPITA COFFEE PRODUCTION (KG) BY CENSUS DIVISION, 1971–72, 1981

1971–72		1981	
Albiges	26.5	Albiges	78.4
Muhiang		Wam	
Wam		Urat	
Urat		Mamblep	
Wora		Muhiang	
Mamblep	14.5	Yangoru	24.3
Maprik		Kumun	
Yangoru		Kombio	
Gawanga		South Wosera	
South Wosera		Wingei	
North Wosera	6.8	Wora	9.2
Kombio		Urim	
Yamil		Yamil	
Tamaui		Nindepolye	
Kumun		Gawanga	
Urim	3.5	Maprik	3.6
Nindepolye		North Wosera	
Kaboibus		Tamaui	
Wingei	0.5	Kaboibus	0.2

SOURCE: Weinand, Young, and Lea (1972); Sepik Producers' Co-operative Association receipt books, 1972; SPCA computer records, 1981.

producer makes a direct comparison between the minimum wage received by a laborer and the income he receives from a cash crop. He also compares himself with other wage and salary earners, including government officers. As the Tumam councillor observed, unprompted,

In the days before independence, there was one kiap at Dreikikir and two policemen. They used to patrol everywhere and do all the work. Now there are three kiaps and twelve police and we never see them. The kiap has a house and a car given to him by the government and he gets paid. For doing what? We should get paid for building our own houses and growing our own food.

The fluctuations of the market are beyond the comprehension of most producers, and the suspicion that outsiders, including SPCA coffee buyers, Port Moresby bureaucrats, and Chinese businessmen, are exploiting them is widespread and deep-rooted among village people.

This situation of apparently permanent and deepening inequality between villages and the outside world, in communities where a very strong ethic of equality exists, goes a long way toward explaining why so many people became

emotionally and financially involved with the Peli Association between 1972 and 1978. The late Kokomo Ulia, policeman, rice leader, councillor, SPCA director, and Member of Parliament, observed in 1975 that it was the loss of control over the affairs of the SPCA, which he and others had been instrumental in starting, that finally led him to reject bisnis after thirty years of involvement and lead his people into the Peli Association.

Peli created yet another niche for aspiring leaders. Few of the now aging bisnis leaders were as agile as Kokomo, and most defended the coffee industry and cash as the only means to major social and economic change. Old cargo leaders were rejected because the mass hysteria of the 1956 movement had frightened many people. Peli was not a "cargo cult," they said, but something different. The Evangelical mission rejected the movement as the "the Devil working through native spirits" and lost 80 percent of its adherents overnight; physical scuffles occurred between those who left and those who stayed. Some councillors quietly joined and helped their villages' Peli komiti, but others, often at the urging of government officers, resisted, to the point of near nervous breakdown. Coffee had given women ac-

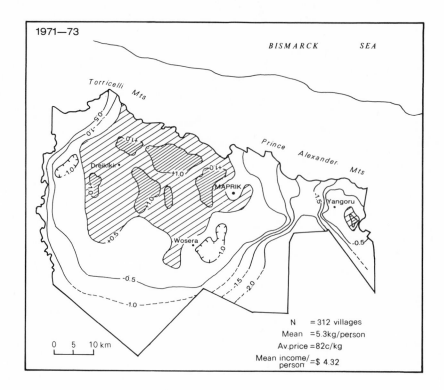

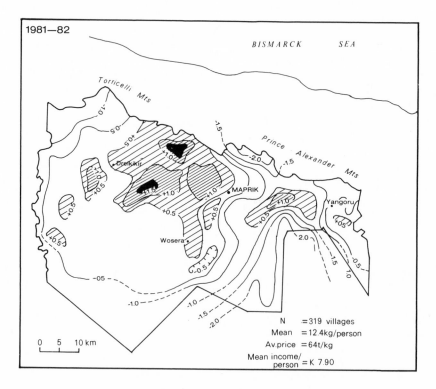

Fig. 1. Village coffee production in the Maprik District, 1971-73 and 1981-82, expressed as standard deviation scores from the district mean (Weinand, Young, and Lea 1972 and Sepik Producers' Co-operative Association records).

cess to cash, many keeping the money they received for coffee picked and processed for themselves. Peli gave the young a special place, as the money to be created in the "power houses" was literally in the hands of young unmarried females and their adolescent consorts. They took their jobs very seriously. At that time coffee production and membership in the Peli Association were highest in those villages with the best access to the Sepik Highway. Villagers were still not distinguishing between the "work" of marketing export crops and the "work" of bringing about the millennium. The goals were similar in the two cases, and, as in the previous case of rice and the 1956 cargo movement, people followed those who claimed they had the knowledge to achieve them.

Although the Peli Association and other movements which grew out of it were opposed by the national government, they were not suppressed by police action as other cargo movements had been in the past. The Peli Association painfully died away as increasing numbers of supporters lost faith. The "power houses" were slowly reclaimed by the forest, the "flowers" and "workers" returned to everyday life.

Then in late 1977, at Daihungai village, in the middle of the night, the slit-gongs boomed out. Men came hurriedly out of their houses to find the old bisnis leader Haptas with a huge dead cassowary at his feet. He made a speech in which he accused his ritual opponents of being like women who had been hurried back into their houses. Blithely ignoring the fact that for thirty years he had vigorously discouraged traditional activities in favor of bisnis, he told the men that he had been waiting for a long time for them to repay the debt his father had created. If they couldn't kill their own cassowaries, here was one for them. Within weeks other villages had announced plans for the staging of an exchange or an initiation. Flutes were again heard in the area, the spectacular masts with their cane rigging went up, and moiety leaders urged greater garden production from their followers.

It seemed to me at the time that a full circle had been turned. Men born in the late 1930s and now in their fifties had participated in these rituals as youths, but they had also experienced World War II, worked on plantations and in mines, planted rice and coffee, and participated in two major efforts to bring about the millennium. Their overarching goal had been to create a situation in which they would be able to meet with and enter into relationships with outsiders on an equal footing. At the same time men and women had continued to try to better their individual positions. Some had been successful, but the major communal goal had never been reached. Did the revival of the old ways indicate a withdrawal, an admission of defeat in the face of a vastly superior force?

Some men suggested that this was the case. Had not Prime Minister Somare himself said *kastom* (tradition) was of value? The origin of their traditions and their rituals was their ancestors, who had given the traditions directly to them. In contrast to bisnis and kago, nobody could come and tell them how to carry out the rituals. Nobody in the whole world knew better than they how to paint the decorations, sing the songs, carry out the ceremonies. Government extension officers excused the failure of the programs by saying that the people were interested only in kastom.[6] Indeed, this seemed like the final rejection of the modern world, at least by the last of the prewar generation who had been so radically innovative during their lives. Since Independence they have shown a marked reluctance to accept information or advice from government agents, and the return to kastom might be interpreted as part of that rejection.

But as always, matters are not as simple as they first appear. Late last year I made a brief visit to the area. There were no plans for further ceremonies. Land was being cleared in many villages along the Maprik road for twenty-hectare cacao and coffee blocks. Kastom was good, but it was hard work, harder than growing coffee, and it didn't bring in money; it was no longer possible to live without money. The Lus Corporation[7] was helping to plan the large coffee blocks and was planning a wet-processing factory on the Amuk River. At Tumam the men had decided that they had to maintain their membership with the SPCA, so all the women in the village had become members of the Lus Corporation. The SPCA had employed an extension worker who was working *in* villages. Many people were talking about planting cacao so that if the price of coffee fell, they could sell cacao, and vice versa. Meanwhile everyone was producing coffee. After two years of traditional activities they were short of money, they said. Less than halfway through the season 1983 production had surpassed that of 1982. Young men trapped in their villages by the recession, who had said a year earlier that the first chance they got they were leaving for the cities, were now marrying, having children, and apparently settling down to life in rural Papua New Guinea. The old men, having discharged their responsibilities to their fathers, seemed prepared to retire from public life. If not the turning of a full circle, it was surely the end of an era.

One could employ a range of approaches to the study of colonial history in the Sepik. These days one pays one's money and takes one's choice. A neo-Marxist analysis, even given the problems which remain in applying concepts such as "articulation" (see, e.g., Foster-Carter 1978), would seem to offer great scope and has been attempted elsewhere in Papua New Guinea by Godelier (1982*b*) and Modjeska (1982). Goulet's (1971) arguments, however, have more appeal for me. To him "development is no abstraction, but a historical reality situated in time and place" (p. 13). The "context and matrix" within which change occurs must be identified. His analysis rests on two points: "vulnerability" (the exposure to forces one cannot control) and "existence rationality" (the strategies employed by societies to process information and make practical choices designed to ensure survival and satisfy the need, according to Goulet universal, for esteem and freedom). Thus we can observe the Dreikikir village communities attempting to employ strategies which will at once free them from outside domination of all kinds (even benevolent domination), provide them with a material standard of living equivalent to those enjoyed by outsiders, and allow them to enter into equal and balanced relationships with them. Yet their goals contain within them fundamental contradictions. Their first set of strategies, cash crop production, brings about increased outside domination and lack of control over their own affairs (in the form of extension workers, cooperative managers, and fluctuating world markets) and increased reliance on world commodity markets, which is equivalent to increased vulnerability. The other set of strategies, millenarianism, does not work but has a powerful psychological attraction when the contradictions of the first set periodically became too painfully obvious.

Sepik villagers live in a country that is becoming increasingly reliant on the export of minerals and agricultural commodities to support a top-heavy and expensive bureaucracy. This bureaucracy is unlikely to redistribute power as it was forced to do in 1977 with decentralization and will probably become entrenched in urban areas. Services to rural areas are unlikely to improve. If we are to contribute in a way which will assist Sepik villagers to come to terms with such a world and to make the least cruel of a number of possible cruel choices, I believe we must use our skills to analyze how Sepik villagers have handled change in the past and how they are dealing with their present situations. To do otherwise will be to become increasingly irrelevant to a modern Papua New Guinea.

Notes

1. Loa says he was "recruited" by Ah Sing. This is probably Ning Sing, the father of Una Ning-foo, now of Brisbane, and the adoptive father of Sangu Leong of Madang. In 1983 they told me that Ning Sing was himself an indentured laborer who left his Canton homeland because the Germans promised that every step in New Guinea left one's boots covered with gold dust.

2. Perhaps such a sweeping generalization is unfair, but studies by, for example, Gell (1975) and Tuzin (1976, 1980) do not, in my opinion, give enough emphasis to the changes which have occurred since colonial contact.

3. In Tau village, south of Tumam, Brigit Obrist (personal communication) has heard an oral account of a pre-European epidemic which killed many people and had symptoms described as being "like scabies."

4. For example, Numbuk Kapok, who began the Erap Mechanical Farming Project in the Markham Valley, was a policeman serving under Simogun in the Sepik from 1945 to 1951 (Hogbin 1963).

5. Nalowas had been taken by blackbirders and sent to Rabaul at such a young age that he did not know the name of his village. He had to stay there for ten years until laborers from his home area recognized him and told where he came from.

6. Some measure of the failure of agricultural extension work in the East Sepik is provided by the ignorance among Urat villagers of the East Sepik Integrated Rural Development Project. This project was, among other things, supposed to have rejuvenated tree crops in the province. Although staff has been appointed, houses built, and vehicles purchased, very little village-level work seems to have been accomplished.

7. The Lus Corporation is not owned by Sir Pita Lus; it is a locally based cooperative now being largely managed by young Sepik university graduates. Its membership is concentrated west of Maprik but is spreading.

15/ The Bishops' Progress: Representations of Missionary Experience on the Sepik Frontier

Mary Taylor Huber

The singularity of a "vocation" is never better displayed than when it is contradicted—but not denied, far from it—by a prosaic incarnation: this is an old trick of all hagiography.   [Barthes 1972:31]

A careful reading of the papers in this volume will uncover many allusions to aspects of modern village life which attest to the impact of Christian mission activity in the Sepik region of Papua New Guinea but few which deal directly with missionaries themselves. The issue of missionary impact, however, like that of government impact, raises many elusive questions, some of which can be addressed by turning the problem around. What aspects of *missionary* work have been affected by the missionaries' experience in the Sepik? What changes have appeared problematic to missionaries, and how have they managed the dilemmas which these changes posed? I have chosen to discuss the Catholic missionaries of the Society of the Divine Word because they have been working in the region since 1896 and because they still comprise the large majority of priests, including the bishop, in the Diocese of Wewak in the East Sepik Province today.[1]

Recent attention to the problem of "law and order" in Papua New Guinea has encouraged some researchers to ask about the "social arrangements" that appear to have made the colonial *kiap* (government officer) system so effective in its time (see Gordon 1983). As any reader of the memoirs of the quintessential Sepik kiap, G. W. L. Townsend, will recognize, however, the very system that made the kiap "an organization of one" in the field (Gordon 1983:220) also pitted him against the "powers that were" in the colonial capital, be it Port Moresby (after World War II) or Rabaul (before). Like kiaps and many of the other emissaries of change who have traveled through Sepik history, Catholic missionaries of the Society of the Divine Word have also had to manage the often conflicting requirements of working effectively in local circumstances while

maintaining the authenticity of their project, i.e., its relation to official or ideal forms (cf. Burridge 1960, 1978). I suggest that by looking at the ways in which such agents have represented their experience we can come some way to understanding the historical processes by which some of the Sepik's most important regional institutions have taken on the character which they have today.

While this paper is intended as a contribution to Sepik history, I follow Beidelman (1982) in my conviction that mission studies are relevant to other issues in colonial culture and society as well. Certainly, few Europeans who have come to New Guinea have been able to represent their experience without contrasting it to Western models in order to render the place and the people intelligible to themselves and to those back home. This may have been especially so for missionaries and others who were enmeshed in large organizations which exercise control over their agents by upholding these models as goals for their activity and as measures of their success. The problem of justifying the inevitable detours that conditions forced on their projects could be especially critical for agents who had internalized the goals of their sending agencies, and it is no surprise that their memoirs and reports are frequently cast in an ironic mode. Catholic missionaries who have worked in the Sepik are no exception, for they have been well aware of the fact that to be effective, their work had to take directions which appeared to contrast with authentic forms.

The ironic expressions through which so many colonists have represented their experience have had political import as well as literary effect. In the words of a young American priest who had recently joined the Catholic mission in the mid-1930s, New Guinea was "a land of the unexpected," a theme as frequently illustrated in letters, reports, and memoirs by the peculiarities of its European denizens as by the exotica of native life. Traveling in the Sepik in the 1920s and 1930s, for example, one might meet a Catholic bishop in shirt-sleeves unloading cargo from a coastal steamer (Marshall 1938:221), a government officer on a tax raid outside his jurisdiction (Townsend 1968:159), a planter roaming the interior to recruit labor (Mead 1977:103), or an illiterate drifter running the district's major store (McCarthy 1963:137).

Perhaps nothing was so frequently used to characterize colonial life in the Sepik as such "standard" deviations from the proprieties of the division of labor that underlie European ideas about the status quo. McSwain (1977:29) has said that Europeans in the Madang District "saw the economic, political, and religious systems as discrete entities," that "individuals involved themselves in only one aspect of the economy," and that "the missions restricted their activities almost entirely to religious and educational change." This is certainly an adequate rendering of social ideology among colonial Europeans, but it is not an adequate rendering of the facts of their life on the Sepik frontier. The Catholic mission's first bishop had written home in the 1890s, "No matter what kind of job comes up, if we don't take care of it ourselves, no one else moves a finger . . . " (Wiltgen 1969:340). And so they did take care of things. In the Madang vicinity itself, the Catholic mission headquarters at Alexishafen soon had not only a church, a school, a printing press, and a hospital but a coconut plantation, a copra factory, railway tracks, a timber mill, a carpentry, a machine shop, a tailor shop, a boot factory, a dry dock, and warehouses as well (see Hagspiel 1926:115–24; Marshall 1938:221–22).

Understandably, such a display of self-sufficiency violated the model of organic solidarity implicit in the European social ideal and had external political consequences for the mission which will receive brief mention later on. What I shall focus on in this paper, however, is the internal contradictions generated by such adaptations, how they have been expressed, and how they have been managed within the mission itself. I focus on bishops because the missionaries themselves do. This is not necessarily because they have been "great men" but because their office has made them responsible for both the effectiveness and the authenticity of the church as it develops in the mission field. Episcopal imagery has been used by the missionaries both to articulate and to

resolve the contradictions that the mission has faced over time. I have organized this paper, then, in terms of successive periods in mission history represented in mission literature by bishops known for their practical skills and manner. For the first two periods, especially, I have worked with fragmentary materials. I thus present my findings as only an outline of what appear to have been the major emphases of the times.[2]

Background

I must assume some familiarity with the history of Papua New Guinea: that the northern part of the country was colonized by Germany in the 1880s, that Australians occupied the colony during World War I and assumed responsibility for civil administration in 1921, that Japanese invaded and occupied lowland parts of the territory from 1942 to 1945, and that Australia again administered the area until the northern territory of New Guinea and the southern territory of Papua achieved independence as a single country in 1975. As most specialists know, the Sepik region itself was long a frontier in relation to the political and commercial centers of the colony and, with the exception of the Catholic mission, attracted little in the way of foreign capital investment until after World War II, when a wealthier and more development-minded administration assumed control. The infrastructure required to support specialized sectors was simply lacking in the Sepik for a very long time.

I cannot, unfortunately, assume much familiarity with the details of Catholic ecclesiastical organization, nor am I competent to present them in strict conformity to canon law. A few points, however, may help the reader to interpret some of the historical material that follows. Catholic missions, like Protestant missions, generally stand somewhat outside the normal structures of the church. In Catholic practice, responsibility for mission territories has generally been "entrusted" by the Vatican to special religious orders, whose operations in the mission field are coordinated by a special curial body long known as Propaganda Fide. A mission society, however, retains a great deal of independence in administering, staffing, and financing the territories to which it has been assigned. The Society of the Divine Word was entrusted with the ecclesiastical territory created for mainland New Guinea in the 1890s in part because it was a German missionary society and the German administrators of the colony wanted to contain the French missionaries of the Society of the Sacred Heart to the Bismarck Archipelago, where their work had begun before Germany assumed control. Needless to say, the German origins of so many of its missionaries have affected the Sepik mission's "spirit" and style. During the periods around World War I and World War II, their nationality complicated their political relations within the Australian colony.

Although the pioneer missionaries had as their territory the whole of mainland New Guinea that was under German administration, they naturally confined their efforts to the coastal region and, for reasons to be mentioned later, focused on the area between Aitape and Madang. Like government districts, however, Catholic mission territories have a complex history of division. I have attempted to outline this history for the New Guinea territory in figure 1. The three bishops to be discussed became, respectively, the Prefect Apostolic of Kaiser-Wilhelmsland, the Vicar Apostolic of Central New Guinea, and the Bishop of Wewak. Each presided over a successively smaller jurisdiction that could be more thoroughly evangelized because of its smaller size. Parts of the original territory were eventually assigned to other mission societies, leaving four of the region's seven jurisdictions in 1966 in the hands of the Society of the Divine Word.

The changes in the bishops' titles are as important in theory as are the divisions of territory and their entrustment to various mission societies in practice. The prefect, vicar, and diocesan bishop are progressively higher offices in the church, and indeed the transition to diocesan status is the climax in a mission territory's official career. From a single undifferentiated territory, the jurisdiction is successively divided—each unit receiving its own prefect or vicar—until finally a hierarchy is established with an archdiocese and several suffragan sees. This event was timed in New Guinea to coincide with the seventieth anniversary of the arrival of the first missionaries of the Society of the Divine Word.

The First Bishop: Eberhard Limbrock and the Material Base

It is significant that the missionary historian Ralph Wiltgen wrote his article on the origins of Catholic mission plantations on the north coast of New Guinea *after* the deliberations of the Second Vatican Council and the papal encyclical "On the De-

velopment of Peoples" (Wiltgen 1969:360). The latter, especially, enabled Wiltgen to depict the first prefect apostolic of Kaiser-Wilhelmsland, Fr. Eberhard Limbrock, architect of the mission's impressive material base, as a man ahead of his times. The combination of enterprise and evangelism that Limbrock pioneered during his tenure as bishop of mainland New Guinea had been highly controversial both within and outside the mission community. For Wiltgen the concept of "integral salvation" that derived from Vatican II brought the "spiritual" and "material" aspects of mission work into a closer relationship than they had been before, thus blunting arguments used by earlier critics of Limbrock and his mission.

A glance at the history of Catholic views on the role of economic development in mission work may illuminate the internal context in which Limbrock's policies received their initial interpretation. Arbuckle (1978:284) provides a useful summary of theological emphases on this issue over the past hundred years: post–Vatican II, "development is an essential part of mission work"; Vatican II, "development is useful to show people that the church is relevant"; pre–Vatican II, "development helps the missionary to make pastoral contact with the people"; and even earlier, "development work is dangerous; it distracts the missionary from his real work." One must move to the end of this list to characterize the dominant emphasis in Catholic opinion in the 1890s, when the mission to New Guinea was officially conceived. It is important to note, however, that in contrast to those of some evangelical sects of the nineteenth century, Catholic views on the dangers of development work did not necessarily entail an ascetic orientation to the cultural world as a whole. Although the Society of the Divine Word had already experienced its own history of dissension and compromise in defining a mode of spirituality for its members by the time it began sending missionaries to New Guinea, missionary work was clearly conceived by the Society as requiring concessions to ways of life "in the world" (Bornemann 1975:166–75). Indeed, the previous failure of two undersupplied Catholic missions to the area near mainland New Guinea motivated the Society's founder and first superior general to pay special attention to the provisioning of his missionaries and to encourage them to develop local sources of financial support as soon as possible. Prior to their departure they not only had ready for shipment a prefabricated house, kitchen, carpentry, foundry, and blacksmith shop but planned to begin a coconut plantation in the area near the co-

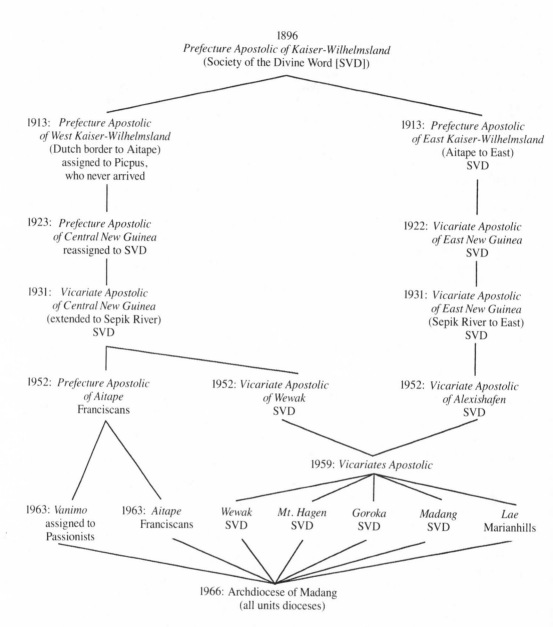

1896
Prefecture Apostolic of Kaiser-Wilhelmsland
(Society of the Divine Word [SVD])

1913: *Prefecture Apostolic*
of West Kaiser-Wilhelmsland
(Dutch border to Aitape)
assigned to Picpus,
who never arrived

1913: *Prefecture Apostolic*
of East Kaiser-Wilhelmsland
(Aitape to East)
SVD

1923: *Prefecture Apostolic*
of Central New Guinea
reassigned to SVD

1922: *Vicariate Apostolic*
of East New Guinea
SVD

1931: *Vicariate Apostolic*
of Central New Guinea
(extended to Sepik River)
SVD

1931: *Vicariate Apostolic*
of East New Guinea
(Sepik River to East)
SVD

1952: *Prefecture Apostolic*
of Aitape
Franciscans

1952: *Vicariate Apostolic*
of Wewak
SVD

1952: *Vicariate Apostolic*
of Alexishafen
SVD

1959: *Vicariates Apostolic*

1963: *Vanimo*
assigned to
Passionists

1963: *Aitape*
Franciscans

Wewak
SVD

Mt. Hagen
SVD

Goroka
SVD

Madang
SVD

Lae
Marianhills

1966: Archdiocese of Madang
(all units dioceses)

FIG. 1. The history of the New Guinea mission territory (*The Word in the World* 1969: 49-57).

lonial capital of Friedrich-Wilhelmshafen, now known as Madang (Bornemann 1975:309; Wiltgen 1969:331).

These elaborate arrangements were in tune with the theological temper of the times because they were clearly subordinated to the essential spiritual work of saving souls. Limbrock was chosen as prefect of the mission not only because he had a farming background and was "practical-minded" but also because he was "devout"

(Wiltgen 1969:330, 360). Limbrock had already served for thirteen years in China, "had a friendly disposition, was prudent in his conduct and speech, and was an able administrator. Genuinely religious, he was at home in the Scriptures and was every inch a priest" (Bornemann 1975:309). This latter was especially important because in this mission, the division of labor made priests responsible for "spiritual upbuilding," while brothers were responsible for "building the mission up materially" (Wiltgen 1969:330).

Limbrock's first problem in organizing the new mission came from local authorities of the Neu Guinea Kompagnie, who took umbrage at his request for plantation land. Although this firm, which then enjoyed a land monopoly in return for its services in administering the territory, clearly confused the categories of commerce and government itself, it was determined to brook no confusion between commerce and religion, especially when the result would mean admitting a competitor to its own interests in the fledgling plantation economy along the north coast. For five years the Neu Guinea Kompagnie obstinately confined the mission to the offshore islands around Aitape, "275 nautical miles up the coast" from the colonial capital (Wiltgen 1969:331). This problem was resolved only after the Neu Guinea Kompagnie had relinquished its privileges and the imperial governor, Albert Hahl, had been convinced that mission enterprise was consonant with the government's own program for extending German influence along the coastal frontier (cf. Wiltgen 1969:345).

Yet if a frontier can be defined as a zone where normal boundaries between government, commercial, and religious institutions could be so easily confused, it appeared to colonists as a zone which in itself was hostile to serious attempts to constitute these fields as separate domains. From Limbrock's point of view (as quoted by Wiltgen 1969:339), at any rate, there were few supports for the specialized evangelical work which he hoped his priests would pursue:

> Poor, poor New Guinea! Here every foot of ground still has to be cleared, every road has to be made, every bridge built, every really worthwhile plant imported, every hen, every duck, and every other domesticated animal including the horse, has to be brought in from the outside. . . . Every thread on our backs has to be gotten from Europe or elsewhere. . . . Here we have to establish the first school in every area. More than that, we have to use exceptionally great patience and effort to make people even somewhat understand the very notion of schools and their usefulness.

Rosaldo (1978:240) has maintained that "civilized society is most likely to infer the social character of indigenous peoples from those acts that impede commerce and that are completely at variance with civilized norms." In similar fashion, Limbrock's conception of the frontier came to be based on the ways in which its economy impaired the functioning of his own project and threatened the structural integrity of the mission itself.

Limbrock's letters, in fact, speak constantly of the overwhelming burden of the material tasks that faced the mission and of the burdens on time and finance that they imposed (as quoted in Wiltgen 1969:340):

> The most diversified demands are made on us. . . . We have to be farmers and planters; we have to import, care for, and breed cattle. For sea journeys we must understand sailing and steering. There are many wounds to bind, sicknesses to study, and sick colleagues to care for. . . . Then we have to study accounts and find places where we can buy things at a low price. . . . As soon as we leave the mail steamer, we need our own ships, our own surfboats, our own oarsmen, our own landing places, boathouses, and piers with cranes and winches. . . . What cost and trouble and work is caused by these boats alone and all that goes with them. . . . We ourselves have to unload the steamers and bring our cargo ashore, and put it where it belongs. . . . In addition to this there is the usual work of caring for souls . . .

Clearly, Limbrock was losing control over the critical relation between spiritual and material work that defined his mission as a religious enterprise and gave it specific denominational and spiritual form.

Beidelman (1982:61) argues that for the first fifteen years that the evangelical Church Missionary Society was in Tanzania "missionary life corresponded to their idealized notions of their calling" and that it was only after their initial success that the material requirements of running a complex organization came into conflict with their ascetic ideals. The Catholic missionaries of the Society of the Divine Word did not find their first years in New Guinea to be in tune with their calling, and Limbrock seems to have decided that if what was lacking was infrastructural support, they would simply have to provide it themselves. The heroic period for these missionaries, then, was not one of spiritual prowess unencumbered by material concerns but one of unprecedented material upbuilding, which resulted in a base of plantations, workshops, and stations that served the mission well until it was destroyed in World War II.

Mission writers become rather breathless in their descriptions of the pace of mission achievement in the years after 1904, when their political fortunes had turned. Hagspiel (1926:115–24, 132–38), for example, reviews the development of the new mission headquarters that Limbrock had established at Alexishafen after the major shipping line in the region had canceled Aitape as a port of call. Limbrock, he reports, had made a contract with the indigenous owners for about a thousand acres of land in June 1904, and by the end of the month the missionaries had cleared an acre of forest and built a rough two-story residence. The next major improvement was a sawmill, imported from Europe, including a steam locomotive and sawing machinery that were installed by December 1905. The sawmill hummed "from six o'clock in the morning until six o'-clock in the evening," utilizing the best of the wood cleared from the site. No longer dependent on the costly importation of building timbers, Alexishafen was soon graced not only with its original residence and the mill but with a residence for native and Chinese workers, a machine room, two timber sheds, a carpenter's shop, a locksmith's shop, and a chapel. In 1907, other woodworking machines were imported and installed along with a machine shop, and there were rails on which wagons could haul timber from the receding forest. Thousands of new coconut trees were planted at Alexishafen, interspersed with yam, taro, and sweet potato for the support of the workers. A new warehouse was erected in 1907, as were a convent and a central school to which some one hundred boys arrived in 1909. A catechetical training center was added soon thereafter, and a central hospital replaced the original dispensary in 1912. Missionaries went abroad to study methods of rice cultivation; a dry dock was constructed, and by 1911, a new and finer house was built for the brothers and the priests.

No kind of heroism comes without sacrifice, however, and in the process several of the mission's most distinctive features became victims. As no further brothers had come to New Guinea in 1904, when it became possible to proceed with the plantations, industries, and new stations, Limbrock was obliged to assign priests to the task of supervision. Wiltgen (1969:352) notes that by 1906 priests were managing plantations at Aitape and Alexishafen and that "other priests too had to do much manual work, and all did not like the idea." Indeed, when questioned by his Society's superior general about his policies, Limbrock (quoted in Wiltgen 1969:352) admitted that his program had certain drawbacks:

Someone might well object . . . and state that we missionaries ought to withdraw ourselves more from material occupations. . . . Of course, we try to let the Brothers do as much of this work as possible, so as to keep ourselves free for divine services and evangelizing. But unfortunately the good brothers are just not numerous enough. . . . If a house is to be built, then a foundation is also necessary. For better, then, or for worse, we have had to accommodate ourselves to what was unavoidable and to take over the work ourselves. It pained us deeply, however, that in the meanwhile the mission work had to suffer greatly.

In one of the more stunning series of reversals wrought on a colonial institution in the Sepik, then, priests became as brothers, material work temporarily took precedence over spiritual work, and in a few years the bishop himself resigned his office and reverted to the status of a priest. Embattled both by his staff and by the commercial community in Kaiser-Wilhelmsland, Limbrock submitted his resignation to the Society's second superior general, who accepted it, allowing Limbrock to retire from public life and live out the rest of his years "as any other priest" in the mission he once had led (Wiltgen 1969:356).

At one point in the mission's internal struggle, the Society's first superior general had supported Limbrock, proposing that "physical work is an honor for the first missionaries and a great example for those that follow" (Wiltgen 1969:352). Although it was not until after Limbrock's "farming system" had enabled the mission to survive the isolation of World War I relatively intact that dissenters within the mission had "changed their minds" and begun to refer to their former bishop as "the man of Providence" (Hagspiel 1926:127), this episode thenceforward had a long legacy in the New Guinea mission not only in regard to finance but in regard to rhetoric, reputation, and style. This model for accommodating a contradiction by making it display the principle that it seems on the surface to negate is found in the next period of mission history as well. The problem, however, now shifts from hierarchy of means to hierarchy among mission personnel.

The Second Bishop: Joseph Loerks and Mission Solidarity

Wiltgen's article on the interest of "land" to the early mission is nicely balanced by the emphasis that Fr. Bruno Hagspiel, writing in 1926, places on the sea. Hagspiel, an American member of the Society of the Divine Word, had toured the New Guinea mission in 1922–23 as chronicler and publicist for the third superior general's grand tour of the Society's Pacific missions. While he devotes one long chapter of his book on New Guinea to the plantations and industries along the north coast—"a feature which distinguishes [New Guinea] from most of the other mission fields in the world" (1926:125)—the reader is treated to far more detail when the subject is the sea. More precisely, the object of interest is the boat that dominated the traveler's world.

The *Gabriel*, a steamer obtained by the mission in 1910, receives pride of place because "she proved to be one of the principal performers in bringing to pass, as far as transportation goes, the greater part of our missionary experience in New Guinea" (1926:28–29). Her dimensions are reported, and so are the arrangement of space on board, her storage capacity, fueling needs, machinery, navigational equipment, crew, etc. In contrast to Limbrock, for whom the frontier was economic and ships represented a great deal of trouble and expense, Hagspiel saw the frontier as clearly political, and in his travelogue the ship undergoes a subtle transformation as the passage proceeds. From a very literal copra- and cargo-carrying workhorse, the *Gabriel* soon becomes a vehicle of communication, connecting the widely scattered missionaries, and finally emerges as a metaphor for the mission itself. The *Gabriel*'s monthly round of the eighteen stations holds the mission together—a "binding characteristic" that is absent "among the people" themselves (pp. 37–38, 69).

It is significant that Hagspiel, a representative of central authority, should choose to emphasize the integrative capacity of the *Gabriel* and, indeed, to select for praise all aspects of mission practice that might serve to contain diversity within the mission field. An earlier missiologist, writing about the New Guinea mission, had already regretted that the spatial arrangement of its stations isolated the missionaries from one another and that ethnographic and linguistic diversity in the area made centralization of the mission impossible (Schmidlin 1913). Hagspiel is more explicit: "What is meant," he writes, "is that each mission [station], being so entirely segregated from the others, has its own distinct problems to such an extent as to be almost a distinct mission by itself" (1926:69). It is clear that if Limbrock saw plantations as a means to resolve the prob-

TABLE 1

MISSION STATIONS AND LOCAL LANGUAGES IN 1922

STATION	LANGUAGE
1. Aissano	Sissano
2. Arop	Sissano
3. Malol	Sissano
4. Tumleo	Tumleo
5. Aitape	Ali
6. Ali	Ali
7. Yakamul	Ali
8. Ulau	Ulau-Swein
9. Swein	Ulau-Swein
10. Boiken	Boiken
11. Yuo	Kairiru
12. Wewak	Boiken
13. Murik	Murik
14. Marienberg	?
15. Manam	Manam
16. Monombo	Monombo
17. Bogia	Other[a]
18. Mugil	Other[a]
19. Alexishafen	Other[a]

[a] Other Madang-area language.

lems of supply and finance that hampered the mission's capacity to get on with its spiritual work, Hagspiel saw the *Gabriel* as a means to resolve the problems of fragmentation that later dominated mission concerns.

Although the mission's external relations with the new Australian administration were then a cause of great concern, Hagspiel's main interest was the obstacles to internal solidarity which he saw arising from ethnographic and linguistic fragmentation in the region itself. Table 1, locating the mission's stations in 1922 by reference to Laycock's (1973) linguistic survey of the Sepik, may help to ground Hagspiel's remarks. It is clear that if dialect variation is taken into account, as well as the fact that missionaries traveled out from their stations to villages beyond its immediate locale, Hagspiel's estimate that between twenty-five and thirty languages were spoken in the mission's area of operation is reasonable. No doubt he is also right in claiming this region to be culturally diverse as well. Hagspiel's point is that each single missionary was irreplaceable within the area of his linguistic and ethnographic competence and was thus limited in his capacity to benefit from the companionship and advice of confreres located elsewhere in the mission field (pp. 57–70).

Of course, Hagspiel believed that mission activity itself had already ameliorated some of these unfavorable conditions along the coast. The German taught in mission schools, for example, "has established a first bond of intercourse and the sharing of common interests among the tribes," and the plantations and industries too had "contributed their quota of influence to bring the people more and more into a common relationship" (p. 70). Mission stations provided models of order for the natives in their vicinity, and there was also the *Gabriel* to enable some degree of communication among these stations themselves. Hagspiel noted ominously, however, that all of these improvements were much limited in their geographical extent and that pioneer work would soon begin again when missionaries moved into the "vast interior" behind the coastal range (p. 70).

It was the church in ideal form that defined the state of nature that Hagspiel found on the frontier. Instead of one language and common interests, the frontier was characterized by many languages and diverse interests. Instead of an organization that oriented individuals to a common center, "there is nothing like a confederation or unifying principle among the several tribes" (p. 69). Hagspiel's spirits were lightened by the stateliness of the mission's headquarters at Alexishafen, where the fruits of disciplined labor were evident and where he witnessed a processional rite in which "the order maintained throughout was splendid" (p. 213). Yet the forces separating missionaries from such "edifying and dignified" spectacles were potent. Hagspiel viewed isolation not as a spiritual opportunity but as a spiritual disaster (p. 130):

> Proportionately remote from one another lie the mission stations: so that it is seldom that the missionaries are able to come together for a friendly conference. And this consciousness of remoteness, of solitude, of standing quite by oneself in the midst of the low cultural state of the heathen, of being severed from every good influence which serves to uplift and to elevate—this consciousness, I say, tends in the long run to weaken the missionary, both in spirituality and humaneness. "In the midst of the wild surrounded by the wild," declared a missionary priest, "one runs into danger of becoming more or less wild and lawless."

Clearly, the mission's organizational capacity was in question at the time of Hagspiel's visit, when the first new missionaries were arriving after the long years of war and expansion beyond the coast became possible. It is thus no coincidence that just before evangelization in the high-

lands and in the Sepik hinterland began, the territory was effectively divided to create two ecclesiastical districts with two centers to facilitate communication and control. The eastern territory remained in possession of the most profitable plantations and the old headquarters of Alexishafen. Although it was from Alexishafen that missionaries began to travel to the distant highlands, Lutkehaus (1983:29) reports that in this mission district "the traditional Catholic hierarchy was replicated in miniature," with Alexishafen "its 'Vatican City' where the [bishop] resided" and where, according to a contemporary observer, its cathedral was designed after the model of St. Peter's in Rome (Marshall 1938:222).

The new jurisdiction created for the Sepik, however, was less well-off than the territory to the east and was capable of meeting only one-third of its financial needs locally (Angelus 1936). The region within which this mission worked still had no real towns and only a rudimentary commercial sector. Although the mission itself possessed some impressive stations, such as those on Tumleo and at Wewak, they were considerably smaller than Alexishafen in scale. Indeed, it appears that while the eastern district could support a center set apart from the frontier, the western district could not. In the Sepik, neither the old center at Tumleo nor the new headquarters on Kairiru Island appears to have taken on the "miniature Vatican" role. The integrating images in the Sepik were more like the *Gabriel*, partaking of the frontier's rustic character, and the bishop's seat in the Sepik was not as important an image as its bishop, Fr. Joseph Loerks, himself.

Loerks's job was to establish the Sepik as a new and separate jurisdiction, a task to which he brought thirty years of experience in New Guinea, at least ten of which he had served as captain of the *Gabriel* and twenty as mission procurator. Loerks had, it was said, an unrivaled knowledge of the state of mission operations, of conditions on far-flung stations, and of the commercial and administrative powers with which the mission had to deal. If Limbrock's reputation as "the man of Providence" reflects the economic nature of his frontier, Loerks's reputation as "the fighting bishop" (Angelus 1936) reflects the political problems that became his to solve.

Despite Loerks's epithet, his style was not always confrontational. Townsend (1968:226), chief administrative officer of the district during Loerks's tenure as bishop, maintained that Loerks had always cooperated with him to manage "the inevitable conflicts with young field staff who hoped to bring the District under 'complete control' by Christmas; and earnest young, and not so young Fathers who hoped to convert the whole population by Easter at the latest." In Townsend's opinion, it was "thanks to [Loerks's] tolerance and wisdom [that] no conflict between persons ever had to go beyond our conferences" (p. 225). While Loerks's willingness to contain such crises may not have endeared him to some of the more "earnest" missionaries on his staff, his cooperation with Townsend resulted in advantages to the mission when, toward the end of the 1930s, Australian suspicions of German nationals in the territory began to rise (see p. 243).

To outsiders like Townsend and the British memoirist and naturalist A. J. Marshall, Bishop Loerks's special qualities were exemplified through the secular skills that brought the bishop into contact with their own world and distinguished him from the stigmatized "otherworldly" missionary type. Marshall (1938:221), for example, reports that

> on steamer day, so the story runs, you'll see him there on the beach checking the mission cargo, lending a hand, shifting the cases, coatless, in shirt-sleeves. Perhaps the South Seas is the only place where you can see a bishop's shirt-sleeves. But it makes little difference what Bishop Lorks [sic] wore, for he has a noble bearing, a fluent scholarly tongue, and the look of the world in his frank direct eyes.

Townsend also appreciated Loerks's appearance and his skill as a boat captain and raconteur. Loerks, Townsend (1968:224–25) concluded, was a "fine figure of a man who bore little resemblance to the conventional idea of a missionary bent on converting Pacific Island heathen." Indeed, so far did Loerks deviate from the conventional missionary type that, as one priest tells it, the Australians wanted to imprison him when they occupied the territory during World War I. "From his excellent [horse] riding," the priest explains, "they thought he was a German officer. He had to prove to them that he was only a missionary priest" (Laumann 1939–40).

Within the mission, of course, Loerks's manner contrasted less with an image of fervent impracticality than with the traditional hierarchical stereotype of a prelate set apart from his priests by ceremony, servants, and wealth. In one article reporting on a confirmation trip taken by the bishop from Kairiru Island to Sassoya, in the hills behind the coast, we are treated to a bishop saddled with a skittish horse, sliding down muddy hillsides, delayed by tardy carriers, and poured upon relentlessly by rain. "His Excellency" is distinguished from his companions in this account only by the grace with which he encounters the many frustrations of a typical Sepik scene. Clearly, conditions were not favorable to the conventional expressions of dignity that bishops in less rustic areas might be able to afford. And clearly, the bishop's refusal to force the situation was approved as appropriate by at least some of the priests on his staff.

A long letter in which a young American priest tells his former classmates about his first five months in the Sepik mission in 1936 is valuable not in that it represents what individual missionaries believed but in that it reflects collective representations within the mission, coming as it does from a newcomer whom more experienced missionaries are just "breaking in." If we recall that the pioneer missionaries had used the confusion between spiritual and material work to represent their frontier, it is notable that while Fr. Angelus spends much time talking about material matters, he turns to hierarchy and community when he wishes to characterize New Guinea as a whole. "Plans seldom materialize in New Guinea," he writes, and instead of becoming a junior member of the headquarters staff as he had expected, he is suddenly left alone:

> When the schooner pulled out, I remained behind with a three-fold title, namely pastor of a flock that speaks Pidgin, German, and the Tumleo languages; newly appointed procurator of the Vicariate, and Rector of the Central Station. *That's New Guinea all over* [emphasis mine]. It surely seemed strange to hear Fr. Blas on his return asking me for permission for certain articles and to arrange the order for confession, etc.—he is ten years my senior and ordained six years before me.

Angelus has been instructed about the dangers of isolation, but, significantly, the effects are now displaced to secular Europeans, who, "having little social life and many servants," become idle and either take ill or to drink. Although he echoes Hagspiel in his conviction that communal support saves the missionary from such a fate, he speaks not of the warm companionship in which Hagspiel had such faith but of internal discipline to "the orderly life that is prescribed by the rule of the Society [of the Divine Word]." Indeed, in Angelus's account, the gravest dangers to the missionary lie not in relaxing the barriers between oneself and the milieu but in failing to relax them. He even suggests that the proper attitude can be learned from New Guineans themselves:

> Take things calmly. . . . Yes, calmly, in Pidgin, *maski*. One soon learns some of that from the natives for if one would allow oneself to be disturbed as easily and frequently as one does in a cooler climate he would be an apt victim for malaria. . . . Our graveyard contains the graves of two Sisters and three Brothers whose service did not exceed two years, and six priests with only one year to their credit. They were either unacquainted with the proper method of taking quinine or had not learned the *maski* philosophy.

Nowhere does Angelus better express the new views on mission solidarity than in his remarks on Bishop Loerks. He had been told that as bishop, Loerks was the "father of the mission," while as procurator, he—Angelus—was the "mother." He claims to see the logic in this designation, "since all the needs and requests must pass through the procure." Yet the model of solidarity expressed through such familial (and sexual) imagery apparently struck neither Loerks nor Angelus as appropriate to the situation. Both prefer alternative designations instead:

> The bishop calls himself the Servus servorum Dei. One soon sees that the title becomes him well. Ever alert from 4:00 A.M. till 9:45 P.M. pondering over the many problems that present themselves daily. . . . Besides the spiritual cares of his flock he is especially vigilant about the clothing, food, and housing conditions being aware that good tropical missionary work cannot be accomplished without them. While at the table with newcomers he sees that each has the kind and the amount necessary. Denying himself, he will pass on the last of some dish with the remark, "the rest for the best" or something similar. The shirts and helmet wanting to my gear were supplied from his private wardrobe.

If the title preferred by the bishop was "the servant of the servants of God, " the title that Angelus would prefer is "servant to this servant of the servants of God." Like the bishop himself, then, Angelus would affirm hierarchy as the principle of mission organization by inverting the models that express hierarchy in socially conventional form. The community has been etherealized; its

leader is not a father but a servant, its center less a place than a state of mind.[3]

The Third Bishop: Leo Arkfeld and the Local Church

I have so far dealt with changes in the mission's economy and with changes in the mission polity that were deemed necessary by the missionaries in New Guinea if they were to bring the church into a productive relationship with the place and people of the Sepik frontier. I have also argued, however, that these changes had appeared to contradict authentic forms, even within the mission itself. For some of the pioneers, the extent of material work involved in establishing the mission seemed to deflect the missionaries from their "real work" of saving souls. Somewhat later, we have seen Hagspiel expound on the dangers of the "loose organization" forced on the mission by the exigencies of a field situation in which linguistic and ethnographic diversity prevailed. Yet while the heroic images of the bishops which emerged from these periods articulated these contradictions, they also denied their force. I shall argue here that missionaries in the Sepik have continued to use such apparent contradictions to generate coherence in their accounts of recent mission history and to articulate mission practice with a different set of theological concerns.

If Hagspiel began his account of the Catholic mission in the 1920s with a boat, virtually all accounts of the mission in the era following World War II focus on the airplane instead. This is not to say that boats are no longer used in mission work: indeed, on the island circuit from Wewak, missionaries still captain a ship named the *Gabriel*. The plane, however, has without doubt superseded the boat both in practical importance and in symbolic role. Not only was Leo Arkfeld, bishop of the Sepik mission from 1948 to the late 1970s, an honored aviator, but planes are different from boats in ways which have enabled missionaries both to act on and to define a new kind of frontier. Hagspiel's *Gabriel* could only follow existing waterways, and, of course, the nature of a boat passage is to focus attention on the transit rather than on the points which mark the beginning and the end. Loerks had to wend his way through the infamous bends and twists of the Sepik River, but the flying bishop can soar over all all the ambiguous and limiting elements that still symbolize a frontier.

Among the themes that aviation imagery allows are the virtually unmediated capacity of the church to reach the people and the heroism of the lone pilot, overcoming external resistance to "devour" space and to bridge time (cf. Barthes 1972:71–73). Stories developing these themes circulate within the mission community and are also presented in publicity features for those outside. Some are prepared specifically for the general public, who might not understand that aviation is less a business than an integral part of mission work, while some are prepared for "friends" of the mission abroad because aviation is an expensive operation, requiring continual infusions of funds. Descriptions of difficult flight conditions, treacherous terrain, and precarious airstrips dominate the stories and articles in my collection and evoke a primitive country steeped in nature over which the plane, a product of culture, can prevail. Of course, Wirui Air Services, like other mission air services, employs lay pilots, but most of the stories concerning aviation in the Diocese of Wewak focus on flights by their missionary pilots, with those featuring the bishop taking pride of place. As one publicist put it, recalling the pilot-heroes of an earlier age, "[The bishop] flies on a wing and a prayer. This formula has always brought him back home unscathed— even when the wing was flapping a bit."

Perhaps the most favored image that aviation admits is the juxtaposition of space and time that is summarized in the notion of speed: from here to there, and from then to now, with nothing in between—an image best displayed in the archetypical photograph of the plane and pilot on a primitive strip with indigenous admirers in traditional costume looking on. As Barthes has said of the pilot-hero, speed is an experience of "space devoured." In mission representations, the space devoured is cultural (moral) space, and, when the pilot is the bishop, the time flying by is the distance between foreign mission and local church.

Clearly, Arkfeld's contributions to the mission as a pilot can encompass themes appropriate to earlier mission frontiers. Yet the postwar frontier in which the problems of material support and internal solidarity were resolved was not the empty frontier of Limbrock's time or even the rustic frontier of Loerks's. Whereas in earlier years, the colonial government and the commercial sector had been weak, the government after the war took the lead in the field of public works, while business responded to the increasing opportunities in the Sepik by providing shipping, transport, import, and retail services. In short, the conditions that would permit organic solidarity between the political, economic, and religious sectors of colonial society were developing at the same time that the mission was trying to reconstitute its own system after the devastation that it suffered in the war. Although the mission retained an important role in providing secular services, especially in outlying areas, its new "material base" was not designed for total self-sufficiency, while the plane, radio, and later the roads made internal communication more frequent and reliable than had been possible in the years before the war.

The postwar frontier was not, in essence, an economic or a political frontier for the mission, but now it posed a cultural challenge of major proportions. Of course, there were powerful ideological forces both within and outside the church that led later missionaries to view their frontier as a cultural frontier. Yet I believe that missionaries in the Sepik recognized this to be the case long before the impact of anti-imperialism and Vatican II. When the missionaries returned to New Guinea after the war, they not only built stations inland among unmissionized peoples but also found it hard to recognize those whom they had known before. Gerstner (1952:799), ethnographer of the "Wewak-Boiken" people, for example, wrote with awe about the reformer Yauiga, who, like the more widely known Simogun, was urging people to bury their old ways and to engage in *bisnis* instead: "Yauiga is a modern type who in the old days would not have been conceivable at all. . . . Although still heathen, he is a man with a sympathetic, respectable character, with sound judgement, astonishing farsightedness, and quite unusual initiative."

The indigenous people of the region, in fact, could no longer be taken for granted. In this regard, the influence of cargo cults on missionary perceptions was probably even greater than the influence of modernists like Yauiga, who, though surprising, conformed to missionary values, or of traditionalists in the vicinity of new mission stations, whose nonconformity was no surprise at all. For the missionaries, cargo cults seemed to combine the surprise of the new with the nonconformity of the old in particularly disturbing ways. The general interpretation emerging among the missionaries was (*a*) that natives had misinterpreted European society and thought they could obtain its material benefits by magic and without hard work and (*b*) that cargo cults were genuine expressions of native religious orientations and that the church had not yet tapped the cultural roots that gave cargo cults their indigenous appeal.

It is one thing to recognize cultural differences and another to try and bridge a cultural gap. Earlier missionaries, of course, had spent much effort on linguistic and ethnographic studies in order to communicate their message and bring people into the church. With the discovery that the obstacle to real success lay in the *relation* between native and Western cultures and not simply in native culture itself, however, new roads were opened for "spiritual" work that had not been seen before. Naturally, missionaries continued to see to the sacramental needs of their congregations, but many also turned to the task of addressing problems in the articulation of indigenous people and their communities to the modern world. Spiritual work, previously conceived as a Catholic version of preaching and teaching, now differentiated into a myriad of specialized ministries, just as material work had done long before.

When I asked one elderly German priest about the changes that had occurred within the mission community after the war, he noted that American missionaries had arrived in great numbers and that these Americans would talk only about tractors. Although he was referring literally to the reconstruction years, he was also referring to the technical orientation of mission culture after the war. Indeed, I was told by another missionary that today the brothers best exemplify the spirit of the Society of the Divine Word, for they can single-mindedly devote themselves to the practice and perfection of their technical skills and crafts. The priests, however, are members of the Society of the Divine Word too. Just as new stations in the Diocese of Wewak were built after the war near possible airstrip sites, so missionaries began to build ministries around problems that might respond to a craftsmanlike approach. The 1966–67 Annual Report of the East Sepik District, for example, commends the Roman Catholic mission for taking an "active part in community development projects and youth work" at its (then) thirty-six outstations.

The communal repercussions of mission work in these years deserve brief mention, for it has been largely an individual's game. Some missionaries look back nostalgically to the 1950s, when a trip to the central station at Wewak was still an occasion for celebration as well as for business and obtaining supplies. Yet the same improvements that enabled missionaries to expand into the interior and to maintain communication through improved roadways and radio networks also made it possible for them to pursue projects at their own stations with less support from the wider mission community. New sources of finance have also facilitated the relative autonomy of the modern priest, for along with the diocese and the Society and the "friends" that support a priest from back home, international agencies can now be approached to fund projects for certain kinds of social and economic development. The bishop himself is said to encourage such experimentation. His philosophy, I was told, is that "the good will out," and to this end he will support a priest's project even against the critiques (if there should be any) of other priests at the mission's periodic convocations.

The situation has naturally permitted the proliferation of projects of many different kinds, varying from parish to parish according to the sociological imagination and entrepreneurial skill of the individual priest involved. For example, a missionary at Maprik began a club for civil servants there who were attempting to give up alcohol, while a missionary at Sassoya once initiated a full program of events at his station designed to stem the tide of urban migration and the consequent demoralization of the rural countryside. One priest in Wewak decided that unemployment among youths was a problem in his parish and instituted a Young Catholics organization, several small-business development projects, and a new hall for sports, while the priest in a neighboring Wewak parish, concerned about the loss of community spirit among migrants, designed a settlement on mission land with "blocks" laid out for families from different home regions.

Certainly there have also been projects aimed specifically at the articulation of indigenous people with the church. In the 1950s and 1960s, several missionaries initiated training schools for catechists at their stations; some missionaries introduced lay organizations such as the Legion of Mary to the people in their station areas; bible study groups form from time to time; and recently, groups of church leaders have been created, with representatives from the different communities in a parish or station area, to meet periodically to discuss parish affairs among themselves and with the priest in charge. On the diocesan level, congregations for indigenous sisters and brothers were established in the 1950s, as were the first sustained efforts to educate young men to be priests. The latter projects, especially, connect current mission goals to those of an earlier era. Angelus, in 1936, hoped to live to see the day when the first native priests would be "raised to the altar," but he was true to his times as well, taking great delight in hearing Tumleo children sing two-voice motets.

It is clear that in the years after Vatican II, missionaries began to reformulate their ideas about the kind of church that they were attempting to build. Some missionaries have been enthusiastic about the use of indigenous motifs and styles in church architecture, music, vestment, and ceremony. Yet my impression in talking to missionaries in Wewak in 1976–77 was that they felt great humility in the face of the tasks before them. Indeed, for some the sense of a "flapping wing" was quite acute. The Catholic mission has been slower than other missions in "localizing" its personnel, but even more than others it is a clerical organization, with priests required for critical sacramental functions and in charge of many important policy decisions. In 1976–77 there were only two indigenous priests in the Diocese of Wewak, and one was on leave to serve as a government official, while the other was only ordained while I was there. For those missionaries who were relying on indigenous clergy to articulate Catholic spirituality with Melanesian culture, the picture looked a bit grim. Indeed, even the more conservative missionaries, concerned primarily with the church's capacity to deliver the sacraments, had cause for worry, because they did not believe that overseas vocations could be counted upon to fill the growing need in the diocese for priests.

For practical as well as for ideological reasons, then, the future was pegged by many on developing increasingly broad roles for indigenous brothers and sisters, and especially for lay men and women. One of the mission's oldest and most valued catechists gave a speech at the new diocesan catechetical center in 1976 on the theme that, as in the country at large, so in the church, now was a *taim bilong fri* (time of freedom). No more were lay personnel to rely solely on the priests for direction; now they must learn to take the initiative and think how to build the church for themselves. Clearly, though, the effort was only beginning, and in Wewak, at least, it was evident that it would be a while before both priests and people would accommodate to such a major shift in control.

The Second Vatican Council officially recognized the authenticity of the direction taken by missionaries like those in the Sepik. This, of course, is why the historian, Wiltgen, anachronistically associates the first bishop, Eberhard

Limbrock, with Vatican II. Yet even with the enhanced value it gave to development work, post–Vatican II mission theology retained some of the traditional tension between "spiritual" and "material" directions for mission work. As Burridge (1978:27) has observed, however, this tension is harder to maintain in practice than in theory, and rather than promoting such goals as localization and indigenization, development ministries may divert the larger project from those ends. Spiritual intercommunication is hard, Burridge argues:

> Traditionally, evangelical frustrations were overcome by attacking them in intellectual pursuits; recording and learning the languages and customs and reflecting on what was being discovered. . . . Today, however, most of the creative fire in that intellectual, spiritual, and moral effort is absorbed into the impersonal routines of bureaucracies and channeled into a variety of practical skills which, even in innocence, place a missionary in a position of power over his charges. They come to rely on his knowledge of bureaucracies and on his skills as a social worker and technical expert. They begin to enjoy advantages quite disproportionate to the contribution they have made themselves.

This pathology of technically oriented mission work clearly involves an ironic reversal of the situation which the image of the flying bishop mythically resolves.

Conclusion

Catholic missionaries in the Sepik have represented their bishops by juxtaposing them as agents with acts drawn from a seemingly contradictory domain. We found first a bishop who developed plantations, then a bishop who captained a boat (among other things), and finally a bishop who flies planes. Yet in all these cases the force of the image is to deny that the juxtaposed domains are contradictory in more than an apparent sense. Irony of this kind, of course, is an ancient device for the expression of religious ideas in the Judaeo-Christian tradition, but we should not forget that it is also the most characteristic means of expression for a "disenchanted" and even revolutionary orientation to the established social or cultural world (cf. Clifford 1981, Fussell 1975). In both cases, the aim is to expose the artificiality of the established order and to suggest its insufficiency in relation to a more natural or transcendent truth. How, then, do we account for the use of irony by colonists intent on establishing the very kind of cultural order that is discredited by both religious and modernist uses of the same device?

To most colonists, the frontier itself has been represented as the prime force for the confusion of projects which aimed to reproduce in the colony the ideal-typical order found at home. The organizational problems encountered by the Catholic mission to mainland New Guinea were understood by the missionaries in terms of economic, geographical, linguistic, political, and cultural characteristics of the region and people in which and among whom they worked. It should be clear, however, that these characteristics emerged as obstacles only in relation to the organizational values of the mission itself. In order to function successfully in the circumstances in which they were placed, missionaries—like other colonists—had to contradict in practice the very values which were upheld to them as ideals. Hence the political, if not actually revolutionary, force of the apparently ironic images in which so many colonists have represented their work.

The moral ambiguity of this move, however, should be noted. The frontier is a place where business cannot proceed as usual or, better, as planned. The ideals are upheld by the status, the humor, or the pathos of those forced by circumstances to depart from them but are shown nonetheless to be inadequate as a guide for life and work in a situation which cannot support them. The latter is what made the frontier a liberating experience for so many Europeans, but—although I have not touched upon the theme here— it is also responsible for many of the abuses wrought in the name of high ideals upon the land and peoples of the frontier.

Townsend, who "had the reputation of being an 'outside' man, who waged a life-long war with . . . headquarters" (McCarthy 1963:84), clearly used irony in his memoirs as a weapon against the idiocies of excessive bureaucratic regulation on the administrative field staff. From several of his references to the Catholic mission in the 1920s and 1930s, one is led to infer that he thought their way of running a frontier operation far more effective than the government's. Bishop Loerks, for example, could manage most of his affairs without orders emanating from afar, and his priests even had horses at their disposal. Townsend himself—in his own opinion, of course—was constantly bedeviled by rules and regulations and,

because of penny-pinching in Rabaul, had to trudge along endlessly on foot in the mud (1968:95, 221–22). As we have seen, however— and as Townsend apparently did not—the missionaries have had uses for irony that paralleled his own.

The pioneer bishop had seen the frontier as preeminently economic in nature, and the "material upbuilding" with which he responded was eventually presented by the missionaries not as a deflection from their spiritual work but as both the condition and the sign of their capacity to conduct it. The interwar frontier was, in essence, a political frontier, and, in the Sepik, the secular expertise and individualistic style of the second bishop were presented not as negations but as guarantees of the mission's capacity to maintain itself as a centered, religious community. The final period is the most difficult to summarize, in part because it was only coming to an end as I left the country in 1977. The third bishop had already been appointed archbishop of Madang, and although he still spent much of his time in the Diocese of Wewak, everyone knew that a new bishop would soon be appointed and would establish his own policies and his own style. I have, nonetheless, argued that the postwar frontier was seen by the missionaries as a cultural frontier and that the technical ministries in which so many engaged were seen not as departures from the spiritual goals of their mission but as means of serving the people by helping them to articulate their lives to the modern world and to the church.

The outline that I have presented for mission history is thus a record not only of successive frontiers but of progress toward the constitution of a distinctive Sepik church. The final irony, of which many missionaries themselves were aware in the mid-1970s, is that while their project had clearly been shaped in a process of interaction with the region, it did not yet exhibit much of the spirit of the indigenous people to whom it had been dedicated for over eighty years.

Notes

1. Fieldwork on Catholic missionization in the town of Wewak was conducted from August 1976 to June 1977 and was made possible in part by a grant from the National Science Foundation (BNS-15269) and by a fellowship from the University of Pittsburgh. I am grateful to Carl E. Thune for critical comments on earlier drafts of this manuscript and for discussions in which many of the ideas presented in this paper were clarified and developed. Ivan Karp and John Barker

provided valuable advice for revisions, and I also thank Peter B. Huber, Richard Scaglion, and T. O. Beidelman for critical advice and encouragement in various stages of my analysis of Catholic missionization in the Sepik. Responsibility for errors in fact and interpretation is, of course, my own. A version of this article appeared in the *American Ethnologist* 14(1987):107–25.

2. I have not been able to undertake archival research on the history of the mission. Most of my sources on the periods before World War II are published works, the major exception being the letter of Fr. Angelus which provides such valuable insights on the mission led by Bishop Loerks. There is some ambiguity about the name of the author, so I have simply called him Fr. Angelus. The bishop's secretary in Wewak allowed me to make a copy of this letter, which, to the best of my knowledge, remains in the files in the office of the Bishop of Wewak. Translations from German sources are my own.

3. It is fitting to note here that "the fighting bishop" died in the war that engulfed New Guinea in 1942. The Japanese, unlike the Australians, could not be convinced that the missionaries were neutral. Loerks and 38 other missionaries were shot at sea while ostensibly en route to imprisonment in Rabaul, while the missionaries in the Alexishafen region suffered heavy losses when the ship taking them to a Japanese camp in Hollandia was strafed by Allied planes (*Wantok* 1974; Townsend 1968:225). In all, 122 of the 230 missionary priests, brothers, and sisters of the Society of the Divine Word who had worked in New Guinea since the beginning of the mission in the 1890s lost their lives during the war (Divine Word Missionaries 1969:55).

16/ Business and the Romance of Community Cooperation on Kairiru Island[1]

Michael French Smith

Kragur village lies on Kairiru Island's rugged northwest coast. Villagers produce all of their own shelter, most of their own food, and many of their tools. But in the decades since the first European intrusions, which began on Kairiru shortly after the turn of the century, a few items of Western clothing, metal tools and cookware, and a variety of other commercial goods have become virtual necessities. Villagers also need money for such new necessities as local government council taxes and their children's school fees. And it is painfully obvious that in the larger world that encompasses the village it is those with the most money who enjoy the most prestige, power, mobility, and security. New standards of prosperity have left Kragur behind (see Allen in this volume). Referring to a traditional source and measure of prosperity, a renowned old leader sums up the change simply and eloquently: "Taro is finished."[2] Many villagers would like to see Kragur transformed from a community of largely subsistence horticulturalists and fishermen to a community of cash producers and businessmen (cf. Allen, Schindlbeck, Schmid in this volume). But if taro is finished, money has not yet really begun for Kragur. Not counting remittances from migrant kin, I estimate that the per capita income in the village in 1980 was less than twenty kina, at that time equivalent to about twenty-five U.S. dollars.

When they explain their lack of success in the new economy, villagers frequently speak of their lack of cooperation and unity and suggest that European societies enjoy great wealth because Europeans cooperate harmoniously. In 1976 a middle-aged village man had this to say about a plan for joining with other Kairiru villages to buy a boat for commercial use: "Now we'd like to buy a boat. But the way we New Guineans are, one village wants to work alone, another village wants to work alone. They don't think of working together to start a business with a boat or something. The whites don't have that kind of idea."

When I returned to Kragur in 1981 there was still much talk of investing in a commercial vessel, though the villagers were then planning to go it alone. Explanations for the slow progress of this plan sounded familiar. As one young man put it: "We're thinking of buying a boat, but we don't have good cooperation." Similarly, a vigorous middle-aged leader opined that too many people were trying to start business enterprises which included only the members of their patrilineally based residential groups (*koijeng*). This, he said, was wrong and could not lead to success because Kragur was really "one family." And referring to the slow pace of commercial and other material progress in Kragur, a young man recently returned from several years as a wage laborer in an urban area offered this opinion: "If we worked hard, the village would really amount to something . . . but . . . we aren't unified yet."

One can, however, observe numerous obstacles to Kragur's success in the cash economy other than community disharmony. One can also observe numerous instances of effective communitywide cooperation in activities other than business, and one can observe the failure of community business ventures and the existence of ventures that embrace only a part of Kragur's population. These observations raise several questions. Why do villagers favor explanations in terms of the quality of community cooperation? What ails business in Kragur aside from whatever problems villagers have in sustaining a collective effort? To what extent is lack of cooperation itself an obstacle to business success in Kragur, and how are problems of cooperation related to the existing system of social relations?

I will begin by examining the explanations villagers offer for current lack of progress and considering the sociocultural and historical circumstances that account for their preoccupation with village cooperation and unity. Following that, I will survey business activity in Kragur, focusing on two community ventures. After examining various other obstacles to business success in Kragur, I will consider the implications of social structure for cooperation. Assessing the problem of cooperation in business ventures, I will note not only how aspects of the existing social organization inhibit more effective villagewide cooperation but also how business failures, which are the results of many factors, react upon longstanding weaknesses in the fabric of community solidarity. I will suggest that while collective approaches to business are not unreasonable in Kragur, the romanticization of communitywide effort may, in fact, be an obstacle to both more successful experimentation with business and more effective cooperation.

Explaining Lack of Progress

In 1976, having heard a great deal of public oratory on the subject of Kragur's failure to progress, I surveyed the opinions of twenty-one adult men and ten adult women, about 23 percent of the resident population above primary-school age. I asked each, in Tok Pisin, some version of the question "What do you think is needed if Kragur is to become a better place to live?" A summary of the responses arranged in general categories (table 1) indicates the emphasis that villagers place on various aspects of community unity and cooperation.[3] This emphasis appears more pronounced if we include responses concerning cooperation among leaders and better relations between leaders and other villagers.

What about progress in the cash economy? Of course, villagers know that copra prices are chronically unstable. Some blame this on the ineffectiveness of the managers of the Cooperative Society or the Copra Marketing Board or the failure of copra producers themselves to demand better prices. Some have no opinion. But a good number of village men are able to relate a fall of copra prices to a glut on the world market. Similarly, if villagers compare Kragur with other villages in terms of success in the cash economy, they tend to point to factors outside their control rather than to the quality of village social relations. For example, they say that the people of south coast Kairiru villages have more money because they are closer to mainland markets and have more flat land suitable for growing coconuts.

But it seems that villagers are less concerned with such uncontrollable obstacles than they are with why they do not do better with what they have, for, as we have seen, they frequently ignore other issues and focus on the question of harmony and cooperation. An educated young villager, home in Kragur for a brief visit, echoes the opinions of many residents when he speaks, in English, of Kragur's difficulties. In Kragur, he observes: "It's a bit hard to start up . . . business, because people are still wild. If you ring the bell, you can't expect anybody to attend. They will find silly excuses . . . . If everybody agrees and attends the meeting, it would be very good. Things would run smoothly."

When villagers engage in such self-criticism, what is the standard by which they are measuring themselves? The contrast that concerns them most is the glaring contrast between their poverty and the wealth of European or white society as they know it. The comparisons they draw with European society often go beyond the obvious disparities of wealth and power to moral contrasts which they often present as at the root of the material gap. These comparisons picture Europeans or whites as more cooperative and harmonious in a wide variety of ways. For example, villagers may say that whites are not as prone to disputes inspired by suspicion and jealousy over women. Or they may ascribe the good health and longevity whites allegedly enjoy to the relative absence of rankling grievances that give rise to sorcery and illness meted out by ancestral ghosts. Similarly, villagers commonly contrast the temporal coordination and regularity of the European institutions they have observed with the temporal irregularity and imprecision of activities in the village, and they find here an important source of European superiority in the cash economy. Their concern is not simply that their own conduct is less efficient in a Western instrumental sense but that it is a manifestation of a deeper lack of social harmony and cooperative spirit (Smith 1984).

Where have Kragur villagers gotten the notion that Europeans are so extraordinarily cooperative and harmonious and that this is an important source of their prowess in the money economy? One can easily imagine Kragur people's being impressed with the bureaucratic order and regularity of European institutions, which is in clear contrast to villagers' own forms of organization and activity, but there is much more to it than that. Motives more familiar to Westerners intertwine with indigenous notions concerning the relationship of social harmony and solidarity to supernatural aid and supernatural obstacles in the pursuit of material well-being.

TABLE 1
NEEDS FOR VILLAGE PROGRESS OR IMPROVEMENT

NEED	NUMBER OF MENTIONS	PERCENTAGE OF TOTAL
Unity, cooperation, and harmony (more cooperation, a more communal approach to work, more communal social gatherings, less gossip and jealousy, etc.)	21	30
Leadership		
Better leaders	2	
Less dispersion of authority, less factionalism, more cooperation between elected and customary leaders and among all leaders	9	
Willingness to follow village leaders	6	
No more use of sorcery and malign magic by customary leaders	6	
Leaders who support cash production more vigorously and who won't stand in the way of innovation by the younger generation	2	
Total	25	37
Economic change		
More cash production	5	
Reduction of traditional exchange, gift giving, and obligation to kin	4	
Other (a village guest house run on a cash basis, move village to better land)	2	
Total	11	17
More personal freedom		
More freedom of choice for women in marriage and other aspects of life	3	
More freedom for young people in social activities	2	
Less compulsory work (e.g., council work) and more freedom to work independently on business ventures	2	
Total	7	10
Miscellaneous	4	6

Villagers believe, for example, that much serious illness is the result of disputes and unsettled grievances within the community, for a person's deceased ancestors may act on his behalf, bringing illness to those with whom he is angry, even if he does not consciously will it. A healthy village is therefore a sign of harmonious and cooperative social relations. Maintaining social harmony is also an important dimension of productive activities in the indigenous view. Producing taro and catching fish, for example, are conceived of as in part magicoreligious enterprises. At the very least, it is necessary to avoid magicoreligious interference with one's physical efforts. Villagers worry that those few who possess rights to the magic for controlling the growth and health of the taro will competitively impede each other's efforts or that they will use their knowledge maliciously as an expression of anger or sorrow. Successful taro husbandry thus requires harmony of goals among the relevant village leaders and between those leaders and other villagers. Similarly, successful fishing depends on more than physical effort. The individual fisherman who is too stingy with his catch risks supernatural interference with his efforts as the deceased ancestors of the living act on behalf of their disgruntled descendants. Certain kinds of

magic for increasing the numbers of fish in Kragur waters can be carried out successfully only if the village is free from rankling disputes (Smith 1978: 207–41; Huber-Greub, Tuzin in this volume).

The circumstances of Kragur's encounter with the European world have encouraged the elaboration of familiar principles and their application to the problem of money wealth and business enterprise. While Christian missions have played a major role in the process of European contact and domination in much of Papua New Guinea (see Taylor Huber in this volume), Kragur has been subject to greater than average mission influence and has forged exceptionally close ties with Catholicism (Smith 1978, 1980, 1982b, 1984). The result has been that many villagers have tended to see Catholicism as the vital core of the wealthy European society. The kind of Catholicism to which villagers have been exposed has emphasized not only Christian brotherhood but also the paramount importance of maintaining proper relations with powerful supernaturals through collective ritual, that is, weekly services and daily prayer gatherings. Catholic institutions have also promoted the superficially more cooperative Western industrial forms of temporally regular and coordinated conduct (Smith 1984).

All this has exacerbated an indigenous concern with the magicoreligious relationship between social relations and material wealth. Many villagers have come to see superior European wealth as rooted in a superior form of harmony and cooperation, and they tend to see such cooperation as having magicoreligious as well as directly instrumental effects. Many younger villagers entertain more secular notions of the benefits of cooperation, but to some extent such secular notions are plausible and compelling because of their resemblance to the indigenous and syncretic magicoreligious ones. The young people who speak of the need for cooperation have often heard their elders give a very similar prescription.

Business and Obstacles to Business in Kragur

As I have said, per capita cash incomes in Kragur are very low and derive mostly from copra sales. Copra production rises and falls with fluctuations of copra prices (Papua New Guinea Copra Marketing Board, Wewak Office 1976–80). But villagers have been disappointed by their years of effort with this cash crop, and they do not expect copra growing to bring them a major economic breakthrough. A few families have begun to plant coffee and cacao, but as of 1981 these plantings had not produced any income. Aside from copra production, the most common way of earning money in the village is selling produce in the market in Wewak, at a small market near the boarding school on the south coast, or to the school itself. These sales are usually spurred by specific immediate needs for cash. When I visited Kragur in 1981, for example, one village family was living temporarily on the other side of the island, producing sago to be sold on the mainland for cash to pay the son's high-school fees.

Over the years there has been a trickle of experimentation with other sorts of small business. There have been several trade stores in Kragur, but when I first arrived in late 1975 there was only one. Two more opened during the following year, but by 1981 they had both come to an end. The owner of one store had died, and the other store had gone bankrupt. In 1976 a fraternal segment of one koijeng was planning a piggery, to be financed by a migrant brother, though by 1981 little had been accomplished. In 1981 a household in another koijeng had begun selling kerosene in a venture owned and financed by a migrant kinsman. A few men were also talking about getting

a license for a village beer club. Recent reports from Kragur indicate that nothing has come of this.

I have seen the beginning and end of two attempts at villagewide cooperation in business. In the late 1970s villagers initiated what was called the Community Development Youth Club. Using a small aluminum boat with an outboard, obtained with a government grant, they engaged in a number of money-making projects, including market gardens and purchase and resale of garden produce to boarding schools and the hospital on the mainland. In 1976 villagers established a village development fund or village account and succeeded in collecting several hundred kina from residents and migrants for the purchase of a boat to carry passengers and cargo between the islands and the mainland.[4]

In 1981 the club still existed, but it had been inactive for several months. The development fund was still in the bank, and its organizers were still meeting and contemplating their next move. I am not certain that the club is now completely defunct, but at the very least it has lost its villagewide membership and support. After I had begun to write this paper in 1983, I received a letter from the man who had been chairman of the club in 1981. In it he reported that he had given up that position because there was too much dissatisfaction: "Ol man i complain nambaut," he wrote in Tok Pisin. His letter, and another which came at the same time, also described a new business venture on which some villagers had embarked, buying green copra from other island villages to dry and market. They were trying to raise money, through government loans, grants, and the contributions of migrants and recently returned migrants, to buy a boat. The list of participants included a number from various koijeng who had been active in and enthusiastic about the club in 1981 and suggests that they were putting their efforts into this new venture. In 1983 I also learned that the village development fund had been dissolved and redistributed to the contributors because, as my informant wrote in Tok Pisin, "em ol man long Kragur . . . i krai nambaut . . . " That is, everyone was complaining.

What went wrong with these two efforts? The club clearly suffered from bad financial management. The accounts were nearly useless, and the club could easily have been operating at a loss without knowing it. The leaders of the development fund lacked experience in planning a venture such as a passenger or cargo business. They did not have clear plans, and they let the fund languish between sporadic bouts of activity. Though some villagers were enthusiastic about the club and the fund in 1981, there was also much grumbling, including talk that the leaders were interested only in self-aggrandizement and that they were misappropriating money. In both cases, the leaders did appear to be conducting things in a closed and high-handed way.

Cooperation does seem to have been a problem here, but it was certainly not the only problem. In considering obstacles to business success in Kragur, we should start by asking if villagers' goals themselves present an obstacle to success as an outside observer might define it. Schwimmer (1979:308–9), for example, speaking of the striking rate of failure of small businesses among the Orokaiva, concludes: "it is only the White observers and social scientists who see anything tragic in these failures. If the Orokaiva thought them tragic, they would stop setting them up again and again. . . . You gain status even by, and especially by failing. Your business dies, its limbs and assets are spread among the multitude and increase exceedingly. It is a religious practice." It is not safe to assume that, when people appear to be doing business, they are doing what we think they are. Kragur villagers *are* interested in making money, and this interest is increasing. But that is not all they are interested in, nor do they necessarily understand the mechanism by which money increases in the way that Europeans do. I think that, like the Manus villagers whom Schwartz (1982) describes, Kragur villagers take pleasure simply in participating in some of the artifacts of European wealth and power—boats and outboard motors, stores, and "bisnis groups." And simply having something that others do not—a speedboat, a youth club, a new copra dryer—is surely a source of invidious satisfaction in an atmosphere of competitive political relations. The existence of such motives accounts in part for the poor quality of financial management, for they can be indulged in the absence of financial success and thus do little to encourage acquisition of greater business expertise (cf. Guilford 1982).

But villagers also want to see cash, both for what it will buy and for its confirmation of their moral or characterological adequacy. In a prevalent view of things, moral achievements in the shape of harmonious social relations are translated into material prosperity through the aid of such supernaturals as deceased ancestors, God, and the Virgin Mary. And villagers speak of prosperity not only as evidence of social harmony but

as itself one basis of that harmony. Such a perception of the intertwining of moral and material issues has probably been heightened by the role of Catholicism in European contact, just as European contact has made confirming moral adequacy and ensuring further prosperity in such a way more problematic. Even when villagers manage to attain a satisfying level of material well-being by traditional standards, the comparatively enormous wealth and power of the Europeans remain an inescapable suggestion that villagers are somehow morally deficient. This contributes to their desire for success in the cash economy, and the strength of their desire for money for whatever reason is likely to contribute to an increasing propensity to engage in business on something like its own terms.

Even so, a major problem for business enterprises of any kind in Kragur is poor understanding of the nature of business enterprises and lack of business skills. Many members of the older generation still find modern money a mystery. For example, one man speculates that Papua New Guinea is so poor in comparison with Australia or America because, though now independent, it does not have its own factory for manufacturing currency. There have also been a number of cargo cult episodes in Kragur over the years. Even in the absence of active cargoism, belief in the possibility of acquiring money from the dead lingers on in certain circles. The nature of indigenous temporal perspectives is also relevant here. In the indigenous view the past is shallow, all history and change compressed into a few generations (Smith 1978: 111–22). This colors views of the nature of progress and inclines villagers to imagine a future in which dramatic change is similarly compressed.[5]

Given a better prevailing understanding of the fundamental nature of business and economic change, lack of basic business skills would remain a problem. Many villagers have only limited competence with either the indigenous numerical system or Tok Pisin and English numbers (Smith 1978:115–17). Those who handle numbers with relative ease are unfamiliar with the conventions of bookkeeping (cf. Jackman 1977), and they are hampered by "narrow economic horizons" (Epstein 1970), for example, lack of knowledge of any but very local markets and lack of the kind of experience that would facilitate recognition of new market opportunities.

Kragur villagers must also deal with limited and unsuitable land, infrequent transport to the mainland, and the poor harbors on Kairiru's rugged northeast coast (see Philpott and the Central Planning Office 1974; Haantjens, Reiner, and Robbins 1968). The Wewak Islands lag far behind most other areas of what used to be called the Wewak Sub-District in coconut plantings per capita (Territory of Papua and New Guinea, Department of Agriculture, Stock and Fisheries 1969) because of such difficulties. Many villagers at least anticipate that labor availability will also become a problem because of the high rate of migration among those in the prime of life. The time allocation study I conducted in 1976 did not indicate any substantial reservoir of discretionary man-hours in the present. Thus, even given better business skills, villagers have much to contend with.

Cooperation and Social Structure

The preceding is not to deny the problem of cooperation, and in order to understand this problem better we must examine some dimensions of social structure. The most obvious social units in Kragur are the koijeng. Villagers themselves speak of a tendency toward koijeng exclusiveness as a major obstacle to collective community effort. When proposing the establishment of the village development fund, for example, one young migrant inveighed against koijeng sectarianism: "Forget about koijeng, all of us together!" The term koijeng refers in one sense simply to a residential area, but each residential area is identified with one or more patrilineal lines of descent. Patrilineal lines in different koijeng are linked by affinal ties, and some even share patrilineal ancestors. In addition, a man may have more than one residence option, and which he chooses may depend on a variety of factors; disputes, shifting political alliances, obligations to affinal kin, or the availability of land. But despite the nexus of ties between koijeng and the flexibility of residence in relation to patrilineal kinship, koijeng affiliations do draw villagers apart. The differential prestige and influence that koijeng enjoy, as well as whatever kinship links or political or economic advantages may be involved, serve to cement koijeng loyalty and foment koijeng rivalry.

One also finds in Kragur the remnants of a tripartite division of the population that in the past was part of the structure of men's cult activities and marriage exchange. Two of these divisions, Seksik and Lepelap, seem to have been the most significant. The crosscutting ties that these divisions created undoubtedly functioned to maintain the cohesion of the community, but there is feud in the peace as well as vice versa. Villagers speak of serious rivalry between the two major divisions within living memory. Participation in recent cargo cult episodes fell out along these lines. In the realm of business, villagers are divided into two copra marketing groups having separate accounts at the Copra Marketing Board in Wewak. These groups roughly mirror the Seksik/Lepelap division, with the third group, the Kusulingyar, rather evenly divided between the two. Lists of those who pooled money to establish two recent trade stores also reflect this division. When I examined the membership of the new business venture described in recent letters from Kragur, I rather expected to find this pattern again. But though the majority of the membership was Lepelap, more than one Lepelap fraternal group was missing and an entire Seksik koijeng was conspicuously present. Nevertheless, it is apparent that while their impact is not necessarily predictable, the structural divisions of the indigenous social order define lines of schism and spheres of trust and cooperation that in a sense subvert attempts to sustain communitywide cooperation.

What about the lack of cooperation among leaders that villagers often complain about? Customary leaders in Kragur are referred to as *ramat walap*, literally "big men." Their leadership is based largely on possession of heritable rights to esoteric magicoreligious knowledge for control of food production, weather, curing, and other areas of general concern. Particular leaders are strongly identified with particular koijeng and a source of koijeng prestige and influence. Both customary leaders and their constituents often speak of the former's power over food production and other activities as a responsibility to the community. But I also found that customary leaders speak of their superior knowledge and power with imperious self-satisfaction. Customary leadership is at least as much a matter of private pride as one of public trust.

I have discussed the nature of the relationship between village leaders and their followers at some length elsewhere (Smith 1985). Villagers take pride in the accomplishments and power of their customary leaders and unequivocally express their dependence on them for ritual assistance in food production and other enterprises in which physical effort alone is not enough. Yet, the big men are also thought to be quick to anger and quite capable of using their knowledge for selfish ends, for example, magically impeding another big man's ritual work in order to diminish his prestige. Customary leaders wield a great deal of power and enjoy a great deal of authority. But villagers' respect for and dependence on their customary leaders coexists with a demand that they continually prove themselves and a readiness to suspect them of selfish motives.

Attitudes toward noncustomary leaders—for example, the councillor, the leaders of Catholic religious life, or those who manage the copra marketing groups—are similar, except that these leaders have less traditional sanction for their authority. Further, they often find themselves trying to exert hierarchical control over spheres of activity that were never before subject to such constraint—for example, hygienic practices or intervillage trail maintenance—or organizing endeavors which have yet to live up to their initial promise—for example, copra production or daily prayer. The limited and uncertain tangible rewards for compliance with their demands add to the predictable suspicion that they are primarily interested in making their individual "names" or reputations.

Customary leaders tend to be arrogant and autocratic in their exercise of power and authority. Noncustomary leaders employ the same methods, but they encounter more resistance because of their lack of traditional precedent and the often questionable benefits of their leadership. The competitive nature of leadership, marked by a pattern of "competitive innovation" (Schwartz 1976), probably does in fact militate against maximum cooperation among leaders and diminishes the likelihood that leaders and aspiring leaders will give their full support to enterprises to which they cannot lay some personal claim.

There is, then, ample evidence of sources of chronic disharmony in the pattern of social organization. One also finds in Kragur a psychocultural orientation reminiscent of what Schwartz (1973) has called the "paranoid ethos," in which pervasive suspicion of others is an important element. Such a psychocultural climate of course has a circular relationship with atomistic social structural tendencies. Taking the long view, Kairiru villages are not stable entities. The series of short migrations that peopled Kragur within recent generations was the result of the fragmentation of other Kairiru communities. If we look at Kragur as part of an ongoing process of fragmentation and recombination, villagers' preoccupation with cooperation and harmony appears both more at odds with reality and more understandable.

Business and Community Cooperation

Some students of social change conclude that forms of social organization found in small face-to-face preindustrial communities are inherently incompatible with the kind of conduct and organization needed for success in a modern economic system. Bailey (1971:298) makes such an argument with regard to economic development in European peasant communities:

> The diversification of ways of making a living which comes about through incorporation into a larger economy automatically cuts down the frequency of exchanges, restricts the flow of information, and so increases ignorance about one's neighbor and thus promotes the paradoxical ignorance and indifference which decreases jealousy and opens the way toward various kinds of cooperation. . . . The kind of development which is needed is not community development, so much as a development which leads toward the destruction of community life.

These are hard words, but one cannot ignore the fragility of trust and the chronic tensions in Kragur that pose real obstacles to new economic ventures. Yet neither can one ignore the many successful forms of cooperation in which Kragur villagers *do* engage. All koijeng cooperate in building houses for all village residents. I have seen people from all koijeng cooperate effectively in amassing taro to be used in a mortuary exchange with another community. I could multiply examples, but the question all this raises is how such cooperation differs from the kind of cooperation needed in commercial ventures. Certainly most villagers dislike attempts to institute Western industrial-style temporal regularity and alter indigenous work habits (Smith 1982a, 1984). They are also confused and ambivalent about the proper role of money in relations with fellow villagers (see Smith 1982b). At the moment, however, it seems that the greatest difference between community cooperation in business and more familiar types of community cooperation is simply that in the latter villagers tend to get the results they expect, whereas in the former they usually do not. Failure of any collective enterprise in Kragur inevitably sets off an outburst of recriminations and accusations of sabotage, selfishness, and hidden opposition. In contrast, success inspires confidence in one's leaders and one's fellows and is taken as itself evidence of harmony and cooperation. Thus, all the conditions other than lack of trust and cooperation that make successful business enterprise difficult in Kragur also exacerbate structurally based tendencies toward mutual mistrust (cf. Schwartz 1966–67:38–39).

The leaders of business enterprises in Kragur are subject to an extra measure of the mistrust that is a constant potential in villagers' attitudes toward all leaders. Lack of quantitative skills and poor understanding of money (cf. Sexton 1982:186) and perhaps actual instances of misuse of funds aggravate the suspicion born of repeated failures in the cash economy. The precedent for autocratic leadership seems to contribute to leaders' indifference to public accountability.[6]

In addition to the effect of a new kind of failure on old tendencies toward disunity, business offers a new field of endeavor, relatively unencumbered by precedent, in which the individual, family, or koijeng may seek prestige and accomplishment. No one has the exclusive rights to business that one has to control of taro production, performance of traditional songs and dances, or ownership and use of particular types of canoes. The centrifugal pull of individual assertion has long been held in check by the uncertainty of life outside the community and the paucity of novel areas of endeavor. The appearance of new forms of economic opportunity, like the increase in possibilities for geographic mobility, upsets this shaky equilibrium.

Is there, then, any point at all in attempting to establish enterprises which embrace the entire community? One thinks of the problem of accumulating significant amounts of capital or marshaling sufficient labor over and above the needs of subsistence production. And there is villagers' own attachment to such an approach for its implications of magicoreligious efficacy and for fear of sorcery and the supernatural repercussions of smoldering anger. Memories of intervillage raiding passed down from parents and grandparents also incline older villagers to see a large and unified village as a source of security.

But this is not the final word. Some of those involved in the new copra-buying-and-drying enterprise were vehemently denouncing village fragmentation in business in 1981. There is no doubt that villagers are willing to take the risk of community fragmentation if there is promise of greater monetary success, but I suspect that they have misgivings. The romanticization of collective community business endeavor that grew out of the circumstances of Kragur's encounter with the European world has surely made villagers more reluctant to experiment with other forms and exacerbated the tensions that such social and economic experimentation might be expected to arouse under any circumstances. Ironically, it may also make villagewide efforts themselves more volatile by promoting unrealistic expectations that lead to disappointment and recriminations.

Bailey (1971:298) suggests that economic change and development in small communities may require that people be "shaken out of the net of community relationships." If achieving some success in the market economy requires experimentation, trial and error, then freedom from preconceived expectations concerning the most effective and the most virtuous form of organization will be an asset. In Kragur a series of more limited failures might do less damage to community solidarity and trust than repeated communitywide fiascos.

Bailey also argues persuasively that the dissolution of extant community relationships need not lead to the demise of community life but may open the way to the development of new forms of cooperation, more voluntary and more adaptive. But to argue against romanticizing community ventures or the present form of community life is not to recommend anticollective policies. When they break away from communitywide efforts, Kragur people tend to choose some form of collective organization, still defined in terms of traditional forms of relationship though embracing a more limited circle. To find this a potentially positive development is a far cry from advocating explicitly anticollective policies such as those described by McKillop (cited in Good 1979), which in the Eastern Highlands encouraged consolidation of land and other resources in a few hands at the expense of the majority.

Indigenous hierarchical tendencies, novel economic opportunities, and development policies which encourage such an outcome have led to increasing economic differentiation—not simply in incomes but in access to land and other resources—in many parts of Papua New Guinea (Good 1979; cf. Grossman 1983). Some form of increasing economic differentiation is a possibility in Kragur, partly because of the edge that traditional elites have had in taking advantage of novel resources in the postcontact world (Smith 1985; cf. Lutkehaus in this volume). Unlike the indigenous "investors" in business ventures in the Hagen area described by A. Strathern (1972a:501), Kragur villagers do not seem to be content with the prospect of sharing only in the nonmonetary benefits of a business venture, including the privilege of basking in the reflected glory of its "promoter." But as cases from elsewhere in Papua New Guinea (Finney 1973, Grossman 1983) illustrate, simply organizing collectively per se does not ensure equitable distribution of benefits any more than it ensures business success.

Increasing economic differentiation is only one among many unanticipated consequences villagers may encounter in their pursuit of business, discussion of which is beyond the scope of this paper (cf. Allen in this volume). Just how they fare in years to come will of course depend greatly on the state of the national economy and the nature of rural development policies and programs. Choosing the village as a whole as the unit on which business enterprise is to be built is not necessarily going to help avert either business failures or unpleasant unanticipated consequences of success. Cooperation is indeed a problem for business enterprise in Kragur, but it must be considered in its specific social context and its reciprocal relationship with other problems. Communitywide business ventures are not out of the question, but their romanticization may actually be an obstacle to their success as well as an obstacle to exploring alternatives and facing other issues.

Notes

1. This paper is based on research conducted from November 1975 through December 1976 and in April and May 1981. Financial support for the latter period was provided by the Institute for Intercultural Studies.

2. In Tok Pisin, "Taro i pinis." Unless otherwise noted, all quotations from villagers are translated from utterances largely in Tok Pisin.

3. Some informants gave more than one response, and I made no distinction on the grounds of response order.

4. Kragur was involved in a cargo and passenger boat enterprise in the early 1960s in which several villages invested. The venture failed.

5. Errington's (1974a) and McDowell's (1980b) discussions of episodic views of history may also be relevant to the Kragur case (and see Josephides in this volume).

6. This topic deserves much more attention. Schwartz (1966–67) provides useful comments on the social context of corruption in the management of Manus cooperatives.

17/ Economic Development at the Grass Roots: Wagu Village 1963–83

T. Wayne Dye

The three hundred–plus Bahinemo-speakers inhabiting the Hunstein Mountains and surrounding plains southwest of Ambunti in the East Sepik Province are the undisputed owners of more than thirteen hundred square kilometers of rain forest but actually utilize less than half of that. When I began fieldwork in 1964, they lived in eight villages; these have since coalesced into four. One village (Nigilu) had its own language; the rest spoke Bahinemo. Both are Sepik Hills languages (Dye, Townsend, and Townsend 1968). The focus of this study is Wagu village, which now comprises seventy Bahinemo-speakers, forty-eight Nigilu-speakers, and sixteen speakers of other languages.

Traditionally, these people ate sago, forest greens, fish, game (principally pigs), and garden foods, in approximately that order of importance. The disease rate is very high, as are both infant and young-adult mortality (cf. Townsend 1983).

There is a strict male-female division of labor and a good measure of antagonism between the sexes. Women have full responsibility for vegetable foods, including sago. Men hunt and fish and clear gardens. Because houses deteriorate rapidly, they spend much of their time building new ones.

In the short run, nuclear and polygynous families are self-sufficient production units. It is not unusual for a household to live alone in the forest for weeks at a time while gathering food, though more typically two or three families will live together. Traditionally, the members of a village would gather a few times each year at the main village site (*yuwei bedo*, "big village") to continue friendships and fulfill social and ceremonial obligations. In recent times the desire to be present when there are visitors from outside has resulted in much more time spent in the main village site. The extreme may be at Wagu, where most people live at the main site almost year round.

Individual autonomy is highly valued; parents do not expect even young children to obey them.

Decisions made by the village must be by consensus, usually at "town meetings," simply because no one feels obliged to obey a decision with which he or she does not agree. Those who disagree are likely, however, to move away temporarily or permanently to reduce interpersonal tensions (see Townsend 1978).

Adolescents and young adults usually remain in their home villages, but they are also free to move to any village where they have close relatives (in practice nearly any Bahinemo- or Bitara-speaking village). Young men especially are encouraged to strike off on their own by attaching themselves to a leading man in their own or another village. The basis of choice is ostensibly kin ties, but it is clear that friendships with other youths, possibilities of obtaining a bride, and, especially, economic opportunities largely determine actual choices. This process forms the basis of much of the variation in importance of leaders.

Traditional religion is a relatively simple variation of the men's cult, with bamboo pipes and carvings with spirit power (both called *gela*), slit-drums (*nebu*), and an emphasis on secrecy. Boys are initiated into the cult soon after puberty. This initiation is the high point of the ceremonial system; it reinforces the authority of older men, reestablishes social relationships, and fosters toughness and camaraderie. There are no later stages of initiation, though the pipes or slit-drums are played at girls' puberty ceremonies and at other high points in the annual cycle.

Social structure is simple and highly flexible. The family comprises a man, his wife or wives, his and their children, occasionally an older widow, and those teenage boys living nearby who are fed by the women of his household. Polygyny has traditionally been the ideal: in 1964 seven out of ten families in Wagu were polygynous.

The largest and most important political unit is the village. Technically, land belongs to particular clans. In practice, however, the land within a day's walk of a village is essentially assigned to that village. Anyone living in the village for any length of time has rights to it, whether he is with his father's relatives, with his mother's or his wife's relatives, or simply among friends. The clans are named, but they are of little importance. Kinship terminology is Iroquois in pattern. Bride-price, child payments, and death payments are given to relatives on both the mother's and the father's side, the amount of previous interaction apparently being an important determining variable.

The only important social unit intermediate between the family and village is the work group. This comprises one big man, a few other married men, some unmarried youths, and, of course, the women and children attached to them. Women and children are not counted in this social structure, though their voices are sometimes heard in village discussions. Members of a work group tend to live together, both in the village and in the forest. They help each other with work, though the basic economic unit remains the family (or household). A big man's work group is his basic influence base; its size largely determines his importance.

The Hunstein Mountains are generally infertile, and diseases are common; this is not an attractive area for development. Travel by motor canoe is expensive, and roads are impractical in the swampy terrain. Mechanical equipment and even wooden objects suffer from the humidity, insects, and fungus and require constant maintenance. According to the officers resident there, in the 1960s the colonial government saw little hope for economic development anywhere in the Ambunti Sub-District. A few projects were introduced, but the consensus was that once crocodiles had been hunted out, the area would be best seen as a labor pool for more prosperous parts of the country. Since Independence, and especially with the advent of provincial government, there have been more efforts to foster development, but economic change has come very slowly. (This situation could soon change; gold deposits have been found along the upper April River.)

Socially, Bahinemo-speakers were long considered backward and crude, "living like dogs and pigs," by members of the more complex societies along the Sepik River that were their trading partners. Gewertz (1978b:39) suggests that a similar attitude of Chambri toward their Sepik Hills trading partners was simply a way of compensating for their dependence on the hill peoples. My data from the 1960s suggest that the Bahinemo-speakers had less to offer those on the

Sepik, and as a result self-esteem in Wagu was generally low.

It is in this context of slow economic development and low self-esteem that the persistent and partially successful efforts of the Wagu villagers toward "progress" must be understood. In the following description and analysis of the history of Wagu since 1963, I shall summarize the economic situation, the social and religious situation, and the leadership pattern.

Experimentation and Confusion, 1963–68

In 1963 Wagu was still two villages. Wagu proper comprised ten families and nine youths. Its leader was Kokomo, who had three wives, two *imawu* (married men of his work group), and five *yenbo* (young unmarried men) and was clearly the most important man in the village. In Nigilu, however, Lasu Baga had a larger following, two imawu and six yenbo. Houses were being built at a new lakeshore site. So far all the children born there had died, but villagers hoped that moving the strange-looking *kwontu* (head killing spirit) stone they had found on the site might break the pattern. All the young men were back from the plantations, and Wafiyo (the future leader of Wagu) now had a shotgun, the first in this language group. The Nigilu villagers were considering a move to Wagu in order to be in touch with the outside world, but Lasu did not seem to favor it.

In 1964 my wife and I moved to Wagu and built a house. We employed people to teach us the language and as household help, and we opened a small trade store at their request. We had three preschool children so needed plenty of help. With this new prosperity coming to Wagu, it took the people of Nigilu only a short time after the death of old Lasu to move permanently to Wagu. Begai, the young *tultul* (messenger and interpreter of the chief), experimented with our medicine, but no one believed we could really slow the infant death rate.

By early 1965, however, the first babies were living more than a year. The government ship had finally brought the long-stemmed coconut seedlings promised to Wafiyo in coconut school eighteen months earlier. However, when he and I went to pick them up, the new agricultural officer (an Australian) told him that none would be distributed because coconuts were no longer considered a money-making crop. We protested that the village needed coconuts for food, but he insisted that the sprouts were to be thrown in the river and could not be used. He did, however, arrange for two other young men to attend a coffee course there at Ambunti.

The most important event in 1965 was the attack on the Sanio-speaking hamlet of Begabegi by Bahinemo-speakers from five different villages who believed the Begabegi were causing the deaths of their leaders by sorcery. For this most of the men of Wagu were jailed for some eighteen months, as were men from other villages and all of the men from Gahom. The wives of these Gahom men came to live in Wagu, protected by its nearness to Ambunti, our presence, and its distance from the Begabegi. Several Gahom babies died during their first few months in Wagu, before our return.

When we returned in 1966 we were able to keep all the babies alive, primarily through rapid diagnosis and treatment of falciparum malaria. Otherwise Wagu had a difficult year, with inadequate housing and a shortage of men. Begai, who had been living with us in the highlands during the fight and so had not been involved, was made the *luluai* (government-appointed chief). The old luluai, Bagi, had been permanently deposed for having used the shotgun in the raid, but this only cemented his position of real leadership. When the men were released from jail in 1967, he became the acknowledged leader of Wagu.

Upon their release from jail, four married men and six singles decided to remain in Wagu, the four married men forming two work groups of their own and the singles attaching themselves to Wagu big men. Leadership in this period meant respect but not control. Leaders were generally too wise to ask anyone to do anything; there were no community projects.

By 1967 my principal linguistic field assistant, Naba, was experimenting with coffee growing. His first attempt failed before it started; a jealous villager prematurely burned his clearing so that it could never be clear enough to plant. During this period crocodile hunting was the most profitable enterprise for others in the area, but the people of Wagu benefited little from it. They were too afraid of the water spirits to go on the lake at night and did not trust one another to divide the profits fairly if a crocodile were killed.

In 1967 a government agricultural officer taught them to harvest copal. The kauri pines that produced it were on a steep hillside a day's journey from the village. The resin had to be taken to Ambunti for sale—a day's travel by motor, two by paddle canoe. The money could not be paid

upon receipt of the copal but had to be sent from Wewak later. A trip to Ambunti was a major undertaking, and often the office was closed when villagers arrived to sell copal or collect money. The payment for all this work was five toea per pound, a pathetically small reward for so much effort. The final blow to this project came when the trees died and villagers learned that the officer had shown them the wrong way to cut the bark.

Up until this time, only Naba had begun to follow the Christian teachings which I was hoping to introduce. The others listened to him at length, however, and by early 1968 they were eager to listen as I haltingly explained the Christian Gospel. In fact, their first experimental prayers (at which we were not present) were that we would have the discipline to stay with them long enough to be able to clearly explain these new ideas.

By 1968, Wagu had grown significantly but had made little economic progress. Villagers had, however, begun to see their infants survive the first year of life; a few were learning to read, and they were learning many things about the outside world. In short, they were ready for religious conversion.

Integration and Florescence, 1968–72

Conversion to Christian faith was a community activity with a high level of participation. Fifty out of a possible seventy-five adults and youths were baptized by Buria, an Assemblies of God evangelist from the village of Meliwai, in July 1968. The villagers' hopes were both religious and practical. They wanted to move the village to a larger and better site. Their location at that time had too little flat ground above high-water level, and its soil was too shallow for well-placed house posts. Water was scarce in the dry season, and the waterfront was muddy most of the year. The site they were considering was ideal: plenty of flat ground above high water, deep soil, a sandy waterfront, and plenty of good water. It had been considered unusable because of signs of previous habitation—peculiar stones that looked like parts of the canoes used by spirits (but were typical of Iatmul tambaran shrine stones). There were also a number of potsherds; Wagu is now listed by the National Museum as an archaeological site. Since no one had ever known of people living there, the villagers believed it must be inhabited by foreign spirits. Therefore their first act as Christians was to clear the new village site, counting on their new "older brother" Jesus to protect them from these spirits.

As kinsmen (*kan*) of Jesus, they felt new strength (*bininyu*) and pride in themselves. At this time the Ambunti local government council was formed, but the sub-district officer would not let Wagu villagers become members because of the 1965 raid. They showed no signs of demoralization, however, and set about vigorously building such a neat, well-kept village that everyone would know they deserved to be included. At the urging of Garu, the councillor from the Manambu-speaking village of Yambon, many of the men began planting coffee, and they told the young men not to go away to plantations but to stay and help with these coffee projects.

The village almost immediately became more unified. A previously little-used system of village meetings (*behi tohwa*, "discussion" [Tok Pisin *kot*] were substituted for the arguments and club fights which had been the more common way of airing disputes. Nevertheless, disagreements were not always settled, and three of the less important leaders (Isakweli, Begawi, and Naintu) built a half-hour's walk away at Metetemei, a site they liked better.

When we returned late in 1969 (in answer to their prayers, they felt), the villagers were meeting for prayer and teaching four times a week, a pattern they themselves had developed. They sang their hymns (with Bahinemo words and music) wholeheartedly. In 1970 an additional twenty-five persons were baptized, including most of those who had been reluctant in 1968. Many of the new group did not continue to show signs of real change of belief, suggesting the primarily sociopolitical focus of their new loyalty. That Wafiyo carefully preserved the *ba doma* (canoe stones) was another sign that villagers were still ready to seek power wherever it was available. Their use of terms reflected this; "repent" was, they insisted, best translated by the verb *yakwa* (set aside until needed) rather than *hali* (get rid of completely).

The first to build on the new site were Kiyawi and his brother Keniyofo, young singles who to this day are not leaders. The first leader was Wafiyo; his house was also one of the largest in the village. In more subtle ways also, Wafiyo was recognized as the leader of this new development (though not the overall leader of the village). Next to build were Wafiyo's close friend Kikwali, then Yafei, and only then Bagi. When we returned we also built on the new site, this time a large semi-permanent dwelling. For convenience we chose to live down near the waterfront across from Bagi rather than in the upper end of the village where Wafiyo wanted us to. Thus, without realizing it, we struck a blow to Wafiyo's leadership and reinforced Bagi.

The spiritual power in their new religion was demonstrated almost as soon as we returned (Dye 1984). Hong Kong flu was sweeping through, killing many of the Sepik Hills people. Wagu lost no one, primarily because they readily took our penicillin shots and when necessary went to the Ambunti clinic. The infant mortality rate continued to decline, partly because of the special birth room in our new house, which gave infants a chance against malaria. Mosquito nets were increasingly used for children, and there was a new willingness to take medicine. With increased cooperation and less fear of the water spirits, they were able to hunt more crocodiles. This was the main source of income over the next few years.

The most important change for their food supply was probably the coincidental influx of tilapia (Tok Pisin *makau*) into the lake, coupled with our introduction of cheap steel spear points. This may also have been the principal reason for their better health; it is likely that steel spear points were the most effective change we introduced. Next most effective were gill nets (in 1972), used to harvest the fast-growing tilapia. We also brought in a water tank for everyone in 1971. A washhouse was built over the stream in 1972. The women's washing greatly contributed to community health; boils, scabies, and fungus became much less frequent, and the large abscesses and intestinal diseases caused by ingested dirt decreased dramatically.

By early 1971 Wafiyo, with help from the village, had purchased the first outboard motor. Within two years Yafei had purchased the second, after an unusually dry year had provided a rich harvest of crocodiles. These motors added immense prestige to the village, as well as enabling their owners to visit Ambunti whether or not we happened to be resident. By 1971, leaders of Sepik River villages and other Bahinemo-speaking villages were coming to visit and see the remarkable change in Wagu. The villagers' health, many children, well-built houses, general cleanliness, and obvious prosperity all showed the strength of the new way. In 1971 Naintu died, and the rest of the Metetemei satellite village people moved to Wagu. At fifty-five, Isakweli had begun to prepare for death, but with this new strength he rallied, built a new house in Wagu, and lived another five years.

During this period the villagers carefully followed Christianity. All attended weekly services, and daily problems were handled, in part, by prayer. They did not build a men's cult house, though many carvings were made to satisfy the new influx of tourists from Sepik Safari. At this time they perceived the men's cult as a kind of worship of the carvings. There had been no prayers or sacrifices to the carvings, but the playing of bamboo flutes was felt to be in obedience to the carvings, which in turn were expected to bring fertility and hunting success. Dances continued as celebrations of God's bounty and His creation rather than of the power of the *wulyal* (creator spirits). The largest dance was the Christmas celebration, which followed a portrayal of the creation and of the life of Christ. They would not dance for the tourists, however, arguing with Wayne Heathcote that "we would be like animals in a zoo" (their idea, not mine). There was experimentation with a Christian variant of the girls' puberty ceremony, and a few brave men were allowing their wives to stay in a corner of the house instead of secluding themselves in a hut apart during menstruation. The boys' initiation ceremony, however, was not so easily disentangled from the men's cult, and it was therefore simply dropped.

During this period most of the adults tried learning to read, and most of the younger men and a few women succeeded. Naba and Begai had both failed to learn English through the crash course to which we had sent them, but they had learned much about the outside world. The Assemblies of God established a station at Ambunti and offered to board a number of primary-school boys. Wagu was the only Bahinemo village to send boys, though Kakilu and Begabegi also sent some. This project is having an increasing effect on Wagu fortunes, since these boys and four from the other villages are now young men living in Wagu and contributing to its ability to cope with change.

By 1972 Wafiyo was the recognized leader of the village. His astute part in village discussions, his friendship with Councillor Garu (the avenue to eventual participation in the council), and his many trading relations with other villages seem to have been his principal assets. He seemed to have just the right balance of traditional leadership qualities and willingness to innovate for the situation. Next in importance was Yafei, who was benefiting from association with the church and his skill in mediating disputes. Bagi was still respected but no longer influenced events. This was

a period of change in Wagu, and those who moved with the changes were establishing themselves.

Considering that Christianity was the integrating ideology of this florescence, it is remarkable how little it helped anyone to become influential. Yafei benefited, to be sure. Other cotranslators did not gain influence, however, and those who took time to evangelize other villages actually lost influence. The villagers did not dislike evangelism; the problem was that no one would pay any church leader, so the evangelist's time away simply diminished his ability to provide food for others, still a crucial basis of influence. Naba, my principal assistant, suffered most. Not only did he make evangelistic trips but, with my capital and advice, he also set up a small store in the village. I taught him to calculate markups on goods to provide himself an income and eventually replace the capital, and by doing so he convinced others as well as himself that he was no longer an upright man; in Bahinemo society, good people never make a profit on transactions. Those who sought leadership later recognized this problem.

Consolidation and Council, 1972–79

By 1972 the easiest improvements in village life had been made. Further developments brought problems as often as progress. Some villagers were raising pigs, but these interfered with the efforts of others to enlarge their gardens. There were now three shotguns in the village, and with most people living there year round the local population of wild pigs was being depleted. In 1972 a Rotary Club in New Zealand gave the village money to fence off the entire peninsula from pigs. It was hoped that this would facilitate pig raising as well as gardening, but we soon observed that local pigs can jump a five-foot fence and swim a kilometer of open water.

In 1974, the villagers' first coffee was sold. In 1975 the Ambunti council gave them an aid post, with young Andrew Wamine from Yambon as the first medical officer. In 1976 they were at last allowed into the council, and Wafiyo was elected councillor of Wagu and Yigai (with implied responsibility for Gahom and Meli) almost by acclamation.

A local government councillor was a new kind of leader for Wagu. He had at least a measure of real authority, not just influence. Villagers felt obliged to obey his orders for "council work," such as cleaning the village, widening paths, and making guest houses. Both Wafiyo and his appointed judge Yafei were able to make judgments in village court sessions rather than merely acting as mediators. This new power in turn gave them new respect and influence in other affairs.

Throughout the 1970s the villagers continued to raise a few pigs for sale, but they usually priced them too high to sell any. Crocodile hunting and sales of carvings to tourists were probably their principal source of income, though coffee also contributed. Some small crocodiles were raised, but inadequate feeding usually resulted in too slow a growth rate for good sales. In 1978 my daughter Edith taught some of the children how to salt and sell tilapia, the income project then being fostered by the government. Until the lake became clogged this was, according to most informants, the most lucrative business they had tried.

My wife and I were on furlough from March 1973 through December 1974, and after that we spent most of our time on a dissertation unrelated to village work. From 1977 through 1979 our two daughters taught a vernacular preschool of their own. Cooperation was slow to develop, but in the end the village was sold on schooling for children. Thereafter villagers' principal lobbying efforts at the local and provincial levels were for a government primary school. (These efforts were rewarded with a "feeder school" beginning in 1984.) Political maneuvering in the council eventually produced a permanent medical building with a water tank for the village but nothing else. The Summer Institute of Linguistics provided a course in development and literacy teacher training for several of the men that improved their ability in metal work and possibly in gardening.

Uneven economic success was paralleled by uneven enthusiasm for Christianity. Even by 1973, interest in Christian things was flagging; people who had no real interest no longer bothered to come to church. Throughout the late 1970s Wafiyo seldom came to church, objecting that Yafei was using the fact that services were in his house to build his position. But neither he nor anyone else offered to hold them, and he adroitly avoided the obvious solution, to build a church/school building. Such a building was finally completed with his approval in 1979.

During our 1973–74 furlough a new men's-cult building was built and cult activities were resumed. The reason villagers usually gave was that they liked the bamboo flute music. Indeed, outside observers also recognize its beauty. A re-

cent study by the ethnomusicologist Graham James uncovered considerable musical complexity and sophistication in the design and musical techniques used to obtain the beautiful harmonics. This complexity had always validated the cult. Flutes could only be played by the power of the gela and according to rules that they had given to the ancestors. A second reason for returning to the cult, therefore, was to restore communion with the gela spirits. This communion could be sensed in the long night sessions of harmonious flute playing, times of harmony with other men, with the creation, and probably with oneself. (This celebration of harmony may have been one reason for the heavy pressure for everyone, even the staunchest Christians, to join in.) Christianity as villagers knew it offered them no similar experience of harmony.

Yet another reason was that representatives of the newly independent government were fostering the men's cults as part of a return to *kastom* (tradition). On the national scene this was a way to build a new national unity (see Schindlbeck in this volume); locally, it had as much to do with the desire to promote tourism. With the demise of huntable crocodiles, the sale of tambaran carvings to tourists had become the principal source of local income. As was the case in Yensan on the Middle Sepik (see Schmid in this volume), tourists came and bought much better when they saw the carvings as part of an active local religion. Government interest in the old ways (some called it government demands) joined with economic interest to justify the cult. After all, if it helped economically and the government was in favor, surely God was in favor also.

The fourth and possibly crucial reason was sociological. There were small payments to the mother's relatives to be made at a boy's initiation. These payments and the ceremonies reestablished the social order and reaffirmed the leadership structure. It appears to have been for this reason that all village leaders except Yafei have encouraged the men's cult in proportion to their importance in the village.

During 1972–79 periods of enthusiasm for Christian things alternated with periods of lack of interest and/or of men's cult activity. In 1977 a surge of interest in the cult was followed by a period of very poor hunting success and then by renewed interest in the church. A similar flurry of interest in the church in 1978 followed a special retreat at Ambunti attended by Yafei and others. In 1979 Wafiyo led a delegation which went with my wife and me to spread Christian teaching to the most remote Bahinemo village. The overall trend, however, was of decreasing interest in Christianity.

Throughout this period Wafiyo's leadership remained undiminished. By 1979 Bagi had lost his last few followers through old age. Yafei gained some teen-aged followers, but his most important follower, Begai, became independent.

When the East Sepik Provincial Assembly was formed, Garu argued that a special electoral district should be set up for the hill peoples, on the quite reasonable grounds that culturally and economically they were so different and so few that no one chosen by Sepik River peoples would adequately represent them. This was Begai's big opportunity. Although his only "education" had been the various Summer Institute of Linguistics courses I had arranged for him and the one failed year at the English school, he was nevertheless the best-prepared person in the electoral district for the office and won it unopposed. Begai was suddenly the most important person in the area, but he and the village now faced some difficult times.

Challenge and Response, 1979–84

When Begai was elected, everyone expected a new surge of economic growth. Several men had set up pig houses, feeding the pigs the tilapia that had become so easy to catch with gill nets. The government had introduced rubber trees, which it was anticipated would be more profitable than coffee. (Coffee had never done as well for them as for other villages, since they had treated it like a traditional crop, not to be pruned or weeded.) Crocodile farming had been given up; the strict regulations put on size and means of capturing in order to develop the crocodile population greatly reduced the economic advantages of crocodiles for villagers. Salted fish were bringing a good return with little effort. Wafiyo purchased a new, larger outboard motor in 1979 with help from nearly all of the villagers, and Begai purchased another in 1980.

In 1980 the tiny floating fern *Salvinia* reached Wagu Lake. Native to a small area of Brazil, it had spread to the Sepik via Wewak and had already caused much harm in the Lower Sepik before it reached the Ambunti area. According to the government biologist Jack Cox, though it is a hybrid that bears no seeds, it doubles by cloning every ten days as long as there is space to expand,

then dies and rots. Therefore a lake that is one-eighth covered will be entirely covered in thirty days. Because it floats freely and is springy enough to spread and be compacted by the wind, it may mass so densely that no canoe can move in it. A canoeist can be trapped for many hours when the wind shifts. By 1981 there were several months when canoe movement was difficult or impossible; by 1982 this had extended to most of the year. The village's location on a long central peninsula, which heretofore had facilitated movement to various shore areas for hunting and sago working, now brought an increased burden. Sago, pigs, and building supplies now had to be laboriously hand-carried around the lake and along the peninsula to the village. Furthermore, fish could not be caught under the *Salvinia*, so the village's protein supply was greatly reduced. Daily life quickly became much more difficult, until by 1983 the villagers were noticeably thinner and hungrier.

Under the leadership of Wafiyo and Begai, the villagers soon cleared a wide trail along the rugged peninsula. They cleared many more food gardens and began harvesting the sago already planted around the village for emergencies. Families went back to spending long periods in the forest, and garden houses were built or rebuilt in strategic locations. Nevertheless, the quality of life diminished. One by one the enclosed pigs starved to death, as the villagers hopefully fed them only the little extra food still available. Since one could not always go to Ambunti to sell coffee, many villagers stopped picking it. Coffee yields were already smaller because many branches had dried up from lack of pruning. The new sheller that Begai had purchased stood idle. The medical officer tended to stay away for longer periods, since traveling to Ambunti for supplies or government business had become so difficult.

Wafiyo seems to have lost more than others. In 1980 he had moved to Ambunti so that Mowi, his only son by his favorite wife Faisowa, could attend the government school. This might have been workable, though expensive, if he had been able to return frequently to cultivate his gardens and guide his followers. The *Salvinia*, however, made trips back and forth fatiguing and often impossible. His gardens became progressively poorer, and his followers, no longer benefiting from his leadership, became progressively independent. By late 1983 his gardens were being harvested by others, and no one was providing him with food when he came to the village.

Late in 1979 my wife and I went on another extended furlough, not returning until 1983. During this period the village became covertly divided between those who still considered the Christian way best and those who felt it had been tried and found wanting. Yafei is now the only leading man following the Christian way, although Gwami, Kokomo (namesake of the original leader), and Kiyawi command increasing respect. Begai began his work as a Provincial Assembly member with strong Christian convictions, but the heavy drinking and cynicism in Wewak left him feeling that he had failed as a Christian. He is now one of the most outspoken supporters of the men's cult, though still sympathetic to Christian ideas, especially of peace and order.

Despite these tensions, religious division is not strong in Wagu. Both sides are careful to compromise in the planning of village activities, and working groups do not divide along religious lines. A more serious cause of division for a while was the question of whether and where to relocate. A few of the older, weaker people resisted the idea of moving at all. The vigorous ones, however, were committed to building at least a satellite village. Some of those with affinal ties to Gahom wanted to relocate at Metetemei. A few of the Nigilu villagers wanted to return to their old village, a day's journey into the forest. They grumbled that their children were speaking only Bahinemo and their heritage was being lost. The most popular option was to move to the end of the lake, where there was a good stream and plenty of garden land. Leaders of each faction built houses there.

The preferred site could also support an airstrip with relatively little effort. Most of the villagers were enthusiastic about that possibility, though some doubted that such a big project could really be completed by their small village. The provincial government expressed interest in funding it, and the Summer Institute of Linguistics had experts to advise and help with construction. The question was complicated by the hope that government efforts to control the *Salvinia* with an insect would soon be successful, which made it seem best to wait out the ordeal, spending as much time in the forest as possible. All of this uncertainty and the frustration of their new poverty brought confusion, division, and new patterns of political influence.

By the end of 1983 Andrew had become old enough to hold office, and he had lived in Wagu long enough to qualify as a resident of the electoral district. In the October 1983 provincial election he overwhelmed Begai to become representative to the Provincial Assembly. By Christmas he had already arranged for a new patrol post and school not far downriver from Gahom and was ready to offer real hope of government help on the Wagu airstrip. The patrol post largely resulted from the gold development near Gahom, but Andrew was extremely quick to grasp and act on the new situation. Since then he has continued to strengthen his leadership by hard work not only in Wewak but also in community projects in Wagu itself.

A complete turnaround in the fortunes and resultant attitudes of the Wagu people began with an exciting announcement in 1984. After years of pleading by Begai, the government was putting a school in Wagu. The villagers pitched in to build the needed building and teacher's house; my wife and I let his family use our house while his was being built. The school was located across the lake to make it accessible to Ambunti, and Begai, Yafei, and three others built houses and gardens at the school site so that many of the children could live there. This school is very important to the future of Wagu, since it is meant to serve several villages and therefore parents from other villages must now build in Wagu. As the months passed, it appeared that the introduced weevil was indeed killing the *Salvinia* . By August the lake was clear. The villagers rejoiced, built new canoes, and immediately resumed their traditional ways of obtaining food. They are currently building new school buildings and two teachers' houses near the main village site. The first school site will become garden land.

Once again Wagu is growing as people who quietly moved away return. Two families from Yigai-Namu and one from Gahom-Meli have moved to Wagu to allow their children to attend school, and it is expected that more will do so. Not even a whooping-cough epidemic that killed four babies has dampened spirits. The current challenge is to set up a trade store. In the past, stores have foundered on the traditional belief that profit making is inherently unethical. Now that unsophisticated view is gone, and villagers are concerned that too much money is going out of the village to Ambunti entrepreneurs. Furthermore, a few local men are now in a position to purchase and manage a store. Begai seems to have lost most of his influence, and Yafei is now old and fading rapidly. Wafiyo, surprisingly, was recently reelected to the council despite his continued absence from the village and the loss of nearly all of his immediate following. He lives near Ambunti to enable his son to attend grade six; it may be that his ability to deal with the council is now his special contribution.

Observations and Conclusions

Development in Wagu has been very slow and intermittent; most innovations have been unsuccessful. To show in part why this is so, I will describe the villagers' approach to development and then look at factors in the external situation and in the village social structure and ideology that have affected the process.

The Wagu approach to development is guided by concept of mana, an emphasis on personal well-being, and individualism. Bahinemo-speakers use the term *bininyu* ("strength," Tok Pisin *pawa, strong*) for both physical and spiritual power. Our electric generator (*pawamasin*) was perceived as having this power, and a helicopter was thought to fly by it. The central meaning of "power" is "that which enables one to succeed in life." In a physical environment which even outsiders recognize as difficult and hostile, success is no small accomplishment. Conversely, power is demonstrably present in any successful person or group. Since the supernatural world is an important (though not the only) source of power, religion is an integral part of development efforts.

Their traditional values and their sense of failing to do well left the Wagu villagers eager for change, and this in turn led to their embracing Christianity. While the men's cult has been strongest when Westernization was least fruitful, they did not simply equate Christianity with progress and the men's cult with tradition, as did the Boroi (see Josephides in this volume). Yet unlike the Kwanga (see Schindlbeck in this volume), those who are now taking up the men's cult see no conflict between it and economic and political change. Neither have these villagers developed a syncretistic combination of traditional religion and Christianity. The reason for this may lie in my own efforts to convince them that no viable ideological combination exists, at least in terms of a relationship of loyalty and dependence to God and the spirits at the same time. At the same time, I have tried to help them find a form of Christianity suitable to their customs and intelligible in terms of their world view.

The goal in life is neither spiritual progress nor Westernization; it is simply physical well-being. There are many perceived paths to that well-being, and each individual tries to examine his options and plot a course to reach it. All relationships and ideological constructs, including religious ones, are potentially adjustable by a Bahinemo-speaker if it will help him reach his goal. Religion is seen as a kind of technology, and any religion that does not contribute to well-being is judged false.

Individual autonomy is, as McDowell (1980*a* and in this volume) has pointed out for Bun, always balanced by the need to be involved in social relations. However, simply put, each person *always* does what he or she wishes; the Wagu villager says, *An yu na neheisi*, "I [customarily] follow my own heart." The need to relate to others affects one's behavior by making it seem necessary or to his advantage to do what they want him to part of the time. Supernatural sanctions such as fear of ghost retribution and the need for others to help with bride and child payments and house building have traditionally balanced this individualism. Even today, unity is an important value, and villagers avoid publicly going against the opinion of the community. Nevertheless, in their ideology and in observed social behavior, individualism plays an important role. No Bahinemo-speaker can ever rule. He can only lead and influence others who choose to follow him.

These attitudes have combined to produce a consistent approach to development: each family engages in that set of religious, economic, and social activities that seems to promise the best contribution to its well-being. For the people of Wagu this means finding the path to economic, political, and sometimes religious change, while in other Bahinemo-speaking villages it means following traditional ways with a small admixture of change. The people of Gahom-Meli, for instance, have tried to stay out of a local government council and have avoided growing coffee because they perceive both activities as involving more work and expense than the gains to be expected. Wagu is the Bahinemo village most committed to change. Therefore individuals from any Bahinemo-speaking village and from several other villages where people are willing to learn Bahinemo gravitate toward Wagu. Conversely, those people in Wagu who tire of Westernization tend to leave it. It is this self-selection process, made acceptable and easy by individualism and a flexible social structure, that has guaranteed that development would be the continuing goal of the Wagu people.

The response to a school is only the latest in a long series of examples of this process. A few of the more progressive people from each of two other villages moved to Wagu as soon as the school was opened, and more are expected. Possibly even more than Redfield's (1950) Chan Kom, Wagu is a village that literally has chosen progress.

Individualism, flexibility, a drive to get ahead, a felt need for change, and a conscious choice to Westernize should be a potent combination for change. Why, then, has development proceeded so slowly? Indeed, the dominant impression to a long-term visitor is not change but continuity. The following are some of the hindrances to Wagu's concerted and continued efforts to "progress."

First, the physical environment has been extremely difficult. All Western goods, from needles to books to radios to outboard motors, quickly rot, rust, are eaten by insects, or break down in the local climate. Considerable skill is required to preserve them. Malaria is a constant cause of debilitation, and pneumonia, tuberculosis, and various viral diseases also take their toll. *Salvinia* for a while threatened to destroy the village entirely.

Government services have been slow to come to an area of such low population density (more than three square kilometers per person). The nearest government post, Ambunti, is two days' round trip by paddle canoe or twenty kina in gasoline. Yet Ambunti is the center for purchases of goods, political activities, and marketing of products. All these activities, which are the core of development efforts, therefore involve transport costs.

Relationships with other villages have been hindered by language differences, especially in the sixties in Wagu and into the eighties for the more distant Bahinemo-speaking villages. Wagu was also hindered by being a combined village; the 30 percent who were not Bahinemo-speakers have learned the language since their arrival. At the beginning of this period few villagers spoke Tok Pisin. Now, everyone in Wagu can speak it, and it is frequently heard in village conversation.

The villages all around Ambunti are culturally quite different, so much so that Wagu villagers are not comfortable staying there. They believe (with some justification) that sexual morals are much looser along the river and refuse to consider intermarriage with the river villages. As a result, they have no foothold in Ambunti, no place to stay on visits, no place for their children to live while attending the Ambunti school. Only Wafiyo's concerted efforts have resulted in a passable

living situation near Ambunti, but not even he can make a Bahinemo-style living there, and getting food has been a major problem.

Government policies have often hurt Wagu. Turnover of personnel has led to many changes in direction for development. Sheer incompetence (e.g., killing the kauri pines while harvesting copal) has ruined several projects. Misunderstandings, including the sharp distinction between Bahinemo concepts of justice and colonial law, have often kept Wagu villagers from seeking government help. The colonial government focused on cash crops during a period when better diet from new food crops was the greatest need. It forbade local officers to pay cash for the crops it bought, and it prohibited the collection of payment for someone else; this meant that the same person had to make two trips to Ambunti just to sell a few kina's worth of goods.

The situation is much better since Independence, and having a councillor and Provincial Assembly member in the village is making a difference. The principal hindrances at this point are the absenteeism of government officers and, once, the embezzling of designated funds by someone in the council office.

Many of the hindrances to development lie in Wagu culture. Village-level cooperative undertakings were impossible until the local government council was instituted and even today take place only on a small scale. Every coffee planting, every outboard motor, every fish net, and every shotgun must be owned by some individual. If he has enough influence to get his followers to help cultivate, fish, or otherwise use the asset, then it can bring a return. But he may find himself putting in most of the effort, while his followers try to get the maximum personal benefit without it. Followers, on their part, argue that big men tend to keep the income for themselves while expecting their followers to do the work. Coffee growing, in particular, seems to have foundered on the expectation that women would do the daily work while their husbands kept the income.

The high traditional value on sharing, so functional for traditional hunting and gathering, has hindered development by taking from the hardworking and rewarding the lazy. Sharing was until recently a principal form of "civic-mindedness." For instance, in 1979 my daughter would reward her vernacular-school pupils with a cookie for good behavior, and each would invariably share the cookie with the others. By 1984, however, this pattern is breaking down. Wild pigs, for instance, were traditionally shared throughout the village, but today are eaten by the hunter's extended family. My informants claim that the sharing rule only applied to hunting with dogs, but my field notes show otherwise. More likely, a weakening of belief in supernatural sanctions and a general increase in individualism to reward the economic producers have brought this change.

Bahinemo ideas about gardening and animal husbandry have hurt them severely. A traditional garden is cleared and planted, then left alone. One returns from time to time to harvest it, but it is not cultivated. This is good policy for swidden plots but disastrous when followed with coffee or rubber trees. Animals are sometimes fed a little, but generally they fend for themselves. As a result the two significant attempts to raise penned animals (crocodiles in the seventies, pigs in the eighties) ended with the animals starving to death.

In the 1960s, fear of water spirits kept villagers off the lake at night. Only after their conversion to Christianity did they have the courage to begin, and by this time the lake was nearly hunted out by main-river peoples. Their move to the present good village site was similarly hindered by a fear of the spirits, and even now I hear arguments against one innovation or another on the grounds that the ancestors might find it offensive.

These internal and external factors have been strong enough to thwart most development schemes. They are a large part of the reason that, for all its commitment to development, Wagu has been changing only slowly.

18/ Tradition and Change in Kwanga Villages

Markus Schindlbeck

The preservation of traditional culture has long been a political issue in Papua New Guinea. In his message to the South Pacific Festival, Michael Somare (1979) said:

> I have spoken to Papua New Guineans all over the country about the importance of preserving our traditional culture because I believe that our traditional cultures and values are the basis for our society and in fact portray the image of our identity. . . . I ask you all to preserve the cultures of your forefathers for you will be persons without identity if you depart from them.

As an anthropologist working in various villages in the Sepik area, I was frequently confronted with questions arising from this concern about traditional culture. Asking questions about the past and the traditional in a changing world, I undoubtedly encouraged village people to reevaluate the world of the past. Nevertheless, I was puzzled when I heard the use of the word *kastom* for the first time in a Middle Sepik village in 1973.[1] Discussing with various men the meaning of this quest for the past (Tok Pisin *painim kastom*), I found that the main question that concerned them was: What is kastom? Typically for the Sawos culture, all this ended up with a debate in the men's house, not about present-day life, rituals, or taboos but about the mythological past, the origin of their culture and of their ancestors. There, on the local level, I observed how different leaders of the village made use of the concept for their own ends. Tonkinson (1982:302), in his introductory remarks about kastom in Island Melanesia, discerns two levels on which different functions of kastom can be seen: "In the local arena the most common uses of *kastom* as a body of lore reflect its utility in defining differences and marking boundaries among competing groups. . . . At the national level . . . its most common political use is in the service of the solidarity and unity of the nation as a whole . . . " I observed this unifying function at the regional festival in Wewak in 1980.

My discussions with village people and missionaries in the Kwanga area in 1979–80[2] left unanswered the question of the content of kastom. It was obvious that reviving kastom could not mean a return to pre-European times. What parts of tradition should be kept up? And how could Christianity and kastom be reconciled? In the relationship between kastom and Christianity there are possibilities for conflict but also for combination and adaptation. Sir Tore Lokoloko (1979), speaking of the traditional culture of Papua New Guinea, includes Christianity: "When we speak of our traditional culture we are referring to everything which is truly Papua New Guinean in origin—languages, dances, songs, drama, music, arts and crafts, personal decoration, legends, myths and magic and our adoption of Christianity."

Kwanga today are having to make choices concerning the future of their village life. Some Kwanga leaders see the choice as being between kastom and *bisnis* (economic development). The concept of kastom is exemplified by the reintroduction in some villages a few years ago of the traditional cult system of male initiation. The cult system determines a large part of the villagers' daily life, and the taboos associated with it create major difficulties in people's adjustment to the demands of modern life. I shall examine this revival of tradition and other responses to new influences in Kwanga villages.

Ethnographic Background

The Kwanga (see Allen 1976) live in the southern foothills of the Torricelli Mountains in northeastern New Guinea (fig. 1). They are the northern neighbors of the Kwoma and Nukuma and together with them constitute the Nukuma language family (Laycock 1973). The Kwanga numbered twelve thousand in 1980 and occupy an area of approximately 650 square kilometers. The area of Bongos, which is rather densely populated, has twenty-four hundred inhabitants. Kwanga villages (fig. 2) are situated on mountain ridges at an altitude of 100–200 meters above sea

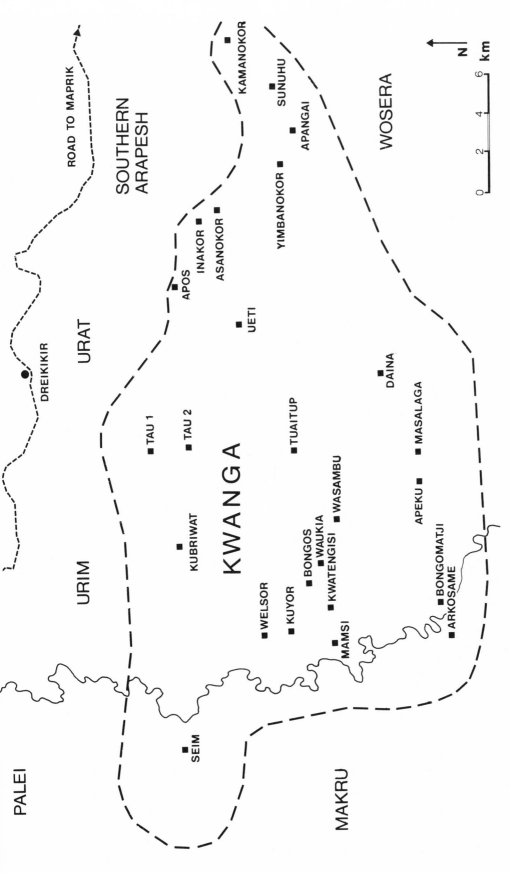

Fig. 1. The study area, showing the locations of the Kwanga and their neighbors.

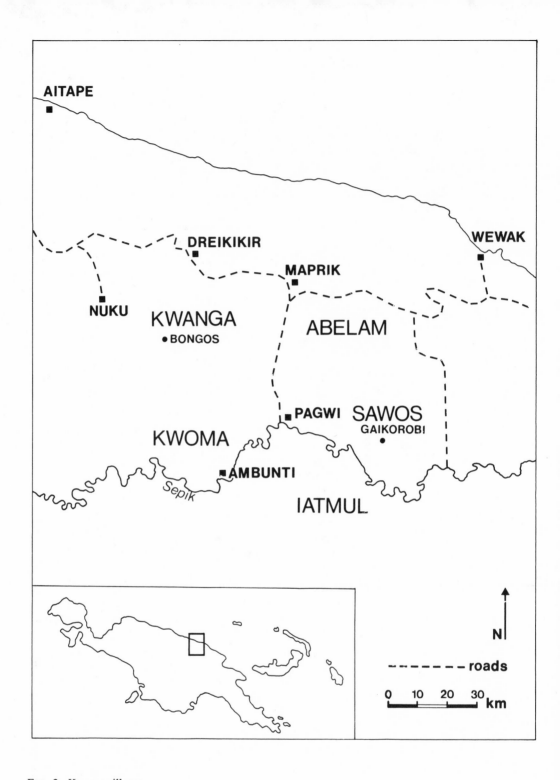

FIG. 2. Kwanga villages.

level. The villages are composed of a great number of dispersed hamlets. There are no centrally dominating cult houses to be seen, as in Abelam villages, because the cult house and the ceremonial ground are hidden from the sight of noninitiates on the edge of the village. The Kwanga are yam cultivators like their neighbors the Abelam and Arapesh. The southern Kwanga, however, rely more heavily on sago exploitation. Differing from the Abelam, the Kwanga have no special plots for ceremonial yams, and their yam magic is concentrated on the species of *Dioscorea esculenta*. Besides gardening, their activities include some hunting and collecting, though these are of minor importance only. Each year they have large yam exchanges which sometimes involve the playing of bamboo flutes (see Schindlbeck 1981). In everyday life the hamlet is more important as a social group than the clan. Clans are exogamous in most Kwanga villages and are always patrilineal. The moiety system, which is interrelated with the initiation system, has its main function in the exchange of garden products and pigs. Unlike the dual system of the Iatmul and Sawos, Kwanga moieties have no mythological or totemic significance. Another function of this dual system is the organization of the garden cycle and political life of Kwanga villages.

History of Contact

The Kwanga had almost no direct contact with the outside world until World War II (see Allen in this volume). During the war Japanese soldiers advanced only as far as the northern Kwanga villages. Besides some missionary work in the northern Kwanga area and a few government patrols, there was no contact at that time. In 1951 the first permanent mission station was established in Bongos, in an area which was then regarded as not under full government control. After the war there was still tribal fighting in the area, but change came quickly. After ten years of intensified contact with the outside world the traditional cult system began to crumble. Schools, aid posts, roads, and airstrips were built. Although an increasing number of men left the villages to work on plantations, in recent years the rate of out-migration has been very low. At the end of the sixties the Kwanga started to plant coffee, and today most of the adult men in the Bongos area have their own coffee gardens. In 1973 an oil company started experimental drilling near Bongos and built a long, wide road running

through the entire Kwanga area, destroying many village sites. Road building has a very lengthy and complex history among the Kwanga; unfortunately, none of the various roads that have been built have lasted very long.

Reintroduction of the Cult System

In most Kwanga villages the traditional cult system (Tok Pisin *tambaran*, Kwanga *kwaramba*) had been abandoned in the late fifties and early sixties. In 1980, however, there were again kwaramba cult activities among the eastern Kwanga (in the village of Inakor) and in Bongos. In the northern Kwanga villages of Apos and Tau the beginnings of a movement toward reintroducing the cult could be observed.

Large food distribution feasts were held in Tau. The preparations for the distribution were shrouded in kwaramba secrecy, and on several occasions noninitiates had to hide in the bush to avoid observing them. This occurred despite an agreement among the villagers some years before to continue public food exchange feasts but to abandon the secret kwaramba cult.

In Apos the reintroduction of the kwaramba cult was marked by a violent conflict among villagers. A group of men had started preparations for the construction of a kwaramba cult house, fencing off a ceremonial ground in the middle of the village and assembling the posts for the new house. At the same time, some of the younger men who were to be introduced into the kwaramba cult wanted to celebrate with their own feast for a new slit-gong. This was forbidden by the initiators. When the younger men claimed that sorcery had been connected with the kwaramba cult of their fathers and therefore they were opposed to their own initiation, a fight started between the two initiatory moieties. As a solution to this conflict, the younger men proposed fleeing to the out-stations and thus depriving the initiators of the chance to give them food during the period of the cult activities. (These gifts of food are an important part of the village's exchange system.) The initiators' moiety claimed that these younger men were ignorant of true kastom.

In the Bongos area, the reintroduction of the cult started in the village of Kwatengisi in 1975.[3] There had been no initiations in the area since 1965. After the initiation in Kwatengisi there were four others, in the villages of Waukia, Bongos, Welsor, and Mamsi. This cult revival was connected with the influence of a man from Bongos who had left his village after the war to work on plantations in New Ireland and New Britain. Returning to the village and marrying, he had trained as a medical orderly (*dokta boi*) and worked in that capacity in various villages in the area. In 1965 he had been elected village councillor. His great concerns at that time had been the construction of roads and the introduction of cash crops, mainly coffee. Elected a member of the House of Assembly in 1972, he began to show more interest in national goals. As a member of Parliament he used the concept of kastom for its unifying function at the national level. On visits to his village he spoke of the importance of kastom and thus promoted the reestablishment of the traditional cult.

Today it is rather difficult to estimate the interlude between initiations before European contact, but we may assume that even in pre-European times the performance of initiations met resistance among villagers and thus was often delayed. For instance, Tuzin (1980:128) says of the cult of the Ilahita Arapesh, the eastern neighbors of the Kwanga, that "the Tambaran has always . . . had to fight for its life. All evidence suggests that the inertia of the system tends against undertaking anything so vast as a Tambaran initiation." The mechanism of reciprocity which pervades all kwaramba cult activities is probably one of the strongest guarantees of the continuity of the tradition. Exchange partnerships are the same in everyday and in ritual life. Thus exchanges during kwaramba ritual are a condensation and culmination of exchange activities in daily life. Exchange partnerships are inherited patrilineally. If a man does not join in an initiation, his exchange partner may break off their relationship. Even more influential, however, is the fear of sorcery if one does not return gifts. There is therefore continuous pressure to hold an initiation, as each one reciprocates for one held in the past.[4]

The Kwaramba Cult and Its Taboos

The cult system of the Kwanga must be seen in a wider context of cultural interchange in the region. The Kwanga do not constitute an isolated, sharply delimited cultural group. It is my impression that cultural differences are more marked between distant Kwanga villages than between Kwanga and neighboring villages of different language groups.[5] Tuzin has presented a detailed

analysis of the tambaran cult of the neighboring Ilahita Arapesh. He gives a very general definition of tambaran: "In its most abstract aspect the Tambaran stands for the totality of Arapesh tradition. . . . it signifies a unitary and unifying dimension informing all categories of the cultural heritage" (Tuzin 1980:24). In interpreting the data on Kwanga culture, we can say that here too the kwaramba system functions as a very strong unifying and classifying instrument in a society with an inclination toward fission.

During my fieldwork I took part in an initiation which lasted for several months. Although I was more participant observer than initiate, I had to obey several of the taboos and thus was able to experience some of the difficulties and complexities of the daily life of the initiated man. The Kwanga have no men's houses like those of the Middle Sepik peoples, and they lead a quite harmonious family life. The separation in daily life between initiates and noninitiates that is imposed by the taboo system is, however, very demanding.

Probably the most influential taboo for initiated men is the one concerning the preparation of food. Forbidden to peel yams or other such food, they are completely dependent on women. If they are widowed, the duty falls to one of their children. Besides this there are many other taboos pertaining to specific garden products such as certain varieties of banana and pandanus fruit and any bulky food. Both initiated men and their wives are forbidden to produce sago. Although for most Kwanga villages sago is not the staple crop, at certain times, especially during the months after planting yams, it acquires a more important position in the diet. Thus it may be necessary for children to produce the sago starch for their families or for one of the very old men, liberated from these taboos, to do it. These rules for initiated men cover not only the type of food they may consume but also the way they may receive it. For example, a kwaramba man is not allowed to drink water carried in a very large bamboo tube. Some of the food taboos last only a few years after initiation. A certain degree of individual flexibility is possible, and one may try formerly forbidden food at the risk of getting sick. Other rules, such as those against producing sago, cutting meat in public (it is allowed in secret gatherings of initiators), and carrying food from gardens, last until an individual has completed the whole initiation cycle. Even in pre-European times, this cycle covered an extended period. In Bongos only a few men were credited with having gone through the whole initiation cycle, including the initiation of their exchange partners.

Kwaramba men are regarded suspiciously when they move around in the village. Even months after their participation in cult ceremonies, they are still dangerous to noninitiates. They have to be very careful in their movements, particularly when they are near firewood, fire, cooking pots, knives, food, water containers, and net bags. A kwaramba man may never step over these things, and anxious warnings were always uttered when I approached them. When playing with children, a kwaramba man has to be very careful that they never pass under his legs. These rules about the movements of kwaramba men are even more extensive if one considers the moiety system which coincides with the initiation moieties. Thus, a man may never enter the house of a man of the opposite moiety if he has been an initiator to that group. Similar rules relate to the entering of gardens. All these rules are still very strictly followed in the Bongos area today. In villages such as Tau, where there has been no kwaramba initiation for many years, only parts of these prohibitions are still observed.

Conflict

Various aspects of the kwaramba cult present the possibility of conflict. Common to all of these is a sense of inequality. The most important complaint about the cult is the inequality in food distribution. According to the structure of the cult system, there are two main barriers in food distribution connected with kwaramba cult activities. The first separates initiates from noninitiates, mainly adult men from women and children; the second separates higher-grade initiates from lower-grade ones. The main reason that initiates give for the existence of the cult is that only through kwaramba will there be plenty of food. These ritual practices, initiates say, increase the productivity of gardens and the number of pigs. Noninitiates know that food plays a major role in the secret cult, but they often reject this explanation and point out that kwaramba men themselves consume most of the food.

Another set of complaints refers to the restrictions in freedom of movement during the period of cult activities. The preparations for initiations are not limited to a sacred area; they may take place anywhere in the village territory. Therefore noninitiates have to be warned and sent away in advance of any kwaramba activity. Women, children, and noninitiated men have to stay in the village while initiated men roam the forests and gardens. Thus I sometimes observed women having to return to the village in the morning because the paths to their gardens were blocked by men making preparations for the cult. If kwaramba men pass through a village, noninitiates have to leave their houses and hide in the nearby bush. In Bongos a whole hamlet has been relocated because it was too near to the kwaramba ceremonial ground.

Cult participants and noninitiates agree that economic development and the kwaramba cult cannot be combined. When kwaramba men of Bongos discussed the timing of subsequent initiations, they often said that road building should be the next step, before any new ceremonial activities. Village meetings with the councillor were occasions for discussion of measures to be taken for the development of the village. One of the leading men in cash-crop matters (among the Kwanga exclusively coffee) said that in the first place they should do bisnis and only in second place "culture," by which he meant the kwaramba cult. The younger men who were accused of doing nothing for bisnis said that the elders should lead the way.

The gap between the generations has assumed new dimensions. In the traditional society a certain degree of separation existed between fathers and sons, especially if the sons were not initiated. Today these sons have sometimes had several years of formal education or worked in far-off places. Back in their own villages they have no tasks and feel that their fathers are preventing the villages' development. Tuzin has mentioned the resistance of Ilahita Arapesh cult partners to repaying ritual debts, calling it "an example of how contact with another culture can generate unprecedented situations which subvert and eventually bring to ruin traditional institutions" (1980:123). He lists cash-cropping, business affairs, and local government council activities as the activities important to younger Ilahita Arapesh men.

Probably of equal weight with the conflict between modern and traditional interests is the incompatibility of kwaramba cult and Christian education. Though I never heard any condemnation of the cult by Catholic priests, I know that no one who wanted to participate in church activities could join in the traditional ceremonies. The first missionary in Bongos observed kwaramba initiations. The missionary in Bongos in 1979–80 never dared to see the more secret parts of the initiation ritual because of possible conflicts in delimiting the spheres of traditional religion and Christianity, but he visited the final public dancing by the novices. One who wanted to be baptized a Catholic and therefore had to go to church weekly for three years as a catechumen was forbidden to take part in kwaramba rituals. An adult Catholic man who was not initiated told me that the magical practices connected with penis bloodletting were the main obstacle. Much stronger opposition to traditional culture occurs in villages under the influence of the Protestant mission. There not only the kwaramba cult but also food exchange feasts and girls' puberty rites have been abandoned. This varying mission influence accentuates the disparity between neighboring villages regarding their adherence to the past.

The kwaramba cult provided not only food but also the means to power. Men of the higher initiation grades made decisions about village matters, among them the timing of major steps in gardening work. Those few initiated men who knew the *ukwasumbu* songs, coded in a secret language, possessed the greatest authority. Newly created positions and institutions now provide other means by which Kwanga may acquire influence and power.[6] The new positions created in the Bongos area during the last few decades include village magistrate, village policeman, councillor, medical orderly, agriculture officer, coffee buyer, catechist, prayer leader, teacher, and member of the provincial government. These positions do not coincide with the kwaramba system. The Bongos village councillor has never participated in a kwaramba initiation, and others have only heard or seen parts of the initiation. Once two of these adult men with grown children complained to me that the cult leaders had never told them any "stories," by which they meant the hidden meanings of the ukwasumbu texts. The cult leaders explained their reluctance to interpret cult meanings by reference to the texts' connection with the higher grades of initiation. These men with new positions and without authority in the cult system find it difficult to carry out their own ideas and projects. They fear the power of initiated men, without whose approval they face threats of sorcery and economic sanctions. Nowadays, many offenses against the rules of kwaramba are sanctioned by the offering of domesticated pigs to the group of initiated men concerned. Complaints about inequality in food distribution and power come mainly from younger adult men who have experienced different cultures and places. One of these men, who had not (yet) been initiated, ex-

pressed this sentiment, with all its implications, in one sentence: "Our fathers oppress us."

Pressure to enter the cult is exerted not by men's own fathers but by the men of the opposite initiatory moiety, their fathers' exchange partners not only in ritual but also in daily life. In the past, men who wanted to evade initiation ran away into the bush. Today some men do not participate in the cult system even though their hamlet neighbors and men of their age-group are undergoing the initiation cycle. The most common objections I heard were that they are afraid of the food taboos connected with initiation, that it is too much work or that some of the initiation duties are women's work, that they do not want to eat so many yams, that their modern official position (e.g., medical orderly) is incompatible with kwaramba ritual, or simply that they do not like it. Even men who had been in one initiation and were quite convinced of the importance of the cult did not want to do the same thing again in a subsequent initiation. Sometimes a man will have missed an initiation by absence from the village, but generally outmigration is rather unimportant and has little influence on men's attendance at initiations. During the last initiation in Bongos in 1978, 30 men entered the kwaramba cult and 19 men did not. Of the 139 adult men in Bongos, 59 percent—76 percent of Moiety A and 42 percent of Moiety B—are initiated. In other villages, where the cult has been abandoned for more than twenty years, the situation is very different. In village of Tau I, with 98 adult males, only 34 percent are initiated; Moiety A has 8 cult members and Moiety B 25.

Conflicts between initiates and noninitiates also arise from the fact that noninitiates—men and probably women too—know what happens in the secret cult, although they are uncertain about the details. They consider the official explanations of cult members to be lies. Opponents of the cult say that it destroys the human being and call it "rubbish." They often said, as a reason for giving up the cult, that they wanted schools instead.

Adaptations to New Situations

In other cultures of Papua New Guinea there have also been changes in traditional initiation complexes. Among Middle Sepik cultures a fundamental change has been a shortening of the seclusion period and its manifold activities, such as the production of ritual objects and ornaments. Among the Sawos of Gaikorobi, bloodletting practices changed in response to mission education, though lately they seem to have been resumed. Cane swallowing as a purification rite in initiation has been abandoned among the Sambia of the highlands; "men say they took it upon themselves to give it up because it was 'bad' and 'too painful' (Herdt 1981:223). The Baruya have abandoned the homosexual practices of their initiation and rituals connected with preparation for warfare (Godelier 1982a:92, 300). Godelier thinks that male initiation has lost its sacred character for the sake of ethics (p. 315) and become a new instrument for men to use in facing new situations outside their traditional culture.

In Bongos there has been an attempt to combine kwaramba ornament and Christian imagery; one of the leading young mission activists once tried to incorporate some pictures from the church into the huge feather headdresses of the novices. His action was severely criticized by the elders, and a heavy thunderstorm at the time of the feast gave them further strong evidence that it was wrong. Another such attempt was observed among the Kwanga of the Seim area in the West Sepik Province, where have been no initiations since about 1965. People from the area used to come as visitors to kwaramba rituals in the Bongos area, but during my stay in Bongos none ever did so. On a journey through the area, I saw a house representing a very individual and fantastic mixture of a kwaramba house and a Christian church. Its owner and builder declared it a tambaran house, and on entering it he would kneel and make the sign of the cross. A kind of table serving as an altar stood at one end, and it was covered with different kinds of carvings and clay figures. I had elsewhere seen almost no carvings in Kwanga villages. Some of them I recognized as genuine kwaramba figures, while others were fashioned in Maprik style or even bought in Wewak. There was also a booklet filled with mysterious handwriting, a kind of bible. This man lived isolated from the rest of the village; he said that he had left it because the villagers were always quarreling and fighting, and because they ate meat and betel nuts. The villagers thought that the man had gone crazy and said that he had had to leave the village because they were afraid of him. In this case, we see how a new cult might begin, in an individual effort to combine traditional elements with modern ones. This experiment has, however, remained isolated, for the moment at least. On the mythological level we can find more

points of contact between tradition and Christianity. For example, one of the Kwanga's ancestors became their "God." The Catholic church seems to foster these experiments. The churches in Arasili (in the Wam area northeast of Dreikikir) and in Tau have facades painted like those of Maprik cult houses.

Finally, I shall mention one instance in which kastom and modern culture met in an extraordinary way. As everywhere in the area, local string bands play an important role in the lives of the younger Kwanga generation. The *pilai gitar resis*, competitions in songs and decorations, represent the culmination of weeks of preparation and training, and have become a sort of kwaramba for this generation. Once some boys from Kwatengisi decorated themselves like novices in the final public dancing ceremony of the kwaramba, with long shell necklaces and headdresses. There seems to have been no criticism by their elders of this combination of traditional and modern culture.

Conclusion

The preservation of local traditions is of increasing importance for the identity of groups and cultures in Papua New Guinea. Part of the reevaluation of the traditional past is the concept of kastom. On the national level the content of kastom has remained vague and imprecise, but villagers have seized upon this concept and tried to give it more detailed meaning. We have seen how the use of kastom has had far-reaching consequences among the Kwanga. While they have only lately come under Western influence, we find changes of varying degrees in almost all aspects of their culture. One of these changes, the abandonment (or interruption) of kwaramba cult activities, has recently been reversed with the reevaluation of kastom. Economic, social, and religious changes in the meantime have set new boundaries for the performance of initiations. The main economic change consists in widespread cash-cropping, which gives villagers new goals and is not linked to tradition. The most important social change may be seen in the consequences of formal education, in particular, the growing gap between the generations and a decline in the authority of the elders. This has had an impact on younger men's attitudes toward initiation. The teachings and practices of the various missions have substantially changed the belief systems of villagers and given rise to skepticism about the ideas and practices of the past.

The traditional taboo system for initiates creates contemporary difficulties. General food taboos and restrictions on the production and preparation of food are a problem for young people who want to maintain the traditions of their culture. This taboo system is, however, one of the main components of the initiation complex. Infringement of taboos may result in illness and death, and this becomes a powerful argument for discontinuing the cult. Probably one of the most strongly felt aspects of kwaramba is its inequality. Contact with Western civilization has given rise to the hope of equal participation in hitherto unknown activities, and in this context the restrictions of one's own culture can only be seen as a burden. The cult's very strict taboo system and its inequality combine to produce the idea that economic development and the kwaramba cult are mutually exclusive. At the same time, there is a wide gap between kwaramba and Christianity. Only on the individual level has there been any attempt to combine the two. It is therefore an open question whether any mixture of kastom and Christianity, tradition and economic development, is possible.

Travel and contact with different cultures offer the opportunity to compare one's own institutions with those of one's neighbors. Kwanga men sometimes compare their own secret cult with that of other villages. Thus Kwanga men in Masalaga maintain that their cult has been more hidden and has lasted longer than the cult of the Nukuma. Initiated men in Bongos consider their kwaramba "hotter" than that of the eastern Kwanga because of its very long periods of taboo. In this way the Kwanga use the institution of kwaramba to express a feeling of identity. This search for identity in traditional terms is not very strong among young Kwanga men, however, and kwaramba has a very doubtful position in their thinking. Godelier (1982a:314, my translation) describes a very different situation for young Baruya men: "All or nearly all are today in favor of

maintaining male and female initiation, which they describe as their deep roots, their identity." Tuzin (1980:325), however, says of young Ilahita Arapesh, "Today's generation of young adults grew up with an easy awareness of the outside world, and it is impossible for them to share the bewilderment and suspicion of their elders in the face of radical alien cultural forms. Increasingly, their concerns and activities lie where the Voice of the Tambaran cannot reach them." Kwanga men are still experimenting with both ways, doing bisnis one season and dancing for kwaramba the next.

Notes

1. Fieldwork among the Sawos was carried out in 1972–74 with the financial support of the Swiss National Research Foundation. Sawos villages were revisited in 1979–81.

2. Fieldwork among the Kwanga was carried out in 1979–80 under a scholarship from the German Research Society. I am grateful to that body for its financial support during the past several years.

3. Allen (1976:30) writes: "The only *haus tambaran* observed in the study area was one built in Kwatengisi in 1975. It was smaller in all dimensions than the well-known Maprik-area houses. The ridge was more level. The facade was covered with bark paintings, but they were not organised into an integrated design." In 1978 Allen observed an initiation at Kwatengisi (see Allen in this volume).

4. Roscoe and Scaglion remark in this volume that internal structure is a significant factor in determining the fortune of the male initiation ceremony in the Sepik area.

5. Some of the papers in this volume (e.g., that of Tuzin) particularly stress the need for an understanding of regional cultural differences or similarities.

6. Discussions at this symposium of traditional and new forms of power and politics in Sepik societies have revealed that in many cultures of this area knowledge has traditionally been recognized as a basis of power. Today this knowledge (and power) is expected to be obtained by individuals through formal education.

19/ The Response to Tourism in Yensan

Jürg Schmid

Yensan, on the bank of the Middle Sepik, is the most recent offshoot of Palimbei. Overshadowed by powerful neighboring villages, it has nevertheless, by cunning, impudence, and stubbornness, succeeded in holding its own. Even when the village was completely destroyed by the Western Iatmul at the turn of the century, the people of Yensan managed to survive by a timely escape. The appearance of the Germans and later the Australians brought quieter times but unmanageable difficulties in understanding the Europeans' ways. When World War II reached the Sepik, its physical threat was managed by submission, but its psychological threat was much more profound. It was clear to the Yensan people that the goodwill of their ancestor spirits (*wagan*) protected them from the bombs and shells; the war itself remained incomprehensible to them and beyond their traditional realm of influence. They were shocked to find their religion incapable of providing efficient survival strategies in an environment that was becoming increasingly unintelligible. In the aftermath of the war, which reinforced the colonial influence of Australia, they were forced to devise new strategies for survival. A period of experimentation began that seemed to toll the doom of Iatmul culture. The so-called cargo cults, ingenious ideas based on wrong assumptions, were falsified by historical developments they should have served to explain. The villagers' active response to the appearance of tourists represented another attempt at mastery of the new situation.

Yensan and Its Neighbors 1972–73

Population Structure and Mobility

Before World War I, mobility almost everywhere in mainland New Guinea was confined within the territorial boundaries of one's own and allied villages. With the increasing demand for plantation labor during the German and Australian colonial periods, migration of men began to have its effects. Tasks traditionally belonging to the male sphere such as the building of houses and canoes

were almost completely abandoned. A 1951 patrol report describes Yensan as a dirty, dilapidated village inhabited only by women and children and urgently warns of the consequences of excessive labor recruitment. Because wages were extremely low, the return for migrant labor was small, but work on the *stesen* ([Tok Pisin] plantation) was a source of prestige and came to represent a new form of initiation. Recruitment continued at a brisk pace until the end of the fifties, and at the same time villagers under the influence of the Catholic mission began to lose their fear of leaving their hereditary territory (having been taught that God the Father is omnipresent). Migration of whole families to the rapidly growing centers on the coast and in the highlands replaced the migration of single men.

At first the traditional social structures of the villages were scarcely touched by this transplantation. In Madang, a squatter settlement called Bikus (after a single dominating tree) is inhabited exclusively by Yensan people and in 1972 even had a men's house. What is more, it is surrounded by settlements of squatters from Kandingei, Palimbei, Malingei, and Sotmeli, Yensan's neighbors in the Middle Sepik. The scarcity of land in the Madang area precluded any substantial subsistence activity, and in 1972 men with salaried jobs had great difficulty in meeting their obligations. Yensan villagers' supplying the Bikus residents with sago and smoked fish, without which they would have been forced to rely on purchased rice, constituted an important economic link between the two communities. Villagers moved back and forth between them, and in 1973 net migration was zero and the populations were nearly balanced (Yensan 140, Bikus 174, other settlements 65). Yensan, however, was characterized by an excess of women and children and especially the absence of young men with education. Education was the first step toward abandonment of the village; an older informant drily asserted that in the end only the stupid ones, who had no alternative, remained. Among older men, those who were more important because of their knowledge of mythological lore tended to be more mobile. These developments pointed to the disintegration of the Yensan social system.

Intervillage Relations

Yensan was the smallest village of the Central Iatmul group that originated in Palimbei. Half of its clans had so few members left that the maintenance of their land rights and religious functions was no longer guaranteed. Its location on the very bank of the Sepik increased the pressure on its territorial boundaries; without the support of the authorities it would not have succeeded in retaining its fishing grounds and garden plots on both sides of the river. Thus the relationship of Yensan to its neighbors before independence was characterized by economic conflict with Palimbei (where fish was in short supply because of limited access to the river and overfishing of the lakes) and the Sawos village of Nangusap in the bush. Backing for its claims came from a loose alliance with Kanganamun. Three times a week, Yensan women bartered surplus fish for the sago of the Sawos women of Nangusap in a clearing in the bush between the two villages. The mission at Kapaimari was the regional center, with a busy airstrip, a hospital, an elementary school, a store, and a modern market that also served as a news agency for the region.

Self-Esteem and the European Presence

Over the years, representatives of the colonial administration—missionaries, art dealers, government officers, linguists, anthropologists, and tourists—had made their presence felt in the Middle Sepik region. The local people had come to consider their own culture, social structure, and religion profoundly and unalterably distinct from and inferior to that of these Europeans. Their resignation and hopelessness had some economic basis; nearly all the development schemes undertaken at the village level had ended in failure. The production of cash crops on the Sepik plains was impossible because of periodic flooding; for example, a coffee plantation bearing for the first time in 1972–73 was completely destroyed by a flood. Timber production was out of the question in the sparsely wooded riverine area. Cattle management proved problematic on the poor soils of the grassland, and the technical and financial difficulties of transport to slaughterhouses turned out to be insoluble. A project to market fresh Sepik fish failed for similar reasons. The once-lucrative trade in crocodile skins came to an end because of a lack of crocodiles. The moderate amount of tourism produced little cash; the government rest house offered accommodation free

of charge, and the dilapidated men's house was scarcely a tourist attraction. The newly produced carvings, mostly of poor quality, could be sold neither in the village nor in the coastal towns. In the end, it seemed that the only alternative to the traditional subsistence economy was wage labor in the cities.

The survival of the village seemed doubtful, and the old men worried about cultural continuity. They saw the young drifting into a world that had nothing in common with traditional Iatmul values, and they considered initiation (then still mandatory) the only effective means of disciplining them and thus binding them to the village. The awareness that cultural continuity and autonomy for the village were possible only on the basis of the traditional social structure played a crucial role in their thinking. As national independence approached, the future seemed increasingly gloomy. Some villagers were convinced that Michael Somare, as the nation's first prime minister and a product of the Sepik himself, would vigorously promote the development of rural areas—roads, cash-cropping and processing industry, and direct subsidies to the villages. Others believed that the existing infrastructure would break down soon after independence and traditional warfare and a reversion to a purely subsistence economy would be the consequences. The two groups agreed that independence was coming much too early.

Yensan and Its Neighbors 1976–83

A New Self-Esteem

Shortly after independence, the mobility of Yensan villagers to and from the coastal cities began to decline. Some men decided to stay in the village and try to earn income through motor canoe transport, the operation of trade stores, tourism, and the production and sale of artifacts. A *bisnisgrup* ([Tok Pisin] business group), with membership conditional on purchase of share certificates, was established in 1976 to explore opportunities for collective as well as individual enterprise. Its first undertaking was the replacement of the disintegrating men's house.

Since the last change of age-grades had occurred long ago, the men of the age-grade to which the house belonged were too old to perform the actual work of building, and this had to be done by whatever men were available. The men of the business group considered a new house not only traditionally important but also of potential commercial value. On its completion two years later, the new men's house assumed a prominent position in the business group's marketing strategies, although not without arousing misgivings in some of the older men. Members reasoned that, whereas the brief visits of tourists were then likely to produce only a few toea in payment for photographing privileges, the establishment of a complete service structure, with transport, lodging, excursions, and guides, might increase the yield from tourism. In the years that intervened before this conception could be realized, these men, most of whom had made their way to the business group by way of various cargo cults, persisted in their aim to understand and make use of the "new time."

By 1980, the lodgings for visitors in the new men's house were frequently occupied, for a fee of five kina per night. Included in the fee for lodging was a reasonable supply of firewood and help with meals, water carrying, and dishwashing. For an additional sum tourists could enjoy guided excursions to other villages, boat rides, and singsings and guitar concerts in the village. The tourist boat *Melanesian Explorer* regularly delivered an audience for a thirty-minute sing-sing that was splendidly rewarded. Though the income from transport on the Sepik at prices recommended by the provincial government and the sale of artifacts proved disappointing and the return of empty beer bottles for the deposit impractical because of transport costs, the business group had earned a considerable sum of money and had reinvested some of it in a number of individual projects (for example, outboard motors) and a trade store with a license for beer and a small stock of gasoline. The twice-weekly regional market at Kapaimari had been attracted to Yensan and grown large and important.

None of these ventures would have been possible without a new sense of self-esteem. Independence and postcolonial development politics had had a stimulating effect. During a long night session in October 1982, the men involved discussed their motivations as follows:

We follow the forceful customs of the past. You've seen—if tourists come inside the men's house and set down something belonging to them, it is forbidden to steal it. That is because this men's house still has power. Do you think that it is the same at other villages on the Sepik River? Oh, George, let me tell you! They do all kinds of annoying things to the tourists. Last month they stole all the shirts and trousers off the tourist boat that they had washed and hung on the line. Now all the tourists are fed up and have left altogether. We don't understand this way of behaving.

Some notion of the obstacles to the introduction of the "new way" can be gained from the discussion of the use of the men's house to accommodate tourists. White female tourists were permitted to stay there, not being classified as "female" in the traditional Yensan sense of the term, and the fee of five kina was viewed as compensation for the possible pollution of female presence and such thoughtless blunders by visitors as the placing of photographic equipment on the ceremonial chair. Thus brilliant mental acrobatics threw a bridge between traditional taboos and new economic ends.

Prosperity, Setbacks, and New Ideas

The peak of Yensan prosperity was reached in 1982. With the increasing circulation of money in the village and the capital accumulated by the business group, ideas for new enterprises were springing up like mushrooms. At the same time, discussion of the use of the men's house was renewed over the issue of tourists in bathing suits. The device of considering the fee compensation for possible damage to the house's sanctity now seemed to threaten the authority of the elders, and they pointed out that the men's house should have been the religious, political, and social center of the (male) community rather than a commercial venture. In response to their concern, it was decided to build a guesthouse for tourists, and money for materials was handed over to an agent and subsequently disappeared. Rumors of misuse of the business group's capital (for example, for bride-price payments and debt repayment) and incompetence began to spread through the village.

In 1983 the number of overnight lodgers in the men's house suddenly declined, partly as a consequence of a nationwide decline in tourism for which no one had an explanation but in which rising prices and transport costs certainly played an important role. In general, the Sepik area was losing its appeal for short-time visitors; too many commercialized men's houses crammed with artifacts had badly scratched the image of the "last untouched paradise." Luckily, the Yensan people had little money invested in ambitious enterprises, and the empty men's house incurred no debts. Nothing was lost, but quieter times ensued.

In the fall of that year the village received a substantial development subsidy from a fund in Port Moresby, and two alternatives for its investment were being considered when I left at the end of October: a houseboat to serve tourists, art dealers, and officials as lodging and means of transportation or a guesthouse with a bar and meeting rooms as well as sleeping quarters. It was clear that real improvement in the village's situation depended on faster transport, and this had led to a reactivation of an earlier plan for a road direct to Yensan, for which, it was said, funding had already been guaranteed and part of the survey work accomplished.

Conclusion

In the mid-seventies, the binding power of traditional culture in Yensan began to fade. A small, extraordinarily active group of villagers undertook a survival strategy in deliberate opposition to the disintegrating life in the towns. To legitimate their pursuit of economic ends they selectively combined elements of Christian and traditional ethics into a new ethic—featuring honesty, discipline, diligence, and observance of traditional obligations—that supported the individual and was considered the key to success. Their success has strengthened their self-esteem. The difficulties they have faced in the realization of their plans have sprung from the loose organization of the group and from lack of information due to rural isolation.

Events such as these have been occurring in many villages all over Papua New Guinea, where people are searching for new strategies for survival in response to the rapid change of the last decade. Since the subsistence economy still provides a reliable basis of existence, this is less a matter of economics than one of mental well-being—a struggle against cultural and social disintegration. Those who manage to combine a ready grasp of new ideas and resilience in the face of repeated failure with firm roots in the *graun bilong tumbuna* ([Tok Pisin] ancestral land) and a sense of intimate connection with the past will likely be the victors in this struggle.

20/ Cultural Changes in Gargar Society[1]

Hanns Peter

In 1969 I had occasion to spend some time with the Gargar of the Green River area, doing field-work in social anthropology (see Peter 1969–70). In 1973 and 1980 I returned with my wife for further studies (see Peter 1973–74, 1979a, b, 1981, 1982, 1983–84). With each visit we saw evidence of rapid change, and I decided to make this a special concern of my research.

Western influence had reached the Gargar comparatively late, and if they were to catch up with the other peoples of Papua New Guinea economically and politically, change was bound to be rapid. The Gargar settlements are remote and inaccessible except by air via the Green River patrol post and the tracks and narrow bush paths that lead on from there. The border separating Papua New Guinea from Irian Jaya cuts right through Gargar territory. Most of it now belongs to Papua New Guinea; about a tenth lies on the Indonesian side. The pacification of the Gargar was carried out in the mid-fifties, and for the next fifteen years the patrol officer was practically the only European with whom they came into contact. During the preparations for self-government and independence, basic political training was given to some of the village men, who in due course passed the new ideas on to the other villagers. These proceedings naturally had a bearing on the old traditions and changed, to a certain extent, the established social order. The remoteness of the region made it difficult, however, for the region to be developed and integrated into the new state.

The Gargar, numbering approximately twelve hundred live in ten to twelve settlements located six to twelve hours' walk from the Green River patrol post. Their staple food, sago, is supplemented mainly by garden crops. Hunting is of little importance in contributing to the food supply, but it is a favorite pastime of males and, above all, is of great cultic significance. The pigs kept in the villages are killed only on certain ceremonial occasions; their meat is not part of the daily diet.

The sago palms grow in swampy valleys surrounded by hills and mountain ranges that are densely covered with rain forest. The gardens are situated as close as possible to the settlements.

However, the soil is exhausted after a year's growth, and a new clearing is therefore necessary. Over a period of several years, the distance between village and gardens increases, and, as a result, the settlement is eventually abandoned and a new one established in an area of primary or mature secondary forest. Where the distance between garden and settlement is great, it is more economical for the people to stay in the garden during the planting and harvesting periods. Special garden houses are built and habitually used by one family, sometimes by more. Barring special occasions such as ceremonies, meetings, etc., up to 80 percent of the villagers may be either in the gardens, in the sago swamps, or in the forest on hunting trips, and settlements often give the impression of being deserted. Apart from economic motives, there may be other reasons for the shifting or abandoning of a village, such as a great number of deaths caused by an epidemic. Occasionally the inhabitants of two villages may build a single new settlement or those of one settlement may build two. Thus, for one reason or another, the number of villages within Gargar territory is not always the same and their locations are constantly changing.

In 1969 the Gargar area on the Papua New Guinea side of the border, the Yuri Census Division, was part of the West Sepik District, and the officer responsible for the division was based at the Green River patrol post. The patrol post had been established in 1950 in the sparse grassland of the sandy Sepik Plain. During World War II an Australian army camp had been located in the same place, and the local authorities and our informants agreed that there had been no contact between the Australian soldiers and the Gargar. Since 1950, more than one census has been carried out in the districts administered by the Green River patrol post. The first census with the Gargar was carried out in 1956–57, but it was not until 1961 that the Yuri Census Division was reported as being "under influence." In the same year a medical aid post was established at Green River. In the mid-sixties, the Christian Mission in Many Lands (CMML) started its activities in the area, but during this early period its influence remained restricted to the inhabitants of Green River itself and the villages nearby.

Foreign Influences Recognizable in 1969

By 1969, the Gargar had already undergone a period of regular, although perfunctory, contact with Western civilization. The presence of the *kiap* ([Tok Pisin] government officer) and his police troop at Green River and the new order they set up in connection with the pacification caused a number of changes which had a lasting effect on traditional Gargar culture. In the settlements of Yuri, Auya, and Troali, comparatively close to the patrol post, outside influences could be recognized more clearly than in the village of Kamberap, where we took up residence, more than twelve walking hours away. Hardly any influence had reached the inhabitants of the villages even farther from the station. However, one of the first steps taken by the administrative authorities had changed the appearance and character of even these remote settlements. Thus, no traditional community houses remained anywhere in the Gargar area controlled by the Australian government in 1969. The traditional villages had all been replaced by new ones made up of a number of smaller family houses, a guest house (*haus kiap*), and a spare guest house (*haus polis*) for the policemen to use when they passed through the village. Most families provided a special menstruation hut for their female members; this might be part of the existing house but with a separate entrance or an individual building apart from the rest of the village. A further innovation was the introduction of toilets, also built at some distance from the village.

Funerals with their traditional stages were still being performed. In earlier times, the corpse was wrapped in leaves and left to decay on a wooden platform near the house. This was not being done any longer; the body was buried instead and the grave, located in a special burial ground near the village, covered with logs and sealed with earth. Some time after the burial—usually six to eight months—the grave was opened and the bones were collected and carefully stored in the house. The final stage of the death ceremony involved ritual singing and dancing, after which the bones were deposited in a mountain cave.

In 1969 the material culture of the Gargar had undergone little change. Here and there modern tools were used instead of or in addition to the traditional implements made of stone or bone. Approximately 50 percent of males and 20 percent of females were in possession of a *laplap* ([Tok Pisin] loincloth) or some other piece of clothing of Western provenience. Paper money was not appreciated, but coins were accepted and sometimes used as ornaments. Barter was generally preferred to any other form of payment.

Within the village the councillor, usually one of the younger men, was regarded as the official authority. He maintained contact between the villagers and the administrative officials, made sure that regulations were being observed, and assigned villagers to community work such as clearing the bush tracks of undergrowth or cleaning the village plaza. The former big man was still respected, but his influence was restricted to traditional activities.

In 1969 there was no school in the Gargar area. In Kamberap, three men and one woman spoke Tok Pisin.

The patrol officer at Green River who was responsible for the Yuri Census Division was an Australian. His patrol troop consisted of ten policemen from the east coast of New Guinea.

Cultural Changes 1969–80

During the years immediately before and after Independence, great efforts were made by the administrative authorities to achieve a frictionless continuation of the Australians' agenda. In many places all over the country, experienced Australian officials were replaced by newly trained local people who, in most cases, had to be more or less self-supporting, often without any possibility of obtaining help or advice. Particularly in an area as remote and underdeveloped as the Yuri Census Division, the authorities had to face a number of difficulties, and to cope with the most urgent problems measures had to be taken that led to fundamental changes in the local society.

These changes were most conspicuous with regard to the material culture. Western clothes, on the whole neat and well-kept, are now generally worn throughout the area. With the exception of bast skirts, which are still occasionally worn by a few women while working in the garden, traditional clothing has more or less disappeared. Penis sheaths are considered extremely old-fashioned and even ridiculous. In Kamberap, pupils wear school uniforms. Watches and sunglasses are worn more or less for reasons of prestige. Umbrellas are frequently used, mainly for protection from the sun, the old shady bush path from Green River to the Gargar villages having been replaced by a broad track with no natural shade at all. Ornaments made of shells, teeth, or feathers were possessed by most Gargar in 1969; now only a very few items are kept by some of the older generation.

Hardly any Gargar still have *kundus* (hand-drums), formerly used almost every night in almost every Gargar village to accompany the old songs and dances. Instead, every Gargar village now has a slit-drum. The first rough slit-drums were introduced into the area many years ago. They were and still are used for calling people to meetings and now summon them to school and to church. Traditional songs are heard very occasionally; in general, people have to be given special encouragement or offered some sort of payment. Old men singing verses of the old songs on such occasions are apparently embarrassed and shy in the presence of the younger people, who often laugh at the old chants and prefer modern songs accompanied by guitar or ukulele.

Stone axes and bone implements have completely disappeared; steel axes, adzes, and bush knives are used in their stead. Sago hammers and digging sticks are still in use, but in addition to the latter modern spades are used. Hunting methods, too, have changed. Bows and arrows, though often carried, are rather sporadically used for hunting, since at least one man in each village owns a shotgun. Thanks to the fact that cartridges are expensive and not easy to come by, game has not been too much reduced by the new way of hunting. Already during the period of Australian administration, transistor radios were given to each village with the intention of gaining influence over the villagers to prepare them for independence. In 1980 cassette recorders were also in use. Most of the above-mentioned products of modern industry as well as batteries, tobacco, and groceries were at that time already available at the two stores which had been set up at Green River. Even in the villages, individual men tried to run their own little stores, but they lacked the necessary training to make the business profitable. Apart from the fact that the range of goods was limited, hardly anybody was able to pay for them.

Beside all these material changes, there were profound changes of other kinds. Great progress had been made with regard to education. The instructional work begun by the missionaries was intensified during the following years by the government. In the early seventies, a young man from Kamberap who had been trained as a missionary teacher set up a school in his native village and began training adults in Tok Pisin and basic mathematics. At about the same time, a school was built at Yuri I, while at Troali one of the local men, who had also had some previous training from the missionaries, opened a kind of Sunday school in which he read from the Bible to his village audience. Two members of the Summer Institute of Linguistics had started their work at the beginning of the seventies, but in spite of their constant contact with the local people in connection with their linguistic studies, their influence remained restricted to the village of Auya, where they had taken up residence.

Shortly after Papua New Guinea became independent, a government school was established at Kamberap, offering the chance for all Gargar children to become educated. At the same time, the settlement was relocated a six-hour walk away in the direction of Green River and in a less hilly area to make it more easily approachable from all directions and give the school a more central location. Part of the new village was designated as school grounds, and six school buildings—one for each grade—were built around an athletic field. Houses for the teachers and their families were built nearby. The guest house and the first-aid station, which temporarily accommodates the medical orderly, also belong to this part of the village. A number of houses are used for boarding pupils from other Gargar settlements, who live at Kamberap during school terms and are looked after by relatives from their own villages.

In 1980, an agreement between the Papua New Guinea and Irian Jaya governments was under discussion according to which the Gargar on the Irian Jayan side of the border would be permitted to send their children to school with the children of their relatives in Papua New Guinea. In 1973 the Gargar were still strictly forbidden to maintain contact with their relatives living across the border, but this prohibition was not strictly observed. When the opportunity arose, we paid a visit to Auyingarab, one of the Gargar settlements in Irian Jayan territory. Here, for the first time, we were able to see one of the old community houses built in the traditional style, many meters above the ground and big enough to accommodate sixty to eighty people, using as a central pole a huge hardwood tree. There were no toilet facilities. Near the main building, there were two little huts where food and firewood were stored, and at the back of the house was a wooden platform on which lay the corpse of a recently departed member of the family.

At Green River, a six-grade primary school had been established years before. This school is mainly attended by children who live in Green River or in one of the surrounding villages. If the villages are too far away for children to walk to school and back every day, pupils have to stay in Green River during the week. Here they live together in several houses (Tok Pisin *haus kunai*) built by their parents a short distance from the main settlement. They take their weekly food supply from home, and, in addition, there is usually some food prepared at the school and given to children who are in need of it.

The government contribution for building and maintaining the school houses is rather small. Therefore only a few buildings are made of modern materials such as concrete or corrugated iron. To earn money to maintain the school, pupils are encouraged to plant gardens, the harvest of which is sold at the Green River market.

One of the school buildings is equipped with an antenna, making it possible to receive the school broadcast, which is part of the educational program and obligatory for all grades. English is now taught right from the beginning. Apart from spelling, reading, and basic mathematics, pupils are also taught "community life," including local history and geography as well as sociology. The girls are taught needlework and the boys crafts. According to age and sex, pupils learn the traditional skills, such as carving, weaving, etc. Political education is given in high schools; in primary school, children receive only basic training. Books, tables, indexes, pictures, are made available by the school. For one hour a week each pupil is expected to do practical work such as repairing the school buildings, gardening, and cleaning.

Occasionally, shortage of staff makes it necessary for a teacher to instruct two forms at the same time. The more intelligent children are asked to help the others. The main object is not the achievement of a certain educational level but learning how to study.

At the end of grade six, the best of the pupils (up to a quarter of them) are selected to go on to secondary education. Success in studies, intelligence, and character are considered equally important as qualifications for further education. However, a basic requirement for high school attendance is parents' ability to pay the school fees, and often this is lacking.

There are only a very few jobs available in the region, and local people mostly lack the qualifications for such jobs as administrative officer, teacher, and medical orderly. Even the administrative center can offer only a limited number of money-making opportunities. The jobs there range from public service (power supply, maintenance of roads, airstrip, etc.) to social service (assistant work at the hospital and the mission). A few people work as shop assistants in one of the two stores. To earn money, then, young men from the villages are more or less compelled to find work in other parts of Melanesia. Many of them, recruited by itinerant labor contractors, hire themselves out to work on the big plantations— mostly on Manus or Rabaul—on contracts which usually run for two or three years.

Most of the modern products to be found in the Gargar area have been imported by village men on their return or bought by them later in one of the local stores. Besides the modern goods, they bring with them a wealth of foreign ideas, the effect of which on the original culture, perhaps not noticeable at first sight, is more lasting than that of the material goods. Unlike that of the majority of Sepik peoples, the traditional culture of the Gargar did not involve sacred carvings, masks, and men's houses. They did not practice any spectacular initiation ceremonies, nor were their ritual dances distinguished by any display of splendor. Their only durable ornaments for ceremonies and other festive occasions were strings of nassa and kauri shells, teeth (dog, flying fox), tusks, and feathers. Most of the materials used for decoration, such as leaves, fruits, fruit husks, and seeds, as well as the pigments for body decoration, were perishable. The wrappings worn by certain dancers at the funeral ceremony were made of and/or decorated with bast, grass, leaves, twigs, and other ephemeral materials, as was the central pole on the dancing ground. After the ceremony, these decorations were no longer of any use, for even with the most careful attention it would have been impossible to preserve them. Dancing boards, similarly, were made of bark and decorated with particular designs and patterns depending on whether they were being used for a funeral or the magical healing of a sick person. When the ceremony was finished, they were thrown into the bush, the pigments soon fading away and the patterns losing their meaning. There was never anything left, then, to remind people of a particular ritual or a traditional ceremony, and this complete lack of any visible symbols of the spiritual aspect of the culture contributed to its decline. There is no manifestation of a culture hero or ancestor or any other spiritual being to remind or encourage the old men to keep up the traditional ceremonies and rites, and young men have no mythical carvings and emblems to guide them in reviving the lost tradition.

Trends and Prospects

Overcoming the disadvantage with regard to economic development caused by the area's peripheral situation is the object of intense effort on the part of the local authorities, and this accelerates the process of acculturation enormously. At the same time, lack of visible symbols of Gargar spiritual culture promotes the continual loss of that culture and the adoption of foreign cultural elements. In addition, the repeated visits of two ethnologists—my wife and I—may have contributed to cultural change. While it is difficult to forecast further cultural changes, certain trends can be recognized.

For instance, it would hardly be good policy to regard the Gargar as isolated from their neighbors. It is to be expected that the various populations of this area will become more integrated with the administrative division as a whole. Some hints of a development in this direction may be gathered from words of Joe Dugouri, who, in 1980, was officer in charge of Green River. In connection with the then-current census, he said:

> I have already completed three census divisions, and I have another three to go. I have to do this because of the provincial election in November. I have to plan for that election as well. It's up to the provincial government in Vanimo. They have just tried to adopt a system of secretaries and deputy secretaries and assistant secretaries, and all that way, and then in a district like this we'll have a district coordinator who becomes the district administrator's secretary respective. He will coordinate all the activities amongst all the divisions. This place is planned for a district, and it will care for Yapsi, Idam, etc., and the rural place station at Kamberap. We are trying to decentralize the administration. . . . It is a subdistrict now. We come under Amanab, and there is now a plan before the district government to upgrade it to a district.

Gargar may also be expected to participate in the economic development of the area. A number of experimental projects to this end were initiated as early as 1977. In this connection, an agricultural research station was established near Green River, with an agriculturalist from Morobe named Buru in charge. To increase the chances of success, the station is working on a number of projects at the same time, ranging from the cultivation of cereals, spices, and rubber trees to the breeding of crocodiles, indigenous birds, and butterflies. As the new station offered jobs to a number of men, its establishment must be regarded as an economic improvement for the local people in any case. According to Buru,

> We have got two laborers permanently employed on wildlife, one on crocodiles at the moment, and three over there we have planted on butterflies. We try butterfly farming also to sell the butterflies overseas. We have to have a farm to encourage people around here to have *their* farm. Then they will have their own butterflies, and they will come here and bring them to us, and we will market them to overseas.
>
> We have laborers working at the rubber farm—we also have rubber research. We have rubber from Malaysia coming in, and we have four laborers on that. Then fishery development is coming up, and we have two laborers on that; we are helping the people on the Sepik River especially on fishery industry. And we have two laborers to keep the station clean, so all together we have fourteen laborers. As soon as we get butterflies on, we might have cassowary.

However, the research station faces a number of problems, shortness of money being the most urgent. Early profits could come from crocodile farming, although the necessity to dispatch the skins as quickly as possible always involves a certain risk. As Buru described the process,

> As soon as the crocodile is slaughtered off, we skin it off, it has to be washed out, cleaned and dried up. Get the water off, dry it up, then we have to salt it. We use common salt, just salt it twice. The first coating is in the morning, then we leave it for tomorrow morning, when we have to remove all the salt. And then there is another coating with salt. Then we have to pack them—timber is recommended for packing—and we have to send them away immediately.
>
> We get about hundred crocodile skins in a month. But at the moment we are having difficulties with transport. Our cash officer here does not get enough money. If we get in

hundred crocodile skins, it takes a lot of money to send them away.

The future will show which, if any, of the various experiments are going to confer the fresh impetus hoped for on the local economy. Whatever happens will estrange the Gargar more and more from their own traditional culture. This is a development necessary with regard to world politics and irresistible, but a complete loss of their traditional culture would be equivalent to an abandonment of their identity. This is something ethnological research should seek to prevent.

Notes

1. Translated by Brigitte Peter.

Part Four
Social Relations and Authority

Introduction

Nancy Lutkehaus

The 1976 symposium "Sepik Politics: Traditional Authority and Initiative"[1]—surprisingly, the first of its kind—took as its theme the ways in which traditional political institutions have shaped the world views and actions of individuals in Sepik societies. Like the contributors to this volume, participants hoped that their work would contribute to the self-understanding of the new nation of Papua New Guinea, which had gained independence the preceding year. The six papers in this section continue lines of inquiry that those researchers initiated, among them the study of the role of exchange in establishing and maintaining specific types of social and political relations, the effects of change on social and political organization, and the region's diverse political forms. These papers extend the analysis of Sepik social organization and political authority in new directions, examining culture-specific concepts of value and power, relations of production and reproduction, the relations between gender and social organization, gesture as a culture-specific means of establishing social cohesion, and key cultural metaphors concerned with power, authority, and social structure.

Like those in the earlier symposium, the political systems represented here take both egalitarian and hierarchical forms. David Lipset notes that authority becomes more diffuse as one moves inland from the Schouten Islands of Wogeo and Manam, with their hierarchical systems of hereditary village leadership, to the hinterlands of the East and West Sepik Provinces, with such extremely egalitarian systems as those of the Wape and the Gnau. Both he and I describe hierarchical political forms (in Murik and Manam society, respectively), pointing to the importance of primogeniture and the relationship between siblings, the flexibility within such systems of authority, and the role of ritual and exchange in the demonstration of power and authority. In contrast, the others describe local variations in what traditionally were basically egalitarian political systems.

In this comments on the 1976 symposium, Bateson (1978:77) described the Sepik as the appropriate setting for a study of cultural evolution, by which he meant the study of the processes whereby "each culture supposedly made its specific picture out of the same jumble of pieces of the jigsaw puzzle." From a similar perspective, some of these papers attempt to delineate Sepik-specific social and political configurations. Thus, despite cultural differences, Lipset posits basic structural similarities in the forms of ascription found in the social organization of the coastal Murik and the island societies of the Schouten archipelago, and in my discussion of the activities associated with the men's house and the performance of the tambaran flutes I describe the Manam variant of a quintessential Sepik cultural institution. Another common element differentially elaborated from culture to culture is exchange as a source of bonds between individuals and groups and of social identities. Several of the papers discuss the exchange of food and items of wealth (pigs, yams, shells, and ornaments made of dog's teeth and pig's tusks) in the competition for status and leadership in Sepik societies. Gilbert Lewis echoes this theme when, in discussing hospitality as a sign of moral support in Gnau society, he points to the importance of generosity in offering food. Finally, the general characteristics of the classless society that Milan Stanek identifies in Iatmul social structure hold true for all of the societies discussed in this volume; whether hierarchical or egalitarian, they are all classless.

Frederick Errington and Deborah Gewertz's description of the politician Yambumbe's rise to power as "chief" of the traditionally egalitarian Chambri presents a picture of the way social change happens and illuminates a number of important issues. The Chambri are willing to experiment with a new form of authority in an attempt to maintain control over their environment. Having tried to make use of relationships with individuals whom they consider more powerful than themselves, they eventually seek to appropriate the power itself. Errington and Gewertz's analysis, drawing on unpublished material from Mead and Fortune's field notes and Gewertz's own longitudinal study, is based on their interpretation of Chambri notions of power and of the meaning of their relationship with Europeans, including not only Mead and Fortune but Errington and Gewertz as well.

My discussion of the traditional and modern Manam leaders called *tanepoa* aims to explain cultural continuity in the midst of political change. Somewhat ironically, for the Manam, faced with a national political ideology that emphasizes egalitarian rather than hierarchical relations, the persistence of the tanepoa represents the perpetuation of their cultural identity.

Lewis presents fascinating microlevel data from the Gnau on gestures, such as the welcoming gesture of stroking a person's chin, and the bodily metaphors of moral support that they engender. He argues that gestures such as these are important in maintaining social cohesion in a small-scale society like the Gnau by demonstrating loyalty and responsibility toward members of the community, particularly members of one's own kin group.

A number of the papers discuss the relationship between a society's material conditions and ideological aspects of its culture. Stanek, for example, analyzes the ways in which the social relations of production and reproduction in Iatmul society articulate with myth and ritual knowledge. Barbara Huber-Greub views land as both a key economic resource and a central metaphor of Abelam culture. She describes the interrelationship between social relations of production and exchange (in particular, male-female relations and relations between old and young) and the cultural lore of spirits, names, and ritual knowledge that links humans with particular plots of land.

Variations in the cultural meaning of value and power and the social nature of the production and exchange of items of value are two topics related to the issue of authority that have been the focus of theoretical attention in recent analyses of the political economy of highlands societies (see, e.g., Modjeska 1982, Feil 1984, Lederman 1987). Unlike these societies, in which pigs remain the items of value par excellence, Sepik societies value both durable items such as shells and boar's tusks and intangible ones such as esoteric ritual lore (see Lutkehaus and Roscoe 1987). Lipset discusses the central symbolic and material role of boar's tusks in the demonstration of status and authority within Murik kin groups and describes the social value of sponsorship of Murik rituals of office. Although boar's tusks are status symbols in Manam society as well, here it is control over the performance of bamboo flutes and the exchange of pigs associated with that performance that demonstrates authority. And, according to Errington and Gewertz, for the Chambri power entails a concept of entropy—a gradual diminution of an individual's power through the loss of esoteric knowledge as it is transferred (or fails to be) from generation to generation. Notions of value and power in Sepik societies contrast with those of highlands societies in interesting and provocative ways. The analysis of differences in political economy between highland and lowland societies should be an important arena for future comparative and theoretical work by Sepik scholars.

Note

1. The participants (and their subjects) included Rhoda Métraux (the Eastern Iatmul), Deborah Gewertz (the Chambri), William Mitchell (the Wape), Nancy McDowell (the Bun), Patricia Townsend (the Sanio-Hiowe), and Donald Tuzin (the Ilahita Arapesh). Margaret Mead and Gregory Bateson commented on the papers presented, and Rhoda Métraux edited the papers for publication as a special issue of the *Anthropological Quarterly* in 1978.

21/ Gestures of Support

Gilbert Lewis

The subject of this paper is the expression of moral support in a particular setting. I will record here some gestures of welcome observed in the Lumi-Nuku area of the West Sepik and go on to describe ways in which Gnau-speaking people show their loyalty to and support for friends and kin. Their villages are small, and the moral value they set on social ties is great. This is hardly surprising; McDowell, Smith, and Stanek, in this volume, refer to village loyalties and their problems. Kinship, common traditions of origin, reciprocity, proximity, and cooperation are familiar grounds for support, but the advantages of local loyalties may now be put in question by new opportunities for individual self-advancement and new forms of association that are more widely based. Smith speaks of the romanticization of the idea of village harmony. My description may seem to do this because it is about expectations and ideals for behavior; I have not balanced it with a statement of the more formal ways in which the people in these villages would break off social ties, bring their disputes forward, and justify themselves against others.

I do not know whether the gestures which have attracted my attention will be familiar to people elsewhere in the Sepik. As the contributions to this symposium show, material culture has been collected and recorded, and we can analyze some aspects of the distribution of artistic and architectural styles. Gestures, in contrast, are insubstantial. Recording behavior and ideas is harder than collecting objects or kinship terminologies. There is no ethnographic survey to turn to, and in any case, because interests and theories change, items that one generation of anthropologists considered essential to record may look foolish to the next. Could we reach some agreement about the inventory of basic data we would wish to have recorded about the different societies of the Sepik? Filer suggests in this volume that we reexamine our assumptions about the fit between language and culture. I wonder what would be the map of gestures in relation to culture or language, technology, and proximity. Allen has asked the symposium to consider the resilience or vulnerability of different institutions: some of the gestures I describe are connected with particular institutions

and purposes. The gestures are, I think, destined to disappear. However striking to see or hear, they are tricky or tedious to describe. They tend to be left out of the record and forgotten.

The oddities of gesture caught my attention early. I made slow progress with the language, but I could see the gestures, and slowly I assembled idioms and expressions that referred to the body or to gesture. The sense of idioms was sometimes elusive, but gradually my data on the presentation and representation of the body in word, image, and gesture grew. Though I could not set out an encyclopedia of Gnau gesture here, I did collect some of the makings of one. For example, men in the Gnau-speaking villages where I worked had a curious breathy whistle produced by protruding the upper lip, pursing the lower one so that it almost touched the edge of the upper incisors, keeping the tongue hollowed and retracted in a mid-to-low position just behind the upper teeth, and then sucking the breath in sharply. They used it to call their dogs and to send each other messages when hunting. They said that game might be tricked into thinking no people were there. They could transpose speech into these whistles, though it was harder to do so than to transpose it into ordinary whistles as everyone could. Some men never got the trick of the other whistle. I wonder where else this whistle might be found.

Again, Gnau men in heated conversation often marked their assertions by bouncing in a posture as though they had drawn an invisible bow and held it, left arm outstretched tensely, forefinger pointing, left foot thumping the ground, the whole body bobbing, the right arm bent pulling the invisible string, hand at the angle of the jaw, until they reached the point of their remarks, when this right arm would whip round in an arc to thwack the buttock with a loud smack. Such assertive thwacks punctuated their hot debates and their animated conversation. They were brought up to make the thwacking gesture whenever they shot an arrow; the gesture belongs to people who use the bow rather than the spear. Bateson (1958 [1936]:225) describes the debating style of the Iatmul with fronds laid on the stool, Forge (1966:23) the Abelam show of support in debate by jumping up, arms outstretched, and glaring round at the participants, portraying the totemic bird defending its young.

In the area where I worked, Lumi Subdistrict (Au East census division), the social units (villages) were small, containing two hundred to three hundred fifty people in most cases, and had formerly been roughly independent political units. Accents differed in the three Gnau-speaking villages, and people sometimes caricatured them when they told a story or related some event. Little differences of dress, custom, and character were subjects for casual comment. People stressed differences, but they recognized that they had picked up ideas, manners, and rites, games, and techniques from each other. People of different villages dress more or less the same now, at least in front of strangers. The obvious outward signs of village or cultural identity have been almost given up. Tok Pisin flows across old language barriers and disguises boundaries. People are ambivalent about change: they would like to resist some changes, want others. The small scale of social units which were once distinct makes the loss of their distinctiveness more noticeable.

Before, when there were risks of war to think of, the villagers might need allies and also need to maintain ties for refuge. And I would also imagine that the transmission of some bits of knowledge could be uncertain because the preservation of it would depend on so small a number of individuals. One can guess at this uncertainty from observing how fragile the record of a lineage can be. A lineage depended on a few men for continuity. If they died, the genealogy would tend to be effaced because there was no one left to remember it. If a man's father happened to have died when he was young, he might never have learned the details his father had known. Obviously, personal qualities of interest, memory, and ability played a part in the preservation of knowledge. One might expect a priori the scale and independence of social units to stimulate diversity of idea and practice. But perhaps, if there are gaps to fill, people copy ideas and borrow practices from neighbors (reducing variation), or perhaps they invent something to fill the gap (increasing it). There was always overlap between the political units: there was intermarriage, knowledge of the language of neighbors, knowledge of their customs. Yet the wish to assert identity and exclusiveness still crops up in boasting and in denigration of the ways of other villages.

Gestures of Welcome

People at Rauit kept up ties with a few villages that were distant and spoke no language they could understand. These places offered, I think, a distant possibility of refuge. A few older men at Rauit could recall once going to help in a fight near Yemereba. They were supposed to share an origin from an ancient site of settlement with people of some lineages at Yemereba, and on that occasion the people at Yemereba had called for help. There being no common language between them, men from Laeko (to whom both were related) acted as intermediaries and translators. (Now they can use Tok Pisin.) Yemereba was on the edge of what had been known country before white control was imposed. The names of ancient settlements near what is now Yemereba occur in myths at Rauit and in some of the great songs (which almost serve as inventories of the world that they had known before white people came [Lewis 1980:59–65]).

I went to Yemereba with Səlaukei, who was taking me on the path mentioned in the great song of Tambin. His coming had been announced, and when we reached the village, there above us, standing to welcome us, were his relatives. Two were old and wore fur head-rings and leaves in their armlets. They stood kicking forward, scuffing the ground, their arms held out to us, palms upwards, smiling, calling his name. As he came up to them they took him by the wrist, put their arms around him, stroked him under the chin, and then stood back and began calling out the names of the ancient settlement sites their ancestors had shared, with the drawn-bow gestures I have just described, their feet still shuffling. The rest of us did things in a modern way; we shook hands.

The one of the two who did not speak Tok Pisin took Səlaukei by the wrist to where the food was to be set and called for it. We followed, and food was brought and set down individually before us. Each bringer squatted down face to face with the guest, the food on a leaf between them. We ate, each exhorted loudly to do so by the man opposite. At the finish, the host took the hand of his guest to rub it clean of food scraps between his own, which he then wiped over his own body, putting his guest's dirt on himself. This wiping clean was accepted as a courtesy, but to the people I was with it seemed peculiar. They did not do it at Rauit, and food scraps are exactly the sort of thing they think can be used for harmful magic or sorcery. But the welcome was unmistakable. To eat under such a gaze—intense, benign, each mouthful watched as it went in and down—was an experience I will not forget. Welcome, food, generosity—the link between these things and friendly intentions speaks for itself to most of us. The Gnau people, like others in New Guinea (Strathern 1973), speak of giving food as something that can express and create a bond and perhaps with time even a tie of substance: food contributes to make the person, and those who eat food that comes from the same place long enough come to share a bond of substance, for they are made from the same stuff.

Most of the gestures with which we were welcomed were easy enough to recognize because Gnau people welcome in much the same way. Presumably it is wise to make welcome unambiguous when there is such a mixture of independent groups and different languages. The gestures comprised several components, and some components occur in more than one sort of situation. Gnau phrases can single them out:

Natəbu' ən, "he greets him": The Gnau say that they extend the gesture of stroking under the chin and the embrace as far as sitting the visitor on his host's lap:

He would pull him by the wrist to come and sit down together. The two of them would sit in one place [the visitor across the other's legs]. Or he would bring midribs of sago leaves and put them down for him to sit on, would light a fire for him. If he [the visitor] lived far away, and he hardly knew his face as he had come only once or so before, he would do everything well for him, fetch him game, cook it for him to eat. In the past, he would come and pull him by the wrist, he would come and sit him on his lap, the two together, he would stroke his chin, saying to him, "You live far away, I have watched out for you, watched out for you, but you did not come. Only once in a while, you come." He would sit cheeks together, arms around him, then they would go and sit down.[1]

This was the way to greet a rare visitor, a long-lost relative, but I did not see it done. The stroking under the chin (*nagiyen lalut*, "he strokes his chin") is a sign of approval as well as welcome. Sometimes older people would make as if to stroke me under the chin, sketching the start of the gesture in the air, when they approved strongly of something I had said. One might see this done as a comment in a noisy conversation.

Nasəlilupən, "he dances that way for him": The term for the shuffling step of welcome describes a dance step and is based on the verb *nasəli*, "to swing." The welcoming step is almost the same as the woman's stepping forward and back, her feet brushing the ground, in dancing, though in welcome it is done in place or backing away so as to draw the person welcomed toward one. The step is one of a complex of actions having to do with praise, welcome, and encouragement that I associate with the verb *nabawɔpən*, "he praises or encourages him." It can be used with reference to a variety of situations. For example,

When a young man goes and shoots a pig, or some other game, he goes off to see his mother's brother taking the game. He comes to give it to his mother's brother, or to his sister. She stands and praises him (*wəbawɔpən*): "You keep to good ways like that. You have a good thinking center (*wuna' at*), keep like that, and I shall tell my nephews and nieces, sisters and brothers, cross-cousins what a good man you are. You come to see us, stand in our doorway, we look up and see you and we praise you. We praise you. You have strong arms and good thoughts (*wuna' at*)."

She must praise him for these early visits that open the path and clear it so that it leads wide and clear to her doorway; this is their metaphor. They commented that if it were the mother's brother who praised him (*nabawɔpen*), he might do it by ululating *elei! elei! elei!* as he saw him coming. Indeed, when people report that men *labawɔpa* ("praise it") while singing, what they mean is that at the end of a verse all ululate loudly, *elei! elei! elei!*[2] They praise the song or verse because it is good and they like it. The spirit in the song (Lewis 1980:61) hears them and is pleased and therefore will bring them game when they hunt.

If it were the mother's brother's wife who received the young man, or his sister, she would praise him (*wəbawɔpən*) by scuffing the ground and holding out her arms to him as if to stroke his chin. This is the welcome that draws someone toward one. When young men emerged decorated from long seclusion in the Tambin initiation, when someone had performed a great feat in war or hunting, and now, most characteristically, when young men return from work away on a plantation or in town, they are greeted by the women dancing to draw them in (*lasəli langu' el*):

The women praise him when the plantation laborer comes back. His mother's brother's wife, his mother, or his sister gets ferns, *tel-*

tati sprouts [of the tulip tree, *Gnemon gne-tum*]. She gets a bow and arrow, places the arrow resting in position on her finger, and goes and stands waiting for him on the path to draw him with the dance step. She praises him, she stretches her hand to stroke his chin as she backs dancing to draw him in, dancing backwards facing him as she draws him into her hamlet, to the doorway of her house, leans the bow against her house, and goes to embrace him (*watəbu' ən*). She holds the fern, the teltati sprouts [to remind him] to shoot pig for her because she cooks pig with ferns and teltati sprouts. She carries her father's or her husband's bow so he will think of the bow he will use.

This welcome and reception involves, then, both praise and reminder of a man's duty to give meat to female relatives. A mother might dance in praise of her son, pulling at her withered breasts to recall to all that she had suckled him, raised him, singing as she danced, "I, your mother, stand here. You come now! What a fine man!"

The movements of the feet give the body a rhythmic bouncing, up-and-down movement that is accentuated by the outstretched arms. Gnau refer to this movement as *nəragapən*, "he dances for him." The same verb (*nərag*) is used for dancing and for singing. The body movement as a whole, or just the head nodding or the outstretched arms might suffice to qualify as "dancing for someone" (*nəragapən*). The bobbing up and down is often shown by men when excited in debate or argument. The bounce then comes from slightly flexed knees, hips, and ankles, pivoting on the ball of the foot, the heel rising up and down just off the ground (*lagəl dərabəg*, "they bend at the hips" [perineum?]). The bobbing movement has an obvious association with joyful celebration and excitement, as the link with singing and dancing suggests. Perhaps the rhythmic movement itself produces exhilaration. We have all felt the infectious power of gestures. We learn most gestures by imitation: some become habits and have feelings strongly attached to them. The gestures seem to call the feelings up.

Head-bobbing and bobbing of the whole body also belong to fierce excitement and joy. The Gnau said that someone who had killed a person in war, coming home in triumph, might proclaim his achievement by standing bouncing with his tongue lolled out and his arms held in the gesture of drawing a bow—in fact, standing almost as those greeting us at Yemereba had stood.

Duwʌt walilu' ən belpi, "the tongue lolls out of his head": The tongue lolls out, the mouth half-open, head nodding in time to the bounce of the body. Another use of the tongue, *nilaupən duwʌt*, "he sticks out his tongue at him," is to startle someone who has not seen one in the shadows of the forest. The message flashed is "I could have shot you—you didn't spot me!" Approaching the village of Mandubil (Maiambel) up a steep hillside, I once looked up and saw, 20 feet above, a man standing silent who suddenly lolled out his tongue twice and started moving his feet, holding out his hand in the stroking gesture, bobbing up and down, saying nothing but matching the startle to other gestures meaning "You come now! You come to see us. Good. You come on up. Ah! Ah! Ah!"[3]

The throaty noise just mentioned–"Ah! Ah! Ah!"—imitates the soft grunts that a mother pig uses to call her piglets to follow her.[4] The verb *wəbawɔpa* refers in its narrowest sense to that soft grunting call, and *nabawɔp* used of men has associations with greeting, praise, approval, and encouragement. In the welcome to the young man returned from the plantation and in the greeting praise for the man who has killed someone, the bouncing, the tongue lolled out, the sound "Ah! Ah! Ah!," and the shuffling feet drawing him on show approval and admiration, and the gestures are emblems of the meaning of the phrases that may be chanted in welcome: *Dji gatiyen gatiyen yiliga! Dəg dadadji (mandadji) yiten! Dji yiliga, gatiyen yiliga!* "Come carefully, carefully! I, your father (your mother), I am standing here! Come, carefully, come!" Also implied are protection, pride, concern: "I, your father, am standing here, come, you are not alone." This reflects a Gnau view of the need for caution in doing things in which one is not experienced[5] and of the responsibility of senior people for the young. The words for welcoming the son who has killed were said to go like this: "Come carefully, carefully! I, your father, I am standing here! Who has shot you? Are you left all alone? No! I, your father, I am here! You come. Come carefully now!" He receives him with praise and pride and stands to guard him.

Perhaps there is an echo of this in the welcome shown the visitor from far away. In the past it required some courage to go outside one's own territory and run the risk of ambush and attack. It is hard to judge just how hazardous travel was before the imposition of administrative control. Certainly older people said that they had rarely entered other villages; some had only done so a handful of times before white people came. The welcome contains a note of praise and warmth for someone who has taken the risk of coming. To visit someone is to "descend on him," and the common, almost cliché phrasing of one's visit from far off is *dəg garil gali gəwagapyi*, "I fled, I come, I descend on you," calling to mind another possible reason for a visit—refuge, protection.

Both men and women, when they do the full chant and praise, bob up and down with their arms outstretched and their whole body bouncing in time, and as they do so, some make the breathy throat-clearing noise—"Ah! Ah! Ah!"—between the chants. It expresses concern for the safety of the person as well as admiration.

There is also encouragement. The mother pig grunts softly to her piglets to encourage them to follow her. The Gnau consider that children need praise and approval. If one scolds children harshly, people will stare appalled (literally, "their eyes will jump out at you") and growl "You are treating them [the children] like a dog or a pig. Think! These are human beings. You must look after them so that they keep well. If you go on like that, lice will foul their heads." They added:

A child's mother should not hit him. She should praise him (*wabəlupən*). She should praise her son, not hit her children. They will grow up and quickly grow big, grown-up, and they must keep their blood in good condition. For if she keeps striking them, she will damage their blood (as happens in bruising someone) and so they will get ill, they will have bad blood.

Praise is encouraging. It may prompt others to emulate the things that are praised. Someone who is well-known for his generosity sets an example for others. People praise him and go to visit him:

The good man (*wuyin*): they call him their own great tree (*wult*, a huge forest tree—*Ficus* spp., I think). Birds come to fill its branches; he gathers all to him; they gather at his house doorway. He brings them in. They fill his house. His relatives from everywhere round, they keep coming to see him. He, though alone, has food for everyone; he is generous. His wife follows his way of doing things. She shows them her hands, palms upwards (open-handed) so they can see she has given them everything. His children grow up and follow their father's example. He chooses the in-laws; they come

and now they follow his ways too; they catch on to their daughter-in-law's way of doing things. . . .

One praises people to encourage them, to show approval, to indicate good examples.

Generosity and Hospitality

Open-handed generosity and hospitality are the virtues of the good man. The value set on generosity and sharing food was loudly evident, for instance, in the insistent repeated calls to others to come and help eat up food that would be heard almost every time people ate in company. No one would want to be seen eating alone like a greedy dog, an outcast, or someone with a foul skin disease. Abundant food is part of the image of the good life: people speak proudly of the food they can give others that they may eat well. They promise food and great abundance of it to persuade someone to settle with them. They offer to give one land, trees, plants. The histories of different lineages and clans are full of details about movements and settlement. Some had been persuaded to come, some had come as refugees and been welcomed with offers of food and land. They spoke of being "pulled" (*nətə'aiyen*, "he pulled him" as you might pull on a rope; *na-ŋgupən*, "he pulled him" as you might draw an object to you). The stories are partly about who came first, who first settled and cleared the site—claims to priority—but there is also pride in having persuaded others to join them and, on the other side, readiness to acknowledge the refuge offered and the generosity or loyalty of those who took them in. The simple verbs for pulling someone to stay express ideas which they also elaborate in more lively images. Here we find metaphor and symbolic reference openly used and clearly understood: "My ancestors were the tree, they the birds who have come to alight on it"; "Mine is the tree, theirs the lianas which hang from it"; "They are cooking pots, we the stones that support them."

Those who return late from a visit will often excuse their lateness by saying that their hosts would not let them go. The verb they use for this is idiomatic: *natelapən wulagi*, literally "he cuts or clears[6] for him many people." It means "he detains him," "he makes him stay by kindness, gifts, and generosity." It implies being urged, pressed, or coaxed to stay. They use the phrase to describe how lineages were prevailed on to come and settle in a new place when they tell the history of a lineage.

Numbers and the Solitary

There was strength and security in numbers. The ideal was the village filled with people, crowded, black as the blackened betel-stained teeth of the warrior (*baningən rupətəgapa*)—suggesting strength and fierceness, crowded as if swarming with ants (*subat nalbati*, "water, ants"),[7] crowded like bats in a fruiting *Ficus* tree (*udati niyiwug*). These are images of something desired, for a small village with few people was weak. At the end of many long sings they did something as the finale to the ending dance Wɔlpililiwa; they called it *latel subat*, literally, "they cut water." It referred to a ceremony in which all the young people were gathered together and a very large piece of bamboo filled with specially scented water was cunningly broken over them so they were all sprinkled with the herb-scented water; it was intended to make them have many children and multiply like the ants (*subat nalbati*). The value they set on numbers and company will hardly seem remarkable (cf. Tuzin 1976) or need great emphasis. It serves to bring out by contrast their concern about the solitary person and the orphan.

In Gnau myths one recognizes a recurrent motif: the person left alone to face danger, be it from a demon witch or from human attack. It may be the woman left alone in her house, the door shut, the fateful cough outside as the demon spirit announces itself: "Eh-hei! I thought you had gone, but here you are!" Or it may be the lone warrior, solitary in his village awaiting his enemies:

> He alone stayed at his place, Mami Albaiyel sat there, and his sister who had gone to marry at Nəmbugil, she came and said to him, "You are alone here. You must not kill people from all these places. You are one man alone here and they are many. They will come to kill you." "I am one. Let them come and shoot me. I will stay here. I shall not run from them." . . . [He makes secret preparations and tells his sister to give them this message] . . . "I am one but I am enough. Let them come and I shall kill them and finish them off" and he beat out this message on the slit-drum: I am standing here at my place. You come and shoot me. My blood will spill out over this place to clear it, to go void and leave it. . . . [and of course he pre-

pares his magical, devastating support. His sister pleads with his enemies, but they say,] "But he shot some of us, and after all, who is with him on his side? He is all alone [*lin butabasi*, "he is one man all alone"; the suffix *-si* stresses the solitary, pitiable state]. Let us go off to shoot him. He is all alone. Come on, let us go off to shoot him now!"

Butabasi, "the one left on his own," must survive or his lineage will be ended. He is, as they say in Tok Pisin, *wanpis*, last survivor of his line. And therefore they sometimes said that such a man should marry more than one wife because he has no brothers to help him to keep it going. A sense that people at a place have a duty to support the *wanpis* and the orphan appears in several forms. Like the last survivor, the orphan is someone left behind; the word for him, *tənapil*, is often accompanied by the adjective *wɔlasi*, meaning "poor old." *Tənapil* is "someone who stays behind," and the word contains the echo of a loose classification of people into those who are, roughly, the original inhabitants of a place (*gapil*, "the people who stay put") and those who flee or disperse (*garil*). Other categories of this loose social classification indicate some of the criteria which seem important to Gnau: there are enemies and strangers, lumped together as "nothing people," *gipi'il*; there are *wuyil*, "good people," those who are friends and more specifically relatives (the word refers to both friends and relatives but in context may mean, specifically, close relatives within the range of those forbidden as marriage partners); there are people who often come to visit, *beiya nawul nawul*, literally "who go along paths and go along paths," and people with whom gifts are exchanged, *matelyil*. These are not all mutually exclusive categories. The orphan is the person who has been left behind by his parents. The image of the father implies a person who gives support, as in the cry "Come carefully, carefully! I, your father, I am standing here! Who has shot you? Are you left all alone? No! I, your father, I am here!" A dying person is sometimes said to be filled with the thought that he or she is leaving the living behind, abandoning them; the conventional last words are "Ah! I leave you now. Who will look after you?"

Idioms of Support

Friends and brothers provide support and help; the idiom for this is *ləwum tapi'it*, "they sit at his back," or *latət tapi'it*, "they stand at his back."

Another idiom of support is more obscure: *ləgatən tapi'it*, literally "they break his back/backbone." This refers to the ceremony in which relatives and friends gather to give honor or praise to someone who has done something well, typically the gathering to celebrate hunting achievement and the performance of hunting rites. Specifically, *ləgatən tapi'it* refers in this context to the celebratory meal in which all (including ancestors, for whom some token food is hung up in the men's house) share except the one person for whom it is being celebrated. The phrase therefore indicates someone's abstention from a communal meal eaten to honor him and secure his future prosperity. He is singled out; others do him honor.

These phrases for support draw on the body and the imagery of simple actions. Gnau say-*nəgatəpən su'əp*, "he opens his thighs for him," meaning "he supports him," the reference being to the way a mother supports a baby in the sitting position by propping it between her thighs. A man may offer assistance by saying *dəg təwupyi*, "let me hoist you up" (as one hoists and carries a child piggyback). More complex is the one for support given to spare someone from taking the whole burden of some duty on himself: *natelapən bangi (akə məna wigət)*, literally "he clears for him a shoulder (so that some may be left)." It derives from the way men carry burdens on their shoulders. One man might help another carry a heavy burden by lifting it up to place it on the other's shoulder (*nasinpən bangəp nagərən*), or he might go farther by taking the burden, or some of it, on his own shoulder. When a man must pay the prestation for the birth of his first child or give compensation for injury, his friends or relatives, seeing him lay out all his money to meet his obligation, will take up some and return it to him, replacing what they take with their own contributions. They will say that they are "clearing a shoulder for him so that he will have some of his own left. What, is he one man alone? Has he no friends to spare him?"

Sparing the Young

In the past it sometimes happened that a death, especially from a fight within a village, demanded immediate revenge. The people of a hamlet knew that they would all be at risk of revenge until one of them had died to pay for the killing. In such circumstances, a father or an old man might choose to offer himself in order to spare his sons or younger men from untimely death. He exchanged his life for that of his son: *lyinəm ʌla nyitel ta'aŋ bangi*, "they would kill him so that he might clear his sons' shoulder":

> For instance, suppose you had shot one of them first and they said they were coming to shoot you. . . . You would fight and they must kill someone, but let them kill someone senior and let it end there so that you, the young people, keep well [remain alive]. . . . Then they are fighting with spears and your father comes and stands up for them to shoot him on the path so as to spare you, his sons, so you will stay alive in the village. They continue, they miss, no one is hit. He, the father, stands up and calls to them: *Lyipər subla'ap, lawut witət* ["Clear away the ferns, let the sago palm stand"]. He challenges them [*nabawɔpel*]: "Elei! Elei! Elei!" He dances [*nasəli*] out along the path, coming up to them, "Let me go in place of my sons. Ah! Ah! Ah! Hu! Hu! Hu! Who dares to shake/topple this wild fighting-taro-aroid!" He stands up on the path blocking the way. The women and children stay in the house. His grown-up sons stand outside behind him in support. . . . The men seeking vengeance, those who have come to kill someone, line up in two lines on either side of the path, and he goes along it. First he dances out to draw them up in line on each side of the path, then he fights his way back along it, like that, and they shoot him as he reaches the cleared place [near his house or where his sons are standing]. They shoot him in the chest just by the armpit [*nalgiti*, a lethal spot] or split his belly and burst his kidneys, and then he tries to rush back to his sons, crying out to them, calling out the names of his children. He comes, looking to see them. Are they standing there? And he falls down dead on the ground in front of them. It is over. They pull him to them, take him, weeping. They carry him to where his house is to cry for him. They weep greatly for him.

Villagers described occasions on which this had been done. The motive always given was desire to save the young, who still had their lives before them. The idea of succession as replacement of the old by the young is evident in their view of the passing on of blood (Lewis 1980:176) and knowledge. They said that women might also offer their lives and used the same phrase for this (*lyipər su-*

bla'ap, lawut witət). I first heard it as the verbal equivalent for the actions of two women during a fight I witnessed. As a confused melee of fist-fighting broke out and men rushed to intervene, two older women suddenly started to dance, turning quite slowly round and round with their arms raised curving in the air, with almost the gesture and grace of ballet dancers. Both women were related to both antagonists as sister to one and wife to the other. Their movements were interpreted for me as begging that they be struck rather than that the men go on striking each other; it was a plea for them to stop. The particular movements were known as *latəgil yitigəm*, "they 'come up' their brothers."[8] They were drawing attention to the cross-sex consanguineal relationship. Loyalty, help, even self-sacrifice are expected of the tie of kinship. The contrast between "good people,"— *wuyil*—the chief of whom are kin—and "nothing people," *gipi'il*, sums up a view of responsibility which is heavy with implications and ramifies throughout the elaborate web of rights and duties.

Loyalty and Responsibility

There are far too many customary obligations between kin to attempt to summarize them here. Through gifts, sharing, speech, and act, ties are given substance and meaning. The overlap, the mesh and interweaving of ties within the village creates a solidarity of interest, duty, and affection; it includes remembered gains and remembered losses. Words like solidarity and loyalty may sound pretentious, but they indicate what it is that people may show in innumerable ways— in little things as well as in dramatic gestures. Concern, advice, sorrow or shame, warnings, teaching, companionship, help, all express attitudes toward social ties. To my foreign ear, Gnau people seem to have many ways to stress by syntax or vocabulary that actions were reciprocal or done in company: they change *p* or *t* in a verb to *k* to indicate reciprocal actions, as when *larapel*, "they married them," becomes *larakel* to indicate the exchange of sisters; they use dual forms in declining verbs, and they say X--*ənə'am* Y, "X in company with Y," and X -*aru* Y, "X together with Y."

In addition to ties of kinship and marriage, people establish ties because they have been through puberty or initiation rites together (*wusai*, "ritual friend or coinitiate") or have

worked on the same plantation (*wanwok*) or out of sheer friendship and liking, as when two people, usually children, decide to seal their friendship by sharing a twin or double fruit and address each other from then on by the name of the fruit (in fact, usually by a deformation of it—e.g., *tila'at* becomes *tila'am*) to mark their close bond. In several situations, people linked as friends, *wusai*, or siblings choose to observe the same taboos, say, on smoking or betel chewing, when one of them must do so because, for example, he or she has a newborn child. The observation of such taboos is a potent reminder of a bond. Indeed, the idea that those who are close to each other as friends will choose the same fate is a theme in stories and is expressed like this: *dau wibarugəl witelgel, wibʌg da'at witelgel*, "we two now together, we shall be inseparable, even sharing the same fate" (literally, "if we go through fire, we shall be together").

If one were persuaded to go with someone, say, to help him with work in his garden, and one by some mistake or clumsiness cut oneself, he might in a warmhearted, and perhaps hotheaded, way immediately do himself the same injury. Now the motive of his action might be to match one's hurt with his own, a kind of literal sympathy, but there might be something else behind it as well. People say that they are ashamed or embarrassed by the sight of someone else's (a friend or a kinsman's) blood or hurt, especially if in some way they think they are the cause of it. By persuading someone to come to work with one, one becomes responsible for what may happen to him:

> If they were to blame me, they would be angry with me because their son was a fine healthy man, and he should have grown up and stayed in the place. They blame me and what, should I get up and answer them back? No, I feel ashamed [*dəg gawulili*, "I am dried out"]. I sit down, I hang my head there. Because you in your thoughts [*wuna'at*] are grieving for your own [kinsman], go on, show your anger against me, blame me. I am ashamed here. But did I want to harm him? We two together, off we went, both so well, so well. He came that night; we got up, we two together, before it was light. The dog chased an *udagi* lizard that ran off and climbed up high, and he climbed after it saying he would get it. He pulled on a branch. Grubs had been at it inside, and the branch broke under him. So he fell, right down, and was killed. We two set off from here. No, we got up in the small

dark hours because he came to tell me he had had a dream [about finding game], so I, we two together, set off.

The general view of such a situation is that the person who initiates or invites the other to do something is responsible for the accident, and that liability may be taken seriously. Out of grief, people have at times attacked the person they thought was responsible.

Responsibility for the welfare of one's friends and relatives reflects the general view of duty. Relatives have a strong obligation to visit someone sick and spend the day where the sick person is. People describe this as coming to sit in company with him so that he may get well or sometimes as sitting in company with his family to surround him (which suggests shielding the sick person). In severe and sudden crises, people may rush to where the sick person lies and sleep the night where he is, fasting to show their concern, but the normal pattern for these sympathy visits is for the family to provide a meal for the visitors and spend the day with them. If someone were distinctly ill or continued ill for long, the obligations of hospitality and the frequency of the visits might put a great strain on the family's resources. Friends and relatives feel bound to come; the family feels bound to receive and entertain them. This can build up into a series of exhausting days. Sick people sometimes (I have heard them say it occasionally) wish that they could slink quietly off to hide or to visit someone else, even though they feel so ill, because they want to spare their family the obligation of entertaining so many visitors. But despite these burdens of hospitality, people feel very strongly that it is good and right to show concern in this way and are glad and grateful for it. Visits for sickness and other misfortunes, just as much as gatherings to celebrate achievements, returns, and rites, bring people close together. The ordinary run of daily life is punctuated often by these sociable occasions.

Mourning

Responsibility for kin is strikingly shown by Gnau behavior at some funeral rites. Distant relatives are expected to come to mourn; it is their duty. They may turn up armed, smeared with mud, sobbing aloud, and crying out reproaches against the mourners at the home of the dead person for having let their kinsman or kinswoman die. The weeping shows their grief, but the reproach to their own relatives who have lived with

the person now dead is sometimes expressed very fiercely. They may shoot at the house or the men's house or the trees. They may even shoot toward the mourners, aiming to miss. The home mourners are supposed to sit, grief-distracted, regardless of the arrows flicking by them. The women and children may well run to hide, but the men are expected to act as though they no longer cared anything for their own skins. The sobbing chant of the visitors is reproach and self-reproach: "Where was I when you needed me? They have let you die. If only I had been with you. I was far away." The chant of the home mourners is usually the moaning cry, "Father! Father! my son/my daughter! Aaoo! Aaoo!", interspersed with sobs, or "Father, come and look on us—your son—who will be left now with him in the village? Father! Father!" Even between home mourners there may be differences. Those who were with the person when he died, who looked after him, stayed with him, will mourn immediately after the death but without putting on mourning clay or mud; a member of the village who happened to be away, perhaps staying in the bush, will return as soon as he hears the slit-drum announcing the death and put on mud or mourning clay on the way. He is likely to chant blame against those who have failed to protect and preserve the person who has died. Sometimes a mother or a wife will be beaten or hit or even stabbed for such asserted neglect, even perhaps as she is bent weeping over her dead child. There is something conventional about the expectation that she should be to blame, should suffer like that; and it also sometimes seems to be half-expected for the mother or the wife to cry out, "Strike me, kill me. Let me follow my child!" I do not mean to imply that her grief is not intense and sincere, only that the words she uses to express it owe something to custom, just as do the reproaches. And when the distant relatives turn up with their fierce show of anger and reproach, it is not resented. Quite the contrary, it is approved, a matter for talk about how loudly and wildly they showed their grief, and they are also, later, given payment for having come to show their grief and for having fouled themselves with mud.

Few of the duties I have referred to are formal and obligatory. Most are looser expectations that leave it up to the individual to decide how to respond. To be with someone so that in distress he will not be left on his own is one value that is strongly maintained. This is expressed in myths in the taunt "So you think I'm all alone. Come on! You come! You will see!," and in everyday life: someone is suddenly ill, and his friends and relatives come, despite other calls on them, other plans, or their own private interests. In sudden catastrophe, the whole village may gather to sleep the night, surrounding the afflicted person. They fast in sympathy. They watch over him (*lənarapən*). To watch over others, to have responsibility for those one lives with, is the sentiment that runs through many of their actions and attitudes. The other side would, by antithesis, point up the strength of these attitudes. This would be an account of the rupture of social ties—the idioms and the formal gestures by which it is done; it must wait for another occasion.

Notes

1. The quotations come from conversations mainly with Tuawei and Kantyi of Rauit village.

2. They may either ululate by calling like that in high-pitched voices or falsetto or they may do its equivalent as a series of staccato high whistles.

3. There are many other ways of using the tongue in gestures. For example, the tongue flicked out may indicate surprise or wonder or appreciation of a joke (*nanuŋgəl duwʌt*, "he puts out his tongue"). A different sense is conveyed when a girl suddenly protrudes her tongue, her jaw slightly drops, the corners of her mouth drawn down and her eyebrows raised (something like pulling a long face and sticking out one's tongue at the same time). This is called *wəraupel duwʌt*, "she bares her tongue at them": it is clearly an expression of dislike, rejection, a rude face. Women sometimes turned their heads sideways to make such a comment, an eloquent but silent aside. Typically it was the riposte to friends' teasing that she would marry so-and-so. Tongue flicks are also part of showing excitement, pride, and assertion. Men who are boasting of their ability to do something or of their readiness to fight may do it, perhaps with the complex mixture of bombastic skipping bow-drawing movements that is called *samsam* in Tok Pisin, *lyigə'alp* in Gnau. *Nəgə'alp*, "he skips," refers to the whole pattern, especially to the war-skipping with the heels kicking up to avoid arrows, the body slightly flexed, the bow drawn. Part of this behavior may include the tongue flicking out, sometimes with twitching flicks of the head. Flicking the tongue quickly, just the tip (*natel duwʌt lawibʌp*, "he shows the tongue at his lips"), indicates fierce excitement or pride. I heard stories about the way this rapid tongue flick was used to signal secretly to companions the intention to kill someone surprised in the forest. I saw it used by older men boasting excitedly of their strength and energy, saying that they could easily clear enough ground for an airstrip. The twitching and flicking head movements mark a state of tense alertness, the eyes which miss nothing. Some

men said that they had eaten a special stone (*səgədat*) found in the crop of the goura or crowned pigeon to give them this watchfulness. They compared being always alert to the tense quivering of the crest of the crowned pigeon. Men who had swallowed this stone were said to be restless, to sleep little.

The tongue might be differently shown in fiercely threatening *ləgə'alp/samsam* behavior to indicate anger, excitement, and readiness to fight. Then the tongue was clamped between the teeth, showing only as a thin pink line. There was a set of threat signs based on the clamped biting jaws; bones, fight-magic materials, rubbish, dirt, and weeds, certain crotons and cordylines, or pigs'-tusk homicide ornaments might be clamped between the teeth (*nʌg da'at nagələm*); the lower lip might be held between the teeth (*nagəl da'ap* or *na'apən da'ap*) as most people did when they drew a bowstring (Lewis 1975:203), made an effort, or prepared to fight (in a photograph I took of a small crowd watching or trying to control four or five men fighting, quite a few of the spectators have their lips clamped between their teeth, either in excitement or in sympathy with the fighters—rather as people watching a boxing match may clench their fists); or the hypothenar eminence of the left hand might be bitten in a peculiar gesture of rage and taunting challenge. The gesture went from biting the hand to sticking it straight out at the person challenged and had the sense "So you think you can match me! You come and try to take my [homicide] ornaments away from me! So you think I'm child's play for you! [literally, So I'm child to you]. Tell me who you've eaten wild fight-taro for."

4. Animal behavior provides Gnau with a number of parallels for human behavior. When they like a verse they are singing, men may snarl (*lanərpa*) with a loud, throaty imitation of a dog growling; the noise suggests threat and menace. They do it partly to express their delight with their singing and partly to impress distant listeners; they growl so that people in other villages will fear them. I was told that people fighting might growl in unison at enemies when they had missed them with shots; threat and challenge were implied. In fact, they also used the ululation form of *labawɔpən* (*elei! elei! elei!*) to taunt the enemy who had shot and missed. They said, for example, "If someone were cross over the theft of crops or land or trees that he thought someone was stealing or taking from him, or if he thought someone was trying to seduce his wife or daughter, and he grew angry, grabbed his bow to shoot him, comes, shoots, misses him, then the other man [might] stand up and *nabawɔpən* [*elei! elei! elei!*, implying "come on! come on! come on! let's fight"], he comes bringing his bow and the two fight together." They also liken people's grunts of anger and fear to the pig's snorts, compare people's state of desire to the tense quivering of a dog watching someone eat and hungering after scraps, etc.

5. Whereas *naven* ceremonies (Bateson 1958 [1936]) celebrate new achievement, the Gnau show caution toward new experiences: avoid eating first

fruits, try new foods carefully, delay if in doubt, impose the food taboos earlier and more stringently for the first child than for subsequent children. There is also the idea of the person who is new, full-grown, complete, untarnished, untried by experience (*bigəp nəmblim*, "hands whole, complete"), with the complementary idea of being toughened, dried out, and used up by experience (Lewis 1980:138, 164, 176).

6. The verb in it (*natel*, "he cuts,") is one of those which crop up in many highly idiomatic phrases, and the more examples of it I found, the more obscure its meaning grew: *natel wigət*, "he clears a place or village site"; *natel təbəgan*, "he cuts off a lump of sago jelly"; *malwi watel tuwi*, "the river cuts across the bush"; *natel malwi*, "he crosses the river"; *natel tambit arən*, literally "he cuts his skin"; figuratively, in the context of singing, "he sings about himself"; in context of shame, "he clears his skin," i.e., he clears himself of shame, makes himself feel all right again; *natel tambig bigəp*, literally "he cuts skins hands"; this is one common euphemism for "he penis-bleeds himself"; it may be contracted to *natel tambit*; *natel nambəg*, "he clears the eyes"; this is a euphemism referring to the

rite in which a father puts his penile blood on his newborn child to "clear its face"; *natelen nambəg*, "he clears his eyes," can refer to this rite or to the effect of hunting rituals, as though they wiped one's eyes clear so that he is alert and awake to things, clear-sighted; the phrase is also used for smearing the blood of game on the bow that shot it so that the bow will "see straight"; *natelapən wulagi*, "he detained him, he persuaded him to stay" (see above); *natel duwʌt lawibʌp* (see n. 3); *latel subat* (see above).

7. *Nalbati* is a kind of little ant which swarms on some kinds of tree, and *subat*, "water," implies the idiom *lar subat*, "they are like water, overflowing," hence swarming. Someone who is *nar subat* is someone who is very generous.

8. The verb root used here seems to be *-təgil*, "to reach" or "come up to" a village, but I am not sure of this. It may instead be a verb that has special importance in the language of kinship, *-təgl*, which indicates the matrilateral relationship. It is translated into Tok Pisin as *em i-kamap long en* (*-natəglən*), as in "the sister's son 'comes up' from the mother's brother" (Lewis 1977:41, 44).

22/ Social Structure of the Iatmul

Milan Stanek

In this paper I shall attempt to identify the basic characteristics of the Iatmul social system. In accordance with the internal logic of an undertaking of this sort, defining the type of society we are dealing with is unavoidable. The basic characteristics of this type of society, in turn, can be determined only in contrast with the societal type that represents its historical negation, distinguished by its highly sophisticated scientific and artistic culture and highly developed class structure. In saying that the Iatmul are or belong to a classless society I mean that prior to the establishment of the colonial administration there were no centers of power or centers of culture on the island of New Guinea. Every village community governed itself and possessed its own cultural identity. There was no structural inequality on the island in precolonial times: every settlement maintained economic, kinship, and hostile relationships with a few surrounding communities and was autonomous within this network. The community was egalitarian with regard to the relations among households or among kin groups. Exploitation and the dominance of a ruling class were unknown—which is not, however, to say that there were no social conflicts, friction, violence, power struggles, hierarchy, authority, or bitterness.

I shall discuss Iatmul social structure in terms of three dynamic relationships: that between the production process and its immediate institutional forms, cooperative groups and households; that between the structures of production and exchange and the institutions of kinship and marriage, i.e., the clan structure; and that between the above-mentioned institutions and mythology.

The Production Process and Its Immediate Institutional Forms

The cooperative groups that assemble for one purpose or another in the everyday life of a classless community may vary greatly in size and composition. It is precisely the fact that they possess no fixed organizational or institutional form that makes the conditions of work so different

from those in the highly developed European class society, where cooperative groups have taken on a rationalized, rigid form in response to the demands of technology and efficient control of the workforce. In classless communities, more or less transitory working collectives form and disintegrate, depending on the current relationship structure. Apart from the technological and minimal organizational requirements that must be fulfilled, there are other factors that play a decisive role in their composition, among them personal attachments and moods, matrimonial alliances or neighborhood relationships, friendships and enmities. Whether a task is to be done or not, where it is to be done, how long it may take, how large the group is to be, and whether particular persons are to take part are matters to be decided by the individuals concerned in accordance with the situation at the moment.

No one is entitled to dictate the tempo at which a job is to be done, how much is to be done, or when the work must be finished; every working individual determines this himself. Communal decisions of short-term validity are reached in loose cooperation with other members of the group and in direct relation to technical necessities or personal needs. Work may be interrupted by intervals of relaxation, joking, or ritual, as desired.

The forms that cooperative groups take differ greatly from culture to culture and society to society; how impermanent and open or rigid they are varies considerably according to whether we are dealing with a collecting, fishing, cattle-breeding, or agricultural economy. The more intimately the structure of production is intertwined with the vegetative cycle of a useful plant, the more stable and repetitive the form of cooperative groups becomes. But as long as the community is an autonomous, classless one, neither the structuredness of the cooperative group nor the organizational coercion needed for the accomplishment of its productive task ever achieves the degree characteristic of both modern and archaic class societies.

Sahlins (1972:41–148), using numerous ethnographic examples, has convincingly demonstrated that it is not in fact cooperative groups but households that must be regarded as the fundamental structural units in a classless community. In classless communities there is normally no professional specialization (and if present, its significance remains marginal); the whole broad spectrum of economic activities is divided into two large groups and assigned to the man and the woman. These two major economic roles presuppose that a husband and wife or, by way of exception, simply a man and a woman collaborate in a disciplined way over a long period of time, exchanging their products and services with one another day after day. Which tasks are reserved for one sex and which for the other is of secondary importance; what is decisive is that, given this division of labor, subsistence remains impossible without a continual exchange between the sexes. In the institution of the household, the outputs of two persons, a man and a woman, are linked; by fulfilling their obligations under mutual control, they see to it that production is maintained at the level required for their subsistence.

In the household, the separate products of its members, including the children and the old, are continually pooled and divided up again for consumption. It is the household which forms a fixed point in the dynamics of the wider relationships that run through the classless community as a whole; when members of a household leave their intimate circle to go about their productive tasks, be it independently or as participants in a cooperative group, their economic thinking and performance will predominantly be determined by the needs of their household, and their product—if they do not consume it themselves—will become part of the common fund of the household.

It is of decisive significance to the egalitarian power structure of classless communities that their constituent units, households, are structurally identical although, as a result of the elementary family's stages of development and the vicissitudes of mortality, they may periodically assume different sizes and compositions. A household always sees itself surrounded by other, similar households and is never confronted with economic units of a different order; its members' cooperative and exchange relationships are all with partners who come from similar households. Thus in establishing relationships one need never reckon with a structurally superior economic potential. In short, on the economic level, the constituent units of a classless community are as alike as potatoes in the well-known sack.

As a result of this structural identity, the real exchange of goods (one category of goods for an-

other category) plays a secondary role in the exchange relationships between households. As every household can produce most of what it needs itself, from a formal point of view most acts of barter have a tautological character; in reality they would be more accurately called acts of mutual aid. If one needs a particular product or service at a certain moment, one can receive it from members of other households after corresponding negotiations and then return a product or service of the same kind to them at a later date. This fundamental characteristic of exchange relationships manifests itself in a spectacular manner in the ceremonial exchange cycles.

Structures of Production and Exchange and Institutions of Kinship and Marriage

How the institutions we call the kinship system are connected with the economic structure of classless communities is a question that has not yet been satisfactorily answered. The formal study of kinship is not much interested in the problem; earlier ethnology, from Morgan to Fortes, overestimated the importance of kin relationships for the structuring of society as a whole; Marxist research, such as Meillassoux's (1975), tries in vain to deduce the distinctive features of kinship systems directly from economic and technological facts, taking a mechanistic view of the relationship of the societal basis to its superstructure. It is too early to make general statements about the kinship systems of classless societies, since no one has yet succeeded in delineating the functional fundamentals in this immense multiplicity of systems. I have restricted myself to societies with clan structure, which means ones composed of several related, exogamous unilineal descent groups, and among those to the Papuan type, with a compact matrimonial area and relatively small exogamous units.

The institution we call the clan primarily fulfills two functions. On the one hand, as a body that continually renews itself through the generations while retaining its structural and symbolic identity, the clan guarantees its members the basic right of free access to natural resources within the range of the clan's specific claims to a portion of the village lands and waters; there are no landless persons in Iatmul villages. On the other hand, the clan is an instrument of marriage regulation: clan brothers and sisters (this includes parallel cousins) may not marry one another. Thus every marriage connects two clans in a familial, economic, political, ceremonial, and religious alliance. The marital relationships and matrimonial alliances of a clan are always manifold, depending on the number of its married members. A clan of average size is connected with almost all the other clans in a village community both through the marriages of its deceased members and through present marriages. At a given time, however, a few matrimonial alliances are of greater significance from the point of view of a particular person.

As a rule, a patrilineal Iatmul clan joins together a few households whose male members are related by descent, i.e., brothers who have a common male ancestor (father or grandfather). As a result of the exogamy rule, the wives of these men, i.e., the female members of the same households, belong to other patrilineal clans which, in turn, also form a fabric of households. From the point of view of a specific household, then, there are always several other households with which cooperation of all kinds can be maintained on the basis of close sibling relationship: on the husband's side the households of his brothers (his patrilineal clan) and on the wife's the households of her brothers (her patrilineal clan). Relations among the descendants of sisters are no less important or less conscious, but they are conceptualized outside the patrilineal clan structure.

These three types of ties between households represent a network of kin relationships, a field in which potential partners for all the different kinds of cooperative groups can be found. But the simple fact of consanguinity does not determine the choice of particular partners and the materialization of a working group with a specific composition; it is the previous development of relationships among the persons involved and the current relationship structure that are decisive. At the same time, the definition of clan structure as a semantic and ideological structure is based entirely on naturally given kinship links: the constitution of the individual clans, i.e., the relationship of the individual to his own clan, and the relationships among the clans, either by marriage or by descent, are represented as kinship relations. Nonetheless, the two most important functions of clan structure, the regulation of inheritance (i.e., continuity in the distribution of natural resources) and marriage regulation, are not simply determined by the given descent structure. The regulation in question here (be it fundamental institutional structures or particular solutions varying from case to case) is merely expressed in terms of the naturally given kinship structure. It is always a matter of deliberation, i.e., of conscious organizational measures taken in view of the distribution of natural resources and the distribution of marital partners; it is a matter of decision-making processes that have led to institutional solutions. The naturally given links of descent serve merely as a medium of expression, a semantic level of correspondence, a means of representation allowing the description and communication of both the established results of the decision-making processes, i.e., overall structures, and the operative structural details of the institutional solutions. This can be clearly seen in the way the exogamy boundary is manipulated by clan elders, in the fact that no fewer than three different marriage rules coexist, the suitable one being chosen according to concrete needs, and in the maintenance of a well-balanced distribution of resources despite the very irregular growth of individual clans.

Decisive to the functioning of the institutions we term the kinship system and to the forms they assume in accordance with their functions are the concrete, practical tasks of the productive cooperation and exchange relationships among the members of individual households and, above all, the distribution of resources and marriage partners among the clans. It is thus the social dynamics of interactions among the basic social units (i.e., the way households or clans deal with one another) that are decisive, not simply the fact of kinship. Nevertheless, the latter determine the semantic structure that allows the basic characteristics of these institutions to be expressed in the Iatmul system of thought and thus enables them to function.

Depending on the vicissitudes of human fertility and mortality, the number of members of individual clans may increase or decrease greatly. A clan may under certain conditions die out in the male line or even in both lines of descent. If a clan greatly expands, an increasing number of young people are forbidden to marry. In such a case, the clan elders may decide to divide the clan in two. Thus the size of exogamous patrilineal descent groups is kept within limits that make the arrangement of new marital relationships as easy as possible. Previous clan divisions are reflected in the institution of the clan association: after a division into two, the resulting two clans consider themselves brother clans, since they have actual common ancestors. After further divisions, clan associations that number several brother clans develop. Several clan associations form a men's-house community, which is at the same time a local unit and can also be termed a village district. The marriages and subsequent matrimonial alliances among the clans intersect the structure of these relationships by descent or reinforce them (i.e., run parallel to them).

A clan is incapable of securing either its subsistence or the procreation of children by itself. There must be a constant supply of marriage partners for its adolescent members so that households can be formed, for this is the only way that a new generation can be born and everyone's livelihood guaranteed by the concerted efforts of the parents. It is difficult for Western observers like ourselves to understand that finding a marriage partner could be considered a prime social problem. Westerners familiar with conditions on family-run farms, which also depend on two complementary economic roles, would be most likely to appreciate the situation of a Iatmul clan. Those like myself, with a bourgeois urban background in which the marriage partnership or the family has lost most of its productive functions, lack the necessary personal experience. In our mass society, the problem, if it poses itself at all, appears as an individual, subjective one. From an objective standpoint—considering the individual's high degree of mobility—there are always enough potential marriage partners.

Meillassoux (1975), in the wake of Washburn and Lancaster (1968), was able to recognize the special structural significance of the problem of marriage in the classless society. It is probably one of the most important basic characteristics of this type of society. Considering the basic biological facts of human fertility, a community that gets no marriage partners from outside requires approximately a hundred couples to ensure that enough children are born and that the proportions of boys and girls are somewhat balanced. This condition is fulfilled only if a community numbers around five hundred members, including children and the dependent aged. At the same time, relying on the existing technical equipment and the corresponding social forms of production, far smaller classless communities can have an autonomous economic existence. A few households, perhaps only five or six, can found a village community and secure their economic survival through their own efforts. A community of this kind, numbering some eighty individuals, cannot, however, be endogamous, since if it were the majority of its adolescents would be unable to find marital partners of the appropriate age and

sex. For the reproduction of such a community to be guaranteed, either the incest prohibition will have to be relaxed or alliances with other communities will have to be formed in order to foster marriage links.

The larger Iatmul village communities, one of which is Palimbei, number between five hundred and a thousand members, including those who have left the village for plantations or colonial towns (who continue to belong to the matrimonial sphere of the village); these communities are composed of sixty to a hundred households and twenty to thirty patrilineal clans. Communities of this size have no pressing problem of reproduction, and in fact less than 2 percent of the married inhabitants of Palimbei come from neighboring villages. Nonetheless, marriage negotiations, wedding ceremonies, and all the social conventions connected with them are a focal point of social life: the regularity or irregularity of a union, how much time and energy to invest in marriage rites, the number of ceremonial gifts to introduce into the exchange cycles are extremely important issues that must be discussed and settled and that sometimes lead to friction. A marriage provides the occasion for revealing animosities among the clans involved. The older generation may try to influence youngsters to marry or not to marry a particular partner but is never really interested in forcing them to marry according to a marriage rule.

The Iatmul kinship system incorporates symmetrical and asymmetrical marriage structures and the corresponding behavioral models. The symmetrical rule (formulated from the male point of view) says that one should marry a woman from a clan that a woman from one's own clan has joined as marriage partner. The asymmetrical rule says that one should marry a woman from the clan that one's paternal grandfather's wife came from. Ideally this solution would presuppose five exogamous units in turn supplying one another with marriage partners in a circular pattern: $A \rightarrow B \rightarrow C \rightarrow D \rightarrow E \rightarrow A$.

In reality there are no such one-way streets, and a clan's marital ties are irregular and multilateral, the total marriage structure of a village community complex. The concept of reciprocity in matrimonial relations does, however, supply an ideological framework for the elders' discussions of concrete unions. According to a Iatmul proverb, a clan's loss of a woman by marriage can only be compensated by the gain of another woman whom a male member of the clan takes as a wife. Since the older generation exercises only limited influence and young people establish their relationships quite independently, efforts to maintain an orderly, balanced exchange of women among the clans are more like a bookkeeping system that merely registers the permanent imbalance and then declares every new marriage to be a compensation for one of the pending past claims. In the closed system of the matrimonial area, the compensation of any registered claim will automatically take place sooner or later.

A smaller village community such as Yindabu, founded only a few decades ago, numbers approximately a hundred members, i.e., ten to fifteen households, three to four patrilineal clans. The founding group, which left Palimbei at the end of the 1940s to start a new settlement, was half the size, numbering only six households and two clans. Even if a community of this kind prospers economically, solving the problem of reproduction may become a tedious task. As a result of this situation, Yindabu is half-jokingly, half-seriously denounced as a hotbed of incest all over the Middle Sepik area. When small groups leave to found a new village it is normally as a result of serious conflict, which means that relations with the mother-village are strained at first and arranging marriages practically impossible. The elders of the newly founded Yindabu saw themselves confronted with the necessity to form new alliances with clans from Malingei and Yensan, an undertaking which required a great deal of effort, political circumspection, and patience. These new marital links were designed according to the symmetrical model: when a woman from Yindabu married someone from Malingei, it was assumed that a woman from Malingei would move to Yindabu during the same or at the latest the next generation. But the older members of the group cannot simply force their children to marry, even in cases of this kind; their task is to bring about new alliances in such a way that the young people themselves have sufficient opportunity to establish relationships.

The periodic fission of a community and branching-off of a segment to found a new settlement is probably one of the very basic features of the classless society's historical dynamics and represents the fundamental mechanism by which it spread across continents and archipelagoes. The problem of reproduction that surfaces periodically must, accordingly, be regarded as one of the central contradictions of this type of society. Even if it does not, at a particular moment of development, represent a pressing problem, it leaves its mark on the ideological systems that belong to it.

Mythology and the Kinship System

The articulation of the community structure into clans, clan associations, and men's-house communities is intimately linked with the extensive fund of myths. The genealogies of all the Palimbei clans lead back to one primordial being; thus all the members of a village community regard themselves as related by descent. This primordial being spontaneously caused itself to divide, which led to the creation of series of male and female ancestors (from the point of view of their descendants). These anthropomorphous ancestors are highly individualized, immortal, and possessed of all sorts of superhuman powers. The original community of ancestors is composed of the members of this first level of differentiation; their stories are linked in a conflict-laden relationship structure. They are regarded as the ancestors of today's clans and clan associations. Their special character traits and their fates are the topics of clan-specific narratives.

The second stage of differentiation comes into being through a tremendous mythical upheaval. As if explosively, the primeval ancestors are transformed into the elements of the present-day world: the earth, stars, plants, animals, and people in their present-day form. All of these are animated by the motive force of the primordial being, which differentiates itself and takes on various shapes. The motive force leaves dying forms to set new objects, new issue, and new seeds in motion. All the phases of this process occur simultaneously. Infinite, branching series of transformations lead from the primordial being through the society of primeval ancestors to man and the other objects of his world but also from the moribund back to the ancestors and the primordial being.

In each clan or clan association a repertory of mythical motifs constituting the clan-specific part of the mythical whole has been passed down from generation to generation. We encounter these motifs in various forms: esoteric communications, stories, ritual chants, systems of names, topics of daily conversation or public argument, works of art, and musical compositions. Certain aspects of this mythological culture are secret, others widely known; the narrative tradition is mainly perpetuated by women, with men concentrating on the systemic relationships in this multitude of motifs. Everyone in the village is familiar with the clan-specific ancestors; men, women, and even children know their names, their manifestations (i.e., the different shapes they may assume), and the main events of their stories, if only fragmentarily. Adults, too, may have only fragmentary knowledge, depending on how gifted they are or how their particular interests have developed. Every clan has one or two specialists who know a great deal about this labyrinth of motifs; only a very few men in a village community have equal command of the quantitative and systematic aspects of the mythological whole.

As opposed to the publicly known stories, the mysterious, esoteric details are guarded by older men and passed on only under special conditions. Friends trade them as a sign of trust, fathers gradually confide them to chosen sons. These esoteric communications are generally short; the publicly known stories, which are mainly told by women, are longer and literary in form, by which I mean chiefly that they are characterized by a unity of plot revolving around one main figure. These stories are thrilling, sometimes funny, sometimes strange, and often told with theatrical skill. The esoteric communications, on the other hand, are intentionally fragmentary. They may consist of a single secret name or the suggestion but not the naming of some atrocity committed by an ancestor. They refer to the same motifs found in the narratives, but they add a detail or illuminate a link between seemingly unconnected motifs.

The complete repertory of a clan's motifs is brought together in one or more long series of songs sung during certain clan-specific rituals. The figures of primeval ancestors make their appearances in these songs; their transformations and various shapes are described, one after another, as are their migrations, the places they settled, and their deeds and fates. The distinctive stylistic trait of these series of songs is their elliptical, cryptic mode of expression. To the uninitiated they are incomprehensible, an endless collection of catchwords, unconnected phrases, lists of names and places, stereotypic invocations. For the initiated participant they tell profound, meaningful stories and convey strong lyrical images while providing a practical compendium of the whole body of myths.

The system of proper names fulfills a singular function. As the names of people and places (plots of land, lakes, streams, and other conspicuous topographical features) are systematically rooted in the clan-specific repertory of mythological motifs, they constitute a semantic network connecting living persons and parts of the village lands with primeval ancestors. Every ancestor, or rather every single manifestation of an ancestor, has a long list of proper names: these names, which may be up to ten syllables long, are composed of elements that suggest the mythical fate of the ancestor in question, that is, refer to important events in his story. If one knows this story, one can read it out of the sequence of names in the list. A clan's fund of names usually numbers some sixty such lists, each of which contains several dozen names.

In the same way that the totality of mythical motifs is divided among the clans in a village community, a clan's portion of them is divided among the individual patrilineal segments of a clan. If a clan has, for example, three or four segments, each segment has about twenty ancestor manifestations and the same number of lists of names allocated to it. Within a segment, the father divides the mythological fabric up further among his children; he nullifies the allocations of the dying generation and transfers the lists of names to the members of the new one. Every little girl and boy receives one or sometimes even several lists of names, and this is regarded as an identification with the corresponding ancestor. Only one of the several dozen names a child receives from his or her father becomes the name he or she is known by. The lists of names also include the names of parts of the village lands where the ancestors in question stayed and where important mythical events took place. Thus every clan member is linked firmly not only with an ancestor but also with a specific part of the natural environment exploited economically by his clan.

Again and again there are opportunities in the social life of a village community to discuss this immense network, exposing its focal points. Its outlines reappear in the arrangement of larger rites, the main configurations of the mythical story being staged during the ritual performances; minor parts of the network become clear at smaller ceremonies or in the course of everyday events. The spectacular debates at the men's house, meetings that all the adult males of the village community attend and to which mythology experts from neighboring Central Iatmul villages may also be invited, represent the highest-ranking forum. Here the complex relationships in the mythological system are publicly discussed, contradictory opinions compared, and conflicts thrashed out. Nevertheless, owing to the considerable wealth of Iatmul village communities (there is no shortage of land in general and no inequality of access), these ceremonial debates are more of an intellectual and social concern than a manner of settling conflicts.

Every clan traditionally exploits a portion of the natural resources of the village community, and its connection with this particular portion is expressed through linkages in the mythological system. The subdivision of land and the parallel subdivision of the fabric of the mythical stories and ancestor figures is carried further within the portion connected with a particular clan and continues down to the individual clan members and individual plots of land. In any given period of time the whole universe of the village community is clearly and unambiguously divided up among its constituent units. Portions of the village territory of various sizes are allocated to concrete groups of persons on all levels of segmentation, from the men's-house community through the clan associations and the clans to the minimal patrilineal segments. But at the same time everything is in flux: on the individual level these allocations may change annually (within the framework of a clan's claim); on the clan level such changes take place in the course of generations.

If a clan dies out, it continues to exist as a portion of the mythology. Even if a clan no longer has any male members, the elders of its brother clans will continue to pass down the piece of the mythical fabric linked with it. Its ancestral figures and their various manifestations, the myths that relate their eventful life-stories, their lists of names, and the ritual chants, all the clan-specific mythology, including the links with a particular part of the natural resources of the village, continues to be passed on. The Iatmul compare this empty semantic construction to a mask: it is a dead frame waiting to be animated by real persons. If another clan in the same clan association grows substantially, the elders may decide to allow one or more of its patrilineal segments to slip into the empty spiritual shape that tradition has preserved and take over both the mythical motifs and the accompanying lands.

The village territory, divided as it is into clan-specific portions, represents a finite quantity with clear divisions that are reflected and embodied in the mythological system. Clan-specific plots of land and the mythology that goes with them represent a kind of shell inhabited by living persons, the new generations that continually appear. If the system according to which people are linked with

the dead shell were absolutely rigid, like a land register stating individual rights of ownership, the equilibrium in the distribution of resources would ultimately break down. Clans that increased considerably in numbers would have less and less land per head, and clans that decreased would have more and more. If the first case meant impoverishment, as in a money economy, and if the owners of uncultivated land could make a profit by farming it out, significant differences in economic power would soon develop; the situation would resemble that of societies where there are wealthy farmers on the one hand and poor ones or even landless persons with only their labor power to sell on the other. Under the conditions of the original classless society, developments of this kind remain merely a utopian scheme, and the distribution of natural resources continues to be more or less equal.

The system of interconnections I have described is very flexible: land whose former holders have died out is simply allocated to clans that have become much larger; clans that have decreased in size cede some of their resources to others, as they know that their own descendants will have enough land assigned to them should they multiply greatly in the future. There are numerous crosscutting connections within the mythological system among the clan-specific sections of the whole, and a transfer of resources along these lines can always be undertaken if there is consensus among the people involved. The primeval ancestors of every individual clan are somehow related, be it by descent or by marriage, to the ancestors of all the other clans, and all of them stem, after all, from the same primeval hole. What we would regard as a transfer of land rights from one clan to another appears in the Iatmul system of thought, this network of mythical, economic, and legal interconnections, as a transfer of persons. The clan-specific section of the mythological system belonging to an extinct clan—this mere semantic construction, a sort of dead shell that has lost its inhabitants—accommodates new ones.

It is, of course, not this admirable flexibility of the Iatmul mythological system that guarantees the equal distribution of natural resources but the structural identity of the constituent social units, all struggling for a position in the village community but all with comparatively equal opportunities to achieve approximately equal positions. Neither households, on the level of production and exchange activities, nor clans, on the level of marriage and inheritance regulation, ever had to reckon with structurally superior social units in precolonial times. The clan as a unilineal, exogamous unit is not superior to the household, because it always includes one marital partner only. The household, founded on the marriage of two persons who always belong to two different clans, is the institutional place where two clans counterbalance their respective influences, cooperate and compete with one another.

Under the conditions characteristic of a classless community (simple technical equipment, corresponding social forms of production, and a corresponding type of ecological relationship to the natural environment), there was no way for households or clans to accumulate means of production or products, materials or commodities; thus there were neither the means nor the need to concentrate economic and military power. Should this happen one day, the whole intellectual construction of the mythological system will be adapted to the new situation and from then on, if it is of any use at all, exhibit the cleavage characteristic of the class society. Whatever shape it takes, it will be utilized by the ruling class, on the one hand, and the ruled, on the other, to conceptualize their contradictory positions.

In all the various forms we know of the classless society, we find inequality in its most basic form: the inequality between children and adults, between the young and the old, which is intensified by the prolonged, profound dependence of the human infant and child. If they also exhibit an established, irreversible inequality between the sexes (i.e., men's domination of women) or a more or less developed chieftainship (i.e., men's domination of men and women), these relationships of dependence remain truly personal relationships allowing the dependents a considerable direct influence on those in authority. The exploitation and highly developed control of the ruled characteristic of the social structure of class societies belong to a completely different world of social forms.

23/ Land in the Abelam Village of Kimbangwa[1]

Barbara Huber-Greub

Land (*kəpma*) is fundamental to the life of the Abelam; their central ideas and interests are linked with it or refer to it metaphorically. Land will therefore be taken here as the focus for a consideration of various manifestations of Abelam culture. A study of land leads inevitably to the study of religion, of the (former) importance of the initiation ritual for everyday life, of the (now) overwhelming importance of cultivation of the long ceremonial yam (*wapi*), of the way of looking at conception and sexuality, and of relations between men and women and between young and old. These manifestations (and others not mentioned here) do not, of course, exist in isolation from one another. Thus the study of an Abelam community through a focus on land does not necessarily distort the picture of the culture as a whole and accords well with the Abelam's own striking tendency to make "interdisciplinary" correlations in the spheres of thought, knowledge, and action. This awareness of significant relations between all sorts of things, facts, beings, ideas, and cultural spheres (what Forge [1973:190] has called "punning chains") touches such vital philosophical aspects of their culture as mystery, coherence, sense, and incentive. The distinctive significance of and manifold correlations between such important entities as man, woman, land, ancestors, coconut, and flying fox form a cardinal point for the understanding of the mysteries and certitudes of the environment and their shared life. Moreover, planting season (approximately from September to February) and ceremonial season (from March to August)—sing-sings, displays of yams, yam competitions, the building of ceremonial houses, the shooting of pigs, initiations, birth, marriage, death, and funeral rites—seem to form a continuous cycle without beginning or end. None of the spheres mentioned exists for its own sake; each is a sort of sounding board for all the others. For the Abelam none of these spheres is outstanding, but for the observer the ceremonial-yam complex and the initiation cycle seem to stand out clearly.

Smooth and prosperous social interaction during the planting season is essential for a success-ful harvest. A successful harvest of long yams makes possible the yam festivities—a sing-sing inside and in front of the ceremonial house and the exchange of yams and pigs (*mbalewapi*, "yam competition")—that characterize the ceremonial season. Thus successful planting of ceremonial yams guarantees social contact, which again guarantees prosperity for the community. Unless many people from neighboring villages attend the festivities and are properly offered hospitality, the next season's yams cannot prosper. Thus the yam festivities end the planting season and lead to the next planting season. But the yam festivities not only (as a sort of thanksgiving) bring to an end the past planting season and lead to the new one but fulfill obligations incurred earlier. Through the yam competition, the "fire of a new ceremonial house is extinguished," i.e., the name of the new ceremonial house is strengthened, and therefore the construction of a new ceremonial house needs to be followed by a competition. Yam festivities and yam competitions are the foundation of coming initiations, and initiations require new yam festivities and yam competitions to satisfy unfulfilled requirements of reciprocity.

The Abelam of Kimbangwa, a Shamu-Kundi-speaking village of Northern Abelam,[2] have a comprehensive term for "earth," "soil," "land," "ground," "territory": *kəpma*. Kəpma is the soil from which subsistence grows, the ground on which one walks, land as opposed to sky (*mii*) or water (*ngu*), the abode of the ancestors and special spirits (called *kəpmandu*, "earth beings"), and the region in which one feels at home and in which one's ancestors felt at home, the territory in which the known rules and sanctions of one's own dialectal subgroup hold sway.[3]

Besides the importance of kəpma as provider of food and as the last dwelling place of the dead, who are buried in the ground (and once were buried inside their dwellings), the various ideas somehow connected with kəpma symbolically cover the whole life cycle of every individual, of the community as a whole, and even of Abelam culture. In mythical times, mankind came up from a hole in the earth. Man receives from the earth the food that helps him to grow and become strong. At the same time, it is the earth that furnishes the most important ingredients of the magical substance (kəpmanamusi, "something of the earth," or traditional sorcery) that can kill people. Underground, in the earth, dwell ancestors and spirit beings who "on their side" control the life of the living and are able to send sickness and even death. As dead persons, people will again dwell underground, as in mythical times, and will, from this other side, help their descendants to prosper while constantly supervising their conduct. In this connection Abelam often say, "Our kəpma will hear and then do something." For every new generation living on earth, a new cycle of exchange with kəpma starts. The quality of this exchange influences in a real as well as a symbolic way the prosperity of the people and their community. In the broader terms of cosmology, well-being is guaranteed, but ruin also threatens the people and the world, in this case from heaven and earth combined. A myth tells how Kokumbale, the god of heaven and of the clouds, and Aniktagwa, the goddess of earth and of earthquakes, hold heaven and earth together; should they ever let go, the world would perish.

History of the Village

The ancestors of the people of Kimbangwa (and of all the Abelam) did not always live in the territory they now inhabit. There is a myth relating how the ancestors of the Abelam and of all mankind came up from their dwellings underground through a hole. They came to the mountain Yambukandja and the place called Dumeni in the southern Wosera region. From there many pairs of men went off in different directions. They settled down at different places, places which now belong together as brothers and sisters belong together. In this way Kimbangwa is mythically closely related to the villages of Barnga, Waignakum, Kalabu, Suambukum, Tiendekum, and Kwarngu (and other villages, depending on the history of the journey its ancestors took from Dumeni to the territory now inhabited). These villages are seen as sisters (eldest, middle, younger, or youngest) and half-sisters.

Many stories tell us about later changes of settlement by the direct ancestors of Kimbangwa. All the other Abelam villages have similar stories of the different stages of settlement from Dumeni to the present. Two brothers are said to have fled the half-mythical, half-historical Upite-Tarkwo

because they found its residents too belligerent and, having discovered the territory of today's Kimbangwa, returned to Upite-Tarkwo to bring their wives and children to settle there. The stories tell of the movement of settlements north and back, south and back, until the ancestors finally settled definitively in today's territory.

In the course of Kimbangwa's history, new hamlets were repeatedly built and old ones abandoned. Death, jealousy, and attacks by enemies from surrounding villages drove people from their familiar hamlets, sometimes even to other friendly villages. Five stages of settlement in different zones of the territory can be identified. Even today, the flow of people between hamlets is striking. Rarely has anyone lived all his life in the same hamlet. Equally striking is the knowledge displayed by many inhabitants of the history of once-inhabited hamlets. Wherever in the area a family or a couple has lived, people will still remember it.

Not all hamlets are equally valued. There are principal hamlets (called "coconut-palm hamlets," "bone hamlets," or "ancestor hamlets") with histories important for the village and small hamlets (called "bush hamlets") that have newly (and this can mean as many as thirty years ago) emerged out of former bush. There are some principal hamlets that were bush hamlets not long ago. These two kinds of hamlets have different importance for different events in the social life of the villagers. A planter of ceremonial yams should live, at least during the planting season, in a coconut-palm hamlet. The most fundamental difference between the two categories of hamlets is the positive presence of many helpful, benevolent ancestors in the coconut-palm hamlets; these are hamlets whose "kəpma knows." In a coconut-palm hamlet people's memory of past individuals and of spirit beings will never be lost. Here one works for the glory of the whole community. Living in a principal hamlet means having ties with the community of the living and the dead, while living in a faraway bush hamlet can be understood as flight and separation from the community.

Landowning Clans and Omniscient Ancestors

Every man and woman belongs primarily to the clan in which he or she is born, his or her father's clan, but through adoption one can achieve affiliation to or even full and primary membership in another. Many villagers have loyalties to different clans. Apart from adoption, for women it is marriage and divorce that change clan membership or allow different affiliation to clans. For men, attachment to the circle of followers of a big man (*nəmandu*) of another clan (especially today, in connection with the planting of ceremonial yams) can mean a temporary principal affiliation to the big man's clan. For all these reasons, the picture of villagers' membership in one of the seven named principal clans (or one of the ten clan groups with ten differently named totems) is constantly changing.

The most important reason for change is adoption, which is often undertaken because of an unfavorable ratio between available clan land and male members of the clan. Inheritance of land is closely linked to clan membership. Everyone has a right to use land of the clan with which he feels most closely related by birth, by marriage (men and women), or by adoption and whose big men are ready to assign him a place in the clan and on its land. The ideal situation would be for a man to inherit the rights of the clan of his own father (or his own father's eldest brother), who for his part had, as firstborn son, followed his own father (or his own father's eldest brother) in the role of "father of the land." Every clan contains one or more such "fathers (or guardians) of the land," who are at the same time the heads of the (unnamed) lineages within the clan. They are "guardians" in that they are not exclusive owners of parts of the clan's land but look after particular parts of it during their lifetimes and decide who may plant on particular plots. They are not always real firstborn sons of firstborn fathers; their elder brothers may be dead or may have moved to other villages. Even men born into other clans can become fathers of the land in their adopters' clans. Sometimes sons of a father of the land divide up their father's part of the clan's land, each becoming father of the land on his own portion. All the fathers of the land (and so all the lineages) of a principal clan are looked upon as issuing from the clan rather than as combining to form it.

The villagers distinguish two kinds of usufruct rights to land: the primary usufruct of land of one's own natal clan and the secondary usufruct of land of other clans, for example, the clan of one's mother, wife, adopter, *naui* (formal friend), or father's *naui*. The ultimate owner of the land is the clan. Today it is very rare for part of the land of one clan to pass into the possession of another. In the past, changes were more frequent because

originally only two clans owned the whole of the village's present territory. These two original clans first gave land to two other clans; then, little by little, new clans split off or appeared, all ultimately receiving their land from the original occupants. People's knowledge of the two primordial clans still forms an important part of village politics. The former division of the village's territory between the two historical founding clans is reflected in the two "geographical" halves *kumun* and *kwien* (both names of bird species). Each of the founding clans is the principal clan of one of these halves. Grouped with one or the other of them are all the other clans, depending on which one was directly or indirectly the original grantor of their land. In former times these halves were probably two parties in opposition within the village territory.

Changes in usufruct relationships to parts of the land today are never changes in the clan's rights over these parts. The name of the clan remains attached to the land; only the guardianship changes. What is important is that "kəpma knows." The ancestors and the important spirits know the primary users of the land of the clan. They "smell" when someone has no right to plant on the land and in consequence do harm to him, to his family, or to his harvest. To plant in secondary usufruct on another clan's land requires the approval of the father of the land and his lineage, the so-called coconut-palm people. Two things are vital for village harmony: knowledge of the history of the land of all the clans, former holders of land, clan affiliations and divisions, adoptions, and grants of parts of the land in usufruct and the concept of omniscient ancestors (metaphorically "knowing, smelling, and hearing kəpma") and the sanctions issuing from them against anyone who breaks the laws of landed property and usufruct.

The diversity of kinship relationships, with their corresponding rights and duties, clan memberships and the frequent adoptions, the position of women in marriage, the ideal position of the eldest son within the family, and the many concrete possibilities of younger sons all point to a life full of claims and of real problems. Rather than definitively regulating the shared life of the people, all these rights and duties must themselves be regulated over and over again. Time and again quarrels arise or sickness, death, or poor harvests call attention to the possibility that someone has broken a rule, has not sufficiently attended to the common welfare. Living together peacefully is an ideal that is always at risk. Sickness, death, and poor harvests are signs of conflict. To cure sickness or understand a death the villagers search for causal conflicts and means of propitiation or counteraction.

For the Abelam, the responsibility for a wrong does not always lie with the sick or dead person. Often the latter is the victim of another person's wrong. Again, it is not always the one offended or attacked who calls forth the sickness or death of the offender; authorities not directly involved will often recognize a conflict and provide for punishment. Such third-party authorities include the *waumamu* (the living mother's brother, mother's father, and others on the mother's side) and ancestors and spirits. These persons and spirits are, in respect to the centrifugal tendencies of village life, interested opposing parties, and they try to intervene in social life in the interest of harmonious coexistence.

Besides relying on these moral authorities, anyone who feels wronged has the opportunity to use force directly. In former times, such a person often took up arms; now he will do harm by charms and, above all, by sorcery (either the principal traditional kind or "first-color" sorcery). This sorcery is closely connected with social organization. Outside observers often think that acts of sorcery are purely arbitrary and simply available for the asking, but in fact there is a very complicated system of competences regulating sorcery. Sorcery is not intended primarily to threaten the peaceful social life of the villagers by arbitrarily striking terror into them but, first of all, represents an omnipresent threat of sanctions against offenses and mistakes, thus indirectly fortifying the ideal conception of a good life.

Cooperation

Secondary usufruct gives every individual a variety of opportunities to cultivate land belonging to a clan other than his own. This right is closely related to the phenomenon of cooperation, which in the case of Kimbangwa cannot be explained solely in terms of economics or the scarcity of clan land (although some clans currently do possess significantly less cultivable land than others in proportion to their male members). Behind the mutual right to use others' land are impulses of a social nature. Cooperation makes it possible to give help to others, strengthens relationships between friends and relatives, gives pleasure, and allows people to know other cultivators nearby; in short, it allows *gris wantem* ([Tok Pisin] jokingly and playfully keeping company).

Helping others is a matter of course in daily life. To plant gardens alone or even as a married couple is tiresome and troublesome work and unnecessarily prolongs every stage of planting. Villagers stress that they do not like to plant alone. Cooperation takes various forms, among them cooperation between husband and wife, the mutual help extended in all domains of life within the narrower circle of a family or lineage, and, finally, help between friends and relatives in general, above all in the planting of yams.

Cooperation between man and woman, especially as a married couple, is seen as self-evident. If this cooperation does not function smoothly it can become the source of public nuisance, and married couples are quite often set right in public discussions. There is a law that a man has to help his wife and a woman her husband. If a man is lazy, his wife can easily leave him. A woman who has worked hard for a man cannot easily be driven away. This is intimately connected with the important fact that the woman has reared pigs that have later been cooked and distributed in competitions and festivities. She has acquired a name because of her pigs, and having become somebody, she has to be treated well. Just as a man gains a good name for his cultivation of ceremonial yams and so gains prestige for himself and the community, a woman gains prestige for herself and the community by rearing pigs, the so-called *poroman* ([Tok Pisin] companion) of yams.

There are many motives for cooperation in Kimbangwa, some more or less practical (the other person is a good worker), others more or less emotional (I like him). Solidarity within a household does not seem to be connected with the idea of restitution, but for solidarity within the lineage one expects, though not immediately and never overtly, a later gift or help in return.

Cooperation with well-disposed persons is important, but it can be no less important to cooperate in special situations with the right people. It may happen that a lineage or even a whole clan dies out. It is taboo to lay hands on this "fatherless" land. But if someone urgently needs this land or is convinced that he has a legitimate claim to it, he must take care to cooperate with one of the most directly related descendants (who may just as well be related through a woman) of the clan or lineage under discussion if he hopes to receive good harvests from it.

Cultivation of Land and Long Yams

The choice of the right kind of soil for the cultivation of yams, taro, sweet potatoes, bananas, vegetables, and sugarcane in gardens is important, but for the Abelam it is not good soil alone that, combined with the right cultivation technique and knowledge of magic, leads to a successful harvest. Equally important is the correct observance of the rights of primary and secondary usufruct that is indispensable for obtaining the positive participation of the ancestors.

The year is subdivided economically into two periods. The planting season, starting approximately in August and coinciding partly with the wet season, and the ceremonial season immediately after the harvest, starting around March and coinciding partly with the dry season. The Abelam also subdivide the year into the period of plenty or of food (*katule*) and the period of hunger (*kwitule*). Kwitule corresponds more or less with the second half of the planting season, in which people have to eat mainly sago because the crops have been eaten up or newly planted and the storehouses are empty.

The long yam is central not only to the division and planning of the year but also to the flourishing of all food crops. The laws which concern the planting of ceremonial yams are the laws of cultivation in general. All the admonitions uttered in the planting season, for example, that people must behave correctly and not quarrel, especially pronounced in connection with the cultivation of ceremonial yams, are valid for the cultivation of all food. A special ceremony for the planting of long yams at the initiation of the planting season is an important event for the transference of special power (*ina*) and of good thoughts for the cultivation of all food. Two or three pigs are cooked and distributed on this occasion. The men assemble for a whole day to sing special songs and converse in the central plaza of a principal hamlet. In the evening every man takes specially prepared water home with him. This water will stand guard for him and transmit force to the food to be planted. The harvest would be at risk unless as many people as possible from the village and other villages first assembled and conversed in this way.

The gardens for the Abelam's daily food are subdivided into new ones and old ones. The spot for the clearing is selected according to the availability of fallow ground to which one has primary right of usufruct as father of the land or a near relative of one, the location of still-cultivated old gardens, the location of nearby gardens of other villagers, and the expressed desires of friends and relatives to cultivate particular plots adjacent to one's own fallow ground. Thus cooperation with other villagers is often discussed in connection with the choice of fallow ground for clearing and cultivation of new gardens.

Shortly before the stars Kwengral and Mengral can be seen on the horizon, the harvest begins in the older gardens. Soon afterward the new gardens, especially the new taro, will be harvested. The appearance of these stars and the harvest of taro, which is so important for the termination of the taboo-laden planting season, are consistently mentioned in the same breath. There is a song called *Kwengral-Mengral* that is often sung, as it were, in introduction of the period of new food. At that time all yams still in the soil of the gardens should be well enough developed that no breach of taboo can destroy them. Only after this song has been sung may planters of ceremonial yams again eat taro; the planting period, with its many taboos, is officially ended. Later the long yams are harvested and the yam festivities prepared. After these festivities, yam and pig competitions take place throughout the ceremonial season.

Kimbangwa sees itself as a village of planters of *mambutap* long yams and possessors of special knowledge and special myths concerning that species of yam and an important role in the fortunes of that species in other villages.

The most important tuber besides the yam is taro. While yams are generally seen as male and associated with men (although some species of yam are associated with female gender), taro is generally seen as female and associated with women (although certain species of taro are associated with male gender). While yams are exclusively planted by men, taro is women's domain. It is in this connection that we have to understand the above-mentioned taboo for planters of ceremonial yams on eating *mai* taro before they harvest their yams (mai taro being the prototype of the different species of taro). A man explained, "To eat mai taro is the same as to make love with a woman." This is the most discussed taboo of the planting season. From this point of view, it is astonishing that in the special gardens for ceremonial yams, some mai taro (especially perceived as female) is also planted between the small hills of mambutap yams (especially perceived as male). The planters do not see any problem with this; the tubers are looked upon as husband and wife. The planters say that mambutap can only prosper if mai prospers as well. Even the magical stone that aids the growth of the ceremonial yams and that is secretly cared for in a special house by a special man has its companion within this house, a magical stone that aids the growth of the taro. Whenever the planters talk of the yam's magical stone, the taro's magical stone is also remembered. The idea is that the mai taro helps the mambutap yam and the mambutap helps the mai exactly as human beings do.

Ceremonial yams are a sort of luxury yam planted only by men in specially cultivated gardens that are the prerogative of those who observe the appropriate taboos. The cultivation of ceremonial yams not only plays a decisive role in the conduct of daily life but also helps shape villagers' ideas about aspects of their social life. The ceremonial yam and its cultivation have central significance in the Abelam's view of the companionship of the sexes, of the ancestors and spirits, of initiation ceremonies, of social rights and duties, and of power and political relationships within the village and between villages. Ceremonial yams stand symbolically not only for ample food but also for wealth, renown, and prestige. Together with shell rings and pigs, they are the most important object of value in exchanges with special partners or persons whom one wants to challenge or to humiliate. A successful harvest of ceremonial yams brings their grower fame and power and authority over others who have less success in planting them, but most important, it brings prestige and renown to the village as a whole.

Some of the ritual knowledge for the successful cultivation of long yams is acquired by men during initiation; some of it, however, is merely hinted at or transmitted in keywords, to be fully communicated only in the actual planting of the yams. A young man who joins an older, experienced planter must do so in the way least likely to allow antagonisms to develop. To have a name as a planter of ceremonial yams does not automatically mean that a young man can easily build up a position of authority, first, because the prestige that an individual gains is primarily the prestige of his lineage, his clan, his *ara* (ceremonial half), or his village, and second, because a planter with too much success sooner or later risks having sorcery aimed at him out of envy and apprehension.

The competition in ceremonial yams (and pigs) often becomes a fight with different weapons and serves as well for the settlement or public display of conflict or the fulfillment of the most important law of Abelam society—to stand in constant exchange with one another in order not to fall into nothingness. In a cycle of exchange without beginning or end, obligations are dispatched and new ones assumed by the giving of ceremonial yams to others.

During the planting season, a man's interest should be focused on yams, and he must maintain a certain distance from women, especially if he is a planter of ceremonial yams. It is said that during the planting season men may only "touch the skin of the yam," and only during the ceremonial season are they again allowed to "touch the skin of women." This does not mean, however, that ceremonial yams are a matter exclusively concerning men. It is true that ceremonial yams primarily bring prestige to men, but to every villager, male or female, it is clear that ceremonial yams and male renown and prestige can exist only if women cooperate with men on several levels—cultivating food, cooking for the men and their guests, observing the taboos connected with the planting of ceremonial yams and those directed at the planters. That men and women are dependent on each other is extraordinarily clear to villagers in the planting season, when women more obviously than at other times have to keep away from men and are oftener judged noxious to the secret domain of men and even responsible for all sorts of planting failures and damage. The whole complex of ceremonial yam cultivation for the villagers of Kimbangwa involves men and women in a way typical of the Abelam, occupying a sort of middle ground in the contradiction between considering women worth nothing at all and considering them worth much more than men.

How is the relationship between the sexes in Kimbangwa to be judged? Must we consider only the categorical view, often expressed by men, that women know less, are weaker, are nothing, can only cook, and that men alone know the true secrets? Or is there something in the more veiled allusions (even by men) to the striking and admirable faculties of women? Are these veiled allusions to be understood as only covert demonstrations of the strong position of men, or have they a deeper meaning? Is women's position to be judged insignificant because of the cult of ceremonial yams (interpreted by many observers as phallic), because women stand in marked contrast to and at a great distance from ceremonial yams and their gardens, and because men are the legitimate and obvious guardians of all the knowledge connected with the cultivation of ceremonial yams and the stages of initiation? The ambiguity mentioned in the valuation of women is related to the divergence between ideal conceptions of the relationship of the sexes in terms of their mythical and symbolic character, on the one hand, and the real position and importance of women, on the other. The degree of divergence varies from one sphere of life to another, and therefore so does the degree of stress on mutuality and the complementarity of men and women. In the sphere of the men's secret cult proper, the sphere of initiations, complementarity of men and women is primarily found on an ideal, mythical level. In the sphere of the cult of ceremonial yams one finds a more pronounced real inclusion of women, and the complementarity of the sexes is more directly lived. In the sphere of daily life linked with kəpma—the cultivation of land, the life cycle, the regulation of relations between the living and the dead, the confrontation of sickness and calamities—the real, lived companionship and complementarity of men and women are in the foreground. Here the recognized inclusion of women is clearest and the divergence between the ideal conception of the complementarity of the sexes as a necessity for the prosperity of social life and the actual, lived relationship between the sexes is least.

Tripartite Division of the Territory

Life within the territory of the village takes place between the principal areas of house (*nga*) and hamlet (*nge*), garden (*yaui*), secondary forest (*apate*), and primeval forest (*mbəgətale*). The Abelam believe that in all these areas ancestors and spirits are always invisibly present. Not only the living but all invisible beings are related to kəpma. Besides the ancestors and the kəpmandu there are the *ngundu* (water beings), which can transform themselves into earth beings, and the *miindu* (sky/cloud beings), for which human beings have built centers of attraction and abodes in the form of the *mbabmutagwa* (moon-woman) stones in the plazas of their principal hamlets.

The relationship between the living, the newly dead, the ancestors, and the various spirits is differently shaped in the three principal domains of house/hamlet, garden, and bush/primeval forest. In each domain one of the beings mentioned stands out as principally responsible actor alongside other actors. In the house/hamlet domain, the newly dead are most threateningly present and determine people's behavior; this domain can

therefore be seen as the domain of human responsibility and the principal human field of activity. In the garden domain, the famous ancestors are the mightiest helpers present, and this is their principal field of activity; everything a human being does in this domain depends on the ancestors. Finally, in the domain of bush and primeval forest, spirits of all kinds are principal actors; everything that men remove from this domain is granted to them by spirits. People fear the presence of spirits most in this domain. They are especially aware, however, that the activities of the spirits extend to the domain of the hamlet; this is something they learn during the various stages of initiation. At the same time, they learn about the less threatening aspects of these beings and the power that men possess as responsible human beings in dealing with them.

As I have pointed out, a central idea about kəpma is that it overhears, knows, and if the "laws of the ground" are not followed, refuses the cooperation that is necessary for the growth of food. In this sense, kəpma exercises a decisive influence on human beings and their subsistence. Between kəpma and living beings there is an active exchange, a sort of cooperation. If human beings follow kəpma's laws, help will not be denied them. Every responsible father of the land has to be a mediator between the beings "of the other side" (ancestors and spirits) on his part of the clan land and the living members of his own and other clans. He has to make sure that members of other clans (and villages) can use his clan's land and his clan's waters without detrimental effects and with the knowledge of the beings "of the other side." Every clan is ultimately responsible for the behavior of its ancestors and spirits toward members of other clans. In turn, the ancestors and spirits on a certain part of the land of a certain clan (thus belonging to this clan) watch over the behavior of the living members of the clan and make sure "on their side" that the ancestors and spirits of all the other clans attend to the welfare of the people on their own clan's land.

Special Sites

In the three principal domains of the territory there are sites that are considered special zones of danger or significance and associated with special requirements concerning the sexual behavior of men and women and the attitude toward each other of young and old (who differ in the "threat" posed by their sexuality). These special sites are, in the extreme case, segregated domains for one sex (e.g., ceremonial houses, central plazas at special times of the year, ceremonial yam gardens [for men] and menstruation houses [for women]) or domains that are open to both sexes but in which increased attentiveness is demanded (e.g., burial places, sleeping places, cooking places, "pathways of the ceremonial yam," waters, stones, tabooed bush and hunting grounds). In all these special places the threatening and beneficent presence of spirits of the newly dead, ancestors, and all other spirits is felt particularly strongly.

The cooking place and the sleeping place are special taboo sites within the house. In former times, when every villager still lived in a house built directly on the ground, everybody always had to remember that to step over these places meant danger to older people, babies, planters of ceremonial yams, and domesticated pigs. This taboo is linked with ideas about the dependence of older people and the relationships between different age-groups and periods of life. The latter ideas are again linked with ideas about sexuality, procreation, and the "quality of blood" of men and women.

Burial places have central importance for the Abelam in that unless the newly dead, who will later become beneficent ancestors, are correctly buried there is a risk that they will not help their living descendants in their gardens and will be a threat to their prosperity. In connection with burial places (both the former sites/graves within the houses and the new ones outside the domain of the hamlets), the relationship between human beings, subsistence, and the dead stands out. With the prohibition by the Australian administration of burial inside the house, the idea of the transfer of power between the living and the dead lost its importance.

That women have to withdraw to special houses on the outskirts of hamlets during menstruation implies that their menstrual blood has inimical qualities, especially for men. Actually, however, ideas and behavior with regard to women's blood (and blood in general) are not so straightforward. Women's blood is inimical (cold) not only to men but to women (especially those of another age-group) and to children and animals as well. Men's blood, under certain circumstances, is also judged as inimical (cold) to other people or to things and activities. Women's blood, on the other hand, if the woman in question is young and vigorous, may be considered

strong (warm), even including at times menstrual blood. There are three qualities of blood of men and of women, and the negative influence of the blood of a person depends very much on its quality. However, it is ultimately not just the blood of one person, man or woman, that is seen as dangerous but the blood of two persons having intercourse together; sexuality is dangerous to certain essential activities and domains. Talking of blood, in a way, always means talking of sexuality and of its dangers to everyone, man and woman, young and old, but to everyone in a special way for different reasons. That menstrual blood is mentioned mostly in connection with the dangers of sexuality and blood in general is due to the idea of the prominent function of menstrual blood in conception. Behind all statements about the noxious influence of menstrual blood to food and to human beings and their activities one can detect the idea of menstrual blood as the incomprehensible power of women to create, a power that is responsible for the creation of new human life ("skin of the woman" is a metaphor for love, sexuality, and, indirectly, conception) and stands opposed to the vital power of men, which finds its most important expression in the growing of ceremonial yams ("skin of the wapi" is a metaphor for man's total absorption during the growth of long yams).

The Abelam say of especially striking stones that Walesakitagwa (also called the Cassowary Woman), who, together with her husband Walesakindu, is the prime creator of all things and of men, made them and gave them to men so that men might adore them and in consequence receive much food. Because these special stones are connected with spirits, the Abelam believe that they have the power to assist fecundity and to transmit sickness.

Water, likewise, is in the mind of the Abelam intimately connected with spirits. Many waters, springs, water holes, and streams are accordingly called *walengu* (water of the *wale* [spirits]) or simply *wale*. Water and stones are especially important in growing ceremonial yams, the corresponding spirits, like the ancestors, helping the planters to raise a successful crop.

Symbolic Significance of Kəpma

I have already mentioned how important the laws of the ground are for the Abelam. One of these laws, as they say, is related to women. It is said that women destroy the ground or expose it to danger. It is not, however, the woman as an individual who endangers the ground and the crops. Rather, she stands symbolically for the dangers of male and female sexuality (and the associated menstrual blood) that threaten the food growing in the ground. The ground and the beings "of the other side" that are implicitly but naturally connected with it smell if someone "jumps the little river" (in this case, sleeps with a woman at the wrong moment or comes into contact with menstrual blood or with the blood of a younger person of either sex). Then the ground withholds its cooperation from the guilty person because, the Abelam say, it feels angry, disappointed, and discontented. Another law relates to the clans as landowners. No one can allow the history of the development of his own clan's land to be forgotten. To maintain the peaceful coexistence of clans it is necessary for at least someone, perhaps even a member of another clan, to "know." At the same time, all members of a clan have to give away parts of their own clan's land in usufruct to others to maintain solidarity within the village. Moreover, only the observance of the rights of primary and secondary usufruct of land makes cooperative exchange possible between the living members of the clans and the beings "of the other side." Ancestors and spirits know about those who "jump the little river" (in this case, usurp land of other clans without having asked permission) and, once again, will withhold cooperation from the guilty persons because they feel angry, disappointed, and discontented.

Besides these laws of the ground, there are other essential implicit statements about kəpma that deal with the principal actors of village life, including the relations between the living and the ancestors and spirits and the character of the relationship between the sexes and between young and old. The ideas about the essence of the relationship of the two sexes and about sexuality and menstrual blood can be seen in exemplary fashion in the taboos and rules which concern the segregated domain of women, the menstruation house, but are most evident in the whole complex of rules and behavior surrounding the cultivation of ceremonial yams. In the latter, the menstruation house (as indirect protection of men from women) and the directly protected domains of men—the central plaza, the ceremonial house, and the ceremonial yam garden—are connected. Ideas about the relationship between young and old have to be seen in connection with sexuality, the relationship between the sexes, and ideas of

blood quality and procreation. The taboos concerning the sleeping place, the cooking place, and the menstruation house call for adherence to the principle of seniority; older people (older blood) must be protected from younger people (younger blood), which primarily means direct or indirect protection from the younger people's still healthy and strong sexuality.

The Human Actors of Village Life

Forge (1971:141–42) pinpoints the fundamental ambiguity of judgments about women when he says that "women are treated as inferior by men, who nevertheless believe them to be basically superior." Kaberry (1940–41:252) is correct in saying that "in spite of the rigorous exclusion of the women from the yam and tambaran cults, the daily relationships between the sexes are characterized by ease and friendliness." Actually, the truth about the power and weakness of women and about women's relationships with men in the social, economic, and religious domains is complex. Whatever the real economic and social position of women, there is an idea of mutuality and complementarity of the sexes at a deeper level.

Clan totems (*djambu apwi*, "totem birds") are considered partly male, partly female. A certain male-female pair of totem birds stands for the Abelam at the origin of the village as a social organism. Figuratively speaking, a male and a female element had to cooperate, to enter into exchange, for the social life of the village to emerge. A further sign that men and women belong together, that they are directly related to each other as sun and moon in the moon-woman stone, is to be seen behind the two principal crops of yams and taro. We have seen that the mambutap yam is viewed as the husband of the mai taro and the magical stones for each as spouses. At first sight only yams, intimately connected with man himself as principal planter and keeper of yams, stand out, but just as a man cannot do without the active participation of a woman, yams cannot do without mai taro or the magical stone for yams without the magical stone for taro. Everything has its poroman. As one Abelam said, man and woman are poroman, and poroman are like man and woman.

Within the most exclusive male domains of activity (cultivation of ceremonial yams, initiation, building of ceremonial houses, and painting of *mbai* (the gabled painted facades of the ceremonial houses), there is a symbolically and mythically based female element in the magical use of pubic hair (*yuwi*). For the Abelam, yuwi is seen as closely related to *saykenayuwi* (cassowary feathers). In songs one hears of saykenayuwi when woman as mistress, as seductress, is meant. For the Abelam, Sayketagwa, the mythical Cassowary Woman, is identical to Walesakitagwa, the female prime creator who brought fire and food to men. It was out of the pubic hair of Walesakitagwa (or Sayketagwa) that fire originated, and the word saykenayuwi is a metaphor for fire. Fire, along with red color, hot blood, and female pubic hair, is one of the strong, vital elements. The proportion of these vital elements seen as linked to femininity is striking.

In some of the motifs of the paintings on the facade of the ceremonial house one can again recognize how important the interrelatedness of men and women is for the Abelam, not only for the procreation of children but for the prosperity of the whole community. Many of these elements refer to the woman as female poroman of the man, albeit on different levels of meaning. The topmost motif, Matbetagwa, is primarily a female spirit, a sort of wild woman, but it also refers, many Abelam believe, to woman in general. Another motif, *kwandjitagwa* (female flying fox), may characterize the situation of someone who has newly come into the village from the outside, who is not an old, established inhabitant of the village and a rightful successor to land, but it also relates to woman in general. The female being on the *tikit* (the wooden carving just below the painting) relates to a female *ngwalndu* (spirit), but once again, it also refers to an ordinary woman. Behind all the observations of the villagers of Kimbangwa concerning the above motifs is the idea that man and woman have meaning only if joined together and that man and woman together, insofar as they stand in a complex exchange with one another, are the source of daily social and cultural life and originally of culture itself.

Two myths point in the direction of this interpretation. One of them tells how a man (the divine sun in the form of the *mange*, the principal ridgepole of the ceremonial house) helped women acquire their mystery or secret cult, childbearing, without making inevitable their own death. The other myth tells how women, as "original men," the original keepers of today's male secret cult, helped man acquire initiation and the cultivation of ceremonial yams. It is, so to speak, analogous to the myth of the first happy delivery, in which man helps woman. The implicit idea that man and

woman in their complementarity are the beginning of all things and all actions is a central subject in the life of the villagers of Kimbangwa. It stresses the exchange between the two sexes more than their differences and dissociation. The prototypes of this complementarity are the two supreme divine beings, sun and moon, but also Walesakindu and Walesakitagwa, the latter passing for the true creator of all things. (When people talk of the creation, they mention her much more often than her male partner, who, however, is naturally thought of together with her as her husband.)

Besides the relationship between men and women, the relationship between people of different ages is a recurrent theme of Abelam daily life. The relationship between men of different ages has to be seen in connection with ideas about sexuality and procreation. Sexual intercourse means for every man and every woman a weakening of their vital essence and is seen indirectly as causing men to grow old. An adult who does not observe the many taboos connected with the period in which one is sexually potent risks growing old prematurely, becoming blind, white-haired, bent, and weak in the legs and thus incapable of participating actively in village life. The older a person grows, the less blood or strength he has; he has given away his power to younger people, by virtue of which they have become strong. The causal facts behind the separation of young and old are most clearly recognizable in the perilous relationship between parents and children. This relationship is a sort of prototype for the relationship between different generations in general and for the principle of seniority, the relationship of older people (*nəmandu*) to younger people (*waigna*). The principal duty of younger people to care for older people so that they will not get sick may be attributed to the already weakened constitution of older people, who have given away much of their vital power to younger people and who, in a metaphorical as well as in a real sense, live on in the younger people and are themselves slowly dying.

Apart from this duty to care for the elderly—which has to be seen as a response to their own earlier care for their children—an equally important aspect of the relationship between old and young is that older people (primarily men) have the duty to transmit their knowledge to the younger generation. The population of the village can be said to be divided into those who are able to instruct others because of their knowledge and those who are still ignorant. The opposition between young and old can also be seen as opposition between those who know and those who are ignorant, just as the opposition between men and women is sometimes viewed. (This naturally does not mean that women in principle cannot be knowledgeable). Old age can thus be seen from two different points of view—negatively as a loss of one's own vital essence and positively as a gain of knowledge.

Exactly as a father (together with the mother) renders life physiologically possible for his children by giving away his own vital essence, blood, a father (with the help of the mother) renders possible the social integration of his children by his efforts to fulfill his role in social life—primarily by passing through the different stages of initiation, which makes him a knowledgeable man without fear and allows him for the first time in his life to be "without name," i.e., without any obligatory incorporation into a debt-creating exchange. This could be interpreted as social death; only now can a son theoretically be equal to his father. In fact, however, the old man in question continues his social life in that he now helps his children to create their own social life cycle. He continues to live socially primarily in and through his children just as he continues to live physically (thanks to his own expended vital forces) in his children. For the Abelam, all old people, the dead (ancestors) and the living, are seen as originators of one's own physical and social life. In daily life the weaker old people often feel unbearably dependent on younger persons. But what every villager learns in daily life—in cultivating land, in supplying food, in the relationship between parents and children, in village discussions—is the fact of the interdependence of younger and older people alongside the fact of the interdependence of men and women.

The social life of the Abelam reveals itself as a sequence of social cycles of individuals connected with each other. A man passes through his own social life cycle from youth to old age. In passing through this cycle he is involved in an exchange of mutual help, a constant giving and receiving with people of the other ceremonial moiety, with his relatives and friends, and with his wife's relatives. He learns that no one can cultivate with success in isolation; everyone plants effectively for the whole community, in a direct or a figurative sense. He has to think of all the people of the other ceremonial moiety and give them pigs; he has to think of his relatives and give them land to cultivate in usufruct; he has to think of his children and help them become good members of the community; and he has to think of the ancestors and act as they demand. In everything he does, he has to think of all the others; this is a principal law of the ground.

All these facts and ideas directly or indirectly related to kəpma (and thus to daily life in the village in general) demonstrate the fundamental importance of mutuality and complementarity. The Abelam recognize complementarities between different things and beings, between men, ancestors, spirits, animals, plants, and things. This recognition is closely linked to another characteristic of Abelam life, the constant involvement in exchange with each other or with the beings "of the other side." The laws of the ground are especially directed toward the maintenance of this exchange, toward peaceful coexistence instead of competition, and toward mutual help and solidarity. Likewise, all ideas of complementarity between different beings and things allude to some hidden struggle against tendencies toward disintegration, fission, and conflict. Among all the possible complementarities recognized by the Abelam, the one between man and woman is the most essential; it is the necessary starting point and foundation of successful, satisfying, productive social life.

Notes

1. This paper is a summary of a Ph.D. thesis to be published in German, "Kokospalmenmenschen: Boden und Alltag und ihre Bedeutung im Selbstverständnis der Abelam von Kimbangwa (East Sepik Province, Papua New Guinea)" (Basel, 1983). It is based on eight months' fieldwork, between October 1978 and June 1979, under a fellowship from the Swiss National Foundation. The thesis describes an example of land use in a single rather privileged Abelam community—privileged in that, unlike many other communities and regions of the country, it has no shortage of land. The many different aspects of land highlighted in it show how a flexible and thus adaptive system of land use may guarantee continuous integration of new economic features, for example, coffee growing, business and village initiatives, the use of "fatherless" land for community purposes, and the smooth integration of men from outside the immediate Abelam area. My material also indicates the importance of land for the viable integration of a community. The linking of a flexible but nevertheless clearly structured (but not legally fixed in a modern sense) system of land use and conservation with the prosperity of the whole community is important, as a guarantee of self-awareness for the small-scale community, in relation to the ongoing adaptation to new life-styles in the context of the country as a whole. It should be borne in mind that land in

Papua New Guinea does not always form such a basis for viable self-awareness (cf. Lipset's and Barlow's descriptions of the Murik Lakes people in this volume and elsewhere). It would be interesting to know more about different systems of land use in the two Sepik provinces as determinants of the transitional situation in a wider political framework.

2. Of the 355 inhabitants in 1979, 86 lived and worked away from home in different regions of Papua New Guinea; the remaining 269 lived in the 18 scattered hamlets of the village.

3. Kimbangwa belongs, together with Djame and Bainyik, to the Shamu-Kundi dialect group proper; villagers call the larger language group Ba-kundi.

24/ Boars' Tusks and Flying Foxes: Symbolism and Ritual of Office in the Murik Lakes

David Lipset

In the Murik Lakes, where a trading-and-fishing society is located at the mouth of the Sepik River, traditional and Western ideas about political authority have been debated and melded syncretically throughout the twentieth century.[1] The process is difficult and has no end. In early statehood, neither men's-cult leaders, cargo-cult leaders, businessmen, nor village councillors prevail politically in the villages. Men's secret *brag* religion is nearly secularized, its most sacred exchanges no longer made; the secret spear images rot in the moist air. The cargo cult and even cargoism now recall an obsolete set of socioeconomic expectations. Murik businessmen and women bank money in interest-bearing accounts in the provincial capital to save what they can from fishing and children's remittances. Reversals in intertribal exchange rates and the high cost of gasoline to fuel the outboard motors that today power outriggers to and from market seventy-five miles away reduce the profits they can make through their fishery. Nor does election to leadership positions lend credence to claims of authority. As men's-cult and cargo-cult authority have declined, village councillors have struggled to remain independent of the claims of the kinship and jural-political systems, which, though not thriving institutions, still provide, for the majority of villagers, the most meaningful terms and tactics for achieving their ends.

Although coastal political systems in this part of the Sepik tend to differ from island ones in the direction of those of the middle river, Murik is essentially similar to Wogeo (Hogbin 1978) and Manam (Wedgwood 1934, Lutkehaus 1982) in material culture, kinship, gender relations, and leadership system. All three are Hawaiian in kinship pattern and sexually egalitarian, and political authority is not typically Melanesian (Sahlins 1963). Leaders are not "big men." They inherit rights to occupy miniature offices which preside over descent groups. In Murik, firstborn elders mount feasts competitively to maintain order and regenerate status. As succession is formulated and practiced, each heir must claim the incumbent's senior status by staging a premortem tributary feast for him. While headmen here rely on many of the classical resources of inequality reported in Melanesia, such as indebting followers through economic/domestic production, competitive pig exchanges (Sahlins 1972:136), and knowledge (Lindstrom 1984), the Murik jural system turns on exchanging detachable symbols of status and wealth (M. Strathern 1985:199)—named boars' tusk and shell ornaments (*suman*) (fig. 1).

In this article I describe the exchange of boars'-tusk ornaments during the life-cycle rituals that are one of the perduring institutions in the society. A key symbolic equivalence is shown to obtain in this ritual cycle between generosity and superior status (Barlow 1985*b*). Superiority is denoted by giving feasts and symbolic ornaments, inferiority by receiving food and insignia. If "boars'-tusk sons" (*suman gwan*) symbolize firstborn citizens in Murik, who give feasts, lastborns (*dam gwan*) are "flying-fox sons" (*nabwag gwan*), who only eat at feasts. Illegitimate sons are also called "flying foxes." They are bastards, without mother and father to feed them, who come at night to steal fruit.

Discussion of this ritual cycle is relevant to Modjeska's (1982) stress on the social value of pig production in traditional Melanesian politics. Value in central Papua New Guinea is produced not by the object itself—the pig—but by the social relations, defined by kinship, that produce it. Pig exchange, Modjeska argues, articulates rights in people during mortuary, compensation, or marriage payments. "The accumulation of social capital [in pigs] . . . would seem to go hand in hand with an increased tolerance for mediated responses in social behavior" (1982:57). Although pig exchange is critical to Murik jural relations, wider political and economic relations do not depend directly on pig production. Central

Murik villagers do not raise pigs but travel by outrigger canoe to purchase them with money or traditional goods and currencies. Wider political relations depend on purchase and distribution rather than production of pigs, among other commodities. Because of overseas trade relations and the prestige system described below, the notion of equivalence of different goods is important in Murik. One of the most important equivalences is transacted with Schouten Islanders: one circular boar's tusk = one pig. In the Murik prestige system, this exchange also articulates the sibling and descent groups.

Economic Change

The Murik Lakes are part of the vast intertidal environment at the mouth of the Sepik River. They consist of 135 square miles of shallow lagoons and mangrove swamps just west of the river. They are barely divided from the sea by sandbanks broken through in two places by wide channels. At some points, the coastline has receded and is little more than two hundred yards wide. Land, house-building materials, and fresh water are scarce, but the mangrove swamps are a particularly rich marine ecology in which dozens of species of fish and shellfish feed and spawn.

The Lakes society, ecologically interstitial, also occupies an intermediate position on the sociolinguistic boundary which stretches along the north coast of Papua New Guinea.[2] Island Austronesian-speakers here have long-standing trade relations with the many groups of non-Austronesian-speakers of the mainland (see Harding 1967). The Murik speak a non-Austronesian Sepik River language that Laycock (1973) has called Nor, but as middlemen and traders they have trading partnerships in both inland and island societies that are institutionalized as the hereditary rights of fictive siblings.

The social relations of production continue to be phrased in traditional ways, although both traditional trade rates and cash are now in use. Men use drift nets and spearfish in the lakes. Women gather: they use droplines to pull in the subsistence catch and, at low tide, collect clams and crabs. Villagers still paddle canoes across the lakes to reach inland trading partners, their sago suppliers, who provide their staple carbohydrate in exchange for fixed amounts of smoked fish or cash. Obtaining jural resources—pigs and *Canarium* almonds—continues to involve overseas travel in motorized outrigger canoes to the Schouten Islands. Murik baskets, shellfish, dances, and

FIG. 1. A suman holder attending an outrigger consecration feast in Mendam village in 1936, wearing the boars' tusk ornaments. Photo L. Pierre Ledoux.

tooth ornaments are still highly valued among the islanders, but today, except between the most senior trading partners, pigs are bartered for money (see Barlow 1985a, Lipset 1985, Lutkehaus 1985).

Overall, the direction of change in the social relations of production is toward a lesser role for men and a greater one for women. The most common goods used in overseas trade—seafood and baskets—are still produced, for the most part, by women, who retain rights in the proceeds. Some couples regularly fish together, but bringing home and smoking the bulk of the subsistence catch is women's work. Men participate in fishing sporadically, using either spears or drift nets, both for trade and for domestic consumption. Men build canoes and do the traveling for most of the trade. However, since military defense is no longer necessary, women today may safely accompany men to town and to the islands or paddle across the lakes to meet the sago suppliers alone. Not only has women's role in trade increased, but the introduction of cash into traditional exchange relations has reduced men's prestige resources. The demand for ornaments, which Murik men and women used to manufacture and sell for pigs to intertribal trading partners, has diminished, while their demand for pigs, etc., has not abated.

Aspects of Social Organization

The 1,400 Murik occupy five villages (*nemot*), which in 1982 ranged in size from 96 to 376. Villages stand on or near the beach.[3] Each village is divided into several politically autonomous hamlets, each with one or two men's cult houses and many lagoon canoes. Ideally, each hamlet is a composite of six to fifteen small autonomous localities (*pwap* or *mot*) occupied by senior sibling groups (*nag*). In two villages, the hamlet and locality divisions have broken down, but each senior sibling still lives in a separate nuclear-family dwelling near one or two junior generations of offspring and their affines.

A conception of sibling leadership permeates inheritance, succession, domestic exchange, and affinal conduct, all construed and negotiated in terms of primogeniture. The firstborn is supposed to hold title to the property of the sibling and descent group but to use this privilege to redistribute goods among junior kin. Ideally, he is generous to younger siblings and children and avoids making requests of them. He specifically avoids the wife of his younger brother by not entering the younger brother's house and not eating her cooking if it makes him ill. Reciprocally, she stays on her knees while inside his house and keeps to the opposite end of the room. Should the elder brother and the younger brother's wife approach each other on a path, she will leave the path until he passes. The two observe name avoidances and behave respectfully toward each other. The asymmetry of sibling exchange is phrased in terms of the younger brother's most important (economic and affective) resource: the elder brother should not take resources from the wives of junior kin.

Contemporary elders believe that they are descendants of refugees (*nagam*) who fled the Middle Sepik River, resettled on the coast, and married into other groups of coastal refugees or indigenous lake peoples. These groups maintained their political identities in terms of rights in and over people and things asserted through both male and female categories. Ethnohistory reflects social structure and the landless environment: Murik men and women cite multiple origins based on movement and exchange in space rather than single autochthonous—i.e., landed and reproductive—ones. *Pwong* (descent group) elders make no cosmogonic claims to their marine "territory." Instead, they call themselves *haphap* ([Tok Pisin] "part-part") men. Rather than creating a world *de novo*, their migration stories construct a network of exchange relationships throughout a preexisting region.

Nor do the elders claim political priority over one another; rather, they compete as political equals, representing homologous sibling (nag) and descent (pwong) groups. They make and manage feasts that dramatize the pwong and momentarily assemble it as a group. Minimal organic division of property obtains among the Murik leadership. Each man controls and distributes a set of rights to insignia, lake resources, networks of trading partners, etc., that is essentially identical to those of others in all respects except name.

The reputation and prestige of any one descent-group leader in a Murik village, as in the Sepik region in general, at a particular time depends on the relative level of his activity as feast maker among rival feast makers. No one descent group forms a permanent elite. I could find no ideological or linguistic evidence that one senior-sibling office is formally superior to any other. No terms distinguish nobility and commoners as on Manam (Wedgwood 1934:384). "There are . . . no chiefs in each village," observed Father Joseph Schmidt, a Catholic missionary who lived on the Murik coast between 1911 and 1941. "The people are organized in several pwong. One pwong does not stand above the others" (1926:41).

Murik villages are occupied by segments of as many as fifteen dispersed, nonunilineal pwong, each led by a group of senior firstborn siblings. The Schouten Islands villages, on the other hand, are led by the headmen of elite lineages (Hogbin and Wedgwood 1953:243; cf. Lutkehaus 1982:85). Moving from island to coast, then, leadership becomes more diffused. As Murik elders like to say, "There, only one man holds the boars' tusks. Here, we all hold them." I argue, however, that Murik descent-group headmen and Schouten Island headmen hold essentially similar offices despite the differences in village structure.

Although leadership in Murik is less diffuse than elsewhere in the Sepik (see e.g., Forge 1972*b*), marriage is not an opportunity for the expression of jural authority. Bridewealth is not paid, and I gather that it was not paid traditionally. Bride service is expected of the groom. Apart from a notion of sister exchange that is, except in rare instances, today ignored, prescriptive marriage rules do not exist. Sibling and descent groups are exogamous. Primary claims are that marriage should not take place between young people with rights to the same suman or with a common grandparent. The right to polygyny is said to be inherited through patrifiliation.

Murik marriage emphasizes choice, flexibility, and an outward orientation. The village is not an endogamous unit. In four villages, 30–60 percent of existing marriages in 1981–82 were between villages. Intertribal marriages (except with sago suppliers), are frequently reported in genealogies. In an intervillage marriage, the woman generally moves to the husband's village. Within villages, residence is pragmatic, open to personal preference. Patrisiblings tend to live together in the same locality, but matrilocal residence is not uncommon.

Marriage is defined by sexual intercourse. When it becomes evident that a couple are having sexual relations, they have married. Parents may object, depending on how hardworking they consider the bride or groom to be, and their objection may take the form of affirming one of the two proscriptions on marriage. But descent and sibling groups are occasionally endogamous, and this creates a curious overlapping of statuses when kin are also affines. Affinal avoidances usually supersede kinship relations, although such changes are subject to personal choice and are not always honored.

Sex and sexual jealousy are seen as frequent in social life. Desire and romantic love determine marriage selection. When a man desires a woman from another village, he may abduct her, take her to his house, and rely on his own kin to guard against her escaping or being rescued by her brothers. Usually the abduction is done with the connivance of the woman. Both single and married women are stolen in this way. A cuckolded husband feels that he must retaliate if his wife has been abducted, and intervillage warfare once arose from such wife-capture.

If a sexual liaison constitutes marriage, Murik young people may "marry" a dozen or more times before settling down with a long-term spouse. A more stable relationship gradually emerges as spouses share a house, work toward its upkeep, and raise children together. But the grounds of first marriages—passion and sexual intercourse—create an initial basis for instability and divorce. Divorce is extremely common among youth, amounting to little more than the return of either partner to the house of his or her parents. Because no bride-price is involved, the major dispute following divorce is over custody of the firstborn child. One solution is to give the firstborn to a spouse's elder sibling who is ready to feed it (see Barlow 1985*c*). Another is for the mother to go on nursing the child while its father and his kin try to alienate its affections. In either event, remarriage and the birth of a new "firstborn" child make the status of the earlier firstborn ambiguous. The frequency of first-marriage divorce and firstborn adoption thus makes primogeniture highly optative and contested. Rather than competition to allocate rights in women's services by sponsoring marriage payments, a significant component of Murik leadership is competition to allocate rights in children by sponsoring firstborn rituals and exchanges.

The Ritual Reproduction of Status and Descent

Before discussing the ritual cycle through which status is transferred, mention must be made of a set of feasting partnerships called the *mwara yakabor* (valuables path) or *pilai kandere* ([Tok Pisin] play cross-kin). Classificatory mother's brothers and sister's sons do not eat together in Murik. Whereas the commensal mother's-brother–sister's-son relationship is a respect relationship that takes the same form as the elder-brother–younger-brother exchange described above, the classificatory mother's brother is a competitive joking partner who becomes a benevolent intermediary only during ritual and danger by providing services and investing money or ornaments (other than the suman) in the name of the classificatory sister's son. In return for this contribution, he receives cooked pigs and other foods to eat. These exchanges legitimate the display of descent insignia on behalf of the firstborn.[4]

Firstborn children are termed *suman gwan* or *ngasen* (insignia son or daughter), *kombatok* (head), or *apo* (big). As heirs, they are honored by descent-group elders through a ritual cycle marking the development of their jural personhood that is scaled down or omitted entirely for subsequent children. For simplicity, I will describe the cycle for a son, although the same rites may also be staged for a daughter.

When the firstborn can laugh and recognize a person at a distance, his classificatory mother's brother takes him from the arms and purview of his mother and carries him through the village (*nemot arekomara*) for the first time. Suman are displayed around the infant's neck, and villagers break coconuts in his honor. Until this point, he has been in his mother's exclusive care, considered too weak to joke with his mother's brothers.

For the subsequent rite on the appearance of his first tooth, a star-shaped platform (*go'een maig*) is constructed in the cult house or some other public venue and decorated with sticks of tobacco, sago breads, fruits, etc. The classificatory mother's brother takes the firstborn from his dwelling to the platform and there feeds him his first taste of ceremonial porridge (*aragen*), thus ending a taboo on coconut products and foods other than sago and mother's milk. A suman is exhibited, and the porridge is divided up among all the households in the village.

When the firstborn becomes mobile and is able to climb up and down the house ladder independently of his mother, the ladder rite (*waik*) is performed. A suman is displayed, and the classificatory mother's brother carries the child up and down the ladder, which has been decorated with imported delicacies, as if teaching him how to climb.[5]

Although none of these initial rites requires pigs, each is slightly more complicated and expensive to mount than the one preceding it. Protocol requires more trade goods and coordinated labor to pay the mother's brother. In each case, the food used as decoration is given to the mother's brother in the name of the firstborn, and the mother's brother distributes it among his own commensal kin. The elder who purchases and prepares this food decorates the child with his own insignia and begins to claim rights in him for his descent group.[6] But the child may be claimed by several descent groups at once. Patrilateral and matrilateral suman holders have equal rights to claim the firstborn and compete to do so. Ritual rivalry thus reflects domestic rivalry for adoption of children. In both cases, elders compete by giving plates of food. In the domestic arena, claims are signified by feeding; in the ritual one, they are signified by the display of suman.

Murik leaders attribute social personhood to the firstborn when he begins to play a role in ex-

changes outside of and beyond mother and dwelling. At first appearance, first public commensality, and first climb up and down the house ladder, the classificatory mother's brother helps the firstborn make the transition. The ornaments mark these early nodes in the development of jural linkages between firstborn and community. He is not further ritually differentiated until puberty, when several rites may honor him.

Male initiation in Murik used to be mounted in three phrases, coordinated with two rituals for women. These were extremely significant events at which headmen exhibited their insignia (see Lipset 1984). Two of the phases are more or less defunct today (see Roscoe and Scaglion in this volume). For the descent-group phase of initiation, called the "loincloth feast" (*nimbero gar*), the classificatory mother's brother continues to give valuables and services to his firstborn sister's son in exchange for celebration and pig feasting from the child's sponsor. Male initiation costs one pig per initiate.[7] The firstborn, who has been subjected to the earlier displays of single insignia, is now bedecked in the complete suman outfit of all the sponsors—loincloth, vest of shells, dogs'-tooth necklace, armbands, leglets, headdress plumage, suman basket, and other paraphernalia—by the mother's brother. For example, Michael Somare, the first prime minister of Papua New Guinea, has described the jewelry given him to wear as a firstborn during his initiation in exquisite detail (1975:36–37):

> I was dressed in all the magnificent ornaments of Sana [father's father]. This beautiful decoration is known as *yamdar*. I wore a crown of bird-of-paradise feathers on my head, and on my forehead I wore the *doatakin* band. This was a headband made of human hair. . . . Round my neck was a *tarer*—a band of dogs' teeth. A *numboag* covered my chest. This was *tapa* cloth with large mother of pearl shells. I wore armlets and wristlets covered with dogs' teeth. On my forehead and shoulders were *usiegs*—pairs of pigs' tusks. . . . Perhaps the most spectacular ornament I wore was the *nemberon*—a tapa cloth apron on which a face had been embroidered with cowry shells. . . . My insignia of office were a tall walking stick decorated with bird-of-paradise feathers, *usiegs*, and a painted basket. . . . Two days later I went to Wotam to be decorated by my mother's family. Here I was given the shells and decorations of *mindamot*.

Younger siblings, regardless of birth order, may also be decorated and initiated, but rituals for them are less elaborate and stress their incompleteness and inferiority as jural persons. During the initiation of Bruno, a last-born son, in 1982, three of his senior commensal mother's brothers (uterine mother's brothers, not joking partners), each representing a different descent group, came into the cult house and presented him with named ornaments made of single boar's tusks to wear in the coming weeks as he walked through each of the lake villages where pwong members lived. "You receive only one boar's tusk [*Kuja usieg ave*]," one of them told Bruno with discernible scorn in his voice. "You may not carry the suman basket. You are just a last-born son![*Suman suun ungwende. Mi gwan kaikoro!*]"

Several different matrilateral suman gwan gave Bruno insignia during his initiation, but a single man was his leading sponsor. He had done the work of organizing his ritual development, and Bruno's elder brother had worn his particular suman during the earlier childhood rituals. One of the commensal mother's brothers was the suman gwan in Bruno's case. In Somare's case, in contrast, the decorations represented patrilateral claims, and my impression, based on genealogical data, is that a patrifiliative bias to suman sponsorship has been shifting in this century toward a matrifiliative one. Birth order and gender are in any case rival idioms in Murik that do not seem to generate or sustain an ideology of unilineal descent. Instead, the ritual cycle articulates incumbent-heir relations between generations and among siblings.

The firstborn son is said to be indebted to his leading sponsor and is expected, at some point prior to the latter's death, to begin to worry about how the senior suman gwan had to work to keep him clean of his own feces when he was small and to seek to reciprocate the ritual work done on his behalf. He gives pigs to his suman holder, who gives them to his mother's brother and retires. The suman holder yields rights to the insignia to his heir, who signals his new incumbency by putting a circular boar's-tusk ornament in each of his armbands.

Mounting the succession feast requires a great deal of organization and work. A new outrigger and cult house should be built and consecrated during separate pig exchanges. The succession celebrations, which may go on for several weeks, must then be catered. In addition, the heir should build a dwelling for his suman gwan to live in during his retirement. House-building is itself a politically complex project, given the environment, and the presentation of the house requires further pigs for the mother's brothers.

Whereas on Wogeo succession ritual (*warabra*) is an initiation staged by the father for his heir, selected from among his wives' firstborn sons to bear the boars' tusks of his lineage (Hogbin 1978:153), in Murik succession is both fraternal and filiative and *the heir stages the ritual for the incumbent*. He mounts a pig feast and then "takes his elder brother's place" (*tatan kaban osanget*) (cf. Young 1972:109)—assumes the position of genealogical seniority, with its associated privileges and duties. The end of the suman holder's incumbency is signaled as he sits down on a platform with his younger brother's wife and the two publicly eat betel nuts together (cf. Fortes 1962:59). Affinal avoidances between them are lifted as a result of the succession: the elder brother is no longer a senior person to be avoided.

Potential heirs may take rights to each other's inheritance, but their feast-making priority is limited by gender-phrased considerations and more precisely by genealogical seniority. Although most suman holders are men, rights to suman do not, in ideology or practice, descend according to sex-specific rules. By means of competitive feast-making (*gar*), (1) a younger sibling may take the suman of his eldest sibling, (2) the eldest son or daughter may take the suman of his or her father or father's eldest sibling (if the latter is childless), and (3) the eldest son or daughter may take the suman of his or her mother or mother's brother (as in the example just given). Although patrifiliative succession is solicited through a more elaborate feast (*yagar*) than that which is called for to solicit rights to an elder brother's or mother's brother's suman, sibling succession (*tatagar*) is more frequent than patrifiliative or matrifiliative succession (*pwapwagar*). Cross-cousin sibling groups are held to be equal rivals for suman rights. In each case, the arbiter is the achievement of the pig feast, which petitions the insignia holder or his stand-in or replacement to pass on the rights to them. A strong sister or firstborn daughter, if she has the support of a hardworking husband and her younger brothers, may mount a succession feast for her suman. Men, that is, may work for women's statuses and prestige. A younger brother, for example, may solicit the suman of his father in the name of his firstborn sister to prevent them from falling into the hands of a rival sibling group.

In 1981, Pita Kanari, an adopted last-born son in his fifties, mounted the tributary feast for

Pa'een, his elder sister, in order to take her title to the suman insignia (see fig. 2). Kanari honored Pa'een, although she was not his eldest sibling, because Wanunge, the firstborn brother, had spent most of his adult life working for the Catholic missions in Wewak and Marienberg; Pa'een had replaced him by mounting the succession feast for their father. Kanari had bought two pigs from Wogeo Island trading partners, one for Pa'een, who had legitimate claim to the suman, and the other for Wanunge, who had lost his birthright. Kanari gave pigs to both siblings, he told me, in order to protect himself against criticism by the pwong that his claim to the suman was incomplete because he had not succeeded his "true elder brother" (*nago tatan*).

Two days after Pa'een had paraded through the village in full Sait regalia for a final time, the ornaments were disassembled in her house, her younger brother's house having recently been devastated by a storm. About thirty senior men and women of the dispersed pwong, local residents as well as those visiting from other Murik villages, gathered to retrieve the boars' tusks and bird-of-paradise plumage they had brought to adorn a walking stick studded with a dozen pairs of tusks and their ornaments. Kanari had a meal for the descent group with rum and a little sweet liqueur. The guests of honor were the senior suman gwan, visiting from two eastern Murik villages, who received the liver of the pig.

Ginau, the senior man from Darapap, stood up

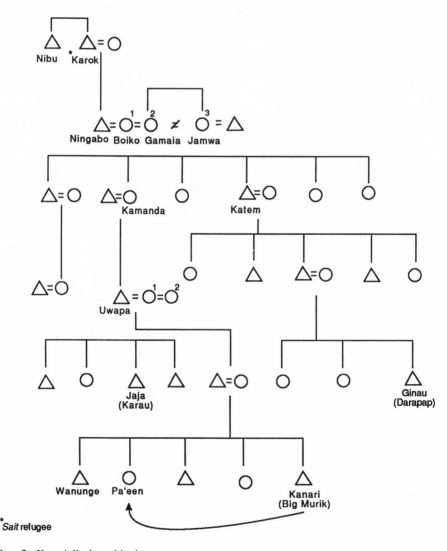

FIG. 2. Kanari displaces his sister.

and praised the events of the past weeks for having gone on without incident and for having raised the name of their pwong above those of others. He then discussed the movements of Nibu and Karok, brothers who had migrated to the Murik Lakes some five or six generations ago. Their grandchildren had settled in different Murik villages. Kanari was the great-grandson of Kamanda, Karok's son's daughter. Ginau admitted to being the grandson of Katem, Kamanda's younger brother. Kanari's claim to the Sait suman in Big Murik was just, Ginau concluded, and then sat down to his plate of liver.

While the suman were being dismantled, much chatter went on about who had brought which boars' tusks. Jaja, the other senior Sait suman gwan present, from Karau, explained to me that the purpose of Ginau's speech had been to make Kanari feel free to decorate children of the pwong or do whatever ritual work he wanted because he had fulfilled his obligations and become a legitimate suman holder. Another implicit point of the speech was that the new suman gwan should not be afraid of sorcery, having no further ritual debts to repay. Insignia holders believe that rivals within the descent group will kill a feast maker who is seen as overstepping his genealogical prerogatives. The careers of such leaders, it is believed, typically end in unexpected death because of sorcery attack rather than succession feast.

In addition to presenting suman to youth during life-cycle feasts, Murik elders also have the right to exchange suman for major gifts of pigs, etc., from intertribal trading partners. From the perspective of dispersed pwong elders, such transactions amount to the initiation of the trading partner into the donor's sibling group and should be subject to their consent. In 1982, Kaango and Daninko, young grandparents, attempted to give a suman basket to a trading partner outside the Murik Lakes area to whom, it was rumored, they owed a great debt for sago. Both husband and wife had attenuated claims to the suman basket they wanted to give (see fig. 3). They were both last-born. As Daninko had woven the basket herself, nothing was said publicly, but gossip went around the villages of Karau and Darapap that the couple were challenging the seniority of their elder siblings. Younger women thought that the basket was merely being made for tourists. More senior women, who held rights to the basket, were particularly agitated and unanimous that what the two were doing was very dangerous. After several months of gossip, Kaango stood up before an audience of a hundred men gathered in the cult

house to conclude another feast, which also had to do with suman display. Demanding an explanation of the rumors that what he and Daninko were doing with the basket was wrong, he vigorously denied any wrongdoing. He insisted that he knew what was necessary to compensate such an exchange: a pig feast for the senior suman gwan in the descent group.

A bony old man who was one of Kaango's mother's brothers did not feel it necessary to rise to his feet to respond. Muttering of his fear that Kaango might mishandle the suman, he worried that the younger man might die (as a result of sorcery). Kaango interrupted: "Why didn't you, my mother's brother, say something directly to my face? Nobody said one word to me!"

A younger brother of Kaango's [adopted] father then leapt to his feet. He said that he had also felt unable to speak publicly about this suman. It was true that, when his older brother had died, he had married Kaango's mother. However, her children, Kaango and the others, were already adults at the time of the second marriage. "You are not my true son," he concluded. "What could I say to you about such a thing?"

A third man said that his father also had a claim to the Sait suman but he himself had not been decorated with it during initiation. His father had been too fearful of the dangers of his holding rights to this particular suman. The problem, the third man went on, was this: none of the senior suman gwan holding the Sait insignia were in the village to direct proper management of the basket. Kaango's elder brother Kem, who had the right to exchange their suman because he had already decorated [succeeded] their father, was visiting a son in town.

An interminable silence enveloped the hall as men studied their cigarettes and feet uncomfortably. A man of Kaango's own age eventually pointed out that he had not yet decorated his elder brother. Both he and his wife were still last-born siblings, too junior to give suman. And another, slightly younger man added that neither had a second pig feast been given so that the elders in the pwong could sit down and discuss the genealogical right of the trading partner to hold the basket. Senior men began to discuss stories about fatalities that they related to sorcery arising from disputed insignia. Among these deaths was that of Kaango's father (genitor).

Kaango went on complaining that he should have been confronted directly rather than through gossip. Although he had already shown the basket to his trading partner, he swore, as he resumed his

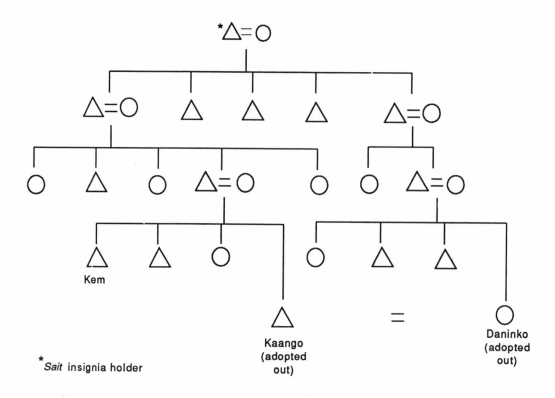

Kem

Sait insignia holder

Kaango
(adopted
out)

=

Daninko
(adopted
out)

Fig. 3. A suman basket for a trading partner. Starred male at top is the Sait suman holder.

seat, that he had since returned it to his house, where it awaited word from the pwong elders.

The absence of Kaango's elder brother and the other suman gwan had created a temporarily empty office in the pwong, and Kaango did not hold rights to it. During the meeting, he tried to gloss over this point by arguing that trading the basket only necessitated getting a pig to feed the descent-group elders so that they might sit down and assess the genealogical credentials of his trading partner. The response of the elders present was to warn Kaango with stories of suman-related sorcery deaths: suman are private, dangerous treasures which do not concern outsiders. The most direct criticism was leveled by an elder sister of Kaango's living in a neighboring village, but she too did not directly confront either him or his wife.

Though the suman gwan becomes a focus of the descent group by organizing expressions of its identity during feasts, this integration is conceptualized as quite frail. Although they stand for peace, the suman are said to be "hot." Suspicion about suman-related sorcery thefts is heightened and sexual jealousies are intensified during feasts

when they are on display. Attending the major adult rites are kin otherwise separated, young and old, male and female. In the days before the dancing "comes down," rumors of trysts and confrontations between jealous rivals are rife. The feast itself is seldom completed without some conflict between sexual rivals. In stories we collected from informants about rituals they had attended, as well as in rituals we observed, more often than not events collapsed into violence. The values of Murik society—generosity, nurturance, celebration, and kinship amity—that are invoked during the display of suman insignia have as their immediate purpose checking the potential for violence that permeates the occasion.

A notion of law and compensation is associated with the suman. The suman gwan are supposed to be men of peace. Should they get into a fistfight, or should their insignia be on display during the outbreak of physical conflict, the suman are said to be "broken" until the antagonists restore their unity by exchanging pig feasts. Until the exchanges are made, the suman are not to be displayed for the firstborn, the dead, new outriggers, etc. The tendency among suman gwan is thus to try to protect their insignia and the continuation of their own careers by getting them in and out of the limelight as quickly as possible. The unity of the suman is not threatened by conflict once they have been returned to their baskets, and compensation for domestic conflict does not call for pigs. The suman gwan will hurry to disassemble his insignia after his feast has ended. The protocol of disassembly calls, as I have suggested above, for convening the senior sibling group in the dwelling of its firstborn member for a meal before putting the suman away.

Following the succession feast, funerary rites and the subsequent end-of-mourning rite (*arabopera gar*) are the last major rites of passage at which suman are displayed. When a person dies, the suman holders, representing the composite identity of the deceased bring their insignia in baskets to the house of the deceased and hang them from the ceiling while mourners keen. The spirit of the deceased pwong son or daughter, it is believed, needs to take one of his insignia baskets with him to one of the spirit places (*pot kaban*) of the descent group in order to be recognized and accepted there.[8]

Following the burial of a suman holder and disassembly of his suman, the three eastern Murik villages fall into a brief period of ritual antagonism between the sexes (*naganaga sarii*). Women and men fight and wrestle with each other. Cross-sex affines (e.g., younger sisters and elder sisters' husbands, younger brothers and elder brothers' wives), who otherwise engage in obscene joking relations, chase each other around the village. Only half playfully, men and women search each other out, carrying behind their backs coconut shells filled with a concoction of animal feces, wet ashes, or mud. The goal is to stuff some of the mixture into their alters' mouths. The fighting goes on until every adult man and woman in the village has been pulled down into the mud and fed the concoction. A number of otherwise celebrated values are reversed in the course of this interlude; here I shall only point out that on the death and loss of a suman holder, who has embodied peace and nuturance throughout his life, society suddenly divides according to sex and takes an antagonistic turn: nurture becomes excremental.

The suman appear one further time in life-cycle ritual. Following the end-of-mourning feast, the closest kin of the deceased resume active involvement in everyday affairs. They wash in the sea and then resume normal life. Pigs and celebration compensate the mothers' brothers of the deceased for services rendered during mourning and burial. The suman baskets of the deceased are hung on a post in the midst of the dancers, who encircle them from dusk to dawn. At dawn, in some cases, the suman baskets of the deceased are burned. Today, the end-of-mourning feast is often combined with suman succession: rights of office go to the heir who purchases the pig to compensate the mother's brother of the deceased.

Conclusion

The Murik suman gwan is an importer-exporter, an organizer of pig feasts expected to be constantly at work preparing them. Pig mandibles, a standing count of the number of major feasts he has mounted, dangle from his porch. His hospitality extends to everyday life, where he is expected to "have plates" (*baka' eenaro*) for his children and younger siblings or for visiting guests, be they trading or feasting partners. The basket of the eldest brother, it is held, is always open to the hand of the younger brother. It is therefore important that a suman gwan's female relatives, who prepare the plates, be industrious, skilled fishwives and quick basket weavers. If the suman gwan is a canoe, goes the Murik saying, his wife is his outrigger, protecting him from eating polluted food (prepared by sexually active young women) or from the theft of food scraps for purposes of sorcery by rival suman gwan.

While the younger brother is permitted to take from the elder brother's basket, he is expected to *carry* that basket on ritual occasions. In his inferior and dependent role, the younger brother is expected to seek out his suman gwan and volunteer his labor unrequested so as not to dishonor him with having openly to request something from a junior person. The influence of the insignia holder is indirect and is based on maintaining fraternal dependence through sentiment created by generosity with food rather than through confrontation or force. Somare speaks clearly of the power of food (1975:23):

> When people come to fight us, we call them to eat first. We sit down together. We talk. We eat. Then we say to them: "All right, if you want to fight, take your spears and stand over there. We also will take our weapons, and will stand on this side." But we believe that after eating, their minds will be changed. They will not want to fight us any more.

The suman gwan must also keep trading partners indebted, which means that he must be generous to them, hospitable to a fault when they visit and ready to give them anything they want. "They can come all at once and try to attack me [with their requests]," swore one of our senior male informants about such visits. "But I always win. I give them everything. No debt can stay with me. I always pay back every one." Together with domestic and ritual acts of nurturance to junior siblings and trading partners, the suman gwan must excel in the many minor feasting rivalries in order to maintain the indebtedness and inferior dependence of his classificatory mother's brothers, whom he is expected to feed when they are visiting from other villages by "killing" (*topre*) them with small "spears" (*ningeg*), gifts of fruit or tobacco, when they are ready to go home. In addition to affording the small pleasure of making them suffer these indignities, this gift-giving ensures that the recipients/victims will perform ritual services at appropriate times.

The first ritual duty of the suman gwan is to mount the succession feast, assume the status of his elder brother or parent, and then begin to decorate (mount life-cycle rites for) children. He gains status and then maintains it, in other words, through generosity with feasts and ornaments that have the effect of reproducing status. The ultimate act in a career of feeding, giving, nurturance, and social regeneration is to be ready, when his younger brother requests permission to mount the succession rite that will retire him, to give in to that as well. Thus the figure cut by the suman gwan is one of politicized generosity. In rivalry to mount ritual feasts within his community, he wins. His generosity reproduces jural children for his descent group and not others.

Hierarchy in Murik, then, is phrased in cultural idioms that are maternal: dominance nurtures while subordination consumes. The design and tactics of power draw for their model not upon male-male relationships—warfare or father and son—but upon a feminine one, mother and child. As I see it, in order to legitimate himself, the suman gwan must continually give feasts and yield to the requests of juniors and guests. He becomes like a mother to them so that when labor is required for some larger project, they will come to him out of a sense of indebtedness and dependence and volunteer their services. His influence consists not in direct force but in kinship sentiment and control over property that he manipulates generously in order to sustain these affective attachments. Incumbent-heir relations strive to

fulfill the same tasks as mother-child ones, nurture and reproduction, in order to maintain the same type of filial dependency. Leadership and authority, although a predominantly male domain, have distinctly feminine overtones in Murik culture. During major dance performances, notably, when dancers wear suman, both men and women wear skirts. But the virtues of motherhood—abundant nurture and peace—elude political leaders just as they do Murik mothers. The sexuality of women and the insignia themselves subvert the noble causes of political leadership, unity and exchange, by stimulating rivalry and sorcery attacks.

Modjeska (1982) argues that the degree of rationality in political relationships among groups—e.g., in marriage and conflict mediation—in highland New Guinea may be indexed to the level of pig production. Social complexity is therefore constrained by wealth, poverty, and the organization of pig production. Since pig husbandry is largely women's work, the integration and industry of a leader's domestic group largely determines how powerful or influential he may be. On the Sepik River and Murik coast the situation appears to be rather different. Here political leadership depends not on pigs directly but on intertribal exchange, and symbols of pigs—the tusks—may be exhibited and themselves exchanged. The Murik prestige system, in which the suman are assigned the highest social value, is based on age differentiation and exchange rather than sex differentiation and pig production. Preeminence is won by denying one's rivals prestige, defined in terms of generosity with insignia rather than in terms of pigs and the exclusive superiority of men. While the Modjeska thesis seems to be a major contribution to the study of political systems in much of Melanesia, it does not explain why authority is construed hierarchically in Murik, nor does it explain the specific form these hierarchical relationships take. As pigs pervade Duna politics, women, both real and metaphorical, pervade Murik.

Collier and Rosaldo (1981), examining marriage exchange among hunter-gatherers, have discussed societies in which services and features of women are of key import in local-level politics. In tribal societies in which goods carry rights to marital privileges, they argue, young people depend on their elders for the resources with which to marry. Affinal politics are construed in terms of debt and payment, and women are the object of profound male ambivalence. Women's labor, values, and personhood are deprecated while reproduction is cosmologically and ritually stressed. Women, as mothers, are lauded by men, although their "blood" is metaphorically rejected as polluting and dangerous to masculinity. By contrast, in hunting-and-gathering societies in which the groom gives his labor in order to claim marital privileges, sexuality, rather than debt and goods, provides the main terms of political life. Politics center on men's rival claims to wives rather than on elders' claims over juniors, and there are no prestige systems independent of marriage. Men are reluctant to assert power directly. Lacking the means to enforce compliance, leaders depend on generosity and altruism. Politics are intimate: a wife's adultery is a direct challenge to a man's personhood because his status depends on his access to her. There is "a recurrent association between sexuality and violence both in the relations of men and women and in competition among men" (Collier and Rosaldo 1981:292). Marriage is achieved gradually through donation of services to the bride's family ensured by an appreciation of women's everyday services. But other than between affines, there is little inequality between men. Contests in which equality goes to the victor prevail. The exchange of identical entities, as in sister exchange, is central. "Political processes . . . lack 'big men' and settle disputes through contests rather than moots" (Collier and Rosaldo 1981:323n).

Murik is clearly such a society; fishing is a muted surrogate for male hunting, and marital privileges are acquired through bride service. Claims made in terms of sexuality are certainly a key idiom for social relations in Murik, establishing marriage rights and causing conflict. Authority is indirect, exerted through nurture. The point of the prestige system, however, is neither marriage nor equality. The suman holders do not allocate rights in women; they compete to reproduce social personhood through acts of ritual nurture (exchange) and the deployment of suman. Reproduction and exchange/nurture are most clearly embodied in the cultural figure of woman-the-mother in Murik (see Barlow 1985b). Analytically, then, the prototype of authority in hierarchical relationships is the mother-child dyad as it is construed here.

Notes

1. Seventeen months of field research in the Murik Lakes were carried out with Kathleen Barlow in 1981–82. The study was supported financially by the Wenner-Gren Foundation, the Kenneth Hill Fellowship for Pacific Studies, the Office of Graduate Studies of the University of California, San Diego, and Sigma Xi. The work was conducted in Tok Pisin. Quotations appearing in the text were translated from the Murik vernacular with help from informants.

2. Two different phyla of non-Austronesian New Guinea languages are spoken by mainland peoples. In enclaves along the coast and on the offshore islands, Austronesian is spoken. The Murik themselves speak a non-Austronesian Sepik River language (Laycock 1973), while to the inland side of the lakes Murik sago suppliers speak a non-Austronesian language which is related to Mead's (1938) Mountain Arapesh and Tuzin's (1976) Ilahita Arapesh rather than to river languages.

3. Actually, in 1981–82, only one of the five villages did in fact stand on the beach, the others having been rebuilt on the lakefront after storms had destroyed them.

4. In addition to the representations of centralized authority, nonunilineal descent and primogeniture, which differentiate ritual politics around the mouth of the Sepik from those among Middle Sepik peoples described by Bateson (1958 [1936]:6–10), exchanges made by mothers' brothers for first achievements of sisters' sons are reversed. There the mother's brother gives food and receives ornaments.

5. Barlow points out that Murik mothers do not permit the child to crawl before he walks, which means that the achievement of climbing up and down the house ladder is also a very important moment for the mother, who may resume a life more independent of her house.

6. Inherited ritual debt also determines the right of a suman gwan to mount these initial rites.

7. But one pig suffices to pay for the services of patrikin for several generations of female novices.

8. The winds of the dead (pre was) may also blow during the last days of a final illness, sometimes reversing direction without warning. The winds are said to be the breath of the person's ancestor spirits contesting claims to the new ghost (nabran). They blow from the various directions in which the deceased's ancestors lived. The wind blowing at the moment of death, whether onshore from the islands, from the southeast, or from elsewhere, indicates which of the ancestors has won the new spirit.

25/ The *Tambaran* of the *Tanepoa*: Traditional and Modern Forms of Leadership on Manam Island

Nancy Lutkehaus

Like many Sepik societies, the Manam have secret flutes (Manam *embeki*, Tok Pisin *tambaran*), kept hidden from women and children, that are associated with male power and authority (see Bateson 1958 [1936] and Tuzin 1980, among others). Manam differs from most other Sepik societies, however, in that political authority is vested in hereditary village leaders called *tanepoa labalaba*. The discussion that follows describes the relationship between this form of leadership and the tambaran flutes and analyzes some of the Manam responses to colonial and mission intervention that contributed to the perpetuation and the contemporary transformation of both tanepoa and their tambaran.

Manam is the easternmost of the Schouten Islands, the archipelago of small volcanic islands inhabited by Austronesian-speaking peoples that extends along the coast of the East Sepik Province from slightly northwest of Wewak to just east of the mouth of the Sepik River. Although the Manam have traditionally been linked socially, culturally, and economically with various groups along the Sepik coast and the lower reaches of the Sepik and Ramu Rivers (Barlow 1985a, Lipset 1985, Lutkehaus 1985, Tiesler 1969–70), politically they belong to Madang Province. The administrative association of Manam with the Madang region began in 1898 with the arrival of the German Neu Guinea Kompagnie at Monumbo on the mainland across from Manam. However, in her description of the Sepik as a culture area, Mead (1938:157) includes Manam along with the other Schouten Islands. Among the "traits" (Mead's choice of term) she describes for the area are special men's houses (*haus tambaran*), ceremonial masks (*tumbuan*), and a variety of objects considered to have supernatural powers (*tambaran*), prominent among them bamboo flutes (p. 172).[1] All three are found on Manam.

Several of the articles in this volume discuss the nature of the political, economic, and social changes that have occurred over varying periods of time in different Sepik societies (see, for example, Dye, Peter, Schindlbeck, and Smith) and call for more detailed studies of the responses of different groups of New Guineans to colonial and mission intervention (Allen, R. J. May). Other contributions discuss aspects of the relationship between indigenous forms of village leadership and social organization and traditional means for the legitimation of authority (Lipset, Stanek). Because Manam is culturally similar to yet structurally different from the politically egalitarian societies characteristic of the Sepik region, its traditional form of political organization and its unique adaptation of the tambaran flutes—a key cultural symbol throughout most of the Sepik area—are of particular interest.

There are two named social groups in Manam society, the aristocracy (called *tanepoa*), from which the hereditary village leader (also called the *tanepoa* or, more precisely, the *tanepoa labalaba*, "the big *tanepoa*") comes, and the commoners (*gadagada*). Membership in these two groups is based on birth. When the British anthropologist Camilla Wedgwood worked on Manam in 1933, people told her that since the advent of Europeans in New Guinea the power of the tanepoa had been greatly reduced. Previously, tanepoa had controlled both warfare and sorcery (Wedgwood 1934:383–84):

> In Manam the village *tanepwa* was not only the pivot around which all social and economic activities revolved, but he also had, it seems, a part to play in preserving law and order, for I was told that he used to have the power of life and death over his fellow villagers, had the right to arrange or forbid marriage, and sufficient authority to settle disputes within the village and to lead his people to war.

Although sorcery still existed in 1933, the colonial administration and the Catholic mission had effectively put an end to warfare some years before Wedgwood's arrival on Manam. There was competition for local authority between the traditional tanepoa labalaba and the government representatives in the village, the *luluai* (Tok Pisin), and Wedgwood was surprised that the tanepoa labalaba still maintained as much power and prestige within the village as he did (p. 384). The tambaran flutes, Wedgwood noted, were closely associated with the tanepoa (p. 400):

> If anyone of these suffers any misfortune, "the *mbei' i [embeki]* come," and for a night the men blow them and beat slit gongs and sing *mbe' i* songs. The *mbe' i* are also blown when any event of importance, such as birth or initiation, occurs in the life of a man or woman of *tanepwa* rank, and on the death of such a one "the *mbe' i* bury him or her."

Since women and children were forbidden to see the tambaran, Wedgwood never actually saw the flutes perform herself. Although she recognized the danger in generalizing, she expressed the opinion that "strong religious feeling is alien to the Manam and is not recognized in their culture" (p. 188). Thus, even though she rightly perceived that the tambaran formed part of a set of activities that was primarily associated with the institution of rank in Manam, she considered these activities of relatively little significance (1937:188):

> If, as seems possible, it dies out as a result of missionary interference, there is a danger probably of the authority and status of the *tanepwa* being damaged yet further; but I doubt whether the loss of the sacred flutes will have the same devastating effect upon the society as would the loss of a vital religious cult.

With the benefit of hindsight,[2] I believe that Wedgwood misperceived the significance of the tambaran and consequently underestimated their persistence as well as the resiliency of the leadership of the tanepoa in Manam society. Although their role within Manam society has changed considerably since Wedgwood's time, tanepoa today are not merely figureheads or satraps; they continue to play a dominant role in the leadership of their villages. Despite the presence of local government councillors, tanepoa still usually control the outcome of village disputes. They are the major force in the organization of public events and the primary initiators and organizers of various economic and exchange activities.

The transformation of the tanepoa and their relationship to the tambaran has been a gradual process of secularization accompanied by a decrease in their power over their villagers. Both the church—the German Catholic missionaries of the Society of the Divine Word—and the state have been influential in this transformation. Paradoxically, these same institutions have also contributed to the perpetuation of the tanepoa as leaders on Manam. The result is that although the power of the tanepoa has declined, there is greater economic inequity between the tanepoa and the gadagada than in the past. The same forces that have helped to perpetuate the leadership of the tanepoa have fostered the development of this form of social inequality.

The discussion that follows presents a necessarily cursory overview of the contradictory and complex relationship between the influence exerted by the church and the state and the responses to them by the Manam in the past and at present. As a result of this discussion, it should become clear why neither the tanepoa nor the tambaran have completely disappeared from Manam (as they have in some neighboring cultures, such as Wogeo [Hogbin 1978] and Karkar [McSwain 1977]).

The Traditional Tanepoa System

By "the traditional tanepoa system" I mean the political organization and supporting ideology that existed in Manam during the early 1930s, when Wedgwood and the missionary Böhm (1983 [1975]) recorded ethnographic data about Manam culture. In that system, aristocratic rank was above all a matter of birth. Whereas one could (if a woman) become a member of the Manam elite through marriage or could enter it through adoption (a possibility for both males and females), the status thus achieved did not have the same prestige associated with it as tanepoa rank acquired by birth. Theoretically, succession to the position of tanepoa labalaba was by primogeniture. When this ideal could not be realized, various compromises came into play (Lutkehaus 1985a).

The authority of a tanepoa labalaba was based on a combination of factors both sacred and profane. Foremost was the irreducible fact of birth. Prestige was inherent in the position of tanepoa labalaba and automatically accrued to his offspring as well. Tanepoa were believed to have inherited special *marou* (Tok Pisin *powa*, "power") from their ancestors. Marou is essentially a form of *mana*, the type of supernatural power found in many Oceanic cultures (Codrington 1891, Goldman 1970), and has both benign and malign aspects. Its benign form was manifested in a tanepoa's ability to produce abundant taro in his gardens, to protect his village against illness and strife, to promote his village's reputation through the organization of large and munificent pig-exchange celebrations (*buleka*), and to ensure his lineage's superiority through success in amassing large numbers of dogs' teeth (*giri*) and boar's-tusk valuables (*zongo*) from mainland trading partners (Lutkehaus 1985). The dark side of marou was its association with malign powers of *naboa* sorcery (Tok Pisin *sangguma*) that tanepoa were believed to control. A tanepoa was not necessarily considered to practice sorcery himself but had the authority to command others to perform it for him.

There was no form of regular tribute to tanepoa. A tanepoa's ability to amass large quantities of food for intervillage exchanges rested on his local reputation and was determined by a combination of factors, including his generosity toward his own villagers and the fear he instilled in them because of their belief in his control over sorcery and other forms of clandestine physical violence. A final element was a tanepoa's own personality. Thus, to the extent that his success as a leader was based on personal factors, such as a forceful and generous personality, and his ability to organize and engage in numerous exchange activities, the tanepoa was similar to the big man of more egalitarian societies throughout Papua New Guinea.

Traditionally the inherent inequality in social status of commoners and aristocrats in Manam was mediated by a series of complementary exchanges between the groups. These usually took the form of labor provided by the gadagada in exchange for food from the tanepoa and the exchange of zongo, slit-drums, and masks—the insignia and sole prerogative of the tanepoa—for pigs, dogs' teeth, and shell ornaments. The performance of the tambaran flutes in honor of a tanepoa or a member of his family constituted a form of exchange as well, since a tanepoa was expected to reciprocate for the performance with gifts of food.

The tambaran flutes in each village belonged solely to that village's tanepoa labalaba. The actual bamboo flutes were kept in the village's tambaran house, which was also considered to belong to the tanepoa labalaba. The playing of the flutes celebrated important events in the life cycle of the tanepoa labalaba and his family. This "appearance" (the flute players always remained hidden on such occasions) of the tambaran meant something much more profound than simply a heralding of the elite with the sound of trumpets, for the tambaran were considered to be powerful spirits called *nanaranga* (Tok Pisin *masalai*). One of the most important of these was the nanaranga of the tambaran, the embeki. Adults, both male and female, told me that when they were little they had believed that the tambaran was a spirit that took the form of a beautiful bird with a long, flowing tail, the sound of the flutes being its cry as it flew through the air. Even now, when the flutes are first heard in the distance, Manam will say, "The tambaran is flying."

Wedgwood (1937:187) commented that "despite the contact with Europeans and the influence of the missionaries, the flutes are still revered and the women are deeply in awe of them." The men, too, she felt, regarded them as a type of "mystery," in the religious sense of the term. The awe the tambaran flutes inspired in the women must have derived in large part from fear, as they were warned by the men that the tambaran would kill them if they should be so bold, or unfortunate, as to see them.[3]

The embeki was also linked to more general acts of violence against both males and females, as the tanepoa was said to "enlist the help of the tambaran" when he wanted to have sorcery or other covert acts of physical violence performed. Thus the threat, and sometimes the actual evidence, of the tambaran's vengeful nature served as a means of social control wielded by the tanepoa. For example, I was told that under the guise of the tambaran a tanepoa's henchmen had once been sent in the dark of night to chop down betel palms and nut trees belonging to a gadagada family whose child had insulted the tanepoa's child.

Young men first learned the true identity of the embeki—that it was merely the effect of the playing of two long bamboo flutes—during the course of their initiation into adulthood. They also first began to play the flutes themselves while they were in seclusion at this time. An additional source of beliefs that attributed supernatural power to the tambaran was the ideas associated with the practices men had to follow in order to play the flutes. Not every man acquired the ability to play the tambaran, nor could the flutes simply be blown without performing the necessary ritual. In submitting to the ritual taboos (sexual abstinence and the avoidance of certain foods) and performing the correct magic rites, men became ritually pure and thus capable of effecting the transformation of the flutes from mundane bamboo instruments into the magically potent tambaran.

Another aspect of male initiation provided an additional fearful image of power and violence associated with the tambaran. During one stage of initiation, youths were forced to crawl through wickets made from thorny vines and branches, and while they traversed the length of this spiked corridor the men beat them with stinging nettles. This ritual beating was metaphorically referred to as being "eaten by the tambaran."

Thus a series of associations formed through the process of male initiation linked men's playing of the flutes with beliefs in the supernatural power of the tambaran and the political authority of the tanepoa. The fact that the revelation of the mystery of the tambaran and the survival of being "eaten" by this spirit formed a central part of the personal process of male initiation—of turning youths into men—is not insignificant. Adult males were aligned symbolically with control over the power of the tambaran and with the patriarchal authority of the tanepoa.

European Influence on the Tanepoa System

The German Neu Guinea Kompagnie first established a base at Hatzfeldhafen on the north coast east of Manam in 1885,[4] but within five years this base had been abandoned. It was not until 1898, when a plantation was started directly across from Manam at Potsdamhafen (Monumbo), that foreigners (in the form of a European trader and his Chinese assistants) would have been seen with any regularity by the Manam. Manam itself was not brought "under control" by the Germans until 1910, when luluai were first appointed in some of the villages on the island (Sack and Clark 1979:322).

The annual reports of the German colonial administration indicate that they were pleased to find a system of "hereditary chiefs" on Manam, in contrast to the leadership by elders common in the villages immediately surrounding Madang (Sack and Clark 1979:279). The stories the Manam relate about the arrival of the Germans indicate that the tanepoa of Zogari was the first tanepoa on the island to be given "the hat and the stick," the luluai's insignia. He then accompanied the Germans to other villages on Manam to help them appoint additional luluai. Not surprisingly, these men were all tanepoa as well. The position of *tultul* (Tok Pisin), assistant to the lu-

luai, seems to have usually been given to gadagada, thus replicating the hierarchic relationships of traditional Manam society.

Although their direct contact with the Germans was infrequent, the Manam recall being terrified by examples of their destructive power such as the German gunboat that steamed into Hansa Bay and fired on the belligerent Awar people along the coast (Sack and Clark 1979:224). The Germans' wealth (in terms of material goods such as axes, knives, and cloth) also impressed them, and initially the association of the tanepoa with the Germans in their official capacity as luluai must have enhanced their prestige and authority within their own villages. The direct material benefits they received from the Germans were few (they were not paid a regular salary) but valuable. People still recount how their ancestors carefully shared the one precious ax that the Germans had given the Zogari tanepoa in appreciation of his services. Indirectly, what few advantages there were to be gained from the foreigners went to the aristocracy; it was, for example, the sons of the tanepoa who were the first Manam to be sent to Madang to learn Tok Pisin.

By the time Wedgwood was on Manam, the tanepoa had become disillusioned with the position of luluai; they personally gained less and less from it materially, yet were responsible for the onerous task of collecting taxes and enforcing communal labor. When the tanepoa labalaba no longer wanted to be luluai themselves, junior members of the aristocracy began to occupy the position (a similar pattern was repeated later with the office of local government councillor). Wedgwood (1934:384) comments that rivalries sometimes developed between the tanepoa labalaba and the luluai in individual villages, but from people's statements it is apparent that they always considered the tanepoa labalaba to have been the more powerful and legitimate authority in their villages.

Members of the Society of the Divine Word mission arrived at Potsdamhafen soon after the German traders, having been invited there by the Neu Guinea Kompagnie to "subdue" the hostile natives. The missionaries' contact with the Manam during this early period was more direct than that of either the traders or the colonial administration and gradually, as it became more frequent, their effect on Manam culture more pervasive.

Although the first mass was celebrated on Manam in 1917 (Böhm 1983[1975]:214), a permanent mission station was not established until

1925. Like the colonial government, the missionaries found it both familiar and advantageous to work through the tanepoa of each village. This form of hereditary leadership conformed to their own understanding of authority as being vested in a single individual within a hierarchy. When they translated the Bible and prayers into Manam, God became the Tanepoa Biabia ("the Great Tanepoa") and all humans gadagada; in relation to God even the Manam aristocracy became mere commoners. (One wonders how easily or literally the tanepoa accepted this idea.)

In addition to introducing a new set of hierarchical relations, the missionaries tried to alter the Manam's belief in nanaranga. God became the Supreme Spirit, the Nanaranga, replacing all lesser nanaranga. Although there is no supreme spirit, no leader among the many spirits, in traditional Manam theology, the description of God as both tanepoa and nanaranga must not have been inconceivable to the Manam, given their own close association between the tanepoa and the tambaran.

The missionaries strongly opposed a number of Manam practices and beliefs. They attempted to stop infanticide, abortion, polygamy, and male initiation rites. The latter they found offensive not only because of the cruelty of the ritual beating but also because youths were taught to perform penis incision, similar to the form of "male menstruation" Hogbin (1970) says men practiced in Wogeo. The beliefs surrounding the tambaran seemed to them idolatrous, and they attempted to prohibit the playing of the flutes.

Although they did not succeed in eradicating all of these traditional practices and beliefs, the missionaries' campaign against the Manam beliefs in the tambaran flutes and male initiation rites gradually had its effect. When talking about the thirties, older Manam men say that some of them, influenced by the missionaries and their own experiences as contract laborers, refused to learn the esoteric lore of the tambaran and other nanaranga that their fathers wanted to teach them. Other men now express regret that their fathers, fearful of divine punishment in the hereafter, were afraid to teach them the secret names of the nanaranga and the special magic rites associated with them.

In contrast to the situation on Karkar Island to the east, there were never any foreign-owned plantations on Manam, and with the exception of a very small amount of land sold to the mission and government, there is no land permanently alienated from the islanders. Prior to World War

II the Australians did not encourage villagers to produce their own copra, preferring to use the New Guineans as a source of labor on their own plantations than to have them as competitors in the production of the same cash crops. Both the Germans and the Australians were careful, as Fitzpatrick (1980:76–77) points out, to enforce the return of contract laborers to their homes— not out of any concern for the laborers but because in the long run it was in their best interests politically and economically to do so. On the one hand, maintaining the traditional communities ensured them a continuing supply of laborers; on the other hand, it kept "finished-timers" from settling in the towns. New Guineans were also prohibited from engaging as middlemen in the purchase of cash crops, such as copra, or the operation of trade stores (Fitzpatrick 1980:77). This combination of factors helped to preserve the traditional patterns of land tenure and production on Manam, as well as to promote the tanepoa's continued control over the organization of communal exchange activities within and between their villages.

Well into the 1960s, even labor migration tended to follow the pattern of traditional Manam hierarchical social relations. Thus, for example, a son of a tanepoa labalaba would be the leader of a group of gadagada who signed on together to work at a plantation or, later on, in the goldfields and timber factories around Bulolo and Wau. Since as workers tanepoa and gadagada were not differentiated by their employers, each receiving the same wages and terms of agreement in their contracts, this form of wage labor in and of itself did not promote any major changes in economic status between tanepoa and gadagada once they returned to Manam.

However, as Wedgwood (1934:384) observed, their experiences away from Manam did alter the attitude of some of the young gadagada men toward the tanepoa's authority. Men who had seen a bit of the world and had had contact with Europeans, as well as with New Guineans from elsewhere, were reluctant to adhere to the various ritual taboos and practices forced upon them by their elders, such as those relating to the performance of the tambaran. They had begun to question the necessity and the validity of these traditions. The doubts about these beliefs first raised by the missionaries were reinforced by their wider knowledge of the world. Fueled by their skepticism, young men began to challenge the authority of their elders and leaders.

During the forty-five years of colonial influence on Manam through World War II, major incursions into the tanepoa's prestige, power, and authority were made by the mission and the colonial administration. The cessation of warfare and the curtailment of sorcery undercut their traditional sources of power, and the presence of a colonial government, however remote from Manam, meant that they were no longer the ultimate authorities within their villages. Eventually, the experiences of young men who had gone away as wage laborers also contributed to the erosion of the respect formerly accorded to the tanepoa by the gadagada. The tanepoa did not, however, become mere "instruments of the state." They gradually withdrew their support of the government, although not opposing it directly, by declining to fill the position of luluai. To the extent that the colonial government was interested in maintaining the traditional village social structure, the tanepoa were able to continue to dominate political, economic, and social affairs internal to their villages and to the island as a whole.

Both gadagada and tanepoa were acutely aware of the loss of autonomy and status symbolized by the decline in the tanepoa's authority. Wedgwood (1934:384) reports of some gadagada men that they seemed "to resent the fact that the white man expects men of *tanepwa* rank to work, as though they were commoners." For these men, the Europeans' disregard for their tanepoa was evidence of their more general disregard for them all and for the values and integrity of their culture.

During this same period there was a gradual "secularization" of the tambaran flutes. While the greatest impetus toward this change came from the missionaries' denunciations of pagan beliefs in evil spirits and the efforts of both the church and the colonial government to curb violence and sorcery, it was augmented by a change in the attitudes of young Manam men, who were beginning to challenge the authority of their elders and to question the necessity of following the traditional practices associated with the tambaran performance.

The Secularization of Authority

The changes in the nature of leadership and authority on Manam since the end of World War II can be best understood in terms of changes in the policy of the Australian government toward the administration of New Guinea from the gradual development of the 1945–59 period through the accelerated development of 1960–75 to independence. Soon after the end of World War II, Australia was induced to change some of the policies encoded in the Native Regulations Act in order to begin to prepare the colony for eventual independence. Sir Paul Hasluck's goal of "gradual development" meant that New Guineans were to begin to learn how to manage their own economy. Reversing prewar policy, agricultural extension officers were sent out to help villagers, who were now encouraged to plant cash crops. Cooperatives were established in rural areas to market these crops, and New Guineans were permitted to be licensed to buy and sell commercial goods (Fitzpatrick 1980:130).

Many Manam men had had experiences during the war, especially in working for American troops, that led them to question the authority and superiority of the Australians. When they returned to Manam, these men were no longer content with the restrictions placed upon them by the Australians that they had accepted before the war. In particular, they wanted to have the opportunity to earn more money in order to have more material goods and to attain social, as well as economic, parity with Europeans. A period of experimentation ensued, and the experiments took two forms: *bisnis* ([Tok Pisin] business) and *kago* (cargo). Commercial ventures included the use of war indemnity payments to set up a scheme to plant and mill rice (which failed miserably), the organization of two cooperatives for the marketing of copra (both of which dissolved because of mismanagement), and the expansion of the planting of coconuts and the production of copra.

During this initial period of experimentation and change two outstanding individuals, one from Manam, the other from the Rai coast east of Madang, became influential leaders among the Manam. The former, Irakau, became a very wealthy and successful entrepreneur, while the latter, Yali, was infamous for the so-called cargo cult activities he inspired throughout the Madang region (Lawrence 1964). In different ways each of these men encouraged the preservation of the tanepoa as leaders on Manam; at the same time, they held antithetical views as to the significance of the tambaran flutes.

Yali's influence on the Manam had its antecedents in the activities of earlier millenarian leaders in the Bogia area, such as Mambu (Burridge 1960). Yali himself came to Manam in the early fifties, during a period of strong antimission sentiment (Fr. Kuhn, personal communication). Belief in supernatural intervention in the provision of material wealth for the living and in the imminence of a "new world" persists in attenuated form today with the participation of some Manam in an organization called the Bodabia Bisnis Grup. In contrast to such recent attempts to fuse business activities and cargo beliefs (Lutkehaus 1981), in the beginning a major effect of people's adherence to Yali's ideology was a renewed appreciation by many older Manam for the traditions of their ancestors. *Lo bilong tumbuna* ([Tok Pisin] the "law" of the ancestors) became the catch phrase of their movement. The ancestors, rather than the nanaranga, came to figure as the more important supernatural beings. The tambaran, while no longer believed to be spirits, were revered as cult objects because of their former importance to the ancestors. Even though men no longer performed many of the rituals associated with the playing of the flutes, the tambaran were still kept secret from women and children, and the youths who were learning to play them, although they were no longer undergoing formal initiation, were still taught off in the bush.

By the mid-sixties the Australian administration had begun to perceive the popular response to Yali's message as a threat not only to the missions but to the government itself. Yali and some of his more vocal followers were arrested for "seditious" behavior,[5] and others began to doubt that the goals of the movement would be achieved in the foreseeable future. Meanwhile, in Baliau village Irakau was establishing his own reputation. Unlike Yali, Irakau was a businessman and a pragmatist. Burridge (1960:236) writes of him as an example of "the new man." In contrast to the charismatic religiopolitical leadership of Yali, Irakau's style was that of the entrepreneur. Between the late 1950s and his death in 1975, Irakau amassed a fortune large enough to make foreign planters envious and to enable him to travel to Australia.[6] Two important factors contributed to his success: the help he received at various stages from Europeans, such as planters, government officers, and the missionaries on Manam, and his status as a tanepoa. Even though he was only a member of a junior lineage of the aristocracy, Irakau was able to use his elite status to help him procure land for a coconut plantation near Baliau and to mobilize labor. Both the mission and the government helped him obtain loans that enabled him to purchase a truck and a boat. He was the only indigenous buyer of copra on Manam (the mission was the only regular alternative). The missionaries were proud of him, and the govern-

ment hailed him as proof that New Guineans could achieve success in Western terms and as an example for others to follow (Burridge 1960).

Soon after he had begun to develop his plantation on Manam in the early fifties, Irakau held a momentous meeting in Baliau attended by leaders from all over the island. At this gathering he declared that the Manam should abandon the "bad" customs of their past—by which he meant fighting and the practice of sorcery—and wholeheartedly embrace the "good" practices of the Europeans—by which he meant planting coconuts and producing copra. To underscore his message and to indicate the importance of a complete break with the past, Irakau declared that the Baliau tambaran would no longer be associated with sorcery and that from then on women would be permitted to see them.

This was a dramatic moment for the Manam. Although it had happened more than twenty-five years before my arrival, when men described it to me they conveyed a sense of wonder at Irakau's boldness that implied the import the event held for them. Not all villages on the island followed suit (at present, more than half still keep the flutes hidden from women and children), but the status of the flutes throughout Manam was irreparably altered. The tambaran were no longer sacred spirits to be feared, and even though they might still be respected, they were known to be only bamboo flutes. The transformation of the tambaran from sacred to mundane was now complete.

Irakau's financial success established him as a leader in two different positions: that of tanepoa and that of councillor. His style of leadership on Manam represented an innovative attempt at synthesizing the old and the new. Even though he was by birth only a junior member of the elite, he became the tanepoa labalaba in Baliau.[7] Like the familiar example of highland entrepreneurs who have used their monetary wealth to expand their involvement in traditional exchange activities, Irakau used much of his money to sponsor buleka. In 1959, after the establishment of the new Yabu Local Government, he was elected council president. Initially other tanepoa were also interested in being elected to serve in the newly created positions of councillors. By the early 1970s, however, most of the older tanepoa had become disillusioned with the work of the council, and indeed, at that point it had accomplished little other than the operation of a boat carrying passengers between Manam and the mainland. Since independence some of the younger tanepoa labalaba have become interested in participating in the local government council again, aware that it gives them access to grants from the provincial government and facilitates obtaining bank loans.

With the exception of a group development project in the one Manam village that is primarily Seventh-Day Adventist, all major Manam commercial ventures are controlled by tanepoa. These include the operation of two workboats that transport copra and passengers between Manam and the coast and the ownership of two trucks that operate on the mainland (there are no roads on Manam). Copra is the only important cash crop that the Manam produce (attempts at introducing cacao and coffee have not been successful). Tanepoa, especially those who also operate the boats and trucks, are the major buyers of copra on the island. (Although there are also missionary-based marketing societies, these are not always as convenient for villagers to get to as are the buyers in their own villages.) Not only have tanepoa used their elite status to enable them to get loans for major capital investments, but they have also used their aristocratic prerogative to acquire land for planting coconuts and have sometimes coopted small businesses, such as trade stores, established by gadagada. Gadagada sometimes operate small trade stores that serve their own hamlets, and youth groups have also organized their own stores, but such stores are not usually successful enterprises. Thus, the few viable commercial ventures operated by Manam are either wholly owned or controlled by tanepoa.

At the same time that the tanepoa have come to dominate and control commercial activities in Manam, they have also maintained their traditional role as leaders within the subsistence economy as organizers of exchange activities. There is a complex interrelationship between the playing of the tambaran flutes from other villages in honor of a tanepoa and the staging of intervillage pig exchanges. When a neighboring tanepoa sends his village's flutes to play for an occasion, such as the celebration of the completion of a new tambaran house, the tanepoa who is the recipient of the honor and his villagers are obliged to reciprocate. The proper form of reciprocity is a large buleka at which the guests, after having performed a special dance, receive gifts of live pigs and baskets of taro and sweet potatoes. The pigs are given to the tanepoa, the vegetables to the gadagada.

When people are asked what tanepoa are expected to do as leaders, their most frequent response is to sponsor buleka. It is the sole prerogative and responsibility of a tanepoa to initiate and coordinate the participation of his villagers in these events. This intimate connection between the playing of the tambaran and collective exchange reinforces the prominent role the tambaran play in the local Manam political economy, for what is at stake at a buleka is the prestige of the tanepoa and by association that of his villagers. Although there have been some changes in the content of the gifts (bags of rice and cartons of beer are now included), the buleka still seems to function much as it did when Wedgwood was on Manam.

At present tanepoa dominate both old and new forms of economic and political activity in Manam. Whereas their role as the organizers of buleka does not result in any material differences in status between them and gadagada (a tanepoa never keeps the pigs he receives at a buleka; he kills them and distributes the meat to the gadagada in his village), this has not been the case with their participation in entrepreneurial activities. Thus, as a result of their monopoly over commercial ventures, there is greater economic disparity between the two groups than in the past.

New Challenges to the Tanepoa's Authority

When I was first on Manam I sometimes heard gadagada complain, guardedly, of the autocratic behavior of some tanepoa. These complaints focused on their refusal to let gadagada develop their own business activities within the villages, the fear of reprisal in the form of sorcery for having more material wealth than a tanepoa, and, in one extreme case, resentment of a tanepoa's demand that villagers supply him with bags of copra (in this case, fear of overt violence led them to refuse to press charges against the tanepoa with the district government).

When I returned to Manam in 1983, I was intrigued to learn that a meeting had recently been held to which all the tanepoa on the island had been invited. The meeting, referred to as the "Kukurai Workshop" (the Tok Pisin term *kukurai* is often used to refer to the tanepoa), had been organized by the *kiap* ([Tok Pisin] government officer) now resident on the island. Since his permanent settlement on Manam (prior to 1982 there had been no resident kiap), the kiap told me, he had continually received complaints from individuals (mostly gadagada) about the misbehavior of certain tanepoa. In particular, the gadagada resented the efforts of the tanepoa to keep them from managing their own commercial activities.

The kiap, who had been surprised to find that the Manam had hereditary leaders, told me that he was impressed with the effectiveness of the tanepoa. He was convinced that the traditional Manam political structure was fundamentally sound and that clearly defined leaders like the tanepoa were necessary to get things going in the villages and to keep people in order. A solution to the problem of the gadagada's complaints, according to him, lay not in doing away with the tanepoa but in getting them to correct their own mistakes. The Kukurai Workshop was his attempt to provide a forum in which the tanepoa, through "self-examination" (as he expressed it), could change themselves. The workshop was seen as a means of "consciousness-raising," the goal being to make the tanepoa more sensitive to their abuse of their position and their need for reform.

The idea for the workshop had not been the kiap's alone. Two others who were major forces behind the event were a young former seminary student and the councillor from his village, who was also the Manam member and Speaker of the Madang Provincial Assembly (significantly, both these men are members of the Manam aristocracy). The workshop had been supported by the Madang Provincial Government's Department of Provincial Affairs and had been videotaped by the Office of Information. Although there had been publicity about the workshop throughout the province and on Manam, not all the tanepoa labalaba on Manam attended the three-day event. Both tanepoa and gadagada, all men, took part.

The event was very formally structured. The participants sat outdoors on benches facing a podium and two blackboards. Introductory speeches were made by the Secretary for Provincial Affairs, the Speaker of the Assembly, and the kiap. Before these obligatory addresses began, the Manam tambaran flutes were played. It was explained to the visiting dignitaries that because the flutes were the privileged possessions of the tanepoa and were played to honor the tanepoa and their endeavors, it was fitting that these accoutrements of their office should appear to mark the commencement of the workshop.

The first part of the workshop was devoted to a presentation by the organizers of an analysis of the past and present structures (this was the term used in Tok Pisin) of the Manam tanepoa system. It was shown that in the past the system had been more diffused and egalitarian than it was at pres-

ent. The past system, in which tanepoa were said to have worked in conjunction with individuals called *bagi lasa* (a term used to refer to the heads of the individual clans in a village), was, the organizers claimed, similar to Papua New Guinea's current system of decentralization and provincial government. They claimed that over the years the tanepoa had begun to ignore the bagi lasa and had become increasingly autocratic in their leadership to the point that some of them were acting like totalitarian, even communist, leaders. The solution to this situation, they said, was for the tanepoa to reinvest the bagi lasa with authority and for the leadership of the villages to become more representative.

Some participants agreed that the bagi lasa should be given a more influential political role, but most men spoke about the changes in their lives brought about by the arrival of Europeans. Their comments included discussion of the role of the *niupela kukurai* (a reference to the combined role of tanepoa and councillor) and the effects of changes brought about by colonialism on the position of the tanepoa.

Gadagada were primarily concerned with their relationships with the tanepoa and their desire to become more involved in their own commercial activities. As gadagada, they said, they had to follow the initiative of their village's tanepoa. If a tanepoa was not supportive of economic development in his village, then the gadagada were prohibited from becoming involved in development projects themselves. A similar complaint was voiced by other gadagada in terms of the dilemma they faced in choosing whether to follow "the bell of the government" (a reference to the gong used by the councillors to summon villagers to council work) or "the slit-drum of the tanepoa." Whose commands, and which mode of work, should they submit to? The tanepoa, on the other hand, often enumerated the various problems they faced as leaders—the insubordination and disrespect shown them by educated young Manam and the conflicting demands of their several wives in promoting their sons' careers. They were also intent on stressing that they too had power as well as the government. The councillors, they felt, ought to remain subordinate to the tanepoa. Thus, while the gadagada were concerned with trying to eliminate the disparities in their relationships with the tanepoa, the tanepoa were concerned with maintaining their traditional authority against the incursions of the state. The nexus between these two sets of relationships is control over participation in entrepreneurial activities. Despite the fact that people distinguish between tanepoa who are councillors and businessmen (usually the younger tanepoa labalaba) and those who have remained more traditional leaders (some of whom, although they are not directly involved in business activities, often have sons or younger brothers who are), both are fearful of losing their position of dominance in their villages. Each type of tanepoa wants to maintain control over who engages in business activities and to what extent.

What was being voiced by the gadagada at the workshop was not the faint beginnings of a political revolution aimed at upending the status quo on Manam but the initial attempts at political reform. Thus, even though by the end of the workshop less had been accomplished than he and the other organizers had hoped for, the kiap said that they had felt encouraged by what had been discussed and had decided to hold a second workshop in the near future.

Conclusion

The Kukurai Workshop signifies a new phase in the ongoing process of reinterpretation and renegotiation of the authority and status of the Manam tanepoa. As the workshop was convened by the government, it is not surprising that not all the tanepoa felt obliged to attend. Remaining aloof was one, albeit passive, means of self-defense. It is also not surprising that it was the more progressive, younger tanepoa—those who are also councillors—who agreed to the idea. This was a wise move on their part toward a more active form of self-defense. It is also understandable why the kiap was eager to organize the event, with the hope that self-examination would generate the necessary changes from within and quell discontent among the gadagada while allowing the tanepoa system, the traditional form of local leadership, to continue. The irony of the situation is that the policies and activities of the government itself, such as its tendency to favor councillors in lending for capital investment, have been the primary cause of the increasing economic disparity protested by the gadagada.

From what Böhm and Wedgwood have written and the information I have gathered from older Manam informants, I am not convinced that in the past (that is, in the 1920s and '30s) the bagi lasa played as important a role in Manam politics as the organizers of the workshop suggested. It may well be that they did so prior to the arrival of the Europeans, especially since rivalry between clans for elite status was probably more fluid than it later became (see Lutkehaus 1985). What is more significant is the way in which those individuals who are interested in reforming the contemporary political situation on Manam have chosen to reinterpret their own past and to present it as a model for a new future. In so doing they have attempted to validate this model by describing it as compatible with the structure and values of the larger national government.

The transformation of the Manam tambaran from sacred to secular objects is not an isolated process among Sepik cultures. Tuzin (1980) has described a somewhat parallel phenomenon with the Ilahita, in which a transformation in their religious beliefs, from a former emphasis on magical to more ethical thinking, is manifest in changes in the beliefs and behavior surrounding their tambaran. For the Manam, the changes in their tambaran symbolize changes in the nature of the power and authority of their tanepoa. That both the tambaran and the tanepoa remain preeminent in Manam culture was demonstrated by the appearance of the tambaran at the opening of the Kukurai Workshop. Long-simmering dissatisfactions within Manam society are today being more explicitly and urgently stated. It remains to be seen for how long, and for whom, the tambaran will sing in the future.

Notes

1. The extent to which the general features Mead lists as characteristic of the Sepik region are useful or valid indicators of "the Sepik" as a culture area distinct from other such areas in Papua New Guinea is an issue that remains to be resolved by Sepik and other Melanesian specialists.

2. I carried out research on Manam Island in 1978–79 and returned there briefly in December 1983, working in the same village as Wedgwood had in the thirties. My initial research was supported by a Fulbright Fellowship (Australian-American Educational Foundation) and Training Fellowship no. 5 F31 MHO 595202 from the U.S. National Institute of Mental Health. During my research I was affiliated with the Research School of Pacific Studies, Australian National University, and the Department of Anthropology, University of Papua New Guinea.

3. Despite the threat of violence, Wedgwood (1937:88) did not feel that the men used the flutes to terrorize women. Neither Wedgwood nor I recorded evidence of any female deaths attributed to the tambaran.

4. The Manam had trading partners in nearby villages, and people today recount stories of their ances-

tors' having gone to visit these mainland friends soon after the Germans arrived, curious to see and learn more about these new people. People still sing songs that commemorate the name of the island near Hatzfeldhafen where the Germans landed before settling on the coast.

5. I do not know the exact sentences given these individuals. One man told me that he was jailed because he possessed a copy of Lawrence's (1964) book *Road Belong Cargo*.

6. More details about Irakau's career are presented in Lutkehaus (1984). According to records kept by the Copra Marketing Board in Port Moresby, between 1962 and 1975 Irakau produced a total of 969 tons of copra, an average of 75 tons per year.

7. After Irakau's death, the position of tanepoa labalaba in Baliau reverted to the rightful heir (Lutkehaus 1984).

26/ The Chief of the Chambri: Social Change and Cultural Permeability among a New Guinea People

Frederick Errington and Deborah Gewertz

In what must be one of the most poignant moments captured on film, a New Guinea woman, experiencing "first contact" in the mountainous interior, implores a native carrier hired by the gold-prospecting Leahy brothers not to leave her for a second time (Anderson and Connoly 1983). She thinks the carrier is her dead son, brought back to the land of the living by the white men, and refuses to loosen her grasp upon him. The carrier, apparently embarrassed by the woman's mistaken interest, smiles sheepishly into the camera.

As humanists, we are likely to be moved by the scene largely because we see the woman's personal tragedy as foreshadowing and symbolizing the general tragedy of her society. We believe that as its members are forced to adapt to, and comply with, Western social, economic, and political institutions, they will eventually realize with disappointment that the Europeans and that which they bring with them are not what they appear to be. In contrast to the New Guinea woman who sees "first contact" as a revivifying release from an existential dilemma, many of us view it as akin to the contraction of a fatal disease.

Significantly, our opinion of the general consequences of "first contact" is rejected by many Papua New Guineans. These men and women, often the children of those first contacted, do not regret the European intrusion. Indeed, they believe that their society has already become healthier and think that it will be even stronger in the future. In this paper we explore their perspective by examining a political innovation as it has developed among the Chambri, a group of fifteen hundred living in the East Sepik Province.[1] We employ data collected over a fifty-year period, first by Reo Fortune and more recently by ourselves, to demonstrate that the Chambri are using their encounter with Europeans to overcome a basic contradiction in their cosmology between the intensity of power and the density of social life.[2]

The Social Context

We first became aware of the emergence of a new political form when, on December 28, 1983, Mathias Yambumbe rose to address the throng crowded into his house to watch him raise a bride-price for the son of his elder brother. In the presence of his own clansmen as well as of his political rivals from other clans, Yambumbe proclaimed to all that he was "chief" (the word used) of the Chambri people; moreover, he continued, he *was* Chambri Island. Significantly, we heard no one dispute his claims, either there or elsewhere. In fact, we heard only praise for him. In the context of a society in which adult males compete with each other for patriclan leadership and in which each clan attempts to maintain its autonomy by emphasizing its particular role in a totemic division of labor (see Gewertz 1977*b, c*), that anyone would make such a claim, much less have that claim acknowledged, and with enthusiasm, was startling. Never before, as far as we knew, had the members of this highly competitive society accepted any single individual as their leader.

That the Chambri were so full of admiration for their new chief that Christmas was additionally surprising to us because they were also in the midst of a grave environmental crisis. Since 1977 Chambri Lake has been choked by *Salvinia molesta*, an aquatic fern indigenous to South America. Brought, the Chambri think, to a Catholic mission station in the area by a European priest, it was accidentally introduced into the Sepik River, perhaps as early as 1971. Because the fern doubles in size approximately every eleven days,[3] it subsequently spread quickly throughout the waterways of the region. In Chambri Lake it eventually formed a mat so dense that fishing as well as travel to and from Chambri Island became exceedingly difficult. Since the Chambri normally subsist upon the fish they catch and upon the sago they buy and import from communities on the other side of Chambri Lake with money raised through the sale of their fish, the presence of the fern threatened their physical survival. In response, by the time of our field trip in 1983, nearly 50 percent of the Chambri had moved to coastal towns in search of wage labor, leaving primarily the old and young behind on Chambri Island. Moreover, the appearance of *Salvinia* had raised the possibility that the Chambri no longer had the totemic power necessary to regulate the most immediate environment, that of their lake.

It was the consequences of this environmental disaster that we intended to study when we planned our field trip. Our prior knowledge of the extent of the social and cultural disruption led us to view *Salvinia* as an appropriate metaphor for the European intrusion: the effects of the fern were exactly the sort of affliction likely to follow European penetration.

However, most Chambri with whom we spoke, both at Chambri Island and in the towns of Wewak and Port Moresby, did not share our pessimism. Although they were upset by the presence of the fern and regarded it as European in origin, they were not demoralized, nor did they lament or resent the European intrusion.[4] Indeed, they were not only excited about their chief but full of questions about us: about the achievements of Western society ("Is it true that the Russians were able to have a dog walk on the moon?" "Have the Americans built a bomb so powerful that it can blow up everything?") and about the new ethnographer, Frederick Errington.

Their interest in Errington was particularly aroused when he told them that he had previously done fieldwork in the Duke of York Islands, close to Rabaul (see Errington 1974*a, b*). As the Chambri expected, he already knew that many of them had worked on plantations in this area, and he agreed with them that the local Tolai were formidable sorcerers. They were surprised, however, that he did not know that the two large rocks which rise prominently above the surface of the Rabaul Harbor are the sisters that the mythic figure Arione left behind there on his travels. Nor did he know that Arione eventually traveled to the land of the Europeans, where he taught them, for instance, how to construct large boats with powerful motors. Gewertz had heard the story of Arione twice before in her early work; this time, we were both told the story some eight times, often by the same narrators.

Eventually we came to understand that the Chambri were not as readily distracted from their environmental plight as we had thought. Further-

more, far from accepting themselves as socially and culturally moribund as the result of the *Salvinia*, they were actively combatting the threat it posed to their life by creating a new social position—that of "chief." They thought a chief would be able to induce us and other emissaries of European culture to apply to Chambri society the power conveyed by Arione. That the Chambri so often recounted the story of Arione to us, we came to conclude, was not only a response to Errington's prior research but an expression of the expectation that we, as Europeans, should use our power on their behalf. As the students of Arione, we would undoubtedly have the power to eradicate the *Salvinia molesta*.

This project, we came to recognize, was in its implications extremely ambitious from the Chambri perspective. Their inability to control the *Salvinia* provided the impetus for a major Chambri effort to overcome the fundamental contradiction inherent in their social experience. Until this period in their history, the Chambri had not been able to see any way to reverse the process by which power is dissipated over time—a process of totemic entropy which arises from the impossibility of both remaining absolutely powerful and living in society. To understand their enterprise and the significance to them of Arione, Europeans, and the chief, we must examine the nature of this process.

The Chambri Concepts of Power, Society, and Entropy

Chambri Island and, to some extent, the world beyond (including the rocks in Rabaul Harbor) are filled with signification: The features of the physical landscape and the kinds of processes which take place there embody the activity and presence of both ancestral spirits and *masalai* (nature spirits). Furthermore, the natural world can be read by the Chambri as revealing the activity of living Chambri who, through their capacity to effect an identification with their ancestors and their masalai, control this world for good or for ill.

As part of Errington's introduction to Chambri Island and Chambri culture, he was shown a number of rocks on the clan land where Tambwi Kwolikumbwi's house stands. Each of these rocks is a particular ancestor of Tambwi Kwolikumbwi and carries the name of that ancestor. Each of these ancestors has, in addition, a variety of other forms and may be embodied in and become, for instance, a tree, a bird, or a crocodile. Moreover, each of these entities is a masalai which may also exist apart from any of these particular forms. During the period while a man is alive—before he dies and becomes an ancestor—he will, through the use of the secret names of his own ancestors, of the rocks, of the trees, of the birds, of the crocodiles, and of the masalai, become himself all or some of these (see Bateson 1958 [1936]).

The merging of an individual into this line of identity through specific ritual actions and through the knowledge and utterance of secret names gives him particular kinds of power (see Harrison 1982b). In its most general form, this power consists of the capacity to attract (to pull) and to repel (to expel). Tambwi Kwolikumbwi, for example, through his capacity to become his ancestors, their masalai, and their forms, is able to pull the big-mouth fish into Chambri Lake; he is also able to pull the west wind which expels the water lilies blocking the fishing channel. Unfortunately, the loss or dispersal of the knowledge of these names and the consequent diminution, dissipation, and misuse of power are virtually inevitable in the normal course of social life.

The Chambri make a great effort to keep these efficacious names secret (see Barth 1975 and Jorgensen n.d. for comparable discussions of secrecy). Most men prefer to retain the power that comes with exclusive knowledge of their names until just before their deaths. Although they do intend eventually to pass these names on—they wish their clans to remain strong after they have died so that they will be invoked as ancestors in the ritual activities of their still-living clansmen—many old men, the Chambri think, frequently miscalculate their strength and so die without transmitting all that they know.

Moreover, those secrets which are conveyed are likely to become so widely known over time as to lose a portion of their power. Even if a father transmits ritual knowledge to only one son, each of the members of a male sibling set is thought eventually to have the same degree of ritual knowledge. Those who did not learn the secret names through direct paternal transmission are likely to hear them uttered during ritual performances or perhaps muttered during sleep. Moreover, names can be stolen by members of unrelated clans. Once the names are known by more than a very few, their efficacy is often weakened as a consequence of rivalry.

Rivalry between those who know the secret names—siblings, members of different lines within a clan, or members of different clans entirely—can result in less effective or otherwise impaired regulation of the world. This rivalry may lead one man to tap the same source of power as another, thereby diluting it, or to interfere with the efforts of another to achieve an effective identification with the line of power. In this latter event, through a process of competitive garbling, the utterance of secret names may be sufficiently disrupted that no one can use the power effectively.

Chambri political theory, therefore, sees a contradiction between the concentration of power and participation in social processes. Moreover, to have power without social action would not strike the Chambri as a viable alternative: power, after all, is a necessary but not a sufficient good, for the names that provide power are useless without the people to implement that power and to provide the context for its exercise. As a consequence, because Chambri actually find themselves living within a society in which males compete with both agnates and others for prestige, labor, wives, and valuables, they are subject to a process of entropy which leaves each generation weaker than the last (see Jorgensen 1985 for a similar discussion of entropy).

Thus, for example, we were told the following story to explain the loss of autonomy of a once powerful patriclan and the death of Wapiyeri, its one-time leader:

> Kalambansui was the first man who held the power of everything. He made power happen. He gave most of his power to Mariwansik. Mariwansik belongs to Wombun village. Later, other men got some of the power. They are Yamko, a big ancestor of Wombun; Japawai of Wombun; Sandar of Indingai; Komario of Indingai; Kimbinmeri, a leader of Kilimbit. All of these men who had some of the power died at the same time that the grandfather of Wapiyeri died. The five sticks Wapiyeri has in his house are what is left of the power these men had.

And, as is implied by the context in which this story was related, the residual power available to Wapiyeri after several generations of transmission proved insufficient to ensure the political autonomy of his clan. All clans are subject to this process of entropy, although some lose more power than others.

The Chambri assumption that power diminishes as it is transmitted to the next generation must have made the arrival of the Europeans, with their impressive degree of power, particularly perplexing. Eventually the Chambri concluded that Europeans had acquired their remarkable capacity to concentrate power from the departed Chambri hero, Arione, who, they often say, taught Europeans everything of importance that they now know. Their myth about him suggests that he had enormous power because he absorbed all of his kin relationships into himself and so dispensed with kinship. Arione, we were explicitly assured, would not have been troubled by *Salvinia molesta* or by anything else, including Europeans.

The story of Arione is as follows:

One day a man and a woman went into their garden to make love. A snake passed by, a female snake who ate the man's sperm and became pregnant. She, Pan, had her baby, a boy named Arione. She slept near him in the garden, winding herself around his feet.

During a storm, the man and the woman, Apan and Yeris, heard the baby crying. He was crying because his mother was cleaning him. They found him, wrapped him in a mat, and took him to their canoe. Pan followed. They put her in their canoe as well, and paddled home to their village.

The couple hung a basket from the ceiling of their house. Arione slept there. Every night his mother, who spent her days in the tall grass, came back to the couple's house, crawled into the basket, and slept near her son, wound around his feet.

One night, Arione woke up and found the snake wound around his feet. He called to the man, who told him to leave the snake alone. On the following day, the man and the woman left their village to go and catch fish. Arione, left at home to cut the grass, came upon Pan and killed her with his bamboo knife.

When the man and the woman returned, they told Arione that he had killed his mother. He held her body to his heart and cried. He decided to keep her with him, so he made a palm-bark basket in which to place her body. He used the basket as a pillow, so that his mother slept with him at night. He did this until her body was just bones and stank. Then he made another palm-bark basket and put her bones inside it. He took this basket with him to the top of the men's house and sat there for some days

without eating. The man and the woman cried for him to come down, but he ignored them. He just sat there.

When he came down, he did so to get an ax and a knife. He took these to the bush, where he cut trees, made bush ropes, and built a ship with a house on its deck. He then returned home, where he met the man and the woman; they begged him to eat, but still he refused. The next day he went again to the bush in order to provision his ship with sago seedlings, earth ovens, and everything. On the third day he tried the ship out. He stood in front of it, and it rocked back and forth. He knew then that it worked.

At his men's house, he hung the basket in which he had placed his mother's bones around his neck. He then went in search of the man and the woman to find out if he were an only child. They told him that he had two grown sisters, both of whom were married to the same man. Arione wanted to see his sisters and asked the man and the woman to send for them. They came, and Arione took his sisters into his men's house. One sister sat on his left and the other sister sat on his right. He showed them the bones of his mother, the snake, and told them that he hadn't eaten for four weeks. He asked them to bring him food, and they did so, bringing him betel nuts, sago, lime, and everything else. He ate what they brought, vomited, but then was all right. "Now I am a man," he said.

His sisters found out that the man and the woman would be going to market the next day but that they planned to return the next afternoon. Arione told his sisters that when the man and the woman returned from the market, he would say goodbye to them. He cut three betel nuts, three ginger leaves, and three coconuts and put them in the net bags of his sisters. He cried: "I must leave you. I don't have sisters. I was born of a snake."

Morning came, and, at the fifth cock's crow, Arione and his sisters conveyed the man and the woman down to the water, where Arione put firewood and the basket in which he kept his mother's bones into his ship. He asked his sisters to leave him, because he was not their brother but the son of a snake. He then sang out these magic words: "Eels, I go now, carrying snake wombs. This is how I was born." These words said, his sisters turned into part of the ship's motor, and the ship began to move with the sound, "tin, tin, tin." Arione then called out more magic words: "Suwarkaman [a patrilineally inherited name]; Pandio [a matrilineally inherited name]; Marikaman [another patrilineally inherited name] . . . " These words said, the man and the woman became the rest of the motor.

The ship went around the world. All the people who now know how to build ships [i.e., Europeans] have learned how to do so from Arione. The people of New Guinea don't know how anymore because Arione left this part of the world. He traveled to Rabaul, where he lost his sisters. They became the two big stones near the port there.[5] That is all.

The Chambri, we believe, were preoccupied with the story of Arione—telling it to us in various contexts and with varying degrees of completeness on eight occasions during the three months we were engaged in fieldwork[6]—because they were using it to make sense of the social and environmental circumstances they were facing. Their acceptance of Mathias Yambumbe as chief, their response to the environmental degradation produced by the European-introduced *Salvinia molesta*, and even their interest in their new ethnographer all accord with what seem to be the lessons of Arione about the process and effects of containing power. Unfortunately, because our interest in the myth of Arione developed after we had left the Sepik, we have not directly verified our analysis of its images with any Chambri. Our explication of their meaning to the Chambri must proceed, therefore, from our general understanding, acquired over the past ten years, of Chambri mythic concerns and associations.

The snake in this myth, we argue, is an image of united relationships: while connoting a phallus for the Chambri[7]—as it does for us—it is also a mother who bears Arione after consuming the sperm spilled by the man making love to his wife in the garden. A "snake womb," as Arione himself describes her, Pan is a man-woman whose bones he carries with him throughout his life. The significance of bones to the Chambri lies in their belief that, whereas the blood and flesh of a child are the contribution of its mother, the bones are the contribution of its father. Bones are built, in the Chambri view, by the father during the many episodes of sexual intercourse necessary for the proper gestation of an infant. Arione, however, not only acquires bones from his mother but carries them in the palm-bark basket that he hangs around his neck and uses as a pillow. This kind of basket is made by Chambri women generally to transport sago, a food which is associated with women and was, moreover, "married" to male fish at barter markets (see Gewertz 1980b). By carrying his mother's bones within this female basket, Arione becomes an inversion of her. As a man-woman whose womb is external to his body, he gestates not the bones of his children but those of his parent, the snake who bore him. It is hard to imagine a more complete compression of images, with one's mother being one's father, one's parent being one's child, and oneself being a child-bearing male.

The image of the ship, although not nearly as complex as that of Pan-Arione, is equally the expression of compressed relationships. Indeed, the ship's source of power—the motor that enables Arione to travel throughout the world—is created from the union of the man, his wife, and their daughters. Its power emerges when Arione collapses the distinction between himself and his kin to create a circumstance of asocial sufficiency. In the first of Arione's magic chants, through reference to his essentially kinless birth from the snake womb he carries, he absorbs his sisters. In the second of his magic chants, by referring to both agnatic and matrilateral relationships in the same utterance, he collapses the distinction between them and between them and himself. No Chambri would merge these relationships in normal circumstances, but in so doing Arione further empowers his ship by absorbing his mother and father. His kin become indistinguishable from himself and are bound to him to form a single, undifferentiated force.

Both the image of Pan-Arione and that of the powerful ship are, thus, of undifferentiated and autonomous strength, comparable in fact to the Chambri descriptions of their founding ancestor, Emosuie Apankay, before he dissipated his powers by endowing his three sons with portions of his repertoire of magical names. Arione, unlike Emosuie Apankay, is able to avoid this process of dissipation—of entropy—by remaining disengaged from those relationships on which Chambri social action depends. The response of the Europeans to Arione was to emulate him: by remaining apart from social action in order to contain their power, they could, for instance, build ships as powerful as his. Of most immediate interest to the Chambri, Europeans have been able in this way to maintain sufficient power to control phenomena such as *Salvinia molesta*.

That the Europeans were both extremely powerful and largely asocial had long intrigued as well as bedeviled the Chambri: for decades, they had been impressed by, and subject to, the superior power of those who refused to accept the constraint of relationships of social obligation. As we will see, the Chambri were willing to acknowledge Mathias Yambumbe as their chief because they thought he would be able to pursue a strategy at this time of crisis that could, for the first time, harness European power for Chambri society.

The Europeans: Fortune and the Kiap

Our earliest evidence of Chambri reactions to Europeans and their power comes from Reo Fortune's 1933 field notes (Fortune n.d.).[8] In these notes Fortune recounts a discussion in which a group of Chambri, awaiting a visit by the kiap, appraised the relative powers of the kiap, of Fortune, and of themselves. Significantly, the Chambri refer to Fortune not only by the Tok Pisin term for a European man, *masta* ("Master" in his notes) but by the name of their own founder, "Emosuie." Fortune's informants also liken him to the kiap. The discussion ends with these statements:

> Moi: "All the time you people talk of the Kiap filling you up into calaboose [jail]. . . . You people must not be afraid of the Kiap. Master here can talk to the Kiap now." . . .
> Tumbunaui: "The Kiap cannot ask you to talk much. A Master stays here. In another place men who pull and copulate with women can be gaoled, but not here. A Master stays here." . . .

It was the Chambri conclusion that the ethnographer and the kiap were evenly matched—that Fortune would be able to prevent the kiap from sending any Chambri to the calaboose. They knew, according to the conversation Fortune records in his notes, that before Fortune's arrival the kiap, learning of recent disturbances, which they enumerate (the rape, Kwolui's fight with his brother, and Kabiwon's assault upon the Aibom), would have placed several of them in his pinnace and taken them to jail. But now the Chambri had a white man of their own—a masta had come to them (as Mead's [n.d.] field notes tell us) in a motorboat of his own.

The boats used by the kiap and by Fortune are important because they help us to understand how Fortune's informants came to view the powers of these men. That Europeans like Fortune and the kiap had been able to travel to New Guinea was evidence that they must have learned about the empowering of ships from Arione. Presumably, they were powerful in this and in other ways for the same reason as their mentor: they had not entered into a complex of social relationships.[9] White men such as Fortune, the kiap, and the priests who came later did indeed appear self-contained: usually without children and certainly without an extensive network of agnates, they were apparently able to retain their secret names, their magic powers. Indeed, they were not really comfortable operating within the social world and thus were more akin to ancestral spirits than to living Chambri. Perhaps this is why both Mead and Fortune were asked on several occasions to transmit messages to the dead kin of Chambri (Mead, personal communication).

The Chambri came to accept and, with the story of Arione, explain the European presence and the superiority of their power. However annoying it might be to the Chambri that they could not on their own prevent the kiap from weakening their clans in times of trouble by incarcerating kinsmen, they did until recently find their own totemic power largely sufficient for regulating their lives.

Chambri had now, however, to confront two increasingly obvious indications that their own power had become inadequate. No longer could all natural phenomena in the world—even the world of Chambri Lake—be controlled as part of a single totemic natural system. Concerted and repeated efforts had been made to use totemic powers to control the *Salvinia*: the magic names and attendant ceremonies designed to control the currents, the winds, and the growth and dispersal of aquatic plants had all been employed by the members of the totemically relevant patriclans to little avail (see n. 4 and Gewertz 1983). The most that had been possible was to create a favorable wind that opened up an area near Chambri Island for a few days of fishing. Moreover, no longer could all those who considered themselves Chambri be controlled as part of a single totemic social system: because of the economic disruption caused by *Salvinia*, the Chambri were becoming increasingly dispersed as ever greater numbers left Chambri Island to live in Wewak, Madang, Lae, and Port Moresby.[10] From the Chambri perspective, the wrong sorts of things were both entering and leaving Chambri Lake: the power of Chambri to expel and to pull had become inadequate.

Eventually the Chambri concluded that the *Salvinia* and, by extension, the exodus from Chambri Island must be under European control—Europeans were, after all, responsible for the introduction of the fern. Once they realized that they were no longer cosmologically self-sufficient, even in their own territory, they faced the urgent problem of trying to use European powers for Chambri ends. For some time this had been regarded as a desirable although elusive objective; now it was regarded as an imperative.

It is against this background that their response to our arrival on Chambri Island in late 1983 must be seen. The story of Arione, we came to realize, was not an interruption to or a digression from but a continuation of the topic of *Salvinia*. It suggested a solution to the Chambri of their predicament while, at the same time, serving as a petition that we act as did Fortune, by using our self-contained power on their behalf. Indeed, the account of Arione was frequently followed by a series of direct requests that we immediately put our knowledge and power to work to eradicate the fern. ("Ah, Frederick, you have white man's power; why haven't you helped us yet?")

At the same time, however, Chambri were exploring another alternative. Rather than trying to induce Europeans to help them—rather than relying on the whims of European patronage—Chambri were trying to gain direct control of Europeans and their power. Whereas Arione, Fortune, the kiap, and most other Europeans the Chambri had encountered were powerful, they were also peripheral. Each formed a social autocosm and was rarely willing to use his power for Chambri ends. What the Chambri now sought was a way to encapsulate these autonomous Europeans and their power within Chambri life. They hoped, in this way, to have both concentrated power and society. But to achieve this objective they would first have to accumulate sufficient power of their own to pull the necessary Europeans to them. This was a more ambitious enterprise than they had ever before attempted, and its success depended upon their becoming more powerful than ever before. Thus, they were looking for someone who could embody and concentrate their hitherto dispersed powers. They were looking for a chief.

The Chief

When Mathias Yambumbe proclaimed himself chief, his credentials as a socially significant Chambri were impeccable (see Burridge 1960 and 1969 and Lawrence 1964 for comparable discussions of postcontact Melanesian leaders). He had just assembled the largest bride-price in Chambri memory, a sum of almost K2,200 (approximately, U.S. $2,850). He was in this way proving himself by traditional standards to be the most impressive of any in his clan—more impressive even than his elder brother and others who were his genealogical seniors. Moreover, this achievement was taking place at Christmas, the season for Chambri of greatest political, economic, and social activity, when many Chambri living in the towns return home to visit. Consequently, the achievements of Yambumbe and his clan could be measured directly against the achievements of other big men who were also engaged at this same time in amassing bride-prices. In the context of this competition, Yambumbe was able not only to surpass all others in the amount of money he and his clan could raise but also to contribute conspicuously to the efforts of other big men to raise bride-prices for their agnates. His triumph was all the more apparent in that, despite his help, no bride-price assembled by another approached his own in size. For these occasions of cooperation with other big men, he would choose the most direct kinship link available to him out of the tangle of possibilities created by generations of intermarriage in this endogamous community. Through his judicious use of wealth, he strengthened his connections to most, if not all, segments of Chambri society.

In these respects Yambumbe was behaving as any Chambri big man would like to. When he proclaimed himself chief and Chambri Island itself, he was not, however, simply acting as a very big man might within Chambri society. His claims to transcendence actually rested on the links he had been able to establish as a big man with the external world. It was because of his travels abroad that he could claim the status of chief and be regarded as the embodiment of Chambri Island.

Indeed, after proclaiming that nearly K2,200 had been raised as bride-price and that he was the chief of Chambri, he began recounting his foreign travels. The previous Christmas he had been in Singapore, and next year at this time he would again be in some distant city. He then described at length his trips to Manila, Singapore, Australia, New York, and Rome. From Gewertz he demanded confirmation that he had visited her in New York City (which he had done) and acknowledgment that she had never been to Rome. In

Rome, he said, he had seen St. Peter's Cathedral and many miracles. Rumors that he had used clan money collected for this bride-price on these trips were not true, as all could see by looking at the money now on display.

These themes were familiar to his audience: he had frequently discussed his travels with others and with us. Many had seen the photographs of him posed in foreign places with figures of political, economic, and religious importance; many had noted that he kept his wristwatch running two hours early, not on local time, as he explained, but on Manila time.

Travel per se is regarded as impressive by the Chambri, and the more distant the journey, the more impressive.[11] Many older Chambri, including Yambumbe, have gone to various parts of Papua New Guinea to work. Even though Chambri soon recognized that much of this work was regarded by European employers as menial, their capacity to survive away from home became a source of prestige. Chambri felt weakened when away from their kinsmen and ancestors and, moreover, at a considerable disadvantage when they had to contend with locals such as Tolai who were regarded as potent sorcerers. The response Gewertz encountered in 1975 when she met a Chambri visiting in Port Moresby was, we think, typical of a Chambri on his own. When she asked him how he was liking Port Moresby, he recognized that the town was impressive but admitted that he wanted to go home because no one in Port Moresby knew his names: no one there knew his totemic identity as a person within a particular kinship context who had access to particular magic powers. For Chambri, whose primary personal identity is social, it is difficult to support this identity away from the social context by which it is conferred. Only those individuals who are able clearly to envision and activate their totemic names and powers can sustain themselves as strong individuals away from home for long periods of time, especially when living among potentially hostile aliens.

Thus, many Chambri through their own survival abroad were, and still are, able to prove themselves as men of power, men to be reckoned with on their return home, especially if they also accumulated trade goods or, more recently, money. Yambumbe is happy to talk about his own experiences as a labor migrant and of his subsequent visits to various parts of Papua New Guinea. It is not these domestic travels, however, that he stresses to his audiences, since these may render a man impressive but not singular. Only he

has been able to embody the powers of Chambri necessary to travel to, and to survive in, a truly foreign country.[12] His travels are of particular significance to the Chambri, moreover, because they also suggest that his power can be used on their behalf.

Yambumbe has for several decades served as the Chambri political representative, initially as president of the Gaui local government council, then as a member of the national Parliament, and, most recently, as minister for lands in the East Sepik provincial government. Throughout his career he has been able to convince the Chambri that he is about to pull enterprises to them—coffee plantations, tourist hotels, fishery and timber projects—which will bring them prosperity. Although none of these projects has yet materialized, Chambri maintain their confidence in his capacity to help them: through his international travels as the Chambri representative, Yambumbe continues to demonstrate to himself and an attentive audience not only that he can sustain himself abroad but that he knows and can utilize the pathways that link the different parts of the world, pathways along which the sources of wealth and power can be attracted.

Yambumbe's travels show that for the first time a Chambri other than Arione can pass freely into and through foreign realms. This in turn suggests that Chambri may acquire the knowledge and power to use these pathways for thir own benefit. Europeans have always come and gone as they chose; now, however, Chambri may be able to pull Europeans and their resources to them. Indeed, Yambumbe embodies the possibility of introducing and encapsulating some of these extraordinarily powerful, asocial Europeans within Chambri society. In this way Europeans might be treated as a type of natural power, under the control of particular Chambri.

Yambumbe's first major demonstration that he was able to use the pathways which link cultural worlds came when he traveled to Australia as Gaui council president in 1971. Then he induced Gewertz in 1974 to choose Chambri as her field site. Subsequently, he visited her in New York City, where, in a new three-piece suit, he was escorted to the World Trade Towers by subway, ate prawns at Beefsteak Charlie's, witnessed other urban marvels, and addressed the United Nations. His most recent triumph—after further travels—was to induce another European named Brian Taylor, the personnel manager of Burns Philp in Port Moresby, to become a Chambri (see *Post-Courier* [Port Moresby], February 13,

1981). Taylor was an Australian who had decided to become a citizen of Papua New Guinea and wished to acquire a local identity. He became a member of Yambumbe's clan and, while visiting Chambri Island in 1981 during his annual leave, was initiated under Yambumbe's direction. Since Chambri initiation requires a lengthy period of seclusion and the infliction of hundreds of incisions on the back and arms, this was a painful experience which left an indelible physical imprint. Chambri, and particularly Yambumbe, talked frequently about how remarkable it was for them to have initiated a European. According to Yambumbe, he plans to accompany his new initiate when the latter visits his Australian family; each is to be attired in traditional Chambri male dress consisting primarily of a penis sheath.[13]

These are perhaps Yambumbe's most dramatic demonstrations of the interpenetrability of worlds—demonstrations that power can flow between them. Whereas Arione, Fortune, and the kiap were extremely powerful but socially disengaged, Mathias Yambumbe and Brian Taylor are emerging at this time of sharp Chambri need as a contemporary pair through which substantial power can actually be channeled into the Chambri world for the benefit of Chambri themselves. If power in the form of Brian Taylor can be brought into Chambri society, then it may prove possible for the Chambri to have both concentrated power and a society. Chambri power, particularly if augmented by that of Brian Taylor, as well as by that of the anthropologists, may be sufficient to control those who control the *Salvinia*.

As we have mentioned, Chambri men eventually concluded that they did not have totemic power over this fern. It was a European introduction and thus subject only to European control. What the Chambri had to do, therefore, was to use their own power to pull to Chambri those Europeans who would use their power to help them. Yambumbe's specific strategy in the case of the *Salvinia* was to bring the European in charge of the (FAO-funded) control project to Chambri. He envisioned the two of them landing together on Chambri Island in a helicopter filled with bags of the weevil *Cyrtobagous singularis*, which would then be released into the lake. (This weevil has been an effective agent of biological control over *Salvinia* in other areas and was about to be introduced into Chambri Lake when we left the field [see Thomas 1983].)[14]

Yambumbe, it seems, had become a chief inasmuch as the Chambri were content when he spoke for them, gave strong support to his projects, and identified themselves with him and his activities. In part their support stemmed from a perception that it was important that they harness more power for their own ends: Yambumbe was able, they thought, to bring the power home in a usable form. But their support also was given because he was skillful in maintaining cordial relations with other powerful Chambri men. This in turn arose from his own perception that he very much relied on their power.

During the long periods of his absence, Yambumbe periodically had his sister convey gifts of money to the more important men in appreciation and recognition of their use of totemic powers on his behalf. He and other Chambri believed, for instance, that his safety when he traveled in a plane required that those Chambri responsible for controlling the winds keep his plane aloft. Similarly, some Chambri used their specific powers to protect him against sorcery. On his return to Chambri, he met his constituents and publicly praised these powerful men. They were in turn strong in their praise of him. One very important man, for instance, stated emphatically to us that Mathias Yambumbe was different from most government officials, who, although they spoke English and were university-educated, really knew nothing and had little concern for their people. Another important man described to us the success that Mathias Yambumbe had had in terms of the traditional totemic division of labor. Because Mathias was the descendant of Walintimi (one of the three sons of Emosuie Apankay, the ancestor of all Chambri), he was of the line concerned with government and thus had the power to induce people to "like" him. Our informant continued by saying that his own line, in contrast, was of fighters and that, if he were the Chambri leader, there would be continual conflict. It was better that Mathias be their leader, for then there would be peace and tranquillity. He was, however, giving Mathias his active totemic support by helping him defeat any who wished to circumvent his programs.

Chambri do not at this time expect to have the power to create the helicopter which may come to their rescue. Nor do they expect to control directly the forces which affect *Salvinia*. They certainly do not wish to gain European powers if it is at the cost of experiencing the social disconnection which they still see as characteristic of European life. But they do aspire to control, or at least to influence those who have these powers. Mathias Yambumbe has been able to become a chief by achieving, or perhaps by presiding over, a synthesis of Chambri totemic powers. In this way, the Chambri hope that he has been able to accumulate enough power to attract European power.

It remains important, however, to all of the Chambri that Yambumbe be socially engaged during his enterprises. It would do them little good if he were simply to become another detached Arione. It is appropriate, therefore, that he announce himself as chief at the moment of his most intense involvement in Chambri social interaction. If he is successful in his efforts to pull those who do control such phenomena as helicopters and *Salvinia* into the Chambri realm, he may, the Chambri think, become chief of more than the Chambri. His power, from their perspective, has become a meta-power, perhaps capable of overcoming the basic contradiction, one which they assume characterizes the lives of all humans, between intensity of power and density of social life.

Conclusion

Many cultures—indeed, most cultures—specify not only the objectives of life but the likely impediments to their realization. When the Chambri encountered Europeans, they were greatly impressed by their power, although, as the myth of Arione implies, they concluded that European culture suffered from the same fundamental contradiction that faced Chambri culture. Nonetheless, the arrival of Europeans provided the Chambri with the possibility of resolving this contradiction for themselves. (This contact may also have increased the degree to which the Chambri were explicitly aware of their cultural dilemma.) If, through the intervention of their chief, they could domesticate European power, then they might no longer be limited as effective agents in the world by the very nature of their social life. Thus, in their encounter with European power the Chambri saw a solution to their own difficulty.

Cultures, we suggest in conclusion, vary in their attitudes toward social change depending on their own degree of self-satisfaction—their perception of the extent and gravity of their cultural limitations. One reason cultures may incline toward change is to resolve traditional sociocultural conflicts. From the perspective of members of these cultures, "first contact" presaged not sociocultural degeneration but sociocultural opportunity. With the arrival of the Europeans, Chambri

realized that contemporary humans—in contrast to Emosuie Apankay, their founder—could concentrate great amounts of power. For the Chambri, even as they are now surrounded by *Salvinia molesta*, the sense of possibility provided by the advent of the Europeans remains undiminished.[15]

Notes

1. The Chambri, who, along with all the peoples of Papua New Guinea, achieved political independence from Australia in 1975, live in three villages on a mountain south of the Sepik River. Every year during the wet season from December through March, two Sepik River tributaries overflow their banks, becoming Chambri Lake and changing the mountain into an island.

2. The Department of Anthropology of the Research School of Pacific Studies at the Australian National University sponsored our 1983 field trip to the Chambri, which was Errington's first visit there. Gewertz had made two previous trips. The first, from 1974 through 1975, was sponsored by the East-West Center's Population Institute, the National Geographic Society, and the Graduate School of the City University of New York. The second, during the summer of 1979, was supported by Amherst College and by the National Endowment for the Humanities. Gratitude is expressed to each of these agencies, as it is to the Wenner-Gren Foundation for Anthropological Research, which allowed Gewertz to investigate archival material during 1981. We also wish to thank Leslie Haviland, Mervyn Meggitt, Marie Reay, Edward Schieffelin, Krystyna Starker, James Wiener, and the anonymous reviewers of the *American Ethnologist* for commenting on earlier versions of this paper. We are extremely grateful to Carolyn Errington for invaluable editorial assistance. A version of this paper was published in the *American Ethnologist* 12(1985):442–54.

3. This figure is based upon recent data collected by Phillip Thomas of the Salvinia Control Project, Wewak. Earlier studies suggested that *Salvinia* doubled in size even more frequently, perhaps as often as once in four to seven days (see Mitchell 1979).

4. During 1979 the Chambri were preoccupied with analyzing the causes of the environmental disaster they had just begun to face in terms of a set of cultural associations between priests and out-marrying women (see Gewertz 1983). By 1983 this set of associations seemed of little interest to them.

5. Marie Reay has asked us to account for Arione's travel once he lost two crucial components of his motor at Rabaul. Unfortunately, we cannot.

6. Chambri frequently use mythology didactically; for other examples, see Gewertz 1985 and Errington and Gewertz n.d.

7. Evidence for this statement can be found in the many Chambri carvings of male humans with snake penes.

8. We thank Ann McLean, Reo Fortune's literary executor, for granting us permission to consult and publish her uncle's field notes.

9. We do not know precisely when the story of Arione originated. It may date from the early 1920s, when, shortly after Europeans were initially encountered, Chambri labor migrants had already seen the Rabaul Harbor. Even if the story originated later, it would still serve as an explanation of the characteristics of Europeans as first noted.

10. There are now more Chambri-owned houses at the Kreer squatter settlement in Wewak than there are at any of the three Chambri Island villages.

11. In the distant past some Chambri big men refused to travel, fearing foreign sorcery, but controlled followers who would travel on their behalf.

12. Yambumbe's younger brother, Ralph Wali, is also well-traveled. A graduate of the University of Papua New Guinea, Wali received his M.A. degree at the University of Hawaii, was secretary to the national minister of law, and now works for the United Nations in Samoa. He has not, however, returned to Chambri Island for over ten years, and most local Chambri attribute his successes to Yambumbe's powers.

13. Although Chambri now recognize that Europeans do have families, they still do not consider them to be members of kinship networks of sufficient size and importance to lead to the significant dissipation of power.

14. Phillip Thomas has recently given us the welcome news that *Cyrtogabous singularis* appears to be eradicating *Salvinia molesta* in Chambri Lake.

15. In another publication, Gewertz (1983) suggested that the *Salvinia* infestation had caused certain Chambri to doubt the wisdom of embracing Europeans as allies. These particular individuals, however, were among those who, in 1983, celebrated Yambumbe as their chief. They had doubted their ability to cope with *Salvinia* but had discovered their culture more resilient than they had earlier thought.

Part Five
Person and Socialization

Introduction

Nancy Lutkehaus

Beginning with Mead's (1935) examination of temperament among the Arapesh, Mundugumor, and Tchambuli (Chambri), Bateson's (1936) description and analysis of Iatmul ethos and eidos, and Whiting's (1941) work on socialization among the Kwoma, Sepik societies have long been a focus of anthropological inquiry into individual psychology, the cultural expression of emotion, and socialization. The five papers in this section continue and expand this inquiry. They are, however, representative of new analytic developments in the study of cultural psychology, the relationship of the individual to society, and the individual life cycle—more closely associated with "ethnopsychology" (see White and Kirkpatrick 1985:4) than with the psychoanalytic orientation of Mead's culture-and-personality studies or Whiting's social-learning approach. Thus their concern is less with individual behavior and its motivation than with the concepts and interactive processes involved in the construction of social meaning (McDowell, Tuzin) and domains of social action (Harrison, Weiss) or the acquisition of specific cultural roles (Barlow). Another emphasis characteristic of these studies is their explicit attention to the experiences and social worlds of children (Barlow, Weiss, and Tuzin). This emphasis again is one pioneered by Mead (1928) and also of interest to Whiting (1941), but the present studies, especially Tuzin's, adopt a more complex theoretical framework for an understanding of the process of enculturation. Rather than seeing socialization as unidirectional, there is acknowledgment of interaction between the individual personality and specific experiences of the child and the social forces directed at producing a culturally defined ideal social person.

Kathleen Barlow's work on siblingship focuses on the relationship between childhood experience and the adult's exercise of authority. It is through learning how to be a good sibling, especially an elder sibling, that men and women learn to exercise the authority appropriate to their adult roles in Murik society. Social authority in Murik cultures—which Barlow characterizes as "nurturant authority"—is based on seniority and generosity. Power is associated with the role of giver and based on a model of the good mother who generously provides food for her children. As with parenthood, learning to be an elder sibling entails learning to give, and sometimes to give in, to those in junior positions.

When Florence Weiss first went to the Iatmul village of Palimbei to study the relationship between childhood and society, she noticed that, in contrast to European children, Palimbei children were very independent. To understand the social conditions that contributed to this situation, she concentrated on the Palimbei economy and children's position within it. The summary of her findings that she presents here describes the division of labor by sex fundamental to the subsistence economy, children's ability to master adult economic tasks at an early age, their easy access to resources and the products of their labor, and the relative abundance of leisure time available to both children and adults that makes children's labor expendable rather than essential. Weiss notes that, while ethnographies often describe the lives of children, they seldom present actual children's voices. In contrast, she recorded daily conversations with seven Palimbei children and presents not only their points of view but their own words in her ethnographic writings.

Nancy McDowell begins her discussion of reciprocity and the relationship between the individual and society in Bun—a small community on the Yuat River—with reference to K. O. L. Burridge's (1979) *Someone, No One: An Essay on Individuality*. According to Burridge, in societies with subsistence economies, such as Bun, emphasis is placed on the person, who reproduces the norms of a given social order, while in market economies, especially those of Western societies, emphasis is on the individual, who is capable of changing that order. Burridge's concern, the tension between individual autonomy and the requirements of social order, is also a central concern of the strongly egalitarian Bun. A human being, according to the Bun, is independent of other human beings but must engage in specific social relations. The cultural resolutions of this paradox are based on the notion of balanced reciprocity. McDowell shows how two basic modes of social transaction—sharing and formal exchange—allow individuals in Bun to forge alliances and yet maintain their autonomy. She concludes by discussing the difference between the type of autonomy valued by the Bun and Burridge's concept of the individual.

In his analysis of two basic aspects of personhood in Avatip culture that he glosses as Spirit and Understanding, Simon Harrison discusses several theoretical issues important not only for the study of Sepik societies but for that of society more generally, among them male-female relations and the nature of culture. He describes the constructs of Spirit and Understanding as key elements used by people in Avatip to articulate two contradictory—indeed, incommensurable—systems of social relations. These two aspects of personhood are broadly associated with two distinct social domains: the domain of ritual hierarchy, in which males are dominant over females, and the secular-domestic domain, characterized by sexual equality. Spirit is the dominant aspect of the person in the context of ritual hierarchy and Understanding the dominant aspect in the domestic context. One of the important theoretical points that Harrison makes is that, rather than representing separate male-female worlds, the two domains include both men and women but in each a different aspect of the person is dominant.

In the final paper in this section, Donald Tuzin begins by asking what, if anything, characterizes the Sepik as a distinct cultural region. His answer is "a common fascination with symbolic forms [that] amounts to a kind of regional metalanguage—a shared, intellectualist orientation which . . . enjoys novelty for its own sake." Following this line of thought, he suggests that tambaran "cults" and cargo cults are alike in that they are both symbolic statements about cultural authenticity, "a mythic state which is best attained—and then only momentarily—in ritual action." Tuzin links the concern of Barlow and Weiss—childhood experiences—with that of Harrison and McDowell—concepts of personhood in relation to society—in his hypothesis about the dynamics of cultural authenticity: "that cognitive and emotional associations originating in childhood, mainly within the nexus of family and peer-group relationships, directly affect one's adult sense of self, person, and cultural authenticity." He suggests that future research on the development of the self and the self's relation to socially defined notions of the person focus on middle childhood (ages five to ten) and on children's culture—concepts shared among children themselves. Quoting Sapir on the nature of art, he points out that if cultural traditions are to be perpetuated it is essential that they continue to have emotional salience and meaning in everyday life, but this is difficult to maintain as people's lived experience and social environment change. Hence the significance of his title—"Fighting for Their Lives"—and his identification of cultural authenticity as a problem facing people in Sepik societies today.

27/ The Dynamics of Siblingship: Nurturance and Authority in Murik Society

Kathleen Barlow

Sepik cultures display a variety of types of social organization—patrilineal, matrilineal, and non-unilineal—in which the prominence and influence of father, mother, and mother's brother vary in complex combinations. Variations in social organization at the level of domestic and familial arrangements coincide with different expressions of public and ritual authority, suggesting that there are systematic relationships between these domains of social activity.

My purpose in this essay is to explicate the relationship between the familial, domestic context and the public and ritual construction of authority in one Sepik culture. Lipset (in this volume) describes the specifics of social organization and authority relations among the Murik, a group of approximately fourteen hundred located in the mangrove and lake region at the mouth of the Sepik River. I discuss the way in which Murik concepts about authority and leadership are learned within the context of sibling relationships in the nuclear and extended family.[1] The things children learn about the roles of older and younger siblings eventually become important understandings about seniority, cooperation, and respect in adult authority relations.

It is especially appropriate that an investigation of the relationship between social organization and authority should lead to an examination of sibling relationships in the experience of children and adults. The sibling relationship is a potentially fruitful area for cross-cultural comparison within the Sepik region. Recently, some anthropologists (Burridge 1959, Kelly 1976, Goodale 1981) have suggested that descent may have perseverated, somewhat inappropriately, in ethnographic analyses of Melanesian societies—a preoccupation carried over from earlier African studies that focused on patrilineal, segmentary lineage systems (Barnes 1962). In some Melanesian cultures, the principle of siblingship may be at least as important as descent as an organizing principle of social life (Schneider 1981, Kelly 1976, Marshall 1981, Read 1959, Wagner 1967). The norms of siblingship may provide more coherent explanations of behavior in multiple contexts than the proscriptions of descent. The Sepik region exhibits an interesting series of cases for examining the importance of siblingship. In particular, sibling seniority is already known to be important among the Arapesh (Tuzin 1976, Mead 1935), Abelam (Forge 1972c), Avatip (Harrison 1982a), Kwoma (Whiting 1941, Whiting and Reed 1938), Iatmul (Bateson 1932, 1958 [1936]; Métraux 1978), Mundugumor (Mead 1935, McDowell 1977), Murik (Lipset 1984), and Manam (Wedgwood 1953 [1927]; Lutkehaus 1982). In these cultures an emphasis on the sibling relationship is present in conjunction with a variety of authority and leadership styles, ecological and economic adaptations, and systems of kinship, descent, and inheritance.

I begin by reviewing the distinctive features of authority in Murik society as it is expressed in sibling relationships. Then I describe, on the basis of observations of ongoing daily life in domestic and public settings,[2] how this form of authority is learned in childhood and enacted in adulthood. The observations indicate that there is a close association between legitimate authority and senior sibling status in public and ritual as well as private and domestic groups. They also substantiate Mitchell's statement (in this volume) that cultural norms are powerfully imbued with positive and negative value at the level of individual personality.

Authority in Murik Society

A Maternal Metaphor

Murik society is characterized by an interesting and unusual arrangement of power relations that Lipset and I have called "nurturant authority." The prototype of power and influence is the mother-child bond, in which the mother has many resources and much to give and the child is dependent and inferior because unable to reciprocate. Those who exercise legitimate authority are said to be "big" (influential) by virtue of their ability to indebt by giving and feeding. They are "mothers" to their dependents and should be generous, indulgent, harbingers of peace and social unity, and patient teachers. These qualities are exhibited by mothers, fathers, mother's brothers, and father's sisters on different occasions, but in each case, Murik say, they are acting like a mother. Aside from actual mothers, the most consistent representative of these qualities across a broad range of contexts is the senior sibling, called *tata*.[3] This role is institutionalized in the status of *suman* holder, as described below. Its most frequent occupants are the firstborns, male or female, of a sibling set.

The basic metaphor for social relationships is an asymmetrical one.[4] The superior party is a generous giver, the inferior party a dependent recipient. Age is the main criterion for establishing expectations about givers (senior) and receivers (junior). Sex is of secondary importance, since men or women may fill the role of food giver. The intergenerational metaphor of parenting (mothering)[5] operates intragenerationally among siblings. The achievement of control and power through giving, feeding, and manipulating others' dependence is the openly acknowledged prerogative of senior siblings. In the domestic realm, giving food and feeding are the hallmarks of motherly affection and generosity, but in the public domain these acts are the competitive and aggressive means of achieving personal prestige and enhancing the reputation of one's sibling group with respect to other such groups.[6] The Murik say that one is "killed" or "speared" by a plate of food. On ritual occasions, the sibling group that makes the greatest show of plates (and of pigs for certain events) is said to carry the day and advance its name above those of its competitors.

Social Organization

In Murik society the sibling group (*nag*) is the basic social unit. Descent is traced through both mother and father, and sibling sets trace their filiation through either or both parents to ancestral sibling groups (*nagam*) from various parts of the Lower Sepik. Such related sibling sets are called *pwong*, dispersed descent groups that jointly own particular insignia (*suman*) and ritual property. Individuals inherit property and rights (to organize ritual activities, initiate the next generation, make decisions about peace and war, etc.) ac-

cording to their position in the birth order of their sibling group. Decision-making authority within the sibling group rests with the eldest member, male or female. He or she legitimates the claim to this status by retiring the parent from whom senior status is claimed by giving a succession feast in his/her honor.

The eldest sibling inherits family property such as land in the village, garden land, mature coconut trees, the dwelling, oceangoing canoes, and suman. In addition, he or she has the right to organize ritual and trading activities and to make decisions about work obligations and goals on behalf of the sibling group. These rights are exercised for the benefit of the entire sibling group. The prestige of the eldest sibling depends on the well-being of the set of siblings and entails heavy responsibilities for their welfare.

The achieved status of *suman gwan* (insignia son) or *suman merogo* (insignia woman) is preferentially held by the oldest sibling in each generation. If he or she fails to perform the legitimizing ritual work, the eldest sibling may perform the role of suman holder, but his or her efforts may be challenged by rival younger siblings. They may simply be insubordinate or they may perform the necessary ritual work to assume the leadership status as described below. The position of suman holder may be acquired by a younger sibling only if he or she is able to mount the retirement feast of the elder sibling and any intervening siblings who have prior claims to the status (see also Lipset in this volume).

Ritual work and prestige competition among rival pwong are supported by an infrastructure of senior-junior sibling relationships. Within each sibling group there is a continuum of responsibility and dependence which each person must keep in mind with respect to each senior and junior sibling. Older siblings have the most responsibility for and authority over others, and younger ones have least. The eldest is expected to be most like a suman gwan or suman merogo and the youngest least like the ideal.

Sibling Seniority among Adults

Murik regard certain personality characteristics and social skills as the outcome of birth-order position within a sibling group. The ideal image of a firstborn child or eldest sibling is someone who is proficient at advancing his/her prestige by giving and caretaking. The image of the last-born child—demanding, indulged, and dependent—is more envied than admired. The responsibility to feed, give, and caretake falls on the older of any pair of siblings, whether real, classificatory, adoptive, or step-. Middle children are perhaps most proficient at both sides of the sibling relationship. Often they are able to achieve their goals in social interaction by performing the role of either older or younger sibling, depending upon which of their siblings are present.

Expectations about sibling interaction are well defined. There are ideal images of older- and younger-sibling behavior. The older sibling is responsible for the welfare of the younger one(s) and may not refuse the younger's requests for food, tobacco, betel, fishing equipment, and other goods. To maintain the image of abundant provider, the older sibling should be ashamed to refuse a younger brother or sister's request for help. Older siblings are taught that if they perform their duties well, their younger siblings will eventually give freely (when they are able) out of a sense of gratitude. The tatan has authority to request that younger siblings work in the name of the family—to help cut a canoe log, build a house, mount a trading expedition, provide food for a feast, and so on. Younger siblings have a debt to the older sibling(s) who helped raise them. This is the same as the debt owed to parents for their hard work.

The role of younger sibling combines freedom to make requests for help and needed articles with an obligation to be supportive and loyal and to work on behalf of the entire sibling group.[7] The group's prestige depends on members' ability to work cooperatively. A younger sibling who does not recognize and appreciate his/her older siblings' efforts is subject to disdain and disapproval. Adults speak of their sense of indebtedness to older siblings who tolerated them while they were young and obstreperous. They say that the senior siblings shared the often exasperating job of parenting and must be cherished for it. Verbal acknowledgment is replete with promises to give food and to do work to honor one's older sibling in repayment of one's debt from childhood. These obligations are formally expressed in the terms of the suman succession.

The ideal scenario is somewhat altered in practice by the distribution of resources within the family. In fact, older siblings have greater resources. Younger siblings often continue to expect and demand, while older ones continue to provide. Junior siblings tread a fine line of exploitation and gratitude. The relationships are sometimes kept in balance by gossip that conveys an older sibling's complaints and reminds younger ones of their obligations indirectly. A senior sibling is humiliated if he or she has to ask for something from juniors and will go to great lengths to avoid this. This complex negotiation is illustrated by the following sequence of events:

One older sister with a large family repeatedly gave away the last of her fishing line and hooks to a younger brother's wife who frequently asked for them. As a result, she was sometimes forced to ask for fish from her own mother and mother-in-law, who scolded her for not working hard enough. Eventually she mentioned this predicament to a friend in her age-group outside of the family. When the rumor finally reached the younger woman that she was creating a hardship for her husband's oldest sibling, she began asking for such assistance from her mother-in-law instead. Her husband, the younger brother, began to offer to set the older sister's net for her more often.

It is important to individuals to represent themselves well in front of their older siblings. Public fulfillment of the image of the "good sibling" is widely viewed as desirable. For older siblings this means generosity and indulgence. For younger ones it means public behavior that will make the older sibling proud of them. Younger siblings wish to appear competent, generous, and appreciative of the older siblings' efforts to help them grow up properly. For an adult to be chastised by an older sibling is one of the most humiliating experiences imaginable. This sensitivity is expressed in behavior, interpretations of events, and myth. Many stories, both mythical and historical, account for suicide as a response to the wrath of an older brother or sister.

The following incident demonstrates the remorse of a younger brother who failed to perform according to his older brother's expectations. The reasons for his feeling of humiliation and subsequent self-punishment were understood immediately by the villagers who heard of the events.

At his older brother's request, sixteen-year-old T.[8] was supposed to shove down the family canoe so that the family could leave in the afternoon to go to their house in the mangroves and fish. He was off spear fishing with companions when the tide went out, and the canoe was left high and dry. When he and his friends returned, his older brother was just finishing shoving the heavy canoe across the mud flat. The older brother said nothing, but T. was ashamed. Crying silently, he took his fishing spear and paddle into the house. His mother offered him food and tried to console him. Without a word, he left the house again and went far down the beach, where he sat by himself throughout the night and the next day. The story was told to her daughter-in-law by the boys' mother as a group of women sat stripping leaves for thatch. Both women cried and cried in sympathy with T. for his terrible shame. When I inquired why they were crying, a woman sitting near me said with mild surprise at my ignorance, "Why, because he was so ashamed before his ta-tan!"

It is clear that T. understood his obligation to do the work his older brother requested and that there was no need for the older brother to confront him with his failure. T.'s response to seeing his brother doing work that he should have done for him was extreme; he punished himself by withdrawing from the family and refusing food. No one failed to understand the meaning of his penitence, and no one interfered, although his mother and sister-in-law were very sorry for him. In order for such a sequence of events to take place, senior and junior siblings must share understandings about what each is expected to do for the other and how to communicate about these expectations. T. knew that he had failed to live up to expectations of him as a younger brother. For his older brother to be seen by the community doing such a task was reproach enough. The older brother treated him as an irresponsible child who could not be relied upon for real help, and he maintained his image of generosity and forbearance by shoving the canoe down himself without being openly angry or resentful.

This kind of response to others' insufficiency is referred to in Tok Pisin as *soim pasin* (to show how, to show by example). In the family situation just described, it is impossible to tell whether the older brother was deliberately humiliating T. or just happened to be completing the task as T. arrived. When the reproach is intended for a rival descent group or involves the official transfer of suman, the intent to humiliate by performing the failed obligation is flagrant. On one occasion, a second-born woman should have been decorated with suman valuables before the retirement of a certain senior man, as promised. When she was not, she appeared in the village in the full initiation regalia to which she was entitled but which she had not received. Her ritual sponsor was appropriately stung by the incident and exclaimed in tears that he had intended to complete the ritual work on her behalf soon. This technique of demonstrating what should have been done is learned within the sibling relationship but finds powerful expression on other occasions as well. These examples illustrate how the dynamic of authority within sibling relationships is paralleled in the exercise of authority by senior men and women with respect to the descent group, ritual activities, and prestige within the community. In public and domestic contexts the interaction is laden with powerful emotional messages that are easily understood by participants and observers. Individuals become proficient at this and other techniques for communicating about responsibility and obligation through experience in the proper conduct and obligations of siblingship. Training begins in early childhood but continues throughout a lifetime.

Learning Siblingship: From Rivalry to Caretaking

The ideal sibling relationship is one in which the elder's nurturance and concern are received with appreciation and respect. Lack of confrontation and strategies of indirection are characteristic means of communication among mature siblings. This indulgence and deference stand in sharp contrast to the initial problem of sibling rivalry that begins with the birth of a second child and continues as the family grows. When a new child is born into the family, the next older child is displaced as the focus of the mother's attention. Yet at this point the older child is stronger, more skilled, and certainly more competent to express his or her desires than the weak and dependent infant. From the Murik point of view, this competitive advantage may not be expressed as direct aggression or dominance but must be transformed into a specific pattern of social authority and responsibility, on the one hand, and respect and cooperation, on the other.

Learning Nurturance

In a metaphorical sense, maternal indulgence is the prototype of legitimate authority and power. In the domestic setting it is the mother who reverses the initial rivalry and competition between siblings. When a new baby is born, the older siblings' approaches may be suspicious, wary, and occasionally hostile. The mother watches carefully for opportunities to interpret an older sibling's advances as interest, concern, and affection (see Barlow 1985c). She also interrupts and inhibits any direct aggression from older siblings by making proximity to her conditional upon an affectionate attitude toward the new younger sibling. She responds warmly when the older children imitate her nurturance and caretaking and ignores or wards off any other kind of approach. Often she informs older siblings that they must behave like parents to a younger brother or sister. To a daughter she will say, "You are a mother."

Throughout childhood, mothers consistently enforce a younger child's interests. In general, they do not insist on quick obedience from their children. Murik mothers often give orders, make requests, and complain loudly about stubborn and insubordinate children. They threaten them with monsters, fishing spears, beatings, and shark attacks but seldom act on these threats or enforce their requests in any way. They spring into action, however, to swat or chase away an older child who refuses something to a younger one. Children learn very quickly that they can count on their mother's quick response to interrupt aggression toward a younger sibling, and this response stands out against her usual indulgence.

Mothers' insistence takes several forms. One of the central issues of sibling caretaking is sharing food. Mothers make sure that younger children receive their fill and often serve them first. An older child of four or five may be given a plate of food and instructed to feed a younger child from it. When both children are capable of feeding themselves from the same plate, the older one is punished if he or she causes the younger one to cry or whine for its share. A snack must be shared or wholly given away if a younger child sees it and cries for it.

Older children find it hard to give when they are hungry and a little brother or sister whines for the tidbit they long to eat. Adults remember the difficult lesson well and recall how they argued with siblings and were punished for it. Perhaps because this kind of sharing is so difficult, parents, grandparents, and older siblings are adamant that the rule be obeyed. The younger child soon feels entitled to whatever the older one has to eat. The expectation that an older sibling, especially an older sister, should give food is an important element of siblingship that is laden with mixed emotions. For the younger sibling, it is the basis for affection and gratitude as well as suspicion that the older one secretly begrudges giving the food. The older sibling takes pride in his or her generosity and the younger's health and well-being but expects that the younger one always harbors resentment over what is being withheld. These contradictory feelings are openly acknowledged in the following incident:

When school was in session, the children came home to eat at mid-morning, usually very hungry because they had not yet eaten anything at all. On this morning a group of women were sitting around a heap of clams, shelling them, when two sisters came back from school and went into their house. Their mother, working with the women outside, called to them that their food was on the rack above the fire. Soon the older girl (aged fifteen) came down and sat near her mother. The younger one (aged eight) appeared in the doorway with two pieces of roasted sago. The older girl complained that her younger sister had taken some of her sago. A woman sitting nearby nodded in approval: "If only I had an older sister here, I would steal her food, too!"

She was acknowledging the older girl's frustration and assuring her that there was no relief for her as an older sibling. Her audience laughed warmly at the remark, acknowledging the paradox of affection and abuse which she expressed. Her wishful tone of voice conveyed longing and pleasant memories of her older sister. That she would still "steal" from her older sister if she were there spoke volumes about younger siblings' constant desire to have what belongs to the older ones. Food is a central issue in a general attitude of insubordination among younger siblings. This undercurrent of resentment, suspected or real, often upsets cooperative work efforts and hinders ritual work within the larger pwong (see Lipset in this volume).

A similar dynamic of obligation and resentment pervades other aspects of sibling interaction. The necessity to give extends to possessions, help, and attention. Mothers encourage children to want to give things to younger siblings by pointing out to them their special place in the younger child's world and affections. Toddlers and small children are eager to accompany their older brothers and sisters, but older children become adept at slipping past them. If an older sibling comes into view, the younger ones often call to them or cry to get their attention. Mothers quickly call out to make sure that the older child recognizes this attachment. They do not try to comfort or distract the younger child; rather, they attempt to evoke the older's sympathy ("He is crying for *you*"). If the smaller child tries at some point in the day to call the older one or speaks about him/her, the mother is sure to report this when the older one returns. She teaches the older child to enjoy the younger one's dependence, affection, and admiration, thereby emphasizing the potential enjoyment the two can derive from imitating her indulgence and affection.

Learning Responsibility and Cooperation

The tatan must overcome feelings of jealousy and rivalry toward younger siblings from an early age, but younger siblings remain aggressively rivalrous. Following closely upon the heels of older siblings, they imitate their activities and strive to equal or surpass them in skills and accomplishments. Rivalry from younger siblings is most evident between adjacent siblings, who are closely matched in terms of physical and psychological maturation and often belong to the same peer group. Given the requirements to give to and tolerate younger siblings' demands and incivilities, an older sibling is "enslaved" by the younger unless he or she can learn to get the younger sibling to cooperate.

There is only one legitimate threat that can be used to get a younger sibling's cooperation, but like the background threat of sorcery in adult interaction it is vague and unreliable. This is the invocation of Gaingeen, a leafy, masked figure impersonated by adolescent boys who appears sporadically to chase and beat younger children. When a child misbehaves, mothers and siblings often call for Gaingeen: "Gaingeen, you come o! X is messing up the house (eating someone else's food, wanting to nurse *again*, etc.)." Occasionally there happens to be a costume available and a wearer near enough to hear the call and put it on. More often Gaingeen is called to no avail. Even quite small children are willing to risk that he is not anywhere near and persist in their misbehavior.

Faced with weak resources for control—a younger child's willingness to be entertained or the unreliable threat of Gaingeen—an older child must learn when to insist on cooperation despite the younger's protests and how to maneuver the younger into cooperating when resistance seems imminent. Knowing they will be held accountable, older children are unwilling to offend younger ones, at least when parents and other supervisors are likely to hear of it.

The mother, other members of the family, and the community in general contribute support and direction for learning to handle potentially insubordinate juniors without resorting to force. The following descriptions of observed events illustrate some of the techniques and understandings that are part of the role of senior sibling.[7]

Taking responsibility. One source of help is guidance from those who know the older sibling's role and responsibilities. Parents, grandparents, and others point out when older children may be directive and support their efforts. These occasions mostly involve protection and care of the younger child; authority is exercised *on behalf of* the junior sibling. In the following example, a grandmother encourages her grandson to take responsibility for a little sister:

Rinson (aged ten), his grandmother, and his classificatory younger sister (aged two) were visiting at a neighbor's house. The grandmother sent the little girl home and watched her go down the house ladder. Rinson was sitting in the doorway and reported after a few minutes that she had gone to play at the water tank. His grandmother said, "You scold her. Send her home." (The village is only a few feet from the edge of the lake and has many shallow pools and footbridges along the paths. A child of two cannot wander around alone safely.) Rinson sat watching and said nothing. His grandmother said again, "Scold her. Tell her she cannot play there." He then said, "You go home. You cannot play there in the water. Grandmother says." His grandmother reinforced his directions by calling out, "You go home! Gaingeen, you come o!"

The grandmother was near enough to the little girl that she could have told her not to play in the water and to go home, but she used the situation to instruct Rinson in his role as an older brother. He was perhaps reluctant to displease the little girl or indifferent as to whether she went home. In either case, the message from his grandmother was that he should intervene to make the younger girl do what she had been told to do and that he had a responsibility to act rather than sit idly by. As an older brother he was responsible for her even though others who could also look after her were present.

Companionship and imitation. Parents and grandparents often do more than insist that older children take responsibility for younger ones. They teach sibling caretakers special techniques for getting a young child to cooperate. First, they insist that the older child accompany a younger one rather than direct him/her to come to them, to do something, or to go somewhere alone. Second, they encourage older children to use the younger child's tendency to imitate them. The following example includes both of these techniques:

Bujon (aged six) was taking care of her brother, Jangeinor (aged one), while their mother was fishing for the day. Their great-grandmother, Saimbu, sat in their house weaving a basket and generally making sure that all went smoothly in their mother's absence. Bujon tried to get Jangeinor to lie down and have a nap by calling him to come to where she sat on the sleeping mat. He was on the other side of the house and ignored her. When she raised her voice to insist that he come right away, Saimbu interrupted her sharply.

"Jangeinor, come! Jangeinor, come!" she mimicked sarcastically. "What is he? A grown person? Can you call him and he will come? No! He is just a little boy. You don't want to take his hand. Don't just call him and get mad at him for not coming to you."

Bujon then led him to the mat and he went with her willingly. She told him to lie down, but he just looked at her. Saimbu suggested that she lie down as if she were going to sleep and he would imitate her. This worked.

In insisting that Bujon take Jangeinor's hand and lead him to the sleeping mat, Saimbu was expressing the general feeling that people should be accompanied rather than directed. When visitors arrive or leave, out of courtesy someone goes with them to the house they are visiting or the landing from which they are departing. It is expected also that people will balk at doing something that the person directing them is unwilling to do. At village council meetings, for example, some people complain that the grass is getting too long because others are too lazy to cut it. The "others" respond with an aside among themselves, "Yes, and you never see them cutting grass either, do you?" It is important for those giving directions to demonstrate their willingness to follow their own instruction.

Distraction. Another important technique is not directly taught but is frequently used by adept caretakers and attempted by those who are learning. This is the technique of distraction. Young children learn from watching their mothers and other women that a crying baby will often stop if one jostles and soothes it, saying, "Look, look!" and pointing out some feature of the landscape or putting an interesting object in the child's line of vision.

When the infant is old enough to understand the names of a few people and objects, distraction is even more useful. People often point out dogs, chickens, and flowers. Calling the name of someone whom the baby finds important is also effective. It is not necessary for the person to be present or approaching for someone to call out, "Look! Here comes Papa!" Bystanders also look to see if the person is coming. The caretaker will say to them, "I am tricking him. His father is not coming." Child caretakers quickly learn to adopt

this technique by imitation. They also learn that it is not necessary to be truthful as long as it works.

Infants learn to look around for the promised object or person. The ruse has to become more sophisticated as the child becomes more perceptive. For example, when a child is able to understand more complicated explanations and to wait a little for the promised reward, other offers are used to distract him/her. A grandmother soothed a fussy three-year-old whose mother was off working sago as follows: "Hush, now. Just a minute. I will wash this plate. Then we will walk to the point. Is the boat coming? Will they bring us bananas? I don't know. Maybe." They did go to the point for a little walk, but no one was expecting the boat or bananas that day.

The distraction routine has further elaborations. In order to take something away from an infant or toddler without his objecting, one might distract him by handing him something in the other hand. This is often done just as a child reaches for something fragile or dangerous in order to change his focus of attention and lift the forbidden object out of sight. As a child becomes more verbal, it is possible to distract him with conversation and promises of what one will do with or for him as soon as the crying stops. Caretakers often promise to go for a walk, meet the canoes coming in from fishing, find a green coconut to drink, etc. The promises are not necessarily kept, but if the child stops fussing they serve their purpose. Of course, some of them must be fulfilled in order to retain credibility.

A similar technique for obtaining a younger child's cooperation is to offer to do something *for* the child. This distracts the child from the fact that one is telling him what to do by coopting him into a joint project or pointing out how the activity serves his interests. This is often useful for taking away something like a sharp knife or an ax. Offers such as the following are common: "Come. I'll fix (make, do) this for you," "I need the (knife, stick, ax, etc.). I am doing something," and "Give it to me and I will give you X."

This approach is not only useful for small children. Often adults use it on each other to gain access to another's tools or other resources. A woman who needs a bit of basket dye to finish her basket handles will offer to make some for her sister, too, if the sister will supply the dye. A man who wants to make a trip to town but has no gasoline for his outboard offers to pick up the kerosene his brother wants if the brother will supply the gas.

The distraction technique, first learned as caretakers, is practiced with skill by adults. The routine amounts to offering another person something that he or she likes, wants, or needs before that person can refer to some indebtedness or forestall the impending request. Adults ward off others' expected complaints over what they have failed to do or done wrong by making the first offer. For example, having borrowed her mother's canoe but not brought a fish when she returned it, a daughter prefaced a new request with an extended excuse: "I caught a red snapper yesterday, the kind you like. When I pulled it in I decided it was for you. But when I arrived at the wharf, older brother's wife was out walking with the baby. The baby cried for the red fish, and I gave it to him." An older brother's wife must be treated with the respect and appreciation due the older brother, but she is also unable to ask directly for a fish because of her seniority in the family. The older brother's baby is also the canoe borrower's classificatory son, and she has a responsibility to maintain the family's claim on this child by feeding it. Therefore it is appropriate for her to say the older brother's child wanted the fish. In fact, as the mother later found out from her older son, the snapper had been taken home for the daughter's own family, but by the time this information came to light the latter had left to go fishing again that day after borrowing her mother's hooks and canoe. When she returned the second day, she forestalled criticism over both her failure to give fish and her deceit by giving her mother a large mullet.

The explanations become more artful as the situation requires. Credibility depends on fulfilling at least some of one's promises. Individuals carefully calibrate the extent to which their distraction techniques are apparent to their listeners in the same way that older children gauge their younger siblings' gullibility.

The skills learned in childhood for gaining cooperation from younger siblings eventually constitute a repertoire which adults employ in social interaction with siblings and others. The expectations of senior-junior relationships pervade social life within and among extended family groups. Requests are made indirectly. Obligations and cooperation are expressed through an idiom of generosity. One senior woman explained this mode of interaction as follows: "If someone has bad feelings toward you and talks behind your back, you must invite that person to your house. Give him/her the best things that you have. Betel nut. Tobacco. Food. Whatever good thing you

have. Give it. If that person wants to speak ill of you again, he/she will remember this and be silent." Skill at this kind of one-upmanship is acquired gradually over a long period of time, but it is the hallmark of a "big" man or woman. These skills are used to coordinate the work of the pwong in ritual, trade, and feasting. They are first learned from the mother and within the domestic setting, but the wider community is also important as a supporting network of people and activities who recognize and reinforce the tenets of sibling seniority.

Family and Community

In general, the sibling relationship is first learned within the family context, and later interaction routines associated with siblingship are enacted in the wider contexts of public and ritual life. But the process of learning how to behave occurs in both family and community contexts from the time a child is just six months old. The community supports the family learning environment, just as the family prepares the child for later competence in public life.

The following series of incidents occurred among Manjimara's children during the year and a half that we lived in Darapap village. The sequence shows some aspects of the process of learning siblingship, including the participation of extended-family members and the importance of a supportive community environment. The sibling group included Yai (aged thirteen to fourteen), the firstborn daughter, and Bujon (aged six to seven), the third-born daughter. The second-born son was living with his mother's brother, a prison warden in the highlands. Both older girls were well trained as caretakers of their younger brothers, Kwega (aged three to four) and Jangeinor (aged one to two).

When we arrived in the village, Kwega seemed to be going through a transition from spending most of his time in his mother's company to learning to play with peers and to venture out into the village on his own. He was often angry and frustrated at his mother's attentions to his younger brother. She was adamant that he learn to be a proper older brother. Yai and Bujon were adept at handling the demanding last-born brother. Aunts, uncles, grandmothers, and grandfathers living nearby were eager to coach and coax Kwega to be indulgent toward Jangeinor. He made impressive progress toward understanding the role of older brother and gradually learned how to cajole Jangeinor into cooperating with him at least some of the time.

In the first example, Kwega uses one of the distraction techniques described above without success. He does not correctly gauge what kinds of statements Jangeinor is capable of understanding, and he inadvertently reveals his intention to take something away by his gestures:

Kwega came back to the house one afternoon to discover that Jangeinor had dismantled his toy. Earlier in the afternoon their grandfather had made Kwega a small push car with a stick handle and axle and little wheels made of round green fruit. Kwega had run happily through the house with it for a while and had then left it on the floor and gone outside. Jangeinor had picked it up and tried to push it across the uneven bark floor. Unable to get it to roll, he had taken it apart and now was walking around the house waving the two parts.

Kwega, on seeing what Jangeinor had done to the toy, started to reach for it. Jangeinor frowned and pulled his hand back. Kwega then said, holding out his hand palm up, "Come, I'll fix it for you." Jangeinor refused to give it to him, and Kwega stamped his foot and cried, "Mama, you look at Jangeinor here." She looked up and said nothing. Kwega sat down and cried, but his mother yelled at him loudly, "Eeyeh!" He went down from the house.

The eventual outcome was clear to both Kwega and his mother, and he knew to leave the house rather than insist. He was furious at his little brother and unhappy that the toy was spoiled and he could do nothing about it. His attempt to get the toy by offering to fix it was unsuccessful, probably because Jangeinor understood his gestures better than his words and was reacting to Kwega's initial attempt to reach for the toy and take it away. Jangeinor did not understand Kwega's offer to put the toy together again and give it back to him. At this point, he was best at responding to one- and two-word sentences.

A few months later, Kwega again struggled to control his feelings:

Manjimara, the children's mother, had taken them to their grandmother's house to visit. Jangeinor had a little puppet that he played with for a while; then he sat on his mother's lap to nurse. He whined when Kwega picked up the puppet. Their mother demanded that he give it back. Kwega did so, then sulked, sitting with his back to everyone. Jangeinor clung triumphantly to his mother, nursing and holding the puppet with a pleased expression on his face. He looked from person to person, blinking coyly.

Bujon, their older sister, came in then and began to distract Jangeinor from nursing with a marble from her pocket. She would hide it and then give it to him. When it fell through the floor, she retrieved it for him. Jangeinor then teased her with the marble by pretending to bring it to her and running away again. Kwega continued to sulk until his mother, temporarily relieved of Jangeinor by Bujon's play, gave him a piece of coconut to eat.

Jangeinor was openly rivalrous with Kwega over the puppet and expected to be given it. Kwega's mother enforced the seniority obligations and eventually rewarded Kwega with food for having done the appropriate thing even though it was accompanied by some sulking. Bujon had adjusted to having younger siblings when Kwega was born and knew that she would receive more positive attention if she entertained Jangeinor than if she ignored or annoyed him. She readily gave him something of her own and was quite willing for him to have it, at least for a while. She made the issue of possession into a game. Possibly she was competing with Kwega for her mother's approval. She had heard the scolding from down below; and perhaps she was showing how well she knew how to do what Kwega found most difficult, an act akin to the soim-pasin technique described above.

In these two situations, Kwega struggled to meet the expectations placed on him as an older brother. In the first example, he had learned one technique by seeing others use it, but he did not quite succeed in executing it. In the second, he was able to give in to Jangeinor with difficulty and, having done so, showed his displeasure by sulking. His mother responded not to the sulking but to his appropriate act of generosity.

The full role of older sibling includes patience and tolerance. It also requires that the older child be able to match the techniques he or she knows for managing a younger child with the child's abilities and understanding and the situation at hand. Kwega learned some of the techniques for dealing with Jangeinor and at the same time learned the general rule that older children must be caretakers of younger ones. He was not immediately able to put these things together in such a way that he could avoid punishment while achieving his own goals. There is some evidence that his emotional involvement (namely, jealousy and resentment over the preferential treatment his young rival received) made it more difficult for him to use what he already knew in family situations.

Separate elements of what Kwega would need to accomplish this appeared in his repertoire first. He learned to be solicitous to younger children. He would greet a two-year-old from the next house sweetly and invite the little neighbor in, showing appropriate hospitality. He requested food from his mother for his guest and escorted her to a place to sit down. He interested her with conversation and gave her small objects to examine and play with.

Kwega mastered the various request and distraction techniques and used them successfully with younger children in play. A boy almost the same age as Jangeinor lived nearby. Kwega learned to recognize his cry and to alert the little boy's mother. He sometimes brought him home if he got hurt while playing or was unhappy. He knew to lead him by the hand and often tried to be helpful in ways that he was not with his brother. Some of these caretaking techniques he learned from Bujon. However, when frustrated by an uncooperative Jangeinor, he quickly lost his temper and would appeal unsuccessfully to his mother or leave the house in angry confusion.

The next example illustrates both the difficulty of acting as an older sibling in spite of a younger's provocations and the consistency with which the rule is enforced:

Yai sat in the doorway to her grandmother's house and watched her brother Kwega, who stood down below. When he reached up to break off a stem of orchid blossoms from the plant their grandmother had tied to a post, she told him to stop. When he did not, she reported what he was doing to her mother and grandmother inside the house. One of them yelled at him to stop, which he did not. Yai commented that he had broken it off.

A few minutes later Kwega was called in to eat his sago pancake, and on the way in the door he hit Yai on the shoulder for reporting his misdemeanor. She swatted him back, and her mother immediately got up and hit her hard on the shoulder with a broom.

Of the misdeeds here, breaking the plant was the most damaging in terms of property, but neither Manjimara nor her mother was much concerned. Yai was immediately punished for hitting her younger brother, but he was not reprimanded for hitting her.

These few instances illustrate several things about the process of learning to act like an older sibling. It is one thing to have observed a technique for getting cooperation from a younger child and another to use it successfully in the appropriate situation. Kwega had to learn not to give himself away when he wanted to conceal his intentions and get his way with Jangeinor. His feelings sometimes disrupted his efforts to perform according to expectations. In the case of relinquishing the hand puppet, he controlled his resentment at least partially. With younger children outside the family, he could practice the benevolent-older-sibling role and seemed to enjoy the little neighbors' responsiveness and his success at entertaining and directing them. Bujon was more proficient, having been working on these social skills for several years more. She was able in many instances to achieve her own goals, please her younger siblings, and receive her mother's approval all at once. Yai was often responsible enough to be in charge of all of the younger siblings for the day and knew very well her prerogatives and responsibilities. But occasionally she failed to check her impulse to hit back and had to be reminded that there were no exceptions to the rule.

The last example concerns another set of siblings who were playing a game in which one brother pretended to be Gaingeen. Gaingeen explicitly reverses the norms of siblingship that prohibit aggression from older to younger. The person wearing the costume may chase and belabor anyone younger than he. Children sometimes wish aloud that they were old enough to wear the costume and harry their younger sibling. In the game among these children, their awareness of sibling norms is quite evident both from the way they play the game and from their response to a disturbance of it:

Thompson (aged nine) helped his younger brother, Wesley (aged seven) put on a miniature Gaingeen costume. Wesley then proceeded to chase their younger brother and sister, Maxwell (aged five) and Clancy (aged three). They ran away from him, squealing and laughing. Clancy stopped to pick up a stick from the ground and handed it to Wesley, and they proceeded to dash around the sand flat in front of their house. At different times the costume came undone, or Wesley tripped on the leaf fringe and fell down. Each time, his playmates stopped running and helped him reassemble himself and the play began again.

Three older boys (between eight and ten years) saw their play and wanted Wesley to chase them, too, but they were also carrying sticks, and the younger children felt threatened. Clancy called in alarm to her older brothers in the house, Thompson and Andip. "They are coming to fight us!

They want to fight us!" The three little players scurried to arm themselves with pieces of wood and coconut husks, and they crouched warily behind a small platform for firewood under their house, pitching little missiles out at the intruders.

Then one of the older boys saw a third older brother of the Gaingeen players coming toward the house and said casually to his companions, "Let's go." They sauntered off looking very indifferent, but Clancy and Maxwell followed them furtively, throwing little bits of wood to scare them off. When the "danger" was past, they resumed their game.

Within the play frame of Gaingeen, aggression is limited by the cumbersome costume and the skill of the players. But the children followed the rule that Gaingeen should be played by the oldest sibling. The game created great hilarity among them, and they increased his threatening qualities by helping him with the costume and giving him sticks to throw at them. Had Wesley simply chased them with a stick, they would probably have called for help from another older sibling. Such aggression would have been real, unbounded by the rules of Gaingeen interaction and contrary to the norms of sibling behavior. It would have been unpredictable and dangerous.

When the game was threatened, the children turned to their older siblings for protection. Clancy immediately called to her brothers in the house. The presence of another older brother was enough to keep the three intruders from harassing the little ones any further. They left when they saw him approach, indicating that they knew he would not allow them to make trouble for his younger brothers and sister.

The norms of siblingship seem well understood by all of the children involved, from youngest to oldest. Nevertheless, the threat from the older children shows that these norms are best upheld within a context of community consent. There were no enforcing adults obviously present, and Clancy hastened to appeal to her older brothers as potential protectors and enforcers of the prohibition on aggression from older to younger. Younger children are frequently encouraged to stand up to and hit older siblings who threaten them.

Conclusion

In Murik society, legitimate authority is vested in the eldest sibling, whether male or female. Within sibling groups there is a hierarchy of responsibility (from oldest to youngest) and of dependence (from youngest to oldest). The siblings' rivalry is constrained, though not eliminated, by an idiom of nurturant authority in which older siblings provide food, caretaking, and protection in return for respect and help with work. The relationship is characterized by lack of confrontation and strategies of indirection. As adults, older siblings exercise authority through generosity (especially food) and tolerance.

The norms of siblingship organize social life in public and ritual settings. The tatan's obligation to give food is repeated in the competitive presentation of plates of food as a way to gain prestige. The humiliation of being fed and the triumph of feeding are lavishly burlesqued in joking relationships. There is an occasion, called *baas*, at which joking partners compete to "kill" each other with plates of food, inviting their partners to enjoy the misery of being overfed. These are a few of many instances in which dominance is displayed through feeding.

The idea that cooperation and goodwill are achieved through giving food and companionship and indulging others' wants and desires is the basis of Murik hospitality and their philosophy for successful trade. A visitor must be fed, and whatever other needs he or she may have must be met if at all possible. If a visitor to the village shows the slightest hesitation about finding another house he wants to visit, the right path to the beach for bathing, etc., someone will accompany him. And when anyone leaves or arrives, he must be accompanied to the farthest point possible before sending him on his way.

Overseas trading partners receive this hospitality and more. One must give to them generously to make them want to return lavish quantities of goods. The Murik say that they always give the most that they can, so that the partners' gratitude and goodwill are great. This is similar to the appreciation which elder siblings intend to receive from youngers as suitable recognition of their patience and generosity.

Perhaps most striking is the extension of this philosophy even to enemies. Individuals who gossip meanly must be disarmed with generosity. Attacks by hostile groups may be averted by inviting the attacker to stop, eat, talk a little bit; then, say the Murik, we will see about fighting.

Learning to be a tatan is a complex challenge. Older siblings must overcome strong emotions in order to meet others' expectations of them, and their feelings of rivalry sometimes interfere with their acting appropriately. Some are able to fulfill the expectations of the older sibling role first with respect to nonsiblings and only later in actual sibling relationships. By the age of six to seven years, children learn to be quite effective in managing younger siblings at the same time that they manage to do what interests them. With time, they become able to help others conform to the tatan role. For young adults, much of the communication about expectations and evaluations of success or failure need not be verbalized but is implicit in other aspects of older and younger siblings' actions.

The adult relationship is achieved after long years of learning through experience. Parents actively teach children what their responsibilities and prerogatives are. The injunction to feed and give food is strenuously enforced with even very young children. Aggression toward younger children is not tolerated, but younger children are encouraged to stand up to older ones. As a result, the older sibling learns to defuse the younger's aggression and rivalry and to obtain his/her cooperation in specific ways—through distraction, anticipation of need and wants, exemplifying desired actions for the younger to imitate, companionship rather than direction, and play rather than assertion. Eventually children become proficient at caretaking and achieving cooperation through indirect means. These techniques become a repertoire for handling others which expresses the general attitude that the most powerful position is that of giver.

The sibling relationship is an important arena for the formation of attitudes about the self and the requirements of social personhood. Sibling roles entail complex communication about self-presentation and the evaluation of others. Some of the norms of "good siblingship"—notably those concerning respect, generosity, and appreciation—are quite inflexible. Others, such as obedience and truthfulness, are more context-dependent and negotiable in ongoing interaction. The skills necessary to exercise authority and to critique others' performance are acquired in the crucible of domestic sibling interaction. They are further honed in the arenas of public and ritual ac-

tivity as complex elaborations of the basic sibling relationship.

Notes

1. For a detailed description of senior-junior and cross-sex sibling relationships in the family, see Barlow (1985*b*).
2. The fieldwork on which this discussion is based was done with David Lipset from February 1981 to August 1982 in the villages of Darapap, Karau, Mendam, and Big Murik in the Murik Lakes region. It was supported by grants from the Wenner-Gren Foundation for Anthropological Research, the Institute for Intercultural Studies, and the Office of Graduate Studies and Research of the University of California, San Diego.
3. The terms *tata* (for address) and *tatan* (for reference) are used for older siblings of either sex. *Yeteman* means "younger sister" and *dam* means "younger brother." The kinship terminology reflects the importance of seniority over gender.
4. For a description of a contrasting emphasis on "balance" or "sameness," see McDowell's discussion (in this volume) of exchange relationships among cross-cousins in Bun.
5. The Murik concept of fathering is a modified version of maternal indulgence rather than a contrasting one such as one finds in Western culture. Thus the dominant theme of parenting is a maternal one (see Barlow 1985*b*: chap. 4).
6. Young (1972) describes a similar complex of competitive feasting among a Massim group.
7. Because I am considering those aspects of siblingship that relate to authority in Murik society, this discussion focuses on senior siblingship. My observations suggest that the ability to appreciate one's older siblings dawns on junior siblings rather slowly and usually only when they themselves become senior siblings. At this point they experience directly the difficult demands of this role. Often understandings about how to conduct oneself exceed the ability to perform accordingly. Even in adolescence older siblings who enforce the correct behavior between two junior ones may yet have difficulty fulfilling the role themselves from time to time.
8. The ages used are approximate, based on combined information from multiple sources, including mother's reports, mission birth records, school enrollment records, birth order and spacing within the family, and succession of births in the village birth houses.

28/ The Child's Role in the Economy of Palimbei[1]

Florence Weiss

The three hundred inhabitants of Palimbei, a village on the Sepik River, belong to the Iatmul, known through the works of Bateson (1932, 1958 [1936]) and Mead (1947, 1949).[2] My main interest was the relationship between childhood and society. As I examined the daily life of the children of Palimbei, I was struck by three things that contrasted with the situation of children in Europe:

1. The children were perfectly self-confident and independent; none of the relationships that developed between us came about through the good offices of their parents or other adults. I received the impression that children were brought up to be self-reliant from a very early age on.

2. The children spent much of their time in autonomous groups. They occupied themselves in a variety of ways, playing, having picnics, or working. Adults did not interfere with these group activities.

3. Even small children were in a position to carry out economic tasks. Nonetheless, I did not have the impression that children worked a great deal. The economy of Palimbei did not seem to depend on the full exploitation of child labor.

Of the many possible ways I might have investigated the social structures responsible for the situation as I experienced it or, in more general terms, the social conditions that shaped the children's lives, I am convinced that analysis of the economic system and the children's position in it was most suitable, especially since neither Bateson nor Mead was interested in the Iatmul economy.[3] As a rule, ethnologists seem to be interested in the relationship between economic conditions and children's lives mainly when the children have to work hard and long (see, e.g., Nag, White, and Peet 1978). This is, however, not the case even for Iatmul adults, let alone children. But the fact that neither adults nor children in Palimbei work very much is directly connected with the economic system as a whole. In other words, the freedom the Palimbei Iatmul have for activities unrelated to work depends on their economy.

The Palimbei do not divide their time into two distinct blocks of "work" and "leisure." Whether and how long one works are determined by the specific task. A boy leaving the village to go for a swim in the lake encounters a group of men who are pulling a tree trunk onto the shore; if he feels like it, he will help them. Work may supersede nonwork and vice versa at almost any time. Without exhaustive knowledge of all sorts of children's activities, their participation in the economic system cannot be judged.

My analysis of the economic system is based on three sets of data: my own observations, conversations with adults, and daily conversations with children from six families. As Goodman (1973:2) has so keenly observed, there is a great deal written about children, but they themselves are rarely given a chance to speak. Children's statements constitute the focus of my study. I hope that my report on their life will thus be authentic, concrete, and consistent with Iatmul cultural structures. Every day for a week I met seven children of a particular elementary family and listened to what they had done and experienced. The children talked about practically all aspects of their daily activities. I shall first describe the individual work processes as they are carried out by adults and then evaluate the information about their participation in this work obtained from the children's daily reports and from my own observations and conversations.

Aspects of the Economic System

The Iatmul live in a region of grassy swamps, lakes, rivers, and streams. Before the colonial conquest they obtained everything they needed to live from their environment or by bartering with neighboring peoples at markets. The subsistence economy of Palimbei remained intact until 1976. Owing to the spread of *Salvinia molesta*, an aquatic plant that covers lakes and streams and makes fishing and transportation difficult or impossible, it has since undergone radical change. I shall describe it as I found it in 1972–74.

The two chief roles in the economic sphere are that of fisherman and that of craftsman. Taking care of the children and providing the family's daily food (through fishing and barter) are a woman's work, and she also produces some of the implements she needs, such as plaited fish traps, fishnets, etc. A man builds houses, carves canoes for himself and his wife and children, lays out gardens during the low-water period, and sometimes does some fishing. In contrast to woman's work, the man's tasks are less regular, being at most determined by the season (flood and low water).

Apart from this division of labor by sex, there is no individual occupational specialization. Every man and every woman is in a position to acquire or produce the necessities of life. Specialists such as the ones that exist in the sphere of myth and ritual and used to exist in the field of head-hunting fulfill their specialized roles only for a limited period of time and normally do what other men and women do.

The people of Palimbei do not divide a work process up into a series of elementary units each of which may be assigned to a particular person. Everyone is in a position to carry out practically every stage of a work process necessary to produce an object by him- or herself.

The complementarity of the tasks of wife and husband makes the married couple the most important production unit; a larger one is rarely necessary. This division of labor by sex means that the cooperation of a woman and a man is always needed to accomplish the tasks of life. Without the contribution of the other partner, the material basis for life is not secure. The man's dependence is a daily one: he needs a woman to feed him. The woman, on the other hand, may use products made by her husband or by another male person, such as house, canoe, paddle, and fish spear, every day, but she is not dependent daily on the man's working.

The population of the village is divided into two groups in these terms: women and men. Each sex fulfills certain productive tasks, and each marriage creates a cooperative unit with the partners exchanging their work and their products with one another, taking care of themselves and their children. Before marriage most woman's work is done for a boy by his mother and sisters and most man's work for a girl by her father and brothers. Through the institution of the family as living, production, and most important consump-

tion unit in one, the population of Palimbei is divided into structurally corresponding socioeconomic cells.

A further result of the division of labor is that the products of an individual's work are consumed by others, most frequently by other members of the elementary family who, because of their sex or age, are not in a position to do this particular productive work themselves.

More extended cooperation is necessary only for a few work processes: some stages of building a house, certain fishing and hunting techniques, transport of material to build houses or canoes, marketing, and above all ritual. If one considered work processes alone, one could justifiably term the vast majority of them individual, but many of these processes acquire a collective character when, for example, groups of women go to the lake together to fish, each for herself.

Because of the division of labor, most of the extended cooperating units are composed of members of the same sex. If there are not enough members of an elementary family, for instance, a father and his sons, to do a certain job, first brothers and then brothers-in-law and sons-in-law will be called to help; when a house is built, for instance, more distant relatives up to the whole neighborhood will be asked to help. In accepting this help the owner of the house incurs the obligation to help the others on similar occasions.

The initiative to do a job comes from the individual who wants to produce something for himself, his family, or someone else. This also holds true for work that requires cooperation. Even ritual, for example, a celebration for a canoe or an initiation, is rooted in individual initiative. The participation of others is based on emotional ties or on the obligation to return a service already rendered or expected in future. It is never compulsory.

The Role of the Child in the Economy

Mastery of Production Processes

According to their age and sex, children may take part in all economic activities including the collection of materials and food production itself. The ability to execute work processes independently is a matter of age; the children first have to learn them.

Work is done in public in Palimbei. Like other Iatmul villages, Palimbei is a compact settlement without fences or hedges, and, as many jobs are done outdoors, they can be watched by everyone.

Children start taking part in adults' work or in the work of older children very early. At first this takes the form of play, the child beginning with the simplest stage of a work process and eventually mastering the whole. Although work is not divided up in the sense of specialization, most work processes consist of several stages. For example, the production of a net bag of the kind that women, above all, use to transport wood is divided into two stages: twining and looping the cord. Twining is a relatively simple task and can be done by little girls; looping requires more skill. Not all work processes can be so clearly divided, however. Making a plaited fish trap is a case in point, for it can only be made larger (taking longer to make) or smaller. All tasks demanding skill and steady aim, such as hunting birds or spearing fish, consist of a single work process. But here, too, gradual acquisition takes place, as there are playful forms of all these tasks.

A further characteristic is important. Most work processes have forms demanding more or less strength and skill. In the cultivation of a garden, for example, planting, tending, and especially harvesting yams are the hardest work there is. It is done only by youths of at least sixteen. Sweet potatoes, on the other hand, are so easy to plant that children of five to seven can already do it.

Successive additions to the repertory of tasks take place over a relatively long period of time. Playful forms are gradually superseded by responsible ones. The children are never put under any pressure, however, for they do not have to have mastered certain work processes by a particular point in time. The content of the work basically does not change; in principle, children do the same work as adults. There are only two jobs mainly done by children: fetching and carrying for someone and running errands. These are among the most important tasks little children carry out.

Children are capable of doing work important to the community at the relatively early age of four or five. By the age of fourteen, a girl has mastered the whole repertory of woman's work. Boys, in contrast, can only do all a man's tasks from eighteen upwards, for the heavy work men do, such as building canoes and houses, requires more strength.

In a society with so clear a role division between man and woman, one is curious to know when children begin doing role-specific jobs. The vast majority of jobs done by children of seven and below are not tied to their sex. A boy of this age does far more of these unspecified jobs for his mother or sister than for his father. This is because many women's jobs have to be done every day and because small children are with their mothers more than with their fathers. The sex-related division of labor takes place in the following years, and by about fourteen boys and girls are in as good a position as adults to exchange their services and products with one another, in other words, to do work for others who cannot do it because of their sex or age.

Access to Resources

Little boys of five plant tiny gardens, girls catch fish, and the children of a neighborhood band together to go collecting. Most of the products acquired independently in this way are eaten by the children at picnics they have.

Iatmul women provide food for their husbands and children every day. After they have prepared a meal, they divide the food into portions and put them aside for the various members of the family, who eat when they are hungry. There are no fixed mealtimes. Apart from these main meals, snacks play an important role, especially for children, who depend for them on their own resources.

Everyone, woman, man, or child, may freely use a sector of village territory as a member of a particular clan or village sector. The land the Iatmul cultivate is divided up among the various members of the clan, but because there is enough land, every child who wishes to can plant a garden of his own. Children have the right to use water, land, and raw materials for their own purposes, independent of the will of their parents or anyone else. This free access to the means of production allows children to acquire goods independently or to produce them from raw materials and use them for their own purposes.

Control over Products

Closely related to this access to the means of production is control over the products. If everyone has a right to use everything in the natural environment, it is only consistent that he should be free to do what he likes with what he acquires or produces. This is equally valid for adults and children. Where cooperation is needed to acquire a particular product, everyone concerned has a right to it. For example, if a girl collecting wood in the forest finds a piece suitable for carving, she will carry it to the village and give it to an older boy, who will make a carving out of it. The boy will give her the carving, and she may try to sell it to an art dealer or tourist, giving the boy a share of the money received.

Villagers are extremely careful to respect a person and everything that belongs to him. Infants are given their own spoons and plates, which may not be taken away from them. Even if a woman has not caught any fish and her daughter comes home with some, the mother will never take the fish and prepare it for the family without asking. Parents do expect their children to share their products, but the decision is left to the children.

Production of and Control over Tools

Palimbei villagers use few implements, and they are all simple: canoe, paddle, spear, ax, fish trap, and various knives are the most important. All adults and most children possess their own implements. There are many products for whose acquisition or production no implements are needed, for example, fish traps; even for garden cultivation, just a wooden stick may do. Children are able to make their own implements or exchange something for them at a comparatively early age. Nevertheless, it is in this respect that a child is most dependent on others. One of the reasons for this is the division of labor by sex. A girl cannot, for instance, produce her most important tools—canoe and paddle—herself; that is her father's or brother's task. As many Palimbei men do not simply set to work carving a canoe on their own, the girls and women pester them and threaten not to give them any more food if they refuse.

To sum up: The ability to carry out individual work processes independently at a fairly early age and free access to natural resources are prerequisites for children's autonomous economic activity. Their independent economic activity allows them to develop close relationships with various people on their own—relationships based on the principle of reciprocity. Even the smallest services and gifts play an important part in the maintenance and strengthening of this network of relationships. If a six-year-old boy occasionally gives some of the fruit he has collected to his aunt, she will not simply appreciate it; when she does something for him she will consider it an exchange.

Work and Leisure

For a long time the prevailing view was that primitive societies, above all hunters and gatherers, could guarantee their survival only through the greatest exertion; these societies, it was argued, did not live but rather managed to stay alive. Their existence seemed to be a never-ending struggle against hunger, for because of their technological and other cultural insufficiencies they were unable to produce surpluses (Clastres 1978). Through Sahlins's studies (1972, 1976), among others, this image has been called into question.

With our highly developed technology and our forceful exploitation mechanisms, we still have a forty-four- or forty-hour work week, and it includes neither transportation to and from work nor the work that remains to be done at home, which makes up an additional ten to fifteen hours. An adult in Palimbei works a total of forty hours per week on the average, *everything included*; children work far less—a twelve-year-old girl an average of three hours per day, a seventeen-year-old four to five hours. The children spend about half of these working hours doing things for themselves. Palimbei adults think that childhood should be a carefree time. The situation of Palimbei children is a structural feature of this economic system; whereas they can carry out all work processes at an early age, there is no necessity to exploit these skills and children's labor fully.

The autonomous groups so characteristic of the children's lives emerge out of the social structure which endows them with so much freedom, for it seems obvious that these children should get together to pursue their interests.

The Child's Viewpoint

Children talk indiscriminately about working, celebrating festivals, lazing about, and playing. Work is an integrated component of daily life and is understood as one activity among others. On the last day of our meetings it was still worth their mentioning that they had chopped wood or done some cooking; that they did this every day was no reason not to report it.[4] At the same time, children's statements contain no such rigid, hierarchic value judgments as that work is not always pleasant but from a moral point of view is better than play.

That we can determine some preferences in the children's reports—for instance, that some things are talked about in greater detail than others—is dependent not on the type of activity being described but on its emotional content or on what else happened while it was being done, what interactions took place.

From the following report on a day's activities by Kapmakau, a seven-year-old boy, we can glean that even the small amount of work he is expected to do seems too much to him: he does not feel like cutting grass. We also see that he is more dependent than his elder sisters and brothers. Kapmakau wants something to eat from his mother. He behaves according to the norm and whines until he gets fish from her, but that is still not enough for him; he also wants the fish his mother has put aside for his brothers and sisters. Kapmakau's behavior also shows us that the cultural norm of sharing is not yet natural to him; it is obviously contrary to his wishes and needs.

In the morning the others are still asleep, I get up . . . , extinguish the lamps, and put them away. I go under the house and chop firewood. Then Kawanagwi [my younger sister] comes down the stairs and goes to pee. She comes back, and we carry the firewood up into the house together.

[Later] we cut grass: I, Simbari [my elder sister], Jimmy [Mansi's son], my [paternal] aunt, and Kumbui [my eldest brother] cut grass together. A small bit is left to be cut when Kumbui says: "If you hurry up, you will soon be finished." He says that and walks away. We hurry, and when we are finished with the work, we put our sickles in the water and clean them. When they are clean we lay them in the sun in the grass to dry. We carry the dry sickles up to the house.

We are together in the house when Simbari suggests we go to the forest to fetch wood [my elder brother] Kumbal has chopped. [We go there and tie the wood up in bundles.] Simbari carries a bundle of wood on her head. I want to carry one over my shoulder, but Karu [my eldest sister] does not agree to that, and then we return home again.[5] Then Kawanagwi begins to tease Kumbal. . . . I tease Kawanagwi, Kumbal helps, and then she begins to cry. We sit there, teasing each other. Later we play. Kumbui comes home in a very good mood and plays with us too. . . . I mow the grass with Jimmy. I'm fed up and want to leave. He says, "Come back!" I've heard what he has said to me, but I just go away. I don't turn around. I walk away and he stays behind silently and goes on mowing. He finishes mowing the piece of meadow by himself.

That's the end of my story.

[I: Did you cry today, Kapmakau?]

After the mowing I go up to the house and scream for fish. I scream and cry without stopping; then my mother roasts me a fish, gives it to me, and I eat it up. She roasts me another, bigger fish; I eat it up too. Now I start crying because I want the fish she has roasted and put aside for Karu and Kumbal. She does not approve. She says: "Your meal is over!" She doesn't want to give me the fish, and so I just take my sago pancake and get up. I notice Kawanagwi, who is sitting on the top step of the stairs. I throw the sago pancake at her; it flies past her and lands on the ground in front of the house. Then a chicken comes by, picks up the pancake and carries it away. . . .

[I: Did you give your father any help?]

Mbarangawi [my uncle] asked if he could have my father's whetstone. Kinsinagwi [his daughter] comes by and fetches it. We go to her house to play; we beat the slit-drum. When Mbarangawi has sharpened all his tools, he gives me the stone, and I take it home. I put my father's whetstone in the house. . . . That's all.

Conclusion

Iatmul children, in striking contrast to their European counterparts, are independent and autonomous; in principle, they have the same rights as adults. Their labor power is exploited neither by their parents nor by any other adult. Children work mostly on their own initiative and retain control over the results of their work. Their work is an integral part of the daily life of the Iatmul.

Postscript

When I returned to Palimbei in 1979, the spread of *Salvinia* was already far advanced, and the subsistence economy of the eighty thousand inhabitants of the Sepik plain was endangered. The most disastrous result of the spread of *Salvinia* is that fish, the most important commodity of Palimbei's subsistence economy, can now be caught only in very limited numbers. This scarcity of fish has brought with it numerous consequences, one of the more harmless of which is the increased necessity for land cultivation. Fathers of large families in particular are trying to compensate for the lack of fish by growing crops; in the low-water period fish and sago are replaced by sweet potatoes, bananas, taro, and yams. During my stay, there was no famine in Palimbei, but without sago and fish people feel hungry even if they have eaten a quantity of sweet potatoes: only fish and sago are regarded as real food.

To move on to the grave consequences, the scarcity of fish has furthered the development of the money economy to an extent previously unimaginable. Instead of spearing fish, people buy fish canned in Japan. Freshly caught fish have become a rare and highly desired commodity that can be bought in the village from those women who happen to have had a good day fishing and do not have many people at home to feed. Whereas women used to help each other out with surplus fish, this seldom happens today, since reciprocity is no longer guaranteed: no woman with many children has been able to catch enough fish in the past two years to have enough left over to give away. Money also plays a major role at the market with the Sawos. The forest women are loath to trade sago for tobacco or cultivated crops; they want fish, and as they do not receive enough from the river women, they want money so that they can buy canned fish. Import companies and storekeepers are doing an excellent business; for them, the decline of the subsistence economy means increased profits.

The mood in Palimbei has changed. Daily life, particularly for the women, seems to have become harder, often even depressing (see Morgenthaler, Weiss, and Morgenthaler 1984). They told me that on their daily fishing trips, though they traveled longer distances and used more complicated techniques, fishing only with store-bought nets, they rarely brought home enough. Their pride and strength have suffered. Objective need is experienced as personal failure. This became especially clear in the reverse case, when I could see how content and self-confident a woman was when she came home with plenty of fish. In the long term, this difficult economic situation is bound to have an effect on migration to the towns:

more Palimbei than ever will prefer life in town to life in the village.

Notes

1. This note is an extract from my *Kinder schildern ihren Alltag: Die Stellung des Kindes im ökonomischen System einre Dorfgemeinschaft in Papua New Guinea (Palimbei, Iatmul, Mittelsepik)* (Basler Beiträge zur Ethnologie 21 [1981]).

2. I lived in Palimbei for seventeen months, October 1972 through March 1974. At this time New Guinea was a Trusteeship Territory administered by Australia. Together with the territory of Papua, New Guinea achieved independence in September 1975. My research was conducted within the framework of an expedition of the Ethnological Seminar of the University of Basel, Switzerland. It was supervised by Meinhard Schuster and provided financial support by the Swiss National Research Foundation.

3. Thus Mead (1947) writes that, in contrast to Balinese children, Iatmul children begin occupying themselves with and being responsible for their younger brothers and sisters at a very early age. She ascribes this to adult expectations and role assignments and treats it as purely attitudinal matter, with no reference to the basic material conditions of life. She says nothing about the fact that the structure of the economic system plays an important, codeterminate part in this connection. Iatmul women could not fulfill their roles as providers unless others, especially children, looked after their infants when they went fishing or to market. Thus women are dependent on children's knowing how to care for infants.

4. In his work on daily life, Michel (1974) shows how difficult it is for us to describe everyday events and things—how the everyday has to be made into something special before it acquires communicative value.

5. I believe that Karu refused Kapmakau's offer to carry wood because it was typically woman's work. Kapmakau's suggestion was already a compromise, because girls carry burdens and net bags on their heads and only men and boys carry them over their shoulders.

29/ Person, Reciprocity, and Change: Explorations of Burridge in Bun

Nancy McDowell

In *Someone, No One: An Essay on Individuality*, Burridge (1979) discusses the nature of self, person, and individual and explores the relationship between the concept of the individual and the shape of the social order, reciprocity, and change. This paper tests the applicability of Burridge's model to one society, that of Bun, on the Yuat (or Biwat) River in the East Sepik Province. I neither challenge nor adopt the model[1] but use it as a heuristic device to explore such themes as reciprocity, transaction, person, self, separation, autonomy, control, replacement, dialectic, and change in Melanesian, particularly Sepik, sociocultural organization. Although much of the discussion may seem too theoretical and esoteric to be relevant to the contemporary problems and needs of Sepik peoples, I argue that the issues raised by this exploration have a profound impact on the nature and direction of change and development.

Burridge

Burridge begins by somewhat idiosyncratically defining the self, the person, and the individual. Although these are all potential components or achievable states for a single representative of the human species, he differentiates them in unusual ways. He defines the person (p. 5) as a "conformist who, in reproducing in word and deed the norms of the given traditional social order, manifests the relations of that tradition." The person occupies specific roles and statuses, achieves social recognition within the values of the tradition, and is the intersection of the variety of relationships in which he/she participates. The person is significantly different from the individual, defined by Burridge as "one who manifests relations opposed to those indicated by the person. . . . the moral critic who envisages another kind of social or moral order, the creative spark poised and ready to change tradition. . . . one who manifests relations potentially capable of changing the given or traditional moral order." Thus the individual transcends, operates outside of, the normal and accepted social order and becomes a

critic of what Burridge calls the accepted moralities. Finally, Burridge defines the self (p. 6) as a form of energy that integrates various features: "the self now becomes an integrative/disintegrative energy which gathers particular relations either into the person or into the individual and, also, an energy which either inhibits or makes possible the movement between person and individual." It is possible, then, for a single instance of the species to be person at one time and individual at another, and it is this movement between the two that Burridge calls "individuality" (p. 5).[2]

A major focus of Burridge's work is the basic philosophical problem faced by all human groups: the tension between the assertion of autonomy and the demands of the social order. The idea that the will or needs of the single instance of the species and those of the group are at odds is, of course, an old one, certainly predating the musings of Rousseau and Hobbes on the topic. Anthropologists have discussed it in the context of Papua New Guinean societies at least since Reay's (1959) classic description of "freedom and conformity" among the Kuma of the highlands.[3] The tension between autonomy and the social order may be observed in many Sepik societies. It is especially apparent among the Chambri (Errington and Gewertz in this volume) and Avatip (Harrison in this volume), and other papers point to its importance elsewhere in the area: Dye, for example, notes how autonomy is prized among the Bahinemo, and Lutkehaus describes how the coming of Europeans led to a loss of autonomy and therefore feelings of resentment and inferiority on Manam.

Burridge explores and phrases the problem compellingly: how is it possible to "resolve at a stroke both operational difficulties and the paradoxical ideals of being as gods, equal and free, yet subject to discipline and order in social and moral relationships" (p. 59), to "satisfy the assertion to autonomy on the one hand and the need for ordered social relations on the other" (p. 60)? He recognizes that every culture achieves some resolution: "if, given the assertion to autonomy, the human organism and society are antithetical, becoming a person represents a reconciliation" (p. 67). "Every culture may be presumed to offer opportunities for realizing the self: an integrative transcending or reconciling of the opposition between the behests of the cultural categories and the natural or biological proclivities" (p. 74). How the tension is framed or resolved differs from one culture to another. The extent to which the problem is central to a cultural structure must also vary. Furthermore, Burridge suggests that the way in which a sociocultural system deals with this tension may be a central factor in determining the nature of the system and of change within it.

Burridge seems to assume that the assertion of autonomy is a human universal and biologically given.[4] He sometimes uses "self-willedness" as a gloss for autonomy and clearly associates it with nonconformity (e.g., p. 35). "Assertions to autonomy, working against the processes of socialization which create the person, are opposed to and negate a given moral order" (p. 33). Burridge argues that autonomy is critical to achieving the status of individual, but this autonomy is of a special sort, based on some truth that stands in opposition to given moralities: "They [assertions to autonomy] incubate the individual, but they also give rise to mere nonconformities, arrogance, the criminal, or the insane. What distinguishes the individual from his likenesses manqué is a stand on a truth revealed or perceived in the event . . . " (p. 33). Thus, if autonomy is related to a transcendence or critique of the given moral order or the construction of an alternative one, it forms the individual.

The concept of the individual, he argues, comes directly from Christianity. Western societies have what he calls "generalized individuality," the expectation that each member of the society can or will attain that transcendent state. Because of this expectation of movement from embedded person to separate individual who acts as moral critic, the frequency of individual-inspired questioning of given moralities, and the dialectic induced by external-to-the-system individuals, Western societies are characterized by continual social change. Furthermore, such change is expected and accepted as routine.[5] In contrast, individuals are rare in non-Western societies, and when they occur they do so in institutionalized positions (such as shamans). Their relative absence and the absence of generalized individuality have a significant impact on the nature and frequency of change. Furthermore, the development of individuals is inhibited by the very nature of the society, in particular the importance in it of reciprocity.[6]

Reciprocity is, Burridge (p. 64) recognizes, universal in human societies, but in some it is essential in defining persons and social dyads (e.g., pp. 40–41, 85) necessary for the social order (p. 26):

> Anyone becomes someone, a person, in virtue of mutually acceptable exchanges with those who have a defined identity. What is exchanged—a message, an emotion, a good, a service, an idea—has a general and recognizable currency, a place within an order that the exchange itself reaffirms and reestablishes as proper. Though the manner and style of negotiating an exchange reveal selves in interaction, they are dominated and bounded by rituals and routines of form and procedure without which we would not know what to do with ourselves.

This is especially true in Melanesia (p. 230):

> among Melanesians dogmas of descent, kinship, and group membership are of minor importance when set against the event, particularly the transaction, the exchange of foodstuffs and valuables: events whose relevances are inherently ambiguous, and whose rationalizations must differ with viewpoint and interest in the situation. Yet just these events mediate social relationships, make their nature manifest.[7]

Burridge argues that in subsistence economies, based on reciprocity and without the transcending medium of money, the requirement to exchange inhibits the generation of individuals (p. 150): "in Subsistence communities the moralities are continually regenerated and reexpressed by exchanges and other interactions within a context determined by traditional constraints and the situational objectives and agreements of interested others." Reciprocity traps persons in the traditional social forms and prevents transcendence to a new morality.

Upon this foundation, Burridge builds his case about the nature of change: "By prescribing individuality or its parts to selected positions, individuality—and so the seeds of change and moral innovation—is controlled, and a traditional structure is maintained and renewed but not necessarily changed. Generalized individuality, on the other hand, implies continuing restructuring and change" (p. 139). Burridge relates not only the nature of historical change but also concepts of history to the presence of generalized individuality. Without it, change is rare and unexpected, and the reciprocities and moralities continually regenerate the self and person. With it, change is inherent and expected: "the European or Western tradition . . . cannot rest content with things as they are, but is impelled to change and develop" (p. 211). The contrast with subsistence economies is great (p. 210):

> A metanoia [associated with Christianity and the West] connotes a change of state, a change of being, a transformation. Truth and reality are not what they were, the change predicates a different kind of being, the change in being feeds back into and confirms the change in truth and reality. Further, indelibly stamped as it is with a notion of linear time, an idea of History unfolding itself, a true metanoia is unlikely in a Subsistence economy where cyclical notions of time predominate or are decisive.[8]

A final theme from Burridge will complete this cursory summary. The notion of transcendence, especially that of transcending the given moralities and structures, plays an important role in change and individuality. Burridge claims that the idea comes from Christianity and goes on to relate individuality to transcendent love and (borrowing from Turner [1969]) communitas. Thus, while the individual is autonomous, he/she is autonomous in the sense of being separated from social categories and united with all others above social and cultural form (p. 207): "movement between on the one hand a knowledge and experience of obligation and opposition inherent in the roles and statuses of community . . . and on the other hand a sense and experience of unobligedness, freedom, and at-oneness is, in principle, fraught with infinite possibility." Furthermore, Burridge incorporates not only communitas but also antistructure and a variety of other significant concepts; person and individual are interdependent, structure requires an absence of structure, etc. (pp. 234–35):

> In all cultures, even though their references are by no means identical, analytical oppositions such as sacred/profane, mysterium/prosaic, *satori*/science, self-willedness/morality, nonreciprocity/reciprocity, antistructure/structure, communitas/community, spiritual/moral, animal/moral, anomie/order, someone/no one, individual/person yet converge in the intuition, articulated and institutionalized in a variety of id-

ioms, that though the ordered and moral and safe should always be asserted against the unordered and nonreciprocal and dangerous, the authenticities of the former are in every context dependent on the latter.

I have described the sociocultural system of Bun in terms of many of the themes Burridge (see esp. McDowell 1978a, 1980a, 1984) elaborates. Drawing heavily on previously published work, I shall discuss the applicability to Bun of his model and thereby draw out further implications of both the model and the data.[9]

Bun

In Bun, the opposition between autonomy and social demand, between what social-contract theorists might call the individual (not Burridge's individual) and the group, is of prime importance. In fact, it is the central philosophical problem addressed by the cultural structure, and the attempt to resolve it is what generates social form, provides cultural meaning, and structures experience.

The problem is revealed and contained in the Bun concept of the human being, *barajik*. In order to attain the status of barajik, it is necessary to accomplish two different things, and it is logically impossible to do both. On the one hand, one must be free, unfettered, and separate—an independent agent unindebted to others and not subject to anyone else's control or will. The Bun place a central value on freedom and independence. To be controlled, indebted, dependent is to be somewhat less than human, a "rubbish person."[10] (Barlow and Lipset in this volume mention a similar notion in Murik, and surely the idea is common throughout not just the Sepik but Melanesia as a whole.) On the other hand, one must participate in social relations, take on social roles, act as kinsperson in a variety of settings—to be uninvolved with other human beings is also to be less than human. If one does not participate in social relations, has no relatives, interacts with no one, then one is just as much a "rubbish person" as one who fails to achieve and maintain independence. One simply cannot be a human being outside the context of human society. The difficulty arises because all social relations, roles, statuses, and activities involve rules, norms, and obligations, and these must to some extent always impinge on freedom and autonomy.

The Bun attempt to structure and, in part, resolve this paradox by basing *all* their social relations on balanced and equal transaction. In this way, they can relate to one another yet remain relatively autonomous, free, and unindebted. As Burridge argues, this phenomenon probably exists to some extent in most if not all societies, and it is certainly common throughout Melanesia. Forge argues in this volume, for example, that the important flexibility of Abelam social organization is dependent on the use of "equality-seeking exchange in preference to lineal principles." But just as the tension between autonomy and social control may be a human universal but differently emphasized in different societies, so the solution to the paradox in terms of transaction is also differently emphasized. In Bun the solution is strict *egalitarian* reciprocity[11] as the basis for all interpersonal ties.

The structuring of this solution is more subtle. Basically, two separate transactional modes are recognized, each linked directly to one aspect of the paradox. It is necessary to participate or transact in both modes, to balance them, in order to be human. These two modes serve to order all social relationships.

The first of these modes I have labeled sharing (see McDowell 1978a, 1980a). One shares with close kin. However, this kind of transaction is still based on egalitarian reciprocity, because although no precise accounting is ever kept, one's close kin are expected to share back when they are able to do so. A mother cares for her child but expects that child to care for her when she is old. It is this mode which encompasses most relations of positive affect. This is not the generalized love for unspecific other that Burridge argues accompanies Christianity and the transcending individual, but positive affect attached to specific persons. There is a certain identity and closeness, intimacy in relationships based on sharing. Sharing corresponds to the relational aspect of the human paradox. One is embedded in these human ties. If one shares with no one, then one is less than human.

The second mode is that of formal exchanging. Relationships based on exchanging contrast markedly with those based on sharing. In exchange, precise accounts are kept and equivalent returns are expected. Name taboos apply to all with whom one exchanges. These relationships are characterized by formality, respect, and distance. It is essential that all of the transactions be balanced and equal, for they allow one to establish autonomy and freedom and equality, to demonstrate that one is not indebted or controlled by another. In this way, they relate to the autonomy/

freedom aspect of the paradox. If one fails to maintain equal and balanced exchange relationships, then one fails to be human. Furthermore, it is within this mode of formal exchanging that one asserts one's equality and separateness. It is in the act of exchanging that the self as an autonomous being is defined.[12]

In the abstract, one must be free yet related in Bun; in the concrete, one must share with some and exchange with others. A human being must balance sharing/relatedness with exchanging/autonomy in order to attain full status as human being.

A further complication exists in that there are two mutually exclusive types of exchange. One involves marital transactions, the other the exchange of tangible and intangible items between specific relatives called *kamain*. Kamain are exchange partners who formally exchange a variety of items, especially feast foods (see McDowell 1975, 1976). Most people have a kamain relationship with another; it is not restricted to managers or big men. All transactions between them are balanced and equal. The equivalence extends not only to transactions of material goods but also to intangibles. For example, if a man accidentally breaks a tool, his kamain will break his own tool.[13] The dynamic of the relationship is to remain equal. Any kind of closeness or denial of separation is strictly taboo. Kamain may not share, nor may they marry; indeed, informants were adamant that sexual matters were not even mentioned in the presence of such a relative. It is by maintaining one or more kamain relationships that a person has the opportunity to establish herself or himself as a separate, autonomous, and equivalent human being.

The other transactional mode is marriage. The ideal form of marriage, and usually the reality, is brother-sister exchange, especially with second bilateral cross-cousins (see McDowell 1978b). Egalitarian reciprocity is central. There is no need to mask the reality of affinal inequality with symbol or mythical resolution as the Chambri do (Gewertz 1978a), because affines are equal. The relationship between same-generation affines is one of equivalence, separation, formality, respect, and name taboos. Yet it sharply contrasts with the kamain relationship because it rests on what is basically a sexual tie.

These three—sharing, kamain exchanges, and marital exchanges—are the basic modes in which each person must transact in order to be fully human. By participating in all three, one can achieve autonomy and equality yet engage in social relations.

It is tempting to associate the autonomous individual in Burridge's terms with the freedom, autonomy, and exchange aspect of the Bun paradox and to relate the person to the socially embedded, sharing, relating aspect. There is a sense in which this association fits, but the Bun solution involves a somewhat different kind of autonomy—autonomy from hierarchy and control, autonomy in the sense of being separate from others, not separate from the system itself. Indeed, three kinds of autonomy are analytically distinguishable: freedom from specific control and hierarchy, the "self-willedness" inherent in each member of the species, and a lack of articulation with the social system. In the first, the separation is from a particular other or others and is achieved in such a way as to produce what I call individuation; in the second, it is a seemingly biological assertion; and in the third, it is a disengagement or opposition to social form.

The kind of autonomy built into and valued in the Bun system is not the same as the autonomy Burridge declares essential to the individual. Although autonomy is necessary for the achievement of human status, it is an autonomy embedded within the given moralities and social forms. It does not transcend but embodies traditional and established values and structures. In Burridge's terminology, the barajik is not an individual but a person. Despite the achievement of a degree of freedom from the control of others, the successful human being does not transcend the given moralities to become a moral critic. The barajik/person is deeply embedded in the social system.

Burridge's assertion that individuals (as he defines them) are rare in subsistence economies seems to hold true in Bun. It is the person who plays the central role here. This does not mean, of course, that there have never been individuals in the society; it only means that generalized individuality is not culturally central. It is also true, as Burridge suggests, that change in Bun is rare and unexpected.

The two transactional modes not only structure experience, social form, and cultural ideology[14] but also give form and meaning to Bun life over time, and they do so in such a way that change is not only unexpected but undesired. Examination of the cross-cousin relationship reveals the way they operate over time.

The cross-cousin relationship is an inherently ambiguous one in Bun. There is no single prescribed, appropriate behavior pattern for cross-cousins. Instead, people choose from among three sets of relationships in the particular case. First, cross-cousins may be transformed into kamain. Traditionally a kamain relationship was created by presenting a cross-cousin with a feast that included the head of a slain enemy; today, feasting between cross-cousins establishes a kamain relationship between their children. These relationships are then inherited, theoretically forever; there is no way to convert a kamain back into a cross-cousin. Name taboos take effect, and the cross-cousin terms (*vavadabwi* for a female, *vavadaveut* for a male) no longer apply. Second, cross-cousins may be defined as close relatives by sharing with them. In this case they are treated as siblings, and sibling terms replace those for cross-cousins.[15] Finally, the ideal marriage is with a cross-cousin (preferably a second bilateral cross-cousin), an option which converts cross-cousins into affines. Until one of these three paths is taken, cross-cousins are ambiguous, and joking is the main behavioral component of the relationship. Once one of these three is chosen, joking ceases; it is highly improper to joke with a sibling and taboo to joke with a kamain or an affine.

I have argued elsewhere that the cross-cousin relationship is central to the operation of Bun society through time:

> The cross-cousin relationship is a key *symbol* in Ortner's (1973:1240) sense because it is a symbolic mediator between sharing and exchanging, female and male, relatedness and autonomy. But it is in reality more than a symbol. It is also a key *institution* because it is the main mechanism for relating and maintaining the system through time. It does this by generating relationships from which new and necessary ties can be derived. . . . The cross-cousin relationship is especially significant because it performs both of these functions, symbolic and behavioral, simultaneously, and thereby provides the context within which all complementary elements—both behavioral and conceptual—can articulate as a systemic whole. [McDowell 1984:49]

The cross-cousin relationship is the fundamental mediator in the paradox the Bun face in being human, that of being between autonomy and human participation. The choices implicit in the cross-cousin relationship establish the central role of human initiative and exchange in mediating the compromise—people *choose* to exchange [transact]. One neither shares nor exchanges with cross cousins *per se*. One must choose to redefine them as something else, and by so doing the Bun reaffirm that they do, indeed, control their own individual lives and collective society.... The distinction between affines and *kamain* becomes critical. By transforming a cousin into a *kamain*, a person establishes a relationship of exchange and distance/distinctness that is binding on, and continues through, future generations.... The affinal relationship is significantly different because, in the next generation, affines are converted back into close kin; they are in a sense "recycled" back into the sharing mode as siblings or "close" ... cross cousins. (Thus, in another context, affines also mediate between close and sharing relatives and more distant ones.) In future generations, new cross cousins are generated and the whole process begins again. The result of these processes over time is a complex interweaving and cycling of people in an effort to maintain a proper balance and to continue as human beings [persons], and it is thus that exchange gives form, shape, and meaning to Bun life over time. [McDowell 1980*a*:67–68]

The essential movement in Bun life, both from the perspective of the person and from that of the social form as a whole, is the process of maintaining personhood and regenerating this social form through time. It is a dynamic process that involves choice, balance, critical cultural conceptions and meanings, and social structure, but the desired end is to maintain equilibrium. It is difficult to discern how this system could change from within. Without an external source of change (colonial intervention, environmental alteration), the internal dialectic which describes the form and process seems incapable of throwing up the antithesis required to generate movement; gradual, driftlike change remains. Although Bun life and society are based on process rather than structure, the process is a relatively stable one and one dedicated to the maintenance of balance. In this sense, Bun share what increasingly seems to be important in many Melanesian societies: a concern with replacement and regeneration (Jane Goodale, personal communication; see also Weiner 1976). It resists change in order to ensure that people can continue to achieve the status of human being and make sense of their lives. Reciprocity creates, enriches, and traps the

person. As long as meaning can be achieved through the workings of the processual form, without external intervention a basic stability results—just as is predicted by Burridge.

Significantly, the Bun *expect* stability, not linear or evolutionary change. This repetitive and regenerative system fits well with their cultural conceptualizations of change and the way they structure the past and future. I have previously (1980*b*) described Bun concepts of history as "episodic" in contrast to the Western linear or evolutionary. Bun do not conceive of their past as a series of interrelated events, connected together, culminating in the present and leading into the future. Rather, they structure it in terms of a steady state in which persons come and go but the process, the system, the balance remains unchanged. Only radical, total, pervasive, catastrophic change is possible. When change does occur, it is complete and total, almost a reversal of the way things were before, and such change is an extremely rare event. (Josephides, in this volume, notes similar concepts of history among the Boroi of Madang Province, and I suspect that it is pervasive throughout Melanesia [see McDowell 1980*b*].)

The Bun concept of history is probably "accurate" in the sense that it fits the past of the society, and it is quite congruent with Burridge's model. Without generalized individuality, Burridge argues, change is rare; when a society without generalized individuality does produce an individual—a rare event—the change seems drastic and overwhelming.

Burridge (e.g., pp. 163, 164) frequently addresses the necessity for a transcendent, out-of-society individual to initiate change. In doing so, he calls on the societas/communitas, structure/antistructure oppositions of Turner's (1969) model. The individual disengages from societas or structure and initiates a dialectic of change.[16] By separating from social form, by becoming no one (everyone?), one can perceive new moralities and formulate new combinations of old elements. Liminality, during which the individual presents and articulates new formulations, separates the old and new: "overcoming the inertial momentum of traditionally patterned modes of rationalization so that new data will engender new rationalizations and new moralities requires a movement into the liminal or unstructured, whence inspiration comes" (p. 164).

Again, what is interesting here is the congruence of the Weber/Turner/Burridge model with Bun conceptions of history and change. The Bun conceive structure as punctuated by brief moments—Burridge (e.g., p. 231) might say "events"—of radical and monumental change, moments when structure ceases to exist (see McDowell 1980*b*) and things till then undreamed of are possible.[17] As for Burridge, for the Bun liminality is the source of change.

Conclusion

Far more important than the applicability of Burridge's model are the themes that have arisen in the discussion: concepts of human being and person and individual, the central role of reciprocity and exchange, the nature of change, the conceptualization of history, and the tension between egalitarianism and hierarchy. We must explore these issues and the articulations among them if we are to understand the dynamics of sociocultural form and meaning. Further, these issues are not irrelevant to contemporary concerns such as the nature and direction of change in the Sepik. I have elsewhere argued (1978*a*) that one of the most profound impacts of colonialism in Bun was a consequence of the intruders' failure to participate in moral transactions of reciprocity, which defined the Bun as less than human. Lutkehaus (in this volume) notes a similar phenomenon on Manam, and Allen (also in this volume) underscores the deep and unsettling nature of the challenge to world view: "foreigners refused to enter into balanced and equal relationships and instead maintained, commonly by force, a superior and dominating position. This situation set in train a series of practical and intellectual crises in Sepik societies that continue into the present. . . . "

The "intellectual crisis" in Bun pertains to achieving moral as well as material equity and thereby the status of human being or person, and the pervasiveness of cargo cult ideology indicates that the concerns are far-reaching. Furthermore, attempts to achieve equity are coupled with the expectation that if any change occurs, it will be rapid and radical. People in Bun quickly adopt almost any new method of obtaining cash that presents itself, but they just as quickly lose interest in and abandon a project when it fails, as it almost inevitably must, to trigger the drastic changes they expect. The erosion of self-esteem begun by the failure to maintain equity with others is exacerbated by what the Bun perceive to be repeated failures in economic development. Development planners, too, must be frustrated by what appears to be the people's failure to follow through with

projects such as rubber, rice, coffee. Thus cultural notions of the sort Burridge discusses are central to the understanding of contemporary events in the Sepik.

Notes

1. I have reservations especially with regard to its narrowness about the relationship between the individual and Christianity.

2. Perhaps it is necessary here to stress again that these are Burridge's definitions, not necessarily widely accepted ones.

3. I am indebted to Andrew Strathern for pointing out that autonomy and conformity are old, if not thoroughly explored, themes in Melanesian ethnography. Furthermore, anthropologists have not completely ignored issues surrounding the person, as Read's (1955) classic article illustrates.

4. For example, in saying "if we take the assertion to autonomy to be a universal which different cultures view and deal with in their several ways . . . "; see also pp. 27, 34.

5. This idea is similar to Gellner's (1964) depiction of the West as having an "evolutionary" view of history. It is also relevant to Kuhn's (1962) discussion of the nature of the history of science. Burridge seems to be after something similar to the distinction between "hot" and "cold" societies. See also McDowell (1980*b*).

6. In this discussion Burridge reveals a deep commitment to Western, particularly Christian, ideology. I think it is possible to get at some of the differences he attempts to examine without tying them to the presence or absence of Christianity and an abstract "truth." For example, earlier descriptions of societies as "hot" or "cold," although awkward, were attempts to get at some similar things. A full discussion of these issues is, however, beyond the scope of this paper.

7. These are some of the factors that have led to the characterization of some Melanesian societies as having "loose structures." Process simply takes precedence over structure.

8. The similarity of these views to those of Weber and Geertz on social change is apparent here as elsewhere in the book.

9. I thank the National Institute of Mental Health and the Institute for Intercultural Studies for the financial support they provided for my first field trip to Bun (October 1972 through November 1973) and the National Endowment for the Humanities and Franklin and Marshall College for support for the second (July and August 1977).

10. The association between "rubbish person" and "less than human" is explicit; when describing a "rubbish person," informants often used phrases such as *barajik na* (not a human being) or, in Tok Pisin, *em i no man [meri] tru* (he [she] is not a real person). Burridge suggests that demotion to nonhuman is perhaps char-

acteristic of subsistence cultivators in general: "one who did not or could not honor his exchange obligations abdicated moral status and, being in that sense less than human, was so treated" (p. 90). He (p. 127) explicitly links the failure to exchange in Melanesia with the "rubbish person."

11. The tension between hierarchy and egalitarianism is another theme that I suspect is central to understanding most Melanesian societies and that is directly pertinent to the issues discussed here. I hope to address it in a future publication.

12. Anthropologists have not adequately noted that exchange operates in two ways in Melanesia (and probably elsewhere). In the first, usually recognized by those who espouse either a social anthropological or an alliance approach, exchange establishes alliances between persons and groups. Transacting forms a tie between two entities. Exchanges establish connections between clans, ceremonial exchange systems foster regional integration, prescriptive marriage rules set up permanent relationships between transacting groups. However, exchange is not just a way of bringing together or conjoining but also a means of differentiating or separating. The process itself differentiates the parties to it, makes them separate. Probably the most familiar example of this second way in which exchange operates occurs in the context of clan or lineage segmentation. The constituent units of an exogamous clan, for example, are unable to engage in marital exchanges; however, when the clan begins to split apart, such exchanges occur and help to define the units as separate and differentiated. This separation mode of exchange also operates on another level: the process is a major way of individuating the person and thereby helps to define the self. Thus exchange can promote autonomy and separation, not just alliance.

13. This relationship is reminiscent of the *tshambela* relationship among the Iatmul (Bateson 1932:272–73).

14. Although there are matrilineal clans, they are of little significance in generating the shape of Bun society, experience, and meaning (see McDowell 1975, 1977).

15. The Bun sometimes combine kin terms to refer to persons who are not quite one thing but not completely something else. For example, a woman may refer to a male cross-cousin with whom she shares as *jimwan-vavadaveut*, "brother–cross-cousin." Such a term may also be used by someone who wants to acquire something—a favor, an item—from a cross-cousin; doing so merely stresses the possibility of and desire for sharing.

16. Again, Burridge's scheme is reminiscent of Weber's. Individual-induced change might be conceived to be a breakthrough that increases rationalization. Charisma is also central in Burridge's argument.

17. A people's experience of colonialism is clearly relevant here. The extent to which it is interpreted or experienced as liminality may be very significant in analyzing change.

30/ Concepts of the Person in Avatip Religious Thought

Simon Harrison

In anticipation of a study of religion and initiatory ritual at Avatip, a community on the Sepik River in the East Sepik Province of Papua New Guinea, I would like to examine here the concepts which Avatip people use to describe and conceptualize the individual as religious subject. In the past, this issue was paid relatively little attention in studies of Melanesian religion (though see Leenhardt 1979), but I argue in this paper that it is central to an understanding of Avatip ritual.

It has become increasingly apparent in recent years that Melanesian initiatory systems pose something of a challenge to traditional Durkheimian perspectives on religion (Keesing 1982). There has been a growing recognition of the powerful effects of the experience of initiation upon the development of personal self-concepts, and this has led to a number of studies exploring the subjective or psychological dimensions of ritual (Herdt 1981, 1982; Gell 1979; Poole 1982; Tuzin 1982). Another development has involved an increasing awareness that these ritual systems are, at a sociological level, essentially concerned with power relations based on age and—especially—gender (Keesing 1982, Langness 1974). Both of these approaches indicate, from different perspectives, that constructs of personhood may well have major symbolic and political significance in Melanesian male cult ritual. It is this issue that I would like to explore in this paper: I try to show that these constructs articulate the subjective and institutional aspects of Avatip initiatory ritual and are central to the conceptualizations of power displayed in these rituals.

Avatip[1] is a largely endogamous community of some thirteen hundred speakers of Manambu, a language of the dominant Middle Sepik Ndu family (Laycock 1965). Avatip is closely related socioculturally to its downriver neighbors, the Iatmul (Bateson 1932, 1958 [1936]). Its economy is based on fishing and sago exploitation supplemented by swiddening; some individuals nowadays earn wages or salaries in towns. The main political units of the community are sixteen exogamous patrilineal subclans, each identified, through a rule of patrivirilocal residence, with a ward in which its domestic houses and men's cult buildings stand. The community is politically decentralized, and the authority of leaders rarely extends beyond their own subclans. Leadership is achieved, though with some elements of ascription, through a combination of male ritual seniority and expertise in myth, magic, and oratory (see Harrison 1982a).

The realm of ritual and that of mundane or secular life are not only relatively distinct at Avatip but involve differing conceptualizations of the overall nature of social relationships. Avatip religion, like many in Melanesia, centers on a male initiatory cult having a series of ritual grades. During these rituals, relations between the sexes and between men of different grades are regimented and prescriptively hierarchical. Inequalities in ritual status are stressed, dramatically displayed, and underwritten by graded mystical powers associated with increasing ritual seniority. In secular contexts, in contrast, relations between men and between men and women are governed by a familial or kinship ethos and are considerably more relaxed, informal, and egalitarian. The ideal, in this paradigm, is of equal moral accountability between persons in which their differences in ritual status are minimized or held in abeyance.

Ultimately, these two formulations are equipollent, and this is largely because the values they embody are not so much opposed as incommensurable. But my point here is that rather than view Avatip ritual as a summation of axiomatic cultural values, I take the approach that the values and conceptualizations embodied in ritual are in a number of important respects the antitheses of those of nonritual social life. Secondly, I would argue that the relation between "ritual hierarchy" and "secular equality," as they might be called, is dynamic or dialectical. From the ritual perspective, egalitarianism is viewed as a tendency toward a kind of amorphous state of societal entropy; from the secular perspective everyone, including men, would view a complete or permanent state of ritual hierarchy as intolerably repressive. In social interaction, actors regularly shift contextually between these two frames of reference, and in fact the community as a whole moves continuously through alternating periods of ritual and secular time. As this occurs, these two alternative schemata are invoked, each destined in the end to call forth the other so that each is only partially or temporarily realized.

Tuzin (1982) has made what I think is a comparable observation of the Ilahita Arapesh, a group some thirty miles north of Avatip in the Torricelli Mountains. In a study of violence in Ilahita ritual, Tuzin argues that the domestic and ritual domains of Ilahita society are governed by "two mutually abhorrent ethical doctrines" (p. 352) whose irreconcilability poses an enduring moral dilemma for men. The problem, exacerbated by tendencies on the part of men toward religious skepticism, is that of justifying the ritual aggression which their religion ordains against noninitiates. Tuzin has raised a number of important issues here, and one which I would particularly like to develop is the antithesis he posits between a domestic and a ritual ethos. I shall try to show that at Avatip, however, the dilemma is not between two irreconcilable moral codes; rather, it lies in the fact that religion and morality are distinct, embodying values of wholly different orders.

I would particularly like to focus on the way in which the antithesis between what I have called ritual hierarchy and secular equality is connected with Avatip conceptions of the person. All human beings, male and female, child and adult, are viewed as possessing, though in varying and differential degrees of development, two basic dimensions of selfhood, which I shall call Spirit and Understanding. Understanding is the faculty by means of which the individual is aware of social obligations and conventions and apprehends them as having moral force. It is the source of all forms of identification with others: sociability, compassion, respect, "amity" in Fortes's sense, and all the "Apollonian" virtues involved in the ethos of secular equality. Spirit, on the other hand, is the individual's life-force, a kind of élan vital conceived as the source of physical growth and well-being, of self-assertion and self-will, and, in the course of the life cycle, of certain mystical powers over others. Spirit is the aspect of the personality to which Avatip religion addresses itself; the ritual system has the overall aim of intensifying or augmenting the Spirits of males, and the ritual grades represent the increasing "degrees" of Spirit which men are viewed as acquiring as they become more senior. It is of

course by no means unusual for a system of religious ideas to revolve around a dualistic conception of personhood, and the Spirit/Understanding dichotomy is as central to Avatip religion as, say, the flesh/spirit dualism is in the Christian tradition. But the point I would like to stress, itself by no means novel, is that the subjective dynamics of religion originate in the lived and felt tensions between the terms of such dichotomies.

Avatip religion does not celebrate moral consensus or the submission of the individual ego to the conscience collective. These ideas—or at least ideas resembling them—are indeed important values at Avatip, but they are connected primarily with the aspect of personhood which I have called Understanding. That is, they are associated primarily with the domain of everyday social relations and stand in counterpoise to the concept of Spirit and the scheme of ritual values identified with it. Male ritual values, encapsulated in the notion of Spirit, have to do with the development by the individual of an increasing autonomy from the constraints imposed by others, with a kind of transcendence of the moral conditions of existence. Men are regarded as open, by means of their Spirits, to a dimension of living "above" the secular domain and one in which essentially "aesthetic" values predominate over moral ones.

I call these values aesthetic because they are concerned above all with the power of signification. This power is viewed as inherent in human individuality as the capacity to strike admiration, fear, desire, or other types of powerful affect into the subjectivities of others. It is regarded as the ability of a more intense life-force to influence a weaker one and as a power which can be augmented by ritual and magical means. In a ritually heightened state, a man's life-force can, for instance, strike desire into women or, in warfare, incapacitate his enemies with fear. With increasing ritual seniority, a man becomes able to impart something of the power of his Spirit to others or, alternatively, to harm or kill them by attacking their life-force; in short, he gains the ability to bless or bewitch his ritual juniors. All forms of immediate interpersonal influence—from the capacity to evoke emotional responses in others to the ability to harm or benefit them mystically— are treated as varieties of the same phenomenon: the power inherent in the individual's Spirit. To Avatip people, witchcraft is simply an augmented form of the "natural" capacity of individuals to affect one another's emotions; to put it the other way around, the effects people have on each other's subjective states are treated as miniature acts of witchcraft. In short, Avatip people attribute expressive and instrumental powers to the human life-force and make no distinction between them except in degree.

It is in the context of ritual, when the initiatory grades emerge as salient social categories, that the powers attributed to the life-force come to the fore. A principle basic to the ritual domain is that there are fundamental inequalities between individuals, according to their ritual status, in their powers of signification, that is, inequalities in the degree to which their Spirits have power over and autonomy from those of others.

I spoke earlier of male ritual as a kind of transcendence of the moral order, and an important point here is that the primary focus of this transcendence is the individual's body and those aspects of personality which the villagers would view as immanent in the physical self. Spirit is conceptualized as essentially *embodied* life-force: it manifests itself in physical size, strength, and health, fecundity, physical courage, self-display, and the forceful pursuit of personal ends. In contrast, those aspects of personhood treated as wholly immanent in the individual's social relationships—what I have called the Understanding—comprise the purely "profane" or this-worldly dimension of the self.

Avatip men regard their life-force as attaining, in the actual performance of rituals, such intensity that they and their actions are in effect assessable not by moral criteria but only by aesthetic ones. This idealized state of ritual potency represents, I think, the ultimate aim which Avatip religion establishes for men. It is, one might say, in the nature of men to rise—precariously and only for brief periods—above the status of moral subjects and attain that of objects of spectacular display and intense significance. All Avatip male ritual expresses this aspiration and attempts to demonstrate that it has, if temporarily, been achieved.

Central to Avatip religion is the idealized aim—reminiscent of Nietzsche's philosophy of the Will—of a "Dionysian" aggrandizement of the self reserved for a select few (at Avatip, adult men). But in contrast to the German philosopher, Avatip people do not view this as the attainment of a hypertrophied subjectivity, but rather the reverse: the depersonalization of oneself into a human equivalent of a ritual object, like the masks, wooden statues, and other objects that figure in Avatip ritual as physical embodiments of vital force. The actors in ritual temporarily suspend their ordinary social identities but gain instead power in the form of the impact which highly charged symbolic objects have upon the subjectivities of others. The power of men is not *reflected* in ritual, as though its real basis lay elsewhere, but constituted in the act of being displayed. It is fully realized only during the periods of its dramatization, and outside of the context of its ritual display its tendency is to dissipate.

Spirit and Understanding

Avatip people distinguish between two basic aspects of the personality, which I have called Understanding and Spirit but which they themselves call *mawul* and *kaiyik* respectively. The term *mawul* has a number of meanings, all of which have in common the idea of the "soft" inside or core of something. The soft pith at the center of a tree trunk, for instance, is the *mawul* of the tree, and *mawul* is the term for the human or animal liver. But it is also the term for what we would call the "mind" or "understanding," and it is this sense that I would like to examine here.

First, the mawul is the seat of the individual's affective responses: to be happy or satisfied, for example, is *mawul viyakət təna* (lit. "my mawul is good"), to be troubled or perplexed is *mawul samasam təna* (lit. "I have much mawul"), and despair or frustration is *mawul pukana* (lit. "my mawul rots"). The mawul is also the seat of thought and knowledge. After proposing some course of action to a public meeting, for example, a man might conclude by saying *wuna mawul ata wana* (lit. "my mawul speaks thus," i.e., "that is my opinion"); people might say of a taciturn individual *ndəka ma' andj mawulam rəna* (lit. "his speech remains in his mawul"); and the secret aspects of myth, ritual, and magic are often described as *mawulam rənandi ndja' av* (lit. "things to remain in the mawul," i.e., "things not to be spoken of openly").

The mawul is thought of as the quintessentially "moral" or "social" aspect of the personality, the hallmark of the properly socialized individual. To have a mawul is to be rational, to possess all appropriate adult skills and knowledge, and to be conscious of one's obligations and the rights of others. But more than this it involves above all an empathic disposition toward others. At Avatip there is little in the way of an explicit code of ethical prescriptions (cf. Read's [1955] similar observations on the Gahuku-Gama); instead, the villagers view morality, much as did Rousseau in his concept of natural compassion, as lying in the generalized capacity for empathy. The predicate most commonly used of mawul is the verb *wukəna*, the primary meaning of which is "to hear" but which, depending on context, can carry any one of a number of linked senses: to hear, listen to, obey, understand, sympathize with, long for, admire, respect, and regret. The mawul is the aspect of the self predisposed above all to "hear" others, the notion of "hearing" covering a range of ideas—comprehension, obedience, pity, desire—all of which have in common the implication of the capacity to identify with others.

When asked to illustrate what a person would be without a mawul, people refer to insane, stupid, or senile individuals, whom they describe as being in a condition known as *kwam*. But in quarrels and disputes, it is common for people to accuse each other of lacking mawul. A parent chastising an unruly child or an orator disputing in public debate with a political rival may make the angry reproach *mən mawul ma'a tə; kwam tənandəmənək?* ("Do you not have a mawul? Are you kwam?"). The implication is simultaneously one of lack of sense, of knowledge, and of a right disposition toward others.

Kaiyik—the counterpart of mawul in Avatip constructs of the person—means shadow, reflection, or any type of image of something: a carving or painting, for instance, or nowadays also a photograph. In relation to the person it means what I called earlier the life-force. It is the Avatip version of the widespread and long-familiar notion which Tylor (1873) described as the "soul." The kaiyik is the source of the individual's capacity for motility and spontaneous action and of physical and mental energy. It can wax and wane in strength, and it can be removed by sorcery or spirit attack, causing lassitude, illness, and eventually death unless magical measures are taken to retrieve it. Out of the body, it usually appears as the individual's double, though it can also impersonate others. A kaiyik on the loose is a public nuisance, as it plays irresponsible and sometimes frightening pranks: scaring travelers in the bush, ruining the luck of hunters, or capsizing canoes. Detached from the mawul it is amoral and mischievous, being the pure animating energy of human individuality temporarily disincarnated and unconstrained.

When it is thriving and securely attached to the person, however, the kaiyik is the source of one of the most admired qualities an individual— particularly a man—can possess. This quality is called *ka'aw*, which literally means "sharpness," for example, the sharpness of a knife blade. Applied to a man it means physical courage and a vital and self-assertive style of behavior. To have ka'aw is to show that one places greater importance on one's own aims than on the rights of others, and it also involves a readiness to face impassively hardships such as the privations and physical pain which men undergo in initiatory ritual. In short, ka'aw can manifest itself in a wide range of behavioral forms, from belligerence to ascetic self-denial, but the element common to all is that they signify an enlarged personal autonomy, the impulse of the sheer energy of selfhood to free itself from the conditions of its existence: sickness, danger, physical needs, the rights and claims of others. The concept of ka'aw represents the ideal of living life as it were wholly in the active voice, of the self-determining individual acting upon the world but not himself acted upon. Examples which Avatip men give of individuals with little or no ka'aw include cowards, women to some extent, and men described as "those who do not cut their own paths." The image here is of a man too lazy or frightened of ambush to cut paths into new sago-palm areas, one who just uses established trails and exploits sago stands discovered by others. In other words, he lives off the work and initiative of others and creates nothing new of his own.

The terms Spirit and Understanding are, I think, useful labels to cover not just the concepts of kaiyik and mawul but also the two distinct orientations of the self toward the world which they define and the complementary schemes of values connected with them; and it is in this sense that I shall use the two terms in this paper. Like kaiyik, the term "spirit" can convey the ideas of "soul," "mettle," and "self-will," while the term "understanding" carries variously the notion of "mind," "comprehension," "agreement," and "empathy" and so has something of the same range of associations as mawul.

I explained earlier that a central disposition ascribed to the mawul is "hearing," and in fact in many expressions *mawul* can be replaced idiomatically by *wan* ("ears"). Someone reproaching another with lack of mawul, for instance, might ask *mən wan ma'a tə?* ("Do you not have ears?") or, alternatively, *mən wan təpənandəmənək?* ("Are your ears blocked?"). The kaiyik is more often associated with the mouth and with speech. A man of forceful character may be described as a man with a "mouth" (*səpakwundi*) or with "speech." The term for speech, *ma'andj*, is in fact virtually a synonym for "dispute" or "quarrel," and it is these common associations with fractiousness that conceptually link Spirit and speech. The Understanding "hears" in the sense of being passive in its orientation toward others: responsive, dependent, solicitous, and so forth. The Spirit, on the other hand, "speaks": it is active, autonomous, assertive.

From birth onward, the individual's Spirit and Understanding are regarded as developing in tandem and more or less in equilibrium. An infant's Understanding is virtually nonexistent, manifested if at all in its complete dependence on others. Its Spirit is similarly weak, and only loosely attached to its body; hence the feebleness of infants and their easy susceptibility to illness and death. As its Understanding grows, the child becomes aware of others and of the need to adjust its behavior to theirs and begins to acquire the knowledge needed to conduct relations with them. The growth of its Spirit is manifested in increasing strength, size, and physical coordination and in its developing capacity to assert its rights and independently pursue its aims. Children are looked upon as gaining Understanding through more or less informal socialization in the context of everyday life, but the development of Spirit is viewed as requiring magical and ritual assistance. The first ritual meant to strengthen the child's Spirit takes place during the first year of its life, as part of the annual ceremony inaugurating the cultivation of yams (see Harrison 1982b). But an overall aim of the ritual system as a whole is regularly to generate funds of Spirit and apportion them out to individuals in increasing quantities as they rise in ritual seniority.

Attitudes toward Spirit and Understanding, as two complementary yet in some respects antithetical ideals, are ambivalent. I have occasionally heard a father praise his small son's growing self-assertiveness by saying "He has no ears at all" and, not long afterward, use exactly the same phrase in anger at the child's disobedience. Encouraged from childhood to develop and display both qualities, individuals begin at an early age to sense a tension between them. By the time they are adults, most individuals have learned to negotiate these potential conflicts with some skill. Adults of the same sex—and this is particularly true of men—tend to treat each other with a kind of affectionate belligerence or aggressive sentimentality, a manner that is both affectively intense yet curiously neutral. But this highly charged equivocation is, I think, the essence of Avatip etiquette. On the one hand, adults must

show themselves responsive to one another's subjective states. On the other hand, to affect someone deeply—with fright, pity, shame, admiration, or any other powerful emotion—is viewed as an attack upon that person's Spirit and a mild form of witchcraft; it is said to loosen the person's tie with his Spirit and so diminish his vital force. It is treated, in other words, as an affront to his autonomy, subjecting him to a force outside himself. Depending on the type of emotion provoked, it could disrupt interaction in a number of ways: perhaps by creating an unwelcome emotional intimacy enervating both participants' Spirits or by setting off a quarrel or fight equally inimical to the ideal of Understanding.

There are of course many contexts in which Spirit and Understanding complement each other and can be freely displayed at the same time. I am thinking here in particular of the large-scale work bees which men organize for major tasks such as house building. These are basically "secular" events, which men speak of as calling for a display of a "single Understanding" (mawul nak), in other words, coordinated unanimity. But they also involve ritual preparations meant to strengthen the men's Spirits, and they are treated as opportunities for male self-display; men may, for example, wear their finery for the sake of effect. They perform the work fast, shouting orders which go ignored because they all know exactly what to do. Everyone plays at dominating the affair, and while these attempts to exercise a totally imaginary control over it escalate and grow increasingly noisy, the work gathers a furious pace. The women stay on the sidelines preparing food and commenting appreciatively on the men's collective strength and energy. Men claim that the success of the impression they make on the women (and also, I think, on themselves) is due to the power of their Spirits to incite admiration.

There are, however, situations which call for an exclusive emphasis on either Spirit or Understanding. Male initiatory ritual, brawls, warfare (now of course defunct), and, to some extent, the ceremonial debates which form the main political forum of the society are all contexts which license in one way or another dramatic expressions of Spirit. Significantly, these are all contexts connected with the ritual system and involving more or less explicit displays of power. An important situation in which people are expected to express Understanding is that of bereavement and mourning. During the months of mourning, people say they "hear" their dead kin—that is, they pity and long for them—and this "weakens" them and vitiates their Spirits. During this period it is customary for the bereaved to sleep without protection from the mosquitoes, a practice which, on the Sepik River, is a deliberate form of self-mortification. They do this, they say, in identification with the dead person: "Why should we sleep in comfort while our kinsman's body is rotting in the earth?"

I might also note that either Spirit or Understanding can be behaviorally "marked" by means of dress and adornment. At one extreme is the deliberately spectacular attire men wear for warfare or ritual and both sexes don for ceremonial debates: oil and body paints, shell ornaments, a feather headdress, and other accouterments meant to dazzle and, as Simmel would have put it, enlarge or intensify the sphere of the wearer's personality.[2] At the other extreme is the appearance of someone in mourning: virtually naked, with dirt-smeared skin and unkempt hair, and (in the case of a man) unshaven. The stylistic range of normal attire lies between these two extremes of self-aggrandizement and self-abasement, expressing a more or less balanced commitment to Spirit and to Understanding. But quite subtle gradations of dress and adornment are possible and carry significance. At a court case, for example, a litigant might wear a feather stuck jauntily in his hair as a visual warning that he is intransigent; a shabby and unadorned appearance, on the other hand, might hint at contrition or express a sense of injury.

In interaction between individuals of the same sex, a display of either Spirit or Understanding tends to call forth responses in the same vein, in what Bateson (1958 [1936]) in his study of the neighboring Iatmul called symmetrical schismogenesis. For a man to exhibit Spirit in some way is a challenge to other men and incites escalating displays of Spirit by those involved. Similarly, the behavior of mourners not only expresses grief and pity but invites them; the Understanding they evince calls forth Understanding from others, particularly members of their own sex. In interaction between the sexes, on the other hand, this symmetry tends to be replaced by a form of what Bateson called complementary schismogenesis: Understanding calls forth Spirit and vice versa.

Spirit and the Ritual System

With increasing age, the individual's Spirit is regarded as gaining certain mystical powers, to a small degree, more or less naturally and without ritual assistance. The most basic of these is the power to curse and bless, which both men and women acquire in increasing intensity as their social status rises with age. But these powers are viewed as inherently superior, in both range and potency, in men. A man's status as household head gives him these powers over his entire domestic group, while a woman's powers are weaker and extend only to her own children. Moreover, men's powers are further augmented by their initiation into the men's cult and their successive ritual promotions. In the case of the ritually most senior men, they extend to virtually all their ritually junior kin, at least within their own lineages.

Men and women bless (*wurumbasawlana*) their dependents to ensure their success in important undertakings: a trading expedition or, in the past, warfare, and nowadays even a school examination, a sports contest, or a term of labor migration. Similar benedictions are also made to cure or assuage illness, which is almost always ascribed to supernatural causes. As senior men explained to me when I was ill, "You always give us lots of sugar in our tea, and when we drink that sugar our Spirits drink it too. They are therefore well-disposed toward you and will make you well." The blessing is a simple optative statement spoken while blowing lightly on the patient: *Sei, wunandə kaiyik, mbar kwusikwa, yera kwakwand* ("My Spirit, let the illness end, let him be well"). The patient in turn propitiates his benefactor's Spirit by briefly placing a shell ornament on him, an act called "adorning" (*sawtakana*) his Spirit.

The maledictions I referred to are conditional curses (*wambawi ma'andj*) made in the heat of disputes—within the household or outside it—as a partial or complete annulment of relations with the offending party. If a husband and wife accuse each other of laziness, their quarrel often ends with their both pronouncing curses on any future cooperation between them in food production. In an argument with another household, a woman may lay a curse on any subsequent association between the two domestic groups. In all cases the sanction is the same: if the curse is ignored, the Spirits of the curse-makers will visit sickness on anyone in their household group over whom their powers of cursing extend—including, and perhaps especially, themselves. When tempers have cooled, the curse is usually lifted, in a sacrificial offering to the curse-maker's ancestral ghosts.

People can also convey these maledictions by a number of means other than the power of their own Spirits, and these are freely and equally available to men, women, and even children. These are curses, known as *sa'al*, sworn on a variety of objects having some degree of ritual potency, the most commonly used of which are yams. Anyone can pronounce a conditional curse by biting into a raw yam and tearing a piece off it, and this is considered a very powerful curse affecting all the members of the person's household. Parents tend to keep raw yams out of the reach of children, particularly if the latter are in a temper, for fear they might endanger the household with irresponsible curses.

My point here is that the high ritual status of men, expressed as the superior potency of their Spirits, in fact gives them little if any special coercive power at the level of domestic relations. In some circumstances, it can actually put them at a disadvantage. The Spirit of an initiated man is considered so powerful that his wife and children can use it to make a special type of curse, called *wasunggwulna*, with a view to coercing *him*. If, for instance, he is lazy, his wife may lay this curse upon his eating any food she contributes to the household, and even his children can do the same with any food they produce. Affliction would fall on any member of the household, including him, if he ignored the curse.

I said earlier that the villagers treat the power of cursing and blessing as an intensification of a power of signification inherent to some degree in all human beings. Men possess this power permanently, and to a degree which women and children can achieve when they need to but only by appropriating, briefly, the power in ritual objects such as yams. Men, in a sense, *are* ritual objects; what distinguishes them from women and children is that ritual potency is intrinsic to their personhood.

When a man is initiated into the men's cult, his Spirit is said to grow in strength and gain a number of special mystical powers. This specially augmented form of Spirit, exclusive to initiated men, is known as a *nggəlaka'aw*. This term derives from *ka'aw*, which I discussed earlier, and *nggəl*, the black face paint worn ceremonially by homicides. As the etymology of the term suggests, the nggəlaka'aw is closely associated with warfare and aggression. The special powers of the nggəlaka'aw operate in two contexts: male initiatory ritual and, in the past, warfare (and nowadays, I might add, in the modern substitutes for warfare: intervillage brawls and sports contests).

There are hereditary ritual leaders called *simbuk* who administer to initiated men—during rituals and, previously, before head-hunting raids—a form of magic which temporarily places their Spirits in a state of heightened ritual potency; this state is known as *səpanəmbi takwun* (lit. "bristling skin").

Men say that in this state, their Spirits shielded them from harm in warfare, filled them with ferocity, and sowed terror and confusion among their victims. Their Understanding was suspended or, as they say, "blocked" (*təpəna*); they were incapable of fear or pity and had no thoughts except of killing. After the raid, when the spell was removed, the power of their Spirits would dissipate, their Understanding returned, and, as one informant put it, "Our eyes became clear again, and we would look around and see all the fine men and women we had killed." Killing in warfare is treated as the ultimate demonstration of the power of one's Spirit over others, and the Spirits of homicide victims, symbolized in their captured skulls, were in fact said to attach themselves to their killer's Spirit and henceforth treat him as their "owner" (*asa'ai*, lit. "father").

Male ritual is closely connected with war making, and a similarly aggressive ritual potency is imparted to men's Spirits during initiations. I cannot describe here all the elaborate prescriptions which in ritual contexts govern relations between initiates and noninitiates, but, to give an example, during any ritual, the women and uninitiated must keep away from the cult house in which it is taking place and must have minimal contact with the men performing it. Depending on the precise ritual or the particular episode within it, they may simply have to give a wide berth to the initiates whenever they emerge from the cult building, or they may have to remain in their houses in silence or even completely abandon the village for a few hours. Men stress that their Spirits would quite automatically kill, even against their own wishes, anyone who broke these rules; they point out that their Spirits would attack even their own wives and children in this way. Men's Spirits stand above the morality of kinship and make no distinctions between individuals except those of ritual status.

An important point here is that the ritual hierarchy is a relation not between whole persons but between persons considered solely under the aspect of their ritual status. Considered simply as conscious subjects—that is, at the level of their Understanding—people remain equally morally accountable to each other irrespective of their ritual status. For example, initiated men are themselves obliged during rituals to keep their distance from women and the uninitiated so as not inadvertently to harm them, and I have seen women become very angry with men who carelessly failed to do so.

It is significant in this connection that in the course of a man's ritual career his Spirit is conceived as taking on not only an increasing power but also an increasing autonomy. Beginning its existence simply as the force animating him, his Spirit is thought gradually to project itself out of him into the form of a mystical guardian or alter ego, a conscious and intelligent agency independent of his will. The significance of this, I think, is that because of the dissonance between religious and secular values, it is necessary to absolve ritually senior men of personal responsibility for their possession of special ritual powers. The solution is to attribute to a man's Spirit an inherently ambiguous status; while always remaining a part of his identity, it becomes increasingly "other" than himself.

There is evidence for this in the fact that a man's Spirit is regarded as becoming in the end quite literally an item of attire. When a man joins the ritual elite—the third and final initiatory grade—his female kin present him with a string bag (*kwasembi*). This is a larger and finer version of the ordinary string bag worn by men, except that it has a distinctive pattern in the weave and a flexible rod inside to splay it out, giving it a crescent-shaped appearance. This bag is regarded as the material form of his Spirit; it is thought of as animate and highly dangerous to others. As he goes about his daily affairs, the bag remains hung unworn in his house; similarly, his Spirit, though still in contact with him, draws off and lies dormant. To wear the bag in everyday contexts would not only suggest overweening pride; it would be treated as a public menace. He is expected to wear it only in ritual situations, when his Spirit is allowed to become active and volatile.

A man keeps his ordinary string bag with him at all normal times, and it is one of his most personal possessions. While gossiping in their cult houses or relaxing after work, men rummage in their string bags for tobacco and betel nut and share them out; smoking and betel chewing are an indispensable part of male leisure and informality. At these times string bags are often the focus of horseplay; someone might subject another to an aggressive search of his string bag for tobacco, which the victim responds to with absurdly affected disdain. It is in these sorts of situations that

differences in ritual status between men are at their most submerged; horseplay signals a temporary state of equality, a suspension of the roles that divide them in the more formal atmosphere of ritual. A man's initiatory string bag, in contrast, is sacrosanct. His Spirit would attack anyone who reached into it or even touched it without permission. If he asks someone to fetch him the bag from his house, for instance, the latter must address the bag before he touches it and inform it that its "father" has sent him; otherwise the owner's Spirit would automatically attack him.

A string bag of either kind is a possession so intimate as to be a kind of tangible metonym for its owner's social identity. One might suggest, drawing on the ideas of Leach (1964) and Douglas (1966), that the sacred or "taboo" attributes of the initiatory string bag derive from its ambiguous conceptual relation to the person. But this would fail to explain why the same taboos do not apply to the ordinary string bag, and a slightly different approach seems to be needed. I would argue that the powers men assume in ritual pose a dilemma that is at the same time conceptual, moral, and political, and the solution has been to represent this power as an aspect of their personhood yet separable from them. Hence the ambiguous status ascribed to a man's Spirit: it is a part of himself but also an agency independent of his will. The string bag has been made the symbol of this power, I would suggest, because it has a similarly equivocal relation to its owner's identity. A man's Spirit is thought of, quite literally, as an item of adornment, a detachable or wearable part of himself.

These conceptualizations make it possible for men, in situations in which the ritual ethos threatens to obtrude in some unwelcome way into secular life, to take deliberate measures to dissociate themselves from their Spirits. For example, it often happens that victims of sickness or other misfortune make offerings—of a pig or a fowl—at the men's cult buildings to propitiate the spirit-beings they believe to be afflicting them. In theory, the sacrifice is eaten only by the ritual grade associated with the spirit-being in question; if others ate any of the meat they would automatically be attacked by the Spirits of the men of this grade. In fact, these men invariably share the meat out equitably to all the ritual categories, consuming some themselves and setting some aside for their wives and children and the rest for their male ritual juniors and their families. As they do so they announce loudly—as a subterfuge to deceive their Spirits—that they are "just throwing away rubbish" or "giving some scraps to the dogs" (cf. Tuzin 1982:349). In fact much of secular life at Avatip has this atmosphere about it, of men conspiring with their ritual inferiors against the ritual system in defense of an egalitarian social order.

With increasing age and ritual advancement, a man's Spirit is viewed as becoming associated or fused with other spiritual agencies: his agnatic ancestral ghosts, the Spirits of his head-hunting victims, the forces he invokes in ritual, the totemic ancestors figuring in his growing store of myths, and the beings addressed in his expanding repertoire of magic. It is said that some exceptional men internalize the power of such a vast array of spirit-beings that, when old, the potency of their Spirits begins to waste them physically and destroy their Understanding: "their Understanding no longer hears; they speak as if mad." Old ritual leaders do sometimes begin in time to show signs of senility, and when this happens it is assumed that their ritual careers have, as it were, gone *too* far, and their successors use this pretext to retire them from ritual life. I regret that I never told the legend of Faust to my Avatip informants, as I think it would have struck a chord. To them too, inordinate powers have their price: not the damnation of one's soul, but ending life confined by infirmity to one's house, a demented, awesome, almost inhuman object of immense ritual potency, revered by everyone and firmly excluded from the life of society.

Spirit, Understanding, and Gender

In ritual contexts at least, Spirit is regarded as a quintessentially "male" attribute, and this raises the question of whether Understanding might correspondingly be associated with women. There is perhaps evidence for this in the fact that the terms for Spirit and Understanding (*kaiyik/nggəlaka'aw* and *mawul*) are grammatically masculine and feminine in gender respectively. But I would stress that both capacities are assumed to be innate in all normal individuals, male or female, if in varying proportions and degrees of development. Nevertheless, in certain respects Understanding is implicitly portrayed as a "female" attribute, particularly in the domestic roles central to women's lives. Motherhood, for example, is extolled as an important exemplar of Understanding. Mothers are seen as identifying with their children so closely as to neglect themselves, and children must repay them with life-long respect and loyalty. The physical aspects of this identification are particularly stressed, especially the fact that, as the villagers put it, "When we are infants our mothers let our feces and urine fall onto their laps." "We must treat our mothers well," men in particular often say in a highly ambiguous idealization of womanhood, "for are they not our latrines?" The altruism attributed to mothers is held up for admiration by both sexes, yet—especially by men—seen from another perspective as slightly abject, even a little contemptible. As a result of the general attitude that too much contact with women, children, and domesticity weakens a man's Spirit, a father's relations with his children tend to be reserved and distant. Yet, curiously, men often speak of this with regret and even bitterness when discussing their relationships as children with their own fathers.

In addition to motherhood, an important responsibility of a married woman is to ensure that her husband looks after the welfare of her parents. Usually, parents foster the affections of their daughters from an early age and maintain close ties with them after marriage, for it is through their daughters' influence over their husbands that the parents will be assured, as they put it, "of growing old in the hands of our sons-in-law." The bestowal of a daughter in marriage is often managed by her kin with a good deal of tact and well-aimed flattery, for fear of alienating her if they used compulsion. Daughters, it is said, naturally "hear" their parents, and their loyalty and solicitude must be encouraged. On the other hand, Avatip parents perennially complain that their adult sons neglect them; their sons are, indeed, often too preoccupied for reasons of prestige with their obligations to their affines.

In sexual relationships as well, Understanding is treated as a "female" characteristic. There is a kind of erotic dogma at Avatip to the effect that while a woman may become infatuated with a man, the reverse is either impossible or disgraceful. This is institutionalized in the exclusively male prerogative of learning and performing love magic. Men are capable of magically empowering their Spirits to cause women to "hear" them, but women have no such power over men. It would be unthinkable, men say, to allow women the use of love magic, for it would enable women's Spirits to hold sway over their own. Women's Spirits are, and must remain, weaker than men's, for men are autonomous and women dependent, men act and women are acted upon (see Harrison 1983).

Another indication of the association between women, Understanding, and the domestic ethos is that there are legends of women so grief-stricken on the death of a husband or brother that they chose to join them in the world of the dead. It is believed possible for bereaved individuals to send a message, via a bird called the *yambukei*, to the ghosts of their dead kin, bidding them to come and fetch their Spirits away. One simply throws the bird a leaf, knotted for the number of days to pass before the rendezvous, and the bird will fly off with it to the land of ghosts. It would not be held unthinkable for a man to end his life in this way, and in fact there is always some concern after a death that distraught mourners of either sex might try to throw leaves to the yambukei. But there is a sense in which this is seen as a peculiarly female weakness, and it is significant that the only individuals regarded as ever actually having done this were women. Men, with their stronger Spirits, are less prone than women to excesses of Understanding. Spirit, as the power of life within the individual, allies itself with life, while Understanding is viewed, in some situations at least, as having a dangerous affinity with death.

Avatip women tend implicitly to endorse the view that Understanding is a distinctively "female" disposition. They often see men as unconcerned with their children, wives, and parents and chronically disloyal to the domestic morality in which women's own lives are centered. Men themselves sometimes concur with this and admit that it is lamentable, but they also tend to regard Understanding—particularly as it manifests itself in women—as bordering too closely on docility and dependence, as involving too ready a tendency to accommodate to others or identify with them, in short, as representing everything inimical to the masculine virtues of Spirit (cf. Chodorow 1974).

Having said all this, I must now point out that in some contexts at least, both men and women implicitly speak of Understanding as a characteristically "male" attribute. Men, for example, pride themselves on an ability to settle their disputes—for instance, the disputes between subclans played out in ceremonial debates—by patient discussion and with a generous willingness to compromise. They contrast this with women's ways of handling disputes: "When two women argue," men claim, "they just shout and swear at each other, neither listening to what the other is saying." In fact, men deride as a "woman" any man who loses his temper in a debate. Under-

standing, in this formulation, is an attribute of men and Spirit an attribute of women—but a peculiarly feminine Spirit which expends itself uselessly in petty strife. Although they do not speak in debates, the women of opposing sides—more so in the past than now—often brawled with each other, and this was expected by the men and even encouraged. While this is virtually the only opportunity permitted to women to publicly display Spirit and so demonstrate an equal status with men, it is in effect a kind of object lesson set up by men to demonstrate women's inferiority and to act as a foil to their own displays of exemplary moral responsibility. I might note that there is in fact a strong need in debates for a foil of this kind. A typical Avatip debate is almost continuously on the brink of collapsing into a brawl among the men themselves. The brawling of the women provides the men with a kind of antithesis against which to uphold the ideals of masculine conduct; any man who fought would show himself, by implication, to be no better than a woman.

Women, too, sometimes lay claim to Spirit as an attribute distinctively their own, but in a very different sense. When crises occur in their domestic or kinship relations, women are capable of defending what they see as their own familial interests vehemently and if necessary violently. But in these altercations they often view their husbands and close kinsmen—who are usually concerned to restore peace—as conceding too easily to their antagonists and too ready to appease, and they interpret this as disloyalty and cowardice. Only women, in their own view, have the interests of their own immediate kin truly at heart and are prepared at all costs to defend them, while men simply give in in these crises. The superior courage on which men pride themselves is sometimes regarded by women with a certain cynicism.

The point here is that women live their lives largely within the realm of domestic relations, with which their interests are more or less completely identified, while men participate both in this domain and in wider social and political concerns of varying degrees of scale (cf. Ortner 1974:79). Men as social actors are continually mobile, much more so than women, between organizational domains of greater or lesser inclusiveness and abstraction, with the familial at one pole and that of initiatory ritual at the other. The conflicting demands which these different orders impose lie at the root of the conflicts of interest between the sexes and of the tendency of the sexes to define themselves in interaction as each other's antitheses. They also lie at the root of a moral and existential tension which, I think, many men keenly if inarticulately feel between the ideals of Spirit and Understanding. It is through their Understanding that men are susceptible to the morality which has its paradigm in familial relationships; it is through their Spirits that they are open to extricating themselves from this and possessing freedom of political action.

There is a strong tendency, in short, to assimilate the Spirit/Understanding dualism to the dichotomy of the sexes; but this assimilation is made in two contradictory ways, and the only constant factor is that whichever of these two faculties men arrogate to their own sex they represent it as the "higher" or superior of the two. In some contexts, particularly in ritual, men arrogate Spirit to themselves and assign Understanding to femininity. In this formulation the worst offense a man can commit is to be weak, while the worst a woman can do is to be disloyal. Although this is perhaps the predominant schema, it cannot by itself provide men with a comprehensive representation of, or model for, the behavior of the sexes, and so to compensate for the deficiencies of this paradigm men sometimes invert it and speak of Understanding as the distinctively "male" attribute. From this perspective, men represent the common interests of the community, while women are the source of strife and division. The whole constellation of ideas is, in short, unstable and equivocal, but I think it is in this that its significance lies.

For example, Avatip men assume that when a woman acts in a way expressive of Understanding—say, in the nurture of her children—she is simply acting according to her nature and deserves no special commendation. But when a man evinces Understanding—in forgoing, for instance, his ritual rights to sacrificial meat—it is a magnanimous renunciation of his innate freedoms and so possesses greater ethical depth. On the other hand, when a man displays Spirit in some way, he is simply being faithful to the impulse to self-determination innate in men; when a woman does so it is treated as a characteristically female repudiation of the moral responsiveness attributed to her sex and so deserves all the more censure. My point here is that the categories of Spirit and Understanding in fact undergo subtle changes of meaning, depending on whether men apply them to themselves or to women, and these are structured in such a way as either to earn men greater moral dividends from their conduct or to give them greater freedom of acceptable action.

To the extent that these conceptualizations form part of what Ardener (1975) would call a "dominant structure," they implicitly govern the way in which women perceive themselves and their relations with men. But one can discern, in the perspectives women develop within the much smaller canvas of the domestic sphere, a muted model, as Ardener would call it, a counter-formulation of the Spirit/Understanding dichotomy. This is their tendency to contrast their own commitment to familial values with a habitual disloyalty to these on the part of men, a disloyalty they attribute to callousness (i.e., deficiency of Understanding) or weakness (i.e., deficiency of Spirit). And this is a perspective to which men—in the privacy of their relations with their wives and female kin—are themselves by no means impervious.

An important point on which I would take issue with Ardener is that it would be misleading to view the religious and domestic perspectives as "models" held respectively by men and by women. The ritual and familial ideologies are properties not of two social groups but of two organizational domains. Just as women are certainly capable, especially in the context of ritual, of subscribing to the ritual ethos, so men are capable of subscribing to the domestic ethos in the context of their own domestic relations. The two perspectives are a function not of gender but of social relationships contextually formulated in two alternative ways.

Conclusion

In recent years, a number of observers have pointed to the difficulties of interpreting Melanesian initiatory systems from traditional anthropological perspectives derived from Boas or Durkheim (Keesing 1982, Langness 1974). The social polarities these ritual systems express in the exclusion and deception of women and non-initiates make it difficult simply to assume, for example, that religious symbols are necessarily part of an integral "culture" shared by a total society or that they express its commitment to a unifying set of values and sentiments.

A recent shift of focus toward a psychological perspective has, I think, been one reaction to these problems, and it has resulted in a number of valuable and fine-grained studies of the subjective experience of initiation (Herdt 1981, 1982; Poole 1982). My only criticism of this approach is that it leaves what I see as a central problem—

that of providing an adequate sociological paradigm for the interpretation of these rites—still unresolved. But in its attention to the powerful impact which the experience of ritual has on personality structure and individual psychosocial development, this approach has implicitly recognized what I think is one of the key sociological features of these rituals: the great—if often traumatic—physical and psychological attention they focus on the individual. This is one reason I have examined the relation between ritual and constructs of the person, for while these constructs enter into individuals' subjective experience of ritual, they are publicly accessible ideas and related systematically to Avatip social organization.

A second recent approach to these initiatory systems has been to view them as centrally concerned with power relationships (Godelier 1976, Keesing 1982, Langness 1974). It is in this, I think, that the potential lies for developing an adequate sociological interpretation of them, and this is the second reason for my focus on Avatip concepts of personhood. It has been noted of many Melanesian societies that they place a high value on the individual and on personal autonomy (see, for example, Read 1955; Strathern 1980:209; Weiner 1976:212–14), and, as Read (1955) was perhaps the first to imply, this is certainly connected with the small political scale of these societies and the tendency for male power and status to be based on personal achievement. Although it is not based on ceremonial exchange and a "big man" pattern of leadership and has a certain ascriptive bias, Avatip political organization is of the general Melanesian "type": it is personalized, charismatic, and weakly institutionalized. In societies of this kind, I would suggest, the sources of power and inequality are viewed as lying not so much in the social order as in the individual; power is thought of as immanent in human selfhood rather than vested in social institutions. This is the conceptualization of power dramatized in Avatip ritual, and for this reason the central preoccupation of this ritual system is more with symbolic idealizations of the self than with symbolic idealizations of an encompassing social order. Avatip ritual is an attempt, above all, to set up a particular ideal of male individuality and to endow it with charismatic power and an absolute value.

In representing power as "nonstructural," the ritual system of course makes a statement about the social order; it implicitly defines it as a loosely organized, essentially egalitarian system in which the means of institutionalizing inequality are weakly developed. The paradox here is that, objectively, the ritual system is itself the central complex of institutionalized inequality within the society. It is this paradox which lies at the root of the separation and pervasive tension between the secular and ritual domains.

A view of these ritual systems as instruments of senior male domination points in a useful direction, but it is misleading if formulated too simply. The central concern of Avatip ritual is the attempt by men to demonstrate or achieve power; but the next step is to examine the mechanisms through which this power does actually have effects beyond the context of ritual itself. I have not tried to answer this issue here but simply raised it by indicating that the ritual and secular spheres of Avatip society are relatively separate. To portray Avatip society as having some single, definitive "ideology" of which male ritual is the canonical expression would be more than just an ethnographic distortion. It would be a repetition of precisely those assumptions which these initiatory cults should surely cause us to rethink, that is, that culture is in some simple sense a uniform and collectively shared whole.

I have tried to show that a central shared construct of Avatip culture is the idea of personhood as a relation between Understanding and Spirit, the former drawing individuals together in empathy and mutual identification and the latter setting them apart as the force perceived as driving selfhood to fulfill itself in power and autonomy. But the consensus as to these categories does no more than pose for the society a set of permanent and essentially unresolvable ideological questions, for example, of the relative valorization to be given these categories, of their articulation with gender, and of the forms of social and political organization they imply.

There are, very broadly, two antithetical sets of implications deriving from this concept of personhood, two alternative ways of envisioning society: one more or less tied to the politico-ritual organizational structures and the other to the structures of the domestic-secular domain. This, and not the dichotomy of the sexes, is the central disjunction within Avatip society. A tendency to assume that gender is a central or irreducible organizational dichotomy in Melanesia has, I think, sometimes caused confusion in the debate on the status of women. If I had made this assumption, I would have been left with an intractable problem: to put it quite simply, relations between the sexes at Avatip involve elements of both egalitarianism and male domination in different contexts.

A more general but related problem bedeviling the study of male-female relations in Melanesia has to do with certain theoretical preconceptions in our view of culture and society. According to this view, culture is an integral whole shared by a social group of some kind. This perspective either ignores the possibility of contradictions within culture or else treats them as ideological conflicts occurring between social categories based on gender, class, and so forth. In either case, my problem—that there are at Avatip two broadly opposed views of male-female relations, but tied to context and not to gender—remains intractable.

My suggestion is this: We have known since Marx and Durkheim that all modes of consciousness are a function of particular systems of social relations (cf. Lawrence 1970), but a point we sometimes overlook in this connection is that systems of social relations may or may not in fact correspond to, or be coterminous with, social groups and categories. One might, for instance, have a group whose overall organization rests on different principles in different situations, as Leach (1954) showed for the Kachin, and—as is an anthropological commonplace—groups salient in one organizational context may dissolve and be replaced by other alignments in other contexts. Both, I have argued, are the case at Avatip. Neither the ritual nor the secular domain is exclusive to any particular social group, but both involve the whole of the society and in fact define in alternative ways what the significant divisions within the society are. There are important ideological divergencies within Avatip culture; but these are not between segments of the society but *of the society with itself.* Thus while it may be true that the ritual ideology serves the political interests of senior men, it is also tautological, for the ritual ideology constitutes senior men as a relevant social category in the first place, and outside of the context of ritual the household, the conjugal dyad, the kindred, and so forth are entities at least as significant and probably more so. In short, we need a theory of culture able to accommodate contradictions of a deeper kind than even Marxism envisages: one which would, first, make it quite acceptable to describe a society as having ideals of male domination and sexual equality, of hierarchy and egalitarianism, simultaneously; second, enable us to do so rigorously by tying these ideologies to contextually defined systems of social relations; and, last, identify the constructs which articulate these opposed formulations with each other. I have tried to show that at Avatip these constructs are those relating to the nature of personhood.

Notes

1. Twenty-two months' fieldwork were carried out at Avatip between 1977 and 1979, under a scholarship in the Department of Prehistory and Anthropology of The Australian National University. I am grateful to that body for its financial support. A version of this paper was published in *Man* 20 (1985):115–39 and is reprinted here by permission of the Royal Anthropological Institute of Great Britain and Ireland.
2. "The radiations of adornment, the sensuous attention it provokes, supply the personality with . . . an enlargement or intensification of its sphere: the personality, so to speak, *is* more when it is adorned" (Simmel 1950:340).

31/ Fighting for Their Lives: The Problem of Cultural Authenticity in Today's Sepik

Donald Tuzin

The phrase "cultural authenticity," intentionally ambiguous, usefully subsumes a number of issues that, in some measure at least, are begging to be resolved by this historic gathering. The first and oldest of these bears on the very justification for our presence here: to what extent may the Sepik be authentically described and studied as a "culture area" or, indeed, to borrow Schwartz's (1963) more ambitious concept, an "areal culture"? It is an interesting and perhaps ethnologically significant fact that Sepik researchers, to a remarkable degree, have been drawn to problems of ethos, ethnic interaction, and regional cultural systems. Thurnwald (1916), for example, conjectured about the effects of Austronesian contact on groups on the Lower Sepik tributaries. Likewise, Mead (1935, 1938, 1947a) devotes a considerable portion of her Sepik corpus to patterns of temperamental variation and cultural diffusion among local groups; Bateson (1936) revives the idea of "ethos," joins it with the notion of "eidos," and uses them to conceptualize the emotional and intellectual features of the culturally hegemonous Iatmul; Newton (1971) explores the continuities of artistic and architectural styles in the Upper Sepik region to demonstrate, inter alia, the existence of a distinctive regional form; Gewertz (1983) analyzes Chambri society, in some of its aspects, as a precipitate of historical (political, economic, cultural) interactions centered on groups of the Middle Sepik; my own work among the Ilahita Arapesh (Tuzin 1976, 1980, 1982) emphasizes the need to understand local social and ritual forms as derived from foreign sources; finally, our esteemed hosts are without peer in their attempt to gain ethnographic mastery of the Middle Sepik subregion (e.g., Hauser-Schäublin 1977, Schindlbeck 1980, Wassmann 1982). Such has been the intensity of cultural interchange throughout the region that ethnographers must take special care to conceptualize village and tribal boundaries not only as cultural barriers but also as cultural conduits (McDowell 1983).

The recognition of this necessity, widespread though it has been in Sepik symposia and informal discussions, has yet to produce a clear statement of the dynamics of *areal culture* in this region; neither has it yielded a comprehensive or defensible account of the Sepik's ethnographic distinctiveness. In a paper written shortly before her death Mead (1978:69) asks, "To what extent can it be said about the Sepik region that we are here dealing with a culture area that can be defined in any except negative terms?" It is a question she would be asking if she were with us today, and it echoes her earlier call (Mead 1973) for a program of Sepik research that would lead to an authentic, ethnological understanding of the region:

> To what extent this cluster of dynamic generalized tendencies, which can be handled either as highly eclectic traits, as pervasive themes, or as very deep area characteristics, are unique to the Sepik area, and how they relate to other areas of New Guinea and island Melanesia, is an area of research for the next decades. Whether there is a pervasive cultural style which may provide some uniformity of response to the demands made on the peoples by localization and self-government will also be a fruitful subject for field work and subsequent synthesis.

The challenge, then, is to overcome our monographic myopia long enough to visualize research problems of broad regional import. But areal cultures are poorly attended by anthropologists, and a skeptic might argue that "the Sepik" is merely a label—at best incidental in ethnographic importance to the parts which comprise it, at worst nonexistent. I would prefer to think that our raison d'être as a Sepik conference is less arbitrary than that. More significantly, the studies cited above powerfully suggest that local cultures in the Sepik cannot be understood without reference to the region and that accordingly, knowledge of the part ultimately rests on knowledge of the whole. What this "whole" is and how it is to be known about are questions perhaps more easily asked than answered, but for now I propose that a satisfactory response entails more than a summary of regional trade, migration, war, and other societal interactions; it involves an understanding of the psychocultural dispositions which facilitate the movement of ideas, practices, and matériel between distinct, sometimes warring social groups.

For example, in characterizing the Mountain Arapesh as an "importing culture" Mead (1938) may have hit upon a tendency that typifies most Sepik groups and in its intensity may even be a distinctive feature of the region. Diffusion exhibited on the Sepik scale requires more than the juxtaposition of different groups, more than their social interaction; it also requires regular cultural mechanisms through which meanings originating in one system can be translated (or transliterated) into terms consistent with meanings already inherent in the importing system. This process, which I have termed the "naturalization of meaning" (Tuzin 1980), appears to be fostered by the almost playful experimentation manifested by Sepik peoples toward symbols encoded in art, mythology, ritual, and other self-expressive realism. At the risk of overgeneralizing from my Ilahita Arapesh observations, I suggest that this common fascination with symbolic forms amounts to a kind of regional metalanguage—a shared, intellectualist orientation which, within limits, enjoys novelty for its own sake and craves discourse with like-minded others who have something new to offer. Instances of transmission may be isolated and trivial in themselves, but in the aggregate they are the means by which the reality of the Sepik as an areal culture is continually reaffirmed and recalibrated. This is why it is possible to speak of the Sepik in unitary terms despite its internal and seemingly fundamental diversity of settlement and subsistence patterns, marriage, kinship and descent forms, and the like. Indeed, the one institution that does enjoy broad regional agreement—the tambaran cult—is also the one that most directly embodies symbols of personal and cultural identity, symbols which are nonetheless eagerly manipulated. I will return to this point shortly.

The fact that we were brought here to consider studies both in and *for* modern Papua New Guinea supports an additional reason for taking as our object the Sepik as an areal culture. I refer to the emic significance of this concept and its modern vicissitudes. In Papua New Guinea and elsewhere the idea that large geographical regions possess groups of certain cultural types began, like the concept of "the tribe" (Leaf 1979), as an invention of administrators, missionaries, and anthropologists, who in the early days of contact had the special vantage point to notice these patterns. The people themselves were limited by immobility and military insecurity to an awareness that their immediate neighbors were either more or less like themselves in language and custom; strictly speaking, in *their* world areal culture did not exist. The radical penetration of these physical and conceptual barriers in the modern era has established the indigenous, politically entailed reality of entities such as "the Sepik," "the Southern Massim," and "the Western Highlands" and has led to their becoming provincial districts and/or major components of an emergent national consciousness. Within both national and provincial jurisdictions culture policy aims to distill and preserve traditional essences which have a place in the modern world, thereby injecting into the future of these people a measure of cultural authenticity. But this presupposes that policy makers know what the character, conditions, and costs of cultural authenticity *are*, and I am not confident that they do—any more than we do! If it is to be rational, humane, and effective, the kind of policy that everyone agrees is needed deserves to be informed by an understanding of the psychocultural bases of local and regional identification. In my view, Sepik research has matured to the point at which this issue might be addressed, and it appears that some of my fellow contributors are thinking along similar lines.

Only a Philistine would dispute the value of, for example, the prodigious work being done by Mack and Ruth Ruff and Christian Coiffier to survey, preserve, and encourage manufacture of artistic and architectural masterpieces of the Sepik, but it is perhaps worth asking what the continuation of these traditions might accomplish, other than attracting affluent tourists to the area. The problem of cultural authenticity arises when we admit that many of these objects belong to a world that is now dead or dying, which is another way of saying that the expressive needs which gave birth to these forms are in the process of radical eclipse or redefinition. As Sapir (1924:425) wrote,

> the highest manifestations of culture, the very quintessence of the genius of a civilization, necessarily rests in art, for the reason that art is the authentic expression, in satisfying form, of experience; experience

not as logically ordered by science, but as directly and intuitively presented to us in life. As culture rests, in essence, on the harmonious development of the sense of mastery instinctively sought by each individual soul, this can only mean that art, the form of consciousness in which the impress of the self is most direct, least hampered by outward necessity, is above all other undertakings of the human spirit bound to reflect culture. To relate *our* lives, *our* intuitions, *our* passing moods to forms of expression that carry conviction to others and make us live again in these others is the highest spiritual satisfaction we know of, the highest welding of one's individuality with the spirit of his civilization. Were art ever really perfect in expression, it would indeed be immortal. Even the greatest art, however, is full of the dross of conventionality, of the particular sophistication of its age. As these change, the directness of expression in any work of art tends to be increasingly felt as hampered by a something fixed and alien, until it gradually falls into oblivion. While art lives, it belongs to culture; in the degree that it takes on the frigidity of death, it becomes of interest only to the study of civilization.

Keeping the art, then, even ensuring its continued manufacture, poses only technical difficulties; the real problem is keeping it alive to the changing experiences of the present and future Sepik. The architectural training program described by our co-contributors (see Ruff and Ruff in this volume) is promising as a practical link between artistic tradition and artistic modernity. From the standpoint of more general theory, however, Sapir's emphasis on art as a vehicle and expression of human spirituality leads toward questions concerning the dynamics of self and personhood as major constituents of the methodological individual featured in the passage—the one whose intuitions discriminate between the genuine and the spurious under conditions of cultural change and dislocation.

Cast in contemporary anthropological terms (see papers by Harrison and McDowell in this volume), the experience which Sapir exalts is the intrinsically meaningful fusion of self and person—the graceful union of our subjectively felt, existential center and our socially constituted profile as a morally competent being. Art may be, as Sapir says, the noblest expression of this plenitude, but in principle the measure of cultural authenticity is surely the degree to which all acts

and artifacts, down to the most mundane, are suffused with this self-affirmative quality. By this view the demoralizing effect of rapid cultural change, the depression of cultural collapse, results from the progressive experiential divergence of elements of person from elements of self. That is to say, values and activities associated with unfamiliar technological, economic, political, religious, and other exigencies may quickly alter the constitution of personhood, thus depriving the self of recognizable opportunities for expression and placing the individual in a condition of spiritual under- or malnourishment. This does not imply that harmony between self and person is ever ideal; as sentient beings we achieve such perfection only in myth—and, as Adam and Eve's actions suggest, the result can be exceedingly boring. At the other extreme, perfect disharmony—null expression—is achieved only in death, since even the suicide's final act is an expression of sorts. Cultural authenticity does not free the individual from these contradictions, but it does lighten their burden by codifying means by which they can be recognized and managed. The movement described therefore begins at a point of normative contradiction. Disjunctions in the traditional order may in fact be an incentive for welcoming change. A few individuals may flourish under the new regime, but most will discover that the loss is far greater than the gain and that the gates to the Garden have locked behind them.

Inspired by the examples of Sapir, Leenhardt, Hallowell, and others, the person-self framework has, I think, the special virtue of promising insights into traditional cultures that are assimilable to the analysis of change, leading perhaps to an understanding of why and how the Sepik is developing a cultural identity in its own right. I shall illustrate this point with three brief examples, each of which may be worth further research.

In Ilahita at the time of my fieldwork (1969–72), life was becoming partitioned by the rapidly changing definitions of personhood. The crisis—if I may call it that—was largely centered on men, and to a much lesser extent their female coevals, between twenty-five and forty. Traditionally, these are the years during which the greatest investment of time and effort is made to ensure maximum social, political, and economic standing during the subsequent period. This was the career course that had been expected and valued since the enculturative years of middle childhood. Intrasocietal and intrapsychic conflict arose because the demands of cash-cropping and business enterprises—the allure of money—were presenting individuals with the painful choice of where to invest their limited energies. Stated crudely, the changing constitution of personhood was at war with their perduring sense of self. In an earlier work (Tuzin 1980) I argued that this conflict was addressed and momentarily resolved in favor of the latter by the dramatic resurgence of the tambaran cult. Aided by the timely reversal of some of the village's economic schemes, the elders of the cult succeeded in convincing their juniors that the only solution to the general sense of community malaise was to recapture, through appropriate ritual performances and supportive collective activities, the values that had served them (especially the elders!) so well in the past. Although it was widely agreed that this would probably be the last full-dress initiation, complete with a monumental spirit house and trappings, everyone admitted that this sort of finality had been assumed for every major cult ceremonial within memory. Will this one truly be the last? Possibly so. The middle-aged men of today will carry their conflicts into old age and will not be as convinced and willful as their fathers were in defense of ritual traditions. On the other hand, predictions of the imminent demise of the cult have been around for a long time; future contingencies may hold compelling reasons of their own for the men to recapture that sense of themselves to which only the performances of the tambaran can give recognizable expression.

The men could have joined a cargo cult. During the period in question a movement imaginatively fixed on the stone survey marker atop Mt. Turu, near Yangoru, was sweeping the entire Sepik region. In the face of dire warnings that on the day the marker was ceremonially removed the heads of those who had not paid their dues would be blown away by a "great wind," it took considerable courage to resist joining the movement. And yet, to my knowledge only one man in Ilahita (pop. 1,500) subscribed, though many were painfully apprehensive as the Day approached. They resisted, first, because local enemy villages had already joined, and the people of Ilahita wanted no part of a millennium that included them; secondly, because it would have meant abandoning their tambaran activities, the objectives of which were seen to be obscurely identical to those of the cargo cult. The latter reason hints that the reunification of person and self sought in traditional ritual performances may also be a component of cargo cult aspirations, both in the Sepik and elsewhere.

Students of cargo cults and other millenarian movements have not, in my opinion, satisfactorily answered the question why, after prophecy fails, adherents in large numbers continue to believe that the cargo will come. Contrary to expectation, "Sydney" did not appear when the Mt. Turu marker was removed, and yet adherence to the movement was barely affected by this technicality. Those who explain this by appeal to the human need to eliminate cognitive dissonance (e.g., Festinger, Riecken, and Schachter 1956) neglect to notice that the inevitable disparity between the real and the ideal, between illusion and truth (Tuzin 1980), is the central metaphysical point of virtually all ritual action. Not the elimination but the culturally fulfilling *contemplation* of this dissonance is what ritual and certain other symbolic acts are all about. Rather than taking the cargo as a literal—and therefore deeply irrational—object of these collective exercises, we might consider it as an idiom through which people are saying something about themselves.

One clue that favors this line of analysis is the widely reported notion that, as a precondition of the cargo's arrival, it is necessary for the aspirants to achieve a community of complete harmony and mutual good intention, often accompanied by the need to create purity and order in their moral and physical conditions. This idea has a precedent in traditional ritual contexts. In Ilahita and elsewhere, ritual success depends on the purity and goodwill of all participants. If something goes wrong with the preparations—inclement weather, repeated failures to net a sacrificial pig—the assumption is that someone is consciously or unconsciously harboring an antisocial thought that is obstructing the collective effort. A meeting is held to ferret out the problem and, by payment or other inducement, resolve it. Similarly, precautionary peace markers are typically erected before any gathering that includes parties who may fall into quarreling or fighting. Aware of the shortcomings of their regulatory mechanisms in controlling the "natural" human impulse to hate or strike out against an enemy but adhering nonetheless to what Michael Smith (in this volume) has aptly termed "the romance of community cooperation," the organizers proceed in the hope that all will be well. The success of ritual—and usually it is successful, since its goals are intangible things such as species fertility, the masculinization of youths, or the rededicated patronage of cult spirits—is exhilarating because it implies that the ideal of community unity has been achieved and that the harsher realities of everyday existence can be faced with renewed confidence.

Applying this perspective to the question of what the cargo signifies, I suggest that it is an image of self-person unity amidst and in defiance of circumstances that are driving these elements of experience apart. That the cargo is to be taken in a mythic rather than literal sense follows from the odd fact that, as the people themselves are somewhat aware, the preconditions for its arrival are impossible to achieve. Given the indigenous recognition of the fractiousness and disorder that beset social life, is the attainment of perfect local or regional accord any less miraculous than the advent of the cargo? The persistence of the idea that the cargo will come might therefore be seen as an expression of the age-old hope that spiritual harmony, the "romance" at both personal and collective levels, will be attained. In yearning for the cargo, they yearn for themselves. And, since cargo is not really what the cults are about, it is not surprising that sightseeing tours by cultists to the factories of Australia and Japan have little effect on their (misunderstood) aspirations.

I am proposing that forms such as the tambaran cult and the cargo cult are alike in being indigenous statements about cultural authenticity, a mythic state which is best attained—and then only momentarily —in ritual action. The final issue to be addressed here concerns the etiology of this image in the life of the individual. The question is, how does experiential authenticity come to rely on the psychocultural integration of subjective self and socially constituted person? The source lies, I suggest, in the experience of middle childhood, between the ages of approximately five and ten. This is not to deny that important enculturative events occur before and after these years; rather, it is to focus analytically on that formative period during which the individual first encounters serious demands of social responsibility and cultural competence (Rogoff 1981). This is a topic for serious future study in the Sepik. Anthropologists have often reported what is said and done to children by adults, but from an ethnographic standpoint we know very little about what children say and do to one another, about the interpretations which children place on cultural understandings as they receive and transmit them, or about the lasting feed-forward effects of these interpretations on adult belief, behavior, and ideation.

My hypothesis is that cognitive and emotional associations originating in childhood, mainly within the nexus of family and peer-group relationships, directly affect one's adult sense of self, person, and cultural authenticity. To be sure, childhood experience is constrained by a sociocultural context. But this truth should not obscure the fact that the child *interprets* this context in an independent, creatively childlike way, using the resources of knowledge, logic, and above all, imagination that are available at this stage of life. Moreover, by virtue of their timing these interpretations are interwoven with the emotionally involved formation of personal identity during latency. Later socialization may subsume, modify, or intellectually reject these interpretations and their affective overtones, but it is very unlikely to obliterate them. Thus, the fact that one's cultural life begins when one is a child carries the important implication that adult understandings, despite certain discontinuities, are referable to and derive part of their meaning from understandings instilled in childhood (cf. Crapanzano 1981). By this act of reference, the ego investment of the child is repeatedly deployed as the adult's commitment to the cultural values and percepts which he or she now commands. Accordingly, the phenomenon known as "cultural identity" represents the projection of childish (in the strict sense) significances into the adult world of meaning and action (Tuzin 1980:216). If part of the anthropological program is understanding the wellsprings of cultural signification, we should consider that Wordsworth may have been correct in saying, "The Child is father of the Man."

An example from my Ilahita fieldwork may help to clarify these points. In eliciting opinions as to the character and ontological status of senior tambaran spirits, I found that initiated men variously emphasized their abstract, mystical attributes, women professed a fearful incuriosity, and children conceived them to be horrifying, people-eating monsters. Where do children obtain these primitive images? Not from adults, but from older children, whose fantasies are sublimated through devising lurid accounts with which playfully to torment their younger, more credulous peers. Adults disapprove of this cruel amusement and will intervene if they see it happening; but most children's play is unsupervised and unnoticed by adults, and hence such teasing is rarely restrained. Moreover, the persistence of these childish images in adult mental life is confirmed when dream reports, psychological projective tests, and ritually contrived illusions bring them back to the foreground of consciousness. In other words, despite having distanced themselves intellectually from these boyhood images, men retain and refer to them through the emotional expressions of religious consciousness.

This example suggests that, when it comes to the emotions which we invest in adult beliefs and practices, it is often children, not adults, who are the naive *agents* of enculturation. Middle childhood is the time, it is said, when society begins its concerted program to instill knowledge, cultural routines, normative compliance, and moral values in its next adult generation. But any observant parent would probably realize that this abstraction neglects an important, albeit informal, enculturative fact, namely, that many of a child's introductory understandings about the world are taught to him or her *by other children* and are thus subject to a host of imaginative infusions originating in the cognitive and emotional sets of both tutor and pupil. Some of these never proceed beyond childhood: they are the jingles, jokes, sayings, and games that are handed down by continuous generations of children—a "children's culture," or, as the Arapesh say, a "children's tambaran," which owes little or nothing to adult assistance. Other lessons, however, perhaps most of them, involve values, judgments, ideals, beliefs, procedures, and other elements of adult society. While later years will perfect these understandings in line with adult forms, the individual's lasting attachment to them—their value as signs which bind a person's sense of identity to a body of received custom—derives from the fact that one first encounters them during childhood, when the acquisition of personal identity and the acquisition of culture proceed as two aspects of the same developmental process.

It is important to emphasize that the emotional qualities of these adult forms are not merely ornamental. For example, in adult attitudes toward authority figures, toward the opposite sex and certain types of kin, toward supernatural agencies, the correct emotional stance is *criterial* to the customary form itself. The integration of these dispositions is manifest as a distinct cultural ethos, the acquisition of which begins under the peculiar conditions of childhood. For this reason, the satisfaction gained through feeling and acting "correctly" is, in a sense, regressive; it is an experience which recaptures the prototypic childhood equivalence of personal and cultural worth. It is the fusion of self and person defined earlier as the subjective content of cultural authenticity. Obversely, the exaggerated disapproval or cathartic amusement so often evoked in response to the culturally alien indicates that its very existence is (regressively) perceived to be an assault on the integrity of the respondent—an integrity that is never as unassailably perfect as we would like it to be.

I have tried to argue, briefly and tentatively, that future studies in and for modern Papua New Guinea would do well to examine the dynamics of cultural authenticity. While I worry that the terms self and person may oversimplify this complex phenomenon, I have used them because they are current in the literature and because they are minimally adequate descriptors of two of the poles (there may be more) of psychocultural integration. It is neither trite nor uninteresting, I think, to say that the future shape of this integration in the Sepik is now being decided by the children of the region. Their experiences are determining what the future terms of cultural authenticity will be. Although these terms will certainly include novel elements such as regional and national identity, there are enough continuities in formative experience to make the final result recognizable to the ancestors. Sapir is inclined to sneer at civilization as deracinated culture, a husk, a mockery. I would prefer to regard it as a continuation in objectified form of what has always been valued, there to be reassigned to whatever *cultural* needs may emerge. The future expressive fit between civilization, culture, and the individual in the Sepik will not be perfect, but then life was never perfect anyway.

Part Six
Engendering Gender

Introduction

William E. Mitchell

The anatomical difference between males and females is rarely ignored by human societies in organizing the psychological and instrumental lives of their members. The papers in this section examine some of the ways in which gender as a social category is culturally conceived in the Sepik region. Patricia K. Townsend documents that Hiyewe women, compared with women in many other Papua New Guinea societies, have high status vis-à-vis men in terms of their ability to engage in trade, inherit strategic resources, and participate in economic decision-making. She relates this finding to the fact that leadership among Hiyewe men is weakly developed and decentralized. This correlation between weakly developed male leadership and relatively high female status, she notes, is one that holds for other parts of the world as well.

Bernard Juillerat's symbolic analysis stresses the importance of the Yafar marital couple, in their private domain of "connubial complicity," as the primary "cell" for transgressing the society's dominant male ideology. He points to a recent millenarian cult that permits women's partial participation as further indication of the gradual breakdown of male dominance in Yafar society in the context of Western contact.

Diane Losche identifies the contrasting views of Marilyn Strathern and Annette Weiner on the status of women in Melanesian society and, on the basis of her own ethnographic material on the Abelam, develops a third position that dismantles the issue of gender hegemony by emphasizing the ideological and behavioral fluctuations of gender relations depending upon the social context.

Margaret Holmes Williamson is similarly concerned with gender ideologies but approaches the problem from a different perspective. In an attempt to avoid what she identifies as circularity in the use of the concepts of "sex" and "gender," she focuses on an analysis of the life-cycle rituals of Kwoma men and women and examines the relationships between "persons," i.e., both men and women, and their cosmos.

Paul Roscoe reconstructs the male initiation rituals of the Yangoru Boiken, who abandoned the practice in the late 1940s, and discusses contemporary Boiken views regarding the significance of male initiation. In Roscoe's and Richard Scaglion's comparative analysis of colonial and postcolonial male initiation in the Sepik area, they consider why the practice has persisted in some societies and disappeared in others. They conclude that missionary opposition, millenarianism, and labor migration have all contributed to the decline of male initiation but that these factors have been least effective in those societies in which the social organization of the rituals was based on a pattern of alternation and complementary opposition of groups and individuals.

32/ *Our* Women Are Okay:
Aspects of Hiyewe Women's Status

Patricia K. Townsend

Not getting anywhere with my discussions of menstruation with Hiyewe women in 1967,[1] in desperation I asked a teen-aged boy, "Why is it that Saniyo women use menstrual huts but I never see women around here using them?" Waro replied, grinning slyly, "Oh, *our* women are okay (*fara'u*)." It was not until last year that I finally understood that he was saying that Hiyewe women did not menstruate. At the time, his reply had seemed to me a summing-up of a kind of smug "feminism" that Hiyewe men quite often expressed. For example, several men claimed to have worked sago when their wives needed help (while a visiting Sio man listened shocked and said that Sio men *never* worked sago). Despite a generally strict sexual division of labor, women who mastered a man's skill, such as sewing thatch or understanding clan slit-gong signals, were pointed out to me by men with approval. Other men grumbled mildly, but with a certain pride, about their wives' independence in going off to other communities to participate on their own in feasts and other public events.

I tended to dismiss men's assertions of such feminist sentiments as intended for my ears only, but as have some other ethnographers in recent years I noted that women's participation in decision making and public affairs was greater than I had expected from the reading of male-biased ethnography. This paper does not attempt anything like a systematic comparison of Hiyewe women's overall status with that of women elsewhere in the Sepik or beyond. It is simply an overview of some of the ways in which Hiyewe women's participation in activities beyond the household is encouraged or constrained. Women's participation in the public sphere is facilitated by several key factors, including a fairly balanced control over strategic resources and the pattern of bilocal or even multilocal residence.

Control over Strategic Resources

For the people living along the Miwei River, there is no single, all-important strategic resource

equivalent to pigs in the highlands or yams in the Trobriands. Food, shell valuables, and pigs all have some importance, but none is overriding. In managing the continuous stream of everyday interhousehold transfers of food within the hamlet that helps to even out the vagaries of luck and health, women have complete control over the disposal of the sago that they produce, just as men control the fish and game that they obtain. Women as well as men may have distant trading partners on the Sepik River, outside the language group.[2] Although the main item Hiyewe women have for trade is sago, this trade has not developed into regular markets as in the Middle Sepik and takes place only infrequently. In exchange for their sago they receive not fish, as in the Middle Sepik, but manufactured goods such as baskets.

Domestic pigs are a strategic resource which men and women manage jointly. The ratio of pigs to persons is very low (of the order of one to eight) and their use restricted to rare ceremonial occasions. When a pig is killed, the decision is jointly made by the man, who in part owns the pig, usually by virtue of capturing a piglet from the wild, and the woman, who feeds the pig. Neither will be able to eat any of its meat. Pigs are killed mostly for curing ceremonies. A pig may be killed for an occasional marriage or mortuary feast, but more often game, sago grubs, or vegetables suffice, along with the sago pudding always made in large quantities for feasts.

Shell money is an equally important type of wealth. Bride-price (*taunei ma'aru*, "wife cowries") is paid in 1–2-meter-long strings of cowries, with secondary gifts of other shells, beads (which have replaced dogs' teeth and buttons), and other items such as bows. Money in small amounts is now beginning to come into bride-price. So far only one marriage, that of a man on salary for the mission, has involved a large amount of money. One hundred kina were distributed among thirty-seven persons, of whom fifteen were women and girls. The largest single amount, twelve kina, went to the bride's mother. This bride-price also included approximately twenty strings of cowries, of which only one went to a woman.

Shells (and now, money) are controlled by both men and women individually. Although the amounts controlled by women are smaller, they are managed in the same way. A woman may contribute a string of cowries to the bride-price of a kinsman, and other women receive bride-price for their kinswoman. In this respect the Hiyewe differ significantly from highlands societies, in which women's influence in exchange is typically behind the scenes, and from other lowlands societies, in which they participate in separate systems of exchange using different types of valuables. Within the Sepik, the participation of women in this way is not unusual but is declining with the monetarization of bride-price (Hauser-Schäublin 1977:94).

The Hiyewe view is that the pay given for a woman directly compensates those who contributed to her mother's bride-price. These investments in a woman's future offspring are passed on to one's children, and the child is taught, "When that little girl grows up, you will get part of the pay."[3]

Although the amounts of bridewealth are typically small, there are strong sanctions against omitting it. Disgruntled men who are dissatisfied with the pay received for their sisters are believed to have caused barrenness or even their own sisters' death through sorcery. The amount of bride-price expected is not affected by the failure to arrange a brother-sister exchange. Most marriages do involve some immediate or delayed reciprocity in women, if not an actual sister exchange, as well as payment.

A man getting married may contribute one or two strings of cowries, but usually it is an elder brother who takes the responsibility of getting as many as possible of their bilateral kin (including their brothers-in-law) to contribute, until the number reaches at least the total agreed on in prior discussion with the bride's kinsfolk. The wider the network they can tap, the more recipients there will be among the bride's kindred.

Most of the cowries are massed for display, and women are almost as active as men in deciding who will get which valuables. The recipient chosen often has some other link of kinship, residence, or friendship with the giver of his or her string. Few men will have more than one string to contribute, and few women own any. The number of cowries is small, and they circulate quickly. However, women have recently been particularly quick to convert cowries purchased from more remote hamlets to the east and west, since the building of the airstrip at Mapisi has made small

amounts of cash available through work for the mission and the sale of food.

It is not a straightforward matter to quantify the relative place of women as givers and recipients of bride-price. In the retrospective accounts given by male informants, women tend to drop out entirely, with the occasional exception of the bride's mother as a recipient. Even when talking about very recent events, men tend to speak as though a string of cowries given by a woman were given by her husband. Female informants, in contrast, are seldom able to give a coherent account of an entire bride-price, even one in which they have been major participants.[4] For this reason it is necessary to confine the analysis to the few bride-price payments I observed.

Sera's bride-price, paid at Yaputawi in January 1983, included thirteen strings of cowries. Two of these were given by women, the groom's father's sister's daughter and his father's father's sister's daughter, and the recipients of these two strings of cowries were women. As usual, women were as active as men in the exchange of smaller items such as beads and small amounts of money. These smaller items were flung back and forth so rapidly in the heated discussion as the payment reached its climax that to follow or reconstruct it all became impossible.

For Karopa, a bride-price of fifteen strings of cowries had been agreed upon in advance. At the feast and distribution in January 1984, the major items given were seven *tipesi* (the most valuable cowrie strings, in which the cowries are placed crosswise on the woven band), five *mei* (cowries sewn lengthwise on a band), and three *feipi* (pig's tusk–cowrie ornaments). Three items were given by older women, all distant cross-cousins of the groom. On this occasion the bride's elderly father's sister took a more prominent role in the distribution of cowries to their relatives than either the bride's father or mother. Three of the fifteen strings were distributed to female relatives of the bride.[5] The bride's father had decided not to take any cowries himself but had brought a bowl to keep all the money, comprised of small contributions of one to two kina each from several men. In addition to the cowries and cash given for Karopa, on a recent trip to the trade store at Frieda River the groom's brother's wife had added masses of beads (predominantly of the favorite color, red). Most of these went to wives and daughters of men who had received other items. But this was not the end of the story. Two women who had received only beads were very angry. They were daughters of two men, now dead, who had contributed to the bride-price for the girl's mother twenty-five years earlier. Each had a younger brother who had received a string of cowries, and the women asserted that they too should receive cowries. (The implication was that the bride-price needed to be larger, not that others were not entitled to cowries.) The two claims were resolved differently. One brother good-humoredly turned his string over to his sister later. The other woman went home in anger, smearing herself with mud to show her distress, and a few days later a distant kinsman of the groom living in the village into which she had married gave her a string of cowries.

These accounts show that the participation of women in bride-price is somewhat less than that of men. Women also tend to get involved later in life: all the women mentioned here were over thirty-five, while single men as young as eighteen received some cowries. More important, however, the women's participation, although less frequent, is on exactly the same terms as that of men.

Residence and the Organization of Production

The Hiyewe move frequently in a complex cycle to maintain claims to natural resources in several areas and to renew ties of cooperation with various sets of relatives (Townsend 1978). The implication of this residence pattern for women will be our only concern here. Although descent groups are strictly patrilineal, in 1966–67 only part of the time were families actually living in hamlets that were predominantly agnatic in composition. Instead, they were shifting from hamlet to hamlet to live with various of the wife's and husband's kin. The settlement pattern has changed significantly since 1967,[6] with fewer, larger, and more permanent settlements, but because people spend correspondingly more time in bush houses they continue to exploit resources controlled by both partners as well as collaborating with kin on both sides.

Even when families are not physically moving to maintain a kinship network and a set of scattered resource claims, women within a hamlet are continually forming and rearranging their networks of working relationships. Unlike many Papua New Guinea women, who work alone or with their husbands, Hiyewe women work sago together. They are invariably accompanied by a breast-feeding child, but weaned children are usually left at home, most often in the care of their father. The working partnerships between women may last for only the few days needed to work a short log of a variety such as *nau tare* or for many years. I believe that these networks form a significant basis for women's solidarity in a society which has relatively few collaborative group activities.[7]

Close analysis of sago work in Yaputawi village for thirty-five days in December 1982 and January 1983 revealed that even over such a short time there is considerable shifting. Most women made at least one change during that time; only two of twenty-three women continued working together steadily for the whole time. The woman who made the most changes was Mo'une, who in fifteen days of working sago worked on five logs. The first two were short palms that her husband had inherited from his mother. She worked them alone while he was building a bush house near by. Then she worked with the mother of Mark, a kinsman of her husband. Next Mark's wife joined them on a large palm inherited from Mark's father. All of these palms were in the tract of swamp controlled by Yimiri Ni'iyei lineage, to which Mo'une's husband's mother and Mark's father both belonged. Next she went off in the opposite direction from the village to work with her own Arasu Iruwaya lineage-mate Tapay (her father's father's brother's son's daughter), but the sago they worked was some that Tapay had inherited from her mother, of Iya Na'asu lineage. Into this short period Mo'une compressed many of the same kinds of working relationships that other Hiyewe women form. Reflecting the patrilineal bias of the community, the most common sago-working groups are linked through husbands, such as the wives of two lineage brothers or a mother-in-law and daughter-in-law, but direct links between the women, such as mother and daughter, sisters, and cousins, are nearly as common. Because women simply work side by side on the same log, using separate sago-washing troughs and not pooling their product, they do not have a product to be distributed jointly. There is, however, considerable coordination involved in decisions about whose logs to work and when. This can in itself be seen as another field for considerable female independence in managing relationships between households.

The Tambaran Cult

Throughout the Sepik, the tambaran cult makes a major contribution to community integration

(Tuzin 1980). At the same time, it effectively excludes women from its ritual. Thus it is significant for the involvement of Hiyewe women in community life that the tambaran cult is rather weakly developed here. The Hiyewe are at the southern margin of the cult. In the next Sepik Hill language to the south, Paka or Niksek, on the upper April and Leonhard Schultze Rivers, there is no cult with slit-gongs or flutes. In addition, a significant boundary runs right through the middle of the language group. In the eastern part of it, including Bukabuki, Sio, and the hamlets of the Nuwe River, slit-gongs are played along with flutes in the men's cult. In the western part, including the Hiyewe dialect groups and the Saniyo villages on the Mapuwe River, only the flutes were played, and these were discarded in the late 1970s. Slit-gongs were used for signaling but not in ritual. The paired bamboo flutes were called *nahe awe* (literally "ancestor") and the long bamboo trumpet *nahe ta'u* (literally "ancestress").

The flutes in Yaputawi village were thrown away in 1975 after only the most cursory work by Assembly of God evangelists. "The flute spirits were killing too many babies," explained Kerapi, "so we threw them away in the bush to follow God's talk." In contrast, the cult has remained active from the Nuwe River eastward, although the Seventh-Day Adventists have done a little work at Sio. Even before first contact and pacification of the Hiyewe, the cult may have lapsed from time to time. Usually small groups of one, two, or three boys in a hamlet were initiated as they reached puberty, but in what is now the senior generation of Yaputawi village, seven men were initiated together. The youngest of them, who are now in their fifties, were teen-agers, but others, now dead, were already married and had children, suggesting that the cult had not been practiced for several years.

The sacrifice of pigs to the spirits of the flutes in mortuary feasts and curing ceremonies continues now as a sacrifice to God and is believed to be effective in exactly the same way. The social dimensions of the events are thus little changed except for the elimination of the parts of the ritual from which women were excluded.

Change

The abandonment of the flutes without a struggle was not the only abrupt change affecting gender relations in the 1970s. I returned to the field in 1980 to find that houses were being built with a single door rather than separate entrances for men and women. "Why?", I asked. "Because *you* do it that way," I was told. An important blunder of ours in our first month in Yareno in 1966 had been to build our house with a single door. Though we had quickly discovered our error, we had never bothered to alter it, because we were amused to observe that men simply climbed in through the window and left the door to the women.

An apparently casual suggestion from an outsider had also led to the abandonment of restrictions on male contact with newborn infants. I was told that the Kwoma man who directed the construction of the airstrip at Mapisi in 1979 had said that it was all right for fathers to see their infants, and this had led to the change. It is not clear to me how exclusively the practice had to do with male concern for childbirth pollution. Even now, a father's own hunting spirits are the most frequently cited cause of infant death, and this may have been as much the basis for his avoidance as fear of female pollution.

Another gender-related practice discarded in the 1970s was infanticide, now known to be punishable by jail. Although females killed outnumbered males by a ratio of three to one (Townsend 1971), the practice had always been justified in terms of the survival of an older, closely spaced sibling; the sex bias had not been acknowledged. Female infants in the population do suffer higher mortality from disease as well, but one would be hard-pressed to discern any neglect in the care of baby girls. It is possible that the bias toward female infanticide merely reflected an assessment of their lower probability of survival. Until 1984 there were no aid posts, immunizations, or maternal and child health clinics in the area. Infant mortality remained high at 400 per thousand (Townsend 1983).

In other ways the pace of change from 1966 to 1984 has been slow. There is still no community school. There is no cash-cropping. There is no local government council, though an abortive move to get one started was made in 1983. Even labor migration, which took out most young men at the end of the 1960s or early 1970s for at least two years, had minimal impact. Because the men stayed together, some of them managed to get through their work experience in East New Britain without even learning Tok Pisin. Similarly, some aspects of gender relations remain unchanged.

Restrictions:
Menstruation and Widowhood

Although Hiyewe women's participation in events beyond the household is relatively unrestricted, this is not to say that they meet no gender-specific restraints. The widespread Melanesian view of menstrual pollution as dangerous to men is found here as well, though the effect of menstrual taboos is mitigated by the denial that most Hiyewe women menstruate. Menarche (*sa'i huwei*, "washing") is celebrated by seclusion lasting several days, followed by a coming-out ceremony and feast for which the girl washes and is dressed up in new skirts and beads. Subsequent menstrual periods for a teen-ager involve a day's seclusion, usually sitting in a shady spot just outside the hamlet under a bush or near a stream. Married women deny that they menstruate (as did a young widow who was neither pregnant nor lactating), and they do not restrict their activities once a month as girls do. Despite these denials, there is still some sense that women can contaminate through leaving traces of menstrual blood. Decontamination is easy, however: once, after a rain, women beckoned to my husband to enter a house by the nearer women's door, saying that the rain had made it all right.

Whatever the ambiguities in the Hiyewe treatment of menstruation, the fact is that it does not result in any restriction of a woman's activities outside the household. Although she is not accustomed to monthly restriction of her activities, a woman's role is drastically altered when her husband dies. Initially she is completely secluded, hidden in a back room (*tevi wesi*) of the main house, and subjected to the most severe food taboos, even being prohibited the staple sago. The most severe taboos were traditionally removed when the deceased's bones were removed from the platform for secondary burial, but for several years afterwards a widow had to keep a very low profile, particularly if her husband had died young. Insufficiently submissive widows have been killed as suspected cannibal witches by either their husband's bereaved kin or men from other communities seeking vengeance for another death.

The widow Heniye will serve to illustrate the restrictions on a widow's public role. Three years and three months after her young husband's sudden death of respiratory disease, she was still wearing a widow's long skirt. She was forbidden to wear cloth or ornaments or to eat meat or fish (except canned fish), to attend even as public a gathering as a church service, or to work sago, though her husband's sister had recently given her a saucepan symbolizing the granting of permission to make sago pudding. Later the sister or brother of her dead husband would give her a sago pounder symbolizing the granting of permission to work sago. She would be expected to make a small return payment of cowries in exchange for each removal of a restriction, but this might well be omitted. Meanwhile she was dependent upon other women for sago for herself and her two small children. Her own sisters' sago, however, she was not yet allowed to eat.

If it were not for the widow's taboos, women like Heniye would be in a strong position to be active producers and exchangers. The women able to be most active in both production and exchange are married women past their mid-thirties who are barren or at least no longer breast-feeding. The wives of polygynists (many of whom are remarried widows) are in fact the most independent women of all. Like widows, but without taboos, they are free to travel, produce, and exchange on their own.

Conclusions

The firm division of labor in production between sago-working women and hunting, fishing, and house-building men might lead one to talk about complementarity of sex roles in Hiyewe society. The notion of complementarity, however, does not so readily apply to Hiyewe gender roles in exchange. As transactors Hiyewe women are expected to behave like men. In decisions about whom to marry, where to live, and what resources to exploit, women are expected to have an equal voice as well.

The Hiyewe have changed slowly since first contact in the early 1960s. They have been quickest to change in ways that have made their society even more sexually egalitarian, discarding exclusively male cult activities and practices based on concepts of female pollution. This direction of change is unlikely to continue, however, as new institutions with exclusively male leadership, such as the church (already training young men to be pastors) and local government, are beginning to emerge.

A pattern of subordination of women like that described for the highlands (e.g., Modjeska 1982) would be inconsistent with several aspects of Hiyewe society. Most important among these are bilocal residence and the inheritance of sago palms and other resources by both men and women from both parents. The fact that women form strong female peer relationships not only as preadolescents but in adulthood with their sago-working partners is also significant.

Perhaps many of these aspects of Hiyewe society are features of Sepik or lowlands societies in general. But as more systematic comparisons of Sepik societies are made, it should be possible to test the proposition that certain aspects of women's status are associated with key differences in political structure even within the region. In other parts of the world, where organization above the household level is weak or decentralized women tend to have a stronger role in decision making (Schlegel 1977:351). One would expect that within the Sepik as well, in the societies on the fringes, with less developed supra-household organization, women would participate more equally in such affairs.

Within the Sepik, the Hiyewe represent an extreme in their lack of political development. Rigorous egalitarianism among males is the rule, and leadership is weakly developed. The term "big man" (*ru erasi*), when used by the Hiyewe, means merely "full-grown man." The ideal personality is soft-spoken and unassertive, avoiding most conflict by moving away from it (Townsend 1978).[8] Gewertz's (1981) characterization of the Sepik Hills people as submissive certainly applies to the Hiyewe. For the Hiyewe, that submissiveness not only implies a preference for withdrawal rather than confrontation with outsiders;[9] it also means a certain mutual submissiveness among men and women.

Notes

1. Fieldwork was conducted in Yareno hamlet in 1966–67. Between December 1980 and January 1984, I was able to spend a further five months in Wourei, Mapisi, and Yaputawi hamlets. For practical support in this later work, squeezed into vacation periods, I am greatly in debt to Bill and Alison Townsend and Ron Lewis. I owe thanks to Mary Rei for typing. In previous publications the spelling of the language name has been changed several times to correspond with changes in the orthography as it has been developed by the Summer Institute of Linguistics. The Hiyewe or western dialect of the Saniyo language is centered above the junction of Heiwei tributary with the Miwei (Wogamus) River. The /w/ is pronounced /v/ in the westernmost hamlets, where I have lived, but not elsewhere.

2. Trading partners call each other *nati*, a term which includes fictive kin of the same sex and generation. Its core meaning as a kin term is "offspring of the same sex of any two cross-cousins of the same sex" (i.e., second cross-cousins).

3. In contrast with these investments inherited by children, any valuables which are actually held at time of death are inherited by a same-sex cross-cousin (*ofai rame*). These are the *u ma'aru* ("sickness cowries").

4. Similarly, Hiyewe women are unable to give coherent accounts of clan and patrilineage structure. (The only exception was Re'i-Peraupe, who was also the woman who knew the lineage slit-gong signals.) If one studied Hiyewe social organization with women informants alone, the picture that would emerge would be one of a cognatic society.

5. Only one of these three had been given by a woman, so it is not invariably the case that women receive the valuables contributed by other women. Also, two additional women later received cowries that had been contributed by men.

6. Yareno has been abandoned, and its residents are now divided between Yaputawi, Mapisi, and Wourei.

7. Most Hiyewe men's major activities, including house building, fishing, and hunting, are optionally carried out alone or in collaboration with one or two other men.

8. This is not to say that killings did not and do not occur. Prior to 1960 the Hiyewe engaged in regular payback killings with their Yabio-speaking neighbors to the south. These were, however, sneak attacks by small parties rather than the large coordinated assaults they attribute to Sepik River peoples. A woman or child was considered an equally suitable target for a revenge killing. Bride-price payments and other group gatherings also frequently exploded into violence, hence the custom even now of feasting and dancing first, then quickly dispersing as soon as the payment is made before dissatisfaction can lead to violence. The only homicide by a Hiyewe in the 1970s was the killing of a suspected female Saniyo witch by a man acting alone.

9. My most memorable experience of this occurred in June 1967, when Mervyn Meggitt and John Barnes visited us in the field. Before going to get them we explained that they were my classificatory kin. (This was a major concession, as we had spent a year vigorously denying suggestions that the *kiap* [government officer] was my brother.) After two days of difficult river travel, we brought them to our hamlet, which quietly emptied of people. When we came back the next week from returning our guests to Ambunti, our house was crowded with people. "Where were you when my 'father' and 'brother' were here to meet you?" I asked. "We were too shy; they were big men," they replied.

33/ Male Ideology and Cultural Fantasy in Yafar Society

Bernard Juillerat

The Border Mountains are only marginally part of the Sepik region, and the societies settled there (see Huber and Peter in this volume and Gell 1975) are culturally more closely related to the Irianese groups to the west than to the communities of the Upper Sepik plain. The Yafar live in Amanab District, some 15 kilometers northwest of the Amanab station. They reside in three hamlets with a total population of two hundred and share a territory of 40–45 square kilometers surrounded by similar territorial communities. Tribal unity is based on a name, a territory, dual organization, and a strong sense of collective identity and solidarity. Exchange and marriage occur as much with neighboring groups as within the society. The family or domestic group lives in a one-room house on stilts. There are no separate men's houses.

In this paper, I propose a somewhat contradictory and, to a degree, hypothetical approach to the now classic problem of the relations between the sexes and the manner in which a society utilizes and manages the difference between them. Anthropologists have often analyzed the balance of power between men and women. They have tried to explain the sexual division of labor and the limits of male domination and have examined how a given culture symbolically transposes sexual antagonism and complementarity in its myths and rites. Questions about the not easily perceptible role of women in social and domestic life have been formulated mostly in reaction to a more conventional anthropological view of radically opposed male and female statuses (see Losche in this volume). This improvement in the evaluation of sex roles has led to a consideration of the notion of ambiguity or perplexity (see Townsend and Williamson in this volume) as an integrative element in the social and ideological interaction between men and women. Nevertheless, "man" and "woman" are most often envisaged as social categories, while the focal point of male/female relations in the couple remains inexplicit. Indeed, it seems that whereas the community obeys the norms it has imposed to codify the relationship between the sexes, in intimacy the couple may be allowed to violate them.

In a changing world, social transformations have a strong impact not only on the society as a whole but on individuals as well and, consequently, on private marital life and intrafamilial socialization. In the case of a rather recently contacted group like the Yafar, profound modifications of this nature are still largely in the future, and the only analysis one can now provide depends on an understanding of the potential evolution of the couple in its sociocultural context. From the Yafar viewpoint the dichotomy between the sexes is mainly founded on the perpetuation of a male-dominated cult and male possession of sacred knowledge. I shall try to show the ambiguity which characterizes the couple's miniaturized version of sexual antagonism set against the background of sexual discrimination at the collective and cultural levels.

The Yafar data led me to approach the problem of the relations between the sexes through the identification of a correlation between three orders of reality: fantasy, ideology, and transgression. *Fantasy* is the most basic; it consists of partly unconscious, maternally dominated mental representations. *Ideology* is the result of a defensive male reaction to fantasy that has both imaginary and socioeconomic dimensions. *Transgression* is restricted here to reaction against ideology; it may take the form either of a partial resurgence of fantasy or of an episodic liberation of the individual from the social norms by exercise of one's free will.[1]

Fantasy

Fantasies constitute imaginary material expressed in cultural terms, especially in myth, ritual exegesis, or belief. Yafar myths—which they call "true stories" or "hard speech"—repeatedly reveal themes of feminine procreative power (suprahuman pregnancies and twin births) and of a Mother Earth as central in cosmology, with the masculine character playing a secondary role. This is because "woman" is strongly fantasized in terms of her reproductive and nutritive functions. She alternates between these two biological roles in relation not only to the man but also to the child, not only in a sexual role but also through filiation (see Green 1977). However, sexual identity intervenes in the latter relationship, since a daughter enters into the continuity of the procreative function through identification with the mother, whereas the son is seen as connected to the mother mainly through breast-feeding and is eventually separated from her. The dual nature of this relationship according to sex appears clearly in the Yafar totemic ceremony *yangis*,[2] as well as in various myths. It emphasizes the fact that the sexual dialectic must be considered within the larger context of filiation. Faced with this alternative, Yafar fantasy makes its choice: a mythical mother either reproduces herself in her daughter or gives birth to a son and dies as a result. In the latter case, exegesis reveals that the mother is identified with a seed and the son with the germ: the latter frees itself and grows while the former decays.

On the male side, the father is "displaced" in relation to the role incumbent upon him in the reproductive process. Maternal figures in myth become pregnant parthenogenetically and then are "opened" by male sexual intervention; a man puts an end to the pregnancy, liberating the woman from the product of her womb. The metaphor of vegetal reproduction here expressed in a human analogy does not restore man to his procreative role. Feminine principles take precedence over masculine, maternal over paternal. The male is the object of a form of "castration" through the denial of his reproductive function, which is, however, rationally recognized. Moreover, he incurs the danger of seeing his "self" (*sungwaag*) become prematurely "ripe" by contaminating itself during sleep with cosmic feminine blood and fluids which are concealed within the chthonian depths. The male appears weakened by his contact with female cosmic forces and is threatened with a return to the primordial Mother. This fear of regression is expressed in the *gungwan* ritual,[3] which appears as an institutionalized defense against the persistence of a maternal imago. Although she is the agent of that double peril, a woman is not safe. Because she is the bearer, and potentially the victim, of her reproductive powers, she is at the mercy of an "excess of blood," which may be fatal to her in childbirth. Hampered by the physical weight of her pregnancy (a recurring mythical image) or by her nursing role, in fantasy woman is an immobile and passive being awaiting her deliverance.

The contents of male secrets refer mainly to these socially repressed mental images of motherhood and filiation, but secrecy as a strategy is the expression of male ideology.

Ideology

In capsule form, the heart of Yafar fantasy, upon which a defensive process simultaneously develops, gives rise in the social domain to a dominant masculine ideology, which must in turn be validated. The mythical theme of male appropriation of the control of reproduction recorded in numerous societies throughout the world is its most obvious expression. Among the Yafar and their neighbors, the inversion of the balance of power between male and female principles is supposed to have been realized through violence and the reestablishment of sexuality, previously interrupted during a period of physical segregation of the sexes (women in the village, men in the forest). Men spy upon the women, then return to couple with them, steal their masks, paints, and trumpets for use in their yangis performance, which ensures the reproduction of both totemic palms and cosmic sexual principles (see Gell 1975, Huber in this volume, and Juillerat 1986), and finally murder them (Juillerat n.d.). Masculine social order replaces the feminine "presocial," or natural, order and establishes the two moieties of Yafar society. The ritual function of the moieties today is precisely to perform yangis. This mythical construct shows clearly that ideology, as an intermediate term, is coupled both with fantasy and with transgression. It is built up in reaction to the former and in perpetual danger of being unsettled by the latter.

At a deeper level, the maternal figure is central and the father a sort of "satellite." The validation of the social order of male dominance inverts this structure, which, without this validation, would imply regression. Thus legitimized, male ideology holds that whereas only women have the natural power of childbirth, only men have social and symbolic control of it.

In real life, a pregnant woman sees herself as being desocialized and separated from men in order to give birth in isolation. With the newborn at her breast, she remains in seclusion for several weeks, ignored by the rest of the community with the exception of some female relatives. She finally comes out from underneath the house and, after bathing, is reintegrated into the domestic group. The father then confronts his child for the first time and establishes his social paternity through unilineal descent. First desocialized and then resocialized, a woman gives birth inside the village but outside society, since the power that she alone possesses is, by definition, unsocializable.

By exercising their magic on female and natural fertility, men keep women outside the realm of esoteric knowledge, even though "femaleness" is its principal object. The male monopoly on hunting and meat distribution places game (which, according to one myth, is the "child" of Mother Earth) exclusively under their control in the same way that patrilineality places the wife's child within the male descent line. The public yangis ritual portrays the reproduction of the totemic species and shows men acting in a phallic way through the performance of a dance with clicking phallocrypts in which the divine "pregnancy" of the original coconut tree and sago palm is dramatized. More generally, only men wear masks, paint their bodies, pronounce spells, play musical instruments, and sing. In terms of spatial representation, men occupy central and upper places. Their public speech is tinged with a certain contempt for the female sex. Thus, masculine ideology, to which women themselves implicitly contribute,[4] gives rise to a normative organization of social behavior which includes the sexual division of activities, the allocation of the content and form of speech and exchange, the shared occupation of space (village, house, garden, etc.), and specific sexual and kinship attitudes. The public domain is the obligatory setting for the expression of these norms. The maternally dominated fantasies have no place there. The fantasy stereotyped in public ritual and profane mythical speech remains unrecognizable to those who do not have the "key." One may attend, even participate in, the most important ceremonies or listen to public versions of the most sacred myths without grasping any of their esoteric meanings. The code is kept secret in exegesis controlled by a male elite, among whom I eventually succeeded in identifying semianonymous "priests" whose titles are inherited.

Transgression

The breach of social norms may proceed from individuals who occupy various social categories: women, young men and children, or older men who do not respect secrecy. It may also be produced by outsiders: by missionaries, with the more or less acknowledged aim of disrupting the traditional balance of power that constitutes an obstacle to evangelization, and, less often, and more unwittingly, by other visitors passing through and by anthropologists themselves.[5]

I have arbitrarily chosen here to situate transgression at the level of the married couple, paradoxically, at the core of sexual duality. The simplest and most banal social unit, the couple is also the most impenetrable. This fact probably accounts for the silence about it on the part of anthropologists. What sort of behavior do married men, men who publicly claim their autonomy from the feminine world, who do not dare to speak with their wives in front of other men or if recently married, display a total lack of interest in their young spouses, adopt in the intimacy of the couple? At the outset the economic cooperation between spouses attests to the existence of a complementary and coordinated exchange of labor (see also Losche in this volume). The sharing of a room or garden, the organization of domestic duties, often based on reciprocity, the exchange of plots after planting, the husband's prompt intervention in feminine chores (such as the preparation of sago jelly, child care, and the carrying of burdens) constitute evidence of the couple's socioeconomic integration, as well as its independence. This is even the case with the magic that accompanies a young married couple's first sexual intercourse, in which the spells spoken by the man simultaneously conjure up game appearing from the forest and children to be procreated. Socially repressed in public life, fantasy reappears within the intimacy of the couple. For example, although any magic about natural female fertility is normally performed out of the reach of women's ears, a man shares his fertility magic with his wife. While male ideology declares women polluting and dangerous, hunters secretly gather menstrual blood to be transmuted into magical ingredients that will attract wild animals on their paths.

When a man and woman find themselves alone at night by the fire in an isolated garden, or when a husband chants the incantations about the growth spirits or the "blood" of sago in his wife's presence, without witnesses, what then of male control of knowledge and the alleged ignorance of women concerning the nature of the masks and the secret names of ritual plants and mythical characters? Is not transgression the indispensable complement of taboo, and are not women the most suitable recipients of men's secrets (see Zempléni 1976)? The protagonist's personality, especially the man's, is obviously a determining factor with respect to the norm; a husband can reproduce it at the core of the family and limit his communication with his wife to domestic needs; but he may also allow himself to become a transgressor, whether through a taste for conjugal complicity or as compensation for feelings of rejection by the male community. Just as conjugal secrets are susceptible to disclosure in the public domain, the knowledge harbored by the male elite can be passed on to the female community by way of that "bottleneck" of social communication, the couple. In their intimacy, a man and a woman can communicate outside the bounds of social control and allow some resurgence of the suppressed fantasy. However, no outsider can have access to the minimal and essential unit without destroying it. Anthropologists in search of the truth concerning relations between the sexes will always remain excluded from this privileged place of complicity and transgression. This is unfortunate, since the couple, as an essential arena for the articulation of male/female social relations, might constitute a way of opening up the ideological system. This is implicitly alleged for the Abelam by Losche (in this volume), who emphasizes the contradictions between the couple's sexual and economic harmony and the male cults, as well as mentioning the fact that "ideology is honored in the breach."

It has often been said that the anthropologist in the field, male or female, from abroad or from the same country, is a victim of the male ideology of the society he or she studies. Although ideology constitutes one object of an ethnographer's interest, he or she should also leave a place, even if it remains empty, in his or her reconstruction of the social system for what may be communicated between a man and a woman when the society around them is momentarily forgotten.

Change

The recent social transformations brought by Australian colonization, for the Yafar effective only since 1960, and the creation of the Papua New Guinea government have not yet modified the relationship between fantasy, ideology, and transgression.[6] During the 1960s young men worked on plantations in the Bismarck Archipelago, but these prospects for work are now closed. The entire society feels imprisoned in its traditional socioeconomic space and for several years has been trying to find a new identity through millenarian activity. Things seem to have changed slightly as a result of this cult.[7] For the first time, women are participating, although rather passively and under male control, in a community effort at ethical and social restoration to further the advent of the millennium. But women continue to be excluded from traditional religious knowledge and from recent cultic extensions, which express a hope for the return of the dead and access to cargo. There is direct communication between the sexes during meetings in which the leaders set forth the new morality's principles (actually a reinforcement of the former ones). One might ask whether this pragmatic building of a new solidarity between men and women does not simultaneously increase the risk of domestic transgression against ideology. As the new ethic encourages stronger conjugal cohesion, should we not again see the couple as the Achilles' heel of male ideology, the flaw through which men's secrets can surreptitiously worm their way out of their confinement? In fact, this will occur less easily than in the customary cultural context, since this time the stakes are considerable: the global and permanent control of the original source of the wealth as well as the abolition of death through the return of the dead. The cult once again allows the resurgence of fantasy in all its force, but more than ever it is under the men's vigilant control. The cult's ideology strengthens men's power over women, but it needs them to remodel a social identity acceptable to the guardians of the underground maternal abyss (as it is fantasized by the cult's followers) into which men may or may not be admitted. The distinction between the public sphere, of which women are an integral part, and the private domain of the cult, where a few men secretly manipulate the ancient fantasies which constitute the symbolic material of their messianic expectations, was never before so clear-cut in such a communal enterprise. The danger of a return to female control of cosmic fertility (cf. Juillerat n.d.) is revived in this reconstruction, but for the first time there is at least an open dialogue taking place between the sexes. The new cult allows Yafar women to participate in social life on a communication level at least partly free of both male exclusivity and the atomization of the domestic unit. The cult, as a reactualization of fantasy under exclusively male control, once again relegates women to the secular field.

In this context, the couple seems to have strengthened its social and affective unity only to foster the efficiency of the renewed male cult. Under these conditions, and until the millennarian ideology weakens, it can hardly serve as a conduit for secret knowledge. Actually, the situation can only change when people abandon their belief in the stakes posited by the cultural fantasy. Educational programs, contact with the outside world, the development of a market economy in which women play a role, and the opening of the Sepik-Vanimo road are already effecting some changes. Ideas will be renewed, sexual antagonism will relax, but marriage will perhaps also lose its present stability. No longer believing in the veracity of their myths and rites, Yafar men of a younger generation will perhaps one day have nothing to hide from their women. The couple will then no longer be a potential secret place for transgression, or, to put it another way, the communication of formerly secret knowledge between spouses will no longer be considered a breach. Again, this shows that ideology and transgression are complementary. Men will then have to seek other monopolies, particularly in economic and political activities, if they want to keep active in some way their dominance over women.

Conclusion

This paper has had as its object to propose a discussion of the married couple as an indivisible social unit, autonomous against the background of sexual antagonism. Its potential as a locus for the violation of social norms and male dominance may appear to be mostly theoretical. I acknowledge this point, in spite of the fact that I acquired some evidence in the field that elements of male esoteric knowledge were passed to women in the intimacy of the couple and that certain elder women shared some of men's secrets.[8] Even if this is not the rule, I would argue that the possibility remains valid, especially for older couples,[9] since sexual antagonism is based on men's symbolic control of female fertility. In view of the radical transformations affecting rural societies in Papua New Guinea, and to the extent that Yafar social management of sexual antagonism and se-

crecy is not specific to the Border Mountains, I venture to hope that the present argument may find a place in the broader examination of the evolution of the family in the Sepik area.

Notes

1. In the latter case, using Burridge's (1979) concepts as discussed in this volume by McDowell for the Bun, I would categorically oppose the "person" as subject to social order and the "individual" as originator of change. Each member of any society is at once a person and an individual to varying degrees. In this view, the couple is the locus of similar tensions between submission and individual initiative. However, here I shall consider the spouses not as opposed to each other but as forming a dual unit in which two individuals (in Burridge's sense) may sometimes take the liberty of escaping from social constraint.

2. The Yafar name for the *ida* ritual of the Umeda analyzed by Gell (1975). The Yafar adopted this cult several generations ago from the Punda, the Umeda's neighbors.

3. The aim of this public ritual is to protect the "selves" of all community members from going down into the earth, from "eating ghosts' food," and from sorcery.

4. Women's participation in male domination is not formally recognized in female initiation as it is, for instance, in some highland societies (see Godelier 1982*a*).

5. I am aware that this paper is a breach of Yafar ideology, even though it is perpetrated outside of the society.

6. Until very recently the Christian Mission in Many Lands, based at Amanab, has had little influence.

7. It was introduced from Irian Jaya through affinal relations (see Losche in this volume on other cultic movements coming into the Sepik from Irian Jaya).

8. In contrast to the situation in other New Guinea societies (see, for example, Meigs 1976 on the Hua), there is no formal introduction of elder women to male knowledge, and no such special status as existed in some New Britain groups (see Jeudy-Ballini 1985) required that a woman receive that knowledge.

9. Age is a determining factor for transgression between spouses; older men are less persuaded than the young of women's ignorance and of the necessity for male vigilance.

34/ Gender and the Cosmos in Kwoma Culture[1]

Margaret Holmes Williamson

Among many other characteristics, Sepik River cultures share what is perhaps best called a perplexity about the relationship between men and women. Any culture displays a variety of kinds of relationship between the two. Depending on the context, they may be antithetical, complementary, or undifferentiated. These peoples seem to be trying out, so to speak, different arrangements to see which is most satisfactory. One consequence of this experimentation is that one cannot offer a conclusive definition of man and woman for Sepik cultures, as seems to be possible in other areas (e.g., Southeast Asia, North America). This is an unsatisfactory state of affairs if we assume that at some level there must be a set of cultural premises that serve as the guide and justification for the actions of those who participate in the culture.

In this paper I approach this problem through an analysis of the Kwoma rituals associated with the life cycles of men and women. These are of a familiar kind, involving the separation of boys from the female sphere of life by means of initiation and the differentiation of men from women in a number of ways including ceremonial societies for men from whose secrets women and uninitiated boys are excluded. The Kwoma data suggest that there is no constant relationship between person and gender such that men always exemplify maleness or women femaleness. Initially we may assume that "male" and "female" are abstractions to which individual men and women conform more or less closely at different periods of their lives.

This is not an application of Mead's (1971) ideas about sex and temperament to the Kwoma material, although obviously I agree with her insistence that "temperaments" are culturally ascribed to genders and that these ascriptions influence the raising of children. She characterizes Arapesh as "feminine" or Mundugumor as "masculine" by reference to American definitions of male and female. I am trying to understand

Kwoma men and women purely in Kwoma terms, much as Bateson (1958) tried to do for the Iatmul. Nor do I assume that the relative "masculinity" of a postmenopausal Kwoma woman involves any sort of deviation from the norm or any change in temperament. Postmenopausal women are not necessarily fiercer than women of childbearing age, nor are they perceived as such. Kwoma do recognize, and even delight in, the idiosyncrasies of individuals and may remark that someone is "like a man" in having a hot temper or "like a woman" in disliking to hunt pigs. (Neither is an expression of approval.) But because this is a practice regarding individuals only, it differs from what I address in this paper, which is collective and affects everyone. The two are related, though, in that both involve the identification of persons in terms of abstract ideas of gender.

Even studies explicitly based on the premise that gender is cultural rather than biological and therefore a collective phenomenon not reducible to anatomy include a circular argument that I am trying to avoid in this analysis. The circularity is this: "gender" has replaced "sex" in such studies because it reflects the realization that "sex" (read "biology") is not all that important in justifying occupations, dress, supposed mental abilities, and so on. "Gender" is therefore to be divorced from "sex," that is, sexuality and reproduction; it is purely cultural. But the terms we use to designate gender, male and female, are in fact terms that refer to sex. These terms have the connotation of reproduction by sexual union. Consequently, their use as glosses for a common theme among disparate kinds of phenomena, persons included, introduces the sense that sex is after all the basis for classifying things.

To avoid this I have tried to set out the relationships in Kwoma culture between persons (men and women) and the cosmos. The anthropologist's conventional verbal link between these two is gender—some "things" are male, others female, if only by association. In making that link, however, we intrude the notion that the order of the world proceeds from the cultural identification of men and women, as well as that the identification depends on biology. In this analysis I have tried to identify in Kwoma thought a set of opposed characteristics that persons and nonpersons share and so arrive at definitions of gender that do not depend on biology, or sexuality, for their motivation. By this means it is possible to show that the identification of anyone with one set of characteristics or the other alters during a life-time.

All of this is leading up to one of those unrea-sonable demands that anthropologists make on their readers, namely, to attach rather unfamiliar meanings to familiar words. Because it is con-ventional and convenient, I use "male" and "fe-male" throughout this paper, but in the sense of "gender" as defined in the *Concise Oxford Eng-lish Dictionary*: "Grammatical classification . . . of objects roughly corresponding to the two sexes . . . property of belonging to such a class." The identification of characteristics in such terms should not be taken to imply that any one of them is the model for the rest. Rather than thinking of male and female as ideas generated by the nature and appearance of men and women, respectively, I have taken them as categories in which various phenomena, including men and women, may be more or less appropriately included.

Kwoma accomplish the symbolic association of a person with one gender or another by remov-ing him or her from a genderless state, identifying him or her in terms of gender, and establishing that that gender is complementarily opposed to the other. In order to be sure how Kwoma define male and female, we should consider not just what happens to boys and girls or what is typical of men and women, which would beg the ques-tion, but also those nonhuman aspects of the world for which Kwoma clearly make an associ-ation with gender. The result is a set of meta-phorical associations among various phenomena that suggests the order that Kwoma perceive in the world, men and women forming part of the world so ordered.

Kwoma make certain geographical associa-tions with gender. The most obvious is that high = male, low = female. In reference to humans these equations find expression in such customs as making the men's house the highest building in a village or in women's being physically lower than men as a rule—sitting in canoes while men stand, watching men climb trees but never doing so themselves, avoiding stepping over men or their belongings, and so on. In narrative women are usually carrying out some activity in a swamp, while men are working in gardens or resting in villages, both located on ridges or up-per slopes. The women's activities in these sto-ries are always the same—fishing or working sago. Both are activities necessarily confined to swampy or low ground. Men are always garden-ing, smoking in the men's house, or fighting.

Related to the high/low opposition, but in a different geographical plane, are the equations center = male, periphery = female. The two planes intersect because ridges (high and "cen-tral") are the property of patrilineal groups, while streams (low and "peripheral") are the bounda-ries between them. Swamps mark the end of hab-itable territory, and the Sepik is ultima thule. A hike with a Kwoma, whether man, woman, or child, produces a fund of information about the terrain one passes through: geographical, histor-ical, genealogical, mythological. From such ac-counts it is clear that Kwoma fight over ridges, not valleys; valleys, or swamps, are fit only for ani-mals. Ownership of swamp land (necessary for working sago) is contingent upon ownership of the adjacent ridge. Each ridge is a repository and stimulus for the collective memories of a patriline and its history of villages, gardens, alliances, and enmities. A ridge, like the ideal patrilineage, per-sists; it ensures continuity in the presence of change. Water, of course, has no such stability. The Sepik rises and falls, and when it rises it makes hard ground mushy before inundating it al-together. Swamps are trackless, rain is unpredict-able, streams run away. Ridges, or hills, stand out as solid and enduring reference points, giving a form to the land just as patrilineages and com-munities give order and form to society in spite of the come and go of wives and sisters, daughters-in-law and daughters. Kwoma women are, in a sense, socially peripheral as streams and swamps are geographically peripheral. Their status is ev-ident partly in the fact that they take little part in public events. In rituals they are more visible than men, but this again is due to their being literally outside while the men are concealed in the men's house. Partly it is due to their being members of two patrilineal groups and thus marking the sep-aration between them at the same time as they act as liaisons between them.

Like women and water, fish are peripheral, in fact rather alien. Unlike land animals, they can-not be domesticated. The Kwoma get most of their fish from the women of Yambon and Avatip on the river in exchange for sago flour. This inten-sifies the foreignness of fish and strengthens their resemblance to women, or at least to wives, who should always be "strangers." Fish are also cold, a characteristic that Kwoma say is more female than male.

Another clear gender association is made of hardwoods, which are male. These grow on ridges; they are harvested and used by men, who turn them into houseposts, carvings, slit-gongs, and tools (including weapons); in narrative, hardwoods turn into men or men into hardwoods. Kwoma refer to sons as *akakwata*, "the posts of the house," because they are embedded in their father's land and will not stray and because they are a prop in one's old age. Kwoma men distinguish themselves verbally (and presumably conceptually) from river people like the Yambon or Malu (whom they despise) in terms of their relationship to hardwoods, which, Kwoma say, river people do not understand and cannot work properly. The woodworking adze is the preeminently masculine tool.

The dominant swamp tree is the sago palm. Although one would expect a tidy opposition between hardwoods and sago, the Kwoma do not make one. They divide sago into male and female varieties, basing the identification on the average size of the mature palm and whether it has spines. Large, spined species are male; the smaller, smooth species are female. There are more male palms than female. A narrative tells of a spirit who caused a forest of sago to grow overnight so that two children in her care could feed themselves. The children found only water in the trunks, however. The spirit then told them to work the spined sago, and this time they found pith. This story suggests that the only useful sago is male, but my informants said that both sorts were productive and good. Two other narratives identify sago as female. One tells of the origin of sago from a woman, who returned to her vegetal state after being caught in a rainstorm. The other attributes the origin of a large descent group, the Nuntakau, to sago pith, from which the first Nuntakau emerged as from their mother.

On the basis of these distinctions we may suggest that Kwoma define "male" in terms of large size, hardness, and the capacity to wound. Female palms are small and harmless. The attributes of male sago are, of course, those of a warrior. A few women become homicides, but only in self-defense, and then with someone else's spear.

Among cultivated foods the yam (*Dioscorea esculenta*) is clearly associated, not surprisingly, with maleness. Although Kwoma do not grow long yams, they have the same sort of yam cults as those who do. Only senior men with the right knowledge can plant yams. They must be sexually continent and, while the gardens are young, abstain from tobacco and coffee. Their behavior, even more than their wives', determines the value of the harvest.

Kwoma appear to think of the bush as a whole as female when they assign a gender to it at all. This is consistent with the center/periphery distinction in that Kwoma talk about villages and gardens as isolated areas under human control, wrested from the bush that surrounds them and threatens to take them over again, as ultimately it will succeed in doing. Among the denizens of the bush perhaps the most important are the bush spirits, *sikilowas*. Some of these are male, but most are female. When the females appear in dreams they take the form of a woman known to the dreamer, and their names can be given to girls. A few sikilowas have daughters, but none is married or has sex relations, and they do not form a community as humans and ghosts do. They are important to Kwoma as providers of food, both wild (game and fish) and cultivated (yams), as well as for protection from all sorts of harm. The sikilowas' ability to provide food in abundance is a reflection of the Kwoma attitude toward the bush generally as an abundant, self-regenerating place. Bush plants such as sago do not need to be planted or cultivated; they grow and flourish spontaneously. Garden plants, though, are different—if they were not tended and given light and space, they would die.

Animal life is similarly spontaneous. Although Kwoma say that there are male and female animals, identifying specific animals by reference to genitals, they appear to regard the males as unimportant to animal reproduction. They know that animals copulate because they have seen them do it, but there are no fathers in the bush, only mother's brothers. Like spirits, female animals bring forth young by themselves. Animals, then, are matrilineal, and so distinguished from humans.

All this suggests that the ability to reproduce is peculiarly female, evidence of reproduction being evidence of feminity. For Kwoma, however, there is more to reproduction than simply having a baby or hatching an egg: one must also raise the infant produced. More important than conceiving a child is feeding it—i.e., producing an abundance of food. One of the Kwoma words for mother is *nokwapa*, "plenty." Mother's milk, like life in the bush, springs from nowhere—it is spontaneous. Uncontrolled, indeed uncontrollable, fertility in this double sense is the hallmark of femaleness.

The fairly concrete distinctions between ridge and swamp with which I began are thus part of an inclusive set of oppositions of varying degrees of abstraction: high/low, center/periphery (which in human terms becomes public/private and collective/individual), hot/cold, garden (village)/bush, land/water, nonreproducing/reproducing, familiar/alien, and, finally, male/female. The identification of men as male and women as female is made in terms of these oppositions, which are symbolized in the various Kwoma rites of passage, especially those associated with puberty.

Conception, Birth, and Childhood

I have discussed Kwoma ideas about conception in detail elsewhere (Williamson 1983). Here an important point about conception is that Kwoma say that neither placental blood nor semen forms a specific part of the fetus: the combination produces the entire baby. The *mai*, or breath, is imparted by the mother, who gives some of her own *mai* to her baby without, however, diminishing her own in doing so.

The rituals associated with childbirth are not elaborate and receive no public attention. Afterbirth, like menstrual blood, is held to be dangerous to men, so only women attend the birth. The baby's father's mother usually cuts the umbilical cord, and she washes the baby in warm water, often with soap, immediately following the delivery. The mother washes herself also. The afterbirth is buried in a corner of the kitchen, away from the fire. Kwoma say that it must be buried here because otherwise wild animals would eat it and thus make the child weak and sickly and cause the death of subsequent children. Fire can likewise destroy life; burning bones, for example, will destroy that person's ghost. For this reason Kwoma used to bury bones outside houses so that if the village were burnt by an enemy the ghosts would still survive.

Mother and newborn are in a liminal state for about six weeks, until the child's skin darkens or its eyes can focus. Then the mother gathers various special leaves (unidentified) and adds them to warmed water with which she washes both herself and the baby, removing the impurities associated with childbirth. The mother's activities are now the same as before the delivery, but there is a postpartum taboo on intercourse for a further nine or ten months.

The child is incorporated into society when it is named. There is no indigenous ritual associated with naming. Human names form a category distinct from those of animals and places. Only human names are gender-specific. Naming thus makes a baby an actual, instead of a potential, person. The death of an unnamed baby is not mourned, and, more significant, unlike the death of anyone with a name it requires no funeral payment.

Except that their names (Kwoma usually have at least two) are gender-specific, all babies receive the same treatment at birth and for some time thereafter. Differentiation into boys and girls involves teaching children the occupations proper to their sex; this occurs when the child is old and strong enough to do the work, that is, about five or six years old.

The statement that children have occupations appropriate to their gender implies a contradiction, but in fact there is none. Kwoma identify gender in children at birth just as they identify it in animals, by reference to the genitals. Parents name their babies on this basis. Although distinguished by gender-specific names, children are primarily children, not boys or girls. Kin terms, for example, do not distinguish boys from girls in generations below one's own. Thus in a sense children are genderless, or neuter, but it is a neutrality with, if I may put it so, a feminine tinge. Children, like women, are rather private actors. The events of birth, just described, are familial rather than communal. While men stamp and argue in public meetings and conduct noisy, flamboyant ceremonies, women and children watch on the sidelines. Children, like women, are officially ignorant of men's ceremonial secrets. Children share with women a comparative immunity from such legal pressures as can be created in Kwoma culture. A sorcerer, for example, will attempt to kill a man because of a grievance against the man himself, but he attacks a woman or a child only because her husband or the child's father has harmed him. Conversely, a man is held responsible for injuries his wife or children may have done to others. Although there are these associations between children and the feminine, there are also differences between children and women and the feminine generally, as the rituals associated with puberty make clear. Until maturity, then, anyone's gender is implicit rather than explicit.

Observation of Puberty

Kwoma say that girls reach puberty earlier than boys and that the boys' puberty ritual is an imitation of menarche. Therefore I shall discuss girls' maturation first.

A Kwoma girl reaches puberty (that is, Kwoma cease to regard her as a child) with the beginning of her first menstrual period. When the period has ceased she must build a fire of her own, supply it with wood which she has cut herself, and cook in pots which have been made specifically for her by her parents or—if she is betrothed and living with her in-laws—by her father- or mother-in-law. She may not cook on her mother's fire or eat food cooked on it until she has had four or five children. A mother may cook food on her daughter's fire only for her daughter to eat. The girl's parents and their siblings must not eat food cooked on her fire. The Kwoma say that if a woman eats food that her daughter has prepared, the mother's skin will be "weak," she will be cold after washing, and she will waste away to skin and bone, but not die—in other words, she will age prematurely. The girl must sleep alone in her own bed, which is at the opposite end of the house from her parents' bed. Usually her father builds a partition around it as well. Previously, I was told, she may have slept in one bed with her father.

With puberty a girl becomes a suitable object of male interest. Kwoma say that an immature girl is "green," but a mature one is "ripe." She is informally segregated from all men except her father and brothers, with whom she has limited contact. Her companions, other than children, are almost always her sisters and her mother.

Sometime during the long period between first menstruation and her first pregnancy, usually just before marriage, a girl is given an elaborate scar tattoo on her stomach (for more detailed discussion, see Williamson 1979a, b). Although the operation cannot be called a rite of passage in the classic sense, since no change of status results from it, it is an important part of a girl's maturation and a significant part of her self-image and of the way other people perceive her. The recent revival of this custom, at the girls' request, shows its significance to them. The custom is favored by both sexes for the same reason: it provides direct evidence of the moral and physical strength of the woman. Men admire such women; the women like the admiration, and they value such fortitude in themselves. Men and women with whom I discussed this custom repeatedly sneered and joked about the substandard scars on two Bangwis women. Indeed, these women were the only ones reluctant to display or discuss their scars. Usually women seem quite complacent about the sufferings they have undergone as girls and about the ornamental value of the resulting scars.

Strength is a desirable quality of men and women, but the Kwoma associate different sorts of strength with each. They distinguish between physical and moral strength, and only in connection with women have I ever heard the second mentioned. In such conversations the tone is approving, even admiring. Physical strength, also, is different in men and women. Men, it is said, are "strong for" climbing trees, cutting them down, carrying logs, planting yams. Women who display this kind of strength are only grudgingly approved. A man may be grateful for a wife who can help him build his house. A proper man will not need to rely on his wife (house building is a community affair) because a proper woman will help him by providing the feast that is the primary inducement to help a man with his house. Women are "strong for carrying" everything but logs in the ubiquitous net bag.

That a woman's scar demonstrates physical endurance is easy to appreciate. This endurance has moral connotations also because scars are supposed to be beautiful, and the girl's cooperation is necessary to the beauty of her scar. Beauty in all forms pleases the bush spirits, who reward the beautiful with prosperity and health. A woman who has suffered to be beautiful is thus morally good as well as strong. As evidence of strength scars appear, however, to contradict the identification of swampland and water with the feminine. This identification has more to do with the marginal nature of such areas in space and in political organization than with the quality of the land or of water itself. The moral strength of women exemplified by the scar resonates with the idea of sikilowas as the enforcers of the primeval law.

Kwoma boys used to undergo a formal initiation similar to those reported from elsewhere in New Guinea. This ceremony has not been performed at Bangwis, where I did most of my fieldwork, for about forty-five years. Today, in the absence of the ritual, the distinction between boy and man is relatively vague, but Kwoma still make it. One criterion is the boy's physical maturation: a deeper voice, body and facial hair, and more adult proportions. Another is his return from school. His ability to do men's work is also important. Boys of about fifteen accompany and assist their fathers more and more as the older men go to cut trees and make gardens, visit other villages, and so on. Men of twenty or so usually have their own gardens, and some may build their own houses. Such industry shows a potential wife that the young man would be a good husband. Kwoma also judge a boy's discretion when deciding his status. A grown man is one who does not betray men's secrets to his wife.

Although the initiation, called *handapia-sug-wia*, appeared to be obsolete during my fieldwork, I include it in this discussion for several reasons. The memory of it is still vivid among older men. In view of the recent revival of many other customs that I had thought gone forever, it seems possible now that male initiation may also be revived. Handapia-sugwia symbolically expressed a definition of maleness found in other aspects of Kwoma culture, but, being a ritual, it presented the definition in concentrated and redundant form. Approaching the idea of "male" by means of a discussion of this ritual is thus the most convenient method. A comparison of this ritual with the events of girls' puberty and maturation shows also the complementary opposition between male and female in Kwoma.

In the course of this ritual, the older married men of several neighboring hamlets collected the nearly or newly matured boys in a stream, drained them of what appears to have been a fair amount of blood (perhaps a pint) through cuts in the penis, fortified them afterwards with hot food that the men had cooked themselves in the men's house, and then isolated them for several months in a specially built house near the men's house, where the older men began to teach the initiates the stories and songs belonging to their descent groups.

For the novices this ritual was the culmination of many years of secret bloodletting. Whiting (1941:64) reports that a boy was

> taught that growth depends upon the renewal of blood, and that food produces blood, which promotes growth as long as it is fresh. When blood has been in the system for a time, however, it begins to grow stale and finally rotten, and then growth ceases until the bad blood is removed from the body. . . . the best method of removing this bad blood is through the penis. . . . Boys frequently go into the bushes and scrape their penises with nettle leaves so that the blood may flow out. . . . boys performed this act only in private and were ashamed if they were discovered.

Apparently men performed the bloodletting on themselves at approximately five-year intervals after the initiation in order to restore their strength by renewing their blood.

The observation of menarche and the boys' initiation make adults of children—or at any rate they begin the change—by producing or recognizing an association of a boy or girl with a particular gender definition. Kwoma men are male, therefore, because they conform to Kwoma ideas of maleness, and Kwoma women are female because they conform to the ideas of femaleness. The two rituals described above use the same elements—food, fire, blood, water, and space—but juxtapose them in different ways in order to assert the nature of, and resulting differences between, male and female. Men and women thus represent different elaborations on a fundamental principle. They are not identical, but they are consubstantial.

Menstruation makes a girl a woman because it announces that she is cold, fertile, and produced by extrahuman forces. She herself elaborates on these qualities by asserting her individual, peripheral, and private status. She shares food and fire with no one and sleeps alone.

The idea that women are private persons, limited members of a collectivity, is manifest in the individual and familial celebration of the event. A girl's withdrawing from her accustomed society in the various ways described above foreshadows her eventual physical separation from her father's household when she marries and her resulting peripheral social status.

The fact of menstruation itself illustrates the coldness of women at the same time as it gives evidence of her fertility. Menstrual blood represents a failure to conceive. As such it is absolutely dead, and cold, as well as the epitome of dirt and decay. Kwoma say that a menstrual period is a woman's means of purifying herself. Healthy blood will conceive a child and become part of it, as well as forming the afterbirth (which is an essential part of a person). When a girl has her first period she becomes a woman because she is fertile; her failure to conceive is due to sexual continence, not a lack of femininity.

The liminal status between first menstrual period and marriage is best expressed by what a girl can do with food. Kwoma women identify themselves primarily as producers and distributors of food. During menstruation—also a liminal state—a woman performs neither of these female tasks but turns the cooking over to someone else, usually her husband. A postpubescent but unmarried girl takes a middle course between these extremes. She produces food that is almost entirely for her own consumption, although she may (when not menstruating) feed her brothers or her younger sisters. She may feed no one in the generations senior to her and —with the exception noted above—may not accept food from them. If she has a fiancé she may not feed him at all, since doing so initiates the actual marriage. In terms of food she is neither child nor adult; she has more control over food than a child but less than an adult. This is parallel to her sexual and reproductive status in that she is physically attractive and capable of conceiving a child but as an unmarried girl should neither engage in sexual activity nor have a baby.

At the end of her first period, and all subsequent ones, a woman bathes in a stream and so removes from her person the dangers associated with menstrual blood. The blood itself is burned, together with the bark or rags in which she collected it, and the ashes are scattered.

Kwoma regard menarche and menstruation as inevitable and uncontrollable, like the renewal of life in the bush. They have no explanation for the origin of the blood—it just happens. Likewise, periods just happen—there is no means of inducing them, and preventing them is possible only by conceiving, which is not an inevitable consequence of sex relations.

Using the same symbols, handapia-sugwia establishes both a relationship between boys and maleness and their complementarity to femaleness.

Boys' initiation was performed collectively, a group of men operating on a group of youths. The blood of men and boys flowed into one stream, which carried it out of Kwoma land to the Sepik. Here, as in menstruation, water purifies. This group of men shared food that men cooked, and together the initiates learned the stories and songs that are the property of their descent groups.

Space was as important as collectivity in this ritual for establishing maleness. The boys' rotten blood was lost in a stream. This was a female aspect of themselves, replaced later, in male surroundings—the men's house or its temporary outbuilding, at the top of a ridge. Grown men's blood rots with time, and with action, most of which occurs in the relatively female everyday world. Men must regain their masculinity periodically, just as boys must first acquire it. When purged of bad blood the men moved from the peripheral, low area of the stream to a high central area and there completed the transformation of boys into men.

The food the boys ate replaced the blood they lost and became male, or "hot," blood. The Kwoma stress even now that this had to be *hot* food, whereas ordinary cooked food is tepid or cold when eaten. The food is unambiguously male because men cook it in the men's house, out of range of female influence. Although hot, and therefore cooked, it is in fact hardly changed in texture. It remains hard, again unlike ordinary food, which is soupy. Hardness is a male quality, as we have seen. Probably this food also reflects, wryly, the Kwoma notion that men cannot cook.

The men's bloodletting is an imitation of menstruation. As one informant said, "Women lose bad blood every month. That's their nature. We have to do this instead, otherwise it'll never come out." The boys' initiation is male menstruation performed in a intensely male world: more communal than the everyday world, with hotter food cooked by men performing what is otherwise a preeminently female task. The everyday world becomes relatively feminine in contrast. It is also a sexual world, while the male world is asexual. But unlike women's menstruation, men's bleeding is something humans can control—or at any rate used to think they should control. Men, in short, are not produced by extrahuman forces as women are.

The opposition between male and female expressed in these rituals is not antagonistic. The intense masculinity of the boys' initiation seems to have expressed not fear of women or female pollution but rather an exaggeration of the differences between men and women that make the fact of their subsequent cooperation in marriage more evident.

Marriage

Marriage is in fact the next status change that Kwoma experience. Like maturation it is a lengthy process, taking in some cases ten years from the first negotiations to the payment of bridewealth which finishes them.

Marriages may be arranged by the parties involved or by their fathers. The former sort of marriage usually involves the boy's courting the girl, but it may involve the girl's moving in with an already married man, subject to his wife's consent. When marriages are arranged the fiancés are still children, and the girl goes to live with and be raised by her betrothed's family. Girls have absolute control over their marriages, however. Even a betrothed girl may leave her fiancé before her bride-price is paid, and no one can cause her to return.

The marriage ceremony involves a ruse planned by the fiancée and her mother-in-law; it is a woman's prerogative to decide when a man marries, as well as whom. On a day when he is absent and cannot see who is cooking, his fiancée for the first time prepares his food, which his mother gives him to eat on his return without, however, identifying the cook. Until this time his mother has cooked for him, and so he accepts this food from her without suspicion. She waits until he has consumed about half of it and then informs him that his fiancée has cooked it. At this news he is supposed to rush away and try to throw up (cf. Whiting 1941:125; I have never seen this, although I have had it described to me several times). The motivation for this is variously said to be that the groom thinks that if he can void his stomach he can escape marriage, or that since wives are supposed to be in league with their brothers or lovers to poison their husbands the groom is trying to eject a deadly meal. My own observation of Kwoma men leads me to suspect, however, that there is a measure of buffoonery in this performance, as there is in much else that they do. But the performance, if serious, is futile, because eating his fiancée's food obliges a man to behave as a husband.

The symbolic importance of cooked food which we have already encountered in puberty observances appears in this rite of passage also. Sharing food implies a relationship in which there is no suspicion of sorcery, i.e., hostility, and offering food is an act of incorporation. The wife is admitting her husband to the female domain. Sharing food is the sign of a viable marriage and cooking the preeminently wifely task. Women describe wifely devotion almost entirely in terms of cooking for their husbands; men enlarge on their attachment to their wives in terms of culinary energy and skill. Kwoma say that a man returning from a long journey hastens homeward when he sees the smoke of his wife's cooking fire rising against the evening sky.

If the bride initiates the married state, her husband's patriline confirms it several years later with the payment of bride-price. With this payment, which is the first to which the groom has ever contributed, both husband and wife become fully adult members of the community, clearly distinguished from children.

The wife is more definitely incorporated in her husband's lineage and separated from her own. Both husband and wife are now able, and even obliged, to participate in exchanges of shell valuables with affines. A wife acquires the control of her household's wealth (previously controlled by her mother-in-law) and contributes to her brother's wealth by trading sago for shells at Avatip. She is able to distribute food more widely than before. A husband presents most of the shells on public occasions and delivers food from his garden to his sister and mother's brother to solicit shell valuables from them. Besides these responsibilities, fully married persons, especially men, are responsible to others for damage they may cause to them or their property. Women are responsible for the health of their families, including providing food and regulating marital sex relations.

In Kwoma thought, the human relationship that best exemplifies the opposition between male and female is that between husband and wife. Marriage thus completes the identification of men and women with male and female by effecting a union between them. In so doing, marriage mediates public and private, individual and collective; it mediates the asexual male world and the sexual female world; it joins to the past, represented by the patrilineage and its traditional knowledge and by the patrilineal gender pair brother/sister, which is always nonreproducing, the possibility of the future, represented by the gender pair husband/wife, which is by definition a combination capable of producing a new generation and thus of perpetuating the past.

The taboos associated with conception concisely illustrate the nature of marriage. The pregnant woman must remain sexually continent to prevent miscarriage, and she avoids certain foods that cause birth defects. The expectant father need not be sexually continent, but he cannot make carvings or slit-gongs. Kwoma say that if he were to make a slit-gong, it would have no "voice," and if he were to work on a statue, all the carvings in the men's house would fall down and break. Contemplation of such an event is distressing because the men's house represents the community and, more important, its relationship to the spirit world. The wood used in carvings and slit-gongs is especially hard and durable; Kwoma men boast about the fact that their great-grandchildren will see the carvings they make today. Carvings are analogous to children, male and female products respectively: both represent a continuity between past and future, and both may be destroyed by improper activities during a crucial time. The important difference between them is, of course, that statues—produced in a male, asexual environment—are not alive (in fact, they usually represent purely fictional beings, my informants told me) and babies—produced in a female, sexual environment—are. Babies will eventually reproduce themselves, but statues will not. The restrictions appropriate to expectant parents thus reflect the idea that bestowing life is a female power that men can only imitate, just as they imitate menstruation by slitting their penes. But men's "children" and women's are mutually necessary, just as men and women are, even for conception. Wives give husbands access to their reproductive world, but husbands reciprocate with access to the spirit world. Husband and wife form a fruitful household, while humans and spirits make a fruitful world. Kwoma marriage is a microcosm.

Aging

Advancing age, like puberty, has different effects on women and on men. Women reach menopause, a change without ceremonial observation but allowing somewhat more freedom than before, notably in connection with food. They have more time now to make net bags, which are important items of wealth in funeral prestations. Old women retain many female associations. They participate in reproduction, if only vicariously, by assisting at births; old men cannot do this. Their association with cooking persists also. They contribute to debates only when a close relative has been threatened or harmed in the meeting. They may never enter the men's house during a ceremony. They remain largely peripheral to the body of men that forms the community and its constituent lineages.

Older men are invited to join the senior yam cult, nogwi. Nogwi men are the adepts who know how to plant yams. The knowledge involves, I gather, certain spells and actions that are essential to the maturation of yams. None of these will be successful unless the man avoids all sexual contact with women, especially his wife. (She, incidentally, may refuse to allow him to join nogwi if she is unwilling to share his celibacy.) The restriction is not particularly onerous, however, because in Kwoma opinion people lose interest in sex as they age, as well as becoming less and less appealing to the opposite sex.

An aged couple is thus asexual and nonreproductive, its creative energies devoted to the welfare of yams, which are male by association. The separation of men and women into male and female becomes of less and less account as the couple ages, until they are similar to the immature brother and sister who cooperate economically but cannot reproduce. Kin terms reflect this change; they make no gender distinction in the second and third ascending generations (except for father's father's sister).

It is tempting to see the resolution of two genders into one at this age as the resolution of female into male, opposed to the separation of male from female at puberty, despite the fact that old women still retain some female associations. The fact that an elderly couple is supposedly celibate, like men who are "hot" because they are performing a ceremony, is consonant with this interpretation. Old women have more authority than younger ones, and they are less shy about speaking in public. Only postmenopausal women smoke, although not all of them do so. (All men smoke.) In general, only older women participate in nogwi (although outside the men's house), while younger women watch. Occasionally one of these women shakes a spear as she dances—a mild form of transvestism—instead of a fishing net or a string bag stiffened with sago skin. Several informants said that an old woman could help her husband plant yams. Whether this is true or not, it suggests (as do these other facts) that older women are less female, and more male, than women of reproductive age.

Death

That the gender associations made at puberty, as it were, cling to the aged is evident in Kwoma ideas about death. Just as Kwoma give no clear primacy to either parent in conception, they make no unambiguous gender identification of dead bodies or the parts thereof.

Kwoma have always practiced double burial. In the past they exposed the body on a tree platform down the hill from the person's house until only the bones were left, at which time mourning ended and the bones were buried in or near the kitchen. Today the body must be buried within twenty-four hours of death, but it is later disinterred and reburied when mourning ends. Sons may keep a long bone in a bag in the house to ensure that the ghost will look after them and their families.

Since bones are hard and permanent, and these are male qualities, the conclusion that a completely dead body is male is plausible. The slight elevation of the decomposing body suggests this as well. Ghosts, *nggamba*, are the postmortem form of mai, the breath of life conferred by women. Kwoma do not, however, make a neat association between these two pairs of oppositions; in fact, the funeral customs together seem to confuse the question of gender identification to the point of obliterating it. The initial deposition of the body, whether on a platform or in a grave, is in a liminal space, neither village nor bush but decidedly peripheral compared to the men's house. Moreover, the bones are reinterred in a female area. Ghosts are said to retain the gender they had in life. They live in agnatically based communities like those of the living except that they are beneath hills rather than on top of them. At the same time, they may hover about their relatives' houses, especially at night, and they are supposed to take an active interest in the welfare of the living. The fact that Kwoma do not represent death in a tightly structured way is, I think, a reflection of the fact that for them death is largely a mystery.

Conclusion

Two points may be made here, one ethnographic and one theoretical.

The many parallels between this analysis and Losche's (1982) analysis of Abelam gender will not have gone unnoticed. Kwoma and Abelam are not identical, of course, but they do seem remarkably alike in their perception of the life cycle. The fact that Losche and I have arrived independently (and by somewhat different routes) at very similar conclusions about the relationship of gender to human life cycles suggests, encouragingly, that these are objective, not subjective, analyses.

Losche suggests that for Abelam, as for Kwoma, the life cycle moves from a period in which gender differentiation is unimportant to one in which it is essential and back to one in which it is again unimportant; but the whole cycle seems to involve a slight shift from female to male. (As is usual in the Sepik, the differences are not clear-cut, but the evidence is suggestive.) These changes themselves reflect fundamental cultural concerns having to do with the continuity from the past to the future. That Kwoma care about their posterity will have become obvious. Three things are necessary to ensure continuity,

children, food, and the benevolence of spirits, and these are closely interrelated. Food (yams) makes children grow, and food grows only with the help of spirits, whose benevolence is secured by older persons. The Kwoma life cycle, then, involves a shift from the production of children by male men and female women to the production of food (yams) by "male" humans and female spirits. The parallel with Abelam may not be exact, but certainly there is the same shift in emphasis: younger people (or sexually active women) have children, and older people (or sexually inactive men) have yams.

The approach in this paper, though, is not quite the same as Losche's, for the reasons outlined in the introduction. Whereas she tends to use gender and person as interchangeable categories (a usage that may reflect Abelam ideas), I have preferred to explore the possibility that they are separate. Undoubtedly the relationship between the abstract gender definition and the concrete person is circular, but because gender definitions involve and affect so much more of the world than men and women I am reluctant to assume that only humans inform them—they do no more than confirm them. In any case, it is as well to get away from a style of analysis in which the only terms are "people" and "everything else" and these mutually define each other. In concrete terms, I am not suggesting that men are male because they are like ridges, any more than that ridges are male because they are like men. Rather, I am suggesting that, in Kwoma thought, ridges and men share an attribute that distinguishes them from water and women: the shared attribute, not either item in itself, provokes the association. Our convention of glossing the association in terms of gender attributes a conceptual eminence to one item and presents culture as a set of mechanistic causes and effects in which the embodiment is more than the idea. This analysis suggests that reversing the relationship may be a more useful procedure in the long run.

Notes

1. My fieldwork among Kwoma was carried out between October 1972 and August 1973 and in June-July 1981, primarily in Bangwis village. I am grateful to the American Council of Learned Societies for a grant in aid that made the 1981 trip possible. I am also grateful to Ross Bowden for supplying me with descriptions of men's secret ceremonies. Finally, I thank Peter Huber for his penetrating criticisms and constant encouragement.

35/ Utopian Visions and the Division of Labor in Abelam Society

Diane Losche

Ideas produced in academia are often marked by what has been called dichotomous theorizing, "a tendency to present two positions often in a highly simplified or abstract form, as mutually exclusive . . . . with the implied injunction that it is necessary to choose one or the other" (Barret et al. 1979:18). As with other products in a competitive marketplace, the aim is to cause the consumer to choose one over the other. Perhaps this competition increases the production of ideas. It certainly produces entertaining rhetoric. The problem is that the process of choice in these situations forces us to eradicate some portion of perceived reality. This paper is an attempt to escape this impasse within the bounds of the debate generated by the metropole's collision with one of the outliers of the colonial empire, Papua New Guinea.

During the 1970s, apparently contradictory models emerged from different analyses of women's roles and gender relations within Papua New Guinea. According to one model, women in some societies are viewed by all members of those societies as inferior to men. According to the other, anthropologists have underestimated the value of women and the cultural domains which they control. Implied by the debate over these models is that they are mutually exclusive. I will suggest that this assumption is related to an unwarranted notion of the holism of small-scale societies and the sharing of models within them. I will discuss some of the issues involved in this debate, comparing the work of Marilyn Strathern, Annette Weiner, and Daryl Feil, and then provide material from a village in the East Sepik Province suggesting that one can discern elements of both models in one ethnographic situation.

Studies of intersexual relations in Papua New Guinea can be divided into two phases. In the first phase, researchers concentrated on the analysis of an antagonism which they perceived as prominent in intersexual encounters. Many anthropologists (e.g., Meggitt 1964; Langness 1967; Lindenbaum 1972, 1976) took as their point of departure the observation of Read (1952) that there is marked antagonism between the sexes in the highlands. Until the early 1970s, this observation was not critically examined. The emphasis was rather on the isolation of the variables which produce this hostility. Some of the writers involved in this early phase of research have moved from an examination of the ecological variables to an examination of the symbolic and psychological dimensions of sexual antagonism (e.g., Brown and Buchbinder 1976). From many of these studies there emerges a model of highland societies bifurcated into opposed domains of public/domestic or domestic/wild. These domains are linked via metaphor with a male/female opposition such that the female-associated domain is lower in status than and often polluting to the male-linked one. They also form part of an exchange system in which men dominate prestigeful activity while women make major contributions to food production.

A meticulous analysis of Melpa-speaking women in the Mt. Hagen area by Marilyn Strathern, *Women in Between* (1972), can be seen as transitional to a new phase of research. Strathern emphasizes that, while women have little power in exchange relative to men, they sometimes perceive and pursue their own interests as distinct from those of men. Since the mid-seventies, the model of highland societies generated by the research of the fifties and sixties has been challenged (see, e.g., Faithorn 1976). Feil (1978), in his analysis of exchange among the Enga, emphasizes the influence of women whatever the ideology of male Enga. Weiner (1976), in her analysis of Trobriand exchange, suggests that if we reconstitute what we mean by power (and in the Trobriands the notion of power must extend to the cosmological domain), then women as well as men control objects central to the continuation of society. She offers the strongest critique of male-centered views of culture in Melanesia, criticizing Strathern for not recognizing the significance of net-bag transaction by Melpa women (p. 13). Weiner implies, as Strathern (1981a) herself has pointed out in a recent talk, that because of theoretical bias earlier analyses, in particular that of Strathern (1980), have not seen what is there. She suggests that Strathern ignores a potential domain of control by women in the exchange of net bags in the Hagen area because of a Western male-centered view of power. Feil (1978) contends that Strathern's analysis is biased toward the male Hagener's view of society and that this bias is bolstered by an opposition between domestic and public that elevates the status of men versus women.

This clash of views is tangled within a web of ethnographic specifics. It is obvious, for example, that the highlands and the Trobriands are quite different from one another in social structure. Weiner herself recognizes crucial differences in women's position between Kiriwina and the highlands (pp. 117–18). It is of course possible that each model is appropriate to each society. Further, the dichotomy I draw between the models does some violence to the work of those concerned. If Strathern suggests that women are categorically "rubbish" compared to men, she does not ignore the extent to which women pursue interests divergent from those of men. Nor is Weiner unaware of hierarchies of power: "Within their own domains, men and women control different kinds of resources and hence effect different degrees and kinds of power over others. A hierarchy of power develops from the structure of these two domains as men borrow from the female domain" (p. 18). As Austin (1983:223) has said of another debate in the anthropological literature, "These writers are involved in a juggling of apparently opposing themes, without a consistent language for both."

Strathern's recent rejoinders to the criticisms of Weiner and Feil provide a lucid analysis of the nature of the models we use to translate the structure of foreign societies. Her point is that, in some instances, ethnographers have glossed certain oppositions in the society they study with oppositions such as "nature/culture" which are grounded in Western historical development. She suggests that the conflation of Western oppositions with indigenous ones has led to mistaken conclusions about the position of women in parts of Papua New Guinea. For example, in the case of the Hageners with whom she worked, the nature/culture opposition is inappropriate to gender categories because it involves notions of an object worked on by a subject and of property and control that are foreign to Hagen. While not denying that there are oppositions relevant to the female/male split among Hageners, she points to the semantic domains that oppositions cover and the dialectic between different opposing pairs. Wei-

ner's criticisms, she maintains, are based on an opposition of nature and culture which involves a denigration of domestic life and food production and doubt as to whether women may be regarded as full persons. Whereas Weiner's reconsideration of the concept of power stems from the need to prove that women have some domain of power, the notion of control may not be central to the gender domains which other societies create (Strathern 1981b). Strathern's work suggests that successful anthropological inquiry needs an analysis of our own native categories as well as those of our informants.

While Strathern criticizes the application of a Western model of nature/culture to Hageners, her data suggest that in Hagen there are oppositions in which female is ranked as inferior to male (Strathern 1980:209):

> Females may be categorically "rubbish" by contrast with males; household chores and horticultural labor do not carry the prestige of group enterprise. When they define themselves as interested in prestige . . . males set their gender off from the irresponsible and "wild" propensities of females. Categorically (though not in terms of individual ascription—quite another matter), females are of lower status than males.

The problem is precisely with the notion of cultural category. With the notion of culture currently shared by Strathern, Weiner, and most other anthropologists, cultural categories are shared representations, notions about which members of the society are in agreement. To say that members of a group share a system of representations is not, however, to imply that they agree as to the value of these representations. The notion of culture as shared representation leaves out crucial elements of conflict. This notion is, however, deeply imbedded in the current debate, which opposes a hegemonic Western model to an equally hegemonic native one. In comparing a unified "us" with an undifferentiated "them," it obscures the process by which oppositions are formed. Oppositions are the subject of debate and questioning in other societies as well as in our own.

I do not wish to imply that the authors involved in this debate are unaware of conflict in the contexts that they write about. Strathern (1972:287) in particular is at pains to emphasize potential points of conflict and struggle within Hagen society:

> Until now I have refrained from assertions about women's status as such if for nothing

else than to avoid the implied assumption of harmony or complete integration between aspects of one role or between the several roles which women might play. . . . the very fact that it is limited participation in exchanges which enables women to combine wifely and sisterly duties as an intermediary leads to its own difficulties.

My point is that the debate itself, with its implied and unexplored dichotomy of models, suggests a holistic notion of culture. From the evidence of our own society, the implication that one model or the other is appropriate is absurd. Strathern's model lends itself to metaphorical comparison to the "politics of similarity" produced at one stage of the recent feminist movement, while Weiner's model bears some resemblance to the "politics of difference" generated in a different stage. These models have arisen from particular contexts of struggle. Our reading of the debate, then, tends to reify the concept of culture. As Werbner (1977:ix) has suggested;

Essential relations with a wider context get stripped away when a small group, little community or tribe is studied as an isolated whole. This idea is virtually a commonplace and it is now conventional, also, to reject the method as a fault of earlier studies. Yet relatively little advance has been made beyond naive holism. . . . the challenge remains . . . to analyze change in fields of relations that cross political economic and ethnic boundaries. . . .

Bloch and Bloch (1980:39) have suggested that the very notion of nature and culture be viewed as produced not within a "great" tradition or effortlessly, in the absence of conflict:

Anthropology is heir to a polemic where the opposition between nature and something else is part of the attempt to understand society and at the same time to criticize it, it is not heir to a set of organized concepts, clearly defined. . . . when therefore we see other cultures in terms of these concepts of nature, as inevitably we must, we should perhaps look more for the ideological polemic which uses this type of notion rather than make the sterile attempt to match our categories to theirs. . . .

This notion can be extended to many cultural categories. It suggests that what appears to be a hegemony of representations at any moment in time is in fact the very momentary product of a tumultuous history.

To clarify my point that we must look at cultural representations as matters of debate and struggle, I now turn to an example from the East Sepik Province. The material presented here comes from twenty months spent over a period of four years between 1976 and 1980 in the village of Apangai, northwest of Maprik. The population of the village is approximately 550. People in Apangai speak a dialect of the Abelam language that they call Samu-Kundi.

Villagers live in clan hamlets which, while patrilineal in ideology, are also formed by matrilateral and affinal ties. They live by gardening supplemented by some hunting, arboriculture, cash-cropping, and the purchase of some trade store products. The staple of the diet is yams, some varieties of which are grown only by adult men in separate gardens. About three nuclear families have been residing away from the village for ten years. Most adult men have spent some time away from the village, and some younger women have lived away for several years. A number of young people now go occasionally to Maprik or the provincial capital, Wewak, to work in hotels or as drivers. The village has a spirit cult in which carvings and paintings are produced when men are initiated into it. Some of these art products are now sold to collectors, tourists, and museums.

Prior to the 1930s there was some sporadic contact with whites in the form of labor recruiting of men to other areas of New Guinea and occasional visits by gold prospectors. Even in the 1920s artifacts were being collected from the area. The earliest known artifact to be collected from the Torricelli–Prince Alexander region of the Sepik was acquired in 1898 in Aitape. Gold was discovered in the area in the 1930s, and this may have prompted the Australian administration to set up a permanent post on land bought from the village of Maprik. A Catholic mission at Kungingini was established in 1938.

The Australians fled when the Japanese invaded the territory. Toward the end of the war, relations between villagers and Japanese soldiers became violent and bitter, since the soldiers, cut off from supplies by an Allied blockade, were trying to live off the land. When Allied soldiers came into the area, villagers saw black Americans who subsequently became important symbols in cargo cults. Administrative apparatus was restored by 1953, and since then missionaries, administrative personnel, researchers, artifact dealers, and tourists have entered the area. Two of the most significant events for villagers in the last twenty years have been the completion in 1972 of the Sepik Highway, a two-lane dirt and gravel road that has made travel much faster, and the establishment of Papua New Guinea as an independent state in 1975. Missionaries move into the area—and out—with great ease. In 1974 there were representatives of thirty-six denominations working in the East Sepik; however, the choice is not so magnificent at the village level. Apangai is nominally Assembly of God; it has a native Assembly of God deacon, and a small house serves as "church." Some villages nearby are nominally Catholic. However, this order gives way on closer acquaintance to an at first rather bewildering variety of affiliations to and interests in other religious denominations, cargo movements, and what seem idiosyncratic beliefs.

Three "roads" or ways of improving life are perceived by the people of Apangai. These roads might be called conflicting ideologies in that people are continually trying to decide which is best. One road may be called "traditional" and is concerned with the proper maintenance of the long-yam cult, initiations, etc. A second is that of the missions and/or cargo cults; taking this road entails giving up initiations and the practice of sorcery (in theory) but not long-yam cultivation, the sine qua non of male status, since apparently neither cargo-cult leaders nor missionaries have ever pinpointed long yams as an expression of paganism. The third road is the governmental one, involving the maintenance of traditional ways in a modified form. Initiations, for example, are to be continued but without the ordeals of penis incision and beating. This road rejects cargo cults, is skeptical of missions, and aligns itself with the ideas of the newly independent government of Papua New Guinea as broadcast over the radio and in local speeches made by government leaders.

These roads are by and large not chosen once and for all by individuals; rather, there is continual shifting from one to another. There is, however, a very small core of senior men who appear to have followed the way of mission and cargo cult for ten and sometimes twenty years. Three of the men (aged fifty to sixty, approximately) who are the most fervent believers in cargo cults and/or missions appear to have acquired their passion for such activities during World War II, when all three were caught out of the village and underwent a series of more or less traumatic experiences. Again, the present councillor is the leader of the governmental road, and a small group of men in his own clan hamlet appears to echo his

beliefs. The clan elders who follow the traditional road are much less vociferous in espousing their views but are extremely important precisely because they side with neither of these two factions and can always shift their allegiance. The crystallization of factions can be traced to the disturbances of the Peli Association, which reached its peak in the early seventies. The central men of the two factions are respectively the previous and present councillors. The previous councillor is now the most committed and vocal of cargo-cult leaders. He has been jailed twice for a month at a time at the instigation of the present councillor for his participation in cargo activities. One may not infer from this that he is or feels he is fighting a losing battle, for the oscillations of belief in the East Sepik are rapid. Viewing the situation from only one point in time will give a false impression. Villagers have not chosen one path or another; rather, they are in the process of wondering, experimenting, and evaluating and will probably remain so all their lives.

When I entered the village in 1976, the village court had just been established, and there was great interest in it on the part of villagers. The councillor appeared to have a large support group. An initiation was held in which he was one of the prime movers. His rival, the cargo-cult/mission leader, acknowledged the councillor's temporary hegemony but remained optimistic: "The councillor and I are on opposite sides. He has belief in government, and the village court gives him power now, but I have my own road and will never change."

In 1977, word of a new movement began to spread through the village. Apparently some refugees from Irian Jaya living in Aitape (the capital of the West Sepik Province) had persuaded men from some of the surrounding villages to collect money from the villagers to buy uniforms and guns for their "cousins" (the word used by the men for cousin was *kandere*, Tok Pisin for either cross- or parallel cousin). I assume that the Irian Jayanese organizers of this movement intended the money to be sent to Irian Jaya, but the village men thought all this military paraphernalia was meant for them. One may argue that this sounds like an attempt to form a guerrilla army, and it is certainly a far cry from Vailaila madness, but the men from the village who attended meetings about this activity perceived it as having supernatural efficacy. They thought that the contribution of money and the acquisition of uniforms would lead to their seeing their dead relatives, who were thought to be living in some form on an island somewhere in the direction of Irian Jaya. The leaders of this movement never came into the area; rather, they spoke to village men in Aitape, who returned to their villages and spread the word. The incipient movement was very short-lived. In 1978 the councillor had the cargo-cult leader jailed and alerted the Maprik authorities, who apparently saw to it that the refugees were expelled from Papua New Guinea.

When I returned to Apangai in 1980, the first news I heard was that everyone in the village had joined a mission that villagers were calling the New Apostles. The councillor told me glumly, "Everyone has joined this new mission, this rubbish." When I asked who actually had joined, I was surprised by a number of members besides the cargo-cult/mission faction. On my visits to the villagers whom the councillor had mentioned as taking part in the new mission, I found that one Apangai elder who had formerly not committed himself to either government or mission had joined it with fervor, and so had most of his extensive clan. In 1976, the government road had seemed to be strongest in the village; in 1980, the mission road appeared to have gained in popularity. To assume that either picture is an enduring state of affairs would be wrong. Experimentation and flux in belief systems are the norm. For example, the cargo-cult leader who had ostentatiously declined to participate in the initiation that took place in 1977 had, when I returned in 1980, just organized the construction of one of the largest and most beautiful tambaran houses in the area in his own hamlet. In response to my questions about his change of heart, he coolly said, "I decided that culture is good—just like missions." A wily man, he had evidently decided that it was in his own interest to beat the councillor at his own game.

Factions are emerging, one might suggest, as a result of the interaction of the political organization of competing patriarchies with the state apparatus. The point I wish to make here is that the courses advocated by the two factions at any point in time may be similar to one another. The cargo-cult leader is not irrevocably committed to abolishing tambaran houses. Rather, his rejection was temporary, the result of a dispute with the pro-tradition councillor. Perhaps a better way of characterizing the situation is to recognize that there are factions whose members seek the power to transform society and simultaneously to establish hegemony within the village. Because no one is yet sure of the road to transformation, ideological commitment shifts.

The common ground of the competing factions is a desire for power to transform village society. But what is the goal of this transformation? I will suggest that it is framed in terms of utopian elements in village life that are seen in myth and expressed in formal debate by orating men and in individual statements by women and men in the course of conflict. Such statements represent individuals' questioning of the premises of their own society, and this questioning is not simply the result of colonial incursion but to a significant degree also indigenous.

It is fairly easy to elicit from most adults a series of myths which posit a transformation of the social order in terms of exchange, food production, and reproduction. In one myth a woman is changed from a woman into a cassowary and back again and in the course of her personal transformation creates fire, houses, and food gardens. In another myth, which accounts for the origin of certain flutes, we are presented with a reversal of the present division of labor; women hunt, are warriors, and grow long yams while men bear and nurse children and cook. In a third myth, which recounts the origin of the long yams, a young man creates this yam species and institutes the sexual taboos operative during its cultivation. His father, a senior man, drives the young hero to suicide by persuading his wife to break the sex taboo necessary for long-yam growth. In this myth the present-day authority structure of the long-yam cult, in which senior men attempt to keep younger men in line on sex taboos and are responsible for the successful growth of the yams, is reversed. In a fourth myth, a woman receives from a male spirit a spell that enables her to give birth through the birth canal, infants previously having had to be cut out of their mothers' wombs. Such myths, which in certain ways transform the social order in terms of responsibility for food production and reproduction, are not uncommon among horticultural societies and have provided the basis for many structural analyses of cultural categories. From the point of view of many of these analyses, they are projections of contradictions within the social order. This type of analysis tends to depolemicize the myths, to remove them from the arena of struggle against the social order. Structural contradictions and struggle are reified, and contradictions become only logical inconsistencies. The assumption is that any such struggle has been won, that the cultural hegemony which is both transformed and mirrored in these myths is total.

I would suggest that such transformations as are reflected in these myths arise from combat against aspects of the perceived social order. In fact, myths such as those briefly outlined here are related to situations in which the valuations attached to categories are altered by individuals in particular contexts and in which individual women and men take a polemical stance against some aspect of their own social organization. For villagers this social order is constructed around a particular form of sexual bifurcation in the production and exchange of food. I will argue that the paradoxical set of postulates which the myths form about reproduction, food production, and exchange must be seen in relation to a social reality in which opposition between the domains of women and men in terms of production, exchange, and reproduction is interwoven with an identity of interests between women and men. The myths reflect not a hierarchical set of categories about male and female, food production and exchange, nature and culture, but a questioning of power relationships.

This polemical stance can only be understood by reference to a social life in which individual women and men are placed between two orders of exchange and production. Within the village women and men are not neatly bifurcated into two separate realms of production and exchange; rather, both participate in two separate but interconnected orders of exchange and productivity. On the one hand, we see sets of nuclear-family households maintaining blocks of garden land. There is a division of labor between women and men in these gardens, but it is not regulated by taboos and is relatively flexible. The everyday pattern of village life is organized around daily trips to the gardens, where wife, husband, and children spend most of the day. These nuclear-family households are linked to each other by ties of marriage. Affinal exchanges of food, shell rings, and money take place at times of birth, first menstruation, marriage, and death. Women prepare the food, but the division of labor is somewhat flexible and varies from household to household, depending on the personalities of the individuals. Women show an interest equal to that of men in such exchanges and are actively involved. Associated with this order is an ideology of amicable and harmonious interdependence of wife and husband: sharing a fire, sharing food, sharing concern over food production, the nurturance of children, and exchange relations are important to both women and men. That the ideal of harmonious interdependence is often honored in the breach does not lessen its quality as a compelling vision. The ideal is, one might say, created in the breach as relatives intervene in an attempt to resolve disharmony between wife and husband.

Running parallel to this order, in which women and men are interdependent, is the contradictory one comprised of the long-yam and spirit cults. The long-yam cult is restricted to men. Taboos prohibit sexual intercourse and food sharing on the part of the long-yam grower and others for four to five months at a time. Men exchange yams with partners within the village and with other villages, gaining renown based on the size and shape of the harvest. The ability to grow long yams is linked to the ability to observe taboos and perform powerful magic, including sorcery. When men gather on the plaza for meetings about long yams, women may not be present, but they are expected to prepare cooked yams or rice to be delivered to the men by boys. Associated with the yam cult is a spirit cult into which men are initiated throughout the life cycle and in which carvings and paintings are produced. Women are excluded from much of the activity of this cult. In both of the cults, women related to men involved are obliged to cook food and observe the same food taboos as their male kin. Associated with both these cults is an ideology of misogyny and authority of older men over younger. This ideology, again, is often honored in the breach. Senior men are regarded with ambivalence by younger men and women because they control sorcery. If one wants to kill anyone over the age of five through sorcery, one must apply to a senior man who has access to the paint which, besides being used to decorate carvings, is used in magic.

Individual women and men move with unease between these two orders and their associated ideologies. One promises renown at the possible sacrifice of marital relations. The other has what many believe to be a potential for sexual harmony at the sacrifice of renown. Nowadays there are mass desertions from and polemical tirades by men against the yam and spirit cults. Many women also voice rejection of these structures. At most deaths there are gatherings in which the wisdom of maintaining the cults is debated. Part of the reason for the public polemic is undoubtedly the incursion of Christian sects into the area. Many Abelam villages show oscillations between participation in the long-yam and spirit cults and mission beliefs. It is entirely possible for households to maintain themselves outside these cults. It appears that some villagers are trying out various forms of what we would call millenarian beliefs promising a Utopia of sexual harmony and redemption from death—beliefs that are conducive to their choice of ensconcing themselves in the household economy, with its hope of sexual harmony in nurturance and production. One woman, when I asked why she became a Christian, grinned and said, "So my husband and I can be like Adam and Eve in the magic Garden." Promises of Utopia embedded within their own social order are now wedded to the utopian elements of incursive religions.

One might speculate that the villagers were led to the present crisis of customs by the incursion of colonialism, that is, by systematic comparison of their life-style with that of the intruders, and there is certainly some large truth in this. However, this interpretation does not do justice to what little we know about their history. If we accept the evidence of glottochronology and burned grasslands, Middle Sepik peoples sometime in the last two thousand years moved north and west into the area formerly occupied by Torricelli-phylum groups such as the Arapesh. Forge (1972a) describes this as a gradual jostling rather than an organized military conquest. In their incursion into the area, they may have developed a number of cultural products, particularly magically efficacious materials for use in fostering the growth of yams and in spirit cults, to export in exchange for such scarce items as stone tools and stone for tools (Forge 1977). Thus, as Forge has suggested, the Abelam emphasis on the yam and spirit cults may have been exported to other peoples as magic. Villagers, both women and men, certainly still regard their possession of magically efficacious techniques of transformation, including the spirit cult, as of prime importance in the production of yams. This powerful export is based on gender antithesis. This separation and opposition has, I suggest, entailed a protest from within the society itself, produced by women and men not entirely comfortable with the contradictions between the household and the male-dominated cults. It is at this state of play that Europeans may have first entered the area.

This case study suggests that assumptions of the hegemony of a categorical association of men with prestige and the exchange of valuables including food and women with production and the domestic economy are, for the area I worked in, incomplete and misleading. Here the hegemony of cultural categories about the proper realm of women and men in regard to food production, reproduction, and exchange is constantly being dismantled by individuals struggling to attain utopian visions within the contradictions of their own social order.

I would argue that, from the point of view of villagers, recent changes in the material base of their society have presented the possibility of transforming utopian visions into programs of reform via such activities as cargo movements and Christian sects. Some individuals are beginning to realize that the pursuit of these visions may lead to the destruction of their way of life and an unwanted dependence on the apparatus of world trade. This realization may produce changes in the visions, but that is the subject of another paper. People recognize that incursive elements allow for certain types of material changes, for example, in transportation, previously unknown in their society. They are, however, not materialists in that they have not, for the most part, given over efficacy and prime-movership only to material conditions. Rather, they are continually trying out different sources of power, change, and transformation. Utopian elements in their own society, such as the desire to see their dead ancestors, the desire for unification of the living and the dead, and the desire for more harmonious communication between women and men are motivating villagers in some of their choices.

The current debate on gender relations in Papua New Guinea assumes that the ideologies and social structures of small-scale communities form relatively undifferentiated cultural hegemonies. It has been argued that either women are structurally and ideologically peripheral or they are central to the production and reproduction of their own society, despite the ideology of men, and this has been obscured by our own presuppositions. I have attempted to suggest a third possibility: that the relative positions of women and men are the subject of debate and struggle in small communities. This possibility dismantles the hegemony and to some extent alters the terms of the debate. While we must compare our own categories with those of the people we study, we must also view these people as potentially as puzzled as we are by the problem of sexual differentiation and identity.

36/ Male Initiation among the Yangoru Boiken

Paul Roscoe

For some time now, it has been apparent that male initiation in the Sepik differs in crucial respects from initiation elsewhere in Papua New Guinea, most notably the highlands (e.g., Hage 1981, Keesing 1982). Unfortunately, the wealth of detail available on highlands initiation is matched in relatively few Sepik accounts (though see, e.g., Tuzin 1980), thus complicating the opportunities that these differences offer for cross-cultural analysis. Furthermore, despite evidence of a renaissance in some quarters (see, e.g., papers by Allen and Schindlbeck in this volume), these rites have now disappeared from many parts of the Sepik (see Roscoe and Scaglion in this volume), raising the specter of imminent loss of their details forever.

On this score alone, then, attempts to salvage what is still remembered of these rites serve the purpose of research in and for Papua New Guinea. The exercise is of academic value in adding another "datum" to an ever-growing cross-cultural file. And, at the risk of arrogance in assuming the role of purveyor of cultural tradition, preservation of these details remains one of the central services that anthropologists can furnish the communities they study (a service which, it might be added, these communities frequently request). Many Melanesians already evince a burgeoning pride and interest in their passing ancestral heritage, and unless Papua New Guinea proves different from other areas of the world, this interest can be expected to grow with future generations.

The exercise has virtue on other scores besides. On the one hand, the analytical disadvantages of studying a complex now in decline are considerably offset by the opportunity of studying a system under change (see, e.g., Roscoe and Scaglion in this volume). On the other, the hope can be extended that these analyses may one day constitute more than mere epiphenomena of Papua New Guinea's interaction with the anthropological world. Despite a growing awareness of the adaptability of culture, the possibility that massive ritual change might have psychosocial consequences cannot be casually dismissed.

While it is certainly naive to suggest that theory yet provides more than an occasional glimpse of the nature of these phenomena, it is to be hoped that their deeper comprehension will ultimately produce a more accurate appreciation of the consequences of cultural interaction and change.

With these ends in mind, I shall attempt to reconstruct the male initiation rites of the Yangoru Boiken, rites which were last held in the late 1940s. Following a brief introduction to Yangoru ethnography, I shall describe the aims of Yangoru Boiken initiation, its conduct, and certain predicaments created by its decline. Finally, I shall examine some current theories of initiation for their relevance to these data and sketch an argument that the focus of the Yangoru complex lay less in cross-sex or age-related concerns than in politics. From this perspective, the "decline" of the complex in modern times can be interpreted as an intriguing transformation impelled by the incorporation of the urban world into the mills of village politics.

The data for this account come from interviews with six men from Sima, a village lodged in the high foothills above Yangoru government station. When the last initiation ceremonies were completed, these men had achieved different levels in the ritual hierarchy. Cross-checking establishes a high degree of reliability in their accounts, but the following reconstruction must be qualified on several grounds. First, of course, the information must inevitably have suffered with the passage of over thirty years. Secondly, this period has seen the deaths of all of Sima's exegetical masters, the fully initiated men who organized the last ceremonies. Thirdly, an informant requested that certain data concerning initiation into the final ritual grade be withheld as ritually dangerous to the uninitiated. Fourthly, World War II conspired with missionary opposition to delay the last initiation, the one to which most informants alluded in their accounts, distorting it at least to the extent that several participants were hustled through two grades instead of the usual one. And finally, few data could be obtained on the contemporaneous seclusion of initiates' wives. Male informants were neither privy to these details nor felt they should be, and the old women who possessed this knowledge were uncomfortable discussing it with a young European male.

The Yangoru Boiken

The Boiken-speaking people of the East Sepik Province command one of the most varied terrains to be found in northwestern Papua New Guinea. Dominated by the eastern fall of the Prince Alexander Mountains, it drops steeply on the north to the Bismarck Sea, spreading out to envelop the offshore islands of Walis, Tarawai, and parts of Muschu. To the south, it fades through rumpled foothills deep into the rolling grasslands of the Sepik plains. Of some forty thousand people claiming residence within this territory, about a third speak the dialect found in the southern foothills around Yangoru government station. Predominantly horticulturalists, these Yangoru Boiken base their economy on the slash-and-burn cultivation of yams and taro, supplemented with bananas, pigs, a variety of bush and trade store foods, and a "feast and famine" dependence on sago.

Before the advent of Europeans, when male initiation was still a vibrant feature of the social landscape, the Yangoru Boiken were divided into several great war confederacies named either Samaong or Lebuging. Although fighting was common within these confederacies, pains were taken to avoid deaths, and women and children were always spared injury. Similar strictures governed any fighting that might break out between confederacies of the same name, for these were considered allies. Confederacies of different name, however, were enemies, and wars were launched to secure deaths regardless of the age and sex of the victim.

Stripped by the colonial peace of their warlike functions, these confederacies now endure largely in the memories of older men. Nevertheless, their social substrate survives relatively unchanged. Political, economic, and social life is still founded on relatively shallow patrilineages united by stipulated descent or legendary connection into subclans and clans. Sima and neighboring villages are slightly atypical in further uniting these units into two phratries, Homung and Sengi. Ceremonial organizations devoted to the competitive exchange of pigs crosscut this kinship base, usually embracing two or three villages, with odd participants drawn in from farther

afield. Each exchange system is divided into two moieties, also having the names Samaong and Lebuging, and some systems are linked to others by a second, overarching network of exchanges based on food.

The Goals of Initiation

By every account, the rigors of initiation were necessary for men to become "strong"—to be motivated to the tasks appropriate to their gender and to possess the talents necessary for success in these tasks. The foundations of this view are ethnophysiological conceptions about blood (*wing*) as innervating both the body (*penga*) and the breath (*yamembi*). Physically, blood fills out and fires the body: it is bodily substance, it is the fuel for activity, and it supplies the motivation for activity, the willingness to exert oneself. With a plentiful supply of blood, youthful bodies are fleshed out and smooth of skin. They have the capacity for energetic activity and constantly indulge it. Half a century later, however, when the years have all but exhausted this blood supply, the human body is reduced to pitiable state. The skin is slack on the bone, and there is little energy and even less motivation. Quantity of blood is also vital to the "strength" of the breath, gauged in terms of rootedness in the heart (*huizik*) and by the loudness of the speech to which it gives substance. Thus, the young can indulge in energetic activity without gasping for breath. They can— and, to their elders' envious annoyance, constantly and raucously do—yell and yodel to one another across the ridgetops. By contrast, their enervated seniors remain close to home, unable even to cross the courtyard without gasping for breath, their grumbles seldom able to rise above an undertone.

If quantity of blood were the only factor in Boiken ethnophysiology, then youth might be the envy of old age. Sadly, though, for the young, success in life depends on social as well as physical grace, and social potency is dependent on quality as well as quantity of blood. "Good" blood, that is, blood which is "hot," is essential if a man is to be motivated to the tasks necessary for sociopolitical eminence and if he is to possess the capacity to carry these tasks to successful conclusions. On the one hand, "good" blood ensures that he will be courageous in battle, ardent for the hunt, devoted to his gardens, eager to obtain shell wealth and currency, and anxious to shower pigs on his exchange partner. On the other, it ensures him a powerful breath—one which will envelop the audience at moots, drawing them to his cause, and which, expelled over a fistful of magical ingredients, will sway others to his desires, snare the game in the bush, cause his crops to flourish, and attract shell wealth in abundance from his relatives.

Good blood, however, is not a genetic endowment. It must be won over a lifetime of vigorous combat against the debilitating effects of the "cold," "bad" blood associated with pollution (*sara*). "Bad" blood is physically and socially debilitating. It induces lassitude, a lack of motivation for the tasks necessary to social eminence, and, because it is cool and in turn cools the breath, it removes the ability to perform these tasks successfully. In both sexes, its primary source is a spontaneous generation in early adolescence, shortly before puberty. This upwelling renders teen-agers the most polluted members of society, and contact with their blood, saliva, or perspiration is therefore a secondary source of pollution for their elders, who, through ritual, have achieved relative purity. Menstrual blood, being expressed bad blood, is a third source of pollution. Though direct contact with such blood is especially dangerous, even indirect contact, such as consumption of food prepared by a menstruating woman or improper sexual behavior, can have serious consequences.

If men were forever polluted, they would always "wander in the bush," lackadaisical and handicapped destitutes (*fatchik*). Male initiation reduced this danger. At each initiatory stage, its rituals and observances removed more of the initiates' pollution, turning the cold blood of youth into the hot blood associated with the sociopolitical eminence of late middle-age. The process was a lengthy one, spanning some thirty years of a man's life and involving him in three ceremonies some fifteen years apart. Around the age of thirteen to fifteen, shortly after he had become polluted, he entered the *sumbwi* initiatory grade. Around the age of twenty-eight to thirty, by which time, ideally, he would have one or two offspring, he entered *kwuli*, the second grade. Finally, around the age of forty-five, when active sexual life had finished and when, in theory, his first son was due to be initiated into sumbwi, he entered the final ritual grade, that of *suwero*. Now fully initiated, he had achieved the state of purity known as *pana* and could enter upon his most glorious period of sociopolitical potency, focused of will and confident in the knowledge that impurity would no longer thwart his ambitions. It is to charting the details of this ritual progress that we turn in the sections to follow.

The Myth of Men and Their Initiation

As in many other quarters of Melanesia, Yangoru Boiken myth attributes the origins of male initiation to women.[2] Two women cutting *pitpit* (*Saccharum edule*) sliced their hands. Seeing a hole nearby, they spread wild taro leaves at the bottom and let the blood drip onto them. Some time later, they returned to discover two male infants in the pit. They departed, and when they returned they found that the infants had grown. Each subsequent visit found the children bigger until eventually they were young adolescents, at which point the women set about preparing feather decorations and body paints for them. Finally, the youths became young men. The women started up songs of celebration, built a large fence, and placed the pair behind it. The singing attracted other villagers, who asked whence the young men had come and why the women were singing. The women explained the pair's genesis, adding: "Now they have grown, and we are celebrating." The others joined the festivities and then returned to their villages.

The Construction of the *Hworumbo*

The initiation ceremonies created by these culture heroines traditionally drew most of their participants from a pig-exchange system: people who exchanged pigs combined for the initiation of their sons. Even in the days of warfare, however, some initiates would be drawn from beyond the system and even the confederacy. The occasion was a time of temporary truce (*hohwale*), and any village—even an enemy one—could send along young men who had reached initiatory age without any immediate prospect of initiation by their own system (see also Gesch 1985:177). Regardless of origin, though, there was a demand that the number of initiates from the two exchange moieties—Lebuging and Samaong—balance one another.

The decision to hold a ceremony lay with those responsible for organizing and orchestrating its rituals, men who had already passed into the final, suwero grade. Naturally enough, the decision was primarily prompted by growing numbers of youths and men ready to move into the next initiation grade, but failure of the harvests required to underwrite the festivities, unresolved sorcery accusations, or an outbreak of hostilities could all delay a ceremony. Once a decision was reached, however, the news was announced on the slit-gong, and village attentions turned to construction of the *hworumbo*, the initiation enclosure.

In contrast to the Abelam and Arapesh, who initiate their youths in graceful, soaring tambaran houses, the Yangoru Boiken conducted their initiations behind a large, palisaded fence running some 18–20 yards along the edge of an abandoned ceremonial ground. The fence, which had side walls at either end descending into the bush, was constructed of stout posts, perhaps 9–12 inches in diameter and some 30–60 feet high. These were set flush against one another, with an occasional tall post spacing the rows of smaller ones.[3] Sago and coconut palm fronds adorned the frontage, partly for decoration but partly to guard against prying eyes. More fronds covered three openings in the fence, one at either end and another in the center.

Behind the fence, a shallow ditch ran back from the center aperture for some 20–30 feet. A row of sticks embedded in either side of this channel formed a riblike tunnel whose height could be varied by scissoring the sticks across one another. The ditch terminated at a small shelter built on stilts some 12 feet high,[4] which some informants asserted was the hworumbo proper. Close by was a small hut housing the *malingatcha*, the bespelled and ritually powerful carvings reserved for initiation,[5] and behind these two structures was a large pit, 6 feet or more in depth, spanned by several logs. Other logs were scattered around inside the enclosure as seating. Outside the palisades, small huts were erected around the ceremonial ground to house initiates during the early stages of their initiation.

The initiates themselves began the construction of the hworumbo. Assisted by male relatives and other men from the sponsoring villages, each had to cut and transport a post for the palisade, his name being hallooed around the ceremonial ground as it arrived. Older, fully initiated men undertook the actual construction, digging a series of narrow, deep holes into which the posts were tipped with the aid of vines employed "like a winch." When the enclosure was finished, a magician bespelled each of its three apertures, and henceforth, on pain of serious illness, only individuals consuming food strictly from their own families' cooking fires could pass through them.

During the day, women and children were barred from the hworumbo site. In the evenings, however, they joined their menfolk for the *hworumbowanga*, a night of singing and dancing to celebrate the rising structure and the impending initiations. For the most part, the ballads were time-honored airs celebrating memorable events of clan history. Others, though, commemorated initiation itself: one old favorite tells of pigs entering a fenced enclosure, the parallel with initiates and the hworumbo being explicitly recognized. The songs and celebrations continued for several nights after the hworumbo was completed—in some informants' memories, for as long as two or three weeks. The enclosure then stood ready to receive the first initiates, the young men about to enter the sumbwi grade.

Induction into the Sumbwi Grade

Induction began with the formal nomination of initiates for the sumbwi grade. Shortly after the hworumbowanga period was finished, the fully initiated men gathered at dusk and ascended into the stilt house behind the initiation palisades. Below them, the fathers of the sumbwi novices assembled, each with a coconut representing his son. One by one, the fathers pitched the nuts up at the stilt house, calling out their sons' names. When all the initiates had been identified, the suwero descended from their chamber, and the stilt house was never again entered.

The *lemohlia*, a festival of triumph and defiance, began at dusk the next day and continued till dawn. The young initiates were then summoned by name to the hworumbo, and, when all had mustered, the frond covering the central aperture was removed. Each was then bidden to crawl through, upon which he found himself in a narrow tunnel formed by the ditch and crossed sticks, the latter attended by several fully initiated men. The ditch was liberally plastered with mud, and as the initiates attempted to squirm along it, the crossed sticks were lowered to ensure that he was pressed deep into the mire.

When all had passed down the ditch, the young men were escorted onto the ceremonial ground in front of the palisades, where they confronted a gauntlet of men armed with whips of cane, stinging nettle, and supple tree branch. The younger initiates entered the gauntlet first, carried piggyback by older youths. When their own turn came, the latter draped their arms over a pole passed behind their necks and walked down the lines. Though younger boys were spared the rod in some degree and blood was seldom drawn, all informants emphasized the pain involved. Nevertheless, their pace was supposed to be unhurried, for the beating was a ritual with therapeutic intent, a first step in driving out the pollution that had recently arisen within them. Thus, there was no stigma to sobbing under the whip, but the longer the initiate could endure the pain, the purer he would become. After he had emerged from the gauntlet, he walked or was carried down to a nearby stream and was bidden to wash and await the others. The group was then conducted back to the hworumbo and fed a ritual soup containing ginger (lekiya) and fern root (ningi) designed to purify their blood and make their heads "clear as water" (i.e., receptive and agile). For the remainder of the day, they rested in the huts surrounding the ceremonial ground.

The events of the next two days were less traumatic. The lemohlia was performed at night, and the following morning the initiates were brought out to view a small leafed enclosure, constructed behind the palisades of the hworumbo. Inside, they could hear something moving around, making noises. Their initiators, who knew that one of their own number was inside, nonetheless derived great amusement from telling the initiates that it was a pig. On another occasion, the young men were shown the wala or tambaran of sumbwi,[6] a man painted black with a net bag slung from his head across his back. This, they were told, was kilanuwa, "the black mother."

The fourth and last day in the hworumbo marked the most arduous of the initiates' ordeals—the mutilation of their penes. Early in the morning, after the drums and flutes of the night's lemohlia had been stilled, the youths were assembled before the palisaded enclosure and informed of what lay in store. They were exhorted to bravery: the operation was to their benefit because it would purge them of bad blood. As the lemohlia again struck up, each initiate in turn was sent through one of the two openings at either end of the initiation fence. Youths belonging to the Lebuging moiety were directed to the opening attended by a Samaong man. Initiates from the Samaong ranks were directed to the other aperture, guarded by a Lebuging man. Lebuging initiate alternated with Samaong initiate. As each emerged on the other side of the enclosure, he was conducted to the pit behind the stilt house, where he

was bidden to squat on a log spanning the hole. An initiator from the opposed moiety[7] then thrust a sharpened flying fox bone laterally through his penis, causing the "bad" blood thus liberated to flow into the pit.[8]

Up to this point in his life, the youth had gone nude around the village. Now, for the first time, he was allowed to don a small bark loincloth (sungwun) to cover his wounds. He was taken down to a nearby stream to wash and then conducted away to a small shelter in the bush near his natal hamlet. Here he waited several days, while those previously in sumbwi underwent initiation into the kwuli grade.

Induction into the Kwuli Grade

On the morning of sumbwi's departure from the hworumbo, initiates into kwuli, the next ritual grade, were assembled. They were led off to a stream close by the hworumbo, where two initiators—one from each moiety—awaited them. Before the assemblage of coinitiates and fully initiated men, each was conducted in turn into the stream to confront the initiator from the moiety opposite his own. The initiator drew a long, sharpened cassowary bone, thrust it deep into the initiate's urethra, and with a sideways jab pierced the flank of the penis. The "bad" blood thus liberated was allowed to drip into the stream, to be diluted and carried safely away from malefactors who might use the ichor for sorcery.

When all was finished, the group was led back up to the hworumbo, seated on logs, and fed a ritual soup similar to that consumed by sumbwi. They were then shown the malingatcha carvings, which, newly painted and decorated, were displayed in the hut next to the stilt house or, if the weather was fine, against one of its outer walls. Each initiate in turn was instructed to stand before the array, where the ritual guardians of the carvings informed him of their identity—wangiwandauwa,[9] the kwuli wala or tambaran—and listed a series of taboos that must be observed for several months hence on pain of serious risk to health.

For the next two or three days, the kwuli initiates rested in the houses by the hworumbo, recovering from their ordeal. They were then taken to a nearby hamlet and ceremonially decorated with loincloth, amulets, red body paint, and parakeet and hawk feathers. Back at the hworumbo, they were joined by the sumbwi initiates, each wearing a *walarauwa*—literally "female wala spirit" but actually a strip of wood worn as a helmet, garlanded with parakeet and chicken feathers. Before an audience drawn from far and near, the two grades then embarked upon the hworumbowanga. According to some, these celebrations lasted from dawn to dusk for several nights. In other opinions, they went on for weeks or even months. When the final night of celebration drew to a close, those entering the sumbwi grade were deemed fully initiated.

Kwuli initiates endured several more weeks of seclusion aimed at their further purification. Returning to their villages, they were led into circular enclosures, some 15 yards in diameter, with a sleeping shelter let into one side. Some 6–9 feet high, these enclosures were constructed of poles covered with sago and coconut palm frond. In Sima, four would be constructed: two for the males of each phratry and two for their wives, the latter contemporaneously entering seclusion as part of their own initiation sequence.

Modern estimates of the length of this seclusion vary from ten days to three months, though most put it at one to two months. Whatever its duration, life in the enclosure followed a daily routine. Each initiate was attended by a guardian—an older man, usually a brother or other near relative but not one's father—who was responsible for feeding the initiate a meager, "rubbish" diet of yams, taro, and sago, with no meat for leaven. Each morning, the initiates were released from the enclosure to hunt food "to pay for the hands" of their wardens. Taking pains to avoid being seen by women, they were supposed to bring back at least some meat, be it only lizard or fish. Failure roused a guardian's ire, and the initiate could expect little or no food for the rest of the day. At night, decorated with the feathers and amulets furnished them on leaving the hworumbo, they were joined by their wives for a lemohlia outside the enclosure. The wives of kwuli appear to have enjoyed a less arduous seclusion than their husbands: they were not, for example, under the same strict food observances. Only one event of their initiation was described to me in any detail: at one point during their stay within the fenced enclosure, they were shown a masked dancing figure, the wala of the kwuli wives.

On the afternoon of their last day in seclusion, the guardians presented each initiate with a lime gourd and spatula—the insignia of political potency—and demonstrated how the spatula could be rasped against the mouth of the gourd for theatrical effect in singing and dancing. In return,

the fathers of kwuli feasted the guardians with pork. That night, the villagers performed the *bukreku*, another variety of song and dance employing the entire musical repertoire of the village—slit-gongs, hand drums, and flutes.

With the dawn, the initiates retired. In the afternoon, a feast was prepared to end their gustatory privations, and they were fed another ritual soup. The following day, after a repeat performance of the bukreku, relatives gathered to pay the kwuli guardians, and the day after, at yet another ceremony, they presented wealth to the initiates' maternal and affinal relatives. It is not clear whether kwuli were joined on this occasion by sumbwi or whether sumbwi's wealth payments had been made previously.[10] Either way, the conveyances were essentially the same. The agnates of each initiate laid shell wealth on a hardwood palm spathe set in the center of the ceremonial ground, with prestations from his sisters' husbands and father's sisters' husbands following. (The valuables presented by agnates were loans; those from the sororal relatives were gifts.) When all contributions had been gathered, the father then divided the principal sum among the initiate's mother's brothers, reserving smaller sums for his own maternal relatives and, if the initiate had a wife, presenting further small sums to her brothers. These payments were believed literally to remove much of the initiates' pollution. Once completed, the initiates were deemed "big men," fully initiated into the kwuli grade and ready to embark upon a political career proper. That night, another lemohlia took place in front of the fenced enclosures, and at dawn the initiates returned to their own hamlets and to their new ritual life.

Induction into the Suwero Grade

For reasons previously explained, limited detail can be provided about initiation into suwero, the final ritual grade. Suffice it to say that it was rather less elaborate than those for sumbwi and kwuli, and the period in the hworumbo was brief, limited to a day or two. The initiates were not beaten, and there was no genital mutilation. In the main, initiators were preoccupied with expositions on the significance of secret ritual paraphernalia such as the bullroarers, "the voice of the tambaran." The only event of note occurred toward the end of their initiation, when initiates were shown the wala of suwero.[11] For the duration of their initiation, initiates' wives were also secluded. When the two groups emerged, they were considered pana for the first time since childhood, although there is a contemporary opinion that some were nevertheless purer than others, depending on the number of their children—in particular daughters—who had been initiated. Total purity was achieved with the initiation of all daughters or, if there were no daughters, with the initiation through sumbwi of all sons. If there were no children at all, the "adoption" of a young man entering the hworumbo was arranged.

Pollution and Taboo

Pervaded by a pollution which had "risen like smoke" from nowhere, the hworumbo was left to decay, its site avoided by passers-by for many decades following. The fenced enclosures for kwuli initiates, their wives, and the wives of suwero initiates were also polluted, but to lesser degree. Once they had been burned and the ground ritually cleansed with fire, the site could be reused for residence. These events marked the end of the formal ceremonial sequence, but initiates into all three grades remained under taboo for months, even years, afterwards. In the month following the final hworumbowanga, and on pain of blindness in later life, sumbwi initiates were barred from consuming tobacco, betel nut, cold water, and food prepared at any cooking fire other than their mothers'. For several years, they were prohibited from the traditional male task of working sago, and their new status required that they sleep apart from their parents, in a house of their own.

In the month or two following their seclusion, kwuli initiates were forbidden tobacco, betel nut, cold water, and food prepared at fires other than their wives'. Because they had viewed the malingatcha, they avoided flying fox meat and *lapwa* (a potato-like tuber) until the ritual guardian of the carvings formally removed these proscriptions by feeding them a cold soup, and for several years they were barred from sago processing and intercourse.[12] I was unable to establish the nature of the taboos observed by suwero initiates.

The Present

Along with the ritual flagellations, genital mutilations, seclusions, and payments of shell wealth,

these observances contributed to the expressed goal of male initiation—the removal of the polluted blood blighting youth's social abilities and motivation. When these practices disappeared, however, it was not at the expense of beliefs about purity and pollution. Adolescent males are still believed to be dangerously polluted, their elders are still designated pana, and the latter still vigorously avoid pollution by the former and by women. How, then, in the modern day, do the Yangoru Boiken reconcile these beliefs with the disappearance of the hworumbo, the major mechanism for removing male pollution? How can young Boiken males aspire to sociopolitical eminence if they are deprived of the main means of purifying their blighted physiology?

Quizzed about their predicament, young men are apt to say, with a diffident laugh, that they are just "rubbish" men: they know nothing about such matters. Given the length of time since initiation passed away, there is little reason to doubt their protestations. Older men are rather more forthcoming, and in the not infrequent moments when they become exasperated with what they perceive to be their indolent youth, the demise of male initiation provides a ready explanatory scapegoat. "Now there is no hworumbo, young men don't work any more!" declaimed one influential Sima man, annoyed by the raucous outbursts of a nearby card circle. "They just sit playing Laki, drinking beer, strumming guitars, and singing. They don't work hard to get pigs and give them to their exchange partners!" "Before," reflected another man wistfully, "the ancestors were big, powerful men. Now, there is no initiation, and there are only little men. They still have initiations down on the Sepik River. Men are still strong down there."

Nevertheless, such moments of denigration sit ill with Sima's general pride about itself, and, in less irritated moods, older men offer several explanations for why men are still able to grow to sociopolitical eminence. Not surprisingly, their most elaborate theoretical innovations concern achievement of pana. Nowadays, parents are said to achieve this purity primarily through the initiation of their daughters, a custom still vigorously pursued in Yangoru (Camp 1979). At menarche, when a young woman is secluded because of her dangerously polluted state, her parents also become polluted by virtue of her father's giving blood and her mother birth to her. They sleep in a rough shelter, unwashed and dependent on relatives to cook their food. They forgo betel nut and tobacco and must eat their food without touching it, using leaves or small sticks as utensils. Dereliction in these observances results in serious harm to their health. As their daughter's pollution starts to diminish, however, so does theirs, until, about a week later, it has gone.

In the days of the hworumbo, it will be remembered, the initiation of daughters removed the final taints of pollution from their suwero parents. Nowadays, however, the initiation of daughters *replaces* the initiation of their parents. Initiation of the eldest daughter now marks entry into the suwero grade, and complete purity is achieved with the initiation of the youngest. (The degree of purity attained is independent of the number of daughters available for initiation; parents with only one daughter are said to achieve the same purity at her initiation as parents with three at the initiation of the last.) Nor is all lost if there are no daughters. Parents will await the birth of several children to their eldest son and then declare themselves fully purified.[13]

Rather less theoretical consideration is given to the position of younger men, those who previously would have moved toward purity by their initiations into the sumbwi and kwuli grades. One view, however, is that young men are now purified as their children are born. Traditionally, parents are considered polluted for one to four weeks after the birth of a child, and they therefore enter seclusion for a short period. Just as female initiation assists older people in removing pollution, one man claimed, this rite of passage now assists younger parents in their progress toward purity. Another view, however, equates urban absenteeism with seclusion in the hworumbo. "Before, a young man had to enter the hworumbo. Nowadays, he goes to work in town. When he returns, people say, 'He went away, and now he has returned a big man.'" This view is intriguing for the several congruences between urban absenteeism and initiatory seclusion. During their absence in town, young men reside with age-mates from the Yangoru area. If they are married, they are not supposed to take their wives with them. Typically, therefore, they are absent from their spouses for three years—approximately the duration of kwuli's sexual taboos. Like initiates in the hworumbo, their seclusion is spent in the abode of the wala—that is, the European. Like wala, Europeans had (and are believed still to have) the capacity to ordain custom and law. Like wala, they created aspects of the universe—machines, for example, and, more important, a new form of wealth. Like the wala (in the guise of sisters' husbands and sisters' sons), they supply this

wealth in return for labor, land, and food; and, like the wala that appear in dreams, they are white. For these reasons, the European is known as the wala and town is quintessentially his abode. Finally, if the youth manages to secure urban employment, he will return from "seclusion" in the wala's abode with cash savings, a share of which his maternal relatives claim on the grounds that he is polluted and has to pay for his skin/body.

One final view of how ritual purity is achieved today emerged under exceptional circumstances. The views expressed above were frequently inconsistent, either internally or with reference to other spheres of Boiken belief.[14] When pressed on these problematic points, two informants separately resorted in exasperation to the notion that, as a man grows older, pollution automatically leaves his body until, around late middle-age, he has become ritually pure. It might not be surprising if, in the future, this simple and encompassing belief achieved much wider circulation in the Yangoru area.

Some Analytical Conclusions

Until this point, I have described Yangoru initiation largely in its own terms, setting forth the emic view of its goals and the means by which they were realized. In shifting to the etic frame, we leave consensus and conviction for a situation in which perhaps the only secure ground is Van Gennep's (1960 [1909]) thesis that rites of passage effect changes of social identity. It would be unnecessarily tedious to spell out the implications of the symbolic "swallowings" and "rebirths" that characterized Yangoru initiation. Suffice it to say that the demise of the elaborate and public method of marking social transition was attended by the rise of new, equally public symbolic modes—urban absenteeism and the seclusions attending childbirth and female initiation.

Beyond Van Gennep, the analysis of male initiation fans out into a multiplicity of approaches which, given the multifaceted nature of the phenomenon and the probability of cross-cultural variation, are for heuristic purposes probably best considered complementary rather than mutually exclusive (Keesing 1982). Of these several approaches, though, some at least appear to be of limited relevance to the Yangoru case. Lindenbaum's (1972) ecological argument that male initiation in concert with ideologies of sexual antagonism regulates population growth is difficult to justify on demographic grounds. The decline of Yangoru's initiation coincided with a rise of some 40 percent in the rate of natural increase, a rise attributable almost entirely to reduction in mortality (Roscoe n.d.*a*). In other words, male initiation disappeared at exactly the time when, if it had any population regulation functions at all, one would have expected them to be called into play.

Neither is there substantive evidence that Yangoru initiation represented an attempt to preserve military secrets, foster military solidarity, and secure the loyalty of the community's males against powerful cross-sex ties to wives and mothers from enemy groups (cf. Keesing 1982:24; Langness 1977:18). In contrast to those of some highland groups, Yangoru affines were overwhelmingly drawn from among allies, not enemies, and the argument lies uncomfortably with the fact that temporary truces enabled youths to join the ceremonies of their enemies. The latter datum, together with tales of coinitiates' stealing one another's exuviae for sorcery during their seclusions, also raises questions about the interpretation of these rites as dramatizations and reinforcements of adult male social cohesion (e.g., Cohen 1964, Young 1965).[15]

A further analytical strand sets male initiation against an ideology of sexual antagonism and depicts it as instrumental in the subordination of women and the appropriation of their labor. The prestige of Papua New Guinea's men and the reputation and well-being of their groups depend heavily on women's doing what is required of them when it is required. Male cults, it is argued (e.g., Keesing 1982, Langness 1977), play a fundamental part in securing this end: they may reinforce an implicit consensus among men about the rectitude of their actions against women; they may ritually and often traumatically sever affective bonds that men have with the women they must dominate; and they may keep women in check by propagating asymmetric ideologies of gender and by placing the supposed secrets of growth, maturity, and other matters fundamental to female existence in the hands of males.

This argument would have appealed to Gerstner (1952:807), who felt that the whole purpose of the Nagam Boiken "spirit cult" was to frighten women and keep them in check. In the Yangoru case, a material form of the tambaran, under male control, could be called upon to intimidate a woman who had disparaged her husband's sexuality. But, on other grounds, the argument is less convincing. On the one hand, one searches in vain for the hypothesized means of subjugation. The tambaran was not called, for example, to punish lazy or unruly wives. Nor did initiation confer on males control of the means of female growth and maturity. Instead, these were (and still are) relatively public, their secret aspects being passed down through *women*. Nor did initiated elders appear to enjoy power by virtue of knowledge which might be construed as the secrets of existence itself (cf. Tuzin 1980:26–27). At least, if they *were* initiated into such knowledge, women and junior males seem to have been ignorant of the fact—a crucial point, since the value of secret knowledge as a means of subjugation depends on the subjugated's *knowing* that the secrets address concerns of importance to them (as well as believing that they are valid). In fact, there is no compelling reason to believe that males were initiated into secrets that were any more important in women's eyes than were women's initiatory secrets to men. In the words of informants of both sexes, male initiation was something concerning men and female initiation was something concerning women.

The facts attending the demise of Yangoru initiation also embarrass the argument. If male initiation formerly served the cause of subjugating women and exploiting their labor, then its demise should signal either a reduction in the importance to men of women and their labor, the evolution of new methods for controlling women and their labor, or a reduction in men's control of women and their labor. Needless to say, women and their labor are at least as important to men now as they were before the demise of male initiation. Traditionally, men's tasks consisted of cutting bush, fencing gardens, and planting and harvesting yams. The remaining garden tasks and all of the community's portering were the precinct of women. At an ideological level, this division of labor survives, but the rise of labor migration has modified practice considerably. By the early 1950s, when the first census figures become available, Yangoru Boiken male absenteeism was already running at some 20 percent of the male population and by 1978 it had risen to 31 percent. The consequence is that the modern Yangoru woman now bears not only her own, traditional "women's" work but a sizable portion of her male kinfolks' besides (see also Curtain 1980:357–58). In other words, despite the demise of male initiation, women continue to contribute their labor to fulfill demands which, if anything, have risen rather than fallen. Unless new methods of subjugation have evolved to replace initiation, we must conclude that the complex had a marginal role, if any, in subordinating women and appropriating their labor.

There may be little need, in fact, to invoke the possibility of new methods by which women are subordinated and their labor controlled, for what appears to have been the old means—female initiation—has survived the demise of its male counterpart. Politically unemancipated, women have transformed their onerous place in life into a virtue, evaluating one another's qualities against the standard of a "good" woman who labors hard at her tasks and is dutiful to a "good" husband. If anything serves men's interests in women, it would seem to be women's subscription to this ideology. And it is through female initiation that these qualities are dramatized, exalted, and magically conferred on the youthful initiate. In other words, if any ritual effects the subjugation of Yangoru women and the appropriation of their labor, female, not male, initiation must be considered the prime candidate.

If Yangoru male initiation had little directly to do with subordination of women and the appropriation of their labor, then perhaps, as Keesing (1982:26) suggests, it is the labor and fighting power of young men that were the focus of ritual exploitation? The fighting prowess that young men furnished the purposes of their elders was certainly considerable; the means of male growth and maturation undeniably lay in the hands of these elders; and the argument accounts for the demise of initiation in the wake of the Paces Germanica and Australiana and for the exasperation elders now sometimes express at the "laziness" of modern youth. On the other hand, the labor that youths contributed to the behalf of their elders was limited and declined further with the increase in their responsibilities to families of their own. In fact, a son's labor contributions only became critical to his parents in their old age—by which time, of course, he was fully initiated. The fact that he owed his successful initiation to his father might contribute to the moral obligation he felt to care for his parents. But children feel obligated enough in this respect by virtue of the care they themselves received in childhood (Roscoe and Wais-Roscoe n.d.)—the continued well-being of Yangoru's elderly in the absence of initiation being adequate testimony. In sum, the argument relating male initiation to the exploitation of young Yangoru men seems a partial explanation at best.

Psychoanalytic interpretations of male initiation have also enjoyed considerable attention. Dundes (1976), for example, construes the ritual homosexuality of some highland cults as an unconscious expression of male envy of female procreative powers, while Bettelheim (1962), addressing a phenomenon of more relevance to the Yangoru Boiken case, similarly interprets genital mutilation in imitation of menstruation (see also Mead 1975). These approaches have not escaped criticism on theoretical grounds (see Hage's [1981] summary). However, in the Yangoru case, the important point is a classificatory one. The blood liberated in genital mutilation is not menstrual blood but "bad" blood—blood that issues from women without human intervention and, with human intervention, from men. That the act and event are analogous is undeniable. But the *intent* behind genital mutilation is not, I think, emulation of menstruation from envy but rather achievement by surgical means in men of what menstruation effects in women—namely, social grace. (Hage [1981] makes a similar point, but places the emphasis on *physical* growth.)

By questioning a psychoanalytic interpretation of Yangoru male initiation, I am not suggesting that the complex was without a "psychological" dimension. As Van Gennep hinted, initiation appears to have subjective as well as social entailments, and analysis of some highland complexes indicates that the subjective implications may be quite dramatic. Poole (1982), for example, describes the "ritual forging of identity" among the Bimin Kuskusmin, while Herdt (1981:305) refers to "behavioral surgery" among the Sambia. The Yangoru Boiken appear to have shared with such groups an initiatory preoccupation with traumatic ordeal and also perhaps—in the androgynous forms of the tambaran—with ritual expressions of gender contrast. But among the commonalities, one also senses two crucial differences—in emphasis at least. First, set against highland initiations, Yangoru initiation seems a relatively gentle affair. Informants emphasize the solicitude of their initiators and the fact that, before their trials, they were apprised of what could happen and reassured of the ultimate benefits. There are no reports of the anger, verbal abuse, trickery, and unanticipated violence characteristic of initiation in many highlands areas and in at least some Sepik groups.[16] A second significant difference is age. Typically, highland initiation begins around the ages of nine to twelve (sometimes earlier) and crams a series of initiatory stages into the ensuing ten to fifteen years (e.g.,

Hays and Hays 1982:208; Herdt 1982:53; Langness 1977:6, 9; Newman and Boyd 1982:243; Poole 1982:107; Reay 1959:173). By contrast, Yangoru youths escaped the hworumbo until they were thirteen to fifteen years old and were not again initiated until they were twenty-eight to thirty.[17] Taken together, these data portray highlands initiation very much as an anvil on which adolescence and early adulthood are exposed to the ritual hammer, while Yangoru initiation emerges more as a gradual focusing than a rude forging of identity. In part at least, this difference might be correlated with Yangoru's reduced emphasis on sexual polarization. A limited residential segregation of the sexes, for example, has boys sleeping with their fathers as well as mothers, reducing whatever "need" there may be to "break" them from the latter (cf. Whiting, Kluckhohn, and Anthony 1958).[18]

Hage (1981:274) suggests that the type of initiation rites found in the Sepik constitutes "a subset of possible magical acts designed to induce male growth." For the Yangoru Boiken at least, this misses the important point that male initiation has little to do with physical growth and everything to do with imbuing youth with political motivation and oratorical and magical ability. Men, it is recognized, vary in their political preoccupation and powers. Some prefer the tranquility of their gardens to the turmoil of the public forum. Others have ambition but lack talent. Yet ambitious and able men are of importance to the well-being and prestige of clan, moiety, and village. Given these concerns, then, Yangoru's initiation rites and their associated ideologies can at least be viewed as dramatizations of desirable male qualities—with the magical aspects assuming the Malinowskian guise of attempts to subjugate uncertainty rather than to subjugate women and young men.

Strathern (1970:378) observes that the qualities emphasized in male initiation can also be expressed and inculcated in other contexts and through other institutions. Without diving too deeply into the theoretical quagmires of functional equivalence, I would suggest that the history of Yangoru initiation, with its apparent functional shift to rites associated with birth and female initiation, seems to bear this out—though in a manner which Strathern did not perhaps intend. But the case is of further interest for the modern emphasis on urban absenteeism and the possibility that the "other contexts and institutions" may therefore have been appropriated from beyond the traditional boundaries of Yangoru so-

ciety. In a new political world, where urban finesse is now a quality indispensable to success in village politics, it would certainly be fitting that Papua New Guinea's European legacies should be plundered for a solution to the problems they engendered.

Notes

1. The data on which this paper is based were collected in the course of fieldwork funded by the Emslie Horniman Scholarship Fund, the Ford Foundation, and the University of Rochester. The Department of Community Medicine at the University of Papua New Guinea sponsored my visit. The assistance of these institutions is very gratefully acknowledged. In addition, I am grateful to David Lipset for criticism of an earlier version of the paper. As always, my greatest debt is to the kind people of Sima for the hospitality and assistance I enjoyed throughout my stay with them.

2. Among the Nagam Boiken, the origins of male cult flutes, masks, and dances are mythically attributed to women, while the origins of initiation ceremonies are attributed to spirits and to men (Gerstner 1952:810–13).

3. Gesch (1985:177), writing of initiation in the Negrie area of Yangoru, mentions that carvings were affixed to each post. Sima informants made no reference to carvings on their enclosures, but I did not specifically quiz them on the matter.

4. I was given to believe that this shelter was fashioned in the style of a Boiken dwelling—with walls of sago frond ribs and thatch of sago or coconut palm frond. However, Gesch (1985:177) asserts that in the Negrie area it was made of sago leaf mats.

5. In the main, these carvings were locally produced, though some were obtained in trade from the Sepik River region. The local product was usually manufactured as a male/female pair, humanoid in form, with large head, arms akimbo, and legs apart.

6. The concept of the *wala* is perhaps the most profound in Yangoru Boiken thought and is difficult to summarize because it embraces several spiritual and conceptual dimensions. I am, therefore, indebted to my good friend Peter Wavingare, a Yangoru Boiken man fluent in English, for offering in translation, as the crux of the term's meaning, "important agent, patron."

7. Gesch (1985:255), by contrast, was told that Lebuging was initiated by Lebuging and Samaong by Samaong.

8. Gesch (1985:255) was told that excrement was then wiped over the initiates. This would seem to tally with a separate account from the Yangoru village of Nindepolye (Aufenanger n.d.:230).

9. The carvings also boasted individual names.

10. At some point during their initiation the brothers and father's sisters' relatives of a sumbwi initiate contributed shell wealth on his behalf to his mother's brothers. According to some informants, these pay-

ments occurred on the morning that the hworumbo-wanga began. According to others, it was held on the day that similar payments were made in kwuli's behalf. Those cleaving to the former view had each been pushed through two grades at once in the last of Sima's initiations, indicating that the latter opinion might reflect traditional practice more accurately. Since the arrangement of payments in the case of both grades was essentially the same, description of sumbwi's payments is addressed with kwuli's.

11. An informant request for confidentiality prevents me from publicizing the few details I obtained about this tambaran.

12. An examination of birth spacing prior to the early 1950s indicates longer spacing between earlier than between later births, suggesting that initiates did indeed observe the taboo on intercourse.

13. In 1980, it was not entirely clear whether, in fact, the initiation of daughters and sons *had* contributed to the purity of parents in the days of the hworumbo or whether this belief had since been projected onto the past. Either way, a shift in belief is evident. If male purity was solely dependent on male initiation, then the formulation represents a theoretical innovation. But if the initiations of children *were* once part of the path to purity, then evidently a shift in emphasis now makes them vital to purity.

14. The inconsistencies may of course exist only in the ethnographer's mind, reflecting a lack of persistence in teasing out the skeins of belief that would reveal the sense in the apparent nonsense. In this case, however, there is some justification for believing that informants were venturing tentative theoretical innovations. First, there was some lack of consensus in the beliefs advanced. Secondly, in a majority of instances where confusion or inconsistency was pointed out by the ethnographer, informants attempted to modify what they had proposed, sometimes withdrawing it entirely. Thirdly, there was some lack of concern over inconsistencies and ambiguities, indicating perhaps that people are not much interested in logical nitpicking. The details offered here, then, are beliefs that Yangoru Boiken men venture in response to questions about purity and pollution today and with which they might be content were it not for the presence of a pestilential anthropologist.

15. Without these rites, of course, there might be even less social integration, but this point raises rather too many questions about operationalizing these functional theories (see Graber 1981).

16. I would be prepared to admit that the memories of modern informants might have stripped the old rituals of their more traumatic aspects were it not that Mead notes essentially the same character to Mountain Arapesh initiation (1938:170; 1963:67). This is especially significant in that the Yangoru Boiken have so much else in common with the Mountain Arapesh, with whom linguistic evidence suggests they enjoyed sustained intercourse (D. C. Laycock, personal communication, cited in Tuzin 1976:73).

17. I have the impression that highland initiation is also accompanied by a markedly greater degree of exegesis.

18. It is worth noting that informants categorically resist all attempts to persuade them that "bad" blood is maternal blood.

37/ Male Initiation and European Intrusion in the Sepik: A Preliminary Analysis[1]

Paul Roscoe and Richard Scaglion

Sepik ethnographers have long shown an interest in the region's elaborate cults of male initiation, and with the papers presented to this symposium a data file now emerges that is sufficiently rich and varied to support some cross-cultural exploration. Stimulated by the goals of this symposium, we have therefore chosen to initiate the venture with a preliminary analysis of the impact of European intrusion on Sepik initiatory complexes. This subject has received surprisingly little scholarly attention to date,[2] yet research is strongly warranted not only for the contribution it can make to Papua New Guinean history but also for the light it may cast on more theoretical issues. As natural scientists will attest, the perturbation of a system provides valuable information on its nature. Since European contact proved something of a disturbance to most if not all Sepik initiatory systems, an examination of the consequences may be expected to yield at least some insights into their nature.

Mindful, as is Allen (in this volume), that European intrusion has affected all Sepik traditional life to some extent, one is still struck by the degree to which Sepik initiatory systems have differed in their response to European intrusion (table 1). The Kwanga and several Sepik River societies, for instance, still induct their youth in styles that apparently have manifold similarities to their ancestral forms, but in other societies initiation has either disappeared entirely or undergone radical truncation or transformation. What little remains of Kwoma male initiation, for example, is now apparently supported by the yam cult (Bowden 1983a and personal communication, 1984). On Manam Island,[3] members of the hereditary elite alone are still initiated, and the ceremonies are but pale reflections of the traditional form (N. Lutkehaus, personal communication, 1985). Likewise, among the Murik Lakes, only the occasional flute or loincloth rite is still performed, and then only for firstborn sons (D. Lipset, personal communication, 1985).

Nowhere, however, is the contrast between the persistence and decline of traditional Sepik initiation more vividly and provokingly apparent than among the southern foothills of the Prince Alexander–Torricelli cordillera. Here, systems of male initiation among the Abelam and Boiken, two groups closely related culturally and linguistically, experienced radically different fates in the face of European contact. Yangoru Boiken male initiation now survives only to the extent that some of its functions have been sloughed off onto other rites of passage and onto urban absenteeism (see Roscoe in this volume). Farther east, initiation disappeared many years ago from Kubalia and Nagam Boiken territory, though government encouragement of traditional custom has recently spurred one or two Kubalia villages to revive the old ceremonies (J. Wasori, personal communication, 1984). By contrast, Abelam villages everywhere were still inducting their youths well into the 1970s.

The societies with which we are both best acquainted thus provide an admirable starting point for the examination we propose. In what follows, we shall examine several explanatory possibilities in the light of Abelam and Boiken data. In each case, we shall then expand the ethnographic focus to the extent the record permits in order to examine how each explanation fares in the general historical context of Sepik initiation. Finally, we shall attempt to draw the strands of this investigation into a preliminary conclusion about the nature of Sepik initiatory response to European influences.

The Influence of Missionary Opposition

In 1909, Catholic missionaries became a permanent part of Boiken history with the establishment of a mission in the coastal village of this name. Within a few years, the mission had begun to extend its influence with occasional tours of the hin-

TABLE 1
THE STATUS OF SEPIK INITIATION

Group	Last Reported Initiation In Traditional Style	Interruptions	Source
Abelam			
Central	Early 1970s	?	Scaglion, field data
Eastern	Early 1970s	1950s	Forge (1972c:259–60)
Western	Present	1960s, 1970s	Losche (1982:287); Scaglion, field data
Wosera	Present	1950s	Whiteman (1965:114–15); Lea (1964:161); Scaglion, field data
Arapesh			
Ilahita	1972–73	?	Tuzin (1980)
Kaboibus	1980	?	B. Meckel and B. Meckel, personal communication, 1980
Boiken			
Coastal	Pre-1950	?	Gerstner (n.d.: 2–3)
Kunai	1980	1950s, 1960s	Gesch (1985)
Nagam	1947	?	Gerstner (n.d.:3)
Yangoru	1947	World War II	Gesch (1985), Roscoe in this volume
Chambri	1974	?	Gewertz (1982:287)
Iatmul			
Palimbei	Present	?	C. Coiffier, personal communication, 1984
Tambunam	Present	Early 1940s– recently	C. Coiffier, personal communication, 1984; Métraux in this volume
Timbunke	Present	1940–75	C. Dambui, personal communication, 1984
Yentschen	Present	?	C. Coiffier, personal communication, 1984
Kwanga			
Bongos	1978	1965–75	Allen, Schindlbeck in this volume
East	1980	Late 1950s/early 1960s	Schindlbeck in this volume
North	1980–81?	Late 1950s/early 1960s	Schindlbeck in this volume
West	1965	?	Schindlbeck in this volume
Kwoma	1935	?	Bowden (1983a:2), Williamson in this volume
Manam	1940–45	?	N. Lutkehaus, personal communication, 1985
Manambu	1980	?	S. Harrison, personal communication, 1984; see also Harrison in this volume
Murik	Early 1950s[a]	?	D. Lipset, personal communication, 1985
Urat	1977–78	Late 1970s	Allen in this volume

[a] Possibly continues in one village.

terland, though it was not until the distant turmoils of World War I had subsided that these tours assumed any regularity (Roscoe 1983: chap. 4). In addition to conducting mass, these early Europeans also denounced traditional customs like male initiation as *pasin bilong Aitan* (Satanic custom). To begin with, villagers seem to have taken little notice, for the initiations of the mid-1920s went ahead as usual. Fifteen years later, however, as the next stages were being set in motion, the Boiken missionaries sped to the area and succeeded in having the enclosures destroyed. The advent of World War II delayed any further attempts to induct the growing number of

uninitiated youths until the late 1940s. Ceremonies in several villages were then successfully concluded before the Boiken priests could get wind of them. Unable to do anything about these *faits accomplis*, the missionaries apparently collected the women and children and deliberately exposed the bullroarers to them.[4] Later, in the years following the establishment of a permanent Catholic presence in Yangoru, the resident missionary and his catechist encouraged village leaders to continue the work of exposing initiation paraphernalia to women and children (Gesch 1985).

Asked why they abandoned male initiation, the

Yangoru Boiken invariably respond that it was because the missionaries forbade it,[5] a plausible assertion given early village perceptions of these
visitors. From an early time, missionaries of all
denominations had been equated with the *gavman*
(government), a term which Boiken villagers still
principally identify with firepower rather than
administration. In other words, missionary in-
terdictions were assumed to have the backing of
European arms.

It is doubtful, however, if the demise of initiation can everywhere be laid at the church door:
among the Abelam, for example, missionaries
also inveighed against the rites, yet they continued with little interruption. Significant missionary activity had come later to the Abelam than to
the Boiken. When the Townsend-Eve mapping
expedition of 1933 dropped Father de Bruyn off
at Bainyik, he was one of the first missionaries to
work in the Maprik area (Townsend 1968:210).
By 1937, however, the year in which the Kunjin-
gini Catholic mission was established, missionaries had become active throughout the area, and
several observers commented on their combative
attitude to Abelam ritual activity. According to
Kaberry (1940–41:366), Catholic missionaries
passing through the Central Abelam village of
Kalabu in the 1930s had ordered their ritual carvings burned. The Eastern Abelam encountered
opposition from the Catholic mission and later, in
the 1950s, from the Assemblies of God at Wingei
(Forge 1972*c*:259; personal communication,
1984). Lea (1964:62) and Whiteman (1965:106)
report that the Wosera missions discouraged initiation, going so far as to burn men's houses and
sacred objects. One missionary was even charged
with arson and appeared before the Supreme
Court at Wewak (Maprik Patrol Report no. 2,
1951, p. 13). Yet in none of these areas does missionary opposition appear to have effected more
than a temporary suspension of initiation. Indeed, in the area of the aforementioned arson
case, "It was found that the natives had rebuilt
their initiation bush houses and were carrying on
their initiation ceremonies."

Expanding the focus of the inquiry beyond the
Abelam and Boiken, we find a similar variability
in the response to missionary opposition. On the
one hand, Manam Islanders and Murik Lake
dwellers, whose initiation sequences declined
several decades ago, attribute their demise at
least in part to the missions (Lipset, personal
communication, 1985; Lutkehaus, personal communication, 1985). On the other hand, missionary opposition appears to have been no less strong

in areas where initiation persists to the present.
Kaberry (1940–41:366) noted, for example, that
the Kaboibus Arapesh had experienced "an even
greater degree of interference" from missionaries
than had Kalabu, yet these people were still initiating their youths in 1980. West of Maprik, the
Ilahita Arapesh were still holding initiations in
the early 1970s, despite the opposition of South
Seas Evangelical missionaries resident in the village for some twenty years (Tuzin 1976:33).

It could, of course, be argued that it is not the
existence of missionary opposition that is at issue
but its nature and degree. If opposition amounts
only to verbal denunciation, it may have rather
less effect than exposure or destruction of ritual
paraphernalia. More precise data on this point
would be desirable, but the information at hand
gives little basis for considering it critical. Yangoru Boiken informants consistently identified
missionary pronouncements rather than the exposure of their bullroarers as the important factor
in abandoning their initiations. We have already
noted that the destruction of Abelam and Arapesh
ritual objects and the burning of Abelam initiation houses did little to quell initiatory enthusi-
asms. Moreover, a German missionary in Urat
territory had exposed secret paraphernalia to
women in the 1930s (Allen 1976:82), yet by the
late 1970s these same villages were again initiating their youths. In sum, missionary activity
may have contributed to initiatory decline, but on
the evidence to hand it does not appear to constitute a complete explanation.

The Influence of Millenarian Movements

Among the Boiken, missionaries were not the
only opponents of male initiation. In the late
1940s, just as the Catholic mission began to extend its permanent presence inland, the eminent
Kusaun villager, Yauiga, was undertaking "en-
lightenment trips" around the Wewak, Boiken,
and Kairiru areas. According to Gerstner
(n.d.:4):

> After his arrival in a new village, Yauiga
> first delivered a speech. He ordered all the
> men to hand over spirit cult and magical im-
> plements and all things which could cause
> battles and feuds. In one of these speeches
> to his countrymen he said something like:
> "As long as you possess the old things, you
> only think of them. You threaten with
> magic, battle and assault. A new time has

come. We want to better our ways and follow the lead of the government and mission." The men who heard him talk like this were quite willing to hand over cult and magical things. . . . It is without doubt that in most villages Yauiga was able with his "enlightening" to get rid of the last remains of the old spirit cults [i.e., initiation] without much opposition.

Yauiga paid at least one visit to the Yangoru area, where his movement enjoyed considerable popularity under the direction of ex-Sergeant Beibi Yembanda (Yangoru Patrol Report no. 6, 1949– 50, p.3).

Gerstner and the Yangoru patrol officers evidently believed that these ceremonial abrogations of initiation and the like were prompted by a dawning recognition among villagers of their backwardness. But to anyone acquainted with the long history of cargo-related activities in Yangoru, they have an unmistakable air of millenarianism. Talk of abandoning traditional customs in preparation for a "new time" has accompanied prophecies of several Yangoru millennia, including the now notorious Peli cult, in which Yauiga and Yembanda were later to play prominent roles. In the early 1960s, for example, when villagers were again contemplating initiations, one prominent Yangoru figure publicly urged that the custom cease altogether in preparation for the advent of cargo (Dewdney 1965:184, cited in Gesch 1985). In such instances, it would seem that at least a temporary suspension of induction is likely. Millenarian expectations, then, may have played at least some role in the demise of Yangoru initiations.

Evidence from other quarters of the Sepik seems to support this argument. Allen (1981:122) notes that the slackening of Dreikikir and Wosera hopes in the Peli movement was accompanied by a return to initiation. On Manam Island, as among the Yangoru Boiken, an early initiatory decline was accompanied by periodic and significant millenarian activities that were under way by the late 1930s or early 1940s (Lutkehaus, personal communication, 1985). Conversely, the Central and Eastern Abelam, who retained their initiations into the 1970s, apparently evinced "remarkable tenacity in . . . resisting the temptations of the cargo cults that have swept in waves through the Sepik ever since the end of the Japanese occupation" (Forge 1970b:271). The Arapesh village of Ilahita, which was still conducting elaborate initiations in the early 1970s, showed a similar lack of interest in millenarianism: only

one person out of fifteen hundred joined the Peli movement (see Tuzin in this volume), a remarkable state of affairs when one considers that, by some estimates, the movement embraced one to two hundred thousand inhabitants of the Sepik (May 1975:15).

Other evidence, however, shows that millenarian activities do not always correlate with a decline of initiation. As Gesch (1985) points out, the Kunai Boiken were as engrossed as any other Boiken villagers in the Peli movement of the early 1970s, yet they retain their initiation ceremonies to the present. A decade earlier, this same group had enjoyed the millenarian delights of a movement known variously as the "Angoram Ex-Serviceman's Club" and the "Angoram Sports Club" (Yangoru Patrol Report no. 3, 1964–65, and accompanying letter of the assistant district commissioner). Likewise, the Western Abelam continued their initiations into the 1970s despite some serious flirtations with millenarianism (Scaglion 1983:481–83). On the basis of the limited data available, then, there is reason to suppose a general association of millenarian activity and initiatory decline but not to explain the one wholly in terms of the other.

The Influence of Migration

At an early date in New Guinea's history, the Sepik, in particular the immediate river region, became one of the most fruitful areas in the Territory for labor recruiting. From a total of 4,375 in 1925, the number of laborers from the (then) Aitape and Sepik Districts working away from their villages grew to 12,222 in 1938 (*Report to the League of Nations* 1924–25:55; 1937–38:40). As table 2 indicates, absenteeism from many Sepik villages has continued to rise up to the present.

To early Sepik observers, the decline of male initiation seemed directly related to the siphoning of young men from villages into the European labor camps. Bateson (1958[1936]:136) identified what seemed an obvious connection when he remarked of Mindimbit in the early 1930s: "The boys were going away to work on plantations, leaving the village too weak in numbers for any great ritual to be attempted." Though they do not attribute the decline of their own initiations to absenteeism, Yangoru Boiken informants also point to the difficulties of initiating absent young men. Still, the importance of this factor is debatable. As Neligum Abelam point out, and as the last

TABLE 2
ADULT MALE ABSENTEEISM FROM VILLAGES IN THE SEPIK BY ETHNOLINGUISTIC GROUP

| | ABSENTEEISM | | | | LAST REPORTED INITIATION IN TRADITIONAL STYLE |
GROUP	1928–39	1958–59[a]	1970–71	1974–75	
Abelam					
Central	Low	14.3	11.6		Early 1970s
Eastern	Low	17.0	26.8	30	Early 1970s
Western	Low	16.0	19.0		Present
Wosera	Low	11.4	19.7		Present
Arapesh					
Ilahita	Low	19.0	18.1		1972–73
Kaboibus	Low	24.9	39.0	33	1980
Boiken					
Yangoru	Low	29.7	41.5	36	1947
Kunai	Low	20.2	16.8		1980
Chambri	Low	High?		59	1974
Iatmul	High			58[b]	Present
Kwanga	Low	18.8	18.5		1965–81
Manam	High?	30–35	30–35		1940–45
Manambu	Medium			35	1980
Urat	Low	18.1	17.7		1977–78

SOURCES: For Manam, Lutkehaus, personal communication, 1985; for Chambri 1958–59, Gewertz (1983:111); for Kwanga and Urat 1958–59 and 1970–71, data on relevant ethnolinguistic groups in Kwanga and Urat Census Divisions. Otherwise, 1928–39 data derived from figures for villages closed to recruiters because of overrecruiting by Curtain (1980:180); 1958–59 data from Maprik/Yangoru census reports; 1970–71 data from Seiler (1972:360–83); 1974–75 data from Curtain (1976:23).

[a] Absentees as a percentage of total adult males. Inspection of detailed data for the Yangoru Subdistrict indicates that in most villages absentees were all adult males in these years. In some villages women made up part of the absentee lists, but they seldom comprised more than 10 percent of all absentees. Essentially, then, these figures represent adult male absentees as a percentage of all adult males.

[b] Gewertz's (1983:126) data for 1977, however, indicate a figure nearer 22.1 percent.

Yangoru ceremonies confirm (see Roscoe in this volume), ceremonial stages can sometimes be collapsed into one another to cope with demographic or historical exigencies (see also Tuzin 1980:337–38). Further, the argument assumes that absenteeism is an independent variable, when it may in fact be dependent: absenteeism may be coordinated around initiations instead of being independent of them. Even in traditional times, for example, Murik males were able to organize an elaborate three-stage initiation system around their periodic, extended absences on trading voyages along the coast (Lipset, personal communication, 1985). In postcontact times, Anthony Forge (personal communication, 1984) found that when the Wingei Abelam held initiation ceremonies in the late 1950s, everyone returned from the plantations to attend. In fact, one foreman insisted on remaining for their duration despite two radio calls to the Patrol Office requesting his return. A Iatmul absentee in Lae told Christian Coiffier (personal communication, 1984) that he would soon interrupt his stay to re-

turn for the upcoming initiations in his village; if he did not, he claimed, he would never be able to attract a wife. In fact, such strategies may be widespread in Papua New Guinea: the chairman of the Law Reform Commission in 1980, a Tolai, arranged leave to coincide with the Dukduk initiation ceremonies of his group. Of course, the relationship between absenteeism and initiation might also go the other way. Yangoru Boiken informants claim that labor migration furnished more timorous youths with a convenient means of escaping the pains of initiation.

A second influence of urban absenteeism on initiatory decline may be an indirect one. Keesing (1982:16) notes that cult ideologies can become increasingly difficult to sustain in the face of exposure to the alternative ideologies of other groups and to the ideas and influences of industrial colonialists. Significantly, Bateson (1958[1936]:136) had remarked that the youths returning in Mindimbit "did so with a scorn of the initiatory crocodile." Gerstner (n.d.:3), observing that Nagam Boiken initiation had disappeared by 1947, held a similar view: young men "on their return to the villages were unwilling to take part in the old customs." Manam elders too complain that their youths returned to the villages with a disdain for initiation—its strict taboos, its beatings, its arduous apprenticeship to the flutists, and its forced consumption of bitter leaves and grasses (Lutkehaus, personal communication, 1985).

However, a cross-cultural comparison of Sepik societies for which data are available (table 2) demonstrates at most a partial correlation between absenteeism and the historical fortunes of initiation. In support of the thesis, we observe that some societies—such as the Yangoru Boiken and the Manam Islanders—had high rates of absenteeism from early times and were among the first to abandon their initiations. On the other hand, in some societies with rates rivaling these—for example, the Kaboibus Arapesh, the Iatmul, and the Manambu—initiation persists to the present. We might add that most of these figures represent whole ethnolinguistic groups and may mask considerable local fluctuation. In some parts of the Wosera, for example, a large proportion of the male population was absent in the years immediately following World War II (in one village, 46 percent [39 out of 85] of the "male labor potential" was absent [Maprik Patrol Report no. 3, 1949, p. 4]), yet these villages persist with their initiations today. Taking these data together with the opinions of informants and early observers, there would seem to be some grounds for supposing a relationship between male absenteeism and the fortunes of initiation, but if one exists, it is not a straightforward one, and many more and finer-grained data will be required for definitive conclusions to be drawn.

The Influence of Pacification

Several students of highland societies have attributed the demise of initiatory complexes to the Pax Australiana. Godelier (1976), Keesing (1982: 33), Langness (1967; 1977:20), and Watson and Watson (1973, cited in Langness 1977:20) all argue that, at least in part, initiation cults were instruments of war. They prepared young men ritually for the demands of war, promoted the solidarity of a warrior group faced with conflicting loyalties to wives and mothers drawn from enemy groups, and/or ensured senior control over the fighting power of juniors. Consequently,

when pacification robbed them of these purposes, they declined.

This thesis seems applicable to at least some Sepik cases. Murik seniors, for instance, explain that initiation was meant to create warriors and declined partly because there is now no such need (Lipset, personal communication, 1985). We question, however, whether pacification was as important a factor in Sepik initiatory decline as it seems to have been in the highlands. In the first place, as Keesing (1982:24) points out, Sepik warriors were probably not as concerned with solidarity as their highland counterparts, since wives and mothers were more likely to have come from allied groups. Moreover, a comparison of pacification and initiatory decline shows little evidence of correlation (table 3). Most telling perhaps is the contrast between river and coastal societies, the first regions to be pacified. Societies on the coast or with close contacts to it, such as the Manam, Murik, and Yangoru Boiken, were among the first to abandon their initiations, while systems on the river, where pacification came almost as soon, persist to the present.

In fact, by dividing the societies in table 3 into those that ceased initiation before 1955 and those that continued initiation into the 1970s, we find the median date of final pacification to be approximately 1930 for the former group and the late 1930s–early 1940s for the latter. Yet the median date of the last known initiation is approximately 1945 for the former group and the late 1970s for the latter. A difference of just a decade in date of final pacification seems insufficient to account for a difference of at least a quarter of a century in the dates of final initiation.

The Influence of World War II

Perhaps the most traumatic external influence on the Sepik was not the eradication of tribal fighting, missionary opposition, or contact with the European milieu but the war among the industrial nations. Because of German New Guinea's rapid surrender to the Australian Expeditionary Force, World War I had comparatively little effect on New Guinea society in general and Sepik societies in particular (Rowley 1958). World War II, by contrast, was devastating, the more so as 1945 saw the Sepik transformed into the final and terrible theater of the New Guinea campaigns.

TABLE 3
PACIFICATION OF THE SEPIK BY ETHNOLINGUISTIC GROUP

GROUP	PACIFICATION	LAST REPORTED INITIATION IN TRADITIONAL STYLE	SOURCE
Abelam			
Central	Late 1930s	Early 1970s	Kaberry (1941–42:81)
Eastern	?	Early 1970s	
Western	1937–45	Present	Scaglion (1984:6)
Wosera	Late 1930s	Present	Lea (1973:66)
Arapesh			
Ilahita	1944–45	1972–73	Tuzin (1976:32–33)
Kaboibus	1910–20s	1980	Fortune (1939:27)
Boiken			
Yangoru	1905–35	1947	Roscoe (1984:3)
Kunai	1941	1980	Gesch (1985)
Chambri	Early 1930s–mid-1950s	1974	Gewertz (1978c:578), Mead (1963:243–44)
Iatmul	Late 1920s–30s	Present	Bateson (1932:422), Griffith, Nelson, and Firth (1979:50)
Kwanga	Late 1940s–early 1950s	1965–81	Schindlbeck in this volume
Kwoma	1940s	1935	Bowden in this volume
Manam	1905–25	1940–45	N. Lutkehaus, personal communication, 1985
Manambu	1920s–30s	1980	Griffith, Nelson, and Firth (1979:50)
Murik	1918	Early 1950s	D. Lipset, personal communication, 1985

In some parts of Yangoru, initiations that were already overdue were further delayed by the war, initially because of the fighting, later because of the need to build up a necessary surplus of crops and pigs from depleted stocks of seed tubers and a ravaged bush. In some areas, the effects of the war took much longer to overcome. In Timbunke, the Japanese had lined up and shot for collaboration so many young men that there were not enough left to sustain initiations for many years after. Coupled with missionary opposition, these losses were enough to keep ceremonies in abeyance until 1975 (C. Dambui, personal communication, 1984). On Manam Island, the disruptions caused by the war were also sufficient to start the decline of initiation (Lutkehaus, personal communication, 1985). However, where detailed data are available, no marked correlation emerges between the disruptions of the war and the decline of initiation. Though Wingei, Kaboibus, and the Eastern Urat were among the most devastated areas in the Sepik (Allen 1983:223; Curtain 1980:197–202; Roscoe 1983:83), their initiations continue to the present day. By contrast, initiation disappeared from Central and East Yangoru shortly after the war, even though the surrender of Japanese forces had saved them

from the level of devastation experienced farther west (Roscoe 1983:83–85). Perhaps the most that can be said, then, is that World War II may have been a significant factor precipitating initiatory decline in systems that were somehow less "resistant" than others.

The Influence of Initiatory Organization

At an early stage in our comparison of Abelam and Boiken initiation, we noticed a difference that might explain how some complexes could be less "resistant" than others. Abelam and Boiken initiations differ markedly in their organizational structures. Abelam initiation is part of an ongoing reciprocal arrangement between two exchange moieties (ara). Once Moiety A has initiated Moiety B, Moiety B is "in debt" to Moiety A and remains so until the next ceremony. Moiety B can only eradicate its debt by initiating Moiety A, and in so doing it then places Moiety A in its own debt. This cycle repeats ad infinitum, and since there is no consensus about which moiety originally started initiations in train, one moiety is always in debt to the other (Forge 1967:69;

1970*b*:278; Kaberry 1971:42, 54; Scaglion 1976:85; Whiteman 1965:115). The implications of this indebtedness are profound, for, in an "egalitarian" society like the Abelam, to delay returning an initiation is to risk constant ridicule. Allen's example from the Urat (in this volume) will strike a chord with all who have worked in the Sepik:

> Then in late 1977, at Daihungai village, in the middle of the night, the slit-gongs boomed out. Men came hurriedly out of their houses to find the old bisnis leader Haptas with a huge dead cassowary at his feet. He made a speech in which he accused his ritual opponents of being like women who had been hurried back into their houses. Blithely ignoring the fact that for thirty years he had vigorously discouraged traditional activities in favor of bisnis, he told the men that he had been waiting for a long time for them to repay the debt his father had created. If they couldn't kill their own cassowaries, here was one for them. Within weeks other villages had announced plans for the staging of an exchange or an initiation.

The risk of ridicule engendered by this alternation of initiatory roles lends a powerful momentum to an initiatory system, a consequence that has not gone entirely unnoticed in the literature:

> In Arapesh perceptions the overall cyclical aspect [of initiation] resolves itself into a multitude of reciprocal actions: "We initiated them, now they must initiate our sons!" The system, so to speak, takes care of itself, unfolding as the reciprocity principle regularly conjoins with the knowledge of which initiation is triggered step by step through the sequence. [Tuzin 1980:32–33]

> The mechanism of reciprocity which pervades all kwaramba cult activities is probably one of the strongest guarantees of the continuity of the tradition. . . . There is therefore continuous pressure to hold an initiation, as each one reciprocates for one held in the past. [Schindlbeck in this volume]

If the organizational structure does not involve this oscillating indebtedness, the momentum born of reciprocation that keeps initiation systems like those of the Abelam, Arapesh, and Kwanga in motion will be missing. Yangoru Boiken initiation was such a case. Initiates of one moiety depended on members of the other for the performance of many aspects of their initiation, but both moieties were initiated *simultaneously under principles of strict equivalence*. Each moiety thus emerged from the initiation enclosure under no obligation to the other (see Roscoe in this volume). It hardly seems coincidence, then, that Yangoru Boiken initiation was one of the earliest of Sepik systems to disappear.

In fact, a survey of initiatory organization in the Sepik (table 4) shows that where initiation systems involve an oscillation of ritual obligation, they have persisted in the majority of the group's villages at least into the 1970s. The only contrary case is the West Kwanga, whose departure from expectation could be due to the fact that, in former times, some villages at least did not hold their own initiations but attended those in Bongos (see Schindlbeck in this volume). Conversely, initiation sequences that do not provoke delayed indebtedness appear to have declined at early dates in Sepik history. The only exception known to us is the Manambu, who are still initiating their youths even though initiates do not incur any obligation by their initiation (S. Harrison, personal communication, 1984). We can only speculate that this exception may owe something to the apparent lack of political emphasis this group places on competitive exchange (Harrison 1982:143 and in this volume).

In order to examine this relationship more closely, we constructed a 2×2 contingency table, dichotomizing societies according to organizational form and persistence of male initiation (table 5), and an exact test indicated that the observed relationship is unlikely to be due to chance alone ($p < .05$). In interpreting this table, we are, of course, sensitive to Galton's problem, which issues from the fact that, strictly speaking, culturally related groups do not constitute statistically independent cases. Because of historical relationships and/or diffusion, associations between variables may be duplicated, leading to inflated trait counts. For example, if we considered each Sepik village to be a unique case, our observed relationship would be extremely significant in the statistical sense. In table 5, data are displayed for groupings down to the dialectal level. In view of Galton's problem, we reexamined these data with regard only to the eleven major language groups formed by disregarding dialect differences and coding for the prevailing pattern of the broader linguistic group. The results (table 6) remained significant. This is strong evidence that the organizational structure of initiation is a major factor influencing its historical fortunes.

TABLE 4
ORGANIZATION OF MALE INITIATION IN THE SEPIK

GROUP	ALTERNATING INITIATION	LAST REPORTED INITIATION IN TRADITIONAL STYLE	SOURCE
Abelam			
Central	Yes	Early 1970s	Kaberry (1971:42), Lea (1964:144)
Eastern	Yes	Early 1970s	Forge (1970b:278)
Western	Yes	Present	Losche (1982:298): Scaglion, field data
Wosera	Yes	Present	Whiteman (1965:115)
Arapesh			
Ilahita	Yes	1972–73	Tuzin (1980:32–33)
Boiken			
Kunai	Yes[a]	1980	Gesch (1985)
Nagam	No?[b]	1947	Gerstner (n.d.)
Yangoru	No	1947	Roscoe in this volume
Chambri	Yes[c]	1974	Gewertz (1982:291–92)
Iatmul	Yes	Present	Bateson (1958[1936]:244–46)
Kwanga			
Bongos	Yes	1978	Schindlbeck in this volume
East	Yes	1980	Schindlbeck in this volume
North	Yes	1980–81?	Schindlbeck in this volume
West	Yes	1965	Schindlbeck in this volume
Kwoma	No	1935	Whiting (1941:66, 106)
Manam	No	1940–45	N. Lutkehaus, personal communication, 1985
Manambu	No	Present	S. Harrison, personal communication, 1984
Murik	No[d]	Early 1950s	D. Lipset, personal communication, 1985
Urat	Yes	1977–78	Allen in this volume

[a] Kunai Boiken initiation involves a complex interdependence on one another of four ritual groups (Gesch 1985).

[b] Gerstner (n.d.:16) makes no specific comment on whether or not Nagam Boiken initiation alternates between moieties over time. However, circumstantial evidence, e.g., reference to "all" adolescent youths' being taken to the spirit house at the same time, indicates the absence of any such alternation.

[c] The Chambri appear to initiate their two moieties simultaneously (Gewertz 1982:292), but Gewertz's account makes it clear that debts are here too created: "At each initiation a young man incurs a debt to the older man who lies beneath him [as he is scarified]. Although this debt cancels the identical obligation incurred by the older man to the younger man's father, it can itself be canceled only during the initiation of the older man's son" (pp. 289–90).

[d] In Murik initiation, there is an alternation of senior and junior grades, but there is also a second set of counterbalancing debts (Lipset, personal communication, 1985). In consequence, there do not appear to be alternating reciprocal obligations of the type under discussion. Whatever obligations Moiety B may incur in being initiated by Moiety A are counterbalanced by debts created by the gifts of food and sexual services that Moiety B makes to Moiety A prior to their initiation.

Conclusion

For several reasons, this analysis is only a preliminary one. First, we have yet to review the literature for all Sepik societies for which adequate data may exist on initiation and on the variables associated with its decline. Second, we have treated missionary opposition, millenarianism, and so on as though they were independent of one another, which is almost certainly an erroneous assumption. It is highly likely, for example, that missionary activity and labor migration were dependent to some extent on pacification. However, the data so far available to us are both too crude and too limited to make a detailed analysis of

these dependencies feasible. Finally, we readily concede that if male initiation happens to serve different ends in different societies, then these ends may play a central role in explaining the response of initiation complexes to external influences. Unfortunately, an analysis of what these ends might be would necessarily assume monumental and exhausting proportions. Moreover, since the nature of male initiation is still very much a matter of debate, it is unlikely that any definitive conclusions could be achieved, and for this reason we have also refrained from basing any comparison of initiatory function on analyses by other researchers.

Despite these caveats, we believe some prelim-

TABLE 5

ORGANIZATIONAL FORM AND PERSISTENCE OF MALE
INITIATION IN THE SEPIK

ORGANIZATIONAL FORM	PERSISTENCE	
	Pre-1970	Post-1970
Alternating	1[a]	12
Other	5	1

$p = .0029$, 2 × 2 exact test[b]; χ^2 with Yates's correction for continuity[c] = 7.65, $p = .0057$

[a] The Kwanga are here considered to comprise the four
groups that Schindlbeck mentions in discussing the status
of Kwanga initiation. In fact, there are six Kwanga dialect
groups (Laycock 1973:24), and had we coded for each
separately, the relationship would have become even more
significant.

[b] The precise test used here is the Olivetti P652 Statistical
Significance Program, Test 5.08, a somewhat conservative variation of Fisher's exact test.

[c] Yates's correction for continuity is preferred when expected frequencies are small and is considered a conservative modification to the χ^2 test.

inary conclusions can be advanced about the effects of European intrusion on Sepik male initiation. Our examination of missionary opposition,
millenarian activities, labor migration, pacification, and the effects of World War II indicates that
each probably provided some hindrance to the
continuance of initiation cults. Separately or together, however, they seem insufficient to account
for the entire mosaic of responses to European-
inspired influences. The more striking finding is
that an organizational pattern of alternating, reciprocal obligation is a significant predictor of the
historical fortunes of initiation. We suggest,
therefore, that some systems of initiation may
have been more vulnerable to European influence
than others. In broad terms, missionary opposi-

TABLE 6

ORGANIZATIONAL FORM AND PERSISTENCE OF MALE
INITIATION IN THE SEPIK (GROUPS OF TABLE 4
REDUCED TO LANGUAGE GROUPINGS)

ORGANIZATIONAL FORM	PERSISTENCE	
	Pre-1970	Post-1970
Alternating	0	6
Other	4	1

$p = .0152$, 2 × 2 exact test; χ^2 with Yates's correction
for continuity = 4.48, $p = .0343$

tion, millenarian activities, labor migration, pacification, and the war may have all provided some
resistance to initiation complexes, but their impact was sufficient to bring to a permanent end
only those that lacked the momentum of alternating, reciprocal obligations.

Notes

1. We gratefully acknowledge the support of the in-
situtions that funded and sponsored the field research
among the Abelam and Boiken on which much of this
paper is based: the National Institute of Mental Health,
the Faculty Research Grants Committee of the University of Pittsburgh, and the Law Reform Commission of
Papua New Guinea (Scaglion); the Emslie Horniman
Scholarship Fund, the Ford Foundation, the University
of Rochester, and the Department of Community Medicine at the University of Papua New Guinea (Roscoe).
We are grateful to Kathy Barlow, Ross Bowden, Christian Coiffier, Fr. Cherubim Dambui, Anthony Forge,
Simon Harrison, David Lipset, Nancy Lutkehaus,
Donald Tuzin, and John Wasori for supplying us with
supplementary information and/or criticisms of an earlier draft of this paper. We also thank Barbara Wais
Roscoe for the numerous mind-numbing hours she
spent transcribing Yangoru Subdistrict Patrol census
data. Finally, we each owe vast debts to our patient and
long-suffering Abelam and Boiken informants.

2. One reason for this neglect may be that researchers specifically interested in male initiation have sought
out places still practicing it, a situation in which European influences are likely to seem attenuated. By
contrast, communities where such substantial ritual
complexes have disappeared have tended to attract the
labels "acculturated" or "declining," a taint which, in
the past, has tended to identify a community as no
longer worth studying.

3. Though Manam Island lies just inside Madang
Province, we include it here because of its close ethnographic links to the Sepik.

4. According to a Sima informant, the priests involved were "Pata Kessa" and "Pata Mai." It appears
that Fr. A. Gerstner passed through the area with Fr. P.
May sometime prior to the 1950s (Gerstner n.d.:26).

5. Gerstner (n.d.:3) hints that missionary opposition was responsible, at least in part, for the demise of
male initiation among the Nagam Boiken. For their
part, the Kunai Boiken—who still initiate their
youths—also played host to early Catholic missionaries (Gerstner n.d.:26; Müller 1935–36), but it is not
known to what degree they incurred missionary displeasure.

Part Seven
Sickness and Health

Introduction

William E. Mitchell

This section opens with a paper on the ethno-therapy of the Taute Wape of the Torricelli Mountains in which I compare their indigenous therapeutic system, involving, e.g., curing practitioners, demon curing societies, and self-treatment, with the therapeutic system introduced by Westerners, involving, e.g., medical aid posts, the Catholic mission, patrol officers, and police. In a concluding discussion I highlight the ideological, structural, and political differences between the two systems, emphasizing the ideological schism between the village's egalitarian therapeutic system and the hierarchical Western one.

Chris Haiveta, while similarly concerned with contrasts between indigenous and introduced culture, focuses primarily on the health care alternatives open to residents of the coastal village of Maindroin. Adopting a historical perspective, Haiveta shows the impact of the Catholic mission, in particular its medical services, on indigenous beliefs and healing practices.

Sanguma, a form of sorcery believed to cause severe illness resulting in death, is found in much of the Sepik region as well as in other parts of Papua New Guinea. Within the context of village life, Antje Kelm examines sanguma beliefs and practices in the villages of Abrau and Kwieftim, between the Torricelli Mountains and the Sepik River.

All Sepik societies have local pharmacopoeias. Werner G. Stöcklin reports that the Abelam, although long in contact with Westerners and Western medicine, still recognize and use a large number of indigenous plants for medicinal purposes. He describes how traditional healers employ various of these plants and the therapeutic values the Abelam attribute to them.

Brigit Obrist is also concerned with indigenous plants, in this case in their nutritional value for Sepik villagers. She reviews published subsistence data from ten Sepik societies and analyzes them in terms of, for example, local beliefs about particular kinds of food, including taboos, the organization of food procurement, the distribution and exchange of food, and food preparation and consumption. She concludes by noting the difficulty that nutritionists sometimes have in comprehending beliefs about food and the useful role anthropologists can play in helping them to understand the larger cultural context of which food beliefs are often a part.

38/ Therapeutic Systems of the Taute Wape

William E. Mitchell

The Torricelli Mountains, a part of Papua New Guinea's north coastal range that lies between the West Irian border and the mouth of the Sepik River, are the homeland for almost 10,000 Wape, who live on the inland side of the range in fifty-five villages in the West Sepik Province. One of these villages, Taute, with a population of 220, served as my fieldwork base for eighteen months in 1970–72. In this paper I am concerned with the ethnotherapy of the Taute Wape and have limited my inquiry to those interventions directly applied to humans.[1] Specifically, I examine the place of evil in Taute society and attempts to eliminate or weaken its power.[2] The data are organized around the two therapeutic systems that impinge on the everyday life of Taute villagers. One is indigenous or intrinsic to the village's traditional culture; the other is extrinsic and was introduced into village life by Westerners beginning in the late 1940s.

Theoretical Orientation

The central concern of ethnotherapy, the cross-cultural study of therapeutic systems, is, as I envision it, the analysis and comparative understanding of (1) cultural events defined as wrong, bad, or improper, (2) therapeutic interventions designed to rectify these offending events, and (3) the precepts and rationales on which the interventions are based.[3] The offending events may relate to almost anything—for example, human beings and their artifacts, the surrounding flora and fauna, the physical environment, spirit forms, and, of course, the weather.

The empirical and observational focus for the study of a therapeutic system is on the wrong and the bad, not the right and the good, but the problem is more complex than this might imply. Knowledge of what is bad and good is, itself, a contrastive process; the one helps to define the other. Although cultural beliefs about the good and the bad may be polarized, they are, paradoxically, locked in an intimate ontological embrace. The behavioral dialectics that derive from this ep-istemic engagement between the good and the bad are at the affective core of every culture or, to put it another way, of each member's personality and are expressed both in everyday actions and in rituals of great emotional and dramatic intensity.

Because of the human neurological system's capacity for incorporating complex forms of judgment and evaluation, the moral patterning of thought and behavior is a primary concern of all human societies. Each society has deeply felt and strongly supported beliefs—only in part articulate and within the awareness of most individuals—about what is good and bad, what is right and wrong. As humans are rarely neutral about their existence or their cosmos, this strong ethical stance permeates cultural behavior. Consequently, anything that a group holds dear or that is vital for living may be subjected to corrective intervention when things go wrong.

A significant part of enculturation is learning to identify threatening events. A drought, an infant's rising fever, rice that won't grow, a landslide, a gun that misses its mark, a wasting pig, or a hunting spirit that refuses to send game is observed and acted upon. Whenever a deleterious event threatens something of importance, a diagnosis is made and a countering therapy introduced.

Such threatening events may be interpreted, in the broadest sense, as "evil" in that they are in opposition to the culturally desired. In this usage, "evil" refers to an abstract class of phenomena that a society considers harmful and, therefore, in need of correction. Thus all corrective interventions are basically *moral* acts, acts that are integrally related to a society's views about what is right and good.

As moral acts, therapeutic interventions that are *intrinsic* to the culture are essentially conservative. They attempt to rectify, restore, repair, reclaim, or remedy manifestations of evil. They are conservative because, even though the intervention itself may be innovative and radical, the intent is to reestablish a real or idealized cultural status quo. It is also testimony to the boldness—even arrogance—of *Homo sapiens* toward the cosmos that humans feel capable of correcting whatever they dislike or fear. Thus, when the diagnosis is appropriate and the therapeutic act is of sufficient power, a transformation occurs. The drought is broken, the fever drops, the rice grows, the land becomes firm, the gun kills, the pig gets fat, and the game returns.

Therapeutic interventions that are *extrinsic* to the culture, imposed upon the society by alien authorities, tend to be not conservative but radical and revolutionary. Some of these interventions may be welcomed by the society, but others will be seen as intrusive and disruptive and therefore deeply resented. Such is the situation when a colonial government extends its authority over the indigenous inhabitants and, projecting its own ideas of good and bad onto the local culture, attempts to reform it.

In an earlier paper (Mitchell 1977*b*) I indicated that some of anthropology's own cherished concepts and analytical categories have unwittingly retarded the study of therapeutic systems. The concept of "ethnomedicine" is a case in point. Studies in ethnomedicine tend to rely upon concepts such as "medical" and "disease" to focus the research inquiry. Both concepts are important in Western society and used by specialist and lay person alike with a minimum of referential ambiguity. They are, however, essentially culture-bound. When they are used as major organizing concepts for *transcultural* research, problems of meaning arise. "Medical" and "disease" are concepts related to naturalistic theories about illness, for example, Western biomedicine or Indian Ayurvedic medicine, and are intellectually distorting when applied to the supernaturalistic theories about illness that abound in Papua New Guinea. One important advantage of the therapeutic-system model in the study of evil is that it is less culturally loaded than those intimately related to the Western medical model. It has the further advantage of collapsing anthropology's traditional analytical categories (e.g., religion, economics, medicine, politics, and kinship), categories that reflect Western sociocultural organization, to organize ethnographic data about a society's problem of evil in a more holistic way.

The change agents with which Taute villagers are involved, ranging from government courts and village meetings to demon curing societies and medical aid posts, and the modes of intervention characteristic of each may be organized as shown in table 1. Modes of intervention may be instructive, punitive, or curative; instruction attempts to induce change by benign corrective

TABLE 1
CHANGE AGENTS AVAILABLE TO TAUTE WAPE BY
THERAPEUTIC SYSTEM AND MODE OF INTERVENTION

THERAPEUTIC SYSTEM	MODE OF INTERVENTION	
	Punitive-Instructive	Curative-Instructive
Extrinsic	Patrol officer/police Judiciary	Medical aid post Maternal–child health clinics Hospital Catholic mission Ethnographer
Intrinsic	Village meeting Harangue Sorcery/Witchcraft	Curing practitioner Exorcist Demon curing society Self-treatment

teaching, punishment by inflicting suffering, and curing by alleviating suffering. Change agents in the village's intrinsic and extrinsic therapeutic systems variously combine instruction with punishment or curing.

Wape Society and Culture

The broken hills and mountains of Wapeland are composed primarily of siltstone and mudstone covered by largely secondary forest. The main produce of a Wape garden is sweet potatoes, taro, and bananas. Gardens are generally unfenced and subject to the marauding of pigs. The population of domesticated pigs is small, and they are butchered only on ritual occasions. Sago flour is the major food. Although the sago palm is not native to the mountains, it is planted in moist ravines and swampy areas, where it thrives, nurtured by an average rainfall of 104 inches per year. Hunting is culturally important in terms of male interest and ritual, but little protein is obtained in this way because of the paucity of game. While people rarely go hungry, the Wape diet is deficient in protein, a fact that is reflected in their small stature and slow rate of physical maturation. The Wape birth weight is one of the lowest in the world, and the mean age for the onset of menses is 18.4 years (Wark and Malcolm 1969).

Wape villages are traditionally situated along ridges and comprise several hamlets with a total population of from one hundred to three hundred. Married couples and their children reside in separate houses, while unmarried men and youths live in a bachelors' house. Most hamlets have a separate ceremonial house restricted to men as the center for their extensive ritual activities. Village society is organized agnatically, with un-named exogamous patrilineages and dispersed named patriclans. Cousin terms are Omaha. Marriage is by bridewealth, and postmarital residence is virilocal. Polygyny is permitted but unusual. The Wape have a strong egalitarian ethos and an elaborate exchange system in which wealth cannot be accumulated. Their language is Olo, with the most speakers of any of the forty-seven languages comprising the Torricelli phylum. According to Laycock (1975a:768), the phylum appears to be genetically unique; no other languages on the island seem to be even distantly related to it.

One of the most striking characteristics of Taute village life in comparison with that of many New Guinea societies is its placidity. The physical expression of aggression is strongly disapproved and rare. Verbal expression of anger is allowed but viewed as regrettable. Aggression is rarely symmetrical; the usual response is stolid inertia. For example, when a child has a temper tantrum, it is simply ignored. It is not surprising, then, that Wape culture, overall, is defensively oriented. Instead of centering their ceremonial life on the initiation of warrior youths or the competitive display of giant yams, the Wape have centered it on the pacification of the ancestral ghosts and demons that strike them down with illness and death. Much of their intellectual and behavioral energy is dedicated to the social elaboration of a complex therapeutic system that includes curing practitioners, curing societies, and curing festivals with extensive social and economic intervillage ties.

In 1947, Franciscan priests from Australia established the first mission station in Wapeland near the village of Lumi. Shortly afterward a government patrol post was opened and a local hospital constructed. In 1951, Christian Brethren missionaries opened the first of several stations. Although both missions have been unsuccessful in their attempts to suppress Wape healing and hunting festivals, they remain, with the government, a significant presence in Wapeland.[4]

The Intrinsic Therapeutic System

Punitive-Instructive Mode

Two important and highly visible change agents are the village meeting and the harangue. A third, which is exceedingly private, is sorcery or witch-ery. All three use punishment and/or instruction to effect a desired transformation.

The village meeting. The village meeting is the community's most influential means for publicly defining and correcting wrongdoing. When a villager has a serious problem whose cause may be attributed to another, a meeting is called. It may be spontaneous or announced in advance. Everyone in the village involved in the problem is expected to attend; not to attend is prima facie evidence of guilt.

A central feature of every hamlet is a dance plaza encircled by family houses. In front of each house is a covered verandah where family members work, relax, and visit with neighbors and relatives. When a meeting is called, the women, small children, and a few men assemble in and around the verandahs while most of the men go to the verandah of the ceremonial house. Someone presents the problem rather informally—the Wape do not go in for oratory as do some Sepik societies—and the villagers begin to speak to the issue or, as is frequently the case, other issues they consider related to it. Individuals are blamed directly or by innuendo, and each must answer the accusations. It is a slow process; meetings may last two or more hours. Eventually the problem is resolved by a consensus, and the acknowledged offender, if there is one, must pay damages or in other ways publicly make amends.

It is crucial that the meeting end on a harmonious note with no visible ill feelings. Otherwise there will be more perceived wrongdoing, fresh accusations, and another meeting. This is partly because the powerful ghosts of villagers' dead ancestors observe the deliberations and, if their living descendants are dealt with unjustly, send misfortune to the offenders. Therefore, when a man's hunting fortunes dim after being involved in a meeting, he may assume that his adversary's ancestral ghosts are to blame. If after appealing to his adversary to call off the ancestral ghosts his hunting does not improve, there will be cause for another meeting.

Thus a new offense is often related to an older one, and the village meeting becomes an episodic event in a continuous cycle of blame and punishment. In any small face-to-face society like Taute, where the emphasis is on "getting along," slights and offenses are often seemingly ignored, but, in time, resentment grows. The meetings deal not only with the problems of the key adversaries but, because of the villagers' tight intermeshing network of kin ties and everyday experiences, with other affronts and wrongdoings that are flushed out in what might be called "catharsis networking." Affronts that appear to an outsider completely irrelevant when first presented are revealed to be an integral part of the presenting problem. Thus a village meeting may result in a villager's covert problem's becoming overt, and, if not completely resolved, it becomes part of the public record, a known problematic quantity that may be dealt with later.[5]

The harangue. When someone is wronged by another, an early resort is a haranguing lecture that is usually a combination of punishment and advice. The wronged individual goes to the offender's house and, standing on a path or other public ground, begins a long, loud, ranting lecture about the wrongdoer and the specific wrong. The social intent of the harangue is to give pointed instruction in behavior to the offender and to embarrass by publicizing the offense. If property is involved, there also may be hope of compensation. Unspoken, but known by all, is that the powerful dead ancestors of the offended person are listening and may inflict punishment, such as sickness, upon the offender or a family member. Throughout the stormy lecture, there is no interaction between the two parties. The offending person remains within the house and does not respond. Eventually the haranguer, energy spent and voice gone, returns home.

Before Western contact, a more serious recourse when wrongs went unrighted was a stick fight between two men. Such fights were often over the violation of sexual rights to women. Now fighting of any kind among men is extremely rare. While living in the village, I did not see or hear about a single skirmish between men. "Living in peace" is a major part of the Wape ethos, and most villagers work hard to maintain it.

Sorcery and witchcraft. While the harangue and village meeting are public events, the use of sorcery and witchcraft to punish a wrongdoer is private. This was true even before Westerners came to live in Wapeland but is even more so today. Both the government and the missions have been dogged in their denunciation of these practices and have imposed strong negative sanctions against them. Nevertheless, most, if not all, adult Taute villagers know spells for controlling and affecting the physical and emotional life of others. Not all of these spells are intended to harm. For example, ginger leaves may be charmed and placed under the ladder of the village rest house so that the descending patrol officer will be tranquil and kindly disposed toward the villagers, and there are spells for making a

possible lover desire one. When one has been wronged, however, there are spells, usually performed with a bit of the victim's exuviae, to bring sickness or death.

Traditionally, the Wape also had male witches (*numoin*)[6] who were paid to kill a victim with witchcraft. The last resident numoin in Taute died shortly before I arrived. Because witchcraft is outlawed and the missions consider a witch to be linked with the forces of Satan, young men no longer seek instruction in the art. But many of the villages to the south of Taute still have witches, and deaths in the village are sometimes attributed to them as hired killers.[7] The Wape believe that there is no antidote once a witch has struck, death being inevitable and swift. The numoin is also a curer.

Curative-Instructive Mode

Human sickness, always a grave cultural event, is of serious concern to all societies. Each has devoted considerable imagination to the understanding of sickness and the devising of corrective therapies. The Wape have an especially deep cultural concern about illness. It is, as I indicated earlier, part of their conciliatory ethos and related to their conservative and defensive stance toward human experience and the cosmos. To counter the injurious attacks of ghosts and demons, the Wape have created an armamentarium of curing practitioners and curing societies as well as other less dramatic forms of therapeutic intervention.

Curing practitioners. The Taute Wape recognize three types of practitioners involved with the diagnosis and treatment of illness. The most powerful and feared of these is the numoin, a male shaman-witch who gains his healing abilities by killing persons whose ghosts give him his special powers. As a shaman-witch, he is both a killer and a curer who is feared and respected. His special powers include making himself invisible and flying. He also is adept in the removal of small objects shot by forest demons into a victim to cause sickness. A numoin is summoned only when a person is seriously sick. First he questions the patient about his illness; then he begins to probe for offending articles. After he has removed them by hand, he is paid a small fee. If the patient recovers, the numoin receives the credit, and his reputation grows. If the sickness continues, other causes of the illness will be explored and new therapies imposed.

A *wobif* is a shaman who is expert at massage and sucking out bad blood and bits of tabooed food that have caused illness. Unlike the numoin, he has no supernatural powers and is not feared. He is taught his skills by an older wobif and is paid a very small fee for his curing services. Whereas the numoin is called in for life-threatening illnesses, the wobif is more an everyday practitioner.

The third type of practitioner is the *glasman*. This is a Tok Pisin word, and, as this suggests, the *glasman*'s curing role was introduced into Wapeland from the coast after Western contact. He is clairvoyant, a diagnostician with second sight. By looking into a patient and asking questions, he can divine the cause of the sickness and prescribe an appropriate treatment. He receives a small fee for this diagnostic service, but he himself does not treat patients.[8]

One or more of these three types of practitioners are involved with most illnesses depending upon the symptoms, seriousness, and duration. They are the indigenous primary care givers and are almost always consulted before a patient seeks help from a Western therapy.

Exorcists. The practitioners discussed above are institutionalized part-time specialists. They are few and perform their services in addition to the usual subsistence activities of a Wape male. But *all* adults, men and women alike, are potential exorcists of the ghosts and demons who reside on their patrilineal lands. Each patrilineage, for example, owns tracts of forest land wherein dwell the ancestral ghosts who protect its lands and the rights of its members. Related to the ancestors in a mystical way are the vengeful and unpredictable demons who live on the lineage land in places of strange appearance such as waterfalls, still ponds, and landslides. When angered, an ancestral ghost or demon may enter into the body of the offending person and cause sickness. Adult males of the lineage or, in their absence, their wives are then called upon to exorcise the pernicious spirit.

These exorcisms are common occurrences in the village and often one of the first therapies utilized. If a man goes hunting with a friend on the latter's land and then becomes sick, he will send for his friend to exorcise him. Such a request is never refused. The exorcism itself is informal and simple. While lightly brushing the afflicted body area with some ginger leaves, the exorcist silently appeals to the intruding spirit to cease its exploitation of his friend and depart. The spirit, embarrassed by the chastisement, readily leaves. Of course, if the illness persists or worsens, it is obvious that the interpretation was erroneous and a new diagnosis must be made.

Demon curing societies. Some of the forest demons are the center of curing societies whose exclusively male membership cuts across lineage lines. Men initiated into a society are taught the demon's secret name and thereby have the power to exorcise it from a person it has afflicted. Members may also wear a mask personifying the demon at its curing festival. Such a festival may involve a series of reciprocal exchanges based on ties of kinship and marriage that includes a network of persons extending to the surrounding villages.[9] Curing festivals provide the only traditional occasion in Wape society for such large intervillage gatherings.

Whether a demon society has a large or small curing festival depends upon its traditions. Some stage a single-day festival that ends by sunset. Other festivals are months in preparation and may last a week or more with all-night singing and dancing, parading of masks, and, almost as an anticlimax, the exorcism of the victims.

As most persons become afflicted by a demon between its curing festivals, they are immediately exorcised by one of the members of the society in the informal manner already described. However, they are expected to participate in the festival's formal exorcism, even though seemingly healthy, to give their sickness the *coup de grâce*. Even at future festivals a former victim of the demon may rub his or her skin against the sweating back of a mask carrier as a kind of "inoculation" or preventive therapy against future attacks.

Self-treatment. The agents I have briefly described represent the major socially external forms of intervention to correct a deleterious event. The first line of therapeutic strategies for sickness, however, is self-treatment with home remedies. Every adult villager is responsible for her or his own health maintenance. When a person first feels ill or has an accident she or he decides, sometimes in consultation with another family member, on a home treatment, a therapy that does not involve the formal services of others. For a headache, a tight band may be tied around the forehead; if a leg hurts, it may be superficially cut; if a boil is ripe, it may be lanced. In Wape cultural terms, these interventions are, at best, palliatives. Although they may provide some immediate relief, they do not deal with the *cause* of the problem. Thus most home remedies, like Western aspirin, are symptom-oriented; they do not provide an ultimate explanation and cure for the affliction. Villagers expect a certain amount of suffering as part of the human condition, and their cultural tolerance for pain appears greater than that of Westerners. But if a home remedy does not help and the suffering worsens, then a cause for the affliction must be determined so that a treatment that will act directly on the cause may be applied. For this, one must seek the assistance of others.

The Extrinsic Therapeutic System

When the Australian government and missions established themselves in Wapeland after World War II, they brought with them some strikingly exotic notions about the nature of evil and how to transform it. This was especially true in the realm of human action. Their Western ideas about right and wrong behavior were often in direct conflict with Wape standards of conduct and morality. Although strangers to Wapeland and its culture, the newcomers had both the political and the military power to impose their views of evil on village life.

This was a difficult time for the Wape. The Westerners were welcomed into Wapeland because they brought access to valuable goods that the Wape wanted, but, at the same time, the villagers were subjected to new and sometimes offensive ideas about "justice," "religion," and "health." The Westerners also were emphatic that these new ideas must be accepted and followed. If the Wape would not submit, they would be punished. Villagers who openly challenged or disobeyed the new morality were threatened, flogged, or jailed. The Wape had analogs in their own culture for the threats and beatings, but involuntary confinement was unknown to them and perceived as bizarre and inhuman.

Taute is located across the Sibi River, far enough from Lumi station to avoid the regular scrutiny that closer villages had to endure. When police or medical officers visited Taute, the people dutifully lined up for roll call and cooperated with their program. When a Franciscan priest visited, they would gather to listen as he condemned their elaborate curing festivals and explained about the wrath and love of "papa God." Once the Westerner had left the village, they would relax. They accommodated in their outward behavior to these powerful strangers, but they did not give up the ideology of their ancestors.

An aspect of evil that the Westerners and villagers did agree about was the dread of sickness. For both cultures, sickness was an evil that must be continually confronted and overcome. But the congruence stopped there. The Western and Wape theories about sickness and related therapies were contradictory. This did not, however, prevent the Wape from observing the efficacy of Western medicines. Even the earliest Western medical practitioner in Wapeland noted the Wape's receptiveness to Western medical therapies.[10] Now as then, however, they show little interest in their rationale. Wape culture provides a powerful belief system that is clear about the causes and cures of sickness. While the Wape acknowledge that Western medicine may ease the pain or ameliorate a sickness, they consider it ineffective against the ghostly or demonic forces that have caused the affliction. Only Wape therapies have the power to cure.

Western therapies, then, are used in conjunction with Wape ones. While sitting at a government medical aid post with a Taute friend waiting for treatment, I watched an old woman silently, almost imperceptibly, exorcise her visiting kinsman before he went inside for a shot of penicillin.

Curative-Instructive Mode

According to the Western medical officer in Lumi (Wark 1971:2), the major life-threatening health problems of the Wape are respiratory-tract infections, malaria, and malnutrition. To deal with these and other Western-defined health problems of the Wape, the Department of Public Health, a bureaucracy with almost twelve thousand employees, has instituted three forms of medical services to which the villagers have direct access: medical aid posts, maternal–child health clinics, and a local hospital in Lumi. Each relies on both curative and instructive strategies to effect positive change. Although these three services were established at different times (ranging from 1949 for the hospital to 1962 for the maternal–child health clinic), each was well received by the people. From a villager's perspective, however, the most important of these Western-inspired services is the aid post.

Medical aid posts. In predominantly rural Papua New Guinea, the aid post is usually the nearest source of Western medical care and by far the most important general medical service in the country (Radford 1971:4). In Wapeland, as elsewhere, aid posts are located in geographically strategic villages serving a regional population and are staffed by an indigenous male medical orderly called a *doktaboi* (Tok Pisin). Most of these men are literate in Tok Pisin and have completed a two-year training course in the principles of hy-

giene and public health, first-aid procedures, and
the treatment of common illnesses and injuries including acute respiratory- and alimentary-tract
infections, malaria, tuberculosis, leprosy, common skin conditions, burns, and wounds. Patients requiring skill beyond the doktaboi's competence are usually referred to the nearest
hospital. The building for the aid post is maintained by the villagers, and the Department of
Public Health provides the medical and office
supplies and the orderly's salary of A$4 bi-
weekly.

The aid post nearest Taute is an hour's walk
away in Wilkili village. The orderly, a native of
Wilkili, is related to a number of Taute villagers
and is a respected and trusted therapist. Occasionally he comes to Taute if a person is too sick
to walk to the aid post. He has minimal understanding of the theories that lie behind his interventions, however, and, like his patients, accepts
them on the empirical level. During my stay in
Taute, the villagers made frequent use of his services.[11]

Maternal–child health clinics. The maternal–child health clinics subsidized by the Department of Public Health are staffed by three
Western women—a physician and two nurses—
with the Christian Brethren mission. The goal of
these clinics is to prevent serious sickness among
pregnant and lactating mothers, their infants, and
small children and to teach health care methods
based on Western medicine. Staff members make
periodic foot patrols to each village, where they
examine babies and toddlers, maintain growth
records, give immunizations and medication, examine women when necessary, and instruct
mothers in diet and hygiene.[12] Mothers and children needing special medical care are referred to
the hospital at Lumi, where a ward is devoted to
their medical problems, usually nutritional ones.
The staff has good rapport with the Taute village
women, and the clinics are well attended. These
are important social occasions, as they are the
only time when women from the village gather
for an activity that is exclusively theirs.

Lumi Hospital. The Department of Public
Health's hospital in Lumi has a daily average in-
patient population of sixty-five with a median
length of stay of eleven days and treats over seventy-five hundred outpatients a year.[13] The hospital is staffed by a male New Guinean assistant
medical officer, the three clinic women, eight
male Wape hospital orderlies, who perform much
of the routine nursing and outpatient care, and
several young Wape women trained on the job to
assist with routine tasks in the maternal and child
health unit.

Although villagers in the immediate vicinity of
Lumi tend to use the hospital as the Taute villagers use the Wilkili aid post, the latter use the
hospital as a last resort unless referred to it by the
aid post orderly or one of the clinic staff. If a patient is too ill to walk into Lumi, she or he must
be carried, and this requires two teams of four
men each, all of whom must be paid unless they
are close kin. This is a big investment in a therapeutic service that, in Tautean eyes, may help
but not cure. While I lived in Taute only one adult
patient, a pregnant woman who fell out of a tree
while gathering food, was carried to the hospital.[14] When a problem demands more sophisticated care than can be provided by the hospital,
the patient is flown out to the coastal hospital in
Wewak.

These three therapeutic agencies are the most
important providers of Western curative-instruc-
tive interventions. Two others of minor importance are the Catholic mission and Taute's ethnographer.

The Catholic mission. If one believes in a
Catholic God, then one may appeal to Him
through personal or priestly prayer to transform
an evil. Although many Tauteans are declared
Catholics and have baptismal names as well as
Wape ones, their commitment to the Catholic
faith is a nominal one. They may pray with the
priest when he visits the village, but there is no
evidence that the Catholic religion is a significant
part of their lives. Through the authority of his
church offices, a visiting priest can hear confessions and administer penances, but this aspect of
the church's intervention is almost nonexistent in
Taute. More important is the priest's homily,
which usually treats an aspect of church doctrine.
These talks are important in shaping the villagers' view of Western morality and may be referred to for reinforcement of a villager's own
opinion. Sometimes interpersonal complaints are
brought to a visiting priest's attention. If the matter involves Catholic doctrine, he will certainly
respond. Otherwise, it depends upon the specific
priest. Today, priests are less intrusive into village
affairs and customs than formerly. The church has
even developed a kind of tolerance for the elaborate curing festivals. Once shunned as the devil's
work, curing festivals are now sometimes attended by Franciscan priests and nuns as interested spectators.

The ethnographer. Most ethnographers
feel more closely identified with the foreign com-

munity they are studying than with the expatriates living on outstations (e.g., officials, missionaries, and tradespersons) with whom they share a cultural tradition. Villagers, however, are not as idealistically inclined toward their ethnographer as she or he is about them. The ethnographer's presence in a village may be desired and appreciated by villagers for a variety of reasons, but he or she is still an "outsider" living "inside" who looks more like a patrol officer, nurse, or priest than a fellow villager. When I came to live in Taute with my family, I publicly disavowed any role taking in the village as a Western arbitrator of disputes or as a first-aid worker. But I had been correctly identified as a representative of the powerful expatriate culture and therefore a strategic contact person. It is a common fieldwork experience. As I was making a study of the village's therapeutic systems, I considered it methodologically inappropriate to become any kind of therapeutic agent. I did not want to study myself. So I successfully refused to arbitrate disputes and did not establish a daily first-aid clinic as some ethnographers and missionaries do who live in remote areas. There were emergency occasions when I gladly gave first aid to a hamlet neighbor, but we were not a formal resource that villagers could count on like those just discussed.[15] I mention this to acknowledge my own participation, however limited, in Taute's therapeutic systems.

Punitive-Instructive Mode

The patrol officer and police. In Wapeland, the patrol officer and his indigenous policemen are men of prestige and power. They are influential carriers of the new Western morality and, unlike the missionaries, have the authority to enforce it. Government officers visit most villages once or twice a year for a variety of reasons, among them to stage an election, explain a new policy, update a census, inspect the village, or collect taxes. Regardless of the reason for the official's visit, he usually hears villagers' complaints as a matter of course. These complaints are often of an intervillage nature, because warfare, the traditional way of settling such complaints, is outlawed. If the official agrees that there is a problem, he will call the accused into Lumi with the accuser to resolve the dispute informally. The official's decision is not binding as in an official court of law, but it is perceived as such by the disputants.

Officials, like the missionaries, take good advantage of their village visits to lecture the people on the new morality, with special emphasis on village hygiene, avoiding disputes, maintaining village paths and government rest houses, supporting and obeying the government, and formal education. These lectures, when placed alongside actual experiences with expatriates through time, provide a large corpus of data on expatriates' views about what is right and wrong.

The judiciary. Cases involving villagers are heard in local courts, district courts, and the Supreme Court. The Tautean's most common experience is with the Lumi local court, which has "civil jurisdiction over matters involving up to $200, and criminal jurisdiction over minor offences for which the penalties are not greater than a fine of $100 or six months' imprisonment" (Commonwealth of Australia 1970:56). Taute villagers prefer to keep the government and its judiciary out of village conflicts because of their uncertain understanding of expatriate culture and the unpredictability of expatriates' behavior. However, threatening to report a fellow villager to the government is not uncommon and is a strong incentive for solving problems at the village level. Generally, only serious traditional offenses such as child rape and adultery are brought to the government's attention by Tauteans. The government, of course, uses the various courts to enforce its regulations about village life. These are set forth in English in the "native" administration regulations (Territory of Papua New Guinea 1968), a statutory instrument adapted from Anglo-Saxon law via Australia. The regulations are very specific and range from a requirement to cover the genitalia when in town to the prohibition of stealing and assault.

Discussion

I have outlined the therapeutic agents of the intrinsic and extrinsic therapeutic systems of the Taute Wape as these systems impinge on the villagers as resources to combat manifestations of evil. I have not examined the relationship of these agents within a system or the relationship between the systems, nor can I within the scope of this paper. Instead, I will make some comparative observations about the two systems to highlight their ideological, structural, and political differences in a situation of accelerated cultural change.

It is obvious that the extrinsic system is an expression of expatriate culture and was invented and put in place as a moral response to the colonial experience with the indigenous cultures of

Papua New Guinea. I say "moral response" because the expatriates' response to the indigenous culture is in terms of right and wrong as they define it. Operationally speaking, their goal in relation to the indigenous society is to remake it in their own image. In this sense, induced cultural change and therapeutic intervention are simply different terms for the same process. This is hardly a revelation to the fieldwork-trained anthropologist, but a therapeutic-systems approach emphasizes the culturally universal problem of evil and focuses on culture change as fundamentally ideological. Thus a culture undergoes change when new ideas of right and wrong arise within it or are imposed from without, and to enforce the new morality therapeutic agents are installed to rectify offending events.

For example, in Wapeland the role of an indigenous policeman or aid post orderly is initially shaped by Western values, not those of his own culture. He is an active agent of change helping to establish the new morality. He is also a role model for village boys, who may see him as closely associated with the sources of external political power and the glamour of modernity. Since Papua New Guinea's achievement of independence in 1975 and the acceleration of the "localization" job program to replace expatriates with nationals, the visibility of New Guineans within the extrinsic system has greatly increased, as has the importance of their role in the process of cultural change.

A related difference is that the languages of the extrinsic system are English and Tok Pisin, both symbols of expatriate culture and its political power, while the language of the intrinsic system is an indigenous one that, while spoken by everyone, is not a prestige language. Here the males of Taute have considerable edge over the women. While no villager speaks English, all of the men and boys speak Tok Pisin although few of the women and girls do.[16]

When the Taute Wape's extrinsic and intrinsic therapeutic systems are contrasted from a Western viewpoint, the former becomes an alternative model for the latter and, as I have noted, should eventually replace it. The two systems are viewed as symmetrical in their competition to accomplish the same ends. They are also oppositional in that the extrinsic system is seen as sophisticated and learned, the intrinsic system as primitive and unenlightened. While the intrinsic system is not utilized by the expatriate, nor is she or he subject to it, the extrinsic system is used, in part, by both villagers and expatriates. The important differ-

ence here is that villagers do not initiate actions that impose an extrinsic therapeutic agent upon an expatriate. Expatriates use the extrinsic system to cure or discipline Taute villagers; the reverse rarely occurs.

The villager's view of the two therapeutic systems is radically different from the expatriate's. The villager perceives them as complementary, not symmetrical; the one begins where the other leaves off. The intrinsic system explains as well as intervenes to confront evil. The extrinsic system does not explain, but it has some powerful tools for combatting evil that greatly augment the villagers' therapeutic armamentarium. Thus from the village perspective the two systems are relatively harmonious, each offering something the other lacks. There are differences, however, in the ways in which villagers utilize agents of the two systems. As one might expect, the services of the intrinsic system are utilized before resorting to the services of the extrinsic system. This appears to be true whether an individual is trying to right an injustice or cure a sickness. The intrinsic system has explanatory power that the extrinsic one lacks, and it is basic to enculturation, but there is another reason for choosing it that relates to the ties of the extrinsic system to a powerful external government. The villager does not understand all of the premises of the expatriates' culture and therefore cannot predict with certainty the outcome of an interaction. The danger of the expatriate's using his or her political power against the villager is ever-present. One may be friendly, but wary.

In terms of the ideological premises of the two systems, the extrinsic system is primarily secular, the intrinsic one primarily religious. This is why the rationales of the extrinsic system are so unconvincing, even irrelevant, to the villagers. Their beliefs in the magical powers of ancestral ghosts, demons, and curers give them unassailable knowledge. Every member of Taute Wape society has relatively quick and easy access to absolute knowledge regarding the causes of sickness and deviance. It is the kind of knowledge about evil that is tightly interwoven into the dense fabric of everyday life. There are few loose threads, few dangling unknowns. There may not be unanimity about a particular issue, but there is rarely ignorance. Thus the ideological stances of the two systems are contradictory. There is, however, no evidence that this ideological discontinuity is disjunctive in the social or psychological lives of the villagers.[17] To them, the extrinsic therapeutic system is an exotic creation. To utilize it for one's benefit does not require one to believe or even understand its underlying principles.

An ideological difference of greater significance pertains to the organization of social relationships. The therapeutic agents within the intrinsic system reflect the strong egalitarian ethic of Wape society, buttressed by a relentless exchange system based on kinship and marriage that prevents the accumulation of wealth or power. In traditional Wape society there are no headmen, and personal influence is circumscribed by one's kinship statuses. Power is diffused throughout the society, just as it is within the intrinsic therapeutic system. By contrast, the extrinsic therapeutic system is strongly hierarchical, with clearly marked power centers in which kinship and marriage are relatively unimportant and race, class, and education major concerns. This contrast between the two systems is deep and irreconcilable. It poses a fundamental problem for the Taute Wape and the larger indigenous society. As more Wape men and women are educated and begin to move into government-paid occupations as teachers, administrators, and health workers, the ideological schism between Wape egalitarianism and Western hierarchialism becomes increasingly grave. Although the new morality includes the attainment of concentrated power and wealth, this is impossible for a Wape person who must, at the same time, maintain toward kin extensive economic obligations that systematically siphon off wealth. The most viable solution may be to work in another region and rarely return home.

While I have based this paper on the conditions that prevailed during my 1970–72 fieldwork, much that I have written about the therapeutic systems of the Taute Wape remains directly relevant today. The cultural problems have not significantly changed with independence. The independent government of Papua New Guinea is solidly built on the Western institutions established first by Germany's, then Australia's colonial administrations. The extrinsic therapeutic system available to the Taute Wape, while somewhat eroded, continues to work toward the eventual transformation of the intrinsic therapeutic system, which remains, even today, highly resilient.

Notes

1. The research was supported by a National Institute of Mental Health Grant (1 RO1 MH 18039) entitled "Studies of Culturally Contrasting Therapeutic Systems: A Comparative Field Study of Interacting Traditional and Modern Therapeutic Systems in New Guinea." I was accompanied by Joyce Slayton Mitchell, who assisted with the study, and our two preschool-age children. An earlier reconnaissance of the Sepik area was financed, in part, by a grant from the Wenner-Gren Foundation.

2. As this paper goes to press, the idea of evil is the subject of a new book edited by Parkin (1985).

3. See Mitchell (1977b) for a more extended discussion of ethnotherapy as a field of inquiry and Mitchell (1975) for a partial example of its practice.

4. For more detailed information on Wape culture, see Mitchell (1978a, b, c, 1973).

5. See the articles by Dye and Haiveta in this volume for a discussion of the village meeting in the villages of Wagu and Maindroin respectively.

6. For a phonemic and grammatical description of Olo, see McGregor and McGregor (1982).

7. The form of witchcraft prevalent among the Wape and in other parts of the Sepik is called *sanguma* (Tok Pisin). For an account of sanguma among the Lujere of the Yellow River, see Mitchell (1977a), and see Kelm in this volume on sanguma in Abrau and Kwieftim.

8. On the Aitape coast, however, Haiveta (in this volume) reports that the glasman treats as well as diagnoses but does not accept fees. He also appeals to God during the consultation. I did not observe this among the Wape.

9. See McGregor (1982) for a detailed description of the *niyel* curing festival by a Christian Brethren missionary who had lived in Wapeland for fifteen years and was fluent in Olo.

10. Interview with L. R. Healy, medical assistant, who came to Lumi in September 1949 to build a government hospital.

11. For example, during February 1971, Tauteans made forty-nine visits to the Wilkili aid post. Fifty-seven percent of the visits were for the treatment of sores, 24 percent for the treatment of malaria.

12. For more information on the clinics at the time of my fieldwork, see Biddulph (1969).

13. According to Wark (1971:3), in 1970 the ten most frequent diseases treated were malnutrition, 21 percent; acute respiratory-tract infections, 20 percent; skin infections, 5 percent; maternity, malaria, anemia, and gastroenteritis, each 4 percent; and tropical ulcers, measles, and wounds, each 3 percent. The relatively high percentage of malnutrition cases is related to the very active maternal–child health clinics. In 1966, when but half of the present population was patrolled, only 8 percent of the patients were admitted for malnutrition.

14. See Joyce S. Mitchell (1973) for an account of this event.

15. The only exception, small but important, was a bottle of mercurochrome that I kept on the verandah for anyone who wished to use it.

16. The opportunity for women to become more directly involved in the new morality is increasing, however, even in rural villages like Taute. When I revisited the village in 1982, there was a government primary school, and all the boys and girls in attendance knew Tok Pisin and were learning English.

17. This may not be the case for educated Wape men and women, who are caught in a dilemma of following old feelings or new learning.

39/ Health Care Alternatives in Maindroin

Chris Haiveta

Maindroin is situated on the coast thirty-five kilometers west of Aitape in the West Sepik Province.[1] Together with the villages of Amsor, Mainar, and Nimas, it forms the Sissano ethnic group, numbering 1,271 in the 1980 census. Villagers speak Sissano, an Austronesian language linked to Malol. With Warapu, the villages lie on the northern bank of a brackish channel that runs east-west parallel to a coastal strip of undulating beach ridges, some ten kilometers long and two to five hundred meters wide, that stretches to the mouth of the Rainbrum River. Inland, across the channel, are swampy plains, a few limestone hills, and mid-height forests that converge with mangrove and nipa tidal flats on the fringes of the lagoon and extend to the foothills of the Torricelli and Bewani Mountains.

Maindroin, the second largest and westernmost of the Sissano villages, consisted of sixty households with a total resident population of 361 at the time of my research. The population is evenly divided between the sexes, with a large proportion (44.8 percent) under the age of fifteen. Young people who work outside of the village tend to return home for most of their holidays. Further, surprisingly, the nearby towns of Wewak, Aitape, and Vanimo have failed to attract many young men and women. (In contrast, many Lumis and Nukus have moved across the ridges to squat on the outskirts of Aitape and Vanimo townships.)

The village is divided into six small localized landowning patrilineal clans: Raintenien, Airoin 1, Airoin 2, Tarperin, Nowul, and Luniv. Raintenien and Airoin 1 both trace their origin to Amake, the founder of the village, while the other clans are immigrants. Clan leaders are considered the keepers of clan spirits or *parak*, in constant communication with them and deeply knowledgeable about their powers, both beneficial and malevolent. They act as mediators, high priests, and spokesmen for the spirits in meeting the needs of their clans and regulating the social life of the clans and the village as a whole. In addition to attending to the welfare of the group, clan leaders have the power to heal and to call upon clan spirits to punish wrongdoers. Clan leadership is inherited, usually patrilineally.

While clans are very important in village life, the nuclear family is the most important unit of production. Most subsistence needs are met on this level; the few exceptions include house building and group hunting or fishing. Subsistence is based on hunting, gardening, and sago exploitation. Economic activity in the cash sector is low-key. The village has two trade stores, a kerosene dealer, and a clan-owned copra-drying shed. Copra is the main export crop. There is also a cattle project, initiated under a village development fellowship scheme, that now has fourteen head of cattle; this venture is organized along clan lines and collectively owned by members of a clan. There are two outboards and an aluminum dinghy, individually owned, and an outboard repair shop. Most villagers get money by marketing surplus fish, garden foods, greens, sago, and green coconuts to one another or to the mission schoolteachers and patrol post staff. Remittances are another source of income.

With the other Sissano villages and Warapu, Maindroin enjoys a number of services provided by the Catholic mission, staffed by a priest and five nuns who run a clinic and teach at the mission community school and girls' vocational center near the village. The mission airstrip is used by Franair plans to bring mail and supplies. The patrol post at nearby Raintapot, staffed by a patrol officer and an agricultural officer, provides assistance in keeping law and order in the village and advising the various economic projects undertaken by villagers.

Health Care in Maindroin since First Contact

Oral accounts of local history indicate that Malay traders were the first foreigners to come into contact with the Sissano people. Four years after the earthquake of 1907, which destroyed the old Warapu village, the Catholic Society of the Divine Word (SVD) from Germany established the Sissano mission at its present site. From 1911 to 1916, two white men had prolonged contact with the people of Sissano: the first parish priest, Father Jaesche, who soon died of malaria, and Father Hoerlein, who replaced him, assisted by a lay brother. From 1916 to 1918, the station was closed by the British as a result of their war with Germany. As soon as the war was over, the missionaries were allowed to return to Sissano, and they remained there until 1943, when the priest Father Fastinrath was taken into custody by the Japanese. He returned only in 1947, and two years later Franciscan missionaries took over control of the station. Franciscan nuns arrived from Queensland to establish a convent and start medical work in Sissano in 1962.

Contact with modern drugs and an awareness of a medical care system different from their own apparently began for villagers much earlier, however. When the SVD missionaries established their station at Sissano, they built a house for the local parish priest, and on its verandah was kept a little box, looked after by a lay brother, in which there were bandages, cotton swabs, gentian violet, iodine, antiseptic ointment, gauze, wood splinters for applying ointment to sores, and syringes and needles for injections. Medicine for injections was kept inside in a room forbidden to all except the cook and the priest or lay brother. Once a year all the children would be lined up in front of the priest's house for inspection, and he would select those with large sores or other acute ailments for treatment. The injections he gave them are said to have been very painful and strong; small children had to be carried home afterward and developed swollen lumps on their buttocks that lasted a day or two. The priest would visit them in their villages later, and older people with health problems identified during these visits might also receive injections.

Medical supplies came in once a year from Wewak or Madang, the mission's headquarters. Especially the older people came to believe that these boxes contained mysterious magical elements that the white man carefully guarded. Afraid that the medicine would kill them, most people never went to the priest voluntarily, relying instead on local remedies and hit-or-miss identification for treatment during his visits. The mission catechist at Sissano kept an eye on people and informed the priest about seriously ill adults. The priest would then visit the village and try to persuade the sick persons to come and see him at the mission station. The critically ill would be sent by canoe to Malol and then carried on

stretchers to the old hospital in Aitape. There was no motorized transport and no good road, although the priest at Malol did have horses, used mainly to carry medical supplies.

Around this time, the German administration introduced the *dokta boi* ([Tok Pisin] medical aide), a village man trained in Aitape in the use of the basic medicines and the dressing of sores. On completion of the course he would be given a letter indicating that he had received this training and a cap similar to the one worn by the *luluai* (local appointed government official) with a white band and a red cross on its peak. The dokta boi treated villagers mostly for cuts and abrasions, using antiseptic ointment or iodine and bandages. If a person's condition was serious and he favored using the introduced medical care system, he was more likely to go to the priest. After World War II, the dokta boi, together with the luluai and the *tultul* (interpreter), was called upon to hand in his cap at the government office in Aitape. From 1954 on, training as aid-post orderly was offered at the Aitape hospital. No such orderly was ever stationed in Maindroin itself; the villager who has become an orderly works in Warapu.

The Franciscan nuns who arrived in the sixties were perceived as kind and friendly, giving sweets to the children and newspapers for rolling cigarettes to their mothers to encourage them to use their health-care services. The nuns' own initial reactions to the circumstances in which they found themselves were quite negative (Agnella 1972:63):

A few nights after our arrival we had our first night call to the beach. A woman was giving birth to a child and needed help. Two sisters set off with their lantern. The beach was quite close to us but each woman went to that part of the beach nearest her own village. After an hour or so the sisters were back. They were appalled that any woman should give birth to a child in such conditions on the open beach on the sand, without even a clean towel or a drop of clean water. We were yet to get used to this as time went on. . . .

The lack of any form of hygiene was appalling. The babies were so dirty and covered in sores around which the flies gathered. Yaws are horrible sores. Would it ever be possible to teach these people to be clean?

The sisters got down to medical work quickly, one look at the children covered in dirty sores made us all want to run for clean bandages. The natives came every morning for treatment. Great big tropical ulcers covered with leaves! Babies covered with yaws from head to foot! Neglected cuts and abrasions! Conjunctivitis was very common. Many women were blind or nearly so.

The sisters set about their work with energy, concentrating on maternal and child health mainly because of the rules governing intimate contact between males and females and fear of the effects of the white man's magic medicine. Young children were generally in the care of their mothers and other females, and, during this time when the healing powers of the clan spirits were being challenged by the agents of a seemingly stronger God with greater healing powers and material wealth, they became the major users of these new services.

Over the years the people's attitude has changed to one of general trust in the efficacy of medicine, and social barriers between the sisters and the men have lowered sufficiently to allow men to be touched and treated for minor complaints by them. Elderly men are usually afraid to allow treatment or discussion of major illnesses by the nuns and may even walk to the Warapu aid post as an alternative.

Indigenous Healing in Maindroin Today

In their early years at Sissano, the Catholic missionaries destroyed all the physical paraphernalia of clan identity, which they considered harmful to their teachings. Men's sleeping houses and parak houses in the village were destroyed, and crucifixes were erected on the sites. The people simply built replicas of the old houses in the forest, and men began to live with their wives and children. In another attempt to suppress traditional beliefs in the 1930s, the missionaries had the forest parak houses destroyed and brought all the sacred ceremonial objects they contained to the church, where, after a brief ceremony, they burned them in front of the villagers to show that the power of the Christian God was greater than that of the parak.

At the same time, a nontraditional healing cult arose whose adherents vigorously opposed the traditional healers and employed Christian beliefs and practices alongside traditional ones. They claimed that the parak had been superseded by the Christian God. Even after all the physical

TABLE 1
CLANS AND THEIR ASSOCIATED ILLNESSES

CLAN	TOTEM	PARAK	ILLNESS
Raintenien	Troklau (eagle)	Nisawain, Trui Hamoni, Niwalai (stars)	Headache, crippling ailments
Airoin 1	Troklau (eagle)	Melai (ginger)	Aches and diarrhea
Airoin 2	Sultun (croton)	Melai (ginger)	Aches and diarrhea
Tarperin	Pao	Tarperin (tuber with medicinal and magical properties)	Sore ribs and respiratory ailments
Nowul	Noyun	Nowul (magical vine)	Sore ribs and respiratory ailments
Luniv	Luniv	Nurlpanas (magical vine)	Aches and diarrhea

traces of the parak had been removed, however, belief in and identification with them persisted. Clan groupings traditionally centered around parak houses are still very important in ordering social relations and influencing beliefs and practices in relation to health care. Clan leaders are one of the two main groups of healers who provide medical care alternatives to the clinic today. These traditional healers combine knowledge of medicinal plants and concoctions with ritual. In contrast, the *glasman* ([Tok Pisin] seers) combine Christian faith healing and exorcism with some elements of traditional healing.

The traditional healer derives his power to cure illness from his clan parak. Although claiming to be the medium of the parak, he does not in any way manipulate them for malevolent purposes, for instance, to cause illness in an innocent person. He is, however, credited with the power to do so. Anyone can cause the parak to afflict another if he is wronged, and the parak may also act on the wronged person's behalf even if he or she is unaware of it or does not seek retribution. Children are considered more vulnerable than adults to parak affliction, and therefore parents and relatives try to live according to the rules so that children need not suffer for wrongs committed by their elders.

Certain major or common illnesses are associated with particular clans (table 1). The belief that each clan has its particular illness may mean that some illnesses are more common among their members. It certainly means that some illnesses have an easily comprehensible cause over which the society and the individual have some measure of control. Clan illness is caused only by the clan parak, and it occurs when a rule or law of the village is broken. The parak, the guardian spirit of the clan, oversees and regulates reciprocal relations and ensures egalitarianism by the use of rewards and punishments. A person may be made ill by the parak for not following the rules of reciprocity (e.g., not sharing a food surplus with clan members and relatives) or for breaking other rules (e.g., not keeping his yard clean, especially if his house is near a former parak or *masalai* [(Tok Pisin) nature spirit] site, or stealing).

During my research, for example, a subclan had promised to give one of its members a pig before he left for a teaching job. As the time for his departure approached and hunts were repeatedly unsuccessful, subclan members came to feel that the parak was displeased with them for failing to keep their promise. Since the parak is believed to confer good luck in hunting, fishing, and gardening, it had to be appeased. It was therefore decided that the ladder of the bush house that is now generally recognized as the clan parak house would be repaired. When the repairs had been completed, a little platform was built in the village near the clan leader's house, and food was prepared by females of the group. In the evening, the food was shared and eaten by all the male members of the clan, and afterward the village string band played. People came from all the Sissano villages to watch or participate in the dancing. Females, both young and very old, and young boys made up the majority of the dancers, while everyone else watched and joked throughout the night. In addition to appeasing the parak, the party served to strengthen clan morale and goodwill among members and in the village as a whole, and the hunt the next day was successful.

If a person is sick, the clan leaders and elders are informed, and they meet to consider the cause of the sickness. The patient's actions are recalled, and an effort is made to pinpoint actions that might have angered the parak. This discussion usually produces a consensus as to the cause. In some instances, if the person implicated is a group member, he will get up and admit his guilt. Then the sick person is washed with a cup of water by the guilty person, who tells the spirit to leave him. Later he is expected to try to mend the broken social relationship that is the ultimate cause of the illness. It is said that if the person identified in this way is truly guilty, the spirit leaves the sick person and he gets well. Continued illness, then, implies some other cause. At this point a small meal of meat is prepared for the elders, who gather again to discuss the case. This is seen as a direct offering to the parak, which is believed to guide such discussion and reveal the true cause of the sickness. If the patient's condition is very serious and clan discussions have not helped, the mother's clan group may be asked to participate in the discussion.

In the past, the drawing of foreign objects such as pieces of bone or human hair out of the body by hand, using bark and leaves, was common, but today most traditional healers regard it as dirty, harmful, and farcical. Practices that persist, along with group discussion and washing with water, include steam baths and the spitting of herbal mixtures into the air around the sick person to drive out the parak. The herbs used in healing are also used by the healers to induce dreaming. Events from such dreams are recalled during the discussions and linked to specific human actions and actors. (Induced dreams are also used to predict events, such as death or luck in the hunt.)

From the table of clan illnesses it is clear that they are all ailments without clear physical causes; sores, wounds, and cuts are not included. There is also no mention of boils, fever, and malaria, which may have been endemic and common to all regardless of clan membership. For these ailments, there were traditional herbal medicines. For example, for the skin infection of grille, *aitisis*, a flowering bush usually found near fresh water, was rubbed on the affected area. For fresh cuts and wounds, the bark of the betel palm and the *palpal* tree was scraped and the mixture boiled to form a paste that was applied to the wound. For large sores, the broad, fleshy leaves of a local tuber called *woight* were heated until tender and then rubbed between the hands to extract the juice, which was poured onto the sore. Another woight leaf was then put over the sore as a covering or dressing and tied in place with a piece of string. For small sores, the sap of the *airopa* was used. For severe headaches, incisions were made on the forehead to let out the bad blood that was causing them. Although this knowledge remains in the village, especially among members of the older generation, modern medical services and drugs have entirely replaced this facet of traditional medicine. Plants are, however, still used as protection against evil procured by an enemy through *poisin* ([Tok Pisin] sorcery) or the parak.

The other main type of healer, the glasman, differs from the traditional healer in methods, position in the village, and belief system in terms of which cures are effected. Glasman first appeared in Maindroin after World War II and later spread to the other Sissano villages and to Warapu, Arop, and Malol. The first glasman from this area told me that they were the new generation of healers who helped stop many of the traditional ways of healing, such as the spitting of chewed betel nut and herbal mixtures onto the sick person and the extraction of foreign objects thought to have been introduced into his body by the parak. These practices associated with the parak had been condemned and aggressively stamped out by the early missionaries, whose Christian God the glasman believed had the ultimate power to heal any type of sickness.

The first glasman, now in his early fifties, says that he got his power at the Aitape hospital, where he was looking after a child of his who had been born with a twisted leg in 1947. During the war he had served as a carrier for the Allied troops in the Sepik region, and he had had extensive outside experience before returning home to settle down and marry. The birth of his first child with a malformed leg led him to seek the services of the doctor at Aitape, where the child was hospitalized for about six months. One night around midnight, he felt something fill him spiritually, as if his parak had entered him (an experience apparently similar to religious and spiritual awakenings being experienced in Christian revival and charismatic movements today). He began to speak in tongues, and he had a vision about happenings back home during his absence. Eyewitnesses later told him that he had spoken of God and talked as if he were very learned and preaching from the Bible.

After this occurrence, he stayed on at the hospital for the rest of the time required for his son's leg to be straightened and then left for home. He claims that although he was given the power to heal at the time of the incident, he was not aware of its purpose until he returned home. His first case was that of his own wife, whom he diagnosed as afflicted by her patriclan parak. He was moved by her condition, upon the directive of a more powerful entity and without really realizing the significance of his action, to undertake the first-ever act of glasman diagnosis and ritual of spiritual healing. Word of it spread, and villagers who were not really satisfied with either the tra-

ditional practices or the modern medical services began to come to him for cures. The ritual of diagnosis and healing was the same for all ages and sexes and transcended clan boundaries. Other men from Sissano, especially from his own age-group and younger, started following him around in the hope of being taught the secrets of the practice and acquiring the power. Most of his original disciples had had similar experiences and exposure to Australian, German, and Japanese administrations and mission, trader, and plantation influences both within and outside of the Sissano setting. These apprentices accompanied the glasman, observing and acting upon his directions in ministering to the sick. No other qualification was necessary than the wish to acquire the glasman's gift of healing powers and adherence to the code of ethics embodied in his actions and advice. The phenomenon or cult of the glasman spread from Maindroin throughout Sissano, along the coast from Serra to Matapau, and into the interior behind the Torricelli Mountains,[2] but it is at Sissano that one finds the largest group of acknowledged glasman on the north coast.

The glasman has been described as "a seer, anyone who claims the gift of seeing the spirits or communicating with them, anyone who sees future events in his dream" (Mihalic 1971:88). (The term *glasman* may have something to do with the examination through a microscope of blood samples on glass slides observed by local people in hospitals.) In the Maindroin context, he is a person with the ability to see *past* events that point to the cause of sickness and the power to heal in a state of trance. Today glasman are the more influential group of healers, although the situation has become confused as some traditional healers have adopted glasman techniques. They tend to be called in when an illness has resisted attempts at a traditional cure.

Glasman believe that most illnesses are caused by parak or masalai, *sanguma*[3] ([Tok Pisin] witchcraft), or poisin. Illnesses that do not respond quickly to the available curing practices, especially when the sick person is an adult, are attributed mostly to poisin. Poisin is performed in secret by a specialist, and people in the village are not sure who is a *poisinman*. Because of the short duration of my stay, I obtained no firm evidence about sorcery. Sorcerers were reportedly mostly male, inherited their positions, and acted as a social control mechanisms in village life. The absence of any recognized sorcerer and the proliferation of healing practices indicate a leaning toward benevolent magic for social control, but acknowledgment of the existence of sorcery in itself acts as a deterrent, especially after a death.

Sanguma is also acknowledged to exist, although it is reputed to be practiced by inland people whose services are utilized by Sissano who need them. Their role is similar to the poisinman's, although sanguma is said to be more deadly and effective. Illnesses through to be caused by either sanguma or poisin are brought to traditional healers or glasman, who confirm or reject earlier diagnoses and recommend treatment. Poisin is reported to be treated with some success, especially by glasman; sanguma is very rare and usually fatal, glasman assistance being sought very late.

With illness caused by spirits, the glasman's task is to identify the type of spirit and drive it out in the appropriate manner. (It is not clear whether spirits possess the sick person. Parak traditionally did possess clan members, especially older men who had undergone initiation, during traditional dancing and singing.) If the spirit is a good spirit, he gently coaxes it out of the sick person, but if it is a bad spirit he banishes it violently. The urgency and sense of drama involved in a healing session vary with the nature of the illness. If a person is very sick, the glasman displays a state of high nervous tension, emotion, and excitement. Glasman say that the power to drive out spirits is not inherent in them; it is only released through them by God in these healing episodes. They say, and people in general agree, that even after a healing session in which the sick person gives the appearance of recovery, he is still vulnerable to spirit affliction until all the other recommended activities are completed. A spirit that has been driven out goes to an unknown place and stays there with others of its kind until a wrong is once again committed.

The following account is typical of the glasman activities in Maindroin to which I was an eyewitness. Late one night, as I sat conversing with a glasman in front of his house, a young father came to us carrying his child of one to two years of age, who was crying loudly and unceasingly. The father explained to the glasman that his child, who was slightly feverish, had been crying since evening and he wanted the glasman to cure it. The glasman got up and went into his house to fetch his bottle of holy water and his rosary. In the meantime, the child's mother arrived and tried to feed it to no avail.

When the glasman returned, he lifted his face to the dark void of a starless night, made the sign of the cross, and began to pray in Tok Pisin to God to help him *rausim spirit nogut* (drive out the evil spirit). After praying loudly for about five minutes, he opened the container of holy water and sprinkled some on the child. Then he asked the mother to hand him the child and blew all over it, saying soothing words to it and calling upon God to drive away the evil spirit and cure it. When he gave the child back to its mother, its crying had decreased noticeably; it vomited for a few seconds and then quieted down against its mother's breast. The glasman sat down and held up the rosary and holy water again as before, praying much more fervently. Then, as if speaking to God in a trance, he said that he understood very well what he was being told and would tell the parents the course of remedial action to be followed.

After this episode, he again returned to the child, blew on it again, and sprinkled more holy water on it. During this interaction the baby cried much louder, but it quieted down again after the glasman had finished. He said that the baby was all right now, and he explained why it had been crying: the mother had ventured into a forbidden place where two masalai lived, and they had become angry and consequently made the child sick. He advised her not to go there again and to take the child to the clinic the next day, and the couple thanked the glasman, said goodnight to us, and left. (No gifts were given to the glasman.) Early next morning I went to the couple's house and inquired about the child, and they said that all the crying and fever had stopped during or after our meeting and they and the child had had a good night's sleep. Later in the day the mother took the child to the clinic for a checkup.

There is only one glasman in Maindroin, but people consult glasman in other villages if he is unavailable. In these sessions glasman seem to enter into a trance that symbolizes an open line of communication with God. The ultimate causes of the illness they cure are always phrased in terms of human actors and their social relations, the physical environment, and the spirits. The code of ethics to which they must adhere to retain their healing power is rigidly biblical, including strict observance of the Ten Commandments, regular (preferably daily) attendance at mass, refusal to accept payment for services,[4] and availability to any needy person at any time of the day or night. There is no sign of capital accumulation among glasman; their ideology does not allow it.

Conclusions

Traditionally, Maindroin men generally left the health and welfare of their children to the women, being preoccupied with defending their territory and regulating village life. They played their prescribed roles during pregnancy and birth ceremonies and observed restrictions on their activities, including postpartum sex taboos, while the children were young. Healing was explained in terms of spiritual and social causation in a framework of clan-specific illnesses that had developed over generations, and men played an important role as healers. When modern medical services were introduced into this situation, their effects on the health of the population, especially the young, were held in awe, and magical properties were sometimes ascribed to the drugs used. The introduction of the dokta boi, a local male from the village, provided an avenue for more understanding and better utilization of the services provided. The arrival of the sisters heralded the beginning of more systematic and intensive care for children and their mothers. Men, by the general rules governing contact with females, could not bring their children to the sisters for attention and therefore played a very limited role in child health care.

Catholic mission suppression of local culture in the initial stages of contact, other European influences, and the mission's strong advocacy of and association with the maintenance of a medical service that at first seemed magical in its efficacy but was materialistic in its approach all contributed to the rise of the syncretic glasman cult. In the long run, glasman weakened the grasp of traditional clan healers on their practice. Glasman used the Christian belief in God as the overarching power to adapt the traditional ideology of clan illnesses and parak affliction to their own practice. Because glasman live in the village, they can be reached much more quickly than the clinic personnel, and when a person is very ill the glasman is called in. Glasman diagnosis and treatment are within the grasp of the Maindroin villager, and the social causes identified tend to perpetuate the overall social order or structure of village life. Glasman have shown greater flexibility in changing times than the traditional healers, who have now begun to use some glasman practices although not the Christian elements of their ritual. Traditional healers, being clan leaders, though not so important in health care, are still quite important in other social, political, and economic affairs in the village.

The use of the health care alternatives to the modern medical services always involves the father of a sick child as well as the mother. The presence of both parents is prompted by the fact that parak-affliction explanations for illness are usually based on the social behavior of a parent or a member of his matri- or patriclan. The remedy, which includes an act of appeasement, is communal and usually involves the mending of reciprocal relations, in which both parents must also participate. The glasman is often sought in cases for which modern medical treatment is considered ineffective. The participation of the father in the attempt at curing underlines the importance he places on his relationship with his child and also the value of the service the glasman provides.

Males have on the whole suffered alienation from the health care services provided by the mission, but they make key decisions during times of serious illness in their children. The failure of the modern clinic to recognize and deal with this has contributed to the persistence of traditional and glasman healing. It is clear that, as modern health care is extended to rural communities, there needs to be a careful examination of local health care strategies and of the local social conditions under which these services are provided.

Notes

1. Research in Maindroin was carried out over a period of five weeks from January 4 to February 20, 1982. I stayed with a family in the village and carried out observations, informal discussions, and interviews with members of the community, mostly males, to gather data for this essay, which formed part of my B.A. Honours thesis at the University of Papua New Guinea. I wish to express thanks to the following individuals who helped with this work: in the field, Melchior Kapaith, Father Urban, Sister Martina, Kiap Edward, Brother Garry, Giles Aiyari, Bonny Lissai, and the many others who helped me be a part of the Maindroin community; at the Institute of Applied Social and Economic Research, Louise Morauta, Pat Townsend, Richard Jackson, Michael Walter, Mandy Pratt, Robert Makai, the accounting staff, and the typists, including my wife; at the University of Papua New Guinea, Ruth Latukefu, Maev O'Collins, and Marc Schiltz.

2. See Mitchell in this volume for a brief description of glasman in the Lumi area of the Torricelli Mountains.

3. The local practices of poisin and sanguma are similar to those found in many north-coast societies. Poisin involves taking a piece of dirt or a possession of the victim, mixing it with special herbs, sealing it, and uttering spells over it to cause the victim's illness or

death. Sanguma involves a planned attack on the victim, who is first blinded by spells and lime, by a professional sanguma man. The victim's intestines are removed and his stomach stuffed with leaves before being sewn up; then he is released from sleep to return home, unaware of the attack, after the sanguma man has suggested to him the time and place of his death.

(See Kelm in this volume for an account of sanguma beliefs in Abrau and Kweiftim.)

4. Though no cash payment or substantial material reward is involved, the long-term social rewards of status and influence are important. A glasman may share an occasional meal, chew betel nut, or smoke with participants in a healing episode.

40/ *Sanguma* in Abrau and Kwieftim

Antje Kelm

In 1969 and 1970, my late husband, Heinz Kelm, and I carried out ethnographic fieldwork in the Lumi region of the West Sepik Province, where we spent several months in the villages of Abrau and Kwieftim. Until then the two villages had had very little contact with Europeans. A Christian Missions in Many Lands missionary had worked in Kwieftim for several years in the sixties, but he had left the village in 1967 or 1968. The inhabitants of Abrau had always resisted any kind of Christianization. Around 1968, a native teacher from one of the Yellow River villages had started a school in Abrau that quite a few children had attended. After some months, however, this teacher had hurriedly returned to his home village because, our informants explained, he was afraid that the Abrau might practice *sanguma*, a special kind of witchcraft, upon him.

Although the people of Kwieftim, under the missionary's influence, had given up some of their traditional rites (especially initiation and, of course, war festivals), life in both villages in 1969 and 1970 could be regarded as rather traditional. This was one of the reasons we selected them for our fieldwork. In addition, Abrau had been recommended to us because its inhabitants were feared throughout the region as practitioners of sanguma. The Wape (see Mitchell in this volume) of the Lumi region are said to have been afraid of the Abrau on this account, and Lynn Wark, an Australian doctor stationed at Lumi at the time, told us that fear of sanguma prevailed even among the Christianized and educated staff of the Lumi hospital. Once when she had had to stay overnight in Abrau, the medical assistants accompanying her had asked to be allowed to share her house, saying that they were afraid to sleep alone in the house reserved for them because of the possibility of a sanguma attack, and then had been unable to sleep even in the presence of a European.

The distribution of sanguma from the Torricelli Mountains to the villages on the lower course of the Yellow River is confirmed by the work of Mitchell (1977), who studied it among the Lujere, neighbors and traditional enemies of the Abrau. (Having revisited the region in 1983, he reports [personal communication, 1984] that the fear of sanguma among the Lujere has not altered and may even have increased.)

Sanguma is the special kind of malevolent or destructive magic that in German ethnography is called *Todeszauber*. Whereas most researchers writing in English have referred to it as sorcery or assault sorcery (see, e.g., Glick 1982:1029), Mitchell (1977:1) has convincingly argued that it should be considered witchcraft because it involves the possession of personal magical powers, a characteristic of witches and not of sorcerers. It would not, however, be appropriate to use the German *Hexerei* for sanguma, because it is *Zauber* that involves the control of secret powers or spirits by the practitioner. Furthermore, *Hexerei* refers only to destructive magic, whereas *Zauber* may be either negative or positive. This seems important because Mitchell shows that the Lujere view sanguma practitioners as curers as well and describes them as shamans or witch-shamans. Our field material also points to a dual role for sanguma men.

In Kwieftim, the existence of sanguma was generally known, but people did not seem to fear it very much. In Abrau, in contrast, everyone not only knew about but greatly feared it. Here sanguma was closely connected with the Kari (Mitchell's Lujere), with whom the Abrau had long lived in a more or less continuous state of war and whom since the cessation of warfare under the Australian administration they had continued to regard as enemies. The hostility between the two groups at the time of our fieldwork found its expression in continuous accusations of sanguma.[1]

A few weeks after our arrival in Abrau, Aitäpu, a woman of less than twenty, died in childbirth. Immediately everyone in the village explained this death of a young and healthy person as the result of sanguma, and everyone was ready to tell us that the Kari were responsible. The death had occurred in the hamlet of Arieki, about a mile from the house where we were staying, and therefore we only became aware of it after the fact. During the night, when the delivery had turned out to be difficult and many people had assembled in the house, some had wondered whether it would be useful to go and get help.

Two men from the neighboring village of Yakel-tim (of the same language group as Abrau) had argued in particular that we might be able to help with our Western medicine. But, as these men explained to us the next morning, all the others had maintained that only sanguma could explain the young woman's difficulties, and Europeans would be unable to influence sanguma in any way.[2] Besides, to the Abrau it was clear who was responsible for the sanguma: a group of men from the Yellow River villages who had passed through Abrau on their way to Lumi a few days before.

Some days later, we asked our informants, among them the husband of the young woman, to explain the unexpected death. They told us that a few days before the delivery the woman had been working alone outside the village. At a certain place near an areca plantation, the above-mentioned men from the Yellow River had lain in ambush and assaulted her. She had lost consciousness at once, and they had opened her belly with a little bamboo knife (Auwon *leko*) and removed flesh and bone. Then they had pushed the embryo into a corner of the uterus and put many little black kunai worms (Auwon *imoku*) into the uterus alongside it to kill it. (The baby had been stillborn.) Then they had filled the victim's belly with leaves, closed it, and rubbed the wound with kunai grass so that it could not be seen afterwards. Finally, they had packed the flesh and bones into palm-leaf sheaths and left. Later on, in a hidden place, they had cooked and eaten the young woman's flesh with sago pudding. The woman had returned to the village, where she had died a few days later.

A few months later we discussed sanguma with Saine, one of our main informants from Kwieftim. In contrast to the situation in Abrau, where quite a few men who were said to be sanguma men were still alive, we were told that in Kwieftim there were no longer any sanguma men. All its inhabitants knew about sanguma, however, although they had no such traditional enemies as the Kari to accuse of performing it. According to Saine, sanguma can be performed only by certain specialists called *naukuitetú* (in Ak) or *auwaiye ölmon* (in Auwon). Before undertaking a sanguma attack these men assemble and prepare themselves by chewing betel for hours and drinking human blood. Then they fly to a certain lonely place and hide near a path where someone is expected to come along. (Sanguma men have special wing bones hidden in their arms that they can allow to protrude from their elbows when they want to fly.) When they see a solitary traveler

(whether man or woman) coming along the path, they attack from behind, beating the victim with clubs until he or she falls unconscious. Then they cut open the victim's belly with a small bamboo knife, take out the flesh, and fill the hole with kunai grass or leaves. Then they carefully close the wound so that no scar or any other sign of the attack remains. Next they hide nearby and wait until the victim regains consciousness to watch him or her gather up his or her belongings and return home. The person attacked will be unable to remember what has happened, and he or she will die within a few days.

When we asked the reason for such attacks, Saine assured us that it was not revenge. (On other occasions, we had been told by others that blood vengeance was one of the main reasons for sanguma murders.) Sanguma men had to kill in this way from time to time, he said, because in eating human flesh and drinking human blood they believed themselves to be strengthening the powers they needed for their special tasks, for instance, healing the sick.

Sanguma is widespread in large parts of Papua New Guinea, and many anthropologists have described it and have tried to understand the connection between physical violence and magic. In particular, they have been interested in the reason for the victim's death, and there has been some controversy as to whether any aspect of the sanguma assault is actually practiced (see Patterson 1974:143). One definition of sanguma considered valid by the majority of scholars is the "minimal" definition of Schmitz (1959:47): "the victim is attacked secretly and made unconscious; a series of violent actions is performed on him; then he is restored to consciousness again and sent home; in most cases he is told how long he has left to live. Death then follows immediately." A more detailed definition is that of Höltker (1964:237), who lists the elements of sanguma as follows: ritual preparation (taboos, rites, fasting) of the sanguma men before the attack, aimed at making them invisible; a violent attack on the victim (without witnesses); intentionally suggestive application of physical terror and hypnosis; brutal sadism; violent insertion of objects, especially thorns and bone needles, into the body of the unconscious victim; revival of the victim and the command to return to his village; loss of memory and speech on the part of the victim; and absolutely certain death of the victim within a few days.[3] The ethnographic data leading to Schmitz's and Höltker's definitions were collected in different parts of the East Sepik and Madang Provinces and on the Huon Peninsula many years before our fieldwork in the West Sepik, but the accounts of sanguma attacks given us by our informants are very similar. The main difference is that in relating the cases mentioned above our informants did not refer to the insertion of any objects into the victim's body. In both villages they spoke of the use of small bamboo knives to cut open the body. However, in both villages we were able to collect myths explaining the origins of sanguma, and these myths mention sago thorns in connection with sanguma attacks.

In Abrau we were told the following myth:

A member of the clan of the Tutu, together with his wife, is cutting sago in the bush. While they are working there, they see a lizard. The man takes sago thorns and sticks them into the body of the lizard. He sticks a lot of thorns into the lizard's body. The lizard flees and climbs a sago palm, higher and higher, until it reaches the very top. Suddenly its legs become stiff and it falls, right in front of the man.

"Why, what's that?" the man asks himself. "All the thorns that I stuck into the lizard's skin have disappeared, and there are no wounds or scars to be seen."

Now the man gets tired and dreams. In his dream the spirit (*aukai*) of the lizard shoots him with a tiny bow and arrow. He shoots sanguma all over his body—into his head, his neck, his breast, all parts of his body. Then he says to the man, "You must give me back my legs. Go and kill a man."

"Yes," the man answers. "I'll bring you back your legs."

On awakening, the man reflects on his dream. Then he goes and kills a man. He does exactly what the spirit has shown him in his dream. He shoots the man with a tiny bow and arrow, and the man gets sick and dies. From then on sanguma exists. A lizard has brought sanguma to the clan of the Tutu. Then people from all over the world come and get sanguma from the Tutu.

A similar story was told to us in Kwieftim:

Two men living in mythical times once caught a little lizard. They stuck sago thorns into its skin. They caught the blood that came forth from its wounds and kept it in leaves. After that they let the lizard climb a tree. When after a short time the lizard fell out of the tree, the men found that it had died and began mourning for it. Then they

thought that this was a wonderful way of killing. They wanted to try it with men. On their way to the village they met a dog, and they tried the new method on it. This time they only pointed at the dog with a sago thorn. The dog ran for a little while and then fell dead. Finally, the men tried their new method with an old woman. Pointing at her with a sago thorn, they drew blood from her body, and along with the blood they drew out her soul. Then they cooked the blood, and when it exploded in the heat the old woman got sick and soon died.[4]

In these descriptions there seems to be some confusion about the weapon used to injure and later kill the victim. In the myths, sago thorns are employed, whereas in all the accounts of "real" sanguma attacks bamboo knives are used for the operation. Superficially it may seem as if some of these weapons—the thorns and the little bow and arrow—were being used to shoot the cause of death into the victim's body, and Schmitz (1959:44) and Sterly (1965:207) draw this conclusion from their materials. The Kwieftim variant of the myth allows, however, another explanation: that the weapons (whether arrows or thorns) are used to draw blood from the victim's body, and with the loss of blood the victim also loses his soul and is therefore condemned to die within a few days. The same holds true for our informants' accounts of "real" sanguma cases. With their bamboo knives the sanguma men cut out essential parts of the victim's body, thereby condemning him or her to die within a short period of time. As can be seen from the Kwieftim variant of the sanguma myth, the sanguma assaults with thorns are not to be interpreted as having really happened—the sago thorns are only supposed to have been pointed at the waylaid person. The same conclusion is drawn by Schmitz (1959) and by Sterly (1965); they are convinced that the victim is only magically shot with little arrows or pierced with thorns. Again, it seems to me that in the sanguma cases reported to us in Abrau and Kwieftim, the victims' bodies were only magically cut open, if there was any sanguma assault at all.

Death, in the view of the Abrau and the Kwieftim, comes to the magically condemned person in some other way. The young Abrau woman who died in childbirth was in labor, and therefore not in a normal condition, when death struck her. The Abrau are convinced that the actual cause of her death was the loss of vital parts of her body through the sanguma operation, but they feel that to kill her completely a secondary cause was necessary. While in general women are able to give birth without difficulty, after the sanguma assault this woman did not have the strength to survive this special condition. Other "real" causes of the deaths of persons considered to have been attacked by sanguma men include snakebite, a blow from a falling branch, attack by a wild boar, and a fall over a root in the bush. Prior to the prohibition of warfare, the death of a man in battle might be explained in terms of sanguma, it being held in some cases that the enemy's arrow could only strike a man whose soul had previously been drawn from his body in a sanguma assault.

The case of Aitäpu reveals yet another essential aspect of sanguma beliefs in Abrau and Kwieftim: sanguma is considered an independent spiritual power, and sanguma men are believed to be able to perform their assaults because at certain times they are able to use this power. After Aitäpu's death, the adult men, who up to then had been sitting around in the village, suddenly took their weapons and hurried into the surrounding bush to meet their wives and children, who were working there in their gardens or in the sago swamps. A short time later all the women and children were led home by armed men, and not a single inhabitant of Abrau remained alone in the bush. When we asked the people why they did this, they explained that there was sanguma in the air, and it might strike again, so it would be very dangerous for a person to remain alone in the bush. The most sanguma, in their opinion, was around the house in which Aitäpu had died, and therefore her relatives, especially her husband, had to stay away from it. In my opinion, this means that the Abrau believe that sanguma men can only carry out their assaults when there is sanguma around that they can command for their malicious purposes. If they believed otherwise, the Abrau would always hide in their houses or remain in the village when Kari men were passing through.[5]

Later, in Kwieftim, we were told that sanguma was an independent power. The sanguma men are believed to command part of this power, which can be bound to certain objects—for example, dried human flesh (parts of man's arms and legs) or a mixture of ginger root and human flesh that the sanguma man carries with him in his bag. These magical objects can whistle and in so doing impart certain knowledge to their "masters." Since the ability to whistle is one of the main characteristics of spirits according to Abrau and Kwieftim belief, I think that we can interpret these magical objects (Ak *naukuit inés*, Auwon *auwaiye yen* ["sanguma son"]) as auxiliary spirits of the sanguma men. From myths we also learned that the Kwieftim consider the naukuit inés children and advisers of the sanguma men (Kelm and Kelm 1975:192, 198). For example, the naukuit inés can see certain things that their master cannot and inform him about them, thus influencing his actions.

Because command over spirits is one of the characteristics of the shaman, this brings us back to Mitchell's identification of the Lujere sanguma man, both witch and curer, as a witch-shaman who "not only typifies but symbolically mediates the fragile balance between productive and destructive magic reflected in the tenuous ties of Lujere community life" (1977:187). It is clear from our field materials, especially those collected in Kwieftim, that the possession of sanguma power and command over spirits enables the sanguma man to do things beyond the capabilities of ordinary men—heal the sick, practice magic against the sanguma of foreign sanguma men, foresee deaths, and (very important in a hunting society) be especially successful in hunting. Therefore I agree with Mitchell that sanguma cannot be seen as merely a destructive power and that sanguma men are believed to use personal supernatural power for their ends. I would, however, hesitate to call the sanguma man a shaman, at least in the sense of the term (*Schamane*) employed by most German scholars, which is closely connected with the Siberian material.

In my opinion, the belief in sanguma among the inhabitants of the region between the upper course of the Sepik River and the Torricelli Mountains must be seen as one of the means used by the big men, most of whom are said to be sanguma men, to maintain political power. It is the big men who create the fear of sanguma among the villagers, not only by accusing others (in the case of Abrau, the Kari) of having practiced sanguma against members of their society[6] but also by producing evidence of sanguma assault in the course of their curing ceremonies. We learned that when healing a sick person a sanguma man spits red saliva on a piece of sago sprout and places it on the afflicted part of the patient's body; when he lifts the sago sprout from the patient's skin, there is a sago thorn or splinter of wood in the saliva that is shown to spectators and declared to be the projectile (Auwon *auwaiye pi*) shot into the patient's body by the foreign sanguma man. This thesis would explain why we found the fear of sanguma much greater in Abrau than in Kwieftim, where it was practically nonexistent. As I have said, there were a number of big men in Abrau who were said to be sanguma men and who at the same time were politically the most powerful personalities in Abrau society, both feared and esteemed. In Kwieftim there were no big men in the traditional sense of this term—individuals with so much power that they could ignore social values with impunity as the big men in Abrau did in many ways.

With regard to whether sanguma assaults ever actually take place in this region,[7] for two reasons I think that now and then they do. First, individuals intent on murder may use the belief in sanguma while trying to stab their victims.[8] Second, big men seeking to foster the fear of the terrible power of sanguma may now and then ambush a solitary traveler, and the shock of such an assault by fierce-looking men in whose ability to perform sanguma he deeply believes may be sufficient to cause the death of the victim within a few days. Stumpfe (1973) presents case materials drawn from all over the world suggesting that it is relatively simple to cause the psychogenic death of someone who is absolutely convinced of the lethal consequences of certain actions performed upon him.

Notes

1. Mitchell investigates Melanesian *sanguma* "within the framework of a general psychosocial theory regarding the human predisposition to create images of the 'Omnipotent Other'" (p. 187), and it is in this sense that he interprets sanguma men as witches, the classic omnipotent other. It may be of interest that from the viewpoint of the Abrau, it is not so much the sanguma men of their own society as the Lujere as a group who play this role. For the Abrau the Lujere indeed constitute a kind of "red danger": "They are mighty, they have everything, they have sanguma, they can kill. But we, we have nothing, we cannot defend ourselves against them, we are helpless."

2. The Lujere seem to believe that sanguma can also kill Europeans (Mitchell 1977:185). The Abrau clearly stated that sanguma neither constitutes a danger for Europeans nor can be influenced by them.

3. A similar summary is given by Patterson (1974:132–33), who calls the phenomenon *vada* or *vele* sorcery.

4. Mitchell (1977:184) reports being told that young men who wish to be initiated as sanguma men must accompany an experienced practitioner on his expeditions, in the course of which "they must kill in succession a lizard, a dog, and finally an old woman."

5. Perhaps it should be mentioned in this connection that the Abrau know a string figure that refers to sanguma; it is called, in Tok Pisin, *sanguma was long rot* (not *sanguma men . . .*).

6. Mitchell (1977:185) reports that among the Lujere sanguma men do not hesitate to kill members of their own local group, although they never attack their agnates. In Abrau, sanguma is believed to be invariably directed against neighboring groups.

7. Patterson (1974:143) reports that Craig witnessed an attempted sanguma attack in Telefomin in which the assailants were able to stick needles into a man's body before he could escape.

8. This may have been the case in the event reported by Craig (n. 7).

41 / Plants in Abelam Medicine[1]

Werner H. Stöcklin

Having reviewed in detail the plants used in so-called primitive medicine, Drobec (1954:56) proposes the following set of categories to order them: (1) plants with specific healing power for certain diseases and ailments; (2) plants with obvious effect which, however, may be considered useless from a European point of view; (3) plants with doubtful effects only; (4) plants without any healing effects in terms of Western medicine but extraordinary with regard to smell, taste, color, or shape; and (5) poisons and secret drugs unavailable for scientific evaluation. Though these categories may seem quite suitable for the experienced observer, they disregard the fact that it will probably always be extremely difficult to demonstrate the usefulness of plants for medical purposes.

Hippocrates is said to have known of only about 60 plants worth mentioning as medicinal. Pliny, some four hundred years later, enumerated 1,000 plants considered helpful for medical treatment. By the nineteenth century no fewer than 15,000 plants were considered of some healing value. Since then, however, scholars have become more and more critical, and today we find the number of medicinal plants in the 6th *Schweizerisches Arzneibuch* reduced to 101. Even with modern methods of research, it is time-consuming and costly to trace the healing capacities of a plant or drug or to describe and analyze the chemical structure thought to be responsible for its effects. Given these difficulties even within well-established Western medicine, making correct statements with regard to an exotic medical system is certainly problematic. Therefore Drobec's idea of grouping plants according to their effectiveness from a European standpoint seems a vulnerable approach to this problem. In attempting to classify the plants of primitive medicine, we should be careful to concentrate not on our own scientific criteria but on those offered by the people we are dealing with. As Sterly (1970:70) has pointed out, "The power [*Macht*] of medicinal plants is not identical with the effectiveness that can be demonstrated."

In this paper I would like to point out some of the uses of plants in the medicine of the Abelam. In order to avoid judgments such as "effective," "ineffective," "unnecessary," or "of merely psychological value," I shall try to discuss these plants with an eye to traditional belief and cultural background. This approach yields a classification quite different from Drobec's: (1) plants used as mechanical instruments; (2) plants with primary (genuine) healing power; (3) plants with secondary (induced) healing power (e.g., impregnated by the healer); (4) plants capable of attracting souls and spirits; and (5) plants capable of repelling spirits.

Abelam Medicine

In spite of several decades of contact with Western civilization, the Abelam manage to preserve many essential parts of their Neolithic way of life. Even the knowledge of traditional medicine appears untouched by modern influence.

With the exception of the minor ailments called *sik nating* in Tok Pisin, accidents and illness are usually considered sanctions for violation of tribal laws. Sometimes they may also be thought of as the results of human revenge or jealousy. The inducers of ill health and misfortune are in the first place sorcerers and witches but also spiritual beings such as *kwalwale* (waterhole spirits), souls of newly deceased persons, or even spirits that are normally harmless and friendly but are in this case responding to insult.

For traditional medical treatment as it is still carried out in the villages, the Abelam call upon a number of specialists who take part in the curing process according to their roles within a kind of diagnostic-therapeutic hierarchy.

First, of course, the *marasin bilong lain*, the simple medical secrets of the patient's family, will be tried, perhaps following the advice of an experienced grandmother. If no improvement is noted, a *nimandu* (big man) may be asked to offer his more extensive knowledge of plants and songs representing healing power.

In more serious situations, the value of the nimandu's intervention may be limited, and a specialist called *kumbundu* (blowing doctor) may be brought in to transmit some of his extraordinary curing capacity by means of his breath. If his treatment is unsatisfactory, there is still a chance that another expert, the *njugrandu* or the *njugra-tagwa* (stone doctor; both sexes are equally accepted in this category of healers) will be able to extract the aching "stone" or other magic "foreign body" from the patient. The list of specialists can be completed by the *babmondu* (moon man), who employs an impressive kind of steam treatment, and by the *yukundu* (good man), who specializes in the detection and appeasement of sorcerers.

If in spite of all these endeavors the patient's condition does not improve, hope may at last be concentrated on the *win bilong ples*, the breath (and goodwill) of the most important people in the village. This powerful breath can be collected and swallowed by the patient with a few sips of water.

Plants Used in Abelam Medicine

For nearly all the healers and treatments just mentioned, plants seem to be of some importance, and it is said that even the *kusndu* (paint man, or sorcerer) needs a certain degree of botanical knowledge for his work. The different ways of using plants in medicine are as follows:

Plants Used as Mechanical Instruments

Plants, or rather parts of plants, are used in Abelam medical practice for puncturing, scratching, splinting, and strapping. The scratching of the swollen skin after contusions and bone fractures or or painful swellings due to infections is common. Headaches, abdominal pain, or arthritis in a knee may be influenced by a tightened string made of *nyangele* bark. Apart from these everyday methods I learned of a lifesaving operation performed by a young Abelam mother whose baby was born with its anus closed by a membrane; she managed to open the baby's intestinal outlet with the sharpened rib of a coconut palm leaf.

Plants with Primary (Genuine) Healing Power

Most of the plants designated as medicinal by the Abelam may be considered to have primary healing power, but it would be very difficult to evaluate their effectiveness in terms of Western medicine. According to Schofield and Parkinson (1963:6),

Herbal medicines are used in the treatment of illness, but we have no good evidence on their therapeutic efficiency. Many are used in such a way that any active principle they might contain could not reach the site of the disease. They are thus essentially magical rather than pharmacological. However, nettles or other irritants may be employed and leaves may be used for dressing sores.

A review of the more or less complete assortment of medicinal plants described to me by several informants makes it clear that the leaves and herbs employed for the treatment of abdominal trouble and tropical ulcers are more varied than the plants used for other ailments. There is also, however, a variety of plants considered effective against earache, stuffy nose, abscess, fungus, or pain caused by the poison of a centipede. The usefulness of *Cassia alata* against *Tinea rubra* (a fungus of the skin) and of heated mushrooms (*tebmak-wanga* or *naankwanya*) against tropical ulcers can hardly be explained by magical or merely psychological influence.

Plants with Secondary (Induced) Healing Power

Healers such as the kumbundu, the njugrandu, and the babmondu use a number of plants that they invest with healing power themselves. The kumbundu may occasionally blow directly upon the painful part of his patient's body, but usually he collects his healing power first in the sponge-like fibres of a rotten banana tree or in a handful of leaves, with which he will massage the patient. The njugrandu also uses certain leaves, both to hide the stone or distract the relatives who are watching and (after careful preparation) as carriers and transmitters of his personal healing power. Finally, in the steam treatment of the babmondu it is evident that the plants involved have no primary therapeutic value. The babmondu impregnates *kanda* leaves with his breath, with sweat from his armpits and neck, and with his good wishes. Moments later he puts the leaves into a coconut shell and adds water and heated stones. The steam produced by this old-fashioned method apparently contains the collected healing power, and having inhaled it the patient may recover within hours.

Plants Capable of Attracting Souls and Spirits

Plants play a role both in the causation of serious illness by black magic and in its diagnosis. The most common and most dangerous type of sorcery is performed with a *gikus*, a cigar-shaped bundle containing a small piece of the patient's *ginyan* (bundle soul). When the captured ginyan is mistreated, the patient's *wuranyan* (main or breast soul) suffers, and physical illness (such as pneumonia or severe diarrhea) is the result. In order to extract the ginyan from the wuranyan, the kusndu uses a magic paint mixed with scented leaves and the excrement of the future victim. The leaves used for this procedure are said to have a lemon-like smell that souls and spirits approach joyfully. Soul-attracting leaves are also used (without the additional help of magic paint) in a special performance for revealing the cause (or agent) of a person's death. Herbs with a lemon-like smell are placed in the thick end of a stick of bamboo. The stick is then placed near the dead relative or in his grave (provided he has not died more than three days before). A speaker asks the soul to enter the bamboo, and the odor of the soul-attracting leaves causes it to do so. The deceased, now trapped, can communicate with clan members through the stick, which he directs (while several men lightly support it) toward the house or village of the sorcerer, sanguma man, or witch who has killed him (see Stöcklin 1976, 1977).

Plants Capable of Repelling Spirits

Certain plants with an extremely unpleasant smell resembling sulfur or garlic are considered capable of repelling spirits (and therefore neutralizing the effect of the spirit-attracting plants or even of the powerful magic paint mentioned above). *Kaamen* (*Enodia* sp.) leaves are the best-known of this group. Their therapeutic usefulness was described to me in connection with the traditional treatment of a baby suffering from pneumonia. Pneumonia, like other serious diseases in small children, is often thought to be caused by kwalwale. As the sick child grows weaker, the kwalwale comes back to fetch its soul. If, however, the baby smells of kaamen, the spirit will not be able to return to his victim. Therefore, as a lifesaving procedure, a bunch of

kaamen leaves is placed under the young patient and a string of odorous leaves around his neck.

The same leaves are also used to neutralize a gikus bought back from the sorcerer and thus set free the captured bundle soul. Kaamen can occasionally be helpful in deactivating a sorcerer's whole gikus archive. This procedure is, of course, only acceptable when the sorcerer has been behaving in a criminal, unpredictable way instead of sticking to the traditional rules by which he is expected to be the instrument of village justice.

In this context, finally, croton leaves should also be mentioned, though their soul-repellent effect is limited. In the southern and eastern parts of Abelam territory, bad luck, accidents, and illness are often thought to have been arranged by witches. The Abelam believe that witches, while pretending to sleep peacefully in their houses, allow their souls to leave their bodies and penetrate such creatures as a wild pig, a cassowary, a flying fox, a poisonous snake, or a centipede. These animals are now made to act as the witch's instruments in doing mischief such as ruining gardens, stealing fruit, injuring people, etc. At daybreak the witch's soul reenters the sleeping body and reestablishes the friendly and normally behaving villager—who, however, may take another evil ride within a wild animal on subsequent nights. The least violent way of getting rid of a witch is by putting a croton leaf across the path in front of her cottage during the night. When the witch's soul attempts to return to her sleeping body, the croton will stop it, and the witch will never wake up from her pretended sleep, instead dying within hours.

Notes

1. This paper was presented in German at the 5th International Technical Conference on Ethnomedicine held November 30–December 3, 1980, in Freiburg im Breisgau, Federal Republic of Germany, and was published with the conference proceedings. It has since been reprinted in *Ethnobotanik: Beiträge und Nachträge zur 5. Fachkonferenz Ethnomedizin* (Curare 3[1985]).

42/ The Study of Food in Its Cultural Context

Brigit Obrist

The study of food first aroused my interest during a three-months' training period in Tauhundor village (Kwanga language group, Dreikikir Sub-District, East Sepik Province) in 1980. After my return to Switzerland, I learned that almost every school of academic anthropology has at one time or another investigated food in relation to its sociocultural context. Montgomery's (1978) review and two recently published readers (Fitzgerald 1977, Jerome, Kandel, and Pelto 1980) illustrate various approaches. Different currents in anthropological thought are also reflected in the food-related studies conducted in the Sepik, for example, Schindlbeck's (1980) functional analysis of sago among the Sawos, the ecological investigations of Lea (1964), Townsend (1970), and Dornstreich (1974), and the symbolic studies of Tuzin (1972, 1978).

If food is considered in terms of nutrition, it becomes, as Pelto and Jerome (1978:322) put it, "a biocultural issue par excellence." Anthropologists and nutritionists take different approaches to a common interest. In a 1981 paper Jerome and Pelto explore the ways in which the two disciplines can learn from one another, thereby opening new perspectives for applied anthropology. Such collaboration is already a reality in Papua New Guinea. P. Heywood, head of the Nutritional Division of the Institute of Medical Research in Madang, is coordinating a multidisciplinary program to investigate maternal child feeding practices and beliefs and their effects on child growth. C. Jenkins is an anthropologist on his staff, and I have been affiliated with it to conduct a year's fieldwork (October 1984–September 1985) on child feeding in the cultural context of Kwanga-speakers. In preparation for this research, I have reviewed the major studies on food in the Sepik. Some of the results are presented in this paper in an attempt to identify issues of particular interest for nutrition-related research.

Sepik Food-getting Activities

Most monographs contain general information on how people obtain their food, usually in a chapter

on the "subsistence economy." Thorough investigations have been carried out among the Abelam (Lea 1964), the Sawos (Schindlbeck 1980), the Siano-Hiyewe (Townsend 1970), and the Gadio Enga (Dornstreich 1974). In attempting to compare these data, however, we face two major problems: the classification of food-getting activities varies somewhat from one researcher to another, and particular activities have been studied in varying degrees of detail. In his study of the Gadio Enga, Dornstreich (1974) presents a classification which is more refined than most: (1) gardening, (2) sago making, (3) silviculture, (4) gathering of food plants, (5) animal husbandry, (6) trapping, (7) fishing, (8) collecting of animal foods, (9) hunting. His interest in the nutritional aspects of subsistence prompts him to look at the overall food pattern and set up categories that he can later correlate with the nutritive quality of the returns. To see whether his classification could also be used to analyze other Sepik subsistence patterns, I tested it on ethnographic reports about nine ethnic groups occupying different ecological zones: the Mountain Arapesh (Mead 1938:219–225, 281–94), the Abelam (Lea 1964, Hauser-Schäublin 1983), the Gnau (Lewis 1975:41–75), the Abrau and Kwieftim (Kelm and Kelm 1980:55–165), the Kwoma (Kaufmann 1972:124–25; 1982a, b, c), the Sawos (Schindlbeck 1980:69–153), the Iatmul (Schuster and Schuster 1975; Hauser-Schäublin 1977:19–27; Weiss 1981:65–66, 213–54), the Siano-Hiyewe (Townsend 1970:15–69), and the Yimar (Haberland and Seyfarth 1974:223–51). This test revealed that each of these groups engages in at least eight of the nine listed food-getting activities.

Gardening and sago making often produce the staple foods in the Sepik and therefore receive the attention of many researchers. Silviculture is rarely treated as a separate category, although most groups plant food-bearing trees such as coconut palms, breadfruit trees, *tulip* trees (*Gnetum gnemon*), or *Pandanus*. It overlaps with sago making because some groups plant sago palms, but because the returns of these two activities differ in quantity and quality a distinction seems advisable. Similarly, it can be difficult to draw the line between tree cultivation and the use of wild-growing trees. Gathering of food plants includes the harvesting of tree products as well as of parts of shrubs, grasses, bamboo, and other plant species. Their nutritive quality is strikingly different from that of grubs, insects, and small animals, and the collecting of these therefore constitutes a separate category. The term "animal husbandry" rarely occurs in this literature and refers mainly to the raising of village pigs. The groups living on the banks of the Sepik River and its tributaries heavily depend on fishing, but in fact most groups occasionally fish. Trapping is distinguished by Dornstreich because the Gadio Enga obtain large quantities of animal protein by this activity. In most other groups it has a less prominent position, and I suggest subsuming it under "hunting." Two activities not listed by Dornstreich are mentioned in the sources consulted: traditional trading in food in the Middle Sepik area (see Schindlbeck 1980:154–248; Hauser-Schäublin 1977:51–64; Gewertz 1977a,d, 1978b) and acquiring of store foods in more accessible areas (see Lea 1964:128–29; Hauser-Schäublin 1977:235–36). My modified classification, therefore, would be (1) gardening, (2) sago making, (3) silviculture, (4) gathering of food plants, (5) animal husbandry, (6) fishing, (7) collecting of animal foods, (8) hunting, (9) trading in food, and (10) acquiring of store foods.

This brief discussion shows that with minor modifications Dornstreich's classification serves well as a frame of reference for the analysis of the food patterns adapted to various ecological settings in the Sepik. Every food-getting activity, however unobtrusive, is represented in the classification, and this guarantees a well-balanced investigation of the overall food pattern. As we shall see, the categories can also serve as a key to further analysis of the sociocultural context.

In the description of each activity, special attention should be paid to variations within it; for example, little boys may go fishing more frequently for the mere excitement of it, some men may be more successful hunters than others because they own one of the village shotguns, and some families may spend more time pounding and washing sago than others. The ultimate objective is, of course, an assessment of the subsistence pattern, but intragroup variations can be illuminating. Such an assessment is usually based on the ranking of food-getting activities according to their relative contributions to the diet,

and therefore data will need to be gathered on food consumption.

Local Concepts of Food Procurement

So far I have taken an etic approach to food procurement in the Sepik. To see what the local people themselves have said about food-getting activities, I again searched the same sources.

The Ilahita Arapesh (Tuzin 1972:234) and the Kwoma (Kaufmann 1982b:16–17) believe that yams have inherent spirits. The harvesting of short yams among the former involves magical invocations of ancestral spirits. Tuzin offers a vivid description (p. 234):

> Thus, while to an outsider, a short yam garden immediately before harvest is a desolate place, with leaves shrivelled and no trace of former lushness, to the Arapesh it is now really coming alive. Under the earth the yam spirits are moving about . . . leading active lives which are in most respects human. . . . Short yam spirits do not communicate with men, but it is understood from experience that they do not want to be harvested. If the spirits get an inkling that the owner is about to unearth them, they will flee the garden and leave the harvest team to poke about in the empty soil. To ensure that this does not happen ancestral spirits are magically invoked on the eve of the harvest to use their influence in keeping the unruly yam spirits contained in the garden.

It would be interesting to investigate Ilahita beliefs associated with yam growing further. It might be asked, for example, where the cultivator learns the invocations and whether there is any evidence that yam growing is conceptually linked with the men's cult. Among the Kwoma (see Kaufmann 1982b:32–34), only the men of a certain initiation grade possess the right and the knowledge to plant yams; their planting allows yi (children) of the seed yam nokapa (mother) to develop in the earth. Among the Kwanga, neighbors of the Kwoma and the Southern Arapesh, initiates claim that their rituals increase the productivity of gardens and the numbers of wild pigs (see Schindlbeck in this volume). These fragments indicate that in this area gardening activities are linked to the men's cult. Unfortunately, it is increasingly difficult to investigate these relationships systematically because the belief systems

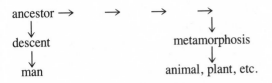

ancestor →   →   →   →

descent   metamorphosis

man   animal, plant, etc.

FIG. 1. Man-environment relationships among the Sawos (Schindlbeck 1980:409).

are showing cracks produced by social and economic change.

Quite different concepts of man-environment relationships exist in the Middle Sepik area. Here, plants and animals are totemistically associated with particular clans, which own the right to perform the rituals that ensure their fertility. Among the Manambu of Avatip (see Harrison 1982:143) the yam (*Dioscorea alata*) is associated with a descent group, and the specialists of this group perform fertility rites before clearing and planting yam gardens and a first-fruit ritual before harvesting. In his study of the Sawos, Schindlbeck (1980) inquired into the mythological background of these beliefs. The central theme emerging from his inquiry is the "metamorphosis of ancestors," the natural environment (trees, birds, grass, stars, fish, etc.) in the last analysis representing the transformed substance of ancestral beings (see pp. 335, 409). The association of a plant or an animal with a particular clan is deduced from its creation from one particular ancestor, and Schindlbeck suggests the graphic representation of figure 1 for these man-environment relationships. The Sawos interpret daily food-getting activities with reference to their mythology. Sago, for example, is closely associated with a mythic ancestor of the Moni clan called Moem (Schindlbeck 1980:97–107, 215–31, 366–72, 410). Referring to myths about the first sago making, the Sawos say that women have intercourse with Moem when they sit on the sago-palm log and that through this act sago starch is produced. In eating sago, then, they "eat the ancestral substance of Moem."

Food taboos often offer clues to local concepts, but they rarely form a coherent belief system. One type of taboo frequently mentioned in the literature is that the "producer" of certain foods may not consume them himself. In some groups (Kelm and Kelm 1980:120; Schindlbeck 1980:146; Schuster and Schuster 1975), the person who planted a sago palm must not eat of its starch. The Kwoma planter is not allowed to eat any of the tubers that develop from the seed yam (Kaufmann 1982*b*:32–33), and similar concepts

are found among the Abelam (Lea 1964:59) and the Mountain Arapesh (Mead 1940:412). The hunter is sometimes forbidden to eat any portion of the pig he has killed (Mead 1940:412; Kelm and Kelm 1980:57; Kaufmann 1982*c*:13; Schindlbeck 1980:127). The meat of village pigs may not be eaten by the persons who have fed and raised them (Mead 1940:412; Lea 1964:59; Kelm and Kelm 1980:16). Each of these taboos must of course be interpreted in the cultural context of the group in which it occurs, but the comparison shows a pattern that Mead (1940:412) observed among the Mountain Arapesh—a widespread belief that the growing of certain plants and the capture of certain animals required ritual knowledge and that performing the ritual to produce or obtain certain foods forbids the planter or hunter to eat of them. Such a belief may, as we have seen, be embedded in a totemistic system or a men's cult.

This sketchy discussion reflects the fact that we know very little about the conceptual background of food procurement. It also shows that yam growing, hunting, and sago making seem to have more ritual significance than other food-getting activities. The attitude of local people toward these ritually important activities is often difficult for a pragmatic Westerner to understand because it is deeply embedded in the group's world view.

The Organization of Food Procurement

Food procurement can be further examined in relation to its social context. Following Dornstreich (1974), I have selected the following aspects for an intergroup comparison: rights to food resources, division of labor by sex, and other forms of labor organization. In the subsequent paragraphs I shall attempt to generalize the data compiled from the sources mentioned above.

Information on land rights is abundant. Usually clans own portions of the group territory and clan membership determines which sections of the forest, sago swamps, lakes, ponds, or rivers a man and his family can put to their use. Matrilateral and affinal ties sometimes add flexibility to this system based on patrilineal descent (see Lea 1964:64–75; Schindlbeck 1980:306–23). Rights to trees and garden crops have received far less attention. Planting materials can be regarded as the "true 'capital' of the cultivator" (Dornstreich 1974:197) because garden crops (and trees) are propagated vegetatively. What happens to the parents' stock of yam, taro, banana, and other garden crops when their children come of age or marry or when the parents die? One answer to be found in the literature refers to the inheritance of yams in the Maprik area (see Tuzin 1972:236). Among the Ilahita Arapesh, the newlywed couple receives a supply of yam tubers from each set of parents. These tubers not only provide food until the newlyweds can harvest their first garden but also form the basis of the new family's yam cultivation. At successive harvests, each tuber must be carefully marked as to whether it descended from the wife's lot or the husband's. If death or divorce separates the couple before the children are married, the surviving spouse or the responsible agnatic descent group must hold the yam line in trust and prevent its extinction. I do not know whether similar rules are observed in other yam-cultivating groups.

The division of labor by sex has become a favorite subject of inquiry over the last two decades. In all the groups reviewed, men, women, and children all participate in subsistence activities. However, what is considered a typically female or male contribution to an activity differs from group to group (see Lea 1964:89; Lewis 1975:55–56; Kelm and Kelm 1980:212–17; Kaufmann 1982 a, b; Schindlbeck 1980:69–72; Weiss 1981:66–69; Townsend 1970:102–4; Haberland and Seyfarth 1974:291–99).

Husband and wife cooperate in many activities, but it is usually the woman who is responsible for the daily provision of food, while the husband's contribution alternates with other social, economic, and ritual tasks (see Mead 1947a: 213–14; Kelm and Kelm 1980:212–17; Schindlbeck 1980:153; Hauser-Schäublin 1977:34; Weiss 1981:214; Townsend 1970:102; Dornstreich 1974:296). Adolescent children often help their parents. In Palimbei, children assume their age-specific roles in food getting between age six or seven and age twelve or thirteen (Weiss 1981:213–54, 315–19), and this is probably the usual pattern in most groups.

Apart from working with other family members, men and women tend to form working partnerships with persons of the same sex. Abelam men help each other on a reciprocal basis in the clearing of secondary forest (Lea 1964:83–84), Gadio men collectively organize fish poisoning (Dornstreich 1974:259–60), and Iatmul women cooperate in the building of fish weirs (Weiss 1981:217). Collaboration is voluntary in most cases and depends on the type of work involved. Some activities can more effectively be carried out in collaboration, as the examples illustrate. Sometimes, however, what looks like collaboration turns out to be coordinated activity of several individuals. A group of Iatmul women may be seen fishing together, but in fact each woman tends to her own business. (She may afterward exchange some of the fish she has caught.) Similarly, two or three Siano-Hiyewe women may wash sago side by side, each using her own apparatus (Townsend 1970:104–5).

On some occasions associated with ritual events, coordination of activities on a large scale is observed. Lewis (1974:88) documents, for example, how an impending ritual feast acts as a spur to coordinated hunting among the Gnau. The Abelam of Yenigo village coordinated their gardening activities in view of a large yam distribution to be held after a new cult house had been completed (Lea 1964:88); it is an interesting detail that on such occasions extra gardens had to be planted at least seven months in advance. The third example has already been mentioned in another context—the descent group that "owns" the ritual knowledge coordinates the cultivation schedule among the Manambu of Avatip (Harrison 1982a:143).

Information on the social context of food procurement can be used in the planning of rural projects. Traditional rights to food resources should be integrated as well as possible with any new form of ownership. It should further be asked whether the bulk of a newly introduced activity falls to the women or the men according to the traditional division of labor. At this stage of development, a project that takes the family as a basic unit and builds upon the coordinated activities of families can be expected to be more successful than a project involving the regular collaboration of many individuals.

Food Distribution and Exchange

Many special events in the Sepik are marked by the pooling and distribution of food. Indeed, precisely regulated giving and receiving can be regarded as characteristic of Sepik and many other Melanesian food patterns. Lea (1964:135) reports that he paid more attention to the ceremonial and dramatic than to the everyday events, and a look at the literature confirms that his remark about himself holds true for many field researchers. Two examples help to balance this general picture.

In Gaikorobi, a systematic survey by Schindl-beck (1980) revealed that women distribute some of the sago they produce. The mother-daughter relationship dominates in this network, but women also give sago to real and classificatory sisters and affinal kin. Further investigation revealed the existence of a distribution network which includes other food types as well. In fact, both men and women give away food but always to persons of the same sex. Schindlbeck points to a symbolic link between food giving and sexual intercourse.

Iatmul women do not distribute the sago starch they obtain from the Sawos; they informally exchange fish instead (Hauser-Schäublin 1977:25–37, 43–51). Every woman maintains exchange relationships with several other women living in the same part of the village. The most remarkable feature of this system is that women give and receive fish at the same time. Even a woman who can barely provide enough fish for her own family not only accepts fish but also gives it away. In times of need, for example, after childbirth or during illness, these exchange relationships serve as a support network. Here again, food changes hands exclusively between persons of the same sex.

The often tedious task of recording the daily giving and receiving of food can help us to answer such questions as: Who takes over when a mother is incapable of providing the family's daily food? Who can/cannot accept cooked food from whom? What are the symbolic connotations of food giving and food sharing?

Returning to ceremonial food transactions, it is important to keep in mind that a central theme in Melanesia is *bekim bek* (repayment). What a visitor witnesses as a unique event is often one stage in such an exchange relationship. Two examples, one from the Ilahita Arapesh, the other from the Gnau, serve as an illustration.

I have earlier mentioned the large amount of yams distributed after the construction of a new cult house had been completed in the Abelam village of Yenigo. Among the Ilahita Arapesh, the building of a house for Nggwal, a paramount figure of the men's cult, is the preparation for the fourth initiation stage (see Tuzin 1980:116–67). On several occasions during the construction period, the two initiation classes exchange prescribed food items. Once the house is finished, the initiation class responsible for the house construction gives a feast for the helpers. The various transactions throughout the initiation period must be interpreted in the context of obligations between initiation classes. The initiators return all the "gifts" they receive during their own initiation by taking care of the sons of the men who in an earlier sequence initiated them.

Among the Gnau, marriage creates another exchange sequence (Lewis 1975:29–31). The transfer of bridewealth is followed by several exchanges between the husband's agnates and their affinal and matrilateral kin. The exchange items consist of money (formerly shell valuables), game, and particular vegetable foods. The relationship between the kin groups is recognized at certain stages of the family's life, for example, the birth of the first child, the child's first eating of meat, the puberty of the first child, the return from the plantation of the first son (formerly a certain stage in male initiation), the death of the wife, and the death of the first son. In each instance, payment is made to the mother's brother's agnatic group. By this payment rights in respect of all the children born of this marriage are established by the husband's agnatic group. Each of these exchanges is beyond the resources of a nuclear family. In addition to these payments, every family must recognize the relationship established by marriage by giving *wadagep* (taro and yams) and meat after the annual ceremony of first eating *wadagep*. The demands of these smaller exchanges can be met by the nuclear family. The sister's son continues to confirm this relationship after he is married by giving food and other payments to his maternal kin at the birth and puberty of his first child.

In a nutrition-oriented study, food exchanges and distributions must be taken into account in the assessment of the people's diet. Many groups make a distinction between daily foods and ceremonial foods (Mead 1938:298; Lea 1964:59, 146; Tuzin 1980:27, 38, 42, 44, 58, 102; Kelm and Kelm 1980:163; Kaufmann 1975; Schindlbeck 1980; Schuster and Schuster 1975:13; Townsend 1970:34–35, 54: Haberland and Seyfarth 1974:232–33; Dornstreich 1974:253). Sometimes ceremonial foods are prepared in a special way; sometimes certain types of food are reserved for ritual consumption. The researcher should note who eats what portions of these foods and how often. Do all age- and sex-groups benefit from these special treats, or are they prerogatives of certain segments of the community?

Food Preparation and Consumption

In their reports on the groups reviewed, the researchers describe the "daily foods," but only a few make an additional effort to obtain a range of recipes and to document cooking methods (Kaufmann 1972:127; Schindlbeck 1980:249–54; Hauser-Schäublin 1977:48; Weiss 1981:261–63; Dornstreich 1974:372–74). Kaufmann (1982c, 1975) and Schuster and Schuster (1976a) filmed the preparation of some common Middle Sepik meals. This lack of data contrasts with the long lists of or scattered references to plant and animal foods known to different communities (Lea 1964:186–92; Kelm and Kelm 1980:55–65; Townsend 1970:181–83; Dornstreich 1974:417–18). In this context we may quote an experienced nutritionist who has conducted many surveys in Papua New Guinea. According to Oomen (1971:4), "A definite characteristic of the New Guinea diet is its extreme monotony," and "the great diversity of food plants reported by ethnologists should not detract from the fact that few varieties of plants are present in the daily diet in significant quantities" (p. 3) This statement can neither be verified nor falsified on the basis of the literature consulted, and it certainly presents a challenge for future researchers. This brings us back to a problem briefly mentioned earlier. Instead of simply describing each food-getting activity, the researcher should attempt to assess its relative importance within the subsistence pattern. The ranking of the categories is not an easy task. The anthropologist is tempted to use cultural criteria, but the activities to which the people themselves attribute most importance do not necessarily coincide with the ones supplying the largest proportion of food to the daily diet. The Abelam serve as an excellent example. Lea (1964:111, 136) calculated that the total returns of long yams cultivated in Yenigo in 1961 and 1962 provided no more than 30 metric tons of food. The production of short yams in the same village in 1962 totaled 285 metric tons, of which approximately 100 tons were eaten, 28 tons used as seed, 16 tons fed to pigs, and 141 tons used as surplus. Food-intake surveys conducted in the same village at two different times of the year showed marked seasonal variation in the diet (see Lea 1964:139–41). There was a yam-eating period around August and a sago-eating period around March. Even during the yam-eating period, however, this food type contributed only 34 percent of the total calorie intake and 38.9 percent of the total protein intake. Taro and sago supplied 19.8 percent and 24.5 percent of the total calorie intake and greens 22.1 percent of the total protein intake. To call the Abelam yam eaters is therefore wrong, despite the prominent role the yam plays in their culture. Sago is their second staple food, and in March it even ranks first. In the assessment of their subsistence pattern, sago making must be considered equally as important as the cultivation of yams.

This example also shows the advantage of correlating data on food-getting activities with those on food consumption. Most investigators have estimated how much one or the other activity contributes to the diet (see, e.g., Mead 1938, Kelm and Kelm 1980, Schindlbeck 1980, Hauser-Schäublin 1977, Weiss 1981, Haberland and Seyfarth 1974). A few have weighed all the food obtained by each activity and computed the nutritive values of the respective returns (Townsend 1970, Dornstreich 1974). Quantifying the returns of consumption requires sound training and is perhaps best left to the nutritionists. Whereas most food-intake surveys are carried out in a patrol situation, the anthropologist has the advantage of spending a long time in close contact with the people and is therefore in an excellent position to keep records on each food-getting activity and on the daily diet over several months. These records are valuable documents of seasonal variation, frequency, and regularity, and they will, of course, include information on the impact of feasts on the diet. On the basis of these data, food-getting activities can be ranked according to their contribution to the diet.

Diet records form the core of any investigation into food patterns. We should always bear in mind that a nutrition-oriented study focuses on what people actually eat or, more precisely, what different age- and sex-groups consume. The body's requirements change in the course of the life cycle, and different methods of preparation change the nutritional value of food. Our data on food preparation and consumption should therefore be as detailed as possible.

Methods of food storage and preservation can only be briefly mentioned here. Various methods of sago storage have been reported from the Gnau (Lewis 1975:92–94), the Abrau and Kwieftim (Kelm and Kelm 1980:129–30), the Iatmul of Aibom (Schuster and Schuster 1975), and the Siano-Hiyewe (Townsend 1970:32–33). The Abelam and probably many other groups store yams (Lea 1964:100). Several groups smoke fresh meat and fish and usually cook it again before consumption (see Lewis 1975:92; Kelm and Kelm 1980:85; Kaufmann 1982c:12; Schindlbeck 1980:254; Hauser-Schäublin 1977:37; Dornstreich 1974:373). Greens, fruit, nuts, sugarcane, bamboo sprouts, grubs, small marsupials, and other foods are in most cases collected and consumed on a day-to-day basis.

Meal patterns seem to be quite irregular and depend on the woman's daily routine. In most groups she cooks the main meal of the day when she gets back to the village (see Lea 1964:138; Schindlbeck 1980:255; Weiss 1981:261). During the day, she may cook a snack when the children are hungry or they themselves may roast some food in the fire. These snacks are especially difficult to record because they are often eaten away from home.

Food Beliefs

Many groups in the Sepik have beliefs about food expressed in food taboos. This label is as vague as our understanding of these phenomena but usually means that certain persons observe food proscriptions or restrictions.

A major problem for the investigator is distinguishing between idiosyncratic and systematic beliefs. Mead (1980:400–410) renders a vivid account of her experience in this matter. One day an informant walked up to her and announced, "I don't think you understand enough about food and who can eat it." He then lectured her spontaneously on taboos connected with 235 food items customarily eaten by the Mountain Arapesh. When Mead cross-checked this list she found that most Arapesh were "less well informed"; there was great disagreement between localities and even between individuals. She finally succeeded in identifying ten classes of food taboos that were generally acknowledged. Another question, of course, is whether food proscriptions and restrictions reported as rules are actually practiced, but this is often difficult to investigate.

Examining Ilahita food taboos, Tuzin (1978:84) identifies two major categories which he calls "situational" and "existential":

Situational taboos are normally self-imposed and are applied as necessary adjuncts to magic governing such activities as gardening, hunting, war-making, courtship and sorcery. . . . existential taboos relate to status assignments that are long-term or even life-long, further implying certain qualities of the individual. . . . Violating these taboos effects nothing so trivial as the failure of some enterprise; it means death or grievous injury to oneself or one's children.

In other words, the ingestion of food is believed either to affect certain activities for better or worse ("situational taboos") or to affect the health of the person or the person's children directly because of his or her status ("existential taboos"). Examples of both categories have been reported from other groups.

There are other kinds of taboos that do not fit into these categories. I have earlier mentioned that the producer of certain foods may not consume them himself. Some cases of this could perhaps be subsumed under "situational taboos" (where performing the magic involved in producing the food prevents the planter or hunter from eating it), but this does not apply to all of them. Still other beliefs concern the preparation of food. In many groups the husband's health is believed to be endangered if he eats food cooked by his wife while she is menstruating. In the Kwanga area initiated men must not peel any tubers. Should they or their wives or children eat a meal containing such tubers, they would be "held by the tambaran." In Tauhundor village, parents must not eat any food prepared by a daughter who has passed the menarche, and they never accept food which has been stored in the house of a (real or classificatory) married son or daughter. This list is by no means comprehensive, but it demonstrates the difficulty of finding general categories.

As McDowell (1979) shows for the Bun, it cannot be assumed that food taboos form a unitary system in any given group. Beliefs such as the ones just mentioned must be seen in their cultural context, for example, in relation to the men's cult or concepts surrounding sexuality. Others, as Tuzin has shown, form part of a general notion that magic, including the observation of food restrictions or proscriptions, can influence the outcome of an activity, and still others refer to ideas about personhood.

Even if one is not a follower of Sigmund Freud, the symbolic association of food and sexuality is often striking. I have mentioned the conceptual link between food giving and sexual intercourse as it has been reported for the Sawos and the Iatmul. Many other examples hint at a similar connection. Mead (1940:350) relates the numerous Mountain Arapesh food taboos to "the rhythm of sex growth within an individual of either sex." Among the Ilahita Arapesh, Tuzin (1978:83) also found a link between sex and eating. In another paper, he examines the conceptual links between conception, food production, and consumption. Semen and untapped menstrual blood are thought to form the fetus. The fetus at the same time represents a spiritual amalgam of the parents and is an essential link between the infant and his ancestors. Throughout a person's life, the link which originated in conception is fortified by the ingestion of yams which themselves descend from yams planted and eaten by the ancestors. During the process of digestion, part of the yam is absorbed by the physiological system of the body, part is excreted, and the "spiritual essence of the yam is released and finds its way to the *okom* (heart), the source of being and emotion" (Tuzin 1972:235)

Although the Melpa culture is different from Sepik cultures in many respects, Strathern (1977) elucidated similar beliefs. The Melpa term *kopong* (grease) conveys the notion of nourishment and fertility. The mixing of the father's kopong with the mother's blood ensures the conception of a child. The kopong of the mother's milk makes him grow until he can eat the kopong of good food after he is weaned. Later, the child gets kopong from good foods and pork fat. The adult draws his sustenance from plants which are cultivated on the land of his ancestors. Their influence ensures that the ground has kopong or fertility. Strathern concludes (p. 506) that "in a culturally very real sense . . . food is ancestrally provided. In eating it one is simply using external sources of sustenance which are also internally passed down through the bodily 'grease' (semen, milk) of one's parents."

These last two examples, although perhaps exceptional in their consistency, illustrate the complexity of food beliefs. The researcher should not limit himself to the identification of food avoidance and preferences but search for their conceptual foundations.

The nutrition-oriented researcher is particularly interested in local explanations of how food affects the human body and the qualities attributed to certain foods. Such findings as those of Tuzin and Strathern are exciting because they constitute local interpretations of human growth and nutrition. With regard to food proscriptions and restrictions, the researcher needs to know whether they are shared by the majority of the group and which segments of the community are affected by them. The most vulnerable groups, because of their special nutritional requirements, are young children, pregnant and lactating women, and the old and the sick. Lewis (1975:89–92) studied the order of introduction of foods to Gnau infants in relation to growth stage. During the first six months of life, the infant depends entirely on breast milk. Once he can sit or once his first teeth have appeared (at about six months), he receives plain sago jelly. At the age of about ten months, when he begins to stand, water, coconut milk, and coconut are introduced to his diet. At fourteen to sixteen months, breadfruit, bananas, and *pitpit* (wild sugarcane) are added. He is not allowed to eat tubers, beans, or meat until the age of approximately two years, when he begins to talk. The leaves of the *tulip* tree (*Gnetum gnemon*) and the seeds of *Pandanus* are introduced in the third year, when he begins to walk on paths to the garden and can go to the toilet independently. According to Lewis, the late introduction of protein-rich foods may be one of the causes for the retarded growth pattern of these children. Similar findings have been reported from other regions of Papua New Guinea, and, along with a deficient total food intake and various ecological factors, they may lead to the development of a form of malnutrition in these children (Malcolm 1974). Since childhood malnutrition is a problem in both Sepik provinces (see Townsend 1982), particular attention should be given to beliefs affecting the diet of children under five years of age.

Summary

In societies with a subsistence economy, food plays a central role in daily and ceremonial life. Cultural anthropologists have, however, been "remarkably uninterested in the nutritional systems of the communities they study" (Pelto and Jerome 1978:322). With few exceptions (see Lea 1964, Schindlbeck 1980, Townsend 1970, Dornstreich 1974), this statement applies to Sepik anthropology. As a result, we know less about Sepik foodways than about other areas of anthropological research. In an attempt to balance this picture, I have examined selected sources on ten groups occupying different ecological zones for information on food acquisition, allocation, and consumption and the beliefs associated with them. On several points of interest, no field data are available, and I have proposed these as possible subjects of future inquiry. My approach is nutrition-oriented, and I believe that collaboration with nutritionists will open new perspectives for applied anthropological research.

Food-getting activities provide an excellent key to the study of food procurement. Many researchers have observed subsistence activities in varying detail, but there is little agreement in the choice of categories. Dornstreich's (1974) well-balanced classification can, with minor modifications, be used as a frame of reference in various ecological settings. Most studies of food patterns begin with a description of each food-getting activity. Some researchers have gone a step farther by reporting the way people experience these activities; their data are as fascinating as they are fragmentary. Only Schindlbeck (1980) has considered local concepts of food procurement in the wider context of man-environment relationships.

Many investigators have looked at land rights and their legitimation. Their findings can be interpreted in terms of access to food resources. Less is known about rules governing the inheritance of food-bearing trees and planting materials. If we look at the group as a whole, food resource areas and the availability of planting materials to a large extent determine the pattern of food acquisition.

Another aspect of food acquisition is the organization of labor. Within the nuclear family, specific tasks are assigned to each member according to age and sex. Nuclear families (and their variant forms) are the smallest economic unit in most Sepik societies. Certain activities call for collaboration, usually among persons of the same sex, but this should be clearly distinguished from coordinated activity of several individuals. Ritual events, in particular, often involve a coordination of activities on a large scale.

The Tok Pisin expression *bekim bek* characterizes many food distributions and exchanges. To receive means to give back, either now or later. This idea can be found in informal fish exchange among Iatmul women—one of the few recorded examples drawn from everyday life—and cul-

minates in prestigious transactions between initiation grades continued over generations, for example, among the Ilahita Arapesh.

Studies of food acquisition and its organization, food exchange and distribution contribute to an understanding of the cultural context of food. However, a more pragmatic subject forms the core of a nutrition-oriented study: the local diet. Participant observation enables the anthropologist to collect recipes and to document seasonal variations in the diet, but very few have done so. The correlation of data on the diet and data on food-getting activities is an easy method of assessing the overall subsistence pattern.

Nutritionists find food beliefs a tough nut to crack and turn to anthropologists for expert advice. Many Sepik societies observe food taboos, but they have rarely been subject to thorough investigation. The first step is to distinguish between idiosyncratic and systematic beliefs, the second to determine whether commonly acknowledged food proscriptions and restrictions are actually practiced. Food beliefs often do not form a unitary system in any given group, and different sets of beliefs must be interpreted in their cultural context. A conceptual association of food and sexuality has been reported from several groups. Future investigations of this relationship may perhaps lead to a generalization. Local explanations of how food affects the human body and beliefs concerning food qualities seem particularly relevant. The most vulnerable groups are young children, pregnant and lactating women, and the sick and the old, and beliefs affecting the diet of these groups should be a priority of future research.

Part Eight
Visual and Aural Arts

Introduction

Douglas Newton

It is powerful testimony to the pervasiveness of what we call "art" in Sepik cultures that while these papers address aspects of it directly, a number of others (for instance, those by Forge, Ruff and Ruff, Lutkehaus, Tuckson, Eoe, Roscoe, and Craig) also refer to its functions in more or less depth and length.

Western acquaintance with Sepik art is by no means a recent phenomenon: its material products have been known to us for over a century. The first exporters of it were probably the Malay traders along the north coast, whose main targets were birds of paradise. The masks they acquired from the north-coast islands and even some Abelam figures were sent to Dresden and Paris during the 1870s and 1880s by an agent in Ternate. Other traders participated in such sporadic, not to say random, efforts. The scene changed when the Neu Guinea Kompagnie took over the territory in 1885: the 1890s saw the establishment of a number of trade and mission stations along the coast, increasing patrols by the Kompagnie's vessels, and even exploration inland. Personnel of these ventures and the officials of the Kompagnie made collections as a profitable sideline. In one way or another an appreciable quantity of ethnographic material found its way onto the market.

Official explorations up the Sepik River took place in 1886 and 1887; during the second, in 1886, the ubiquitous R. Parkinson obtained a Iatmul basketry mask now in Dresden, but pickings, it seems, were otherwise slim. The export of Sepik objects had, however, increased from a trickle to a modest stream in twenty-five years; ten years later it had become a torrent. From 1909 to 1914 German scientific expeditions collected extensively in the river area, and private collecting continued as well.

Following World War I, the late 1920s and early 1930s saw continued adventures to the Sepik River but also, more important, the anthropological research of Bateson, Fortune, Mead, and Speiser, who began to view art in some sort of context. The onset of World War II put a stop to this; other populations, other landscapes claimed anthropological attention when peace returned. Subsequent scientific work, as well as the pertinacity of local dealers, augmented the sheer quantities of art objects brought into museums and private hands. What has actually been done with this massive quantity of raw material? The only realistic answer must be very little. Great collections have remained unpublished and even unvisited—though, with what appears to be an increasing interest among anthropologists in the potential of museums as resources, this deplorable situation is changing (see, for instance, Kaufmann in this volume).

Until about thirty years ago, anthropologists felt uneasy with the idea of "art," except as a kind of ornamental frill to the concerns of social studies. Their strategy was to tuck it under some innocuous heading such as "Decorative Art," or "*Bildende Kunst,*" at the end of an ethnographic report, to compile leaden inventories, such as those of K. T. Preuss, of design motifs, or, more dashing, to describe its economic setting. Would-be art historians all too regularly lapsed into the fatuities of baseless speculation. Today, anthropologists are far more conscious of the integration of art into culture as a whole, and art historians understand that they cannot be ignorant of the elements of anthropology and remain effective. Released from attempts to isolate the arts, and no longer limiting their work to the documentation of "collectibles," researchers have become engaged with the expansive roles of all the arts, including architecture and music.

Among the themes running through these papers is the perception of change as it has occurred in the past and, more obviously, is taking place in the present. Both Patricia May and Dirk Smidt report on areas which are either little known or quite unknown. Although the Boiken are a large, accessible Ndu-language-speaking group, until recently they have been poorly recorded (but see Roscoe in this volume); May sets out to redress this situation with a systematic inventory of what is known about the work of the several Boiken groups, drawing upon her own fieldwork and published sources. Beyond this she discusses such topics as the associations of color with totemic dual organizations and painted house facades as markers of political alliances. A consideration of the distribution of designs, objects, and building styles leads to an account of the even less

well-known speakers of Torricelli-phylum languages living around the Boiken. Smidt's fieldwork among the Kominimung, a small Ramu
River group, records a rich sculptural tradition
that may be waning: of three types of mask formerly made, only one may be current. Carving
techniques are reported in detail, as is the symbolic content of the masks, which includes both
totem imagery and moiety-based color associations. The performances by the masks express aspects of male hunting and female gardening activities, while the conformation of the masks as a
whole expresses integrative aspects of the social
structure.

Three papers—by Ross Bowden, Brigitta
Hauser-Schäublin, and Christian Coiffier—are
on architecture, another subject that has been
badly neglected even though the structures have
long been one of the most admired sights of the
Sepik. All three writers discuss the positions of
the house (or houses) in village layout and the
ways in which they reflect social systems and
concepts. Among the Kwoma, Bowden shows,
the village layout expresses the view held by men
of the essential attributes of gender and their implications. Hauser-Schäublin and Coiffier describe Iatmul settlement patterns as based on
dualities overlying an immanent triadic system.
Hauser-Schäublin goes on to contrast this pattern
with those of two other Ndu-speaking groups,
Sawos and Abelam, and to discuss the historical
and environmental considerations involved.
Bowden continues with the analysis of Kwoma
ceremonial houses, detailing the mythological
charter of all such buildings and the specific nature of the references to myth conveyed by the
materials of the buildings' construction and their
placement. These references are also present in
the bark paintings that conspicuously decorate
the houses and in themselves, through the manipulation of standard designs, convey (and dis-
guise) symbolic meanings. For Hauser-Schäublin the detailed account of the Abelam ceremonial
house, its form and engineering, is the stimulus
for the construction of a hypothesis about the
course of Ndu architectural history and its influences on non-Ndu groups (particularly the Ilahita
Arapesh): this, in turn, has implications for population movements in the area. Coiffier describes
the symbolism and traditional technology of Iatmul houses, ceremonial and domestic. The ceremonial house remains surprisingly durable as an
institution, with apparently an increasing number
having been built between 1960 and 1980. While
the principles of their construction have remained

constant, their form has undergone considerable
change from those of pre-Western times, size and
decorative schemes both showing diminution.
The principles of traditional settlement patterns
are maintained even in emigrant urban communities. The introduction of new ideologies and
technologies is, however, having profound effects.

The immersion of Sepik cultures in music is
conveyed by Rhoda Métraux in a survey of Iatmul
music in Tambunam. The fieldwork period,
1967–73, saw the coexistence of traditional music, harmonica music (an instrument introduced
in the 1930s), "new" music sung and danced by
young people to guitars (a 1960s innovation), and
church and school music. The radio was a constant stimulus to innovation for the young and, in
its broadcasting of other Papua New Guinea traditional music, a reinforcement to their elders.
The repertoire of instruments is large, including
idiophones (slit-gongs), membranophones (hand-
drums) and aerophones (flutes). Some of them, or
certain performances with them, are restricted to
males. Vocal music is performed by both sexes,
with or without instrumentation, and by anything
from a soloist to a chorus of a hundred. Accordingly, suitable occasions for performances are innumerable, from private expressions of emotion
to full-scale public ritual. A specific ritual performance at Aibom, also a Iatmul village, is analyzed in detail by Gordon D. Spearritt. It was
originally mounted, with dancers and a mask effigy, in honor of the Aibom pottery "goddess"
Yumanwusmangge; but has now been adapted,
without dancers and mask, to other notable village events. A complex series of rhythms and
melodies played by seven flutists led by a single
drummer, it corresponds to Iatmul usage in many
respects but shows influences from the nearby
Chambri. As does Métraux, Spearritt points to
Iatmul music's relationship to fundamental aspects of social structure complementarity and the
cross-cutting of age-grade and moiety systems. A
special feature of Sawos slit-gong playing, described by Thomas C. Aitken, comprises signals
for individuals. Melody as well as rhythm are apparent in them and may be onomatopoeic of "totemic" beings' calls.

Most of the writers in this section, then, interpret works of art as materializations of nonmaterial conceptions of the interaction of cosmology
and society. Operationally, the works of art, simply by existing, voicelessly reify society's tenets
both in the simplest terms (for those who are informed simply) and at a higher order of complex-

ity. As one might expect, given human nature, some of these nonverbal messages (as in the Kwoma case) are lies. This assumption about Sepik art to a certain extent takes it for granted that the objects, actions, and sounds it describes are "authentic," that the homology of the material and the nonmaterial is exact, and that both exist in a state not unduly tainted by external influences. But external influences are increasingly powerful and may tend in several directions. Conservatism in either the art or the social forms may signal a radical distinction between them or an adaptation of one or the other to create a new synthesis.

In any case, while current interpretive methods are valuable, even essential, they leave unapproached the fascinating problem of the nature of Sepik aesthetics: what the artists think they have been doing and why and how we respond to their works. A consideration of formal qualities is rewarding; one can perceive and think about a good deal of Sepik sculpture in very much the same way as one does about African, Western, or Asian sculpture. This applies very well to the smaller, repetitious works, but it is not enough. We cannot escape the fact that the impression made by the greater works of Sepik art is evoked by certain qualities deriving from the artists' motives accepted or even demanded by their audiences that are literally foreign to us. The "affecting presence" of Sepik art, we can hardly doubt, goes beyond the "magic" toward the numinous, the awesome, and the terrifying. The idea is so foreign to us, in fact, that in the present climate of opinion many may well resist it on the grounds that it revives or perpetuates an image of savage man cringing before demonic idols. This would indeed be one way to dismiss a very real problem.

The perception of the highest art as not necessarily emollient and amiable is not new to European thought. It was stated nearly 250 years ago in Edmund Burke's now neglected essay, *Philosophic Enquiry into the Origin of Our Ideas of the Sublime and the Beautiful* (1757). Burke considered the roots of the Sublime to be horror, fear, astonishment, and terror, as they are inspired in art by such masters as the Greek dramatists, Shakespeare, Michelangelo, and Milton. Thus he offered us a traversable road into Sepik aesthetics, as he would no doubt have been surprised to hear: there can have been no image of the South Seas in his mind as he wrote, for there was still none in Europe for anyone to have. Burke was, in fact, a prophet.

43/ In the Swamps and on the Hills: Traditional Settlement Patterns and House Structures in the Middle Sepik

Brigitta Hauser-Schäublin

In the course of several years of social anthropological study that resulted in a book about women in the Iatmul village of Kararau, I became more and more uneasy about the growing number of publications on New Guinea societies that described and interpreted complex systems of belief and ritual on such a high level of abstraction that the conclusions could not be verified by the reader. This uneasiness increased when I did fieldwork among the Abelam, who are known for not giving elaborate answers (as, for example, the Iatmul do) to anthropologists' questions. As Forge (1979) has said, they almost never verbally express ideas about the meaning of visual aspects of their culture. At first this impeded my studies of the function, symbolism, and meaning of Abelam *korambo* (spirit houses). Then I recognized that I had to start not on the abstract level that seemed to me most exciting but by studying the concrete material facts. This meant not only mapping the whole village of Kalabu carefully but also analyzing korambo from the point of view of architecture and collecting the names given to various parts of the building. From this starting point two different directions for further research arose: one providing initial clues for a better understanding of Abelam meaning and symbolism and the other leading to comparative studies of ceremonial houses in a larger area, including not only other Abelam villages but also Iatmul and Boiken settlements. This latter followed from my recognition that some elements of the Abelam korambo that cannot be explained in terms of current architectural requirements nevertheless have meaning attached to them. Guessing that such elements as the low, narrow entrance, the piles inside on both sides of the roof, and the sago thatching underneath the plaited mat below the carved crossbeam on the front had histories of their own, I undertook comparative synchronic studies in the hope of coming to understand them. It was only after examining spirit houses among neighboring groups that I discovered hints as to their possible explanation. In this article I want to focus on some of the results of these comparative studies; I shall not deal with function and meaning (but see Hauser-Schäublin n.d.).

Building Traditions and Language

My premise was that house construction in a traditional society is never an ad hoc act springing from a single ingenious brain. Since a house must conform to certain rules of statics that are not calculated in Western architectural terms, it is always the result of cooperation. It is based mainly on practical knowledge and skills handed down from one generation to another. It is subject to change through adaptation to a new environment (if the group migrates to a new area), as a result of external influences, or—to a lesser extent if the group remains in the same setting—as a response to internal factors. This is especially true for ceremonial houses, which are the most elaborate buildings in all Middle Sepik societies. These represent, in their shape and structure, the consensus of most of the important men of the village. Individually owned dwellings are more subject to change. In the Abelam villages in which people still build korambo, they do it in basically the same way they did when Thurnwald passed through Maprik in 1913, but quite a number of Abelam nowadays have abandoned the traditional A-shaped-front dwelling with sloping ridge and construct rectangular houses instead. Ceremonial houses may also be more attached to tradition than dwellings because they are usually the locus of rituals held to link, in one way or another, the present with the past.[1]

The data I have collected convince me that building traditions are as much a specific cultural heritage of a group as is language (see also Leroi-Gourhan 1973[1945]:245) and perhaps music. Buildings are not traded between villages as artifacts may be. It is not enough simply to see such a house on a trading or war party in order to copy it. Building traditions are shared by all the men of a village. Boys and young men learn them by helping more experienced men and being taught by them; then, when they feel competent, they perform them themselves. Building traditions are more stable than interpretations of them. They cannot be changed completely within a short time in response to, for example, new considerations of aesthetics. The technical knowledge to which practical experience is vital evolves only step by step, new elements being integrated and old ones abandoned. Construction of a ceremonial house is aimed at producing a place to hold meetings, discussions, and certain rituals; its appearance must suit its purpose in a traditional way and conveys meaning to those who see it. The meaning of a house may change with the acquisition of new elements, e.g., masks or carvings captured during a raid on an enemy village (as I observed several times among the Abelam), just as the meaning of a word may alter (e.g., *wapi* means "long bamboo flute" in Iatmul and "long yam" in Abelam; *ngussa* means "paddle" in Iatmul and "digging stick" in Abelam).

That language and building traditions may be compared in these ways does not mean that both follow the same paths. The Ndu language family and Middle Sepik building traditions do not correspond completely, the latter extending beyond the boundaries of the former. In Ilahita, for instance, the shape of Abelam ceremonial houses has been copied, although not the structure evolved step by step by the Abelam (see Tuzin 1980). The Kwanga seem to have lost their own building traditions for ceremonial houses and borrowed a perhaps similar type from the Arapesh or the southern Abelam (Wosera). This leads us too far afield, but it is important to remember that the Ndu language family is a linguistic construction based on data available today; we have no way of knowing whether some of its former members lost their language and adopted another (as I know happened with an Abelam group that migrated to Nagripaim) or outsiders adopted a so-called Ndu language. The same applies to building traditions.

Settlement Patterns

Houses should not be analyzed separately from the settlement patterns of which they are part. I shall therefore begin by summarizing the pub-

lished material on Iatmul, Sawos, and Abelam villages.

Iatmul

As Bateson (1932:258) describes it, the Iatmul village is dominated by the dancing ground and its men's houses. Nowadays these have declined in number, size, and elaboration. Iatmul villages are mostly linear, along the bank of the river, with little depth compared with their length (see maps in Hauser-Schäublin 1977, Ruff and Ruff 1980, Wassmann 1980). Villages such as Palimbei, situated some distance from the river, tend to be a bit broader (see Ruff and Ruff 1975), but the linear concept is still apparent. In all the villages documented, even if there are no longer any men's houses the dancing ground (*wombuno*) forms the elongated center of the settlement. Dwellings are oriented either toward it or toward the river, which runs parallel. Although Kararau now has its wombuno near the shore of the lagoon, pictures from the German expeditions show that in the former main settlement (now the smaller settlement called Kwedndshangge[3]) it was situated away from the river. There are no Iatmul villages with the rather circular layout that Stanek (1983:32) mentions.

Whereas one side of the village is on the water, the others are bordered by patches of forest. Within the village there are, in addition to shrubs with edible leaves and those used in rituals, mainly coconut palms, lining both sides of the wombuno and separating clusters of houses that correspond to clans. The visual impression of boundaries is accentuated by the fact that the palms grow on dikes. These boundaries end in right angles at the wombuno. Tracks lead from the main village paths on the two sides of the wombuno to the plots owned by particular clans. There is no rule as to the number of plots in a village; it depends on the number of clans.

Traditionally, there seem to have been three men's houses in most villages, and there were boundaries between the village sections named for these houses. Weiss (1981:35) and Stanek (1983:63) mention three such sections for Palimbei, and two still have men's houses (recently built). In Kandingei, three men's houses are built along one axis on the dancing ground (Wassmann 1982:20–22), and most of the houses are located between the dancing ground and the shore. In the main village of Kararau (Hauser-Schäublin 1977), built after World War II, the three small structures used as men's houses are located near the shore, all built on one axis, but nothing resembling the former dancing ground is recognizable between them. The old posts of one of the first *gaigo* (men's houses) built there indicate that it faced the lagoon. My informants told me that it was oriented toward the then-surviving men's houses of Kwedndshangge, thus forming a line with them. When the old buildings collapsed both in the former main village and in the new settlement, the present small men's houses were erected along the shore. Holden (1975) and Ruff and Ruff (1980) report two men's houses in Kanganamun, located on a curved dancing ground that follows the course of a creek. Haberland (1966:23) mentions three main sections of the village, one separated from the other two; we do not know whether they were assembled on a wombuno in former times. Schuster (1970) mentions two important men's houses and one less prominent one, all apparently built along a single long dancing ground, for Aibom. According to early German reports, Tambunum had "at least three men's houses which were named after the sections of the village" (Behrmann 1950–51:341). For other Iatmul villages Behrmann just mentions those ceremonial houses that he or one of his colleagues had photographed forty years before.

In summary, Iatmul villages were situated on riverbanks at a slight elevation. Normally, they were the last areas to be flooded during the rainy season. The Iatmul adapted their habitat to the natural environment to the extreme, with villages consisting of rows of houses stretched along the shore. There is consensus that the names of sections were identical with the names of the men's houses, and since there were usually three men's houses in a village there must have been three sections in each. This seems to have been the case for all three Iatmul groups. Although the Iatmul tend to think in dualities and classify themselves and the world around them in terms of this principle, they have also produced the concept of the triad, which applies not only to sections of the village but to the group as a whole as they perceive it.

A further principle of village organization is expressed in Iatmul settlement patterns.[4] According to the moiety system, all clans are classified as either *nyamei*, "mother," or *nyaui*, "heaven." The importance of this classification in everyday life and in ritual contexts varies from one group to another. In the recent settlement of Kararau, no clear moiety distinction is recognizable, most of the land being owned by nyaui clans. Members of the nyamei clans settled on parts of it reported that it was allocated to individual clans rather

than to nyamei as such. In Kwedndshangge, one of the former three men's houses was owned by nyamei, one by nyaui, and one by both, one moiety having the front section and the other the back. Wassmann (1981:37) gives evidence of a similar situation in Kandingei, where the boundary between nyaui and nyamei divides the men's house in half. Thus the village is divided into two large sections, which are sometimes (e.g., in Aibom) marked off by stones. This is probably the reason that Schuster (1970) reports that the "classical Middle Sepik village has two men's houses"[5] and mentions longitudinal boundaries in the men's houses indicating where members of each moiety may sit, according to a shore/mountain opposition.[6] Obviously less important is the division of front and back of the men's house that prevails in other Iatmul villages. As far as I can gather from my notes and Wassmann's maps, most of the men's houses had two ceremonial mounds with sacred stones (connected with headhunting), one in front and one in back. For Palimbei the situation is unclear, as the maps seem to have been drawn from photographs and not much attention has been paid to the ceremonial mounds; both their number and their positions remain uncertain. Stanek considers the moiety system of lesser importance for village layout, and his analysis of clan structure within the village (1983:75, 157) omits the question of which moiety owns which part of it. Attempting to reconstruct it on the basis of his data, one discovers that one of the two main sections of the village (Nambariman) is owned by nyaui and the other (Payambit) by nyamei. The only exception is the Nangusime clan, which belongs to nyaui but lives in Payambit. In Kandingei, where the most rigid classifications seem to exist, it is clear from Wassmann's map that the village has two parts, one owned by nyaui clans and the other by nyamei clans.[7]

Sawos

Little is known about Sawos villages[8] except for Gaikorobi, documented by Schindlbeck (1980). Located north of the river villages of Kanganamun and Yenshan, it is surrounded by sago swamps. Whereas Iatmul villages are compact, Gaikorobi is rather dispersed, lacking a longitudinal ceremonial ground around which dwellings are clustered and not being located on a riverbank. Only the main dancing ground, which extends from the eastern part of the village to the center, is reminiscent of the Iatmul situation. The people of Gaikorobi subdivide their village into three sections. Unlike Iatmul villages, Sawos settlements have more men's houses than sections. Ruff and Ruff (1975) mention six for Nangusap, and Schindlbeck gives the same number for Gaikorobi in 1972; he was told that there had always been a large number of (probably smaller) men's houses. In the preceding settlement, Ngətəpmə, there seem to have been nine gaigo (Schindlbeck 1980:62), and all bear names that are common for Iatmul village sections and men's houses. Whether the settlement had as many sections as men's houses or just three (two of which have same names as gaigo) as is the case today is unknown. Schindlbeck views the three sections as results of historical constellations—migrations of different groups that settled in the same villages—and the middle section as the oldest of the three. As the social system is very flexible (Schindlbeck 1980:33), the Sawos could probably have adopted newcomers in some other way than by creating a three-sectioned village, but evidence from other Sawos villages would be necessary to demonstrate this. I am inclined to consider the Sawos three-sectioned village equivalent to the similarly structured but more compact Iatmul villages. I also find it difficult to understand why the sections should be survivals of migrations when all clans are classified into several moiety systems (some of which have no Iatmul equivalents) and the so-called original section of the village is nowhere opposed to the other two. Having three sections (rather than two or four) combined with different moiety systems probably helps to avoid the formation of permanent alliances that might result in fission. As in the Iatmul village, part of the men's house is owned by nyamei and part by nyaui, and this was the case in the much earlier Sawos settlement of Mivimbit as well (Schindlbeck 1980:37).

Generally speaking (if Gaikorobi can be taken as typical), in Sawos settlements the clans seem to be more independent units than in a Iatmul village, where they are more strongly subject either to a prominent moiety system or to the section, dominated by a men's house. Gaikorobi shows a perhaps rather loose settlement pattern compared with that of the rigid Iatmul villages. This may be due not only to social organization but to the environment, here a relatively safe place, hidden in the sago swamps and accessible only on foot at least during the dry season. In the dry season, then, people would not have to fear raids by the Iatmul,[9] who relied on their canoes for warfare and do not like walking at all. In the Iatmul village, in contrast, the location in the open, accessible to raiders by canoe from almost all sides, calls for a more compact settlement pattern. Behrmann (1918:335) actually saw watchtowers (i.e., tree houses) near Iatmul villages, which sometimes also had fences with gates. Iatmul men's-house communities had their equivalents in warfare, each men's-house group having its canoe.

Abelam

Abelam settlement patterns[10] seem at first glance to have little in common with those of the Sawos and Iatmul. The Abelam area is densely settled, and there were fights over land long before the Europeans arrived. Mainly for strategic reasons, most Abelam villages are sited on ridges. Before pacification, parts of the village liable to be raided were fenced, and the gates were locked at night. Villages consist of a great number of hamlets and seem to have nothing like a single main center. Dwellings and storehouses are situated according to natural conditions, landownership, and personal predilection. Ceremonial houses are built where there is space for a round dancing ground in front of them.

Kalabu is about 7 kilometers long, its hamlets situated on various small hills that are part of the main ridge. Apart from the broadly defined common site, there are almost no clues in the settlement pattern to the organization of the village. The main division is the one between two sections, upper and lower,[11] separated by a narrow strip of no-man's-land that has been the site of minor fights between members of opposite sections. In each half of the village there is normally more than one ceremonial house (korambo). Where a korambo will be built depends on the strength of the clan or clans that own the land and live on it. Traditionally, a new clan splitting off from another has demonstrated its influence and defied the other clans by constructing a korambo. There are, however, two hamlets in each section of the village that are considered the most important ones from the point of view of history and their role in yam festivals and initiations. Actually, it is not the hamlet as such to which importance is attached but the ceremonial ground (amei) for which it and its ceremonial house are named. The two amei in each section have different tasks, being responsible for the cultivation of certain varieties of yam, for sorcery and healing, and for yam displays, and they are in constant competition. Each amei allies itself with the amei of the other section that has the same tasks. Thus the division into sections, which certainly contains the possibility of complete separation, is overcome by alliances between the founding hamlets. This cooperation is, however, intersected by a different one that is probably stronger, a nonlocalized moiety system to which all males are actively attached (and females more passively). The function of the moieties (*ara*) is the organization by one of yam festivals at which decorated tubers are given to members of the other and of initiations. The competition between ara is much stronger than that between hamlets. Ara do not own land or ceremonial houses, nor are clans classified by moiety[12] as is the case among the Iatmul and the Sawos.

The structure of a settlement may be roundish, following the natural contours of the site. On a long, narrow ridge, the pattern may be linear. The only thing that Abelam settlements have in common (besides being sited on ridges) is the almost round dancing ground in front of the korambo. There are no ceremonial mounds such as are found in front of the men's houses of the Iatmul and the Sawos, but there are peculiarly shaped stones placed near the korambo, each stone standing for an important man or woman of the village who has died or an enemy killed during a raid. Sometimes dwellings and storehouses are clustered around the korambo and sometimes not.

The obviously common cultural heritage of the Iatmul, Sawos, and Abelam postulated by their inclusion in the Ndu language family has almost no correspondence in settlement patterns. The similarities between Iatmul and Sawos settlements can be explained as a result of these groups' living in immediate proximity to each other and being linked by a vital barter system. Except for the fact that some Abelam hamlets bear the same names as Iatmul and Sawos village sections, the Abelam might be regarded as a completely alien group. From this we can conclude that settlement patterns are variable, depending mostly on the environmental conditions and modes of subsistence to which they are adapted.

Abelam Spirit Houses

To demonstrate that, whereas settlement patterns vary with the environment, house structures show a continuity greater than that of any other cultural trait except language, I shall show that Abelam ceremonial houses are related in structure to Sawos and Iatmul men's houses. Since I have done

this in detail in a forthcoming work (Hauser-Schäublin n.d.), I shall be as brief as possible.

An Abelam ceremonial house looks like a huge roof set on the ground. It is A-shaped in front view and rather trapezoid in ground plan. The ridgepole slopes downward toward the back. While there are a number of minor differences from one Abelam region to another, the ceremonial houses in them are almost identical in their main points. All have four posts (fig. 1, *1*), two on each interior side, the front posts higher than the back. On them rest horizontal poles (*2*) which are said partly to carry the roof (this is why, according to Abelam, the postholes are so deep). It is surprising, however, although a korambo may be up to 25 meters high and the horizontal poles may indeed help to stabilize it, that in ordinary dwellings and storehouses constructed almost identically there are no such lateral posts and horizontal poles. I doubt that they are crucial to the statics of the korambo, and there would be more efficacious means of supporting the heavy roof.

The ends of the horizontal poles almost touch the spot where on the outside the carved crossbeam (*3*) is fixed. Looking at korambo from the side, one notes that in some parts of the Abelam area their roofs rise almost vertically from the ground to the point where the crossbeam (*tikit*) is fixed and then slant to the top of the house. After mapping several in detail, my husband and I realized that the plaited lower section (*4*) of the front was not strictly vertical but slanting; the bottom edge always stuck out farther than the top, ending at the crossbeam. Most of the earliest photographs of Abelam ceremonial houses, taken by Thurnwald in 1913, show this feature, the bottom edge sometimes protruding farther than both sides of the main roof and thus leaving no room for the men to sit in a sheltered place in front of the korambo. ("Plaited lower section" is not quite accurate; although only a plaited mat is visible from the outside, the whole of the lower section is first covered with sago-leaf thatch just as is the main roof and then the mat is attached to it.) In the korambo photographed by Thurnwald the tunnel-like entrance (*korekore*) started low as it does today but ascended toward the interior, following the slope of the plaited section.

Traditionally, Abelam ceremonial houses were not closed at the ends as they sometimes are today. My informants said that closing the back was a new thing that they had copied from the Arapesh (who had in turn earlier copied the shape of the Abelam korambo). They had varied it to the extent of closing the back completely. Abelam

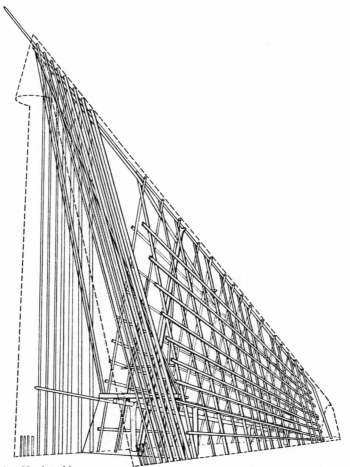

FIG. 1. *Korambo*, Kalabu, Yambusaki.

ceremonial houses had traditionally had to be open at the back because this was an exit to a sacred ceremonial place (*toiembo*) to which only initiated men were permitted to go.

The question that interested me was how the singular shape and the peculiarities just mentioned could be explained in terms of gradually evolved building traditions and in ethnohistorical perspective. The main clues to an answer came from a trip to Kinyambu, a Boiken-speaking village on the southern edge of Boiken territory, where we saw a men's house on piles similar to the Sawos men's houses photographed by Alfred Bühler twenty years before. The piles of the old building were lower than those of the well-known Iatmul gaigo of Kanganamun, and the building itself looked a bit more sturdy. Nevertheless, it had an elegant saddle roof. There was an upper floor where ritual instruments and skulls were kept, and a ladder on the front side ascended to it. The building, in poor condition in 1979 and probably no longer standing since the earthquake a year later, had painted facades both front and back.

From the ridgepole the facade descended to the point where the piles carrying the roof and those of the upper floor (which were on the same level) ended. There a carved crossbeam was attached horizontally. Below it there was a short roof linking the two sides of the main roof; it ended about a meter above the ground. When we mapped the house we realized that the front of the house was not only higher than the back but also more inclined.

Having studied this house, I gathered all the data on men's houses that I could get hold of, both during our fieldwork (where we were confined to a rather small area) and when we returned home. Thanks to Bühler's and Gardi's photographs and the German archives in which I was permitted to work, I was able to gather documentation on ceremonial houses covering a span of seventy years and an area from the Sepik to the southern foothills of the Prince Alexander Mountains. The conclusions of this research are as follows:

The Abelam korambo has evolved from a house on piles with a saddle roof that had two almost identical sides (front and back). These sides were decorated with paintings filling the gable frame completely. Below the paintings were carved horizontal crossbeams, masks arranged in a row, or skulls (and I consider this latter the original form); the masks or skulls[13] were placed on top of the frontal lean-to roof. The house had an upper floor to which a ladder ascended either on the inside (immediately behind the frontal roof) or on the outside; both possibilities are recorded among the Iatmul from the time of the Germans. Where access to the upper floor was from the outside, there was often a narrow entrance sheltered by a small roof. Along the eaves small paintings were attached. Except for the house I saw at Kinyambu, the only such house I know of was photographed in Muschu, in an Austronesian-speaking area, by Parkinson at the end of the last century (Meyer and Parkinson 1894).

As the Abelam moved northward[14] from the Sepik plains to the hills, they adapted to a new, much drier environment than in the swampy plains, and it was no longer necessary to build houses on piles. The main posts of the ceremonial house became shorter and shorter—a process that Thurnwald documented in Ambatigi in 1913 and Bühler in Numbungai in 1956. More or less simultaneously, the upper floor was abandoned, probably first in dwellings and later in ceremonial houses. Finally, the posts that carried the roof and those destined for the floor—typically distinct throughout northern New Guinea, especially among non-Austronesian groups—became indistinguishable, and only one pair was built on each side of the house. The lower the supporting part of the house became, the closer to the ground came the roof. The entrance, formerly on the first-floor level with a ladder ascending to it, now dropped to the ground, and this is why the lower section, now covered by a plaited mat, has sago-leaf thatching and why the whole lower section is still slightly protruding. Thurnwald's photographs, which show an even more exaggerated lower section, having much in common with the frontal roof of a house on piles, tend to confirm my thesis. Viewed from the side, some korambo still show a division into a lower supporting part and an upper part consisting mainly of the roof and the forward-leaning painted facade. That the edge of the roof first ascends almost vertically and then, at the point of the carved lintel, slants testifies to this clearly.

I have mentioned that the carved crossbeam corresponds in height to the horizontal poles carried by the posts on both sides of the interior. Both crossbeam and horizontal poles once belonged to an inner structure, probably the first floor. Traditionally, until the first permanent contacts with the Australians, the Abelam did not build floors either in dwellings or storehouses or in korambo, and they have no term for "floor." There was, however, a spectacular exception to this: at one stage of initiation, they built a floor into the korambo at the height of the horizontal poles, and the initiators would hide on it while the novices crawled into the house. I therefore suppose that the four posts, the horizontal poles, and the crossbeam are indications of an earlier upper floor. I do not know how the lateral posts and poles supporting the roof became extinct; there are today only elements reminiscent of these posts and poles. In Kalabu there is a carved and painted black-palm beam on each inner side of the roof at the height of the poles (2) that starts at the back of the house and extends beyond the plaited mat to near the front edge of the roof. I could find no further evidence supporting my hypothesis and can therefore only speculate on the subject.

I have said that the Ilahita tambaran house has only the superstructure and not the internal structure (I would call it syntax) of the Abelam korambo. I now want to explain briefly what I mean by this. In the Ilahita house there is no correspondence between horizontal poles and carved crossbeam; they are at different levels. There is no visible "organic" division between the lower, supporting part of the house and the upper part. There is no sago-leaf thatch under the mat, and the entrance is simply a hole in it. The little round roof at the peak of the house is not part of the main roof as it is in the Abelam korambo; instead it looks like a hat set on the ridgepole. These and other hints indicate that the tambaran house of the Ilahita Arapesh was imported from the Abelam; thus the shape is similar but the basic structure is lacking.

I have not yet discussed the problem of the reduction of a building with a saddle roof and a gable and painted facade on each side to a one-sided building like the korambo. I have pointed out that the front of the men's house in Kinyambu was higher than the back and leaned forward. The same was true of all the Sepik men's houses we mapped except that elsewhere the relationship of front to back was less disproportionate. As far as I can gather from Bühler's photographs, the ridgepole of some Wosera ceremonial houses was less sloping than in those of more northern Abelam villages. I think that a process of reduction of a two-sided to a single-sided building must have taken place; we can see the starting point and the result[15] of this process but know nothing about what happened in between. To solve this problem it will, I think, be necessary to return to settlement patterns.

Houses, Settlements, and Migrations

As I have shown, the layout of an Abelam village differs fundamentally from that of a Iatmul settlement, and Sawos settlements are somehow between the two. I have indicated that the differences have to do with their environments; what I have not yet said is that mode of production also has its effects on settlement patterns here. Iatmul villages are mainly fishing communities, depending for their sago supply on barter with the Sawos. Their daily life is oriented toward the river, and their means of transport is the canoe, which allows a relatively quick return to the village even from a long trip. Hunting and gathering are more common among the Sawos, who are not confined to their sago swamps as the Iatmul are to the river. The canoe is less important to them, and most of their activities in the bush are dependent on walking. They are therefore accustomed to spending the night in temporary shelter when far from home. Because their villages are not as readily accessible to enemy raids as the Iatmul, they are not constrained to build them as compactly. Abelam settlement patterns have, I think, much to do with their shifting, extensive cultivation. Unlike the Iatmul and, to a lesser extent, the Sawos, who dispose of permanent resources, the Abelam use their gardens intensively only for a season, and the fallow period is rather long (up to twenty years in former times and now from six to eight). A clan needs a great deal of land, and if people were to live in a compact village it would soon be a long way to the garden for everyone as the land around the settlement was used up. Living dispersed in a great number of hamlets, they have more land to use, each clan having its gardens in its own neighborhood.

The ceremonial house I have described as the one from which the Abelam korambo has evolved must have stood in a more compact village containing more than one or two clans. There were certainly groups (perhaps moieties) that shared it, one owning the front and the other the back. Oral traditions that I found in many villages recount that in the beginning of Abelam history all the people lived together; then a dispute arose and fighting followed, with various groups leaving the place in different directions. If we think of the cases of Kandingei, Kararau, and Gaikorobi, where the men's houses are divided between moieties, we can perhaps imagine how the house was divided when the groups split, each clan or moiety claiming part of the building it owned. I do not think that social change—whether induced by changes in subsistence or internal or external social or environmental factors—would overnight have created a situation in which people built only the part of the house that belonged to them. I think that the Kinyambu men's house, with its unequal front and back sides, may be not only a good example of regional change (being situated between the Sepik swamps and the Abelam and Boiken hills) but also an indicator of the transformation over time to which Abelam ceremonial houses were subjected. There must have been a gradual accentuation of the front part of the building and a gradual neglect of the back that ended in a one-sided building, the Abelam korambo. Perhaps this process was accelerated by the change from a house on piles to one on the ground.

I do not think that Sawos and Abelam men's houses evolved from the Iatmul ceremonial houses of German times. As I have explained, the Abelam korambo must have derived from Boiken or perhaps Sawos men's houses. Laycock takes house forms as a "cultural indication" of his hypothesized south–north migration:

> the characteristic decorated gables of the Iatmul, Abelam and Boiken[16] spirit houses show features which suggest a northern movement. For instance, on the river, where timber is plentiful, the gables reach their greatest height; in the plains areas, however, where timber is less plentiful, the spirit houses are lower, but an obvious attempt has been made to obtain the greatest height possible. Tradition of high buildings is the obvious explanation of the erection of these structures with unsuitable materials. Only in the Maprik mountain areas, where timber is again plentiful, do the spirit houses again approach the dimensions of those of the Sepik River.

Laycock implicitly assumes a need to build high houses that could be satisfied on the river and in the mountains but not in the plains and a persistence of that need while people lived on the plains (perhaps driving them into the mountains).

My data suggest that the groups must originally have lived somewhere north of the Sepik, the Boiken probably remaining in almost the same area in which the groups split.[17] From there, some groups went down to the Sepik, crossed it, and went on to the southern foothills (including the Krosmeri and the Blackwater) and westward to the Bahinemo, where influences from other areas are as strong as those from the north. Chambri, documented by Kirschbaum in the early thirties, shows three different regions of influence, one having great affinities with the Blackwater, one with Malu/Avatip,[18] and one with the Sawos. It looks as if there were relations between the northern and southern swamps for a long time and these were cut by the Iatmul, who came into the area only later. The latter had evolved almost vertical gables and therefore abandoned painted facades. They placed the roof on piles that were much higher than those for the floor (see also Forge 1966:25). There is of course the possibility that changes in building traditions took place more rapidly on the river than in the northern hinterland, but I doubt this; the Sepik plains between the mountains and the river were much more an area of transition from east to west than the river, which was one only for the colonial impact.

I have found no indication of any influential movement from the Sepik northward. On the contrary, I found one from the Middle Sepik up the Korewori, where in certain regions similar men's houses are built that can obviously be understood only as influences from the river and not the other way around. Apart from these considerations based on the facts of construction, I cannot imagine how the first Ndu-family groups, which are said by the linguists to have entered the Middle Sepik from its southern tributaries (whether the Krosmeri or the Korewori as Laycock [1965] has assumed and as Gewertz [1983] has argued in her "historical ethnography"), could have come from that direction. I see no way of explaining how they acquired there a building ancestral to the present ones. I also doubt that, as Gewertz (1983:29) would have it, the Iatmul "arrived at the river to find that its fish and communicational advantages allowed the establishment of permanent villages." I cannot believe that advantages caused them to settle on the river; in their oral histories they tell how they first drifted on rafts down the river because they had not yet learned how to make canoes.

My comparative studies indicate that Middle Sepik men's houses cannot be discussed without taking into consideration the whole north coast and its passages into the Middle and Lower Sepik. I cannot imagine that the three Ndu-family groups discussed here came into the Sepik before they had acquired these building traditions that have so little in common with those of the highlands. Theoretically, after the Ndu family had split, each group could individually have picked up similar house forms, but if this were the case there would be no such structural correspondence between them as I have indicated and no such gradual changes as I have suggested for the Abelam korambo could be reconstructed. And it is the korambo that testifies that the Abelam had been bound for a long time to a building tradition from which the ceremonial houses of other groups in the Middle (and Lower) Sepik derived. It is impossible to say how long ago the present-day Middle Sepik groups adopted it,[19] but I think I have made it clear that they had already integrated it before they split. Calculations in centuries or millennia like those of the linguists are beyond the means of this study.

Before concluding, I would like to return to the ongoing discussion of the ethnohistory of the Middle Sepik cultures. Gewertz (1983:24) has asserted that "the social and ritual complexity of Iatmul villages is not even approached by most of the Sawos counterparts, for the large and elaborate men's houses and well-kept dance [grounds] so characteristic of the former are absent from many of the latter." There can be no question, however, that the Sawos had men's houses as elaborate as those of the Iatmul, and I think they may even be older. It is true that Iatmul gaigo were higher and larger, but this is no indication that they were the prototype for Sawos ceremonial houses.[20] It is, I believe, Western-centric and a result of Bateson's (1936) brilliant study that the Iatmul are regarded as the group that dominated the Middle Sepik. The river is the easiest route into the area (by motorboat, of course) for administrators, art dealers, and anthropologists, but life on its banks is marginal, threatened not only by disastrous floods (the village of Maimdangger was destroyed by one overnight) but also by a shortage of sago. The abundance these people dispose of consists of fish, water, and mosquitoes. Their life required courage, and the Iatmul cultivated it superbly, but it is rather daring to argue that the Sawos had "hope[d] to transform themselves into Iatmul" (Gewertz 1983:124).

I have attempted to reconstruct Middle Sepik history on the basis of facts of technology, that is, building traditions, presuming that their development and spread largely correspond to those of the groups concerned. I have done so knowing full well the responsibility I have assumed not only for myself but also for Middle Sepik societies. My conclusions are not intended to be final or irrefutable. I conceive anthropology as a scholarly discipline whose conclusions can be falsified or verified rather than an ingenious art of theory that obeys not the facts of reality but only its own laws.

Notes

1. Cargo cults link the past with the future; therefore ceremonial houses influenced by cargo cults are intentionally changed in shape and/or structure.

2. Ruff and Ruff (1980) print the same map upside down.

3. In my book (1977) I wrote "Quedndshange," using German orthography.

4. Schuster (1970:3) confirms one of my main points in reporting that "the village itself is lavishly structured; its structure can be gathered from the whole conception of the village."

5. In his paper in this volume, Schuster states that in former Aibom settlements men's houses existed "mostly in groups of three."

6. This seems to have been true also for Malingei (Bateson 1932:256).

7. Besides nyamei and nyaui moieties, to which clans are linked not only totemically but also by landownership within the same boundaries, there is another moiety system that is of importance among the Eastern Iatmul. In Mindimbit (Bateson 1932:256–57) it is called *kishit/miwot,* and similar moieties that are not locally fixed in Kararau are called *yambunde* and *bombiande*. Their function is confined to rituals such as exchanges of large amounts of food and initiations.

8. Many more anthropological data should be added to Ruff and Ruff's (1975, 1980) map of Nangusap.

9. According to Gewertz (1983:10), "It is the Iatmul, however, who have achieved control of the Sepik, thrusting their Sawos cousins into the backswamps of the flood plain where, living in their small villages,

they have been vulnerable to Iatmul headhunting forays."

10. Most of the information is based on the work of Kaberry (1940–41:239–44; 1971:42–51) and on my own fieldwork (sixteen months between 1978 and 1983); two of my three field trips were supported by the Swiss National Research Fund, Bern.

11. Kaberry (1971:46) erroneously puts the border between the two sections between Mabmeia and Yambudjaki instead of between Dueningi and Wabinda.

12. I suspect that ara membership and membership of upper or lower Kalabu were once identical.

13. There is evidence of this from the eastern Abelam.

14. Almost all the researchers who have done fieldwork there mention the general south–north migration of most of the Abelam groups.

15. There is evidence of this from other parts of Papua New Guinea, for example, the Lower Sepik, Milne Bay, and the Gulf of Papua. I consider these analogous historical processes.

16. He certainly means the Abelam type of Boiken house.

17. Forge (1966:n. 3) also thinks that there are closer connections between the Abelam and the Iatmul than between these and the Boiken.

18. Newton (1971:64) has collected some oral histories confirming relations between the two areas but in the opposite direction.

19. I think that it is not only the ceremonial house that should be discussed in this context but also, closely linked to it, the megaliths erected nearby.

20. Gewertz (1983:34) considers the Sawos, "sandwiched between expanding populations of Iatmul in the south and Abelam in the north," to be constantly threatened by Iatmul hegemony, but the relationship between the two groups is much more complex than this. Whenever a Iatmul village (as I can attest from Kararau) felt threatened by another Iatmul village or by flood (and not only by World War II), it fled into the bush, because the Sawos are considered not merely as women (Gewertz 1983:27) but as nyamei, "mother," which is something very different (at least for Iatmul). The statement she attributes to "the Iatmul"—"The Sawos, like women, are weak and inferior"—can only be understood in the context of her queries on dominance and subordination.

44/ The Architecture and Art of Kwoma Ceremonial Houses

Ross Bowden

Among the most important and certainly the most spectacular art objects found in Sepik societies are men's ceremonial houses (Behrmann 1950–51, Newton 1971, Forge 1966; see also Coiffier, Ruff and Ruff, and Hauser-Schäublin in this volume). Indeed, these buildings, especially when they are fully decorated with carvings and paintings, constitute some of the most impressive forms of vernacular architecture not only in the Pacific region but in the entire tribal world. But despite their importance aesthetically and ethnographically, they have not yet received the attention they deserve either from anthropologists or from Papua New Guinea's own students of architecture (see Ruff and Ruff in this volume). The purpose of this article is to contribute to the ethnography of this neglected aspect of Sepik culture by providing a summary account of the architecture and art of the ceremonial men's houses of the Kwoma, a non-Austronesian-speaking people numbering approximately two thousand in the Washkuk Hills of the Ambunti Sub-Province of the East Sepik (Bowden 1983a; see also Whiting 1941, 1970; Whiting and Reed 1938; and Kaufmann and Williamson in this volume). In particular, I wish to examine the sculpture, painting, and mythology associated with the building named Waypanal in Bangwis. At the time of fieldwork (October 1972 to January 1974) this was the only fully decorated ceremonial building in the village and one of only three in the society as a whole.

In common with those of most other Middle Sepik societies, Kwoma ceremonial houses are located (generally) at the center and also the highest point of a clan settlement (see site plans in Coiffier and Ruff and Ruff in this volume). As elsewhere in the Sepik, these buildings are the focus of the social and ceremonial lives of the adult male members of the communities in which they are located (see papers by Hauser-Schäublin, Lipset, Lutkehaus, and Schindlbeck in this volume). In them men spend part of almost every day of their lives either chewing betel nut, sleeping, or conversing with other men; in them they publicly debate matters of clan and village concern

and formerly prepared for war; and in them they perform the rituals believed to be of vital importance to the economic and political well-being of Kwoma communities (see Bowden 1983a). Because they provide the focus of men's ceremonial lives, such buildings are appropriately referred to in the literature as "men's houses." The term that Kwoma use for them, korob,[1] has no readily translatable meaning (such as "men's house"), but when speaking Tok Pisin people refer to them either by the equivalent term haus boi ("boy's house"; the vocabulary is a legacy of the colonial period) or, more commonly, by the term haus tambaran ("spirit house" or "house in which spirits are located").

As is the case generally in the Sepik, Kwoma women have no equivalent structures in which they congregate for social or ceremonial purposes. Furthermore, women were traditionally prohibited from entering men's houses or even from approaching them except on certain ritual occasions. Today the rule excluding women from such buildings has been relaxed to the extent that they may now enter them during the all-day moots that men hold periodically to discuss matters of village concern, but they must enter from the back and sit at the back, in marked spatial contrast to the men, who sit in a group at the front. On ceremonial occasions, women are still rigorously excluded from men's houses and are only permitted to approach them, and then only to dance outside at the front, on one or two occasions during the year. Before they are permitted to do so, however, men place tall screens across the front of the men's house to prevent the women from seeing anything of what is going on inside (see Bowden 1983a: chaps. 3 and 4).

Kwoma men rationalize the exclusion of women from ceremonial buildings (and from the rituals performed inside them) in terms of the different natures or essences of the two sexes. Men say that they, as a category, are intrinsically "hot" (hiyutow), whereas women, as a category, are intrinsically "cold" (niikiiriyaw). The "coldness" of women, however, is not thought of simply as a passive quality, a mere absence of heat; if a "cold" object were to come into contact with a "hot" object, the former would drain the heat out of the latter and destroy its physical, mental, and ritual potency. Since men believe that all ritual and magically powerful objects are "hot" like themselves, and must be so to be ritually efficacious, they must protect them from women. Thus, they believe that if women were to come into direct physical contact with ceremonial carvings—or even *see* such objects—the "heat" would be drained out of the sculptures, the spirits they represent would flee from the scene, and the ritual would be rendered ineffectual. To ensure that a ritual serves its purpose, therefore, men believe that they are duty-bound in the interest of a community as a whole rigorously to exclude women from men's houses on ceremonial occasions and prevent them from seeing or even knowing anything about the art objects displayed.

The preceding remarks indicate that in the context of ceremonial houses and the rituals that are performed within them, Kwoma women are very much "on the outside," socially, spatially, and symbolically. This peripheral position that women occupy vis-à-vis men in relation to men's houses can be correlated with the way in which villages are physically structured. All Kwoma villages are composed of a number of localized exogamous clans (*magwil*), each of which contains a *residentially stable* core of agnatically related men. Normatively, and in practice, men stay where they are born (unless their clan as a whole moves) and live in stable, solidary groups—physically, genealogically, and socially. Since clans are exogamous and patrilocal, women born into these groups, unlike the men, do not remain resident members of them but leave them on marriage to take up residence with their husbands in other clan settlements. Women, in other words, *move between* groups. Since divorce in Kwoma society can be obtained relatively easily and since women commonly marry more than once, women are even thought of as being continually on the move, shifting from one clan to another throughout their adult lives as they enter or leave marriages. Unlike men, therefore, who constitute the residential, and hence social, cores of the groups of which the society is composed, women link groups, occupying, as it were, the spaces between them (M. Strathern 1972). To phrase the matter slightly differently, from the point of view of the *resident* members of any one clan, men are the *insiders*, whereas women (in the form of wives) are the *outsiders* (Meggitt 1964).

This opposition between insiders and outsiders

can be developed even further. Kwoma men regard the members of all clans other than their own, including those in the same tribe, as "enemies" (*ow*). Traditionally men only fought against clans in other tribes, but clans belonging to the same tribe were, and still are, widely thought to practice homicidal sorcery against each other, and traditionally a clan was not above avenging an injury committed by another clan in the same tribe by getting an enemy tribe to attack the group in question. Since clans are exogamous, men by definition obtain their wives from "enemy" groups—"we marry our enemies," they say. Furthermore, in marked contrast to their attitudes toward outmarrying clan sisters, men are highly ambivalent about their wives. Not only do the latter derive from outside, or "enemy," groups but in important ways they remain permanently identified with those groups. For instance, married women regularly visit and are visited by their brothers, "enemies," who have an obligation to "look after" (*aboboy hawa*) them throughout their adult lives, and all men believe that if they alienate or persistently antagonize their wives the latter will not hesitate either to divorce them or secretly to send some of their leavings to their brothers with instructions to perform sorcery against them. A clan settlement or larger village, therefore, is composed of a group (or several groups) of closely related men and married women who both derive from and are identified with outside or enemy groups.[2]

The important differences, socially and structurally, between the men and women who compose clan settlements can be correlated symbolically with the physical layout of villages. Ceremonial houses, as I have already indicated, are normally located at the center of clan settlements. Being the structures that men build and occupy to the exclusion of women, they form a clear spatial counterpart to the central, and indeed pivotal, position that men occupy, socially and structurally, in clan communities. The dwelling houses which in-marrying wives occupy (and in which men actually sleep with their wives at night), on the other hand, are scattered around the clan's ceremonial house (see Whiting 1941:5; 1970:3), occupying, literally, the margins of the settlement (cf. Gell 1975:43, 133–37). But more than this, resident females not only occupy marginal or peripheral positions spatially in settlements; unlike men, they never form solidary groups. Physically, in-marrying wives (and daughters) remain divided among themselves in their separate and often widely scattered dwell-

ings (see Mead 1972:211), and socially they neither constitute a single kin group (the marriage
rules specifically prevent this) nor act as a group,
even economically. Indeed, the adult women resident in a clan settlement (or larger village) physically come together only to dance outside a
men's house during a ceremony, and then they
only form a group—and an extremely ephemeral
one at that—in relation to the men whose wives
(or daughters) they are. Spatially, socially, and
symbolically, therefore, men are at the center of a
community, as is a men's house. Women are on
the margins, their marginal position structurally
corresponding both to the fact that the houses in
which they live are on the periphery of clan settlements and to the fact that they are *kept outside*
the ceremonial buildings in which men perform
the rituals that, potentially at least, females are
thought to threaten.

Given the clear correlation between the central
position that men's houses occupy spatially in
clan settlements and the central position that men
occupy spatially and structurally in clan communities, we should not be surprised if we were
to find that men, in Kwoma collective representations, are tacitly *identified* with men's houses.
This is in fact the case, and later I will mention
one way in which such an equation is expressed
architecturally.

In any study of Kwoma art, men's houses must
occupy a prominent place. Broadly speaking,
Kwoma plastic art (i.e., painting and sculpture)
falls into two categories. On the one hand, there
are the portable sculptures in wood that men display in men's houses during ceremonies. These
sculptures are never seen by women or children,
and allegedly they know nothing about them. On
the other hand, there are the carvings and paintings that decorate the ceremonial buildings themselves. Because women traditionally never ventured into men's houses, in all probability they
would have known little in detail about the artworks that decorated the interior of these buildings; but women have never been formally prohibited from seeing such objects, and nowadays
they have the opportunity to inspect them regularly during village meetings. Because this material is not prohibited to women, men classify it
as "public" or "free," in contrast to the private
and "secret" ceremonial sculptures that most decidedly are intended for men's eyes only. Before
examining the art associated with one of these
buildings in detail, I will comment further on the
architecture of men's houses.

The Architecture of the Korob

Structurally, a korob consists of nothing more
than a steeply pitched thatched roof supported by
posts (Bowden 1983a: pl. 2; see also Whiting
1970:171–75). Unlike their Abelam and Iatmul
counterparts (Forge 1966, Behrmann 1950–51;
see also Coiffier, Ruff and Ruff, and Hauser-
Schäublin in this volume), they are open at both
ends and for this reason are not used to store ceremonial sculptures (since women and children
might see them during public meetings). All such
paraphernalia are stored in the attics of private
dwellings or in storehouses. The size of a korob
varies according to the numerical strength and energy of the clan that builds it.[3] Waypanal, the
largest structure in Bangwis, measures approximately thirty meters in length, ten meters in
width, and ten meters in height. To be used ceremonially, a men's house need not be decorated
in any way. A fully decorated building, however,
is a source of immense prestige to the clan(s) that
own(s) it and a sign of its prominence in village
and tribal affairs.

The visual art found in men's houses is of two
broad types: the painted carvings and incised designs that decorate the various posts and beams
and the bark paintings that line the ceilings (see
Bowden 1983a: pl. 2 and 3). The carvings for the
most part represent personages from myths or
clan spirits, the ceiling paintings totemic species
of plants and animals. Myths are owned by particular clans, and only members of the clan (or set
of clans) that owns a myth are entitled to carve
representations of the human or quasi-human personages who figure in it. Totems (*sabo*) and spirits (*sikilowas*), like myths, are owned by particular clans, and only members of the clans that
own them may carve or paint representations of
them. Kwoma say that if a man were to depict in
a painting a totem belonging to another clan without first obtaining the owners' permission, members of the owner clan(s) would be entitled to
come into the building in which it was displayed
and tear it off the ceiling.[4]

All ceremonial houses have a designated front
(*ma*) and back (*yen*), right (*mamu*) and left (*yej*)
(as seen from the perspective of a person standing
inside facing the front). Sculptures depicting the
best-known mythological figures tend to be found
in the front half of such a building; less well-
known figures and "meaningless" decorative
carvings tend to be concentrated at the back. In
buildings that several clans have constructed

jointly, sculptures depicting mythological and other figures belonging to the clan(s) most active in its construction, which nominally "own(s)" it, similarly tend to be located at the front, while those belonging to other clans will be at the back. In contrast to Polynesian societies but like those of the rest of Melanesia, Kwoma do not possess an elaborate lateral symbolism (though a slight preference symbolically is given to the right), and to my knowledge there is no significant difference between the kinds of sculptures found on the two sides of such a building. The term for the front of a men's house, *ma*, is a homonym of that for "man" or "male"; in keeping with this (as noted earlier), men sit at the front during public meetings. The term for front is probably also a cognate of the term for "right": *mamu* (*ma*, "man, male"; *mu*, "foundation, base"). The term for back (*yen*) is distinct from the term for female (*mima*) but is probably a cognate of the term for "left" (*yej*, pronounced "yenj"). In contrast to Abelam men's houses (Forge 1966), Kwoma korob are grammatically male. In plan men's houses are basically symmetrical, laterally and longitudinally (see Bowden 1983a:48).

I indicated above that in Kwoma collective representations men are tacitly identified with men's houses. One way in which this identification is expressed architecturally is through the rules governing the kinds of timbers that may be used for specific parts of the building. Customarily the two sets of longitudinal side beams (*pay* and *mes jiraba*, respectively; see Bowden 1983a:47), the composite ridgepole (*tow*), and the ridgepole finial (*yaba*) are made of *mes* wood (*?Homalium foetidum*, Tok Pisin *malas*). Similarly, the four central uprights—and especially the two termed *nowkwapa kwat* ("mother posts")—are customarily made from the hardwood *nyebi* (*?Vitex confossus*, Tok Pisin *garamut*). (If insufficient timber is locally available to make all four uprights from nyebi, this type of wood should at least be used for the front post, the *ma somar*. In small korob, which have only two central uprights, nyebi wood similarly should be used at least for the foremost of the two posts.)

I have argued elsewhere (Bowden 1983a, 1984) that in the art and ritual of the yam harvest ceremonies—the only large-scale public rituals still performed in all Kwoma villages—men can be seen to be communicating information to themselves about themselves. Two very important ideas which men communicate to themselves (and implicitly to others, viz., women) relate to masculine fertility in the context of both human reproduction and yam cultivation, on the one hand, and homicidal aggression, on the other. Men represent themselves, that is, both as creators of human beings and yams and as killers. These two ideas are actually related in Kwoma thought, since it is by killing enemies in battle that men are believed to acquire the capacity to plant and grow yams. If a man who had not killed were to plant yams, people say, the tubers would simply rot in the ground.

Through the use of mes and nyebi timbers for different parts of these buildings men are effectively attributing similar qualities to men's houses themselves; they may thereby be seen to be tacitly *identifying* themselves with these structures. How do the two timbers, mes and nyebi, bring out the two ideas of fertility and homicidal aggression?

First, the tree named mes provides the wood from which yam-planting dibbles are customarily made. If any other type of wood were to be used, Kwoma believe, the growth of the yams would be jeopardized. Mes wood, in other words, is directly associated with garden fertility in the context of yam cultivation. But more than this, in a myth entitled "Mes," the eponymous hero of which is a tree of this species, yam-planting dibbles are explicitly associated with masculine sexuality and procreativeness. The narrative tells how a man goes into the forest, cuts a swidden, and plants yams. At the end of the day, when the planting is completed, the gardener throws the dibble he has been using into the bush at the side of the swidden. Shortly afterward, a female *howpukos* snake finds the freshly cut dibble and drinks some of the sap that it is still exuding, whereupon she becomes pregnant with and gives birth to a male human child. In the myth, therefore, mes timber is directly associated with masculine fertility, for the sap impregnates the female snake. Implicitly, of course, the myth is also equating the dibble with the penis, and the connection is explicit in art associated with men's houses. In Waypanal, for instance, there is a slit-gong with a carving on its end which depicts this very incident in the myth of the mes tree (see Bowden 1983a: pl. 32). The carving shows the howpukos snake drinking sap from the digging stick and simultaneously giving birth to a (male) human child. Most significant in this context, however, is the fact that the artist has carved the dibble in the form of a penis: it has an unmistakable glans at the end from which the snake drinks.

In the second half of the same narrative, the association between mes wood and masculine procreativeness is reinforced. The child who is born to the snake, when he grows up, is killed by a group of "enemy" tribesmen on their way to the village in which he lives to participate in a ceremony. They bury him beside the forest track, and following this a huge mes tree springs from the grave. Some of the tree's thick roots lie across the track, and whenever a woman steps over them she automatically becomes pregnant. So great are the tree's procreative powers that it impregnates even tiny prepubescent girls, all of whom, because of their immaturity, die in childbirth. So in the myth the timber that is customarily used for the ridgepole and side beams of men's houses is unambiguously associated with masculine sexuality and procreativeness and also with garden fertility.

The timber that is used for the central uprights is associated with homicidal aggression (and also masculine sexuality) in the following way. There is a myth, one of several dealing with the origin of men's houses, which tells how a group of villagers construct a ceremonial building named Dowamu. Unbeknown to the villagers, the men's house they construct is in reality a violent homicidal and cannibal spirit. Whenever the adult members of the village go hunting or gardening, the men's house jumps on any children who wander into it and kills and eats them. To hide the evidence of its crimes, it mops up their blood with the bright red bodi fruit that men customarily hang in newly constructed ceremonial buildings. Eventually the villagers discover why their children are disappearing, and to avenge the killings the men decide to burn the building down. But the spirit, named Dowamu, avoids being killed by escaping underground in the form of the front post made of nyebi wood and hides in a nearby stream. There it is later found by women from the village when they are wading around in the stream fishing with hand nets. The post darts around under that water like a large fish, prodding them phallically between the thighs. (In some versions of the narrative, the women become pregnant as a result of this action.) The women immediately tell their husbands what they have found and with their assistance catch the post in their hand nets—the term for which is a common euphemism for "womb"—and drag it up onto the bank. The men thereupon vent their anger on the cannibal spirit Dowamu by hacking at the post with their adzes. Pieces of wood fly in all directions. The men then drag what remains of the post far off into the forest and dump it there. They have not killed Dowamu, however, and although the myth does not say so, it implies that he lives

on in men's houses in the form of central posts made from the same type of timber, nyebi.[5]

This association in myth of central posts of men's houses with the homicidal and cannibal spirit Dowamu underlies the respect with which men treat these uprights in everyday life. In contrast to the side posts, they may not be touched. Any contact with them at all would cause Dowamu and the other spirits that are thought to inhabit (and, in a sense, are) the building to punish the offender with a debilitating disease. The only way supernatural punishment can be averted is by immediately making a pig sacrifice (poy poyiik, "pig soup") inside the building. This entails providing a pig, cooking it, and sharing it in a meal with all of the men who occupy the house (see Bowden 1983a:59–61). The association between the central posts and homicidal aggression is brought out even further by the fact that when they are constructing a men's house, the owners of the building bury skulls of famous warriors beside these posts. Men say that this imparts added strength (hapa, "bone") and aggressiveness of disposition (ow katawa) to the building—qualities which are also greatly admired in men. Thus in the architecture of these buildings men give expression to ideas of creativity in the context of both yam planting and human reproduction, on the one hand, and homicidal aggression, on the other.

Carvings

In the korob called Waypanal, the upper sections of the two central uprights at the extreme front and back of the building—the ma somar ("front somar") and yen somar ("rear somar"), respectively—are enclosed by vaulted arches termed "wasp's nests" (hem aka; see Bowden 1983a: pl. 2). These are formed from bark paintings attached to a timber frame. The arches resemble and are named after the nests built on branches of forest trees by a type of wasp (hem) that is a totem of the clan that owns this building. "Wasp's nest" vaulted arches are a "copyrighted" feature of men's houses built by this clan, and no other group may incorporate them into their buildings. Both arches are hollow, and during the mija ("minja") ceremony, when women dance outside the building immediately in front of the ma somar, two men climb inside the front "wasp's nest" through a trapdoor made from one of the paintings and play flutes, which the women dancing below are supposed to think are the voices of spirits present at the ceremony (cf. Tuzin 1980).

The larger-than-life sculpture that is attached to the lower half of the ma somar (see Bowden 1983a: pl. 2) represents the youthful culture hero Nalawen. Nalawen and his younger brother Moychey (an equally large sculpture of whom stands in front of the rear nowkwapa kwat) are the two persons credited, in myth, with building the first men's house named Waypanal. A myth entitled "Wale" tells how Nalawen and Moychey go hunting in the forest and come across a road previously unknown to them. They follow the road and soon find themselves at a village in the land of the dead. The ghosts who normally occupy the village are all temporarily absent, having returned to the land of the living (along the road that Nalawen and Moychey found) to collect the soul of a man who has just died. The two brothers enter the ghosts' village and there discover a fully decorated men's house named Waypanal. The building's design and splendid decorative artworks so impress them that they resolve to build an identical one when they return home. Before they leave the village they encounter two ghosts in the guise of beautiful young girls—the only people left in the village. The girls flirt with them and provide them with a meal. Once back at their own village in the land of the living, the two culture heroes build the first men's house named Waypanal, modeling it exactly on the building they have just seen in the land of the dead. Ever since then, Kwoma say, all men's houses named Waypanal have been built and decorated in precisely the same way. After they complete the building, Nalawen and Moychey decide to return permanently to the land of the dead to marry the two beautiful young girls they met there, but the only way they can do this is by dying. So the two brothers take up weapons, commence fighting, and kill each other.[6] Ironically, when they get back to the land of the dead, this time as ghosts, they discover that the two women, far from being beautiful young girls, are really wizened old hags and that they had appeared to the brothers as young girls only to trick them into killing each other.[7]

This myth is noteworthy for two reasons. First, it indicates explicitly that men's houses named Waypanal have a *supernatural* origin.[8] By attributing a supernatural origin to such men's houses, the myth thereby invests them with a sanctity and authority in social and ritual life that is beyond question. Men's houses, that is, form part of the divine order of things. Second, the myth unambiguously (but indirectly) depicts "culture," in

the form of men's houses named Waypanal, as a "gift" of the spirits (even if, like the fire of Prometheus, it had to be stolen),[9] and gifts must be repaid. Nalawen and Moychey—who represent humanity vis-à-vis the ghosts/spirits from whom they steal the designs—pay for them with their lives. (Men commenting on the myth make clear that the ghostly owners of Waypanal, being spirits, know in advance that Nalawen and Moychey are going to steal the design of their building and to ensure that they will pay for it set a trap for them in the shape of the two illusory beautiful young girls.)

Two other members of Nalawen and Moychey's family are also depicted in Waypanal. On the central *kisiikiis* post (see Bowden 1983a:48) on the left-hand side of the building there is a carving of the boys' mother, Mowsor, shown weeping uncontrollably after learning that her sons have killed each other. Directly opposite, on the central kisiikiis on the right-hand side, there is a carving depicting the two heroes' younger brother Mabor. In the myth Mabor attempts to stop his two older brothers from fighting, and to prevent him from doing so Nalawen and Moychey tie him to the same post on which his portrait sculpture is carved. The figures of Nalawen and Moychey are depicted in the act of killing each other. Nalawen carries a spear under one arm, and Moychey holds a dagger in his raised right hand. These and other sculptures in Waypanal, incidentally, provide an exception to Forge's (1979:279) assertion that sculpture in Papua New Guinea never portrays scenes from myths.

Like the ma somar and rear nowkwapa kwat, the shorter *tapatobo kwat* ("short posts"; see Bowden 1983a:48) on either side at the front of Waypanal are decorated with carvings of mythological figures. The two rear tapatobo kwat, by way of contrast, are carved with "purely decorative" figures, or totemic animals. The life-sized sculpture that stands against the front left tapatobo kwat depicts a mythological figure named Madakapmes. Madakapmes suffers from elephantiasis of the scrotum and hence is depicted with greatly enlarged testicles (*mad*). This grotesque male figure represents one of the best-known but at the same time most puzzling characters in Kwoma myth. One of the two narratives in which he figures tells how he lives alone deep in the forest. His only companions are a fierce man-eating hunting dog named Nukowur (a carving of which stands beside the sculpture of Madakapmes) and an equally fierce tusked boar named Womogweya. Madakapmes possesses a continuously burning fire, and people from nearby villages out hunting in the forest who require fire for cooking customarily turn to him for it. But like the spirit Dowamu, Madakapmes is both a killer and a cannibal, and whenever possible he kills his visitors when they bend down to get a light from the fire beside him and then cooks and eats them. He stores his victim's bones in one large clay pot inside his house and the contents of their digestive tracts in another.

I am inclined to believe that Madakapmes's significance lies in the fact that he is a symbolic "mediator." To borrow a phrase from Lévi-Strauss, Madakapmes is a "master of fire" (1970:188). He possesses cooking fire, and fire, as Lévi-Strauss has demonstrated (1970:64–65, 335–36 and passim), is an important marker of the transition from nature to culture. As a master of fire Madakapmes can be seen as a mediator between the "raw" and the "cooked"—which, for Lévi-Strauss, of course, are metaphors for nature and culture respectively. He can also be seen as a mediator between a whole range of other conceptual oppositions: between life and death (he is alive like a living human being but, being diseased, is symbolically "dead" [cf. Lévi-Strauss 1970:61]), between this world and the subterranean region from which all humans primordially emerged (unlike normal people, who walk on the surface of the earth, he sits with his grossly swollen testicles resting in a large *hole* he has dug in the ground [Bowden 1983a:18]) between the animate and the inanimate (he can move his limbs and to that extent is animate, but because of his greatly enlarged testicles he is unable to move far from where he sits and hence is effectively immobile, like the inanimate), and so on. Madakapmes's role as a symbolic mediator and symbol of the transition from nature to culture is emphasized even more starkly in another myth, where he appears transmogrified, half man, half rotting log. The narrative tells how Madakapmes lies *immobile* (and face down) across a forest track. People who clamber over him, thinking him to be nothing more than a decaying log, thoughtlessly jab at him with sharpened digging sticks and hack at him with their adzes. Small boys shoot toy arrows into his posterior. Eventually Madakapmes persuades two men passing by to carry him far away from the spot, and in return for their assistance he vomits up the different species of sago palm which now provide Kwoma with their staple food.[10] Like the paired culture heroes (Lévi-Strauss 1970:332–33) Nalawen and Moychey, themselves mediators between the nat-

ural and supernatural worlds, Madakapmes, aided by a pair of males, becomes an *originator* of culture as Kwoma understand it.

The major longitudinal side beams, termed *pay* (Bowden 1983a:47), which the tapatobo kwat support, are carved on their front ends with additional figures from myths and on their back ends with totemic animals. For instance, the personage depicted on the front end of the left-hand beam immediately above Madakapmes is the culture hero Sasap (Bowden 1983a:135–44). The carving shows only Sasap's head and his long tongue, which penetrates the vagina of a woman who lies facing away from him with her legs wide apart. The carving illustrates an incident in a myth which tells how Sasap builds himself a house in the top of a tall tree. One day two beautiful young girls who have been attracted by his singing visit him and ask to be helped up into the tree so that they can live with him as his wives. Sasap, however, has no ladder, and to get around the problem he extends his long tongue down to the ground, inserts the tip of it into the vagina of each of the women in turn, and by getting a grip on them in this way, pulls them up.

The central sections of the same longitudinal side beams are carved not with mythological or totemic figures but with what men themselves describe as purely decorative designs. These consist principally of numerous pairs of *arokamaka*, opposed faces. The two minor longitudinal side beams (*mes jiraba*) are decorated much less elaborately. Both have totemic animals carved on their two ends, but the areas in between are decorated with only a few crudely painted totemic designs. Younger painters typically use the surfaces of these beams to practice their art. It is mainly on such beams that one also finds European-style paintings, e.g., of introduced animals such as cats or biblical figures.

I have already commented on two of the carvings on the kisiikiis that support the mes jiraba, viz., the portrait sculptures of Mowsor and Mabor, mother and younger brother, respectively, of the culture heroes Nalawen and Moychey. Three of the four other kisiikiis are decorated with "meaningless" designs and the other with a portrait of the biblical Goliath.

The two other major forms of sculpture found in men's houses are the carvings on the cross-beams and on the ends of slit-gongs (see Bowden 1983a:pl. 3, 23, 32). Cross-beams (*kwar*) are important aesthetically rather than structurally in men's houses, since undecorated buildings lack them altogether. In Waypanal the undersides of the building's four cross-beams are decorated with copies of secret and sacred sculptures that are displayed during the *yena* and *mija* yam-harvest ceremonies. So as not to give away any ritual secrets, the men who constructed Waypanal in the middle 1960s told me that they deliberately carved and painted the figures slightly "incorrectly." Although they are only copies of ceremonial figures, these sculptures are nevertheless thought to *be* the spirits that they represent. Located as they are above the center of the men's house, the spirits are thought to look down on and preside over the activities that take place in the building. For instance, if a man were to strike another in anger during a meeting in the building (something that is strictly prohibited), these spirits, it is believed, would immediately afflict him with disease. The only way to ward off such supernatural punishment is by making a pig sacrifice in the building in which the offense occurred.

The other main form of decorative sculpture found in men's houses consists of the carvings on the finials of slit-gongs. Traditionally slit-gongs were decorated only on their extreme ends, the stylized carvings conventionally depicting human faces bordered by "decorative" designs. However, nowadays, following the introduction of steel tools which make the carving of the hardwood used for drums very much easier, slit-gongs tend to be decorated more elaborately, and the carvings themselves depict a much wider range of subjects (for instance, the carving on a slit-gong [made in 1973] depicting an incident from the myth of the mes tree). Drums made during the late 1970s are occasionally carved and painted all over.

Paintings

Traditionally, Kwoma paintings were highly stylized and for the most part entirely abstract. Today some artists are experimenting with a more "realistic" European style, but the overwhelming majority of paintings are still purely abstract. Paintings are composed of a relatively small number of design elements, such as circles, ovals, dotted lines, lozenges, and wavy lines. These are combined in different paintings to depict a wide range of totemic plants, animals, and other entities. Because the number of design elements is small and the range of objects depicted large, design elements in themselves do not (and could not) have fixed "meanings." Such significance as they have derives entirely from the "meaning" of a painting as a whole, "meaning" in this context signifying the painting's subject matter as identified by the artist. Thus, depending on the wider pictorial context, a circle might represent (among other things) a coconut or one of several other round fruits, an eye, a testicle, a water-lily seed, an animal's belly or navel, a hearthstone, the moon, a star, or a person's head.

Paintings (*bi*) are made on the smooth inner surface of the midrib (*bi*) of the sago palm branch (strictly, the palm's leafstalk). A section about a meter in length is cut from the lower end of the U-shaped midrib (only dry, dead branches are used), the leaves are cut off, the rough outer surface is smoothed, and the bark is flattened to expose the smooth inner surface. The bark still has a good deal of spring to it, however, and before it can be used it must be permanently flattened by being placed under weights for several days, often after being soaked in water. Occasionally an artist will paint on just one bark prepared in this way, but more frequently he will lash two together, placing the wider end of one against the narrower end of the other, to form a roughly rectangular "double" bark about sixty centimeters wide.

Before it is painted, the bark is smeared with a coating of black clay which serves as the base on which the other colors are applied. When the black base has dried, the artist limns the outline of his intended design in clear water. If he is satisfied that he has the proportions correct, he then quickly traces over the lines with white paint. If he is unsatisfied with his initial design, he simply waits for the watery lines to evaporate, since they leave no trace, and starts again. When he has completed outlining the basic design in white, he builds up the picture by adding the two other colors used in painting, yellow and red. When the painting has been completed, it remains to varnish the unpainted areas of black undercoat with sap from the *shogwiyaw* tree, which is white and opaque when wet but dries to form a clear glistening sheen on the picture surface. The black, white, and yellow paints all derive from earth pigments. Red paint is obtained either from one of several types of earth pigment or from *Bixa orellana* seeds (cf. Smidt in this volume). All paints are mixed with water and, apart from the black undercoat, which is rubbed on with a wad of coconut-husk fiber, are applied with small brushes constructed from chewed fibers of betel-nut husks tied to short sticks. The same small brushes (*siipiikwiina*) are used to apply the varnish.

Figures 1–4 illustrate four paintings made for me by distinguished Bangwis artists in February

FIG. 1. Opposed faces.

FIG. 3. Flying fox (torso and wings).

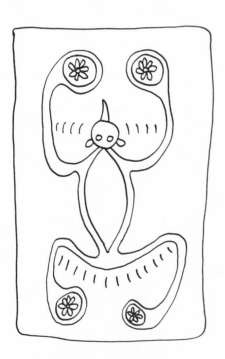

FIG. 2. Flying fox.

FIG. 4. Pumpkin plant.

1982, all of which are now in the Papua New Guinea National Museum and Art Gallery. Each is by a different artist. The first (fig. 1) is a stylized representation of two opposed faces. The artist initially identified this design as a variation of the arokamaka double face that is carved on longitudinal side beams in men's houses (cf. Kaufmann 1979:fig. 21), but he later confidentially informed me that the painting in fact depicted two ceremonial yena carvings, one owned by him and the other by a neighboring clan. The artist remarked (with a sly grin) that he was not formally entitled to depict in his painting a yena figure belonging to another clan, but no one would discover what he had done because he had deliberately represented the two sculptures in a highly stylized manner. This painting is a useful illustration of the fact that without access to the artist's intentions it is not necessarily possible to tell what a painting is "about." Artists, and people generally, speak as if bark paintings had simple unambiguous meanings that could be readily identified by knowledgeable observers solely on the basis of the visual evidence. But in reality they do not, and this is demonstrated by the fact that when different men were asked independently to identify the subjects of paintings made by other artists, their interpretations varied radically.

The best Kwoma artists are never content simply to reproduce existing representations of clan totems (or other entities) but pride themselves on their capacity to modify and embellish them imaginatively. One consequence of this is that no two artists ever depict the same entity in exactly the same way or even paint it in the same way on two different occasions. Some idea of the variations that are found between different paintings that have the same subject can be gained by comparing figures 2 and 3. Both depict the same species of flying fox (apukibi). The first shows the animal's body and four limbs but omits its wings; its head is shown from the top, and its eyes, ears, and nose are clearly visible. Each of its "hands" (tapa) and "feet" (yat) encloses a water lily. The second is more stylized and is composed almost exclusively of the animal's torso and wings. The artist explained that because there was insufficient room at the top of the painting to include its head, he had added its two eyes, in the form of concentric circles, on either side of its body. (Even the most skilled artists routinely offer such seemingly ingenuous explanations for having painted a picture in a particular way.)

In addition to continually modifying designs, the best artists like to incorporate new objects and

motifs into their paintings. The painting illustrated in figure 4, for instance, is one man's impression of a pumpkin plant (an introduced species). The large circles in the four corners of the picture represent fruits and the attached hooked lines the stems. The design that connects and encloses each pair of fruits at the top and bottom of the picture represents the plant's runners and, in the middle, its flower. The circle in the center of the painting represents an elkhorn fern (riibiika), an epiphyte that people bring in from the forest and grow for ornamental purposes on posts around their houses. The two hooked lines inside the circle represent the fern's large cabbage-like leaves, which fold around its base. The artist informed me that the riibiika plant was not a totem of his own clan and consequently he was not formally entitled to depict it in his paintings, but like the artist responsible for the painting of the so-called arokamaka faces above, he privately boasted that since his painting was so highly stylized no one would know what he had depicted unless he told them—something that he had no intention of doing. This painting provides a second striking example of the difficulty of determining what a Kwoma painting is about without access to the artist's intentions.

Notes

1. According to the orthography adopted for Kwoma words in this article, b, d, g, and j are equivalent to mb, nd, ngg, and nj respectively. The spelling of village names is that of the Village Directory for 1969.

2. Since Kwoma women traditionally married as soon as they reached puberty, the adult females resident in a clan settlement would all be in-marrying wives (or widows).

3. Each clan is entitled to build and settle around its own men's house; but Kwoma clans are small—those in the tribe in which I worked contained on average only six married male members each—and more commonly several clans jointly build and use a single men's house for all social and ceremonial purposes.

4. Since the bulk of my field data have been collected in only one of the four Kwoma tribes, the Hongwama, my description of men's houses and the art and mythology associated with them properly applies to that tribe only. Kwoma share their language with several villages immediately to the north of the Washkuk Hills, but following local usage the name "Kwoma" in this article refers exclusively to the inhabitants of the Washkuk range.

5. Kaunga-speaking neighbors of the Kwoma (see Bowden 1983a:11), in their version of this myth, associate the homicidal spirit Dowamu with the central

posts in contemporary men's houses even more directly, for their narrative states that the post which the women capture in their hand nets subsequently gives rise to the nyebi trees from which men now cut the central uprights of ceremonial buildings. Both Kwoma and Kaunga versions of this myth also tell how some of the slivers of wood chipped off the captured men's-house post while the men are attacking it with their adzes land in the stream and are transformed into secret sacred flutes (Bowden 1983a:125–26), replicas of which men now play during rituals in men's houses. Through their association with nyebi wood and the homicidal spirit Dowamu, flutes, therefore, like the buildings in which they are played, are also associated with masculine procreativeness as well as homicidal aggression (cf. Bateson 1934, Forge 1966). Slit-gongs are associated with the same two ideas, since they are customarily made from the same hardwood, nyebi or garamut (the Tok Pisin term for slit-gong), as the main uprights.

6. To the best of my knowledge suicide, in the sense of death by one's own hand, never occurs in Kwoma society. It is significant therefore that the two young men in this myth commit suicide by killing *each other* rather than individually killing themselves.

7. Ghosts, who were once people, are said to resent being dead and out of sheer spite to do everything possible to augment their number with souls from the land of the living.

8. Although the first men's house named Waypanal is said to have been located in the land of the dead, Kwoma point out that all of the beings that figure in myths, whether they are described as people, ghosts, or animals, are spirits. Thus Nalawen and Moychey, although represented in the myth as humans (*ma*) vis-à-vis the ghosts (*gaba*), are themselves spirits (*sikilowas*); hence spirits actually built the first Waypanal in the land of the living.

9. Kwoma understand Nalawen and Moychey to have "stolen" the design of Waypanal.

10. Although yams provide the focus of Kwoma ceremonial, sago is the single most important food in the Kwoma diet.

45/ Sepik River Architecture: Changes in Cultural Traditions[1]

Christian Coiffier

The peoples of the Sepik Basin have been known to the Western world since the turn of the century from the extraordinary artifacts gathered for museums and private collections by merchants, travelers, and ethnologists. The variety of social structures of these tribes of very different languages has interested ethnographers, and their architecture and settlement patterns display the same great variety and ingenuity. I shall limit myself here to the Middle Sepik region, in particular the area between Pagwi and Tambunam, in Iatmul territory (Iapmai to its inhabitants). Of the twenty-four or so villages in the area, about half still have one or more large ceremonial houses: Nyaurangai, Kandingai, Korogo, Suapmeri, Aibom, Yindabu, Yensan, Palimbei, Malingai, Kanganaman, Kaminimbit, Timbunke, and Mumeri (see table 1). Tambunam deserves mention as well because, though it no longer has a ceremonial house, its dwellings merit special attention.

When the Germans discovered the area, there were scarcely more villages with ceremonial houses than there are today, but in general these were not the same ones. Whereas the discoverers expressed admiration for these ceremonial houses, it is difficult to obtain a complete picture of them from the available museum collections or publications.[2] Paintings, pillars, ridgepoles, carvings, and masks from the gables of a building were often dispersed. Construction of ceremonial houses continues in the Sepik. One was completed in Yensan in 1980, and houses were under construction in Mumeri and Nyaurangai. While tourism may explain the construction of the one in Yensan (see Schmid in this volume), it cannot explain that of those in the other two villages, which are not situated on the usual tourist route. Certainly, these new edifices lack the presence of those one sees in photographs from the early twentieth century; they are smaller, and the layout of the decoration of gables and beams has changed. Modes of construction have evolved, as they have elsewhere in the world, following the trading and cultural contacts between the Iatmul villages and their neighbors. For example, the ceremonial houses of Timbunke, Korogo, and Kanganaman, on the north bank of the Sepik River, are similar in shape and technology to those of the Sawos. In Palimbei, the Numbaroman house is similar to Aibom's Nongruimbit and Kosimbi houses. Palimbei's Bayembit house resembles one in Yensan, and the two houses are known to have been built by men of the same clan. The architecture of Mindimbit, Tambunam, and Mumeri, again, has been influenced by that of their neighbors.

The geographical locations of the villages have changed over time with the meanderings of the river and in the aftermath of tribal wars. Kandingai, Nyaurangai, Palimbei, Malingai, Angriman, Tegoi, and Kararau are all situated on abandoned meanders of the Sepik. Kaulagu, formerly called Kolina, was moved six kilometers downstream after quarrels with people from Yensemangua, and its name was changed again, to Korogo. Locations have been chosen for economic and strategic reasons; for example, Kandingai, Nyaurangai, and Suapmeri all control channels connecting the Sepik with the Chambri lakes.

At Malingai, Kandingai, Palimbei, and Kanganaman, the traditional settlement pattern can still be clearly seen. Each has a long, wide area surrounded by coconut palms parallel to the river,[3] either straight, as in Kandingai and Malingai, or slightly curved, as in Palimbei and Kanganaman, on which rise the ceremonial houses for initiated men only. This ceremonial area, the *wompunau*, is usually divided between the two parts of the village. In Palimbei (figure 1), for example, the wompunau, three hundred meters long and thirty meters wide, has two ceremonial houses, one for Numbaroman and the other for Bayembit. The village is linked to the Sepik by parallel paths on each side of a channel called Kurupmui, one belonging to Numbaroman and the other to Bayembit. The wompunau, reserved for men, is paralleled by paths used by women, and a path between the two ceremonial houses allows women to cross it.

The ridgelines of the ceremonial houses (*ngaigo*) are oriented along the wompunau's lon-

TABLE 1
Iatmul Ceremonial Houses, 1980

Village	House	Date Constructed	Condition
Nyaurangai		1979–80	new
Kandingai	Mariruman	1970?	fair
	Wombum	1965?	fair
	Aulimbit	1976	fair
Korogo		1965	poor
Suapmeri		1970–71	good
Aibom	Kosimbi	pre-1972	fair
	Nongruimbit	pre-1972	fair
Yindabu		?	poor
Yensan		1975	very good
Palimbei	Numbaroman	1951–54	fair
	Bayembit	1968–72	very good
Malingai		?	poor
Kanganaman	Worimbi	1945–46	poor
Kaminimbit		1968	poor
Timbunke		1976	very good
Mumeri		1980	new

gitudinal axis. The ceremonial house (figs. 2–4) has two parts: *damageko* (literally "the nose of the house"), which faces the center of the wompunau, overlooking a ceremonial mound (*wake*) planted with totemically significant palmyra palm (*Borassus flabellifer*) and hibiscus, and *gumbumgeko*, which faces away from it. The ceremonial mound was fenced in 1972, but the fence has since disappeared; the only place I saw the remnants of such a fence, carved with anthropomorphic figures, was Malingai. Groups of five megaliths (*mbwan*) often surround mounds of this kind, as in Malingai, Kanganaman, Kandingai, and Suapmeri.[4] At Palimbei there are three groups of five megaliths each near the Numbaroman, Bayembit, and Andimbit houses, respectively, three groups of twin megaliths, and four isolated rocks, a total of twenty-five megaliths (fig. 5). These stones are important for the archaeology of the region, since they may sometimes be the only visible indicators of ancient village repossessed by the forest.[5]

The interior of the ceremonial house is divided both horizontally and vertically. Horizontally, one distinguishes a cruciform division with a central post (*warangka*) and an entrance on each side. The platforms, ninety centimeters high, of the various clans are situated along the walls. (In the western part of the area, there are platforms on all four walls and entrances in each corner.) Theoretically, the youngest initiated men of the clan occupy the outside end of the platform and the eldest the inside, closest to the central post and

the orator's stool. There is thus a progressive shift of generations near the center of the building from which at any point one may determine the social hierarchy. Custom dictates that one not cross the building from one end to the other but go around the central post and leave by one of the side doors.

Vertically, three levels can be distinguished: (1) the ground, always very tidy, on which one finds the hearths of the various clans, surrounded by several three-legged wooden stools, and the big slit-drums (sometimes set on logs) in different places according to the occasion; (2) the platforms, made of *limbum* (areca palm) planks supported on an independent framework, where men rest, talk, and carve; and (3) the upper platform, reached by a ladder that according to Milan Stanek (personal communication) represents for the Iatmul the mythical link between earth and sky. Climbing through the trapdoor of this platform, one passes between the legs of two female sculptures that probably represent the female ancestors of the clan to which they belong. Since the central post represents the male ancestor, the framework constitutes a coherent structure—the central post, the "father," and the two king posts, "mothers," supporting the ridgepole.[6] The ten side posts represent the clans that participated in the construction of the house; each has a name and is associated with a particular clan. Thus the ceremonial house, in addition to its function as protector of beings and sacred objects, has a symbolic dimension. It has evolved as a concrete representation of the villagers' social and cosmic worlds.[7]

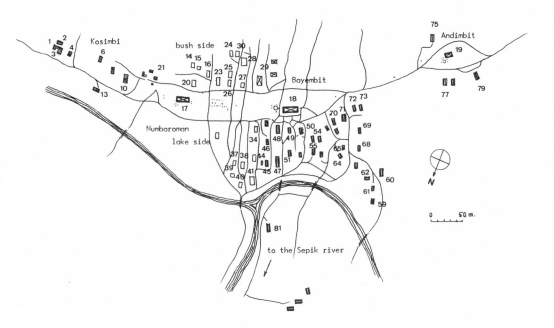

Fig. 1. Palimbei in 1980 (drawing by C. Coiffier). Numbaroman (with bush and lake subdivisions) and Bayembit are the two sections. Andimbit houses members of clans that have broken off relations with the village; most of them have gone on to found a new village at Indabu, five kilometers north on the river. Kosimbi contains recent migrants from Aibom.

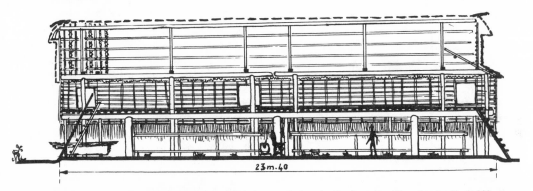

Fig. 2. Numbaroman ceremonial house (length 23.4 meters), longitudinal section (drawing by C. Coiffier).

The construction of a ceremonial house is a collective activity. Whereas the construction of a dwelling may bring together ten or so persons, the construction of a large ceremonial house could traditionally bring together several hundred. The agreement of a number of individuals is therefore necessary for construction to begin. The big men must use their authority and skills to obtain the cooperation of the various participants, taking into account the spirits and ancestors and calculating the right moment for each activity. Each of the clans that plans to participate must bring together enough men for its part of the project.

There is no group specifically concerned with construction, as there is in Polynesia, but there are individuals who, as a result of their experience, are more skilled in certain techniques than others. The construction of a ceremonial house calls for coordination unequaled in any other activity except possibly war. For a certain period of time the men and women of the community must work to their maximum potential, some in locating, transporting, and preparing the materials and others in feeding the participants. The acquisition of essential materials not available in the area obliges the community to activate exchange re-

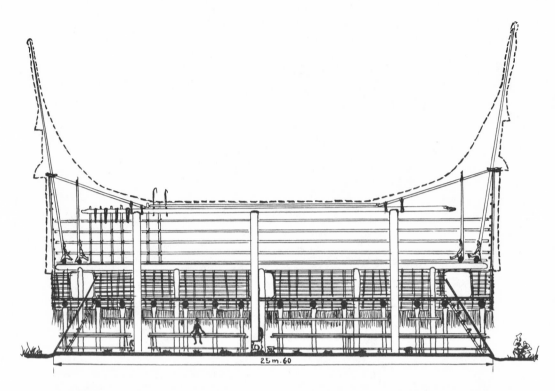

FIG. 3. Bayembit ceremonial house (length 25.6 meters), longitudinal section (drawing by C. Coiffier).

lations with other villages, sometimes far away. This is especially the case for certain posts unobtainable in the forests of the Sepik, where trees are scarce and expensive. The Iatmul frequently buy trees from the Sawos.[8] During the construction of the new Yensan house in 1975, conflict is said to have broken out between Yensan and Marap villagers when the latter demanded the return of the trees used in the construction. Transport of the trees is also a problem; overland it must be done by men, the number of carriers depending on the weight and length of the trunk.

The typical dwelling, like the ceremonial house, has two distinct structures, one supporting a platform and the other the roof. In the oldest houses, the ridgepole is supported by two or three central posts. Shape and materials vary. Generally, houses are rectangular, twice as long as they are wide. Walls may be made of sago-palm leafstalks tied together with rattan cords or of woven coconut-palm fronds; sometimes they are covered with sago-palm fronds applied like slates. The same material is used for roofs, which are two-sided and form canopies over the gables. In Tambunam most dwellings are wider and sturdier than those of the western Iatmul villages. Their

facades on each end are adorned with large basketwork masks covered with sago-palm fronds. Sometimes the whole gable looks like a human face, with the opening for the door taking the place of the mouth. The names for the decorative elements of the gable confirm this anthropomorphism: *pu* (breast), *dama* (nose), *nimbi* (teeth), *kundi* (mouth), *menii* (eyes), *dama-livit* (decorative nose). The ridgelines of dwellings are oriented at right angles to the wompunau or to the nearby river. The openings, without doors, are placed in the center of the gables, often at both ends. Houses are set in rows corresponding to the various clans, and each row is separated from others by a dike (*tuwinumbu*) planted with ornamental trees (coconut palms, bananas, papayas, and other fruit trees). When the river rises, the dikes protect the trees and hold back the water.

Family life in the house is preferably confined to the upper platform, which is shared among a number of closely related persons. It is divided into four areas in relation to the central axis of the building: front, back, right (the most important), and left. These areas are not, however, physically separated. Each woman has her own area of the house with her various cooking utensils—one or

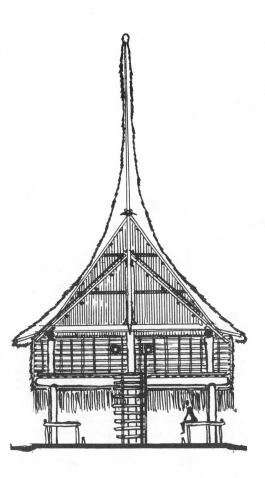

FIG. 4. Bayembit (*above*) and Numbaroman ceremonial houses (widths 5.9 and 8.3 meters respectively), cross-sections (drawing by C. Coiffier).

two pottery bowls from Chambri for cooking sago pancakes, large pottery jars for storing sago flour, and dishes. Foodstuffs are kept in baskets and string bags (*bilum*) hung from hooks attached to the framework. Traditionally these fishermen and horticulturists had no need to store food for long periods, since fruits, vegetables, and fish were brought daily from the gardens and the river (Powter 1975). Along the sides of the house are platforms some eighty centimeters high on which objects that one does not want to set on the floor are placed. People sit on mats or small wooden stools. At night mosquito nets, until recently made of finely woven wicker, are put up. The floor is made of limbum planks and is kept tidy. The hearth is often near an opening through which smoke can readily escape. In addition to the two entrances, there are small windows halfway up the walls. Wood for the fire is often stored beneath the house, which seems to be reserved for men and for children's games.

The wood most often used for construction is *miamba* (Tok Pisin *garamut*), the region's hardest, most resistant to insects, and heaviest; *kwarap* (*kwila*) is confined to sheltered areas because it tends to rot. Limbum, which is also very resistant to insects, is used for floors. A rattan rope is used as a measuring tape. The leafstalks of the sago palm, sewn together with rattan cords, have enough interstices to allow the breeze to circulate. This type of wall is, however, totally ineffective when it comes to keeping out mosquitoes. When it is not too old, the rattan that ties together the various elements of the roofing and walls is sufficiently solid and supple to ensure rigidity and pliability against wind and earthquakes. The sago-palm thatch, if it is thick enough and well made, provides good protection against the heat and the equatorial rains. The slope of the roof is 40–50°, which permits a good flow of rain water into the gutter around the building.

Palimbei houses, with their opposed openings, their sago-palm walls, and their limbum-plank floors, are well ventilated and correspond exactly to the typical equatorial house described by Rapoport (1969). The parallel rows of coconut palms provide much-needed shade for the houses, and the ornamental bushes not only are decorative but form a low barrier to the wind, which is deflected toward the platforms. These traditional solutions coincide with recommendations based on recent climatic studies (see Rapoport 1969). In these houses, the roof is the prevailing element. It is actually an enormous, very light,

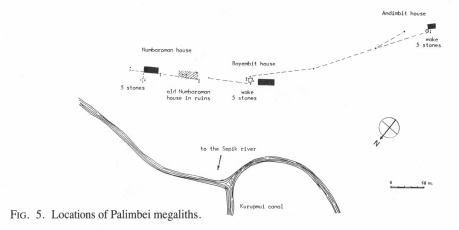

FIG. 5. Locations of Palimbei megaliths.

opaque umbrella that resists the torrential rains and avoids accumulating heat. In every inhabited house, fires burn constantly in large clay hearths set on the floor, reducing the moisture in the air. By coating the framework and the thatch, the smoke from the fires kills vermin; it also drives off mosquitoes. The double-framework structure, supporting the platform and the roof independently, offers the possibility of partially repairing the building without modifying the entire structure. The fact that the principal elements, beams and posts, are placed one on top of the other guarantees the resistance of the building to various natural forces—swelling of materials, earthquakes, wind, flood, etc. Hanging a movable wall from the roof is also an excellent technique. Roofing materials are tied together with a great variety of knots, each with its technical and magical function; for example, the *kwanduk kowo* tightly secures the roof to the ridgepole.

Many factors, both physical and social, contribute to the rapid deterioration of buildings in this equatorial region. Among the physical ones are the annual floods, which break up the soil, loosen the posts, and sometimes carry tree trunks that act as battering rams. House pilings may be underwater for weeks. The daily monsoon rains rot the framework, which is then quickly attacked by mold and insects (termites and other xylophagous insects such as Cerambycidae and Buprestidae). A number of animals—birds, snakes, rodents, and insects—participate in the destruction of the thatching by inhabiting it. Strong winds regularly blow away elements of the roof and, along with floods, may topple a house. Earthquakes may dislocate or break up buildings, as happened, for example, to the Kanganaman ceremonial house in 1981. Fire is rare and according to villagers the result of witchcraft. The only

burned-down house I saw was in Tambunam in 1979, where the fire had been caused by an oil lamp knocked over by a child. The humidity of the wood and the air is generally too high for fires to start.

Among the social factors causing the destruction of houses, wars between villages were once a major one, but today the most important is economic and social change. The majority of young people have deserted the villages to work in the productive centers of the country. Houses can no longer be properly maintained, and some have even been abandoned. Site plans of Palimbei made in 1972, 1975, and 1980 (cf. figs. 6 and 7 with fig. 1) document the loss of fifteen houses over the eight-year period.

Change

Of the many changes that have overwhelmed the local economy and the traditional culture since World War II, the arrival of foreigners and the migration of young people to other parts of the country are especially important. The construction of roads between Wewak and Angoram and between Wewak and Pagwi in the early sixties opened up these areas to police, missionaries, traders, civil servants, crocodile hunters, tourists, doctors, and scholars. Pagwi and Angoram grew. A monetary exchange system replaced the traditional gift exchange. Under the Australian authorities, fighting between villages was stopped. New languages, Tok Pisin and English, became the media for a different culture for youth. Schools and medical facilities were created by missions and government. Population increased. The trading of items such as tools, machines, and boat motors created new exchange systems. The transistor ra-

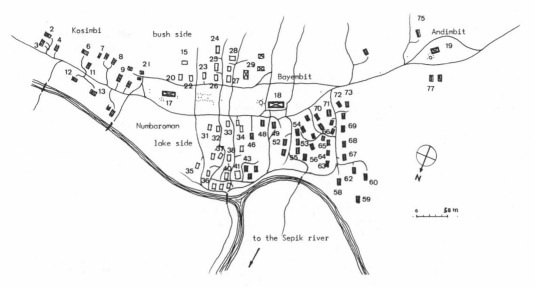

FIG. 6. Palimbei in 1972 (drawing by C. Coiffier from a 1981 survey by Florence Weiss and Milan Stanek).

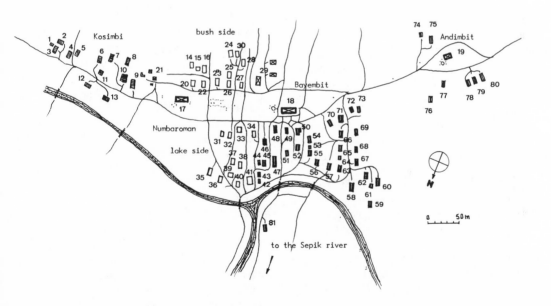

FIG. 7. Palimbei in 1975 (drawing by C. Coiffier from a 1975 survey by W. Ruff and J. Lawson).

dio opened up the area to information about other parts of the country and the world. New stock-breeding and farming techniques were introduced in the Pagwi and Timbunke areas. At the same time, a destructive floating fern, *Salvinia molesta*, invaded the river. Finally, when Papua New Guinea became independent in 1975, indigenous inhabitants assumed public office in the new provincial government, taking over roles formerly occupied by Australian administrators.

Meanwhile, young people were going to work in the plantations on the coast, in Wewak, Madang, and Rabaul, where they were introduced to new ways of life and new technologies. They met people of other ethnic groups with whom they could compare their ideas. They also became acquainted with new forms of housing and brought new products and knowhow back to their villages, and they established important new communities of migrants on the outskirts of the above-mentioned towns. In studying the Bumbu communities on the outskirts of Lae, I found that the people, originally from Sepik villages, had established communities there with the same kinship organization centered on men's houses as before. These houses were oriented traditionally, parallel to the river, but because of the distance from the bush they were made of materials salvaged from the discards of the new consumer society. They were still built on pilings, and the walls were made in the same way, but the doors now had locks. Relations can be traced between native villages and the different points of migration; people move between them in terms of kinship relations. Young people return to their native villages to be initiated in order to marry. Some, however, marry outside of the region and become cut off from their traditions. Young people who have lived a few years away from the village and then return to it are extremely critical of their elders.

The Christian missionaries who settled in different parts of the country brought new types of housing very different from the ones traditional in the villages. Their buildings were models of Western technology, and the construction techniques they employed came from other parts of Papua New Guinea and elsewhere in the world. At first, the missionaries' policy was to destroy the ceremonial houses and replace them with little wooden and corrugated-iron chapels similar to ones in Europe. Later they began to adapt their buildings to the local culture, and many religious buildings, Catholic and Protestant alike, were built in the traditional native style (for example, the old church at Kaningara and the one in Arisili, near Maprik). At Palimbei the Catholic mission built a chapel in the shape of a large traditional dwelling, except that it had openings at mid-height along the sides. The placing of this building on the border between Numbaroman and Bayembit is significant because it is used by people from both parts of the village. During my last stay in the area, large churches, pastiches of traditional buildings such as the new Kaningara church, were being built. Certain traditional motifs have been adapted to Christian notions in the process. For example, over the Kaminimbit mission church the *kau* (eagle) stretches out its wings like the arms of Christ, even though it is a symbol of ancestral warlikeness. Again, in the Kaningara church, this symbol is placed above a human figure with its hands joined like an angel's.

The Australian administration ordered the construction in every village of a building in which government patrols could stay. These houses, called *haus kiap* in Tok Pisin, are no longer being maintained and are falling into ruin. The administration further ordered the construction of an outhouse near every dwelling, and these are well maintained but rarely used. Government and missionaries also imposed burial of the dead and the building of cemeteries. A small post office has recently been built at Kanganaman; previously mail could be received only in Pagwi or through the missionaries. The Pagwi city hall combines traditional elements with techniques of construction employing new materials. Schools, which isolate children from their native environment and teach them new ways of sitting, eating, sleeping, and thinking, tend to alienate them from the ancestral architectural forms.[9] Some schools, however, such as the one in Kaminimbit, have been built like traditional dwellings.

The development of tourism has brought foreigners on organized tours to the Sepik, and some villages, such as Korogo and Yensan, now specialize in presenting staged rituals for visitors. As I have already mentioned, the ceremonial house in Yensan is reported to have been built because of tourism, to compete with the one in Korogo (see Schmid in this volume).

Imported materials have been a force for change in traditional architecture since the turn of the century. Steel axes and nails were probably the first of these, and although the axes were a decided improvement, the same cannot be said for nails. Nails often contribute to the disintegration of buildings. They create holes that, with time and weather, help to split and rot the wood, and, unlike the traditional rattan lashing, which at worst will slip or break under stress, they tend to respond to strong winds or earthquakes by tearing the wood apart. Since New Guineans began using nails, they have taken to employing beer bottle-caps as washers to strengthen joints. Instead of capping the ridge tiling with coconut shells, they now use upside-down beer bottles or pieces of folded sheet metal. Corrugated iron is sometimes used to repair holes in thatched roofs, but because of the heat and humidity all sorts of microscopic fungi and insects proliferate under it. Instead of twine made from local plants, villagers now use string made of polyester fiber, imported rope, or wire, all of which react differently in terms of strength and elasticity in an equatorial climate. The plywood or asbestos panels sometimes used in constructing partitions tend to confine the heat.

Some villagers, thinking that everything brought by the white man is better but also aware of its resistance to twisting, shocks, rust, insects, and fungi, have begun to invest in corrugated iron for roofs. Iron is easy to use, facilitates the collection of rainwater, and is fire-resistant, but it has the important drawback of being expensive to apply properly. For example, villagers never install insulation under it, with the result that their homes soon become uninhabitable ovens. Again, they rarely use washers around the nails that secure the roof, and consequently it often leaks. Proper placement of the metal is difficult because the structure is more or less irregular. Finally, the cost of purchase and transportation of the metal is much higher than for traditional materials.

Palimbei offers an interesting example of the use of new technology. In contrast to the Bayembit house next door, the Numbaroman ceremonial house, rebuilt in 1951–54 under the guidance of a man from the Mbowi clan named Masobabwan (Milan Stanek, personal communication), has a triangulated framework put together with nails. For no apparent technical reason, central posts were preserved only in the lower part of the house. Before becoming a big man, Masobabwan had worked for the Catholic mission and later for the government in town as a carpenter.[10]

Gradually, then, old methods are being replaced by new ones; most striking about the process are the radical use of new materials and the pace of change. Every death of an old man in the village means the loss of tradition and skill. The elders sit on the platforms of the ceremonial houses, which look increasingly like senior citizens' clubs, and recall the past.

In the urban centers of Papua New Guinea, some architects have been directly inspired by Iatmul architectural forms. The bar at the University of Technology in Lae is a good example, since it perfectly combines traditional style and modern materials; basically a framework screwed together and supported by metal posts set in concrete blocks, it is roofed with sago-palm thatch and has its gables decorated with mythological motifs. The roof of the main amphitheater at the university is supported by Sepik-style carved posts. Two government buildings in Port Moresby seem to be inspired by traditional Sepik shapes, perhaps because the prime minister, Michael Somare, is a native of the Sepik. Similarly, the National Museum is a building made of concrete blocks supporting a framework of taut steel cables that reproduces the curved shape of a Sepik roof. The bookshop at its entrance gives a rough idea of traditional ceremonial-house architecture, while the prime minister's house on the hillside above the museum is reminiscent of a Lower Sepik dwelling. Private buildings such as the Karawari Lodge (a hotel on a tributary of the Sepik) seek to offer tourists the originality of a traditional dwelling combined with modern comforts. Finally, the Maprik Law Court, built entirely of traditional materials in the shape of a yam storehouse, must be mentioned. In all these buildings, the choice of traditional shapes, materials, and decoration was made by individuals who were outsiders to Sepik culture, and consequently the original functions of the traditional buildings have been distorted.

The Future

What future can be foreseen for the architecture of the Sepik? Will it be one that bears in mind cultural variants and is carried out by the inhabitants themselves, or will be it one of rapid change imposed from the outside? Will the local people be able to organize things in their own way, or will there be centralized administration? Should the local population be stabilized by preventing youth from emigrating? Can education be prevented from turning youth away from their native environment? Is it not possible for the young people of today to continue to discover a new world and its opportunities and still remain proud of the creative skills of their ancestors?

In any case, Sepik architecture deserves a place in any world history of architecture (see Ruff and Ruff in this volume), and the improvement of Sepik dwellings should begin with a recognition of their architectural values and then go on to a study of the needs of their inhabitants with a view to adapting them to new life-styles. The chances for success in this enterprise will be increased by the use of local natural resources (see Housing Commission 1976).

While Sepik people are very skillful carpenters, it is conceivable that they might benefit from some technical suggestions. For example, the shingle roofing so successfully used elsewhere has not yet been widely adopted in the Sepik. The cutting and laying of shingles is easy to learn, and one or two good trees can produce enough shingles to roof a whole house. A shingle roof may last more than twenty years, the time it takes for a tree to grow to maturity in a tropical climate, and it allows the collection of rain water pouring from its overhanging eaves.

Chemical treatment of the wooden materials used should be avoided (see Te'oo Selarn Nawayap 1975). Efficient and inexpensive ways of protecting the foundations of buildings against termites already exist. Consideration might also be given to improving the choice of tree species. New techniques such as prefabrication might be experimented with. Some new materials might also be identified among the existing local resources. It would be quite easy to create self-sufficient dwellings identical to those of which some Western ecologists dream. In an equatorial climate, no heating is needed (except in the mountains), and hot water could easily be produced by solar energy. Rain water is sufficient for drinking water if caught under the eaves and stored in tanks. Climatic problems are often better solved in villages than in towns, where air conditioning is expensive, requires energy and maintenance, and remains insufficient against humidity as well as unhealthful.

Conclusion

As Ruff and Ruff (1979) have pointed out, "The power of money and collectors' interest have convinced Papua New Guineans of the value of their traditional artifacts, but they have not yet realised the value of their traditional house forms, their ceremonial structures and the settlement pattern of their villages."[11] Fortunately, the Papua New Guinean Constitution proposes the promotion of the survival of traditions. The aim of my study of Sepik village architecture (Coiffier 1982, 1983, 1984) is to establish a baseline inventory that will help young villagers, researchers, and architects of this new nation to become aware of the value of the architectural structures and solutions that their ancestors invented. In countries with stone architecture, the ruins that have survived inform us of their value; this is not the case with Sepik architectural masterpieces, which quickly fall into ruin and vanish. Will they all disappear before future Sepik generations become aware of their cultural value?

Notes

1. Translated by Louisette Rat and Daniel Ford. I thank Wallace and Ruth Ruff for their help and for the valuable information they placed at my disposal.

2. The Berlin Dahlem Museum and the Hamburgisches Museum für Völkerkunde are exceptional in displaying models of houses from Angriman.

3. Hauser-Schäublin (in this volume) reports her informants' explanation of the departure from this rule of the ceremonial house in Kararau.

4. It would be interesting to investigate the source of these stones, which may have been transported from fairly distant rocky mountainous regions (see Schuster in this volume).

5. A systematic study of these megaliths might allow the identification of former areas of settlement in the basin (see Kaufmann and Schuster in this volume).

6. A house is believed to have a life and death just as do human beings, and for this reason a damaged house is not always repaired.

7. In Tambunam many dwellings have enormous masks or faces on their facades (see Métraux in this volume). From Bowden's article in this volume it would appear that there are some very interesting similarities between Iatmul and Kwoma villages in the terms used for certain parts of ceremonial houses.

8. At fifty to a hundred kina per tree in 1979.

9. Before Independence, all teachers were foreign, and most of them transmitted their own ways of thinking about technology to their students. Some of them were not even aware of this influence. This kind of education did not develop a sense of cultural identity. European and local ways of thinking are in fact compatible and should have received complementary emphasis. A number of participants in the Basel symposium expressed regret that research in education and vocational training is no longer being pursued.

10. A house for an important man in the Numbaroman half of the village was also built under the guidance of Masobabwan (Florence Weiss, personal communication), and it also has a special feature: a double roof, like that of a pagoda, without the increased height's representing another floor.

11. As is evident from the market value of the carved posts taken from the Kanganaman ceremonial house (see Eoe in this volume).

46/ Art Styles among the Boiken

Patricia May

The Boiken, numbering about forty thousand in 1980 (Roscoe 1983*a*), live in varied geographical environments, covering the Schouten Islands and a coastal strip northwest of Wewak and fanning out from the coast to the eastern slopes of the Prince Alexander Range and the northwestern grasslands of the Sepik plains. Their language is part of the Ndu language family (Laycock 1965, 1973). Laycock distinguishes seven Boiken dialects (Islands, East Yangoru, Plains, Central Yangoru, Munji, West Yangoru, and Haripmor), and Freudenberg (1976) also identifies seven: Yangoru (twelve thousand speakers), Central (fifty-six hundred), Nagum (twelve thousand), Kunai (one thousand), Kubalia (thirty-one hundred), Island (twenty-eight hundred), and Coastal (thirty-six hundred). (These figures appear to exclude bilingual border villages; not having access to the Freudenberg study, I have not been able to reconcile the two classifications, but see Roscoe 1983*a*.)

Unlike their neighbors the Pukia (Mountain Arapesh) and the Abelam, and surprisingly considering their size and geographic spread, the Boiken have until recently received little scholarly attention. Until the recent work of Roscoe (1983*a, b*), the literature on the Boiken consisted of substantial—though uneven—writings by two Society of the Divine Word missionaries, Gerstner (1952) and Aufenanger (1972, 1975); some other early missionary accounts; the work of the linguists Glasgow and Loving (1964), Laycock (1965, 1973), and Freudenberg (1976); a few studies of recent social and political change; and a study of pottery (May and Tuckson 1982). Virtually nothing comprehensive has been recorded of the material culture of the Boiken.

The object of this paper is to record what is known (and what is not known) about the art of the Boiken. In compiling this record I have drawn on existing studies as well as the fieldwork of my husband and myself (1971–76). But this record is very much a germinal one; moreover, a major area for future research—relating the art styles of the Boiken to those of their neighbors—will be only touched on here.

Information from my research (primarily on pottery but also on art styles and food production) does not always correspond to Laycock's and/or Freudenberg's linguistic divisions; therefore I have grouped villages according to geographical and cultural criteria: (1) Eastern Boiken, including villages located about 12–40 kilometers from Wewak along the Wewak-Maprik road and merging into the Sepik plains to the south and the foothills of the Prince Alexander Mountains; (2) Plains Boiken, including villages located deep in the *kunai* region of the Sepik plains; (3) Toanumbu Boiken, a complex of villages and hamlets located in the hills near Kubalia; and (4) Yangoru Boiken, villages and hamlets located on the slopes of the Prince Alexander Mountains—specifically, Mt. Turu—and around the Yangoru patrol post. (I have excluded the island and coastal Boiken because I do not know enough about their art, but they most certainly need to be included and I hope to follow this up in the future.)

According to Laycock (1965, 1973), about fifteen hundred to two thousand years ago the ancestors of the present Boiken and Abelam separated from the Sepik River Iatmul, and about A.D. 500–700 saw the division of the Boiken and the Abelam and their migration northward—in the process pushing aside, killing, or assimilating the older Torricelli-phylum inhabitants—Mountain Arapesh, Kamasau, Muniwara, and Urimo. The Abelam and the Sawos (near neighbors of the Boiken) speak Ndu-family languages. The Bungain, neighbors of the Sepik plains people featuring in this discussion (Kamasau, Muniwara, and Urimo), have many cultural affinities with them, but the Bungain villages located along the coast and close to the Murik Lakes would seem to have more affinities with the Austronesian-speaking and Lower Sepik peoples. The Boiken language reveals evidence of sustained intercourse with the speakers of Torricelli-phylum languages (Roscoe n.d.*b*). According to Laycock (cited in Tuzin 1976:73), "Absorption processes are clearly in evidence for the Boiken (Ndu-speaking) people who now live in the Prince Alexander Mountains. Their language is an interesting blend of a basically Ndu pattern with Torricelli additives, suggesting that the aboriginal inhabitants were assimilated by the Boiken intruders."

Pottery

Boiken pottery falls into three main categories based on style and technique of manufacture: (1) Eastern, (2) Plains, and (3) Yangoru. There is a fourth mixed industry around Toanumbu, where the picture is not clear. Broadly, these industries have far more in common with those of neighboring groups than with one another. There is no culturally exclusive Boiken industry like those of the Sawos and the Kwoma.

Eastern

Villages producing pottery: Passam, Paliama, Bungaripma, Kumbagora, Paparam, Tandori (now defunct), Nangumarum, Japaraka, Nagusempo.

Function: Working vessels (*au*), sago storage jars (*au*).

Form: Two basic vessel shapes, (*a*) deep, pointed or nipple base, neckless with direct rims, usually used in storing sago, and (*b*) deep, pointed or nipple base, vertical walls with necks and restricted. In general, it is difficult to distinguish between cooking pots and sago storage vessels on the basis of shape alone except in the case of *a*, which has a wide mouth. Larger vessels are mostly used for storage.

Decoration: Fingernail or finger drag marks across unbonded coils, alternating patterns of smooth and unsmoothed coils.

Technique: Made by men; spiral coiling, hand-smoothed.

Comments: The type of pottery produced here is distinct to this group, although related types are found among the neighboring Muniwara, Kamasau, Bungain, and Urimo and the Plains Boiken. Trade to other groups is not widespread—probably because all the neighboring groups make their own pots or import them from the coastal Kaiep and Terebu. Toanumbu does import Eastern Boiken vessels, seeming to favor them over the Yangoru cooking vessels. Serving/eating vessels, imported from neighbors who make them, are scarce. Large wooden platters made locally are probably used instead of pottery vessels in spirit-house activities.

Cooking pots related to those of the Eastern Boiken but distinctive from them are made by some of their neighbors on the Sepik plains to the southeast. In the Bungain villages of Wawat, Namarab, and Yaugiba, there are cooking pots (*mono*), sago storage jars indistinguishable from the former except by function, and eating/serving vessels (*dieni*). All three types are ovoid, with everted necks and pointed or nipple bases. Their decoration is similar to Eastern Boiken. The people of the Kamasau villages of Tring, Wau, and Kenyari produce vessels similar to those of the Bungain except that an eating bowl (*opiai*) is distinguished from the cooking pot (*aus*) by a band of exposed coils along the outer rim. Vessels are made by men by spiral coiling. The shapes, decorative elements, and methods of manufacture of these pots are closely related to those of the Eastern Boiken, though they are smaller and thinner-walled and include another type of eating/serving bowl which is used in spirit-house activities and ceremonies. In the past pots were traded to the Angoram people as well as within the group. The Muniwara-Urimo villages of Timaru, Muniwara, Kowiro, Wamango, Kumburraga, Yari, Mambe, and Pitan produce a cooking and sago-stirring pot (*tau*) and an eating/serving ceremonial vessel (*komogi*). The tau is similar in shape and decoration to Bungain and Kamasau cooking pots. The komogi is unrestricted ellipsoid with a rounded base, a wide mouth, and outward-flaring walls, similar to the serving/eating vessels of the Plains Boiken, Kwoma, and Sawos. It is decorated with chip-carved and gouged curvilinear designs and, when destined for ceremony, painted in red, yellow, black, and white pigments. Vessels are made by men by spiral coiling. The Eastern Boiken import some komogi, although they do not seem to have imported such ceremonial vessels (even through middlemen) from the Plains Boiken.

Plains

Villages producing pottery: Maperinga, Soandogum, Rabundogum, Rabiawa, Barawat, Bima, Yumungu, Kiniambu, Numendogum.

Function: Cooking vessels and sago-storage vessels (*au*), spirit-house cooking pots (*khamanunguin*), eating/serving bowls (*khomogu*).

Forms and decoration: Cooking and storage vessels are similar to Eastern Boiken and Bungain-Kamasau-Muniwara-Urimo in overall form and in decoration, which consists of fingernail or finger drag marks across unbonded coils. The only khamanunguin I saw (now in Wewak Cultural Centre) is deep (about 80 centimeters high) and looks like a common cooking pot except for a "spirit" face, consisting of two round eyes, a cylindrical nose, and a round pursed mouth with a hole in the center, formed by applications of clay coils. Khomogu have three variants: (1) a deep or shallow conical bowl with open wide mouth, with or without a base knob; (2) a shallow, round-based bowl, with or without base knob; and (3) a deep, restricted-ellipsoid bowl, with or without a base knob. All three variants are decorated by chip carving and gouged curvilinear and figurative designs, burnished, and, when used in spirit-house activities, painted.

Comments: There are two distinct pottery traditions here. The cooking/storage pots relate to those of the Eastern Boiken and Sepik-plains language groups but are much less scrupulously fashioned and crudely finished. The eating/serving bowls are closely related in technique of production, form, and application of design elements to those of the Sawos and the Muniwara-Urimo. It is always possible to recognize a Muniwara-Urimo vessel but often difficult to distinguish between a Plains Boiken and a Sawos vessel. The spirit-house cooking pot with applied decoration forming a face is also found in the Eastern Boiken village of Japaraka, but on a smaller scale (15–20 centimeters high). We need to know more about the distribution of this type, but it would appear to be a hybridization of the Eastern and Plains Boiken cooking-pot shape and another specializing in applied-facial types—perhaps the "Kwoma" or the Wosera.

Yangoru

Villages producing pottery: Wamaina and its hamlets, Kworabri, and Mambuk.

Function: Cooking pots (*gelawo*), common eating/serving vessels and ceremonial or spirit-house eating/serving vessels (*khomongu*).

Form and decoration: Gelawo are round-based, deep-proportioned, with conical or straight walls, and unrestricted; they are decorated by thumb-impressed exposed coils along exterior rim. Common khomongu are semispherical, round-based, and slightly restricted; they generally have one lug; the rim coil is left unmarked, and there is a tool-applied band of zigzags, scallops, or diamond motifs; they are sometimes painted white. Ceremonial khomongu are semispherical or ellipsoid and restricted; they may have one or two pierced lugs. The inverted rim is decorated with an unbonded coil, external walls with chip-carved curvilinear designs; they are always burnished and painted.

Technique: Made by men; spiral coiling.

Comments: While the eating/serving vessels are distinctively Yangoru, the cooking pots seem to belong to a cooking-pot tradition widespread throughout the Prince Alexander Mountains and into the Torricellis. Similar cooking pots are made by Abelam, Mountain Arapesh, Bumbita and Southern Arapesh, Kwanga, Kombio,

Yambes, Urim, Urat, and Nuku. Probably the Abelam and the Yangoru Boiken adopted the earlier inhabitants' cooking-pot tradition but looked to Sepik River traditions for their ceremonial eating/serving bowls.

Toanumbu

Villages producing pottery: Toanumbu and related hamlets.

Function: Eating/serving vessels (*khomongu*).

Form: Two variants, (*a*) shallow, conical bowls with knobbed or pointed base and one or two pierced lugs, and (*b*) deeper vessels with rounded bases and no lugs.

Decoration: Chip-carved curvilinear designs related to those on the Plains and Yangoru Boiken eating/serving bowls.

Technique: Made by men; spiral coiling.

Comment: There is considerable variation in shape of vessels and decorative schemes, as well as variation in quality of manufacture and chip carving, from one hamlet to the next. The smaller, conical pots, very similar to Plains Boiken types, are rougher and cruder, while the larger, round-based ones, reminiscent of those of the Yangoru Boiken, are masterful, refined, and of a high conceptual quality. It would seem that these Boiken, sandwiched between the Plains, Eastern, and Yangoru Boiken and the Mountain Arapesh, produce a hybrid type of ceramic vessel (*a*), as well as a generically strong version of their own (*b*). Cooking pots are not made here but imported from the Eastern Boiken; some large, grand ceremonial vessels—similar to Mountain Arapesh examples—are also imported (from where we do not know).

The Mountain Arapesh villages of Malapaiem, Alisu, Kaboibus, Bukinara, Nimbihu, and Kuragamon (and possibly other villages) produce cooking pots (*malep*), individual eating bowls (*sahin*), and communal ceremonial eating/serving vessels (*bitap*). In form and decoration, malep are clearly related to Torricelli–Prince Alexander Mountains cooking-pot types and sahin to Yangoru Boiken common khomongu. Bitap have a painted base, curved walls, restricted mouth, and everted lip. Their decoration varies from village to village and from vessel to vessel but always consists of boldly conceived chip-carved designs, some curvilinear, others more geometric, separated by horizontal zones; they are painted before use in ceremony. Vessels are made by men by spiral coiling. Bitap are readily identifiable as Mountain Arapesh, but the cooking pots reinforce the picture of a widespread cooking-pot tradition.

Abelam ceramics are so mixed that at this stage there appears to be only one stylistically strong industry, the Wosera. Groups to the north and west produce wares quite distinct from these Abelam "hybrids."

There are, then, three pottery traditions in the area: (1) the cooking-pot tradition of the Yangoru and Plains Boiken, Mountain Arapesh, Abelam, Kwoma, Sawos, and peoples throughout the Torricelli Mountains and into the West Sepik as far as Nuku and Lumi; (2) the cooking-pot/sago-storage vessel type found in the Eastern and Plains Boiken and Bungain-Kamasau areas; and (3) the chip-carved-decoration tradition of the Plains, Yangoru, and Toanumbu Boiken, Muniwara, Urimo, Arapesh, Abelam, Kwoma, Sawos, and the peoples of the foothills of the Torricelli Mountains to the extreme west of the East Sepik Province—Kwanga, Urim, Urat, and Yambes. All groups, with the exception of the Sawos, use these vessels in ceremony relating to cults and initiation. While the Plains Boiken vessels are related to the Sawos, Muniwara, Urimo, and Toanumbu ones by shape and the Yangoru vessels differ, the design elements are similar throughout, consisting of curvilinear patterns featuring faces, figures (very rare), and motifs such as leaves, lozenges, and abstractions of faces. In all cases we were told that the designs contained *masalai* (spirits), marks of the masalai, and marks of the clan of the potter.

Wooden Plates, Bowls

Wooden plates and bowls are of two types. The Murik Lakes type is oval and "boat"-shaped, deep or shallow. It is decorated at the tapered ends with lively carved figures, figures entwined with mythological creatures, heads of mythological creatures, and formal abstractions of these. It is found on the Schouten Islands, in the Austronesian-speaking villages along the coast south of Wewak, inland among the Bungain, Muniwara, and Sepik-plains people, and upriver as far as Angoram. The Boiken–Muniwara–Bungain–Mountain Arapesh type can be exceptionally large (50–150 centimeters in diameter) and is shallow (8–10 centimeters deep), round or ellipsoid, and decorated with a serrated rim and often a flying fox or frog motif incised in the center on the outside base. This type is mainly restricted to the areas in which it is manufactured; the center

of production seems to be the inland Eastern Boiken villages of Paliama, Passam, Japaraka, Paparam, and Tandori, the coastal Boiken villages north of Wewak, and Bungain and Kamasau villages. Aufenanger (1972) mentions their being used at Sassoia, and this would indicate either their importation from the plains or Eastern Boiken or their local manufacture.

Mead's description of the bowls and platters of the Mountain Arapesh tallies with our data on the Boiken and plains peoples' bowls. She does say that the Mountain Arapesh seldom export them; they rarely make enough for their own use and import them from the villages nearer to the beach (Mead 1970:162). The decorative schema along the outer rim and the use of individual motifs on the base correspond to decoration seen in a Boiken context.

These plates are used as common food bowls, but some are made exclusively for and kept in spirit houses to be used during dancing festivals, pig exchanges, and initiation ceremonies.

Wooden plates of the second type are manufactured and used by groups that do not make or extensively use the elaborate eating/serving pottery vessels (except for the Mountain Arapesh). Therefore, the sphere of influence of the wooden plate extends up to but does not include the Yangoru Boiken and the Muniwara-Urimo people and only partially includes the Plains Boiken, all manufacturers of and utilizers of pottery eating/serving vessels. The ceramic vessels become dominant the farther one gets from Wewak and the coast and the closer one gets to the Sawos, Abelam/Wosera spheres of influence. Aufenanger (1972) tells us of the use of a wooden plate in the spirit house at Paparam, where it is called *kamunggu*—the same word used to designate the spirit-house ceremonial pottery vessels.

Spirit Houses

Roscoe (1983a) records three types of spirit house. Among the border Boiken villages of West Yangoru, the spirit house is modeled after the archetypical Abelam one. Deeper into Boiken territory, two structures are found, the *hworumbo*, a modest enclosure used for male initiation, and the *ka nimbia*, built on a grander scale and based on the Abelam spirit house but with regional variations. There has been a steady decline of all three types of spirit house, and apparently all have disappeared except for an old one at Kumun that was still standing in 1980. (In 1976, the National Cultural Council promulgated the construction, or rather the resurrection, in the cases of the Yangoru and Dreikikir, at Maprik of four spirit houses, one for each of the regional government stations—Maprik, Yangoru, Wosera, and Dreikikir. The two houses from non-Abelam-speaking groups—Yangoru and Dreikikir—are derivative of the Abelam prototype at least structurally [see Beier 1976].)

While the Abelam and Mountain Arapesh spirit houses are primarily associated with initiation, the Yangoru ka nimbia is bound up with the *wala*, creators of the world, on the one hand, and the male and female entities who dwell in the bush, on the other. The male wala are associated with warfare, pig exchange and wealth, and the descent group and its sororal affines. Representations of wala on the facades of the ka nimbia become, when viewed spatially, structurally, and conceptually, not simply a painted adornment on a facade but intrinsic to its construction; they represent a synthesis of the wala of the builders and the wala of the painters and are therefore both graphic and conceptual idioms for political allies. In summary, the facade is an artistic representation of the alliances enjoyed by the house builders. The association of ka nimbia with shell wealth rests on the ceremonial decoration of the house with shell rings in celebration of stages of warfare and pig exchange. Roscoe's interpretation of the function of the spirit house in Yangoru society provides art historians a focus for the analysis of the artistic manifestations associated with it.

Gerstner's (1952) study of the spirit cult includes the territory of the Nagum (Eastern), the Kunai (Plains), and the Kubalia (Toanumbu) Boiken. He reports that the spirit cult in its original form has almost died out in these areas. There are many reasons for its decline, and the importance of Yauiga in helping lay the "old pagan spirit cults" should not be underestimated (Gerstner 1952). Revivals of sorts are, however, going on all the time. Roscoe reports on an initiation held in Hanyuk in 1978 and one in Kinyambu in 1980–81. The wooden "long nose" mask and plaited eye masks we found in a Plains Boiken village in 1975 were said to have been made for a "festival." Gerstner's description of a spirit house in a Boiken village includes the data that the village people were part of a dual organization, each group having its own totem—the white parrot (*wama*) for the "white" group and the black hawk (*peri*) for the "black." He then directs our attention to Mead's report of the organization of the Mountain Arapesh into two groups, each named for its totem, *kumun* (hawk) and *kwain* (parrot). (Yangoru Boiken societies are divided into two moieties—black and white [Roscoe 1983a].)

I will not go into a comparative study of the physical features and construction elements of the spirit houses of our area but look forward to Brigitta Hauser-Schäublin's publication of her work on this. Gerstner does tell us that the gable and sides are decorated with spirit heads (carved wooden heads?) and figures, while wooden carvings representing hornbills, turtles, and snakes adorn the facades. Cult objects stored inside consist of spirit masks (*wale*), spirit flutes also called *wale*, spears, and skulls. Gerstner mentions only initiation ceremonies associated with the spirit house.

Aufenanger (1972, 1975) reports on spirit houses, ceremony, and ritual objects throughout the Kamasau, Bungain, Muniwara, Urimo, and Boiken areas. The spirit houses are associated with initiation and ceremonial pig exchange; the spirits that abide in and around the houses and the masks are often masalai, although there are also spirits with more universal connotation.

Talipun

Talipun, the shell currency of the Yangoru Boiken, is cut from the giant turban shell (*Turbo mamoratus*). There are two main types: *hwempulli*, a male form, which generally seems to include the base and outer layers of the shell, and *horie*, a female form, from which the base section of shell has been cut away and some of the outer layers removed to produce, when new, a smooth, shiny surface. A third type, called *koliava* ("grandfather"), is apparently physically indistinguishable from the *hwempulli*. Shells from Ambukanja and Marambanja (only?) were obtained by trade with the islands off the coast and brought back to Yangoru for cutting, basically the removal of the last two or three spirals. From Yangoru the shells found their way by trade or exchange to other Boiken groups, to some Mountain Arapesh and eastern Abelam villages, and even to the Sepik River.

After being cut, the shells were decorated with plaited (woven) cane masks. Some men in every Yangoru village made these masks, and men from Soandogum (Plains Boiken) said that they had made them in the recent past. Four types of masks are distinguished: (1) those that represent clan symbols, e.g., the hornbill (*fale*) and the black cockatoo (*maenge*); (2) those that represent masalai (wale); (3) those said to be the face of a man (*man nating*); and (4) abstract representations including *yabi* (bee), said to represent the entrance to the hive of the wild bee. Four distinct forms (which do not always correlate with the four types) are (1) a two-dimensional lozenge shape, which serves as a flat base for a face—with woven elements forming stalklike cylindrical eyes, a cylindrical vertical nose, with or without nostrils, and a round or elliptical mouth, all inscribed within a heart-shaped cane outline (these features are rendered in a variety of ways that determine what it is they represent—hornbill, man, masalai; the masalai types are sometimes depicted with "ears" and vestigial arms; (2) a two-dimensional lozenge shape, from the center of which juts a cylindrical protuberance of basically two forms, one whose features are like birds or animals and another whose elements are abstract; (3) a three-dimensional, volumetric "head" shape with a variety of features, denoting man or masalai; and (4) a series of abstract shapes, from a three-dimensional "taro" form to flat fan-shaped or round forms. These masks are always painted in some combination of brown, red, black, and white. They are usually fringed with cassowary plumes and may be embellished with bone or carved wooden decorations representing birds. Two large talipun masks seen in Maprik in 1975 had skulls and beaks of hornbills attached to the shell (cf. Aufenanger 1972:186).

Talipun are used in conjunction with *Tridacna* shell rings (*weinka*) manufactured by the Mountain Arapesh. The Yangoru Boiken distinguish two classes of shell rings, one obtained from villages near Kaboibus (Mountain Arapesh) and others which they do not recognize as coming from outside Boiken territory and believe were made by wale. The rings and talipun are exchanged in bride-price payments and on occasions such as death, birth, initiation, and (at least in case of rings) the settlement of disputes and payment for sorcery. The koliava seem to have been kept in the spirit house and not used in any form of exchange, and some that bear the mark of the clan or village are never traded.

What is curious is that while the Yangoru Boiken (and at least some of the Plains Boiken) have integrated the talipun with the shell rings, the Mountain Arapesh (who make them) and the Abelam (who import them) make use only of the shell rings (although we have been told that Boiken talipun were sometimes exchanged with

the Mountain Arapesh). Mead does not refer to them, and we do not know what significance they have to the Arapesh, if any.

Masks

At least three kinds of masks were made and used by the Boiken and the Sepik-plains peoples to the southeast of them. The first type is a carved wooden face mask with a characteristic long nose that juts out at about 33° from the concave facial plane; the brow is deeply cut, and the eyes are small, slanted, and slitted. It may be painted in combinations of black, red, and white stripes. This type is most abundant in the Kamasau, Bungain, Muniwara, and Urimo areas (see Aufenanger 1972: pls. 4 and 5). Among the neighboring Plains Boiken and Eastern Boiken, the shape is less cubist—the long nose juts downward and extends beyond the end of the face proper, and the forehead is dome-shaped. These masks are worn during dances and ceremonies and are affixed to a frame carried by the dancer. While there is one predominant formal type throughout the area, its function varies from group to group. Among the Eastern Boiken, the mask represents a *tsimbari* spirit—a masalai—and is used during initiation ceremonies and paraded in front of the whole village (Aufenanger 1972:168–69). Similar-looking dance masks are used in initiation ceremonies by the Kamasau. The masks are kept under guard in the spirit house.

This "long-nose" mask seems to be distantly related to the beak style found in the Ramu River area and at the mouth of the Sepik (Murik Lakes). Its distribution is along a corridor stretching inland from the coast south of Wewak between the Prince Alexander Mountains and the grassy plains and swamps of the Murik Lakes area. The distribution and function of this mask correlates with the pottery data, which points to closer cultural affinities among the Eastern Boiken, Plains Boiken, Muniwara, Bungain, Kamasau, and Urimo than between them and the Yangoru Boiken. The Yangoru Boiken do not use wooden masks in their ceremonies and rituals, and neither do the Mountain Arapesh or the Abelam (although the Abelam do occasionally use a carved wooden one instead of the common plaited cane one).

The second type of mask, the plaited face mask used in dances and ceremonies and worn by men, is, to our knowledge, confined to the Plains and Eastern Boiken and the Abelam (we have no data on its use among the plains people to the southeast or the Toanumbu Boiken). The plaited masks of the Yangoru Boiken not only are different in appearance but are used in conjunction with shell money, while the well-known Abelam "yam masks" are used to dress yams for displays and exchanges and are not worn by the men. The Plains Boiken mask, worn over the eyes, consists of two sections of coiled spirals linked in the center with cane. These are painted in ochres and black and adorned with cassowary feathers. (Aufenanger [1972], describing some of the emblems of the Plains Boiken, says that the spiral is the emblem of a spirit woman; it represents the female breast and appears on "knitted" masks around the eyes.) According to Aufenanger, every Passam (Eastern Boiken) man owned a spirit mask, which was a guardian of the gardens and was kept in the spirit house and worn during dancing festivals. Another mask, called the *yigoropen* spirit mask, lived in the spirit house and was never seen by women and children. Gerstner (1952) reports a plaited-cane ("but sometimes also coarsely carved from wood") face mask from Japaraka and Kusanam (Eastern Boiken) that was affixed to a frame and worn by men on special festival occasions. Masks are given names and are male and female. When not in use they are kept in the spirit house along with the grass skirts worn with them. The generic name for these masks is *wale* or *ware*—words used throughout the Boiken territory for masalai. We have seen four hollow plaited-cane heads from Japaraka. One is now in the Australian Museum in Sydney, and the others were seen in the collection of an artifact dealer in Wewak. These could be the type Gerstner refers to.

From the evidence of our field experience and data from Aufenanger and Gerstner, we suggest that there is a carved wooden "long-nose" mask (related to, but distinct from, the beak style) that is used in spirit-house activity (in most cases, for initiation ceremonies) and is common to the Kamasau, Bungain, Muniwara, and Urimo people as well as to at least the Plains and Eastern Boiken. It is not found among the Abelam, Mountain Arapesh, or Yangoru Boiken. In other words, the diffusion of this type stops at the Sawos to the southwest, the Murik Lakes to the southeast, the Abelam to the north, and the Yangoru Boiken and Mountain Arapesh to the east; in all these areas other mask types take over. A plaited mask type is prevalent among the Plains and Eastern Boiken and the Abelam. (As far as we know, this type does not appear in the Kamasau, Bungain, Muniwara, and Urimo groups.)

The Abelam have specialized in two types: the small "yam" mask and the baba, worn in dances and kept in the spirit house. Both of these are different in appearance from either the Yangoru talipun mask or the Boiken plaited dance mask.

One other mask about which we have few data is mentioned by Aufenanger (1972:88–89): "At *Rovundogun* [Plains Boiken] masks appear at the time when the yams are harvested. Some masks are manufactured from thin clothlike coconut sheaths. They are spoken of as '*kwarum baraga*.' Sometimes they represent black buzzards or hawks."

Figures

Surprisingly, the strong tradition of carved wooden figures made for and used in ceremonies and spirit-house activities, which is found throughout Papua New Guinea and is particularly strong in the Sepik River area, is lacking among the Boiken, Mountain Arapesh, Muniwara, Bungain, and Kamasau. Groups immediately surrounding the Boiken that have strong cultural commitments to figures are the Iatmul, the Sawos, the Murik Lakes people, the Kwoma, and the Abelam. Only two groups from our study area make and use figures in a socioreligious context—the Yangoru Boiken and the Urimo.

The Yangoru Boiken figures, while belonging to the same stylistic tradition as the Abelam, are nonetheless quite distinct from them. The Abelam figures show interesting combinations of angular and curved elements. The Boiken figures are basically two-dimensional and frontally oriented. They have none of the arabesque curvilinear flow found in Abelam figures, nor do their representational elements (arms, legs) reveal the swelling volumes of the Abelam; they are articulated geometric forms. The head may be triangular, ovoid, or diamond-shaped; the torso is elliptical, and the legs and arms are faceted with angular contours. Facial features always consist of eyes, mouth, and nose, the nose being perpendicular to the facial plane; ears and headdress (top knots) are frequently included. These figures come in only two positions, one with upraised arms, the other with the arms extending downward and across, the hands resting on the pelvic area (along the genitals). These figures come in pairs, male and female. There are some examples of single figures with breasts and male genitalia (see Aufenanger 1972: pl. 11). There is some surface ornamentation consisting of incised patterns on the body and painting of the face, the torso, and sometimes the legs and arms.

Aufenanger gives us no clues as to how these figures are used except that they dwell in the spirit house and appear during or are carved for pig exchanges. Describing aspects of a pig exchange at Marambanja village, he tells us that just before the slaughtering, "the master of ceremonies tells the people: 'Mourn for the dead now!' . . . for this occasion all the wooden figures and paintings of the dead [?] stand in front of the spirit house. . . . Afterwards the figures are put back into the spirit house" (Aufenanger 1972:200).

I would suggest that from the uniformity of distribution among the Yangoru Boiken and of artistic style would follow a corresponding uniformity of function. The two different ways of representing the arms, upraised and lowered, probably correspond to two different functions (i.e., significance, representation) of the figures.

The faces of the figures are very similar to some of the faces of talipun masks. This is not just because the artists render all faces and facial features in a characteristic style; it is more likely that some talipun masks and the figures represent the same thing—a particular masalai, an even more powerful spirit.

The only other data we have on figures in the area come from Aufenanger, who describes standing "guardian" figures that were being kept in the spirit house at Wambe (Urimo). These were carved from wood but in such bad condition that some had rotted through (see Aufenanger 1972: pl. 7).

Other

Evidence from the work of Aufenanger, Roscoe, and Gerstner and our fieldwork suggests that a number of other objects should be included in this study. Because of lack of any kind of physical description (except in the case of one hardwood war club, the Yangoru *ponga*), we will do no more at this time than mention them. These are shields, spears, war clubs, bullroarers, and flutes. Hardwood shields about a meter high are used by the Yangoru Boiken in interconfederate warfare. The only other groups reported as using shields are the Kwoma to the southeast and the people of the Torricelli Mountains around Dreikikir. The spear is widespread among the Boiken, as is the hardwood club. Roscoe (1983*b*) describes their use by the Yangoru Boiken, and Aufenanger (1972) notes their use by the Eastern and Plains Boiken

and the Kamasau. Flutes, bullroarers, and slit-gongs are also widely distributed throughout the plains and the mountains.

Summary

The information we have to date suggests that the Boiken and their plains neighbors are not as artistically productive as neighboring groups such as the Abelam, the Sawos, the Murik Lakes peoples, and the Kwoma. There could be several reasons for this: earlier contact with the whites, earlier missionary activity, sparser population, and the absence of anything like the long yam around which the Abelam and Kwoma have woven so much of their artistic and ceremonial paraphernalia. The Boiken do have dance, song, and storytelling, and figures, pots, masks, bullroarers, and wooden plates were once used in ritual and ceremony. Before we can get into the dynamics of the diffusion of styles in this area or come closer to an understanding of how art objects were used, we must collect more data.

The decorations on the ceremonial pottery vessels, the use of masks, and the talipun decorations point to the widespread existence of a masalai cult; many of these designs and forms relate to the masalai and are given masalai names. Also, there seems to be some evidence that while the Boiken are related by a common language with dialect differentiation, their cultural development has not always been homogeneous. Culturally, the Yangoru Boiken stand somewhat apart from the other Boiken groups, whereas the Eastern and Plains Boiken groups and their plains neighbors have more characteristics in common.

From the evidence of the pottery, the Toanumbu Boiken seem to have borrowed something from everyone—serving-vessel shapes and designs from the Plains Boiken, cooking pots from the Eastern Boiken, ceremonial vessels from the Mountain Arapesh—while producing their own distinctively decorated type of eating/serving bowl.

The Muniwara-Urimo, Plains Boiken, Toanumbu, and Yangoru Boiken ceremonial vessels, while distinguishable from one another, have a certain repertoire of design elements in common. The one that appears frequently is called the face of a masalai, but whether it is the same masalai, i.e., has the same connotation in each area, is unknown (the elements making up this face, particularly in the Muniwara and Plains Boiken examples, look very much like the "catfish" seen on

Iatmul carvings). This so-called masalai face consists of dominant "eyes" (in most cases formed by a series of circles) and a nose whose curved outlines flow upward and around to become the elements of the face and downward to form a crescent-shaped mouth. The elements are all connected in a continuous network of curved lines. Since we were assured by all informants that this representation was associated with the masalai, we can assume that these groups have similar ceremony, particularly in regard to initiation. We know of one communal ceremonial vessel from the Mountain Arapesh that bears a related motif, but on the whole, from the examples we saw, it appears that this group uses different motifs and makes use of the space "field" of the pot quite differently (design is mostly restricted to the top portion and is more geometric in concept). This seems consistent with Mead's thesis that the Mountain Arapesh are an importing culture. These vessels have become an integral part of their ritual, and they have adopted their own schema of design motifs, one that corresponds to their beliefs. The lack of data on other objects (bone daggers, coconut cups, hand-drums) prevents us from determining whether this curvilinear style is carried over to other valued objects. A Yangoru potter showed us a carved (incised) coconut cup whose designs were exactly like the ones on a small pot he had also made. Of course, this is not enough evidence to suggest that at least the Yangoru Boiken have a tradition of decorating objects by incising.

This paper is a tentative effort to summarize what we know and do not know about Boiken art and its relations to that of neighboring groups. There is little ethnographic information on the Boiken and virtually no documented visual record of their culture. It is important that, while there are still some Boiken people living who can act as informants, we document what is known and do the necessary fieldwork to fill in the gaps.

47/ Symbolic Meaning in Kominimung Masks[1]

Dirk Smidt

The Kominimung live along the middle course of the Goam[2] River, a tributary of the Ramu, in Madang Province. They speak a non-Austronesian language that is classified as part of the Tamolan family of the Goam stock (Z'graggen 1975:34–35). They are a small group, a mere 330 persons, yet they have managed to create a distinctive art style which is expressed in a wide range of objects (Smidt 1983:140).

In this paper I report on fieldwork undertaken among the Kominimung during a period of about eight months between 1976 and 1980. The research was carried out under the aegis of the National Museum and Art Gallery of Papua New Guinea as part of the so-called Ramu Project. The main purpose of this project was to collect artifacts and to obtain documentation on the material culture and art of the Middle Ramu region. A major result of the project is a collection of 2,000 documented artifacts, of which 570 were collected from the Kominimung.

As little was known about the material culture and art of the Middle Ramu area and the stylistic boundaries between the various language groups were not yet clearly established, my research in the area was initially of an exploratory nature. Survey trips were made which covered five linguistic groups: Rao, Breri, Banaro, Akrukay, and Romkun. Later research focused on the Kominimung (fig. 1). The decision to settle among the Kominimung was primarily determined by the fact that Kominimung culture appeared to be much more intact than the cultures of the other groups mentioned, perhaps largely because of the absence of government and mission agencies. Airstrips and patrol and mission posts have been established among the neighbors of the Kominimung on the Ramu River but not in Kominimung territory (see also Smidt 1983:139).

Kominimung culture has hardly been researched. I have been able to find only the name "Kominimung" in one article (Stanhope 1970),[3] in a survey of the languages of the Madang District (Z'graggen 1975), in some general indexes, such as the 1974 *Papua New Guinea Gazetteer* and the 1973 *Papua New Guinea Village Directory*, and on some maps. It is not to be found in such reference works as the *Ethnographic Bibliography of New Guinea* (Australian National University 1968) and the *Encyclopaedia of Papua and New Guinea* (Ryan 1972). Pictures of Kominimung shields have been published in catalogues of collections, exhibitions, and auctions, but none of these are attributed to the Kominimung; in most cases the provenance is given as "Ramu." Up till now I have not been able to detect a published Kominimung sculpture or mask (with the exception of those published by myself in Mangal and Smidt 1980). In concurrence with this paucity of published material is the fact that Kominimung artifacts are hardly found in museum collections. Thus it has been ascertained that the only representative Kominimung collection is kept at the National Museum and Art Gallery at Port Moresby.

Elsewhere I have presented information on the shields and the role of the wood-carver (Smidt 1983:137–61). In this paper I shall present data on Kominimung masks.

On the basis of the material the masks are made of, one can distinguish two categories: feather masks and wooden masks. Here I will discuss only the wooden ones. Three types of wooden masks may be distinguished: (1) house masks, which are suspended inside the men's house horizontally facing downward; (2) house masks with two faces juxtaposed in the same plane in symmetrical fashion, which are said to be displayed on a sort of fence inside the men's house; and (3) dance masks, which are worn by dancers portraying mythical beings. I will restrict myself to a discussion of the dance masks. This type of mask differs from the other two types in being larger and more two-dimensional and, more important, in having eyeholes and a plaited cap of cane attached to the back to be fitted over the head of the dancer (figs. 2, 3). Masks of this type also are much more common. Whereas the other types of masks are possibly group property and are kept in the men's house, dance masks are individual property and are often kept in dwellings. Significantly, I saw many dance masks being made, but none of the second type and only one of the first.

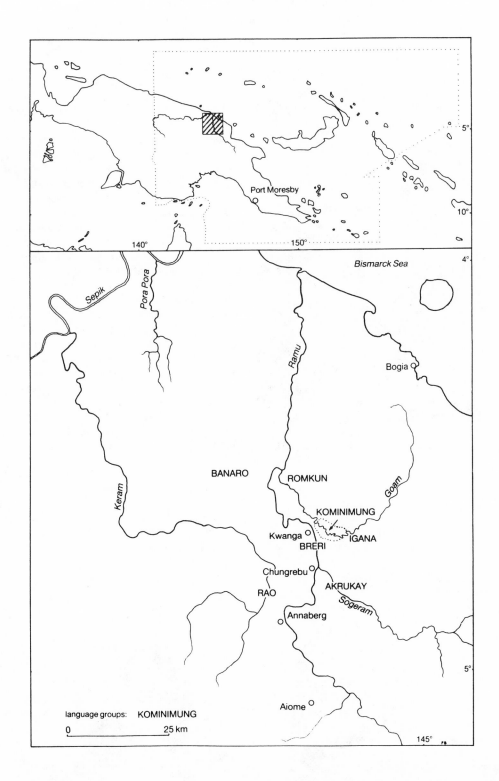

FIG. 1. The Middle Ramu area, showing the locations of Kominimung and other groups mentioned in text.

FIG. 2. Two masks, just completed, being tried out.

Manufacture

Making masks is partly a solitary affair inasmuch as the carver must concentrate on his work. At the same time it is very much a group activity. Several carvers may work simultaneously on their respective carvings, sitting not far apart in a particular spot in the bush a few minutes' walk from the hamlet, on the ground around the men's house, or underneath or (occasionally) inside the men's house. Women, children, and uninitiated boys are not allowed to see the masks being made. Working together allows for social interaction. Verbal communication may be in the nature of gossip—comments on matters of local politics and economic development, on a coming ceremony, on a sorcery case. The interaction is, however, frequently relevant to the work at hand. Working together in a group provides an excellent setting for learning by watching others and for more specific instruction. The communication between master and pupil need not be restricted to verbal advice; the master may actually leave the carving he is working on to guide the pupil through a difficult phase. For the most part, a mother's brother or the father adopts the role of

FIG. 3. The same masks, showing the attachment of a cane cap to fit over the head of the wearer.

FIG. 4. Removal of wood from a nascent mask.

FIG. 5. Thinning of a mask by cutting wood away from the back.

teacher. If such a person is not around (because of death, for example), a young man may be instructed by his elder brother or his father's brother. Wood-carvers do not form a class of specialists; however, a distinction is made between carvers who are excellent and those who have not really mastered the skill. Wood-carvers who are making a poor show are laughed at and frequently laugh about themselves. Aesthetic concepts are consciously applied and discussed. Criticism may be verbally expressed.

In carving a mask, a suitable tree must first be selected in the bush near the hamlet. Wood analysis applied to the masks at Port Moresby reveals that various types of wood may be used: *Gmelina, Trichardenia, Canarium, Elaeocarpus, Polyalthia,* and *Nauclea,* among others.[4] After the tree has been felled with an ax, a piece about 100 centimeters long is cut from its trunk near the base. It seems to be difficult to judge from the outside whether such a piece of wood will turn out to be suitable. Only after cutting away the

bark and slicing off pieces of the wood beneath it is the carver able to gauge the wood's true condition. A wood-carver usually thinks beforehand of making a certain type of carving, but he may change his mind when confronted with a piece of wood which turns out to lack the proper qualities. For example, if a carver has planned to make a figure and the wood shows some defects that make it unsuitable for a figure, he may try to cut it down to a smaller size to make a mask. After the bark has been removed, transverse cuts are made to mark the upper and lower ends. The piece of wood is then cut in half along the vertical axis, and each half may be used for a mask. One carver may use both, or the two blocks of wood may be shared between two carvers. One such 100-centimeter-long piece may be 30 centimeters wide and 13 centimeters thick.

The piece of wood selected is cut into the rough shape of a mask. Initially this is done with an ax (fig. 4). At a later stage an adz with an iron blade is used. The ensuing outline of the mask resembles a window frame from a Gothic cathedral, the bottom edge being horizontal and the sides curving upward and tapering toward the top. A sticklike extension is carved at the top to serve as a handle and as a place of attachment for

FIG. 6. Marking of the outline of an eye.

the cane cap. In the process, the mask is made thinner by slicing wood away from the back. This is done by holding the mask upright and striking downward with the adz (fig. 5). An assistant may hold the wood in various positions to facilitate the work. The front part is carved slightly convex, the rear part slightly concave.

After the general outline has been shaped and the thickness has been reduced to a reasonable degree, it is time to start carving the face. I will not go into the technical details but will simply indicate the order in which the various facial elements are usually carved: (1) the eyes (fig. 6), (2) the nose, (3) the outline of the face, (4) the motif(s) between the eyebrows, (5) the motif(s) on the forehead, (6) the navel and the nipples (fig. 7), and (7) the eyeholes (fig. 8). The actual carving of the mask being finished, the wood is now scraped carefully to make its surface smooth and suitable for painting. Formerly a strip of bamboo was used, but nowadays the larger surfaces are scraped with a flexible metal strip. A pig's tusk is used to scrape the grooves which frame the face, inside the eyes, and along the ridges of motifs carved in relief. For a pig's tusk to be usable it needs to be sharpened; this is done by wetting it in a water container made of the flower sheath of a palm and subsequently sliding it up and down

FIG. 7. Carving out of the area around the navel.

an upright piece of bamboo. Any remaining pieces of tusk are wiped off with a leaf, and the sharpness of the tusk is tested on the thumbnail.

A mask is painted in either black, white, and red or black, white, and yellow. Black is made of charcoal mixed with water, white of clay mixed with water, and yellow and red of vegetable or earth pigments. Vegetable paints are produced locally, but earth pigments have to be obtained through exchange with neighboring groups. For instance, the Kominimung may exchange net bags, lime, and/or *tilapia* for red and yellow ochre from Nodabu and Watabu.[5]

It is hard to say whether the Kominimung prefer the vegetable or the earth pigments. On the one hand, they like the brightness of the vegetable pigments; on the other hand, they appreciate the ease of preparing the earth pigments, considering the preparation of vegetable pigments hard work indeed. If earth pigments are used, a piece is cut off of a ball of red or yellow ochre, crumbled, and mixed with water. With vegetable pigments, yel-

FIG. 8. Piercing of the eyeholes.

low is made by chewing the inner bark and/or leaves of the mango tree (*Mangifera indica*)[6] and spitting the resulting juice into a coconut container, where it is mixed with lime. Red is made by crushing the seeds of the *Bixa orellana* and adding water and sometimes lime. Leaf stems are used as brushes; one end of such a stem may be "sharpened" with a knife, thus rendering it particularly suitable for painting in grooves. To apply paint to large surfaces, the broad end of the stem is used; this end may be chewed a bit to make it soft. The raised parts of the mask are usually first given an undercoating of reddish tree sap; then the black paint is applied over it. The undercoating probably helps to make the black paint stick. The nose and eyes are usually painted first, followed by the facial outline and the motifs. The sunken areas are painted in white, red (fig. 9), and/or yellow. Painting a mask takes about two and a half hours.

A mask is not really complete without the attachment of two additional elements: the sago-leaf tassels and the cane cap. The tassels are made of sago-leaf shoots collected by the men. After the shoots have been shredded (fig. 10) strings of sago fibers are tied together into bundles to make the tassels. Three colors are used for tassels: red, white, and yellow. Red is made by boiling the strings of sago fibers, before they have been cut up, in a pot filled with certain leaves. This may be done by women. White and yellow are made by men, white from clay mixed with water and yellow from a root (*Curcuma domestica*) scraped and mixed with water. Here the color is applied by rubbing the strings of sago fibers in a coconut cup which contains the dye. The dyed tassels are tied to two cane strips and threaded through holes pierced in the sides of the mask (fig. 11).

The cap is plaited from strips of cane. The bottom rim of the cap is made first, and the plaiter

FIG. 9. Application of paint.

gradually works his way upward. When the bottom rim is about a centimeter wide, it is held against the shoulders of an assistant for measuring to ensure that its size will be correct. Plaiting a cane cap is laborious, and some of the younger wood-carvers do not like to do it. Others claim that they have not been able to learn the craft, their fathers having died before transmitting their skills. Upon completion the cap is attached to the back of the mask (fig. 12).

Meaning and Function of the Masks

Like other wood carvings, masks are representations of *bwongogo,* the mythical ancestor spirit called *tambaran* in Tok Pisin. Every man and woman is associated with several bwongogo, and through these individual associations each bwongogo is linked to a certain clan. Bwongogo play an important role with regard to the well-being of the individuals with whom they are associated and their clans. They may be invoked to promote the growth of food crops in gardens, to ensure success in hunting and fishing, to provide protection in warfare, and to help destroy an enemy. They are also influential in the context of rites of passage such as initiation, marriage, and death. The great importance of the bwongogo is illustrated by the fact that they are made tangible and visible by way of wood carvings, particularly when these are manipulated during ceremonies.

FIG. 10. Shredding of sago-leaf shoots for the tassels.

Bwongogo may be grouped into a limited number of categories which correspond to different types of wood carvings.

Each mask is individually named and may be male or female. In general, it is impossible to judge the sex by simply looking at the mask; I saw only one mask on which the female sexual organs were carved (fig. 13). Thus, an indication of the sex of a mask must be obtained from informants. The ceremonial context in which the wooden masks are used might provide further clues, but I have not been lucky enough to witness such a ceremony.

On the whole it would appear that the functions of the male and female masks are different. Most of the female masks for which I obtained information are associated with the gardens, particularly with the yams; these masks are called "mothers of the yams." Performances with them take place at the time of the yam harvest at the end of the dry season. On such an occasion a number of masks, probably from ten to fifteen, may be used in the same performance. Masked dancers leave the men's house one after another and, after dancing within the fence constructed around the men's house, parade through the village in strict order. The bwongogo are not only made visible but also become audible on such ceremonial oc-

FIG. 11. Attachment of the tassels.

casions. Each category of bwongogo has its own type of music. The dancers masked as "mothers of the yams" hold pairs of clapsticks in their hands; in contrast to those representing other bwongogo, they do not hold hand-drums. Inside the men's house, the sacred bamboo flutes are blown and the slit-gongs are said to be beaten.

The masks alone are not to be shown to women, children, and uninitiated boys, but when the masked performers come outside the men's house at the beginning of the ceremony, women and children are allowed to see the bwongogo and may even come inside the fence. The "mothers of the yams" hand out the first yams to them, "saying" (or gesturing), "We have harvested the yams. You must eat these now." Although the masks are associated with the yam harvest, this association does not mean that there is a performance with them at every harvest. Various circumstances may prevent this; for example, ceremonies are not held when a death has occurred and people are still in mourning. I was told that the last performance had taken place in 1972.

While the female masks are associated with gardening, the male masks are associated with hunting, especially the hunting of pigs. If the bwongogo represented by a mask are angry, the pigs disappear in the bush and the hunt fails. In former times the bwongogo also played a role with regard to warfare, stirring up the men to fight their enemies and helping them to be successful warriors. Performances with the masks that ensure successful pig hunts are said to be held at the end of the dry season and the beginning of the wet season, when the pigs are hunted. Some informants indicated that certain male masks play a role in initiation ceremonies in connection with the one-legged figures used to beat the initiates.

Masks and Social Structure

To understand the meaning, function, and symbolic connotations of the masks, it is necessary to have some knowledge of Kominimung social structure. Kominimung society is matrilineal. The ownership of land is based on matrilineal descent. Members of matrilineal clans live together in hamlets or village quarters, and marriage is predominantly matrilocal. The Kominimung in-

FIG. 12. Attachment of the plaited cane cap.

termarry to a limited extent with their nearest
neighbors upstream on the Goam River, the
Igana. Traditionally, marriage between the Kominimung and other groups was prohibited by
strong taboos.

Kominimung society is divided into two exogamous moieties, "black-eye" and "red-eye."
Each moiety consists of a number of totemic
clans. A myth relates how the two moieties originated from a primeval woman who gave birth to
twins, a girl and a boy. The totems and clans of
the red-eye moiety originated in the girl and those
of the black-eye in the boy. Clans of the black-eye
moiety are named for sago, coconut, large bush
rat, fire, crocodile, cockatoo, taro, victory leaf,
betel, flying fox, and eagle and clans of the red-
eye moiety for catfish, pig, cassowary, bird of

FIG. 13. Mask representing a female mythical ancestor, rare insofar as the sex is clearly indicated by
a carved vulva and clitoris.

paradise, hornbill, bamboo, sun, praying mantis,
and croton leaf.

A mask or, rather, the bwongogo represented
by it seems to ensure success in growing yams or
hunting pigs to a group of relatives who belong to
the same clan. Such a mask may be beneficial to
its male owner or guardian and also to his sister,

brother, mother, mother's brother, mother's sister, and mother's sister's children, but there is more to it than this. There are four persons particularly involved with each mask, representing both sexes, more than one clan, and both moieties. The Kominimung use the following terms for them: "mother," "father," "friend," and "child." "Mother" prepares the food for the bwongogo, probably only during the time when it is actually present in the village for a ceremony. She also makes the huge net bag used to store the durable elements of the mask-costume. "Father" looks after the mask and paraphernalia of the bwongogo and may set up the display of the mask in the men's house. "Friend" assists in dressing the masked dancer for a performance and plays a musical instrument representing the voice of the bwongogo. "Child" dons the costume and mask of the bwongogo and performs in it. While performing he may also play a musical instrument— a bamboo tube blown at the upper end in such a manner that it functions as a megaphone and disguises the performer's voice. At other times during the ceremony he may play another musical instrument, either a transverse flute of bamboo or a slit-gong, inside the men's house. "Child" belongs to the moiety opposite to that of "father," "mother," and "friend." "Father" and "mother" are consanguineal relatives, often brother and sister. My data indicate that "child" may often be the mother's brother's son of "father" and "mother." Inheritance of the roles of "father," "mother," and "child" takes place within the clan. The role of "father" seems to pass from ego to his sister's son and that of "mother" from mother to daughter. The role of "child" may be transferred from the father of the mask's owner to his son or from an elder to a younger brother.

The association between masks and social structure becomes even clearer when one looks at the masks themselves. Certain motifs are carved on them which are interpreted by the Kominimung as clan emblems (Tok Pisin *mak bilong bisnis*). A motif usually depicts the totem of the clan with which the mask is associated. Whereas on shields the main motifs are rendered rather large, on masks, where space is limited, they are small and concise and often rendered *pars pro toto* (in which case they are impossible to identify without the guidance of informants). Clan emblems are always rendered on the forehead of the mask. Examples are the poisonous serrated spines of the catfish (fig. 14) and a pair of pig's tusks (fig. 15). Smaller animals, such as the praying mantis, may be rendered in schematic but full form (fig. 16).

FIG. 14. Mask with three catfish spines, emblems of the catfish clan, carved on the forehead. A spine is also carved between the eyebrows in combination with a dotted circular motif which represents the abode of certain insects (possibly bees). This motif is associated with the catfish clan and is frequently used in combination with catfish motifs (see figs. 2 and 17).

Some totemic animals may be rendered in full form on one mask and in a condensed version on another (fig. 17; cf. fig. 14).

More often than not, a carver will carve the motifs of his own clan. This is consistent with the fact that training by the mother's brother seems to

FIG. 16. Closeup of the emblem of the praying mantis clan on the forehead of a mask. The praying mantis is carved in relief (the black lines indicate two pairs of legs, neck, and body). The pair of oval white motifs between the two pairs of legs represents shell ornaments such as those worn on their heads by masked performers.

FIG. 15. Two masks with emblems of the pig clan: a pair of pig's tusks (the slightly raised V-shaped motifs in white) and a pair of pig's teeth (the triangular motifs in white immediately below). An additional clan symbol, a piece of pig bone, is stuck through the "nasal septum."

be the most frequent mode of instruction. However, a carver may also receive instruction from his father and become capable of carving the emblems of his father's clan. A carver may also know how to carve the emblems of his wife's clan. Of the forty-four masks collected by the National Museum, thirty have emblems of the maker's own clan, nine emblems of the clan of the maker's wife and son, one each emblems of the clan of the maker's father and of his sister's son's wife, and three mixtures of clan emblems.

Clan affiliation is further underlined by the way the colors are applied. Where yellow is the dominant color, the mask is likely to be associated with the black-eye moiety; where red is dominant, it is likely to be associated with the red-eye moiety.

Conclusion

A Kominimung mask represents a particular mythical ancestor who ensures the well-being of the people with whom it is associated. It may guide them with regard to the correct way of dealing with nature in order to maintain an adequate food supply, perhaps indicating the right times to plant and harvest yams or the time and place to hunt pigs. The mythical ancestor denoted by the mask may also play a role in rites of passage such

Fig. 17. Closeup of the emblems of the catfish clan on the forehead of a mask. The catfish is rendered in full between motifs representing the nests of certain insects (possibly bees).

as initiation and death, when it may express itself in media other than masks—song and instrumental music, for example. In its masked appearance, its main function seems to lie in the context of gardening and hunting.

A mask also conveys notions of kinship and social structure. Carved on the forehead of each mask are clan emblems, and its colors indicate the moiety to which the clan belongs. However, in the performance of the masked dancer there is indirect reference to the other half of the dual structure, because the wearer of the mask comes from the opposite moiety. Moiety opposition is both stressed, by the visible elements, and dissolved, by the invisible one. Thus the performance enacts the structure of the society and stresses its cohesiveness. Moreover, it makes a powerful statement about the supernatural order of things by which the society of the living is transcended.

Notes

1. I am most grateful to the organizers of this symposium, particularly Meinhard Schuster and Lita Osmundsen of the Wenner-Gren Foundation for Anthropological Research, for inviting me to attend the symposium. The fieldwork on which this paper is based was supported by the Trustees of the National Museum and Art Gallery of Papua New Guinea. In this context I wish to record my appreciation for the encouragement I received from the director, G. Mosuwadoga, and his former assistant, Brian Egloff. During periods ranging from a few weeks to two months I was accompanied by Resonga Kaiku and Soroi M. Eoe, both staff members in the Anthropology Department of the National Museum. They have contributed to the results of this research. At Port Moresby, Maru Kumul (Forest Products Research Centre) kindly identified the various types of wood of which the masks were made. The map was drawn by Paul Bijvoet. The project also benefited from the practical assistance of the Australian Churches of Christ mission at Chungrebu and the Catholic mission at Annaberg. Most of all I am in-

debted to the Kominimung people, who have been very kind to me. Last but not least, I wish to thank Adrian A. Gerbrands for crucial guidance and inspiration.

2. Often spelled "Guam" on geographical maps. I follow the spelling of Z'graggen (1975: map opposite p. 2, 32, 34).

3. Spelled "Kuminimung" (on Map 2, p. 21).

4. Identification by Maru Kumul, Forest Products Research Centre, Port Moresby.

5. Two Rao villages situated on the Ramu River between Annaberg and Chungrebu.

6. Apart from the identifications by Maru Kumul (see n. 4), the botanical names used in this paper are derived from Paijmans (1976).

48/ Music in Tambunam

Rhoda Métraux

The study of music as a set of communications expressive of a culture is still sufficiently new that it is important to place both the research itself and the method of analysis. The music of the Middle Sepik Iatmul of Tambunam was recorded in three time segments: June 1967–January 1968, June–December 1971, and June 1972–January 1973.[1] The research plan called for extensive recording, which had not been feasible earlier, but my original intention had been to study modes of imagery, not music. The decision to concentrate on music was initially taken by Tambunam men, particularly musicians, who had decided that their music must be recorded so that it might be broadcast and one day heard by their children's children—either in the same museum where, they had been assured, written records and photographs of their way of living a generation earlier were safely stored or else in their own country.[2] During the months in which they awaited my arrival, they themselves had meticulously designed a working plan for what I later came to call "concert" versions of some of the principal categories of their music. Although I had had some musical training, I am not a musicologist; nevertheless, the idea of research that was enthusiastically community-initiated captured my imagination.

It is, of course, difficult to present material on a study of music in which no music is heard and no musicians are seen in performance. Here I have had to concentrate on the situation, on the occasions for performance, and on my own deepening awareness of style. I am further handicapped by having had to work so much of the time with music that men held sacred in a community in which, in contrast to many other Sepik communities, they had not been compelled to share their secrets—at least in part—with women and children. However, in all situations but two (that I know of) the musicians and the community made possible my full participation.

Margaret Mead accompanied me to Tambunam in 1967 and remained for a month as a way of bridging the gap of twenty-nine years since she and Gregory Bateson had worked in the village. She made a second two-week visit in October 1971. As I had access to the 1938 records—notes, stills, and films—and Mead was present both at the outset and at the midpoint of the research, we could discuss change in the light of her knowledge of the past and my emerging hypotheses based on current observations.[3] Later, I had long discussions with and played music for Bateson, who dredged up remarkably fresh, vivid images from the 1920s and 1930s, when he had worked in both Central and Eastern Iatmul communities. Comparative material was essential. I had to train myself to hear new sound and rhythmic patterns, variations, contrasts, and individual idiosyncrasies. Luckily the Tambunams enjoyed showing off and stage-managing informal song performances by talented members of the crews of passing boats from as far away as Murik Lakes. On invitation, I recorded ceremonies in Wompun and Timbunke and practice sessions in Mindimbit;[4] later, in 1972, we traveled upriver by canoe a number of times to various Eastern and Central Iatmul communities, as well as others, including Chambri. On one occasion it was explained by my Tambunam companions, in a speech explaining our coming to a new village, that as Bateson was now too busy to return, he had sent me—his sister—in his stead. This stretched classificatory kinship to its utmost. However, as the idea pleased those who, clearly, had loved Bateson and as they enjoyed working with me and my small Tambunam team, he and I decided to let the definition rest. No doubt many were quite aware of its fictive nature.

I have outlined some circumstances of this research to emphasize one point especially, namely, the great advantage of long-term fieldwork in one setting and the enhanced value of overlapping fieldwork involving two or more "generations" of fieldworkers who are intellectually congenial and, in addition, become so identified in the minds of members of the community (or region) studied that the latter, too, begin to plan for new research efforts.

With regard to the method of analysis, Alan Lomax became, in a most important sense, my collaborator, as he advised me from the outset and afterward introduced me to and instructed me in his then newly developed cantometrics, on which my technical analysis of Tambunam music is based (Lomax 1962, 1968, 1976).

The Setting

Everywhere Middle Sepik Iatmul are splendid architects, builders, carvers, and musicians. In Tambunam, the largest village in the three main groups of Iatmul communities, men are the principal musicians, but everyone has an essential part to play in the many kinds of events involving music, whether as musicians, as coaches, as performers (dancers, mimes, impersonators of supernatural beings or of women, etc.), as entrepreneurs, as celebrants or persons celebrated, or as the ever necessary audience, sometimes present and sometimes—and equally important—listening nearby or from afar (see Bateson 1958 [1936]:177–78).

Musicianship—high skill, style, and artistry in the performance of the music that is intrinsic to almost every ritual—is one means by which, through successful conspicuous display, an ambitious man can enhance his prestige in relation to that of others within the lineage and clan and outside them (Métraux 1978). The musician is also necessarily a scholar and even, in some cases, an archivist, for performance involves prodigious feats of memory, and the success of a seldom-produced or long-neglected ceremony depends in large part on the stored learning and ability to reconstruct the past of master musicians (Métraux 1970).

The decision to become a musician lies initially with the individual. A young man who makes this choice takes a gift of betel nut to a senior musician and asks to become his pupil or apprentice. If he is accepted, the two visit the burial place of a former master musician to make a sacrifice and ask for his help and support. At each lesson the master and his pupil must chew betel; the seat of memory is located in the pit of the stomach and must be fed in order for memorization to be accomplished with a minimum of effort. Even so, the effort may fail. Wolimbaan (known familiarly as Mbaan), my teacher in these matters,[5] continually shook his head over the dismal failure of a mature man who earnestly wished to learn and carry on tradition and who, through marriage, had inherited the lore, secret and secular, of an extinct line. Unfortunately, he learned one day only to have forgotten the next. But even

the most accomplished musicians expect to need occasional coaching in the course of a long, complex ceremony. So one often sees, close beside the actual performer(s), one or two other experts, one perhaps a very elderly man who can no longer chant but who follows the chants in his head and is ready with the missing name or the correct sequence at the slightest hesitation or look of doubt. Mbaan, himself a very old man, spent hours alone practicing, keeping up his amazing skills. His greatest grief was that in his long lifetime he had not succeeded in training a full successor; after his death the men of Tavireman, his clan, would no longer be able to perform their special rites.

In fact, the future of traditional ceremonies in Tambunam was already at risk in 1967. No initiation had taken place since the period of the Japanese occupation,[6] and on one occasion when it was decreed that no uninitiated man might enter the men's house that served as tambaran house, men in their middle thirties sat with me, a woman, at the outer periphery. (For the most part, however, all fully adult men were treated alike ceremonially.) Nor had the sacred flutes been played; the high point in the men's original plan for recording was a correctly performed *teva*, an end-of-mourning ceremony in the course of which the flutes played day and night for more than two weeks. In the interim, very much modified versions had been improvised, one of which, on a grand scale but without flutes, was performed in the twin village of Wompun, also in 1967.

During the three fieldwork periods, I witnessed numerous very small *naven* celebrations—usually for a child's first return from a visit to Wewak or on the occasion of a child's arrival in Tambunam, having been born elsewhere. But I recorded only one major naven, this nominally for the purchase, by three adult men, of a powerful outboard motor.[7] There were many other ceremonial occasions; the most common, *tsagi*, involved the performance of a longer or shorter series of chants.

As I soon came to realize in the course of attending ceremonies, the number of fully competent musicians in the community was very limited, and most were elderly. Indeed, in the whole of Tambunam there was, in 1967, only one young man, Kara, who was a serious, committed musician-in-process. He was apparently undertaking the almost impossible task of learning whole chant cycles of clans other than his own. His having become a Christian appeared not to have weakened his will to perform beautifully and knowledgeably the difficult music to which he was heir.

There were several sets of three or four men who liked to perform together and were, it appeared, called upon to perform tsagi for any one of the clans as professional musicians. At times it was necessary or at least desirable for a member of the household in which the tsagi was held to participate in the performance; usually the amateur chanted with difficulty and had to be constantly coached. Kara, who belonged to no one set of musicians, performed with several and worked tirelessly at memorizing the complex chants. For some important events, very senior men took over the leadership of a group. But only once, at the climactic ceremony of the traditional teva, did *all* the senior musicians, each with a small set of performers, act as chant leaders.

Women performed as musicians mainly as mourners, as singers/dancers at certain stages in the building of one of the great dwelling houses, and in the celebration of a naven, particularly one of the minor ones, in which, in my experience, men rarely took part. A very few woman performers, however, often served as organizers and teachers of woman participants in some larger event. Other forms of musical participation, for example, a courtship dance/game that formerly was played by adolescent girls and boys at about the time of planting yams (photographed by Bateson in 1938) and what Bateson (1958[1936]:149–51) called "jolly dances for women only," had been dropped. Women stated categorically that they did not sing lullabies to wakeful infants or small children; they thought it a comical idea. But a mother mourning the death of her newborn child sang to it throughout the night before its burial, telling it in song how much it was loved and projecting into the future the activities of a life that would never be lived. So, too, several age-mates of a very elderly dying woman spent the night singing her gently to her death.

Children seemed to have no special traditional music of their own. Off by themselves in their more or less private play places behind the houses, they could be heard almost daily singing snatches of traditional adult song, just as they had done when Mead studied children in Tambunam. Occasionally one also heard snatches of songs they were learning in school. There was, however, one children's ceremony that had fallen into disuse but that the young woman musician Mindsindua arranged to have performed for the record.

Formerly mothers, when children would not sleep, would tell them that the Gwoliwar, a fearsome supernatural figure, would come to frighten them. When the children persisted they would summon the Gwoliwar, impersonated by a band of slightly older children who came to the house singing and bearing small burning brands, which they afterward dropped in the Sepik. Thus, threatened by a supernatural being, children very soon learned that the supernatural was none other than themselves. Yet adult women, though they smiled at me when I praised the voices of supernaturals speaking through the flutes, acquiesced in the formal belief.

By 1967, popular songs had entered the domain of the young via the little battery radios everyone wanted to have and the singing of boys who had been away at boarding school or on visits to relatives living in towns. At home they taught one another, accompanying themselves on ukuleles (by 1972 mostly discarded) or guitars. Theirs was a strange mixture of the dance tunes heard almost anywhere in the world (sung with English words), pop religious songs with catchy tunes such as "You May Talk to Jesus on the Glory-Telephone," and popular melodies to which the boys themselves composed texts in Iatmul or Tok Pisin almost exactly as men a generation older composed *greset* (Tok Pisin *krai*) on many different subjects to a single melody. Adolescent girls, going about their tasks or sitting together to gossip, endlessly repeated the same few songs they had learned from the schoolboys. By 1971, girls, dressed in the briefest miniskirts, danced with the schoolboys to the music of massed guitars. Yet as in the past, becoming a musician—other than someone who just sang along or danced along—was a matter of individual choice and involved learning to play a new musical instrument, not made in the village, that had to be purchased at considerable cost. The expert from whom one learned, however, was another boy or young man, more experienced but hardly older than the learner.

Music heard on the radio did not lead in one direction only. Listening brought the Tambunams to a turning point. Young people, learning new styles of music in schools and churches, were teaching themselves and one another to perform and to enjoy new musical styles. At the same time, Wewak radio broadcast special programs of traditional Papua New Guinea music recorded in the highlands and in many other places, to which the older musicians listened with envy—and made their plans, into which my coming fitted perfectly. When the senior men had agreed in 1953 to have the children attend school in the mission area between Tambunam and Wompun, they had decided that the past was past and children should not be instructed about it. Now, hearing the slit-gongs, flutes, and chants of other folk, they concluded that it was time for a new generation to learn the music that was unique to Tambunam.

Performance

Beginning the very night of our arrival in 1967, the old men sang, the young men sang, an older and a younger woman sang, and even very young girls, shy gigglers, were encouraged by the men themselves to try, almost every afternoon and evening. On our first night in Tambunam the screen room had been set up in the newly built government house, and beds, two chairs, a table, and a lamp had been installed, but we had neither a kitchen nor a cook. Nevertheless, Kami Asavi, who had taken charge (both because he had been the last *luluai* [government-appointed village head] and, earlier, a boy in the Bateson-Mead household in 1938), arranged for and supervised the initial performance. Mead elected to take notes so that I could concentrate wholly on listening and adapting my new tape recorder (see appendix A) to this unfamiliar style of music.

The men came in a crowd but alternated as audience and performers in a quiet, formal, and apparently confident manner. As I slowly learned, they had spent long hours practicing for this and many future "concert" evenings. First, of course, two of the most senior men led off with name chants in their somewhat frail and slightly quavering voices. Then, with only occasional hesitations and not infrequent coaching, younger mature men performed competently and self-critically. Best of all, they had *yivut* (Iatmul for "liveliness," "esprit," or "movement"), a quality they much admire (Bateson 1958[1936]:128).

On other evenings, the men chanted and recited songs from the crucial name-celebrating cycles. They played their clan trumpets with boundless enthusiasm. They sang songs for the proud tambaran house that was no longer standing, songs for the great raiding canoes that were no longer fashioned, songs once sung in the men's houses by successful head-hunters, and songs from the initiation cycle that was no longer performed. They sang greset, some of them well-known to everyone, others still the property of individual composers of texts, who adapted the universal melody to their own style and mood. Yet the veriest neophytes were permitted to perform, and boy ensembles were ordered to play their modern pop music and sing in English, Tok Pisin, and Iatmul, including texts of their own improvising.

The serious musicians, especially, wanted immediate playback. This gave them a chance to rest their voices; more important, they heard themselves for the first time and almost immediately began to relate to the realities of recording. They learned how easily an enthusiastic beat on the hourglass drum could drown out even a strong voice. The drum had to be moved back and the singers forward, they decided. Blown just below the house, the *mwai* trumpets produced an unrecognizable blast on tape; instead, they had to be blown from inside a house some twenty-five yards away. (As a woman, I was naturally not supposed to see these trumpets, but for convenience they kept a pair in the thatch above my head, where I was supposed to ignore them.) For certain songs of the tambaran house and the initiation cycle (which the men refused to translate or explain to me),[8] there was a great deal of experimentation. The problems were twofold: I was supposed to hear and record but not see the chanters, and their voices were meant to come in alternately softer or louder. The singers were men who had never been initiated and sang now with special joy and enthusiasm. They sang running up and down in the dark next to my house until they panted, breathless. They sang close to the house and at some distance. The older men and the singers themselves listened to the recordings; I varied the sound level and moved the mike in response to their critical comments. Then I sent an early set of these "concert" recordings to Alan Lomax, who listened and hurriedly sent back advice.

The liberating hour came when I explained that the tape recorder was not anchored to the house; it could be moved anywhere to record actual events. As a test, the musicians suggested that we record a *mwolimbango*, a dance performed on that occasion by teams of young men from different clans to harden the earth floor of a very large shelter constructed to protect a big tent that was to serve as an office.[9] The musicians saw new possibilities but also new problems in crowd noises, children shouting, dogs barking, cocks crowing, women chatting. Curiously, such noises had not disturbed musicians intent on their own music making, but on playback, trying to sort out music and noise, they were angered, and it took them some time to grasp that the mike could not discriminate between purposeful and irrelevant sound. It was a problem they solved fully only once, when in the dead of night I was summoned to a men's house in which a teva was being celebrated. There, in total darkness, I recorded for almost two hours music played on flutes that I was not permitted to see. The surrounding silence was profound, yet when a lamp was finally lighted I saw that some forty men were lying on their platforms, listening.

Over the three years that I recorded in Tambunam, Wompun, Timbunke, and Mindimbit, we worked on the problem of noise; in time I convinced the men that surrounding noise was part of the event for which music was made, and occasionally, if they wished a clean recording, they came to the house and recorded for that purpose. I learned and they learned. In some ways they were far ahead of me. Within weeks they would advise me where, out of doors, to set up a microphone, taking into account the direction of the wind and the relation of event to surrounding buildings. They even went so far as to locate mikes at strategic points in a men's house for a debate, while I sat modestly at the entrance controlling the tape recorder, so that all men inside would be heard and recorded equally well. Recording was throughout a cooperative enterprise but one in which the proprieties were mostly observed.[10]

The living music spurred us all on. I taped many tsagi: for the repair of a house, for the building of a new one and for the demolition of a very old one; to announce the beginning of a lengthy ceremony at the house of each participating family and at the house where part of the ceremony was to take place as well as on the *wompunau* (dancing ground) to announce the opening of the ceremony to the men's house that served as tambaran house: for hunting luck; to settle a quarrel between two men; to cure a sick child in a house where quarrels between women had endangered life; to appease a house where sickness and death had led to a series of accidents; to announce to the house the divorce of a wife and, on another occasion, to reinstate an erring and discarded wife; to remove the *tambu* (taboo) on sago palms that had been reserved for a special feast; to celebrate the launching of a new canoe; and so on.

The big Tambunam dwelling house, its facade the face of a woman wearing long earrings, was symbolically a woman, often given the name of a sister of the builder, and in its way as sacred as the *ngaigo* (the men's clan house). Men described

seeing the house as a woman sitting at rest on her own house ladder, and I heard women exclaim, when men got very drunk under the dwelling house, that the dwelling was the woman's ngaigo and men should go to their own when they drank. And as the house was a woman, it had to be informed of all events with which it might be concerned and appeased when things of which it disapproved took place. For such reasons, men performed tsagi very frequently, in this village of more than a hundred houses, to please and appease the houses as supernatural beings.

Over three field seasons I recorded mourning—the solitary voice of a young mother mourning her dead prematurely born first child; the voices of women quietly singing to death a man dying, probably of a heart attack, and after his burial the solitary voice of his only living sister standing alone in an empty court by his house; the voices of some hundred women mourning the tragic death of a young woman in childbirth (an act of revenge by a long-deceased former husband); and a formal mourning of women in the different versions of the teva.

I taped the rededication of a small men's house in Wompun and the dedication of a new "chair" in a Tambunam men's house. In Timbunke, where Tambunam men were invited to perform as mwai dancers, I recorded part of the ceremony (which continued for many days) for the dedication of a new mask to replace one destroyed by the man in whose keeping it was when he raged because his sacrifices to the mwai had not effected a cure of his desperately sick small daughter. In Wompun I recorded, over many days, a complex ceremony in which the creation of the Sepik world and of human beings and other events were symbolized, part of which took place within a high enclosure from which women and children were excluded (as was I),[11] where a water drum was an important instrument, and part on the open wompunau to an audience of women and children and with the participation of certain woman relatives. This ceremony had been recorded on film by Bateson in Wompun in 1938, so we had here comparative visual data. This may have been planned.

I taped jolly evening dances by the young, dances to honor a guest's departure, and dances in which sisters' sons honored mothers' brothers. In 1967, I recorded schoolboy dances from which girls were excluded except as audience, in which the boys danced to their songs, perhaps accompanied by a guitar. In 1971, I recorded crowded Saturday-night dances—the boys in shorts and the girls in miniskirts. Sometimes, late at night, when the young were temporarily resting, men and women in their thirties—too young to have participated in traditional ceremonies and too old to have enjoyed the pleasures of contemporary schoolboys and girls—would get up and attempt to sing and dance to the guitars, heavily, clumsily, somewhat sadly, determined but lacking in yivut.

One night, perhaps the night I enjoyed most for its comradeship, the men invited me to sit in on a nine-hour jam session in a men's house where, against a background of rolling thunder and lightning, wind and lashing rain, the old pros coached the young men who were learning the old music. They also sang about Wai, the supernatural crocodile whose voice was thundering outside. And finally, in 1972, toward the end of my stay, the men invited me to visit a very small house in the woods behind the village where young men were being taught how to play the magic bird melodies of the paired flutes. For several hours I watched instructors and instructed play on flutes and at last—after three years—was permitted to record both flutes and players on film and tape recorder.

The one type of song that was always sung and explicated—if at all—out of public hearing was the *stori* (Tok Pisin, not fully translatable either as "history," "mythical history," "myth," or "tale"). When Mbaan decided we should have a session of stori-telling/singing, sitting on the porch with my tape recorder set up, one of his sons and Tavireman clan men close to the household hovered protectively below. What Mbaan narrated and sang on these occasions was, I believe, derived from exoteric versions of esoteric storis told in the Tavireman men's house; part was also esoteric material, and it was this part that inevitably led to a sudden breakdown in grumbling or silence. Mbaan tried hard, but in the end he could never bring himself to elucidate for a woman what was the privileged knowledge of initiated men—even though he believed this knowledge might die with him.

Yet the power of the women of the community was continually made evident in music and in relation to music—by their very presence, for example, silently going about their tasks or, on the contrary, heedlessly chattering, while men, gathered close to the house ladder, sang tsagi to inform or mollify the (feminine) house. And I recorded one talented and intrepid young woman who composed greset and sang in the style of men.

It was in mourning that women excelled musically. Almost every woman can mourn, but there are certain women whose mourning is a high accomplishment, a skill as specialized as that of an opera singer. Like male experts, they are much in demand, but unlike men they are seldom seen performing. Only their voices are heard. During the teva, the voices of mourning women, often in widely scattered houses, singing solo or antiphonally, compete in a dialog with the voices of men chanting songs that have to do with life and with the birdlike melodies of the paired flutes. Inevitably the men—and life—win out, but listening to the women responding to death and loss one cannot doubt their emotional power or question their ability as artists in their own right.

Traditional music was not only at risk in Tambunam in 1967; there had been already irreparable losses. For example, while there is now no way of judging quality of performance on slit-gong or hourglass drum at an earlier period, Tambunam performance in 1967 was very elementary as compared with the drum performance in any of the Central Iatmul villages in which I recorded. It may be that this difference is not a new one. But when I requested that Tambunam mount a performance of the Wagan djura (see Bateson 1958[1936]:pl.18b) or at least of the music for this ceremony, they first for many months made delaying excuses and then finally admitted that no one then living could cope with the difficult drum rhythms. This was a major loss, and certainly there were other losses of this kind.

The Tambunam men were correct in their insistence on the priority of recording music as a centrally important aspect of their culture as they themselves understood it. Within prescribed limits, music was my entry into their confidence. And living so fully in musical occasions over the periods of three field trips I recognized (as I had earlier in Haiti and Montserrat) that recording and hearing only "concert" versions of the music of a culture severely limits one's insights into its cultural relevance, as any artificial segregation of cultural material must. For this reason I have attempted, very sketchily, to include performance in my description.

Analysis

The analysis of part of the corpus that I shall describe here is based on a method designed by Alan Lomax and his associates for a comparative world survey of song types. Cantometrics, as Lomax (1968:34) has written, "is a method for systematically and holistically describing the general features of accompanied and unaccompanied song performances" and, within limits, instrumental performances, including not only the technical features of the music as such but also "many other expressive and social phenomena which shape all musical productions." The method is rather easily adapted to the study of the whole body of music within one culture, in which one is interested equally in defining the core style and the range of the music and in exploring the range of individual and group performance and the ways in which the music is an expression of the culture.

Tambunam music is only one version of Iatmul music and, in a wider context, of the music of the Sepik area and of Papua New Guinea as a whole. For example, in Tambunam as elsewhere, the emphasis is on the human voice, particularly the male voice, even when men are singing songs attributed to women. Flutes and trumpets are common instruments, and, as elsewhere, drums, slit-gongs, rattles, rasps, and stamping feet may set the rhythm (see appendix B). The rhythm, typically one beat, is very free, with much rubato. The use of one melody with many song texts is common practice in the Sepik area, as is the practice of embedding elements of differentiated text within the framework of highly conventional, essentially meaningless repetitive syllables.

Yet Iatmul music has an unmistakable style—pace, preferences for the use of the voice, preferences in combining voices and instruments, and ways of combining independent forms of music in complex performances—that is highly characteristic and, I believe, expresses very deeply rooted cultural sets. Listening one night to singers from a village much farther up the Sepik, gradually I began to discern similarities to Tambunam songs, But, immersed as I was in Tambunam music, I muttered to myself: "It's all right for once, but I couldn't stand recording such beautiful funereal stuff every day." The change of pace, if nothing else, changed everything. In this brief discussion I can give only a few examples of the details that recur in regular patterned ways to define the local style and of the patterning at different levels of performance that characterizes the organization of the music as a whole.

In an early paper on flutes from Mindimbit, Bateson (1935) pointed out that the flutes were so constructed that a melody could be produced (or, at least, that a Iatmul melody could be produced) only when they were played in pairs and cited this as an example of Iatmul emphasis on pairing that runs through the culture. Tambunam clan flutes,

each set with its distinctive melodies, are also constructed to be played in pairs—some pairs "male" and some "female"—but there is perhaps a subtle difference from the Mindimbit flutes. One of the two extant pairs in 1968 was so constructed that at certain points in the melody (typically near a resting point) the flutes played simultaneously, producing a very close dissonance. This dissonance is recurrent in various of the musical forms.

Many songs and chants are designed for a single voice at a time—not a solo but two (sometimes more) voices, closely matched, that succeed each other so smoothly that the effect is a kind of seamless web of sound. Also, in the songs of the men's house, the emphasis in group singing is on perfect vocal and rhythmic unison—an ideal not always achieved, of course. But in these songs, particularly at the end of a strophe, as the voices move toward momentary rest, they move also toward very controlled, close dissonance. The clan trumpets, into which a pair of singers shouts, produce a melodic line characterized by the same kind of dissonance, ending in a burst like a huge horselaugh.

It may be that this dissonance takes the place of vocal rasp, of which there is relatively little in Tambunam voices. (One tends to hear rasp in the voices of some adolescent boys and some older women who are trying to make their speaking or singing voices more impressive.) When men sing as women—that is, when the song a man is singing is imputed to a woman—their voices tend to be high, even occasionally falsetto, tense, and strongly nasal. Otherwise, as a rule, men sing and chant at mid-register, and their voices, although nasal (for there are a large number of nasalized sounds in Iatmul), are quite wide and relaxed. At the same time, their enunciation of consonants, very important in the chanting of strings of names that vary only in one or two syllables, is strikingly definite and sharp. Rasp does not combine easily with this use of the voice. But one can also see—or rather, hear—the dissonance, usually occurring only at special points, as a statement that there are two, not one, performing—that the group, singing in unison, has many components, not one but acting as one at the time.

The different types of musical performance—tsagi, men's songs, mourning, flutes, trumpets, and so on—exist as independent forms, but they are also combined. For example, when men representing several clans are working side by side at a common task, such as sewing thatch for the roof of a new house, pairs of men play the clan trumpets to make the work more lively. Two, three, or four pairs, each belonging to a different clan and having a different song text, blast away simultaneously, but not in unison. At the same time, a group of men from another clan may march up and down loudly singing a song from their own men's house. The resulting cacophony of all for one for all immensely cheers the listening workers, who periodically break out in shouts of enjoyment. Competition in Tambunam, which can run high and is recognized as very dangerous, is customarily resolved in some such statement as *ol i winim em* (Tok Pisin for "everyone wins" or perhaps "everyone is best"). The climax comes at the high point of participation, not at the point of outcome or rest.

In a different setting, in certain ceremonies independent musical forms are combined to produce antiphonal dialog, as when flutes and women's mourning voices alternate. Or, particularly at moments of climax, several simultaneous performances produce an extemely complex heterophony as more and more performers are drawn into an intense interrelationship.Each group follows its own melodic and/or rhythmic line, but there is evidence of a diffused attentiveness to the performance of all groups. Characteristically, such a climax is followed by a falling away of one voice and then another, one group and then another, into an interval of silence.

Looking at this music simply as music, there can be no doubt of the existence of a pervasive style—in the use of the voice, in the characteristics of the melodic line, in rhythm in relation to phrasing, in the emphasis (except in mourning, and even there in certain situations) on the single voice or on leaderless unison, in the pace of the performance, and so on. Analysis of the types of music shows very clearly the complementary relationships of men and women and some points of overlapping, as well as the special position of adolescent boys. There are no lullabies and (as far as I know) only one children's ceremonial chant. Boys and girls both, in their play groups, sing snatches of adult songs.

It is, however, music in its performance that is crucial for an understanding of music as an expression of the state of integration of a culture and as an activity supportive of that integration. Greset, individually sung and composed, celebrate the individual, living or dead, real or mythical, but also express the complementarity of the sexes; most greset are about events involving women and are sung by men as though they were the women involved. Tsagi, celebrating names, are set up in complex configurations of persons, lineages, houses, places, objects, reminders of the past, and so on, each chant paralleling hundreds of others. Their performance reiterates not only a style of person-to-person interaction— and an extraordinary sensuous delight in virtuosity—but also a continual dependence on others for supportive coaching. The songs of the tambaran house and of the clan men's houses that nowadays celebrate events in the distant past at the same time celebrate the ideal of unity among men. And the complexity of multiple performance gives some insight into the ways in which, in spite of elaborate organization, an awareness of the component parts is never lost or evaded.

No in-depth analysis has yet been made of the performance of the popular contemporary music that today links Tambunam youth to Papua New Guinea youth in general and to members of their generation the world over. Notable is the very rapid expansion of skilled performance of this music and its partial adaptation to village uses. In one modification of a teva, very abbreviated in its performance, the young danced to massed guitars throughout the climactic night outside the house of mourning, while indoors, in the presence of the widows, older men chanted in traditional fashion, but on a very reduced scale, the name chants of the deceased. This was the first evidence (in my experience) in Tambunam of the bringing together—rather than the joining—of two traditions belonging to two different time periods.

It remains to be seen what path Tambunams will take as the older, prewar generation loses its position of leadership and the village becomes— as so many have—a home for the elderly, a few men who run the show, some women, and many children. It is perhaps significant that in 1983, when they put on a tourist performance for a group of American visitors (of whom I was one), they costumed themselves very much as Americans might were they playing at being Plains Indians—that is, with admirable fantasy only slightly related to reality. They danced, if one can call it that, with some yivut, but the music and the dance were not their own; instead they carefully performed the Aimolo, a dance complex that had been twice imported into Tambunam and that gave no real clue to the nature of their own music, which, it seemed, remained their own, uncontaminated.[12]

I conclude this all too brief discussion with a presentation of a cantometric profile (see Lomax

TABLE 1
CANTOMETRIC PROFILE OF A GRESET

Category	1	2	3	4	5	6	7	8	9	10	11	12	13
1. Vocal group (Solo → Leader with chorus → Parts independent)	1	(2)	3	4	5	6	7	8	9	10	11	12	13
4. Vocal organization (Solo → Unison → Heterophony → Polyphony)	1			(4)			7			10			13
5. Tonal blend (Solo → Poor → Very good)	(1)			4			7			10			13
6. Rhythmic blend (Solo → Poor → Very good)	(1)			4			7			10			13
10. Text (Wordy → Very repetitious, nonsense)	1			4			(7)			10			13
11. Overall rhythm (Simple, regular meter → Irregular, free meter)	1		3			6			9		11		(13)
12. Group rhythm (Unison → Many independent parts)	(1)		3		5		7		9		11		13
15. Melodic shape (Arched → Terraced → Undulating → Descending)	1				5				(9)				13
16. Melodic form (Complex → Simple)	1	2	3	4	5	6	7	8	9	10	(11)	12	13
17. Phrase length (Very long → Very short)	1			4			(7)			10			13
18. Number of phrases (More than eight → One or two)	1		3		5	6		8	9		(11)		13
19. Position of final (Bottom note in scale → Top note in scale)	1			4					9		(11)		13
20. Range of melody (Monotone → Two octaves)	1			4			(7)			10			13
21. Interval width (Monotone → A fifth or more)	1			(4)			7			10			13
22. Type of polyphony (Drone → Counterpoint)	(1)		3			6		8		10			13
23. Embellishment (Much → Little or none)	1			4			7			10			(13)
24. Tempo (Very slow → Very fast)	1		3		(5)				9		11		13
25. Volume (Very soft → Very loud)	1			(4)			(7)			10			13
26. Rubato (vocal rhythm) (Completely free → Strict tempo)	(1)				5				9				13
28. Glissando (Constant gliding → Clearly separate tones)	1				5				9				(13)
29. Melisma (note load) (One syllable to many notes frequent → One note per syllable)	1						(7)						13
30. Tremolo (quavering attack) (Much, frequent → Little or none)	1						7						(13)
31. Glottal effect (Heavy and constant → None)	1						7						(13)
32. Vocal register (Very high falsetto → Very low deep-chest)	(1)			4			(7)			10			13
33. Vocal width/tension (Narrow/squeezed, hard → Wide/open, mellow)	1		3			(6)		(8)		10			13
34. Nasality (Constant, heavy → Absent)	1			(4)			(7)			10			13
35. Raspiness (Harsh, noisy, chesty → Clear, limpid)	1			4			7			10			(13)
36. Accent (Many notes strongly stressed → No notes strongly stressed)	1			4			7			(10)			13
37. Consonants (Precisely enunciated → Slurred, hard to hear)	1			4			(7)			10			13

NOTE: Adapted from Lomax (1968:22–24), omitting categories referring to instrumental accompaniment. For discussion see Lomax (1968: chaps. 2 and 3; 1976).

1968, 1976) of a single song, a greset performed by one man on one occasion (table 1). The profile serves to indicate the characteristics that are taken into account in a cantometric analysis, except that for purposes of simplification (and because the greset is sung without accompaniment) I have omitted a few categories that refer to instrumental music. It should be said that only in the final analysis are the ratings subjective. The method of analysis is learned by rigorous training with taped examples of each category. Except in a few categories, for example, that having to do with the precise range of sound on a scale, what is required is a fine-tuned ear but not necessarily musical training. Musical profiles of this kind can be prepared for all types of music performed in a community (or a culture); these will, as they accumulate, show the range and kind of participation—in this way providing links to the way of life of a people.

Of course, cantometric profiles alone, or even the music heard alone, cannot evoke a culture. Music, like all other activities, is embedded—enmeshed—in people's lives and must be analyzed in that context. For the same reason, *all* the music of a people at a particular time is relevant. In the present discussion I have included the all-important popular music; I have not included church music (the sung mass in this Catholic-oriented community and the pathetic attempts at hymns) or the music taught children in school, but these too are part of the whole. The astonishing thing in 1967 was the men's insistence that their traditional music should survive and remain a valuable heritage for new generations; their difficulty was that they could not yet convey much of its inherited sacred—and secret—meanings to a woman, even a welcome outsider.

At every level in the study of Papua New Guinea music, we are in need of strict comparison. Tambunam music is no more than one priceless exemplar.

Notes

1. Funds for the support of this research were provided by the National Science Foundation (Research Grant GS-642, 1966–69, "The Cultural Structure of Perceptual Communication") and by the Jane Belo Fund, American Museum of Natural History, New York (Expedition to New Guinea, "A Comparative Study of Cultural Style in Communication—Music, Speech, and Body Motion").

2. Bateson and Mead had carefully explained to the Tambunams in 1938 how and where the records—written and visual—would be stored for safekeeping.

3. The full set of 1938 Bateson-Mead field notes on Tambunam, on which I have heavily relied but which I could not bring into the discussion in this brief paper, is archived in the Library of Congress, as are Bateson's original films and half of his stills; a complete catalog is in preparation. The library also holds my own original 1967–68 recordings (with a few exceptions), which are not yet available; a copy series of the music recordings was made by me on professional recording equipment in Lomax's studio. Examples of the latter set can be made available. Later tapes—1971 and 1972–73—will be copied within a year.

4. Mindimbit, where Bateson had done some of his earliest Iatmul research, was in 1967 just breaking free from a postwar conversion to Seventh-Day Adventism. Under the guidance of Windsimbu, who had worked very closely with Bateson, the Mindimbits were attempting both to enter the secular contemporary world and to recover what they could of the past.

5. Mbaan was a principal informant and the language instructor of Mead in 1938. In 1967, we estimated that he must be approximately seventy-five to seventy-seven years old. Tiny, frail, and blind, he was still living and talkative at the time of my visit in 1983. One of the last men who could personally recall headhunting raids, he died in 1984.

6. Tambunam was occupied during World War II. Women and children were hidden deep in the marsh country, but men were forced to work for the Japanese. Even so, they attempted to help downed fliers and others. No ceremonial life was possible in the war years; afterward the energy of the village was mainly given over to rebuilding the badly bombed community. By 1967, many new houses had been built; no new tambaran house had been built even by 1983.

7. In fact, this celebration was apparently a cover for another, unacknowledged naven.

8. It took me some time to work out their reluctance to translate or explicate. Their method of withholding information was wholly traditional: they simply ignored any questions. Early in July 1967, the men held a curing ceremony in the men's house that served as tambaran house to cure themselves of ailments (loose joints) caused by women's having seen men's secret paraphernalia at a public performance at Christmas in Angoram. We learned of this only by chance a day or two later. Men protected their privacy in ritual matters by omission and evasion.

9. The mwolimbango was treated as a social, rather than a ceremonial, dance, but it was danced on some ceremonial occasions, for example, when most Tambunam adults, men and women, went to Wompun to dance all night at the high point of a modified teva because, as they explained, the grieving Wompun people could not dance.

10. It is possible that I could have been male-identified, but as I wished to work intimately with women as well and, in most things, was not barred from masculine activities, I kept my feminine identification and trusted to time to win masculine confidence. So, especially on conspicuous occasions, such as public debates in men's houses, I remained outside. Younger men, especially, informed me "secretly" about events in a closed men's house; for example, when flutes were playing, adult uninitiated men, who feasted with the flute players and others in the men's house, came to me, one by one, late at night and whispered accounts of what was going on, what food they were eating, how much betel had been given, and so forth, an activity that gave them a kind of fearful pleasure.

11. Wompun, unlike Tambunam, soon after my arrival invited me into its one men's house. However, on this occasion, in which Tambunam as well as Wompun men and boys took part day after day, the senior Wompun man in charge of the arrangements offered to allow me to enter the men's ceremonial enclosure on payment of a fee. I refused on the grounds that this was, by his definition, a traditionally correct celebration, not a tourist attraction. This is a common kind of confusion in the villages today.

12. The Aimolo, purchased once in the 1930s (Mead/Bateson unpublished notes) and again after

World War II, is a social dance with accompanying song and drumbeat; it was a dance for young men before the modern popular music came on the scene; later it was adapted for men and women to entertain tourists for pay.

Appendix A

Equipment and Recording Conditions

Equipment. Initially two, later three Uher 4000 Report L tape recorders, battery-powered, were used alternately. In 1967–68, when cassette recorders were still almost experimental, a Norelco Carrycorder, battery-powered, was employed in emergency situations; the cassettes were usable for analysis but not for reproduction. Thereafter, a Sony Cassette-corder TC 110 (later replaced by a TC 110A) and a Uher Compact Report Stereo Tape Recorder Model CP124 were used for cassette recording with satisfactory results, particularly on some visits to other villages when traveling by canoe made weather, weight, and bulk considerations. Copies of tapes or cassettes that proved to be very popular were made on a Sony tape recorder; after the musicians had heard their performance on the original, it was not played again in the field. Usually a single microphone, covered with a windshield, on a tripod or hung from a house rafter was used for recording in a fixed position. Hand-held, the Uher mike is invariably noisy. Kodak tapes (Type 21P, 900 ft. on 1-mil polyester base) were used in 1967–68; later Scotch Magnetic Tape (Type 150, 900 ft., silicone-lubricated on 1-mil polyester backing) was used.

Recording conditions. Musical recordings were made in the open air, in front of or in the high, unwalled area beneath a dwelling house, in a large, lofty room with a peaked thatch roof, on my open porch (all excellent for resonance), or at the entrance to or within a men's house, as the occasion required. Events involved an actively engaged audience—sometimes a few children, sometimes three hundred or more persons in addition to many participants. I myself did not attempt to control noise, except occasionally to restrain very small children too close to the microphone. Few, if any, restrictions were placed on making musical recordings in Tambunam, Wompun, Timbunke, or Mindimbit. Elsewhere recording depended on the preference and interest of the men of the village.

Appendix B

Musical Instruments in Tambunam[a]

Aerophones
  End-blown tubular trumpet

Bamboo tube, approximately three feet long, played in pairs by men only. Played by the two male masked figures in the clan-related mwai trio (elder brother, younger brother, and sister), a lengthy, semitheatrical dance ceremony; on other occasions taboo to and hidden from women and children, e.g., during work parties in the bush, during house building or repairs, etc. On such male-only occasions, several pairs of mwai were played by pairs of men of different clans competitively and simultaneously.

Open, end-blown flute
  Slender bamboo tube without stops, played in pairs by initiated men; hidden from women and children, who are said to be ignorant of the fact that the sound is produced by men playing a musical instrument. In 1967 only two pairs existed in more than name and were played during a tewa; the specialists who knew the music for flutes of other clans were said to have died without passing on their skills. In 1972, I was permitted to see, record, and film a training course for selected young men in a small house out of hearing of the village.

Miniature panpipe
  Formerly used for practice and amusement by boys in the junior men's house, which in 1967 no longer existed; today played for amusement, although not exclusively, by both men and boys.

Membranophones
  Hourglass drum
  Usually approximately two feet in height but somewhat variable in size, with or without a handle and with or without decorative carving. Normally played by men, occasionally by a woman singer. Struck by hand. Normally played singly but for certain chants in pairs. Provides rhythmic accompaniment to all tsagi.

  Water drum
  Described by Bateson (1932) as larger than hourglass drum but without tympanum. Not used in Tambunam 1967–68, but part of lengthy ceremony in Wompun in 1971. I was not permitted to see the drum, which was kept within the men's enclosure.

Idiophones
  Slit-gong
  The large, elaborately carved slit-gongs described and photographed by Bateson in 1938 (unpublished notes and photographs) were destroyed when the tambaran house was bombed and destroyed in World War II. Plain slit-gongs of various sizes are used to beat out, with a stick, simple rhythms to accompany dance songs, for example. A large plain one was used to summon men to meetings. Played by men and, for ceremonial women's songs and dances, e.g., in con-

---

[a]Typology follows Sachs (1913) as modified by Lomax (1976).

nection with ceremony for a new house, by women. Invariably called *garamut* (Tok Pisin) in my hearing. A special one (still taboo to uninitiated) played with one pair of flutes had a special rhythm, apparently that used in *wagan* ceremonies (Bateson 1958[1936]:137: Bateson, personal communication, 1970).

Strung rattles, various types

Shell ornaments worn on upper arm, wrist, and, especially, ankles by male dancers. Shell or other ornaments attached to a ceremonial "tree" set in front of men's house and shaken rhythmically during playing of one set of flutes. Also attached to great snakelike figures (Iatmul *kaiśe*) made for teva; may be fifty feet long, suspended from house rafters and shaken rhythmically to playing of flutes, chanting, etc., during ceremony.

Rasp

Carved lime stick rubbed against lime gourd used by some men as a rhythmic accompaniment to dancing.

Stamper

Short woman's paddle, pounded on the resounding floor by women mourners as they circle the corpse in a special dance for the death of a young, vigorous person.

Handclapping and foot stamping

As a rhythmic accompaniment to certain dances, e.g., *laua* dance for *wau* (sisters' sons dance for mothers' brothers) during the playing of one set of flutes.

Jew's harp (Tok Pisin *susap*)

It is denied that this has a Iatmul name. Formerly one of set of instruments played in junior men's house; today played for amusement by men and sometimes women.

Contemporary instruments

Ukulele

In 1967–68 played principally but not exclusively by schoolboys to accompany popular music learned in school, town, over radio, and from other boys; by 1971, played only by those who could not afford to buy a guitar or could not borrow one.

Guitar

In 1967 the schoolboys' delight but played principally by young men. By 1971, when girls as well as boys had learned modern dancing (same as in New York at that period but with greater spirit), music was provided by massed guitars, playing in unison, sometimes as many as twenty simultaneously. In 1972, provided music for a teva outdoors, while older men chanted tsagis in the upper room of the house.

Harmonica

Played by a few boys, popular music only. Perhaps introduced in Sepik villages in 1930s.

49/ The Yumanwusmangge Ceremony at Aibom

Gordon D. Spearritt

Iatmul music is for the most part closely linked with the belief system (see Spearritt and Schuster 1981*a*, *b*). Music plays a preeminent part in honoring the ancestors because the Iatmul believe that the sounds of the instruments (particularly those of flutes and drums) represent the ancestors' voices. Music of this kind is secret and played only by initiated men on specific ceremonial occasions. Much less important is the singing of songs or the playing of tunes in recreational contexts.

The main categories of ceremonial music consist of *sagi*, clan-specific feasts to mark a death or the completion of a house or a canoe; *mbangu*, other feasts to commemorate particular spirits either of clans or of the village as a whole; a group of pieces connected with initiation; and *tavɨk*, a repertoire of drum signals used for communication. There are, of course, variations of this scheme from one village to another, but it probably suffices as a broad classification. The vocal and instrumental forces needed to perform these various ceremonies are also likely to vary from village to village, according to particular village traditions and the presence or absence of gifted instrumentalists and singers at any given time. In general, however, a sagi will usually be performed by a solo singer (one who knows the clan's history well), an hourglass drummer and bamboo beater, and a men's chorus; on some occasions a pair of bamboo flutes will also play at a sagi, provided suitable precautions have been taken to preserve the secrecy of the sound source from women, girls, and uninitiated boys. A mbangu may variously combine solo singer, men's chorus, flutes played independently or in pairs, slit-drums (often played in pairs), one or more hourglass drums, and other percussion instruments. The music for initiation is most likely to comprise a selection of the following: solo singer, men's chorus, occasional flutes, one or more hourglass drums, and other percussion, including two water drums and bullroarers. The slit-drum communication signals are usually sent by one man using one drumstick.

The Yumanwusmangge Ceremony

The ceremony at the Iatmul village of Aibom with which we are concerned here was formerly celebrated in honor of the pottery goddess, Yumanwusmangge.[1] According to legend, Yuman introduced pottery to Aibom. Schuster (1967: 274) reports having been present at a dance and feast held around a masked figure of Yuman at Aibom in 1966 and proposes a relationship between this figure and that of Weikanbanma, a similarly masked figure observed at the neighboring Chambri Lake village of Wombun (like Aibom formerly a pottery-making center). One of his photographs shows the highly decorated masked figure of Yuman surrounded by many men, women, and children, the figure being carried by several men because of its great height (1967: table 2, pl. 4).

The music associated with Yuman is a finely organized set of pieces for seven flutes and an hourglass drum and forms one of the most interesting repertoires of all the Iatmul music I have heard. It should be noted, though, that neither the music nor the masked figure is necessarily associated with pottery today. When Andrew Ngauimali of Aibom was asked in July 1974 about the Yuman mask and flutes, he replied that the music might now be presented at a time when the village was suffering from a wave of sickness or infection or when there was a shortage of good food. At the 1966 ceremony observed by Meinhard and Gisela Schuster (personal communication), celebrations were going on simultaneously for the completion of a new house and for a change in leadership of age-grades. Preparations for the feast stretched over several weeks, culminating in the masked entry of the deity. While the masked figure appeared outside the ceremonial house, moving in a fairly restricted area, the flutes and drum remained hidden in the upper story of the house. On those occasions in the past when the masked figure appeared, only men danced around it; women and children watched the procession and danced

Flute 5•   Flute 3•   Flute 1•

Flute 7•

Flute 6•   Flute 4•   Flute 2•

Hourglass drum•

FIG. 1. Disposition of flutes and drum in a Yuman performance at Aibom.

on the periphery but did not take an active part. Although nominally the Yuman flutes are ascribed to the Mboui clan in Aibom, in practice they are regarded by the villagers as not clan-specific and are played on occasions affecting the village as a whole. In the past ten to twelve years it has been usual for the music to be played without any suggestion of a masked figure's appearing.[2]

Traditionally, the ceremony began not in the secrecy of the upper story of the men's house at night but in broad daylight on a large flat rock situated on the mountainside above the village (see Schlenker 1974). The risk of observation by women or children was obviated by hanging a palm branch or sheaf of rattan over the pathway leading to the rock to warn women and children away from the area. After the performance on the rock, further performances took place in the ceremonial house. The flutes customarily played for a minimum of twelve to fourteen hours and sometimes for several days. If the masked figure of Yuman did appear, it was usually toward the end of the period, marking a climax to the feast.

The upper story of the men's house at Aibom, where the Yuman flutes are most frequently played today, has thatched walls with only a very few small apertures, so there is little risk that anybody outside the house will see the men blowing the flutes. Even so, the men play almost entirely in the dark to ensure the secrecy of the instruments. In addition to the performers there are likely to be ten or a dozen other men sitting around the hut upstairs and a similar number downstairs listening to the music.

In a present-day performance, the seven flute players stand in fairly fixed positions relative to one another and to the drummer (fig. 1). Flutes 1 and 2 play as a pair, as do Flutes 3 and 4 and Flutes 5 and 6; Flute 7 alone has no partner, but his part is very definitely bound up with what is played by Flutes 5 and 6. The hourglass-drum player is not far from any of the flute players, because it is essential that they be able to hear his beat very clearly. As in most cases of Iatmul clan flutes, two of the pairs of flutes have only one name for each pair, Flutes 1 and 2 being named

Angwa and Flutes 3 and 4 Yamba. Flute 5 is named Kapmerbalandu, Flute 6 Yimbisimbah, and Flute 7 Kwashe. The name of the hourglass drum is Yanje.

Each piece in the repertoire is some two to three minutes long, after which the players rest briefly before beginning to play again. From time to time the men who have been watching and listening take their turns at playing the flutes; no one player is expected to keep playing for the entire performance. Similarly, the hourglass-drum player may be relieved from time to time; however, this is a very responsible role and calls for a dependable drummer with a very good rhythmic sense. Frequently one of the oldest, most experienced men in the village is called on to perform this function.[3]

Where the performance will be staged and when it will begin and end are decided at a meeting in the men's house. The decision is usually heavily influenced by the clan leaders, particularly those looked on as the chief men of the village. Similarly, they decide whether the players should decorate themselves with leaves, flowers, and anklets of shells or seeds or just wear shirts and trousers. Decisions concerning permission to record or film the performance are also made in the men's house at such a meeting, and the fee to be requested is determined at this time.

The Yuman Flutes

The seven flutes that form the Yuman ensemble are, like most of the long Iatmul flutes, transverse and without finger holes. Even the two short flutes that have been arbitrarily numbered 1 and 2 have no finger holes, an unusual circumstance in that in most cases the very short Iatmul flute does have a finger hole. Only one of the seven flutes is more than one meter in length. The dimensions of the set of Yuman flutes that I measured in Aibom in 1974 are given in table 1. The shortest of these bamboo flutes (Nos. 1 and 2) are the thickest, being approximately five millimeters in thickness, whereas the longer ones are close to two millimeters. It should be noted that the main difference between the Yuman flutes and the ceremonial flutes in Iatmul villages in general, including Aibom, is in their length, the latter rarely being less than two meters long and often as much as three meters.

The fundamentals of the seven flutes and the partials their players choose to emphasize are shown in figure 2.

TABLE 1
DIMENSIONS OF YUMAN FLUTES AT AIBOM (CM)

| FLUTE NO. | TOTAL LENGTH | LENGTH FROM CENTER OF MOUTH HOLE TO PROXIMAL END | LENGTH FROM CENTER OF MOUTH HOLE TO NODE | LENGTH OF EFFECTIVE RESONATING AIR COLUMN | DIAMETER | | DIAMETER OF MOUTH HOLE |
					Outside	Inside	
1	57.3	14.0	4.7	48.0	6.7	5.8	2.6
2	53.0	14.8	4.7	42.9	6.6	5.5	2.4
3	105.5	13.0	5.3	97.8	4.0	3.6	2.2
4	93.9	11.7	5.2	87.4	4.4	3.8	2.2
5	87.1	14.2	4.8	77.7	3.8	3.4	2.3
6	76.8	10.8	5.3	71.3	3.5	3.0	2.4
7	72.7	13.1	4.4	64.0	3.6	3.2	2.2

FIG. 2. Fundamentals (in brackets) and preferred partials (fourth and sixth) of the seven Yuman flutes.

Structure of the Yuman Repertoire

The Yuman repertoire consists of at least twelve pieces distinguished from each other by the rhythm set by the hourglass-drum player. The twelve rhythms (*njangits*[4]) are shown in figure 3. Each of these njangits is played four times in succession before the players move on to a new one. At the end of the fourth performance of a njangit, the drummer beats a rapid signal on the drum for a couple of seconds while the flutes are silent. This indicates to the flute players that the previous njangit is now finished and that they should be alert to the new rhythm which he will shortly adopt.[5]

Although the njangits of figure 3 are listed in the order considered correct by a reliable informant in the village,[6] they are not always played in this order, and there is insufficient evidence at present to be sure that any particular order is obligatory. In the performance recorded on December 22, 1972, the order of njangits was different: Wainjangit once, Manjanaui four times, Ulawala (c) four times, Gitagitavia (b) three times, Luklukvia (a) four times, Waikataut four times, Namio four times, Kwainkwainkwain four times, Ulawala (a) three times, Ulawala (b) five times, Ulawala (c) four times, Manjanaui once, Luklukvia (b) four times, Gitagitavia (a) twice. A commissioned performance recorded on July 4, 1974, had yet another order of njangits. There is, however, almost certainly a set way to begin the Yuman flute performance.[7] Recordings from other sources lead one to believe that there may be more than twelve rhythms in the repertoire,[8] though in some cases it is difficult to decide whether a rhythm is really new or simply another drummer's version of one of the ones listed above. It is clear, too, from the recording of the

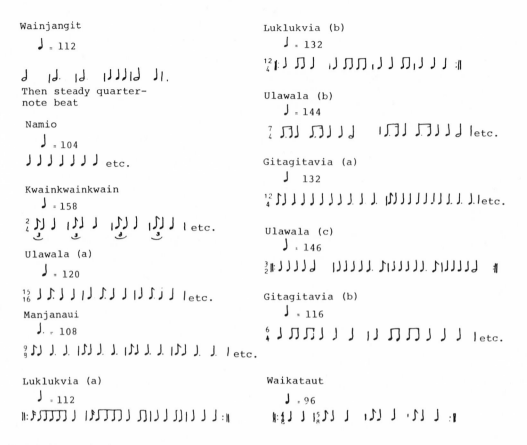

FIG. 3. Yuman njangits.

December 1972 performance that there are variations in the number of times some njangits are played.

The structures of individual pieces in the set are broadly the same. The drum always introduces the rhythm in solo fashion. After a few seconds (i.e., after at least one measure of the music and usually after three or four), Flutes 1 and 2 enter as a pair playing their two notes. A second or two later, Flutes 3 and 4 enter, followed at about the same interval by Flutes 5 and 6. Flute 7 is always the last to enter. Once all flutes have entered, the main central section of the piece begins.

The central section of every njangit except Namio is noteworthy for the emergence of a melodic motif shared by Flutes 5, 6, and 7. This motif broadly takes the shape shown in figure 4, subject to modification depending on the rhythm of the particular njangit. This central section is usually played twice, after which the drum beats out a characteristic pattern (fig. 5) before withdrawing, leaving the flutes to finish alone. This marks the beginning of the final section. The "accompanying" flutes, 1 and 2 as a pair

and 3 and 4 as a pair, begin to speed up their alternate playing, adopting fluttering figures through to the end of the piece, while Flutes 5, 6, and 7 echo the main melodic motif in a rhythmically free manner. Flute 7, the last to enter, is always the first to withdraw; then Flutes 5 and 6 withdraw together, followed by Flutes 3 and 4. Flutes 1 and 2 are always the last to be heard, and Flute 1 has the final sound. This final section, which might be appropriately called a "refrain," is more or less common to all pieces of the repertoire, and there is no attempt here to preserve a rhythm which can be considered characteristic of any one njangit. (A transcription of a performance of the njangit Kwainkwainkwain appears in the appendix.)

All the pieces in the Yuman repertoire can therefore be seen to have a three-part structure of introduction, central section, and final section. The appeal of this range of pieces obviously lies not in the variation of structure but in the subtle way in which the rhythm varies from one njangit to the next and the flutes take their appointed places within that rhythmic design. Perhaps the

FIG. 4. Melodic motif of central section of a njangit (flute numbers above notes).

most interesting aspect of this whole repertoire of Aibom pieces is the tendency for the seven flutes to divide into two teams to give rhythmic impulse to the music. The odd-numbered flutes play as one rhythmic block and the even-numbered flutes as another (fig. 6).

Attitudes toward Performance

Of the eight musicians who make up the team of players of the Yuman repertoire, four may be regarded as having a purely accompanying role, while the other four share in leading the ensemble in some way. The drummer is undoubtedly the "leader" of the ensemble in that he sets the rhythm to be followed by the flute players and keeps the ensemble together rhythmically in the main central section of each njangit. It is up to the drummer to keep count of the number of performances of each njangit so that the ensemble plays each four times. It is also his responsibility to sound the brief reiterated note pattern indicating that one njangit is finished and another is about to begin. He is the one who knows the order in which the njangits should be played. The flute players in general blindly follow the rhythmic lead given by the drummer, each simply sharing the pattern melodically with his partner until the drum ceases. It is, as I have said, usually one of the most senior men in the village who plays the hourglass drum. For one thing, only a senior man would have the secret knowledge concerning Yuman and the distinguishing characteristics of the various njangits; secondly, only a man who has played all the flutes in the ensemble and knows how they must fit the drum rhythm is entrusted with the task of leading the ensemble.

Of the flutes, Flute 7 has the leading role, with Flutes 6 and 5 also having important parts to play

FIG. 5. Drum pattern marking end of central section.

in providing notes of the main melody. It is the player of Flute 7 who has to know the appropriate time to sound his g″, the first note of the melody. Once he does this, Flute 6 has to be ready to follow immediately with his f″ and then Flute 5 with e″-flat, and so on. Similarly, in the closing section after the hourglass-drum beat has ceased, it is Flute 7 who has to know when to begin the series of phrases that echo the melody and how much time should be allotted to his top note. It is therefore understandable that Aibom men are introduced to playing the Yuman flutes in a certain order: first Flutes 3 and 4, then Flutes 1 and 2, then 7, then 5, and last 6. It is only after that that a man may play the hourglass drum.

In performance, the pride that the players of Flutes 5, 6, and 7 have in their special roles is demonstrated by a pronounced swaying movement of the upper parts of their bodies and of their flutes as they play. There is a sense of distinction in their approach to the performance that is as much visual as aural. The tone they use for their melody notes is stronger than the one they use when sharing in the accompanimental figures.

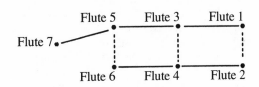

FIG. 6. Rhythmic (*solid lines*) and melodic (*dotted lines*) relationships of Yuman flutes.

Distinctive Points of Interest

The set of pieces that form the Yuman repertoire at Aibom is unique among the Iatmul in that it requires an ensemble of seven flutes and an hourglass drum instead of the usual two flutes and has no solo voice part, an essential element in most other Iatmul ceremonial performances involving the use of flutes. Some of the characteristics that make these pieces of extraordinary interest to the ethnomusicologist include the diversity of the rhythms used to differentiate the njangits; the close coordination needed by the players of each pair of flutes and by each pair with other pairs of flutes and with the hourglass drum; the logical arrangement whereby each njangit is played four times before the "separating" drum signal alerts the players to be ready for a new njangit; the appointed entry of each flute in turn and its withdrawal in reverse order toward the close of the piece; and the participation of three of the flutes in sounding the broad lyrical melody that is common to all of the njangits. Two other characteristics worth mentioning are the unusual harmony of the seven flutes playing together at close intervals and the division of the seven instruments into two opposing rhythmical blocks.

Traditional Iatmul musical performance is preserved in the emphasis placed on paired flutes when it comes to grouping the seven flutes, the paired players standing opposite each other and watching each other closely as they coordinate the notes they play antiphonally to form a continuous melodic line.[9] The fairly strict sequence of musical patterns forming the Yuman cycle tallies with the logical arrangement of njangits in the sagis and other ceremonial music of the Iatmul people in other villages (e.g., *wagen mbangu* in Kandangai [see Spearritt 1979]). The necessity for "secret" performance of the music, away from the gaze of women, girls, and uninitiated boys, is also part of Iatmul tradition.

The ensemble of seven flutes is not part of Iatmul tradition and almost certainly reveals the influence on this southern village of the Chambri villages of Kilimbit, Indingai, and Wombun, which have enlarged flute ensembles (sometimes four flutes, sometimes six or even nine). The leading part played by the hourglass drummer in the ensemble is not part of Iatmul practice either. In sagis, for example, it is the singer and the flute players who have leading roles, while the hourglass drummer and bamboo beater keep up a purely repetitive pattern. In another respect, too,

this cycle of pieces differs from at least two of the other major repertoires of Iatmul music (sagi flute pieces and wagen mbangu at Kandangai) in that less virtuosity is displayed. In the Yuman cycle at Aibom the activity is spread among eight players, whereas in most Iatmul ceremonial music two players carry the main burden of the music and the technical ability and memory required of them are much greater. Furthermore, whereas sagi flute players roam somewhat freely among the upper harmonics of their instruments (at least in Kandangai), the Yuman flute players at Aibom have a fixed, never-varying set of notes to play.

The division of the seven flutes into two rhythmic blocks seems quite unlike Iatmul tradition; to my knowledge no similar division occurs in any other Iatmul village, nor is it a strict practice among the multiflute ensembles of the Chambri villages. It has been suggested (Meinhard and Gisela Schuster, personal communication), however, that the arrangement of the flutes in this sort of rhythmic duality cuts across their arrangement along melodic lines in a way that is similar to the practice in the initiation ceremony, where the age-grade system cuts across the moiety system to which the initiates belong, or to that mentioned by Bateson (1935:159) whereby in a family with a long series of brothers the "first, third and fifth brothers will form an alliance in quarrels against the second and fourth." The Yuman flute repertoire therefore shows some characteristics that are traditionally Iatmul, others that seem to reveal Chambri influence, and still others that reflect aspects of Iatmul tradition that are not evident at first glance.

Notes

1. The local people themselves frequently shorten her full name to Yuman, a practice I shall adopt here.
2. The recordings on which my transcriptions have been based were made on the night of December 22, 1972, at a ceremony attended by Meinhard and Gisela Schuster, Robert MacLennan, and me. There was no masked figure or dancing on this occasion.
3. On the occasion of the 1972 recordings, a change of drummers occurred, but when both the original drummer and the flute players expressed their displeasure at the new drummer's rhythm the original one quickly took over again.
4. A *njangit* is a section of a long piece of music, usually melodically or rhythmically differentiated from other sections, that has its own name and meaning.
5. From recordings made in Aibom ten years earlier, Robert MacLennan realized that on a future oc-

casion it would be necessary to attempt to isolate the sounds of individual flutes from among the seven flutes playing together, not so much to determine the pitch of the notes played by each (which could, in any case, be determined by simply asking each player to blow his notes in turn) as to decide how each player fitted into the ensemble rhythmically. Fortunately, the 1972 recording team had access to a Nagra stereo tape recorder, and for approximately the first hour and a half of recording its two microphones were placed in such positions as to get the best general balance between the seven flutes and the hourglass drum. It was at this time that the flutes were numbered for recording purposes according to the positions in which they stood in the ensemble. Then for approximately twenty-two minutes of the performances, team members held each microphone close to individual flutes either one at a time or in pairs, voice-identifying the flutes by number on the tape.

6. I thank Gisela Schuster for assistance in establishing the order of njangits in the Yuman ensemble.

7. The 1972 recording session did not begin at the very beginning of the performance; I base this statement on the evidence of other recordings of the Yuman flutes. The unwillingness of the chief man of the village to give information about the flutes and their repertoire during my 1974 field visit makes it very difficult to determine some of these matters with confidence.

8. For example, the recordings of Yuman pieces made by Meinhard and Gisela Schuster in Aibom in 1966.

9. Elsewhere (Spearritt 1983) I draw attention to the ways in which the concept of duality in the Iatmul tradition (e.g., the moieties, the alternating age-grade system, the strong differentiation of male and female roles, the symbolism of death and rebirth in the skin-cutting ceremony) finds parallels in the musical practice of the group, especially the emphasis on the pairing of instruments.

Appendix

Transcription of a Performance of the Yuman Njangit Kwainkwainkwain

50/ *Tapets*: Drum Signals of the Sawos

Thomas C. Aitken

Communication by means of patterns transmitted by struck idiophones is well known and extensively documented. In comparison with the complicated drum languages encountered in some parts of Africa, the drum language of the Western Sawos people of the East Sepik Province is basic. The messages relayed are signals, indicating that a particular man or woman is urgently required or imparting such information as that a person has died, a pig has been killed, or bride-price payments are due. These are single-purpose transmissions; for example, in the case of an individual's being summoned, no idea of the reason for the summons is given. They are not, however, made lightly; it is mandatory for the person summoned to return immediately. The seriousness of the personal signal is apparent when we consider the case of the woman working in her garden, which may be as distant as twenty kilometers from the village. The terrain is often dense jungle or dangerous swamp, and always there will be searing heat and high humidity. In responding to the call, she risks losing an entire day's work, at great cost to the family. An adult male, perhaps a long way off collecting betel nuts, would equally be upset to have been frivolously summoned.

Every adult has an individual signal called a *tapet*.[1] This signal has three main sections: an introduction, a main section, and a conclusion. It begins with (A) the rubbing of the inside of a slit in the log, (B) a series of equidistant beats, probably demanding attention, and (C) one (for male) or two (for female) blows indicating the sex of the person summoned; then a slow version (D) of the forthcoming main section is beaten, and this is followed by a repetition of C. Next the main section (E) is beaten and repeated once or several times, and finally there is a repetition of B, C, D, and A.[2]

Although at first these signals appear to be purely rhythmic, on closer inspection pitch is also seen to be of prime importance. The pitches employed are indeterminate and depend on the particular slit-drum used. In simplest terms, they are either high, low, or medium, with no other variation possible. This realization is one of shattering importance for the analysis of all Sawos music.

Most transcriptions of drumming have concentrated on the rhythmic aspects of the signals, little or no attention having been paid to pitch. Yet, in conversation with the African scholar and musician Nketia, I learned that pitch was always uppermost in the minds of African master drummers. While watching Papua New Guinean drummers in performance, I became aware from the striking of different parts of the drum that they were intent upon producing different pitches—high, low, or medium. On the longer drums, considerable movement up and down the surfaces is necessary to produce these different tones, and for some time I wondered whether this movement might be a symbolic imitation of birds, crocodiles, etc. My chief informants quashed this theory, however, by denying any relationship between their movements and those of their chief animal totems. On the shorter slit-drums, no such lateral body movement on the part of the performer is necessary, but the same preoccupation with producing different pitches is obvious.

The importance of pitch was further revealed to me when, attempting to collect the tapets of all the adults in the Sawos village of Torembi III, I asked my chief informant, Raymond Kami,[3] to play his wife's signal for me. He refused, not because she would have answered the call irrespective of where she was and what she was doing but because we were in the tambaran house and female signals may not be sounded from inside it. Since my microphones had been carefully set up there, Kami volunteered to *sing* his wife's tapet, since the sound would not travel outside the house. The mnemonics he used were *keeng*, obviously high-pitched, and two versions of *kung*, one lower than the other.[4]

The melodic element of drumming is in fact aurally evident, especially when the drummers are observed striking different sections of the logs. Since the rhythmic aspect is so immediately demanding of attention, it is not surprising that rhythm has been the main preoccupation of scholars, but to be confronted by a master drummer who offers to sing a signal makes one reconsider the evidence.

My hypothesis is that the melodic element of a tapet is much more important than the rhythmic one, since rhythmic variations occur when a tapet is recorded on different occasions. It is easy to dismiss this seeming lapse of memory on the part of the performer as human error, but having great respect for the prodigious musical memories of my informants I reject this explanation. There is no doubt in my mind that the Sawos drummer is playing a melody and it makes little difference how often he strikes a particular section of the log because the purpose of the repetitions is to sustain this melody on a basically nonmelodic instrument.[5]

I further suggest that the principal aim of each tapet is to imitate the call, shriek, or some peculiarity of the bird, insect, animal, etc., that "belongs" to the family of the person involved, the call having been slowed down so much for ease of performance that it has become unrecognizable as such to the unknowledgeable listener.[6] When we transcribe drum music with the aid of electromechanical equipment, we generally slow the signals to obtain a more accurate realization. If, instead, we speed them up by 100 percent, 200 percent, 400 percent, an exciting transformation takes place, and it becomes possible to perceive the sounds as imitative of those of totemic beings. To support this musical argument, I have produced a short Super-8 film with sound illustrating the performance of tapets and a tape recording that demonstrates their similarity, when speeded up, to bird, animal, or insect sounds.

Notes

1. This paper was originally intended as an analytical discussion of the tapets used by the Sawos departing from the work of Zemp and Kaufmann (1969) on the Kwoma and perhaps comparing the signals of the two groups. However, my findings were so different from theirs (they report that "one summons a person by beating the signal for the patriclan [patrisib] of his father, then the signal for the patriclan of his mother" [p. 42, my translation]) that it proved impossible to do this.

2. Pen recordings of the tapets were made by the following method: An audio tape signal of drumbeats (copied at half speed) is fed to a frequency-dependent detector via a Schmidt trigger. Providing that the input signal to the Schmidt trigger is above the threshold, the input to the detector will be level and the output will vary according to the frequency. This varying output is connected to the pen recorder. The time-base markers are simultaneously recorded at 2.5-second intervals. Each pen recording is preceded by a frequency-test tape at 50, 100, 150, 200, and 250 cycles per second to serve as a bench mark for the recording that follows. To produce a pen recording of amplitude variations, the same audio signal is fed to the pen recorder via a simple detector. Each recording is preceded by the same frequency-test tape, and the tone controls are adjusted for a level output on the pen recorder. It must be appreciated that the recordings thus produced are relative rather than absolute because of the unsophisticated technique used. The pen recorder mechanism has inertia and may overshoot; similarly, the retrace to zero may not always reach zero before the next excursion.

3. Kami is approximately forty years of age, the only male adult of the Baia family in the three Torembi villages, married with three living children (two female, one male). He has worked as cook in the Sepik for several years for David Wall, an academic from New South Wales. I have worked with him since 1977 and found him totally honest and reliable. This impression of him is confirmed by Wall, who still corresponds with him (usually by tape and in Tok Pisin).

4. If the extended drum patterns for two drummers can also be sung, the results may lead to further complications in the notation of this music. The recognition of pitch in drumming throws new light on the repeated assertion that flute music and drum music are *wankain*, *tasol* ([Tok Pisin] one kind only, i.e., no different).

5. Examples of similar processes can be found in the medieval cantus firmus and the *gagaku* court music of Japan.

6. Compare this with the efforts made by many musicians to sustain melodies on plucked stringed instruments.

Part Nine
Conveying the Past

Introduction

Christian Kaufmann

Having sketched the Sepik heritage and its meaning for the present, we ought now to consider its potential for the future. It has long been recognized that documents assembled in the field, published or not, might be very valuable additions to the cultural heritage of an emerging Papua New Guinea society. At the time of the Basel symposium the enduring characteristics of this new society had, after barely a decade of development toward national goals, not yet become apparent.

The Papua New Guinea national elite finds itself in a dilemma that, for lack of the necessary tools, may not easily be resolved. On the one hand there is the heritage from the deep-rooted rural sector, full of traditional knowledge and philosophy accumulated over thousands of years. On the other are the demands imposed by the impact first of colonialism and then of industrial society, which has altered the foundations of social life from the new urban centers to the most remote rural areas. Indeed, postindustrial society, with its electronic approach to work and to communications networks, is already knocking at the young nation's door. Solutions to this dilemma will require that the best of traditional, industrial, and postindustrial strategies be combined. Looking at the cultural heritage of the Sepik region from this perspective means that knowledge about the traditional forms and contents of social life must be organized in such a way as to be accessible to future generations not only locally but also across traditional social and cultural boundaries nationwide.

The symposium did not view anthropology as a purely historical discipline. Without historical depth, however, no scientific study of culture or society can fully serve its purpose. The discussions revealed that the historical depth, however limited, of anthropological and other social studies in the Sepik area provides an important frame of reference for organizing much of the detailed information already collected by specialists or stored in the memories of local people. Helping to establish a comprehensive Sepik archive of some sort, if not physically at least on paper, might constitute our first common task.

A second, concurrent step might be an evaluation of the accumulated material, from which basic insights into the processes governing cultural continuity and change should emerge. Ideally, the systematics of such an analysis would be the result of scientific study and discussion on the basis of a genuinely Papua New Guinean (or, in this case, Sepik) approach to development and tradition. In fact, this might be seen as both a noble and an urgent task for anthropologists at one of Papua New Guinea's national research institutions.

The contributions to this section explore some of the ways of systematically recording, organizing, and analyzing basic data on the traditional background of the two Sepik provinces with a view to their future use. Matters related to traditional technology and visual arts are predominant in the discussion throughout. These cases may serve as models for research in neighboring fields, for example, the study of oral tradition, traditional education, or cultural ecology.

Margaret Tuckson, speaking about her experiences in Papua New Guinea as a researcher and potter working among traditional potters, leads us into the center of the issue. The individual village specialist's knowledge matters more than any ready-made guidelines. Without insight into small-scale differences, ecological, social, or historical in origin, we cannot evaluate traditions for what they might be worth to the next generation. The comparison Tuckson presents with similar experiences in northern Australia, Nigeria, Nepal, Peru, and Laos illustrates this point very clearly.

In their paper on traditional architecture in the Sepik, Wallace and Ruth Ruff show how difficult it is to keep documentation work funded on a long-term basis. Their recording of traditional architectural forms would seem to be of prime interest to a country that has used some of these very forms in its new Parliament building, but for some reason it is not. The Ruffs point, however, to the creative potential that their documentation will help to preserve for future generations.

The objects in museum collections in Papua New Guinea and abroad that remain as material evidence of Sepik cultures need to be placed in their social, cultural, and historical contexts—relating them to the proper periods in their cultures of origin and to the aims of the individuals, usually foreigners, who collected them. In light of this task, I report on work that should ultimately make some such collections in Germany and Switzerland available as open archives to individuals in other countries.

Artifacts play an important role in the Sepik region's economy today, with, according to John Wasori, approximately one-third of the population of the East Sepik Province being actively involved in some way in their production, distribution, or sale. Wasori reports on the provincial government's efforts to coordinate the production and marketing of artifacts as close to the production level as possible.

The art of the Sepik is, alas, certainly the part of the Sepik heritage that is best-known and most appreciated worldwide. Soroi Eoe examines the national government's endeavors to preserve objects of Sepik art as national cultural property with the financial means that government and international agencies have thus far been willing to set aside for this program. Again, there seems to be an impasse. The heritage of the Sepik provinces has become an important part of the world's cultural heritage. Like every heritage, it is at the same time a burden, the sheer weight of which may be more than the nation can bear. The preservation of this heritage as a source of inspiration for future generations throughout the world therefore deserves support from sources that span the globe.

51/ Sepik Pottery Research and Its Relevance for Papua New Guinea

Margaret Tuckson

Andrew Strathern, in his inaugural lecture at the University of Papua New Guinea in 1974, said that "a tremendous amount of anthropological research has been done in this country, and the results of that research, where properly done and published, do form a record which is now a part of Papua New Guinea's general cultural heritage." But he suggested that this is not enough: "Our concern must be with problems of change and continuity in Papua New Guinean society" (Strathern 1974:15). In regard to these two concerns, I will first attempt to assess the value to Papua New Guinea's cultural heritage of a book on the traditional pottery of Papua New Guinea that I was involved in researching and writing (May and Tuckson 1982). I will go on to discuss some pottery "development" projects in Papua New Guinea and compare them with similar projects in other developing countries.[1] One of the things I want to stress is that unless people themselves have asked for help with their pottery, any such project may well be unnecessary. After the main proposals for a project have been thoroughly examined, thought should be given to abandoning the scheme, especially if the village people show doubt about or antipathy toward it. More important than change may be support for the traditional ware, simply through help with marketing. Maintaining the status of the village pottery is not just perpetuating a tradition for its own sake and for that of sentimentalists and researchers but helping individual potters maintain their self-esteem and their livelihood. Continuity may be better than change.

Launching our pottery book at the Australian Museum, Sydney, Alkan Tololo, then the consul general for Papua New Guinea in Australia, said: "In the acknowledgment section of the book mention is made of the debt due to the people of Papua New Guinea for their generosity and assistance. In Papua New Guinea we live by a 'pay back' system. With the publication of this book, may I say, you have paid back this debt. . . . I want to say how grateful Papua New Guinea is for the appearance of such a publication." By showing the importance and standing of its potters in a world

context, the book certainly has made a contribution to Papua New Guinea. A recent review of it in a potters' journal comments that it "is not only a record but a celebration of [Papua New Guinea] pottery making and an appreciation of its makers" (Lewenstein 1983). At the local level, the book has the potential for being widely used in schools, colleges, and libraries; it is reportedly being used in conjunction with a group of local pots collected by Patricia May in a teachers' college and a high school in Wewak. To the potters themselves and to our patient and willing informants, the only immediate result of our activities may be a new pride in their work; on numerous occasions people showed amazement at our enthusiasm and at the praise we heaped on their pots. Occasionally someone in a village would comment on the importance of the study we were doing and be happy that the knowledge of pot making would not be lost. And later, when I presented relevant page proofs of the book to some twenty-five villages in the Sepik Provinces, their pride expanded. Unfortunately, the price of the book in their country will preclude its purchase by many Papua New Guineans. As Specht (1983) says, "a series of cheap booklets or fascicles would be more appropriate for achieving the authors' aims, to stimulate . . . the young people in whose hands lies the fate of the country's ceramic traditions." Perhaps booklets are still a possibility, but even if the price of the book were quartered it would still be beyond the means of villagers and most other Papua New Guineans.

Westermark (1978) says that "the incalculable personal factor of informal information and friendship given and received by the researcher should be considered." My most heartwarming contacts were potter-to-potter (fig. 1); when I revealed that I also made pots, there was disbelief and then a special rapport. But even though I had good relationships with the people in all the hundred or more villages I worked in, the lasting value to them of these associations is impossible to assess. One difficulty arose through my being a potter: it was hoped that I could tell them how they could make their pots smooth and shiny, and

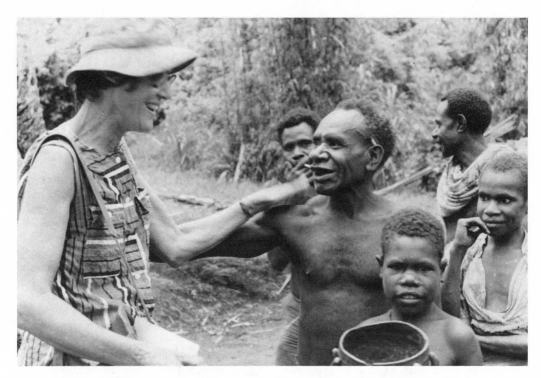

FIG 1. Potter to potter, Wamaina, East Sepik Province, 1972. (Photo courtesy of Patricia May.)

I found it hard to explain that this complicated process takes many years to learn and involves expensive equipment. This could not, unfortunately, be my way of repaying them for all their help.

There has been some worry in Papua New Guinea about foreign researchers' gaining without giving enough in return. For example, when I wrote in 1973 to a Papua New Guinea university student asking if he could help me with information on the occurrence of pottery in his area, he replied by inquiring what I was gaining from this and how many thousands of dollars I was making. It was very difficult to reply. I tried to explain that I understood his attitude and then described the circumstances of my research, pointing out that, even with support from a Crafts Board grant and royalties, the costs of my seven research trips would not nearly be covered and I could expect no Ph.D. Not only is the explanation of such problems difficult but, more important, so are the solutions. Talyaga's (1974) strong criticisms of researchers have drawn many comments and caused much soul-searching. Although some of his criticisms have been countered, I am sure that much more thought is being given now than in the past to ways of repaying villagers for their help.

As a potter I cannot resist quoting Young (1975:57): "Melanesians are right in one sense when they suspect that we mine information and knowledge from them, then depart to rework this raw material into a commodity which we distribute to our profit in the symbolic exchange of the academic market place."

Pottery "Development" Projects

In 1967, at the request of the Australian government, the International Labor Organization employed a Danish potter, Jørgen Petersen, to survey and research Papua New Guinea pottery-making areas and clay deposits, to introduce techniques on the cottage-industry level that would enhance the marketability of various ceramic products, and to inaugurate a training program to this end (Petersen 1970). Petersen was stationed in the Madang area, and over a twelve-month period he visited many of the other important pottery-producing areas, including the West Sepik coast and, in the East Sepik, the Wewak/Maprik area, the Wosera, Washkuk, Aibom, Koiwat, Kamangaui, Dimiri/Marawat, and Keram River. His report

FIG. 2. Jørgen Petersen kiln at Yabob, 1974. (Photo courtesy of Jim Specht.)

discusses the suitability of clay deposits, the type and standard of ware made, and the techniques used in each area and concludes:

> As this survey has shown, there are hundreds of villages and several thousand people involved in making pottery, but only a few artistic pottery villages have a definite future which would ensure economic gain. It is better to help an already established soundly artistic and viable production centre and look at clay deposits generally with an eye to commercial prospects in building materials such as bricks, drainpipes, floor tiles, etc. . . . Only a few villages should be concentrated on to ensure the best impact of a project and to guarantee that something really happens in the villages involved. It would be dangerous to try to cover all potters in the Territory as it is obvious that it would be impossible to assure sales and markets for everybody.

Petersen suggested that existing pottery techniques would enable a woman to produce enough to make at least the minimum male weekly wage if she could market all her products. This, he thought, would help these women "to achieve a higher social standard and prestige." He considered the handmade and traditional element an important marketing point and felt that traditional pottery "should develop into a sound economic enterprise" for villagers, with most of their production being sold to tourists and through trade fairs in Australia. He recommended that the pottery project concentrate on Saragum, Stapigum, Aibom, Kamangaui, Koiwat, Marawat, and Dimiri, East Sepik villages "producing highly decorative pottery well suited to marketing," and on Yabob and Bilbil in Madang Province. Contact was to be maintained with and marketing assistance given to Wanigela in the Northern Province and the Amphlett Island group in the Milne Bay Province. The final objectives were "to produce better and stronger quality pots" by running basic courses in the above villages to teach proper clay preparation and firing techniques.[2]

The first and most influential project was the one at Yabob and Bilbil, typical coastal pottery villages a few miles south of Madang (fig. 2). There, women are traditionally the potters. They use the paddle-and-anvil technique to make cooking pots, sago storage pots, and water pots. The first workshop was established on Yabob land in 1967 (fig. 3). (Later one was built at Bilbil, and a more permanent training center was planned for Madang.) The work and training started immediately, with young men and women coming from Bilbil as well as Yabob. (The report makes no mention of the fact that men were trained to throw on kick wheels, making European-style pots, which is what I understand happened.) Petersen reports that the women worked well and production improved immediately. He mentions that "several modifications, especially in size, were successfully carried out"; presumably, much smaller pots were made to sell to tourists. Though no mention is made of it, Petersen encouraged the women to put three small, ball-like feet on the bottoms of their round-based pots to steady them for the tourists' taste (fig. 4). Many problems were encountered, mostly at Yabob. Some of the women started to earn more money than the Yabob men did in their Madang jobs, and this caused jealousy. Other problems arose over which land should be used and who owned it. Output did increase, however, and the higher-fired pots were said to be easily sold.

Although Petersen stressed the importance of "follow-up work," it seems not to have been undertaken. After he left, the output of hand-thrown work dwindled, and most women gradually returned to their traditional bonfire firing. In 1973, when I briefly visited the two Madang villages, I found a lad struggling to make pots on one kick wheel in a shed. They were small and very badly thrown. He was teaching a group of young people, who crowded around the wheel watching him. On the shelves around him were a few poor-quality pots, badly glazed.

In 1968 Petersen started his training of the Sepik village potters. Sixteen selected potters from the chosen villages were brought to Angoram by boat for the fourteen-day course and installed in a compound near the primary school. For many of them it was the first time they had been outside their village area. The potters brought their own clay in order to demonstrate traditional clay preparation and pot making. Then instructions for sieving the clay were given and certain modifications carried out. Pots made of sieved and of unsieved clay and fired, some in bonfires, some in a kiln built under instruction, were compared. Petersen reports that everyone was favorably impressed with the new pots, and they sold well there in Angoram. Instructions were given to schoolchildren and teachers, and the kiln was left for their use. Petersen judged that only the Aibom clay needed sieving and that there was no need for kilns at Kamangaui and Koiwat, where the fine clay was well fired and became reasonably resistant to breakage. The potters from four of the villages built kilns when they returned home. With the help of a new employee of the Angoram local government council's craft outlet, sales increased greatly, and pots were distributed as far afield as Port Moresby.

At the Wosera villages, Saragum and Stapigum, the headmaster of the Namu River school, Paul Dennett, took a particular interest and assisted Petersen during his visit there. He helped

FIG. 3. The workshop at Yabob. (Photo courtesy of Jim Specht.)

FIG. 4. Small tourist pots with three small feet, drying beside two traditional cooking pots, Yabob, 1973.

the potters make the wooden forms for bricks, which were made using river sand to temper the clay, and he obtained the sheet of marsden matting needed for the kiln shelf. The kiln was built and fired with his help. Dennett reports that Petersen suggested that the potters make smaller versions of the highly decorated and painted bowls and traditional ceremonial whistles and evidently encouraged them to spend less time on the decoration so as to produce them quickly for the tourist market (fig. 5). The marketing worked well with much help from Paul and Helen Dennett. The *Post-Courier* of Port Moresby published a full-page article praising the venture and describing the whistle as being an ideal, easily packed tourist item.

At Dimiri/Marawat near the Yuat River, two kilns were built. No reports were available on their use until an Australian potter, visiting Dimiri in 1974, commented that bonfiring was the only method practiced there (Campbell 1974).

For Aibom, Petersen had realized that there was no use building a kiln because most of the pots were too large. He reports the remark of a patrol officer's wife from Pagwi that the Aibom potters were sieving their clay and therefore producing better pots. Petersen felt that prospects for the Sepik villages were good but that the Department of Trade and Industry should help with technical problems, bookkeeping, and marketing.

One interesting result of Petersen's work—his design of a simple clay sieve, sensibly made of

FIG. 5. Small Wosera tourist pots and a whistle, 1970. Smallest pot height 7 cm. (Photo courtesy of Mike Cockburn.)

easily accessible screen cloth—was that it somehow reached the potters on Tumleo Island and the nearby West Sepik coast. Here its introduction was an easy transition because this is the only place in Papua New Guinea where a sieve—conical and woven of split cane—was traditionally used.

During a brief visit to Yabob in 1984, I found only one kiln still in use (fig. 6), and although most of the potters successfully fire in their bon-fires some of them hope for more bricks to build kilns. Many still use the wire sieves to prepare their clay. In May and June 1984 I visited the Sepik area specifically to locate as many as possible of the potters who had been involved in the pottery project sixteen years earlier. I was able to track down as many as eleven of them but spoke to only seven.

At Saragum, a highly regarded potter, Banga-mali, remembered attending the course in An-goram. (His wife had also been a participant, but she was away in the gardens.) He spoke with en-thusiasm about some aspects of the project. Al-though Petersen had advised that the clay did not need sieving, Bangamali had found it a good way to prepare his clay. He could not explain to us why he had returned to the old method even though he still had some sieve wire. Other men and women in the village joined in the discussion and helped remember building the kiln with Paul Dennett. As recommended, a shelter had been constructed over the kiln, which was built of unfired bricks. (While these become part-fired with the first fir-ing, they remain incapable of withstanding rain.) The shelter had proved to be too close to the kiln, and after two or three firings it had burned down. Rain had then soaked and disintegrated the bricks, and it seems that no further kilns were built at Saragum. Bangamali showed me the ex-act spot where the kiln had been built, close to his house at the edge of his hillside garden. There

was not a single brick remaining. The marsden-matting kiln shelf was now the door of his duck house. He had preferred the even red color of the pots from the kiln to the smudged pots from the open fire but gave as his main reason for not building another kiln the long trek to the river for sand to make the bricks. Two other accomplished potters, Gwoinjon and his wife, Auwi, who had also attended the lessons at Angoram, were still living at Saragum, but Gwoinjon was too ill to join our discussion or to make pots anymore, and Auwi was away working in the gardens.

At nearby Stapigum the people remembered somebody's having come to Saragum to help with pottery but were adamant that no one had come to Stapigum.

At Dimiri, two men—the councillor, Moses, and Edward Akaia—helped rally a group of peo-ple willing to sit down and discuss the pottery project. They were able to list six potters who had been involved: Paulina Oliminda, her brother Nalva and his wife Wanda, Elizabeth Kinimy's grandparents, and Marie. Paulina and Marie helped with our fact-gathering, but Nalva and Wanda were now living at the new Gavien settle-ment near Angoram, where we visited them later. Elizabeth's grandparents had died. At the meet-ing, there was heated talk about the *marasin* ([Tok Pisin] medicine) that Petersen had used at Ango-ram. There was confusion as to what this marasin was, but it seemed to be something mixed with the clay. They believed that it was essential, and

FIG. 6. Liton Pilu's kiln at Yabob, 1984. The sherds are used to cover the pots. (Photo courtesy of Helen Palmer.)

they reported that although they had made bricks and built one or two kilns, the bricks had broken up because they lacked marasin. Perhaps the marasin was sand, without which the bricks would have cracked when drying. However, no shelter had been built over the kiln, so the main reason for ruined bricks was probably that they had been soaked by rain and disintegrated before being fully fired. They said that Petersen did not come back to help them. When the Dimiri potter Nalva (fig. 7) talked with us at Gavien, this was his main complaint. He was also angry about the mysterious marasin that was not supplied to them. His memory of it was that it was red and yellow and was to put on the bricks to make them strong. (It is possible that the potters were shown pigments or glazes and, confronted by so much novelty, became confused about their use.)

At Aibom, near Lake Chambri, a discussion was held on our first night with the councillor, Anska, Pius Wangis, and a third man. After some prompting they began to remember Petersen's project and were able to supply the names of the potters who went to Angoram for the course: Judy Sawi and her son Sisingin and Sanum and his wife, Buendeimbi. The councillor told us that there was a lot of complaining about the scheme

from the big men of the village. The potters took clay from Aibom with them, and the men felt that clan secrets were being given away. Evidently when the potters came back and started to try and make bricks there was so much fuss that the kiln was used only once or possibly not at all. Next day we met two of the potters. Judy Sawi, who still makes some of the best big sago storage jars at Aibom (fig. 8), was eager to talk. She told of the activities at Angoram and of films they were shown by Petersen. Perhaps these only whetted their appetites for things unattainable by them, such as glazed bowls and cups and saucers.[3]

Pot making in general in the Sepik area today is still flourishing, but all the villages are suffering from lack of markets. This is especially the case at Aibom, where *Salvinia molesta*, the water fern that is choking many of the rivers and lakes, is at its worst. The Aibom potters are producing many wonderful pots, especially sago storage jars and hearths. Also, they are making great quantities of small pots for tourists, successfully integrating their traditional decorating techniques and motifs into new forms (fig. 9). But the tourists can seldom get to Aibom now because of the fern, and trading of pots for

FIG. 7. Dimiri potter, Nalva, at Gavien settlement, recalling the problems with the kiln, Sepik River, June 1984.

Fig. 8. Judy Sawi's handsome sago storage jars, Aibom, May 1984.

food has almost ceased for the same reason. Transport and marketing help are desperately needed.

The situation is similar at Dimiri—hundreds of good pots and figures ready for sale but few tourists and not enough help with collecting them to take to tourist outlets (fig. 10). The delightful modeled animal and human figures are still made with very thick sections, but the firing of them seems to be satisfactory. Koiwat potters are still producing beautiful carved conical food bowls of as high a standard as ever (fig. 11), but with high-water problems in this swampy environment they have great difficulty marketing them. At the Wosera villages pot making has slowed down considerably. Bangamali can still sell his pots, but there seem to be few outlets for the other potters.

From these discussions with the Sepik potters, it is obvious that the scheme was not researched thoroughly enough beforehand. All the possible implications should have been considered, and consultations should have been held with the councillors and big men of the villages. The question of the need for a pottery project should have been thrashed out. Then, once a project was decided upon, far more help with problems that arose later and assistance with marketing should have been provided.

At the village level, traditional crafts are best left alone to develop or change from within at their own rate. In Yabob/Bilbil and the Sepik villages, the low-fired pots (at bonfire temperatures of 600° C–900° C) are still entirely functional. Low-fired cooking pots have the shock resistance to withstand direct contact with the flames on a village cooking fire. Many people, of course, are using aluminum saucepans instead, but often villagers say that their food tastes better in their own pots and that they have returned to making them. Low-fired water pots are permeable and therefore keep water cool by evaporation. The same permeability helps with sago storage; people have realized that their sago goes sour more quickly when kept in kerosene tins (as it would in higher-fired or glazed pots) and in some areas are making their permeable sago jars again. These advantages need to be explained to village people before they agree to make changes in their pots. I remember explaining the permeability of water pots to an educated Manus Island man who had been telling me with delight that he could not remember ever having such pleasant cool drinks as he used to have from the water pots in his home village.

Again, the rough, stony clay of Aibom, which Petersen singled out for sieving, is in fact well suited to the making of hearths, frying pans, and cooking pots. A clay with a high nonplastic content helps support these large pots during construction. It enhances heat distribution by leaving an open-textured stony surface on the planed base of the frying pans, and it usually has good thermal shock resistance. As for the fragility of the pots, people are accustomed to handling them carefully during use and transport. Items such as the small whistles and other small tourist items could easily be fired in or among the bigger pots in the hottest part of a bonfire and do not really require a kiln.

FIG. 9. Small tourist pot with well-integrated traditional decoration, Aibom, May 1984.

If people were happy with the stronger pots from the kiln firings, why have they all returned to open firings? One suggestion is that much more solid wood (instead of coconut fronds, etc.) was needed for the kilns, and in some areas there is a shortage; another is that, along with making bricks, it is a lot of extra work. Brick making in the villages was essential for the kilns, as ready-made bricks were unavailable and in any case would have been too expensive. Perhaps people found that the difference in their pots was not great enough to be worth the trouble.

The most appropriate assistance would probably be some guidance for more efficient open firing. The Amphlett Islands firings have been shown to reach temperatures high enough to make strong pots. It is a matter of covering the pots on the outside of the pile well enough with fuel and ensuring that the firing is carried out for long enough (at least half an hour) to reach the required temperature. In his report, Petersen notes that traditional open firing leaves much room for improvement because the thick modeled figures are often unfired at the core. This could be rectified by slightly longer firings. I watched fourteen firings that did fire efficiently, the temperature rising above the 600° C necessary to alter the clay minerals so that the material would not disintegrate in water.[4]

Potters do seem to like the idea of having a kiln, but the fact remains that for their own purposes pots made in the old way are eminently suitable. They do show a liking for the overall red color of pots fired in the kiln. When open firing, they often move pots to brightly burning spots to burn away the smudging. I enjoy the flashings caused by the contact of fuel with pot surfaces and the softness of the colors compared with the harder redness of those from a kiln. Most Australian potters agree and strive to emulate the effect, but if the Sepik potters prefer the red kiln-fired pots it is unfortunate for them that the project came to nothing.

Petersen's addition of three small knobs to the base of the round-bottomed pots was, in my opinion, uncalled for and detracted from the traditional free-moving pots, most of which rest at a slight tilt but do not tip over. Surely even tourists would have been satisfied with a separate small ring of banana leaves or split cane. His idea of smaller pots for tourists had the drawback that the size of decorative motifs in relation to the size of the pot was greatly changed. It seems unfortunate also for him to have suggested spending less time on decoration. However, changes are bound to happen; the form and decoration of some Aibom pots changed well before Petersen's time. A tradition cannot be kept at a standstill just to please those of us who admire it.

It has been suggested that if modified local products are not provided for tourists, the tourist organizations will bring in imported junk. If this is true, the answer may lie in small workshops in urban areas. Why not train unemployed city-dwellers as potters? Nontraditional techniques could be taught these migrants without disrupting the indigenous village methods. One wonders, however, whether there is sufficient tourism in Papua New Guinea to support such workshops, and there is also the problem of very high fuel costs (Lawson 1984).

For the Madang villages the cottage-industry idea had possibilities, as Yabob and Bilbil are very close to Madang by road. Most of the Sepik villages selected, however, are so remote that there seems little likelihood that the projects could have survived. More important, more groundwork on the socioeconomic aspects of the villages chosen should have been undertaken before a pottery expert was brought in.

In 1970 Petersen was asked to advise on setting up the Hohola Small Industries Training Centre in Port Moresby. A clay pit was located on the spot, local materials were used to build potters' wheels, and several kilns were constructed by the trainees. A technical officer in pottery was employed, and the throwing started with flower pots and progressed to glazed domestic ware and tiles. This center functioned with varying degrees of

Fig. 10. Pot being made at Dimiri, May 1984.

success over the years but was almost at a stand-still in 1984, when plans were being made to revive it. In 1970 similar centers in Goroka and Madang had been projected, but they had not materialized. Now, in June 1984, a Volunteer Services Overseas potter has been asked to start a cottage industry in Madang.

The Eastern Highlands Cultural Centre at Kainantu was started in the early seventies by Muriel Larner with local male trainees who were sent for a further course to the Small Industries Centre in Port Moresby. The pottery was later moved to Kainantu and became a commercial venture. Traditional designs are used with hand-painted and carved decorations. Muriel Larner reports (personal communication, 1983) that it has never been successful in sending trained potters home to start their own ventures. Unless more technical staff are employed as supervisors, she says, it will never work. Lawson (1984) reports that this is not a self-supporting project and that high fuel costs are a major problem. He is examining the possible use of sump oil as a cheaper fuel for Kainantu and other workshops.

These small-scale government and commercial workshops may be the best solution for producing domestic ware for townspeople once a more economical fuel is found and a market ensured. One possibility for training workshop managers is to send some Papua New Guineans to do full-time ceramic courses in Australia or elsewhere to broaden their experience.[5]

Fig. 11. Food bowl carefully painted after firing, Koiwat, May 1984.

Pottery Projects in Other Developing Countries

Pottery projects developed in Australia for Aborigines are dealing with people who have absolutely no tradition of pot making. Ivan McMeekin, an Australian potter and lecturer at the University of New South Wales, notes (personal communication, 1983) with respect to the project for Bathurst Island that "the strange new activities we had introduced did not fit easily into existing tribal structures." McMeekin was first involved in feasibility studies and then in setting up a pottery training unit on the Bagot Aboriginal Reserve in Darwin, Northern Territory, in 1967

(McMeekin 1969). This was a joint project by the Welfare Branch of the Northern Territory Administration and the University of New South Wales. He hoped to involve "detribalised Aboriginal residents of Darwin and nearby who really needed to come to terms with their new environment," and he thought that potting might help. But he was overruled, and young tribal Aborigines were brought in from several areas of Arnhem Land. Only one man came of his own accord, a Bathurst Islander named Eddie Puruntatameri, who persisted until he was accepted. He is the only one of the original group still potting.

One of England's leading potters, Michael Cardew, who has had some twenty years' experience teaching pottery in Ghana and Nigeria, was invited to Bagot for six months to set up the training program. By 1968, the workshop had been equipped by McMeekin with kick wheels and wood-burning and low-pressure gas kilns. A materials processing plant had also been set up and bodies and glazes developed utilizing local materials, such as rocks, for glazes. According to McMeekin, "training started off well with Cardew, whose capacity to inspire was immense." McMeekin felt that the program could help the trainees to make the transition from their old way of life more readily "if it took them back into their own country, to the rocks which they already knew and used, and showed them new uses to which these could be put, giving this part of their known world new value and significance" (McMeekin 1969). Pottery was to be introduced to the Aborigines at the artist-craftsman level, to provide the community both with handmade dishes, plates, bowls, etc., and with symbolic or decorative pottery which would provide the craftsmen with a medium of personal expression and a means of personal fulfillment.

The Bagot project slowly declined after a few years. Following Michael Cardew's departure, subsequent supervisors and potters did not stay long. Puruntatameri decided he would only be happy with his own pottery on Bathurst Island. He invited John Bosco Tipiloura, another Bathurst Islander, to join him in setting one up. Under the auspices of H. C. Coombes and the Australian Council for the Arts, McMeekin carried out another feasibility study, and by 1973 the Catholic bishop of Darwin had provided the money for the scheme. Later a number of different government departments were supplying funds, and according to Stephen Anderson, who was supervisor from 1978 to 1981, their need for constant justification of the project caused confusion and

Fig. 12. Bowls made at Yarrabah, Queensland, 1983.

despair. Despite this and other problems, a reasonable flow of functional ware has supplied various outlets. The pottery is still functioning with several local potters, including the original two, although it still needs some financial assistance.

There was considerable misgiving, especially among potters, about introducing a craft that was not indigenous, but most observers will perhaps agree that since Aboriginal culture has been infiltrated by many alien industries, there is no reason that pottery should not be among them. This is especially true for Bathurst Island, where the existing pottery was the result of one Aborigine's love of the craft. Free choice of this sort should be an important aspect of these projects.

In Queensland, two Aboriginal potteries, Barambah at Cherbourg and the pottery at Yarrabah, have also had their ups and downs but are now producing usable pots with painted and carved decorations related to Aboriginal designs (fig. 12). Kevin Grealy, who was pottery instructor at Barambah for two years from 1974, at first suffered from the efforts of the Department of Aboriginal and Islanders Advancement to make a quick "success"—"a phenomenon to be measured in tons of fired clay and balance sheets" (personal communication, 1983). He suggests that the schemes "have failed partially in that they have tried artificially to make pottery a part of traditional culture rather than allowing it to exist as a possible medium for transition from the traditional to the contemporary" (Grealy 1977).

One of the important adjuncts to this studio/workshop training for the future of Aboriginal pottery is college ceramic courses. For example, at least one Aborigine, Thancoupie, who graduated from the ceramics department of the East Sydney Technical College, is working successfully in her own studio in Queensland and is an inspiration to her people (Isaacs 1982).

One of the best-known developing-country pottery projects was Michael Cardew's project in the 1950s at Abuja, Nigeria. The groundwork for it was laid by Harry Davis, also a noted English potter, at Achimota College in what is now Ghana. Davis taught and ran an efficient production unit for five years beginning in 1937. With his trainees, and using all local materials, he made thousands of unglazed terra-cotta water coolers and some building bricks, roof tiles, and water pipes as well as stoneware kitchen and table ware. Cardew joined him there in 1942, and plans were made for expansion, but when the war ended the scheme was abandoned. Taking with him some of the African trainees, Cardew set up a small stoneware pottery at Vumé on the Volta River, where he remained till 1948. In 1950, as pottery officer in the Nigerian Department of Commerce and Industry, Cardew set up a training center at Abuja where, with a team of local people, mud-brick Nigerian-style buildings were constructed for the workshops and kiln. Having become familiar with the low-fired traditional pottery of the country, Cardew (1976) reported that the pots were well-suited to their purpose and needed no improvement. What was needed, given changing life-styles, was good tableware. Stoneware was chosen because all the necessary materials could be collected and prepared locally. Traditional shapes were, in many cases, adapted for the modern wheel-thrown casseroles, jugs, coffee pots, etc., and combed and sgraffito patterns of Nigerian origin were cut through black and white slips.

Aliyu (n.d.) writes that the pots were immediately popular with the European population but rejected by the Nigerians in favor of the cheaper mass-produced pottery imported from Japan and England. The village potter's craft was dying for the usual reasons: children were too busy with schooling to learn the craft, and traditional pottery was being replaced by mass-produced aluminum, enamel, plastic, and ceramic wares. Cardew's was a good idea, Aliyu says, but for Nigeria in 1951 the scheme was premature: "Abuja Pottery was too advanced for the traditional potters: they could not understand the

Fig. 13. The two-pot stove, Nepal, 1983.

chemistry of clay and glazes, and they could not afford to buy the machinery, so they thought that it was something only the Government could own, and they would need to have knowledge of administration to cope with the problems" (p. 187). He feels that the idea could work now if the materials were ground by hand and simple wheels and a simple kiln were used. At first the potters could hand-build pots that the villagers already know and use. If the first step were simple enough, potters would understand and be able to follow as improvements were gradually made. The igneous rocks needed for glazes cannot, however, readily be broken up and ground by hand, and the jaw crusher needed for rapid operation is one of the most expensive pieces of equipment. Cardew had thought of overcoming this problem by crushing and preparing enough at the base pottery in Abuja to supply trainees who were setting up their own potteries. Alternatively, an intermediate hand-operated crusher could be developed.

A smaller project of great importance was recently carried out in Nepal by Bill Lawson, acting head of the Department of Industrial Arts at the University of New South Wales. The project concentrated on one article, a fuel-efficient ceramic cooking stove. The Nepalese government, funded by the World Bank through the FAO's Forestry Department, is establishing seventeen community forests throughout Nepal to combat deforestation (Lawson n.d.). As wood is the main fuel within the reach of the poor, Lawson's task was "to assess the skills of the local potters and their ability to make and distribute the improved stoves, to liaise with the Stove Project staff at local Tribhuvan University and to instruct them in stove design and testing, and to test the suitability of the local raw materials for use in stoves" (Lawson 1983).

The village potters were eager to participate in the project if the new stoves could be produced and sold profitably, but they did not perceive the need to conserve wood as their top priority. They desperately needed a new product for their family potteries because of the decline in demand for their traditional earthenware cooking pots and storage jars. The potters' assurance that the stoves could be successfully fired on their traditional bonfires using rice straw proved correct. Most important, in this situation the open firings did not need precious wood for fuel. The two-pot stoves were made in two sections and joined with slabs (fig. 13). The women approved of the stoves' design, apparently because they were smaller than their previous mud stoves and portable. Distribution of the stoves was greatly assisted by the potters' traditional practice of traveling and making pots in the villages visited in return for food and small cash payments. The stoves were also marketed through village shops and the Kathmandu bazaar. A considerable fuel reduction was achieved, and the stoves are reportedly selling very well. In the mountains, where wood stoves also performed a space-heating function, ceramic liners for the stoves were made to ensure efficient wood use.

In 1984 Lawson carried out similar feasibility studies for the production of these stoves in urban areas in Papua New Guinea, especially around Lae, where hillsides are being stripped of timber for village cooking fires. He found that the wood stoves were not appropriate. Skills were not available, and a suitable metal prototype that can be made in the local foundry has been designed for the low-cost housing market.

In 1971 Harry and May Davis embarked on a pot-making project that was finally established at Izcuchaca, Peru, in 1973. They had decided to attempt a job-creating activity in this remote mountain village that would be "oriented towards local self-reliance calculated to lead the participants to independence and control of their own economic and cultural affairs" (Davis 1983). After searching for a suitable village, planning, testing raw materials, and organizing equipment and machinery at home in New Zealand, they began setting up the workshop at Izcuchaca using water power in a derelict flour mill. The project was privately funded, 90 percent of the expenses coming

from the Davises' own pockets to begin with. Davis writes (1983):

> By stressing an eclectic approach to the technology of today and of yesterday, repetition of such a project will not entail a reliance on imported apparatus or spare parts. These can be made locally. Operating as private individuals, we can modify our style of living to come within sighting distance of that which prevails locally, as we are not status-bound to represent U.N. standards of remuneration. Nor are we compelled to pull out on a date predetermined by some head office outside the locality. If self-reliance in human, economic and creative terms is not possible this year we can stay on until such self-reliance is a reality.

Markets for the ware had to be found. An order for twenty-seven thousand plant pots of various sizes for an agricultural research station was ideal for a start. Candle holders, soap holders, and the flower pots were of unglazed terra cotta and, because they could be fired in the second chamber of the kiln with the excess heat from the first glazeware chamber, could be made and sold very cheaply. Later many dinner plates were in demand. The workshop still provides a living for the group at Izcuchaca, which operates now almost entirely without outside assistance (Davis 1975).

From 1974 to 1980, ceramic training and production projects were undertaken in postrevolutionary Laos. During this period Patricia and Graeme Cheesman acted first as volunteers and later as employees of the International Labor Organization. The objective of the project was to assist the government in the creation of a rural ceramics industry by providing training and research facilities to investigate raw materials for bodies and glazes, improve design of kilns, modernize techniques, and introduce other ceramic production possibilities.

Village life had been disrupted by the war, and very few traditional potters were working. Before the Cheesmans arrived, problems had been encountered in the introduction of an improved kiln and new techniques to the traditional potters at the Ban Done Pottery, sixty kilometers from Vientiane. It was recommended that small-scale workshops be spread throughout the country and run on a cooperative basis, but the government preferred the greater control of centralized workshops. It was also suggested that there be orientation courses to introduce traditional potters to new ideas before student potters were trained, thus preventing the master potters from losing their status.

The Cheesmans particularly worked toward self-sufficiency. A national school of ceramics was established, and Patricia Cheesman was appointed ceramics instructor. She trained the students not only in throwing, kiln building, etc., but in mathematics, chemistry, and glaze technology. Great enthusiasm was shown for this two-year course. At the Phen Panow Center, five kilometers from Vientiane, a forty-five-cubic-meter traditional tunnel or "snake" kiln was built. Traditional ware only was made here, but some new techniques were employed. At one stage there was a labor force of forty-five, but financial problems necessitated reorganization. Modern glazed ceramics were produced only at the Ceramics Institute in Vientiane. These included bone china, stoneware, and fused earthenware utilizing almost entirely local raw materials (Cheesman 1980). The aim most important to Patricia Cheesman was that production be primarily of goods to be used locally by Laotians. The government, in contrast, was hoping for production of porcelain electric insulators, etc., for export and the tourist trade.

Conclusions

Comparison of the pottery projects in Papua New Guinea with those in five other developing societies highlights some common problems. One of these is unrealistic expectations in the short term; it takes several generations to produce good potters. As Grealy notes,

> Real success (the acceptance of the pottery workshop, the occupation of "potter" and of the product inside and outside the community) would take at least a generation— when the sons or daughters of my six workers reached school-leaving age and saw "pottery" amongst other desirable occupations; when they had lived in a household where their parents had exercised the choice between a Barrambah pot and a Woolworth's special at half the price; where they had used (at the risk of breaking) cups, plates, teapots etc. made by other Aborigines.

It seems that financial support will be needed for such schemes for many years before they can hope to be viable. If town potteries are to compete with cheap imported domestic ware, the economic aspects must be carefully planned. This may have to include a tariff to protect to some extent what will be a less efficient industry with a small market. Also, follow-up with technical and management problems is a necessity, both in the group workshops and for individuals who set up their own studios. The problem of pricing at least some of the products within reach of the local people needs to be kept in mind. In the case of the Australian Aboriginal potters, however, Mc-Meekin notes that the people themselves are not interested in using the pots; why use a heavy, breakable pot when you can use a condensed-milk tin? Papua New Guineans would probably say they were happy with Hong Kong enamel for the same reason.

It seems that it would be best to train young people in new techniques separately, leaving the older potters to ask for help only if they desire it. Harry Davis deplores any potting project "in which the aim is to 'upgrade' an existing pottery tradition." He suggests that this should happen only when a tribal community is becoming part of a money economy. In situations where it is suitable for traditional potters to be part of a project, there should be plenty of opportunity for them to put forward their own ideas, as happened with the Nepalese potters, not only in regard to firing but also in product design.

Too much interference from government departments often leads to frustration and misdirection of talents. Cardew has reportedly said that the reason for some success at Abuja was that he was so far away from the government headquarters that they left him in peace long enough to start producing.

Assistance for the Sepik Provinces of Papua New Guinea should be for packing and marketing of their traditional ware from remote pottery villages. Consideration could be given to setting up a small industry in Wewak employing city people. Lawson has provided some guidelines for development of such projects. It is important, he says, (1) that the need(s) which the project is to satisfy be strongly felt by the local people concerned, (2) that the objectives be clear and partly short-term, (3) that the objectives be attainable, and (4) that the project be effectively managed.

Michael Somare is said to be inviting Malaysian investment and participation in developing his country's manufacturing industries, especially in the area of textiles, pottery, furniture, and tiles. I hope that in this process there will be great attention to background information, to real needs, to careful selection of consultants, and to the ideas and feelings of the Papua New Guinean potters themselves. There has been a resurgence among Papua New Guineans since Independence of interest in their cultural traditions, and, as the Ruffs (in this volume) point out, this has been backed up by a South Pacific Commission/ UNESCO symposium entitled "The Preservation of Traditional Living Art in Oceania" in 1979. Perhaps we will see more determination to keep traditional Papua New Guinean pottery as it is.

Notes

1. I thank the following: for sending me requested reports on pottery projects in which they were personally involved, Muriel Larner, Ivan McMeekin, Kevin Grealy, Bill Lawson, Harry Davis, Stephen Anderson, and Patricia Cheesman; for information and photographs, Helen Dennett, Mike Cockburn, Des Clifton-Bassett, Helen Palmer, Janetta Douglas, Barbara Barclay, Sue Bulmer, Gabrielle Johnston, Jim Specht, Patricia May, and John Parker; for assistance on the 1984 Sepik trip, potters and others too numerous to name at Saragum, Dimiri, and Aibom, Helen Dennett, Josephine Bastion, and Milan Stanek.

2. According to Petersen, the clay was to be dried and soaked in water, then sieved through a screen and left to become suitably plastic instead of being cleaned of stones and other impurities by hand. A simple brick-lined, wood-fired, updraft kiln capable of reaching an even temperature of 900° C in a couple of hours was to be built in each of the selected villages to replace the uneven firing in open fires.

3. The kiln that Petersen had designed for them was not intended for firing to glaze temperatures.

4. Of course, some Papua New Guinean pots do fall apart when left in the rain—potters the world over have some wasters. Admittedly, a temperature higher than 600° C is needed, and, as I have said, a bonfire can reach 900° C or more.

5. This may also have its difficulties, such as the common problem of trainees' not wanting to return to their country.

52/ The Village Studies Project for the Recording of Traditional Architecture

Wallace M. Ruff and Ruth E. Ruff

In 1979, a South Pacific Commission–UNESCO symposium on the preservation of traditional living art in Oceania recommended that "governments and administrations in the region be encouraged to establish proper technological facilities for the conservation of the arts of Oceania" and that "an appeal be made to the countries and territories of Oceania to introduce and develop the teaching of indigenous and living arts . . . throughout the respective educational systems." These statements reflected a worldwide concern for the preservation and documentation of art forms rapidly changing and/or disappearing in many developing nations. The Village Studies Project for the Recording of Traditional Architecture was an earlier Papua New Guinean response to this concern.

Initiated in 1973 under the inspiration of Neville Quarry, then head of the Department of Architecture and Building, Papua New Guinea University of Technology, Lae, the program grew out of the department's primary obligation: the teaching of Papua New Guinean students in architecture, who upon graduation were destined to assume influential positions in government departments, particularly those of planning and housing. Quarry (1974a), aware of the many stresses in the urban sector of the country (which impinged directly upon his curriculum and the teaching of architecture), said of its urban building of the present: "Dependence upon recent expatriate [architectural] precedents on the one hand, and traditional precedents on the other, leads to compromise solutions which perform inadequately under the constraints of Papua New Guinea's climate and social and cultural environment." Elsewhere he expressed his views on the need for data collection relating to traditional forms (1974b):

> Although many areas of Papua New Guinea have been investigated intensely by anthropologists, there remains a dearth of quantitative and technical information upon traditional construction methods, materials and distribution of building types within settlement patterns.

Such data is important as an archival record of the built forms of a society in transition. It is also valuable as a stimulus and resources bank of information for future building development which should take into account the existing environment and preferred architectural values of Papua New Guinea culture.

There was no thought that the architectural data and construction traditions, when recorded, would permit the transfer of such techniques and styles intact to the urban scene. As Quarry went on to point out (1975),

> There is no doubt that the spirit of the manmade environment should be rooted in the traditions of the past. But . . . behind this approach must be the will of a people prepared to innovate and bring new responses to new circumstances, maintaining a keen practical sense and social responsibility . . . informed by ingenuity and creative imagination.

This latter, he imagined, would be shaped partly through his department's program. The Village Studies project was to produce an "architectural vocabulary" of traditional and transitional forms and techniques to serve as the underpinning for professional "ingenuity and creative imagination."

It must be added parenthetically, in regard to the aim of recording "traditional" architecture, that researchers were under no misapprehension that they were going to capture in detail unchanged forms and techniques of the 1890s or the 1910s (or even the 1930s, in some areas). As Anthony Forge had indicated in conversation some years earlier, "Even in 1959 we kept saying to ourselves, 'Fifty years too late!'" Therefore the 1970s and early 1980s work by the Village Studies researchers marked an attempt to capture physical details, construction techniques, and design elements of buildings as they existed during those years. It was expected that comparisons with earlier photographs and accounts would be made to identify persisting traits which might be termed "traditional." In one of the earliest reports stemming from the project, Ruff and Ruff (1975) noted its almost total emphasis upon the recording of physical data and, unaware of the tentative nature of funding and personnel which were later to handicap the project, recommended research into an accompanying ethnography, advising of the "need to stage some sort of cooperative project with professionals in other fields, i.e., geography, anthropology, to expand the technical data of village buildings and siting, and document its cultural implications."

Early proposals from the project summarized four immediate objectives: to educate young people in their traditional heritage with regard to the built environment, to encourage preservation of traditional forms, to stress use of patterns of the past as a basis for planning a suitable urban environment for the present and future, and to produce a body of reference materials for future studies. These aims were to be accomplished through the production of measured drawings of traditional and transitional buildings, photographs and slides of traditional and transitional architecture in various areas of the country, freehand drawings of architectural details not available to camera lenses or of special interest, drawings of ritual artifacts in relation to the structures housing them, and site plans illustrating settlement patterns.

Personnel for the project consisted of interested staff members within the Department of Architecture and Building (there were never more than two such in any one particular year; one staff member with the National Art School also conducted three student field trips, which were similarly motivated). Because of teaching commitments, fieldwork was limited to term breaks—twice-yearly periods of two weeks—and six weeks during Christmas holidays. No long-term visits to any one area were possible, both because of teaching schedules (the teaching subsidized researchers within the country) and because of lack of funds earmarked for research. Consequently, rather than in-depth studies of particular areas, a broad survey of many villages was projected—this procedure also dictated by the need to cover many widespread design areas.

Small sums from the Department of Architecture and Building budget were later supplemented by grants from the University of Technology's Research Committee (1977–80). This money financed the field trips. The National Cultural Council of Papua New Guinea assisted in 1979 and 1982; Kodak of Australasia assisted from 1980 to 1982, granting price reductions in the purchase of photographic paper and film supplies; and UNESCO in 1982 granted funds to the Appropriate Technology Development Institute of the university for publication of some Village Studies materials in its "Traditional Technology" series.

In 1981, a project jointly financed by the Department of Architecture and Building and the Department of Surveying examined a declining ceremonial house in the Ramu River area by photogrammetric techniques. Cult houses in Bot Bot village and Boroi, near the Ramu, and the Kanganaman ceremonial house known as Wolimbit were also photographed with this technique. As it turned out, hazards to this sophisticated approach were several. House interiors were in some cases so dark that camera shots into obscure crannies were difficult or impossible (even using the supplementary artificial light carried on the trip) for a photogrammetric camera, which had to be anchored to a tripod. Camera equipment was excessively expensive, and the reading of the data required more expense for the operators' flights to Port Moresby to use the only plotting equipment in the country. All in all, those working on Village Studies were left to conclude that the nature of Papua New Guinea structures and sites, when coupled with these mechanics, lent themselves best to documentation through less intricate and costly systems.

The problems which have beset the Village Studies project are probably no more profound than those which affect fieldwork in general, but some of them should perhaps be highlighted. Before the project was very old, it became apparent that more people, larger expenditures, and, particularly, *sustained* funding over a long period of time would be required for consistent documentation. Except for the two years of the National Cultural Council grant, this funding was never acquired. Very big questions arose as to the eventual use of the data. If the objectives of the project were to be achieved and the data resulting were to be made available for students' use (in the words of UNESCO, if we were to "introduce and develop the teaching of indigenous and living arts throughout the educational system"), how was the teaching curriculum to be altered (see, e.g., Ruff, Ruff, and Loupis 1982)? Both staff and students at the university were generally more interested in the technical aspect of design and in producing buildings in the Australian or American vernacular. Course work involved use of wind tunnels, computers, data on elevators and air conditioning. Government funding to the university was *predicated upon* the offering of courses which instructed in these details. Design courses became a more and more minute portion of the school's offerings as each year passed. Where to find any extra time to include materials on "traditional" building in a curriculum already overloaded with requirements? The same problem applied at the high-school level, where teachers and administrators were trying to educate students to pass the required Australian-based tests, selecting those with the highest test scores for further training. While students were part of each field trip under the project, the main benefit to them seemed to have been to extend their knowledge of areas of the country to which they had not had access and to widen their horizons about architectural forms of which they had not previously been aware. (A few were motivated to do additional taping of myths of their elders when they returned home during school holidays.) Some students, observing the excitement of outsiders about their traditional forms, may have gained some pride in their background. These benefits should not be discounted, but the number of students so affected was minuscule. As of January 1982, all staff members concerned with documentation for the Village Studies project had left the university and the country.

Recently, there have been many positive gains. A few of the Papua New Guinean students who have graduated in architecture are now returning to assume teaching positions at the university. As they do so, they will likely become a united force to implement needed curriculum changes, rearranging course content to reflect Papua New Guinean attitudes and serve traditional concerns. Second, with greater experience in teaching they are likely to recognize that as development continues within the country and traditions disappear, records preserving the past will be a vital resource. As one of our graduates in architecture commented when he returned from training courses in Australia: "At first, I was really impressed by the new techniques and forms of buildings. But, after a few years abroad and in practice, I now realize the gifts of our own ancestors, and the need to be building suitable housing for our own people." A second student commented: "Really, when I first saw the work you were doing in Papua New Guinea architecture, I thought those many hours were a waste of time. Now, I'm beginning to realize the value—and the need for these records. My whole attitude has changed."

A contrapuntal theme during the work of documentation was UNESCO's idea of "conservation of the arts." Buildings studied in 1974 and 1975 often no longer existed by 1978 or 1979. The deterioration of structures just during the course of the project was overwhelming. Time and time again, workers found themselves working hand in hand with the anthropologists and archaeologists of the National Museum and Art Gallery in salvage operations. Documentation for national files became, in some cases, a record of buildings which had left the country for museums abroad or had disappeared because of weather-related problems and neglect. Physical problems of conservation are of course compounded by the ephemeral nature of wood and fiber. Roofing thatch of sago or kunai, with a five-to-seven-year lifespan, cladding of sago stem or rattan strips, of not much more durability, hardwood posts, subject to insect depredations—all of these elements must be subject to constant renewal, replacement, or abandonment and reconstruction on a new site. This traditional cycle—decline and decay and rebuilding—poses almost unsurmountable problems for conservationists and no lesser ones to researchers relying only on present physical details of structures, plus oral traditions recounted by fewer and fewer initiated elders, in order to identify "traditional" building.

During the course of the project, 1974–82, problems were encountered concerning a number of notable structures. The Serakim (Wosera area) ceremonial house (figs 1, 2) was removed from the country by the British Museum; the small Apangai structure was shipped from its site to the Australian Museum in Sydney. Undoubtedly, preservation will be much better in these museums abroad than in the villages of their origin; nonetheless, both richly ornamented structures are no longer available to the people of Papua New Guinea, and it is doubtful that they will be replaced with ones of equal merit. Four tambaran house structures at the Maprik Cultural Center (fig. 3), representing four Maprik and Wosera design styles, succumbed to weathering, neglect, and vandalism between 1979 and 1982. Two small Wosera ceremonial structures on the Maprik High School campus (fig. 4), built with the encouragement of an interested European, were allowed to disintegrate, and a host of bark paintings, a traditional initiation chamber, and the structures themselves have left no trace within Papua New Guinea other than the photographs and drawings recorded by the Village Studies project. The Ambunti council chamber, rich in carvings and ceiling paintings of the Kwoma area, was rapidly falling apart at the time we left the country in 1982. Roof leaks which admitted water to the ceiling were making rapid inroads. Later reports indicated that the building had been dismantled and that the National Museum was taking steps toward conservation. The one remaining Kambot-style ceremonial house (fig. 5) was in need of help if the magnificent bark paintings and facade were to be saved, and the National Museum was assisting villagers in repairs. The last Ramu River ceremonial structure containing a unique style of bark paintings representative of that area was well on its way to total collapse. The Kanganaman ceremonial house Wolimbit (which was declared national cultural property in 1967) was damaged in 1980 by an earthquake, and villagers were debating whether to "restore" or "rebuild" it.

As Swadling (1983b) and Mawi (1983) have pointed out, work on the registration of national cultural property and the publicizing of needs in the conservation of such traditional structures is continuing. The Papua New Guinea Constitution provides for conservation and management of "sites and areas having particular biological, topographical, geological, historic, scientific or social importance," but the difficulties of implementation are considerable. Craig (1983, and as quoted by Crombie 1983) outlines the many problems with documentation of the national cultural property already possessed by the museum and with the conservation, storage, and documentation of traditional artifacts in general. Local government councils of various provinces are beginning to form regional culture centers, and provincial officials frequently wish to assume some of the functions formerly performed by the national government. Whether a provincial system, with dispersed authority, will result in greater or more fragmented conservation and educational efforts remains to be seen. To date both

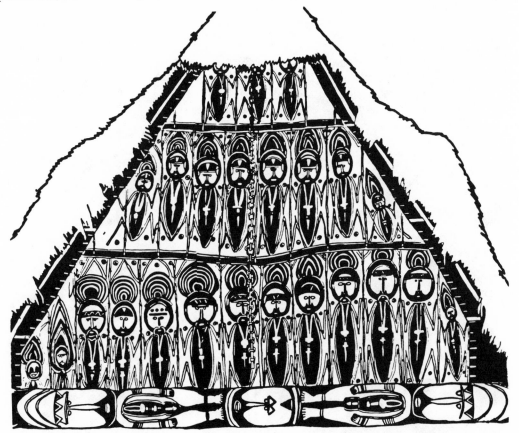

FIG. 1. Facade of Serakim ceremonial house called Rasikil, 1978. According to Nyagera, traditional painter and carver of Serakim, the figures of the top row are *yambingi* and those of the second row *dunguai;* all are male and represent ancestors. The painting was done by Serakim men; men from Stopigum assisted with the carving.

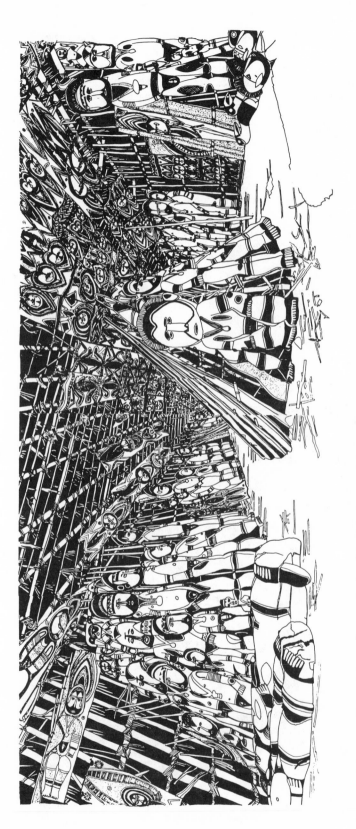

Fig. 2. Interior of Serakim ceremonial house of figure 1, showing bark paintings and carved figures, and (below) details of carved lintels.

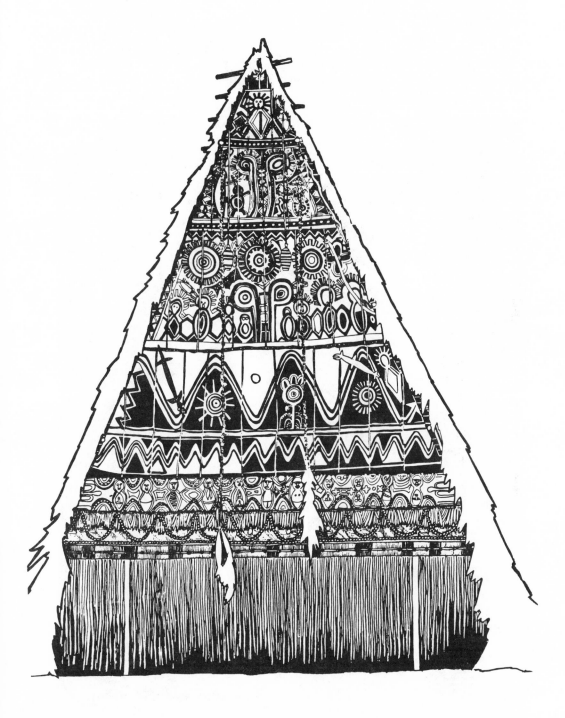

FIG. 3. Facade of small ceremonial house built by men of the Dreikikir area, Maprik, at the Maprik Cultural Center in 1975.

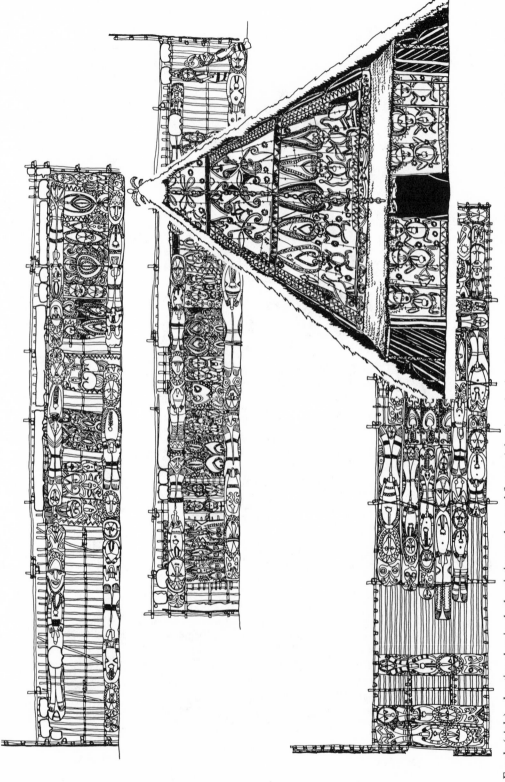

FIG. 4. Facade (*right*), elevation showing bark paintings and carved figures (*above*), and painted ceiling panels and carvings (*below*) of small ceremonial house built by Nala villagers on the Maprik High School campus 1975–76.

Fig. 5. Kambot ceremonial house and (*right*) elevation showing bark paintings on its gable overhang.

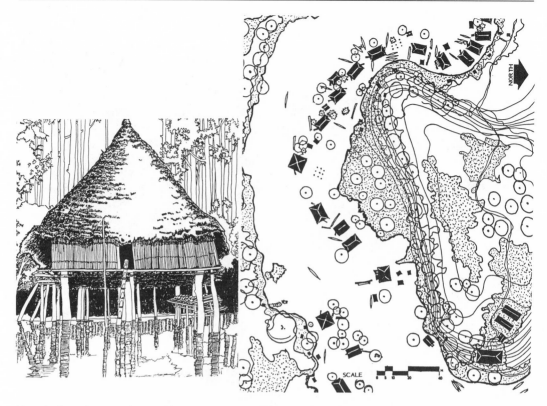

FIG. 6. One of two traditional (square) dwellings remaining in Hauna, Wogumas River, and site plan of village showing placement of men's house over the water and alignment of houses following the flow of the river.

of these functions have been assumed almost entirely by National Museum and Art Gallery personnel.

Some sparks of interest in traditional architecture have been noted by fieldworkers. Researchers in 1980 discovered a spontaneous rebuilding of old longhouse forms instigated by village people. In 1979 the village men of Tetehui, Gulf Province, built a longhouse for their use. A sec-

ond such structure was built and was in use by villagers of Pepeha, also in Gulf Province, as living space for families. While students and staff were recording data on the newly built longhouse in Wowobo in 1980, villagers requested the government to send ethnographers to their Gulf village to record their legends. Mawi (1983) reports (as do Ruff and Ruff 1980) that men of a village near Mendi, Southern Highlands, worried that their

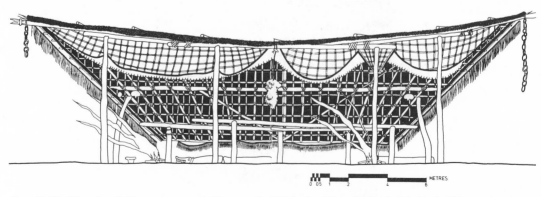

FIG. 7. Traditional-style Kwoma ceremonial house called Molgaivi, Tongwindjamb, Washkuk Hills. Bark paintings cover the ceiling. Large slit-drums are placed near the entrance parallel to the sides of the building. Cassowary-feather-enclosed packet suspended from roof in center contains ritual objects hidden from view of casual observers.

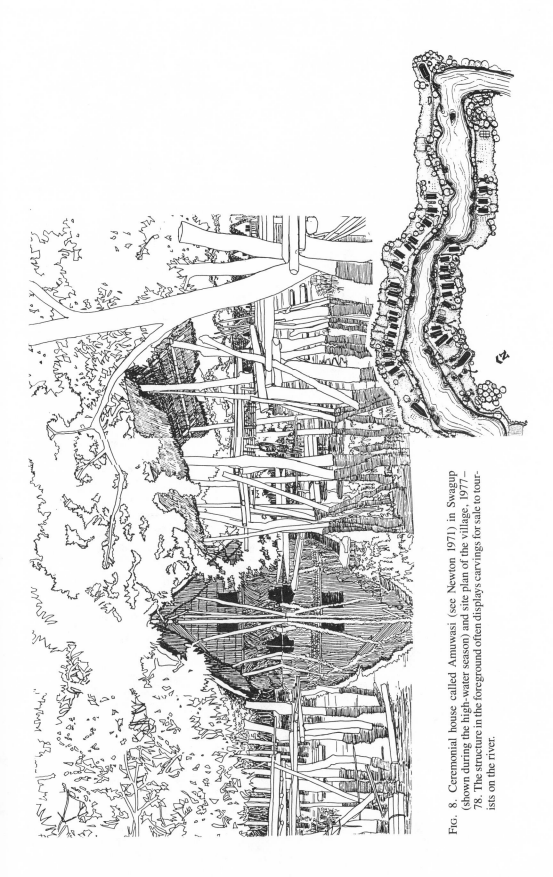

FIG. 8. Ceremonial house called Amuwasi (see Newton 1971) in Swagup (shown during the high-water season) and site plan of the village, 1977–78. The structure in the foreground often displays carvings for sale to tourists on the river.

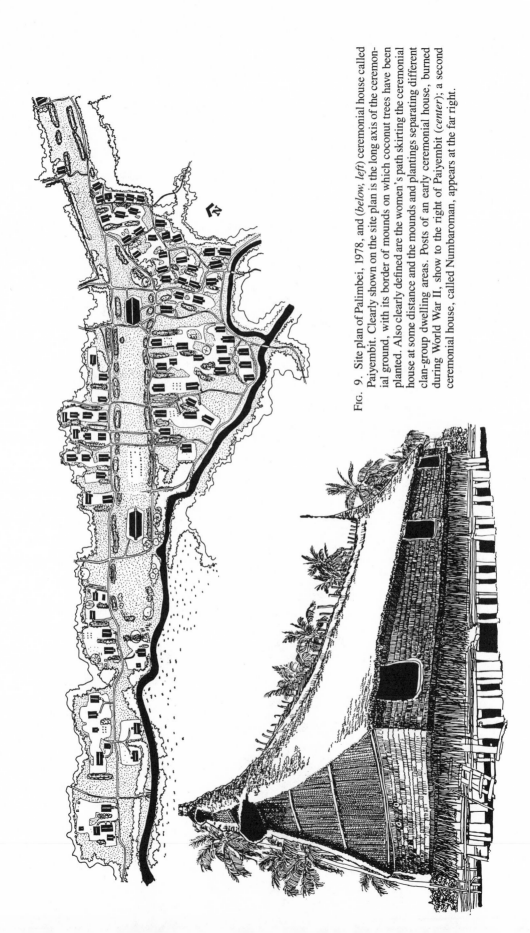

Fig. 9. Site plan of Palimbei, 1978, and (*below, left*) ceremonial house called Paiyembit. Clearly shown on the site plan is the long axis of the ceremonial ground, with its border of mounds on which coconut trees have been planted. Also clearly defined are the women's path skirting the ceremonial house at some distance and the mounds and plantings separating different clan-group dwelling areas. Posts of an early ceremonial house, burned during World War II, show to the right of Paiyembit (*center*); a second ceremonial house, called Numbaroman, appears at the far right.

Fig. 10. Maprik ceremonial house under construction, from a photograph of the 1950s by Anthony Forge.

F<small>IG</small>. 11. Facade of ceremonial house, Jambitanget (Wosera area), 1978.

traditional cult house would disintegrate completely, appealed to the government for financial
assistance to rebuild. They feared that if the structure collapsed, disaster would befall the village
people, and they recognized that a newly restored
structure with a good road leading to it would be
a drawing card for tourists and thus would provide
income for villagers. (Tour operators generally
take visitors to the "scenic" villages, i.e., those
with ritual structures, where a mock "head-hunting" ceremony or sing-sing may be performed for
a fee and carvings may be neatly displayed on the
bank, ready for purchase.)

Village Studies researchers, going about their
business of measuring and drawing, have tended
to be neutral observers to the newer built forms.
Donald Tuzin, however, in this volume, is sharply
critical of the project. Misinterpreting its intent
and procedures (which are certainly not to "encourage manufacture of artistic and architectural
masterpieces"), Tuzin outlines what he considers
more valid research aims. Mead, whom he quotes

in this regard, speaks of "pervasive cultural
styles," and Tuzin says that we must "visualize
research problems of broad regional import." But
how are broad (culturally authentic) traits to be
discovered except through many more narrowly
focused research projects? And how will these be
translated into public policies? Will it be anthropologists or Papua New Guineans who determine
what is "culturally authentic," and will they be in
total agreement? It would seem, furthermore, that
Tuzin might concede some validity to an attempt
to record dying ceremonial architecture when he
himself has recorded what he fears are dying tambaran rituals. Beliefs, universally held and persistent through the years though often hidden,
about power invested in ancestors have stimulated both the architectural forms we have delin-
eated and the rituals he has described.

To date, the project's drawings—a sampling
of which is included here (figs. 6–17)—have had
mostly ornamental use—as logos for newsletters
(Unitech Library) or as cover designs for research

FIG. 12. Facade of ceremonial house, Jama (Wosera area), showing both Maprik and Sepik motifs.

reports/brochures at the University of Technology wherever interest in indigenous culture had to be indicated. Other drawings have been used by A. L. Crawford in his 1981 book on the Gogodala and by Karl Holzknecht in the Morobe Province Historical Society publications. Photographs and drawings of longhouses have been requested by a U.S. publisher for a forthcoming book on "life-space." Various anthropologists have indicated interest in drawings of the Maprik and Murik Lakes areas. Some museum officials in the United States have expressed interest in photographs. Photographs and plans are being used within the Papua New Guinea National Museum for a display of a traditional house facade and interior; various conservation reports have been left with the National Museum for use as background material for conservation efforts. All reports in photocopy form have been placed in the National Museum, the Institute of Papua New Guinea Studies, the National Library, and the libraries of the university and the University of Technology. Interest has been expressed by Europeans and by

students in architecture at the university, where some materials, once they are completed and placed in national files, will be of *direct* assistance to Papua New Guineans other than through teaching or as research sources.

Many of these comments may seem to stress negative aspects of both the educational and the conservation work of the project. There have indeed been persistent problems with funding, and the work does progress slowly. The eventual use of materials is uncertain. It may be that another generation of Papua New Guineans will have to mature before the proper value will be put upon the national heritage. (In the meantime, the work must progress now, while documentation is still possible.) Perhaps the materials should be filed away, labeled "Resources for the Future"? Because architecture is a problem-solving art, these records of architectural forms can be used to understand the past, to define contemporary problems, and, ideally, to stimulate the creation of appropriate forms for the future.

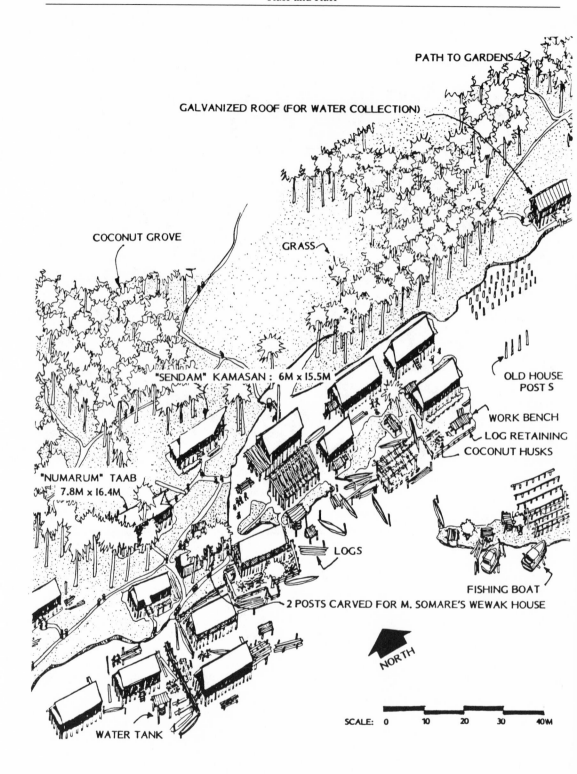

Fig. 13. Bird's-eye view of Darapap, Murik Lakes.

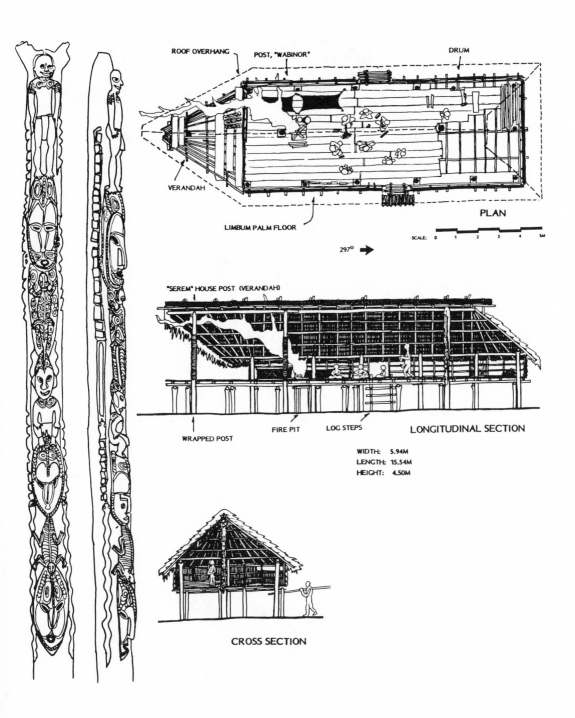

ROOF OVERHANG   POST, "WABINOR"   DRUM

VERANDAH

LIMBUM PALM FLOOR

297°

PLAN

SCALE: 0   1   2   3   4   5M

"SEREM" HOUSE POST (VERANDAH)

WRAPPED POST   FIRE PIT   LOG STEPS   LONGITUDINAL SECTION

WIDTH: 5.94M
LENGTH: 15.54M
HEIGHT: 4.50M

CROSS SECTION

FIG. 14. Ceremonial house called Sendam, Darapap, and (*left*) carved posts from the interior of the structure.

BANFAAB DAUR
(GABLE)

"NOSE" OF THE CEREMONIAL HOUSE   LONGITUDINAL SECTION

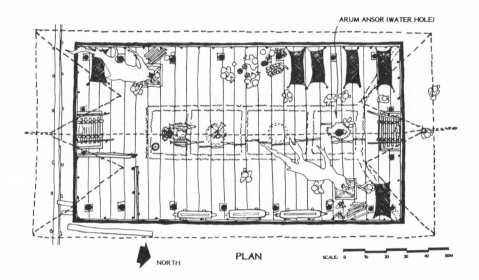

ARUM ANSOR (WATER HOLE)

NORTH   PLAN   SCALE: 0   10   20   30   40   50M

CROSS SECTION

FIG. 15. Ceremonial house called Bungabwar, owned by Peter Kanari, Janeainemot hamlet, Big Murik, 1981. According to David Lipset (personal communication), this style of structure originated in Mushu Island and reached Janeainemot by way of the Kaup (Imul) to the west. The right to build this particular house was acquired as payment for help given the Kaup in warfare.

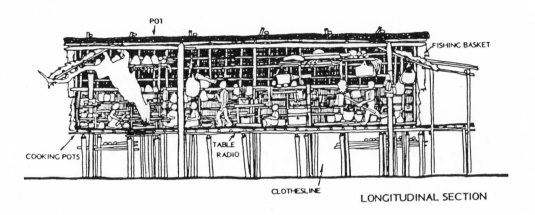

POT

FISHING BASKET

COOKING POTS

TABLE
RADIO

CLOTHESLINE

LONGITUDINAL SECTION

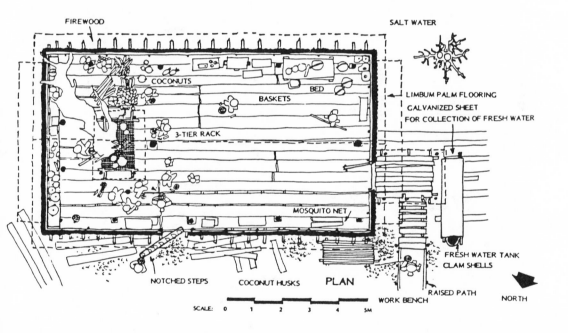

FIREWOOD

SALT WATER

COCONUTS

BASKETS

BED

LIMBUM PALM FLOORING

GALVANIZED SHEET
FOR COLLECTION OF FRESH WATER

3-TIER RACK

MOSQUITO NET

FRESH WATER TANK
CLAM SHELLS

NOTCHED STEPS   COCONUT HUSKS   PLAN

RAISED PATH   NORTH

WORK BENCH

SCALE: 0   1   2   3   4   5M

FIG. 16. Dwelling of Ja Ja Kaneng, big man of Karau, Murik Lakes, 1981.

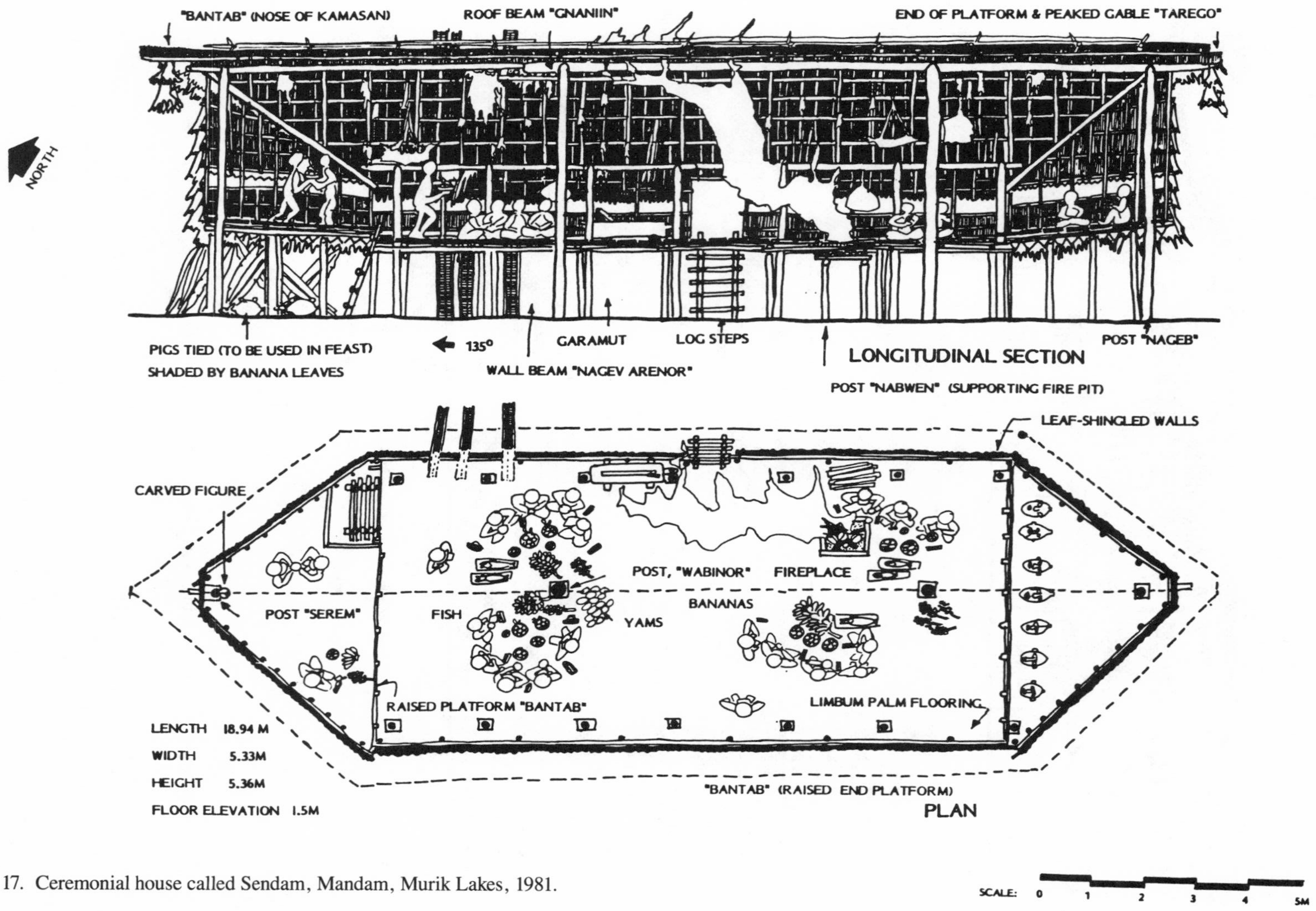

END OF PLATFORM & PEAKED GABLE "TAREGO"

POST "NAGEB"

LONGITUDINAL SECTION

POST "NABWEN" (SUPPORTING FIRE PIT)

LEAF-SHINGLED WALLS

ROOF BEAM "GNANIIN"

"BANTAB" (NOSE OF KAMASAN)

135°

WALL BEAM "NAGEV ARENOR"

GARAMUT   LOG STEPS

PIGS TIED (TO BE USED IN FEAST)
SHADED BY BANANA LEAVES

NORTH

CARVED FIGURE

POST "SEREM"

FISH

RAISED PLATFORM "BANTAB"

YAMS

POST, "WABINOR"   FIREPLACE

BANANAS

LIMBUM PALM FLOORING

"BANTAB" (RAISED END PLATFORM)

PLAN

LENGTH   18.94 M
WIDTH   5.33M
HEIGHT   5.36M
FLOOR ELEVATION 1.5M

SCALE: 0   1   2   3   4   5M

FIG. 17.   Ceremonial house called Sendam, Mandam, Murik Lakes, 1981.

53/ Swiss and German Ethnographic Collections as Source Materials: A Report on Work in Progress

Christian Kaufmann

To appreciate what traditional cultures were like, we should know what they looked like to those who lived them. It would lead us too far afield if I were to explain fully why trying to reconstruct the visual and material record deserves some effort. It is sufficient to say that in a society traditionally unfamiliar with writing there were other ways of storing information and knowledge. Apart from linguistic mnemonic devices such as songs and stories and mnemo-technical aids such as counting sticks and counting ropes,[1] there has always been the possibility of both storing (or, rather, encoding) and transmitting knowledge, feelings, and thoughts by creating sculptures, paintings, drawings, and buildings (among them sacred ones). But it is more than this that I am aiming at. We all know that art always has an aspect of meaning, be it hidden or manifest. I feel, however, that to understand the iconography or, rather (since this is a field of emic study), the "iconology" of any culture fully we should not only try to link oral traditions to permanent works of visual art but also consider the whole range of visually relevant expression. Movements, gesture, dance, the way things are made and used— mostly, if not always, in front of others who are supposed to acquire and learn them—are of equally great importance. It could even be argued that the operation of the "mind" of the community, both its memory and its capacity for projection, depends upon visual stimuli. From a general point of view it may be assumed that the encoding of information and even abstract thinking often take the form of visualized symbols (as Piaget's experiments have shown us). It is safe to assume that all sorts of objects invented by humans are capable not only of serving their particular practical purposes but also of provoking and transmitting visually patterned thought processes.

Those of us who are museum anthropologists should make the best use possible of what has been stored in our institutions' archives and study collections. If we are to gain any understanding at all, we must look at the totality of these documents rather than restrict our study to the artistically most impressive specimens. There is much information that could be used if only we would begin working with it in a systematic way. It is discouraging that no one has achieved a more comprehensive picture of any local culture in the Sepik area than Mead (1938) in her work on the Arapesh. What follows is a report on the rather modest effort at a more comprehensive approach that has been my objective for a number of years and developed into a project involving a number of researchers. From the beginning, we in Basel were able to coordinate our efforts, at least in principle, with the concerns for better documentation of the Anthropology Department of the Papua New Guinea National Museum and Art Gallery. Our aim is to provide that museum with comprehensive documentation (on microfiche) of Iatmul and Kwoma material culture, making use of all the documents available to us, and a complete catalog, including photographs of the relevant specimens in the Basel collection. Such documentation would, of course, be available to any center for cultural activities within the Sepik region. The objective of this paper is to give an overview of what has been done so far on this project and to illustrate some of the results.

The Kwoma Case: From Field Study of Technology to Museum Study of Material Culture

Kwoma culture, viewed with the self-confidence of an anthropology student of the sixties, seemed a simple matter: The traditional way of life was being abandoned. Of all the villages, only Washjkuk had a newly built more or less traditional ceremonial house (*kurumbu*). Ritual had ceased to be performed, and the vestiges of ritual art were being sold, destroyed, or given away. Some of the background stories were being told to the outsider, but more were not. Pottery—my main concern when I first visited the area—was still being made, but for how long? My reports were simple, too: a preliminary description and interpretation of ritual art—incomplete, certainly, and inaccurate in some respects but not completely beside the point, as a comparison with a more recent contribution shows (Bowden 1983*a*, Kaufmann 1968). I saw pottery making as a focal point of Kwoma culture (Kaufmann 1972:123–96). When I left Meno (Saserman) in 1966, I was given a huge net bag, said to be the cover of the *yena* altar, and told to take it to the museum in Basel along with the *yena* and *minza* carvings. The net bag puzzled me: why this typically female artifact in the midst of male ritual objects?

When I returned to the field in 1972, with my wife, I intended to document the material culture of the Kwoma. The focus was a detailed study of selected work processes that yielded primary products (such as yam production), cultural equipment in general use (such as the making of string bags), and products used symbolically and given artistic treatment. The plan was to document these processes (mainly on 16-mm film) and then compare them with what oral tradition might reveal of their invention and development and with Kwoma's views of the role of technical and creative processes in their life. Combined with what was known of Kwoma mythology, at least that of one of the Kwoma groups, the Saserman (Whiting's Koriyasi [Whiting and Reed 1938]), this information was anticipated to lead to a Kwoma "science" of the relations between humans, their works, and their *Umwelt* (the latter seen partly as a creation of the ancestors in mythical times). (It may be worth noting that the research was designed with a view to improving the quality of the presentation of Sepik cultures in the Basel museum.) This program had to be modified both during and after fieldwork. Establishing a comprehensive catalog of tangible culture was seen at the time as less important than documenting the processes associated with their production and use (Kaufmann 1984*a*, 1979), and most of the information obtained from oral tradition remains to be analyzed and edited. It is only now, in the course of analyzing the place of objects made of meshwork (including the various forms of ceremonial shell money mounted onto a mesh-work base), that I have come to appreciate the symbolic aspects of the gesture of entrusting the ritual net bag to me in 1966 (Kaufmann 1986).

Another aspect of Saserman life in mid-1972 proved to be of some importance. Work on a new ceremonial house had begun before we arrived, and we were able to follow the process of constructing such a house under the leadership (or, rather, "authorship") of Yabokoma and Yessomari, outstanding men (*harpa ma* or *his-auəma*) from Meno. It became clear that the ceremonial house was just another, albeit more complicated, artifact of Kwoma culture. Very appropriately, its builders felt that it should be viewed only as an accomplished fact and denied us permission to film the process. We were permitted, however, to take a series of still photographs. Because Yessomari died in 1974, the house was never properly finished, although it served up to 1983 as the stage for a number of ceremonies. In 1984 a new building was on the point of being inaugurated.

In the course of evaluating the documentation accumulated in the field, it became clear that only through research in museums holding Kwoma material—not only the Basel museum but also the Museum für Völkerkunde, Berlin-Dahlem, the Peabody Museum at Yale, the Überseemuseum Bremen, and others—could a full record of the material culture of the Kwoma and their neighbors, the Yassean-Mayo and the Nukuma, be established. A comparative study of the Manambu material, for which the main source is the Roesicke collection from Malu at the Berlin Museum, would also be essential.

So far a total of 1,065 objects of Kwoma, Nukuma, or Yassean-Mayo origin located in six different museums are on record. Approximately 45 additional objects have been recorded during fieldwork or from photographs and notes. In summary, it can be said that Kwoma society produced at least 95 different types of objects (or categories of material culture in the broad sense, including buildings such as ceremonial houses, dwellings, and cooking houses). A number of general-purpose tools may serve in the context of ritual, although in many cases (for example, adzes) there are two varieties of the item, one for everyday use and one for ritual. Once the "catalogue raisonné" is completed, we should be able to use it as a checklist for the analysis of Kwoma culture, past and present. Of course, the catalog will also include the data on the iconography of Kwoma material culture accumulated thus far.

The Iatmul/Sawos Case: A Systematic Approach to Material Culture

General Setting of the Research Program

My involvement with the Iatmul and Sawos material began rather incidentally, since I had only limited personal acquaintance with the Iatmul of Aibom (December 1965) and the Sawos of Torembi, Slei, and Kwaiwut (October and December 1966) while studying pottery making and beginning to document the Basel collection (cf. Schuster 1967). On the basis of my experience with the Kwoma documentation, I developed a postdoctoral program for more intensive documentation of Central Sepik cultures.[2] The aim was to collect as much additional evidence as possible relating to visual cultural aspects (materially represented by items in the museum collections) from field notes, photographs, films, and tapes largely accumulated by a group of younger Ph.D. researchers who had been to the Iatmul and Sawos area between 1972 and 1974 (see Schuster 1979 for an overview and the resulting theses Hauser-Schäublin 1977, Schindlbeck 1980, Weiss 1981, Wassmann 1982, and Stanek 1983; see also Stanek 1982 and Schmid and Kocher-Schmid n.d.). Work started in the spring of 1978.

The task was a double one: to find new ways to analyze and present material-culture items in their functional contexts and to relate the results of this effort to the study of the museum collections. The description of functional contexts was attacked from two points of departure. Markus Schindlbeck took a rather factual approach, examining the role of *wagan* slit-gongs, water drums, female figures, and so on (see the appendix for the titles of these manuscripts on microfiche). Later a more comprehensive approach began to prevail. The plan, mainly inspired by Milan Stanek, was to develop a systematic analysis of daily life (with its economic aspects of production, distribution, and consumption) and then of ritual life and then produce a systematic catalog of cultural items, preferably along emic lines. This plan proved too demanding for any single researcher, and a compromise was therefore reached. We now have a series of contributions that fall into three categories but nevertheless form a structured entity: type catalogs of material culture, texts on the functional contexts of material-culture items, and studies of specific aspects of the cultures in question.

Type Catalogs

Iatmul. A systematic catalog containing every single type of item associated with Iatmul culture, whether produced within Iatmul society or imported from outside, was first conceived by Milan Stanek and later fully established by Brigit Obrist (the first parts of it are now on microfiche; see Obrist et al. 1984). It covers not only the twelve hundred Iatmul objects documented in the collection of the museum in Basel[3] but also the material collected by Gregory Bateson in 1930, 1932, and 1935 and now housed in the University Museum for Archaeology and Anthropology in Cambridge.[4] Reference is also made, where necessary, to the material from the Hamburgische Südsee-Expedition and the earlier part of the Stuttgart collection, both published by Reche (1913). Added to the catalog were objects whose existence can only be inferred from oral information or from photographs. Pending a systematic comparison with the material in the Roesicke collection and the knowledge of Iatmul historians, the catalog cannot be said to be exhaustive. Nevertheless, together with the *catalogue raisonné* of the Basel collection (including photographs of each item) it already amounts to several hundred manuscript pages. Unfortunately, the policy of the Swiss National Research Foundation required termination of the program's funding at the end of 1984. However, limited funds for a translation into English—the ultimate aim in view of the needs of the Papua New Guinea National Museum and the Institute of Papua New Guinea Studies—have been made available (see Kaufmann 1981:229), and translation is under way. For these reasons, the next step in the program—inclusion of neighboring Central Sepik cultures such as Chambri, Kapriman, and Manambu—cannot follow immediately.

The text produced so far by Brigit Obrist, Christin Kocher-Schmid, Sylvia Ohnemus, and me coordinates the visual documentation (photographs of the museum specimens and of the ways they were made and used) with descriptions of what cannot be displayed. Each type is introduced with a definition and a list of the terms used to designate it in the local language and its dialects. Types are generally defined in terms of function and subtypes in terms of form. Information regarding manufacture and use is given with reference to the field observations available. The variation of individual forms represented in the Basel collection is described. Approximately 376 types and major subtypes made from traditional materials and an additional 24 types representing replacements made from more recently introduced materials have been isolated and described so far. Of these, nearly 200 (plus the 24 replacement types) are in everyday (i.e., nonceremonial) use. Types are grouped for convenience in 17 categories: cloth, portable utensils, bags and baskets, canoes and paddles, weapons, tools for food production, tools for crafts, furniture, ceramics, kitchen tools, further household gear, the ceremonial house, general items for ritual use, masks and equipment for dances, initiates' decoration and utensils, musical instruments, and ornaments. The items that serve ritual purposes only have been the object of an additional preliminary study (see below). For a rather important group of objects in which everyday and ritual use overlap, Florence Weiss has contributed an exhaustive list (see appendix).

Four problems deserve specific mention:

1. A remarkable coincidence of formal and functional variation has been found. This should come as no surprise (see Kaufmann 1972:158–70 and n.d.), but it does show clearly that only by careful analysis of every single item in the museum collections and other field documents can we hope to recover the full range of a traditional culture's equipment. Formal variation in a tool or an element of body decoration, repeatedly documented, will with a high degree of probability point to a yet undocumented function rather than to the producer's idiosyncratic creativity.

2. Iatmul culture seems to be marked by a particularly high degree of variation in forms—again, no surprise to the insider, but striking in comparison with, say, Kwoma (with 95 types), Arapesh (for which I count some 110 types and major subtypes, excluding strictly ritual equipment, in Mead [1938:150, 202–319]—a figure that may or may not be appropriate in the absence of her promised "future section on the collection itself" [p. 235]), Eipo (80 types and major subtypes as reported by Koch [1984:23–120, 137], who comments on its "simplicity"), and Melpa (some 108 major types and subtypes [Vicedom and Tischner 1943–48:92–227, 242]). Why is the Iatmul's equipment so much more complex? What historical and/or ecological factors underlie this situation?

3. A rather detailed study of clothing and body ornamentation by Milan Stanek at an early stage of the project brought home to us the fact that inclusion of the wealth of information hidden away in objects and photographs in early collections was essential for a comprehensive picture.

Establishing the historical background of the present situation seems a logical and easy thing to do, but it is a difficult one, partly because of the shortcomings as research tools of the most important museum collections of Sepik materials.

4. An important gap in our information has become apparent with regard to the identification of raw materials and their sources and the routes along which artifacts were traded, although Gewertz (1977:184–225), Hauser-Schäublin (1977:38–64), Schindlbeck (1980:154–248), and Schuster and Schuster (1976b) have recorded data on sago/fish/pottery exchange in the Central Sepik area. A preliminary proposal for a follow-up study has been worked out.

Sawos. Markus Schindlbeck, revisiting the Sawos in 1979 and 1981, provided us with ethnographic documentation for many types of objects that had previously been undocumented and added to the systematic collection of traditional objects once in everyday use (some of which, having since been abandoned, were specifically made for him in 1979). A preliminary count shows that about 125 types and major subtypes can be isolated. The total number of pieces of Sawos origin (excluding Kwaiwut pottery) is about 475. So far, only a very preliminary comparison with the Iatmul material on a type-by-type basis has been possible. At first glance, it can be said that the Sawos-Iatmul relationship deserves attention. We have been told that every Iatmul dialect group has its own Sawos or "people of the bush" (Staalsen 1975:6). It could also be argued, conversely, that the Iatmul are, historically speaking, simply a part of the Eastern and Central Sawos.[5] Study of pottery complexes in the Basel collection hints at the possibility that the differences between the four or five Sawos groups are greater than those between the four Iatmul groups. Differences in cultural inventory between the Western Central Sawos and the Nyaula Iatmul seem to be on the level of subtypes rather than on that of types (except, of course, items determined by local ecological factors, such as the huge nets for hunting pigs common among the Sawos but unknown on the river's southern banks).

Texts

Texts produced by Milan Stanek and Florence Weiss on the functional contexts of material-cultural items include the following four main contributions:

An ideal-type description of an ordinary day in the life of a Iatmul nuclear family as observed in

Palimbei village 1972–74 (Stanek 1984*a*) draws upon Stanek's own field data and Weiss's (1981) published account. Mention is made of all the tools and other items of cultural equipment, beginning with cloth and ending with canoes and paddles, that were used at the time, and the way they were used is described in its context. Going every third day to the exchange market with the neighboring Sawos is a traditional occupation of Iatmul women, and therefore special attention is given to it in the form of a description by an old man of one such event in pre-European times. A new point of comparison for the data already published on this institution is thus established. The text is aimed not primarily at a specialist audience but at anyone looking for a factual and easy-to-understand description of the Iatmul way of life. It will certainly also become a valuable historical document about life in the seventies.

A comprehensive presentation of data relating to the ritual system of the Palimbei Iatmul (Stanek 1984*b*) is based upon the field material, including accounts by village elders of earlier-held rituals and color photographs and Super-8 films of actual ceremonies, gathered by Weiss and Stanek, with reference, of course, to Bateson's published work. Stanek had earlier produced a study of the *pabu*, ceremonial discussions in the men's house (1983:242–75). Other rituals are briefly described under two headings: ceremonies organized by groups (*arɨmbandi*) based on the dual organization into generations characteristic of the different types of men's houses (*mbore, tɨgal, ngeigo*) and ceremonies organized to deal with relationships between clans allied by intermarriage. Under the first heading are descriptions of, among others, cicatrization (*wal mbangu*) and initiation, the *wagɨn* ritual, head-hunting and the ritual fights between arɨmbandi groups, and the *mai, ndumoi, abwan,* and *mengɨnwen* rituals. Under the second are clan rituals including marriage, *navɨn*, death ceremonies, and ceremonies for the inauguration of canoes, houses, etc. Viewed in this context, the navɨn ritual, which may be performed at various levels, takes on new meaning (see Stanek 1983:276–91, 301–13).

An inventory of the objects used in these rituals accompanies the text.[6] It begins with a description of six standard ways of dressing up for ceremonies varying with the status of the participant and the occasion. It goes on to provide, for each type of ritual, a keyword list indicating its location, its specific scenery, and its costumes, accessories, and musical instruments.

A comprehensive typology of Iatmul masks (Weiss 1984*b*) departs from a text on *abwan* masks and a study of the masks in the Basel collection (other than the *mai* masks already studied by Hauser-Schäublin [1976–81]). A further step has involved the mounting of a special exhibit on iconology at the museum in October 1985.

Studies of Specific Aspects of Iatmul and Sawos Culture

Texts dealing with more narrowly defined aspects of Iatmul and Sawos culture are too numerous to mention (but see appendix for a listing).[7] Four deserve attention here. Wassmann (n.d.) has provided a translation of five more clan songs from Kandingei (and see his analysis of the first [Wassmann 1982]) and, on the basis of this groundwork, written an introduction to the cognitive system underlying Nyaula Iatmul culture (Wassmann 1984). Schindlbeck has dealt with, among other things, figures, masks, and musical instruments used in Sawos ritual, and comparison of his 1978–80 data with the material on the Iatmul offers further reason to reconsider the Iatmul-Sawos relationship. Weiss (1984*a*) presents data on the way boys and girls begin making artifacts. Weiss, Schindlbeck, Gisela Schuster, and Christin Kocher-Schmid have provided a detailed description of rituals performed in 1972–74 and documented on Super-8 film (to be made available on microfiche).

Museum Research

The role of museums as archives and research institutions has been so greatly neglected by professional anthropologists that the period since World War II has produced no successors to Haddon, Speiser, and Thilenius. As far as the Sepik area is concerned, special problems arise. One of these is the enormous dispersal of artifacts; having a few Sepik masks or carvings seems to have been a must for almost every museum in the world, including the ethnographic museum in Mexico City, the university museum in Zürich, and such other Swiss museums or special collections of ethnography as those in Neuchâtel, Geneva, Burgdorf, and St. Gall (some of which began collecting Sepik artifacts even before the Basel museum). Another is the fact that an important part of these materials has never been properly documented or has lost its documentation in the course of being dispersed, reshuffled, or sold.

The Sepik area having been part of German Kaiser-Wilhelmsland, the pre-1914 collecting, apart from considerable private curio collecting and dealing by those who went to the Sepik area in search of laborers, bird-of-paradise plumes, or gold, was done mainly by three German scientific expeditions.

Of the six official expedition steamers that carried scientists to the Sepik, two went straight upstream to navigate the Sepik to the area of the then German-Dutch border. One of these, the Schrader expedition, with base camps near Tsenap and Malu/Ambunti, to the best of my knowledge left no trace of having collected systematically except in the field of botany (see Accession 1888 at the Berlin Museum of items donated by the Neu Guinea Kompagnie; see also Hollrung 1887–88), while Schultze-Jena (1914) produced a concise report of his ethnographic activities. Of the remaining four German expeditions, three were excursions of three to fourteen days each on boats belonging to the Neu Guinea Kompagnie that had other tasks to attend to (see Friederici 1909, Schlaginhaufen 1910) or on research vessels (see Reche 1913). Reporting on the results of the collecting activities of the Hamburgische Südsee-Expedition, Reche aimed at a more comprehensive presentation of the material, including samples from museums other than the one at Hamburg, for example, the Lindenmuseum in Stuttgart (the collection of Captain Haug of the *Siar,* a Neu Guinea Kompagnie steamer [see Reche 1913:3, 12]). It was only the last of these expeditions that followed a more precisely set program of research.

This expedition, the Kaiserin-Augusta-Fluss Expedition of 1912–13, aimed at putting the Sepik Basin on the map, in geography as well as geology, botany, zoology, and ethnography or anthropology (the ambiguity as to the direction of the anthropological activities was never properly resolved). The research program had been jointly organized by the German colonial office (with money from the various German states confederated under the emperor) and the Museum für Völkerkunde Berlin, an institution belonging to the Kingdom of Prussia. The proportion of the expedition's costs contributed determined each participant's share of the ethnographic collections (only one of the many fruits of the expedition's research). Accordingly, Prussia (i.e., the Berlin Museum) received, of the total of 5,074 specimens, 4,196 (83 percent), Lübeck (taking first choice among the German sponsors) 136 (2.5 percent), and Saxony (Dresden), Bavaria (Munich), and Württemberg (Stuttgart) lesser numbers (see the documentation of Berlin Museum accession numbers 92/16, 560/16, 990/16). The decision-making process by which the collection was distributed is not clearly documented, except for the efforts of the Berlin curator Dr. Eichhorn and his director to keep all the unique pieces of art, i.e., "the big wooden sculptures, the bark paintings and the splendid masks," for their own institution. Whether on the level of ordinary objects the selection might have been made more haphazardly is hard to judge. The expedition team consisted of Artur Stollé, the expedition leader, who was a mining engineer and had accompanied Schultze-Jena to the Upper Sepik; Josef Bürgers, a doctor, who was to collect the zoological specimens; Walter Behrmann, geographer; C. L. Ledermann, botanist; Adolf Roesicke, "ethnologist";[8] and Richard Thurnwald, "ethnographer," who joined the expedition in the field very late and then remained until after the outbreak of World War I. Most of what Thurnwald collected was lost or, reportedly, destroyed by insects in the crates in which it remained in transit for ten years; what remains, most of it from the Keram River area, is without proper documentation. Another member of the expedition was Captain Hollack of the steamer *Kolonialgesellschaft*, on secondment (or loan) from the Norddeutscher Lloyd. As the terms of his contract were not too elaborate, he (or members of his crew) did some collecting on the side, and these items, many of Iatmul origin, apparently reached the Überseemuseum Bremen together with other materials through an agent at Friedrich-Wilhelmshafen (Madang), unfortunately without proper documentation.[9] They have only recently become available for restudy.

Although Heinz Kelm published substantial material from the core of the Berlin collection, it remains in many respects unknown. Whereas we are fortunate that it was not much damaged or diminished during World War II (Koch 1973:152–53), it is proving rather difficult to track down all the items distributed among the various museums, although a first step has been taken with regard to the Lübeck collection.[10] The main problem is that a number of Sepik artifacts that have passed through the hands of art dealers can be shown to have belonged to the original collection (in some cases even the original field numbers have been preserved). The most serious loss is that of Roesicke's field notes.[11] We are left, however, with his original collecting list and an incomplete copy of his official field diary.[12] This loss is most heavily felt with regard to Malu, the Manambu village near the expedition's base camp at Ambunti, the "Kaulagu camp," that is, the Nyaula Iatmul area ("Kaulagu" being Roesicke's spelling for Korogo, which at that time was still on the right bank of the Sepik below the Nyaurangei inlet), and the Kararau group of settlements and their neighbors. In these three places Roesicke spent a total of some five months of the nineteen months the expedition remained in the Sepik area, most of the time separated from the rest of the expedition.

As the reorganization of the Roesicke collection at the Berlin museum is still under way, a systematic comparison of the Basel and Berlin collections, dating from periods separated by forty to sixty years, has not yet been possible. Preliminary trials have pointed to some additional problems. It has, for example, proven necessary to check Kelm's data on proveniences. In a number of cases specimens presented in an aberrant context (and thus pointing to the possibility of extensive spheres of influence) can be shown to have a much more appropriate local provenience; for example, the "suspension hook" from the Middle Sepik (Kelm 1966a:fig. 18) is definitely Mask No. 3910, collected by Roesicke on September 3, 1913, at Kara (Nggala), Upper Sepik.[13] In the case of the Kwoma, the fact that no major carvings could be traced, despite Behrmann's (1922:257, 260) statements, had led to speculation about the loss of these items. From the description Roesicke gives of his visits to the Kwoma, however, it cannot be inferred that he would have seen a fully decorated ceremonial house of the rich form that is dominant now, in the period of revitalization. Some of Roesicke's fragmentary notes are very important as the earliest firsthand sources; he was, for example, the first European to identify and visit (on May 20, 1913) Aibom as a pottery-making center, and he observed scarification and some of the ceremonies of a Yentschemangua initiation and briefly visited Sawos country (Tschauasche, Numangoa, Wereman). Roesicke also observed activities related to the return to Nyaurangei and Korogo of two headhunting parties against Sengo and the allied Manambus (and possibly Kwoma).[14]

Sepik Research: A Museum Curator's Perspective

Further work along these lines may be expected to stimulate ethnoarchaeological research, to contribute to a new approach to the presentation of Sepik societies to the outside world, and to provide the materials for a reaffirmation of Sepik peoples' cultural identities.

For example, the results of a comparative analysis of pottery-making techniques in the Central Sepik and adjacent centers (Kaufmann n.d.; see also Kaufmann 1984a), linked to elements of oral history, have led me to postulate at least one common Sepik tradition of pottery making, with perhaps an early subdivision into central (Nggala, Sawos), and northern (Kwoma, Kwanga, Abelam), as well as derived intermediate (Dimeri, Aibom-Chambri) complexes, opposed to probably two other traditions documented on the north and northeast coast and elsewhere. This hypothesis needs to be tested archaeologically. Again, the historical knowledge still abundant in the area (see Schindlbeck 1984 for the Sawos, Wassmann 1984 for the Nyaula Iatmul, and Father Cherubim Dambui, personal communication, 1983) needs to be collected and assessed. A program specifically oriented toward an ethnoarchaeological inventory of settlements seems well worth establishing.

Better understanding of the complexities of symbolic action (e.g., exchange systems, rituals, performance of clan songs) could help to dispel stereotypes about traditional Sepik societies (simple technology, fierce head-hunting, etc.). Presenting the material aspects of their cultures in the context of the insights gained through detailed research by a variety of workers over a long period of time should make Sepik societies a very important example for worldwide comparison.

Every document of Sepik traditional life preserved in museums, whether abroad or in Papua New Guinea itself, adds to future generations' knowledge of their past and the roots of their identity. I maintain this position even though one could argue, as Milan Stanek has suggested, that objects kept in museums were from a Iatmul point of view pure form (saba), devoid of life (winsumbu), function, and meaning. Combining the evidence from various sources should clarify the history of the Sepik peoples. More research on museum collections is therefore needed; ours has been too limited so far to do more than suggest the range of possible benefits.

Notes

1. Counting sticks are used by Kwoma men to recall the amounts of bridewealth payments (see Kaufmann field photograph, Basel inventory no. [F]Vb

10792); counting ropes are used by Iatmul (Nyaula) men in connection with the singing of clan songs (Wassmann 1982:113).

2. The program's Swiss National Research Foundation project numbers were 1.593-0.77 and 1.328-0.81.

3. Beginning with a few isolated items collected before his time, the museum's collection dates to the last trip to Melanesia of Felix Speiser in 1930 and has been augmented by Alfred Bühler and René Gardi in 1955–56, Bühler and Anthony Forge in 1959, Forge in 1963, and Meinhard and Gisela Schuster and me in 1966–67. The material collected by Paul Wirz, another ethnographer from Basel, was divided between the museums in Bern (Bernisches Historisches Museum [see Kaufmann et al. 1979:246]) and Amsterdam (Tropenmuseum [see Wirz 1959]) and some private collections, as was his field documentation. The Basel collection also contains materials acquired from others, including missionaries and local timber dealers (see list of accessions in Kaufmann et al. 1979:158–67).

4. I thank Peter Gathercole, then curator of anthropology at that museum, for allowing Milan Stanek and Markus Schindlbeck access to Bateson's collection.

5. I propose a change in terminology whereby the Koiwat (or Kwaiwut-Kamanggaui) group is considered Southeastern Sawos, the Chimbian group Northeastern Sawos, the Gaikorobi group Eastern Central Sawos, the Torembi group Western Central Sawos, and the Burui (Wereman) group Western Sawos, thus realigning the Sawos and Iatmul dialect groups (cf. Staalsen 1975; Wurm and Hattori 1981:map 6; Schuster 1973).

6. Other objects may well have had ritual purposes as well. Weiss's notes on objects used by women in ritual contexts indicate that in the context of navin pantomimes almost any object used by either women or men for everyday purposes may carry symbolic meaning in the ritual. In the more sacred atmosphere of the rituals in men's houses, of course, things are quite different. Stanek (1983:256) rightly reminds us, however, that in the absence of the moving principle, *winsumbu*, material objects are mere form (*saba*).

7. Some texts are devoted to the documentation of the films made by Hermann Schlenker on behalf of the Institute for Scientific Film at Göttingen in 1973–74. A separate catalog of the 16-mm Sepik films made by the Institute is available. Additional films and printed commentaries on them are still in the process of being edited.

8. Adolf Roesicke (1881–1919), the only son of Dr. Richard Roesicke (a member of Parliament and owner of a brewery and property near Berlin), studied economics and law, then chemistry, physics, and geology, and earned his doctorate in chemistry at Freiburg im Breisgau in 1909. He traveled to East Asia and studied anthropology at Berlin, becoming a volunteer assistant at the museum there in 1910. After the Sepik expedition, he saw military service on the eastern front in 1915–18. Having begun work on the publication of the collection (Roesicke 1914), he died rather suddenly

of fever in 1919. (The facts of his life contrast with the belief that he was a lawyer, read his first anthropological book on the journey to Melanesia, and was killed in the first days of the war.)

9. According to a letter of January 1914 from P. Ahr in Friedrich-Wilhelmshafen to the Überseemuseum Bremen, "The carvings are from the village Tschesspandei and its vicinity, 210 nautical miles upstream. The clay pots are from Kararau, 168 nautical miles upstream. The clay plates are from Kaukagu [Kaulagu], 200 nautical miles upstream, right river bank, and from Timbunke. The human heads are all from Kambringi and its vicinity." The names of places refer to Behrmann's preliminary map, by Moisel, on which Kaulagu is not yet mentioned. I wish to thank Dieter Heintze of Bremen for finding this document and making it available to me; the translation is mine.

10. I thank Helga Rammow, Lübeck, and Heide Lienert, Hamburg, for providing me with the results of painstaking checks for collectors' numbers and documents.

11. According to Herbert Tischner (personal communication, 1978), when the war began these notes were taken, together with the bulk of the Hamburg collection, to a safe hiding place at Laufenthal in the Harz area. On one of the very last days of the war, Nazis set fire to the building in which they were housed (an old factory that belonged to Tischner's father). The notion that they were destroyed in the bombing of the Hamburg Museum, based on an assertion by C. A. Schmitz (Kaufmann 1979:313), is incorrect; the Hamburg Museum and the parts of the collection that remained there were not seriously damaged (cf. Zwernemann 1980:77 ff.).

12. These documents, together with all the negatives of field photographs taken by expedition members, are now housed at the Museum für Völkerkunde, Berlin-Dahlem. I wish to thank G. Koch and K. Helfrich for giving me access to the study collections and documentary material, K. T. Teichen, Leonberg, for bringing the Roesicke text to the attention of the anthropological profession, and W. Stoehr, Köln, for redirecting it to its proper place.

13. In the process of reassembling the original Roesicke collection, fourteen pieces acquired from A. Merk-Ikier, most of them Iatmul in style, were traced to Roesicke's original list. One of these, for example, is the male figure from the Central Sepik shown in Kelm's (1966*a*) figures 48 and 49, which had indeed been collected at Kararau, together with its female counterpart (Kelm 1966*a*: figs. 50, 51). Other pieces, however, were found to have been wrongly assigned by Kelm to free entries on Roesicke's list; for example, Roesicke's description does not match the small mask-like carving with apparent Lower Sepik traits said to be from Malu (Kelm 1966*b*: fig. 81). The painting in Kambot style assigned a Sapandei collection number (Kelm 1968: fig. 384) is another case in point, as is the painting said to be from Kubkain (Kelm 1966*b*: fig. 143), which in fact is part of Roesicke's No. 3394, a

suspension hook with painted protective panel acquired at the Kaulagu-Jaurangai camp.

14. Roesicke diary entries for April 15, 25, and 26 and May 9 and 20, 1913. Behrmann (1922) apparently made use of Roesicke's diary for his travel book. It is hoped that an ethnographic key to the Roesicke material will be produced.

Appendix

List of Manuscripts

Microfiches

1. Introduction
Kaufmann, C. Einführung und Aufbau (in prep.). Fiche Sepik-Dok. 1-01.

2. Iatmul collection
Obrist, B., et al. Iatmul-Objektkatalog. Fiche Sepik-Dok. 2-01 to 2-18.

3. Accompanying texts to the Iatmul collection
Stanek, M. Die Rolle der Objekte im Alltag am Beispiel der Iatmul von Palimbei (Mittelsepik). Fiche Sepik-Dok. 3-01.
Weiss, F. Kinder und Jugendliche aus Palimbei (Iatmul, Mittelsepik) als Handwerker. Fiche Sepik-Dok. 3-02.
Weiss, F. Maskenkostüme der Iatmul: Die *abwan*. Fiche Sepik-Dok. 3-03.
Stanek, M. Einführung in das Ritualsystem der Iatmul, Mittelsepik, Papua-Neuguinea (mit Verzeichnis der Ritualobjekte). Fiche Sepik-Dok. 3-04/ 05.
Weiss, F. Frauen und Rituale bei den Iatmul. (20 pp.) Fiche Sepik-Dok. open.
Weiss, F. Filmbeschreibungen und Informationen zu Super-8-Filmen über Iatmul aus Palimbei, Mittelsepik, Papua-Neuguinea, 1972–1974. (23 pp.) Fiche Sepik-Dok. open.
Schuster, M. and G. Filmbeschreibungen und Informationen zu Super-8-Filmen über Iatmul aus Aibom und Sotmeri, Mittelsepik, Papua-Neuguinea, 1972–1973. (6 pp.) Fiche Sepik-Dok. open.

Schmid, J., and Kocher-Schmid, C. Filmbeschreibungen und Informationen zu Super-8-Filmen über Iatmul aus Yensan, Palimbei und Nangusap, Mittelsepik, Papua-Neuguinea, 1972–1973. (5 pp.) Fiche Sepik-Dok. open.

4. Sawos collection
Schindlbeck, M., et al. Sawos-Objektkatalog (in prep.). Fiche Sepik-Dok. 4-open.

5. Accompanying texts to the Sawos collection
Schindlbeck, M. Aufschlagidiophone und Wasserstampfer der Sawos. (5 pp.) Fiche Sepik-Dok. 5-open.
————. Bestattung, Totenfest und *wundjumbu*-Figuren bei den Sawos in Gaikorobi, Mittelsepik, Papua-Neuguinea. (18 pp.) Fiche Sepik-Dok. 5-open.
————. Initiation bei den Sawos in Gaikorobi, Mittelsepik, Papua-Neuguinea. (24 pp.) Fiche Sepik-Dok. 5-open.
————. Krieg und Kriegführung der Sawos in Gaikorobi, Mittelsepik, Papua-Neuguinea. (9 pp.) Fiche Sepik-Dok. 5-open.
————. *wagan*-Trommeln und *abwan*-Masken der Sawos in Gaikorobi, Mittelsepik, Papua-Neuguinea. (7 pp.) Fiche Sepik-Dok. 5-open.
————. Weibliche Giebelfiguren von Männerhäusern bei den Sawos, Mittelsepik, Papua-Neuguinea. (7 pp.) Fiche Sepik-Dok. 5-open.
————. Filmbeschreibungen und Informationen zu Super-8-Filmen über Sawos aus Gaikorobi, Mittelsepik, Papua-Neuguinea, 1972–1974. (17 pp.) Fiche Sepik-Dok. 5-open.

Other Manuscripts
Schmid, J., and Kocher-Schmid, C. n.d. *Initiation bei den Zentral-Iatmul: Männerhausrituale in Yenshan, Palimbei und Kanganaman.* Basler Beiträge zu Ethnologie. In press.
Stanek, M. n.d. Einführung in das Wirtschaftssystem der Iatmul (inkl. Markttag in der vorkolonialen Zeit). (76 pp.)
Wassmann, J. n.d. Fünf Gesangszyklen: Kandingei, Nyaura oder West-Iatmul, Mittelsepik, Papua-Neuguinea. (719 pp.).

54/ Sepik Artifacts in the National and Provincial Framework

John Wasori

The Sepik region[1] has been contributing to the national economy since colonial days, when it was important in supplying labor for the coconut plantations of the New Ireland and New Britain Provinces and the goldfields of Wau and Bulolo in the Morobe Province. Many of the migrant workers stayed on after their contracts had expired and either married or had their families join them there. At the same time, many returned to their villages in the Sepik, bringing with them the knives, axes, blankets, etc., that they had received as payment for their labor, and the items distributed among their relatives encouraged other young men to go to work for the white man's goods. Despite the attraction of foreign goods, however, Sepik people, wherever they were, continued to produce their traditional carvings, increasingly destined not for ceremonial use but for sale.

Sepik art is as old as the cultures of the Sepik themselves, but it is rapidly losing its traditional value. In the course of the last half-century and especially the last decade, as a result of the activities of art dealers and collectors, it has been pouring out of the country like a flood. The National Museum, charged with protecting national cultural property, has for lack of funds and manpower often been unable to do so. It was only in October-November 1982 that Barry Craig, curator of anthropology at the museum, assisted by Wallace Ruff of the University of Technology's Village Studies Project, undertook the first survey of artifacts that might be designated national cultural property in the villages of the Middle and Lower Sepik River from Pagwi to the Murik Lakes (see Ruff and Ruff, Eoe, and Kaufmann in this volume). Reporting on the survey in the magazine of Air Niugini, Craig (1983) wrote, "As the international market for genuine old Papua New Guinea artifacts becomes hungrier, we may expect to see more and more attempts to remove these pieces from villages illegally. We trust we can be ready in time to stop them." Not long after his article appeared, a dealer in Angoram attempted to take a traditional men's house out of the country, but it was confiscated and is now preserved at the Sepik Arts Center in Wewak.

Sepik artifacts have become a commodity, and the demand for them on the international market is a valuable asset for Papua New Guinea. It is calculated that a hundred fifty thousand people throughout the country are involved in producing artifacts either full- or part-time. About eighty thousand of these are in the East Sepik, which produces over 85 percent of the artifacts. At one end of the scale are the true traditional artifacts, objects made within a traditional society for religious or secular use or for trade with traditional partners; sale of these is prohibited. Next come the pseudotraditional artifacts—objects that, though produced by artists brought up in the traditional culture, are intended for sale. A third type of artifact is "airport art"—stylized, mass-produced work, often employing imported materials, whose relation to the traditional culture is tenuous at best. Another is the artifact that combines traditional elements with individual creativity to produce new forms, such as Sepik cane furniture, made with tapa cloth from the Northern District. A final type of artifact is wholly introduced, such as weaving and the work of individual creative artists. All of these kinds of artifacts can be found in the East Sepik, but mass-produced objects are increasingly replacing pseudotraditional ones in the market.

For collectors—representatives of overseas galleries and curio shops, local field-based dealers, and local institutional dealers—the quality of an artifact is defined in terms of its ethnographic authenticity, aesthetic appeal, rarity, or some combination of these. Collectors concentrate on true traditional artifacts and pseudotraditional artifacts. Tourists, in contrast, tend to be looking for something that "captures the spirit of the primitive" or that is decorative, useful, or amusing. These casual buyers tend to be interested in small, inexpensive objects such as bows and arrows and wooden bowls. In the collectors' market, prices often vary widely with the perceived quality of the object, and the supply of objects is increasingly limited. In the tourist market, artifacts are fairly standardized and readily available throughout the country, and prices vary relatively little.

Over the years, national and provincial governments have been concerned with the artifact industry in one way or another. The National Cultural Property (Preservation) Act of 1965 restricts the transfer of "any property, movable or immovable, of particular importance to the cultural heritage of the Territory and including any object, natural or artificial, used for, or made or adapted for use for, any purposes connected with the traditional cultural life of any of the people of the Terrortory past or present" (see Eoe in this volume). The act provides for the acquisition by the government of objects designated national cultural property and requires an export permit before any item of the traditional culture is permitted to leave the country. (A 1970 amendment mandating the licensing of artifact dealers has not yet been implemented.) While the Department of the Prime Minister and Provincial Affairs has been concerned with the artifact industry through its efforts to enforce the act and through its responsibility for the activities of the National Cultural Council, district Departments of Commerce have been involved through the work of business-development officers, sponsorship of cooperatives trading in artifacts, and the promotional activities of the erstwhile Office of Tourism. The Departments of Foreign Affairs and Education have also played a role in the promotion and preservation of the arts.

Drawing on the experience of the Lus Development Corporation, the Sepik Producers' Cooperative Association, and Sepik Cocoa, the East Sepik Provincial Government has recently taken steps to establish a Sepik crafts industry that will link village producers of artifacts, through contract buyers, with workers in processing, packaging, and marketing in Wewak and Port Moresby. Each participant will purchase a single ten-kina share in the company, and there will be dividends estimated at 10 percent, rebates calculated on the basis of primary production by individual shareholders and the percentage of profits available for this purpose, and bonuses calculated on the basis of worker and management contributions to the industry and, again, the percentage of profits available. A maximum of seven directors will be drawn from the various categories of participants as follows: craft producers (two, on a district or a rotating basis as necessary), workers (one), East Sepik Development Corporation (one), East Sepik Provincial Government (one),

private enterprise (two). ESDECO will own one share in the company, hire any overseas staff required during the establishment phase, act as the conduit for any bank loan money and for any provincial or national moneys (to be considered soft loans) employed in the development of the industry, and, in cooperation with the director representing the provincial government, make sure that the company operates in accordance with the government's investment and industrial policy guidelines. The services to the industry of government officials, especially during the establishment phase, are to be strictly accounted for and considered a soft loan; this is especially important to ensure that the withdrawal of government support will not cause any hardship. The possible role of an umbrella management for the project remains to be discussed.

In 1983, K60,000 was allocated to establish the corporation, and the United Nations Development Program Office in Port Moresby was asked to second to it the volunteer who had been dealing with the purchase of artifacts in conjunction with the then Department of Commerce. A shop has since been opened in Wewak, and trial sales have proved encouraging. Direct exports have been made to Hong Kong, Guam, Vanuatu, and Hawaii. Arrangements are now being made to begin selling shares to producers.

Notes

1. What is meant by "the Sepik region" has varied over time. Before 1924, the whole Sepik basin was administered from Aitape. From 1924 to 1933, the area was subdivided into Aitape and Sepik Districts, north and south of the river respectively. In 1933 the two were reunited as the Sepik District; in 1967 they were redivided along the 143d meridian into the East Sepik Province (population 195,000), administered from Wewak, and the West Sepik Province (population 97,000), administered from Vanimo. With the introduction of provincial governments in 1976, the West Sepik became known as the Sandaun Province. The present discussion will focus on the East Sepik. According to the 1980 census, the East Sepik Province has a population of 220,000, of which 196,000 is rural-based. It is subdivided into four districts: Ambunti (pop. 27,553), Angoram (pop. 39,334), Maprik (pop. 99,875), and Wewak (pop. 59,128). It produces cacao, coffee, copra, and artifacts and will very soon be producing rubber.

55/ The National Cultural Property (Preservation) Act and the Art of the Sepik

Soroi Marepo Eoe

Many of the Europeans attracted to the Sepik in the last eighty years have been astonished by the richness and variety of its art, finding in it a combination of realism and extreme stylization with striking visual impact. By the 1930s, Sepik art had caught the imagination of the outside world, and so-called primitive art had become a commodity. It continues so today, to the detriment of Sepik culture. Whether it is being effectively protected is the topic of this paper.

Background

In the last decade or so, the protection of the cultural heritage of the world's peoples against theft, illegal purchase and sale, smuggling, and destruction has become a worldwide concern. The first legislation designed to protect Papua New Guinea's cultural heritage in fact dates to 1913: the Papuan Antiquities Ordinance of the British territory of Papua. How effective it was may perhaps be judged from the paucity of the present holdings of the National Museum and Art Gallery, the bulk of whose Papuan material has come to it through the recent repatriation of the Macgregor Collection (assembled before the ordinance was enacted) from the Queensland Museum in Australia. There is no record of any similar legislation in German New Guinea, and therefore it is possible that the material culture of the Sepik and Madang was subject to wholesale plunder.

The colonial administrators were of course interested in the raw materials the region offered and in civilizing its so-called primitive peoples, and direct colonial intervention to these ends had a profound effect on traditional[1] cultures. Under the new political order, the respect and status once enjoyed by the traditional leaders was undermined. Young men were taken away to work for long periods on plantations or government stations. Ceremonies could not be performed for lack of manpower, and the maintenance of ceremonial houses was neglected. Traditional ceremonial objects sometimes fell victim, moreover, to the extreme measures taken by the authorities to suppress rebellion. Still remembered after fifty-seven years, for example, is a punitive raid by the Australian colonial government on Pinang, a village an hour and a half by motorized canoe from Angoram and ten kilometers northeast of the present-day village of Moim in the East Sepik. In 1927, it is said, a raiding party from Pinang razed a village near what is now the Angoram-Wewak highway, killing several of its inhabitants. The government responded with a raid in which half of Pinang, including a very important tambaran house containing many priceless artifacts, was burned. The loss of these heirlooms, believed to have accompanied the ancestors of the Pinang and Moim people in their migration from Kopar in the Murik Lakes region, had a serious effect on the traditional culture. When I visited the area in 1981, few objects of religious or historical importance survived. All of the eight slit-gongs in use had come from Maramba or the Yuat River. Knowledge of wood carving was absent, as were the ceremonies that had once played a major role in the lives of these people. Rock bands were attracting young and old alike and killing any interest in the traditional songs.

Another source of acculturation pressure was the Christian missionaries, who condemned traditional beliefs and practices that went against the church's teachings. Hard-core converts were responsible for the destruction of tambaran houses and the abandonment of initiation rites in many places. Ritual objects that were discarded as a consequence of new religious convictions were burned, left in the open to deteriorate, or, in some cases, simply shipped to their home countries by the missionaries. (This might help explain why there are so many Papua New Guinean artifacts in European institutions.) Church and government have worked hand in hand, the church educating (or semieducating) manpower for government employment and the state providing the church protection. Neither has shown much concern for the cultural heritage of the host country.

Why Preservation?

Both in Papua New Guinea and among its Pacific island neighbors, the question is being asked why traditional culture should be preserved. As one of the South Pacific's best-known writers, Albert Wendt, has put it, "Is there such a creature as traditional culture? If there is, what period in the growth of a culture is to be called 'traditional'? ... Like a tree, a culture is forever growing new branches, foliage and roots. No culture is ever static and can be preserved like a stuffed gorilla in a museum!" (Wendt 1978:25). Museums are frequently criticized for being temples filled with the remains of dead cultures. It is argued that the artifacts preserved there have no significant role to play in changing societies and that the idea of preserving traditional culture is a Western import being forced upon indigenous peoples. Some of these critics see culture merely in terms of present and future life-styles and consider the traditional a hindrance to personal or national development. Funds for nation building should not be used to preserve traditional culture, they say, because it has no meaning today. Others link traditional culture with cannibalism, head-hunting, and other aspects of indigenous culture condemned by the churches.

From the point of view of the National Museum, preservation of traditional culture (and here we are referring to both its material aspects and the information associated with them) is important because of our obligation to the future and to the past. Museum collections can educate future generations about the way their ancestors lived, and they can be a point of departure for scientific research that leads to better understanding of past societies. Further, we preserve not just to educate or to satisfy scientific curiosity but because the masks, figures, slit-gongs, and tambaran houses bear witness to the history of the culture of Papua New Guinea, whose spirit they perpetuate and renew.

The National Cultural Property (Preservation) Act

The National Cultural Property (Preservation) Act of 1965 was designed to protect Papua New Guinea's cultural and natural heritage from theft, destruction, and illicit export. "National cultural property" includes objects considered to have played a significant religious, ceremonial, or historical role in the lives of the people who produced them: human remains (decorated skulls, fingerbones, tooth necklaces, etc.); ancient pottery or other archaeological remains; carved stone figures, monoliths, and painted or incised rocks; stone tools and weapons (axes, adzes, sago pounders, clubs, mortars, pestles, etc.); carved wooden objects made prior to December 1960; and any artifact incorporating bird-of-paradise plumes or the plumes of other protected species. Acquisition and transfer of such objects are restricted to the trustees of the National Museum, and violation of the law is punishable by a K400 fine or two months' imprisonment. Whether or not an item of national cultural property may be exported is subject to the following standards: (1) Is the object rare? (2) Is it likely to become rare in the immediate future? (3) Is this type of object comprehensively represented in the National Museum? (4) Does the object have aesthetic merit and exhibit a high level of craftsmanship? (5) Is it of significance to the local people? (see Smidt 1970:400).

Certain outstanding examples of traditional material culture (some of them sites of interest to prehistorians) have been designated "proclaimed national cultural property" by formal notice in the government gazette (see Swadling 1983b for a discussion of some problems in the definition of this category). Acquisition and transfer of items in this category are severely restricted.

Some objects currently manufactured for sale, among them pottery, wood, and stone carvings, are exempt from the provisions of the act.

The National Museum, as the institution entrusted with the task of preserving the nation's material culture, has been given the sole responsibility of implementing the act: identifying, designating, documenting, and conserving national cultural property and dealing with infractions of the law. Field research is conducted to inspect and document national cultural property and to recommend purchase if conditions warrant it. In the last ten years, efforts have been concentrated on the Sepik.

More than half of the approximately 26,000 items in the museum's collection come from the East Sepik, and most of these items, having been collected by nonprofessionals, have little or no accompanying documentation. We have come to view the documentation of these materials as a form of salvage research that may constitute the museum's most important contribution to cultural preservation in the next decade. A great deal of information is disappearing; old people are dying without having passed on their unique knowledge to the next generation. In many areas of the Sepik, access to secret knowledge (for example, the ritual for ensuring a good catch of fish or an abundant harvest of yams) depends on completion of initiation rites, membership in a particular kin group, fulfillment of certain obligations, performance of certain roles. Increasingly, the holders of this knowledge are dying without having found a suitable candidate to whom to entrust it. It is our conviction that, though some of the secret knowledge of our forefathers may have no meaning or function in contemporary Papua New Guinea society, it nonetheless should be an important part of the recorded history of the nation.

At the time, the museum has given considerable attention to the identification of objects of cultural and historical significance for designation as proclaimed national cultural property. By 1980 more than three hundred such objects had been so designated, and since 1981 my predecessor Barry Craig and I have documented another three hundred fifty objects from the East Sepik alone that await publication in the government gazette. More than seven hundred items (including archaeological sites, stone monuments, etc.) in all are on file or in the process of being declared proclaimed national cultural property. To safeguard these objects we have launched an effort to photograph and document them all in situ for a publication that will serve to spread information about them to a wider audience, both in the country and abroad, help the museum to monitor their preservation, and provide evidence for any legal action that may be necessary to effect the return of an item of national cultural property that has been taken out of the country illegally. Partial funding for this project has been granted by UNESCO, and the research and documentation aspects of it are under way. Milan Stanek, a volunteer from Basel, and his assistant, Greg Maisen, of Maprik, are photographing and documenting all the items of proclaimed national cultural property, identifying additional items of cultural significance to be recommended for such designation or for purchase, inspecting all items of national cultural property in situ, and enforcing the National Cultural Property (Preservation) Act in the field.

Problems of Implementation

Implementation of the act has been seriously hindered by lack of trained manpower and funds. During the last ten years the anthropology and prehistory departments of the museum have been forced to be content with two or at most three professional employees and inadequate funds for research and the purchase of artifacts. In 1984, for example, the amount allotted the museum for artifact purchase was K20,000. The inadequacy of this sum is apparent from the following example: When several years ago the men's house Wolimbit in Kanganamun on the Middle Sepik, a proclaimed national cultural property, was damaged by an earthquake, the museum sought to assist the villagers in repairing it. In the course of the discussion the owners offered to sell the posts of the house for K80,000, K40,000, or K20,000 each, depending on their size, a total of K900,000. Even after negotiation the price was still far beyond the museum's means. Art dealers are offering sums that the museum cannot match, and the owners of these objects will sell them to the highest bidder whenever they can. In many such cases the museum is forced to pay high prices simply to ensure that the objects will remain in the country. Thus limitations in staff and funds have serious implications for the museum's ability to implement the act to its fullest.

In 1980 an enforcement unit was established within the anthropology department to inspect national cultural property in the field, issue export permits, and prosecute individuals in violation of the act. In the year during which it functioned, this unit established contacts with the law enforcement units of other branches of government, such as the Bureau of Customs and the police, that had not existed before. Several offenders were apprehended and the objects in question confiscated through coordinated action by the museum's enforcement unit and customs officers. When the government declined to supply the museum with extra funds to finance the unit's activities, its functions were returned to the departments of anthropology and prehistory. It is clear, however, that not much can be done in this regard from the office.

Customs officers in centers such as Wewak, Madang, Lae, and Daru often have little or no knowledge about what is prohibited under the act. Furthermore, they can do very little when an export permit is involved, and the substitution of old objects for contemporary ones after a permit has been issued is a major problem. Again, many valuable pieces are leaving the country disguised as contemporary pieces. The technique of artificial aging developed in the Sepik and Madang Provinces to age newly manufactured objects—treatment with betel juice or by the blowpipe method—is now being used to mislead museum officials and their agents.

Organized smuggling of important cultural objects remains the museum's biggest problem. Large numbers of such objects continue to be taken out of the country by private plane and yacht through Daru, Wewak, Madang, Lae, and some highlands centers. The solution to the problem, we feel, is more trained employees with sufficient funds for regular field trips to monitor and control the situation. Despite our best efforts, we have been unable to persuade the authorities (the National Cultural Council and the government) to make this a priority.

Apart from the museum's limited ability to monitor objects of cultural significance is the frequent failure to prosecute offenders—sometimes for lack of sufficient evidence, sometimes because legal action is considered too costly in time and money. If the National Cultural Property (Preservation) Act is to be effective it must be strictly enforced.

Another area of concern to the museum is the destruction of archaeological and historical sites by multinational development projects—mining, logging, fish processing—supported by the national government. The gallant efforts of two archaeologists in opposition to this destruction are minuscule in comparison with the damage being done. Here any legal action by the museum to enforce the act would go against the wishes of the government, and in any case the penalties for defacing or destroying a site of archaeological interest are relatively small (K500 or six months' imprisonment).

A final problem area is tourism. The defunct Office of Tourism has recently been revived by the government under the umbrella of the National Cultural Council. Although an important source of revenue for the nation, tourism generally has a negative effect on its cultural heritage. For one thing, international art dealers, some of them prohibited from entering Papua New Guinea, come in disguised as tourists and smuggle national cultural property out of the country. For another, many tourists, unaware of the act, take protected objects out of the country without the museum's knowledge.

Conclusion

The success of the National Cultural Property (Preservation) Act in protecting the art of the Sepik is doubtful. Many objects of significant cultural value have been lost to the country despite its existence, largely because of a lack of manpower and funds for enforcement that reflects a lack of interest on the part of the government in cultural preservation. Investment in the preservation of its cultural heritage is, however, important to the nation's self-concept in a period of turbulent change. Ten years from now will be too late; men are dying and taking their traditional knowledge with them, and significant cultural objects are leaving the country never to return. The museum is to be commended for its efforts, however limited by lack of resources, but it will need adequate financial support if it is to carry out its mandate.

Notes

1. In recent years concern has been expressed about the use of the term "traditional," which some consider an anachronism. In this discussion it refers to the cultures that are indigenous to Papua New Guinea.

56/ Las Toktok Bilong Ol Masalai

Andrew Strathern

I was prompted to call these comments "Las tok-tok bilong ol masalai" by Milan Stanek's remark to me that the symposium for him had been like a meeting of ghosts—so many of us had not known anything about each other on a personal level before the conference, and one of the great positive outcomes of it is that now we do.

Ron May, who chaired the section that dealt with traditional and new forms of power and politics, made a rather successful job throughout the symposium of reminding anthropologists how narrow-minded they are and forcing us to look at matters at a slightly different level than the one we are used to. I see this business of scale, the level on which our generalizations are made, less as simply a fault than as something that can be converted into a productive tension between ourselves and the future fieldwork that we should do. A major topic raised in this section was signaled by the phrase "changes in the sources of authority," which came up in one of the discussion groups. Almost all anthropologists have said something about these changes and how they affect particular villages or clans. In highlands ethnography, the history of local government councils has become quite a favorite. It is interesting, though, that there appear to be fewer accounts of successes and failures in the council system for the Sepik, and I should like to see more, because this is one way into a discussion of what sorts of people are becoming leaders on the local scene and what sorts of linkages are being created, or failing to be created, nowadays between the local level and the provincial level.

In the 1960s I pointed out that introduced institutions such as councils were at that time often "subsidized" by the funds of power which the individual councillors brought to them from their participation in exchanges and other traditional activities. I should like to know how general that process was in the 1960s and how definite. It is characteristic of the processes of change widely in Papua New Guinea, not just in the Sepik, that, on the one hand, people are painfully keen to take up certain sorts of changes, and, on the other hand, there is enormous resilience in certain sorts of activities which went on before. One of the useful remarks about this was made by Wayne Dye when he said that while various kinds of cults come into and go out of fashion world view tends to be rather stable. This is another one of those generalizations which we should be trying to test on a broad scale in our anthropological work.

Looking at the background to change in this sphere of politics and power, one's attention is attracted by the wide range in the Sepik of different types of political structure, varying along the dimension of hierarchy versus equivalence. This variation must be correlated with different ways in which the new political institutions have impinged upon or have been adapted at local levels. It is an interesting thing for anthropologists to consider, and I would suggest that a sort of Sepik-political-systems volume—shades of other volumes of the past—should be written explicating this theme. Before such a volume could be usefully written, however, we would need, as for so many of these comparative tasks, a careful mapping of what we know.

Again and again we come back to the need for systematic area coverage of data, whatever the topic, from traditional to introduced forms of activity. There is a need, and we are almost to the point of taking up the challenge, to produce an ethnographic survey of the Sepik region—to handle the background data that are needed for so many other studies, to put them into circulation, to persuade people to provide those sorts of data, and to make sure that the things that are in anthropologists' and other people's notebooks but not yet published reach other scholars and people in Papua New Guinea in a form in which they can be used.

The Institute of Papua New Guinea Studies could be deputed to undertake a coordinating role in pushing forward this idea of an ethnographic survey. We could select a number of qualified people who would themselves coordinate particular topics that should be dealt with by all individual studies included in such a survey. One topic that should be included would be systematic sets of studies on land and land problems covering, as far as possible, as many cases within the East and West Sepik Provinces as we know about. After that, questionnaires could be constructed through consultation with people directly involved in this network. These question-naires could then be sent out to researchers with a request that they do what they could to supply unpublished information on the topics or full references to the publications in which they had been discussed. The Institute of Papua New Guinea Studies might assume the role of formally initiating requests for data and coordinating the way in which these data would be put together and then fed back to the scholars involved and, very important, to the national and provincial levels.

A point we have discussed here from time to time is how local and regional identities may be created or are being created. Very few of the papers for this symposium have dealt with mission history and activity, and yet I'm sure that all of you who have worked in particular parts of the Sepik know how significant and important this is in the everyday life and history of the people you have worked with. We seem a bit short of concepts and ideas in terms of which to discuss this, but I should like to suggest that missions and churches have been very important in creating various sorts of identity over time. Whether we agree with the identities that have been created or not is another question, but we have failed to pay sufficient attention to this and to the ways in which these identities are created in ways that run across traditional sorts of groupings. I have in mind that anthropologists should be as ambitious about this as they are about other studies of belief systems and expressive culture. They should aim at a proper internal understanding of what it means to a person to belong to a particular church and of the ritual ways in which that identity is created and supported, including the strong emotional dimension, which exists, especially for those who are taking up adherence to some of the newer churches that are replacing the older ones. Anyone whose fieldwork in Papua New Guinea is fairly recent will know what I'm talking about. The question of the influence of missions requires a more balanced assessment than we have given it.

This study of mission history and church affiliation should be put into counterpoint with the studies of shifts into and out of initiation cults and other kinds of activities that have been popular from time to time. I would like to see a comprehensive understanding by anthropologists of the intermesh of initiation cults, cargo cults, and versions of Christianity in local history. Anthropologists have things to say about this, but their data are a bit sketchy because they have tended to study what they liked themselves and not the

things they reacted against. We should try to overcome this tendency. A most valuable generalization about belief systems, which came out more than once, was that in Sepik societies power is always indigenously seen as based on *knowledge* rather than directly on *wealth*. It may be a bit difficult to make that distinction, but I believe we are thinking here of certain contrasts with the highlands region. If this generalization is correct, it can be a reason on the local level for *either* strong conservatism *or* rapid acceptance of change. This is one way to look at variations in the extent to which people have responded to influences of change. Variations will depend on which sources or kinds of knowledge are seen as possessing the most power to bring about valued results. A lot of comments have been made about this theme from time to time. I would see this, along with the study of what I would call ritual periodicities of various sorts of cults, as forming another interesting thematic volume. Someone interested in the twin topics of ritual and change ought to take up this area and go further with it, along with other conference participants.

Don Tuzin introduced the topic of person, gender, and enculturation as the high spot of the conference, but it seems we had difficulty with it. Looking back to our anthropological ancestors who worked in the Sepik area, we would hope that they would have smiled upon us and given us inspiration in this regard, but it looks as if we might have argued too much with them in the past and made them cross! Tuzin has offered a very interesting speculation that we really haven't followed up. It is about tension again—tension between opposites—a tension which he says is never quite resolved (a very Batesonian remark harking back to some of the early work). This, I think, is something that somehow did not get into all the discussions we had about person and gender. Others stressed, I think, the more familiar point about tension between teaching for autonomy and teaching for group participation. This is not a special feature of the Sepik; one of the very first books of the new wave of ethnography on the New Guinea highlands, by Marie Reay (1959), was subtitled *Freedom and Conformity in the New Guinea Highlands*. On this and many other topics there are excellent opportunities for comparing data from the Sepik with the equally extensive, equally rich, often parallel literature on highlands societies. This is not to say that the Sepik and the highlands are the same—I have discovered at this symposium the ways in which they differ—but simply to point out that there is a lot of useful work to be done, including questions of person and gender, male-female relationships, change in ritual, and so forth, where we could be getting more out of the comparative context.

I'd like briefly to refer to our attempts to explain the retention or rejection of initiation cults. These are obviously artistic performances and seem to have great meaning for people—yet at the same time people have a habit of throwing them away. Again, this is a pan–New Guinea problem. Anthropologists like paradoxes of this sort, and come up with quite good answers, but they should be systematized for a volume on ritual change. The men among us seemed to be the ones coming forward with explanations, mostly to the effect that initiation cults are a sort of cover-up for male inferiority complexes. I think that the women who heard this said, "Yes, that's quite right." I wonder if we shouldn't have argued a bit more about it; there are probably other explanations.

Another very interesting point which came out in discussion was Brigitta Hauser-Schäublin's argument that in the society she has studied, it is the men who keep setting up the oppositions and the women who keep bridging them. We might characterize this as a duality-versus-network ethnotheory of the society. I've searched many times in ethnographic discussions for really convincing examples of a male world view in some sense significantly different from the female one. I'm more inclined to trust this suggestion of Brigitta's because it's already present in some photographs and remarks made by Gregory Bateson with regard to how different the male ethos is from the female. I seem to remember a lovely picture of a couple of Iatmul women in a canoe, looking peaceful, as if they were enjoying themselves and life was in balance for them. How different this is from the volatile and somewhat uncontrolled ways in which men seem to have behaved in that society! More seriously, going back to that sort of psychological anthropology and projecting it onto a wider ethnographic canvas with the aid of Brigitta's more analytical restatement of it would provide some interesting comparative insights.

On the topic of social change, it is interesting how few of our studies have concentrated on socialization. There were only two papers about children, Kathy Barlow's and Florence Weiss's, and yet we have come to realize in our discussion of change how significant education, the introduced educational system, is and, even more significant, how this system spits people out after a certain period of time leaving them with nothing

to do with themselves back home any more. We know very little about the overall pattern of socialization and very little about the effects of formal education and the effects of being thrown out of the educational system, and yet these are matters which are of obvious significance nowadays in the Sepik area.

Running through a lot of our discussions has been a point that also, I think, goes back to Bateson: the importance in general of studies of communication. I'd like to suggest this as a major heading under which various projects for research for the future could be organized. It came out most strongly in the workshop on policy-oriented research, when we discovered that there wasn't really much argument any more that the substantive findings in anthropology and other social sciences can be of great use in policy planning. Everybody seemed to agree about that, but we had a lot of discussion and puzzlement about *how* these findings can effectively be communicated to decision makers. We discussed, for example, how anthropologists do or don't fit well into research teams that are involved directly in making policy suggestions. We discussed how we could set up better communications among ourselves between the national and provincial levels. We discussed how it might be necessary for us to write our findings in plain English—or have somebody else do it for us if we can't—in order that our findings be communicated to the people everybody agrees should hear them. In the course of doing this, it has turned out that we know very little about communication between new social categories of persons and others that have been studied more extensively by anthropologists from the start. A great deal of research waits to be done here on communication between the generations, between the sexes (an old theme of Sepik ethnography), between teachers and pupils, between politicians and constituents, between employers and employees—all sorts of dyads.

Like the others who have perorated, I would like to express my enjoyment of this occasion. It certainly has been a privilege for me, because I'm not a Sepik scholar at all. As one who is concerned with research all over Papua New Guinea and has worked a lot in the highlands, I have found it instructive to learn new details of the ethnography and what you do and don't know about your areas, and also to learn that the problems you have, whether you are academics or administrators or both, are really very similar to those in other regions of Papua New Guinea. This seems to me to indicate that the results of your work should be of significance not just within the Sepik but for anthropologists in general and for the people of Papua New Guinea themselves.

Harking back to more than twenty years ago, when I was a classical scholar of sorts, I want to remind you that "symposium" means "drinking together." We have drunk together in many different ways during this conference—not of the waters of Lethe but of the waters of Mnemosyne, remembrance of the work that others have done. And I think we have heeded Pope's admonition, "A little learning is a dangerous thing. Drink deep, or taste not the Pierian spring."

References Cited

ABRAMSON, J. 1970. Iwam style. *Art Forum* 9:54–57.

AGNELLA, M. 1972. *The story of the missionary Franciscan Sisters of the Immaculate Conception in Australia and New Guinea*. Brisbane: Clark and MacKay.

ALIYU, DANLAMI. n.d. Nigerian pottery tradition and new technique. *Pottery Quarterly* 52:151–89.

ALLEN, B. J. 1976. Information flow and innovation diffusion in the East Sepik District, Papua New Guinea. Ph.D. diss., Australian National University, Canberra, Australia.

———. 1977. Formal and informal information systems and rural change in Papua New Guinea. *Australian Geographer* 13:332–37.

———. 1981. "The North Coast region," in *A time to plant and a time to uproot*. Edited by D. Denoon and C. Snowden, pp. 105–27. Port Moresby: Institute of Papua New Guinea Studies.

———. 1983. A bomb or a bullet or the bloody flux? Population change in the Aitape Inland, 1941–45. *Journal of Pacific History* 18:218–35.

ALLEN, J. 1970. Prehistoric agricultural systems in the Wahgi Valley: A further note. *Mankind* 7:177–83.

ALLIED GEOGRAPHICAL SECTION, SOUTHWEST PACIFIC AREA. 1943. *Terrain study 65: Area study of Sepik District*.

———. 1944. *Terrain handbooks 17 (New Guinea, Wewak) and 18 (New Guinea, But)*.

AMBROSE, W. 1976. "Obsidian and its prehistoric distribution in Melanesia," in *Ancient Chinese bronzes and Southeast Asian metal and other archaeological artefacts*. Edited by Noel Barnard. Melbourne: National Gallery of Victoria.

ANDERSON, ROBIN, and BOB CONNOLY. 1983. *First contact*. New York: Film Makers' Library.

ANGELUS. 1936. Letter from Tumleo Island. MS, Bishop's Office, Diocese of Wewak.

ANTONISSEN, A. 1958. *Kadazan-English and English-Kadazan dictionary*. Canberra: Government Printing Office.

APPADURAI, A. 1988. "Introduction," in *Place and voice in anthropological theory*. Edited by A. Appadurai, pp. 16–20. Cultural Anthropology 3(1).

ARBUCKLE, GERALD A. 1978. "The impact of Vatican II on Marists in Oceania," in *Mission, church, and sect in Oceania*. Edited by James A. Boutilier, Daniel T. Hughes, and Sharon W. Tiffany, pp. 275–99. Ann Arbor: University of Michigan Press.

ARDENER, E. 1975. "Belief and the problem of women," in *Perceiving women*. Edited by S. Ardener. London: J. S. Dent.

ASIAN DEVELOPMENT BANK. 1976. *Appraisal of East Sepik Rural Development Project in Papua New Guinea*. Report PNG:Ap-4.

ASIS SAFIOEDIN, S. H. 1977. *Kamus Bahasa Madura-Indonesia*. Jakarta: Pusat Pembinaan dan Pengembangan Bahasa.

AUFENANGER, H. 1972. *The passing scene in North-east New Guinea: A documentation*. Vol. 1. St. Augustin: Anthropos Institute.

———. 1975. *The great inheritance in North-east New Guinea*. St. Augustin: Anthropos Institute.

———. n.d. *The passing scene in North-east New Guinea: A documentation*. Vol. 2. St. Augustin: Anthropos Institute.

AUSTIN, DIANE. 1983. Culture and ideology in the English-speaking Caribbean. *American Ethnologist* 10:223–40.

AUSTRALIAN NATIONAL UNIVERSITY DEPARTMENT OF ANTHROPOLOGY AND SOCIOLOGY 1968. *An ethnographic bibliography of New Guinea*. Vol. 3. Canberra: Australian National University Press.

BAFMATUK, F., B. EGLOFF, and R. KAIKU. 1980. Islanders: Past and present. *Hemisphere* 25(2):77–81.

BAILEY, F. G. 1971. "The management of reputations and the process of change," in *Gifts and poison*. Edited by F. G. Bailey, pp. 281–301. New York: Schocken Books.

BANKS, D. J. 1974. Malay kinship terms and Morgan's Malayan terminology: The complexity of simplicity. *Bijdragen tot de Taal-, Land- en Volkenkunde* 130: 44–68.

———. 1983. *Malay kinship*. Philadelphia: Institute for the Study of Human Issues.

BARBER, C. C. 1979. *A Balinese-English dictionary*. 2 vols. Aberdeen University Library Occasional Publications 2.

BARLOW, K. 1984. Social aspects of infant feeding in the Murik Lakes. *Journal of Nutrition* 21:342–63.

———. 1985a. The role of women in Murik trade. *Annual Review of Research in Economic Anthropology* 7:95–122.

———. 1985b. Learning cultural meanings through social relations: An ethnography of children in Murik Lakes society. Ph.D. diss., University of California, San Diego, La Jolla, Calif.

———. 1985c. "The social context of infant feeding in the Murik Lakes of Papua New Guinea," in *Infant care and feeding in the South Pacific*. Edited by Leslie B. Marshall, pp. 137–54. New York: Gordon and Breach.

BARNES, J. A. 1962. African models in the New Guinea highlands. *Man* 62:5–9.

———. 1971. "African models in the New Guinea highlands," in *Melanesia: Readings on a culture area*. Edited by L. L. Langness and John C. Weschler. San Francisco: Chandler.

BARNES, R. H. 1972. "Solorese," in *Ethnic groups of insular Southeast Asia*, vol. 1, *Indonesia, Andaman*

Islands, and Madagascar. Edited by F. M. Lebar, pp. 91–94. New Haven: Human Relations Area Files Press.

———. 1974. *Kedang: A study of the collective thought of an Eastern Indonesian people*. Oxford: Clarendon Press.

———. 1977. Alliance and categories in Wailolong, East Flores. *Sociologus* 27:133–57.

———. 1979. Lord, ancestor, and affine: An Austronesian relationship name. *Nusa* 7:19–34.

BARRETT, MICHELE, PHILIP CORRIGAN, ANNETTE KUHN, and JANET WOLFF. 1979. *Ideology and cultural production*. London: Croom Helm.

BARTH, FREDRIK. 1975. *Ritual and knowledge among the Baktaman of New Guinea*. New Haven: Yale University Press.

BARTHES, ROLAND. 1972. *Mythologies*. New York: Hill and Wang.

BASHAM, A. L. 1979. 3d edition. *The wonder that was India: A survey of the history and culture of the Indian sub-continent before the coming of the Muslims*. London: Sidgwick and Jackson.

BATESON, GREGORY. 1932. Social structure of the Iatmul people of the Sepik River. *Oceania* 2:245–91, 401–53.

———. 1935. Music in New Guinea. *The Eagle* (St. John's College, Cambridge) 48:158–70.

———. 1936. *Naven: A survey of the problems suggested by a composite picture of the culture of a New Guinea tribe drawn from three points of view*. London: Cambridge University Press.

———. 1958(1936). 2d edition. *Naven*. Stanford: Stanford University Press.

———. 1978. Towards a theory of cultural coherence: Comment. *Anthropological Quarterly* 51(1):77–78.

BEAZLEY, R. A. n.d. New Guinea adventure. MS.

BECKER, J. 1979. "Time and tune in Java," in *The imagination of reality: Essays in Southeast Asian coherence systems*. Edited by A. L. Becker and A. A. Yengoyan, pp. 197–210. Norwood, N.J.: Ablex.

BEHRMANN, WALTER. 1918. "Die Wohnstätten der Eingeborenen im Innern von Neu-Guinea," in *Festband Albrecht Penck*, pp. 324–39. Stuttgart.

———. 1922. *Im Stromgebiet des Sepik: Eine deutsche Forschungsreise in Neuguinea*. Berlin: A. Scherl.

———. 1924. Die Stammeszersplitterung im Sepikgebiet (Neuguinea) und ihre geographischen Ursachen. *Petermanns Geographische Mitteilungen* 70:61–65, 121–23.

———. 1933. "Die Dörfer im Innern Neuguineas," in *Die ländlichen Siedlungen in verschiedenen Klimazonen*. Edited by F. Klute, pp. 131–42. Breslau: T. Hirt.

———. 1950–51. Die Versammlungshäuser (Kulthäuser) am Sepik in Neu-Guinea. *Die Erde* 2:305–27.

BEIDELMAN, T. O. 1982. *Colonial evangelism: A socio-historical study of an East African mission at the grassroots*. Bloomington: Indiana University Press.

BEIER, U. 1976. *Haus tambarans* in Maprik: Revival or tourist attraction? *Gigibori* 3(1):20–30.

BELLWOOD, P. S. 1978. *Man's conquest of the Pacific*. Auckland: Collins.

BENJAMIN, G. 1976. "Austroasiatic subgroupings and prehistory in the Malay Peninsula," in *Austroasiatic studies*, pt. 1. Edited by P. N. Jenner et al., pp. 37–128. Oceanic Linguistics Special Publication 13.

BENTON, R. A. 1971. *Pangasinan dictionary*. Honolulu: University Press of Hawaii.

BENVENISTE, E. 1973. *Indo-European language and society*. Translated by E. Palmer. London: Faber and Faber.

BERNAL, IGNACIO. 1980. *A history of Mexican archaeology*. London: Thames and Hudson.

BERNDT, R. M., and C. M. BERNDT. 1951. Discovery of pottery in North-Eastern Arnhemland. *Journal of the Royal Anthropological Institute* 77: 133–38.

BETTELHEIM, B. 1962. *Symbolic wounds: Puberty rites and the envious male*. New York: Collier Books.

BIGGS, BRUCE. 1965. Direct and indirect inheritance in Rotuman. *Lingua* 14:383–415.

BISKUP, P. 1970. Foreign coloured labour in German New Guinea: A study in economic development. *Journal of Pacific History* 5:85–107.

BLOCH, MAURICE, and JEAN H. BLOCH. 1980. "Women and the dialectics of nature in eighteenth-century French thought," in *Nature, culture, and gender*. Edited by Carol MacCormack and Marilyn Strathern, pp. 25–42. Cambridge: Cambridge University Press.

BLUST, R. A. 1970. Proto-Austronesian addenda. *Oceanic Linguistics* 9:104–62.

———. 1974. A Muruk vocabulary, with a note on the linguistic position of Muruk. *Sarawak Museum Journal*, special issue, pp. 153–89.

———. 1976. Austronesian culture history: Some linguistic inferences and their relations to the archaeological record. *World Archaeology* 8:19–43.

———. 1977. "Sketches of the morphology and phonology of Bornean languages, 1, Uma Juman (Kayan)," in *Papers in Borneo and Western Austronesian linguistics*, vol. 2. Edited by C. Court, R. A. Blust, and F. S. Watuseke, pp. 9–122. Pacific Linguistics A 33.

———. 1979. Proto-Western Malayo-Polynesian vocatives. *Bijdragen tot de Taal-, Land- en Volkenkunde* 135:205–51.

———. 1980a. Early Austronesian social organization: The evidence of language. *Current Anthropology* 21:205–47.

———. 1980b. Notes on Proto-Malayo-Polynesian phratry dualism. *Bijdragen tot de Taal-, Land- en Volkenkunde* 136:215–47.

———. 1980c. Austronesian etymologies. *Oceanic Linguistics* 19:1–181.

———. 1984. On the history of the Rejang vowels and diphthongs. *Bijdragen tot de Taal-, Land- en Volkenkunde* 140:422–50.

BÖHM, K. 1983. *The life of some island people of New Guinea.* Edited by N. Lutkehaus. Berlin: Dietrich Reimer.

BORNEMANN, FRITZ. 1975. *Arnold Janssen: Founder of three missionary congregations.* Manila: Arnoldus Press.

BOWDEN, ROSS. 1983*a. Yena: Art and ceremony in a Sepik society.* Oxford: Pitt-Rivers Museum.

———. 1983*b.* Kwoma terminology and marriage alliance: The "Omaha" problem revisited. *Man* 18:745–65.

———. 1984. Art and gender ideology in the Sepik. *Man* 19:445–58.

———. 1985. Reply [to Kaufmann 1984*b*]. *Pacific Arts Newsletter,* no. 20, pp. 45–49.

BRAGGE, LAWRENCE. n.d. The evolution of Sepik land tenure. MS.

BRAUDEL, FERNAND. 1967. *Capitalism and material life 1400–1800.* New York: Harper and Row.

BRINEMAN BOVILL, K. J. 1985. Toba Batak relationship terminology. *Bijdragen tot de Taal-, Land- en Volkenkunde* 141:36–66.

BROOKS, J. A. 1965. Earthquake activity and seismic risk in Papua and New Guinea. *Journal of Tropical Geography* 38:1–6.

BROWN, PAULA, and GEORGIDA BUCHBINDER. Editors. 1976. *Man and woman in the New Guinea highlands.* Washington, D.C.: American Anthropological Association.

BÜHLER, A. 1946–49. Steingeräte, Steinskulpturen und Felszeichnungen aus Melanesien und Polynesien. *Anthropos* 41–44:225–74, 577–606.

———. 1957. Schmuck aus Muschel- und Schneckenschalen in Neuguinea. *Kosmos: Gesellschaft der Naturfreunde* 53:231–37.

———. 1960. Sepik: A dying culture. *Graphis* 87:68–75.

BULMER, S. 1973. *Notes on 1972 Wanlek excavations.* University of Auckland Department of Anthropology Working Paper in Archaeology 29.

———. 1977. "Between the mountain and the plain: Prehistoric settlement and environment in the Kaironk Valley," in *The Melanesian environment.* Edited by J. H. Winslow, pp. 61–73. Canberra: Australian National University Press.

———. 1982. Human ecology and cultural variation in prehistoric New Guinea. *Monographiae Biologicae* 42:169–206.

BULMER, S., and W. TOMASETTI. 1970. A stone replica of a bronze socketed axe from the Chimbu District of Australian New Guinea. *Papua New Guinea National Museum Record* 1(1):38–41.

BURRIDGE, K.O.L. 1959. Siblings in Tangu. *Oceania* 30:128–54.

———. 1960. *Mambu: A study of Melanesian cargo movements and their ideological background.* New York: Harper. (Also published as *Mambu: A Melanesian millennium* [London: Methuen, 1960].)

———. 1969*a. New heaven, new earth: A study of millenarian ritual.* New York: Schocken Books.

———. 1969*b. Tangu traditions: A study of the way of life, mythology, and developing experience of a New Guinea people.* Oxford: Clarendon Press.

———. 1971. *New heaven, new earth: A study of millenarian ritual.* London: Oxford University Press.

———. 1978. "Introduction: Missionary occasions," in *Mission, church, and sect in Oceania.* Edited by James A. Boutilier, Daniel T. Hughes, and Sharon W. Tiffany, pp. 1–30. Ann Arbor: University of Michigan Press.

———. 1979. *Someone, no one: An essay on individuality.* Princeton: Princeton University Press.

CABONCE, R. 1983. *An English–Cebuano Visayan dictionary.* Manila: National Book Store.

CAIRNS, I. J., D. TAKENDU, and G. SADLER. 1980. *Internal review of the East Sepik Rural Development Project, Papua New Guinea.* Konedobu: Department of Primary Industry.

CAMP, C. 1979. "A female initiation rite of the Neigrie area," in *Powers, plumes, and piglets: Phenomena of Melanesian religion.* Edited by N. C. Habel, pp. 68–83. Bedford Park: Australian Association for the Study of Religions.

CAMPBELL, JOAN. 1974. Northern neighbours: A Papua New Guinea experience. *Pottery in Australia* 13(2):43–48.

CAPELL, A. 1968. 3d edition. *A new Fijian dictionary.* Suva: Government Printer.

CARDEW, MICHAEL. 1976. *Michael Cardew: A collection of essays with an introduction by Bernard Leach.* London: Crafts Advisory Committee.

CARRO, A. 1956. *Iloko-English dictionary.* Translated and revised by M. Vanoverburgh. Manila.

CARY, I. 1976. *Orang Asli: The aboriginal tribes of peninsular Malaysia.* Kuala Lumpur: Oxford University Press.

CASEY, D. A. 1934. An uncommon type of stone implement from Australia and New Guinea. *Memoirs of the National Museum, Victoria* 8:94–99.

CHAMPION, I. F. 1967. *Across New Guinea from the Fly River to the Sepik.* London: Lansdowne Press.

CHAPPELL, J. 1982. Sea levels and sediments: Some features of the context of coastal archaeological sites in the tropics. *Archaeology in Oceania* 17(2):69–78.

CHEESMAN, [L.] E. n.d. (?1938). *The land of the red bird.* London: Herbert Joseph.

———. 1941. The mountainous country at the boundary, North New Guinea. *Geographical Journal* 98:169–88.

CHEESMAN, PATRICIA. 1980. Ceramics training and production: Project findings and recommendations. MS, United Nations Development Programme, International Labour Organisation.

CHODOROW, N. 1974. "Family structure and feminine personality," in *Woman, culture, and society.* Edited by M. Z. Rosaldo and L. Lamphere. Stanford: Stanford University Press.

CHRISTENSEN, O. A. 1975. A tanged blade from the New Guinea highlands. *Mankind* 10:37–39.

CLASTRES, P. 1977. *Society against the state: The leader as servant and the humane uses of power among the Indians of America*. Translated by Robert Hurley and Abe Stein. New York: Urizen Books.

CLAYRE, I. F. C. S. 1972. A grammatical description of Melanau. Ph.D. diss., University of Edinburgh, Edinburgh, Scotland.

CLIFFORD, JAMES. 1981. On ethnographic surrealism. *Comparative Studies in Society and History* 23:539–64.

CODRINGTON, R. H. 1891. *The Melanesians: Studies in their anthropology and folklore*. London: Clarendon Press.

COEDES, G. 1968. *The Indianized states of Southeast Asia*. Translated by S. B. Cowling. Honolulu: East-West Center Press.

COHEN, Y. A. 1964. *The transition from childhood to adolescence: Cross-cultural studies of initiation ceremonies, legal systems, and incest taboos*. Chicago: Aldine.

COIFFIER, CHRISTIAN. 1982. "Etude du village de Palimbei et des maisons cérémonielles de la vallée du fleuve Sepik," in *Architecture mélanésienne: Un inventaire de l'habitat vernaculaire des îles mélanesiennes*. MS, Unité Pedagogique d'Architecture 6, Paris.

———. 1983. "Maison des hommes: Maison masque ou maison masquée?" in *Océanie, le masque au long cours*. Rennes: Ouest France Université.

———. 1984. *Aspect de l'organisation sociale d'un village Iatmul perçu à travers une description de ses différents édifices*. Memoire de D.E.A., Ecole des Hautes Etudes en Sciences Sociales, Paris.

COLLIER, J. F., and M. Z. ROSALDO. 1981. "Politics and gender in simple societies," in *Sexual meanings*. Edited by S. B. Ortner and H. Whitehead. Cambridge: Cambridge University Press.

COLLINS, J.T. 1983. *The historical relationships of the languages of Central Maluku, Indonesia*. Pacific Linguistics D 47.

Conditions for affiliation to the Department of Anthropology and Sociology, UPNG, by foreign researchers. 1982. *Research in Melanesia* 6 (3–4):5.

CONKLIN, H. C. 1953. *Hanunóo-English vacabulary*. Berkeley: University of California Press.

CONSTANTINO, E. 1971. *Ilokano dictionary*. Honolulu: University Press of Hawaii.

COOK, E. A., and D. O'BRIEN. Editors. 1980. *Blood and semen: Kinship systems of highland New Guinea*. Ann Arbor: University of Michigan Press.

COX, E. 1979. "Gavien and Bagi: Rubber/profit vs. people/community," in *Going through changes: Villagers, settlers, and development in Papua New Guinea*. Edited by C. A. Valentine and B. Valentine, pp. 15–34. Port Moresby: Institute of Papua New Guinea Studies.

CRAIG, BARRY. 1968. Report to the Wenner-Gren Foundation on the Upper Sepik Ethnographic Expedition of 1968. MS.

———. 1969. Houseboards and warshields of the Mountain Ok. 3 vols. M.A. thesis, University of Sydney, Sydney, Australia.

———. 1970. Art styles of the Upper Sepik, New Guinea. MS.

———. 1983. Sepik treasures. *Paradise* 3:31.

CRANSTONE, B. A. L. 1972. "Material culture," in *Encyclopaedia of Papua and New Guinea*. Edited by Peter Ryan, pp. 715–40. Melbourne: Melbourne University Press in association with the University of Papua and New Guinea.

CRAPANZANO, VINCENT. 1981. "Rites of return: Circumcision in Morocco," in *The psychoanalytic study of society,* vol. 9. Edited by Warner Muensterberger and L. Bryce Boyer. New York: Psychohistory Press.

CROMBIE, LES. 1983. Museum mess: "We can't cope—close the door." *Post-Courier* (Port Moresby), September.

CURTAIN, R. L. 1976. *The 1974–75 Rural Survey: A study of outmigration from fourteen villages in the East Sepik Province*. Institute of Applied Social and Economic Research Discussion Paper 3.

———. 1978. Labour migration from the Sepik. *Oral History* 6(9):1–114.

———. 1980. Dual dependence and Sepik labour migration. Ph.D. diss., Australian National University, Canberra, Australia.

CURTAIN, R. L., and R. J. MAY. 1979. "Wewak," in *The Urban Household Survey: Town profiles*. Edited by R. J. May, pp. 52–67. Institute of Applied Social and Economic Research Monograph 12.

———. 1980. *A report to the East Sepik Provincial Government on the social impact of the East Sepik Rural Development Project*. Institute of Applied Social and Economic Research Special Publication 2.

DARK, PHILIP J. C. 1979. "The art of the peoples of western New Britain and their neighbors," in *Exploring the visual art of Oceania*. Edited by Sydney M. Mead, pp. 130–58. Honolulu: University Press of Hawaii.

DAVIS, HARRY. 1975. Guest of honour, from the ABC's broadcast, May 1975. *Pottery in Australia* 14(2):25–29.

———. 1983. Why "projects" in developing countries? MS.

DEMPWOLFF, O. 1969. *Vergleichende Lautlehre des Austronesischen Wortschatzes*. Vol. 3. *Austronesisches Wörterbuch*. Nendeln: Kraus.

DENTAN, R. K. 1970. Hocus pocus and extensionism in Central Malaya: Notes on Semai kinship terminology. *American Anthropologist* 72:358–62.

———. 1979. *The Semai: A nonviolent people of Malaya*. New York: Holt, Rinehart and Winston.

DEPARTMENT OF INFORMATION AND EXTENSION SERVICES. 1972. *Districts of Papua New Guinea 1972*. Port Moresby: Government Printer.

DEWDNEY, M. S. 1965. "The Maprik Open Electorate," in *The Papua New Guinea elections 1964*. Edited by D. G. Bettison, C. A. Hughes, and P. S. van der Veur, pp. 181–93. Canberra: Australian National University Press.

DEXTER, D. 1961. *Australia in the war of 1939–1945: The New Guinea offensives*. Canberra: Australian War Memorial.

DIFFLOTH, C. F. 1974. "Austroasiatic languages," in *Encyclopaedia Britannica*, Macropaedia, vol. 2.

DJAMOUR, J. 1959. *Malay kinship and marriage in Singapore*. London School of Economics Monographs on Social Anthropology 21.

DOCKER, E. W. 1970. *The blackbirders: The recruiting of South Seas labour for Queensland, 1863–1907*. Sydney: Angus and Robertson.

DORNSTREICH, M. 1974. *An ecological study of Gadio Enga (New Guinea) subsistence*. Ann Arbor: University Microfilms.

DOUGLAS, M. 1966. *Purity and danger*. London: Routledge and Kegan Paul.

DOUGLAS, R. S. 1911. A comparative vocabulary of the Kayan, Kenyah, and Kelabit. *Sarawak Museum Journal* 1:75–119.

DREWES, G. W. J. 1968. New light on the coming of Islam to Indonesia. *Bijdragen tot de Taal-, Land- en Volkenkunde* 124:433–59.

DROBEC, E. 1954. Zur Pflanzenmedizin der Naturvölker. *Paideuma* 6:55–59.

DUNDES, A. 1976. A psychoanalytic study of the bullroarer. *Man* 11:220–38.

DYE, T. WAYNE. 1984. Toward a theology of power for Melanesia. *Catalyst*, nos. 1 and 2.

DYE, T. WAYNE, P. TOWNSEND, and W. TOWNSEND. 1968. The Sepik Hill languages: A preliminary report. *Oceania* 39:146–56.

DYEN, I. 1965a (1963). *A lexicostatistical classification of the Austronesian languages*. International Journal of American Linguistics Memoir 19.

———. 1965b. *A sketch of Trukese grammar*. New Haven: American Oriental Society.

ECHALES, J. M., and H. SHANDILY. 1975. *An English-Indonesian dictionary*. Ithaca: Cornell University Press.

EGEROD, S. 1980. *Atayal-English dictionary*. 2 vols. London: Curzon Press.

EGGAN, FRED. 1960. "The Sagada Igorots of Northern Luzon," in *Social structure in Southeast Asia*. Edited by G. P. Murdock, pp. 24–50. Viking Fund Publications in Anthropology 29.

EGLOFF, B. J. 1975. *Archaeological investigations in the coastal Madang area and on Eloaue Island of the St. Matthias group*. Papua New Guinea National Museum Record 5.

EIBY, G. A. 1957. *Earthquakes*. London: Frederick Muller.

ELKINS, R. E. 1968. *Manobo-English dictionary*. Oceanic Linguistics Special Publication 3.

———. 1979. *Batek Negrito religion: The world-view and rituals of a hunting and gathering people of peninsular Malaysia*. Oxford: Clarendon Press.

ENDICOTT, K. M. 1979. *Batak Negrito religion*. Oxford: Clarendon Press.

EPSTEIN, T. S. 1970. "Indigenous entrepreneurs and their narrow horizon," in *The indigenous role in business enterprise*. Edited by Marion W. Ward, pp. 16–26. New Guinea Research Bulletin 35.

ERRINGTON, FREDERICK. 1974a. Indigenous ideas of order, time, and transition in a New Guinea cargo movement. *American Ethnologist* 1:255–67.

———. 1974b. *Karavar: Masks and power in a Melanesian ritual*. Ithaca: Cornell University Press.

ERRINGTON, FREDERICK, and DEBORAH GEWERTZ. n.d. Myths of matriarchy reconsidered: The ideological components of social order. MS.

FAITHORN, ELIZABETH. 1975. "The concept of pollution among the Kafe of the Papua New Guinea highlands," in *Towards an anthropology of women*. Edited by Rayna Reiter, pp. 127–41. New York: Monthly Review Press.

FATIMI, S. Q. 1963. *Islam comes to Malaysia*. Singapore: Malaysian Sociological Research Institute.

FEIL, DARYL. 1978. Women and men in the Enga Te. *American Ethnologist* 5:265–79.

———. 1984. *Ways of exchange*. St. Lucia: University of Queensland Press.

FENNER, F. J. 1941. Fossil human skull fragment of probably Pleistocene age from Aitape, New Guinea. *South Australian Museum Records* 6:335–54.

FESTINGER, LEON, H. W. RIECKEN, and H. SCHACHTER. 1956. *When prophecy fails*. Minneapolis: University of Minnesota Press.

FINNEY, BEN R., 1973. *Big-men and business: Entrepreneurship and economic growth in the New Guinea highlands*. Honolulu: University Press of Hawaii.

FISCHER, J. L. 1971. "Art styles as cultural cognitive maps," in *Anthropology and art*. Edited by Charlotte M. Otten. New York: Doubleday.

FITZGERALD, T. K. Editor. 1977. *Nutrition and anthropology in action*. Assen/Amsterdam: Van Gorcum.

FITZPATRICK, P. 1980. *Law and state in Papua New Guinea*. New York: Academic Press.

FLINDERS, M. 1803. *Voyage to Terra Australia*. Vol. 2.

FORGE, ANTHONY. 1962. Paint: A magical substance. *Palette*, no. 9, pp. 9–16.

———. 1966. "Art and environment in the Sepik." *Proceedings of the Royal Anthropological Institute of Great Britain and Ireland for 1965*, pp. 23–31.

———. 1967. "The Abelam artist," in *Social organisation: Essays presented to Raymond Firth*. Edited by M. Freedman, pp. 65–84. London: Frank Cass.

———. 1970a. "Prestige, influence, and sorcery: A New Guinea example," in *Witchcraft confessions and accusations*. Edited by M. Douglas, pp. 257–75. London: Tavistock.

———. 1970b. "Learning to see in New Guinea," in *Socialisation: The approach from social anthropology*. Edited by P. Mayer, pp. 269–91. London: Tavistock.

———. 1971. "Marriage and exchange in the Sepik: Comments on Francis Korn's analysis of Iatmul society," in *Rethinking kinship and marriage*. Edited by Rodney Needham, pp. 133–44. London: Tavistock.

———. 1972a. "Normative factors in the settlement size of Neolithic cultivators (New Guinea)," in *Man, settlement, and urbanism*. Edited by P. J. Ucko, R. Tringham, and G. W. Dimbleby. London: Duckworth.

———. 1972b. The golden fleece. *Man* 7:527–40.

———. 1972c. "Tswamung: A failed big-man," in *Crossing cultural boundaries: The anthropological experience*. Edited by Solon T. Kimball and James B. Watson, pp. 257–73. San Francisco: Chandler.

———. 1973. "Style and meaning in Sepik art," in *Primitive art and society*. Edited by A. Forge, pp. 170–92. London: Oxford University Press for the Wenner-Gren Foundation.

———. 1977. Internal exchange and external trade in the Sepik. Paper presented to the Symposium on Trade and Exchange in Oceania, The Australian Museum, Sydney, Australia.

———. 1979. "The problem of meaning in art," in *Exploring the visual art of Oceania*. Edited by Sydney M. Mead, pp. 278–86. Honolulu: University Press of Hawaii.

FORTES, M. 1962. "Ritual and office in tribal society," in *Essays on the ritual of social relations*. Edited by D. Forde et al. Manchester: Manchester University Press.

FORTH, G. L. 1981. *Rindi: An ethnographic study of a traditional domain in eastern Sumba*. Verhandelingen van het Koninklijk Instituut voor Taal-, Land- en Volkenkunde 93.

FORTUNE, R. F. 1939. Arapesh warfare. *American Anthropologist* 41:22–41.

———. 1942. *Arapesh*. Publications of the American Ethnological Society 19.

———. 1977 (1942). *Arapesh*. New York: AMS Press.

———. n.d. Field notes, University of Auckland, Auckland, New Zealand.

FOSTER-CARTER, A. 1978. "Can we articulate 'articulation'?" in *The new economic anthropology*. Edited by J. Clammer, pp. 210–49. London: Macmillan.

FOUNTAIN, O. C. 1966. *Wulukum: Land, livelihood, and change in a New Guinea village*. M. A. thesis, Victoria University, Wellington, New Zealand.

FREEMAN, J. D. 1960. "The Iban of western Borneo," in *Social structure in Southeast Asia*. Edited by G. P. Murdock, pp. 65–87. Viking Fund Publications in Anthropology 29.

FREUDENBURG, A. 1976. *The dialects of Boiken*. Ukarumpa: Summer Institute of Linguistics.

FRIEDERICI, G. 1909. Deutsch-Neuguinea: Die Expedition Sapper-Friederici. *Deutsches Kolonialblatt* 20:331–36.

FUSSELL, PAUL. 1975. *The Great War and modern memory*. London: Oxford University Press.

GALIS, K. W., and F. C. KAMMA. 1958. Het fort te Jembekaki. *Nieuw-Guinea Studiën* 2:206–22.

GALVIN, A. D. 1967. *A Kenyah vocabulary*.

GARDI, R. 1958. *Sepik*. Zürich.

GARNAUT, R., M. WRIGHT, and R. L. CURTAIN. 1977. *Employment, incomes, and migration in Papua New Guinea towns*. Institute of Applied Social and Economic Research Monograph 6.

GEERTZ, H. 1961. *The Javanese family: A study of kinship and socialization*. New York: Free Press of Glencoe.

GEERTZ, H., and C. GEERTZ. 1975. *Kinship in Bali*. Chicago: University of Chicago Press.

GELL, A. 1975. *The metamorphosis of the cassowaries: Umeda society, language, and ritual*. London School of Economics Monographs on Social Anthropology 51.

———. 1979. "Reflections on a cut finger: Taboo in the Umeda conception of the self," in *Fantasy and symbol*. London: Academic Press.

GELLNER, ERNEST. 1964. *Thought and change*. Chicago: University of Chicago Press.

GERSTNER, A. 1952. Der Geisterglaube im Wewäk-Boikin-Gebiet Nordost-Neuguineas. *Anthropos* 47:795–821.

———. n.d. "The spirit cult in the Wewak-Boiken area of northeast New Guinea," in *The Boiken people of the East Sepik Province, Papua New Guinea: The writings of Andreas Gerstner*. Edited by R. J. May and P. B. Roscoe; translated by C. Smith. In preparation.

GESCH, P. F. 1985. *Initiative and initiation*. Studia Instituti Anthropos 33.

GEWERTZ, DEBORAH. 1977a. From sago suppliers to entrepreneurs: Marketing and migration in the Middle Sepik. *Oceania* 48:126–40.

———. 1977b. The politics of affinal exchange: Chambri as a client market. *Ethnology* 16:285–98.

———. 1977c. On whom depends the action of the elements: Debating among the Chambri. *Journal of the Polynesian Society* 86:339–53.

———. 1977d. *Exchange spheres among the Chambri people*. Ann Arbor: University Microfilms.

———. 1978a. Myth, marriage, and murder among the Chambri of Papua New Guinea. Paper presented to the 77th annual meeting of the American Anthropological Association, Los Angeles, Calif.

———. 1978b. Tit for tat: Barter markets in the Middle Sepik. *Anthropological Quarterly* 51(1):37–44.

———. 1978c. The myth of the blood-men: An explanation of Chambri warfare. *Journal of Anthropological Research* 34:577–88.

———. 1980a. Report on *Salvinia molesta* in the Sepik. *Cultural Survival*, Winter.

———. 1980b. Of symbolic anchors and sago soup: The rhetoric of exchange among the Chambri of Papua New Guinea. *Journal of the Polynesian Society* 89:309–28.

———. 1981. A historical reconsideration of female dominance among the Chambri of Papua New Guinea. *American Ethnologist* 8:94–108.

———. 1982. "The father who bore me: The role of *tsambunwuro* during Chambri initiation ceremonies," in *Rituals of manhood*. Edited by G. H. Herdt, pp. 286–320. Berkeley: University of California Press.

———. 1983. *Sepik River societies: A historical ethnography of the Chambri and their neighbors*. New Haven and London: Yale University Press.

———. 1985. "The Golden Age revisited: A history of the Chambri between 1905 and 1927," in *The history and ethnohistory of New Guinea*. Edited by Edward Schieffelin and Deborah Gewertz. Sydney: Oceania Publications.

GILES, W. E. 1968. *A cruise in a Queensland labour vessel to the South Seas*. Canberra: Australian National University Press.

GILL, E. D. 1968. Significance of Aitape (New Guinea) radiocarbon dates for eustasy and tectonics. *Australian Journal of Science* 30(4):142.

GILLIARD, E. T. 1969. *Birds of paradise and bower birds*. London: Weidenfeld and Nicolson.

GIMLETTE, J. D. 1971. *Malay poisons and charm cures*. Kuala Lumpur: Oxford University Press.

GLASGOW, D., and R. LOVING. 1969. *Languages of the Maprik Sub-District*. Port Moresby: Department of Information and Extension Services.

GLICK, LEONARD B. 1972. "Sangguma," in *Encyclopaedia of Papua and New Guinea*. Edited by Peter Ryan, pp. 1029–30. Melbourne: Melbourne University Press in association with the University of Papua and New Guinea.

GODELIER, M. 1976. "Le sexe comme fondement ultime de l'ordre social et cosmique chez les Baruya de Nouvelle-Guinée," in *Sexualité et pouvoir*. Edited by A. Verdiglione, pp. 268–306. Paris: Traces Payot.

———. 1982a. *La production des Grands Hommes: Pouvoir et domination masculine chez les Baruya de Nouvelle-Guinée*. Paris: Fayard.

———. 1982b. "Social hierarchies among the Baruya," in *Inequality in New Guinea highland societies*. Edited by A. Strathern, pp. 3–34. Cambridge: Cambridge University Press.

GOLDMAN, I. 1970. *Ancient Polynesian society*. Chicago: University of Chicago Press.

GOLSON, JACK, R. J. LAMPERT, and N. D. ORAM. 1969. "Sources for a history of the Port Moresby region: Introduction." *The history of Melanesia: Second Waigani Seminar*, pp. 401–41. Canberra: Research School of Pacific Studies.

GONDA, J. 1973 (1952). 2d edition. *Sanskrit in Indonesia*. New Delhi: International Academy of Indian Culture.

GOOD, KENNETH. 1979. "The formation of the peasantry," in *Development and dependency: The political economy of Papua New Guinea*. Edited by Azeem Amarshi, Kenneth Good, and Rex Mortimer, pp. 101–22. Melbourne: Oxford University Press.

GOODALE, JANE. 1981. "Siblings as spouses: The reproduction and replacement of Kaulong society," in *Siblingship in Oceania*. Edited by Mac Marshall, pp. 275–306. Ann Arbor: University of Michigan Press.

GOODENOUGH, W. H. 1955. A problem in Malayo-Polynesian social organization. *American Anthropologist* 57:71–83.

———. 1956. Reply to Frake. *American Anthropologist* 58:173–75.

GOODMAN, M. E. 1973. *The culture of childhood*. New York: Teachers College Press.

GORDON, ROBERT. 1983. The decline of the kiapdom and resurgence of "tribal fighting" in Enga. *Oceania* 53:205–23.

GORLIN, P. N. 1973. Health, wealth, and agnation among the Abelam: The beginnings of social stratification in New Guinea. Ph.D. diss., Columbia University, New York, N.Y.

GOULET, D. 1971. *The cruel choice: A new concept in the theory of development*. New York: Atheneum.

GRABER, R. B. 1981. A psychocultural theory of male genital mutilation. *Journal of Psychoanalytic Anthropology* 4:413–34.

GRACE, G. W. 1969. "A Proto-Oceanic finder list," in *Working papers in linguistics*, pp. 39–84.

GREALY, KEVIN. 1977. Barambah Pottery, Cherbourg. *Pottery in Australia* 16(2):3–7.

GREEN, A. 1977. "Atome de parenté et relations oedipiennes," in *L'identité: Séminaire interdisciplinaire 1974–1975*. Edited by C. Lévi-Strauss, pp. 81–107. Paris: B. Grasset.

GREENBERG, J. H. 1971. "The Indo-Pacific hypothesis," in *Current trends in linguistics*, vol. 8, *Linguistics in Oceania*. Edited by T. A. Sebeok, pp. 807–71. The Hague: Mouton.

GRIFFITH, J., H. NELSON, and S. FIRTH. 1979. *Papua New Guinea: A political history*. Richmond, Victoria: Heinemann.

GROSSMAN, LAWRENCE S. 1983. Cattle, rural economic differentiation, and articulation in the highlands of Papua New Guinea. *American Ethnologist* 10:56–76.

GUILFORD, VIRGINIA. 1982. Oksapmin trade stores. Paper presented to the annual meeting of the Association for Social Anthropology in Oceania, Hilton Head Island, S.C.

HAANTJENS, H. A. 1965. Morphology and origin of patterned ground in a humid tropical lowland area, New Guinea. *Australian Journal of Soil Research* 3:111–29.

———. 1969. Fire and wind erosion or earthworms as the cause of microrelief in the Lower Sepik plains, New Guinea. *Australian Journal of Science* 32:52–54.

———. Compiler. 1972. *Lands of the Aitape-Ambunti area, Papua New Guinea*. Commonwealth Scientific and Industrial Research Organization Land Research Series 30.

HAANTJENS, H. A., and P. BLEEKER. 1970. Tropical weathering in the Territory of Papua New Guinea. *Australian Journal of Soil Research* 8:157–77.

HAANTJENS, H. A., J. A. MABBUTT, and R. PULLEN. 1965. Environmental influences in anthropogenic grasslands in the Sepik plains. *Pacific Viewpoint* 6:215–19.

HAANTJENS, H. A., E. REINER, and R. G. ROBBINS. 1968. "Land systems of the Wewak–Lower Sepik area," in *Lands of the Wewak–Lower Sepik area, Territory of Papua and New Guinea*. Edited by H. A. Haantjens, pp. 15–48. Melbourne: Commonwealth Scientific and Industrial Research Organization.

HABERLAND, EIKE 1965. Tasks of research in the Sepik region, New Guinea. *Bulletin of the International Committee on Urgent Anthropological and Ethnological Research* 7:33–44.

———. 1966. Beschnitzte Pfosten des Männerhauses munsimbit (Dorf Kanganamun am Sepik) in den Völkerkunde-Museen Stuttgart und Frankfurt. *Tribus* 15:21–46.

HABERLAND, E., and S. SEYFARTH. 1974. *Die Yimar am oberen Korowori (Neuguinea)*. Wiesbaden: Franz Steiner.

HADDON, A. C. 1947. Smoking and tobacco pipes in New Guinea. *Philosophical Transactions of the Royal Society of London* B232:1–278.

HAGE, P. 1981. On male initiation and dual organisation in New Guinea. *Man* 16:268–75.

HAGSPIEL, BRUNO. 1926. *Along the mission trail*. Vol. 3. *In New Guinea*. Techny, Ill.: Mission Press.

HALL, D. G. E. 1968. 3d edition. *A history of South East Asia*. London: Macmillan.

HAPIP, ABDUL DJEBAR. 1977. *Kamus Banjar-Indonesia*. Jakarta: Pusat Pembinaan dan Pengembangan Bahasa.

HARDING, T. G. 1967. *Voyagers of the Vitiaz Strait*. Seattle: University of Washington Press.

HARRISON, SIMON. 1982a. Yams and the symbolic representation of time in a Sepik River village. *Oceania* 53:141–61.

———. 1982b. Stealing people's names: Social structure, cosmology, and politics in a Sepik River village. Ph.D. diss., Australian National University, Canberra, Australia.

———. 1983. *Laments for foiled marriages: Lovesongs from a Sepik River village*. Port Moresby: Institute of Papua New Guinea Studies.

HARRISSON, T. 1970. *The Malays of South-West Sarawak before Malaysia: A socio-ecological survey*. London: Macmillan.

HAUSER-SCHÄUBLIN, BRIGITTA. 1976–81. Mai-Masken der Iatmul: Stil, Schnitzvorgang, Auftritt und Funktion (mit einem Nachtrag). *Verhandlungen der Naturforschenden Gesellschaft in Basel* 87–88:119–45, 92:47–54.

———. 1977. *Frauen in Kararau: Zur Rolle der Frau bei den Iatmul am Mittelsepik, Papua New Guinea*. Basler Beiträge zur Ethnologie 18.

———. 1983. "Abelam," in *Menschenbilder früher Gesellschaften*. Edited by K. E. Müller, pp. 178–203. Frankfurt/New York: Campus Verlag.

———. n.d. *Kulthäuser in Nordneuguinea*. 2 vols. Abhandlungen und Berichte des Staatlichen Museums für Völkerkunde Dresden. In press.

HAYS, T. E., and P. H. HAYS. 1982. "Opposition and complementarity of the sexes in Ndumba initiation," in *Rituals of manhood*. Edited by G. H. Herdt, pp. 201–38. Berkeley: University of California Press.

HEALEY, P., and A. HEALEY. 1977. *Telefol dictionary*. Pacific Linguistics C 46.

HEMPENSTALL, P. J. 1978. *Pacific islanders under German rule: A study in the meaning of colonial resistance*. Canberra: Australian National University Press.

HERDT, G. H. 1981. *Guardians of the flutes: Idioms of masculinity*. New York: McGraw-Hill.

———. 1982. "Fetish and fantasy in Sambia initiation," in *Rituals of manhood*. Edited by G. H. Herdt, pp. 44–98. Berkeley: University of California Press.

HOGBIN, G. R. 1963. Erap mechanical farming project. *Australian Territories* 3:10–15.

HOGBIN, I. 1935. Native culture of Wogeo: Report of fieldwork in New Guinea. *Oceania* 5:308–37.

———. 1958. *Social change*. London: Watts.

———. 1964. Wogeo kinship terminology. *Oceania* 34:308–9.

———. 1970. *Island of menstruating men*. Scranton, Pa.: Chandler.

———. 1978. *The leaders and the led: Social change in Wogeo, New Guinea*. Carlton, Victoria: Melbourne University Press.

HOGBIN, H. I., and C. H. WEDGWOOD. 1953. Local groupings in Melanesia. *Oceania* 23:241–76.

HÖLTKER, GEORG VON. 1940–41. Einiges über Steinkeulenköpfe und Steinbeile in Neuguinea. *Anthropos* 35–36:681–736.

———. 1951. "Die Steinvögel in Melanesien," in *Südseestudien*, pp. 235–65. Basel: Museum für Völkerkunde.

———. 1964. "Der Todeszauber in Nordost-Neuguinea als Problem," in *Festschrift Ad. E. Jensen*, pp. 233–44. Munich: Klaus Renner.

———. 1968. Altertümliche Steinartefakte aus Neuguinea in Anthropos-Institut. *Ethnologica*, n.s., 4:494–531.

HOIJER, H. 1956. Lexicostatistics: A critique. *Language* 32:49–60.

HOLDEN, G. 1975. *Kanganaman house tambaran*. Lae: Papua New Guinea University of Technology, Faculty of Architecture and Building.

HOLLRUNG, M. 1888–89. Expedition nach dem Kaiserin Augusta-Fluss. *Nachrichten aus Kaiser Wilhelmsland* 4:23–32, 189–92, 223–37.

HORNE, E. C. 1974. *Javanese-English dictionary*. New Haven: Yale University Press.

HOSSFELD, P. S. 1949. The stratigraphy of the Aitape skull. *Transactions of the Royal Society of South Australia* 72:201–7.

———. 1964–65. The Aitape calvarium. *Australian Journal of Science* 27(6):179.

————. 1965. Radiocarbon dating and palaeoecology of the Aitape fossil human remains. *Proceedings of the Royal Society of Victoria* 78:161–65.

HOUSING COMMISSION. 1976. *Materials and building survey*. Port Moresby.

HOWELL, W., and D. J. S. BAILEY. 1900. *A Sea Dayak dictionary, in alphabetical parts, with examples and quotations showing the use and meaning of words*. Singapore: The American Press.

HOWLETT, D. 1973. "Terminal development: From tribalism to peasantry," in *The Pacific in transition: Geographical perspectives on adaptation and change*. Edited by H. Brookfield, pp. 249–73. Canberra: Australian National University Press.

HUBER, PETER. 1973. Identity and exchange: Kinship and social order among the Anggor of New Guinea. Ph.D. diss., Duke University, Durham, N.C.

————. 1975. "Defending the cosmos," in *War: Its causes and correlates*. Edited by M. Nettleship, D. Givens, and A. Nettleship. The Hague: Mouton.

————. 1978. "Organizing production and producing organization: The sociology of traditional agriculture," in *The adaptation of traditional systems of agriculture*. Edited by E. K. Fisk. Canberra: Australian National University Press.

————. 1979. Anggor floods: Reflections on ethnogeography and mental maps. *Geographical Review* 69 (2).

————. 1980. The Anggor bowman: Ritual and society in Melanesia. *American Ethnologist* 7:43–57.

HUDSON, A. B. 1967. *The Barito isolates of Borneo: A classification based on comparative reconstruction and lexicostatistics*. Cornell University Department of Asian Studies, Southeast Asia Program, Data Paper 68.

————. 1970. A note on Seleko: Malayic Dayak and Land Dayak languages in western Borneo. *Sarawak Museum Journal* 18:301–18.

————. 1972. *Padju Epat: The Ma'anyan of Indonesian Borneo*. New York: Holt, Rinehart and Winston.

HUGHES, C. A. 1965. "The development of the legislature: The legislative councils," in *The Papua New Guinea elections 1964*. Edited by D. G. Bettison, C. A. Hughes, and P. S. van der Veur, pp. 8–27. Canberra: Australian National University Press.

HUGHES, I. 1977. *New Guinea Stone Age trade: The geography and ecology of traffic in the interior*. Terra Australis 3.

HYMES, D. H. 1960. Lexicostatistics so far. *Current Anthropology* 1:3–44.

IDE SAID, M. 1977. *Kamus Bahasa Bugis-Indonesia*. Jakarta: Pusat Pembinaan dan Pengembangan Bahasa.

ISAACS, JENNIFER. 1982. *Thancoupie the potter*. Sydney: Aboriginal Arts Agency.

JACKMAN, HARRY. 1977. Some thoughts on entrepreneurship in Papua New Guinea. *Australian Outlook* 31(1):24–37.

JACKSON, R. Editor. 1976. *An introduction to the urban geography of Papua New Guinea*. University of Papua New Guinea Department of Geography Occasional Paper 13.

JACOBS, M. 1972. "German New Guinea," in *Encyclopaedia of Papua and New Guinea*. Edited by Peter Ryan, pp. 485–98. Melbourne: Melbourne University Press in association with the University of Papua and New Guinea.

JAKOBSON, R. 1960. "Why 'mama' and 'papa'?" in *Perspectives in psychological theory: Essays in honor of Heinz Werner*. Edited by B. Kaplan and S. Wapner. New York: International Universities Press.

————. 1968. *Child language, aphasia, and phonological universals*. Translated by A. R. Keiler. The Hague: Mouton.

JASPAN, M.A. 1984. *Materials for a Rejang-Indonesian-English dictionary*. Canberra: Australian National University.

JENSEN, E. 1974. *The Iban and their religion*. Oxford: Clarendon Press.

JENSEN, K-E. 1977–78. Relative age and category: The Semaq Beri case. *Folk* 19–20:171–81.

JEROME, N. W., R. F. KANDEL, and G. H. PELTO. Editors. 1980. *Nutritional anthropology: Contemporary approaches to diet and culture*. New York: Redgrave.

JEROME, N. W., and G. H. PELTO. 1981. Integrating ethnographic research with nutrition studies. *Federation Proceedings* 40:2601–5.

JEUDY-BALLINI, M. 1985. A propos d'une femme remarquable: Le statut de la Kheng chez les Sulka de Nouvelle-Bretagne (Nouvelle-Guinée). *Journal de la Société des Océanistes* 40. In press.

JORGENSEN, DAN. 1985. "Femsep's last garden: A Telefol response to mortality," in *Aging and its transformations: Moving toward death in Pacific societies*. Edited by Dorothy and David Counts. Lanham, Md.: University Press of America.

————. n.d. The clear and the hidden: Public and private aspects of self in Telefomin. MS.

JORGENSEN, JOSEPH G. 1971. On ethics and anthropology. *Current Anthropology* 12:321–34.

JOSEPHIDES, SASHA. 1982. The perception of the past and the notion of "business" in a Seventh-Day Adventist village in Madang, New Guinea. Ph.D. diss., University of London (London School of Economics), London, England.

JOSSELIN DE JONG, P. E. DE. 1980. *Minangkabau and Negri Sembilan: Socio-political structure in Indonesia*. The Hague: Martinus Nijhoff.

JOUSTRA, M. 1907. *Karo-Bataksch Woordenboek*. Leiden: Brill.

JOYCE, T. A. 1912. Note on prehistoric pottery from Japan and New Guinea. *Journal of the Royal Anthropological Institute of Great Britain and Ireland* 42:545–46.

JUILLERAT, B. 1981. Organisation dualiste et complementarité sexuelle dans le Sepik Occidental. *L'Homme* 21(2): 5–38.

————. 1982. Les modalités de l'échange chez les Eri (Nouvelle Guinée). MS, Laboratoire d'Ethologie Préhistorique du Collège de France.

————. 1986. *Les enfants du sang: Société, reproduction et imaginaire en Nouvelle-Guinée.* Paris: Maison des Sciences de l'Homme.

————. n.d. Une odeur d'homme: Matriarchat et ordre social dans un mythe yafar (Nouvelle-Guinée). MS.

JUNOD, H. A. 1927. 2d edition, revised. *The life of a South African tribe.* London: Macmillan.

KABERRY, PHYLLIS M. 1940–41. The Abelam tribe, Sepik District, New Guinea: A preliminary report. *Oceania* 11:233–58, 345–67.

————. 1941–42. Law and political organisation in the Abelam tribe, New Guinea. *Oceania* 12:79–95, 209–25, 331–63.

————. 1957. Political organisation among the northern Abelam. MS. (Subsequently revised and published in *Anthropological Forum* 1:334–72 [1966] and in *Politics in New Guinea,* edited by Ronald M. Berndt and Peter Lawrence [Nedlands: University of Western Australia Press, 1971].)

————. 1971. "Political organization among the northern Abelam," in *Politics in New Guinea.* Edited by Ronald M. Berndt and Peter Lawrence, pp. 35–73. Nedlands: University of Western Australia Press.

KASPRUSCH, A. 1940–41. Der grosse "prähistorische" Steinmörser in Atemble am mittleren Ramu River in Neuguinea. *Anthropos* 35–36:647–54.

KAUFMANN, C. 1968. Über Kunst und kult der Kwoma und Nukuma (Nord-Neuguinea). *Verhandlungen der Naturforschenden Gesellschaft in Basel* 79:63–112.

————. 1972. *Das Töpferhandwerk der Kwoma in Nord-Neuguinea: Beiträge zur Systematik primärer Töpfereiverfahren.* Basler Beiträge zur Ethnologie 12.

————. 1975. (New Guinea, Middle Sepik area): Preparation of a dish of sago, vegetables, and beetle larvae. Film E 1378. *Publikationen zu Wissenschaftlichen Filmen, Sektion Völkerkunde-Volkskunde* 5(4): 412–31.

————. 1979. "Art and artists in the context of Kwoma society," in *Exploring the visual art of Oceania.* Edited by Sydney M. Mead, pp. 310–34. Honolulu: University Press of Hawaii.

————. 1981. "Völkerkundliche Dokumentation aus und für Papua New Guinea," in *Das Museum und die Dritte Welt.* Edited by H. Auer, pp. 224–30. Munich: K. G. Saur.

————. 1982a. Kwoma (New Guinea, Sepik): Clearing a yam garden (slash and burn). Film E 2288. *Publikationen zu Wissenschaftlichen Filmen, Sektion Ethnologie* 12 (3).

————. 1982b. Kwoma (New Guinea, Sepik): Yam cultivation. Film E 2289. *Publikationen zu Wissenschaftlichen Filmen, Sektion Ethnologie* 12 (4).

————. 1982c. Kwoma (New Guinea, Sepik): Preparing a pandanus soup. Film E 2104. *Publikationen zu Wissenschaftlichen Filmen, Sektion Ethnologie* 12 (24).

————. 1984a. Pflanzer und Künstler: Führende Männer bei den Kwoma in Papua-Neuguinea. Film D 1479. *Publikationen zu Wissenschaftlichen Film, Sektion Ethnologie* 13 (25).

————. 1984b. Review of: *Yena: Art and ceremony in a Sepik society,* by Ross Bowden (Oxford: Pitt-Rivers Museum, 1983). *Pacific Arts Newsletter,* no. 19, pp. 14–18.

————. 1984c. "Von den mündlich überlieferten Geschichten zu den Umrissen einer Geschichte des Sepik-Gebietes (Papua-Neuguinea)," in *Diachronica.* Edited by Rupert Moser and Peter Heinrich Kamber, pp. 137–52. Ethnologica Helvetica 8.

————. 1986. Maschenstoffe und ihre gesellschaftliche Funktion am Beispiel der Kwoma von Papua-Neuguinea. *Tribus* 35:127–75.

————. n.d. Töpferei-Traditionen im Sepik-Gebiet von Papua-Neuguinea als historische Quellen. MS.

KAUFMANN, C., et al. 1979. *Völkerkundliche Sammlungen in der Schweiz.* Pt. 1. *Basel, Bern, Genève, Neuchâtel und Zürich.* Ethnologica Helvetica 2-3.

KEESING, R. M. 1982. "Introduction," in *Rituals of manhood.* Edited by G. H. Herdt, pp. 1–43. Berkeley: University of California Press.

KELLY, RAYMOND C. 1976. *Etoro social structure: A study in structural contradiction.* Ann Arbor: University of Michigan Press.

KELM, ANTJE, and HEINZ KELM. 1975. *Ein Pfeilschuss für die Braut: Mythen und Erzählungen aus Kwieftim und Abrau, Nordostneuguinea.* Wiesbaden: Franz Steiner.

————. 1980. *Sago und Schwein: Ethnologie von Kwieftim und Abrau in Nordost-Neuguinea.* Wiesbaden: Franz Steiner.

KELM, HEINZ. 1966a. *Kunst vom Sepik.* Vol. 1. *Mittellauf.* Veröffentlichungen des Museums für Völkerkunde Berlin, n.s., 10 (Abteilung Südsee 5).

————. 1966b. *Kunst vom Sepik.* Vol. 2. *Oberlauf.* Veröffentlichungen des Museums fur Völkerkunde Berlin, n.s., 11 (Abteilung Südsee 6).

————. 1968. *Kunst vom Sepik.* Vol. 3. *Unterlauf und Nachtrage.* Veröffentlichungen des Museums für Völkerkunde Berlin, n.s., 15 (Abteilung Südsee 7).

KIEFER, T. M. 1972. *The Tausug: Violence and law in a Philippine Moslem society.* New York: Holt, Rinehart and Winston.

KILIAAN, H. N. 1904. *Madoeresch-Nederlandsch Woordenboek.* 2 vols. Leiden: Brill.

KING, V. T. 1976. The Maloh language: A vocabulary and summary of the literature. *Sarawak Museum Journal* 24:137–64.

————. 1978. "The Maloh," in *Essays on Borneo societies.* Edited by V. T. King. Oxford: Oxford University Press.

KLINKERT, H. C. 1930(1882). 4th edition. *Nieuw Maleisch-Nederlandsch Woordenboek, met Arabisch Karakter.* Leiden: Brill.

KOCH, G. 1968. *Kultur der Abelam*. Veröffentlichungen des Museums für Völkerkunde Berlin, n.s., 16 (Abteilung Südsee 8).

———. 1973. Hundert Jahre Museum für Völkerkunde Berlin: Abteilung Südsee. *Baessler-Archiv*, n.s., 21:141–74.

———. 1984. *Malingdam: Ethnographische Notizen über einen Siedlungsbereich im oberen Eipomek-Tal, zentrales Bergland von Irian Jaya (West-Neuguinea), Indonesien*. Mensch, Kultur und Umwelt in zentralen Bergland von West-Neuguinea 15.

KOCHER-SCHMID, C. 1980. Preliminary report on the analysis of pottery sherds collected in the Aibom-Chambri region, Middle Sepik, Paupa New Guinea. *Verhandlungen der Naturforschenden Gesellschaft in Basel* 91:35–49.

KOENTJARANINGRAT, R. M. 1960. "The Javanese of Central Java," in *Social structure in Southeast Asia*. Edited by G. P. Murdock, pp. 88–115. Viking Fund Publications in Anthropology 29.

———. 1972. "Javanese," "Sudanese," in *Ethnic groups of insular Southeast Asia*, vol. 1, *Indonesia, Andaman Islands, and Madagascar*. Edited by F. M. Lebar, pp. 48–56. New Haven: Human Relations Area Files Press.

KOEPPING, KLAUS-PETER. 1983. *Adolf Bastian and the psychic unity of mankind*. St. Lucia: University of Queensland Press.

KOOIJMAN, S. 1962. Material aspects of the Star Mountains culture. *Nova Guinea* 10 (Anthropology 2):15–44.

KRULFELD, R. 1972. "Sasak," in *Ethnic groups of insular Southeast Asia*, vol. 1, *Indonesia, Andaman Islands, and Madagascar*. Edited by F. M. Lebar, pp. 65–69. New Haven: Human Relations Area Files Press.

KUHN, THOMAS. 1962. *The structure of scientific revolutions*. Chicago: University of Chicago Press.

LANGNESS, L. L. 1967. Sexual antagonism in the highlands: A Bena Bena example. *Oceania* 37:161–77.

———. 1974. Ritual power and male domination in the New Guinea highlands. *Ethos* 2:189–212.

———. 1977. "Ritual, power, and male dominance in the New Guinea highlands," in *The anthropology of power*. Edited by R. D. Fogelson and R. N. Adams, pp. 3–22. New York: Academic Press.

LAUMANN, KARL. 1939–40. Eine Firmungsreise in den Busch. *Steyler Missionsbote* 67:120–23.

LAWRENCE, P. 1964. *Road belong cargo*. Melbourne: Melbourne University Press/Manchester: Manchester University Press.

———. 1970. "Daughter of time," in *Cultures of the Pacific*. Edited by T. G. Harding and B. J. Wallace. New York: Free Press.

LAWSON, BILL. 1983. Pottery projects in developing countries. MS.

———. 1984. *Report on preliminary visit to Papua New Guinea waste oil burning project*. Sydney: Department of Industry/SPATE.

———. n.d. *Design and manufacture of fuel-efficient ceramic cooking stoves*. Sydney: Department of Industrial Arts, University of New South Wales.

LAYCOCK, D. C. 1965. *The Ndu language family (Sepik District, New Guinea)*. Linguistic Circle of Canberra Publications C 1.

———. 1968. Languages of the Lumi Subdistrict (West Sepik District), New Guinea. *Oceanic Linguistics* 7:33–66.

———. 1973. *Sepik languages: Checklist and preliminary classification*. Pacific Linguistics B 25.

———. 1975a. "The Torricelli phylum," in *New Guinea area languages and language study*, vol. 1, *Papuan languages and the New Guinea linguistic scene*. Edited by S. A. Wurm, pp. 767–80. Pacific Linguistics C 38.

———. 1975b. "Possible wider connections of Papuan languages: Southeast Asia," in *New Guinea area languages and language study*, vol. 1, *Papuan languages and the New Guinea linguistic scene*. Edited by S. A. Wurm, pp. 905–13. Pacific Linguistics C 38.

———. 1978. "Unstudied ethnographic areas of the Sepik Basin, New Guinea," in *Approaches to language: Anthropological issues*. Edited by W. C. McCormack and S. A. Wurm, pp. 245–70. The Hague: Mouton.

———. 1981. "Sepik Provinces (Map 6)," in *Language atlas of the Pacific area*, pt. 1, *New Guinea area, Oceania, Australia*. Edited by S. A. Wurm and S. Hattori. Canberra: Australian Academy of the Humanities in association with the Japan Academy.

———. 1982. "Linguistic diversity in Melanesia: A tentative explanation," in *Gava': Studies in Austronesian languages and cultures*. Edited by R. Carle et al., pp. 31–37. Berlin: Dietrich Reimer.

LAYCOCK, D. C., and J. Z'GRAGGEN. 1975. "The Sepik-Ramu phylum," in *New Guinea area languages and language study*, vol. 1, *Papuan languages and the New Guinea linguistic scene*. Edited by S. A. Wurm, pp. 731–63. Pacific Linguistics C 38.

LEA, D. A. M. 1964. Abelam land and sustenance: Swidden horticulture in an area of high population density, Maprik, New Guinea. Ph.D. diss., Australian National University, Canberra, Australia.

———. 1965. The Abelam: A study in local differentiation. *Pacific Viewpoint* 6:191–213.

———. 1972. "Sepik Districts, East and West," in *Encyclopaedia of Papua and New Guinea*. Edited by Peter Ryan, pp. 1030-36. Melbourne: Melbourne University Press in association with the University of Papua and New Guinea.

———. 1973. "Stress and adaptation to change: An example from the East Sepik District, New Guinea," in *The Pacific in transition: Geographical perspectives on adaptation and change*. Edited by H. Brookfield, pp. 55–74. Canberra: Australian National University Press.

LEA, D. A. M., and H. C. WEINAND. 1971. "Some consequences of population growth in the Wosera area, East Sepik District," in *Population growth and socioeconomic change*. Edited by M. W. Ward, pp. 122–36. New Guinea Research Bulletin 42.

LEACH, E. R. 1950. *Social science research in Sarawak*. Colonial Social Science Research Council, Colonial Research Studies 1.

———. 1954. *Political systems of highland Burma*. London: Athlone Press.

———. 1964. "Anthropological aspects of language: Animal categories and verbal abuse," in *New directions in the study of language*. Edited by E. H. Lenneberg. Cambridge: M.I.T. Press.

———. 1971. "More about 'Mama' and 'Papa,'" in *Rethinking kinship and marriage*. Edited by Rodney Needham, pp. 75–98. London: Tavistock.

LEAF, MURRAY J. 1979. *Man, mind, and science: A history of anthropology*. New York: Columbia University Press.

LEBAR, F. M. 1964. "Akha," in *Ethnic groups of mainland Southeast Asia*. Edited by F. M. Lebar et al. New Haven: Human Relations Area Files Press.

———. Editor. 1972*a*. *Ethnic groups of insular Southeast Asia*. Vol. 1. *Indonesia, Andaman Islands, and Madagascar*. New Haven: Human Relations Area Files Press.

———. 1972*b*. "Alor-Pantar," in *Ethnic groups of insular Southeast Asia*, vol. 1, *Indonesia, Andaman Islands, and Madagascar*. New Haven: Human Relations Area Files Press.

———. Editor. 1975. *Ethnic groups of insular Southeast Asia*. Vol. 2. *Philippines and Formosa*. New Haven: Human Relations Area Files Press.

LEBAR, F. M., et al. Editors. 1964. *Ethnic groups of mainland Southeast Asia*. New Haven: Human Relations Area Files Press.

LEDERMAN, RENA. 1987. *What gifts engender*. Cambridge: Cambridge University Press.

LEENHARDT, M. 1979. *Do Kamo*. Translated by B. M. Gulati. Chicago: University of Chicago Press.

LEROI-GOURHAN, ANDRÉ. 1973(1945). *Milieu et techniques*. Paris: Editions Albin Michel.

LE ROY LADURIE, EMMANUEL. 1974. *The peasants of Languedoc*. Urbana: University of Illinois Press.

LÉVI-STRAUSS, C. 1970. *The raw and the cooked*. London: Jonathan Cape.

———. 1985. *The view from afar*. New York: Basic Books.

LEWENSTEIN, EILEEN. 1983. Review of: *The traditional pottery of Papua New Guinea*, by Patricia May and Margaret Tuckson (Sydney: Bay Books, 1982). *Ceramic Review* 83:35.

LEWIS, GILBERT. 1975. *Knowledge of illness in a Sepik society*. London: Athlone.

———. 1977. "A mother's brother to a sister's son," in *Symbols and sentiment*. Edited by I. Lewis. London: Academic Press.

———. 1980. *Day of shining red: An essay on understanding ritual*. Cambridge: Cambridge University Press.

LEWIS, M. B. 1960. *Moken texts and word-list: A provisional interpretation*. Kuala Lumpur: Museums Department.

LINDENBAUM, S. 1972. Sorcerers, ghosts, and polluting women: An analysis of religious belief and population control. *Ethnology* 11:241–53.

———. 1976. "A wife is the hand of man," in *Man and woman in the New Guinea highlands*. Edited by P. Brown and G. Buchbinder, pp. 54–62. Washington, D.C.: American Anthropological Association.

LINDSTROM, L. 1984. Doctor, lawyer, wiseman, priest: Big-men and knowledge in Melanesia. *Man* 19:291–309.

LIPSET, D. 1984. Authority and the maternal presence: An interpretive ethnography of Murik Lakes society (East Sepik Province, Papua New Guinea). Ph.D. diss., University of California, San Diego, La Jolla, Calif.

———. 1985. Seafaring Sepiks: Ecology, power, and vanity in Murik trade. *Annual Review of Research in Economic Anthropology* 7:67–93.

LLAMZON, T. A. 1979*a*. "Languages of the Philippines," in *Papers on Southeast Asian languages: An introduction to the languages of Indonesia, Malaysia, the Philippines, Singapore, and Thailand*. Edited by T. A. Llamzon, pp. 77–156. SEAMEO Regional Language Centre Anthology Series 5.

———. Editor. 1979*b*. *Papers on Southeast Asian languages: An introduction to the languages of Indonesia, Malaysia, the Philippines, Singapore, and Thailand*. SEAMEO Regional Language Centre Anthology Series 5.

LÖFFLER, E. 1974. *Explanatory notes to the geomorphological map of Papua New Guinea*. Melbourne: Commonwealth Scientific and Industrial Research Organization.

———. 1977. *Geomorphology of Papua New Guinea*. Melbourne: Commonwealth Scientific and Industrial Research Organization and Australian National University Press.

LOKOLOKO, T. 1979. Our Pacific heritage. *Post-Courier,* special issue, September, p. 3.

LOMAX, ALAN. 1962. Song structure and social structure. *Ethnology* 1:425–51.

———. 1968. *Folk song style and culture*. American Association for the Advancement of Science Publication 88.

———. 1976. *Cantometrics: A method in musical anthropology*. Berkeley: University of California Extension Media Center.

LONG, G. 1963. *Australia in the war of 1939–1945: The final campaigns*. Canberra: Australian War Memorial.

LÓPEZ, C. 1939. *A comparison of Tagalog and Malay lexicographies (on a phonetico-semantic basis)*. Institute of National Language Bulletin 2.

LORD, ALBERT B. 1976. *The singer of tales*. New York: Atheneum.

LOSCHE, DIANE SARA BRADY. 1982. *Male and female in Abelam society: Opposition and complementarity*. Ann Arbor: University Microfilms.

LOUNSBURY, F. G. 1969. "A formal account of the Crow- and Omaha-type kinship terminologies," in *Cognitive anthropology*. Edited by S. A. Tyler, pp. 212–55. New York: Rinehart and Winston.

LOVEDAY, P., and E. P. WOLFERS. 1976. *Parties and parliament in Papua New Guinea 1964–1975*. Institute of Applied Social and Economic Research Monograph 4.

LUCE, G. H. 1965. Danaw: A dying Austroasiatic language. *Lingua* 14:98–129.

LUS, PITA. 1970. Autobiography: My life story. *Journal of the Papua and New Guinea Society* 4(1):47–56.

LUTKEHAUS, N. 1981. A constricting web of tradition: The political use of rhetoric in Manam. Paper presented to the annual meeting of the American Society of Social Anthropologists in Oceania.

———. 1982. Manipulating myth and history: How the Manam maintain themselves. *Bikmaus* 3:81–89.

———. 1983. "Introduction," in *The life of some island people of New Guinea*, by Karl Böhm. Edited by Nancy Lutkehaus, pp. 13–70. Berlin: Dietrich Reimer.

———. 1984. The flutes of the *tanepoa*: The dynamics of hierarchy and equivalence in Manam society. Ph.D. diss., Columbia University, New York, N.Y.

———. 1985. Pigs for their ancestors. *Annual Review of Research in Economic Anthropology* 7:94–116.

LUTKEHAUS, NANCY, and PAUL ROSCOE. 1987. Sepik culture history: Variation, innovation, synthesis. *Current Anthropology* 8:577–81.

MABUCHI, I. 1960. "The aboriginal peoples of Formosa," in *Social structure in Southeast Asia*. Edited by G. P. Murdock, pp. 127–40. Viking Fund Publications in Anthropology 29.

MCCARTHY, F. D. 1939–40. Trade in aboriginal Australia and "trade" relationships with Torres Strait, New Guinea, and Malaya. *Oceania* 9 and 10.

MCCARTHY, J. K. 1963. *Patrol into yesterday: My New Guinea years*. Melbourne: Cheshire.

———. 1964. *Patrol into yesterday: My New Guinea years*. London: Angus and Robertson.

MCCORMACK, W. C., and S. A. WURM. Editors. 1978. *Approaches to language: Anthropological issues*. The Hague: Mouton.

MCDOWELL, NANCY. 1975. Kinship and the concept of shame in a New Guinea village. Ph.D. diss., Cornell University, Ithaca, N.Y.

———. 1976. Kinship and exchange: The *kamain* relationship in a Yuat River village. *Oceania* 47:36–48.

———. 1977. The meaning of "rope" in a Yuat River village. *Ethnology* 16:175–83.

———. 1978a. The struggle to be human: Exchange and politics in Bun. *Anthropological Quarterly* 51(1)16–25.

———. 1978b. Flexibility of sister exchange in Bun. *Oceania* 48:207–31.

———. 1979. The significance of cultural context: A note on food taboos in Bun. *Journal of Anthropological Research* 35:231–37.

———. 1980a. It's not who you are but how you give that counts: The role of exchange in a Melanesian society. *American Ethnologist* 7:58–70.

———. 1980b. Concepts of history in Bun. Paper presented to the 79th annual meeting of the American Anthropological Association, Washington, D.C.

———. 1983. Trade and power in the Middle Yuat region. Paper presented to the 82d annual meeting of the American Anthropological Association, Chicago, Ill.

———. 1984. "Complementarity: The relationship between female and male in the East Sepik village of Bun, Papua New Guinea," in *Rethinking women's roles: Perspectives from the Pacific*. Edited by D. O'Brien and S. Tiffany. Berkeley and Los Angeles: University of California Press.

MCGREGOR, DONALD E. 1982. *The fish and the cross*. Goroka: The Melanesian Institute.

MCGREGOR, DONALD E., and AILEEN R. F. MCGREGOR. 1982. *Olo language materials*. Pacific Linguistics D 42.

MACKENZIE, M. A. n.d. Bilum looping. *Fibre Forum* (St. Lucia). In press.

MACKNIGHT, C. C. 1976. *The voyage to Marege*. Melbourne: Melbourne University Press.

MCMEEKIN, IVAN. 1969. The introduction of pottery to the Aborigines of Northern Territory. *Pottery in Australia* 8(2):17–24.

———. 1977. Tiwi pottery, Bathurst Island. *Pottery in Australia* 16(1):45–47.

MCSWAIN, ROMOLA. 1977. *The past and future people: Tradition and change on a New Guinea island*. Melbourne: Oxford University Press.

MAHDI, W. 1981. Some problems of the phonology of Metropolitan Indonesian. *Bijdragen tot de Taal-, Land- en Volkenkunde* 137:399–418.

MAIR, L. P. 1948. *Australia in New Guinea*. London: Christophers.

MALCOLM, L. A. 1974. "Ecological factors relating to child growth and nutritional status," in *Nutrition and malnutrition*. Edited by A. F. Roche and F. Falkner, pp. 329–52. New York: Plenum Press.

MANGAL, PITA, and DIRK SMIDT. 1980. *The Kominimung*. Boroko: National Cultural Council.

MANIK, TINDI RADJA. 1977. *Ramus Bahasa Dairi Pakpak-Indonesia*. Jakarta: Pusat Pembinaan dan Pengembangan Bahasa.

MARAGAU, V. 1973. Pita Simogun M.H.A. of Dagua, East Sepik Province. *Oral History* 1(6):5–10.

MARSDEN, W. 1984(1982). *A dictionary and grammar of the Malayan language*. Vol. 1. Singapore: Oxford University Press.

MARSHALL, A. J. 1937. Northern New Guinea, 1936. *Geographical Journal* 89:489–506.

———. 1938. *The men and birds of paradise: Journeys through equatorial New Guinea*. London: Heinemann.

MARSHALL, MAC. Editor. 1981. *Siblingship in Oceania: Studies in the meaning of kin relations*. Ann Arbor: University of Michigan Press.

———. Editor. 1982. *Through a glass darkly: Beer and modernization in Papua New Guinea*. Institute of Applied Social and Economic Research Monograph 18.

MARTIN, F. W. 1974. *Tropical yams and their potential*. Pt. 1. Dioscorea esculenta. U.S. Department of Agriculture Handbook 457.

MARX, K. 1976 (1867). *Capital*. Vol. 1. Translated by B. Fowkes. Harmondsworth: Penguin.

MATTHES, B. F. 1874. *Boegineesch-Hollandsch Woordenboek, met Hollandsch-Beoginesch Woordenlijst*. The Hague: Martinus Nijhoff.

MAWI, THEODORE. 1983. Statement of problems relating to the preservation of historic places in Papua New Guinea. Paper presented to the UNESCO Regional Conference on Historic Places, Sydney, May.

MAY, P., and M. TUCKSON. 1982. *The traditional pottery of Papua New Guinea*. Sydney: Bay Books.

MAY, R. J. 1975. *The view from Hurun: The Peli Association of the East Sepik District*. New Guinea Research Unit Discussion Paper 8.

———. 1979. *The artifact industry: Maximising returns to producers*. Institute of Applied Social and Economic Research Discussion Paper 8.

———. Editor. 1982a. *Micronationalist movements in Papua New Guinea*. Australian National University, Research School of Pacific Studies, Political and Social Change Monograph 1.

———. 1982b (1975). "The view from Hurun: The Peli Association of the East Sepik District," in *Micronationalist movements in Papua New Guinea*. Edited by R. J. May, pp. 31–62. Australian National University, Research School of Pacific Studies, Political and Social Change Monograph 1.

———. n.d. a. Art as a cash crop: Economics and politics of the artifact industry in Papua New Guinea. MS.

———. n.d.b. "The East Sepik electorates," in *The 1982 elections in Papua New Guinea*. Edited by P. King. In preparation.

———. n.d.c. The colonial impact in the East Sepik Province. MS.

MEAD, MARGARET. 1933–34. The marsalai cult among the Arapesh, with special reference to the rainbow serpent beliefs of the Australian Aborigines. *Oceania* 4:37–53.

———. 1935. *Sex and temperament in three primitive societies*. London: Routledge and Kegan Paul/New York: Morrow.

———. 1938. The Mountain Arapesh: An importing culture. *American Museum of Natural History Anthropological Papers* 36:139–349.

———. 1940. The Mountain Arapesh: Supernaturalism. *American Museum of Natural History Anthropological Papers* 37:317–451.

———. 1947a. The Mountain Arapesh: Socio-economic life. *American Museum of Natural History Anthropological Papers* 40:163–232.

———. 1947b. Age patterning in personality development. *American Journal of Orthopsychiatry* 17:231–40.

———. 1947c. The Mountain Arapesh: Diary of events in Alitoa. *American Museum of Natural History Anthropological Papers* 40:233–419.

———. 1949. *Male and female: A study of the sexes in a changing world*. New York: Morrow.

———. 1963. *Sex and temperament in three primitive societies*. New York: Morrow.

———. 1970. *The Mountain Arapesh: Arts and supernaturalism*. New York: Natural History Press.

———. 1971. Dell Laurel edition. *Sex and temperament in three primitive societies*. New York: Dell.

———. 1972. *Blackberry winter*. New York: Morrow.

———. 1973. A re-examination of major themes of the Sepik area, Papua New Guinea. Paper presented at the 9th International Congress of Anthropological and Ethnological Sciences, Chicago, Ill., August-September.

———. 1975. *Male and female*. New York: Morrow.

———. 1977. *Letters from the field: 1925–1975*. New York: Harper and Row.

———. 1978. The Sepik as a culture area: Comment. *Anthropological Quarterly* 51(1):69–75.

———. n.d. Field notes, Library of Congress, Washington, D.C.

MEGGITT, M. J. 1964. "Male-female relationships in the highlands of Australian New Guinea," in *New Guinea: The central highlands*. Edited by J. B. Watson, pp. 204–24. American Anthropologist 66(4, pt. 2).

MEIGHAN, CLEMENT W. 1984. "Archaeology: Science or sacrilege?" in *Ethics and values in archaeology*. Edited by Ernestene L. Green, pp. 208–23. London, New York: Free Press.

MEIGS, A. S. 1976. Male pregnancy and the reduction of sexual opposition in a New Guinea highlands society. *Ethnology* 15:393–407.

MEILINK-ROELOFSZ, M. A. P. 1962. *Asian trade and European influence in the Indonesian archipelago between 1500 and about 1630*. The Hague: Martinus Nijhoff.

———. 1968. Proto-Oceanic addenda. *Oceanic Linguistics* 7:147–71.

MEILLASSOUX, C. 1975. *Femmes, greniers et capitaux*. Paris: Maspero.

MEISER, L. 1955. The "platform" phenomenon along the northern coast of New Guinea. *Anthropos* 50:265–72.

MÉTRAUX, RHODA. 1970. Iatmul music, a cantometric analysis: A contribution to the theory of cultural integration. Paper presented to the 70th annual meeting of the American Anthropological Association, San Diego, Calif.

———. 1978. Aristocracy and meritocracy: Leadership among the Eastern Iatmul. *Anthropological Quarterly* 51(1):47–60.

MEYER, A. B., and RICHARD PARKINSON. 1894. *Album von Papua-Typen: Neu-Guinea und Bismarck-Archipel*. Dresden: von Stengel and Markbert.

MICHEL, K. M. 1975. "Unser Alltag: Nachruf zu Lebzeiten," in *Kursbuch*, vol. 41. Edited by K. M. Michel and H. Wieser, pp. 1–40. Berlin: Kursbuch/Rotbuch Verlag.

MIHALIC, F. 1971. *The Jacaranda dictionary and grammar of Melanesian Pidgin*. Jacaranda Press.

MIKE, M. 1968. Proto-Oceanic addenda. *Oceanic Linguistics* 7:147–71.

MILES, D. 1971. "Ngandju kinship and social change on the Upper Mentaya," in *Anthropology in Oceania: Essays presented to Ian Hogbin*. Edited by L. R. Hiatt and C. Jayawardena, pp. 211–30. Sydney: Angus and Robertson.

MITCHELL, D. S. 1979. *The incidence and management of* Salvinia molesta *in Papua New Guinea*. Port Moresby: Office of Environment and Conservation.

MITCHELL, JOYCE S. 1973. Life and birth in New Guinea. *Ms* 1:20–23.

MITCHELL, WILLIAM E. 1973. A new weapon stirs up old ghosts. *Natural History* 82(10):74–84.

———. 1975. "Culturally contrasting therapeutic systems of the West Sepik: The Lujere," in *Psychological anthropology*. Edited by Thomas Rhys Williams, pp. 409–39. The Hague: Mouton.

———. 1977*a*. Sorcellerie chamanique: "Sanguma" chez les Lujere du cours supérieur du Sepik. *Journal de la Société des Océanistes* 33:177–85.

———. 1977*b*. Changing others: The anthropological study of therapeutic systems. *Medical Anthropology Newsletter* 8(3):15–20.

———. 1978*a*. On keeping equal: Polity and reciprocity among the New Guinea Wape. *Anthropological Quarterly* 51(1):5–15.

———. 1978*b*. *The bamboo fire: An anthropologist in New Guinea*. New York: Norton.

———. 1978*c*. *The living dead and dying: Music of the New Guinea Wape*. Ethnic Folkways FE 4269.

MODJESKA, N. 1982. "Production and inequality: Perspectives from central New Guinea," in *Inequality in New Guinea highlands societies*. Edited by A. Strathern, pp. 50–108. Cambridge: Cambridge University Press.

MONTGOMERY, E. 1978. "Anthropological contributions to the study of food-related cultural variability," in *Progress in human nutrition*, vol. 2. Edited by Sheldon Margen, pp. 42–56. Westport, Conn.: Avi.

MORGENTHALER, F., F. WEISS, and M. MORGENTHALER. 1984. *Gespräche am sterbenden Fluss: Ethnopsychoanalyse bei den Iatmul in Papua-Neuguinea*. Frankfurt: Fischer.

MORRIS, H. S. 1953. *Report on a Melanau sago-producing community in Sarawak*. London: H. M. Stationers' Office.

———. 1978. "The coastal Melanau," in *Essays on Borneo societies*. Edited by V. T. King, pp. 37–58. Oxford: Oxford University Press.

MÜLLER, A. 1935–36. Drei Wochen auf Pferdesrücken durchs Steppenland. *Steyler Missionsbote* 63:103, 106–7, 123–24, 151–53.

MULDER, B., et al. 1930. A vocabulary of Mukah Milano. *Sarawak Museum Journal* 4:87–130.

MURDOCK, G. P. 1949. *Social structure*. New York: Macmillan.

———. 1959. Cross-language parallels in parental kin terms. *Anthropological Linguistics* 9:1–5.

———. 1964. Genetic classification of the Austronesian languages: A key to Oceanic culture history. *Ethnology* 3:117–26.

MUTHALIB, ABDUL. 1977. *Kamus Bahasa Mandar-Indonesia*. Jakarta: Pusat Pembinaan dan Pengembangan Bahasa.

NAG, M., B. N. F. WHITE, and C. R. PEET. 1978. An anthropological approach to the study of the economic value of children in Java and Nepal. *Current Anthropology* 19:293–306.

NEEDHAM, R. 1954. Batu Belah and Long Terawan: Kinship terms and death names. *Journal of the Malayan Branch of the Royal Asiatic Society* 27:215–17.

———. 1955. A note on some Murut kinship terms. *Journal of the Malayan Branch of the Royal Asiatic Society* 28:159–61.

———. 1966. Terminology and alliance. 1. Garo, Manggaarai. *Sociologus* 16:141–57.

———. 1985. Prescription and variation in Rembong, Western Flores. *Bijdragen tot de Taal-, Land- en Volkenkunde* 141:275–87.

NELSON, H. 1980. Hold the good name of the soldier: The discipline of the Papuan and New Guinean infantry battalions, 1940–46. *Journal of Pacific History* 15:202–16.

NEWMAN, P. L., and D. J. BOYD. 1982. "The making of men: Ritual and meaning in Awa male initiation," in *Rituals of manhood*. Edited by G. H. Herdt, pp. 239–85. Berkeley: University of California Press.

NEWTON, DOUGLAS. 1967. "Oral tradition and art history in the Sepik District, New Guinea." *Essays on the verbal and visual arts: Proceedings of the annual spring meeting of the American Ethnological Society 1966*, pp. 200–215. Seattle.

———. 1971. *Crocodile and cassowary: Religious art of the Upper Sepik River, New Guinea*. New York: Museum of Primitive Art.

———. 1979. "Prehistoric and recent art styles in Papua New Guinea," in *Exploring the visual art of Oceania*. Edited by Sydney M. Mead, pp. 32–57. Honolulu: University Press of Hawaii.

NOTHOFER, B. 1975. *The reconstruction of Proto-Malayo-Javanic*. Verhandelingen van het Koninklijk Instituut voor Taal-, Land- en Volkenkunde 73.

———. 1985. The subgrouping of the languages of the Javo-Sumatra hesion: A reconstruction. *Bijdragen tot de Taal-, Land- en Volkenkunde* 141:288–302.

NYAMEKYE, D. 1983. "East Sepik: Issues, parties, and personalities," in *Electoral politics in Papua New Guinea: Studies on the 1977 national elections*.

Edited by D. Hegarty, pp. 240–54. Port Moresby: University of Papua New Guinea Press.

OBRIST, BRIGIT, et al. 1984. Iatmul-Objektkatalog. Museum für Völkerkunde Basel, Fiche Sepik-Dok. 2-02-2-18.

OMAR, ASMAH HAJI. 1983. *The Malay peoples of Malaysia and their languages.* Kuala Lumpur: Dewan Bahasa dan Pustaka.

OOMEN, H. A. P. C. 1971. Ecology of human nutrition in New Guinea: Evaluation of subsistence patterns. *Ecology of Food and Nutrition* 1:1–16.

ORTNER, SHERRY. 1973. On key symbols. *American Anthropologist* 75:1338–46.

———. 1974. "Is female to male as nature is to culture?" in *Woman, culture, and society.* Edited by M. Z. Rosaldo and L. Lamphere. Stanford: Stanford University Press.

PAIJMANS, K. Editor. 1976. *New Guinea vegetation.* Canberra: Commonwealth Scientific and Industrial Research Organization in association with the Australian National University Press.

PAPUA NEW GUINEA COPRA MARKETING BOARD, WEWAK OFFICE. 1976–80. *Records of purchases from planters/traders/co-ops/individual farmers.* Wewak: Copra Marketing Board.

PARKIN, DAVID. Editor. 1985. *The anthropology of evil.* Oxford: Blackwell.

PARKINSON, R. 1907. *Dreissig Jahre in der Südsee.* Stuttgart: Strecker and Schröder.

PATTERSON, MARY. 1974–75. Sorcery and witchcraft in Melanesia. *Oceania* 45:132–60, 212–34.

PELTO, G., and N. W. JEROME. 1978. "Intracultural diversity and nutritional anthropology," in *Health and the human condition.* Edited by M. H. Logan and E. E. Hunt, pp. 322–28. North Scituate, Mass.: Duxbury Press.

PERANIO, R. D. 1972. "Bisaya," in *Ethnic groups of insular Southeast Asia,* vol. 1, *Indonesia, Andaman Islands, and Madagascar.* Edited by F. M. Lebar, pp. 163–66. New Haven: Human Relations Area Files Press.

PETER, HANNS. 1969–70. Bericht über die Forschungsreise in die Yuri Census Division, West Sepik. *Wiener Völkerkundliche Mitteilungen,* n.s., 11–12:107–8.

———. 1973–74. Vorstellungen über Krankheiten und Krankenbehandlung bei den Gargar im West-Sepik Distrikt. *Wiener Völkerkundliche Mitteilungen,* n.s., 15–16:27–62.

———. 1979a. *Völker in Urwald und Wüste: Kulturwandel in Neuguinea und Australien.* Vienna: Museum für Völkerkunde.

———. 1979b. "Feldforschung bei Papuastämmen in Neuguinea," in *Almanach '79 der österreichischen Forschung,* pp. 151–55. Vienna.

———. 1981. Bericht über die Forschungsreise nach Papua Neuguinea. *Wiener Völkerkundliche Mitteilungen,* n.s., 23:9–14.

———. 1982. Mythologische Hinweise auf historische Kontakte der Gargar mit Nachbargruppen (West-Sepik-Province, Papua Neuguinea). *Wiener Ethnohistorische Blätter* 24:37–55.

———. 1983–84. Akkulturation in der West-Sepik-Provinz, Papua Neuguinea: Ein Zwischenbericht. *Wiener Völkerkundliche Mitteilungen,* n.s., 25–26:27–43.

PETERS, W. 1960. Studies on the epidemiology of malaria in New Guinea. *Transactions of the Royal Society of Tropical Medicine and Hygiene* 54:242–60.

PETERSEN, JØRGEN. 1970. *Pottery in Papua New Guinea.* Geneva: International Labour Organisation.

PHILPOTT, M. M. 1972. *Economic development in the Sepik River Basin: An appraisal of transport needs and potential in 1971–1972.* Port Moresby: Department of Transport in conjunction with the University of Papua New Guinea and the New Guinea Research Unit of the Australian National University.

PHILPOTT, M. M., and THE CENTRAL PLANNING OFFICE. 1974. *East Sepik District Growth Centre Study, second draft.* Port Moresby.

PHILSOOPH, H. 1976. "A note on the election and cargo cult in a West Sepik village," in *Prelude to self-government.* Edited by D. Stone, pp. 160–67. Canberra: Australian National University.

PLUMB, J. H. 1978 (1969). *The death of the past.* Boston: Houghton Mifflin.

POOLE, F. J. P. 1982. "The ritual forging of identity: Aspects of person and self in Bimin-Kuskusmin male initiation," in *Rituals of manhood.* Edited by G. H. Herdt, pp. 99–154. Berkeley: University of California Press.

POWTER, A. 1975. A review of traditional design and construction in Papua New Guinea. Paper presented to Section 9, Topic A, of the Tropical Wood Preservation Training Seminar, Port Moresby, July.

PRENTICE, D. J. 1971. *The Muruts language of Sabah.* Pacific Linguistics C 18.

PRENTICE, D. J., and A. HAKIM USMAN. 1978. "Kerinci sound-changes and phonotactics," in *Second International Conference on Austronesian Linguistics,* vol. 1, *Western Austronesian.* Edited by S. A. Wurm and L. Carrington, pp. 121–63. Pacific Linguistics C 61.

PREUSS, K. T. 1899. Künstlerische Darstellungen aus dem Deutsch-Holländischen Grenzgebiet in Neu-Guinea. *Internationales Archiv für Ethnographie* 12:161–85.

QUARRY, N. 1974a. Patterns and precedents in New Guinea housing. Paper presented to International Conference on Housing for Emerging Nations, Tel Aviv, December.

———. 1974b. *Research and development report.* Lae: Department of Architecture and Building, Papua New Guinea University of Technology.

———. 1975. "Changing attitudes to the built environment in Papua New Guinea," in *The Melanesian environment: Papers from the 29th Waigani Seminar, Port Moresby, May 1975.* Edited by J. Winslow. Port Moresby.

RADCLIFFE-BROWN, A. R. 1971. *Structure and function in primitive society*. London: Cohen and West.

RADFORD, ANTHONY J. 1971. The future of rural health services in Melanesia. Paper presented to the Waigani Seminar, Port Moresby.

RAMOS, T. V. 1971. *Tagalog dictionary*. Honolulu: University Press of Hawaii.

RAPOPORT, A. 1969. *House form and culture*. Englewood Cliffs: Prentice-Hall.

RAY, S. H. 1913. The languages of Borneo. *Sarawak Museum Journal* 1:1–196.

READ, KENNETH E. 1947. Effects of the Pacific war in the Markham Valley. *Oceania* 18:95–116.

———. 1952. Nama cult of the central highlands, New Guinea. *Oceania* 23:1–25.

———. 1955. Morality and the concept of the person among the Gahuku-Gama. *Oceania* 25:233–82.

———. 1959. Leadership and consensus in a New Guinea society. *American Anthropologist* 61:425–36.

REAY, MARIE. 1959. *The Kuma: Freedom and conformity in the New Guinea highlands*. Melbourne: Melbourne University Press.

———. 1982. "Lawlessness in the Papua New Guinea highlands," in *Melanesia: Beyond diversity*. Edited by R. J. May and Hank Nelson, pp. 623–37. Canberra: Research School of Pacific Studies, Australian National University.

RECHE, O. 1913. *Der Kaiserin-Augusta-Fluss: Ergebnisse der Südsee-Expedition 1908–1910*. 2. *Ethnographie: A. Melanesien*. Vol. 1. Hamburg: L. Friederichsen.

REDFIELD, ROBERT. 1950. *The village that chose progress*. Chicago: University of Chicago Press.

REED, S. W. 1943. *The making of modern New Guinea, with special reference to culture contact in the Mandated Territory*. Philadelphia: American Philosophical Society.

REHBURGH, J. 1974. "Social structure of the Sepik Iwam," in *Kinship studies in Papua New Guinea*. Edited by R. D. Shaw, pp. 211–22. Ukarumpa: Summer Institute of Linguistics.

REID, L. A. Editor. 1971. *Philippine minor languages: Word lists and phonologies*. Oceanic Linguistics Special Publication 8.

———. 1976. *Bontok-English dictionary*. Pacific Linguistics C 36.

REINER, E., and R. G. ROBBINS. 1964. The Middle Sepik plains, New Guinea. *Geographical Review* 54:20–44.

Report to the League of Nations on the administration of the Territory of New Guinea. 1921–22. Canberra: Government Printer.

———. 1924–25. Canberra: Government Printer.

———. 1937–38. Canberra: Government Printer.

RHOADS, J. W. 1982. Sagopalm management in Melanesia: An alternative perspective. *Archaeology in Oceania* 17:20–27.

RICHARDS, A. 1981. *An Iban-English dictionary*. Oxford: Clarendon Press.

ROBBINS, G. R. 1968. "Vegetation of the Wewak–Lower Sepik area," in *Commonwealth Scientific and Industrial Research Organization Land Research Series* 22. Compiled by H. A. Haantjens.

ROESICKE, A. 1914. Mitteilungen über ethnographische Ergebnisse der Kaiserin Augusta-Fluss-Expedition. *Zeitschrift für Ethnologie* 46:507–22.

ROGOFF, BARBARA. 1981. Adults and peers as agents of socialization: A highland Guatemalan profile. *Ethos* 9(1):18–36.

ROSALDO, RENATO. 1978. "The rhetoric of control: Ilongots viewed as natural bandits and wild Indians," in *The reversible world: Symbolic inversion in art and society*. Edited by Barbara Babcock, pp. 240–57. Ithaca: Cornell University Press.

ROSCOE, P. B. 1983*a*. Trade stores and tambaran houses. MS.

———. 1983*b*. Of hogs and hounds: The symbolism of exchange among the Yangoru Boiken of the East Sepik Province, Papua New Guinea. MS.

———. 1983*c*. People and planning in the Yangoru Subdistrict, East Sepik Province, Papua New Guinea. Ph.D. diss., University of Rochester, Rochester, N.Y.

———. 1984. The legacy of war among the Yangoru Boiken. Paper presented to the 83d annual meeting of the American Anthropological Association, Denver, Colo.

———. n.d.*a*. "Medical pluralism among the Yangoru Boiken," in *Medical pluralism in Papua New Guinea*. Edited by S. Frankel and G. Lewis. In preparation.

———. n.d.*b*. "A history of the Yangoru Subdistrict," in *The Boiken people of the East Sepik Province, Papua New Guinea: The writings of Andreas Gerstner*. Edited by R. J. May and P. B. Roscoe; translated by Claire Smith. In press.

ROSCOE, P. B., and B. WAIS-ROSCOE. n.d. "Reproductive decision making among the Yangoru Boiken," in *Reproductive decision making and the value of children in Papua New Guinea*. Edited by N. McDowell. In press.

ROSS, M. 1977. Relationships of the Austronesian languages of the Sepik and western Madang coast of New Guinea. MS.

ROTH, H. L. 1968. *The natives of Sarawak and British North Borneo*. Vol. 2. Kuala Lumpur: University of Malaya Press.

ROUSSEAU, J. 1974. "A vocabulary of Baluy Kayan," in *The peoples of Central Borneo*, pp. 93–152. Sarawak Museum Journal, special issue.

ROWLEY, C. D. 1958. *The Australians in German New Guinea 1914–1921*. Melbourne: Cheshire.

———. 1965. *The New Guinea villager: A retrospect from 1964*. Melbourne: Cheshire.

RUFF, WALLACE M., and RUTH E. RUFF. 1975. *Settlement patterns of the Sepik*. Lae: Department of Architecture and Building, Papua New Guinea University of Technology.

———. 1979. Buildings crumble. *Post-Courier* (Port Moresby), September.

———. 1980. *Village studies*. Pt. 1. Lae: Department of Architecture and Building, Papua New Guinea University of Technology.

RUFF, WALLACE M., RUTH E. RUFF, and G. LOUPIS. 1982. *Notes on architecture of the New Guinea highlands: A research program for architecture students*. Lae: Department of Architecture and Building, Papua New Guinea University of Technology.

RUPP, HEINZ, and OSKAR KÖHLER. 1951. Historia-Geschichte. *Saeculum* 2:627–38.

RYAN, PETER. Editor. 1972. *Encyclopaedia of Papua and New Guinea*. 3 vols. Melbourne: Melbourne University Press in association with the University of Papua and New Guinea.

SACHS, CURT. 1913. *Real-Lexikon der Musikinstrumente*. Berlin: Hesse.

SACK, P., and D. CLARK. 1979. *German New Guinea: The annual reports (1886–1913)*. Canberra: Australian National University Press.

SAHLINS, M. 1963. Poor man, rich man, big-man, chief: Political types in Melanesia and Polynesia. *Comparative Studies in Society and History* 5:285–303.

———. 1972. *Stone Age economics*. London and New York: Aldine.

———. 1976. *Culture and practical reason*. London and New York: University of Chicago Press.

SANI, S. A. 1982. From Stone Age to space age: Problems and avenues of business management in a rural Sepik village. *Oral History* 10(4):68–93.

SAPIR, EDWARD. 1924. Culture, genuine and spurious. *American Journal of Sociology* 29:401–29.

SATHER, C. 1978. "The Bajau Laut," in *Essays on Borneo societies*. Edited by V. T. King, pp. 172–92. Oxford: Oxford University Press.

SCAGLION, R. 1976. Seasonal patterns in Western Abelam conflict management practices: The ethnography of law in Maprik Sub-Province, East Sepik Province, Papua New Guinea. Ph.D. diss., University of Pittsburgh, Pittsburgh, Pa.

———. 1981. Samakundi Abelam conflict management: Implications for legal planning in Papua New Guinea. *Oceania* 52:28–38.

———. 1983. The "coming" of Independence in Papua New Guinea: An Abelam view. *Journal of the Polynesian Society* 92:463–86.

———. 1984. Pacification and the reorganization of Abelam settlement patterns. Paper presented to the 83d annual meeting of the American Anthropological Association, Denver, Colo.

———. 1985. "Kiaps as kings: Abelam legal change in historical perspective," in *The history and ethnohistory of New Guinea*. Edited by Edward Schieffelin and Deborah Gewertz. Sydney: Oceania Publications.

———. n.d. Abelam migration and cultural exportation. MS, University of Pittsburgh, Pittsburgh, Pa.

SCHÄRER, H. 1963. *Ngaju religion: The conception of God among a South Borneo people*. Translated by R. Needham. The Hague: Martinus Nijhoff.

SCHEBESTA, P. 1973. *Among the forest dwarfs of Malaya*. Kuala Lumpur: Oxford University Press.

SCHEFFLER, H. W. 1978. *Australian kin classification*. Cambridge: Cambridge University Press.

SCHEFOLD, R. 1966. *Versuch einer Stilanalyse der Aufhängehaken vom Mittleren-Sepik in Neu-Guinea*. Basler Beiträge zur Ethnologie 4.

SCHINDLBECK, MARKUS. 1960. *Sago bei den Sawos (Mittelsepik, Papua New Guinea): Untersuchungen über die Bedeutung von Sago in Wirtschaft, Sozialordnung und Religion*. Basler Beiträge zur Ethnologie 19.

———. 1981. Yamsfest dere Kwanga (Nordost-Neuguinea). Paper presented to the congress of the Deutsche Gesellschaft für Völkerkunde, Münster.

———. 1983. Kokospalme und Brotfruchtbaum: Siedlungs-Vorstellung der Sawos und Kwanga, Sepik Gebiet, Papua Neuguinea. *Geographica Helvetica* 38:3–10.

———. 1984. "Über den mythischen Ursprungsort der Sawos und Iatmul (Papua-Neuguinea)," in *Diachronica*. Edited by Rupert Moser and Peter Heinrich Kamber, pp. 153–60. Ethnologica Helvetica 8.

SCHLAGINHAUFEN, O. 1910. *Eine ethnographische Sammlung vom Kaiserin-Augustafluss in Neuguinea*. Abhandlungen und Berichte des Königlichen Zoologischen und Anthropologischen-Ethnographischen Museums zu Dresden 13 (2).

SCHLECHTER, R. VON. 1903. Reisebericht der Guttapercha- und Kautschukexpedition nach den Südsee-Kolonien. *Der Tropenpflanzer* 7:308–19.

SCHLEGEL, A. 1977. *Sexual stratification: A cross-cultural view*. New York: Columbia University Press.

SCHLEGEL, S. A. 1970. *Tiruray justice: Traditional Tiruray law and morality*. Berkeley: University of California Press.

———. 1971. *Tiruray-English lexicon*. Berkeley: University of California Press.

SCHLENKER, HERMANN. 1974. *Aibom (Neuguinea, Mittlerer Sepik): Flötenorchester auf einem sakralen Felsen (7 Bambusflöten, 2 Schlagstöcke)*. Institut für den Wissenschaftlichen Film, Göttingen, Film E 2462.

SCHMID, J., and C. KOCHER-SCHMID. n.d. *Initiation bei den Zentral-Iatmul: Männerhausrituale in Yenshan, Palimbei, und Kanganaman*. Basler Beiträge zur Ethnologie. In press.

SCHMIDLIN, JOSEPH. 1913. *Die katholischen Missionen in den deutschen Schutzgebieten*. Münster in Westfalen: Aschendorffsche Verlagsbuchhandlung.

SCHMIDT, E. W. 1929. Die Schildtypen vom Kaiserin-Augusta-Fluss und eine Kritik der Deutung ihrer Gesichtsornamente. *Baessler-Archiv* 13:136–77.

SCHMIDT, JOSEPH. 1926. Die Ethnographie der Nor-Papua (Murik-Kaup-Karau) bei Dallmannhafen Neu-Guinea. *Anthropos* 21:38–71.

SCHMITZ, CARL A. 1959. Todeszauber in Nordostneuguinea. *Paideuma* 7:35–67.

SCHNEIDER, D. M. 1981. "Conclusion," in *Siblingship in Oceania*. Edited by Mac Marshall. Ann Arbor: University of Michigan Press.

SCHOFIELD, F. D., and A. D. PARKINSON. 1963. Social medicine in New Guinea: Beliefs and practices affecting health among the Abelam and Wam peoples of the Sepik District. *Medical Journal of Australia* 1:1–8, 29–33.

SCHULTZE-JENA, L. 1914. *Forschungen im Innern der Insel Neuguinea: Bericht des Führers über die wissenschaftlichen Ergebnisse der deutschen Grenzexpedition in das westliche Kaiser-Wilhelmsland 1910.* Mitteilungen aus den deutschen Schutzgebieten, suppl. 11.

SCHUSTER, MEINHARD. 1967. Vorläufiger Bericht über die Sepik-Expedition 1965–1967 des Museums für Völkerkunde zu Basel. *Verhandlungen der Naturforschenden Gesellschaft in Basel* 78:268–[90].

———. 1968. *Farbe, Motiv, Funktion zur Malerei von Naturvölkern.* Basel: Museum für Völkerkunde.

———. 1969a. Die Töpfergottheit von Aibom. *Paideuma* 15:140–59.

———. 1969b. Die Maler vom May River. *Palette* 33:1–19.

———. 1970. Aibom: Beispiel einer Dorfstruktur am Mittelsepik. MS.

———. 1973. "Zur Dorfgeschichte von Soatmeli," in *Festschrift 65. Geburtstag von Helmut Petri.* Edited by K. Tauchmann, pp. 475–91. Köln and Vienna: Böhlau.

———. 1979. Ethnologische Feldforschung in Papua New Guinea. *Geographica Helvetica* 1979, no. 4, pp. 171–80.

SCHUSTER, MEINHARD, and GISELA SCHUSTER. 1975. Aibom (Neuguinea, Mittlerer Sepik): Sago-Gewinnung. Film E 1375. *Publikationen zu Wissenschaftlichen Film, Sektion Völkerkunde-Volkskunde* 5(1):69–78.

———. 1976a. Aibom (Neuguinea, Mittlerer Sepik): Kochen von Klössen (Sago mit Kokos). Film E 1376. Zubereiten von Brei (Sago mit Kokos). Film E 1377. Zubereiten von Kuchen (Sago mit Kokos and Banane). Film E 1733. Backen von Fladen und Sago-Brocken. Film E 1734. *Publikationen zu Wissenschaftlichen Film, Sektion Völkerkunde-Volkskunde* 6(2):157–74.

———. 1976b. Topfmarkt. Film E 1370. *Publikationen zu Wissenschaftlichen Film, Sektion Völkerkunde-Volkskunde* 6(4):387–413.

SCHWARTZ, THEODORE. 1963. Systems of areal integration: Some considerations based on the Admiralty Islands of northern Melanesia. *Anthropological Forum* 1:56–97.

———. 1966–67. The cooperatives: "Ol i bagarapim mani. . . . " *New Guinea and Australia, the Pacific and Southeast Asia*, December/January, pp. 36–47.

———. 1973. Cult and context: The paranoid ethos in Melanesia. *Ethos* 1:153–74.

———. 1976. "Cultural totemism: Ethnic identity primitive and modern," in *Ethnic identity: Cultural continuities and change*. Edited by George DeVos, pp. 106–31. Palo Alto: Mayfield.

———. 1982. "Alcohol use in Manus villages," in *Through a glass darkly.* Edited by Mac Marshall, pp. 391–403. Institute of Applied Social and Economic Research Monograph 18.

SCHWIMMER, ERIK. 1979. "The self and the product: Concepts of work in comparative perspective," in *Social anthropology of work*. Edited by Sandra Wallman. New York: Academic Press.

SCORZA, D. P. 1974. "Au social relations . . . 'and please behave,'" in *Kinship studies in Papua New Guinea*. Edited by R. D. Shaw, pp. 187–209. Ukarumpa: Summer Institute of Linguistics.

SCOTT, N. C. 1956. *A dictionary of Sea Dayak.* London: School of Oriental and African Studies.

SEILER, D. G. 1972. Aspects of movement and socioeconomic development in the Maprik Sub-District of Papua New Guinea. B. Ec. (hons.) thesis, University of Queensland, Brisbane, Queensland.

SEILER, W. 1982. "The spread of Malay to Kaiser-Wilhelmsland," in *Gava': Studies in Austronesian languages and cultures*. Edited by R. Carle et al., pp. 67–85. Berlin: Dietrich Reimer.

SERJEANTSON, S. W., R. L. KIRK, and P. B. BOOTH. 1983. Linguistic and genetic differentiation in New Guinea. *Journal of Human Evolution* 12:77–92.

SEXTON, LORRAINE DUSAK. 1982. *Wok meri:* A women's savings and exchange system in highland Papua New Guinea. *Oceania* 52:167–98.

SHAND, R. T., and W. STRAATMANS. 1974. *Transition from subsistence: Cash crop development in Papua New Guinea.* New Guinea Research Bulletin 54.

SIMMEL, G. 1950. "Adornment," in *The sociology of Georg Simmel*. Edited by K. H. Wolff. New York: Free Press.

SIMMONS, R. T., J. J. GRAYDON, D. C. GADJUSEK, F. D. SCHOLFIELD, and A. D. PARKINSON. 1964–65. Blood-group genetic data from the Maprik area of the Sepik District, New Guinea. *Oceania* 35:218–323.

SINGARIMBUN, M. 1975. *Kinship, descent, and alliance among the Karo Batak.* Berkeley: University of California Press.

SIRK, U. 1978. "Problems of high-level subgrouping in Austronesian," in *Second International Conference on Austronesian Linguistics*, vol. 1, *Western Austronesian*. Edited by S. A. Wurm and L. Carrington, pp. 255–73. Pacific Linguistics C 61.

SKEAT, W. W. 1965. *Malay magic.* London: Frank Cass.

SKEAT, W. W., and C. O. BLAGDEN. 1966. *Pagan races of the Malay Peninsula.* Vol. 2. London: Frank Cass.

SMIDT, D. 1977. The National Museum and Art Gallery of Papua New Guinea, Port Moresby. *Museum* 29:227–39.

————. 1983. "Kominimung shields," in *Art and artists in Oceania*. Edited by Sydney M. Mead and Bernie Kernot, pp. 137–61. Palmerston North: Dunmore Press/Mill Valley: Ethnographic Arts Publications.

SMITH, MICHAEL FRENCH. 1978. *Good men face hard times in Koragur: Ideology and social change in a New Guinea village*. Ann Arbor: University Microfilms.

————. 1980. From heathen to atheist: Changing views of Catholicism in a Papua New Guinea village. *Oceania* 51:40–52.

————. 1982a. Bloody time and bloody scarcity: Capitalism, authority, and transformation of temporal experience in a Papua New Guinea village. *American Ethnologist* 9:503–18.

————. 1982b. "The Catholic ethic and the spirit of alcohol use in an East Sepik Province village," in *Through a glass darkly*. Edited by Mac Marshall. Institute of Applied Social and Economic Research Monograph 18.

————. 1984. "Wild" villagers and capitalist virtues: Perceptions of Western work habits in a preindustrial community. *Anthropological Quarterly* 57:125–38.

————. 1985. White man, rich man, bureaucrat, priest: Hierarchy, inequality, and legitimacy in a changing Papua New Guinea village. *South Pacific Forum* 2(1):1–24.

SMITH, ROBERT PAUL. 1957. *"Where did you go?" "Out." "What did you do?" "Nothing."* New York: Norton.

SNEDDON, J. N. 1978. *Proto-Minahasan: Phonology, morphology, and wordlist*. Pacific Linguistics B 54.

SNOWDEN, C. Editor. 1978. *Accounts of the history of cash crops in the Yangoru area, Maprik District, East Sepik Province*. University of Papua New Guinea and Department of Primary Industry, History of Agriculture Discussion Paper 19.

SOEJONO, P. S. n.d. (1963). The prehistory of Irian Jaya. MS. Translated from the Indonesian by J. H. Siregar. (First published as "Prehistori Irian Barat," in *Penduduk Irian Barat*. Edited by Koentjaraningrat and H. W. Bachtiar. Penerbitan Universitas, 1963.)

SOMARE, MICHAEL. 1975. *Sana*. Port Moresby, Hong Kong: Niugini Press.

————. 1979. Our pride, our strength. *Post-Courier*, special issue, September.

SOPHER, D. E. 1965. *The sea nomads*. (Memoirs of the National Museum 5.) Singapore: Government Printer.

SOUTHWELL, C. H. 1980. *Kayan-English dictionary*. Sarawak.

SPEARRITT, GORDON. 1979. The music of the Iatmul people of the Middle Sepik (Papua New Guinea), with special reference to instrumental music at Kandangei and Aibom. 2 vols. Ph.D. diss., University of Queensland, Brisbane, Australia.

————. 1983. The pairing of musicians and instruments in Iatmul society. *Yearbook for Traditional Music* 14:106–25.

SPEARRITT, GORDON, and MEINHARD SCHUSTER. 1981a. *Music of Oceania: Music of the Middle Sepik*. Bärenreiter Musicaphon 30 SL 2700.

————. 1981b. *Music of Oceania: Music of the Iatmul*. Bärenreiter Musicaphon 30 SL 2701.

SPECHT, J. R. 1969. Prehistoric and modern pottery industries of Buka Island, Territory of Papua New Guinea. Ph.D. diss., Australian National University, Canberra, Australia.

————. 1983. Review of: *The traditional pottery of Papua New Guinea*, by Patricia May and Margaret Tuckson (Sydney: Bay Books, 1982). *Mankind* 13:562–63.

STAALSEN, PHILIP. 1965. Brugenowi origins: The founding of a village. *Man* 65:184–88.

————. 1966a. Iatmul-English dictionary. MS.

————. 1966b. The phonemes of Iatmul. *Pacific Linguistics* A 7:69–76.

————. 1969. The dialects of Iatmul. *Pacific Linguistics* A 22:69–84.

————. 1971. *Clause relationships in Iatmul*. Ukarumpa: Summer Institute of Linguistics.

————. 1975. The languages of the Sawos region (New Guinea). *Anthropos* 70:6–16.

————. n.d.a. Essentials for translation from Iatmul. MS.

————. n.d.b. The pronouns of Iatmul. MS.

STANEK, MILAN. 1982. *Geschichten der Kopfjäger: Mythos und Kultur der Iatmul auf Papua-Neuguinea*. Köln: E. Diederichs.

————. 1983. *Sozialordnung und Mythik in Palimbei: Bausteine zur ganzheitlichen Beschreibung einer Dorfgemeinschaft der Iatmul, East Sepik Province, Papua New Guinea*. Basler Beiträge zur Ethnologie 23.

————. 1984a. Die Rolle der Objekte im Alltag am Beispiel der Iatmul von Palimbei (Mittelsepik). Museum für Völkerkunde Basel, Fiche Sepik-Dok. 3-01.

————. 1984b. Einführung in das Ritualsystem der Iatmul, Mittelsepik, Papua-Neuguinea (mit Verzeichnis der Ritualobjekte). Museum für Völkerkunde Basel, Fiche Sepik-Dok. 3-04/05.

STANLEY, G. A. V., S. W. CASEY, J. H. MONTGOMERY, and H. D. EVE. 1935. Preliminary notes on the recent earthquake in New Guinea. *Australian Geographer* 2:8–15.

STEINHAUER, H., and A. HAKIM USMAN. 1978. "Notes on the morphemes of Kerinci (Sumatra)," in *Second International Conference on Austronesian Linguistics*, vol. 1, *Western Austronesian*. Edited by S. A. Wurm and L. Carrington, pp. 483–502. Pacific Linguistics C 61.

STENT, W. R. 1979. Aspects of the transition from a subsistence to a market economy in the Abelam, Papua New Guinea. Ph.D. diss., La Trobe University, Bundoora, Victoria.

————. 1984. *The development of a market economy in the Abelam*. Institute of Applied Social and Economic Research Monograph 20.

STEPHEN, D. 1972. *A history of political parties in Papua New Guinea*. Melbourne: Lansdowne.

STERLY, JOACHIM. 1965. Kritische Bemerkungen zur Erörterung des sogenannten gewaltsamen Todeszaubers in Melanesien. *Kölner Ethnologische Mitteilungen* 4:205–30.

———. 1970. Heilpflanzen der Einwohner Melanesiens. *Hamburger Reihe zur Kultur- und Sprachwissenschaft* 6.

STEVENS, A. M. 1968. *Madurese phonology and morphology*. American Oriental Society Series 52.

STICKER, BERNHARD. 1958. Zeitmass und Zeitmessung. *Studium Generale* 1:35–47.

STÖCKLIN, W. H. 1973. "Fruchtbarkeitsriten und Todeszauber bei den Abelam in Neuguinea: Neue Aspekte der Farbenmagie." *Ethnomedizin: Referate der Fachkonferenz in München 19. + 20.10.73*, pp. 41–54. Munich.

———. 1977. "Die Farbenmagie der Abelam in ethnomedizinischer Sicht," in *Ethnomedizin*. Edited by G. Rudnitski, W. Schiefenhövel, and E. Schröder, pp. 23–35. Ethnologischer Abhandlungen (Barmstedt) 1.

STOKHOF, W. A. L. 1975. On the phonology of Bahasa Indonesia. *Bijdragen tot de Taal-, Land- en Volkenkunde* 131:254–69.

———. Editor. 1980a. *Holle lists: Vacabularies in languages of Indonesia*. Vol. 1. *Introductory volume*. Pacific Linguistics D 17.

———. Editor. 1980b. *Holle lists: Vocabularies in languages of Indonesia*. Vol. 2. *Sula and Bacan Islands, North Halmahera, South and East Halmahera*. Pacific Linguistics D 28.

———. Editor. 1981a. *Holle lists: Vacabularies in languages of Indonesia*. Vol. 3, no. 1. *Southern Moluccas; Central Moluccas: Seram (1)*. Pacific Linguistics D 35.

———. Editor. 1981b. *Holle lists: Vacabularies in languages of Indonesia*. Vol. 3, no. 2. *Central Moluccas: Seram (2)*. Pacific Linguistics D 44.

———. Editor. 1982a. *Holle lists: Vacabularies in languages of Indonesia*. Vol. 3, no. 3. *Central Moluccas: Seram (3), Haruku, Banda, Ambon (1)*. Pacific Linguistics D 49.

———. Editor. 1982b. *Holle lists: Vocabularies in languages of Indonesia*. Vol. 3, no. 4. *Central Moluccas, Ambon (2), Buru, Nusa Laut, Saparua*. Pacific Linguistics D 50.

———. Editor. 1982c. *Holle lists: Vocabularies in languages of Indonesia*. Vol. 4. *Talaud and Sangiru Islands*. Pacific Linguistics D 51.

———. Editor. 1982d. *Holle lists: Vocabularies in languages of Indonesia*. Vol. 5, no. 1. *Irian Jaya: Austronesian languages; Papuan languages, Digul area*. Pacific Linguistics D 52.

———. Editor. 1983a. *Holle lists: Vocabularies in languages of Indonesia*. Vol. 5, no. 2. *Irian Jaya: Papuan languages, Northern languages, Central Highlands languages*. Pacific Linguistics D 33.

———. Editor. 1983b. *Holle lists: Vocabularies in languages of Indonesia*. Vol. 6. *The Lesser Sunda Islands (Nusa Tenggara)*. Pacific Linguistics D 59.

———. Editor. 1983c. *Holle lists: Vocabularies in languages of Indonesia*. Vol. 7, no. 1. *North Sulawesi: Garontalo group and Tontoli*. Pacific Linguistics D 61.

———. Editor. 1983d. *Holle lists: Vocabularies in languages of Indonesia*. Vol. 7, no. 2. *North Sulawesi: Philippine languages*. Pacific Linguistics D 60.

———. Editor. 1984. *Holle lists: Vocabularies in languages of Indonesia*. Vol. 7, no. 3. *Central Sulawesi, South-West Sulawesi*. Pacific Linguistics D 62.

STRATHERN, A. 1970. Male initiation in New Guinea highlands societies. *Ethnology* 9:373–79.

———. 1972. "Social pressures on the rural entrepreneur," in *Change and development in rural Melanesia*. Edited by Marion W. Ward, pp. 489–503. Port Moresby: University of Papua and New Guinea.

———. 1973. "Kinship, descent, and locality," in *The character of kinship*. Edited by Jack Goody. Cambridge: Cambridge University Press.

———. 1974. Anthropology and problems of social change in Papua New Guinea (Inaugural lecture, University of Papua New Guinea). *Man in New Guinea* 6(3):15–25.

———. 1977. Melpa food names as an expression of ideas on identity and substance. *Journal of the Polynesian Society* 86:503–11.

———. 1982. "Tribesmen or peasants?" in *Inequality in New Guinea highlands societies*. Edited by A. Strathern, pp. 137–57. Cambridge: Cambridge University Press.

STRATHERN, M. 1972. *Women in between*. London: Seminar Press.

———. 1980. "No nature, no culture: The Hagen case," in *Nature, culture, and gender*. Edited by C. MacCormack and M. Strathern, pp. 174–222. Cambridge: Cambridge University Press.

———. 1981a. Women and the denigration of domesticity. Paper presented to a seminar at Sydney University, Sydney, Australia.

———. 1981b. Culture in a netbag: The manufacture of a subdiscipline in anthropology. *Man* 16:665–88.

———. 1984. Marriage exchanges: A Melanesian comment. *Annual Review of Anthropology* 13:41–73.

———. 1985. Kinship and economy: Constitutive orders of a provisional kind. *American Ethnologist* 12:191–209.

STUMPFE, KLAUS-DIETRICH. 1973. *Der psychogene Tod*. Stuttgart: Hippokrates.

SWADESH, M. 1955. Towards greater accuracy in lexicostatistic dating. *International Journal of American Linguistics* 21:121–37.

SWADLING, P. 1979. *People of the West Sepik coast*. Papua New Guinea National Museum Record 7.

————. 1981. *Papua New Guinea's prehistory.* Port Moresby: Papua New Guinea National Museum.

————. 1983a. How long have people been in the Ok Tedi impact region? *Papua New Guinea National Museum Record* 8.

————. 1983b. Major issues relating to the preservation of historic places in Papua New Guinea. Paper presented to the UNESCO Regional Conference on Historic Places, Sydney, May.

————. n.d. Plumes from Paradise. MS.

SWADLING, P., and J. ANAMIATO. n.d. Report on shells found in Sites QBB and MSA. MS.

SWIFT, M. G. 1965. *Malay peasant society in Jelebu.* London School of Economics Monographs on Social Anthropology 29.

TALYAGA, KUNDAPEN. 1974. Should we allow research workers and tourists into the Enga district? *Man in New Guinea* 6(4):16.

TAMMU, J., and H. VAN DER VEEN. 1972. *Kamus Toradja-Indonesia.* Rantepao: Jajasan Perguruan Kristen Toradja.

TAYLOR, RUSSELL D., and PARTNERS. 1973. *Wewak Development Plan: A report prepared for the Papua New Guinea Department of Lands, Surveys, and Mines.* Boroko.

TE'OO SELARN NAWAYAP. 1975. Wood preservation: Its potential as a factor in the progress of the Papua New Guinea rural dweller. Paper presented to Section 9, Topic D, Tropical Wood Preservation Training Seminar, Port Moresby, July.

TERRITORY OF PAPUA AND NEW GUINEA. 1968. *Guide to the Native Administration Regulations (New Guinea) and the Native Regulations (Papua).*

TERRITORY OF PAPUA AND NEW GUINEA, DEPARTMENT OF AGRICULTURE, STOCK AND FISHERIES. 1969. *Wewak Sub-District coconut palms per capita survey.* Wewak: Department of Primary Industry.

THOMAS, K. H. 1941. Notes on the natives of the Vanimo coast, New Guinea. *Oceania* 12:163–86.

THOMAS, P. A. 1983. Semi-annual technical progress report. MS, *Salvinia* Control Project, Department of Primary Industry, Wewak.

THURNWALD, RICHARD. 1914. Von mittleren Sepik zur Nordwestküste von Kaiser-Wilhelmsland. *Mitteilungen aus de Deutschen Schutzgebieten* 27:81–84.

————. 1916. Banaro society: Social organization and kinship system of a tribe in the interior of New Guinea. *American Anthropological Association Memoirs* 3:253–391.

TIESLER, F. 1969–70. Die intertribalen Beziehungen an der Nordküste Neu Guineas im Gebiet der Kleinen Schouten-Inseln. *Abhandlungen und Berichte des Staatlichen Museums für Völkerkunde Dresden* 30:1–122; 31:111–96.

————. 1970. Tragbandschilde aus dem Hatzfeldhafen-Gebiet, dem Hinterland der Berlinhafen-Küste und dem Lumi-Gebiet, Nord-Neuguinea. *Jahrbuch des Museums für Völkerkunde zu Leipzig* 27:185–217.

TINDI RADJA MANIK. 1977. *Kamus Bahasa Dairi Pakpak-Indonesia.* Jakarta: Pusat Pembinaan dan Pengembangan Bahasa.

TONKINSON, R. 1982. "Kastom in Melanesia: Introduction," in *Reinventing traditional culture: The politics of kastom in island Melanesia.* Edited by R. M. Keesing and R. Tonkinson, pp. 302–5. Mankind 13.

TOWNSEND, G. W. L. 1968. *District officer: From untamed New Guinea to Lake Success, 1921–46.* Sydney: Pacific Publications.

TOWNSEND, PATRICIA K. 1970. *Subsistence and social organization in a New Guinea society.* Ann Arbor: University Microfilms.

————. 1971. New Guinea sago collectors: A study of demography in relation to subsistence. *Ecology of Food and Nutrition* 1:19–24.

————. 1978. The politics of mobility among the Sanio-Hiowe. *Anthropological Quarterly* 51(1):26–35.

————. 1982. *A review of recent and needed sago research.* Institute of Applied Social and Economic Research Discussion Paper 44.

————. 1983. *Infant mortality in the Saniyo-Hiyowe population, Walio Sio Census Division, East Sepik Province.* IASER/UNICEF Situation of Children Study Working Paper 5.

TUDOR, J. Editor. 1969. 6th edition. *The handbook of Papua and New Guinea.* Sydney: Pacific Publications.

TURNER, VICTOR. 1969. *The ritual process: Structure and antistructure.* Chicago: Aldine.

TUZIN, DONALD F. 1972. Yam symbolism in the Sepik: An interpretative account. *Southwestern Journal of Anthropology* 28:230–54.

————. 1976. *The Ilahita Arapesh: Dimensions of unity.* Berkeley and Los Angeles: University of California Press.

————. 1977. Reflections of being in Arapesh water symbolism. *Ethnos* 5:195–223.

————. 1978. Sex and meat-eating in Ilahita: A symbolic study. *Canberra Anthropology* 1(3):82–93.

————. 1980. *The voice of the tambaran: Truth and illusion in Ilahita Arapesh religion.* Berkeley and Los Angeles: University of California Press.

————. 1982. "Ritual violence among the Ilahita Arapesh: The dynamics of moral and religious uncertainty," in *Rituals of manhood.* Edited by G. H. Herdt. Berkeley: University of California Press.

TYLOR, E. B. 1873. *Primitive culture.* London: John Murray.

VAN BUITENEN, J. A. B., and J. ENSINK. 1964. *Glossary of Sanskrit from Indonesia.* Poona: Deccan College Post-graduate and Research Institute.

VAN DER SANDE, G. A. J. 1907. Ethnography and anthropology: Results of the Dutch Scientific Expedition to New Guinea in 1903. *Nova Guinea* 3.

VAN DER VEUR, P. W. 1972. "Dutch New Guinea," in *Encyclopaedia of Papua and New Guinea.* Edited by Peter Ryan, pp. 276–83. Melbourne: Melbourne

University Press in association with the University of Papua and New Guinea.

VAN GENNEP, A. 1960 (1909). *The rites of passage*. Translated by M. B. Vizedom and G. L. Caffe. Chicago: University of Chicago Press.

VANOVERBERCH, M. 1972. *Iseng-English dictionary*. Honolulu: University Press of Hawaii.

VICEDOM, G., and H. TISCHNER. 1943–48. *Die Mbowamb: Die Kultur der Hagenberg-Stämme im östlichen Zentral-Neuguinea*. Vol. 1. Hamburg: de Gruyter.

VOEGELIN, C. F., and F. M. VOEGELIN. 1977. *Classification and index of the world's languages*. New York: Elsevier.

WAGNER, ROY. 1967. *The curse of Souw: Principles of Daribi clan definition and alliance*. Chicago: University of Chicago Press.

———. 1975. *The invention of culture*. Englewood Cliffs: Prentice-Hall.

Wantok. 1974. Tingting bek-stori 1. Ami bilong japan i kam long Wewak, no. 100, September 18, p. 16; 2. Sodia kilim ol misinari, no. 101, October 2, p. 12; 3.[by Br. Gerhoch], no. 102, October 16, p. 16; 4. Mipela i fri, no. 103, November 6, p. 13.

WARK, LYNETTE. 1971. *Health and medical care in the Wapei Council area, with reference particularly to the problems of the Lumi area*. Department of Public Health Report D1R 9.

WARK, LYNETTE, and L. A. MALCOLM. 1969. Growth and development of the Lumi child in the Sepik District of New Guinea. *Medical Journal of Australia* 2:129–36.

WARNECK, J. 1977 (1906). Revised and expanded. *Toba Batak-Deutsches Worterbuch*. Edited by R. Roolvink. The Hague: Martinus Nijhoff.

WARNER, W. L. 1932. Malay influence on the aboriginal cultures of North-Eastern Arnhem Land. *Oceania* 2:476–95.

WARREN, C. P. 1959. *A vocabulary of the Batak of Palawan*. University of Chicago Department of Anthropology, Philippine Studies Program Transcript 7.

WASHBURN, S. L., and C. S. LANCASTER. 1968. "The evolution of hunting," in *Man the hunter*. Edited by R. B. Lee and I. DeVore, pp. 293–303. Chicago: Aldine.

WASSMANN, JÜRG. 1982. *Der Gesang an den Fliegenden Hund: Untersuchungen zu den totemistischen Gesängen und geheimen Namen des Dorfes Kandingei am Mittelsepik (Papua New Guinea) anhand der kirugu-Knotenschnüre*. Basler Beiträge zur Ethnologie 22.

———. 1984. "Die Vergangenheits-Konzeption der Nyaura (Papua Neuguinea)," in *Diachronica*. Edited by Rupert Moser and Peter Heinrich Kamber, pp. 117–34. Ethnologica Helvetica 8.

———. 1987. "Der Biss des Krokodils: Die Ordnungsstiftende Funktion der Namen in der Beziehung zwischen Mensch und Umwelt am Beispiel der Initiation, Nyaura, Mittel-Sepik," in *Neuguinea: Nutzung und Deutung der Umwelt*. Edited by M. Münzel. Frankfurt.

———. 1988. Der Gesang an das Krokodil: Die Rituellen Gesänge des Dorfes Kandingei an Land und Meer, Pflanzen und Tiere (Mittel-Sepik, Papua-Neuguinea). Basler Beiträge zur Ethnologie 28.

WATSON, V., and J. B. WATSON. 1973. *Mama samting nating*. Paper presented to the 72d annual meeting of the American Anthropological Association, New Orleans, La.

WAWN, W. T. 1973. *The South Sea islanders and the Queensland labour trade*. Honolulu: University Press of Hawaii.

WEDGWOOD, C. H. 1934. Report on research in Manam Island, Mandated Territory of New Guinea. *Oceania* 4:373–403.

———. 1937. Women in Manam. Pt. 2. *Oceania* 8:170–92.

———. 1953 (1927). Manam kinship. (Compiled by Marie Reay.) *Oceania* 29:239–56.

WEINAND, H., E. A. YOUNG, and D. A. M. LEA. 1972. *Coffee and rice production in the Maprik area, 1970–71: A compilation*. University of Papua New Guinea Department of Geography Occasional Paper 2.

WEINER, ANNETTE. 1976. *Women of value, men of renown: New perspectives in Trobriand exchange*. St. Lucia: University of Queensland Press/Austin: University of Texas Press.

WEISS, FLORENCE. 1981. *Kinder schildern ihren Alltag: Die Stellung des Kindes im ökonomischen System einer Dorfgemeinschaft in Papua New Guinea (Palimbei, Iatmul, Mittelsepik)*. Basler Beiträge zur Ethnologie 21.

———. 1984a. Kinder und Jugendliche aus Palimbei (Iatmul, Mittelsepik) als Handwerker. Museum für Völkerkunde Basel, Fiche Sepik-Dok. 3-02.

———. 1984b. Maskenkostüme der Iatmul: Die abwan. Museum für Völkerkunde Basel, Fiche Sepik-Dok. 3-03.

WENDT, ALBERT. 1980. "Reborn to belong: Culture and colonialism in the Pacific," in *Preserving indigenous culture*. Edited by R. Edwards and J. Steward, pp. 25–35. Canberra.

WESSING, R. 1974. *Cosmology and social behavior in a West Javanese settlement*. Ann Arbor: University Microfilms.

WESTERMARK, GEORGE. 1978. Comment on the "unfair exchange." *Research in Melanesia* 3(3 and 4):10.

WHEATLEY, P. 1973. *The golden Khersonese*. Westport, Conn.: Greenwood Press.

WHITE, GEOFFREY, and JOHN KIRKPATRICK. Editors. 1985. *Person, self, and experience: Exploring Pacific ethnopsychologies*. Berkeley: University of California Press.

WHITEMAN, J. 1965. Change and tradition in an Abelam village. *Oceania* 36:102–20.

WHITING, JOHN W. M. 1941. *Becoming a Kwoma*. New Haven: Yale University Press.

————. 1970. *Kwoma journal*. New Haven: Human Relations Area Files Press.

WHITING, J. W. M., R. KLUCKHOHN, and A. ANTHONY. 1958. "The function of male initiation ceremonies at puberty," in *Readings in social psychology*. Edited by E. E. Maccoby, T. M. Newcomb, and E. L. Hartley. New York: Holt.

WHITING, J. W. M., and STEPHEN REED. 1939. Kwoma culture: Report on field work in the Mandated Territory of New Guinea. *Oceania* 9:170–216.

WILDER, W. D. 1982. *Communication, social structure, and development in rural Malaysia: A study of Kampung Kuala Bera*. London School of Economics Monographs on Social Anthropology 56.

WILKINSON, R. J. 1957. *A Malay-English dictionary*. London: Macmillan.

WILLIAMS, F. E. 1978. *The Vailala madness and the destruction of native ceremonies in the Gulf Division*. New York: AMS Press.

WILLIAMSON, MARGARET HOLMES. 1979a. "La scarification des femmes chez les Kwoma," in *Imaginaires*. Edited by Jean Duvignaud, vol. 2, pp. 153–72.

————. 1979b. Cicatrisation of women among the Kwoma. *Mankind* 12:35–41.

————. 1980. Omaha terminology and unilateral marriage on the Sepik. *American Ethnologist* 7:530–48.

————. 1983. Sex relations and gender relations: Understanding Kwoma conception. *Mankind* 14:13–23.

WILLS, P.A. 1958. Salt consumption by the natives of the Territory of Papua and New Guinea. *Philippine Journal of Science* 87:169–77.

WILSON, R. K. 1975. Socio-economic indicators applied to sub-districts of Papua New Guinea. *Yagl-Ambu* 2(1):71–87.

WILTGEN, RALPH M. 1969. "Catholic mission plantations in mainland New Guinea: Their origin and purpose," in *History of Melanesia: Second Waigani Seminar*, pp. 329–62. Canberra: Australian National University.

WINNETT, B., and R. J. MAY. 1983. "Yangoru-Saussia Open: The disappearance of an 83 percent majority," in *Electoral politics in Papua New Guinea: Studies on the 1977 national elections*. Edited by D. Hegarty, pp. 255–67. Port Moresby: University of Papua New Guinea Press.

WINSTEDT, RICHARD. 1949 (1913). 3d edition. *An English-Malay dictionary (roman characters)*. Singapore: Kelly and Walsh.

————. 1950 (1947). Revised edition. *The Malays: A cultural history*. London: Routledge and Kegan Paul.

WIRZ, PAUL. 1959. *Neu Guinea: Kunst und Kult des Sepik-Gebietes*. Koninklijk Instituut voor de Tropen Amsterdam Mededeling 133, Afdeling Cultureele en Physische Anthropologie 62.

WOLFERS, E. P. 1972. "Political parties," in *Encyclopaedia of Papua and New Guinea*. Edited by Peter Ryan, pp. 935–45. Melbourne: Melbourne University Press in association with the University of Papua and New Guinea.

WOLTERS, O. W. 1967. *Early Indonesian commerce*. Ithaca: Cornell University Press.

WOMERSLEY, J. S. 1972. "Crop plants," in *Encyclopaedia of Papua and New Guinea*. Edited by Peter Ryan, pp. 222–32. Melbourne: Melbourne University Press in association with the University of Papua and New Guinea.

Word in the world 1969, Divine Word missionaries. 1969. Techny, Ill.: Divine Word Publications.

WORSLEY, P. 1955. Early Asian contacts with Australia. *Past and Present* 7:1–11.

WURM, S. A. Editor. 1975. *New Guinea area languages and language study*. Vol. 1. *Papuan languages and the New Guinea linguistic scene*. Pacific Linguistics C 38.

————. Editor. 1976. *New Guinea area languages and language study*. Vol. 2. *Austronesian languages*. Pacific Linguistics C 39.

————. Editor. 1977a. *New Guinea area languages and language study*. Vol. 3. *Language, culture, society, and the modern world*. Pacific Linguistics C 40.

————. 1977b. "Possible wider connections of Papuan languages: Papuan and Australian, Greenberg's Indo-Pacific hypothesis," in *New Guinea area languages and language study*, vol. 3, *Language, culture, society, and the modern world*. Edited by S. A. Wurm, pp. 925–32. Pacific Linguistics C 40.

————. 1982. *Papuan languages of Oceania*. Tübingen: Gunter Narr Verlag.

WURM, S. A., and SHIRŌ HATTORI. Editors. 1981. *Language atlas of the Pacific*. Canberra: Australian Academy of the Humanities in association with the Japan Academy.

WURM, S. A., and B. WILSON. 1983. *English finderlist of reconstructions in Austronesian languages (Post-Branstetter)*. Pacific Linguistics C 33.

WURM, S. A., D. C. LAYCOCK, C. L. VOORHOEVE, and T. E. DUTTON. 1975. "Papuan linguistic prehistory and past language migrations in the New Guinea area," in *New Guinea area languages and language study*, vol. 1, *Papuan languages and the New Guinea linguistic scene*. Edited by S. A. Wurm, pp. 935–60. Pacific Linguistics C 38.

YAP, E. P., and M. V. BUNYE. 1971. *Cebuano-Visayan dictionary*. Honolulu: University Press of Hawaii.

YOUNG, F. W. 1965. *Initiation ceremonies: A cross-cultural study of status dramatization*. Indianapolis: Bobbs-Merrill.

YOUNG, MICHAEL W. 1972. *Fighting with food*. Cambridge: Cambridge University Press.

————. 1975. History or nothing? ANZAAS Congress 1975. *Research in Melanesia* 1(1): 50–59.

ZEMP, HUGO, and CHRISTIAN KAUFMANN. 1969. Pour une transcription automatique des "langages tambourines" melanesiens: Une exemple Kwoma, Nouvelle-Guinée. *L'Homme* 9(2):38–88.

ZEMPLÉNI, A. 1976. La chaîne du secret. *Nouvelle Revue de Psychanalyse*, no. 14, pp. 313–24.

Z'GRAGGEN, J. A. 1971. *Classificatory and typological studies in languages of the Madang District.* Pacific Linguistics C 19.

———. 1980a. *A comparative word list of the Northern Adelbert Range languages, Madang Province, Papua New Guinea.* Pacific Linguistics D 31.

———. 1980b. *A comparative word list of the Mabuso languages, Madang Province, Papua New Guinea.* Pacific Linguistics D 32.

———. 1980c. *A comparative word list of the Southern Adelbert Range languages, Madang Province, Papua New Guinea.* Pacific Linguistics D 33.

ZOETMULDER, P. J., and S. O. ROBSON.. 1982. *Old Javanese-English dictionary.* 2 pts. The Hague: Martinus Nijhoff.

ZORC, R. D. 1978. "Proto-Philippine word accent: Innovation or proto-Hesperonesian?" in *Second International Conference on Austronesian Linguistics,* vol. 1, *Western Austronesian.* Edited by S. A. Wurm and L. Carrington, pp. 67–119. Pacific Linguistics C 61.

ZWERNEMANN, J. 1980. *Hundert Jahre Hamburgisches Museum für Völkerkunde.* Hamburg.

Contributors

T. C. AITKEN is Senior Lecturer in Music at the Brisbane College of Advanced Education. He was educated in Glasgow, Cambridge, and Brisbane and specializes in music education and ethnomusicology. He has produced a number of Super-8 films that are also available on videotape, including three of ceremonies at Torembi in 1980–81, one on Sepik *naven* ceremonies, and one on Sepik musical instruments.

BRYANT ALLEN is Research Fellow in Human Geography of the Research School of Pacific Studies, The Australian National University. Following Master's studies in the Cook Islands from Massey University, New Zealand, he received a doctoral degree from the ANU based on field studies in the Dreikikir District of the East Sepik Province. His main interests are social and economic change in village societies, with particular emphasis on agriculture and the adoption of cash crops. His doctoral thesis, "Information Flow and Innovation Diffusion in the East Sepik," was accepted in 1976. As well as maintaining an ongoing research interest in the Sepik, he is currently working in the Tari Basin in the Southern Highlands.

KATHLEEN BARLOW is Visiting Professor of Anthropology at Gustavus Adolphus College. She was a Research Fellow at the American Museum of Natural History. She has done fieldwork among the Murik, near the mouth of the Sepik River, and received her doctorate in anthropology from the University of California, San Diego. Her dissertation (1985) is "Learning Cultural Meanings Through Social Relationships: An Ethnography of Childhood in Murik Society."

ROSS BOWDEN teaches anthropology in the Department of Sociology at La Trobe University, Melbourne. His first degree was in philosophy, and he holds a doctorate in anthropology from Oxford University. His research interests are in Papua New Guinea and the Maori of New Zealand, and he has done extensive fieldwork among the Kwoma and Kaunga of the East Sepik Province. In 1983 he published a study of Kwoma ceremonial sculpture in its ritual setting entitled *Yena: Art and Ceremony in a Sepik Society*. He is now completing books on Kwoma social organization and on the art and mythology of Kwoma men's houses.

LAWRENCE BRAGGE is a beef farmer, also studying tourism business management. He worked from 1961 to 1978 as a patrol officer/district officer in Eastern, Western, Southern Highlands, Chimbu, Milne Bay, and Sepik Provinces. His main interests are oral history, trade, and migrations. The bulk of his work is recorded in seventy unpublished patrol reports and similar documents. His only published work, written with Sachiko Hatanaka, is "Isolation, Habitat, and Subsistence Economy in the Central Range of New Guinea," which appeared in *Oceania* in 1973.

CHRISTIAN COIFFIER has a degree in fine arts from the École des Beaux Arts (Paris), in architecture from the University of Paris, and in ethnology from the École des Hautes Études en Sciences Sociales. He is currently working under the direction of Georges Condominas on technological changes as they affect Sepik housing. His *Un habitat mélanésien: Dans la vallée du Sepik* will be published in 1987.

BARRY CRAIG was Curator of Anthropology at the Papua New Guinea National Museum 1980–83. During this time he extended his experience in the Mountain Ok area of central New Guinea, begun in 1962, and his Upper Sepik fieldwork of 1968, 1969, and 1972–73 to include the compiling of a photographic record and documentation of national cultural property in the Middle and Lower Sepik region. Several articles arising from these fieldwork experiences include two special issues of *Oral History: Legends of the Amto, Simaiya Valley* and *Legends of the Abau, Idam Valley* (both West Sepik).

ANTHONY CRAWFORD is general manager of the Australian publishing house of Crawford and Associates in Bathurst, New South Wales. He lived in Papua New Guinea between 1972 and 1982 and carried out fieldwork amongst the Gogodala of the Western Province, during which time he was employed by the National Cultural Council to establish a program of cultural development at the provincial level. In 1981 he published an account of his fieldwork, *Aida: Life and Ceremony of the Gogodala*. He is editor of *People of Papua New Guinea*, a continuing series of booklets of which there are now thirty titles.

FATHER CHERUBIM DAMBUI was Premier of the East Sepik Provincial Government from August 1986 through October 1984. Ordained in 1974, he served the diocese of Wewak as priest prior to assuming government office.

T. WAYNE DYE is an international consultant in anthropology with the Summer Institute of Linguistics. He has an M.A. in anthropology from the University of Michigan and a Ph.D. in Inter-Cultural Studies from Fuller Theological Seminary. He spent a total of ten years, spread over a twenty-one-year period, in the Bahinemo village of Wagu and has published several articles on the Sepik.

SOROI MAREPO EOE is Director of the National Museum and Art Gallery in Port Moresby, Papua New Guinea. Formerly Curator of Anthropology at the same museum, he holds a degree in social anthropology from the University of Papua New Guinea and has done fieldwork among the Iatmul of the East Sepik Province, the Kominimung, Raos Breri, and lower Ramu of the Madang Province, and the Western Elemas (Orokolo) of the Gulf Province.

FREDERICK ERRINGTON teaches anthropology at Mount Holyoke College. He received his doctorate in anthropology from Cornell University and has done fieldwork on Karavar in the East New Britain Province, among the Minangkabau of West Sumatra, in a small town in Montana, and among the Chambri of the East Sepik Province. Author of *Karavar* and *Manners and Meaning in West Sumatra*, he has, with Deborah Gewertz, published several articles about the Chambri, as well as *The Interests of Men and Women among the Chambri: Strategies for Achieving Worth in a Sepik Society*.

COLIN FILER teaches in the Department of Anthropology and Sociology of the University of Papua New Guinea. He took his first degree in social and political sciences at Cambridge University, where he subsequently earned a doctorate in social anthropology. He has conducted field research in Nuku District, West Sepik Province, from 1972 to 1974 and at various intervals since then. He taught in the Sociology Department of Glasgow University from 1975 to 1982. His major research interest is the cultural effect of contemporary social change in Papua New Guinea.

ANTHONY FORGE has been Foundation Professor of Anthropology in the Faculty of Arts of The Australian National University since 1974. Before that he was a lecturer at the London School of Economics from 1961 to 1973. He has done some three years' fieldwork, in 1958–59, 1962–63, and 1974, among the Abelam and in the Sepik generally, resulting in publications including "Art and Environment in the Sepik" (1965), "The Abelam Artist" (1967), "Learning to See in New Guinea" (1970), "Marriage and Exchange in the Sepik" (1971), and "Style and Meaning in Sepik Art" (1973). His other research includes studies of the British middle class and of art and ritual in Bali.

DEBORAH GEWERTZ is Associate Professor of Anthropology at Amherst College and currently holds the Elizabeth Bruss Chair of Women's Studies. She received her doctorate in anthropology from the City University of New York and has done fieldwork among the Chambri of the East Sepik Province and in Montana. She is the author of numerous articles about the Chambri and their neighbors and in 1983 published a historical ethnography, *Sepik River Societies*. Most recently, she and Frederick Errington have jointly published *The Interests of Men and Women among the Chambri: Strategies for Achieving Worth in a Sepik Society*.

CHRIS HAIVETA is Secretary to the Gulf Provincial Government in Papua New Guinea. He was educated at the University of Papua New Guinea and the Institute of Development Studies in Sussex. He completed his studies in 1985 and took up his present position in 1986.

SIMON HARRISON is Lecturer in Social Anthropology in the Department of Sociology and Social Anthropology of the University of Ulster. He has carried out fieldwork among the Manambu of the East Sepik Province and received his doctorate in anthropology from The Australian National University. His doctoral thesis, "Stealing People's Names: Social Structure, Politics, and Cosmology in a Sepik River Village," is a study of ceremonial debating in the Manambu village of Avatip.

BRIGITTA HAUSER-SCHÄUBLIN was Curator at the Museum für Völkerkunde in Basel and is assistant professor at Basel University. She received her doctorate in anthropology on the basis of fieldwork among the Iatmul in the East Sepik Province. In 1977 she published her Ph.D. thesis, *Frauen in Kararau* (on women's life in the Iatmul village of Kararau). Subsequently she did fieldwork among the Abelam, where she focused on the architecture, function, and symbolism of

Abelam ceremonial houses (with a forthcoming publication).

MARY TAYLOR HUBER is a senior program officer at the Carnegie Foundation for the Advancement of Teaching in Princeton, New Jersey. She received her doctorate in anthropology at the University of Pittsburgh and has done fieldwork in both the West and East Sepik Provinces. Her book on Catholic missionaries in the Sepik was published by the Smithsonian Institution Press in 1988.

PETER B. HUBER does marketing research in Richmond, Virginia. He received his Ph.D. from Duke University in 1974 and taught at Princeton University until 1981. He has been Visiting Professor at New York University and the University of Virginia and has done fieldwork in the West Sepik Province (1961–71, 1976, 1977). Among his publications are "The Anggor Bowman" (1980), "Anggor Floods: Reflections on Ethnogeography and Mental Maps" (1979), and "Organizing Production and Producing Organization: The Sociology of Traditional Agriculture" (1978).

BARBARA HUBER-GREUB received her doctorate in anthropology from Basel University in 1983. She did fieldwork among the Abelam of the East Sepik Province in 1978–79. The publication of her thesis, "Boden und Alltag und ihre Bedeutung im Selbstverständnis der Abelam," is in preparation.

SASHA JOSEPHIDES was a Research Fellow in the Centre for Research in Ethnic Relations at the University of Warwick where she carried out research on Asian and Cypriot groups in the UK. She received her doctorate in anthropology from the London School of Economics in 1982. Her thesis, based on fieldwork among the Boroi people of the Ramu, is "The Perception of the Past and the Notion of 'Business' in a Seventh-Day Adventist Village in Madang, New Guinea."

BERNARD JUILLERAT is Research Fellow of the Centre National de la Recherche Scientifique (Paris) and is responsible for the unit "Anthropologie comparée des sociétés océaniennes." After fieldwork in Cameroon, from which he obtained his doctorate, he has been doing research in Papua New Guinea since 1970 and has in press a monograph on Yafar society: Les enfants du sang: Société, reproduction et imaginaire en Nouvelle-Guinée.

CHRISTIAN KAUFMANN is Curator for Oceania at the Museum für Völkerkunde in Basel. He received his doctorate in anthropology from the University of Basel on the basis of an ethno-technological field study of several pottery traditions in the Sepik area (see Das Töpferhandwerk der Kwoma in Nord-Neuguinea, 1972. Use has been made of further research results, including films on Kwoma artists, in a number of exhibitions in Basel and elsewhere.

ANTJE KELM is a museum educator at the Hamburg Museum of Ethnography. She was educated in Köln, Lima, and Bonn and received her doctorate in anthropology from Bonn University. Together with her late husband, Heinz Kelm, she has done fieldwork in the villages of Abrau and Kwieftim in the West Sepik Province. She has also done fieldwork among several Bolivian Indian tribes. The results of the Kelms' work in Papua New Guinea have been published in two volumes, Ein Pfeilschuss für die Braut (1975) and Sago und Schwein (1980).

DAVID LEA is Professor and Head of the Department of Geography and Planning at the University of New England, New South Wales. He worked among the Abelam of the Maprik area in the 1960s for his Ph.D. dissertation, "Abelam: Land and Sustenance." He has carried out fieldwork in most other provinces of Papua New Guinea.

GILBERT LEWIS is Lecturer in the Department of Social Anthropology at the University of Cambridge. He qualified as a medical practitioner at Oxford and then did a doctorate in social anthropology at the London School of Economics. He has done fieldwork among the Gnau people of the West Sepik Province and has published Knowledge of Illness in a Sepik Society (1975) and Day of Shining Red: An Essay on Understanding Ritual (1980).

DAVID LIPSET is Assistant Professor of Anthropology at the University of Minnesota. His doctorate is from the University of California, San Diego. He did fieldwork among the Murik Lakes people in 1981–82 and has published a biography, Gregory Bateson: The Legacy of a Scientist (1982), and articles on aspects of Murik society and culture.

DIANE LOSCHE received her doctorate in anthropology from Columbia University after fieldwork among the Abelam of the East Sepik. Her doctoral thesis is entitled "Male and Female in Abelam Society: Opposition and Complementarity." In 1982, as Curator at The Australian Museum, she published *The Abelam: A People of Papua of New Guinea* in conjunction with the opening of the Abelam exhibit. She has taught at Macquarie University and is currently a lecturer at the City Art Institute in Sydney. In the United States, she taught at Hofstra University and Cooper Union for the Advancement of Arts and Science.

NANCY LUTKEHAUS is Assistant Professor in the Department of Anthropology at the University of Southern California. She received her doctorate in anthropology from Columbia University and has done fieldwork on Manam Island and in Enga Province, Papua New Guinea, and in lowland Peru. In addition to her doctoral thesis, "The Flutes of the Tanepoa: Dynamics of Hierarchy and Equivalence in Manam Society" (1985), which focuses on social organization, politics, and exchange, she has written about gender in Manam culture, early anthropological research on the north coast of New Guinea, and the work of the British anthropologist Camilla Wedgwood.

NANCY MCDOWELL is currently Associate Professor and Chair of the Department of Anthropology at Franklin and Marshall College. She received her doctorate in anthropology from Cornell University and has conducted fieldwork among the Bun in the Yuat River region of the East Sepik Province. She is especially interested in sociocultural organization and the symbolic dimensions of exchange.

PATRICIA MAY is Lecturer in the Fine Art Programme at The Australian National University. She received her B.A. degree from Vassar College and her M.A. in art history from the University of Michigan. She lived in Papua New Guinea from 1972 to 1977 and conducted fieldwork in various parts of the East and West Sepik and other provinces from 1969. The results of her study of pottery with Margaret Tuckson were published as *Traditional Pottery of Papua New Guinea* in 1983.

R. J. MAY is currently a Senior Fellow in the Department of Political and Social Change of the Research School of Pacific Studies, The Australian National University. He holds a Master of Economics degree from the University of Sydney and a doctorate from Oxford and was formerly director of the Papua New Guinea Institute of Applied Social and Economic Research. His publications include several articles on recent political and social change in the East Sepik.

RHODA MÉTRAUX is Research Associate in Anthropology at the American Museum of Natural History, New York City. She received her doctorate in anthropology from Columbia University. She has done fieldwork in the Caribbean area (Haiti and Montserrat) and among the Iatmul people of the East Sepik Province. She has also carried out research on French, German, and Chinese cultures. She is the author, with Theodora M. Abel and Samuel Roll, of *Culture and Psychotherapy* (1974).

WILLIAM E. MITCHELL received his doctorate from Columbia University and is Professor of Anthropology at the University of Vermont. He has done fieldwork among the Chinese and Jews of New York City and the Iatmul, Lujere, and Wape peoples of New Guinea's East and West Sepik Provinces. His recent publications include *The Bamboo Fire: An Anthropologist in New Guinea* (1978). A recording, *The Living Dead and Dying: Music of the New Guinea Wape*, and a film, *Magical Curing*.

DOUGLAS NEWTON is Evelyn A. J. Hall and John A. Friede Chairman of the Department of Primitive Art at the Metropolitan Museum of Art in New York City. He was educated in London. Among his several publications on the art styles of New Guinea, *Crocodile and Cassowary* (1971) deals specifically with Upper Sepik art styles and their ritual associations.

BRIGIT OBRIST is a graduate student in the Institute of Ethnology at the University of Basel. She did her fieldwork among the Kwanga in the East Sepik Province. The results of her research on child feeding and other food-related questions are in the process of being analyzed for her doctoral dissertation.

HANNS PETER is Head of the Department of Oceania and Australia at the Museum für Völkerkunde, Vienna. He received his doctorate in philosophy (ethnology/psychology) from the University of Vienna. He has done fieldwork among the Gargar of the West Sepik Province and in New Ireland. From 1975 to 1977 he held a research fellowship from the Australian Institute of Aboriginal Studies, Canberra. Among his several works on the Gargar is a comprehensive work in preparation tentatively titled *Eine Papuagruppe im Wandel*.

HUSHANG PHILSOOPH is a Research Fellow in the Department of Social Anthropology of the University of Edinburgh. He has studied psychology and philosophy as well as anthropology, and his fieldwork, on which his Ph.D. thesis (1980, University of Edinburgh) is based, was carried out among the Au of the West Sepik. His interests include belief systems, universals of the mind, social change, and the history of anthropology.

PAUL ROSCOE is Assistant Professor of Anthropology at the University of Maine at Orono. He received a Master's degree in anthropology from Manchester University and a doctorate in anthropology from the University of Rochester. He has conducted fieldwork among the Yangoru Boiken of the East Sepik Province. His doctoral dissertation, *People and Planning in the Yangoru Subdistrict, East Sepik Province, Papua New Guinea*, appeared in 1983.

RUTH E. RUFF was Curator of the Ruff Gallery of Primitive Art of Papua New Guinea, Eugene, Oregon, and was formerly Curator of the Wallace and Ruth Ruff Artifacts Gallery, University of Technology, Papua New Guinea. She graduated from Kansas State University and did graduate studies in anthropology at the University of Oregon. With her husband, she documented traditional architecture, art, and village site plans in Papua New Guinea.

WALLACE M. RUFF is a Research Fellow in the Department of Architecture and Building, University of Technology, Papua New Guinea and Professor Emeritus of LandscapeArchitecture at the University of Oregon. After the end of World War II, he commanded a search-and-rescue mission for the U.S. Navy in the New Hebrides and Solomons. Under the Village Studies program, he was in charge of recording the traditional architecture of Papua New Guinea, with an emphasis on ceremonial houses of the Sepik region.

RICHARD SCAGLION is Associate Professor of Anthropology at the University of Pittsburgh and a research associate with the Carnegie Museum of Natural History. He holds degrees in both mathematics and anthropology. He has spent several extended field trips with the Samukundi Abelam people of the East Sepik Province. In 1979–81 he was director of customary law development for the Law Reform Commission of Papua New Guinea. His primary interests are in legal development and conflict management.

MARKUS SCHINDLBECK is Assistant Curator in the Department of Oceania at the Museum für Völkerkunde, Berlin. He received his doctorate in anthropology from the University of Basel and has done fieldwork among the Sawos and Kwanga

peoples of the East and West Sepik Provinces. In 1980 he published *Sago bei den Sawos (Mittelsepik, Papua New Guinea): Untersuchungen über die Bedeutung von Sago in Wirtschaft, Sozialordnung und Religion*.

JÜRG SCHMID was trained in ethnology, psychology, sociology, and prehistory at Basel University and did fieldwork in Yensan 1972–73. He has recently been serving as a guide for small-scale tourism in the Sepik, the Southern and Central Highlands, Chimbu, Enga, Gulf, Milne Bay, and West New Britain Provinces. He is the author of "Geben und Nehmen" and "Szenenwechsel eines Ethnologen" (both published in the *Bulletin der Schweizerischen Gesellschaft für Ethnologie*) and, with Christine Kocher-Schmid, *Initiation bei den Zentral-Iatmul: Männerhausrituales in Yenshan, Palimbei, und Kanganaman (Basler Beiträge zur Ethnologie)*.

GISELA SCHUSTER is a teacher of arts and history of art at the *gymnasium* of Münchenstein, near Basel. She did her studies (including ethnology and mathematics) at the University of Mainz and developed particular interests in so-called primitive art, museology with regard to art and anthropological museums, traditional handicrafts and ethnographic filming. Since 1965, she has repeatedly done fieldwork in the Sepik and has produced film scripts and articles mainly on Iatmul art and handicrafts.

MEINHARD SCHUSTER is Professor and Head of the Institute of Ethnology at the University of Basel, after having studied and spent the early postdoctoral years at the Frobenius Institute of the University of Frankfurt. He has done field research among the Waika and Makiritare of southern Venezuela (1954–55) and, since 1961, repeatedly in the Sepik region of Papua New Guinea, mainly among the Iatmul. His publications include two books on South American Indians (*Mahekodotedi* [1974], with O. Zerries, and *Dekuana* [1976]) and articles on North American, South American, general, and, mostly, Sepik ethnology.

JONATHAN SENGI is former Premier of East Sepik Province, Papua New Guinea. He received his teaching certificate at Goroka University Teacher's College and taught for more than five years. He previously served as a member of the Provincial Assembly and was Provincial Minister for Education in the first elected government.

DIRK SMIDT is Curator of the Department of Oceania at the Rijksmuseum voor Volkenkunde in Leiden. He has a degree in cultural anthropology from Leiden University and is a specialist in museum anthropology and the art of New Guinea. Between 1970 and 1980 he was attached to the National Museum and Art Gallery in Port Moresby and did fieldwork in various parts of Papua New Guinea, predominantly among the Kominimung of the Madang Province.

MICHAEL FRENCH SMITH is a consultant with Public Sector Consultants, Inc., a public policy research firm in Lansing, Michigan. He received his doctorate in anthropology from the University of California, San Diego. He has done fieldwork in Manus Province and on Kairiru Island in the East Sepik Province. He has also done research on Appalachian family farms in the U.S.A. His doctoral thesis, "Good Men Face Hard Times in Koragur: Ideology and Social Change in a New Guinea Village," is based on his research on Kairiru Island.

GORDON SPEARRITT is Associate Professor and Head of the Department of Music at the University of Queensland. After completing a Master's degree at Harvard, he carried out fieldwork among the Iatmul and later among the Hahon people of northwestern Bougainville. His doctoral thesis at the University of Queensland dealt with the instrumental music of the Iatmul people (1979).

MILAN STANEK is Lecturer in the Department of Anthropology at the University of Zürich. He received his doctorate in anthropology and Germanic philology from Basel University and has done fieldwork among the Iatmul, Angoram, Murik, Kambot, and Adjorab peoples of the Middle and Lower Sepik River. In 1983 he published his Ph.D. thesis on the mythology of the Iatmul in its relation to social structure; a description of the Iatmul ritual system will be published soon.

WERNER H. STÖCKLIN is a medical practitioner (pediatrics and tropical medicine) in Riehen, Basel, and teaches ethnomedicine at the Swiss Tropical Institute. He received his doctorate in medicine at Basel University and worked as a medical officer of the Public Health Department of the Territories of Papua and New Guinea from 1962 to 1964 (Eastern Highlands and Angoram) and from 1969 to 1970 (Maprik, East Sepik Province). In 1984 he published a book about his medical and anthropological experiences in Papua New Guinea entitled *Toktok: Am Rande der Steinzeit auf Neuguinea*.

ANDREW STRATHERN is Professor of Anthropology at the University of Pittsburgh. He received his doctorate in anthropology from Cambridge University and has done fieldwork among the Melpa and Wiru peoples of the Western and Southern Highlands Provinces. His published books include *The Rope of Moka* (1971), *One Father, One Blood* (1972), *Ongha* (1979), and *A Line of Power* (1984).

PAMELA SWADLING is Curator of Prehistory at the Papua New Guinea National Museum. She was educated at Auckland and has an M.A. in anthropology. Her publications include *Papua New Guinea's Prehistory* (1981) and *How Long Have People Been in the Ok-Tedi Impact Region?* (1983).

PATRICIA K. TOWNSEND teaches at Houghton College and does research as a medical anthropologist with the American Lung Association of Western New York. She received her doctorate in anthropology from the University of Michigan and has done fieldwork with the Saniyo-Hiyewe of the East Sepik Province. Her work as senior research fellow at the Papua New Guinea Institute of Applied Social and Economic Research from 1980 to 1984 produced, among other publications, a review of current health, education, and social welfare conditions, *The Situation of Children in Papua New Guinea* (1985).

MARGARET TUCKSON is a potter and teacher of pottery and in 1974 became an associate of The Australian Museum. In 1971 she began a study, together with Patricia May, of the pottery and potmaking of Papua New Guinea which culminated in the publication in 1982 of the *Traditional Pottery of Papua New Guinea*.

DONALD TUZIN is Professor of Anthropology at the University of California, San Diego. He holds a doctorate from The Australian National University and has conducted field research among the Ilahita Arapesh of the East Sepik Province. His publications include *The Ilahita Arapesh: Dimensions of Unity* (1976) and *The Voice of the Tambaran: Truth and Illusion in Ilahita Arapesh Religion* (1980).

JOHN HULANJIFA WASORI is a graduate of the University of Papua New Guinea and a research officer with the East Sepik provincial government.

JÜRG WASSMANN is a teaching assistant at the Institute of Ethnology at the University of Basel. He received his doctorate in anthropology from

Basel University and has done fieldwork among the Iatmul of the East Sepik Province. At present he is working among the Yupna (Madang Province), with an emphasis on cognitive anthropology. In 1982 he published *Der Gesang an den Fliegenden Hund*; an English translation is in preparation.

FLORENCE WEISS is Lecturer in Anthropology at the University of Basel. She received her doctorate in anthropology from Basel University and has done fieldwork in Papua New Guinea (Iatmul), Burkina Faso (Mossi), and Ghana (Nanumba). In 1981 she published her Ph.D. thesis on "The Child's Role in the Economic System of a Iatmul Village." An ethnopsychoanalytic study of Iatmul women conducted in 1979–80 has been published as *Gespräche am sterbenden Fluss* (with Fritz and Marco Morgenthaler, 1984).

MARGARET HOLMES WILLIAMSON is Associate Professor of Anthropology and Chairman of the Department of Sociology and Anthropology at Mary Washington College in Fredericksburg, Virginia. She received a D.Phil. in social anthropology from Oxford University and has done fieldwork among the Kambot-speakers and the Kwoma of the East Sepik Province.

Index of Subjects

Index of Ethnic and Geographical Names

Index of Personal Names

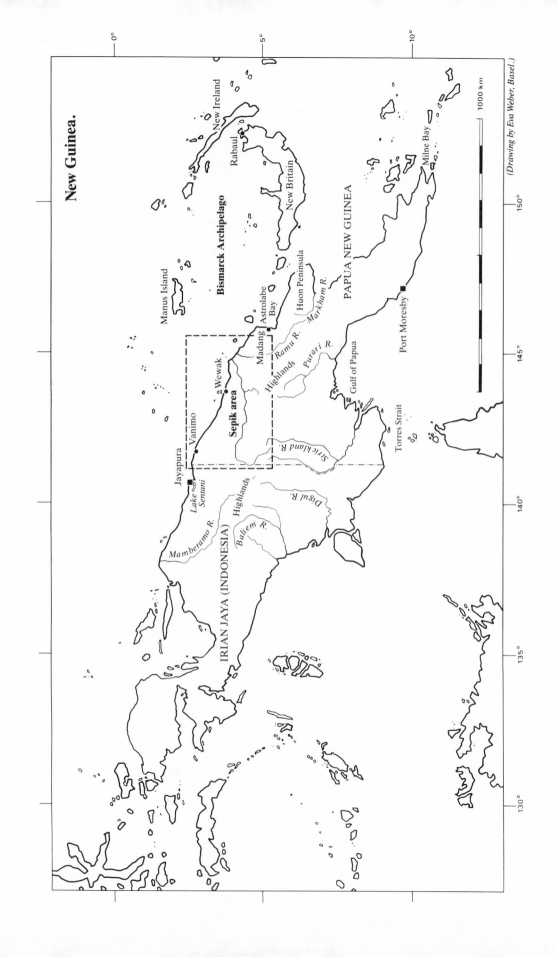

New Guinea.

New Ireland

Rabaul

New Britain

Bismarck Archipelago

Manus Island

Astrolabe
Bay

Huon Peninsula

Madang

Ramu R.

Markham R.

Milne Bay

PAPUA NEW GUINEA

Highlands

Purari R.

Port Moresby

Wewak

Sepik area

Gulf of Papua

Vanimo

Jayapura

Strickland R.

Torres Strait

Lake
Sentani

Highlands

Digul R.

Mamberamo R.

Baliem R.

IRIAN JAYA (INDONESIA)

1000 km

(Drawing by Eva Weber, Basel.)

The Sepik Provinces and their regional centers (former patrol posts and mission stations)

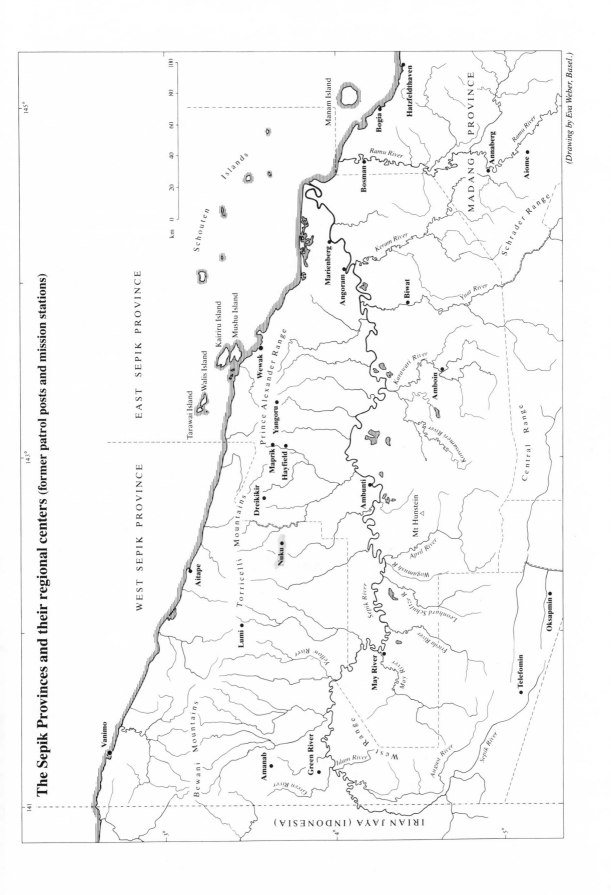

(Drawing by Eva Weber, Basel.)

Languages of the Sepik Area

(Wurm and Hattori 1981:map 6
compiled by D. C. Laycock)

The locations of a number of the language communities mentioned in the text are indicated as follows:
(Numbers are assigned to languages (a) from left to right and (b) in accordance with their classification on the level of language family.)

Abau, 34	Awar, 64	Gamei, 63	Kwoma, 46	Olo, 16
Abelam, 49	Awun, 38	Gnau, 20	Kwomtari, 15	Pahi, 43
Ak, 37	Au, 18	Heyo, 27	Laeko-Libuat, 24	Pasi, 42
Alamblak, 56	Bahinemo, 55	Iatmul, 52	Manam, 69	Sanio, 54
Alu, 17	Bimin, 5	Iwam, 35	Manambu, 48	Sawos, 51
Amanab, 13	Biwat, 60	Kairiru, 68	Mehek, 44	Sissano, 67
Amto, 10	Bo, 11	Kalou, 41	Mianmin, 1	Telefol, 3
Anggor, 12	Boiken, 50	Kambot, 62	Murik, 66	Tifal, 2
Angoram, 59	Bouye, 39	Karawa, 40	Nagatman, 8	Urat, 23
Arapesh, Bumbita, 32	Bun, 61	Karawari, 58	Nambi, 21	Urim, 33
Arapesh, Mountain, 31	Busa, 9	Kayik, 22	Namie, 36	Waris, 14
Arapesh, Southern, 30	Chambri, 57	Kombio, 28	Ngala, 47	Wiaki, 25
	Duranmin, 53	Kominimung, 65	Ningil, 19	Wom, 29
	Faiwol, 4	Kwanga, 45	Oksapmin, 6	Yahang, 26
				Yuri, 7.

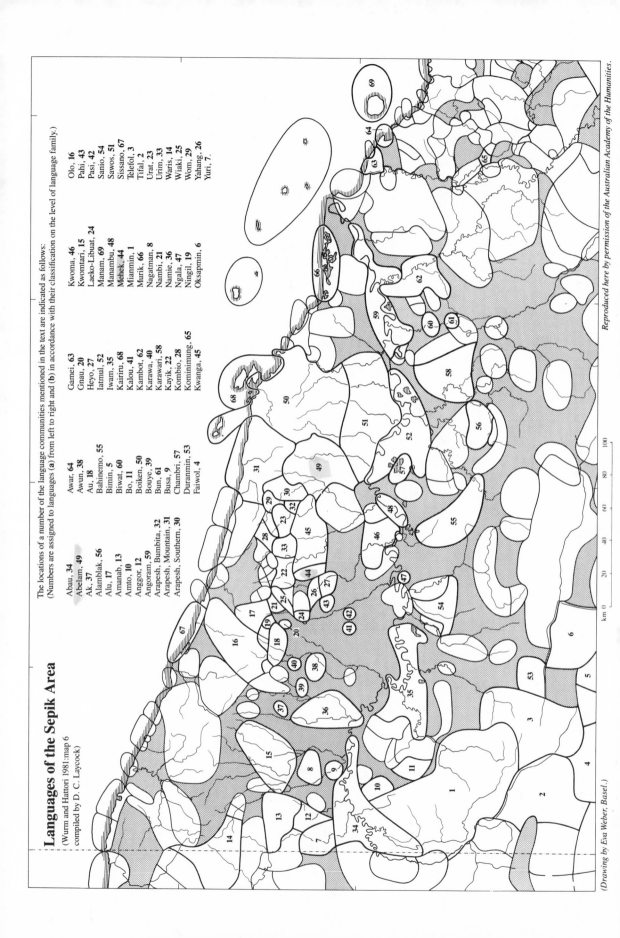

km 0   20   40   60   80   100

Reproduced here by permission of the Australian Academy of the Humanities.

(Drawing by Eva Weber, Basel.)